P9-DOC-513

Contents

Foreword

In show business, every artist likes to complain about awards, but true to the laws of egomania, everyone also covets receiving one. The Grammys in particular have always been a hot button. "It's Grammy time, so it's gripe time again," *Variety* once reported in its follow-up on a Grammy show.

The customary complaint about the Grammys is that they're neither "cool" nor up-to-date. As late as the mid-'70s, a *Variety* headline shouted "Grammy Awards Brush Rock." But while it's indeed true that the awards show seemed to sanctify songs like "Up, Up and Away" by the Fifth Dimension, Tom O'Neil rightly argues that the same ailment afflicts other awards as well: The Oscars snubbed *Citizen Kane* and the Emmys couldn't find the time to recognize Jackie Gleason. Moreover, while the Beatles never won Record of the Year, as O'Neil reminds us, they nonetheless managed to win in other categories.

Recently, the Grammys have worked hard to recognize new categories for rap, hard rock, metal and new age, and voting reforms have been instituted. None of which stifled the griping—complaints that *Variety* certainly helped amplify as far back as 1964 with our "Beatles Play Second Fiddle" headline.

It could be argued that the nature of the music business itself reinforces the impression that the Grammys are out of synch. Irrespective of awards, the mavericks often lead the sales derby. The audience out there seems ahead of the Grammy voters.

All of which, in a way, adds further "edge" to the Grammy shows themselves. They represent the point at which the pop culture intersects the business of pop culture. It's no surprise that at the Grammys, therefore, Rome is always burning.

Tom O'Neil does an excellent job in guiding us through this yearly "gripe time." It's an exciting ride.

Peter Bart
Editor in Chief, *Variety*

Acknowledgments

Compiling this book sometimes seemed like conducting a vast orchestra, all the members of which now deserve their "bravos!" and bouquets.

Both go to the stars who assumed a leading role in making this book happen: our maestro, editor John Duff; copyeditor Bill Betts; cover designer Jill Boltin and those virtuosos at *Variety,* including Peter Bart, Gerry Byrne, Madelyn Hammond, Bruce Brosnan, Peter Cowie, Charles Koones, Joe Sutherland and Bashirah Muttalib. Many thanks also go to Mike Shatzkin and his industrious gang at the Idea Logical Co.

Two deep bows go to Alex Saenz, who assisted with list compilation, and Paula Petrie, whose inky fingers rummaged tirelessly through back issues of *Variety* to make sure we hadn't missed treasured quotables. Other research was headed by two industrious sleuths: the late Edwin Gardner, who canvassed the libraries of New York and Washington, D.C., and Sherie Van Sanford, who performed brilliantly out in Los Angeles. Caroline Kozo and her very efficient staff in the photo department at the L.A. Public Library provided this book with much of its visual accompaniment thanks to its extensive archival collection of old pictures from the files of the now-defunct *Los Angeles Herald Examiner.*

Others who must be thanked include Louis and Pilar Cruz, Hilary Marsh, Sue Dahlinger and Young Kim, who did an expert job pulling together the first edition.

Also deserving huzzahs: America's greatest living editor and my private mentor and good friend, John Mack Carter, Catherine Miller (who pointed the way), Audrey and Gary Clark, Ray Whelan and a ghost I wish to be haunted by forever—Fred Birmingham, the late, great editor of *Esquire,* who once snatched this writer from the Midwest and introduced me to the media dazzle of New York. I am much indebted as well to the warmhearted Mangum family (Nancy, Dianne, Kathy, Ovis, Rodney and Michael), who were supportive and loving during a tragic time that coincided with the compilation of the first edition. I give you the Irish salute: *Sláinte!*

A chorus of other talent contributed hard work and long hours, including Dick Kagan, Dawn Reel, Timothy Marek, Lara Davidson, Karen Clay. Other thanks go to Jeff Miles, Syd and Miriam Cassyd, Lynn Dunn, Ty Wilson, Chandler Warren and Max Alexander.

Among the many people who contributed time for interviews were N.A.R.A.S. founding father Jim Conkling; Priscilla Dunn, wife of cofounder Lloyd Dunn; academy president Michael Greene and Grammy-winning artists Henry Mancini, Herb Alpert, Marvin Hamlisch and others.

Caroline White deserves my deepest bow—and deepest gratitude—for having the courage to pick up the baton on this project. Your contribution echoes on, my friend.

To Frank and Marge O'Neil: thanks for a lifetime of generosity and love. I'm sorry that Bing Crosby nor Andy Williams ever won a Grammy.

• Introduction •

When the Grammys Face the Music:
Safe Sound, Yearly Fury—and Guaranteed Fun

"John is with us here tonight," Yoko Ono said.

The words resonated eerily through the Los Angeles Shrine Auditorium during the 1981 awards ceremony. It hadn't been long since Lennon was gunned down by a crazed fan as he and Ono arrived home one dark December day. The outburst of grief that followed rocked the world—but particularly the music world, which had to deal not only with the loss of one of its greatest artists but also with the guilt over how it had treated him. Ever since the ex-Beatle teamed up with Ono to go traipsing off to explore new musical directions, their billowy clothes and shaggy hair bobbing in defiance as they skipped through strawberry fields for photographers, the recording industry dismissed them as "gurus in drag." Now, at the Grammys, rock's widowed queen led music's leading citizens in a moment of mass meditation as she summoned Lennon's spirit to join them for a triumphant moment of forgiveness that epitomized his peacenik philosophy. She was accepting the Album of the Year award for her and Lennon's *Double Fantasy* as their son, Lennon's "Beautiful Boy" Sean, stood beside her. It was the kind of chilling moment in music history that rarely gets played out in public and it was underscored with a heartwarming standing ovation. "How could you help not crying?" asked a wet-faced Kim Carnes.

It was also a moment of vintage Grammys—because it dramatized what the awards do best. They give us a precious, once-a-year chance to eavesdrop on the music biz and learn what's really happening among the gods empowered

Grammy pantheon members, from left: Art Garfunkel, Paul Simon, Yoko Ono, John Lennon and Roberta Flack backstage at the 1974 awards.

to make our feet tap and sagging spirits soar.

The Grammys tell us who's in (Bob Dylan, Alanis Morissette) and who's out (Hanson—sorry, boys, nice try). They also give us a delicious chance to see showbiz without its script. Who knew what Ono would say when she finally stood before the same music snobs who once mocked her? Eddie Vedder had the gall to trash the Grammys as he accepted the 1995 hard-rock award for Pearl Jam. ("I don't know what this means," he said. "I don't think it means anything.") Remember, in this drama, the whole music community has roles and the inevitable bad boys often provide some of the steamiest scenes. The old pros on hand just put up with it—and usually with wry smiles betraying a wisdom of age. And why not? Who can resist having fun at the Grammys? It's music's greatest show of shows—where Nine Inch Nails meets Tony Bennett and Yo-Yo Ma. It's some of the best of American music all together and it's being presented on an intimate evening during which the music industry shares with us what it privately thinks of itself. In competitive showbiz, everyone keeps secret scorecards on their peers. At the Grammys, we get to peek.

The Grammys also give us glimpses into what makes these stars so great. There are 12 to 16 music performances on the average three-hour Grammycast, the same number as awards given away. Sometimes they're solo numbers that dare to bare an artist's haunted soul, as Eric Clapton did when he sang to his dead infant son, "Would you know my name if I saw you in Heaven?" At other times, two music generations team up, as Stevie Wonder and Babyface did at the 1997 awards, proving how electrifying good music can be when they set off sparks jamming on "How Come, How Long." Just a few minutes later, at the same Grammycast, the producers panicked when they suddenly learned that Luciano Pavarotti was too sick to perform an aria. Don't worry, they were told—*Aretha Franklin will take care of this.* That's just what happened when the Queen of Soul rolled up her sleeves, took on Puccini's "Nessun Dorma" and showed all those spike-haired whippersnappers how an old pro takes care of business—and she knocked everybody out.

Besides being heavyweight entertainment, the Grammys are also the most audacious fashion show of the year. At the Oscars, cutting-edge couture is usually defined by what Cher wears (or doesn't) in any given year. At the Grammys, viewers see a bizarre runway display of torn T-shirts, antique prom dresses, tuxedo travesties, underwear-as-outerwear and gowns that Giorgio Armani might design if he were addicted to eating magic mushrooms. At the 1995 awards, Annie Lennox revealed what Minnie Mouse might look like as a secret dominatrix. When the Red Hot Chili Peppers

> ## The Grammy is music's golden grail. The American Music Award is plastic.

teamed up with George Clinton and the P-Funk All-Stars at the 1992 prizes, the men revealed alternate sides of themselves, too—in a diaper, kimono and wedding dress. *Time* magazine once described the attire of a star attending the 1983 awards: "Stevie Wonder wore a cumulously quilted white satin tuxedo whose upswept lapels formed great angel wings. The costume had the curious effect of making him look like a Puritan headstone." And speaking of heads, Bette Midler once wore something on top of hers that constituted one of the most ingenious Grammy fashion statements ever: a 45-rpm record. "It's 'Come Go with Me' by the Dell-Vikings," she informed the audience. "It was a great record, but it's a better *hat!*"

And what is it like to win music's crowning honor?

"This is too cool," Shawn Colvin said, describing her Grammy victory for 1997's Song and Record of the Year "Sunny Came Home." "We've been doing this a long time, it's been a long road and this does matter."

"It's finger bitin' time," Count Basie once described winning. "If your name is called, a lot of things happen in a few seconds. You're numb, there's an explosion, you're with it, you smile, you think this is the impossible dream come true. For a minute or so you're on a par with all those Oscar winners and those cats who went home with Emmys. It's national television on one hand and a room full of friends and acquaintances on the other."

"It's really a fantastic feeling," Seal said about reaping 1995's Record and Song of the Year awards. Winning is "the ultimate pat on the back," according to 1985 Album of the Year champ Phil Collins. "It just gets sweeter with each one," says Aretha Franklin, who's tasted victory 15 times. Another 15-time champ, Itzak Perlman, says, "I don't remember if I have 13 or 14 or something. I have quite a few, but they look terrific on the shelf." Johnny Cash adds, "When I won my first Grammy that night in the 1960s, I thought it was the greatest thing that ever happened to me—and then they kept coming."

Despite being music's most coveted award, the Grammy is also the most controversial in showbiz—primarily because of such problems as repeat winners and its historic failure to give progressive music its due. *Variety* has often cited voters' fondness for "honoring the hidebound over the fresh" and "the academy's penchant for sentimentalism and Old School ways." Those biases often trigger an uproar, but the annual (and inevitable) hubbub that surrounds the Grammycast simply makes it all the more fun. And even if Beck, Radiohead and Snoop Dog don't win the top awards, at least the music that does triumph is very good.

The Grammy Awards are bestowed by the National Academy of Recording Arts & Sciences, which is funded primarily by individual memberships ($65 per year, often paid by employers), ticket sales ($350 to $950 per seat at the Grammy ceremony) and $20 million a year from CBS for the exclusive broadcast rights. The academy has 13,000 members in eight chapters (New York, Los Angeles, Nashville, Chicago, San Francisco, Atlanta, Memphis, Texas) and exists, in addition to doling out awards, to provide a wide range of services. Its MusiCares Foundation assists artists with health and financial emergencies. The academy also operates the Grammy in the Schools program, which brings music leaders and artists to classrooms in 15 cities, plus the National Coalition of Music Education, which encourages music appreciation nationwide. The academy also sponsors high school concert series and college music festivals—more than 700 events in all each year—including seminars on such topics as songwriting and how to snag a recording deal.

Award winners are decided by 10,000 of the academy's members who've established their credentials by contributing creatively or technically to at least six recordings. Older people already settled in their fields tend to be the ones who join professional organizations like N.A.R.A.S., of course, so they're not always in tune with the times. Given the members' professional expertise, however, it certainly matters what they think is the best music of the year, even if those views have an obvious leaning toward more conservative tastes. The American Music Awards, by comparison, make no such claims. Those prizes go simply to the "favorite" music and artists of the year, which are determined by sales figures, the amount of radio airtime a song gets and polls conducted of frequent music buyers. Which is better? The Grammy is a golden gramophone that's become music's holy grail. The American Music Award—take a close look—is plastic.

But is a Grammy really worth its weight in gold? It's hard to say. Bob Dylan's *Time out of Mind* jumped more than 400 percent the week after the 1997 Grammys, moving from 122nd on the charts to number 27. Prior to the 1994 Grammy race, Tony Bennett's *MTV Unplugged* had only sold 300,000 copies and did not climb higher than 69th on the charts. During Grammy week, it sold only 4,000 copies, then, after reaping Album of the Year, it reentered the charts at number 48, selling 21,000 units in one week—a hike of more than 500 percent. Other examples: Tina Turner's "What's Love Got to Do with It" leapt back into the Top 10 for an additional 12 weeks after being named Record of the Year. Quincy Jones's *The Dude* entered the Top 10 only after it swept up five awards for 1981. Bonnie Raitt's *Nick of Time* peaked at only number 22 just before claiming 1989's Album of the Year, then zoomed to number 1.

"The public has come to look to the Grammys as a signal that a star has really arrived and the impact can be enormous,"

Sony Music President Tommy Mottola says. "Depending on the timing, a Grammy win can increase the sales of an album by anywhere from half a million to 2 million albums."

Not every musical act benefits, however. At the 1995 kudosfest, Naughty by Nature's *Poverty's Paradise* actually sold fewer copies in the week after winning the first Grammy ever bestowed for Best Rap Album.

When gauging music sales, who performs on the Grammycast seems to be just as important as who wins Grammys. (Naughty by Nature did not get airtime at the 1995 awards.) Joan Osborne was nominated for four awards that same year and lost them all, but she performed on the telecast and saw her CD sales leap 47 percent the week after her TV exposure. The average sales hike for winners and/or performers is 26 to 34 percent.

For the most part, the Grammys tend to reward hummable popular music such as past—and deserving—Record of the Year winners "Moon River" by Henry Mancini in 1961 and "Bridge over Troubled Water" by Simon & Garfunkel in 1970. Voters also favor the hits. *Variety* once noted, "Wherever there's a choice between a genuinely innovative talent and a best-selling one, there's no doubt about the outcome—the bestseller wins every time." Voters also like music with strong melodies and a soaring emotional thrust.

Those voting biases have resulted in some pretty puffy choices over the years when the highest honors were swept up by songs like the Fifth Dimension's "Up, Up and Away" and Christopher Cross's "Sailing." But the Grammys have also made some courageous selections in the top categories like Album of the Year winners *Sgt. Pepper's Lonely Hearts Club Band* by the Beatles, Paul Simon's *Graceland*, U2's *The Joshua Tree* and

Alanis Morissette's *Jagged Little Pill*. Those kinds of victories don't happen often enough for critics with progressive tastes, but when they do, they go a long way toward dispelling the accusation that the Grammys are really "the Grannys," as they've often been labeled in the past. "When figures like Stevie Wonder and Paul Simon combine substance and craft within the mainstream tradition, academy members frequently respond with an armful of awards," the *L.A. Times* said. "But the mavericks, from Presley to Bowie and Hendrix, have generally been ignored because their work fell outside that neat tradition."

To arrive at a fair estimation of the awards, one should consider, first, who has won the most. With 31 golden gramophones, it's the late Sir Georg Solti, former conductor of the Chicago Symphony Orchestra, who was one of the leading, and most controversial, figures of modern classical music. But was he America's greatest music artist of the past four decades? Few music experts would claim that.

In the nonclassical fields, with 26 awards, the biggest champ is Quincy Jones, the man who has not only the most impressive Rolodex in the music industry but the most talent in all of music's many aspects. No one is more important on the music scene today than the gentleman who was an arranger for Count Basie as early as 1963 (winning a Grammy for "I Can't Stop Loving You") and collaborated with Michael Jackson as a producer of *Thriller* 20 years later (picking up an impressive four awards in one swoop). In the intervening and subsequent years, Jones has demonstrated extraordinary talent, amazing diversity and incredible staying power. Everybody wants to be a citizen in the country where Quincy Jones rules, and so in Grammyland the natives are content to sing "Hail to the

> *Variety* has often cited voters' fondness for "honoring the hidebound."

Chief" to a class act that reflects well on them.

When Michael Jackson swept the 1983 awards, he set the record for winning the most in one year—eight. Solti not only holds the record for having the most wins overall, he set the record for the longest continuous winning streak, prevailing for 10 years in a row from 1974 to 1983. The second-longest winning streak was achieved by Aretha Franklin, who monopolized the female r&b vocal award for eight years (1967–74) and has picked up an additional seven statuettes as of this writing, making her the most honored woman in the awards' history.

The artist who has won Grammy's biggest prize, Record of the Year, the most is three-time champ Paul Simon for two Simon & Garfunkel singles, "Mrs. Robinson" in 1968 and "Bridge Over Troubled Water" in 1970, as well as his own "Graceland" in 1987. For winning Album of the Year the most times (three), Simon is tied with Stevie Wonder and Frank Sinatra. Sinatra has the most nominations for Album of the Year (eight), followed by Barbra Streisand's seven. Sinatra also has the most nominations for Record of the Year (seven), followed by a tie for second place between Streisand and Paul McCartney with five each. (Paul Simon comes in third place with four; McCartney's best record bids include his work both with and after the Beatles.) Grammy's pantheon may not represent the most daring and pioneering artists of the day, but the biggest winners certainly rank as some of music's most divine talent.

Lesser-known greats have benefited tremendously from victories in the top categories, which often transformed them suddenly into superstars. "Had I been asked three years ago to evaluate the chances of Bonnie Raitt winning four Grammys," *New York Times* critic Stephen Holden wrote about the 1989 awards, "I would have shaken my head and said impossible." The impossible happened when Raitt's *Nick of Time* won

Album of the Year after picking up its three earlier honors, causing its obviously overwhelmed artist to gasp at the Grammycast, "Wake me when it's over!" The awards spotted another real winner in Bette Midler as far back as 1973 when it hailed her as Best New Artist, thereby boosting her fledgling career. At the 1986 awards show, Sting was generous in acknowledging the role his victories played in his and his group finding a wider audience. "The Grammys gave recognition to the Police before we really broke in America," he said. "That gave us a lot of respectability." Since then, the awards have helped the "thinking man's party girl" Sheryl Crow to be taken much more seriously by critics and they've also given a once-little-noticed music trouper, Shawn Colvin, something to celebrate.

When the Grammys are at their best, the choices can be a true credit to America's greatest music. Who could quarrel with the selection of Sinatra's "Strangers in the Night" as the best record of any year? Not even knowing what its competition was in 1966, any rational person would have to believe that such a classic was unbeatable. (It topped, among others, "Monday, Monday" by the Mamas & the Papas and "Winchester Cathedral" by the New Vaudeville Band.) Consider, too, some of the other early and memorable winners: Bobby Darin's "Mack the Knife" (1959), Tony Bennett's "I Left My Heart in San Francisco" (1963) and Herb Alpert's "A Taste of Honey" (1965).

When studying past winners of the top three awards (Record, Song and Album of the Year), certain voting trends become obvious. The Grammys prefer:

• solo artists over groups

• pop divas performing chart-topping power ballads (Whitney Houston, Celine Dion, Bette Midler)

• the megaseller of the moment (*Rumours, Saturday Night Fever, Thriller,*

The Joshua Tree, The Bodyguard, Jagged Little Pill, Falling into You)

- rock veterans long after they're done rocking the boat (Eric Clapton, Bob Dylan, Bruce Springsteen)

- mature female artists who finally break into the Top 40 after long careers performing in honky-tonks or singing backup vocals for stars (Bonnie Raitt, Sheryl Crow, Shawn Colvin)

- veterans rebounding from substance abuse (Natalie Cole, Eric Clapton, Bonnie Raitt) or other tragedies—like Bob Dylan's 1997 heart scare or the 1991 death of Clapton's infant son, Conor.

- artists performing romantic ballads from movies (Whitney Houston's "I Will Always Love You" from *The Bodyguard,* Seal's "Kiss from a Rose" from *Batman Forever,* Henry Mancini's "Moon River" from *Breakfast at Tiffany's*). Broad exposure on the music video channels helps, too. When Seal's "Kiss from a Rose" won 1995 Record of the Year, *Variety* reported that the victory "proved that academy voters prefer soulful, chart-topping ballads supported by elaborate and often-played music videos backed by a film's promotional campaign."

- music "events" for charity (famine-relief fund-raisers "We Are the World" and *The Concert for Bangla Desh* or anti-AIDS anthem "That's What Friends Are For")

When sizing up this list of long-standing voting preferences, something else becomes clear: Grammy selection is not about honoring the best music of the year. It's about acknowledging favorite artists—and they don't always appreciate it. "Man, oh, man, I've had enough already!" Bonnie Raitt chided voters while receiving one of the five additional awards she's reaped since her 1989 grand slam. When Grammy voters like certain artists, they *really, really* like them. Consider the score between the two legendary jazz divas Ella Fitzgerald and Sarah Vaughan: 13 to 1. The polka prize is known as the Jimmy Sturr Award by cynical music critics because Sturr has won it 9 out of the last 12 years. Vince Gill has nabbed the gold for best male country crooner 6 out of the past 8 years. Other unbeatable Grammy grabbers include Mary Chapin Carpenter, Chet Atkins, Shirley Caesar, Take 6, Michael Brecker, Pat Metheny, Tony Bennett, Alan Menken and John Williams. The problem of repeat winners particularly plagues the classical categories, where Sir Georg Solti, Vladimir Horowitz and Leonard Bernstein were once unbeatable and now Pierre Boulez, Yo-Yo Ma and Robert Shaw reign. Largely due to that problem, the *New York Times* recently dismissed the classical awards as *"the other* Grammys, a footnote."

All of these favorite artists and writers do deserve generous attention from N.A.R.A.S., but a problem arises when it comes at the expense of other (often edgier) talent. The academy didn't catch up with the Rolling Stones until 1995 when they finally won their first golden gramophone for *Voodoo Lounge,* a work the *New York Times* called "tired." Alternative rocker Juliana Hatfield recently told CNN, "The Grammys don't really mean anything to me."

The Grammys have other notorious biases. West Coast artists usually have an edge (Toto and the Eagles are good examples; Sheryl Crow proved irresistible to voters as she sang about "the sun coming up over Santa Monica Boule-

> The average sales hike for winners and performers is 26 to 34 percent.

vard.") Country music almost never wins the top trophies. (Among the five exceptions so far are Glen Campbell's 1968 Album of the Year, *By the Time I Get to Phoenix,* and 1982 Song of the Year "Always on My Mind.") Jazz has fared just as poorly. Its few victories include the first Album of the Year, Henry Mancini's *The Music from Peter Gunn,* 1964 Album of the Year *Getz/Gilberto* and Bobby McFerrin's 1988 Record and Song of the Year, "Don't Worry, Be Happy." Classical music—like religious, polka and other genres of less broad appeal—has *never* won in the top categories, which prompted N.A.R.A.S. to introduce a special Classical Album of the Year award in 1962.

The Recording Academy has taken some of the biggest—and undeserved—knocks for its picks in the category of Best New Artist, one of its four highest honors. It's true that some past choices have been real head-scratchers (the Carpenters beat Elton John in 1970; Marc Cohn topped both Boyz II Men and Seal in 1991), while others have music critics shaking their heads (Starland Vocal Band, Men at Work, A Taste of Honey, Debbie Boone, the Swingle Sisters, Christopher Cross). But despite the notorious reputation of this category, many selections have actually been quite good: Bette Midler, the Beatles, Carly Simon, Toni Braxton, Tracy Chapman, Mariah Carey, Bobby Darin and LeAnn Rimes, among them. The voters' worst choice, of course, was those made-for-MTV pop hunks Milli Vanilli, a blunder the Recording Academy is still getting ribbed for—even though it revoked the award as soon as the duo was unmasked as lip-synching front men. It's probably no consolation to N.A.R.A.S., but it's interesting to note that the American Music Awards gave their equivalent prize that same year to Milli Vanilli; so did the Canadian recording academy. Nobody seems to care, though.

The American Music Awards are proud of the fact that their winners are the most popular artists in the country, but when Grammys happen to go to the top pop talent, as they often do, it's not something that academy leaders boast about. The trophies were designed to recognize high artistic achievement. ("Sales and mass popularity are the yardsticks of the record industry," the N.A.R.A.S. credo reads. "They are not the yardsticks of this academy.") Still, more than three-quarters of the winners of Record and Album of the Year were number one at one time or another in the singles or LP/CD charts. Nearly all of them at least have made the Top 10.

Notable exceptions include Henry Mancini's Record of the Year of 1963, "Days of Wine and Roses," which only reached number 33 at its peak. "Graceland" surpassed that failing record in 1987 when it won the same award after having never climbed higher than 81st in the rankings. While the vast majority of Album of the Year champs also reached the Top 10 before reaching Grammy's pantheon, there are a few exceptions: Glen Campbell's *By the Time I Get to Phoenix* (1968), Bonnie Raitt's *Nick of Time* (1989), Eric Clapton's *MTV Unplugged* (1992), Tony Bennett's *MTV Unplugged* (1994) and Bob Dylan's *Time out of Mind* (1997). One of the most convincing and ironic bits of other evidence one can use to counter the pop sales claim (unfortunately, for N.A.R.A.S.) is that, throughout the 1960s when Motown was shaking up the Top 10 with a steady stream of hits, the indie label reaped only one award. And that was slid in, too, just at the decade's end in 1969 (for the 1968 awards) when the Temptations won the best r&b group vocals prize for "Cloud Nine."

Throughout the Grammys' history, the most stinging indictment against them has been the accusation that they took forever to recognize rock & roll adequately. And, unfortunately, on this most serious charge of all, the Grammys are clearly guilty. After several halfhearted attempts to do so earlier, it wasn't until 1979 that N.A.R.A.S. permanently gave rock & roll its own categories, which jazz, rhythm & blues and classical had from the very first awards for 1958 when Frank Sinatra and friends were so terrified that Elvis Presley might be nominated. (He wasn't.) Angry rockers have always suspected that there has been a conspiracy to stop rock & roll from the minute it first twisted and shouted outside the awards ceremony door. And they—plus countless music critics and other progressive Grammy watchers— have never forgiven N.A.R.A.S.

Responding to all the criticism that the awards have fielded over the years, N.A.R.A.S. President Michael Greene once more or less conceded that there really is a little bit of Granny in the Grammy after all when he told *Rolling Stone:* "We're a fat old lady walking down the street and it's easy to throw things at us." But he also seemed to be asking: Doesn't Granny, after all, deserve some respect, too? "Grammy-bashing is one of the easiest sports in the world," he once said.

Under Greene's leadership, the academy has made some significant progress since 1985. Membership has grown from 5,000 to 13,000, with most of the new additions coming from the younger rock and pop worlds. Lots of new categories have been added, too—for metal, alternative, rap, rock gospel, Latin jazz, Latin rock, new age, world music and more.

The perplexing aspect of the constant controversy surrounding the Grammys is why they get flak when compared to the other peer-group entertainment awards. No one bashes the Oscars for picking picture-postcard movies like *Out of Africa* and *Dances with Wolves* as the year's finest. The Emmys still maintain their reputation as the most accurate and fair of all the top showbiz prizes despite having named *Get Smart* and *The Monkees* as past best shows on TV. The Tonys

> "Sales and mass popularity are not the yardsticks of this academy," says the N.A.R.A.S. credo.

once hailed *Cats* as the best piece of musical theater on Broadway and it didn't even have a *plot*. All four awards frequently honor work that is mostly entertaining and beautiful to look at.

Grammy grousers love to point out that some of music's most illustrious talents like Diana Ross, the Beach Boys and Rod Stewart have never won. True, but a comparison to other leading show business awards is appropriate here. Richard Burton went to his grave without an Oscar; TV's "Great One," Jackie Gleason, found the Emmys just as elusive during his lifetime; and some of Broadway's most stellar talent—including Lynn Fontanne and Ian McKellan—have never taken their bows on the Tonys' stage. (Fontanne at least won an Emmy.)

One of the most frequently quoted bits of Grammy trivia is the fact that the Beatles never won Record of the Year, leading many to believe that therefore the Grammys must be *hopeless.* But the Fab Four were victorious in the other top three categories. They were Best New Artist of 1964 and won Song of the Year in 1966 for McCartney's "Michelle" in addition to the Album of the Year prize for *Sgt. Pepper* one year later.

People who quote that trivia fact are really trying to say that often the most obvious and deserving winners get scooped by noncontroversial, mainstream favorites, like what happened to the Beatles when they lost the 1965 group vocals award—in one of the most notorious upsets in Grammy history—to Nashville's Anita Kerr Quartet. The Beatles lost the Record of the Year award on four occasions, but Barbra Streisand, who is just the sort of talented mainstream pop artist that N.A.R.A.S. voters adore, lost it five times. Streisand has nonetheless won an impressive eight Grammys to date.

Still, the criticism is weighted with some additional, hard-hitting evidence. Elvis Presley was nominated for Record of the Year twice—for "A Fool Such As I" in 1959 and "Are You Lonesome Tonight?" in 1960—but the only Grammys that rock & roll's heathen king ever won were in the categories for religious recordings (three times). And he didn't even win the first of those until he got married and had a child.

But, again, comparisons to other awards are relevant. A movie industry poll conducted recently by the American Film Institute declared *Citizen Kane* to be the greatest movie of all time, but the innovative trailblazer lost the Best Picture Oscar of 1941 to the safe but good *How Green Was My Valley*. Do the Grammys therefore deserve to take such a drumming for spurning the frighteningly loud, revolutionary sound of rock?

Perhaps not. But they do deserve their lumps for the problem of repeat winners automatically prevailing over lesser-known artists who are sometimes nominated for their career masterpieces. In those cases, the Grammys are running a race that just isn't fair—since emerging artists have no realistic chance of winning. The Emmys once had the same problem, back in the 1960s when Chet Huntley and David Brinkley were automatically winning all the news awards. The TV networks got so upset about it that they staged an industry-wide boycott, forcing the TV academy to try radical reforms, which meant scrapping Emmy's Oscar-styled voting system. Winners would no longer be chosen by a broad popular vote, but by judging panels forced to watch everything nominated in a given category. The result? Not only did lots of underdogs start pulling ahead, but all the growling in the TV industry over Emmy's lack of credibility suddenly stopped when it became obvious that the best TV was actually winning awards.

It took a similar crisis for N.A.R.A.S. leaders to try radical change. They finally decided to face the music when Tony

Bennett's *MTV Unplugged* won Album of the Year after failing to appear on any major critic's Top 10 list of the best music of 1994. "Christopher Cross and Toto were bad enough," the *New York Times* fumed, referring to Grammy's notorious past, "but Tony Bennett was the last straw."

The top brass of the music industry also sounded off. Sony Music President Tommy Mottola told the *L.A. Times* that the Grammys "do not at all reflect what is going on in music today." Label chief David Geffen agreed: "The Grammys clearly do not reflect excellence with regard to the music that is released each year. It's getting to the point where few people in the music business take them seriously. And if they keep it up, at the rate they're going, it won't be long before they're considered completely irrelevant."

To fix things, Grammy leaders decided to experiment with judging panels, just like the Emmys, but they did so at the other end of the voting system—to determine nominees. Members of the Recording Academy still voted to recommend contenders, but, in the fields of jazz and classical music, the final decision on who actually made the cut was left to national committees that chose nominees from the music that got the most votes. The committees were even permitted to stray and add works overlooked by N.A.R.A.S. voters if two-thirds of the panel wanted to do so. In those cases, one or two works are added to the list of five nominees, expanding the list to six or seven titles.

A similar committee system was introduced in 1995 to pick the five contenders in the top four categories of best record, song, album and new artist. A secret panel of 25 experts now spends two days in seclusion while listening to the top 20 vote-getters endorsed by N.A.R.A.S. members—and then it picks the final 5. (The old voting system was kept in place for most of the other Grammy categories—i.e., the complete

N.A.R.A.S. membership still chooses nominees by broad popular vote.)

The verdict? A hallelujah chorus could be heard across the music biz when the critics' faves suddenly made the race for Album of the Year—Alanis Morissette's *Jagged Little Pill* (1995), Beck's *Odelay* (1996) and Radiohead's *OK Computer* (1997). When *Jagged Little Pill* actually won, N.A.R.A.S. declared that it had finally found the cure for its voting ills.

Others disagreed. Grammy voters, after all, had occasionally embraced hard rock in the same category in the past when faced with such unstoppable music juggernauts as the Beatles' *Sgt. Pepper's Lonely Hearts Club Band* and U2's *The Joshua Tree.* After it rolled through the Grammys, Morissette's *Jagged Little Pill* went on to become the biggest-selling debut work by a solo female artist in music history. It's arguable that it would have won best album under the old voting system, too.

The winner of best record that same year was Seal's "Kiss from a Rose," which was certainly consistent with past winners being a best-selling, romantic ballad that had frequent radio airplay, heavy rotation on the music video channels and was used in a hit movie (*Batman Forever*).

Variety called that 1995 awards night "an evening of mixed results for the new voting procedures," adding, "For all of the attempts to contemporize the awards, the winners for the most part showed a decidedly middle-of-the-road bent. While the academy recognized some of pop's vital currents in its nominations, the awards swayed toward pop songcrafting and lilting ballads."

One year later, the 1996 winners also seemed consistent with past choices—indeed Eric Clapton ("Change the World") had just won Record of the Year

> **More than three-quarters of the winners of best record and album were chart toppers.**

four years earlier and Celine Dion's Album of the Year *Falling Into You* was in the pop-diva tradition of Judy Garland's 1961 victor, *Judy at Carnegie Hall,* and 1963 champ *The Barbra Streisand Album.*

Bob Dylan's *Time Out of Mind* was probably the inevitable winner of 1997's best album trophy, being a critically hailed work by a rock veteran long overdue for a solo salute in a top Grammy category. But what about Record and Song of the Year champ "Sunny Came Home" by Shawn Colvin? As a mature music artist who was finally hitting the pop charts, she fit the Sheryl Crow/Bonnie Raitt/Carole King mold of past champs. "Sunny Came Home" was also one of the year's longest-charting singles and it received wide exposure on radio, MTV and VH1. But it was a sad song about an angry young mother who returns home, grabs the kids and torches the place. In short, it wasn't the typical romantic ballad that Grammy voters love.

Yet lots of sad songs have won best record in years past: Simon & Garfunkel's "Bridge Over Troubled Water," Tina Turner's "What's Love Got to Do with It" and Eric Clapton's "Tears in Heaven."

It'd be interesting to know what was nominated against "Sunny" before the Secret Gang of 25 tinkered with the list. It may very well be the first example of a musical work winning a top award as a result of the recent reforms. Missing among the final five contenders for 1997 Record of the Year were such logical N.A.R.A.S. picks as Elton John's "Candle in the Wind 1997," LeAnn Rimes's "How Do I Live," Jewel's "Foolish Games," Seal's "Fly Like an Eagle" and Sarah McLachlan's "Building a Mystery." The real mystery: Could any of them have beaten "Sunny"? Did any deserve to?

If the correct answer to the latter question is yes, then the new reforms are bad news. If no, then it's great news for the Recording Academy at a time when it's trying hard to improve its procedures and reputation.

Meantime, if nothing else, Colvin's victory was certainly a sunny outcome for N.A.R.A.S.—since the work, if not the best single of the year, was respected widely among the cognoscenti.

The Grammys were born in Hollywood in the 1950s. Tinsel Town was losing some of its sparkle in those days, at least along the main stretch of Hollywood Boulevard where more and more lackluster shops like hardware stores were springing up to remind tourists that even Bing Crosby had a leaky faucet now and then. A Hollywood Beautification Committee was formed to dress up the area by putting stars in the sidewalks to honor the leading talents in film, TV and music. Five top executives from the five leading record labels were tapped to contribute the names of music's finest. In 1955, they gathered together one day in a back room of the Brown Derby restaurant: Paul Weston of Columbia Records, Lloyd Dunn of Capitol, Sonny Burke of Decca, Jesse Kaye of MGM and Dennis Farnon of RCA. As Weston once told *Grammy Pulse,* "There was no thought of an academy at that time."

"One day, the man [from the Hollywood Beautification Committee] who was supposed to be with us was late, and we were talking among ourselves," Jesse Kaye told the same source. "And it was Sonny [Burke] who came up with the idea. He said there were Academy Awards for the movies, and the TV industry had already organized its own academy. He felt that the record business was getting of age and we ought to be thinking about the same thing. We all agreed that it was a great idea. A little starry eyed, but it was a good idea. So,

after that, [at] every meeting for that other purpose, we would talk about forming an academy."

By 1957, the group approached a mutual friend to help them organize the effort, Jim Conkling, who had been president of Columbia Records and the Record Industry Association of Commerce, but who was now semiretired. According to *Variety,* Conkling "agreed to serve in a temporary organizational capacity to launch a national organization which would include reps of vocalists, leaders, conductors, art directors, engineers, arrangers, orchestrators, composers, producers, directors, and instrumentalists." In short, the founding fathers were after the best creative people, or as Conkling said, "We wanted it to be on a higher level." On May 28, 1957, the National Academy of Recording Arts & Sciences was officially formed at the Brown Derby, with Conkling named as the academy chairman.

N.A.R.A.S.'s first regular meeting was held on June 26, 1957, at the Beverly Hilton Hotel, where a board of governors was elected, which included songwriter Sammy Cahn and Nat King Cole in addition to Burke, Weston and others. The board stressed the rule that only creative persons in the industry were allowed to become members. The Recording Academy wanted to remain truly academic in nature, free from all commercial pressures, and functioning as an institution where its members could discuss and pursue—and reward—great music as it *should* be. "That eliminated record companies from participating," Weston told *Grammy Pulse.* "That kept out disc jockeys, promotional people, and publishers." In August 1957, the academy's Los Angeles chapter was incorporated, with Weston serving as its first president. A New York chapter followed early the next year, with Guy Lombardo waving his baton at the top. In 1961, a chapter was formed in Chicago, too, followed by other outlying cities like Nashville, Memphis and Atlanta.

It was a member of the academy's Awards and Nominations Committee, Val Valentin, who came up with the idea of what the new music award should look like: a composite design of the old gramophones once made by Columbia, Edison and Victor. The academy then decided to hold a contest to determine what to call it, offering 25 albums to the person who came up with the winning name. The Associated Press spread the word. About half of the letters that came back in response suggested "Grammy," so the committee took the hint and made it official. (None of the entries, to anyone's recollection, proposed the alternative shortening of "phonograph" so that these showbiz prizes might be known as the Phony Awards). Grammy's first award—those 25 LPs—was thus given to the first person who proposed the right answer: a Mrs. Jay Danna of New Orleans.

The premiere awards ceremony was held in the Grand Ballroom of the Beverly Hilton Hotel where 500 people paid $15 each for a nontelevised dinner gala. A few snafus occurred when there turned out to be a shortage of both statuettes and presenters. ("I was still lining up presenters while people were eating their dinner," Weston told *Grammy Pulse*.) But otherwise things went smoothly as the new golden gramophones were given out to Henry Mancini, Ella Fitzgerald, Perry Como and others who represented the best of the melodic music of the day.

Presenters included André Previn, Frank Sinatra, Milton Berle, Sammy Davis, Jr., Peggy Lee and Weston's wife, singer Jo Stafford. Noticeably missing were leading rock & rollers like Elvis Presley and Little Richard, but this was an industry insiders' party, not a frat house bash. And "it was fun," recalled Conkling's wife, Donna, who was then a member of the King Sisters, "because it was small and you knew everybody in this cozy little group." It wasn't fun for Sinatra, though. His music was nominated 12 times and only ended up winning an award for Best Album Cover. The fun went to victors like Henry Mancini, who told *Grammy Pulse,* "When I think back, I guess the first one was kind of historic although at the time I didn't realize where the Grammys were going. I didn't know it was going to become such a world-wide enterprise."

Sinatra boycotted the second awards celebration and, of course, ended up winning big. This time there were two ceremonies, held simultaneously in both Los Angeles and New York, which were followed by a live L.A.–based TV show that featured winners such as Ella Fitzgerald, Van Cliburn, Jimmy Driftwood, Shelley Berman and the 350-member Mormon Tabernacle Choir. Duke Ellington and Nat King Cole couldn't make it, but sent taped performances instead. Several newspapers gave the show bad reviews, but *Variety* insisted that it "was handled with savvy and imagination." Whatever the case, the Grammys didn't go back on TV until 1963 (for the 1962 awards) when "Best on Record" was born, featuring performances by the artists who had actually won a few months earlier.

N.A.R.A.S. wanted a live awards telecast like the Oscars and Emmys had, but the TV network executives weren't convinced the Grammys could attract the necessary superstar participants needed to draw viewers in large numbers. The execs weren't convinced that they wanted to continue the "Best on Record" show either, but it was tried again in 1965 (for the 1964 awards), and when the reviews stayed positive, the program stayed on the air until 1971, when at last the ceremony itself was broadcast live. The first Grammycast, as we know it today, was also the hardest to pull off. Producer Pierre Cossette told *TV Guide,* "We literally had to go out on the street to get people to fill up the seats in front." By the late 1970s and early 1980s, the Grammys became the second-highest-rated awards show on TV, after the Oscars. "For the 1986 telecast," Cossette asserted, "we could fill Yankee Stadium."

The networks may have been right about an embarrassing shortage of stars occurring in the Grammys' early days. The Beatles failed to show up at the 1965 awards ceremony (for the 1964 awards) and also skipped making a live performance on that year's "Best on Record" show, although they did prepare a taped segment on which they accepted their award for Best New Artist from actor Peter Sellers and performed "I'm So Happy Just to Dance with You." Years later, however, once the Grammys were an established force and the first live show was aired, they were there, more or less. The Beatles had broken up, but Paul McCartney—dressed casually in a blue suit, unbuttoned flower shirt and white tennis shoes—appeared to "shrieks of surprise" to accept the best film score award for the Fab Four's *Let It Be,* saying only, "Thank you."

In those early years, N.A.R.A.S. leaders were caught in a frustrating catch-22. Without the excitement of a live telecast, they had a difficult time rounding up stars for the comparatively sedate awards ceremonies. One of the founding fathers, Jim Conkling, was surprisingly candid about what they had to do in the early years as a result: let the winners know that they'd won before the results were announced. "There weren't any surprises like you have today," he said. "We had to tell the people because they were on the road and we had to bring them in. There weren't any secrets, but the public didn't know that. But we told the winners, 'If it leaks, we might have to take you out of it,' so nobody talked."

The first song to win Record of the Year was "Nel Blu Dipinto di Blu (Volare)," and some critics say that things haven't changed since, as ballads continue to prevail in the top category. But some pretty daring work has won, too. It was Henry Mancini's offbeat and jazzy score to the TV series *Peter Gunn* that beat out Sinatra's *Come Fly with Me* and *Only the Lonely* for the first Album of the Year award. For the most part,

though, in those days the predictable giants of mainstream music reigned in the other leading categories: Ella Fitzgerald, Count Basie, Perry Como, Ray Charles and Judy Garland. The boldest departure N.A.R.A.S. voters made in the early days was picking Bob Newhart's comedy LP *Button Down Mind* as winner of Album of the Year in 1960. Otherwise, safe, mainstream songs like Percy Faith's "Theme from *A Summer Place*" and powerful vocal albums like Garland's *Judy at Carnegie Hall* took the highest honors.

Jazz was the one adventurous sound that N.A.R.A.S. voters were comfortable with, so another exception occurred at the 1964 awards when Stan Getz and Astrud Gilberto shook up the Grammys with Record of the Year "The Girl from Ipanema" and Album of the Year *Getz/Gilberto* just as they were shaking up America with their new bossa nova sound. A breakthrough came for pop rock finally in 1966 when Paul McCartney and John Lennon reaped Song of the Year for "Michelle." The first winners of Record and Album of the Year that can be considered victories for the younger sound occurred one year later when the 5th Dimension won for "Up, Up and Away" (an ironic triumph, considering that such a radical breakthrough was accomplished by a song now regarded as the epitome of lightweight pop; back in 1967, though, it was *groovy*) and the Beatles *really* scored a triumph with *Sgt. Pepper's Lonely Hearts Club Band.*

Grammy's reluctance to recognize rock & roll was evident from the very first year. *Variety* wrote about the debut ceremony, "Over the pomp and circumstance of the festivities hung a cloud. The record academy has sharply snubbed the rock." The academy considered introducing a rock & roll category the next year, but changed its mind at the last minute and instead created Best Performance by a "Top 40" Artist. Nat King Cole won for "Midnight Flyer," which never actually made it into the Top 40 and wasn't, of course, a rock tune.

In 1961, the academy finally introduced a prize for Best Rock & Roll Recording, which went to Chubby Checker's "Let's Twist Again." (N.A.R.A.S. had overlooked the original "The Twist" when it topped the charts a year earlier.) The subsequent winners weren't especially radical choices and weren't really rock music either, but at least the academy was earnest in its attempt to recognize the popular sound of the day, giving the prize to "Alley Cat" by Bent Fabric (1962), "Deep Purple" by Nino Tempo and April Stevens (1963) and "Downtown" by Petula Clark (1964).

After that, the award's title changed to "Best Contemporary (R&R)" and it was bestowed to Petula Clark (again), the Statler Brothers, Roger Miller, Paul McCartney and the Mamas & the Papas. In 1967, the category kept its "Contemporary" label but lost the "R&R" designation. New winners included Glen Campbell, Dionne Warwick and Peggy Lee. And the younger generation was continuing to make inroads. One year later *Variety* wrote that "a host of youths have overthrown the elders in the field. . . . The recording industry has virtually shucked off its past. The Grammy Awards gave an indication of how far the rebellion of the young has gone. There was rarely a prize in the pop field to anyone over 30." Works by young artists may have been winning more awards, but rock & roll was still faring poorly. The *L.A. Times* asked in a headline as late as 1976: "Is Grammy Boycotting Rock?" Finally, in 1979, rock & roll got its own awards again, apparently for good.

Rock isn't the only music genre singled out for oversight. It wasn't until 1975 that *Billboard* ran the headline "N.A.R.A.S. Says 'Sí' to Latin Grammy, Wins Loud Olé." Reggae wasn't added until 1984. Polka joined the lineup one year later. Rock has certainly been the biggest sound in America, though, in addition to being the loudest, so it seems strange that the Grammys chose for so long to turn a deaf ear.

But they did, right from the beginning, because N.A.R.A.S. leaders were afraid of where this new call of the wild might take them. The late N.A.R.A.S. founding father Lloyd Dunn was a senior executive at Capitol Records when the Grammys were born. His wife, Priscilla, said, "He just didn't understand the music. In fact, he *hated* it! The music he knew was from Gilbert and Sullivan and Irving Berlin and on and on through all the great musicals of the '20s to the '50s. He loved all that, but he just couldn't understand all this banging and shrieking. He came into work one day and there was this group with their guitars and things. They were all pimply-faced kids with their hair dyed green and he went over to the reception desk and said, 'What the heck is that over there?' and the receptionist said, 'Wait till I tell you what they call themselves!' He said, 'What? I'm afraid to ask,' and she said, 'They call themselves the Underarm Deodorants!' Lloyd went 'Oh, my God!' and went upstairs and wrote out his resignation, asking 'Where are we going?!'" Dunn, it turned out, didn't go anywhere. He stuck with Capitol—like deodorant—and would eventually help introduce the Beatles to America.

In time, the entire music industry would yield to the revolutionary new sound, of course, but not before becoming engaged in a battle that consumed American culture and blasted the generation gap further apart with each new rock & roll hit single played on the radio. As the Grammys were being born, Frank Sinatra was denouncing rock & roll as "the most brutal, ugly, degenerate, vicious form of expression it has been my displeasure to hear." He not only didn't understand the appeal of the amazing new sound, he and his contemporaries, surprisingly, could never appreciate its true musical artistry either. From its earliest days as an organization, N.A.R.A.S. was thereafter used as a fortress by the most conservative elements of the music industry in their battle against the new music—and the angry young rockers, in turn, used the academy as a target for their rage and frustration over not being recognized as artists. As a result, the entire historic battle over rock & roll—at its rockiest and sometimes even its most ridiculous—ended up getting played out at the Grammys.

The 1969 awards ceremony is a good example of the absurd heights that the battle could reach as the older generation continued to show signs of distrust and paranoia long after they had really lost their fight. Host Merv Griffin introduced a mellow pop/folk group with the half-jest, "Here's Peter and Mary. It's Paul's night at home to work on the dynamite caps."

The Grammys' credibility has been challenged outside of rock & roll, too. Sizing them up in 1987, *New York Times* critic Jon Pareles wrote, "Results range from passable (r&b awards) to tacky (the jazz awards) to out-of-it (the Latin awards)."

In the classical categories, the awards are the victim of "celebrityitis," according to Don Vroon, editor of the classical music magazine *American Record Guide*. "Grammys tend to go to the artists with the most name recognition," he says. "The awards have recognized some beautiful music in the past, but, in nine cases out of ten, I wouldn't even consider those records as nominees for being called the year's best."

Addressing the problem of repeat winners, N.A.R.A.S. president Michael Greene says, "I don't disagree with the criticism. So many incredibly important artists have been ignored by this organization that it's a source of extreme heartache to us. That's why we're being so bold with the experiments we're trying with the voting process."

The one reform that N.A.R.A.S. has yet to try is the one that solved most of Emmy's problems long ago: using judging panels to select winners. But music's highest honors, Greene insists, are "still in the process of being fine-tuned."

The Grammy Awards are such an established force today that it's surprising to learn how long it took them, following their rocky birth, to reach adulthood—at least in the sense that they were regarded on an equal basis with the Oscars, Emmys and Tonys. Probably because the Grammys weren't given an annual telecast till 1971, they spent more than a decade in relative obscurity.

As late as 1966, the *L.A. Times* covered the results of the eighth annual (1965) awards in an article that can be found on page 2 of Part II of that day's paper (March 16). The National Book Awards were announced the same day— on the *front* page of another section.

About this same time, the *New York Times* covered the platter prizes for the first time, probably because a local Broadway tune ("Hello, Dolly!") took 1964's Song of the Year award. Subsequent coverage remained minimal. In 1976, the *New York Times* ran a brief roundup piece on the winners of the 1975 awards on its inside TV page. The article was dwarfed by another one that reviewed a new, and now forgotten, pilot film for a proposed TV series called *Young Pioneers*.

Even if the leading West and East Coast newspapers weren't giving the Grammys much prominence, their coverage was much more respectful. By 1976, critic Robert Hilburn of the *L.A. Times* expressed high praise for all of the Album of the Year nominees, saying they reflected "the academy's most impressive collective judgment" so far. (Stevie Wonder's *Songs in the Key of Life* was the winner.) By the 1979 awards, when the rock & roll categories were reinstated for good and the Doobie Brothers' "What a Fool Believes" took Record of the Year, even the awards' most cynical onlookers, like rock critic Dave Marsh, conceded, "For once the Grammys spent its accolades where they were deserved."

The N.A.R.A.S. awards were clearly onto something and were commanding more respect. By the 1980s, the newspaper articles became more prominent and more extensive. The photos that accompanied them suddenly got bigger, too, and more numerous. On February 28, 1985, a headline in the *New York Times* boldly proclaimed, "Grammy Awards Show Finally Comes of Age."

When the first Grammy noms were announced, *Variety* reported a shocking snub that would continue to haunt N.A.R.A.S. for decades.

Variety's coverage of the Grammys through the years reveals a lot about them, too, particularly how they were regarded in the showbiz industry. Here are snippets:

- 1958 awards—When the first set of nominations came out, the March 18, 1959, edition of *Weekly Variety* covered the news on page 77 under the headline "DISK 'OSCARS' BRUSH OFF R'N'R."

    The first Grammy ceremony was reported on the bottom of page 1 of *Daily Variety* on May 6, 1959, under the headline "First Grammy Awards." Getting more prominent treatment higher up on the page was news of who won UCLA's Creative Writing Awards (senior George Erengis received $1,000).

    At least the first Grammy ceremony received better coverage in *Variety* than the first Emmy Awards show 10 years earlier. Emmy's debut got reported on page 6.

- 1964 awards—Headline: "Beatles Play 2d Fiddle in Grammys to Bossa Nova, Barbra, Mancini & Miller." The article reported, "The Beatles may have swamped the music business during 1964, but that fact was not reflected in the Grammy award ceremonies."

- 1965 awards—*Variety*'s headline reported this year's race began with "lotsa beefs." The nominations "touched off another brouhaha this year," the article added, pointing to

"glaring omissions" from the lineup such as the Beach Boys and Rolling Stones. Another *Variety* headline asked: "Wha' Hoppen to Folk-Rock Hero Bob Dylan in Grammy Nominations?" The article said, "The failure of Bob Dylan, the single most influential figure in the pop field since Elvis Presley, to receive a single mention has raised eyebrows over the judgment of the electorate of the academy."

- 1967 awards—"How the times have changed was shown by the award for Best Sacred Performance," *Variety* reported, noting the first-time win by Elvis Presley. "It was not so many years ago [that Presley] was a dubious moral item on TV because of his swivel hips. That, however, was long before them twist and other sundry exhibitionist dances."

- 1969 awards—Page 1 article is below the fold: "Columbia Records Bags 13 Grammys as 4,000 Attend." A bartender's strike in Las Vegas earned the banner headline above it.

- 1970 awards—On March 17, 1971, the date of the first Grammycast, the kudosfest earned the banner headline while *Variety* reported on Columbia Records' good luck with Simon & Garfunkel: "COL SWEEPS GRAMMYS WITH 18."

- 1971 awards—The Grammys no longer merited banner headline treatment, but the article at least remained above the fold: "RCA Wins Grammies with 7, Col 5 and Carole King Bags 3." The article reported, "As usual, the N.A.R.A.S. vote completely brushed off the hard rock sound" when the Carpenters beat Three Dog Night for the pop group vocals prize.

In a separate article, headlined "That Yrly. Debate Already on over Grammy Awards," *Variety* quoted record exec David Geffen saying, "The Grammy Awards mean nothing to me. There are a lot of better records out every year that never get nominated." Past Grammy grabber Henry Mancini (the award's biggest winner with 20 statuettes) rallied to the prize's defense, saying, "The thing I like about the Grammys is that they always give the new people a shot."

• 1974 awards—"It's Grammy time so it's gripe time again," *Variety* reported when the nominations were announced. "A widespread sentiment in the disk industry, not only limited to the losers, is that the Grammy nominations represent a strictly commercial, play-it-safe name roster."

When the winners were announced, *Variety* reported, "Rock talent may pay the freight for the disc industry, but the Grammy Awards gave rock only one major award [McCartney's "Band on the Run"]. The winners were dominated by rhythm & blues, middle-of-the-road artists and, in some categories, there were some winners who raised questions about the judgment of the academy voters."

• 1975 awards—This year's nominations were "accompanied by a chorus of gripes, squawks and the sounds of crushed sour grapes. The Grammy choices were once again slanted against the hard rock sector of the disc biz and elevated to the fore such acts as Janis Ian, Morris Albert, Brecker Brothers, Linda Ronstadt, Paul Simon,

Captain and Tenille, among others. Among the missing were Bob Dylan, who was even brushed off by the Grammy nominations several years ago when he was at the crest of his career, and Bruce Springsteen, who made the biggest press splash of 1975."

• 1977 awards—Headline: "Grammy Award Nominee List Reflects N.A.R.A.S.' Coming to Terms with Popular Tastes." The article declared that this year's "nominations reflect the academy members coming to terms with popular tastes to the greatest extent in the history of the awards. The list of categories can be seen as the result of an influx of younger blood into the N.A.R.A.S. roster."

• 1980 awards—Grammy coverage remains parked in the same place on page 1 for a decade: in the upper left-

Grammy's biggest overall champ, with 31 awards, is the late Chicago Symphony conductor Sir Georg Solti. Was he the greateast U.S. musical artist of the past 40 years?

hand corner, above the fold but below the banner story. This year's headline: "Christopher Cross Dominates Grammy Awards; Denied Sweep by Kenny Loggins Win." News of the nominations occasionally does grab the banner, as it did this year: "FAMILIAR FACES DOMINATE GRAMMYS."

- 1981 awards—Finally, the awards' outcome earns the banner on a consistent basis: "NIGHT BELONGED TO QUINCY JONES."

- 1983 awards—Review: "Live on stage at the Shrine, Herbie Hancock's performance of his Grammy-winning number 'Rockit,' proved particularly electrifying, as did the appearance of Eurythmics vocalist Annie Lennox, her carrot-red hairdo abandoned for a pompadour and sideburns hair style which suggested slender versions of Wayne Newton and Vegas-era Elvis Presley."

- 1986 awards—When veterans like Paul Simon prevail, the banner reads "GRAMMYS ROCK WITH THE AGES."

- 1988 awards—Announcement of the nominations regularly receives the banner: "CHAPMAN MOVES INTO FAST LANE."

Variety was startled by the inclusion of two "oddball picks" as Best New Artist nominees, claiming that "the soft-gospel group Take 6 and defrocked Miss America-turned-recording-star Vanessa Williams came out of left field. Shut out were such acclaimed new acts as Keith Sweat, Al B. Sure!, Sinéad O'Connor and Edie Brickell and New Bohemians."

When the Record of the Year winner was announced, *Variety* reported, "To the surprise of just about everyone, it was one-man-band Bobby McFerrin."

- 1989 awards—*Variety* calls the Milli Vanilli fiasco "the biggest disgrace in Grammy history."

- 1991 awards—After the sweep by Natalie Cole's "Unforgettable," *Variety* reported, "The fact is, the academy's industry stalwarts have been slow to honor anything other than antiseptic, traditional compositions and performances, and this year was, for the most part, no exception."

- 1992 awards—"Nominations have gotten hipper in the recent past—alternative music kings R.E.M. had seven bids last year—but most N.A.R.A.S. voters still think that Ice Cube is something that floats in your highball."

- 1994 awards—*Variety* noted, "The vital music of '94, in sales and newsworthiness, continued to emerge from Seattle, and yet Soundgarden, Nirvana and Pearl Jam are relegated to the less-important categories of hard rock and alternative." *Variety* did cheer the vote result for best alternative music: "Although many

The Beatles prove that not all of Grammy's choices for the Best New Artist award were as dubious as Milli Vanilli and Starland Vocal Band.

N.A.R.A.S. critics would have preferred that Nine Inch Nails get the honor, the nod to Green Day—which has sold more than 6 million units—may indicate the org's voters are not as far afield as some record label chiefs have suggested."

Variety noted that since the Grammys "often shun changing currents, this year's awards ceremony has come under particular fire from the record labels." Soon thereafter, radical voting reforms were introduced.

- 1995 awards—"For all of the attempts to contemporize the awards, the winners for the most part showed a decidedly middle-of-the-road bent."

- 1996 awards—Referring to the victories of Eric Clapton's "Change the World" and Celine Dion's *Falling Into You*, *Variety* reported: "In a year when it looked like fresh faces and new sounds were finally due for Grammy recognition, key awards went instead to the mainstream pop that sells records and has traditionally earned statuettes."

- 1997 awards—Weighing the integrity of the nominations beyond the top four categories, *Variety* declared, "The mis-

fires suggest the panel approach should be implemented in other categories."

Several things are apparent while reviewing four decades of *Variety*'s coverage: It's just as tough as the consumer media. Obviously, the Grammys seem to invite that kind of controversy naturally, and consistently, so, to enjoy the awards show every year, it's probably best for onlookers to turn down the volume a bit, kick back and wait for the "Soy Bomb" wackos to crash the stage and Aretha Franklin to lift listeners' souls to aria heaven.

What really matters is that these are the Oscars of musicdom. Thousands of the industry's elite are sounding off on the year's music—and if they don't know what the best is, nobody does.

"A Grammy does mean something," the *New York Daily News* once insisted. "You win an American Music Award and you put it with your baby pictures. Tell people you won a Grammy and they're impressed."

"The acknowledgment of a job well done from fellow performers: That's what the Grammy is all about," José Feliciano once said. When Shabba Ranks accepted the statuette for 1991's Best Reggae Recording (*As Raw As Ever*), he addressed what the Grammy is all about to those who win one when he said, beaming, "I'm a star now!"

• The Grammys •
(1958–1997)

• 1958 •
Debut

"**O**ver the pomp and circumstance of the festivities hung a cloud," *Variety* reported on the first Grammy ceremony. "The record academy [has] sharply snubbed the rock. Not one R&R record was nominated in the 28 categories submitted to members."

When the bids were announced, *Variety* called them "a demonstrative brushoff to the prevailing trend in the pop field, i.e., rock 'n' roll. While such artists as Frank Sinatra, Perry Como, Peggy Lee and Ella Fitzgerald were nominated for awards in the top classifications, hot sellers like Elvis Presley, Paul Anka, Bobby Darin, Connie Francis and Conway Twitty, who dominated the pop charts last year, are conspicuous by their absence." Presley's music was responsible for nearly half of RCA's record sales, but it had been recently denounced as "deplorable, a rancid-smelling aphrodisiac" by Sinatra, whose own music led with the most Grammy nominations—12.

Grammy leaders responded to the criticism by stressing that "the main consideration was 'artistic merit,' not commercial success" and urged naysayers to "join N.A.R.A.S. and participate in the voting if they didn't like the results," *Variety* said.

The cloud of disappointment, however, did not end up darkening the bright spirits of those gathered for Grammy's opening night.

The banquet ceremony took place at the Beverly Hilton Hotel in Los Angeles and was supposed to be broadcast nationally. "A TV special was slated to be sponsored by Pepsi-Cola but fell through because there wasn't enough time to get the production in shape," *Variety* reported.

The precedent for ballads winning best record was set by Domenico Modugno's "Volaré."

Nonetheless, 525 music industry insiders paid $15 each to attend the event. "The *creme de la creme* showed up in full force," according to *Variety* columnist Army Archerd. "Lawrence Welk, for example, had to take a rear table in the name-jammed room." N.A.R.A.S. President Paul Weston told Archerd about the turnout, "We had no idea it would be so great. We thought at first we might be able to fill 10 tables at the American Room at the Brown Derby" restaurant.

Reporting on the ceremony, Archerd wrote that it was "disappointing, with the available musical talent, that there wasn't one note of music in the program. Instead, a tired old skit was presented, 'How South Was My Pacific,'" which spoofed *South Pacific* and starred bandleader Billy May.

There were a few other glitches that night, including a shortage of statuettes when a preponderance of groups ended up winning. There was also a shortage of stars scheduled ahead of time to dole out the prizes ("I was still lining up presenters while people were eating their dinner," Weston later recalled), but Weston managed to enlist Sinatra, Dean Martin, Peggy Lee, Henry Mancini, Sammy Davis, Jr., André Previn, Johnny Mercer, Milton Berle and Weston's wife, Jo Stafford. (Elvis Presley was far away—serving on guard duty as an army private in Wiesbaden, Germany.)

Otherwise, *Variety* added, "This first N.A.R.A.S. bash ran smooth as shellac" and "Mort Sahl emceed with his usual glib tongue."

The balloting was done by N.A.R.A.S.'s 700 members who could vote for the nominees and winners in 28 categories. The results were huge surprises, with jazz and pop tunes faring well despite the hard hit taken by hit rock & roll.

Media pundits predicted an easy sweep for Sinatra, whose dozen bids represented more than twice as many as his closest rival, Henry Mancini, whose musical score for the TV detective series *Peter Gunn* received five. Sinatra had two LPs contending for Album of the Year (*Come Fly with Me* and *Only the Lonely*), one single up for Record of the Year ("Witchcraft") and two entries competing for best male vocalist ("Witchcraft" and the "Come Fly with Me" single).

Ol' Blue Eyes faced serious competition in the contest for best record, but he was expected to snare the album and vocalist laurels easily. The chief suspense of the night was considered to be which Sinatra bids would nab the most votes from the elite members of music's inner club who considered the crooner their chairman of the board.

Then the true shocker of the night

> "Over the pomp of the festivities hung a cloud," *Variety* reported.

occurred. When Sinatra's votes split, he was nearly shut out. The only Grammy he won was for Best Album Cover, which even he admitted should have gone to artist Nick Volpe, who drew the sad clown face on the *Only the Lonely* cover.

Sinatra was "so upset about not winning a music award," his date for the evening, actress Sandra Giles, later told biographer Kitty Kelley, "that he refused to let any of the photographers take our picture that night. He was very moody and drank a lot afterwards. I guess I should've been grateful that Elvis didn't win anything."

Considering Sinatra's clout with the conservative music establishment, his Grammy snub had one positive aspect, famed songwriter Sammy Cahn told *Variety*'s Archerd: "I guess that proves that this wasn't fixed."

Instead, the top honors mostly went to the nonrock music that topped the pop charts. The double winner of the awards for Record of the Year and Song of the Year was the number-seven single of 1958: "Nel Blu Dipinto di Blu (Volare)," sung by its cowriter, the romantic Italian balladeer Domenico Modugno, who since then has never won, or even been nominated for, another Grammy. The song title was inspired by an illustration on the back of a pack of cigarettes that once caught the eye of colyricist Franco Migliacci. "Volare" means "to fly." The rest of the title is an intentionally nonsensical phrase referring to the whimsical dream of a man who paints his hands blue and flies through the sky—or "the blue painted in blue."

"Volare" was such a huge hit that *Billboard* reviewed seven versions of the tune in just one issue (July 21, 1958), including renditions by Dean Martin and Nelson Riddle. Martin's version had English lyrics written by Mitchell Parish and was extremely popular, too, peaking at number 12 on the charts.

The first soundtrack for a TV series to sell more than a million copies became Grammy's first Album of the Year. *The Music from Peter Gunn* was the country's number-one LP for 10 weeks and also won a best arrangement Grammy for Mancini, who had previously distinguished himself as an arranger and composer for Hollywood films such as *The Glenn Miller Story* and *A Touch of Evil.* When he was asked to work in television by producer Blake Edwards (after they ran into each other one day outside the Universal Studios barbershop), Mancini used the opportunity to experiment with an innovative jazz beat that ultimately became more popular than the TV show it underscored.

"The idea of using jazz in the *Gunn* score was never even discussed. It was implicit in the story," Mancini wrote in his autobiography, *Did They Mention the Music?* "Peter Gunn hangs out in a jazz roadhouse called Mother's—the name was Blake's way of tweaking the noses of the censors—where there is a five-piece jazz group. . . . The title theme actually derives more from rock and roll than from jazz. I used guitar and piano in unison, playing what is known in music as an *ostinato,* which means obstinate. It was sustained throughout the piece, giving it a sinister effect, with some frightened saxophone sounds and some shouting brass."

More Music from Peter Gunn would bring the composer six more nominations next year, and *Gunn* would even echo longer in Grammy lore. Emerson, Lake & Palmer's interpretation would score a nomination in 1981; the Art of Noise Featuring Duane Eddy would win Best Rock Instrumental Performance for 1986 for its own shot at *Peter Gunn.* Mancini would go on to become such a long-standing Grammy favorite that his total of 20 statuettes would rank him as the fourth-biggest overall winner by the time of his death in 1994.

In the race for best r&b performance, *Variety* quoted disgruntled music leaders who decried the omission of Fats Domino and Ray Charles. The nominations "stretched the meaning" of rhythm and blues by including Harry Belafonte and Nat King Cole, according to one unnamed critic who also maintained that "the only legitimate nomination was the Champs' 'Tequila.'" Happily, that same group turned out to be the Grammy champs, marking their latest stroke of good luck, which began when it was formed hastily from the musicians present when guitarist Dave Burgess recorded a "B" side to his "Train to Nowhere" release for Gene Autry's new Challenge label. (Autry's famous horse was named Champion, thus suggesting the band's name.) "Nowhere" went nowhere, but when deejays discovered "Tequila" on the flip side, the Champs became the first instrumental group ever to reach the top of the charts, and their single ended up as the year's fifth-best seller.

A controversy erupted over the prize for best country & western performance, which went to the Kingston Trio for the year's number-six-ranked "Tom Dooley," a traditional Blue Ridge Mountains folk song about a man hanged for murder in 1868. Critics maintained that its *folk* quality didn't necessarily make it a *country* song.

Perry Como triggered discord, too, when he beat out Sinatra, Modugno and Andy Williams in the category of Best Vocal Performance Male. The victory was considered a major upset, even though "Star" was Como's 16th single to sell a million copies and the year's 17th-ranked disc.

Broadway's *The Music Man* (Best Original Cast Album, Broadway or TV) was the year's third-best-selling album. When sixth-ranked *Gigi* won best film soundtrack, an awkward moment of confusion followed. One of N.A.R.A.S.'s founders, Jesse Kaye, was seated at the same table with André Previn, who composed the movie's score, but not its songs, which were penned by the Broadway team of Alan Jay Lerner and Frederick Loewe. Kaye told *Grammy Pulse:* "We didn't know who should be the one to go up and get it. There was no clear-cut decision at that time, who gets what!" (It was Previn who was finally designated as the winner.)

In terms of sales, however, nothing topped the recipient of three awards, "The Chipmunk Song," which became the fastest-selling record of all time in 1958. It sold 3.5 million copies in five weeks—and 7 million in all.

The Chipmunks were the creation of a failed California raisin farmer, David Seville (born Ross Bagdasarian), who came up with the idea for the cartoon-drawn singing trio after encountering a stubborn chipmunk who refused to budge off the road in California's Yosemite Park. For fun, he named his three Chipmunks Alvin, Simon and Theodore after three executives at Liberty Records (Alvin Bennett, Sy Waronker and Ted Keep) and employed tape-recorder tricks to simulate their voices by distorting his own at different speeds. The result was a Christmas novelty tune, "The Chipmunk Song," that scored four Grammy nominations and won Best Recording for Children, Best Comedy Performance, and Best Engineered Recording, Novelty. The Chipmunks later became a popular TV cartoon series and inspired further songs that sold more than 30 million copies by the time Seville died of a heart attack in 1972 .

Among the other multiple Grammy winners was Ella Fitzgerald, who, like Mancini, would come to dominate the early ceremonies, winning seven awards in the first five years. She scored two in Grammy's debut year: best female vocal performance for *Ella Fitzgerald Sings the Irving Berlin Song Book* (also nominated for Album of the Year) and best individual jazz performance for *Ella Fitzgerald Sings the Duke Ellington Song Book,* which was the first in her "song book" series.

Another veteran jazz great, Count

> ## Nearly half of RCA's sales were due to Elvis Presley, who wasn't nominated.

Basie, also won two awards, both for his musical collection *Basie,* which was voted Best Performance by a Dance Band and Best Jazz Performance Group. Basie's and Fitzgerald's victories were popular on Grammy night, but *Variety* reported considerable discord in the jazz categories when their nominations were announced. "N.A.R.A.S. was charged with riding a few particular hobby horses . . . and ignoring the mainstream of current jazz creativity," the paper noted. "Where, one jazz expert asked, were names like Charles Mingus, Miles Davis, Thelonius Monk, or Gerry Milligan?" One lesser-known, Billy May, did receive a statuette for Best Performance by an Orchestra. May had been freelancing solo as a trumpet player and arranger around Hollywood for several years after dropping out of a band in 1954, but he reassembled a group a few years later to pull off the winning *Billy May's Big Fat Brass.*

The *L.A. Mirror* hinted at provinciality in the classical music competitions, noting, "Local artists made a strong showing in the seven classical categories, winning four trophies: *Gaîté Parisienne* by the Hollywood Bowl Symphony, under Felix Slatkin, for best classical orchestral performance; the Hollywood String Quartet's *Beethoven Quartet No. 13,* for Best Classical Chamber Music Performance, giving Slatkin a second award; *Virtuoso* by the Roger Wagner Chorale, Best Operatic or Choral Classical Performance; and Laurindo Almeida's *Duets with Spanish Guitar* Best Engineered Classical Record."

Critics were mixed on whether or not the prizes were deserved. "These performances by the Hollywood Quartet are not profound," *High Fidelity* wrote, but the magazine did cheer the success of *Gaîté Parisienne*: "There have been a number of glittering *Gaîtés* before, but none that shine as brightly as this from one end of the tonal spectrum to the other."

The winner of best classical instrumental performance was a shoo-in considering the LP was also a contender for Album of the Year. Van Cliburn had created an international stir when he won the Tchaikovsky piano competition in the Soviet Union. Two days upon his return, RCA Victor recorded *Tchaikovsky: Concerto No. 1 in B Flat Minor* when Van Cliburn performed it to a frenzy of "bravos!" at Carnegie Hall. It quickly became the best-selling classical album of all time, a record it would hold for two decades.

Fifty years after guitarist Andrés Segovia appeared in Granada to give his first concert performance, Decca released his *Golden Jubilee,* a three-disc tribute spanning compositions by 17th-century masters such as Roncalli to 20th-century composers like Manuel Ponce, who wrote specifically for Segovia. The reviews were ecstatic. "Nothing can be more alive or humanly expressive than the guitar in Segovia's hands," cheered *High Fidelity*. The magazine also applauded the choice for Grammy's vocal soloist award: Renata Tebaldi, whose *Recital of Songs and Arias* included 13 Italian works and 1 Spanish tune. Noted *High Fidelity:* "Those who maintain that Renata Tebaldi possesses the most beautiful tone of any present-day soprano will find their most potent argument in this recital."

Capitol had the most wins among record manufacturers, taking 10 of the 28 awards. RCA received 4 statuettes,

"The Chipmunk Song," winner of three awards, was the fastest-selling single in music history.

Bagdasarian Productions

Decca and Liberty 3 each. *Variety* said, "Some of the major disc company execs, whose labels were shut out of all categories, voiced some complaints about the voting system, but they, too, will still stick with N.A.R.A.S., hoping the kinks will be ironed out by the time it gets around to voting again next year."

"The Grammy Awards came to be a real party from the start," Mancini wrote in his memoirs, but also noted that many of the early participants, like himself, failed to realize their full importance. "There was this little award that no one had had in their hands before, no one had ever seen before. I thought, that's nice and took [the statuettes] home . . . and they sat there until next year when their brothers arrived. . . . When I think back, I guess the first one was kind of historic although at the time I didn't realize where the Grammys were going. I didn't know it was going to become such a world-wide enterprise."

• 1958 •

Awards were bestowed at the Beverly Hilton Hotel in Los Angeles on May 4, 1959, for music released during 1958.

ALBUM OF THE YEAR
• *The Music from Peter Gunn* (TV series soundtrack), Henry Mancini. RCA.

Ella Fitzgerald Sings the Irving Berlin Song Book, Ella Fitzgerald. Verve.
Come Fly with Me, Frank Sinatra. Capitol.
Only the Lonely, Frank Sinatra. Capitol.
Tchaikovsky: Concerto No. 1 in B Flat Minor, Op. 23, Van Cliburn. RCA.

RECORD OF THE YEAR

- "Nel Blu Dipinto di Blu (Volare)," Domenico Modugno. Decca.
"Catch a Falling Star," Perry Como. RCA.
"The Chipmunk Song," David Seville. Liberty.
"Fever," Peggy Lee. Capitol.
"Witchcraft," Frank Sinatra. Capitol.

SONG OF THE YEAR
(Songwriter's Award)

- "Nel Blu Dipinto di Blu (Volare)," Domenico Modugno (lyrics collaborator Franco Migliacci not noted by N.A.R.A.S.).
"Catch a Falling Star," Paul Vance, Lee Pockriss.
"Fever," Johnny Davenport, Eddie Cooley.
"Gigi," Alan J. Lerner, Frederick Loewe.
"Witchcraft," Cy Coleman, Carolyn Leigh.

BEST VOCAL PERFORMANCE, MALE

- Perry Como, "Catch a Falling Star." RCA.
Domenico Modugno, "Nel Blu Dipinto di Blu (Volare)." Decca.
Frank Sinatra, "Come Fly with Me." Capitol.
Frank Sinatra, "Witchcraft." Capitol.
Andy Williams, "Hawaiian Wedding Song." Cadence.

BEST VOCAL PERFORMANCE, FEMALE

- Ella Fitzgerald, *Ella Fitzgerald Sings the Irving Berlin Song Book*. Verve.
Doris Day, "Everybody Loves a Lover." Columbia.
Eydie Gormé, *Eydie in Love*. ABC-Paramount.
Peggy Lee, "Fever." Capitol.
Keely Smith, "I Wish You Love." Capitol.

BEST PERFORMANCE BY A VOCAL GROUP OR CHORUS

- Louis Prima, Keely Smith, "That Old Black Magic." Capitol.
King Sisters, "Imagination." Capitol.
Kingston Trio, "Tom Dooley." Capitol.

Variety hailed the first Grammy ceremony on the bottom of page one. Coverage of the first Emmy show 10 years earlier had been buried on page 6.

Kirby Stone Four, "Baubles, Bangles and Beads." Columbia.
Lambert, Hendricks & Ross, *Sing a Song of Basie*. ABC-Paramount.

BEST PERFORMANCE BY A DANCE BAND

- Count Basie, *Basie*. Roulette.
Ray Anthony, *The Music from Peter Gunn*. Capitol.
Warren Covington & the Tommy Dorsey Orchestra, *Tea for Two Cha Cha*. Decca.
Jonah Jones, "Baubles, Bangles and Beads." Capitol.
Perez Prado, "Patricia." RCA.

BEST PERFORMANCE BY AN ORCHESTRA

- Billy May, *Billy May's Big Fat Brass*. Capitol.
Buddy Defranco, "Cross Country Suite." Dot.
Esquivel, *Other Worlds, Other Sounds*. RCA.
Jack Kane, *Kane Is Able*. Coral.
Henry Mancini, *The Music from Peter Gunn* (TV series soundtrack). RCA.

Johnny Mandel, *I Want to Live*. United
  Artists.
David Rose & His Orchestra with André
  Previn, *Young Man's Lament*. MGM.
George Shearing, *Burnished Brass*.
  Capitol.

BEST COUNTRY & WESTERN
PERFORMANCE

• Kingston Trio, "Tom Dooley." Capitol.
Everly Brothers, "All I Have to Do Is
  Dream." Cadence.
Everly Brothers, "Bird Dog." Cadence.
Don Gibson, "Oh Lonesome Me." RCA.
Jimmie Rodgers, "Oh, Oh, I'm Falling
  in Love Again." Roulette.

BEST COMPOSITION, OVER 5
MINUTES' DURATION

• "Cross Country Suite," Nelson Riddle.
"Vanessa," Samuel Barber.
I Want to Live, Johnny Mandel.
Victory at Sea, Vol. 3, Richard Rodgers.
"Mahagonny," Kurt Weill.

BEST ORIGINAL CAST ALBUM,
BROADWAY OR TV

• *The Music Man* (Broadway cast).
  Meredith Willson, composer. Capitol.
Flower Drum Song (Broadway cast). Sal-
  vatore dell'Isola, musical director.
  Richard Rodgers, composer. Columbia.
Sound of Jazz, Seven Lively Arts (TV
  series soundtrack). Count Basie, Bil-
  lie Holliday, others. Columbia.
Victory at Sea, Vol. 2. (TV series sound-
  track). RCA Victor Symphony
  Orchestra, Richard Rodgers. RCA.
The Music from Peter Gunn (TV series
  soundtrack). Henry Mancini. RCA.

BEST SOUNDTRACK ALBUM,
DRAMATIC PICTURE SCORE OR
ORIGINAL CAST

• *Gigi*, André Previn. MGM.
Auntie Mame, Ray Heindorf Orchestra.
  Warner Bros.
The Bridge on the River Kwai, Malcolm
  Arnold. Columbia.
I Want to Live, Johnny Mandel. United
  Artists.

South Pacific, Alfred Newman, orchestra
  conductor. RCA.

BEST ARRANGEMENT

• Henry Mancini, *The Music from Peter
  Gunn* (Henry Mancini). RCA.
Billy May, *Come Fly with Me* (Frank
  Sinatra). Capitol.
Jack Marshall, "Fever" (Peggy Lee).
  Capitol.
Billy May, *Billy May's Big Fat Brass*
  (Billy May). Capitol.
Nelson Riddle, "Witchcraft" (Frank
  Sinatra). Capitol.

BEST RHYTHM & BLUES
PERFORMANCE

• Champs, "Tequila." Challenge.
Harry Belafonte, *Belafonte Sings the
  Blues*. RCA.
Nat King Cole, *Looking Back*.
  Capitol.
Earl Grant, *The End*. Decca.
Perez Prado, "Patricia." RCA.

BEST JAZZ PERFORMANCE,
INDIVIDUAL

• Ella Fitzgerald, *Ella Fitzgerald Sings
  the Duke Ellington Song Book*.
  Verve.
Jonah Jones, "Baubles, Bangles and
  Beads." Capitol.
George Shearing, *Burnished Brass*.
  Capitol.
Matty Mattock, "Dixieland Story."
  Warner Bros.
Jonah Jones, *Jumpin' with Jonah*.
  Capitol.

BEST JAZZ PERFORMANCE,
GROUP

• Count Basie, *Basie*. Roulette.
Jonah Jones, "Baubles, Bangles and
  Beads." Capitol.
George Shearing, *Burnished Brass*.
  Capitol.
Four Freshmen, *The Four Freshmen in
  Person*. Capitol.
Basie Rhythm Section, Dave Lambert
  Singers, *Sing a Song of Basie*. ABC-
  Paramount.

BEST CLASSICAL PERFORMANCE, ORCHESTRA (CONDUCTOR'S AWARD)

- Felix Slatkin conducting the Hollywood Bowl Symphony, *Gaîté Parisienne*. Capitol.
- Leonard Bernstein conducting the New York Philharmonic, *Stravinsky: Le Sacre du Printemps*. Columbia.
- Pierre Monteux conducting the London Symphony, *Rimsky-Korsakov: Scheherazade*. RCA.
- Charles Munch conducting the Boston Symphony, *Barber: Meditation and Dance of Vengeance*. RCA.
- Eugene Ormandy conducting the Philadelphia Orchestra, *Prokofiev: Symphony No. 5 in B Flat Major*. Columbia.
- Bruno Walter conducting the Columbia Symphony Orchestra, *Beethoven: Symphony No. 6 in F Major*. Columbia.
- Bruno Walter conducting the New York Philharmonic (Westminster Choir; solos: Emilia Cundari, Maureen Forrester), *Mahler: Symphony No. 2 in C Minor*. Columbia.

BEST CLASSICAL PERFORMANCE, CHAMBER MUSIC (INCLUDING CHAMBER ORCHESTRA)

- Hollywood String Quartet, *Beethoven: Quartet No. 13*. Capitol.
- Budapest String Quartet, *Ravel: Quartet in F Major; Debussy: Quartet in G Minor*. Columbia.
- Pablo Casals, Eugene Istomin, Fuchs, *Beethoven: Trio in E Flat Major; Trio in D Major*. Columbia.
- Jascha Heifetz, William Primrose, Gregor Piatigorsky, *Beethoven: Trio in E Flat, Op. 3*. RCA.
- Jascha Heifetz, William Primrose, Gregor Piatigorsky, *Beethoven: Trio in G, Op. 9, No. 1; Trio in C Minor, Op. 9, No. 3*. RCA.

BEST CLASSICAL PERFORMANCE, INSTRUMENTAL (WITH CONCERTO SCALE ACCOMPANIMENT)

- Van Cliburn (Kondrashin Symphony), *Tchaikovsky: Concerto No. 1 in B Flat Minor, Op. 23*. RCA.

Andrés Segovia, *Segovia Golden Jubilee* (last record in set). Decca.

Emil Gilels (Fritz Reiner conducting the Chicago Symphony), *Brahms: Piano Concerto No. 2*. RCA.

Leonard Pennario, *Rachmaninov: Rhapsody on a Theme of Paganini*. Capitol.

Artur Rubinstein (Alfred Wallenstein conducting the Symphony of the Air), *Saint-Saëns: Piano Concerto No. 2*. RCA.

Isaac Stern (Leonard Bernstein conducting the New York Philharmonic), *Bartók: Concerto for Violin*. Columbia.

BEST CLASSICAL PERFORMANCE, INSTRUMENTAL (OTHER THAN CONCERTO SCALE ACCOMPANIMENT)

- Andrés Segovia, *Segovia Golden Jubilee*. Decca.
- Marcel Grandjany, *Music for the Harp*. Capitol.
- Vladimir Horowitz, *Horowitz Plays Chopin*. RCA.
- Wanda Landowska, *Art of the Harpsichord*. RCA.
- Nathan Milstein, *Beethoven Sonatas Nos. 8 and 9*. Capitol.

BEST CLASSICAL PERFORMANCE, OPERATIC OR CHORAL

- Roger Wagner Chorale, *Virtuoso*. Capitol.
- Maria Callas, Tito Gobbi, *Rossini: Barber of Seville*. Angel.
- Erich Leinsdorf conducting the Rome Opera House Chorus and Orchestra (solos: Peters, Pace, Carlin, Paima, Peerce, Maero, Tozzi), *Donizetti: Lucia di Lammermoor*. RCA.
- Erich Leinsdorf conducting the Rome Opera House Chorus and Orchestra (solos: Cifferi, Mattioli, Moffo, Zeri, Elias, Pace, Carlin, Valletti, Catalani Cesari, Mineo, Corena [Monreale]), *Puccini: Madama Butterfly*. RCA.
- Dimitri Mitropoulos, Metropolitan Opera Chorus and Orchestra (solos: Steber, Elias, Resnick, Gedda, Nagy,

Cehanovsky, Tozzi), *Barber: Vanessa*. RCA.

Dom David Nicholson directing the Choir of the Abbey of Mt. Angel and C. Robert Zimmerman directing the Portland Symphony Choir, *Victoria: Requiem Mass*. RCA.

BEST CLASSICAL PERFORMANCE, VOCAL SOLOIST (WITH OR WITHOUT ORCHESTRA)

• Renata Tebaldi, *Recital of Songs and Arias*. London.

Maria Callas, *Cherubini: Medea*. Mercury.

Salli Terri, *Duets for Spanish Guitar*. Capitol.

Eileen Farrell, *Eileen Farrell As Medea*. Columbia.

Eileen Farrell (Charles Munch conducting the Boston Symphony), *Wagner: Prelude and Liebestod (Tristan und Isolde); Brünnhilde's Immolation (Die Götterdämmerung)*. RCA.

BEST ENGINEERED RECORDING, CLASSICAL

• Sherwood Hall III, *Duets for a Spanish Guitar* (Almeida and Terri). Capitol.

Sherwood Hall III, *Gaîté Parisienne* (Felix Slatkin). Capitol.

Prokofiev: Lieutenant Kijé; Stravinsky: Song of the Nightingale (Fritz Reiner). RCA.

Stravinsky: The Rite of Spring (Leonard Bernstein). Columbia.

BEST DOCUMENTARY OR SPOKEN WORD RECORDING

• *The Best of the Stan Freberg Shows*, Stan Freberg. Capitol.

Great American Speeches, Melvyn Douglas, Vincent Price, Carl Sandburg, Ed Begley. Caedmon.

Green Christmas, Stan Freberg. Capitol.

Improvisations to Music, Mike Nichols, Elaine May. Mercury.

The Lady from Philadelphia, Marion Anderson (Rupp, Morrow). RCA.

Two Interviews of Our Time, Henry Jacobs, Woody Leafer. Fantasy.

BEST COMEDY PERFORMANCE

• David Seville, "The Chipmunk Song." Liberty.

Stan Freberg, *The Best of the Stan Freberg Shows*. Capitol.

Stan Freberg, *Green Christmas*. Capitol.

Mike Nichols, Elaine May, *Improvisations to Music*. Mercury.

Mort Sahl, *The Future Lies Ahead*. Verve.

BEST RECORDING FOR CHILDREN

• "The Chipmunk Song," David Seville. Liberty.

"Children's Marching Song," Cyril Stapleton. London.

Fun in Shariland, Shari Lewis. Victor.

Mommy, Give Me a Drinka Water, Danny Kaye. Capitol.

Tubby the Tuba, Jose Ferrer. MGM.

"Witch Doctor," David Seville. Liberty.

BEST ENGINEERED RECORDING, NOVELTY

• Ted Keep, "The Chipmunk Song" (David Seville). Liberty.

Hugh Davies, *Billy May's Big Fat Brass* (Billy May). Capitol.

Luis P. Valentin, *Come Fly with Me* (Frank Sinatra). Capitol.

Luis P. Valentin, "Witchcraft" (Frank Sinatra). Capitol.

Rafael O. Valentin, *Other Worlds, Other Sounds* (Esquivel). RCA.

BEST ALBUM COVER

• Frank Sinatra, *Only the Lonely* (Frank Sinatra). Capitol.

Ray Heindorf, Ray Rennahan, *For Whom the Bells Toll*. Warner Bros.

David Rose, *Ira Ironstrings Plays Music for People with $3.98*. Warner Bros.

Marvin Schwartz, *Come Fly with Me* (Frank Sinatra). Capitol.

Charles Ward, *Julie* (Julie London). Liberty.

• 1959 •

Sinatra's Revenge

Following the modest success of the initial awards ceremony, N.A.R.A.S. was so eager to move on to the next set of prizes that the second annual Grammys were held just six months after the first. The eligibility period for contending nominees was only eight months long, but it was a time span that included releases of important new music by such big winners from the first Grammys as Ella Fitzgerald and Henry Mancini. And losers, too. The heavily nominated Frank Sinatra suffered a near shutout last year, but now he was back with new bids that didn't compete against each other within the same categories. For the most important prize of all—Record of the Year—Sinatra was up against two nominees he considered particularly irksome: teen idol Bobby Darin, who was often likened to a young Sinatra (much to the elder's dismay) and the greasy-haired King of rock & roll, whom the Chairman of the Board openly despised: Elvis Presley.

Presley's three nominations (the same number as Sinatra) represented a serious new effort on N.A.R.A.S.'s part to acknowledge the growing rock revolution, just as it seemed to ignore it deliberately only six months earlier. N.A.R.A.S. was also serious about reaching beyond its California base to the easterners vital to the record industry and the future success of the Grammy Awards. In what would become a tradition for a decade in the future, the West Coast ceremony was held in concert with an East Coast party at the Waldorf-Astoria Hotel in New York City.

Most of the action was out in L.A., where excitement reigned as the awards were set to be shared with a national TV

Ella Fitzgerald returned as a double winner with "But Not for Me" and *Ella Swings Lightly*.

audience for the first time. The live NBC broadcast took place at the network's Burbank studios immediately following the awards banquet at the Beverly Hilton Hotel. Ten of the year's 34 winners were announced a month earlier so they could be on hand for the program. Seven showed up. Duke Ellington and Nat King Cole were missing, but they had performed on tape in New York a few weeks earlier. Frank Sinatra was unavailable altogether, but the show put on by the remaining nine performers was good enough to deserve a special LP that bore a N.A.R.A.S. label and was underwritten and distributed by the show's sponsor, Watchmakers of Switzerland, which sold the recording in jewelry shops for a dollar. Emcee of both the L.A. awards ceremony and TV broadcast was Meredith Willson, composer of *The Music Man,* which won Best Original Cast Album last year.

Variety applauded the TV show: "With the payola charges currently swirling around the music business, the disc industry put its best side forward in its first TV presentation of its Grammy Awards. The overall approach was handled with savvy and imagination, adding up to a fairly solid hour of entertainment."

Frank Sinatra snubbed the awards ceremony, reputedly because he was sore about his humiliating losses last year. Again he was in the running for both Album and Record of the Year and he needed a win badly. His recent work with Capitol Records, begun in 1953, marked a crucial career comeback for him as he made the changeover from teen idol of the war-torn 1940s to seasoned crooner and screen star of the quieter and safer Eisenhower '50s. Record buyers had discovered him again, but acknowledgment from his industry peers was still elusive.

At the first Grammys, his two top LPs, *Come Fly with Me* and *Only the Lonely,* came up with only one prize between them—Best Album Cover, which was mistakenly awarded to Ol' Blue Eyes instead of to the album's art director. This time Sinatra implored his fans to *Come Dance with Me* instead and his luck changed dramatically.

He not only won the album award but was also lauded for giving the year's best male vocal performance, an honor he lost last year in a major upset to Perry Como. *Come Dance* had the year's Best

> ## Sinatra rebounded from his humiliating defeats last year.

Arrangement, too, a prize that went to Billy May.

By virtue of his absence, however, Sinatra was literally upstaged by the young "imitator" whose music, complained the *L.A. Herald & Express,* was so popular that it was "super-charging the air around any given juke-box" in America.

"I'd like to be a legend by the time I'm 25 years old," Bobby Darin had told *Life* magazine. By 1958, at age 22 and after watching his first half dozen singles turn out to be flops, Darin finally got his first break: "Splish Splash" hit number three in the nation. But Darin didn't want to be known just for pop tunes. "In night clubs I lean to other things," he told *Billboard* proudly. "I even do 'Mack the Knife' from *The Threepenny Opera,*" the Kurt Weill–Bertolt Brecht musical.

Darin based his version of "Mack the Knife" on an earlier rendition by Louis Armstrong and included it in his album *That's All* as an example of his musical versatility. He opposed its release as a 45, but Atco proceeded to distribute it anyway and "Mack" ended up ruling the charts for nine weeks at number one, becoming the best-selling single of the year. It also became Darin's signature song—and Grammy's Record of the Year. By the end of 1959, "Mack" shared the Top 10 with another Darin hit, "Dream Lover," and N.A.R.A.S. acknowledged him with its first Best New Artist award even though he was really a "new artist" when "Splish Splash" was released a year earlier.

The Grammys' Song of the Year turned out to be the year's number-two hit tune, much "to everyone's surprise," noted the *L.A. Examiner,* since the choice was a country & western song. "The Battle of New Orleans" described the final fight of the War of 1812, which saw U.S. General Andrew Jackson defeat the

British on January 8, 1815, two weeks after the war was declared over in far-away London and Washington. To celebrate the victory, fiddlers across America played a catchy new tune called "The Eighth of January."

One hundred and forty years later, Jimmy Driftwood, a schoolteacher from Snowball, Arkansas, penned lyrics to a song that subsequently came to the attention of country singer Johnny Horton. Horton had been struggling for professional kudos since 1951 but had so far failed to score a pop hit. With "New Orleans," his battle would be over. While the trophy for songwriting went to Driftwood, Horton won the prize for giving the year's best country & western performance. It was Driftwood, however, not Horton, who was asked to perform the song on the Grammy telecast.

Duke Ellington won the first 3 of his 11 eventual Grammys for his first attempt at scoring a motion picture. *Anatomy of a Murder* was a gripping courtroom drama directed by Otto Preminger and starring James Stewart, Lee Remick, George C. Scott and the Duke himself in a cameo appearance. Ellington's score was voted best soundtrack album as well as Best Performance by a Dance Band and Best Musical Composition, More Than 5 Minutes.

After a stellar career that first brought Ellington to prominence in 1927 when he performed at New York's Cotton Club, the Duke's popularity had fallen to a low ebb by the mid-1950s. By decade's end, his career experienced a resurgence, however, thanks partly to Ella Fitzgerald's *Song Book* salute that thrilled critics, rallied record buyers and won her a Grammy at the first awards show. This time Fitzgerald was back winning two again: best solo jazz performance for her album *Ella Swings Lightly* and best female vocal performance for her single

"But Not for Me." Trumpet player Jonah Jones and his quartet gave the year's best jazz group performance on *I Dig Chicks*. Dinah Washington was acclaimed for Best Rhythm & Blues Performance for her classic version of "What a Diff'rence a Day Makes," which beat out Elvis Presley's "A Big Hunk O' Love." Veteran Hollywood bandleader David Rose won the orchestral honors for his work with André Previn on the latter's hit *Like Young* LP.

Artur Rubinstein won two classical awards for his Beethoven Sonatas Nos. 21 and 18 (the recording has "moments of delicacy and quiet beauty that merit commendation," said *High Fidelity*). The Boston Symphony Orchestra's salute to Debussy was called "sumptuous" by the critics and won the award for best classical orchestra performance.

Pianist Van Cliburn had a best-selling album in *Billboard*'s Top 20 of 1959: *Tchaikovsky: Concerto No. 1 in B Flat Minor*, which won a classical Grammy last year and was a contender for the top Album of the Year prize. This year he won a new Grammy for Best Classical Performance, Concerto or Instrumental Soloist, for his *Rachmaninov: Piano Concerto No. 3*, which was also a best album contender. Both recordings were made at Van Cliburn's famed Carnegie Hall concert of May 19, 1958, which heralded his triumphant return from the Soviet Union after winning the Tchaikovsky piano competition.

The opera awards went to Swedish tenor Jussi Björling and to the recording of Mozart's *The Marriage of Figaro* by the Vienna Philharmonic with Erich Leinsdorf conducting.

"An amateur musical group of 350 singers walked away with the award for best performance by a chorus," noted the *L.A. Herald & Express*. "It was the Mormon Tabernacle Choir from Salt Lake

> "The Grammy," said *Variety*, "still has to come to terms with rock & roll."

City out-polling such professionals as the Ames Brothers, the Kingston Trio, and the Robert Shaw Chorale to win with its rendition of 'Battle Hymn of the Republic.'" The Kingston Trio did end up with the new award for best folk performance for their album *The Kingston Trio at Large,* which was the fifth-best-selling LP of the year.

There was a tie for Best Broadway Show Album between *Gypsy* and *Redhead,* while André Previn and Ken Darby's rendition of Gershwin's *Porgy and Bess* won the honors for best film soundtrack. The movie featured Sidney Poitier, Dorothy Dandridge and Pearl Bailey in the lead roles and was the last film produced by studio mogul Samuel Goldwyn.

Last year Capitol won the most awards, taking 10 of the 28 categories. This year the champ was RCA, which nabbed 11 trophies in the year's 34 categories, followed by Columbia with 9, Capitol 7, Atco 3 and Verve 3. Clearly, a pattern was already developing: Large companies had an obvious advantage over the smaller record labels. The big firms often paid the annual $15 membership fee for large numbers of employees to join N.A.R.A.S.' and then benefited from their staffers voting—out of loyalty or as a result of corporate pressure—for their own company's music. *Variety* observed, "Predominance of the majors is again evident with the indies virtually shut out."

Saturday Review cried foul. "Of the 40-odd nominations . . . in the eight categories involving jazz and classical performances," it noted, "a total of 30 (or some 80 percent of the whole) are products of RCA." RCA's dominance of the year's competition was actually worse than that: It scored almost 100 nominations, a sum larger than the bids earned by all other record companies combined. The magazine accused N.A.R.A.S. of tolerating "stuffed ballot boxes" and added, "Whatever the causes, the results, plainly, are awards without dis-

Nat King Cole beat Elvis Presley to nab the new "Top 40" award for "Midnight Flyer," which never actually landed in music charts' Top 40.

tinction, to which no well-informed record buyer or critic would attach any significance."

Columbia President Goddard Lieberson agreed and delivered "a hot blast" in an open letter, published in *Variety,* to N.A.R.A.S.'s West Coast and East Coast chapter presidents. The nominations, he said, "in no way reflect either the status, the quality, or the scope of the record industry. . . . There is no merit in self-served awards won by the sort of electioneering and lobbying which I believe must invariably accompany the N.A.R.A.S. method of balloting." N.A.R.A.S. said it would investigate the problem and try to take corrective action by next year.

Some critics accused voters of determining the top prizes on the basis of record sales. "The N.A.R.A.S. membership still seems to be using the best-seller charts to determine Record of the Year," said *Variety,* "and it still has to come to terms with rock & roll."

Rock & roll, however, did somewhat better this year. At least its "King," Elvis

Presley, was nominated in the Record of the Year lineup for "A Fool Such As I," even though the tune ranked only a distant 50 in *Billboard*'s year-end rankings. Presley's musical output was sparse in 1959 because he was still serving in the U.S. Army overseas.

N.A.R.A.S. began this year's Grammy race by making a serious effort to recognize all rock artists by including a new category that was originally to be called Best Rock & Roll Performance. In the end, however, conservative factions within the Recording Academy won out, the acknowledgment was scrapped and the category title was switched to Best Performance by a "Top 40" Artist. The new award went instead to another "King"—Nat Cole—for "Midnight Flyer," which was not a rock song and never even made it into the top 40. The victory is considered one of Grammy's most embarrassing vote results histori-

cally, since Cole beat Presley's "A Big Hunk O' Love," which charted at number 39 for the year.

The year 1959 was a tragic time for rock & roll, seeing the deaths of Buddy Holly, Ritchie Valens and the Big Bopper (J. P. Richardson) in a plane crash after their concert at Clear Lake, Iowa. The sound was still having trouble gaining popular acceptance, too, and not just from bullheaded music listeners. A story on page one of the *L.A. Mirror* on the same day that the Grammy results were announced (on an inside page) reported that dairy cows now joined the ranks of rock detractors. "Rock 'n' Roll Makes Cows Tighten Up," said the paper's grabber headline. "That music tightens the cow's glandular system and deters milking," said a spokesman for the American Dairy Association in the article. "Waltz music produces much better milking conditions."

• 1959 •

Awards were bestowed on November 29, 1959, at ceremonies held simultaneously at the Beverly Hilton Hotel in Los Angeles and the Waldorf-Astoria Hotel in New York for the eligibility period January 1 to August 31, 1959. A post-Grammy show was broadcast live by NBC.

ALBUM OF THE YEAR
• *Come Dance with Me*, Frank Sinatra. Capitol.
Belafonte at Carnegie Hall, Harry Belafonte. RCA.
More Music from Peter Gunn, Henry Mancini. RCA.
Rachmaninov: Piano Concerto No. 3, Van Cliburn, Kiril Kondrashin. RCA.
Victory at Sea, Vol. 1, Robert Russell Bennett. RCA.

RECORD OF THE YEAR
• "Mack the Knife," Bobby Darin. Atco.

"A Fool Such as I," Elvis Presley. RCA.
"High Hopes," Frank Sinatra. Capitol.
"Like Young," André Previn. MGM.
"The Three Bells," Browns. RCA.

SONG OF THE YEAR
(Songwriter's Award)
• "The Battle of New Orleans," Jimmy Driftwood.
"High Hopes," Sammy Cahn, Jimmy Van Heusen.
"I Know," Karl Stutz, Edith Lindeman.
"Like Young," Paul Francis Webster, André Previn.
"Small World," Jule Styne, Stephen Sondheim.

BEST NEW ARTIST
• Bobby Darin
Edd Byrnes
Mark Murphy
Johnny Restivo
Mavis Rivers

BEST VOCAL PERFORMANCE, MALE

- Frank Sinatra, *Come Dance with Me.* Capitol.
Harry Belafonte, *Belafonte at Carnegie Hall.* RCA.
Jesse Belvin, "Guess Who." RCA.
Bobby Darin, "Mack the Knife." Atco.
Robert Merrill, *An Evening with Lerner and Loewe.* RCA.

BEST VOCAL PERFORMANCE, FEMALE

- Ella Fitzgerald, "But Not for Me." Verve.
Lena Horne, *Porgy and Bess.* RCA.
Peggy Lee, "Alright, Okay." Capitol.
Pat Suzuki, *Broadway '59.* RCA.
Caterina Valente, *La Strada del Amore.* RCA.

BEST PERFORMANCE BY A VOCAL GROUP OR CHORUS

- Mormon Tabernacle Choir, Richard Condi conducting, "Battle Hymn of the Republic." Columbia.
Ames Brothers, *Ames Brothers Sing Famous Hits of Famous Quartets.* RCA.
Browns, "The Three Bells." RCA.
Kingston Trio, *The Kingston Trio at Large.* Capitol.
Robert Shaw Chorale, *The Stephen Foster Song Book.* RCA.

BEST PERFORMANCE BY A "TOP 40" ARTIST

- Nat King Cole, "Midnight Flyer." Capitol.
Coasters, "Charlie Brown." Atco.
Elvis Presley, "A Big Hunk O' Love." RCA.
Floyd Robinson, "Makin' Love." RCA.
Neil Sedaka, *Neil Sedaka.* RCA.
Sarah Vaughan, "Broken Hearted Melody." Mercury.

BEST RHYTHM & BLUES PERFORMANCE

- Dinah Washington, "What a Diff'rence a Day Makes." Mercury.

Best New Artist and Record of the Year champ ("Mack the Knife") Bobby Darin wanted to be a "legend" by age 25. He did, then died at age 37.

Jesse Belvin, "Guess Who." RCA.
The Coasters, "Charlie Brown." Atco.
Nat King Cole, "Midnight Flyer." Capitol.
Elvis Presley, "A Big Hunk O' Love." RCA.

BEST JAZZ PERFORMANCE, SOLOIST

- Ella Fitzgerald, *Ella Swings Lightly.* Verve.
Ruby Braff, *Easy Now.* RCA.
Urbie Green, *Best of New Broadway Show Hits.* RCA.
Red Norvo, *Red Norvo in Hi-Fi.* RCA.
André Previn, *Like Young.* MGM.
Bobby Troup, *Bobby Troup and His Stars of Jazz.* RCA.

BEST JAZZ PERFORMANCE, GROUP

- Jonah Jones, *I Dig Chicks.* Capitol.
Duke Ellington, *Ellington Jazz Party.* Columbia.
Henry Mancini, *More Music from Peter Gunn.* RCA.
Red Norvo, *Red Norvo in Hi-Fi.* RCA.
Shorty Rogers, *Chances Are It Swings.* RCA.

BEST COUNTRY & WESTERN PERFORMANCE

- Johnny Horton, "The Battle of New Orleans." Columbia.

Eddy Arnold, "Tennessee Stud." RCA.

Skeeter Davis, "Set Him Free." RCA.

Don Gibson, "Don't Tell Me Your Troubles." RCA.

Jim Reeves, "Home." RCA.

BEST FOLK PERFORMANCE

- Kingston Trio, *The Kingston Trio at Large*. Capitol.

Eddy Arnold, "Tennessee Stud." RCA.

Harry Belafonte, *Belafonte at Carnegie Hall*. RCA.

Jimmy Driftwood, *The Wilderness Road*. RCA.

Ralph Hunter Choir, *The Wild Wild West*. RCA.

BEST PERFORMANCE BY A DANCE BAND

- Duke Ellington, *Anatomy of a Murder*. Columbia.

Ray Anthony, *Sound Spectacular*. Capitol.

Count Basie, *Breakfast Dance and Barbecue*. Roulette.

Larry Elgart, *New Sounds at the Roosevelt*. RCA.

Glenn Miller, *For the Very First Time*. RCA.

Perez Prado, *Pops and Prado*. RCA.

BEST PERFORMANCE BY AN ORCHESTRA

- David Rose & His Orchestra with André Previn, *Like Young*. MGM.

Esquivel, *Strings Aflame*. RCA.

Henry Mancini, *More Music from Peter Gunn*. RCA.

Bob Thompson & Orchestra, *Just for Kicks*. RCA.

Stanley Wilson, *Music from M Squad*. RCA.

Hugo Winterhalter, *Two Sides of Winterhalter*. RCA.

BEST MUSICAL COMPOSITION, MORE THAN 5 MINUTES

- *Anatomy of a Murder*, Duke Ellington.

More Music from Peter Gunn, Henry Mancini.

Prokofiev: The Overture Russe, Op. 72, Serge Prokofiev.

St. Lawrence Suite, Morton Gould.

Shostakovitch: Concerto No. 2 for Piano and Orchestra, Op. 101, Dmitri Shostakovitch.

BEST BROADWAY SHOW ALBUM (Tie)

- *Gypsy*, Ethel Merman. Columbia.
- *Redhead*, Gwen Verdon. RCA.

A Party with Betty Comden and Adolph Green, Betty Comden, Adolph Green. Capitol.

Ages of Man, Sir John Gielgud. Columbia.

Once upon a Mattress, Hal Hastings, conductor. Kapp.

BEST SOUNDTRACK ALBUM OF ORIGINAL CAST FROM A MOTION PICTURE OR TV

- *Porgy and Bess*, André Previn, Ken Darby. Columbia.

The Five Pennies. Dot.

For the First Time, Mario Lanza. RCA.

Sleeping Beauty. Disneyland.

Some Like It Hot. United Artists.

BEST SOUNDTRACK ALBUM OF BACKGROUND SCORE FROM A MOTION PICTURE OR TV

- *Anatomy of a Murder*, Duke Ellington. Columbia.

More Music from Peter Gunn, Henry Mancini. RCA.

Pete Kelly's Blues, Dick Cathcart. Warner Bros.

The Music from M Squad, Stanley Wilson. RCA.

The Nun's Story, Franz Waxman. Warner Bros.

BEST ARRANGEMENT

- Billy May, *Come Dance with Me* (Frank Sinatra). Capitol.

Johnny Green, *An Evening with Lerner and Loewe*. RCA.

Richard Wess, "Mack the Knife" (Bobby Darin). Atco.

More Music from Peter Gunn (Henry Mancini). RCA.
Strings Aflame (Esquivel). RCA.
Victory at Sea, Vol. 1 (Robert Russell Bennett conducting the RCA Victor Symphony Orchestra). RCA.

BEST CLASSICAL PERFORMANCE, ORCHESTRA
(Conductor's Award)
• Charles Munch conducting the Boston Symphony, *Debussy: Images for Orchestra*. RCA.
Morton Gould & His Orchestra, *Tchaikovsky: 1812 Overture; Ravel: Boléro*. RCA.
Kiril Kondrashin conducting the RCA Victor Symphony Orchestra, *Tchaikovsky: Capriccio Italien; Rimsky-Korsakov: Capriccio Espagnol*. RCA.
Pierre Monteux conducting the Vienna Philharmonic, *Beethoven: Symphony No. 6*. RCA.
Fritz Reiner conducting the Chicago Symphony, *Rossini: Overtures*. RCA.

BEST CLASSICAL PERFORMANCE, CHAMBER MUSIC (INCLUDING CHAMBER ORCHESTRA)
• Artur Rubinstein, *Beethoven: Sonata No. 21 in C, Op. 53; Sonata No. 18 in E Flat, Op. 53, No. 3 ("Waldstein")*. RCA.
Festival Quartet, *Beethoven: Piano Quartet in E Flat, Op. 16; Schumann: Piano Quartet in E Flat, Op. 47*. RCA.
Nathan Milstein, *4 Italian Sonatas*. Capitol.
Felix Slatkin, *Cello Galaxy*. Capitol.
Felix Slatkin, *Villa-Lobos: String Quartet*. Capitol.

BEST CLASSICAL PERFORMANCE, CONCERTO OR INSTRUMENTAL SOLOIST (FULL ORCHESTRA)
• Van Cliburn (Kondrashin conducting the Symphony of the Air), *Rachmaninov: Piano Concerto No. 3*. RCA.

Jascha Heifetz (Munch conducting the Boston Symphony), *Mendelssohn: Violin Concerto No. 2 in E Minor, Op. 64; Prokofiev: Violin Concerto No. 2 in G Minor*. RCA.
Vladimir Horowitz (Toscanini conducting the NBC Symphony), *Tchaikovsky: Piano Concerto No. 1*. RCA.
Artur Rubinstein (Krips conducting the RCA Victor Symphony), *Brahms: Piano Concerto No. 2*. RCA.
Henryk Szeryng (Monteux conducting the London Symphony), *Brahms: Violin Concerto in D*. RCA.

BEST CLASSICAL PERFORMANCE, INSTRUMENTAL SOLOIST (WITHOUT ORCHESTRAL ACCOMPANIMENT)
• Artur Rubinstein, *Beethoven: Sonata No. 21 in C, Op. 53; Sonata No. 18 in E Flat, Op. 53, No. 3 ("Waldstein")*. RCA.
Laurindo Almeida, *Danzas*. Capitol.
Glenn Gould, *Berg: Sonata for Piano, Op. 1; Křenek: Sonata No. 3, Op. 92, No. 4; Schoenberg: 3 Piano Pieces, Op. 11*. Columbia.
Jaime Laredo, *Presenting Jaime Laredo*. RCA.
Nathan Milstein, *4 Italian Sonatas*. Capitol.
Leonard Pennario, *Pennario Plays*. Capitol.

BEST CLASSICAL PERFORMANCE, OPERA CAST OR CHORAL
• Erich Leinsdorf conducting the Vienna Philharmonic (solos: Peters, London, Della, Casa), *Mozart: The Marriage of Figaro*. RCA.
Fausto Cleva conducting the Metropolitan Opera Orchestra and Chorus (solos: Stevens, Del Monago), *Saint-Saëns: Samson and Delilah*. RCA.
Richard Condie conducting the Mormon Tabernacle Choir, *The Beloved Choruses*. Columbia.
Erich Leinsdorf conducting the Metropolitan Orchestra and Chorus (solos: Peters, Valetti, Merrill, Tozzi), *Rossini: The Barber of Seville*. RCA.

Fernando Previtali conducting the Accademia de Santa Cecilia, Rome, Orchestra and Chorus (solos: Milanov, Tozzi), *Verdi: La Forza del Destino*. RCA.

BEST CLASSICAL PERFORMANCE, VOCAL SOLOIST (WITH OR WITHOUT ORCHESTRA)

• Jussi Björling, *Björling in Opera*. London.
Maria Callas, *Maria Callas Portrays Verdi Heroines*. Angel.
Maureen Forrester, *A Brahms/Schumann Recital*. Decca.
Zinka Milanov, *Milanov Operatic Arias*. RCA.
Cesare Valletti, *The Art of Song*. RCA.

BEST ENGINEERING CONTRIBUTION, CLASSICAL RECORDING

• Lewis W. Layton, *Victory at Sea, Vol. 1* (Robert Russell Bennett). RCA.
Lewis W. Layton, *Doubling in Brass* (Morton Gould). RCA.
Lewis W. Layton, *Rossini Overtures* (Fritz Reiner). RCA.
Lewis W. Layton, *Tchaikovsky: Capriccio Italien; Rimsky-Korsakov: Capriccio Espagnol* (Kiril Kondrashin). RCA.
Lewis W. Layton, *Tchaikovsky: 1812 Overture; Ravel: Boléro* (Morton Gould). RCA.

BEST DOCUMENTARY OR SPOKEN WORD RECORDING

• *A Lincoln Portrait*, Carl Sandburg. Columbia.
Ages of Man, Sir John Gielgud. Columbia.
New York Taxi Driver, Tony Schwartz. Columbia.
Basil Rathbone Reads Sherlock Holmes, Basil Rathbone. Audio Book.
Mark Twain Tonight, Hal Holbrook. Columbia.

BEST COMEDY PERFORMANCE, SPOKEN WORD

• Shelley Berman, *Inside Shelley Berman*. Verve.

Lenny Bruce, *Sick Humor*. Fantasy.
Stan Freberg, *Stan Freberg with Original Cast*. Capitol.
Andy Griffith, *Hamlet*. Capitol.
Mort Sahl, *Look Forward in Anger*. Verve.

BEST COMEDY PERFORMANCE, MUSICAL

• Homer & Jethro, *The Battle of Kookamonga*. RCA.
Cliff Arquette, *Charlie Weaver Sings for His People*. Columbia.
Betty Comden, Adolph Green, *A Party with Betty Comden and Adolph Green*. Capitol.
Hans Conreid, Alice Pearce, *Monster Rally*. RCA.
Bernie Green, *Musically Mad*. RCA.

BEST RECORDING FOR CHILDREN

• *Peter and the Wolf*, Peter Ustinov (von Karajan conducting the Philharmonia Orchestra). Angel.
The Arabian Nights, Maria Ray. RCA.
Hansel and Gretel, Franz Allers. RCA.
Popeye's Favorite Sea Chanties, Captain Allen Swift. RCA.
Three to Make Music/Cinderella, Mary Martin. RCA.

BEST ENGINEERED RECORDING, NOVELTY

• Ted Keep, *Alvin's Harmonica* (David Seville). Liberty.
Thorne Nogar, *Orienta* (Markko Polo Adventurers). RCA.
Robert Simpson, *Supersonics in Flight* (Billy Mure). RCA.
Robert Simpson, *The Wild Wild West* (Ralph Hunter Choir). RCA.
Luis P. Valentin, *The Bat* (Alvino Rey). Capitol.

BEST ENGINEERING CONTRIBUTION (OTHER THAN CLASSICAL OR NOVELTY)

• Robert Simpson, *Belafonte at Carnegie Hall* (Harry Belafonte). RCA.

Ernest Oelrich, *Strings Aflame* (Esquivel). RCA.

Robert Simpson, *Big Band Guitar* (Buddy Morrow). RCA.

Robert Simpson, *Compulsion to Swing* (Henri René). RCA.

Robert Simpson, *New Sounds at the Roosevelt* (Larry Elgart). RCA.

BEST ALBUM COVER

- Robert M. Jones, *Shostakovich: Symphony No. 5* (Howard Mitchell). RCA.

Saul Bass, *Anatomy of a Murder* (Duke Ellington). Columbia.

Acy R. Lehmann, *Porgy and Bess* (Lena Horne, Harry Belafonte). RCA.

Col. Tom Parker, *For LP Fans Only* (Elvis Presley). RCA.

Robert L. Yorke, Acy R. Lehmann, *The South Shall Rise Again* (Phil Harris). RCA.

SPECIAL TRUSTEES AWARDS FOR ARTISTS & REPERTOIRE CONTRIBUTION

Record of the Year, "Mack the Knife," Bobby Darin. Ahmet Ertegun, A&R producer. Atco.

Album of the Year, *Come Dance with Me,* Frank Sinatra. Dave Cavanaugh, A&R producer. Capitol.

• 1960 •
Grammy's Night at the Movies

Several significant changes were introduced to quiet a growing chorus of complaints after last year's awards. The categories for best vocal performance were separated into honors for albums and single releases for males and females (although, ironically, both would be won by the same male and female). In jazz, a new slot was created for best composition, while the jazz performance prizes were split into categories for large and small groups, with soloists being bunched with the latter. Jazz categories also included nominees suggested by music critics in addition to the five entries determined by N.A.R.A.S. voters. The classical, folk and r&b categories also accommodated the outside recommendations, sometimes swelling the number of contenders to as many as eight nominees in each race.

Nearly all of the Top 10 singles of 1960 were rock & roll tunes (Elvis had three of the top five, including "It's Now or Never"), but again none would win a Grammy, and despite pleas throughout the music industry, no new category was created to give them separate recognition.

N.A.R.A.S. voters were stubbornly loyal either to "serious" music (read jazz or classical) or to the melodic, instrumental sound that tended to dominate the album charts just as rock & roll ruled the singles lineup. Typically, the top LPs of the day were Broadway cast albums, such as *The Sound of Music,* which was the number-one seller of 1960 (and Grammy's Best Show Album), or hit film scores—the more romantic the better.

Record of the Year winner was the year's number-one-ranked single, the

Best New Artist Bob Newhart beat Sinatra and Belafonte to win the Album of the Year Award.

only all-instrumental disc to hold that position in the rock era. "Theme from *A Summer Place,*" performed by Percy Faith & His Orchestra, was from Max Steiner's score for the film starring Dorothy McGuire, Sandra Dee and Troy Donahue. (Faith would later record a disco version of the music shortly before his death from cancer in 1976, but it failed to catch on in the record stores.)

Song of the Year turned out to be from a movie score, too: the "Theme from *Exodus,*" which was written by Ernest Gold and also won the film score honors. *Exodus* was Otto Preminger's movie adaptation of the Leon Uris novel about the struggle of two Jewish refugees, played by Paul Newman and Eva Marie Saint, to reach the newly formed State of Israel. Several versions of the lead theme became popular in 1960, including the original film score recording and renditions by Ferrante & Teicher and Mantovani & His Orchestra. Other movie music winners included André Previn's interpretation of Leonard Bernstein's *West Side Story* score, which was voted Best Jazz Performance, Solo or Small Group.

On only two occasions in Grammy history has the Album of the Year award gone to a comedy LP, in this case one that was also significant for launching the career of the low-key satirist Bob Newhart, previously known chiefly to nightclub audiences. And just like the choice for Record of the Year, album victor *Button Down Mind* was a megaseller, too, landing at number three in the year's LP rankings, thereby fueling critics' accusations that N.A.R.A.S. favored commercially popular recordings. Newhart's huge disc sales also proved that he had a universally appealing touch. In *Button Down Mind,* he poked fun at such diverse workaday folk as bus drivers, real estate salesmen and a Madison Avenue ad executive who gives Abraham Lincoln ridiculous advice on how to buff up his public image just prior to giving the Gettysburg Address. Strangely, the album didn't win the award for Best Comedy Performance. That went to its sequel, *Button Down Mind Strikes Back,* released six months after the original. Newhart was also voted Best New Artist—the only time the prize has gone to a comedian.

The winner of Grammy's first Album of the Year award, Henry Mancini, returned to claim three new awards. Two of them (Best Performance by an Orchestra and Best Arrangement) were for his score to the short-lived TV series *Mr. Lucky,* about a professional gambler, and the third was for Best Jazz Performance, Large Group, for *The Blues and the Beat.* Another alumnus of the 1958

awards came back, too, when Count Basie reprised his win for the best dance band performance, this time for *Dance with Basie.* When the Chipmunks burrowed back as well, this Grammy show started to look like a reunion of the class of 1958. *Let's All Sing with the Chipmunks* became 1960's Best Album Created for Children.

For the third year in a row, Ella Fitzgerald took the best female vocalist award, thereby monopolizing the category since its inception. Her most recent victory was for her own version of "Mack the Knife," a song that won Record of the Year last year for Bobby Darin and now earned Fitzgerald a losing nomination for the same award this year. The recording's parent album, *Ella in Berlin,* also took the equivalent LP kudos.

Generous Grammy recognition went to a newcomer when Ray Charles scored the most awards of the night: four. Although his version of the 1930 Hoagy Carmichael classic "Georgia on My Mind" lost its bid for best record, it reaped the statuette for best performance of a single record or track by a male vocalist; its album, *The Genius of Ray Charles,* nabbed the equivalent LP award. Charles also earned the prize for Best Performance by a Pop Single Artist, which was a repackaging of last year's controversial award honoring a Top 40 artist. The pop single that the Georgia-born artist was hailed for was "Georgia," which he recorded at the urging of his driver, who heard him sing it often while they were on the road together. His fourth Grammy was for "Let the Good Times Roll," 1960's Best Rhythm & Blues Performance.

Another first-time champ of note was Miles Davis, who was up for three awards thanks to the new input of music critics who decried his omission from past Grammy races. Davis was teamed

Best record and song were both from hit films.

up with Gil Evans on *Sketches of Spain* for two bids, but failed to beat N.A.R.A.S. fave Henry Mancini in the jazz group category. *Spain* nonetheless prevailed as best jazz composition. In the soloist performance category, Davis lost to another first-time champ, André Previn (*West Side Story*).

The year's Best Country & Western Performance was given to Marty Robbins for "El Paso," the 10th-best-selling single of the year. Robbins was accustomed to crossover success. Many of his earlier hit country tunes also made it onto the pop charts, such as "Singing the Blues" and "A White Sport Coat (and a Pink Carnation)."

The classical awards were dominated by the works of Brazilian-born guitarist Laurindo Almeida, who emigrated to the United States in 1947 at the age of 30, played as a soloist with Stan Kenton's Orchestra and then made his mark in film music. Almeida's *Conversations with the Guitar* was chosen as Best Chamber Music Performance (Vocal or Instrumental). *The Spanish Guitars of Laurindo Almeida* reaped him the honor for instrumental soloist and also won the classical engineering award.

Aaron Copland's *The Tender Land* was chosen Best Contemporary Classical Composition and was hailed as his "most important opera to date" by *High Fidelity*. The magazine added: "This is Copland, the composer of folkloric lyricism, at his most eloquent, luminous, delicate and restrained." Bestowing the prize for best choral performance to the Royal Philharmonic Orchestra and Chorus for Handel's *Messiah* was less popular with the same source: "Conductor Sir Thomas Beecham went off here on a musical spree. He produced an orchestration in the style of—*Die Meistersinger!*"

The Best Classical Opera Production was Puccini's unfinished *Turandot* performed by Erich Leinsdorf leading the Chorus and Orchestra of the Rome Opera House with accompanying vocals by Birgit Nilsson and Renata Tebaldi. "The presentation as a whole is fine indeed," *High Fidelity* wrote. "The soloists are simply the best that could be found today for their roles. Nilsson sails through the altitudinous title role with even, powerful tone." The recording was also in the running for Grammy's Album of the Year award.

Bob Newhart not only trounced Leinsdorf in the LP race, but when he was voted Best New Artist, he beat American soprano Leontyne Price, who was just then coming to the attention of critics after impressive debuts in San Francisco in 1957 and Vienna in 1958 (where she triumphed as Aida at the Vienna State Opera). Price nonetheless earned a Grammy for Best Classical Performance, Vocal Soloist, for *A Program of Song,* which included works by Gabriel Fauré, Francis Poulenc and Richard Strauss.

Although *Variety* reviewed Grammy's TV show last year favorably, other media gave it mixed notices and no telecast was planned this year. Simultaneous ceremonies were held in Los Angeles at the Beverly Hills Hotel and New York at the

The year's biggest champ scored four trophies for *The Genius of Ray Charles* and "Georgia."

Astor, Hotel where corporate patrons paid $400 per table to attend. Presenters included Leonard Bernstein, André Previn, Rudy Vallee, Margaret Whiting, Louella Parsons and Lawrence Welk (whose *Calcutta* was number one on *Variety*'s album chart that same week; the Grammy-winning *Exodus* soundtrack was number two). In the past, the crowds at each ceremony heard what was happening on the opposite coast via a phone hookup that was broadcast to the audiences. This year, however, the telephone line went dead just as the proceedings were about to begin and confusion reigned until the faraway victors were revealed by N.A.R.A.S. leaders who broke open the secret winners lists.

RCA ended up with 11 awards, Capitol and Columbia with 6 each and Warner Bros. and Verve with 3.

"RCA walked away with the third annual N.A.R.A.S. Grammy awards," *Variety* reported afterward, adding, "and the Artia label walked out of the organization." Artia's beef was that small record companies continued to fare poorly and it wanted to register its complaint dramatically. Artia had a strong case when considering who won the most golden gramophones. Last year "many industryites squawked because Capitol Records ran away with the prizes and [now] RCA Victor practically stole the show. It was said that the awards really weren't representative because the company with the most N.A.R.A.S. members could swing votes to its own product. This has been a sticky problem for the N.A.R.A.S. execs and they feel that recruiting more members would be the surest way to clean it up." Membership currently stood at fewer than 1,000.

N.A.R.A.S. had revamped the voting process considerably this year in order to help smaller labels and lesser-known artists have a better chance. As in the past, nominations were submitted by individual academy members (and five entries each were permitted from record companies), but now contenders could also be recommended by the academy nominating committee, which included a few prominent music reviewers. As before, only N.A.R.A.S. voters picked the winners. Artia Vice-President Peter Sutro told *Variety,* "It's clear that this did not solve the problem."

The voting experiment did nothing to counter the enormous advantage held by behemoth record firms that purchased memberships for their employees, who in turn voted for their own companies' music. "Some N.A.R.A.S. board members from RCA proposed that a bylaw be added which would not allow members to vote for their company's product," *Variety* reported. "The proposition was passed by the N.Y. chapter, but failed to go through a vote at a combined N.Y.–L.A. meet."

There were also some quarrels with the artistic merit of some of the winners. "Some of this year's awards are funny, and some are merely sad," *Down Beat* groused about the jazz awards. "It is amusing to see Henry Mancini's *Mr. Lucky* chosen over Gerry Mulligan's *The Concert Jazz Band* as best performance by an orchestra. It is sad to see André Previn's *West Side Story* called the best jazz performance, solo or small group, when John Coltrane's significant LP *Giant Steps* didn't even reach the final nominations stage, and the fair-minded Previn would probably be the first to admit it.

"But, to keep things in perspective," the magazine added, "we should also note how much more meaningful the awards were this year than last year. Some progress seems to have been made."

Variety described this year's ceremony: "Although the event wasn't televised, the N.A.R.A.S. entertainment committee latched on to the Modern Jazz

The Album of the Year award has gone to a comedy recording twice.

Quartet, Dave Brubeck, Bill Dana and Paul Anka to entertain. Manny Album batoned the orch for dancing and fanfares.

"The Grammys were awarded on both Coasts with dinner-dance fests at N.Y.'s Hotel Astor and Hollywood's BevHills Hotel. Vet recording exec Edward 'Ted' Wallerstein emceed in Gotham and Mort Sahl carried the ball on the Coast."

• 1960 •

Awards were bestowed on April 12, 1961, at ceremonies held simultaneously at the Beverly Hills Hotel in Los Angeles and the Astor Hotel in New York for the eligibility period September 1, 1959, to November 30, 1960. No telecast.

"RCA walked away with the third annual N.A.R.A.S. Grammy awards," *Variety* reported, "and the Artia label walked out of the organization."

ALBUM OF THE YEAR
• *Button Down Mind*, Bob Newhart. Warner Bros.
Belafonte Returns to Carnegie Hall, Harry Belafonte. RCA.
Brahms: Concerto No. 2 in B Flat, Sviatoslav Richter. RCA.
Nice 'n' Easy, Frank Sinatra. Capitol.
Puccini: Turandot, Erich Leinsdorf. RCA.
Wild Is Love, Nat King Cole. Capitol.

RECORD OF THE YEAR
• "Theme from *A Summer Place*," Percy Faith. Columbia.
"Are You Lonesome Tonight?" Elvis Presley. RCA.
"Georgia on My Mind," Ray Charles. ABC.
"Mack the Knife," Ella Fitzgerald. Verve.
"Nice 'n' Easy," Frank Sinatra. Capitol.

SONG OF THE YEAR
(Songwriter's Award)
• "Theme from *Exodus*," Ernest Gold.
"He'll Have to Go," Charles Green, Joe Allison, Audrey Allison.
"Nice 'n' Easy," Lew Spence, Marilyn Keith, Alan Bergman.
"Second Time Around," Sammy Cahn, Jimmy Van Heusen.
"Theme from *A Summer Place*," Max Steiner.

BEST NEW ARTIST
• Bob Newhart
Brothers Four
Miriam Makeba
Leontyne Price
Joanie Sommers

BEST VOCAL PERFORMANCE, ALBUM, MALE
• Ray Charles, *Genius of Ray Charles*. Atlantic.
Harry Belafonte, *Belafonte Returns to Carnegie Hall*. RCA.
Nat King Cole, *Wild Is Love*. Capitol.
Elvis Presley, *G.I. Blues*. RCA.
Frank Sinatra, *Nice 'n' Easy*. Capitol.

BEST VOCAL PERFORMANCE, SINGLE OR TRACK, MALE

- Ray Charles, "Georgia on My Mind." ABC.
Johnny Mathis, "Misty." Columbia.
Elvis Presley, "Are You Lonesome Tonight?" RCA.
Jim Reeves, "He'll Have to Go." RCA.
Frank Sinatra, "Nice 'n' Easy." Capitol.

BEST VOCAL PERFORMANCE, ALBUM, FEMALE

- Ella Fitzgerald, *Mack the Knife, Ella in Berlin*. Verve.
Rosemary Clooney, *Clap Hands, Here Comes Rosie*. Columbia.
Peggy Lee, *Latin a la Lee*. Capitol.
Miriam Makeba, *Miriam Makeba*. RCA.
Della Reese, *Della*. RCA.

BEST VOCAL PERFORMANCE, SINGLE OR TRACK, FEMALE

- Ella Fitzgerald, "Mack the Knife." Verve.
Doris Day, "Sound of Music." Columbia.
Eileen Farrell, "I've Gotta Right to Sing the Blues." Columbia.
Brenda Lee, "I'm Sorry." Decca.
Peggy Lee, "I'm Gonna Go Fishin'." Capitol.

BEST PERFORMANCE BY A POP SINGLE ARTIST

- Ray Charles, "Georgia on My Mind." ABC.
Ella Fitzgerald, "Mack the Knife." Verve.
Peggy Lee, "Heart." Capitol.
Elvis Presley, "Are You Lonesome Tonight?" RCA.
Frank Sinatra, "Nice 'n' Easy." Capitol.

BEST PERFORMANCE BY A VOCAL GROUP

- Eydie Gormé, Steve Lawrence, "We Got Us." ABC.
Brothers Four, "Greenfields." Columbia.
Hi-Los, "All Over the Place." Columbia.
Kingston Trio, "Here We Go Again." Capitol.

Swe-Danes, "Scandinavian Shuffle." Warner Bros.

BEST PERFORMANCE BY A CHORUS

- Norman Luboff Choir, *Songs of the Cowboy*. Columbia.
Belafonte Folk Singers, *Belafonte Returns to Carnegie Hall*. RCA.
Ray Charles Singers, *Deep Night*. Decca.
Pete King Chorale, *My Favorite Things*. Kapp.
Robert Shaw Chorale, *What Wondrous Love*. RCA.

BEST PERFORMANCE BY A BAND FOR DANCING

- Count Basie, *Dance with Basie*. Roulette.
Les Brown, *Bandland*. Columbia.
Henry Mancini, *The Blues and the Beat*. RCA.
Billy May, *Girls and Boys on Broadway*. Capitol.
Perez Prado, *Big Hits by Prado*. RCA.

BEST PERFORMANCE BY AN ORCHESTRA

- Henry Mancini, *Mr. Lucky*. RCA.
Count Basie, *Count Basie Story*. Roulette.
Esquivel, *Infinity in Sound*. RCA.
Percy Faith, "Theme from *A Summer Place*." Columbia.
Gerry Mulligan, *The Concert Jazz Band*. Verve.

BEST SHOW ALBUM, ORIGINAL CAST (Composer's Award)

- *The Sound of Music*, Richard Rodgers, Oscar Hammerstein. Columbia.
Bye Bye Birdie, Charles Strouse, Lee Adams. Columbia.
Camelot, Alan Jay Lerner, Frederick Loewe. Columbia.
Fiorello! Jerry Bock, Sheldon Harnick. Capitol.
The Unsinkable Molly Brown, Meredith Willson. Capitol.

BEST SOUNDTRACK ALBUM OR RECORDING OF ORIGINAL CAST FROM A MOTION PICTURE OR TV
(Composer's Award)
- *Can-Can*, Cole Porter (film score). Capitol.

Bells Are Ringing, Betty Comden, Adolph Green, Jule Styne (film score). Capitol.

G.I. Blues, Elvis Presley. RCA.

Li'l Abner, Nelson Riddle. Columbia.

BEST SOUNDTRACK ALBUM OR RECORDING OF MUSIC SCORE FROM A MOTION PICTURE OR TV
(Composer's Award)
- *Exodus*, Ernest Gold. RCA.

The Apartment, Adolph Deutsch. United Artists.

Ben-Hur, Dr. Miklos Rozsa. MGM.

Mr. Lucky, Henry Mancini. RCA.

The Untouchables, Nelson Riddle. Capitol.

BEST COUNTRY & WESTERN PERFORMANCE
- Marty Robbins, "El Paso." Columbia.

Johnny Horton, "North to Alaska." Columbia.

Ferlin Husky, "Wings of a Dove." Capitol.

Hank Locklin, "Please Help Me, I'm Falling." RCA.

Jim Reeves, "He'll Have to Go." RCA.

BEST FOLK PERFORMANCE
- Harry Belafonte, "Swing Dat Hammer." RCA.

Belafonte Singers, "Cheers." RCA.

Brothers Four, "Greenfields." Columbia.

Jimmy Driftwood, *Songs of Billy Yank and Johnny Reb*. RCA.

Kingston Trio, "Here We Go Again." Capitol.

Alan Lomax, *Southern Folk Heritage Series*. Atlantic.

Ewan MacColl, *Songs of Robert Burns*. Folkways.

Miriam Makeba, *Miriam Makeba*. RCA.

BEST RHYTHM & BLUES PERFORMANCE
- Ray Charles, "Let the Good Times Roll." Atlantic.

LaVerne Baker, "Shake a Hand." Atlantic.

Hank Ballard, "Finger Poppin' Time." King.

Bo Diddley, "Walkin' and Talkin'." Checker.

John Lee Hooker, "Travelin'." VeeJay.

Etta James, "All I Could Do Was Cry." Argo.

Muddy Waters, "Got My Mojo Working." Chess.

Jackie Wilson, "Lonely Teardrops." Brunswick.

BEST JAZZ COMPOSITION, MORE THAN 5 MINUTES
(Composer's Award)
- *Sketches of Spain*, Miles Davis, Gil Evans. Columbia.

"Blues Suite," Bob Brookmeyer. Atlantic.

"Blue Rondo à la Turk," Dave Brubeck. Columbia.

Idiom '59 (Festival Session), Duke Ellington. Columbia.

"Newport Suite," Maynard Ferguson. Roulette.

"Western Suite," Jimmy Giuffre. Atlantic.

Sketch from Third Stream Music, John Lewis. Atlantic.

BEST JAZZ PERFORMANCE, SOLO OR SMALL GROUP
- André Previn, *West Side Story*. Contempo.

Miles Davis, *Jazz Track*. Columbia.

Duke Ellington, Johnny Hodges, *Back to Back*. Verve.

Dizzy Gillespie & His Octet, *The Greatest Trumpet of Them All*. Verve.

Lambert, Hendricks & Ross, *The Hottest New Group in Jazz*. Columbia.

Modern Jazz Quartet, *Pyramid*. Atlantic.

George Shearing, *White Satin*. Capitol.

Art Tatum, *Greatest Piano of Them All*. Verve.

BEST JAZZ PERFORMANCE, LARGE GROUP

- Henry Mancini, *The Blues and the Beat*. RCA.

Count Basie, *The Count Basie Story*. Roulette.

Miles Davis, Gil Evans, *Sketches of Spain*. Columbia.

Quincy Jones, *The Great Wide World of Quincy Jones*. Mercury.

Gerry Mulligan, *I'm Gonna Go Fishin'*. Verve.

Recording Artists, *Spirituals to Swing Concert*. Vanguard.

BEST CLASSICAL PERFORMANCE, ORCHESTRA

(Conductor's Award)

- Fritz Reiner conducting the Chicago Symphony, *Bartók: Music for Strings, Percussion and Celesta*. RCA.

Sir Thomas Beecham conducting the Royal Philharmonic, *Haydn: Solomon Symphonies, Vol. 2*. Capitol.

Leonard Bernstein conducting the New York Philharmonic, *Ives: Symphony No. 2*. Columbia.

Aaron Copland conducting the Boston Symphony, *Copland: Appalachian Spring*. RCA.

Morton Gould conducting the Morton Gould Orchestra, *Grofé: Grand Canyon Suite*. RCA.

Josef Krips conducting the London Symphony, *Schubert: Symphony No. 9*. London.

Pierre Monteux conducting the Boston Symphony, *Stravinsky: Petrushka*. RCA.

Eugene Ormandy conducting the Philadelphia Symphony, *Tchaikovsky: Sixth Symphony*. Columbia.

BEST CHAMBER MUSIC PERFORMANCE (VOCAL OR INSTRUMENTAL)

- Laurindo Almeida, *Conversations with the Guitar*. Capitol.

Clifford Curzon and Vienna Octet, *Schubert: Trout Quintet*. London.

Joseph Eger, Henryk Szeryng, Victor Babin, *Brahms: Horn Trio; Beethoven: Sonata for Horn and Piano*. RCA.

Griller Quartet, *Haydn: Quartets, Opp. 71 and 74*. Vanguard.

Juilliard Quartet, *Debussy and Ravel Quartets*. RCA.

Yehudi Menuhin and Bach Festival Chamber Orchestra, *Bach: The Complete Brandenburg Concertos*. Capitol.

Robert Shaw Chorale, *Bach: Cantata No. 4; Christ Lag in Todesbanden*. RCA.

Smetana Quartet, *Janáček String Quartets Nos. 1 and 2*. Artia.

BEST CLASSICAL PERFORMANCE, CONCERTO OR INSTRUMENTAL SOLOIST

- Sviatoslav Richter (Leinsdorf conducting the Chicago Symphony), *Brahms: Piano Concerto No. 2 in B Flat*. RCA.

Gervase De Peyer (Maag conducting the London Symphony), *Mozart: Clarinet Concerto*. London.

Malcolm Frager (Leibowitz conducting the Paris Conservatoire), *Prokofiev: Concerto No. 2*. RCA.

Zino Francescatti, Pierre Fournier (Walter conducting the Columbia Symphony), *Brahms: Double Concerto (Concerto for Violin and Cello in A Minor)*. Columbia.

Glenn Gould (Golschmann conducting the Columbia Symphony), *Bach: Concerto No. 5*. Columbia.

Jascha Heifetz (Hendl conducting the Chicago Symphony), *Sibelius: Violin Concerto in D*. RCA.

Rudolf Serkin (Ormandy conducting the Philadelphia Symphony), *Brahms: Piano Concerto No. 2*. Columbia.

Van Cliburn (Reiner conducting the Chicago Symphony), *Schumann: Piano Concerto in A*. RCA.

BEST CLASSICAL PERFORMANCE, INSTRUMENTAL SOLOIST OR DUO (Other Than Orchestra)

- Laurindo Almeida, *The Spanish Guitars of Laurindo Almeida*. Capitol.

Julian Bream, *The Art of Julian Bream*. RCA.

Vladimir Horowitz, *Pictures at an Exhibition*. RCA.

Wanda Landowska, *Haydn . . . Landowska*. RCA.

Jaime Laredo, *Bach: Partita No. 3 in E; Brahms: Sonata No. 3 in D Minor*. RCA.

Paul Maynard, *Brahms: Keyboard Music of the French Court*. American Society of Concerts in Home.

Sviatoslav Richter, *Prokofiev: Sonata No. 7; Pictures at an Exhibition*. Artia.

Artur Rubinstein, *Chopin: Ballades*. RCA.

BEST CLASSICAL PERFORMANCE, CHORAL (INCLUDING ORATORIO)

- Sir Thomas Beecham conducting the Royal Philharmonic Orchestra and Chorus (solos: Vyvyan, Sinclair, Vicki, Tozzi), *Handel: Messiah*. RCA.

Moravian Festival Chorus, *Arias, Anthems and Chorales of American Moravians, Vol. 1*. Columbia.

Charles Munch and New England Conservatory Chorus, *Berlioz: Requiem*. RCA.

Fritz Reiner, Vienna Philharmonic Society of Friends of Music of Vienna, *Verdi: Requiem*. RCA.

Robert Shaw Chorale, *Bach: Motet No. 3 ("Jesu Meine Freude")*. RCA.

Maria Stader, Sieglinde Wagner, Hans Ernst Haefliger, Kim Borg, *Dvořák: Requiem*. DGG.

Roger Wagner Chorale, *Vaughan Williams: Mass in G Minor; Bach: Christ Lay in the Bonds of Death*. Capitol.

BEST CLASSICAL OPERA PRODUCTION

- *Puccini: Turandot*, Erich Leinsdorf, conducting the Rome Opera House Chorus and Orchestra (solos: Tebaldi, Nilsson, Björling, Tozzi). RCA.

Boito: Mefistofele, Tullio Serafin (solos: Siepi, Tebaldi, Del Monaco). London.

Britten: Peter Grimes, Benjamin Britten conducting the Royal Opera Chorus and Orchestra (solos: Pears, Pease, Watson). London.

Mozart: Don Giovanni, Josef Krips (solos: Siepi, Danco, Dermote, Corena). London.

Poulenc, Cocteau: La Voix Humaine, Georges Prêtre conducting the Paris Opéra Comique and National Theater Orchestra (solo: Duval). RCA.

Puccini: La Bóhème, Tullio Serafin conducting the Accademia di Santa Cecilia (solos: Tebaldi, Bergonzi, Bastianini, Corena). London.

Verdi: Aida, Herbert von Karajan conducting the Vienna Singverein and Vienna Philharmonic (solos: Tebaldi, Bergonzi, Simionato, Corena). London.

Verdi: La Traviata, Tullio Serafin conducting the Rome Opera Chorus and Orchestra (solos: de los Angeles, Del Monte, Sereni). Capitol.

Verdi: Macbeth, Erich Leinsdorf conducting the Metropolitan Opera Chorus and Orchestra (solos: Warren, Hines, Rysanek, Bergonzi). RCA.

BEST CLASSICAL PERFORMANCE, VOCAL SOLOIST

- Leontyne Price, *A Program of Song*. RCA.

Eileen Farrell, *Arias in Great Tradition*. Columbia.

Dietrich Fischer-Dieskau, *Schubert: Songs, Album 3*. Angel.

Maureen Forrester, *Mahler: Kindertotenlieder*. RCA.

Peter Pears, *Britten: Nocturne*. London.

Joan Sutherland, *Handel: Arias*. L'Oiseau-Lyre.

Salli Terri, *Conversations with the Guitar*. Capitol.

Cesare Valletti, *Schumann: Dichterliebe*. RCA.

BEST CONTEMPORARY CLASSICAL COMPOSITION

- *Orchestral Suite from Tender Land*, Aaron Copland. RCA.
- *Symphony No. 1*, Easley Blackwood. RCA.
- *Sonata for Cello and Piano*, Paul Hindemith. RCA.
- *Symphony No. 2*, Charles Ives. Columbia.
- *La Voix Humaine*, Francis Poulenc. RCA.
- *Symphony No. 1*, Roger Sessions. Composers Recordings.
- *Threni*, Igor Stravinsky. Columbia.
- *Density 21.5*, Edgard Varèse. Columbia.

BEST ENGINEERING CONTRIBUTION, CLASSICAL RECORDING

- Hugh Davies, *The Spanish Guitars of Laurindo Almeida*. Capitol.
- John Kraus, *The Two Pianos of Leonard Pennario*. Capitol.
- Lewis Layton, *Bartók: Music for Strings, Percussion and Celesta* (Fritz Reiner conducting the Chicago Symphony). RCA.
- Lewis Layton, *Berlioz: Requiem* (Charles Munch conducting the New England Conservatory Chorus and Boston Symphony). RCA.
- Lewis Layton, *Prokofiev: Alexander Nevsky* (Fritz Reiner conducting the Chicago Symphony Orchestra). RCA.
- Lewis Layton, *Puccini: Turandot* (Erich Leinsdorf conducting the Rome Opera Chorus and Orchestra; solos: Tebaldi, Nilsson, Björling, Tozzi). RCA.
- Lewis Layton, *R. Strauss: Don Quixote* (Fritz Reiner conducting the Chicago Symphony). RCA.

BEST ARRANGEMENT

- Henry Mancini, *Mr. Lucky*. RCA.
- Don Costa, "Theme from *The Apartment*" (Ferrante & Teicher). United Artists.
- Percy Faith, "Theme from *A Summer Place*" (Percy Faith & His Orchestra). Columbia.

Bill Holman, "I'm Gonna Go Fishin' " (Gerry Mulligan). Verve.
Quincy Jones, "Let the Good Times Roll" (Ray Charles). Atlantic.
Nelson Riddle, "Nice 'n' Easy" (Frank Sinatra). Capitol.
Dick Schory, "Wild Percussion and Horns A'Plenty" (Dick Schory). RCA.
George Shearing, Billy May, "Honeysuckle Rose" (George Shearing). Capitol.

BEST PERFORMANCE, DOCUMENTARY OR SPOKEN WORD (OTHER THAN COMEDY)

- Franklin Delano Roosevelt, *F.D.R. Speaks*. Robert Bialek. Washington.
- Henry Fonda, *Voices of the Twentieth Century*. Decca.
- Sir John Gielgud, *Ages of Man, Vol. 2 (One Man in His Time) Part 2—Shakespeare*. Columbia.
- Archibald MacLeish, *J.B.* RCA.

BEST COMEDY PERFORMANCE, SPOKEN WORD

- Bob Newhart, *Button Down Mind Strikes Back*. Warner Bros.
- Shelley Berman, *The Edge of Shelley Berman*. Verve.
- Carl Reiner, Mel Brooks, *2,000 Year Old Man*. World Pacific.
- Jonathan Winters, *The Wonderful World of Jonathan Winters*. Verve.

BEST COMEDY PERFORMANCE, MUSICAL

- Paul Weston, Jo Stafford, *Jonathan and Darlene Edwards in Paris*. Columbia.
- Stan Freberg, *The Old Payola Roll Blues*. Capitol.
- Homer & Jethro, *Homer and Jethro at the Country Club*. RCA.
- Tom Lehrer, *An Evening Wasted with Tom Lehrer*. Lehrer.
- David Seville, *Alvin for President*. Liberty.

BEST ALBUM CREATED FOR CHILDREN

- *Let's All Sing with the Chipmunks*, David Seville. Liberty.

Adventures in Music, Grade 3, Vol. 1,
Howard Mitchell. RCA.

*Dr. Seuss Presents: Bartholomew and
the Oobleck,* Dr. Seuss. Camden.

Folk Songs for Young People, Pete
Seeger. Folkways.

Mother Goose Nursery Rhymes, Sterling
Holloway. Disneyland.

Stories and Songs of the Civil War,
Ralph Bellamy. RCA.

BEST ENGINEERING CONTRIBUTION, POPULAR RECORDING

• Luis P. Valentin, *Ella Fitzgerald Sings
the George and Ira Gershwin Song
Book.* Verve.

Robert Fine, *Persuasive Percussion No.
2.* Commodore.

John Kraus, *Wild Is Love* (Nat King
Cole). Capitol.

John Norman, *Infinity in Sound*
(Esquivel). RCA.

Robert Simpson, *Belafonte Returns to
Carnegie Hall* (Harry Belafonte).
RCA.

Robert Simpson, *Wild Percussion and
Horns A'Plenty* (Dick Schory). RCA.

Luis P. Valentin, *Louis Bellson Swings
Jule Styne.* Verve.

BEST ENGINEERED RECORDING, NOVELTY

• John Kraus, *The Old Payola Roll
Blues* (Stan Freberg). Capitol.

George Fernandez, *Mr. Custer* (Larry
Verne). Era.

Ted Keep, *Alvin for President* (David
Seville & the Chipmunks). Liberty.

Ted Keep, *Let's All Sing with the Chipmunks* (David Seville & the Chipmunks). Liberty.

John Kraus, *June Night* (Jack Cookerly).
Capitol.

Thorne Nogar, *Spike Jones in Hi-Fi.*
Warner Bros.

Robert Simpson, John Crawford, Tony
Salvatore, *New Sounds America
Loves Best* (John Klein). RCA.

BEST ALBUM COVER
(Art Director's Award)

• Marvin Schwartz, *Latin a la Lee*
(Peggy Lee). Capitol.

Marvin Israel, *Bean Bags* (Milt Jackson). Atlantic.

Bob Jones, *Carlos Montoya.* RCA.

Bob Jones, *Prokofiev: Alexander Nevsky*
(Reiner conducting the Chicago
Symphony). RCA.

Bob Jones, *Stravinsky: Petruchka* (Monteux conducting the Boston Symphony). RCA.

Bob Jones, *Tchaikovsky: Nutcracker
Suite Excerpts* (Reiner conducting
the Chicago Symphony). RCA.

Bob Jones, *Wild Percussion and Horns
A'Plenty* (Dick Schory). RCA.

Sheldon Marks, *Ella Fitzgerald Sings
the George and Ira Gershwin Song
Book.* Verve.

Irving Werbin, *Now! Fred Astaire.*
Kapp.

• 1961 •

"Moon" Walks—and Rock Finally Rolls

"This is the year of Henry Mancini," *Variety* proclaimed.

The past Grammy grabber came back to claim an unprecedented 5 awards in one night, bringing his total tally so far to 10. All of his newest prizes were for his film score to *Breakfast at Tiffany's,* an adaptation of Truman Capote's novella of a small-town girl who turns fabulously hip when she moves to New York City. The movie was directed by Blake Edwards, who hired Mancini to score his TV show *Peter Gunn* back in 1958, a gig that earned Mancini Grammy's first Album of the Year award.

Now Mancini scored the other two top prizes—Song of the Year, with lyricist Johnny Mercer, and Record of the Year—for "Moon River." The same cut from his soundtrack LP also brought him the Best Arrangement prize (for a third time), while the disc won best soundtrack album and best nondance orchestral performance, too. Earlier in the year, *Breakfast at Tiffany's* and "Moon River" shone at the Oscars, winning Best Original Score and Best Song.

Mancini's big night was beheld, noted *Variety,* by "an SRO audience of 700 that turned out at the Beverly Hills Hotel" in Los Angeles, where Carl Reiner presided as emcee and entertainment was provided by the Dave Pell Octet. Tickets cost $17.50, a $2.50 hike over last year. *Variety* added, "Biggest chuckle of the evening came when presenter Bob Newhart remarked, 'I'm up here as a presenter and as an Emmy winner for comedy, which has nothing to do with writing comedy or being funny on records.' " One week earlier, *The Bob Newhart Show* had won best TV comedy series at the Emmy Awards

Los Angeles Library Collection

Chubby Checker's "Let's Twist Again" won the first award for rock & roll music after N.A.R.A.S. voters bypassed the original "Twist" last year.

three weeks after NBC axed the show. But Newhart failed to mention that he also had solid-gold Grammy credentials, having been the previous year's choice as Best New Artist and Album of the Year champ for *Button Down Mind.*

Five hundred people attended a concurrent ceremony at the ballroom of the Waldorf-Astoria in New York, where WNEW radio deejay William B. Williams presided as host. Entertainment was provided by Tony Bennett and Si Zentner & His Orchestra, the latter of which turned out to win the award for Best Performance by an Orchestra for Dancing for *Up a Lazy River. Variety* called the New York ceremony "a long, tedious affair, which needed more lifts than the lone big one it got from a nonscheduled appearance by Buddy Hackett who presented an award and offered a bit of fast and funny patter that broke the place up." The Chicago N.A.R.A.S. chapter hosted a cocktail party at the Sheraton Hotel while its members kept track of the proceedings out east and west via telephone.

The music elite attending the formal Grammy bashes no longer seemed to bar the rock & roll ruffians from the door. In fact, the edgy young artists were even welcomed to participate in a new category—Best Rock & Roll Recording—which was overseen by a specially appointed panel determined to get the selection right. The winner: Chubby Checker's "Let's Twist Again," a curious, conciliatory choice, since N.A.R.A.S. voters failed to nominate the original "Twist" when it shook up America one year earlier.

The winner of Album of the Year was a far more traditional pick and marked the triumphant return of a star who first came to national attention as the little lost Dorothy in *The Wizard of Oz*. Judy Garland seemed to have completely lost her way by the early 1960s after frequent public bouts with suicide attempts, pills and booze. Her hopes for a career comeback hung on a concert at Carnegie Hall. On the night of April 23, 1961, showbiz's glitterati—including Richard Burton, Rock Hudson, Harold Arlen, Henry Fonda and Julie Andrews—packed the seats to witness the result.

The performance they beheld was transcendent. "Never saw the like in my life!" Hedda Hopper roared in her review. "We laughed, cried and split our gloves applauding. . . . She was sensational as she clowned, talked, danced a bit and used the mike as though it were a trumpet." After the two-and-a-half-hour performance of 26 songs, including "The Man That Got Away," "Swanee," "Chicago" and "Over the Rainbow," the *New York World*

Five awards for *Breakfast at Tiffany's* doubled Henry Mancini's tally.

Telegram concluded, "This kid is still a killer." Capitol's two-disc live recording of her performance topped the LP charts for 13 weeks (and was still in *Variety's* Top 10 lineup a year later during the week of the Grammy Awards). In addition to the Album of the Year trophy, *Judy at Carnegie Hall* won three other honors: Best Solo Vocal Performance, Female; Best Engineering Contribution, Popular Recording; and Best Album Cover.

The best male vocal laurels went to Jack Jones, who was hailed by his promoters as the "Sinatra of the Sixties." Jones's clean good looks and melodic light baritone made him something of an anachronism in the burgeoning rock era, but he still found legions of swooning fans for such hits as his Grammy-winning "Lollipops and Roses." Old-fashioned pop music also prevailed with the selection of the year's Best New Artist, jazzy pianist Peter Nero, who beat Ann-Margret and comedian Dick Gregory.

In 1961, singer Jimmy Dean had his own weekly TV series featuring popular country music, but it wasn't until he recorded "Big Bad John" that he had his own first million-selling song and the number-four platter of the year. The success of "Big Bad John" was something of a fluke. Dean needed a tune to fill up the "B" side of a new single he had coming out and wrote it in an hour and a half while on a plane ride to Nashville. It ended up scoring four nominations, including bids for Record and Song of the Year, and won one: Best Country & Western Recording.

Last year's winner of the best male vocal honors (the two awards for album and single performance were combined this year) returned with the Best Rhythm & Blues Recording—"Hit the Road, Jack," Ray Charles's third million-selling single. André Previn came back, too, reclaiming the same award (Best Jazz Performance by a Soloist or Small Group) for his tribute to composer Harold Arlen. Last year Previn won it for *West Side Story*. Stan Kenton and his band gave the same music their own interpretation this year and won the jazz award for large groups. The most sought-after singing team in the jazz world—Lambert, Hendricks & Ross—was honored for Best Performance by a Vocal Group in *High Flying*. Galt Mac-Dermot ended up with two statuettes (for Best Instrumental Theme and Best Original Jazz Composition) for "African Waltz."

A new gospel award went to Mahalia Jackson for her hallelujah vocals on "Every Time I Feel the Spirit." (Jackson scored another professional triumph earlier in the year when she sang at John F. Kennedy's inauguration ceremony.) N.A.R.A.S. also introduced a new Classical Album of the Year award, which went to *Stravinsky Conducts, 1960: Le Sacre du Printemps; Petruchka,* a recording of the two ballets written by Stravinsky for Diaghilev's Ballets Russes. Stravinsky himself batoned the Columbia Symphony Orchestra in what are now considered the definitive performances.

After a double win last year, Brazilian-born American guitarist Laurindo Almeida returned to take two more Grammys, stirring up some controversy, since he was a popular member of the academy's board of governors. In a tie with Stravinsky's Movements for Piano and Orchestra, Almeida shared the award for Best Contemporary Classical Composition for *Discantus*. Beating out Vladimir Horowitz and Andrés Segovia, he was also acknowledged for giving the best solo instrumental performance on *Reverie for Spanish Guitars,* in which he played such works as Maurice Ravel's "Pavanne for a Dead Princess" while playing as many as three guitars on overlapping tapes. The Boston

Symphony Orchestra, under the baton of Charles Munch, also played Ravel, resulting in two Grammys, both for *Daphnis et Chloé*: best classical performance by an orchestra (reprising Munch's 1959 victory in the category) and best engineering.

Music reviewers of Grammy's opera choices were in sound agreement. *High Fidelity* said of Puccini's *Madama Butterfly* performed by the Rome Opera Chorus and Orchestra with Gabriele Santini conducting (Best Opera Recording and Best Album Cover, Classical): "Capitol's new version of *Madama Butterfly* is especially welcome, for it offers not only Victoria de los Angeles as Cio-Cio-San, but Jussi Björling as Pinkerton and Mario Sereni as Sharpless, making this the best sung *Butterfly* in the catalog."

Best Classical Performance, Vocal Soloist, was given to Australian soprano Joan Sutherland, who gained fame in 1959 after singing the title role in Donizetti's *Lucia di Lammermoor* at Covent Garden in London, a role she reprised in 1961 in her New York debut at the Metropolitan. About *The Art of the Prima Donna,* in which she performed works by George Handel and Thomas Arne, *High Fidelity* wrote: "This album exhilarates . . . Joan Sutherland takes 16 tests in Advanced Vocalism, and sails through them with startling freedom, scattering *grupetti* and *volate* as she goes."

"RCA went ahead of the field to cop 12 Grammys," *Variety* reported on the final Grammy tally. "Capitol (and its Angel subsidiary) ran second with 10 prizes and Columbia took show money with eight awards." Grammy critics continued to grouse that smaller record companies still weren't being heard at the awards.

> A ticket to the ceremony cost $17.50.

• 1961

Awards were bestowed on May 29, 1962, at ceremonies held simultaneously at the | Beverly Hills Hotel in Los Angeles and the Waldorf-Astoria Hotel in New York for the eligibility period December 1, 1960, to November 30, 1961. The N.A.R.A.S. Chicago chapter held a concurrent cocktail party at the Sheraton-Chicago Hotel. No telecast.

ALBUM OF THE YEAR
• *Judy at Carnegie Hall*, Judy Garland. Capitol.
Breakfast at Tiffany's, Henry Mancini. RCA.
Genius + Soul = Jazz, Ray Charles. Impulse.
Great Band with Great Voices, Si Zentner, Johnny Mann Singers. Liberty.
The Nat Cole Story, Nat King Cole. Capitol.
West Side Story (soundtrack), Johnny Green, music director. Columbia.

RECORD OF THE YEAR
• "Moon River," Henry Mancini. RCA.
"Big Bad John," Jimmy Dean. Columbia.
"The Second Time Around," Frank Sinatra. Reprise.
"Take Five," Dave Brubeck. Columbia.
"Up a Lazy River," Si Zentner. Liberty.

SONG OF THE YEAR
(Songwriter's Award)
• "Moon River," Henry Mancini, Johnny Mercer.
"A Little Bitty Tear," Hank Cochran.
"Big Bad John," Jimmy Dean.
"Lollipops and Roses," Tony Velona.
"Make Someone Happy," Jule Styne, Betty Comden, Adolph Green. RCA.

BEST NEW ARTIST
• Peter Nero
Ann-Margret
Dick Gregory
Lettermen
Timi Yuro

BEST SOLO VOCAL PERFORMANCE, MALE
• Jack Jones, "Lollipops and Roses." Kapp.
Jimmy Dean, "Big Bad John." Columbia.
Burl Ives, "A Little Bitty Tear." Decca.
Steve Lawrence, "Portrait of My Love." United Artists.
Andy Williams, "Danny Boy." Columbia.

BEST SOLO VOCAL PERFORMANCE, FEMALE
• Judy Garland, *Judy at Carnegie Hall*. Capitol.
Ella Fitzgerald, *Mr. Paganini*. Verve.
Billie Holiday, *The Essential Billie Holiday (Carnegie Hall Concert)*. Verve.
Lena Horne, *Lena at the Sands*. RCA.
Peggy Lee, *Basin Street East*. Capitol.

BEST PERFORMANCE BY A VOCAL GROUP
• Lambert, Hendricks & Ross, *High Flying*. Columbia.
Four Freshmen, *Voices in Fun*. Capitol.
Kingston Trio, *Close Up*. Capitol.
Lettermen, *The Way You Look Tonight*. Capitol.
Limeliters, *The Slightly Fabulous Limeliters*. RCA.

BEST PERFORMANCE BY A CHORUS
• Johnny Mann Singers (Si Zentner Orchestra), *Great Band with Great Voices*. Liberty.
Belafonte Folk Singers, *Belafonte Folk Singers at Home and Abroad*. RCA.
Norman Luboff Choir, *This Is Norman Luboff*. RCA.
Pete King Chorale, *Hey, Look Me Over*. Kapp.
Roger Wagner Chorale, *A Song at Twilight*. Capitol.

BEST ROCK & ROLL RECORDING
• "Let's Twist Again," Chubby Checker. Parkway.
"Goodbye Cruel World," James Darren. Colpix.

"I Like It Like That," Chris Kenner.
Instant.
"It's Gonna Work Out Fine," Ike & Tina
Turner. Sue.
"The Lion Sleeps Tonight," Tokens. RCA.

BEST RHYTHM & BLUES RECORDING
- "Hit the Road, Jack," Ray Charles.
  ABC-Paramount.
"Bright Lights, Big City," Jimmy Reed.
  VeeJay.
"Fool That I Am," Etta James. Argo.
"Mother in Law," Ernie K-Doe. Minit.
"Saved," Laverne Baker. Atlantic.

BEST ORIGINAL JAZZ COMPOSITION
(Composer's Award)
- "African Waltz," Galt MacDermot.
  Riverside.
"A Touch of Elegance," André Previn.
  Columbia.
"Gillespiana," Lalo Schifrin. Verve.
"Perceptions," J. J. Johnson. Verve.
"Unsquare Dance," Dave Brubeck.
  Columbia.

BEST JAZZ PERFORMANCE BY A
SOLOIST OR SMALL GROUP,
INSTRUMENTAL
- André Previn, *André Previn Plays
  Harold Arlen*. Contemporary.
Bill Evans Trio, *Bill Evans at the Village
  Vanguard*. Riverside.
Erroll Garner. *Dreamstreet*. ABC-
  Paramount.
Al Hirt, *The Greatest Horn in the World*.
  RCA.
Modern Jazz Quartet, *European
  Concert*. Atlantic.

BEST JAZZ PERFORMANCE BY A
LARGE GROUP, INSTRUMENTAL
- Stan Kenton, *West Side Story*. Capitol.
Count Basie & Orchestra, *Basie at Bird-
  land*. Roulette.
Gil Evans, *Out of the Cool*. ABC.
Dizzy Gillespie, *Gillespiana*. Verve.
André Previn, *A Touch of Elegance*.
  Columbia.

BEST COUNTRY & WESTERN
RECORDING
- "Big Bad John," Jimmy Dean. Colum-
  bia.
"A Little Bitty Tear," Burl Ives. Decca.
"Hello Walls," Faron Young. Capitol.
"Hillbilly Heaven," Tex Ritter. Capitol.
"Walk on By," Leroy Van Dyke. Mercury.

BEST FOLK RECORDING
- *Belafonte Folk Singers at Home and
  Abroad*, Belafonte Folk Singers.
  RCA.
The Big Bill Broonzy Story, Bill
  Broonzy. Verve.
*The Clancy Brothers and Tommy
  Makem*, Clancy Brothers & Tommy
  Makem. Columbia.
Folk Songs of Britain, Vol. 1, Alan
  Lomax. Caedmon.
The Slightly Fabulous Limeliters,
  Limeliters. RCA.

BEST GOSPEL OR OTHER RELIGIOUS
RECORDING
- "Everytime I Feel the Spirit," Mahalia
  Jackson. Columbia.
Hymns at Home, Tennessee Ernie Ford.
  Capitol.
Jesus Keep Me Near the Cross, Prof.
  Alex Bradford. Choice.

The first concert album to win Album of the Year
marked a dramatic comeback for Garland. "This
kid is still a killer," one critic declared.

Lincoln Hymns, Tex Ritter. Capitol.
Swing Low, Staple Singers. VeeJay.

BEST PERFORMANCE BY AN ORCHESTRA FOR DANCING

• Si Zentner, *Up a Lazy River*. Liberty.
Les Brown, *The Lerner and Loewe Bandbook*. Columbia.
Glen Gray, Billy May, *Shall We Swing?* Capitol.
Quincy Jones, *I Dig Dancers*. Mercury.
Henry Mancini, *Mr. Lucky Goes Latin*. RCA.
Lawrence Welk, *Calcutta*. Dot.

BEST PERFORMANCE BY AN ORCHESTRA (FOR OTHER THAN DANCING)

• Henry Mancini, *Breakfast at Tiffany's*. RCA.
Al Hirt, *The Greatest Horn in the World*. RCA.
Stan Kenton, *West Side Story*. Capitol.
Gerry Mulligan, *A Concert in Jazz*. Verve.
André Previn, *A Touch of Elegance*. Columbia.

BEST INSTRUMENTAL THEME OR INSTRUMENTAL VERSION OF SONG (Composer's Award)

• "African Waltz," Galt MacDermot. Roulette.
"La Dolce Vita," Nino Rota. RCA.
"Paris Blues," Duke Ellington. Columbia.
"The Guns of Navarone," Dimitri Tiomkin. Columbia.
"Theme from *Carnival*," Robert Merrill. MGM.

BEST ORIGINAL CAST SHOW ALBUM (Composer's Award)

• *How to Succeed in Business Without Really Trying*, Frank Loesser. RCA.
Carnival, Robert Merrill. MGM.
Do Re Mi, Jule Styne, Betty Comden, Adolph Green. RCA.
Milk and Honey, Jerry Herman. RCA.

Wildcat, Cy Coleman, Carolyn Leigh. RCA.

BEST SOUNDTRACK ALBUM OR RECORDING OF ORIGINAL CAST FROM A MOTION PICTURE OR TV

• *West Side Story*, Johnny Green, Saul Chaplin, Sid Ramin, Irwin Kostal. Columbia.
Babes in Toyland, Tutti Camarata. Buena Vista.
Blue Hawaii, Elvis Presley. RCA.
Flower Drum Song, Alfred Newman, Ken Darby. Decca.
The Parent Trap, Tutti Camarata. Buena Vista.

BEST SOUNDTRACK ALBUM OR RECORDING OF SCORE FROM A MOTION PICTURE OR TV

• *Breakfast at Tiffany's*, Henry Mancini. RCA.
Checkmate, Johnny Williams. Columbia.
The Guns of Navarone, Dimitri Tiomkin. Columbia.
La Dolce Vita, Nino Rota. RCA.
Paris Blues, Duke Ellington, Louis Armstrong. United Artists.

BEST ARRANGEMENT

• Henry Mancini, "Moon River." RCA.
Bob Florence, "Up a Lazy River" (Si Zentner). Liberty.
J. J. Johnson, "Perceptions" (Dizzy Gillespie). Verve.
Peter Nero, "New Piano in Town." RCA.
George Russell, "All About Rosie" (Gerry Mulligan). Verve.

ALBUM OF THE YEAR, CLASSICAL

• *Stravinsky Conducts, 1960: Le Sacre du Printemps; Petruchka*, Igor Stravinsky conducting the Columbia Symphony. Columbia.
The Art of the Prima Donna, Joan Sutherland (Molinari-Pradelli, Royal Opera House Orchestra). London.
Block: Sacred Service, Leonard Bernstein, New York Philharmonic. Columbia.

Brahms: Symphony No. 2, William Steinberg, Pittsburgh Symphony. Command.
Reverie for Spanish Guitars, Laurindo Almeida. Capitol.

BEST CONTEMPORARY CLASSICAL COMPOSITION
(Composer's Award)
(Tie)
- *Discantos*, Laurindo Almeida. Capitol.
- *Movements for Piano and Orchestra*, Igor Stravinsky. Columbia.
Gloria in 'G Major, Francis Poulenc. Angel.
Music for Brass Quintet, Gunther Schuller. Composers Recordings.
String Quartet No. 2, Elliott Carter. RCA.

BEST CLASSICAL PERFORMANCE, ORCHESTRA
(Conductor's Award)
- Charles Munch conducting the Boston Symphony, *Ravel: Daphnis et Chloé*. RCA.
Herbert von Karajan conducting the Philharmonia, *Bartók: Music for String Instruments, Percussion and Celesta; Hindemith: Mathis der Mahler*. Angel.
Fritz Reiner conducting the Chicago Symphony, *R. Strauss: Don Juan; Debussy: La Mer*. RCA.
George Szell conducting the Cleveland Orchestra, *R. Strauss: Don Quixote*. Epic.
Bruno Walter conducting the Boston Symphony. *Bruckner: Symphony No. 4 in E Flat Major; Wagner: Tannhäuser Overture and Venusberg Music*. Columbia.

BEST CHAMBER MUSIC PERFORMANCE
- Jascha Heifetz, Gregor Piatigorsky, William Primrose, *Beethoven: Serenade, Op. 8; Kodály: Duo for Violin and Cello, Op. 7*. RCA.
Juilliard String Quartet, *Berg: Lyric Suite; Sebern: 5 Pieces for String Quartet, Op. 5; 6 Bagatelles, Op. 9*. RCA.
Leonard Pennario, Eudice Shapiro, Sanford Schonbach, Victor Gottlieb, *Fauré: First Quartet, Op. 15; Schumann: Clavier Quartet, Op. 47*. Capitol.
Gary Graffman, Berl Senofsky, *Fauré: Sonata No. 1; Debussy: Sonata No. 3*. RCA.
Erica Morini, Rudolf Firkusny, *Franck and Mozart Sonatas*. Decca.

BEST CLASSICAL PERFORMANCE, INSTRUMENTAL SOLOIST (WITH ORCHESTRA)
- Isaac Stern (Ormandy conducting the Philadelphia Orchestra), *Bartók: Concerto No. 1 for Violin and Orchestra*. Columbia.
Leon Fleisher (Szell conducting the Cleveland Orchestra), *Beethoven: Emperor Concerto*. Epic.
Pierre Fournier (Szell conducting the Cleveland Orchestra), *R. Strauss: Don Quixote*. Epic.
Jascha Heifetz, Gregor Piatigorsky, *Brahms: Double Concerto (Concerto in A for Violin and Cello)*. RCA.
Andrés Segovia (Jorda conducting the Symphony of the Air), *Boccherini, Cassadó: Concerto for Guitar*. Decca.

BEST CLASSICAL PERFORMANCE, INSTRUMENTAL SOLOIST (WITHOUT ORCHESTRA)
- Laurindo Almeida, *Reverie for Spanish Guitars*. Capitol.
Vladimir Horowitz, *Homage to Liszt*. RCA.
Ruggerio Ricci, *Bartók, Hindemith, Prokofiev: Solo Violin Sonatas*. London.
Sviatoslav Richter, *Beethoven: Appassionata Sonatas; Funeral March Sonata*. RCA.
Andrés Segovia, *Bach: Suite No. 3*. Decca.

BEST OPERA RECORDING
(Conductor's Award)
- *Puccini: Madama Butterfly*, Gabriele Santini conducting the Rome Opera Chorus and Orchestra (solos: de los Angeles, Björing, Pirazzini, Sereni). Capitol.
- *Donizetti: Lucia di Lammermoor*, John Pritchard conducting the Chorus and Orchestra of the Accademia di Santa Cecilia (solos: Sutherland, Cioni, Merrill, Siepi). London.
- *Mozart: The Marriage of Figaro*, Carlo Maria Giulini conducting the Philharmonic Orchestra and Chorus (solos: Schwarzkopf, Moffo, Taddei, Wachter, Cossotto). Angel.
- *R. Strauss: Elektra*, Karl Böhm conducting the Orchestra and Chorus of Dresden State Opera (solos: Borkh, Schech, Madeira, Fischer-Dieskau, Uhl). Deutsche Grammophon.
- *Wagner: The Flying Dutchman*, Antal Dorati conducting the Royal Opera House Orchestra (solos: London, Rysanek, Tozzi, Enas, Liebl, Lewis). RCA.

BEST CLASSICAL PERFORMANCE, CHORAL (OTHER THAN OPERA)
- Robert Shaw Chorale (Robert Shaw conducting), *Bach: B Minor Mass*. RCA.
- French National Radio-TV Chorus and Orchestra (Yvonne Gouverne, director; Georges Prêtre conducting), *Poulenc: Gloria in G Major for Soprano Solo, Chorus and Orchestra*. Angel.
- Roger Wagner Chorale (Roger Wagner, director; Alfred Wallenstein conducting the Los Angeles Philharmonic), *Respighi: Laud to the Nativity*; *Monteverdi: Magnificat*. Capitol.
- Rutgers University Choir (F. Austin Walter, director; Eugene Ormandy conducting the Philadelphia Orchestra), *Walton: Belshazzar's Feast*. Columbia.
- St. Anthony Singers with Pears, Morrison (Colin Davis conducting the Goldsbrough Orchestra), *Berlioz: L'Enfance du Christ*. L'Oiseau-Lyre.
- Westminster Choir (Warren Martin, director; Leonard Bernstein conducting the New York Philharmonic), *Beethoven: Missa Solemnis*. Columbia.

BEST CLASSICAL PERFORMANCE, VOCAL SOLOIST
- Joan Sutherland (Molinari-Pradelli conducting the Royal Opera House Orchestra), *The Art of the Prima Donna*. London.
- Adele Addison (Conant, Russo, Orenstein), *Trimble: Four Fragments from the Canterbury Tales*. Columbia.
- Victoria de los Angeles (Moore, pianist), *The Fabulous Victoria de los Angeles*. Angel.
- Eileen Farrell (Bach Aria Group Orchestra), *Bach: Cantatas Nos. 58 and 202*. Decca.
- Leontyne Price (Defabrutis conducting the Rome Opera House Orchestra), *Operatic Arias*. RCA.

BEST ALBUM COVER, CLASSICAL
(Art Director's Award)
- Marvin Schwartz, *Puccini: Madama Butterfly* (solos: de los Angeles, Björling, Pirazzini, Sereni; Gabriele Santini conducting the Rome Opera Chorus and Orchestra). RCA.
- Robert Jones, *Albéniz: Iberia; Ravel: Rapsodie Espagnole* (Morel conducting the Paris Conservatory Orchestra). RCA.
- Robert Jones, *Gould Ballet Music: Fall River Legend, Interplay, Latin American Symphonette* (Gould and His Orchestra). RCA.
- Meyer Miller, *Golden Age of English Lute Music* (Julian Bream). RCA.
- Marvin Schwartz, *Beethoven: 9 Symphonies* (Klemperer conducting the Philharmonia Orchestra). Angel.

BEST ENGINEERING CONTRIBUTION, CLASSICAL RECORDING
- Lewis W. Layton, *Ravel: Daphnis et Chloé* (Munch conducting the Boston Symphony). RCA.

Robert Fine, *Brahms: Symphony No. 2* (Steinberg conducting the Pittsburgh Symphony). Command.

Heinrich Keiholtz, *R. Strauss: Elektra*, (solos: Borkh, Schech, Madeira, Fischer-Dieskau, Uhl; Bohm conducting the Orchestra and Chorus of Dresden State Opera). Deutsche Grammophon.

Chris Parker, *Prokofiev: Concerto No. 3* (solo: Browning; Leinsdorf conducting the Philharmonia Orchestra). Capitol.

Paul Vavasseur, Walter Ruhlmann, *Poulenc: Concerto in G for Organ, Strings and Timpani* (solo: Duruflé; Prêtre conducting the French National Radio-TV Orchestra). Angel.

BEST DOCUMENTARY OR SPOKEN WORD RECORDING (OTHER THAN COMEDY)

• *Humor in Music*, Leonard Bernstein conducting the New York Philharmonic. Columbia.

The Coming of Christ, Alexander Scourby. Robert Russell Bennett, conductor. Decca.

More of Hal Holbrook in Mark Twain Tonight! Hal Holbrook. Columbia.

Wisdom, Vol. 1 (Sandburg, Shapley, Nehru, Lipschitz), Milt Gabler, producer. Decca.

The World of Dorothy Parker, Dorothy Parker. Verve.

BEST COMEDY PERFORMANCE

• Mike Nichols, Elaine May, *An Evening with Mike Nichols and Elaine May*. Mercury.

Bill Dana, *José Jimenez the Astronaut*. Kapp.

Stan Freberg, *Stan Freberg Presents the United States of America*. Capitol.

Carl Reiner, Mel Brooks, *2,001 Years with Carl Reiner and Mel Brooks*. Capitol.

Jonathan Winters. *Here's Jonathan*. Verve.

BEST RECORDING FOR CHILDREN

• *Prokofiev: Peter and the Wolf*, Leonard Bernstein, New York Philharmonic. Columbia.

Golden Treasury of Great Music and Literature, Arthur Shimkin, producer. Golden.

101 Dalmations, Tutti Carmarata, producer. Disney.

The Soupy Sales Show, Soupy Sales. Reprise.

Young Abe Lincoln (original Broadway cast), Arthur Shimkin, producer. Golden.

BEST ENGINEERED RECORDING, NOVELTY

• John Kraus, *Stan Freberg Presents the United States of America*. Capitol.

Eddie Brackett, *The Soupy Sales Show*. Reprise.

Ted Keep, *The Alvin Show* (David Seville). Liberty.

Rafael O. Valentin, *X-15 and Other Sounds: Rockets Missiles and Jets*. Reprise.

Bruno Vineis, *Cartoons in Stereo* (Bob Prescott). Audio Fidelity.

BEST ENGINEERING CONTRIBUTION, POPULAR RECORDING

• Robert Arnold, *Judy at Carnegie Hall* (Judy Garland). Capitol.

Al Schmitt, *Breakfast at Tiffany's* (Henry Mancini). RCA.

Bill MacMeekin, *Cozy* (Steve Lawrence, Eydie Gormé). United Artists.

Al Schmitt, *Great Band with Great Voices* (Johnny Mann Singers). Liberty.

Robert Fine, *Stereo 35/MM* (Enoch Light). Command.

BEST ALBUM COVER
(Art Director's Award)

• Jim Silke, *Judy at Carnegie Hall* (Judy Garland). Capitol.

Bob Cato, *A Touch of Elegance* (André Previn). Columbia.

Ken Deardoff, *New Orleans—The Living Legend* (Peter Bocage). Riverside.

Robert Jones, *Breakfast at Tiffany's* (Henry Mancini). RCA.

Reid Miles, *Jackie's Bag* (Jackie McLean). Blue Note.

• 1962 •

When the Laughter Died

Variety reported that harmony reigned over this year's Grammy race: "With a fairly large spread of record companies represented with nominations, the squawks that have hounded the academy in the past years have been virtually eliminated." Rock & roll was still downplayed compared to its prominence on American jukeboxes, but otherwise the nominations seemed fairly in synch with the music scene. Even *Down Beat* was upbeat: "Jazz recordings have never been as well represented as they are this year."

The biggest award, Record of the Year, was nonetheless reserved for the kind of romantic ballad that Grammy voters embraced in the past. This year it was Tony Bennett's signature anthem "I Left My Heart in San Francisco," which sold more than 2 million copies in the early 1960s. Bennett's music began the Grammy race with five nominations, including bids for Song, Record and Album of the Year, and ended up with three: best male solo performance and Best Background Arrangement, in addition to the top platter prize.

A loser for best record rebounded to claim the prize for Song of the Year— "What Kind of Fool Am I" from the Leslie Bricusse Anthony Newley Broadway musical *Stop the World—I Want to Get Off.* The tune was such a contemporary hit that multiple recordings competed in multiple Grammy categories. It was Sammy Davis, Jr.'s version that lost Record of the Year and the arrangement awards to Bennett's "San Francisco." Davis's rendition also lost the prize for best male solo vocal performance, as did Newley's own recording.

Two years earlier Bob Newhart proved that the recording business was comprised of more than just music when he won the

Vaughn Meader's LP champ *The First Family* spoofed daily life in the Kennedy White House.

Album of the Year award for *Button Down Mind.* Now the top LP prize, in addition to the award for best comedy recording, went to Vaughn Meader's *The First Family,* a megaselling spoof of President John F. Kennedy's clan. At the Grammy ceremony at the Beverly Hilton, *Variety* columnist Army Archerd reported, "Sheila MacRae accepted for Vaughn Meader—he wanted someone who looked the most like Jackie Kennedy."

Meader is remembered in comedy circles today as a somewhat tragic figure. He was one of the top political parodists of his day, but his career got shot down the same day gunfire felled Kennedy in Dallas on November 22, 1963.

Instead of being yet another stand-up routine, Meader's *First Family* stood out among humor albums because it was one of the earliest audio sitcoms. The record also set a record of its own. When it was released in 1962, it was certified by *The Guinness Book of World Records* as the fastest-selling album of all time.

The LP kidded the Kennedy brood with such silly scenes as young Caroline and John-John taking a bath together, screaming, "The rubber swan is mine!" When French President Charles De Gaulle comes to visit the White House, a budget-conscious President Kennedy orders out for sandwiches instead of giving the French general what he really wants: duck under glass. Meader chose to tweak the First Family more on a cute personal basis than a biting political one. (President Kennedy even tweaked him back once, saying, "I listened to Mr. Meader's record, but I thought it sounded more like Teddy than it did me.") But when Kennedy died, Americans turned on Meader with a vengeance. There were widespread press accounts of people throwing their copies of *The First Family* in the trash, and record buyers refused to give any of his later, non-Kennedy albums a chance. Other comics like Mort Sahl, who also lampooned JFK, rebounded easily after the assassination, but Meader was so closely associated with his Kennedy spoofs that he was never able to rescue his career despite frequent comeback tries that even included changing his name.

The choice of the top rock & roll recording was Bent Fabric's "Alley Cat," which beat out "Big Girls Don't Cry" by the Four Seasons and Neil Sedaka's "Breaking Up Is Hard to Do." Fabric was a notable Danish TV personality, musician and record executive whose real name was Bent Fabricus Bjerre. "Alley Cat" was his only American hit, but it sold more than a million copies and marked the first time that a Danish tune became an American best-seller, which it did for 18 weeks, peaking at number 12 on the charts.

> **Kennedy kidded Meader back, saying his comedy album "sounded more like Teddy than me."**

Peter, Paul & Mary had "Puff the Magic Dragon" in *Variety*'s Top 10 the week of the Grammy contest. The trio was nominated for several awards, including Best New Artist, and reaped two (best vocal group and Best Folk Recording), both for their recording of Pete Seeger's "If I Had a Hammer," which was the year's 10th-best-selling single. Another folk group that also lost the race for Best New Artist won the trophy for choral performance: the New Christy Minstrels, honored for their debut album.

The Best New Artist distinction ended up going to Robert Goulet, the twenty-eight-year-old baritone whose matinee-star looks were literal. He gained renown on Broadway in 1960 as Lancelot in Lerner and Loewe's *Camelot,* also starring Richard Burton and Julie Andrews. Goulet had an album in the Top 20 for the year, *Two of Us,* but it was overlooked by Grammy voters. *Variety* therefore called his one victory an "odd bit," adding, "Goulet copped the Best New Artist honor, but there was no record award to substantiate that accolade. In fact, Goulet didn't even have a disc nomination among the 240 platters in the competition."

Among industry veterans, several came back from past Grammy races to claim even more gold. Ella Fitzgerald nabbed her seventh for giving the best female vocal performance on her album salute to composer/arranger/conductor Nelson Riddle. *Variety* columnist Archerd reported the next day: "N.A.R.A.S. Prexy Van Alexander delivers the Grammy to Ella Fitzgerald at the Flamingo tonight— it was he who arranged her first smash, 'A-Tisket, A-Tasket.'"

Great Songs of Love and Faith won gospel contralto Mahalia Jackson her second consecutive best religious recording award.

Ray Charles received his sixth career Grammy for the year's best r&b recording, "I Can't Stop Loving You," which he included on his first country & western album. In an interview with *Rolling Stone* years later, Charles recalled people warning him against making the LP. He recounted their admonishments: " 'Hey, man, gee whiz, Ray, you got all these fans, you can't do no country-western things. You gonna lose all your fans!' " His *Modern Sounds in Country and Western Music* disc became the first million-seller for ABC-Paramount and scored a nomination for Grammy's Album of the Year. Its "I Can't Stop Loving You" single release was one of the five contenders for Record of the Year.

As *Down Beat* noted, jazz was getting better representation throughout the awards recently, largely because N.A.R.A.S. had decided to redress "such misunderstandings in jazz and other music on the part of the membership," the magazine added. "One should note in passing that even the nominations for these awards are usually made in an open, preliminary balloting of the full membership," but the Recording Academy had polled a number of jazz journalists for nomination recommendations over the past two years.

"This is the first year that a jazz artist, Stan Getz, has been associated in eight categories of nominations," *Down Beat* noted. "Most of the Getz-associated nominations are for 'Desafinado' and *Jazz Samba,* the album from which the former came, both culled by the tenorist and guitarist Charlie Byrd. The 'Desafinado' performance or the album are nominated for record of the year, album of the year, best jazz performance by a soloist or small group and best album cover. Getz's album *Focus,* written by Eddie Sauter, was nominated for best original jazz composition and best instrumental arrangement."

By 1962, Getz had become known as the nation's leading tenor sax player. His frequent collaborator Byrd had recently traveled to Brazil, was impressed by the indigenous music he heard and brought back seven songs he thought might work

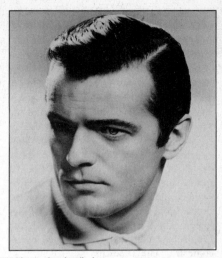

Judy Garland called Grammy's Best New Artist of 1962 Robert Goulet "a living 8-by-10 glossy."

well to a jazz beat. Together he and Getz produced one of the top-selling albums in jazz lore and one that was singly responsible for popularizing the bossa nova sound (bossa nova means "new wave" or "new wrinkle") that engulfed the United States—and the Grammy nominations. Getz won only one award, though—the performance prize for "Desafinado."

The composition award went to pianist Vince Guaraldi for "Cast Your Fate to the Winds." Henry Mancini had been nominated in four categories but won only the Best Instrumental Arrangement trophy for "Baby Elephant Walk."

The Classical Album of the Year was *Columbia Records Presents Vladimir Horowitz,* which also won the virtuoso pianist the solo instrumental award for performing works such as Chopin's Sonata for Piano No. 2 in B Flat Minor and Robert Schumann's Arabeske in C, Op. 18. Columbia's name was prominent in the title because the album was the artist's first release since his break with RCA. After 1953, Horowitz performed only on recordings (he returned to making live performances in 1965), so they were considered particularly valuable, not only for the rare chance to hear the artist play but for his unique interpretation of the classics.

As of 1962, Columbia had recorded more than 40 compositions by Igor Stravinsky and now, in honor of the maestro turning 80, released seven more. Stravinsky's work dominated three of the other classical prizes. He had won Classical Album of the Year last year for new recordings of two dance scores he once wrote for the Ballets Russes (*Petruchka* and *Le Sacre du Printemps*). This year he again conducted the Columbia Symphony Orchestra in another of his Ballets Russes scores, *The Firebird*, which earned him 1962's best classical performance by an orchestra. The maestro was also honored for Best Classical Composition by a Contemporary Composer for *The Flood*, a new musical theater work *High Fidelity* called "a kind of Mystery play." With Stravinsky conducting the Columbia orchestra, Isaac Stern played his Concerto in D for Violin and won the solo instrumental prize for orchestral accompaniment.

Violinist Jascha Heifetz shared the chamber music award with cellist Gregor Piatigorsky for a recording of their four joint concerts with violinist William Primrose held at Hollywood's Pilgrimage Theater. For the winner of the choral accolade, *High Fidelity* had only the highest praise. Bach's *St. Matthew Passion* as performed by a stellar cast including tenor Peter Pears, soprano Elisabeth Schwarzkopf and bass Walter Berry was, it said, "an overwhelming performance, with no weak spots." Soprano Eileen Farrell took the solo vocalist kudos for *Brünnhilde's Immolation Scene* by Wagner, with Leonard Bernstein conducting the New York Philharmonic. (She had performed it once before with Charles Munch and the Boston Symphony.) Sir Georg Solti, who would go on to win

more Grammys than anyone else, garnered the first of his career for Verdi's *Aida,* which was sung by Leontyne Price. "The proportions are beautifully judged," *High Fidelity* said, although "Solti occasionally throws in a highly personal, almost eccentric note. . . . Price's *Aida* is nothing less than a revelation."

In other award categories, Burl Ives won the only Grammy of his long singing career for "Funny Way of Laughin'," which was judged best country & western platter. The theme song to the film *A Taste of Honey,* about a homely white girl who gets pregnant by a black sailor, would come back strong at the 1965 Grammys as Herb Alpert's Record of the Year, but this year won its first award, for Best Instrumental Theme, for writers Bobby Scott and Ric Marlow.

The New York ceremony was held at the Astor Hotel and was emceed by Merv Griffin. *Variety* added: "Count Basie's band dished out the downbeat and Mel Tormé served up several songs. DJ William B. Williams hosted an hour of the overlong affair for broadcast over WNEW radio."

Out on the West Coast, Soupy Sales did the honors at the Beverly Hilton Hotel, although one of his jokes was considered so risqué that it was edited out of the radio broadcast. He said, "Award for best scoring—to Richard Burton," who'd recently begun his notorious affair with Elizabeth Taylor while she was still married to Eddie Fisher. Presenters included Henry Mancini, Les Brown, Connie Stevens, Nelson Riddle and Johnny Mathis. The night's most touching moment involved the bestowal of the prize for best spoken word recording. "An emotional scene was presented when actress Elsa Lanchester accepted the award for her late husband Charles Laughton, for his recording of *The Story Teller,*" *Variety* reported. "This album makes Charles's life a little longer

> **Both Sammy Davis, Jr., and Anthony Newley recorded best song "What Kind of Fool Am I?"**

in a way," Lanchester said, "especially for his friends and family."

"N.A.R.A.S. still has to pull a complete industry turnout," *Variety* added. "Among companies not taking tables were Decca and London."

For the first time since 1959, the Grammys were back on television, but with a difference. Its "Best on Record" roundup show featured winners of the top prizes singing on sequences actually taped months after their victories were announced. N.A.R.A.S. had been lobbying the TV networks aggressively for a live show, but since it couldn't guarantee that celebrity winners would show up, "Best on Record" was the best it could do.

The program had an ominous beginning. It was set to air on November 24, 1963—just two days after the Kennedy assassination. Luckily for the academy, the program was moved to more than a week afterward, giving viewers a chance to cope with the shocking news. The "Best on Record" failed to feature the person who won the best album prize. Kennedy spoofer Vaughn Meader was nixed from the program, even though he offered to substitute his Kennedy routine with a serious personal tribute.

• 1962 •

Awards were bestowed on May 15, 1963, at ceremonies held simultaneously at the Beverly Hilton Hotel in Los Angeles and the Astor Hotel in New York for the eligibility period December 1, 1961, to November 30, 1962.

ALBUM OF THE YEAR

• *The First Family*, Vaughn Meader. Cadence.

I Left My Heart in San Francisco, Tony Bennett. Columbia.

Jazz Samba, Stan Getz, Charlie Byrd. Verve.

Modern Sounds in Country & Western Music, Ray Charles. ABC-Paramount.

My Son, the Folk Singer, Allan Sherman. Warner Bros.

RECORD OF THE YEAR

• "I Left My Heart in San Francisco," Tony Bennett. Columbia.

"Desafinado," Stan Getz, Charlie Byrd. Verve.

"Fly Me to the Moon Bossa Nova," Joe Harnell & His Orchestra. Kapp.

"I Can't Stop Loving You," Ray Charles. ABC-Paramount.

"Ramblin' Rose," Nat King Cole. Capitol.

"What Kind of Fool Am I," Sammy Davis, Jr. Reprise.

SONG OF THE YEAR
(Songwriter's Award)

• "What Kind of Fool Am I," Leslie Bricusse, Anthony Newley.

"As Long As He Needs Me," Lionel Bart.

"I Left My Heart in San Francisco," Douglass Cross, George Cory.

"My Coloring Book," John Kander, Fred Ebb.

"The Sweetest Sounds," Richard Rodgers.

BEST NEW ARTIST

• Robert Goulet

Four Seasons

Vaughn Meader

New Christy Minstrels

Peter, Paul & Mary

Allan Sherman

BEST SOLO VOCAL PERFORMANCE, MALE

• Tony Bennett, "I Left My Heart in San Francisco." Columbia.

Ray Charles, "I Can't Stop Loving You." ABC-Paramount.

Sammy Davis, Jr., "What Kind of Fool Am I." Reprise.

Anthony Newley, "What Kind of Fool Am I." London.

Mel Tormé, "Comin' Home Baby." Atlantic.

BEST SOLO VOCAL PERFORMANCE, FEMALE

- Ella Fitzgerald, *Ella Swings Brightly with Nelson Riddle*. Verve.

Diahann Carroll, *No Strings*. Capitol.

Lena Horne, *Lena . . . Lovely and Alive*. RCA.

Peggy Lee, "I'm a Woman." Capitol.

Ketty Lester, *Love Letters*. Era.

Sandy Stewart, "My Coloring Book." Colpix.

Pat Thomas, "Slightly out of Tune (Desafinado)." Verve.

BEST PERFORMANCE BY A VOCAL GROUP

- Peter, Paul & Mary, "If I Had a Hammer." Warner Bros.

Four Freshmen, *The Swingers*. Capitol.

Hi-Lo's, *The Hi-Lo's Happen to Folk Songs*. Reprise.

Lettermen, *A Song for Young Love*. Capitol.

Limeliters, *Through Children's Eyes*. RCA.

BEST PERFORMANCE BY A CHORUS

- New Christy Minstrels, *Presenting the New Christy Minstrels*. Columbia.

Pete King Chorale, *Consider Yourself*. Kapp.

Norman Luboff, *A Choral Spectacular*. RCA.

Johnny Mann Singers (Si Zentner Orchestra), *Great Band with Great Voices Swing the Great Voices of the Great Bands*. Liberty.

Fred Waring & the Pennsylvanians, *The Waring Blend*. Capitol.

BEST ROCK & ROLL RECORDING

- "Alley Cat," Bent Fabric. Atco

"Big Girls Don't Cry," Four Seasons. VeeJay.

"Breaking Up Is Hard to Do," Neil Sedaka. RCA.

"Twistin' the Night Away," Sam Cooke. RCA.

"Up on the Roof," Drifters. Atlantic.

"You Beat Me to the Punch," Mary Wells. Motown.

BEST RHYTHM & BLUES RECORDING

- "I Can't Stop Loving You," Ray Charles. ABC-Paramount.

"Bring It on Home to Me," Sam Cooke. RCA.

"Comin' Home Baby," Mel Tormé. Atlantic.

"Loco-Motion," Little Eva. Dimension.

"Nut Rocker," B. Bumble & the Stingers. Rendezvous.

"What'd I Say," Bobby Darin. Atco.

BEST ORIGINAL JAZZ COMPOSITION (Composer's Award)

- Vince Guaraldi, "Cast Your Fate to the Winds." Fantasy.

Paul Desmond, "Desmond Blue." RCA.

Quincy Jones, "Quintessence." Impulse.

Henry Mancini, "Sounds of *Hatari!*" RCA.

Charlie Mingus, "Tijuana Moods." RCA.

Eddie Sauter, "Focus." Verve.

Lalo Schifrin, "Tunisian Fantasy." Verve.

BEST JAZZ PERFORMANCE BY A SOLOIST OR SMALL GROUP, INSTRUMENTAL

- Stan Getz, "Desafinado." Verve.

Laurindo Almeida, *Viva Bossa Nova!* Capitol.

Eddie Cano, *A Taste of Honey*. Reprise.

Bill Evans, Jim Hall, *Undercurrent*. United Artists.

Charlie Mingus, *Tijuana Moods*. RCA.

Oscar Peterson Trio, *West Side Story*. Verve.

George Shearing Quintet, *Nat King Cole Sings, George Shearing Plays*. Capitol.

BEST JAZZ PERFORMANCE BY A LARGE GROUP, INSTRUMENTAL

- Stan Kenton, *Adventures in Jazz*. Capitol.

Count Basie, *The Legend*. Roulette.

Miles Davis, Gil Evans, *Miles Davis at Carnegie Hall*. Columbia.

Duke Ellington, Count Basie, *First Time!* Columbia.

Stan Getz, Gary McFarland, *Big Band Bossa Nova*. Verve.

Dizzy Gillespie, *Carnegie Hall Concert*. Verve.

Jimmy Smith, *Walk on the Wild Side*.
Verve.

BEST COUNTRY & WESTERN RECORDING

- "Funny Way of Laughin'," Burl Ives.
  Decca.
"Devil Woman," Marty Robbins.
  Columbia.
"It Keeps Right on A-Hurtin'," Johnny
  Tillotson. Cadence.
"P.T. 109," Jimmy Dean. Columbia.
"She Thinks I Still Care," George Jones.
  United Artists.
"Wolverton Mountain," Claude King.
  Columbia.

BEST FOLK RECORDING

- "If I Had a Hammer," Peter, Paul &
  Mary. Warner Bros.
"The Ballad of Jed Clampett," Flatt &
  Scruggs. Columbia.
Bob Dylan, Bob Dylan. Columbia.
Joan Baez in Concert, Joan Baez. Van-
  guard.
The Midnight Special, Harry Belafonte.
  RCA.
Presenting the New Christy Minstrels,
  New Christy Minstrels. Columbia.
Something Special, Kingston Trio. Capitol.

BEST GOSPEL OR OTHER RELIGIOUS RECORDING

- *Great Songs of Love and Faith*,
  Mahalia Jackson. Columbia.
Black Nativity, Prof. Alex Bradford (Mar-
  ion Williams & Stars of Faith). VeeJay.
Hymns at Sunset, Ralph Carmichael.
  Capitol.
I Love to Tell the Story, Tennessee Ernie
  Ford. Capitol.
*Inspiration—Great Music for Chorus
  and Orchestra*, Norman Luboff Choir
  (Leopold Stokowki conducting the
  New Symphony Orchestra of Lon-
  don). RCA.
*Marian Anderson—He's Got the Whole
  World in His Hands, and 18 Other
  Spirituals*, Marian Anderson (Franz
  Rupp, piano). RCA.
Same Me, Clefs of Calvary. True Sound.

BEST PERFORMANCE BY AN ORCHESTRA FOR DANCING

- Joe Harnell, *Fly Me to the Moon
  Bossa Nova*. Kapp.
Laurindo Almeida, *Viva Bossa Nova!*
  Capitol.
Stan Getz, Gary McFarland, *Big Band
  Bossa Nova*. Verve.
Neal Hefti, *Jazz Pops*. Reprise.
Quincy Jones, *Big Band Bossa Nova*.
  Mercury.
David Rose, *The Stripper*. MGM.

BEST PERFORMANCE BY AN ORCHESTRA OR INSTRUMENTALIST WITH ORCHESTRA (NOT JAZZ OR DANCING)

- Peter Nero, *The Colorful Peter Nero*.
  RCA.
Elmer Bernstein, *Walk on the Wild Side*.
  Ava.
Acker Bilk, *Stranger on the Shore*. Atco.
Henry Mancini, *Hatari!* RCA.
Felix Slatkin, *Hoedown!* Liberty.

BEST INSTRUMENTAL THEME
(Composer's Award)

- "A Taste of Honey," Bobby Scott, Ric
  Marlow. Reprise.
"Baby Elephant Walk," Henry Mancini.
  RCA.
"*Route 66* Theme," Nelson Riddle.
  Capitol.
"Stranger on the Shore," Acker Bilk,
  Robert Mellin. Atco.
"The Stripper," David Rose. MGM.
"Walk on the Wild Side," Elmer Bern-
  stein, Mack David. Ava.

BEST INSTRUMENTAL ARRANGEMENT

- Henry Mancini, "Baby Elephant
  Walk." RCA.
Robert Farnon, *Sensuous Strings of
  Robert Farnon*. Mercury.
Joe Harnell, *Fly Me to the Moon Bossa
  Nova*. Kapp.
Quincy Jones, "Quintessence." Impulse.
Nelson Riddle, "*Route 66* Theme."
  Capitol.
David Rose, "The Stripper." MGM.
Eddie Sauter, "Focus" (Stan Getz). Verve.

BEST ORIGINAL CAST SHOW ALBUM
(Composer's Award)
- *No Strings*, Richard Rodgers (Broadway cast). Capitol.

A Funny Thing Happened on the Way to the Forum, Stephen Sondheim (Broadway cast). Capitol.

Beyond the Fringe, Dudley Moore (Alan Bennett, Peter Cook, Jonathan Miller, Dudley Moore). Capitol.

Oliver! Lionel Bart (Broadway cast). RCA.

Stop the World—I Want to Get Off, Leslie Bricusse, Anthony Newley (Anthony Newley, Anna Quayle and cast). London.

BEST BACKGROUND ARRANGEMENT
- Marty Manning, "I Left My Heart in San Francisco" (Tony Bennett). Columbia.

Marion Evans, "Go Away Little Girl" (Steve Lawrence). Columbia.

Bill Finegan, "My Ship" (Carol Sloane). Columbia.

Antonio Carlos Jobim, *João Gilberto* (João Gilberto). Capitol.

Marty Paich, "Born to Lose" (Ray Charles). ABC-Paramount.

Marty Paich, "I Can't Stop Loving You" (Ray Charles). ABC-Paramount.

Marty Paich, "What Kind of Fool Am I" (Sammy Davis, Jr.). Reprise.

ALBUM OF THE YEAR, CLASSICAL
- *Columbia Records Presents Vladimir Horowitz*, Vladimir Horowitz. Columbia.

Bach: St. Matthew Passion, Otto Klemperer conducting the Philharmonia Orchestra and Choir. Angel.

The Heifetz-Piatigorsky Concerts with Primrose, Pennario and Guests, Jascha Heifetz, Gregor Piatigorsky. RCA.

Mahler: Symphony No. 9 in D Minor, Bruno Walter conducting the Columbia Symphony. Columbia.

Stravinsky: The Firebird Ballet, Igor Stravinsky conducting the Columbia Symphony. Columbia.

BEST CLASSICAL COMPOSITION BY A CONTEMPORARY COMPOSER
- Igor Stravinsky, *The Flood*.

Benjamin Britten, *Noye's Fludde*.

Aaron Copland, *Connotations for Orchestra*.

Lukas Foss, *Song of Songs*.

Lukas Foss, *Time Cycle*.

Edgard Varèse, *Arcana*.

Sir William Walton, *Symphony No. 2*.

BEST CLASSICAL PERFORMANCE, ORCHESTRA
(Conductor's Award)
- Igor Stravinsky conducting the Columbia Symphony, *Stravinsky: The Firebird Ballet*. Columbia.

Leonard Bernstein conducting the New York Philharmonic, *Mahler: Symphony No. 3 in D Minor*. Columbia.

Otto Klemperer conducting the Philharmonia Orchestra, *Bruckner: Symphony No. 7 in E Major*. Angel.

Fritz Reiner conducting the Chicago Symphony, *R. Strauss: Also Sprach Zarathustra, Op. 30*. RCA.

Bruno Walter conducting the Columbia Symphony, *Mahler: Symphony No. 9 in D Minor*. Columbia.

BEST CHAMBER MUSIC PERFORMANCE
- Jascha Heifetz, Gregor Piatigorsky, William Primrose, *The Heifetz-Piatigorsky Concerts with Primrose, Pennario and Guests*. RCA.

Laurindo Almeida, Virginia Majewski, Vincent De Rosa, *The Intimate Bach*. Capitol.

Budapest String Quartet. *Beethoven: The Late Quartets*. Columbia.

Hungarian Quartet, *Bartók: Complete Quartets*. Deutsche Grammophon.

Yehudi Menuhin, George Malcolm, *Bach: Sonatas for Violin and Harpsichord*. Angel.

Artur Rubinstein, Henryk Szeryng, *Rubinstein and Szeryng Violin Sonatas, Brahms: Sonata No. 1; Beethoven: Sonata No. 8, Op. 30, No. 3*. RCA.

BEST CLASSICAL PERFORMANCE, INSTRUMENTAL SOLOIST(S) (WITH ORCHESTRA)

- Isaac Stern (Stravinsky conducting the Columbia Symphony), *Stravinsky: Concerto in D for Violin.* Columbia.

Jascha Heifetz (Sargent conducting the New Symphony Orchestra of London), *Bruch: Scottish Fantasy; Vieuxtemps: Concerto No. 5.* RCA.

David Oistrakh (Klemperer conducting the French National Radio Orchestra), *Brahms: Concerto in D for Violin.* Angel.

Sviatoslav Richter (Kondrashin conducting the London Symphony), *Liszt: Concertos Nos. 1 and 2 for Piano and Orchestra.* Mercury.

Van Cliburn (Reiner conducting the Chicago Symphony), *Rachmaninov: Concerto No. 2.* RCA.

BEST CLASSICAL PERFORMANCE, INSTRUMENTAL SOLOIST OR DUO (WITHOUT ORCHESTRA)

- Vladimir Horowitz, *Columbia Records Presents Vladimir Horowitz.* Columbia.

Leon Goossens, *The Art of Leon Goossens.* Angel.

Robert and Gaby Casadesus, *French Piano Music—Four Hands.* Columbia.

Glenn Gould, *Bach: The Art of the Fugue, Vol. 1.* Columbia.

Sviatoslav Richter, *Beethoven: Sonata No. 22 for Piano.* RCA.

Artur Rubinstein, *Highlights of Rubinstein at Carnegie Hall Recorded During the Historic 10 Recitals of 1961.* RCA.

Andrés Segovia, *5 Pieces from Platero and I.* Decca.

Joseph Szigeti, *Bach: The 6 Sonatas and Partitas for Violin Unaccompanied.* Vanguard.

BEST OPERA RECORDING
(Conductor's Award)

- *Verdi: Aida*, Georg Solti conducting the Rome Opera House Orchestra and Chorus (solos: Price, Vickers, Gorr, Merrill, Tozzi). RCA.

Beethoven: Fidelio, Otto Klemperer conducting the Philharmonia Orchestra and Chorus (solos: Ludwig, Vickers, Frick, Hallstein, Berry). Angel.

Bizet: The Pearl Fishers, Pierre Dervaux conducting the Chorus and Orchestra of Théâtre National de l'Opéra Comique (solos: Micheau, Gedda). Angel.

Puccini: La Bohème, Erich Leinsdorf conducting the Rome Opera House Orchestra and Chorus (solos: Moffo, Tucker, Costa, Merrill, Tozzi, Maero). RCA.

R. Strauss: Salome, Georg Solti conducting the Vienna Philharmonic (solos: Nilsson, Wachter, Stolze). London.

Wagner: Die Walküre, Erich Leinsdorf conducting the London Symphony (solos: Nilsson, Brouwenstijn, Gorr, Vickers, London, Ward). RCA.

BEST CLASSICAL PERFORMANCE, CHORAL (OTHER THAN OPERA)

- Philharmonia Choir, Wilhelm Pitz, choral director; Otto Klemperer conducting the Philharmonia Orchestra, *Bach: St. Matthew Passion.* Angel.

New England Conservatory Chorus, Lorna Cooke de Varon, director; Charles Munch conducting the Boston Symphony, *Berlioz: Roméo et Juliette.* RCA.

University of Utah Chorus, Ardean Watts, director; Maurice Abravanel conducting the Utah Symphony, *Honegger: King David (Le Roi David).* Vanguard.

Roger Wagner Chorale, Orchestre de la Société des Concerts du Conservatoire de Paris, Roger Wagner, conductor, *Fauré: Requiem.* Capitol.

Westminster Choir, Warren Martin, director; Thomas Schippers conducting the New York Philharmonic, *Prokofiev: Alexander Nevsky, Op. 78.* Columbia.

Women's Chorus of Schola Cantorum; Hugh Ross, director of Boys' Choir; Church of Transfiguration, Stuart Gardner, director; Leonard Bernstein conducting the New York Philharmonic, *Mahler: Symphony No. 3 in D Minor*. Columbia.

BEST CLASSICAL PERFORMANCE, VOCAL SOLOIST (WITH OR WITHOUT ORCHESTRA)

• Eileen Farrell (Bernstein conducting the New York Philharmonic), *Wagner: Götterdämmerung, Brünnhilde's Immolation Scene; Wesendonck: Songs*. Columbia.

Adele Addison (Bernstein conducting the New York Philharmonic), *Foss: Time Cycle*. Columbia.

Victoria de los Angeles (Soriano, piano), *Spanish Songs of the 20th Century*. Angel.

Maria Callas (Prêtre conducting the Orchestre National de la Radio Diffusion Française), *Great Arias from French Opera*. Angel.

Dietrich Fischer-Dieskau (Moore, piano), *Schubert: Die Schöne Müllerin*. Angel.

Birgit Nilsson (Solti conducting the Vienna Philharmonic), *R. Strauss: Salome*. London.

BEST ALBUM COVER, CLASSICAL
(Art Director's Award)

• Marvin Schwartz, *The Intimate Bach* (solos: Almeida, Majewski, De Rosa). Capitol.

Marvin Schwartz, *Beethoven: Fidelio* (Klemperer conducting the Philharmonia Orchestra and Chorus). Angel.

Marvin Schwartz, *Fauré: Requiem* (Wagner conducting the Roger Wagner Chorale and Orchestre de la Société des Concerts due Conservatoire de Paris). Capitol.

Marvin Schwartz, *Otto Klemperer Conducts* (Weill, *Threepenny Opera Suite* and others) (Klemperer conducting the Philharmonia Orchestra). Angel.

Marvin Schwartz, *Wagner: Prelude and Love Death; R. Strauss: Death and Transfiguration* (Leinsdorf conducting the Los Angeles Philharmonic). Capitol.

Jim Silke, *Bartók: The Miraculous Mandarin; Shostakovich: The Age of Gold* (Irving conducting the Philharmonia Orchestra). Capitol.

BEST ENGINEERING CONTRIBUTION, CLASSICAL RECORDING

• Lewis W. Layton, *Strauss: Also Sprach Zarathustra, Op. 30* (Reiner conducting the Chicago Symphony). RCA.

William Britten, *Mahler: Symphony No. 9 in D Minor* (Walter conducting the Columbia Symphony Orchestra). Columbia.

Robert Fine, *Copland: Billy the Kid; Appalachian Spring* (Dorati conducting the London Symphony). Mercury.

Robert Fine, *Prokofiev: Concerto No. 3 for Piano; Rachmaninov: Concerto No. 1 for Piano* (Janis, piano; Kondrashin conducting the Moscow Philharmonic). Mercury.

London Recording Team, *Holst: The Planets* (von Karajan conducting the Vienna Philharmonic). Columbia.

Fred Plaut, *Mahler: Symphony No. 3 in D Minor* (Bernstein conducting the New York Philharmonic). Columbia.

Fred Plaut, *Columbia Records Presents Vladimir Horowitz*. Columbia.

BEST DOCUMENTARY OR SPOKEN WORD RECORDING (OTHER THAN COMEDY)

• *The Story Teller: A Session with Charles Laughton*, Charles Laughton. Capitol.

Carl Sandburg Reading His Poetry, Carl Sandburg. Caedmon.

Enoch Arden (music by R. Strauss; poem by Alfred Tennyson), Claude Rains, reader; Glenn Gould, pianist. Columbia.

First Performance: Lincoln Center for the Performing Arts, Leonard Bernstein conducting the New York Philharmonic. Columbia.

Mama Sang a Song, Stan Kenton. Capitol.

Sir Michael Redgrave Reads "The Harmfulness of Tobacco," "A Transgression," "The First Class Passenger" by Anton Chekhov, Sir Michael Redgrave. Spoken Arts.

Six Million Accuse, Yehuda Lev, narrator. United Artists.

This Is My Beloved, Laurence Harvey. Atlantic.

BEST COMEDY PERFORMANCE

• Vaughn Meader, *The First Family*. Cadence.

Alan Bennett, Peter Cook, Jonathan Miller, Dudley Moore, *Beyond the Fringe*. Capitol.

Elaine May, Mike Nichols, *Nichols and May Examine Doctors*. Mercury.

Allan Sherman, *My Son, the Folk Singer*. Warner Bros.

Jonathan Winters, *Another Day, Another World*. Verve.

BEST RECORDING FOR CHILDREN

• *Saint-Saëns: Carnival of the Animals; Britten: Young Person's Guide to the Orchestra*, Leonard Bernstein. Columbia.

The Cat Who Walked by Herself, Boris Karloff. Caedmon.

The Chipmunk Songbook, David Seville. Liberty.

Grimms' Fairy Tales, Danny Kaye. Golden.

Shari in Storyland, Shari Lewis. RCA.

Through Children's Eyes, Limeliters. RCA.

You Read to Me, I'll Read to You, John Ciardi. Spoken.

BEST ENGINEERED RECORDING, NOVELTY

• Robert Fine, *The Civil War, Vol. 1* (Fennell conducting the Eastman

Wind Ensemble; Martin Gabel, narrator). Mercury.

Lowell Frank, *My Son, the Folk Singer* (Allan Sherman). Warner Bros.

John Quinn, *The First Family* (Vaughn Meader). Cadence.

Al Schmitt, *The Chipmunk Songbook* (David Seville). Liberty.

Eddie Smith. *Pepino, the Italian Mouse* (Lou Monte). Reprise.

BEST ENGINEERING CONTRIBUTION (OTHER THAN NOVELTY OR CLASSICAL)

• Al Schmitt, *Hatari!* (Henry Mancini). RCA.

Hugh Davies, *Jonah Jones and Glen Gray*. Capitol.

William Hamilton, *Stereo Spectacular* (various artists). Audio Fidelity.

John Kraus, "*Route 66* Theme" (Nelson Riddle). Capitol.

Bill Putnam, *I Can't Stop Loving You* (Ray Charles). ABC-Paramount.

Al Schmitt, *Great Band with Great Voices Swing the Great Voices of the Great Bands* (Si Zentner Orchestra, Johnny Mann Singers). Liberty.

Carson C. Taylor, *Adventures in Jazz* (Stan Kenton). Capitol.

BEST ALBUM COVER (OTHER THAN CLASSICAL)
(Art Director's Award)

• Robert Jones, *Lena . . . Lovely and Alive* (Lena Horne). RCA.

Loring Eutemey, *The Comedy* (Modern Jazz Quartet). Atlantic.

Loring Eutemey, *Lonely Woman* (Modern Jazz Quartet). Atlantic.

Ken Kim, *My Son, the Folk Singer* (Allan Sherman). Warner Bros.

Bill Longcore, *The First Family* (Vaughn Meader). Cadence.

John Murello, *Jazz Samba* (Stan Getz). Verve.

Jim Silke, *The Great Years* (Frank Sinatra). Capitol.

Ed Thrasher, *Potpourri par Piaf* (Edith Piaf). Capitol.

• 1963 •
Happy Days for Mancini and Streisand

In 1961, the last time that both the Record and Song of the Year trophies were given to one artist, they went to the same artist they did this year: Henry Mancini, who was back to claim 3 more Grammys to bring his career total to an astounding 14. In Grammy's six-year history, only once did he fail to strike gold—at the 1959 awards.

Once again Mancini also won an Oscar for the same music that earned him a golden gramophone. It last happened two years ago when he teamed up with Johnny Mercer on "Moon River." Now he and Mercer triumphed for "The Days of Wine and Roses," which they composed for Blake Edwards, the same director Mancini worked with on the TV series *Peter Gunn* (earning him two Grammys) and the film *Breakfast at Tiffany's* (five more, one shared with Mercer).

The movie *Days of Wine and Roses* starred Jack Lemmon and Lee Remick as a married couple drowning in the horrors of alcoholism. A popular version of the theme song was recorded by Andy Williams, but Mancini's rendition reached only number 33 on the charts, making his Record of the Year triumph one of the rare times that the top award didn't go to a commercial hit. It also earned him a Grammy for Best Background Arrangement. The full soundtrack was nominated for Album of the Year.

Instead of going to a veteran talent like Mancini, the LP trophy went to a twenty-two-year-old upstart who became the youngest artist ever to receive the honor. Before Barbra Streisand became famous for the stage and film versions of

The victory of Henry Mancini's "Days of Wine and Roses" was Grammy's "biggest longshot."

Funny Girl, she gained notice on Broadway for her large nose and "delicatessen accent" in the role of Miss Marmelstein in the Harold Rome musical *I Can Get It for You Wholesale*. Streisand's rave reviews and the success of the cast album convinced Columbia that she might be due for her first solo LP. The result was a standout for her renditions of Cole Porter's "Come to the Supermarket (in Old Peking)" and the slow, ballad version of "Happy Days Are Here Again" that was nominated for Record of the Year. *The Barbra Streisand Album* won three Grammys, including the prize for best female vocal performance and Best Album Cover.

The best male vocalist honor went to Jack Jones, who last won a Grammy at the 1961 awards, and now competed with

"Wives and Lovers," which was also a contender for best record. Another returning champ was Count Basie, who was acknowledged for *This Time by Basie! Hits of the '50s and '60s,* which earned him the dance orchestra award for a third time, bringing his career tally to four statuettes. Reclaiming the prizes they won last year for group vocals and folk music, Peter, Paul & Mary were now honored for their rendition of Bob Dylan's "Blowin' in the Wind."

Quincy Jones won the first statuette of his many-Grammyed career for his instrumental arrangement of "I Can't Stop Loving You."

The choice of best rock & roll platter came as a surprise when it beat out Lesley Gore's "It's My Party," Sam Cooke's "Another Saturday Night," Little Peggy March's "I Will Follow Him" and "Our Day Will Come" by Ruby & the Romantics. "Deep Purple" was a last-minute, desperation release by Atlantic Records, which had been trying for years to popularize the brother-sister team of Nino Tempo and April Stevens. When "Purple" topped the charts for a week in November, it became the crowning record of the combo's career.

Belgium's Singing Nun was up for four Grammys, including Album and Record of the Year, winning only the award for religious music for "Dominique." The Singing Nun was really Sister Luc-Gabrielle (Jeanine Deckers in lay life; dubbed Soeur Sourire, or "Sister Smile," by Philips Records). She became a star by accident after having pressed Philips execs into letting her use their studios to tape some religious songs that were favorites with the students at her convent. The execs were so impressed by her music that they gave it a commercial release that resulted in both "Dominique" and *The Singing Nun* topping the single and album charts simultaneously. Then came the vocalist's fall, in a sense, from grace. A 1966 movie based on her life starring Debbie Reynolds was panned by the critics. Soon thereafter, she left the convent. In 1985, she committed suicide.

Bobby Bare had Grammy's best country & western song of the year. He first gained renown with his surprise hit of 1959, "The All-American Boy," but then vanished from the music scene for a few years while he served in the military. Soon after being discharged, Bare wrote and recorded the Grammy-winning "Detroit City" and went on to croon more than 50 other c&w hits such as "500 Miles from Home" and "Come Sundown."

Allan Sherman gave the comedy performance of the year in his number-one single "Hello Muddah, Hello Faddah," a recitation of a boy's letter to his parents from summer camp, set to the music of Amilcare Ponchielli's "Dance of the Hours." One of the funniest aspects of the win was that Sherman triumphed over a man who took himself very seriously and was not accustomed to losing (Cassius Clay, later known as Muhammad Ali) and another one who would come to dominate the category for six years (Bill Cosby) after Sherman introduced him to record executives.

Several surprises rocked the jazz categories. Music critics were rooting for Charlie Mingus's "Black Saint and the Sinner Lady" for the best composition prize, but instead it went, in a major upset, to musician-composer Ray Brown and comedian and occasional songwriter and pianist Steve Allen for "Gravy Waltz."

At the Los Angeles Grammy ceremony, *Variety* columnist Army Archerd reported, "When the Best New Artist winner was announced as the Swingle Sisters, you could have knocked over with a feather contenders Vikki Carr, John Gary and Trini Lopez." The French

At 22, Streisand became the youngest artist ever to win best album.

pop vocal group formed by singer-arranger Ward Lamar Swingle became popular for jazzing up classical music by scat-singing Bach and Mozart. Their *Bach's Greatest Hits* LP lost its bid for Album of the Year but won the chorus award over such past victors as the New Christy Minstrels and the Mormon Tabernacle Choir.

In another surprise outcome, the orchestra trophy went to "Java," a work that marked a move into the big time for the 6'2", 300-pound bandleader and trumpet player known in the jazz world as "the Monster," Al Hirt. "Java," Hirt's first million-selling single, was a track from *Honey in the Horn,* his first million-selling LP that was also a contender for Grammy's Album of the Year prize.

The laurel for jazz solo work went to *Conversations with Myself* by Bill Evans, who "plays the piano the way it should be played," Miles Davis once said to jazz writer Leonard Feather (who won a Grammy this year himself for the album notes to *The Ellington Era*). The Woody Herman Band garnered the large-group jazz statuette for *Encore.*

The choice of the Classical Album of the Year was Benjamin Britten's recording of his *War Requiem,* which he wrote for the rededication of England's Coventry Cathedral after it was severely wrecked during World War II. The result was an unconventional music work mingling elements of the *Latin Mass for the Dead* with the inspired antiwar poems of Wilfred Owen, a 25-year-old British soldier who died in battle. *Requiem* was also named Best Classical Composition by a Contemporary Composer and took the choral honors.

The winner of last year's Classical Album of the Year award, Vladimir Horowitz, returned to snare a new prize for best instrumental soloist for his new

Variety cheered the ceremony as "the most successful and harmonious affair" yet.

Sound of Horowitz album. Conductor Erich Leinsdorf figured prominently in the other classical categories: He led the Boston Symphony Orchestra in Bartók's Concerto for Orchestra (best classical orchestra performance) and he and the orchestra backed up Artur Rubinstein in Tchaikovsky's *Concerto No. 1 in B Flat Minor for Piano and Orchestra* (best instrumental soloist with orchestra). "Passion rather than frenzy predominates in this splendid performance," *High Fidelity* wrote of the Tchaikovsky work. Rubinstein, it added, "admirably resists the temptation to blow the spark into a conflagration."

Leinsdorf also conducted the RCA Italiana Opera Orchestra and Chorus in the year's top operatic recording, Puccini's *Madama Butterfly,* sung by Leontyne Price (who won the vocal soloist award for *Great Scenes from Gershwin's "Porgy and Bess"*). About Leinsdorf, *High Fidelity* said, "He must share praise with his orchestra, which is every bit as good as hoped." About Price, the magazine's reviewer wrote, "I don't think there's a wrong note within hailing distance of this recording."

N.A.R.A.S. added a new accolade this year meant to be a classical equivalent of Best New Artist and one that would last only a few years. The first winner of the award for Most Promising New Classical Artist (the word "Classical" would be eliminated next year) went to André Watts, the young pianist who had made a celebrated debut with the New York Philharmonic in a televised program in 1962 when he was only 16 years old.

Comic Stan Freberg did a "terrif m.c. job" at the Grammy ceremony at the Beverly Hilton in Los Angeles, according to *Variety* columnist Army Archerd. (The Freberg joke that Archerd liked best: "There was to be a Lyndon B.

Johnson Award for the record that 'Most Grabbed You by the Ears.'") Les Brown and his band "maintained the dignity of the evening by playing good music—no wild, Watusi-type jazz," Archerd added. Other entertainment included Vikki Carr, John Gary and the Swingle Sisters. The West Coast ceremony was plagued by a preponderance of no-show winners, 80 percent by one account. At the Waldorf-Astoria in New York, most of the victors in the classical categories were on hand to receive their laurels.

"Turnouts in both cities were at capacity for the hotel rooms," *Variety* added, "and marked the most successful and harmonious affair in N.A.R.A.S.'s six-year history."

Conductor Erich Leinsdorf's *Madama Butterfly* was hailed as the year's Best Opera Recording.

• 1963 •

Awards were bestowed on May 12, 1964, at ceremonies held at the Beverly Hilton Hotel in Los Angeles, the Waldorf-Astoria Hotel in New York City and the Knickerbocker Hotel in Chicago for the eligibility period December 1, 1962, to November 30, 1963.

ALBUM OF THE YEAR
• *The Barbra Streisand Album*, Barbra Streisand. Columbia.
Bach's Greatest Hits, Swingle Singers. Philips.
Days of Wine and Roses, Andy Williams. Columbia.
Honey in the Horn, Al Hirt. RCA.
The Singing Nun, Soeur Sourire (Singing Nun). Philips.

RECORD OF THE YEAR
• "Days of Wine and Roses," Henry Mancini. RCA.
"Dominique," Soeur Sourire (Singing Nun). Philips.
"Happy Days Are Here Again," Barbra Streisand. Columbia.

"I Wanna Be Around," Tony Bennett. Columbia.
"Wives and Lovers," Jack Jones. Kapp.

SONG OF THE YEAR
(Songwriter's Award)
• "The Days of Wine and Roses," Johnny Mercer, Henry Mancini.
"Call Me Irresponsible," Sammy Cahn, Jimmy Van Heusen.
"The Good Life," Sacha Distel, Jack Reardon.
"I Wanna Be Around," Sadie Vimmerstedt, Johnny Mercer.
"Wives and Lovers," Burt Bacharach, Hal David.

BEST NEW ARTIST
• Swingle Singers
Vikki Carr
John Gary
J's with Jamie
Trini Lopez

BEST VOCAL PERFORMANCE, MALE
• Jack Jones, "Wives and Lovers." Kapp.

Tony Bennett, "I Wanna Be Around." Columbia.

Ray Charles, "Busted." ABC-Paramount.

John Gary, "Catch a Rising Star." RCA.

Andy Williams, "Days of Wine and Roses." Columbia.

BEST VOCAL PERFORMANCE, FEMALE

• Barbra Streisand, *The Barbra Streisand Album*. Columbia.

Eydie Gormé, "Blame It on the Bossa Nova." Columbia.

Peggy Lee, *I'm a Woman*. Capitol.

Miriam Makeba, *The World of Miriam Makeba*. RCA.

Soeur Sourire (Singing Nun), "Dominique." Philips.

BEST PERFORMANCE BY A VOCAL GROUP

• Peter, Paul & Mary, "Blowin' in the Wind." Warner Bros.

Hi-Lo's, *The Hi-Lo's Happen to Bossa Nova*. Reprise.

J's with Jamie, *Hey Look Us Over!* Columbia.

Anita Kerr Quartet, *Waitin' for the Evening Train*. RCA.

Jackie & Roy Kral, *Like Sing—Jackie and Roy Kral*. Columbia.

BEST PERFORMANCE BY A CHORUS

• Swingle Singers, *Bach's Greatest Hits*. Philips.

Henry Mancini & His Orchestra with Chorus, *Charade*. RCA.

Mormon Tabernacle Choir (Richard P. Condie, director; Leonard Bernstein conducting the New York Philharmonic), *The Joy of Christmas*. Columbia.

New Christy Minstrels, *Green, Green*. Columbia.

Robert Shaw Chorale (Robert Shaw conducting the RCA Orchestra), *The Many Moods of Christmas*. RCA.

BEST ROCK & ROLL RECORDING

• "Deep Purple," Nino Tempo, April Stevens. Atco.

"Another Saturday Night," Sam Cooke. RCA.

"I Will Follow Him," Little Peggy March. RCA.

"It's My Party," Lesley Gore. Mercury.

"Our Day Will Come," Ruby & the Romantics. Kapp.

"Teen Scene," Chet Atkins. RCA.

BEST RHYTHM & BLUES RECORDING

• "Busted," Ray Charles. ABC-Paramount.

"Frankie and Johnny," Sam Cooke. RCA.

"(Love Is Like a) Heat Wave," Martha & the Vandellas. Gordy/Motown.

"Hey, Little Girl," Major Lance. Okeh.

"Hello Stranger," Barbara Lewis. Atlantic.

"Part Time Love," Little Johnny Taylor. Galaxy.

"Since I Fell for You," Lenny Welch. Cadence.

BEST ORIGINAL JAZZ COMPOSITION (Composer's Award)

• Ray Brown, Steve Allen, "Gravy Waltz." Dot.

Paul Desmond, "Take Ten." RCA.

Dick Grove, Pete Jolly, Tommy Wolf, "Little Bird." Ava.

Kenyon Hopkins, "East Side–West Side." Backbone Hill.

Newton Mendonco, Antonio Carlos Jobim, "Meditation." Riverside.

Charlie Mingus, "Black Saint and the Sinner Lady." Impulse.

BEST INSTRUMENTAL JAZZ PERFORMANCE BY A SOLOIST OR SMALL GROUP

• Bill Evans, *Conversations with Myself*. Verve.

Dave Brubeck Quartet, *Dave Brubeck at Carnegie Hall*. Columbia.

Miles Davis, *Seven Steps to Heaven*. Columbia.

Al Hirt, *Our Man in New Orleans*. RCA.

Thelonious Monk, *Criss-Cross*. Columbia.

Peter Nero, *Peter Nero in Person*. RCA.
André Previn, with Ray Brown, Herb
Ellis, Shelly Manne, *4 to Go!*
Columbia.

BEST INSTRUMENTAL JAZZ PERFORMANCE BY A LARGE GROUP

• Woody Herman Band, *Encore: Woody Herman, 1963*. Philips.
Miles Davis, *Seven Steps to Heaven*.
Columbia.
Al Hirt, *Our Man in New Orleans*. RCA.
Quincy Jones, *Quincy Jones Plays the Hip Hits*. Mercury.
Gerry Mulligan Concert Jazz Band, *Gerry Mulligan '63*. Verve.
Oliver Nelson Orchestra, *Full Nelson*.
Verve.

BEST COUNTRY & WESTERN RECORDING

• "Detroit City," Bobby Bare. RCA.
Flatt and Scruggs at Carnegie Hall,
Flatt & Scruggs. Columbia.
"Love's Gonna Live Here," Buck
Owens. Capitol.
"Ninety Miles an Hour (Down a Dead
End Street)," Hank Snow. RCA.
The Porter Wagoner Show, Porter Wagoner. RCA.
"Ring of Fire," Johnny Cash. Columbia.
"Saginaw, Michigan," Lefty Frizzell.
Columbia.

BEST FOLK RECORDING

• "Blowin' in the Wind," Peter, Paul &
Mary. Warner Bros.
Green, Green, New Christy Minstrels.
Columbia.
Judy Collins No. 3, Judy Collins. Elektra.
Odetta Sings Folk Songs, Odetta. RCA.
Walk Right In, Rooftop Singers. Vanguard.
We Shall Overcome, Pete Seeger.
Columbia.
The World of Miriam Makeba, Miriam
Makeba. RCA.

BEST GOSPEL OR OTHER RELIGIOUS RECORDING, MUSICAL

• "Dominique," Soeur Sourire (Singing
Nun). Philips.

The Earth Is the Lord's (and the Fullness Thereof), George Beverly Shea.
RCA.
Make a Joyful Noise, Mahalia Jackson.
Columbia.
Makin' a Joyful Noise, Limeliters. RCA.
Piano in Concert, Charles Magnuson,
Fred Bock. Sacred.
Recorded Live! Bessie Griffin and the
Gospel Pearls. Epic.
Steppin' Right In, Kings of Harmony.
Kings of Harmony.
The Story of Christmas, Tennessee Ernie
Ford, Roger Wagner Chorale.
Columbia.

BEST PERFORMANCE BY AN ORCHESTRA FOR DANCING

• Count Basie, *This Time by Basie! Hits
of the '50s and '60s*. Reprise.
Les Brown, *Richard Rodgers Bandbook*.
Columbia.
Page Cavanaugh, *The Page 7 . . . An
Explosion in Pop Music*. RCA.
Joe Harnell, *Fly Me to the Moon and
the Bossa Nova Pops*. Kapp.
Woody Herman, *Encore: Woody Herman, 1963*. Philips.
Quincy Jones, *Quincy Jones Plays the
Hip Hits*. Mercury.

BEST PERFORMANCE BY AN ORCHESTRA OR INSTRUMENTALIST WITH ORCHESTRA (NOT JAZZ OR DANCING)

• Al Hirt, "Java." RCA.
Percy Faith, *Themes for Young Lovers*.
Columbia.
Henry Mancini, *Our Man in Hollywood*.
RCA.
Peter Nero, *Hail the Conquering Nero*.
RCA.
André Previn, *André Previn in Hollywood*. Columbia.
Kai Winding, *More*. Verve.

BEST INSTRUMENTAL THEME (Composer's Award)

• "More (Theme from *Mondo Cane*),"
Riz Ortolani, Nino Oliviero, Norman
Newell. United Artists.

"Bluesette," Jean "Toots" Theilmans.
ABC-Paramount.
"Gravy Waltz," Ray Brown, Steve Allen.
Dot.
"Lawrence of Arabia," Maurice Jarre.
Colpix.
"Washington Square," Bob Goldstein,
David Shire. Epic.

BEST SCORE FROM AN ORIGINAL CAST SHOW ALBUM
(Composer's Award)

• *She Loves Me*, Jerry Bock, Sheldon
Harnick (original cast with Barbara
Cook, Daniel Massey, Jack Cassidy).
MGM.
Here's Love, Meredith Willson (original
cast with Janis Paige, Craig Stevens,
Laurence Naismith; Elliot Lawrence,
musical director). Columbia.
Jennie, Arthur Schwartz, Howard Deitz
(original cast with Mary Martin,
Ethel Shutta, George Wallace, Jack
DeLon, Robbin Bailey). RCA.
110 in the Shade, Harvey Schmidt, Tom
Jones (original cast with Robert Hor-
ton, Inga Swenson, Stephen Douglass,
Will Peer, Steve Roland, Scooter
Teague, Lesley Warren; orchestra con-
ducted by Donald W. Pippin). RCA.
Tovarich, Lee Pockriss, Anne Cromwell
(original cast with Vivien Leigh,
Jean-Pierre Aumont). Capitol.

BEST ORIGINAL SCORE WRITTEN FOR A MOTION PICTURE OR TV SHOW
(Composer's Award)

• *Tom Jones*, John Addison. United
Artists.
Cleopatra, Alex North. 20th Century
Fox.
Lawrence of Arabia, Maurice Jarre.
Colpix.
Mondo Cane, Riz Ortolani, Nino
Oliviero. United Artists.

BEST INSTRUMENTAL ARRANGEMENT

• Quincy Jones, "I Can't Stop Loving
You" (Count Basie). Reprise.
Robert N. Enevoldsen, "Gravy Waltz"
(Steve Allen). Dot.

Peter Nero, Marty Gold, "Mountain
Greenery" (Peter Nero). RCA.
Claus Ogerman, "More" (Kai Winding).
Verve.
Joe Sherman, "Washington Square"
(Village Stompers). Epic.

BEST BACKGROUND ARRANGEMENT

• Henry Mancini, "The Days of Wine
and Roses" (Henry Mancini). RCA.
Benny Carter, "Busted" (Ray Charles).
ABC-Paramount.
Marion Evans, "Blame It on the Bossa
Nova" (Eydie Gormé). Columbia.
Pete King, "Wives and Lovers" (Jack
Jones). Kapp.
Nelson Riddle, "Call Me Irresponsible"
(Frank Sinatra). Reprise.
Gerald Wilson, "Tell Me the Truth"
(Nancy Wilson). Capitol.

ALBUM OF THE YEAR, CLASSICAL

• *War Requiem*, Benjamin Britten con-
ducting the London Symphony
Orchestra and Chorus (solos: Vish-
nevskaya, Pears, Fischer-Dieskau);
David Willocks directing the Bach
Choir; Edward Chapman directing the
Highgate School Choir. London.
*Debussy: La Mer; Ravel: Daphnis et
Chloé*, George Szell conducting the
Cleveland Orchestra. Epic.
*Great Scenes from Gershwin's "Porgy
and Bess,"* Skitch Henderson con-
ducting the RCA Symphonic Orches-
tra and Chorus (solos: Price,
Warfield). RCA.
Puccini: Madama Butterfly, Erich
Leinsdorf conducting the RCA Ital-
iana Opera Orchestra and Chorus
(solos: Price, Tucker, Elias). RCA.
The Sound of Horowitz (works of Schu-
mann, Scarlatti, Schubert, Scriabin),
(solo: Horowitz). Columbia.

BEST CLASSICAL COMPOSITION BY A CONTEMPORARY COMPOSER

• Benjamin Britten, *War Requiem*. Lon-
don.
Samuel Barber, *Andromache's Farewell,
Op. 39*. Columbia.

John LaMontaine, *Concerto for Piano*. Composers Recordings.

Dmitri Shostakovich, *Symphony No. 4, Op. 43*. Columbia.

William Schuman, *Symphony No. 8*. Columbia.

Heitor Villa-Lobos, *Concerto No. 2 for Cello and Orchestra*. Westminster.

BEST CLASSICAL PERFORMANCE, ORCHESTRA
(Conductor's Award)

• Erich Leinsdorf conducting the Boston Symphonic Orchestra, *Bartók: Concerto for Orchestra*. RCA.

Herbert von Karajan conducting the Berlin Philharmonic, *Beethoven: The 9 Symphonies (Complete)*. Deutsche Grammophon.

Fritz Reiner conducting the Chicago Symphony, *Beethoven: Symphony No. 6 in F Major, Op. 68 ("Pastorale")*. RCA.

George Szell conducting the Cleveland Orchestra, *Ravel: Daphnis et Chloé*. Epic.

Arturo Toscanini conducting the Philadelphia Symphony, *Schubert: Symphony No. 9 in C Major ("The Great")*. RCA.

Bruno Walter conducting the Columbia Symphony, *Mahler: Symphony No. 1 in D Major ("The Titan")*. Columbia.

MOST PROMISING NEW CLASSICAL ARTIST

• André Watts, pianist. Columbia.

Abbey Singers, vocalists. Decca.

Regine Crespin, vocalist. London.

Colin Davis, conductor. Angel.

Alirio Diaz, guitarist. Vanguard.

John Ogdon, pianist. Angel.

Fou Ts'Ong, pianist. Westminster.

BEST CHAMBER MUSIC PERFORMANCE

• Julian Bream Consort, *An Evening of Elizabethan Music*. RCA.

Members of Budapest String Quartet with Mieczyslaw Horszowski and

Julius Levine, *Schubert: Quintet in A Major for Piano and Strings, Op. 114 ("Trout")*. Columbia.

Zino Francescatti, violinist; Robert Casadesus, pianist, *Beethoven: Sonatas for Violin and Piano (Nos. 3, 4 and 5)*. Columbia.

Arthur Gold, Robert Fizdale (with vocalists), *Brahms: Liebeslieder Waltzes; Schumann: Spanische Liebeslieder*. Columbia.

Juilliard String Quartet, *Beethoven: Quartet No. 11 in F Minor, Op. 95; Quartet No. 16 in F Major, Op. 135*. RCA.

London Wind Soloists, *Mozart: Wind Music, Vols. 1–5*. London.

BEST CLASSICAL PERFORMANCE, INSTRUMENTAL SOLOIST(S) (WITH ORCHESTRA)

• Artur Rubinstein (Leinsdorf conducting the Boston Symphony), *Tchaikovsky: Concerto No. 1 in B Flat Minor for Piano and Orchestra*. RCA.

Vladimir Ashkenazy (Fistoulari conducting the London Symphony), *Rachmaninov: Concerto No. 3 in D Minor for Piano*. London.

Jascha Heifetz (Sargent conducting the New Symphony Orchestra of London), *Bruch: Concerto No. 1 in G Minor for Violin, Op. 26; Mozart: Concerto No. 4 in D Major for Violin, K. 218*. RCA.

Lorin Hollander (Leinsdorf conducting the Boston Symphony), *Ravel: Concerto in G for Piano and Orchestra; Dello Joio: Fantasy and Variations for Piano and Orchestra*. RCA.

David Oistrakh (Hindemith conducting the London Symphony), *Hindemith: Concerto for Violin*. London.

Rudolf Serkin (Szell conducting the Columbia Symphony), *Bartók: Concerto No. 1 for Piano and Orchestra*. Columbia.

André Watts (Bernstein conducting the New York Philharmonic), *Liszt: Concerto No. 1 for Piano and Orchestra*. Columbia.

BEST CLASSICAL PERFORMANCE, INSTRUMENTAL SOLOIST OR DUO (WITHOUT ORCHESTRA)

- Vladimir Horowitz, *The Sound of Horowitz* (works of Schumann, Scarlatti, Schubert, Scriabin). Columbia.

Glenn Gould, *Bach: The 6 Partitas.* Columbia.

Artur Rubinstein, *Schumann: Carnaval Fantasiestüke.* RCA.

Andrés Segovia, *Granada (Albéniz: Granada; Granados: Spanish Dance in E Minor; Ponce, Tansman, Aguado: 8 Lessons for the Guitar; Sor: 4 Studies).* Decca.

Rudolf Serkin, *Beethoven: 3 Favorite Sonatas (Sonatas No. 8 ["Pathétique"]; No. 14 ["Moonlight"]; No. 23 ["Appassionata"]).* Columbia.

BEST OPERA RECORDING

- *Puccini: Madama Butterfly,* Erich Leinsdorf conducting the RCA Italiana Orchestra and Chorus (solos: Price, Tucker, Elias). RCA.

Bartók: Bluebeard's Castle, Eugene Ormandy conducting the Philadelphia Orchestra (solos: Elias, Hines). Columbia.

Mozart: Così Fan Tutte, Eugen Jochum conducting the RIAS Chamber Chorus, Berlin Philharmonic (solos: Seefried, Merriman, Koth, Haefliger, Prey, Fischer-Dieskau). Deutsche Grammophon.

Mussorgsky: Boris Godunov, André Cluytens conducting the Paris Conservatoire Orchestra and Chorus of National Opera of Sofia (soloist: Christoff). Angel.

Puccini: Tosca, Herbert von Karajan conducting the Vienna Philharmonic (solos: Price, di Stefano, Taddei). RCA.

Wagner: Siegfried, Georg Solti conducting the Vienna Philharmonic (solos: Nilsson, Windgassen, Hotter, Stolze, Hoffgen, Neidlinger, Sutherland). London.

BEST CLASSICAL PERFORMANCE, CHORAL (OTHER THAN OPERA)

- David Willcocks directing the Bach Choir; Edward Chapman directing the Highgate School Choir; Benjamin Britten conducting the London Symphony Orchestra and Chorus, *Britten: War Requiem.* London.

Richard Condie directing the Mormon Tabernacle Choir; Eugene Ormandy conducting the Philadelphia Orchestra, *Brahms: A German Requiem.* Columbia.

Abraham Kaplan directing the Collegiate Chorale; Stuart Gardner directing the Boys' Choir, Church of Transfiguration; Leonard Bernstein conducting the New York Philharmonic, *Bach: St. Matthew Passion.* Columbia.

Hugh Ross directing Schola Cantorum of New York; Leonard Bernstein conducting the New York Philharmonic, *Milhaud: Les Choephores.* Columbia.

Robert Shaw conducting the Robert Shaw Chorale and Orchestra, *Robert Shaw Chorale on Tour* (Ives, Schoenberg, Mozart, Ravel). RCA.

Igor Stravinsky conducting the Chorus and Orchestra of Washington Opera Society, *Stravinsky: Oedipus Rex.* Columbia.

David Willcocks conducting the Choir of King's College and London Symphony, *Haydn: Nelson Mass (Mass No. 9 in D Minor, Missa Solemnis).* London.

BEST CLASSICAL PERFORMANCE, VOCAL SOLOIST

- Leontyne Price, *Great Scenes from Gershwin's "Porgy and Bess."* RCA.

Netania Davrath (orchestra conducted by Pierre de la Roche), *Canteloube: Songs of the Auvergne, Vol. 2.* Vanguard.

Victoria de los Angeles (Prêtre conducting the Paris Conservatoire Orchestra), *Mélodies de France* (Ravel, Debussy, Duparc). Angel.

Dietrich Fischer-Dieskau (Moore, pianist), *Schubert: Schwanengesang*. Columbia.

Maureen Forrester (Prohaska conducting the Symphony Orchestra of Vienna Festival), *Mahler: Des Knaben Wunderhorn*. Vanguard.

Anna Moffo (Ferrara conducting the RCA Italiana Symphonic Orchestra), *A Verdi Collaboration*. RCA.

Joan Sutherland (Bonynge conducting the London Symphony), *Command Performance*. London.

Jennie Tourel (Bernstein conducting the New York Philharmonic), *Ravel: Shéhérazade; Berlioz: Cléopatre (Scène Lyrique)*. Columbia.

Shirley Verrett (Stravinsky conducting the Chorus and Orchestra of the Washington Opera Society), *Stravinsky: Oedipus Rex*. Columbia.

BEST ALBUM COVER, CLASSICAL
(Art Director's Award)
• Robert Jones, *Puccini: Madama Butterfly* (Leinsdorf conducting the RCA Italiana Orchestra and Chorus). RCA.

John Berg, *Beethoven: Symphony No. 5 in C Minor, Op. 67* (Bernstein conducting the New York Philharmonic). Columbia.

Vladimir Bobri, *Granada (Albéniz: Granada; Granados: Spanish Dance in E Minor; Ponce, Tansman, Aguado: 8 Lessons for Guitar; Sor: 4 Studies)* (Andrés Segovia). Decca.

Bob Cato, *R. Strauss: Don Quixote* (Ormandy conducting the Philadelphia Orchestra). Columbia.

Robert Jones, *Beethoven: Symphony No. 6 in F Major, Op. 68 ("Pastorale")* (Reiner conducting the Chicago Symphony Orchestra). RCA.

Dorle Soria, *An Evening of Elizabethan Music* (Julian Bream Consort). RCA.

Dorle Soria, *Puccini: Tosca* (von Karajan conducting the Vienna Philharmonic Orchestra). RCA.

BEST ENGINEERED RECORDING, CLASSICAL
• Lewis Layton, *Puccini: Madama Butterfly* (Leinsdorf conducting the RCA Italiana Orchestra and Chorus; solos: Price, Tucker, Elias). RCA.

Lewis Layton, *Great Scenes from Gershwin's "Porgy and Bess"* (solos: Price, Warfield). RCA.

Lewis Layton, *Mahler: Symphony No. 1 in D ("The Titan")* (Leinsdorf conducting the Boston Symphony). RCA.

Gordon Parry, *Wagner: Siegfried* (Solti conducting the Vienna Philharmonic; solos: Nilsson, Windgassen, Hotter, Stolze, Hoffgen, Neidlinger, Sutherland). London.

Fred Plaut, *Bernstein Conducts Tchaikovsky* (Bernstein conducting the New York Philharmonic). Columbia.

Kenneth Wilkenson, *Britten: War Requiem* (Britten conducting the London Symphony Orchestra and Chorus). London.

BEST DOCUMENTARY, SPOKEN WORD OR DRAMA RECORDING (OTHER THAN COMEDY)
• *Who's Afraid of Virginia Woolf?* Edward Albee, playwright (original cast with Uta Hagen, Arthur Hill, George Grizzard, and Melinda Dillon). Warner Bros.

The Badmen, Goddard Lieberson, producer (Pete Seeger and others). Columbia.

Brecht on Brecht, Bertolt Brecht, playwright (original cast with Dane Clark, Anne Jackson, Lotte Lenya, Viveca Lindfors, George Voskovec, Michael Wager). Columbia.

John F. Kennedy—The Presidential Years, Norman Weiser, producer (David Teig, narrator). Four Corners.

Strange Interlude, Eugene O'Neill, playwright (original Broadway cast with Betty Field, Jane Fonda, Ben Gazzara, Pat Hingle, Geoff Horne, William Prince, Geraldine Page, Richard Thomas, Franchot Tone). Columbia.

We Shall Overcome (The March on Washington, August 28, 1963), Dr. Martin Luther King, Jr. (with Joan Baez, Marian Anderson, Odetta, Rabbi Joachim Prinz, Bob Dylan, Whitney M. Young, Jr., John Lewis, Roy Wilkins, Walter Reuther, Peter, Paul & Mary, Bayard Rustin, A. Philip Randolph). United Civil Rights.

BEST COMEDY PERFORMANCE

- Allan Sherman, *Hello Mudduh, Hello Faddah*. Warner Bros.

Cassius Clay, *I Am the Greatest!* Columbia.

Bill Cosby, *Bill Cosby Is a Very Funny Fellow, Right!* Warner Bros.

Carl Reiner, Mel Brooks, *Carl Reiner and Mel Brooks at the Cannes Film Festival*. Capitol.

Smothers Brothers, *Think Ethnic*. Mercury.

BEST RECORDING FOR CHILDREN

- *Bernstein Conducts for Young People*, Leonard Bernstein conducting the New York Philharmonic. Columbia.

Addition and Subtraction, Rica Owen Moore. Disney.

Children's Concert, Pete Seeger. Columbia.

Let's Go to the Zoo, Fred V. Grunfeld, producer (various artists). Decca.

On Top of Spaghetti, Tom Glazer (and the Do Re Mi Children's Chorus). Kapp.

"Puff the Magic Dragon," Peter, Paul & Mary. Warner Bros.

Winnie-the-Pooh, Jack Gilford. Golden.

BEST ENGINEERED RECORDING, SPECIAL OR NOVEL EFFECTS

- Robert Fine, *Civil War, Vol. 2* (Frederick Fennell). Mercury.

William Hamilton, *Fast, Fast, Fast Relief from TV Commercials* (Bill McFadden, Bryna Rayburn). Audio Fidelity.

John Kraus, *Cheyenne Frontier Days* (Hank Thompson). Capitol.

John Kraus, *Zounds! What Sounds* (Dean Elliott). Capitol.

John Kraus, Hugh B. Davies, *Heartstrings* (Dean Elliott). Capitol.

Phil Macy, Al Weintraub, *Pepino's Friend Pasquale* (Lou Monte). Reprise.

Scotty Shackner, Bob MacMeekin, *Four in the Floor* (Shut Downs). Dimension.

BEST ENGINEERED RECORDING (OTHER THAN CLASSICAL)

- James A. Malloy, *Charade* (Henry Mancini Orchestra & Chorus). RCA.

Harold Chapman, *Exotic Sounds of Bali* (Mantle Hood, director). Columbia.

Frank Laico, *The Barbra Streisand Album* (Barbra Streisand). Columbia.

Frank Laico, *The Second Barbra Streisand Album* (Barbra Streisand). Columbia.

Anthony J. Salvatore, *The Many Moods of Christmas* (Robert Shaw Chorale). RCA.

Albert H. Schmitt, *Our Man in Hollywood* (Henry Mancini). RCA.

Ronald A. Steele, *Politely Percussive* (Dick Schory). RCA.

Ronald A. Steele, *Supercussion* (Dick Schory). RCA.

Luis P. Valentin, *Ella and Basie*. (Ella Fitzgerald, Count Basie). Verve.

BEST ALBUM COVER (OTHER THAN CLASSICAL)
(Art Director's Award)

- John Berg, *The Barbra Streisand Album* (Barbra Streisand). Columbia.

Robert Jones, *Aloha from Norman Luboff* (Norman Luboff Choir). RCA.

Robert Jones, *Honey in the Horn* (Al Hirt). RCA.

Jim Ladwig, *Bach's Greatest Hits* (Swingle Singers). Philips.

John Murello, *Night Train* (Oscar Peterson). Verve.

Jim Silke, *Hollywood My Way* (Nancy Wilson). Capitol.

Edward L. Thrasher, *Carl Reiner and Mel Brooks at the Cannes Film Festival* (Carl Reiner, Mel Brooks). Warner Bros.

BEST ALBUM NOTES
(Annotator's Award)

• Leonard Feather, Stanley Dance, *The Ellington Era* (Duke Ellington). Columbia.

Edward Albee, Harold Clurman, *Who's Afraid of Virginia Woolf?* (original cast). Columbia.

Harold Arlen, *The Barbra Streisand Album* (Barbra Streisand). Columbia.

Sidney Bock, *An Evening of Elizabethan Music* (Julian Bream Consort). RCA.

Bob Bollard, *The Amazing Amanda Ambrose* (Amanda Ambrose). RCA.

B. A. Botkin, Sylvester Vigilante, Harold Preece, James Horan, *The Badmen* (Pete Seeger and others). Columbia.

• 1964 •

"Hard Night" for the Beatles

Variety sized up this year's Grammy race: "The three B's—Barbra, the Beatles and Bossa Nova—have dominated the nominations."

The Beatles were also dominating the overall music scene in 1964. Just days after the longhaired lads from Liverpool arrived in New York on February 7, 70 million people watched their two performances on *The Ed Sullivan Show*. Within two months of their arrival, they set a music record that still stands: Their tunes held all five top positions on the singles charts—"Can't Buy Me Love," "I Want to Hold Your Hand," "Twist and Shout," "She Loves You" and "Please, Please Me."

Even N.A.R.A.S. voters got swept up in "Beatlemania." The Fab Four led with the most Grammy bids (nine) for the music from their debut movie, *A Hard Day's Night,* which grossed an amazing $1.3 million in its first week. The *Village Voice* called it "the *Citizen Kane* of juke box musicals" because of its daring zaniness as it followed the foursome through two fictitious days of gearing up to perform a rock concert. Within two weeks of the movie's release, its title song leapt to the top of the U.S. charts. The LP ended up as the top seller of 1964, although it failed to make the Grammy race for best album.

Three of their noms were for their music performed by other groups. The rest were all the Beatles' own, including shots at Record of the Year ("I Want to Hold Your Hand") and Song of the Year ("A Hard Day's Night," also nominated for Best Rock & Roll Recording), best film score, best group vocal performance and Best New Artist.

The Beatles had the most nominations (nine), but scored only two awards: Best New Artist and best group vocals.

Variety reported the shocking results: "The Beatles may have swamped the music business during 1964, but that fact was not reflected in the Grammy award ceremonies."

The Fab Four reaped Best New Artist and Best Performance by a Vocal Group for "A Hard Day's Night," but that was all. *Hard Day* lost the prize for Best Original Score Written for a Motion Picture or TV Show to the album that later became the chart-topper of 1965, *Mary Poppins,* also winner of the Grammy for Best Recording for Children. (*Hard Day* suffered a worse snub at the Oscars. All of its singles were eligible for Best Song, but none was nominated. The Academy Award went to "Chim Chim Cheree" from *Mary Poppins.*)

Considering all of the adulation they were getting elsewhere at the time, the Beatles didn't seem ruffled at all by the N.A.R.A.S. slight. At Grammy's after-the-fact "Best on Record" TV show, they appeared on a segment taped at

London's Twickenham Studios, where they were filming *Help!* They performed "I'm So Happy Just to Dance with You" and accepted their trophies, apparently quite happily, from actor Peter Sellers.

But what happened? *Variety*'s headline declared, "Beatles Play 2d Fiddle to Bossa Nova."

The bossa nova sound had been introduced to America by 1962 Grammy champ Stan Getz and collaborator Charlie Byrd, whose *Jazz Samba* album became one of the biggest sellers in jazz history and launched a music craze that soon found followers in Eydie Gormé, Dizzy Gillespie and Frank Sinatra.

"In his lifetime, Stan Getz got under our skins," *Esquire* wrote of the famed tenor sax player soon after his death from cancer in 1991. He was, added *Time,* "the master of cool riffs and sultry melodic lines." He was also the first person in Grammy history to win both Record and Album of the Year.

The bossa nova ("new wave" or "new wrinkle") craze was at a low ebb by 1964. Getz considered it was time to stir things up again and so he teamed up for a new album effort with Brazil's leading performer of the genre, guitar player/singer João Gilberto. But their *Getz/Gilberto* collaboration included occasional vocals in addition to instrumental music, presenting the twosome with a problem. Gilberto could sing only in Portuguese. Getz' solution was to ask Gilberto's English-speaking wife, Astrud—a capable singer who had never performed professionally before—to do the album's "Girl from Ipanema" track in both languages. The result: "Ipanema" reigned for two weeks at number five on the charts and was voted Record of the Year. *Getz/Gilberto* also won Album of the Year—plus prizes for instrumental jazz

performance and engineering. (Astrud Gilberto lost her bid for Best New Artist.)

Past multiple winner and classical guitarist Laurindo Almeida was among those who got caught up in the new bossa nova wave that followed. Almeida recorded *Guitar from Ipanema* in 1964 and won a jazz instrumental gramophone.

For Song of the Year, N.A.R.A.S. voters again expressed their appreciation for traditional American melodies when they honored "Hello, Dolly!" by Broadway composer Jerry Herman, which became the third show tune to win one of the top Grammys. *Hello, Dolly!*'s title song was so popular that it was covered more than 200 times by other artists within two years of the show's premiere.

The tune pulled off another amazing coup. Three Beatles songs ruled the number-one slot on *Billboard*'s singles list for 14 consecutive weeks up until May 9, 1964. The Fab Four were then dislodged by an unlikely contender: Louis "Satchmo" Armstrong, the veteran, 63-year-old trumpet player and sometime singer, who, ironically, wasn't even familiar with the song when he decided to record it. Armstrong had been compiling a tribute to Broadway show tunes when he was approached by an associate of songwriter Herman and asked to include "Dolly" in the album. The result was one of the three show tunes to rank number one in the rock era, the other two being Bobby Darin's "Mack the Knife" (Grammy's 1959 Record of the Year) and "Aquarius/Let the Sunshine In" from *Hair* (Grammy's 1969 Record of the Year).

Satchmo did "Hello, Dolly!" with raspish gusto and a jazzy beat, earning him a nomination for best record and a victory for the male vocalist prize. Later Grammy winner Herb Alpert remembered Armstrong's private reac-

> ## Roger Miller scored five Grammys for his humorous hit "Dang Me."

tion to his victory then. "He couldn't believe it," Alpert said. "He told me, 'I've been playing for 50 years and now I've got a f——ing number-one record! I don't know what happened to all those other records. But I'm singin' on this one and winning awards!'" His success with "Dolly" even helped to boost the musical's Broadway attendance and also helped Armstrong land a part in the 1969 film version, which starred Barbra Streisand.

Streisand's newest LP release was *People,* the year's number-six best-seller. The title song came from her long-running Broadway musical *Funny Girl,* winner of this year's Grammy for Best Score from an Original Cast Show Album despite strong competition from *Hello, Dolly!* and *Fiddler on the Roof.* "People" was nominated for both Record and Song of the Year, but, having failed to take either, it at least won a trophy for vocal accompaniment arrangement and the best female vocal performance prize for

"The Beatles may have swamped the music business, but that fact was not reflected in the Grammy award ceremonies," *Variety* reported.

Streisand for a second year in a row. The LP took Best Album Notes, too.

A loser for the female vocalist honor and the Record of the Year trophy, Petula Clark managed to score a surprise victory over the Beatles, Roy Orbison and the Righteous Brothers for 1964's Best Rock & Roll Recording. Prior to 1964, Clark had a solid career as a singer back in her native England, where she first performed on radio in 1941 at the age of nine. Now, twenty-three years later, her upbeat "Downtown" established her as an international star and one of the first British women ever to have a rock hit in America.

But while the Brits, Brazilians and Broadway's best did well at this year's Grammys, the ceremony night really belonged to country singer Roger Miller, who tied Henry Mancini's 1961 record of winning the most Grammys in a single year—five. Moreover, he would return next year to top it.

After several years of difficult negotiations, an eager N.A.R.A.S. finally set up a chapter in Nashville in 1964. Critical observers said the academy gave away too many concessions in the deal: Country & western music now had six categories of its own (more than jazz, rock and rhythm & blues put together), up from only one last year. And Miller, along with his funny and folksy tune "Dang Me," dang near swept all of them—the sole exception being the one for which Miller wasn't qualified due to gender, the best c&w female vocalist prize, which went to Dottie West for "Here Comes My Baby."

Among Miller's five prizes was one for Best New Country & Western Artist. What made Miller special was a lighthearted touch (typical of his early songwriting efforts was "You Can't Roller Skate in a Buffalo Herd") that struck a universal chord. "Dang Me" had whole choruses of humorous lines, and when it sold a million copies, Miller became one of the first country-to-pop crossover stars in music history. At the Grammys, "Dang

Me" was named country's best song and best single and won Miller the prize for giving the best male country & western vocal performance. The *Dang Me/Chug-a-Lug* LP (the latter being his "goofy" musical toast to moonshine) was also hailed as Best Country & Western Album, a new category that would be dropped after Miller won it again next year.

In the comedy category, a historic winning streak was begun when a losing nominee of last year—Bill Cosby for *Bill Cosby Is a Very Funny Fellow, Right!*—returned to topple the same comic (Allan Sherman) who bested him in 1963. (A fitting victory, since it was Sherman who introduced Cosby to Warner Bros. record executives soon after Cosby proved himself in Greenwich Village nightclubs.) By the time the 1964 Grammys were bestowed in 1965, Cosby had distinguished himself as the first black leading actor in a TV drama series when he starred opposite Robert Culp on *I Spy*. But he stayed active in the comedy field. It was his second album, *I Started Out as a Child,* that brought him his first of six Grammy Awards in a row—a record that would not be broken until Aretha Franklin won eight consecutive trophies as best female r&b vocalist from 1967 to 1974. In *Child,* Cosby recalled such childhood scenes as playing street football with his pals and being told by the quarterback, "Cosby, you go down to 3rd Street, catch the J bus, have him open the doors at 19th Street—I'll take it to ya."

After Miller, Stan Getz and João Gilberto, the biggest winner on Grammy night was veteran champ Henry Mancini, "a repeat winner every year," said the mistaken *L.A. Herald Examiner.* (Mancini's amazing winning streak actually skipped one year—1959—but otherwise set a new five-year record, from 1960 to 1964, that no one would surpass until Bill Cosby did so in 1969.) Mancini's classic *Pink Panther* film score was the result of his teaming up yet again with film and TV director

Stan Getz became the first artist to win best record and album in the same year when *Getz/Gilberto* took four awards.

Verve

Blake Edwards and won him three instrumental awards: for composition, performance and arrangement. It was also nominated for Album of the Year.

Mancini's three trophies were matched by three bestowed on the work of English composer Benjamin Britten, whose *War Requiem* garnered several statuettes last year, including Classical Album of the Year. Britten's *Ceremony of Carols,* performed by the Robert Shaw Chorale, now won the choral performance award, while his *Young Person's Guide to the Orchestra* nabbed the classical prizes for best engineering and album cover.

This year's Classical Album of the Year award went to Leonard Bernstein's Symphony No. 3 (*"Kaddish"*—the traditional Hebrew prayer for the dead), performed by the New York Philharmonic. *High Fidelity* called it "a powerful artistic statement," but added, "What we have here is a major expression by a minor composer."

Samuel Barber's *Piano Concerto* was named Best Classical Composition by a Contemporary Composer. "Barber has written a big, splashy, old-fashioned concerto," *High Fidelity* opined. "All the work really lacks, and the lack is only relative to some of Barber's other scores, is distinctive melodic substance." Vladimir Horowitz continued his three-year winning streak by picking up a performance prize for instrumental soloist. Four-time past victor and double champ of last year Erich Leinsdorf of the Boston Symphony returned again to win the orchestral performance kudos for works by Gustav Mahler (Symphony No. 5 in C Sharp Minor) and Alban Berg (the opera *Wozzeck*).

American mezzo-soprano Marilyn Horne had supplied the vocals for Dorothy Dandridge in the movie *Carmen Jones,* but it wasn't until the early 1960s—when she teamed up periodically with diva Joan Sutherland, toured Europe and perfected her coloratura style—that critics and serious opera- goers took equally serious note of her. Horne was a rising star in 1964 (her debut at New York's Metropolitan Opera was still six years off) when she was named Grammy's Most Promising New Artist. Opera superstar and two-time past winner Leontyne Price (1960

and 1963) again took the vocalist's laurels, this time for singing Berlioz with the Chicago Symphony.

Price also performed the lead in Georges Bizet's *Carmen,* recorded by the Vienna Philharmonic with Herbert von Karajan conducting, which lost its bid for best classical album but won Best Opera Recording. Price had not yet played the role onstage, but of her first recording of the music, *High Fidelity* said, "She copes, she handles it smartly."

On hand for the Grammy festivities at the Beverly Hilton Hotel were 750 people, including winners Henry Mancini, Robert and Richard Sherman (composers of *Mary Poppins*) and songbird Nancy Wilson (winner of Best Rhythm & Blues Recording for "How Glad I Am"). In New York, Louis Armstrong, Allan Sherman and Woody Herman entertained 800 at the ballroom of the Astor Hotel. The Chicago and Nashville chapters also held dinners.

Variety judged the year's awards to be "the most successful to date."

> Bill Cosby beat the same person who helped to discover him: Allan Sherman.

• 1964 •

Awards were bestowed on April 13, 1965, for the eligibility period December 1, 1963, to November 30, 1964, at ceremonies held at the Beverly Hilton Hotel in Los Angeles, the Astor Hotel in New York, and at dinners held in Nashville and Chicago.

ALBUM OF THE YEAR

• *Getz/Gilberto,* Stan Getz, João Gilberto. Verve.
Cotton Candy, Al Hirt. RCA.
Funny Girl, Robert Merrill, Jule Styne. Capitol.
People, Barbra Streisand. Columbia.
The Pink Panther, Henry Mancini. RCA.

RECORD OF THE YEAR

• "The Girl from Ipanema," Stan Getz, Astrud Gilberto. Verve.
"Downtown," Petula Clark. Warner Bros.
"Hello, Dolly!" Louis Armstrong. Kapp.
"I Want to Hold Your Hand," Beatles. Capitol.
"People," Barbra Streisand. Columbia.

SONG OF THE YEAR
(Songwriter's Award)

• "Hello, Dolly!" Jerry Herman.
"A Hard Day's Night," John Lennon, Paul McCartney.
"Dear Heart," Henry Mancini, Ray Evans, Jay Livingston.

"People," Jule Styne, Bob Merrill.
"Who Can I Turn To?" Leslie Bricusse, Anthony Newley.

BEST NEW ARTIST
• Beatles
Petula Clark
Astrud Gilberto
Antonio Carlos Jobim
Morgana King

BEST VOCAL PERFORMANCE, MALE
• Louis Armstrong, "Hello, Dolly!" Kapp.
Tony Bennett, "Who Can I Turn To?" Columbia.
João Gilberto, *Getz/Gilberto*. Verve.
Dean Martin, "Everybody Loves Somebody." Reprise.
Andy Williams, *Call Me Irresponsible*. Columbia.

BEST VOCAL PERFORMANCE, FEMALE
• Barbra Streisand, "People." Columbia.
Petula Clark, "Downtown." Warner Bros.
Gale Garnett, "We'll Sing in the Sunshine." RCA.
Astrud Gilberto, "The Girl from Ipanema." Verve.
Nancy Wilson, "How Glad I Am." Capitol.

BEST PERFORMANCE BY A VOCAL GROUP
• Beatles, *A Hard Day's Night*. Capitol.
Browns, *Grand Ole Opry Favorites*. RCA.
Double Six of Paris, *The Double Six Sing Ray Charles*. Philips.
Four Freshmen, *More Four Freshmen and Five Trombones*. Capitol.
Peter, Paul & Mary, *Peter Paul and Mary in Concert*. Warner Bros.

BEST PERFORMANCE BY A CHORUS
• Swingle Singers, *The Swingle Singers Going Baroque*. Philips.
Ray Charles Singers, *Love Me with All Your Heart*. Columbia.

Song of the Year champ "Hello, Dolly!" was recorded by more than 200 artists, including the winner of best male vocalist, Louis Armstrong.

Stan Kenton Orchestra: Chorus by Pete Rugolo, *Artistry in Voices and Brass*. Capitol.
Henry Mancini Orchestra & Chorus, *Dear Heart*. RCA.
Serendipity Singers, *Don't Let the Rain Come Down (Crooked Little Man)*. Philips.

BEST ROCK & ROLL RECORDING
• "Downtown," Petula Clark. Warner Bros.
"A Hard Day's Night," Beatles. Capitol.
"Mr. Lonely," Bobby Vinton. Epic.
"Oh, Pretty Woman," Roy Orbison. Monument.
"You've Lost That Lovin' Feeling," Righteous Brothers. Phillies.

BEST RHYTHM & BLUES RECORDING
• "How Glad I Am," Nancy Wilson. Capitol.
"Baby Love," Supremes. Motown.
"Good Times," Sam Cooke. RCA.
"Hold What You've Got," Joe Tex. Dial.
"Keep on Pushing," Impressions. ABC.
"Walk On By," Dionne Warwick. Scepter.

BEST ORIGINAL JAZZ COMPOSITION
(Composer's Award)
• Lalo Schifrin, "The Cat." Verve.
Dave Brubeck, "Theme from *Mr. Broadway*." Columbia.
Duke Ellington, "Night Creature." Reprise.
Bob Florence, "Here and Now," Liberty.
Quincy Jones, "The Witching Hour." Mercury.
Gerald Wilson, "Paco." World Pacific.

BEST INSTRUMENTAL JAZZ PERFORMANCE BY A SMALL GROUP OR SOLOIST WITH SMALL GROUP
• Stan Getz, *Getz/Gilberto*. Verve.
Miles Davis, *Miles Davis in Europe*. Columbia.
Modern Jazz Quartet with Laurindo Almeida, *Collaboration*. Atlantic.
Pete Jolly, *Sweet September*. Ava.
Oscar Peterson, Clark Terry, *Mumbles*. Mercury.
André Previn, *My Fair Lady*. Columbia.

BEST INSTRUMENTAL JAZZ PERFORMANCE BY A LARGE GROUP OR SOLOIST WITH LARGE GROUP
• Laurindo Almeida, *Guitar from Ipanema*. Capitol.
Miles Davis, Gil Evans, *Quiet Nights*. Columbia.
Gil Evans, *The Individualism of Gil Evans*. Verve.
Woody Herman, *Woody Herman '64*. Phillips.
Quincy Jones, *Quincy Jones Explores the Music of Henry Mancini*. Mercury.
Rod Levitt, *Dynamic Sound Patterns of the Rod Levitt Orchestra*. Riverside.
Shelly Manne, *My Fair Lady with the Unoriginal Cast*. Capitol.
Oscar Peterson, Nelson Riddle, *Oscar Peterson—Nelson Riddle*. Verve.

BEST COUNTRY & WESTERN ALBUM
• *Dang Me/Chug-a-Lug*, Roger Miller. Smash.
The Best of Buck Owens, Buck Owens. Capitol.

The Best of Jim Reeves, Jim Reeves. RCA.
Bitter Tears, Johnny Cash. Columbia.
Guitar Country, Chet Atkins. RCA.
Hank Williams, Jr., Sings Songs of Hank Williams, Hank Williams, Jr. MGM.

BEST COUNTRY & WESTERN SINGLE
• "Dang Me," Roger Miller. Smash.
"Four Strong Winds," Bobby Bare. RCA.
"Here Comes My Baby," Dottie West. RCA.
"Once a Day," Connie Smith. RCA.
"You're the Only World I Know," Sonny James. Capitol.

BEST COUNTRY & WESTERN SONG
(Songwriter's Award)
• "Dang Me," Roger Miller. Smash.
"Here Comes My Baby," Dottie West, Bill West. RCA.
"Once a Day," Bill Anderson. RCA.
"Wine, Women and Song," Betty Sue Perry. Decca.
"You're the Only World I Know," Sonny James, Bob Tubert. Capitol.

BEST NEW COUNTRY & WESTERN ARTIST
• Roger Miller. Smash.
Charlie Louvin. Capitol.
Connie Smith. RCA.
Dottie West. RCA.
Hank Williams, Jr. MGM.

BEST COUNTRY & WESTERN VOCAL PERFORMANCE, MALE
• Roger Miller, "Dang Me." Smash.
Bobby Bare, "Four Strong Winds." RCA.
Johnny Cash, "I Walk the Line." Columbia.
George Hamilton IV, *Fort Worth, Dallas or Houston*. RCA.
Sonny James, *You're the Only World I Know*. Capitol.
Hank Locklin, *Hank Locklin Sings Hank Williams*. RCA.
Buck Owens, *My Heart Skips a Beat*. Capitol.

BEST COUNTRY & WESTERN VOCAL PERFORMANCE, FEMALE

- Dottie West, "Here Comes My Baby." RCA.

Skeeter Davis, "He Says the Same Thing to Me." RCA.

Wanda Jackson, *Two Sides of Wanda Jackson*. Capitol.

Jean Shepard, "Second Fiddle." Capitol.

Connie Smith, "Once a Day." RCA.

BEST FOLK RECORDING

- *We'll Sing in the Sunshine*, Gale Garnett. RCA.

Belafonte at the Greek Theatre, Harry Belafonte. RCA.

Peter, Paul and Mary in Concert, Peter, Paul & Mary. RCA.

The Times, They Are A-Changin', Bob Dylan. Columbia.

Today, New Christy Minstrels. Columbia.

The Voice of Africa, Miriam Makeba. RCA.

Woody Guthrie: Library of Congress Recordings, Woody Guthrie. Nonesuch.

BEST GOSPEL OR OTHER RELIGIOUS RECORDING, MUSICAL

- *Great Gospel Songs*, Tennessee Ernie Ford. Capitol.

Family Album of Hymns, Roger Williams. Kapp.

Gregorian Chant, Dominican Nuns of Fichermont. Philips.

George Beverly Shea Sings Hymns of Sunrise and Sunset, George Beverly Shea. RCA.

Sweet Hour of Prayer, Jo Stafford. Capitol.

Standin' on the Banks of the River, James Cleveland and the Angelic Choir. Savoy.

This I Believe, Fred Waring. Capitol.

BEST INSTRUMENTAL COMPOSITION (OTHER THAN JAZZ)

(Composer's Award)

- Henry Mancini, *"The Pink Panther Theme."* RCA.

Russ Daymon, "Cotton Candy." RCA.

Buddy Killen, Billy Sherrill, "Sugar Lips." RCA.

Jack Marshall, "Theme from *The Munsters*." Capitol.

Charles Strouse, Lee Adams, "Theme from *Golden Boy*." Decca.

BEST INSTRUMENTAL PERFORMANCE (OTHER THAN JAZZ)

- Henry Mancini, *"The Pink Panther Theme."* RCA.

Al Hirt, "Cotton Candy." RCA.

Quincy Jones, "Golden Boy" (string version). Mercury.

Peter Nero, "As Long As He Needs Me." RCA.

Stu Phillips, *The Beatles Song Book* (Hollyridge Strings). Capitol.

BEST INSTRUMENTAL ARRANGEMENT

- Henry Mancini, *"The Pink Panther Theme."* RCA.

Bob Florence, "The Song Is You." Liberty.

Quincy Jones, "Golden Boy" (string version). Mercury.

Richard Hayman, "I Want to Hold Your Hand" (Arthur Fiedler & the Boston Pops). RCA.

Anita Kerr, "Sugar Lips" (Al Hirt). RCA.

Hugo Montenegro, "Theme from *The Long Ships*." RCA

Billy Strayhorn, "A Spoonful of Sugar" (Duke Ellington). Reprise.

BEST ACCOMPANIMENT ARRANGEMENT FOR VOCALIST(S) OR INSTRUMENTALIST(S)

- Peter Matz, "People" (Barbra Streisand). Columbia.

Sid Bass, "We'll Sing in the Sunshine" (Gale Garnett). RCA.

Pete King, "Where Love Has Gone" (Jack Jones). Kapp.

Oliver Nelson, "How Glad I Am" (Nancy Wilson). Capitol.

Don Ralke, "Ringo" (Lorne Green). RCA.

George Siravo, "Who Can I Turn To?" (Tony Bennett). Columbia.

BEST SCORE FROM AN ORIGINAL CAST SHOW ALBUM
(Composer's Award)

- *Funny Girl*, Jule Styne, Bob Merrill (original cast with Barbra Streisand). Capitol.

Fiddler on the Roof, Jerry Bock, Sheldon Harnick (original cast with Zero Mostel, Tanya Everett, Joanna Merlin). RCA.

Hello, Dolly! Jerry Herman (original cast with Carol Channing). RCA.

High Spirits, Hugh Martin, Timothy Gray (original cast with Beatrice Lillie, Tammy Grimes, Edward Woodward). ABC.

What Makes Sammy Run? Ervin Drake (original cast with Steve Lawrence). Columbia.

BEST ORIGINAL SCORE WRITTEN FOR A MOTION PICTURE OR TV SHOW
(Composer's Award)

- *Mary Poppins*, Richard M. Sherman, Robert B. Sherman (Julie Andrews, Dick Van Dyke, with David Tomlinson, Glynis Johns, Ed Wynn). Buena Vista.

A Hard Day's Night, John Lennon, Paul McCartney (Beatles). United Artists.

Goldfinger, John Barry (John Barry, conductor). United Artists.

The Pink Panther, Henry Mancini (Henry Mancini, conductor). RCA.

Robin and the Seven Hoods, Sammy Cahn, Jimmy Van Heusen (Frank Sinatra, Dean Martin, Bing Crosby, Sammy Davis, Jr.). Reprise.

ALBUM OF THE YEAR, CLASSICAL

- *Bernstein: Symphony No. 3 ("Kaddish")*, Leonard Bernstein conducting the New York Philharmonic. Columbia.

Bizet: Carmen, Herbert von Karajan conducting the Vienna Philharmonic (solos: Price, Corelli, Merrill, Freni). RCA.

Mahler: Symphony No. 5; Berg: Wozzeck Excerpts, Erich Leinsdorf conducting the Boston Symphony (solo: Curtin). RCA.

Verdi: Falstaff, Georg Solti conducting the RCA Italiana Opera Orchestra and Chorus (solos: Evans, Merrill, Kraus, Simionato, Ligabue, Elias, others). RCA.

Verdi: Requiem Mass, Carlo Maria Giulini conducting the Philharmonia Orchestra (solos: Schwarzkopf, Gedda, Ludwig, Ghiaurov). Angel.

BEST CLASSICAL COMPOSITION BY A CONTEMPORARY COMPOSER

- Samuel Barber, *Piano Concerto*. Columbia.

Leonard Bernstein, *Symphony No. 3 ("Kaddish")*. Columbia.

Charles E. Ives, *New England Holidays*. Composers Recordings.

Darius Milhaud, *A Frenchman in New York*. RCA.

Igor Stravinsky, *Sermon, Narrative and Prayer*. Columbia.

BEST CLASSICAL PERFORMANCE, ORCHESTRA
(Conductor's Award)

- Erich Leinsdorf conducting the Boston Symphony, *Mahler: Symphony No. 5 in C Sharp Minor; Berg: Wozzeck Excerpts* (solo: Phyllis Curtin). RCA.

Leonard Bernstein conducting the New York Philharmonic, *Mahler: Symphony No. 2 in C ("Resurrection")*. Columbia.

Yehudi Menuhin conducting the Bath Festival Chamber Orchestra, *Handel: Concerti Grossi (12), Op. 6*. Angel.

Eugene Ormandy conducting the Philadelphia Orchestra, *Bartók: Concerto for Orchestra*. Columbia.

Fritz Reiner conducting the Chicago Symphony, *Haydn: Symphony No. 95 in C Minor; Symphony No. 101 in D Major ("Clock")*. RCA.

George Szell conducting the Cleveland Orchestra, *R. Strauss: Symphonia Domestica*. Columbia.

Bruno Walter conducting the Columbia Symphony, *Mozart: Last 6 Symphonies*. Columbia.

MOST PROMISING NEW ARTIST

* Marilyn Horne, mezzo-soprano. London.
Mirella Freni, soprano. Angel.
Igor Kipnis, harpsichord. Epic.
Judith Raskin, soprano. Decca.
Jess Thomas, tenor. Deutsche Grammophon.

BEST OPERA RECORDING
(Conductor's Award)

* *Bizet: Carmen*, Herbert von Karajan conducting the Vienna Philharmonic Orchestra and Chorus (solos: Price, Corelli, Merrill, Freni). RCA.
Mussorgsky: Boris Godunov, Alexander Melik-Pachaev conducting the Orchestra and Chorus of Bolshoi Theater (solos: London, Arkhipova). Columbia.
Puccini: La Bohème, Thomas Schippers conducting the Orchestra and Chorus of Opera House, Rome (solos: Freni, Gedda, Adani, Sereni). Angel.
Smetana: The Bartered Bride, Rudolf Kempe conducting the Bamberg Symphony (solos: Lorengar, Wunderlich, Frick). Angel.
Wagner: Lohengrin, Rudolf Kempe conducting the Vienna Philharmonic, Chorus of Vienna State Opera (solos: Thomas, Gummer, Fischer-Dieskau, Ludwig). Angel.
Verdi: Falstaff, Georg Solti conducting the RCA Italiana Opera Orchestra and Chorus (solos: Evan, Merrill, Kraus, Simionato, Ligabue, Elias, Freni). RCA.

BEST CLASSICAL PERFORMANCE, INSTRUMENTAL SOLOIST(S) (WITH ORCHESTRA)

* Isaac Stern (Ormandy conducting the Philadelphia Orchestra), *Prokofiev: Concerto No. 1 in D Major for Violin*. Columbia.

Julian Bream (Davis conducting the Melos Chamber Orchestra), *Rodrigo: Concierto de Aranjuez for Guitar and Orchestra; Vivaldi: Concerto in D for Lute and Strings*. RCA.
John Browning (Szell conducting the Cleveland Orchestra), *Barber: Concerto for Piano and Orchestra, Op. 38*. Columbia.
Rafael Druian, Abraham Skernick (Szell conducting the Cleveland Orchestra), *Mozart: Sinfonia Concertante in E Flat Major for Violin, Viola and Orchestra*. Columbia.
Yehudi Menuhin (Kletzki conducting the Philharmonia Orchestra), *Bloch: Concerto for Violin*. Angel.
Artur Rubinstein (Leinsdorf conducting the Boston Symphony), *Beethoven: Concerto No. 5 in E Flat*. RCA.
Van Cliburn (Leinsdorf conducting the Boston Symphony), *Brahms: Concerto No. 1 in D Minor for Piano*. RCA.

BEST CLASSICAL PERFORMANCE, INSTRUMENTAL SOLOIST(S) (WITHOUT ORCHESTRA)

* Vladimir Horowitz, *Vladimir Horowitz Plays Beethoven, Debussy, Chopin (Beethoven: Sonata No. 8 ["Pathétique"]; Debussy: Préludes; Chopin: Etudes and Scherzos 1–4)*. Columbia.
Julian Bream, *Popular Classics for Spanish Guitar* (Villa-Lobos, Falla, etc.). RCA.
Glenn Gould, *Bach: Two and Three Part Inventions*. Columbia.
Igor Kipnis, *French Baroque Music for Harpsichord* (Couperin, Rameau, Boismortier). Epic.
Sviatoslav Richter, *Richter Plays Schubert (Sonata in A Major for Piano; Wanderer Fantasia for Piano)*. Angel.
Artur Rubinstein, *A French Program* (Ravel, Poulenc, Fauré, Chabrier*)*. RCA.

BEST CLASSICAL PERFORMANCE, VOCAL SOLOIST (WITH OR WITHOUT ORCHESTRA)

- Leontyne Price (Reiner conducting the Chicago Symphony), *Berlioz: Nuits d'Eté; Falla: El Amor Brujo.* RCA.

Maria Callas (Rescigno conducting the Paris Conservatoire Orchestra), *Callas Sings Verdi.* Angel.

Boris Christoff (Cluytens conducting the Paris Conservatoire Orchestra), *Tsars and Kings (Opera Arias).* Angel.

Regine Crespin (Ansermet conducting the Suisse Romande Orchestra), *Berlioz: Nuits d'Eté.* London.

Dietrich Fischer-Dieskau, *Shubert: Die Winterreise.* Angel.

Peter Pears (Britten conducting the London Symphony), *Britten: Serenade for Tenor, Horn and Strings.* London.

Joan Sutherland (Bonynge conducting the London Symphony and New Symphony of London), *The Age of Bel Canto: Operatic Scenes.*

BEST CHAMBER MUSIC PERFORMANCE, INSTRUMENTAL

- Jascha Heifetz, Gregor Piatigorsky (Jacob Lateiner, piano), *Beethoven: Trio No. 1 in E Flat, Op. 1, No. 1.* RCA.

Juilliard String Quartet, *Beethoven: Quartet No. 15 in A Minor, Op. 132.* RCA.

Igor Markevich conducting the Chamber Group (with narrators Jean Cocteau, Peter Ustinov, Jean-Marie Fertey, Anne Tonietti), *Stravinsky: L'Histoire du Soldat.* Philips.

Jean-Pierre Rampal, Robert Veyron-Lacroix, *Mozart: The Complete Flute Sonatas.* Epic.

Sviatoslav Richter, Mstislav Rostropovich, *Beethoven: Sonatas (5) for Piano and Cello (Complete).* Philips.

Rudolf Serkin with the Budapest String Quartet, *Brahms: Quintet in F Minor for Piano and Strings.* Columbia.

BEST CHAMBER MUSIC PERFORMANCE, VOCAL

- New York Pro Musica (Noah Greenberg conducting), *It Was a Lover and His Lass* (Morley, Byrd, and others). Decca.

Deller Consort, *Music of Medieval France, 1200–1400, Sacred and Secular.* Vanguard.

Hermione Gingold, Russell Oberlin, Thomas Dunn, *Walton: Façade.* Decca.

Golden Age Singers, *Music for Voices and Violins in the Time of Shakespeare.* Westminster.

Le Petit Ensemble Vocal de Montréal, *Dufay Motets.* Vox.

Vocal Arts Ensemble, *Music of the Renaissance (Des Prez, Morley).* Counterpoint.

BEST CLASSICAL PERFORMANCE CHORAL (OTHER THAN OPERA)

- Robert Shaw conducting the Robert Shaw Chorale, *Britten: A Ceremony of Carols.* RCA.

Rene Duclos conducting the René Duclos Chorus; Georges Prêtre conducting the Paris Conservatoire, *Poulenc: Stabat Mater.* Angel.

Elliott Forbes conducting the Harvard Glee Club, Radcliffe Choral Society; Alfred Nash Patterson conducting the Chorus Pro Musica; Lorna Cooke De Varon conducting the New England Conservatory Chorus; Rt. Rev. Russell H. Davis conducting the St. John's Seminary Choir; Erich Leinsdorf conducting the Boston Symphony, *Mozart: Requiem Mass in D Minor.* RCA.

Elmer Iseler conducting the Toronto Festival Chorus; Igor Stravinsky conducting the Canadian Broadcasting Corporation Orchestra, *Stravinsky: Symphony of Psalms.* Columbia.

George Lynn directing the Westminster Choir; Eugene Ormandy conducting the Philadelphia Orchestra, *Verdi: Requiem Mass.* Columbia.

Wilhelm Pitz directing the Philharmonia Chorus; Carlo Maria Giulini conducting the Philharmonia Orchestra, *Verdi: Requiem Mass.* Angel.

BEST ALBUM COVER, CLASSICAL
(Art Director's Award)
- Robert Jones. Jan Balet, graphic artist. *Saint-Saëns: Carnival of the Animals*; *Britten: Young Person's Guide to the Orchestra* (Fiedler conducting the Boston Pops). RCA.
John Berg. Henrietta Condak, designer. *R. Strauss: Also Sprach Zarathustra* (Ormandy conducting the Philadelphia Orchestra). Columbia.
Robert Cato. *Mexico (Legacy Collection)* (Carlos Chavez). Columbia.
Bill Harvey. Lionel Kalish, graphic artist. *Court and Ceremonial Music of the 16th Century* (Roger Blanchard Ensemble with the Poulteau Consort). Nonesuch.
Robert Jones. David Hecht, photographer. *Mahler: Symphony No. 5 in C Sharp Minor* (Leinsdorf conducting the Boston Symphony). RCA.
Marvin Schwartz. *Verdi: Requiem Mass* (Giulini conducting the Philharmonia Orchestra). Angel.

BEST ENGINEERED RECORDING, CLASSICAL
- Douglas Larter, *Britten: Young Person's Guide to the Orchestra* (Carlo Maria Giulini conducting the Philharmonia Orchestra). Angel.
Lewis Layton, *Mahler: Symphony No. 5 in C Sharp Minor* (Leinsdorf conducting the Boston Symphony). RCA.
Lewis Layton, *Prokofiev: Symphony No. 5, Op. 100* (Leinsdorf conducting the Boston Symphony). RCA.
Fred Plaut, *Mahler: Symphony No. 2 in C Minor ("Resurrection")* (Bernstein conducting the New York Philharmonic). Columbia.
Fred Plaut, *Vladimir Horowitz Plays Beethoven, Debussy, Chopin* (solo: Vladimir Horowitz). Columbia.

BEST DOCUMENTARY, SPOKEN WORD OR DRAMA RECORDING (OTHER THAN COMEDY)
- *BBC Tribute to John F. Kennedy*, "That Was the Week That Was" cast. Decca.
Dialogue Highlights from "Becket," Richard Burton, Peter O'Toole. RCA.
Dylan, original cast with Sir Alec Guinness, Kate Reid.
The Kennedy Wit, John F. Kennedy, narrated by David Brinkley, introduction by Adlai Stevenson. RCA.
Shakespeare: Hamlet, Richard Burton (original cast: Hume Cronyn, John Gielgud, Alfred Drake, George Voskovec, Eileen Herlie, William Redfield, George Ross). Columbia.
Shakespeare: Othello, National Theatre of Great Britain, producers (Sir Laurence Olivier with Maggie Smith, Joyce Redman, Frank Finlay). RCA.

BEST COMEDY PERFORMANCE
- Bill Cosby, *I Started Out as a Child.* Warner Bros.
Woody Allen, *Woody Allen.* Colpix.
Godfrey Cambridge, *Ready or Not, Here Comes Godfrey Cambridge.* Epic.
Allan Sherman, *For Swingin' Livers Only!* Warner Bros.
Jonathan Winters, *Whistle Stopping.* Verve.

BEST RECORDING FOR CHILDREN
- *Mary Poppins*, Julie Andrews, Dick Van Dyke with David Tomlinson, Glynis Johns, Ed Wynn. Buena Vista.
Britten: Young Person's Guide to the Orchestra, Hugh Downs, narrator (Arthur Fiedler conducting the Boston Pops Orchestra). RCA.
Burl Ives Chim Chim Cheree and Other Children's Choices, Burl Ives and Children's Chorus. Buena Vista.
Daniel Boone, Fess Parker. RCA.
A Spoonful of Sugar, Mary Martin and Do-Re-Mi Children's Chorus. Kapp.

BEST ENGINEERED RECORDING, SPECIAL OR NOVEL EFFECTS

- Dave Hassinger, *Chipmunks Sing the Beatles* (Chipmunks). Liberty.
Bill Robinson, *The Big Sounds of the Sport Cars*.
Larry Levine, *Walkin' in the Rain* (Ronettes). Phillies.
James Malloy, "Main Theme: *The Addams Family*"(Vic Mizzy). RCA.
John Norman, *Les Poupées de Paris* (various artists). RCA.

BEST ENGINEERED RECORDING

- Phil Ramone, *Getz/Gilberto* (Stan Getz, João Gilberto). Verve.
Bernie Keville, *Pops Goes the Trumpet* (Al Hirt, Arthur Fiedler & Boston Pops). RCA.
George Kneurr, Frank Laico, *Who Can I Turn To?* (Tony Bennett). Columbia.
John Kraus, *Artistry in Voices and Brass* (Stan Kenton). Capitol.
James Malloy, *The Pink Panther* (Henry Mancini). RCA.
Chuck Seitz, *Sugar Lips* (Al Hirt). RCA.

BEST ALBUM COVER
(Art Director's Award)

- Robert Cato; Don Bronstein, photographer, *People* (Barbra Streisand). Columbia.
Robert Cato; Milton Glaser, graphic artist, *The Sound of Harlem* (various artists). Columbia.

Acy Lehman; Olga Albizu, graphic artist, *Getz/Gilberto* (Stan Getz, João Gilberto). Verve.
Acy Lehman; Tom Daly, graphic artist, *Oscar Peterson Plays My Fair Lady* (Oscar Peterson). Verve.
George Osak; George Jerman, photographer, *Guitar from Ipanema* (Laurindo Almeida). Capitol.
Ed Thrasher, *Poitier Meets Plato*. Warner Bros.

BEST ALBUM NOTES
(Annotator's Award)

- Stanton Catlin, Carleton Beals, *Mexico (Legacy Collection)* (Carlos Chavez). Columbia.
Neville Cardus, *Mahler: Symphony No. 5; Berg: Wozzeck Excerpts* (Phyllis Curtin) (Leinsdorf conducting the Boston Symphony). RCA.
Alexander Cohen, *Beyond the Fringe '64* (original cast). Capitol.
Stan Getz, João Gilberto, Gene Lees, *Getz/ Gilberto* (Stan Getz, João Gilberto). Verve.
Rory Guy, *The Definitive Piaf* (Edith Piaf). Capitol.
George Sponholtz, *The Young Chevalier* (Maurice Chevalier). Capitol.
Jack Tracy, *Quincy Jones Explores the Music of Henry Mancini* (Quincy Jones). Mercury.

• 1965 •

It Was a Very Good Year . . . for a Confederate Coup

The 1965 awards triggered, as *Variety* noted in a headline, "lotsa beefs."

Starved for nominations were some of the leading music acts of the year. The Beach Boys and Rolling Stones ruled the charts, but they got no satisfaction in terms of their quests for recognition from the Recording Academy. The most glaring oversight, though, was noted in a sassy *Variety* headline: "Wha' Hoppen to Folk-Rock Hero Bob Dylan in Grammy Nominations?" The article said, "The failure of Bob Dylan, the single most influential figure in the pop field since Elvis Presley, to receive a single mention has raised eyebrows over the judgment of the electorate of the academy."

The list of contenders wasn't a total fiasco. The academy continued its generous recognition of the Beatles by giving them nine bids for "Yesterday" and the music from their latest film, *Help!* (although it would give them a shocking "brush-off," noted *Variety*, once the awards were given out). All of the following were also nominated: the Supremes ("Stop! In the Name of Love"), Herman's Hermits ("Mrs. Brown, You've Got a Lovely Daughter"), Glen Yarbrough ("Baby the Rain Must Fall") and Sam the Sham and the Pharaohs ("Wooly Bully").

Nashville's Anita Kerr Quartet scored one of the most notorious upsets in Grammy history by trouncing the Beatles for the group vocals prize.

Yarbrough and Herman's Hermits were up for Best New Artist, as were the Byrds and Sonny & Cher.

But the chief problem of the year's contest involved *who else* was nominated in the rock & roll categories: country & western artists, who had six slots of their own to compete in, a number many critics thought was generous enough. Their sudden might was all due to the huge new bloc of faithful voters in Nashville.

A number of industry insiders believed that the academy made too many concessions when it negotiated to bring Nashville into the fold last year. Among the irate was Jerry Wexler, executive vice-president of Atlantic Records, who, *Variety* said, "sent off a hot note to N.A.R.A.S. prexy Francis M. Scott, protesting the disproportion between the six categories allocated to country &

western music and the one category given to rhythm & blues discs." Wexler added, "One is to wonder at the nature of the pressure to which [the academy] obviously succumbed when they subscribed to this weird alignment of categories."

Nashville used its clout to shower its record-setting star of last year, Roger Miller, with more nominations than it ever bestowed to one artist or group before: nine. The king of the Grammys was up for his classic "King of the Road" disc, a huge hit that sold more than half a million copies in 18 days. Considering its enormous pop success, the large bloc of Nashville voters judged it a worthy entry in the top rock categories, and when it came to vote for who would take home the golden gramophones, they again rallied behind their own golden boy.

Country artists even swept the rock awards.

Miller ended up with six Grammys, thereby topping the record he set last year when he tied Henry Mancini for reaping the most awards in a single year, and established a new one that would not be overtaken until Michael Jackson's *Thriller* album enthralled both disc buyers and N.A.R.A.S. voters alike in 1983, winning eight Grammys. "King of the Road" took five of the six for Miller: for best rock & roll single and male vocal performance as well as top country & western single, song and male vocal performance. *The Return of Roger Miller* reaped the prize for Best Country & Western Album. A good-natured spoof of Miller's tune won the c&w female vocal honors for Jody Miller (no relation) for "Queen of the House."

Among those Roger Miller trounced was the Beatles' Paul McCartney (for "Yesterday") in the r&r single and male vocalist categories. The entire Fab Four in turn lost their nod for *Help!* in the r&r group performance slot to Nashville boys, the Statler Brothers ("Flowers on the Wall"), who were neither Statlers nor brothers, but a harmony group discov-

ered by Johnny Cash that was also voted Best New Country & Western Artist. It was a defeat the Beatles suffered at the hands of other Nashville talent, though, that triggered the biggest "beef" of all and amounted to what is still considered one of the sourest notes in the history of music's highest honor.

Of their nine bids, the one award the Beatles seemed sure to get was one of the two prizes they took easily last year— Best Performance by a Vocal Group, a category in which they were now up against the Statler Brothers, Herman's Hermits, We Five and the Anita Kerr Quartet.

Anita Kerr was a songstress of moderate success, who had a minor hit with "Joey Baby" in 1962 and was one of the first women to produce c&w albums. She was also a darling of the Grammy crowd, being vice-president of the Nashville chapter and extremely active in the Los Angeles and New York academy branches. Due to her popularity among N.A.R.A.S. voters, no one dismissed her group's nomination for *We Dig Mancini* as lightweight, but when it prevailed over the Beatles' *Help!*, the critics cried "foul!"

So did many of the other Grammy contenders who were at the ceremony. "I felt the same," said multiple nominee Herb Alpert, who recalled his surprise and dismay when Kerr was announced as the winner. "The Beatles made such an unusual statement and touched so many people musically and intellectually that we all felt at the time that they deserved to be recognized."

Not everyone was unhappy about the outcome. Some Beatle-bashing was still in vogue as late as 1965. "American musical tastes are finally creeping upward," jazz critic Leonard Feather wrote in the *L.A. Times*. "Any organization that presents 47 Grammys for 'artistic merit' without acknowledging the Beatles can't be all bad."

After the Confederate foray into pop territory was over, and the smoke cleared, some of pop's top talents were still left with considerable turf of their own. The Best New Artist honors were wrested from the Statler Brothers (who still held on to their Best New Country & Western Artist designation) by Tom Jones, the panties-catching Welsh crooner who got his first big break in the big time when he recorded "It's Not Unusual" after it had been turned down by British singer Sandie Shaw. Another British vocalist, Petula Clark, whose "Downtown" was last year's Best Rock & Roll Recording, returned to claim the trophy for best rock & roll female vocal performance for her latest release, "I Know a Place." Barbra Streisand came back, too, to seize the laurels for best female vocal performance for a third year in a row, this time for her *My Name Is Barbra* album, which had just won five Emmy Awards as a TV special.

Another returning champ, Bill Cosby, took the comedy prize for a second year in a row for *Why Is There Air?*, about a nervous father-to-be who frets over what

Ex-army bugler Herb Alpert won best record after rearranging film song "A Taste of Honey": "It was written as a waltz and I did it as a shuffle."

lies ahead for him as a family man. Recalling his own childhood, he said on the LP, "I was playing with my navel [and] my mother said, 'All right, keep playin' with your navel, pretty soon you're gonna break it wide open, the air's gonna come right out of your body, you'll fly around the room backwards for 30 seconds, and land flat as a piece of paper, nothin' but your little eyes buggin' out.' I used to carry Band-Aids in case I had an accident." It remained a bestseller for an astounding 152 weeks.

Among all the homecomers, none was greeted more generously than Frank Sinatra, winner of the Album of the Year award over Streisand, Herb Alpert & the Tijuana Brass, *The Sound of Music*'s film soundtrack—and, again, the Beatles. Sinatra hadn't been heard from at the Grammys since 1959, when he won the same prize for *Come Dance with Me*. Now the Chairman of the Board was 50 years old and, showing surprising sensitivity to his advancing age, chose to muse candidly about growing older in the winning LP, *September of My Years*. *September* included "Last Night When We Were Young" and the tune that also won him the trophy for best male vocal performance, "It Was a Very Good Year."

Nineteen sixty-five was a very good year for Sinatra for another reason: He was finally singing his own tune on a new label—his own. Back in the late 1950s, during his earlier Grammy reign, Sinatra felt confined by his contract with Capitol Records and wanted to break free. In January 1961, he started up the Reprise label and announced in the trade papers: "Now—a newer, happier, emancipated Sinatra . . . untrammeled, unfettered, unconfined." Two years later, and after signing up such pals as Dean Martin, Sammy Davis, Jr., Bing Crosby and Rosemary Clooney, he sold two-thirds of his stock to Warner Bros. in exchange for several million dollars and various film commitments. Since he still held a sizable stake in the firm, however, his return to the Grammys, for music on his

Reprise label, marked an important career triumph for him. (*September* won Best Album Notes, too.)

Herb Alpert & the Tijuana Brass made up for their loss of the LP honors by nabbing three others, the second-highest tally of the night, after Roger Miller. "The mariachi band with the north-of-the-border sound" (as the *L.A. Herald Examiner* described them) reaped Record of the Year for "A Taste of Honey," in addition to statuettes for best nonjazz instrumental performance and Best Instrumental Arrangement.

Alpert, a former army bugler who played taps for as many as 19 funerals a day, once described his band, saying, "The seven who made up the Tijuana Brass sound were not of Spanish-American descent. We were four salamis, two bagels and an American cheese."

Alpert was one of the "bagels," the product of Hungarian-Russian ancestry. He was born and raised in L.A. and often went down to the Mexican border town of Tijuana to watch bullfights for recreation. "That's where it hit me," he later said. "Something in the excitement of the crowd, the traditional mariachi music, it all clicked." The spectacle inspired Alpert to write "The Lonely Bull," but he wasn't well enough connected in the music business to snare a producer, so he and a friend, Jerry Moss, kicked in $100 apiece to produce it themselves. Their collaboration not only created a a hit but also followed Sinatra's formula for success and launched a major new label. A&M record company subsequently signed up headliners Sergio Mendes and Brazil '66, Quincy Jones, Carole King and the Police.

For "A Taste of Honey," Alpert rearranged the title song from the score of the 1961 British-produced film about a homely white girl who becomes pregnant by a black sailor. There were a number of recordings already extant, including one by the Beatles and another, Latin version that inspired Alpert to try his own interpretation. "I thought it was a wonderful melody," he

Snubbing Dylan, "the single most influential figure in the pop field since Elvis Presley . . . has raised eyebrows" over voters' judgment, *Variety* said.

said. "It was written as a waltz and I did it as a shuffle, which I thought was unique and would have an interesting, original flair to it." Record buyers and critics agreed: The parent album of "Honey," *Whipped Cream and Other Delights,* was so successful that it was still ranked number two by *Variety* on Grammy night, a year after its release. The only LP that surpassed it was Alpert's latest disc, *Going Places.*

The source of the Song of the Year winner was another motion picture, *The Sandpiper,* a sudser about a sordid love triangle that featured extraordinary talent, including Elizabeth Taylor, Richard Burton and Eva Marie Saint. Its equally exceptional love theme, "The Shadow of Your Smile," was written by lyricist Paul Webster and composer Johnny Mandel, the latter of whom also won the Grammy for Best Original Score Written for a Motion Picture or a TV Show. Four weeks after its Grammy victory, "The Shadow of Your Smile" was hailed as the Best Song at the Oscars, too.

Like Frank Sinatra, Duke Ellington hadn't reaped gold at the Grammys since 1959, but now he was back for the large-group jazz instrumental performance salute to his *Ellington '66* collection. The jazz instrumental kudos for small groups went to the Ramsey Lewis Trio, whose *The "In" Crowd* at last catapulted them to fame after nine years of jamming in smoke-filled basement clubs.

The best jazz composition of 1965 was "Jazz Suite on the Mass Texts" by Lalo Schifrin. In the sole rhythm & blues category—best recording—James Brown snagged his first career Grammy for "Papa's Got a Brand New Bag," which he also wrote.

Pianist Vladimir Horowitz made his debut at Carnegie Hall in 1928. When he returned in 1965 following a 12-year, self-imposed retirement from public appearances, the *New York Times* called the evening "one of the most dramatic events in music history." He performed works by Schumann, Scriabin, Chopin, Debussy and others. The album recording won three awards (thus tying Herb Alpert & the Tijuana Brass for garnering the second-most trophies): Classical Album of the Year, best engineered classical recording and Best Classical Performance, Instrumental Soloist (without Orchestra).

The Grammy for Best Composition by a Contemporary Classical Composer was awarded to Charles Ives for *Ives: Symphony No. 4.*, who died in 1954, finished the symphony between 1910 and 1916. It was such a complicated work that it wasn't performed publicly for decades, but the challenge was finally taken up by the American Symphony Orchestra under the direction of Leopold Stokowski, winner of the statuette for best classical orchestra performance. Artur Rubinstein won the instrumental soloist prize (with orchestra) for Beethoven's Concerto No. 4 in G Major for Piano and Orchestra.

Best Opera Recording went to Alban Berg's *Wozzeck,* performed by the Orchestra of German Opera (with Karl Böhm conducting), American soprano Evelyn Lear, German baritone Dietrich Fischer-Dieskau and German tenor Fritz Wunderlich. ("Brilliant," *High Fidelity* declared it.) Three-time past winner Leontyne Price returned to take the vocal honors for her *Salome* by Richard Strauss.

The Most Promising New Recording Artist laurel went to Peter Serkin, a pianist with a mostly modern repertory, who was a student of his famous pianist father, Rudolf.

When the winnings were tallied, they triggered renewed carping in the industry: RCA had 12 awards, Columbia 10, Mercury and its subsidiaries 9 and Warner Bros.–Reprise 7. "MGM Records, one of the hottest pop labels in the business during 1965," *Variety* said, "received no awards outside of a Grammy for *Wozzeck* opera on the Deutsche Grammophon label distributed by MGM." In addition to what some music critics were calling Nashville's "Confederate invasion" this year and what *Variety* was terming "the brush of the Beatles," N.A.R.A.S. was dogged with another problem: the old issue of bloc voting, which would persist for years to come.

"Capitol execs were particularly bitter" over receiving only one award, *Variety* added. "One company exec said that Capitol should walk out of the academy."

Variety predicted that "a basic reappraisal of the methods and structure of the Grammy Awards appears to be likely. Glaring omissions of some outstanding names from the winning roster and the radical disproportion of awards on a label basis sparked widespread comment that something had to be done."

N.A.R.A.S. had its biggest turnout ever for the ceremonies held in Los Angeles, New York, Chicago and Nashville. In Los Angeles, the event took place, as it did the previous year, at the Beverly Hilton, while in New York,

> **Roger Miller's six victories in one year set a new record.**

the academy added some of the glitzy trappings that are traditionally part of other show business events. As *Variety* noted, "The presentation at the Hotel Astor was glamorized with a kleig-lighted entrance for the guests as they stepped out of limousines into the hotel."

• 1965 •

Awards were bestowed on March 15, 1966, for the eligibility period December 1, 1964, to November 30, 1965, at ceremonies held at the Beverly Hilton Hotel in Los Angeles, the Astor Hotel in New York, and at dinners held in Nashville and Chicago.

ALBUM OF THE YEAR
• *September of My Years*, Frank Sinatra. Reprise.
Help! Beatles. Capitol.
My Name Is Barbra, Barbra Streisand. Columbia.
My World, Eddy Arnold. RCA.
The Sound of Music, Julie Andrews and cast. RCA.
Whipped Cream and Other Delights, Herb Alpert & the Tijuana Brass. A&M.

RECORD OF THE YEAR
• "A Taste of Honey," Herb Alpert & the Tijuana Brass. A&M.
"The 'In' Crowd," Ramsey Lewis Trio. Cadet.
"King of the Road," Roger Miller. Smash.
"The Shadow of Your Smile (Theme from *The Sandpiper*)," Tony Bennett. Columbia.
"Yesterday," Paul McCartney. Capitol.

SONG OF THE YEAR
(Songwriter's Award)
• "The Shadow of Your Smile (Theme from *The Sandpiper*)," Paul Francis Webster, Johnny Mandel.
"I Will Wait for You (Theme from *The Umbrellas of Cherbourg*)," Michel Legrand, Norman Gimbel, Jacques Demy.
"King of the Road," Roger Miller. Smash.

"September of My Years," Jimmy Van Heusen, Sammy Cahn.
"Yesterday," John Lennon, Paul McCartney.

BEST NEW ARTIST
• Tom Jones
Byrds
Herman's Hermits
Horst Jankowski
Marilyn Maye
Sonny & Cher
Glenn Yarbrough

BEST VOCAL PERFORMANCE, MALE
• Frank Sinatra, "It Was a Very Good Year." Reprise.
Tony Bennett, "The Shadow of Your Smile (Theme from *The Sandpiper*)." Columbia.

Roger Miller's "King of the Road" was voted both best rock & roll single and best country single.

Paul McCartney, "Yesterday." Capitol.
Roger Miller, "King of the Road."
Smash.
Glenn Yarbrough, "Baby the Rain Must
Fall." RCA.

BEST VOCAL PERFORMANCE, FEMALE
- Barbra Streisand, *My Name Is Barbra.*
Columbia.
Petula Clark, "Downtown." Warner
Bros.
Jackie DeShannon, "What the World
Needs Now Is Love." Imperial.
Astrud Gilberto, *The Astrud Gilberto
Album.* Verve.
Nancy Wilson, *Gentle Is My Love.* Capi-
tol.

BEST PERFORMANCE BY A VOCAL GROUP
- Anita Kerr Quartet, *We Dig Mancini.*
RCA.
Beatles, "Help!" Capitol.
Herman's Hermits, "Mrs. Brown,
You've Got a Lovely Daughter."
MGM.
Statler Brothers, "Flowers on the Wall."
Columbia.
We Five, "You Were on My Mind."
A&M.

BEST PERFORMANCE BY A CHORUS
- Swingle Singers, *Anyone for Mozart?*
Philips.
Paul Horn and Chorus, "Jazz Suite on
the Mass Texts." RCA.
Henry Mancini Chorus & Orchestra,
*Dear Heart and Other Songs About
Love.* RCA.
New Christy Minstrels, *Chim Chim
Cher-ee and Other Happy Songs.*
Columbia.
Robert Shaw Chorale & Orchestra,
*Robert Shaw Chorale and Orchestra
on Broadway.* RCA.

BEST CONTEMPORARY (R&R) SINGLE
- "King of the Road," Roger Miller.
Smash.
"Baby the Rain Must Fall," Glenn
Yarbrough. RCA.

"It's Not Unusual," Tom Jones. Parrot.
"What the World Needs Now Is Love,"
Jackie DeShannon. Imperial.
"Yesterday," Paul McCartney. Capitol.

BEST CONTEMPORARY (R&R) VOCAL PERFORMANCE, MALE
- Roger Miller, "King of the Road."
Smash.
Len Barry, "1-2-3." Decca.
Tom Jones, "What's New, Pussycat?"
Parrot.
Paul McCartney, "Yesterday." Capitol.
Johnny Tillotson, "Heartaches by the
Number." MGM.

BEST CONTEMPORARY (R&R) VOCAL PERFORMANCE, FEMALE
- Petula Clark, "I Know a Place."
Warner Bros.
Fontella Bass, "Rescue Me." Chess.
Jackie DeShannon, "What the World
Needs Now Is Love." Imperial.
Lesley Gore, "Sunshine, Lollipops and
Rainbows." Mercury.
Barbara Lewis, "Baby I'm Yours."
Atlantic.

BEST CONTEMPORARY (R&R) PERFORMANCE BY A GROUP (VOCAL OR INSTRUMENTAL)
- Statler Brothers, "Flowers on the
Wall." Columbia.
Beatles, "Help!" Capitol.
Herman's Hermits, "Mrs. Brown,
You've Got a Lovely Daughter."
MGM.
Sam the Sham and the Pharaohs,
"Wooly Bully." MGM.
Supremes, "Stop. In the Name of Love."
Motown.

BEST RHYTHM & BLUES RECORDING
- "Papa's Got a Brand New Bag,"
James Brown. King.
"In the Midnight Hour," Wilson Pickett.
Atlantic.
"My Girl," Temptations. Motown.
"Shake," Sam Cooke. RCA.
"Shotgun," Junior Walker & the All
Stars. Soul.

BEST ORIGINAL JAZZ COMPOSITION
(Composer's Award)
- Lalo Schifrin, "Jazz Suite on the Mass Texts." RCA.

John Coltrane, *A Love Supreme.* Impulse.

Duke Ellington, Billy Strayhorn, "Virgin Islands Suite." Reprise.

Wes Montgomery, *Bumpin'.* Verve.

Oscar Peterson, "Canadiana Suite." Limelite.

Eddie Sauter, *Mickey One.* MGM.

BEST JAZZ PERFORMANCE BY A SMALL GROUP OR SOLOIST WITH SMALL GROUP
- Ramsey Lewis Trio, *The "In" Crowd.* Cadet.

John Coltrane, *A Love Supreme.* Impulse.

Paul Desmond, Jim Hall, *Glad to Be Unhappy.* RCA.

Bill Evans Trio, *Trio '65.* Verve.

Paul Horn, *Cycle.* RCA.

Gary McFarland Group, *Soft Samba.* Verve.

Clark Terry, Bob Brookmeyer Quintet, *The Power of Positive Swinging.* Mainstream.

Cal Tjader, *Soul Sauce.* Verve.

BEST JAZZ PERFORMANCE BY A LARGE GROUP OR SOLOIST WITH LARGE GROUP
- Duke Ellington Orchestra, *Ellington '66.* Reprise

Kenny Burrell, Gil Evans Orchestra, *Kenny Burrell: Guitar Forms.* Verve.

Stan Getz, *Mickey One.* Verve.

Dizzy Gillespie (Fuller, Monterey Jazz Festival), "Theme from *The Sandpiper*." World Pacific.

Paul Horn, "Jazz Suite on the Mass Texts." RCA.

Rod Levitt, *Insight.* RCA.

Wes Montgomery with String Orchestra, *Bumpin'.* Verve.

BEST COUNTRY & WESTERN ALBUM
- *The Return of Roger Miller*, Roger Miller. Smash.

Father and Son: Hank Williams and Hank Williams, Jr., Hank Williams & Hank Williams, Jr. MGM.

The Jim Reeves Way, Jim Reeves. RCA.

More of That Guitar Country, Chet Atkins. RCA.

My World, Eddy Arnold. RCA.

BEST COUNTRY & WESTERN SINGLE
- "King of the Road," Roger Miller. Smash.

"Flowers on the Wall," Statler Brothers. Columbia.

"Is It Really Over?" Jim Reeves. RCA.

"Make the World Go Away," Eddy Arnold. RCA.

"May the Bird of Paradise Fly Up Your Nose," Little Jimmy Dickens. Columbia.

"Yakety Axe," Chet Atkins. RCA.

BEST COUNTRY & WESTERN SONG
(Songwriter's Award)
- "King of the Road," Roger Miller. Smash.

"Crystal Chandelier," Ted Harris. RCA.

"Flowers on the Wall," Lewis Dewitt. Columbia.

"May the Bird of Paradise Fly Up Your Nose," Neal Merritt. Columbia.

"What's He Doing in My World," Carl Belew, B. J. Moore, Eddie Busch. RCA.

BEST NEW COUNTRY & WESTERN ARTIST
- Statler Brothers. Columbia.

Wilma Burgess. Decca.

Norma Jean. RCA.

Jody Miller. Capitol.

Del Reeves. United Artists.

BEST COUNTRY & WESTERN VOCAL PERFORMANCE, MALE
- Roger Miller, "King of the Road." Smash.

Eddy Arnold, "Make the World Go Away." RCA.

Bobby Bare, "Talk Me Some Sense." RCA.

Carl Belew, "Crystal Chandelier,"
RCA.
Jim Reeves, "Is It Really Over?" RCA.

BEST COUNTRY & WESTERN VOCAL PERFORMANCE, FEMALE

• Jody Miller, "Queen of the House."
Capitol.
Molly Bee, "Single Girl Again."
MGM.
Wilma Burgess, "Baby." Decca.
Skeeter Davis, "Sunglasses." RCA.
Dottie West, "Before the Ring on Your
Finger Turns Green." RCA.

BEST FOLK RECORDING

• *An Evening with Belafonte/Makeba.*
Harry Belafonte, Miriam Makeba.
RCA.
A Song Will Rise, Peter, Paul & Mary.
Warner Bros.
Makeba Sings, Miriam Makeba. RCA.
*Roscoe Holcomb: The High Lonesome
Sound*, Roscoe Holcomb. Folkways.
Strangers and Cousins, Pete Seeger.
Columbia.
There but for Fortune, Joan Baez. Van-
guard.
The Womenfolk at the Hungry 1, Wom-
enfolk. RCA.

BEST GOSPEL OR OTHER RELIGIOUS RECORDING

• *Southland Favorites*, George Beverly
Shea & Anita Kerr Quartet. RCA.
All Day Sing and Dinner on the Ground,
Statesmen Quartet with Hovie Lister.
RCA
Bob Ashton's Songs of Living Faith,
Ralph Carmichael Singers & Orches-
tra. Stylist.
How Great Thou Art, Kate Smith.
RCA.
Just Keep On Singing, Marian Ander-
son. RCA.
Let Me Walk with Thee, Tennessee Ernie
Ford. Capitol.
Something Old, Something New, Black-
wood Brothers. RCA.
What a Happy Time, Happy Goodman
Family. Word.

BEST INSTRUMENTAL ARRANGEMENT

• Herb Alpert, "A Taste of Honey" (Herb
Alpert & the Tijuana Brass). A&M.
Bob Florence, "Mission to Moscow" (Si
Zentner Orchestra). RCA.
Neal Hefti, "Girl Talk" (Neal Hefti).
Columbia.
Horst Jankowski, "Walk in the Black For-
est" (Jankowski Orchestra). Mercury.
Johnny Mandel, "The Shadow of Your
Smile" (Armbruster Orchestra). Mer-
cury.
Jack Mason, "A Hard Day's Night"
(Fiedler conducting the Boston
Pops). RCA.

BEST ARRANGEMENT ACCOMPANYING A VOCALIST OR INSTRUMENTALIST

• Gordon Jenkins, "It Was a Very Good
Year" (Frank Sinatra). Reprise.
Burt Bacharach, "What the World Needs
Now Is Love" (Jackie DeShannon).
Imperial.
Don Costa, "He Touched Me" (Barbra
Streisand). Columbia.
Gil Evans, "Greensleeves" (Kenny Bur-
rell). Verve.
Bob Florence, "Everything I've Got"
(Vikki Carr). Liberty.
George Martin, "Yesterday" (Beatles).
Capitol.
Claus Ogerman, "Day by Day" (Astrud
Gilberto). Verve.
Les Reed, "It's Not Unusual" (Tom
Jones). Parrot.

BEST INSTRUMENTAL PERFORMANCE (NON-JAZZ)

• Herb Alpert & the Tijuana Brass, "A
Taste of Honey." A&M.
Chet Atkins, "Yakety Axe." RCA.
Neal Hefti, "Girl Talk." Columbia.
Horst Jankowski, "Walk in the Black
Forest." Mercury.
Henry Mancini, "The Great Race." RCA.

BEST SCORE FROM AN ORIGINAL CAST SHOW

• *On a Clear Day You Can See Forever*,
Alan Jay Lerner, Burton Lane. RCA.

Bajour, Walter Marks. Columbia.

Baker Street, Marian Grudeff, Raymond Jessell. MGM.

Do I Hear a Waltz? Richard Rodgers, Stephen Sondheim. Columbia.

Half a Sixpence, David Heneker. RCA.

BEST ORIGINAL SCORE WRITTEN FOR A MOTION PICTURE OR TV SHOW
(Composer's Award)

- *The Sandpiper* (Robert Armbruster Orchestra), Johnny Mandel. Mercury.

Help! (Beatles), John Lennon, Paul McCartney, George Harrison, Ken Thorne. Capitol.

The Man from U.N.C.L.E. (Hugo Montenegro Orchestra), Lalo Schifrin, Mort Stevens, Walter Scharf, Jerry Goldsmith. RCA.

The Umbrellas of Cherbourg (Michel Legrand Orchestra), Michel Legrand, Jacques Demy. Philips.

Zorba the Greek (Mikis Theodorakis Orchestra), Mikis Theodorakis. 20th Century-Fox.

ALBUM OF THE YEAR, CLASSICAL

- *Horowitz at Carnegie Hall, an Historic Return*, Vladimir Horowitz. Columbia.

Berg: Wozzeck, Karl Böhm conducting the Orchestra of German Opera, Berlin. Deutsche Grammophon.

Chopin: 8 Polonaises and 4 Impromptus, Artur Rubinstein. RCA.

Ives: Symphony No. 4, Leopold Stokowski conducting the American Symphony. Columbia.

Strauss: Salome (Dance of the Seven Veils, Interlude and Final Scene); The Egyptian Helen (Awakening Scene), Erich Leinsdorf conducting the Boston Symphony (solo: Leontyne Price). RCA.

BEST COMPOSITION BY A CONTEMPORARY CLASSICAL COMPOSER

- Charles Ives, *Symphony No. 4*. Columbia.

Benjamin Britten, *Cantata Misericordium*. London.

Leonard Bernstein, *Chichester Psalms*. London.

David Diamond, *String Quartet No. 4.* Epic.

Morton Gould, *World War I Suite*. RCA.

William Walton, *Variations on a Theme by Hindemith*. Columbia.

BEST CLASSICAL PERFORMANCE, ORCHESTRA
(Conductor's Award)

- Leopold Stokowski conducting the American Symphony, *Ives: Symphony No. 4*. Columbia.

Morton Gould conducting the Chicago Symphony, *Gould: Spirituals for Orchestra; Copland: Dance Symphony*. RCA.

Herbert von Karajan conducting the Berlin Philharmonic, *Bach: Brandenburg Concertos*. Deutsche Grammophon.

Erich Leinsdorf conducting the Boston Symphony, *Prokofiev: Symphony No. 6 in E Flat Minor*. RCA.

Jean Martinon conducting the Chicago Symphony, *Ravel: Daphnis et Chloé Suite No. 2; Roussel: Bacchus and Ariadne, Suite No. 2*. RCA.

Arturo Toscanini conducting the NBC Symphony, *Berlioz: Roméo et Juliette*. RCA.

MOST PROMISING NEW RECORDING ARTIST

- Peter Serkin, pianist. RCA.

Nicolai Ghiaurov, bass. London.

Evelyn Lear, soprano. Deutsche Grammophon.

Raymond Lewenthal, pianist. RCA.

Shirley Verrett, mezzo. RCA.

BEST CHAMBER MUSIC PERFORMANCE (INSTRUMENTAL OR VOCAL)

- Juilliard String Quartet, *Bartók: The 6 String Quartets*. Columbia.

Vladimir Ashkenazy, Malcolm Frager, *Mozart/Schumann Recital*. London.

Erick Friedman, Bruce Prince-Joseph, *Bach: The 6 Sonatas for Violin and Harpsichord*. RCA.
Yehudi Menuhin and members of the Bath Festival Orchestra, *A Purcell Anthology*. Angel.
Isaac Stern, Eugene Istomin, Leonard Rose, *Schubert: Trio No. 1 in B Flat for Piano*. Columbia.
Joseph Szigeti, Béla Bartók, *Sonata Recital by Szigeti and Bartók* (Bartók, Beethoven, Debussy). Vanguard.

BEST CLASSICAL PERFORMANCE, INSTRUMENTAL SOLOIST(S) (WITH ORCHESTRA)

• Artur Rubinstein (Leinsdorf conducting the Boston Symphony), *Beethoven: Concerto No. 4 in G Major for Piano and Orchestra*. RCA.
Gary Graffman (Ormandy conducting the Philadelphia Orchestra), *Tchaikovsky: Concerto No. 2 in G Major for Piano and Orchestra; Concerto No. 3 in E Flat Major for Piano and Orchestra*. Columbia.
Leonard Pennario (Previn conducting the Royal Philharmonic), *Rachmaninov: Concerto No. 1 in F Sharp for Piano; Concerto No. 4 in G Minor for Piano*. RCA.
Rudolf Serkin (Toscanini conducting the NBC Symphony), *Beethoven: Concerto No. 4 in G Major for Piano and Orchestra*. RCA.
Isaac Stern (Bernstein conducting the New York Philharmonic), *Barber: Concerto for Violin and Orchestra; Hindemith: Concerto for Violin and Orchestra*. Columbia.
Isaac Stern, Leonard Rose, Eugene Istomin (Ormandy conducting the Philadelphia Orchestra), *Beethoven: Triple Concerto*. Columbia.

BEST CLASSICAL PERFORMANCE, INSTRUMENTAL SOLOIST(S) (WITHOUT ORCHESTRA)

• Vladimir Horowitz, *Horowitz at Carnegie Hall, an Historic Return*. Columbia.

Vladimir Ashkenazy, *Chopin Ballades (1–4)*. London.
Julian Bream, *Julian Bream in Concert*. RCA.
Glenn Gould, *Bach: The Well-Tempered Clavier, Book 1, Vol. 3 (17–24)*. Columbia.
Raymond Lewenthal, *Alkan: Piano Music*. RCA.
Artur Rubinstein, *Chopin: 8 Polonaises and 4 Impromptus*. RCA.

BEST OPERA RECORDING
(Conductor's Award)

• *Berg: Wozzeck*, Karl Böhm conducting the Orchestra of German Opera, Berlin (solos: Fischer-Dieskau, Lear, Wunderlich). Deutsche Grammophon.
Bellini: Norma, Richard Bonynge conducting the London Symphony and Chorus (solos: Sutherland, Horne, Alexander, Cross). RCA.
Verdi: La Forza del Destino, Thomas Schippers conducting the RCA Italiana Opera Orchestra & Chorus (solos: Price, Tucker, Verrett, Merrill, Tozzi, Flagello). RCA.
Verdi: Luisa Miller, Fausto Cleva conducting the RCA Italiana Opera Orchestra and Chorus (solos: Moffo, Bergonzi, Verrett, MacNeil, Tozzi, Flagello). RCA.
Wagner: Götterdämmerung, Georg Solti conducting the Vienna Philharmonic (solos: Nilsson, Windgassen, Fischer-Dieskau). London.

BEST CLASSICAL PERFORMANCE, CHORAL (OTHER THAN OPERA)

• Robert Shaw conducting the Robert Shaw Chorale, RCA Victor Symphony, *Stravinsky: Symphony of Psalms; Poulenc: Gloria*. RCA.
Benjamin Britten conducting the London Symphony Chorus and Orchestra, *Britten: Cantata Misericordium*. London.
Herbert von Karajan conducting the Vienna Singverein and Berlin Philharmonic, *Brahms: A German Requiem*. Deutsche Grammophon.

Robert Page conducting the Temple University Choir; Eugene Ormandy conducting the Philadelphia Orchestra, *Berlioz: Requiem*. Columbia.

Wilhelm Pitz, chorus master, Philharmonia Chorus; Otto Klemperer conducting the Philharmonia Orchestra, *Handel: Messiah*. Angel.

Wolfgang Schubert conducting the Bavarian Radio Symphony Chorus; Rafael Kubelik conducting the Bavarian Radio Symphony, *Schoenberg: Gurrelieder*. Deutsche Grammophon.

BEST CLASSICAL VOCAL PERFORMANCE (WITH OR WITHOUT ORCHESTRA)

• Leontyne Price (Leinsdorf conducting the Boston Symphony), *Strauss: Salome (Dance of the Seven Veils, Interlude, Final Scene); The Egyptian Helen (Awakening Scene)*. RCA.

Dietrich Fischer-Dieskau (Moore, pianist), *Schumann: Liederkreis*. Angel.

Mirella Freni (Ferraris conducting the Rome Opera House Orchestra), *Mirella Freni—Operatic Arias*. Angel.

Nicolai Ghiaurov (Downes conducting the London Symphony), *Russian and French Arias*. London.

Anna Moffo (Stokowski conducting the American Symphony), *Canteloube: Songs of the Auvergne; Rachmaninov: Vocalise; Villa-Lobos: Bachianas Brasileiras No. 5*. RCA.

Shirley Verrett , *Falla: Seven Popular Spanish Songs*. RCA.

Galina Vishnevskaya (Markevitch conducting the Russian State Symphony), *Mussorgsky: Songs*

BEST ENGINEERED RECORDING, CLASSICAL

• Fred Plaut, *Horowitz at Carnegie Hall, an Historic Return* (Vladimir Horowitz). Columbia.

Edward T. Graham, *Ives: Symphony No. 4* (Stokowski conducting the American Symphony Orchestra). Columbia.

Bernard Keville, *Gould: Spirituals for Orchestra; Copland: Dance Symphony* (Gould conducting the Chicago Symphony). RCA.

Bernard Keville, *Stravinsky: Symphony of Psalms* (Robert Shaw Chorale, RCA Symphony). RCA.

Anthony Salvatore, *Strauss: Salome; The Egyptian Helen* (Leinsdorf conducting the Boston Symphony; solo: Leontyne Price). RCA.

BEST SPOKEN WORD OR DRAMA RECORDING

• *John F. Kennedy: As We Remember Him*. Columbia.

The Brontës, Margaret Webster. Vanguard.

Much Ado About Nothing, National Theatre of Great Britain. RCA.

A Personal Choice, Sir Alec Guinness. RCA.

A Time to Keep: 1964, Chet Huntley, David Brinkley. RCA.

The Voice of the Uncommon Man, Adlai Stevenson. MGM.

BEST COMEDY PERFORMANCE

• Bill Cosby, *Why Is There Air?* Warner Bros.

Godfrey Cambridge, *Them Cotton Pickin' Days Is Over*. Epic.

Earl Doud, Allen Robin, *Welcome to the L.B.J. Ranch*. Capitol.

Smothers Brothers, *Mom Always Liked You Best*. Mercury.

Various artists, written by Bob Booker & George Foster, *You Don't Have to Be Jewish*. Kapp.

BEST RECORDING FOR CHILDREN

• *Dr. Seuss Presents "Fox in Sox" and "Green Eggs and Ham,"* Marvin Miller. RCA.

Love Songs for Children: "A" You're Adorable, Diahann Carroll. Golden.

Patrick Muldoon and His Magic Balloon, Carmel Quinn. RCA.

Supercalifragelistic Expialidocious, Chipmunks (David Seville). Liberty.

Winnie-the-Pooh and the Honey Tree,
Sterling Holloway, Sebastian Cabot.
Disney.

BEST ENGINEERED RECORDING

• Larry Levine, *"A Taste of Honey"* (Herb
Alpert & the Tijuana Brass). A&M.
Richard Bogert, James Malloy, *Latin
Sound of Henry Mancini* (Henry
Mancini). RCA.
Lowell Frank, *September of My Years*
(Frank Sinatra). Reprise.
Frank Laico, *My Name Is Barbra* (Bar-
bra Streisand). Columbia.
Al Pachucki, Chuck Seitz, *More of That
Guitar Country* (Chet Atkins). RCA.
Chuck Seitz, William Vandevort, *That
Honey Horn Sound* (Al Hirt). RCA.

BEST ALBUM COVER, PHOTOGRAPHY
(Art Director's Award)

• Bob Jones; Ken Whitmore, photogra-
pher, *Jazz Suite on the Mass Texts*
(Paul Horn). RCA.
John Berg; Dan Kramer, photographer,
Bringing It All Back Home (Bob
Dylan). Columbia.
Robert Cat; Sheldon Streisand, photog-
rapher, *My Name Is Barbra* (Barbra
Streisand). Columbia.
Ed Thrasher; Sherman Weisburd, pho-
tographer, *The Aznavour Story*
(Charles Aznavour). Reprise.
Acy Lehman; Rudolph Regname, pho-
tographer, *Kenny Burrell: Guitar
Forms* (Kenny Burrell & Gil Evans
Orchestra). Verve.
Jerry Smokler; W. Eugene Smith, pho-
tographer, *Monk* (Thelonious Monk).
Columbia.
Peter Whorf, art director/photographer,
Whipped Cream and Other Delights
(Herb Alpert & the Tijuana Brass).
A&M.

BEST ALBUM COVER, GRAPHIC ARTS
(Art Director's Award)

• George Estes; James Alexander,
graphic artist, *Bartók: Concerto No.
2 for Violin; Stravinsky: Concerto for
Violin* (Silverstein, Leinsdorf, Boston
Symphony). RCA.
John Berg, art director/graphic artist,
Horowitz at Carnegie Hall
(Horowitz). Columbia.
John Berg, art director/graphic artist,
*William Tell and Other Favorite
Overtures* (Bernstein conducting the
New York Philharmonic).
Columbia.
George Estes; Charles White, graphic
artist, *Gould: Spirituals for Orches-
tra; Copland: Dance Symphony*
(Gould conducting the Chicago
Symphony). RCA.
Jerry Smokler; Paul Davis, graphic
artist, *Solo Monk* (Thelonious
Monk). Columbia.
Ed Thrasher; Patrick Blackwell,
graphic artist, *Concert in the
Virgin Islands* (Duke Ellington).
Reprise.

BEST ALBUM NOTES
(Annotator's Award)

• Stan Cornyn, *September of My Years*
(Frank Sinatra). Reprise.
Dom Cerulli, *The Voice of the Uncom-
mon Man* (Adlai Stevenson).
MGM.
Stanley Dance, *Grand Terrace Band*
(Earl Hines). RCA.
Charles Lamb, *Father and Son: Hank
Williams and Hank Williams, Jr.*
MGM.
Gustav Rudolf Sellner, Otto Gerdes,
Berg: Wozzeck (Karl Böhm conduct-
ing the Orchestra of German Opera).
Deutsche Grammophon.

• 1966 •

Ol' Blue Eyes Is Back

The big winner of 1966 was certainly no stranger on Grammy night. Frank Sinatra had five awards so far, including two for Album of the Year—*Come Dance with Me* (1959) and *September of My Years* (last year). This year, noted UPI, "The old pro with the receding hairline left the mop-top, guitar-strumming set at the starting gate when he walked off with three top Grammy Awards."

Sinatra held on to the LP category when *Sinatra: A Man and His Music* took Album of the Year honors. His other two victories were for Record of the Year "Strangers in the Night" and a third best male vocal performance trophy. "Strangers" also snagged trophies for arrangement and engineering. *Sinatra at the Sands* took Best Album Notes.

A Man and His Music was an anthology of Sinatra's biggest career hits that included overview narration by the singer. *Strangers in the Night* was one of his four albums to reach number one (the other three being *Come Fly with Me*, *Nice 'n' Easy* and *Sinatra Sings for Only the Lonely*).

Strangers' title song was by German composer Bert Kaempfert from the score for a forgettable James Garner spy film, *A Man Could Get Killed*. Music industry insiders knew early on that it was a hit tune, and a rush ensued, involving Sinatra, Bobby Darin and Jack Jones, to record it as a single as soon as English lyrics were written. When Sinatra discovered that Jones's version was due out in three days, an orchestra and arrangement were thrown together over the next 48 hours. On the third day, Sinatra stepped into a Reprise recording studio at 8 P.M., finished the taping session by 9,

Frank Sinatra continued to reign as "King of the Swingers" by winning best record and album.

and the song was on the nation's radio airwaves 24 hours later.

"Strangers" turned out to be the first of Sinatra's two number-one singles in the rock era, a pinnacle he hit just 18 weeks after his daughter Nancy was there with "These Boots Are Made for Walkin' " (a losing nominee for two vocal performance Grammys). Nine months later, he and Nancy teamed up for his second chart-topper, "Somethin' Stupid" (a losing contender for 1967 Record of the Year).

The only defeat Ol' Blue Eyes and his music suffered was for Song of the Year, which went to John Lennon and Paul McCartney for "Michelle," thereby redressing the "brush-off" the Beatles got from the Grammys last year. (The Liverpool lads nonetheless got the brush-off from the *New York Times,* which, strangely, failed to note their historic win in its roundup Grammy coverage.) The Beatles and their music were up for seven prizes in all, including Album of the Year (for *Revolver*), and won two more prizes in addition to top song: Best Album Cover (for art director Klaus Voormann) and Best Contemporary (R&R) Solo Vocal Performance, Male or Female, for McCartney singing "Eleanor Rigby." (The r&r vocal honors had been split by gender last year, but were combined for 1966.) Curiously, on the same day that McCartney's ode to loneliness reigned as the number-one platter in America—August 29, 1966—the Beatles performed their last paid public concert at Candlestick Park in San Francisco.

The success of "Michelle" was historic because it marked a major shift in Grammy voting preferences. For the first time ever, one of the top award choices was in tune with the frontline music of the day, which, strangely, came during another tribute year to Sinatra, who was clearly the champion of the old sound. Even better, "Michelle" prevailed over four songs—all stage and screen tunes—that typified the kind of music that usually won: "Born Free," "The Impossible Dream," "Somewhere, My Love" and even Sinatra's "Strangers in the Night."

The breakthrough came at a time when N.A.R.A.S. was actively reaching out for more young blood to join the academy. "Hip" Rev. Norman O'Connor, a noted author and musicologist, was the newly elected head of the New York chapter, and, although a cleric, was apparently less worried about the Rock of Ages than he was about the Grammys' performance in the rock age. "Father O'Connor Tosses Out N.A.R.A.S. Welcome Mat to 'Vital' Rock Makers," said a headline in *Variety.* The priest told the trade paper, "Up till now we have

reached too few of these very productive people." Apparently, he was not as flustered as others were by John Lennon's recent remark that shocked the religiously devout and caused a furor in the press. "The Beatles are probably bigger than Jesus," Lennon had boasted.

But the vital rock makers were still needed as voting academy members in order to correct the Grammys' ongoing failure, despite occasional exceptions, to acknowledge r&r adequately. Again this year, the choice for Best Contemporary (R&R) Recording was controversial: "Winchester Cathedral" by the New Vaudeville Band, which was also a contender for Record of the Year.

"Winchester Cathedral" was deliberately *anti*rock. Its composer/producer/singer, Geoff Stephens, was attempting to re-create the sound of a bygone time when he came up with the idea for the song one day when he spied a calendar photo of the famed medieval church while working as a songwriter at a small British music publisher. Stephens wanted to bring back the bouncy spirit of old vaudeville. When setting up the recording, he had musicians play the same band instruments popular during the late 1920s and sang the lead vocals himself, Rudy Vallee style, by shouting them through a megaphone. The novelty sparked a megaphone fad across America and helped land the song at number two in the year's Hot 100. Within four years, it was covered by 400 artists, including Frank Sinatra.

Another victory that triggered an outcry was the return of the Anita Kerr Quartet, whose triumph over the Beatles last year for Best Performance by a Vocal Group is still considered one of the most shocking results in Grammy vote history. This time the Fab Four wasn't even among the nominees when Kerr, a popular N.A.R.A.S. insider, reclaimed the same trophy for "A Man and a Woman."

> **The Beatles pulled off an upset to win best song for "Michelle."**

The latest losers were the Beach Boys, the Association, the Sandpipers and the Mamas & the Papas.

The Mamas & the Papas were the perfect mix of pop talent for their time: four mellow hippies whose soaring, old-style harmonies made rock palatable to real everyday mamas and papas and to their record-buying teens. Rock's Mamas & Papas were also the first group to include an equal balance between the sexes, being comprised of two women (Cass Elliott and Michelle Phillips) and two men (John Phillips and Dennis Doherty). Although they lost the vocal group honors to Kerr, they did take the prize for Best Contemporary (R&R) Group Performance, Vocal or Instrumental, for a track from their first album, *If You Can Believe Your Eyes and Ears*. "Monday, Monday," a losing nominee for Record of the Year, was so popular that radio deejays started playing it even before its release as a single, creating a clamor for the song that resulted in its selling 150,000 copies on the first day that it was finally available in record stores.

Many of the other Grammy wins went to the kind of middle-of-the-road music that N.A.R.A.S. voters embraced in the past. Eydie Gormé ("If He Walked into My Life" from the Broadway musical *Mame*) managed to break the lock on the best female vocal performance category held since the Grammys' inception by Ella Fitzgerald and Barbra Streisand (both of whom were nominated again this time) and interrupted only by Judy Garland in 1961. Herb Alpert & the Tijuana Brass picked up two instrumental trophies (performance and arrangement) for "What Now My Love."

The song from the TV show *Batman* reaped Best Instrumental Theme. Past Grammy champ Jerry Herman (for 1964's Song of the Year "Hello, Dolly!")

> Ray Charles reaped two Grammys and a standing ovation for "Crying Time."

won Best Score from on Original Cast Show Album for *Mame* (beating out *Man of La Mancha* and *Sweet Charity*). The theme music to *Dr. Zhivago* had won the Oscar for best film score and now garnered the equivalent accolade from the record academy, topping close contender *Born Free*.

Dr. Zhivago snagged a second prize when "Somewhere, My Love (Lara's Theme)" won Best Performance by a Chorus for Ray Coniff & Singers. Coniff and his troupe specialized in what Grammy voters loved: sweeping, instrumental mood music accompanied by equally soaring vocals. Coniff's fare dominated the easy-listening FM channels of the mid to late '60s, although "Somewhere" turned out to be his only Top 40 hit and only Grammy victory.

Bill Cosby continued his dominance of the comedy category when he won for a third year in a row. *Wonderfulness* was only his fourth LP, but it contained some of his most wonderfully funny routines such as "Tonsils," "Chicken Heart," "Go Carts" and "The Playground." (In "Chicken Heart," he recalls being so frightened by a popular radio drama as a child that he smeared Jell-O—a product for which he'd become a spokesman in future years—all over the floor in order to keep the program's monster at bay.) When it was released, *Wonderfulness* set a new record for most comedy albums sold in a day—200,000—and remained on the charts for 106 weeks.

One of the most curious—and least comical—wins of the year involved the Best Folk Recording, which went to a blind street singer who panhandled in downtown Nashville for a living. Cortelia Clark's sole LP, *Blues in the Street,* had been a financial disaster, so he couldn't afford to attend the Nashville Grammy show because of the prohibitive cost of renting a tuxedo. Worse, his moment of glory would be short-lived. Despite his award success and the extensive news coverage that followed, Clark was never again asked to perform on record. The day after the Grammy ceremony, he was seen still hustling spare change on the sidewalks of the honkytonk capital. Two years later he died when a kerosene stove exploded in his trailer home. He has since been immortalized in a Mickey Newberry song called "Cortelia Clark."

Seven-time past winner Ray Charles received a standing ovation on Grammy night when he made a triumphant return to claim two statuettes for his bittersweet "Crying Time," including Best Rhythm & Blues Recording. Charles had dominated the prize from 1961 to 1963 after it replaced the earlier r&b performance award, which Charles won in 1960. Since the start of the Grammys, the genre had had only one annual category, but after the jealous turmoil that followed Nashville's copping of six country & western categories when it joined the Recording Academy in 1964, a comprehensive awards revamping ensued. Charles's second award was for the reinstated performance prize. A new r&b category for group performance (vocal or instrumental) was nabbed by last year's jazz group winner, Ramsey Lewis, for "Hold It Right There."

Jazz ended up losing one of its three categories in the overhaul, leaving only Best Original Jazz Composition (claimed by Duke Ellington for "In the Beginning God") and the instrumental performance slot, which went to Wes Montgomery. (Previously, the category was split between prizes for large group and small group or soloist. Now all performers competed for a single honor.) Ellington's fifth Grammy came with a heartfelt bonus. On the after-the-fact "Best on Record" Grammy TV show, which showcased performances by some of the winning artists, the Duke was given a Lifetime Achievement Award. He accepted it telling the audience and the academy, "We do love you madly."

Wes Montgomery's Grammy success was a welcome win to his fans, but a disappointment to some critics. He was the reigning jazz guitarist of the 1950s and early '60s, having, in the words of *Rolling Stone,* "demonstrated a fluid single-note style brilliantly interfaced with a subtle use of chords." Some critics and musicians turned away from him in the mid-1960s, however, when he pursued more commercial music like his Grammy-honored "Goin' out of My Head," which they dismissed as light pop fare.

Country & western was cut back to four categories, three of which were claimed by David Houston and his "Almost Persuaded" disc about the allure of honky-tonk temptresses.

"Almost Persuaded" almost didn't make it. Houston was looking for a "B" side to his "We Got Love" single even up to the night before the 45 was due to be wrapped up. Songwriters Billy Sherrill and Glenn Sutton worked on it till midnight. The next morning Houston recorded the tune, which was subsequently discovered by an Atlanta deejay and went on to top the country charts for nine weeks. Sherrill and Sutton prevailed over 11-time (over two years) winner Roger Miller and his "Husbands and Wives" platter for Best Country & Western Song. Houston won Best Country & Western Recording and the c&w male vocal performance prize.

Jeannie Seely took the equivalent female honors for "Don't Touch Me," a pioneering Hank Cochran song that epitomized the new soul-searing, woeful tunes that were just then replacing the traditional storytelling c&w music of the past. Country's two-year-old best new artist award was dropped entirely, just as the overall Best New Artist prize was, too—the only time in Grammy history that the category was skipped after it was introduced in 1959.

The choice of Classical Album of the Year was the first recording of Charles Ives's Symphony No. 1 in D Minor, which the adventurous American composer wrote while he was still a student at Yale. (His Symphony No. 4 was voted best contemporary classical composition last year.) Performed by the Chicago Symphony Orchestra under the baton of conductor-composer Morton Gould, Ives's first symphony was "the highest point of Gould's conducting career," in the words of critic Arthur Cohn, who added, "No one has thus far matched the caressing sweetness of his interpretation." Conductor Gregg Smith and the Columbia Chamber Orchestra were among the winners tied for Best Classical Performance, Choral (Other Than Opera), for Ives's *Music for Chorus,* which included works such as "General William Booth Enters into Heaven." The honors were shared with Robert Shaw and his chorale and orchestra for their rendition of Handel's *Messiah.*

Five-time past Grammy winner Erich Leinsdorf reaped the orchestral performance trophy for the Boston Symphony's Symphony No. 6 in A Minor by Mahler. Classical guitarist Julian Bream won the instrumental soloist award for his *Baroque Guitar,* which incorporated works by Bach, Sanz and Weiss. "Bream's art does beautifully by them," *High Fidelity* wrote, "and vice versa."

Leontyne Price stretched her winning streak to four years by holding on to the laurels for vocal soloist, this time for *Prima Donna,* an assortment of arias written by Verdi, Purcell and Barber. The Best Opera Recording went to Georg Solti for conducting the Vienna Philharmonic in the first of Wagner's *Ring* operas, *Die Walküre. High Fidelity* called it "his best work on records," and said soprano Birgit Nilsson as Brünnhilde "does a wonderful job." Regine Crespin as Sieglinde, it added, "is magnificent." The principal soloists, including Nilsson, Crespin, Christa Ludwin, James King and Hans Hotter, received special plaques.

The Grammy ceremonies took place in New York, L.A., Nashville and Chicago. In L.A., the ceremony was held

Metropolitan Opera

Prima Donna earned Leontyne Price the classical vocalist's laurels for a fourth consecutive year.

at the Beverly Hilton, with Bill Dana acting as master of ceremonies and Les Brown's orchestra providing the entertainment. In New York, the festivities were shifted this year from the Astor Hotel to the Hilton where Tony Randall acted as host before a crowd of 500. Nineteen sixty-three Grammy winner Woody Herman and his band provided the entertainment, while presenters included songwriter Harold Arlen, bandleader Skitch Henderson and singer Steve Lawrence. But the presenters didn't have many opportunities to pass out the golden gramophones as planned. Lawrence's wife and frequent vocal partner turned out to be the single highlight of the gala by default. *Variety* noted: "The only winning artist accepting an award at the New York affair was Eydie Gormé.

"The most popular refrain as the prizes were announced was that 'the winner of this award will accept it in Hollywood' or, in the same degree, Nashville," *Variety* continued. "Frank Sinatra's domination of the ceremonies by copping accolades in six of the 42 categories was symptomatic of the shift in accent to the

Coast." Out in Los Angeles, noted the *Herald Examiner,* "an enthusiastic and natty throng of diners applauded the results at the Beverly Hilton International Ballroom," where most of the action was. Key victories by those "California Dreamers" the Mamas & the Papas (who would have been the likely winners of Best New Artist if the category hadn't been scrapped) and other L.A. heroes such as Herb Alpert & the Tijuana Brass confirmed that the West Coast–based N.A.R.A.S. had reclaimed control over the newly humbled rebels in Nashville and the once all-powerful titans of Tin Pan Alley in New York.

• 1966 •

Awards were bestowed on March 2, 1967, for the eligibility period November 2, 1965, to November 1, 1966, at ceremonies held at the Beverly Hilton Hotel in Los Angeles, the Hilton Hotel in New York, and at dinners held in Nashville and Chicago.

ALBUM OF THE YEAR
• *Sinatra: A Man and His Music*, Frank Sinatra. Reprise.
Color Me Barbra, Barbra Streisand. Columbia.
Dr. Zhivago (soundtrack), Maurice Jarre. MGM.
Revolver, Beatles. Capitol.
What Now My Love, Herb Alpert & the Tijuana Brass. A&M.

RECORD OF THE YEAR
• "Strangers in the Night," Frank Sinatra. Reprise.
"Almost Persuaded," David Houston. Epic.
"Monday, Monday," Mamas & the Papas. Dunhill.
"What Now My Love," Herb Alpert & the Tijuana Brass. A&M.
"Winchester Cathedral," New Vaudeville Band. Fontana.

SONG OF THE YEAR
(Songwriter's Award)
• "Michelle," John Lennon, Paul McCartney. Capitol.
"Born Free," John Barry, Don Black. MGM.

"The Impossible Dream," Mitch Leigh, Joe Darion. Kapp.
"Somewhere, My Love (Lara's Theme from *Dr. Zhivago*)," Paul Francis Webster, Maurice Jarre. MGM.
"Strangers in the Night," Bert Kaempfert, Charles Singleton, Eddie Snyder. Reprise.

BEST VOCAL PERFORMANCE, MALE
• Frank Sinatra, "Strangers in the Night." Reprise.
David Houston, "Almost Persuaded." Epic.
Jack Jones, "The Impossible Dream." Kapp.
Paul McCartney, "Eleanor Rigby." Capitol.
Jim Reeves, "Distant Drums." RCA.
Andy Williams, *The Shadow of Your Smile*. Columbia.

BEST VOCAL PERFORMANCE, FEMALE
• Eydie Gormé, "If He Walked into My Life." Columbia.
Ella Fitzgerald, *Ella at Duke's Place.* Verve.
Sandy Posey, "Born a Woman." MGM.
Nancy Sinatra, "These Boots Are Made for Walkin'." Reprise.
Barbra Streisand, *Color Me Barbra.* Columbia.

BEST PERFORMANCE BY A VOCAL GROUP
• Anita Kerr Quartet, "A Man and a Woman." Warner Bros.
Association, "Cherish." Valiant.

Beach Boys, "Good Vibrations." Capitol.

Mamas & the Papas, "Monday, Monday." Dunhill.

Sandpipers, "Guantanamera." A&M.

BEST PERFORMANCE BY A CHORUS

• Ray Conniff & Singers, "Somewhere, My Love (Lara's Theme from *Dr. Zhivago*)." Columbia.

Alan Copeland Singers with Count Basie, *Basie Swingin', Voices Singin'*. ABC-Paramount.

Henry Mancini, Orchestra & Chorus, *Henry Mancini Presents the Academy Award Songs*. RCA.

Johnny Mann Singers, *A Man and a Woman*. Liberty.

Swingle Singers, *Rococo A'Go Go*. Philips.

BEST CONTEMPORARY (R&R) RECORDING

• "Winchester Cathedral," New Vaudeville Band. Fontana.

"Cherish," Association. Valiant.

"Eleanor Rigby," Paul McCartney. Capitol.

"Good Vibrations," Beach Boys. Capitol.

"Last Train to Clarksville," Monkees. Colgems.

"Monday, Monday," Mamas & the Papas. Dunhill.

BEST CONTEMPORARY (R&R) SOLO VOCAL PERFORMANCE (MALE OR FEMALE)

• Paul McCartney, "Eleanor Rigby." Capitol.

Bobby Darin, "If I Were a Carpenter." Atlantic.

Sandy Posey, "Born a Woman." MGM.

Nancy Sinatra, "These Boots Are Made for Walkin'." Reprise.

Dusty Springfield, "You Don't Have to Say You Love Me." Philips.

BEST CONTEMPORARY (R&R) GROUP PERFORMANCE (VOCAL OR INSTRUMENTAL)

• Mamas & the Papas, "Monday, Monday." Dunhill.

Association, "Cherish." Valiant.

Beach Boys, "Good Vibrations." Capitol.

Monkees, "Last Train to Clarksville." Colgems.

Sandpipers, "Guantanamera." A&M.

BEST RHYTHM & BLUES RECORDING

• "Crying Time," Ray Charles. ABC-Paramount.

"It's a Man's Man's Man's World," James Brown. King.

"Love Is a Hurtin' Thing," Lou Rawls. Capitol.

"Uptight," Stevie Wonder. Tamla.

"When a Man Loves a Woman," Percy Sledge. Atlantic.

BEST RHYTHM & BLUES SOLO VOCAL PERFORMANCE (MALE OR FEMALE)

• Ray Charles, "Crying Time." ABC-Paramount.

James Brown, "It's a Man's Man's Man's World." King.

Lou Rawls, "Love Is a Hurtin' Thing." Capitol.

Percy Sledge, "When a Man Loves a Woman." Atlantic.

Stevie Wonder, "Uptight." Tamla.

BEST RHYTHM & BLUES GROUP PERFORMANCE (VOCAL OR INSTRUMENTAL)

• Ramsey Lewis, "Hold It Right There." Cadet.

Capitols, "Cool Jerk." Atco.

King Curtis, "Spanish Harlem." Atco.

James & Bobby Purify, "I'm Your Puppet." Bell.

Sam & Dave, "Hold On, I'm Comin'." Stax.

BEST ORIGINAL JAZZ COMPOSITION (Composer's Award)

• Duke Ellington, "In the Beginning God." RCA.

Bob Brookmeyer, "ABC Blues." Solid State.

Bill Evans, "Time Remembered." Riverside.

John Handy, "If Only We Knew."
Columbia.
Claus Ogerman, "Jazz Samba." Verve.
Lalo Schifrin, "Marquis de Sade."
Verve.

BEST INSTRUMENTAL JAZZ PERFORMANCE BY A GROUP OR SOLOIST WITH GROUP

• Wes Montgomery, "Goin' out of My
Head." Verve.
Ornette Coleman Trio, *At the Golden
Circle*. Blue Note.
Duke Ellington Orchestra, *Concert of
Sacred Music*. RCA.
Bill Evans, Jim Hall, *Intermodulation*.
Verve.
John Handy Quintet, *John Handy
Recorded Live at the Monterey Jazz
Festival*. Columbia.
Woody Herman Orchestra, *Woody's
Winners*. Columbia.
Stan Kenton, *Stan Kenton Conducts the
Los Angeles Neophonic Orchestra*.
Capitol.

BEST SACRED RECORDING, MUSICAL

• *Grand Old Gospel*, Porter Wagoner
and the Blackwood Brothers. RCA.
Bigger 'n' Better, Happy Goodman
Family. Canaan.
Connie Smith Sings Great Sacred Songs,
Connie Smith. RCA.
How Big Is God, Blackwood Brothers.
RCA.
The Oak Ridge Boys at Their Best, Oak
Ridge Boys. United Artists.
Southland Songs That Lift the Heart,
George Beverly Shea. RCA.

BEST COUNTRY & WESTERN RECORDING

• "Almost Persuaded," David Houston.
Epic.
"Distant Drums," Jim Reeves. RCA.
"Don't Touch Me," Jeannie Seely. Mon-
ument.
"I'm a Nut," Leroy Pullins. Kapp.
"There Goes My Everything," Jack
Greene. Decca.

BEST COUNTRY & WESTERN VOCAL PERFORMANCE, MALE

• David Houston, "Almost Persuaded."
Epic.
Ben Colder, "Almost Persuaded No. 2."
Verve.
Jack Greene, "There Goes My Every-
thing." Decca.
Charley Pride, "Just Between You and
Me." RCA.
Jim Reeves, "Distant Drums." RCA.

BEST COUNTRY & WESTERN VOCAL PERFORMANCE, FEMALE

• Jeannie Seely, "Don't Touch Me."
Monument.
Jan Howard, "Evil on Your Mind." Decca.
Loretta Lynn, "Don't Come Home A-
Drinkin'." Decca.
Connie Smith, "Ain't Had No Loving."
RCA.
Dottie West, "Would You Hold It
Against Me." RCA.

BEST COUNTRY & WESTERN SONG (Songwriter's Award)

• "Almost Persuaded," Billy Sherrill,
Glenn Sutton. Epic.
"Don't Touch Me," Hank Cochran.
Monument.
"Husbands and Wives," Roger Miller.
Smash.
"Streets of Baltimore," Tompall Glaser,
Harlan Howard. RCA.
"There Goes My Everything," Dallas
Frazier. Decca.

BEST FOLK RECORDING

• *Blues in the Street*, Cortelia Clark.
RCA.
God Bless the Grass, Pete Seeger.
Columbia.
"Hurry Sundown," Peter, Paul & Mary.
Warner Bros.
Leadbelly, Leadbelly. Elektra.
Oliver Smith, Oliver Smith. Elektra.
Reflections in a Crystal Wind, Mimi &
Richard Farina. Vanguard.
Sound of the Sitar, Ravi Shankar. World
Pacific.
Violets of Dawn, Mitchell Trio. Mercury.

BEST INSTRUMENTAL THEME
(Composer's Award)
• "*Batman* Theme," Neal Hefti. RCA.
"Arabesque," Henry Mancini. RCA.
"Prissy," Priscilla Hubbard. RCA.
"Trumpet Pickin'," D. J. Edwards. RCA.
"Who's Afraid," Alex North. Warner Bros.

BEST INSTRUMENTAL PERFORMANCE
(OTHER THAN JAZZ)
• Herb Alpert & the Tijuana Brass, "What Now My Love." A&M.
Chet Atkins, *Chet Atkins Picks on the Beatles*. RCA.
Neal Hefti, "*Batman* Theme." RCA.
Maurice Jarre, *Dr. Zhivago* (soundtrack). MGM.
Roger Williams, "Born Free." Kapp.

BEST INSTRUMENTAL ARRANGEMENT
• Herb Alpert, "What Now My Love" (Herb Alpert & the Tijuana Brass). A&M.
John Barry, "Born Free" (John Barry). MGM.
Bob Florence, "Michelle" (Bud Shank). World Pacific.
Neal Hefti, "*Batman* Theme" (Neal Hefti). RCA.
Henry Mancini, "Arabesque" (Henry Mancini). RCA.

BEST ARRANGEMENT ACCOMPANYING A VOCALIST OR INSTRUMENTALIST
• Ernie Freeman, "Strangers in the Night" (Frank Sinatra). Reprise.
Don Costa, "If He Walked into My Life" (Eydie Gormé). Columbia.
George Martin, "Eleanor Rigby" (Paul McCartney). Capitol.
Oliver Nelson, "Goin' out of My Head" (Wes Montgomery). Verve.
Billy Strange, "These Boots Are Made for Walkin'" (Nancy Sinatra). Reprise.
Brian Wilson, "Good Vibrations" (Beach Boys). Capitol.

BEST SCORE FROM AN ORIGINAL CAST SHOW ALBUM
(Composer's Award)
• *Mame*, Jerry Herman. Columbia.
The Apple Tree, Jerry Bock, Sheldon Harnick. Columbia.
Man of La Mancha, Mitch Leigh, Joe Darion. Kapp.
Skyscraper, Jimmy Van Heusen, Sammy Cahn. Capitol.
Sweet Charity, Cy Coleman, Dorothy Fields. Columbia.

BEST ORIGINAL SCORE WRITTEN FOR A MOTION PICTURE OR TV SHOW
(Composer's Award)
• *Dr. Zhivago*, Maurice Jarre. MGM.
Arabesque, Henry Mancini. RCA.
Born Free, John Barry. MGM.
Alfie, Sonny Rollins. Impulse.
Who's Afraid of Virginia Woolf? Alex North. Warner Bros.

ALBUM OF THE YEAR, CLASSICAL
• *Ives: Symphony No. 1 in D Minor*, Morton Gould conducting the Chicago Symphony. RCA.
Aaron Copland Conducts ("Music for a Great City," "Statements"), Aaron Copland conducting the London Symphony. Columbia.
Handel: Messiah, Colin Davis conducting the London Symphony Orchestra and Choir. Philips.
Henze: Symphonies (1–5), H. W. Henze conducting the Berlin Philharmonic. Deutsche Grammophon.
Mahler: Symphony No. 6 in A Minor, Erich Leinsdorf conducting the Boston Symphony. RCA.
Mahler: Symphony No. 10, Eugene Ormandy conducting the Philadelphia Orchestra. Columbia.
Opening Nights at the Met, various artists. RCA.
Presenting Montserrat Caballé (Bellini and Donizetti arias), Montserrat Caballé. RCA.

Wagner: Die Walküre, Georg Solti conducting the Vienna Philharmonic (solos: Nilsson, Crespin, Ludwig, King, Hotter, Frick). London.

BEST CLASSICAL PERFORMANCE, ORCHESTRA
(Conductor's Award)

- Erich Leinsdorf conducting the Boston Symphony, *Mahler: Symphony No. 6 in A Minor*. RCA.

Ernest Ansermet conducting the Orchestre de la Suisse Romande, *Ravel: Daphnis et Chloé*. London.

Leonard Bernstein conducting the New York Philharmonic, *Ives: Fourth of July*. Columbia.

Pierre Boulez, Antal Dorati conducting the BBC Symphony, *Boulez: Le Soleil des Eaux; Messiaen: Chronochromie; Koechlin: Les Bandar-Log*. Angel.

Morton Gould conducting the Chicago Symphony, *Ives: Symphony No. 1 in D Minor*. RCA.

Jean Martinon conducting the Chicago Symphony, *Varèse: Arcana; Martin: Concerto for 7 Wind Instruments, Timpani, Percussion and String Orchestra*. RCA.

Eugene Ormandy conducting the Philadelphia Orchestra, *Mahler: Symphony No. 10*. Columbia.

George Szell conducting the Cleveland Orchestra, *Bartók: Concerto for Orchestra*. Columbia.

BEST CHAMBER MUSIC PERFORMANCE, INSTRUMENTAL OR VOCAL

- Boston Symphony Chamber Players, *Boston Symphony Chamber Players* (selections by Mozart, Brahms, Beethoven, Fine, Copland, Carter, Piston). RCA.

Erick Friedman, André Previn, *Franck: Sonata in A Major for Violin and Piano; Debussy: Sonata in G Minor for Violin and Piano*. RCA.

Jascha Heifetz, Gregor Piatigorsky with Leonard Pennario, *Arensky: Trio in D Minor for Violin, Cello and Piano; Martinu: Duo for Violin and Cello*. RCA.

Eugene Istomin, Isaac Stern, Leonard Rose, *Beethoven: Trio No. 6 in B Flat, Op. 97 ("Archduke")*. Columbia.

Gregor Piatigorsky, Rudolf Firkusny, *Prokofiev: Sonata for Cello and Piano, Op. 119; Chopin: Sonata in G Minor for Piano and Cello, Op. 65*. RCA.

Walter Trampler and Budapest Quartet, *Mozart: The 6 Quintets for String Quartet and Viola*. Columbia.

Vienna Philharmonic Quartet, *Schubert: Quintet in C Major*. London.

Weller Quartet, *Haydn: Quartets, Op. 33*. London.

BEST CLASSICAL PERFORMANCE, INSTRUMENTAL SOLOIST(S) (WITH OR WITHOUT ORCHESTRA)

- Julian Bream, *Baroque Guitar* (Bach, Sanz, Weiss, etc.). RCA.

John Browning (Leinsdorf conducting the Boston Symphony), *Prokofiev: Concerto No. 1 in D Flat Major for Piano; Concerto No. 2 in G Minor for Piano*. RCA.

Raymond Lewenthal, *Operatic Liszt*. RCA.

Yehudi Menuhin (Boult conducting the New Philharmonia Orchestra), *Elgar: Concerto for Violin*. Angel.

Ivan Moravec, *Chopin: Nocturnes*. Connoisseur Society.

Artur Rubinstein, *Rubinstein and Chopin* ("Boléro," "Tarentelle," "Fantasia in F Minor Barcarolle," "Bercuse" and 3 nouvelles études). RCA.

Isaac Stern (Ormandy conducting the Philadelphia Orchestra), *Dvořák: Concerto in A Minor for Violin*. Columbia.

John Williams (Eugene Ormandy conducting the Philadelphia Orchestra), *Rodrigo: Concierto de Aranjuez for Guitar and Orchestra; Castelnuovo-Tedesco: Concerto in D Major for Guitar*. Columbia.

BEST OPERA RECORDING
(Conductor's Award)

- *Wagner: Die Walküre*, Georg Solti conducting the Vienna Philharmonic (solos: Nilsson, Crespin, Ludwig, King, Hotter). London.

Bartók: Bluebeard's Castle, István Kertész conducting the London Symphony (solos: Ludwig, Berry). London.

Copland: The Tender Land, Aaron Copland conducting the Choral Arts Society and New York Philharmonic (solos: Clements, Turner, Cassilly, Treigle, Fredericks). Columbia.

Puccini: Turandot, Francesco Molinari-Pradelli conducting the Rome Opera Chorus and Orchestra (solos: Nilsson, Corelli). Angel.

Wagner: Lohengrin, Erich Leinsdorf conducting the Boston Symphony (solos: Konya, Amarca, Gorr, Dooley). RCA.

BEST CLASSICAL PERFORMANCE CHORAL, (OTHER THAN OPERA)
(Tie)

- Robert Shaw conducting the Robert Shaw Chorale and Orchestra, *Handel: Messiah*. RCA.
- Gregg Smith conducting the Columbia Chamber Orchestra, Gregg Smith Singers, Ithaca College Concert Choir; George Bragg conducting the Texas Boys' Choir, *Ives: Music for Chorus* ("General William Booth Enters into Heaven," "Serenity," "The Circus Band," etc.). Columbia.

Richard Condie directing the Mormon Tabernacle Choir; Eugene Ormandy conducting the Philadelphia Orchestra, *Bless This House*. Columbia.

Colin Davis conducting the soloists, London Symphony Orchestra and Choir, *Handel: Messiah*. Philips.

Alfred Nash Patterson directing the Boston Symphony Chorus; Erich Leinsdorf conducting the Boston Symphony Orchestra, *Verdi: Requiem*. RCA.

Wilhelm Pitz conducting the New Philharmonia Chorus; Otto Klemperer conducting the New Philharmonia Orchestra, *Beethoven: Missa Solemnis in D Major*. Angel.

Wilhelm Pitz conducting the New Philharmonia Chorus; Rafael Frühbeck de Burgos conducting the New Philharmonia Orchestra, *Orff: Carmina Burana*. Angel.

David Willcocks conducting the Bach Choir and Choristers of Westminster Abbey and London Symphony, *Vaughan Williams: Hodie*. Angel.

BEST CLASSICAL PERFORMANCE, VOCAL SOLOIST

- Leontyne Price (Molinari-Pradelli conducting the RCA Italiana Opera Orchestra; solos: Barber, Purcell, etc.), *Prima Donna*. RCA.

Janet Baker (Morris conducting the London Philharmonic), *Mahler: The Youth's Magic Horn (Das Knaben Wunderhorn)*. Angel.

Dietrich Fischer-Dieskau, *Schumann: Dichterliebe*. Deutsche Grammophon.

Montserrat Caballé (Cilario, conductor), *Presenting Montserrat Caballé* (Bellini and Donizetti arias). RCA.

Judith Raskin (Szell conducting the Cleveland Orchestra), *Mahler: Symphony No. 4 in G Major*. Columbia.

Elisabeth Schwarzkopf (Szell conducting the Berlin Radio Symphony), *Strauss: 4 Last Songs*. Angel.

BEST ENGINEERED RECORDING, CLASSICAL

- Anthony Salvatore, *Wagner: Lohengrin* (Leinsdorf conducting the Boston Symphony Pro Musica Chorus and soloists). RCA.

Bernard Keville, *Ives: Symphony No. 1 in D Minor* (Gould conducting the Chicago Symphony). RCA.

Bernard Keville, *Varèse: Arcana* (Martinon conducting the Chicago Symphony). RCA.

Ernest Oelrich, *Vivaldi: Gloria in D* (Robert Shaw Orchestra and Chorus). RCA.

Anthony Salvatore, *Mahler: Symphony No. 6 in A Minor* (Leinsdorf conducting the Boston Symphony). RCA.

BEST SPOKEN WORD, DOCUMENTARY OR DRAMA RECORDING

• *Edward R. Murrow, a Reporter Remembers—Vol. 1, The War Years*, Edward R. Murrow. Columbia.

Day for Decision, Johnny Sea. Warner Bros.

Death of a Salesman, Lee J. Cobb, Mildred Dunnock. Caedmon.

History Repeats Itself, Buddy Starcher. Decca.

The Stevenson Wit, Adlai Stevenson. David Brinkley, narrator. RCA.

BEST COMEDY PERFORMANCE

• Bill Cosby, *Wonderfulness*. Warner Bros.

Don Bowman, *Funny Way to Make an Album*. RCA.

Archie Campbell, *Have a Laugh on Me*. RCA.

Homer & Jethro, *Wanted for Murder*. RCA.

Mrs. Miller, *Downtown*. Capitol.

BEST RECORDING FOR CHILDREN

• *Dr. Seuss Presents: "If I Ran the Zoo" and "Sleep Book,"* Marvin Miller. RCA.

Alice Through the Looking Glass, original cast. Moose Charlap, Elsie Simmons, score. RCA.

The Christmas That Almost Wasn't, Paul Tripp and cast. RCA.

For the Children of the World Art Linkletter Narrates the Bible, Art Linkletter. RCA.

Happiness Is, Marty Gold conducting the Do-Re-Mi Children's Chorus. Kapp.

BEST ENGINEERED RECORDING

• Eddie Brackett, Lee Herschberg, *Strangers in the Night* (Frank Sinatra). Reprise.

Dick Bogert, "Arabesque" (Henry Mancini). RCA.

James Malloy, *The Last Word in Lonesome Is Me* (Eddy Arnold). RCA.

Phil Ramone, *Presenting Thad Jones* (Mel Lewis & the Jazz Orchestra). Sid. St.

Phil Ramone, *Joe Williams and Thad Jones* (Mel Lewis & the Jazz Orchestra). Sid. St.

BEST ALBUM COVER, PHOTOGRAPHY

• Robert Jones, art director; Les Leverette, photographer, *Confessions of a Broken Man* (Porter Wagoner). RCA.

Bob Cato, John Berg, art directors; Gerald Schatsberg, photographer, *Blonde on Blonde* (Bob Dylan). Columbia.

Bob Cato, John Berg, art directors; Guy Webster, photographer, *Turn! Turn! Turn!* (Byrds). Columbia.

Robert Jones, art director; Tom Zimmerman, photographer, *The Time Machine* (Gary Burton). RCA.

Ed Thrasher, art director; Tom Tucker, photographer, *Sammy Davis, Jr. Sings, Laurindo Almeida Plays*. Reprise.

Peter Whorf, art director and photographer, *Guantanamera* (Sandpipers). A&M.

Peter Whorf, art director; George Jerman, photographer, *What Now My Love* (Herb Alpert & the Tijuana Brass). A&M.

BEST ALBUM COVER, GRAPHIC ARTS

• Klaus Voormann, graphic artist, *Revolver* (Beatles). Capitol.

Elinor Bunin, graphic artist; Bob Cato, John Berg, art directors, *Color Me Barbra* (Barbra Streisand). Columbia.

Rod Dyer, graphic artist; George Osaki, art director, *Stan Kenton Conducts the Los Angeles Neophonic Orchestra*. Capitol.

Gordon Kibbee, graphic artist; William S. Harvey, art director, *Baroque Fanfares and Sonatas for Brass* (Rifkin directing London Brass Players). Nonesuch.

Mozelle Thompson, graphic artist; George Estes, art director, *Ives: Symphony No. 1 in D Minor* (Gould conducting the Chicago Symphony). RCA.

Allen Weinberg, graphic artist; Bob Cato, John Berg, art directors, *Charlie Byrd Christmas Carols for Solo Guitar*. Columbia.

Peter Whorf, graphic artist; Woody Woodward, art director, *Talk That Talk* (Jazz Crusaders). Pacific Jazz.

BEST ALBUM NOTES
(Annotator's Award)
• Stan Cornyn, *Sinatra at the Sands*. Reprise.

Harvey Cowen, *Ben Colder Strikes Again*. MGM.

Stanley Dance, Ralph Gleason, *The Ellington Era, Vol. 2*. Columbia.

Fred Friendly, *Edward R. Murrow, a Reporter Remembers—Vol. 1, The War Years*. Columbia.

Nelson Lyon, *Dr. Zhivago* (Maurice Jarre). MGM.

• 1967 •

Sgt. Pepper's Coup

No major Grammy triumph has generated more hot air than the 5th Dimension's "Up, Up and Away," the Jimmy Webb Song and Record of the Year about a fanciful balloon ride that soared up the singles charts for 12 weeks, peaking at number four. N.A.R.A.S. voters were trying hard in 1967 to keep their picks in tune with the times, but once again they embraced an easy-listening choice despite the academy's insistence that the awards were becoming more hip.

To critics, "Up, Up and Away" represented the height of sentimentality in music as well as considerable proof that N.A.R.A.S.'s Sinatra-loving old guard still held sway, even though the song's victory as Record of the Year marked the first time that the Grammys' highest honor went to music written for the younger generation. But just as last year when Ol' Blue Eyes and the Beatles split the top awards, the Grammys were again headed toward a schizophrenic outcome.

"Up, Up and Away" was unabashedly cute and breezy. Its obvious appeal to N.A.R.A.S. voters resulted in the 5th Dimension receiving the most nominations of the year—seven, a number tied by Bobbie Gentry. (The Beatles and Glen Campbell followed with six bids each.) The group ended up winning four Grammys. N.A.R.A.S. dropped the "Contemporary (R&R)" awards this year in favor of simply "Contemporary" ones, a slap at r&r that left many progressive music pundits smarting. In addition to the prizes for best song and record, the 5th Dimension also nabbed Best Contemporary Group Performance as well as Best Contemporary Single, a new category that would vanish into the stratosphere next year. An

Best album champ *Sgt. Pepper's Lonely Hearts Club Band* led the charge as music by younger artists swept the top awards for the first time ever.

even *easier*-listening version of "Up, Up and Away" recorded by the Johnny Mann Singers just as easily took the prize for Best Performance by a Chorus.

Like Best Contemporary Single, the award for Best Contemporary Album was also dropped after 1967, but not before being caught this year by the winners of the Album of the Year honors. The Beatles' victories of 1967 were a milestone in Grammy history. The Fab Four had won only one of the top three awards in the past—for last year's Song of the Year "Michelle," a platter well suited to N.A.R.A.S. voters' long-standing preference for strong, safe melodies and romantic lyrics. *Sgt. Pepper's Lonely Hearts Club Band,* by comparison, was everything but safe: Its experimental electronic sound was revolutionary and utilized the latest technological devices like the four-track tape recorder, making it the Grammys' Best Engineered

Recording, too. Lyrics to songs like "Lucy in the Sky with Diamonds" and "A Day in the Life" were psychedelic and deliberately nonsensical, causing fans to scrutinize them carefully for hidden meaning. Its brightly colored, hallucinogenic cover (featuring images of Marlene Dietrich, W. C. Fields and a flower patch spelling out "Beatles") earned it the Best Album Cover award. N.A.R.A.S.'s bold acknowledgment of *Sgt. Pepper*'s importance did not represent a future trend, however. The Beatles, as a group, would reap only one more Grammy in subsequent years despite having such other breakthrough releases as *Abbey Road*. Their final bow would come in 1970 for the film score to *Let It Be*, which was released after the band broke up.

Tied with the 5th Dimension for the most awards of the night—four—was the perfect N.A.R.A.S. music hero. Glen Campbell was squeaky-clean cool. He may have represented more of the western influence in country & western, but Nashville voters, at least for now, considered him their own and ensured his triumph with a wave of votes. His first hit record, "Gentle on My Mind," was the easy victor of Best Country & Western Recording and also brought him c&w's male vocal performance trophy.

But Campbell's support stretched far beyond Nashville. He'd worked in the Hollywood film studios, stood in for Brian Wilson of the Beach Boys for a few months on tour and performed as a loyal session man for Eydie Gormé, Nat King Cole and Frank Sinatra, among others. His many N.A.R.A.S. friends also voted him the overall best male vocal performance prize and the performance award allotted to the new "Contemporary" categories, both of them for his second hit, "By the Time I Get to Phoenix," which he originally opposed as a single release. (Pat Boone, he argued, had

recorded it earlier without much success. Luckily for Campbell, he was overruled by Capitol Records execs.) When he accepted his first award on Grammy night, the *L.A. Times* noted, Campbell "thanked all the people he had backed up on guitar for their votes."

"By the Time I Get to Phoenix" was written by Jimmy Webb, who was nominated for Song of the Year for both "Phoenix" and the victorious "Up, Up and Away." "Gentle on My Mind" was the work of John Hartford, who took the prize for Best Folk Performance, for his own rendition of his hit tune, as well as Best Country & Western Song.

The Best New Artist award was reinstated this year and went, for the first time ever, to a country & western artist. Bobbie Gentry was a Mississippi Delta lass who was born Roberta Lee Streeter and changed her name after seeing the Jennifer Jones film *Ruby Gentry*. She began writing music at the age of 7 (her first tune was "My Dog Sergeant Is a Good Dog") and made her first public appearance at age 11. By the time she was 23, her "Ode to Billie Joe," the year's number-four-ranked single, had nominations for Grammy's Record and Song of the Year.

The "Ode" tells the story of Billie Joe McCallister, who jumps off the Tallahatchie Bridge, a suicide noted only casually by onlookers and even Billie Joe's own family. The song took less than an hour to record, with Gentry doing her own guitar playing (violins and cellos were added later), but it earned her the best female vocal performance award and the equivalent honor in the new contemporary categories. "Ode" also won an arrangement prize.

"How the times have changed was shown by the award for Best Sacred Performance," *Variety* wrote. It was also the most curious victory of the year and, in a

> To critics, best record "Up, Up and Away" represented the height of sentimentality.

sense, the most sacrilegious. Not only had Elvis Presley never won a Grammy before, but many of his fans and N.A.R.A.S. critics believed there was a clear conspiracy to keep him at bay while he reigned as king of the rock & roll heathens. That he'd finally win one was probably inevitable, but that he'd win the prize for a religious recording was certainly ironic. "It was not so many years ago [that Presley] was a dubious moral item on TV because of his swivel hips," *Variety* pointed out. "That, however, was long before them twist and other sundry exhibitionist dances." It was also long before Presley settled down. In 1967, he married Priscilla Beaulieu; their only child, Lisa Marie, was born four weeks before Grammy night. It was now safe for the conservative N.A.R.A.S. to acknowledge the King at last, particularly if it was for his obvious and sincere religious faith. Presley would take two more of music's top awards before his death in 1977—both of those for religious discs, too. His first and last were for two versions of *How Great Thou Art*, recorded first as a studio album and later as a live performance LP.

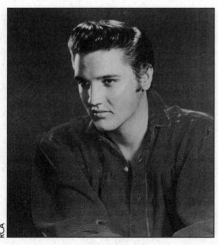

RCA

"How the times have changed was shown by the award for Best Sacred Performance," *Variety* said, noting Elvis' first of three wins for religious music.

Johnny Cash had also settled down by the time the 1967 Grammys were awarded in 1968. He and singer June Carter were to be married within a few weeks and Cash was enjoying success in his private battle against pill addiction. Cash and Carter went on to have five hit duets together, the first of which, "Jackson," earned them the 1967 c&w duet, trio or group vocal honor. Their mutual reading of it, wrote *Rolling Stone,* was "inspired."

Tammy Wynette had only been recording since 1966, but she climbed the charts quickly with such sassy tunes as "Your Good Girl's Gonna Go Bad." The former hairdresser from Tupelo, Mississippi, won her first Grammy (best female c&w vocal performance) for "I Don't Wanna Play House," an interesting choice, since Wynette once walked away from a marriage that resulted in three children.

Members of a Mississippi sharecropping family, the Blackwood Brothers, shared the trophy for Best Gospel Performance with country singer/guitarist/songwriter Porter Wagoner. *More Grand Old Gospel* marked the first of three collaborative works that would bring them three awards.

Aretha Franklin had been signed up with Columbia Records since 1961, but she was primarily given show tunes to sing and was "produced by a series of white pop producers who tried to make her a black version of Barbra Streisand," wrote rock critic Dave Marsh. "This approach was generally disastrous." In 1967, she switched to Atlantic, where producer Jerry Wexler finally gave her the professional respect she craved by letting the former church singer perform the blues and soul music she loved. Her "Respect" single (written and first recorded by Otis Redding) followed, along with Grammys for Best Rhythm & Blues Recording and best r&b vocal performance.

The r&b male vocal honors went to another gospel-trained singer, Lou

Rawls, for "Dead End Street," which became one of his most successful platters of the decade. The group performance honors were bestowed on Sam & Dave for "Soul Man," one of the two 1960s hits enjoyed by the dual champions of Memphis soul, Sam Moore and Dave Prater.

Duke Ellington and his band experienced a renaissance in the 1960s. His "Far East Suite" was inspired by a recent world tour and showed him back in high style, earning him the large-group jazz performance trophy. (The Duke would also likely have won the jazz composition prize for a second year in a row, too, but the category was dropped by N.A.R.A.S.) He also accepted an honorary award on behalf of his late arranger, Billy Strayhorn, who had been with him since 1939 and contributed to, and in many cases composed, such classics as 1941's "Take the 'A' Train."

Sax player Cannonball Adderley suffered a slump in the 1960s as his bluesy jazz style took on a more soulful sound, causing jazz diehards to turn away. When he and his quintet recorded "Mercy, Mercy, Mercy," however, they welcomed a whole host of new fans as it zoomed to number 11 in the pop singles charts and to 14th in the LP rankings. It also garnered an instrumental jazz performance Grammy.

Bill Cosby's five LPs had grossed $30 million for Warner Bros., setting a record for spoken-word discs. His latest comedy recording (and fourth-in-a-row Grammy winner) was *Revenge,* which followed his quest for retribution from a childhood bully who once hit him in the face with a slushball. (The young Cosby keeps one of his own, hidden in the freezer until after winter passes in order to ambush his nemesis come summer.) *Revenge* also introduced one of Cosby's most popular childhood pals, Fat Albert, the "two thousand pound" boy who causes the ground to quake while playing the street game buck-buck.

For the first time since the category

Wide World Photo

Aretha Franklin displays one of her two prizes for "Respect." She'd continue to rule the r&b category for a record-setting eight straight years.

was introduced in 1961, an opera recording was named (in a tie) Classical Album of the Year—and it took Best Opera Recording, too: Berg's *Wozzeck,* performed by conductor Pierre Boulez with the Paris National Opera and recorded in stereo for the first time. (Karl Böhm and the Orchestra of German Opera won Best Opera Recording two years earlier for a monaural version of *Wozzeck.*) "If Böhm's commands the last degree of one's admiration and respect," wrote *High Fidelity* of the two versions, "Boulez's may finally engender a more personal sort of attachment" because of "its romantic emotions and moods." In another first, Boulez's *Wozzeck* tied for the album prize with the recording of Mahler's Symphony No. 8 in E Flat Major ("Symphony of a Thousand") performed by Leonard Bernstein conducting the London Symphony Orchestra. And in yet another Grammy tie, Bernstein's Mahler recording took the laurels for best classical choral performance along with Carl Orff's *Catulli Carmina* (one of his stage works that Orff called "scenic cantatas") performed by the Temple University Chorus and the Philadelphia Orchestra.

Like *Wozzeck,* another Grammy victor of yore returned for more recognition in the form of the 1967 orchestra performance award: Igor Stravinsky conducting the Columbia Symphony in his *Firebird* and *Petrouchka* suites. (His earlier *Petrouchka* recording, paired with *Le Sacre du Printemps,* was 1961 Classical Album of the Year.) American soprano Leontyne Price also came back, reprising her *Prima Donna* victory of last year for best vocal soloist with one for *Prima Donna, Vol. 2,* another collection of her favorite arias. Winner of the instrumental soloist award was Vladimir Horowitz for a two-disc album of works by Haydn, Chopin, Mozart and Liszt that he had performed recently at Carnegie Hall.

When a tally of the year's winning discs was taken, Capitol "ran away with the Grammy sweepstakes," *Variety* wrote, "paced by Bobbie Gentry, the Beatles and Glen Campbell." Capitol's 14 trophies were followed by runners-up Columbia with 12 and RCA with 8. The biggest losers among performers were Vikki Carr and Ray Charles, with four failed nominations each. "Nominations

Bernstein and Boulez scored a tie for the best classical album award.

ignored among the rock groups," noted the *L.A. Times,* included "the Bee Gees, Cream, the Rolling Stones, Jimi Hendrix, Donovan and Buffalo Springfield."

In Los Angeles, 1958 Grammy-winning comic Stan Freberg served as Grammy's master of ceremonies at the Century Plaza Hotel, where Glen Campbell, Bobbie Gentry, the 5th Dimension and Ed Ames performed their nominated works.

In New York, the Grammy party relied more on comic entertainment. In a humorous sidebar article accompanying its Grammy coverage, *Variety* reported the results of the new "Allen Awards," saying, "Steve Allen, emcee of the Grammy Awards dinner at the N.Y. Hilton, took one look at the 48 categories in which the awards were to be made and thought that the list omitted some worthy causes. He suggested awards in the following categories:

"1. For the longest sideburns.

"2. For the longest delay by a diskery in paying royalties.

"3. For the longest beating caused by switching jukebox distributors."

• 1967 •

Awards were bestowed on February 29, 1968, for the eligibility period November 2, 1966, to November 1, 1967, at ceremonies held at the Century Plaza Hotel in Los Angeles, the New York Hilton Hotel, and at dinners held in Nashville and Chicago.

ALBUM OF THE YEAR

• *Sgt. Pepper's Lonely Hearts Club Band*, Beatles. Capitol.
Francis Albert Sinatra/Antonio Carlos Jobim, Frank Sinatra, Antonio Carlos Jobim. Reprise.
It Must Be Him, Vikki Carr. Liberty.

My Cup Runneth Over, Ed Ames. RCA.
Ode to Billie Joe, Bobbie Gentry. Capitol.

RECORD OF THE YEAR

• "Up, Up and Away," 5th Dimension. Soul City.
"By the Time I Get to Phoenix," Glen Campbell. Capitol.
"My Cup Runneth Over," Ed Ames. RCA.
"Ode to Billie Joe," Bobbie Gentry. Capitol.
"Somethin' Stupid," Nancy & Frank Sinatra. Reprise.

SONG OF THE YEAR
(Songwriter's Award)
- "Up, Up and Away," Jimmy Webb. Soul City.

"By the Time I Get to Phoenix," Jimmy Webb. Capitol.

"Gentle on My Mind," John Hartford. RCA.

"My Cup Runneth Over," Tom Jones, Harvey Schmidt. RCA.

"Ode to Billie Joe," Bobbie Gentry. Capitol.

BEST NEW ARTIST
- Bobbie Gentry

Lana Cantrell

5th Dimension

Harpers Bizarre

Jefferson Airplane

BEST VOCAL PERFORMANCE, MALE
- Glen Campbell, "By the Time I Get to Phoenix." Capitol.

Ed Ames, *My Cup Runneth Over*. RCA.

Ray Charles, "Yesterday." ABC.

Frank Sinatra, *Francis Albert Sinatra/Antonio Carlos Jobim*. Reprise.

Joe South, "Can't Take My Eyes off You." Philips.

BEST VOCAL PERFORMANCE, FEMALE
- Bobbie Gentry, "Ode to Billie Joe." Capitol.

Vikki Carr, "It Must Be Him." Liberty.

Petula Clark, "Don't Sleep in the Subway." Warner Bros.

Aretha Franklin, "Respect." Atlantic.

Dionne Warwick, "Alfie." Scepter.

BEST PERFORMANCE BY A VOCAL GROUP
- 5th Dimension, "Up, Up and Away." Soul City.

Association, "Never My Love." Warner Bros.

Beatles, "Sgt. Pepper's Lonely Hearts Club Band." Capitol.

Box Tops, "The Letter." Bell.

Monkees, "I'm a Believer." Colgems.

BEST PERFORMANCE BY A CHORUS
- Johnny Mann Singers, "Up, Up and Away." Liberty.

Ray Charles Singers, "Blame It on Me." Command.

Living Voices; Ethel Gabriel, conductor, "Wish Me a Rainbow." RCA.

Percy Faith Chorus & Orchestra, "Windy." Columbia.

Swingle Singers with Modern Jazz Quartet, "Encounter." Philips.

BEST CONTEMPORARY SINGLE
- "Up, Up and Away," 5th Dimension. Soul City.

"By the Time I Get to Phoenix," Glen Campbell. Capitol.

"Don't Sleep in the Subway," Petula Clark. Warner Bros.

"Ode to Billie Joe," Bobbie Gentry. Capitol.

"Yesterday," Ray Charles. ABC.

BEST CONTEMPORARY ALBUM
- *Sgt. Pepper's Lonely Hearts Club Band*, Beatles. Capitol.

Insight Out, Association. Warner Bros.

It Must Be Him, Vikki Carr. Liberty.

Ode to Billie Joe, Bobbie Gentry. Capitol.

Up, Up and Away, 5th Dimension. Soul City.

BEST CONTEMPORARY SOLO VOCAL PERFORMANCE, MALE
- Glen Campbell, "By the Time I Get to Phoenix." Capitol.

Ray Charles, "Yesterday." ABC.

Scott McKenzie, "San Francisco (Be Sure to Wear Some Flowers in Your Hair)." Columbia.

Jimmie Rodgers, "Child of Clay." A&M.

Frankie Valli, "Can't Take My Eyes off You." Philips.

BEST CONTEMPORARY SOLO VOCAL PERFORMANCE, FEMALE
- Bobbie Gentry, "Ode to Billie Joe." Capitol.

Vikki Carr, "It Must Be Him." Liberty.

Petula Clark, "Don't Sleep in the Subway." Warner Bros.
Aretha Franklin, "A Natural Woman." Atlantic.
Dionne Warwick, "I Say a Little Prayer." Scepter.

BEST CONTEMPORARY GROUP PERFORMANCE (VOCAL OR INSTRUMENTAL)

• 5th Dimension, "Up, Up and Away." Soul City.
Association, "Windy." Warner Bros.
Beatles, "Sgt. Pepper's Lonely Hearts Club Band." Capitol.
Box Tops, "The Letter." Bell.
Monkees, "I'm a Believer." Colgems.
Procol Harum, "A Whiter Shade of Pale." Deram.

BEST RHYTHM & BLUES RECORDING

• "Respect," Aretha Franklin. Atlantic.
"Dead End Street," Lou Rawls. Capitol.
"Skinny Legs and All," Joe Tex. Dial.
"Soul Man," Sam & Dave. Stax.
"Try a Little Tenderness," Otis Redding. Atco.

BEST RHYTHM & BLUES SOLO VOCAL PERFORMANCE, MALE

• Lou Rawls, "Dead End Street." Capitol.
Wilson Pickett, "Funky Broadway." Atlantic.
Otis Redding, "Try a Little Tenderness." Atco.
Joe Tex, "Skinny Legs and All." Dial.
Jackie Wilson, "Higher and Higher." Brunswick.

BEST RHYTHM & BLUES SOLO VOCAL PERFORMANCE, FEMALE

• Aretha Franklin, "Respect." Atlantic.
Etta James, "Tell Mama." Cadet.
Gladys Knight, "I Heard It Through the Grapevine." Soul.
Nina Simone, "(You'll) Go to Hell." RCA.
Carla Thomas, "The Queen Alone." Stax.

BEST RHYTHM & BLUES GROUP PERFORMANCE (VOCAL OR INSTRUMENTAL)

• Sam & Dave, "Soul Man." Stax.
Marvin Gaye, Tammi Terrell, "Ain't No Mountain High Enough." Tamla.
Smokey Robinson & the Miracles, "I Second That Emotion." Tamla.
Booker T. & the M.G.'s, "Hip Hug-Her." Stax.
Carla Thomas, Otis Redding, "The King and Queen." Stax.

BEST INSTRUMENTAL JAZZ PERFORMANCE BY A SMALL GROUP OR SOLOIST WITH SMALL GROUP (7 OR FEWER)

• Cannonball Adderley Quintet, *Mercy, Mercy, Mercy.* Capitol.
Gary Burton Quartet, *Duster.* RCA.
Miles Davis, *Miles Smiles.* Columbia.
Bill Evans, *Further Conversations with Myself.* Verve.
Stan Getz, *Sweet Rain.* Verve.
Bobby Hutcherson, *Happenings.* Blue Note.

BEST INSTRUMENTAL JAZZ PERFORMANCE BY A LARGE GROUP OR SOLOIST WITH LARGE GROUP (8 OR MORE)

• Duke Ellington, "Far East Suite." RCA.
Don Ellis Big Band, *Live at Monterey.* Pacific Jazz.
Woody Herman, *Woody Live, East and West.* Columbia.
Thad Jones, Mel Lewis, *Live at the Village Vanguard.* United Artists.
Buddy Rich, *Big Swing Face.* Pacific Jazz.

BEST SACRED PERFORMANCE

• Elvis Presley, *How Great Thou Art.* RCA.
Browns, *The Old Country Church.* RCA.
Red Foley, *Songs for the Soul.* Decca.
George Beverly Shea, Blackwood Brothers Quartet, *Surely Goodness and Mercy.* RCA.

Dottie West, *Dottie West Sings Sacred Ballads*. RCA.

BEST GOSPEL PERFORMANCE

- Porter Wagoner, Blackwood Brothers Quartet, *More Grand Old Gospel*. RCA.

Blackwood Brothers Quartet, *The Blackwood Brothers Quartet Sings for Joy*. RCA.

Happy Goodman Family, *Good 'n' Happy*. Canaan.

Oak Ridge Boys, *Oak Ridge Boys*. Heartwarming.

Singing Rambos, *Singing Rambos, Gospel Ballads*. Heartwarming.

BEST COUNTRY & WESTERN RECORDING

- "Gentle on My Mind," Glen Campbell. Capitol.

"Cold Hard Facts of Life," Porter Wagoner. RCA.

"Does My Ring Hurt Your Finger," Charley Pride. RCA.

"Pop a Top," Jim Ed Brown. RCA.

"Through the Eyes of Love," Tompall & the Glaser Brothers. MGM.

BEST COUNTRY & WESTERN SOLO VOCAL PERFORMANCE, MALE

- Glen Campbell, "Gentle on My Mind." Capitol.

Jim Ed Brown, "Pop a Top." RCA.

Jack Greene, "All the Time." Decca.

Charley Pride, "Does My Ring Hurt Your Finger." RCA.

Porter Wagoner, "Cold Hard Facts of Life." RCA.

BEST COUNTRY & WESTERN SOLO VOCAL PERFORMANCE, FEMALE

- Tammy Wynette, "I Don't Wanna Play House." Epic.

Liz Anderson, "Mama Spank." RCA.

Skeeter Davis, "What Does It Take." RCA.

Connie Smith, "Cincinnati, Ohio." RCA.

Dottie West, "Paper Mansions." RCA.

BEST COUNTRY & WESTERN PERFORMANCE BY A DUO, TRIO OR GROUP (VOCAL OR INSTRUMENTAL)

- Johnny Cash, June Carter, "Jackson." Columbia.

Liz Anderson, Bobby Bare, Norma Jean, "Game of Triangles." RCA.

Blue Boys, "My Cup Runneth Over." RCA.

Bobby Goldsboro, Del Reeves, "Our Way of Life." United Artists.

David Houston, Tammy Wynette, "My Elusive Dreams." Epic.

Lonesome Rhodes, "The Lonesome Rhodes." RCA.

Some of Chet's Friends, "Chet's Tune." RCA.

Tompall & the Glaser Brothers, "Through the Eyes of Love." MGM.

BEST COUNTRY & WESTERN SONG (Songwriter's Award)

- "Gentle on My Mind," John Hartford. RCA.

"Break My Mind," John Loudermilk. RCA.

"Cold Hard Facts of Life," Bill Anderson. RCA.

"Does My Ring Hurt Your Finger," Don Robertson, John Crutchfield, Doris Clement. RCA.

"It's Such a Pretty World Today," Dale Noe. Capitol.

BEST FOLK PERFORMANCE

- John Hartford, "Gentle on My Mind." RCA.

Judy Collins, *In My Life*. Elektra.

Arlo Guthrie, *Alice's Restaurant*. Reprise.

Janis Ian, *Janis Ian*. Verve.

Peter, Paul & Mary, *Album 1700*. Warner Bros.

Pete Seeger, "Waist Deep in the Big Muddy." Columbia.

BEST INSTRUMENTAL THEME (Composer's Award)

- "Mission: Impossible," Lalo Schifrin. Dot.

"A Banda," Chico Buarque De Hollanda. A&M.

"Casino Royale," Burt Bacharach, Hal David. A&M.

"Hurry Sundown," Hugo Montenegro. MGM.

"Mercy, Mercy, Mercy," Joe Zawinul. Capitol.

BEST INSTRUMENTAL ARRANGEMENT

• Burt Bacharach, *Alfie* (Burt Bacharach Orchestra). A&M.

Burt Bacharach, *Casino Royale* (Herb Alpert & the Tijuana Brass). A&M.

Hutch Davie, *Music to Watch Girls By* (Bob Crewe Generation). Philips.

Bill Holman, *Norwegian Wood* (Buddy Rich Orchestra). Pacific Jazz.

Claus Ogerman, *Wave* (Antonio Carlos Jobim). A&M.

Bill Reddie, *West Side Medley* (Buddy Rich Orchestra). Pacific Jazz.

BEST INSTRUMENTAL PERFORMANCE

• Chet Atkins, *Chet Atkins Picks the Best*. RCA.

Herb Alpert & the Tijuana Brass, "Casino Royale." A&M.

Cannonball Adderley Quintet, *Mercy, Mercy, Mercy*. Capitol.

Bob Crewe Generation, *Music to Watch Girls By*. Philips.

Lalo Schifrin, "Mission: Impossible." Dot.

BEST SCORE FROM AN ORIGINAL CAST SHOW ALBUM

(Composer's Award)

• *Cabaret*, Fred Ebb, John Kander. Columbia.

Hallelujah, Baby, Jule Styne, Betty Comden, Adolph Green. Columbia.

I Do! I Do! Harvey Schmidt, Tom Jones. RCA.

Walking Happy, Sammy Cahn, Jimmy Van Heusen. Capitol.

You're a Good Man, Charlie Brown, Clark Gesner. MGM.

BEST ORIGINAL SCORE WRITTEN FOR A MOTION PICTURE OR TV SHOW

• *Mission: Impossible* (Lalo Schifrin Orchestra), Lalo Schifrin. Dot.

Casino Royale (various artists; Burt Bacharach, conductor), Burt Bacharach. RCA.

Doctor Doolittle (Rex Harrison and motion picture cast; Lionel Newman, conductor), Leslie Bricusse. 20th.

In the Heat of the Night (Quincy Jones, conductor), Quincy Jones. United Artists.

To Sir with Love (soundtrack with Lulu & the Mindbenders), Ron Grainer, Don Black, Mark London. Fontana.

BEST ARRANGEMENT ACCOMPANYING VOCALIST(S) OR INSTRUMENTALIST(S)

• Jimmie Haskell, "Ode to Billie Joe" (Bobbie Gentry). Capitol.

Beatles, George Martin, "A Day in the Life" (Beatles). Capitol.

Tony Hatch, "Don't Sleep in the Subway" (Petula Clark). Warner Bros./Seven Artists.

Bill Holman, Bones Howe, Ray Pohlman, Windy (The Association). Warner Bros./Seven Artists.

Al de Lory, "By the Time I Get to Phoenix" (Glen Campbell). Capitol.

ALBUM OF THE YEAR, CLASSICAL

(Tie)

• *Berg: Wozzeck*, Pierre Boulez conducting the orchestra and chorus of the Paris National Opera (solos: Berry, Strauss, Uhl, Doench). Columbia.

• *Mahler: Symphony No. 8 in E Flat Major ("Symphony of a Thousand")*, Leonard Bernstein conducting the London Symphony with soloists and choruses. Columbia.

Horowitz in Concert, Vladimir Horowitz. Columbia.

Mahler: Das Lied von der Erde, Leonard Bernstein conducting the Vienna Philharmonic (solos: King, Fischer-Dieskau). London.

Puccini: La Rondine, Francesco Molinari-Pradelli conducting the RCA Italiana Opera Orchestra and Chorus (solos: Moffo, Barioni, Sereni, Sciutti, De Palma). RCA.

The World of Charles Ives, "Robert Browning Overture," Leopold Stokowski conducting the American Symphony; "Washington's Birthday," Leonard Bernstein conducting the New York Philharmonic. Columbia.

BEST CLASSICAL PERFORMANCE, ORCHESTRA
(Conductor's Award)

• Igor Stravinsky conducting the Columbia Symphony, *Stravinsky: Firebird and Pétrouchka Suites*. Columbia.

Leonard Bernstein conducting the Vienna Philharmonic (solos: King, Fischer-Dieskau), *Mahler: Das Lied von der Erde*. London.

Sir Adrian Boult conducting the New Philharmonia Orchestra, *Holst: The Planets*. Angel.

Morton Gould conducting the Chicago Symphony, *Ives: Orchestral Set No. 2; Robert Browning Overture; Putnam's Camp*. RCA.

Herbert von Karajan conducting the Berlin Philharmonic, *Shostakovich: Symphony No. 10 in E Minor*. Deutsche Grammophon.

Georg Solti conducting the London Symphony, *Mahler: Symphony No. 2 in C Minor ("Resurrection")*. London.

BEST CHAMBER MUSIC PERFORMANCE

• Ravi Shankar, Yehudi Menuhin, *West Meets East*. Angel.

Eugene Istomin, Isaac Stern, Leonard Rose, *Brahms: Trios for Piano, Violin and Cello (Nos. 1–3)*. Columbia.

Juilliard Quartet, *Ives: Quartets Nos. 1 and 3*. Columbia.

Philadelphia Brass Ensemble, *The Glorious Sound of Brass*. Columbia.

Artur Rubinstein, Guarneri Quartet, *Brahms: Quintet in F Minor for Piano, Op. 34*. RCA.

Yale Quartet, *Beethoven: Quartet No. 15 in A Minor, Op. 132*. Vanguard.

BEST CLASSICAL PERFORMANCE, INSTRUMENTAL SOLOIST(S) (WITH OR WITHOUT ORCHESTRA)

• Vladimir Horowitz, *Horowitz in Concert*. Columbia.

Julian Bream, *20th Century Guitar* (works by Brindle, Britten, Villa-Lobos, Martin, Henze). RCA.

Alicia de Larrocha, *Granados: Goyescas Completo/Escénas Románticas*. Epic.

William Masselos, *Ives: Sonata No. 1 for Piano*. RCA.

Artur Rubinstein, *Chopin: Nocturnes*. RCA.

Andrés Segovia, *Segovia on Stage*. Decca.

BEST OPERA RECORDING

• *Berg: Wozzeck*, Pierre Boulez conducting the Orchestra and Chorus of the Paris National Opera (solos: Berry, Strauss, Uhl, Doench). Columbia.

Handel: Julius Caesar, Julius Rudel conducting the New York City Opera Chorus and Orchestra (solos: Treigle, Sills, Forrester, Wolff). RCA.

Puccini: La Rondine, Francesco Molinari-Pradelli conducting the RCA Italiana Opera Orchestra and Chorus (solos: Moffo, Barioni, Sereni, Sciutti, De Palma). RCA.

Puccini: Madama Butterfly, Sir John Barbirolli conducting the Rome Opera Orchestra and Chorus (solos: Scotto, Bergonzi). Angel.

Verdi: Falstaff, Leonard Bernstein conducting the Vienna Philharmonic Orchestra and Chorus (solos: Fischer-Dieskau, Ligabue, Sciutti, Resnik). Columbia.

Wagner: Die Walküre, Herbert von Karajan conducting the Berlin Philharmonic (solos: Crespin, Janowitz,

Veasey, Vickers, Stewart, Talvela).
Deutsche Grammophon.
Wagner: Tristan und Isolde "Live," Karl
Böhm conducting the Bayreuth Festi-
val Chorus and Orchestra (solos:
Nilsson, Windgassen, Ludwig,
Talvela, Wachter). Deutsche Gram-
mophon.

BEST CLASSICAL PERFORMANCE, CHORAL (OTHER THAN OPERA)
(Tie)
• Leonard Bernstein conducting the
  London Symphony Chorus and
  Orchestra with soloists and choruses,
  *Mahler: Symphony No. 8 in E Flat
  Major ("Symphony of a Thousand")*.
  Columbia.
• Robert Page conducting the Temple
  University Chorus; Eugene Ormandy
  conducting the Philadelphia Orches-
  tra, *Orff: Catulli Carmina*. Colum-
  bia.
Karl Böhm conducting the Vienna
  Singverein and Vienna Symphony,
  Haydn: The Seasons. Deutsche
  Grammophon.
Aaron Copland conducting the New
  England Conservatory Chorus, *Cop-
  land: In the Beginning; Lark; Las
  Agachadas*. CBS.
John McCarthy conducting the
  Ambrosian Singers; Charles Mack-
  erras conducting the English Cham-
  ber Orchestra, *Handel: Messiah*.
  Angel.
Janusz Przybylski and Jozef Suwara
  conducting the Boys' Chorus of Cra-
  cow; Henryk Czyz conducting the
  Cracow Philharmonic, *Penderecki:
  Passion According to St. Luke*.
  Philips.
Gregg Smith Singers, *The Choral Music
  of Arnold Schoenberg*. Everest.

BEST CLASSICAL PERFORMANCE VOCAL SOLOIST
• Leontyne Price (Molinari-Pradelli
  conducting the RCA ltaliana Opera
  Orchestra), *Prima Donna, Vol. 2*.
  RCA.

Adele Addison (Aaron Copland,
  pianist), *Copland: 12 Poems of Emily
  Dickinson*. CBS.
Victoria de los Angeles (Gonzalo Sori-
  ano, pianist), *Victoria de los Angeles
  Sings Debussy and Ravel and other
  French Songs*. Angel.
Dietrich Fischer-Dieskau (Jorg Demus,
  pianist), *Beethoven: Songs*. Deutsche
  Grammophon.
Christa Ludwig (with instrumental
  ensemble), *"Shepherd on the Rock"
  and Other Songs*. Angel.
Peter Pears (Benjamin Britten, pianist),
  Schubert: Die Winterreise. London.
Elisabeth Schwarzkopf (Gerald Moore,
  pianist), *An Elisabeth Schwarzkopf
  Songbook*. Angel.
Fritz Wunderlich (Hubert Giesen,
  pianist), *Schubert: Die Schöne Mül-
  lerin*. Deutsche Grammophon.

BEST ENGINEERED RECORDING, CLASSICAL
• Edward T. Graham, *The Glorious
  Sound of Brass* (Philadelphia Brass
  Ensemble). Columbia.
Edwin Begley, *Mahler: Symphony No. 3
  in D Minor* (Leinsdorf conducting the
  Boston Symphony). RCA Red Seal.
Edward T. Graham, *Rachmaninov: Sym-
  phony No. 1 in D* (Ormandy conduct-
  ing the Philadelphia Orchestra).
  Columbia.
Gunter Hermanns, *Wagner: Tristan und
  Isolde "Live"* (Böhm conducting the
  Bayreuth Festival Orchestra; solos:
  Nilsson, Windgassen). Deutsche
  Grammophon.
Hellmuth Kolbe, *Mahler: Symphony No.
  8 in E Flat* (Bernstein conducting the
  London Symphony). Columbia.
Gordon Parry, *Mahler: Symphony No. 2
  in C Minor ("Resurrection")* (Solti
  conducting the London Symphony
  Chorus and Orchestra; solos: Harper,
  Watts). London.
Gordon Parry, *Mahler: Das Lied von
  der Erde* (Bernstein conducting the
  Vienna Philharmonic and soloists).
  London.

BEST SPOKEN WORD, DOCUMENTARY OR DRAMA RECORDING

• *Gallant Men*, Sen. Everett M. Dirksen. Capitol.
The Balcony, Patrick Magee, Cyril Cusack. Caedmon.
The Earth, Rod McKuen. Warner Bros.
A Man for All Seasons, Paul Scofield, Wendy Hiller, Robert Shaw. RCA.
Mark Twain Tonight, Vol. 3, Hal Holbrook. Columbia.
An Open Letter to My Teenage Son, Victor Lundberg. Liberty.
Poems of James Dickey, James Dickey. Spoken Arts.

BEST COMEDY RECORDING

• *Revenge*, Bill Cosby. Warner Bros.
The Cockfight and Other Tall Tales, Archie Campbell. RCA.
Cowboys and Colored People, Flip Wilson. Atlantic.
Lenny Bruce in Concert, Lenny Bruce. United Artists.
Take-Offs and Put-Ons, George Carlin. RCA.

BEST RECORDING FOR CHILDREN

• *Dr. Seuss: How the Grinch Stole Christmas* (TV soundtrack), Boris Karloff. MGM.
The Carnival of the Animals, verses by Ogden Nash, narrated by Tutti Camarata (Symphonie-Orchester Graunke). Buena Vista.
A Happy Birthday Party with Winnie-the-Pooh, Sterling Holloway. Disney.
The Jungle Book, motion picture cast. Disney.
Jungle Books, Richard Kiley. MGM.
Magic Fishbone/Happy Prince/Potted Princess, Julie Harris, Richard Kiley. MGM.

BEST ENGINEERED RECORDING

• G. E. Emerick, *Sgt. Pepper's Lonely Hearts Club Band* (Beatles). Capitol.
Hank Cicalo, *Mission: Impossible* (Lalo Schifrin). Dot.

James Malloy, *How Great Thou Art* (Elvis Presley). RCA.
Joe Polito, *Ode to Billie Joe* (Bobbie Gentry). Capitol.
William Vandevort, *Chet's Tune* (Some of Chet's Friends). RCA.

BEST ALBUM COVER, PHOTOGRAPHY

• John Berg, Bob Cato, Roland Scherman, *Dylan's Greatest Hits* (Bob Dylan). Columbia.
Bill Harvey, Guy Webster, Joel Brodsky, *The Doors* (Doors). Elektra.
Bob Jones, Jimmy Moore, *Suburban Attitudes in Country Verse* (John Loudermilk). RCA.
Robert Jones, New World Photography, *Earthwords and Music* (John Harford). RCA.
Robert Jones, Howard Cooper, *From Mexico with Laughs* (Don Bowman). RCA.
Ken Kim, *Bravo, Bravo, Aznavour* (Charles Aznavour). Monument.
Ken Kim, *That Man, Robert Mitchum, Sings*. Monument.

BEST ALBUM COVER, GRAPHIC ARTS

• Peter Blake, Jann Haworth, *Sgt. Pepper's Lonely Hearts Club Band* (Beatles). Capitol.
John Berg, Bob Cato, Henrietta Condak, *Haydn: Symphony No. 84 in E Flat Major; Symphony No. 85 in B Flat Major ("La Reine")* (Bernstein conducting the New York Philharmonic). Columbia.
John Berg, Bob Cato, Lasio Kubinyi, *Monk: Straight, No Chaser* (Thelonious Monk). Columbia.
Robert Jones, Jack Davis, *Nashville Cats* (Homer & Jethro). RCA.
Ed Thrasher, Charles White, *The Gold Standard Collection* (Hank Thompson). Warner Bros./Seven Artists.
Woody Woodward, Wayne Kimball, *Up, Up and Away* (5th Dimension). Soul City.

BEST ALBUM NOTES
(Annotator's Award)
• John D. Loudermilk, *Suburban Attitudes in Country Verse* (John Loudermilk). RCA.

Stan Cornyn, *Francis Albert Sinatra/Antonio Carlos Jobim.* Reprise.

Stanley Dance, *Far East Suite* (Duke Ellington). RCA.

Rory Guy, *Extra Special* (Peggy Lee). Capitol.

Rod McKuen, *The Earth* (Rod McKuen, music by Anita Kerr). Warner Bros.

Richard Oliver, *Listen!* (Gary Lewis & the Playboys). Liberty.

• 1968 •
A Smooth Triumph for the New Generation

"The recording industry," wrote *Variety,* "has virtually shucked off its past. It's doing its own thing with a roster of youths who have overthrown the elders in the field. . . . The Grammy Awards gave an indication of how far the rebellion of the young has gone. There was rarely a prize in the pop field to anyone over 30."

The spirited new generation of artists may at long last have won their battle against Sinatra & Co., but they found themselves locked in a different struggle that saw their numbers divided into two camps: smooth pop and cutting-edge rock.

The new showdown was over Record of the Year, pitting the Beatles' "Hey Jude" against Simon & Garfunkel's "Mrs. Robinson." "Jude" had the advantage of being the best-selling single of the year, but "Mrs. Robinson" better represented the middle-of-the-road sound N.A.R.A.S. voters hailed in the past. Also to the folk/pop duo's credit was that they were fairly new on the scene, having had only one top single, "The Sounds of Silence," in addition to smaller successes like "Homeward Bound." The Beatles, on the other hand, warned *Variety,* "may be old hat." Still, the Fab Four had proved their popularity with Grammy voters last year when they took Album of the Year honors for *Sgt. Pepper's Lonely Hearts Club Band.*

The suspense dragged on even beyond Grammy night. N.A.R.A.S. executives decided to delay naming the Record of the Year winner so it could be revealed during the modestly rated, after-the-fact "Best on Record" telecast that was once reserved exclusively for performances by the winners. (For more than a decade, TV network executives refused to air the awards ceremony because they

The flamenco-flavored music of Best New Artist José Feliciano made him a young lovers' favorite.

didn't think the top nominated talent would show up.) The Beatles showed up for "Best on Record," but performed mechanically. Simon & Garfunkel chose to perform "Mrs. Robinson" on tape and submitted an energetic precursor of the modern music video that showed them romping around Yankee Stadium as the song's lyrics asked "Where have you gone, Joe DiMaggio?" in voiceover.

Simon & Garfunkel had the most nominations of the year (five), compared to four each for the Beatles and Glen Campbell. The duo ended up with three awards, including Record of the Year and the group vocals prize for best contemporary pop performance for "Mrs. Robinson," which was written by Paul Simon for the Mike Nichols film *The Graduate.* "Pop" was added to the title of the contemporary categories after N.A.R.A.S. again made drastic changes in the awards lineup, even slashing the total number back from 48 to 40 in a streamlining effort. Gone were last year's laurels for Best Contemporary Single and Album as well as Classical Album of the Year and the general vocal performance honors, among others.

The duo's third Grammy was for *The Graduate*'s film score, which included some of their other pop hits such as "Scarborough Fair." They lost their Album of the Year bid for their latest LP, *Bookends*.

The Beatles also had an entry in the album race, *Magical Mystery Tour*, but the Fab Four lost all of their four Grammy bids this year.

The victorious choice for best album confused many Grammy watchers—Glen Campbell's *By the Time I Get to Phoenix*, the title song of which won two awards for the c&w troubador last year. The reason for the delayed album honor was that the LP was released after the "Phoenix" single and landed in the Grammy's next eligibility period. Campbell's latest victory only underscored his enormous popularity at the time of the 1968 awards ceremony on March 12, 1969. The former regular on TV's *The Smothers Brothers Comedy Hour* had his own hit variety series and new best-selling records like "Wichita Lineman" (Best Engineered Recording) and "Galveston" (ranked number 12 on *Variety*'s chart on Grammy day).

Safe, smooth pop continued its winning streak when the recipient of Song of the Year was named—"Little Green Apples," written by Bobby Russell, who was also nominated in the same category for Bobby Goldsboro's "Honey" (a contender for Record of the Year). "Apples" was popularized by pop/soul singer O. C. Smith, although it had also been recorded earlier by Roger Miller and Patti Page. The tune's past association with Nashville brought it the prize for Best Country Song, too. (Older songs were

> ### Simon & Garfunkel made best record "Mrs. Robinson" into one of the first music videos.

permitted to compete as long as they'd never before been nominated.) As part of the larger awards revamping, "& Western" was dropped from the country prize titles this year. Some critics speculated that the real reason for the change was western star Glen Campbell's victories over Nashville country artists last year.

The smoothest music of 1968 was recorded by Best New Artist José Feliciano, whose *Feliciano!* was then the favorite "makeout" album among teen lovers. It was also considered a strong contender for Album of the Year. Born blind, Feliciano was raised in New York's Spanish Harlem and championed an impassioned form of flamenco-flavored singing that made him popular in Greenwich Village coffee houses where he was discovered by an RCA record executive. (He performed there with his 12-string guitar "not for coins, just for the hell of it," he once said.) By 1968, he was renowned throughout the Spanish-speaking world, but he didn't reach the American pop music market till he covered a recent hit by the Doors. For his own interpretation of "Light My Fire," he combined influences of Latin, soul, folk and rock music, earning him the male vocal Grammy for contemporary pop.

The female vocalist prize went to Dionne Warwick, the signature singer of the melodic tunes of Burt Bacharach and Hal David. Their latest collaboration was "Do You Know the Way to San Jose," which followed earlier hits including "I Say a Little Prayer" and "Walk On By."

Mason Williams's "Classical Gas" won three Grammy Awards, thereby tying Simon & Garfunkel for the evening's most wins: best contemporary pop instrumental performance, Best Instrumental Theme and Best Instrumental Arrangement. But "Classical Gas" was more than classical in nature. It also combined elements of rock, bluegrass and Latin music to achieve a sound Williams once described as "half flamenco, half Flatt & Scruggs and half classical."

Motown and its affiliated Gordy and Tamla labels made a formidable impact on the pop scene of the 1960s with such talent as the Supremes, "Little Stevie Wonder," the Four Tops and Gladys Knight & the Pips, but the only Grammy the company won in the entire decade went to the Temptations for "Cloud Nine," winner of the rhythm & blues group vocal award. The song marked a key turning point for one of the most successful male singing groups of the decade. Shortly before recording "Cloud Nine," the Temptations decided to shake off the old pop style of their earlier hits like "My Girl" and "You're My Everything" to pursue the same "funk" terrain being explored by Sly & the Family Stone. The result was a cerebral soul recording with a daring, two-level narrative that left listeners wondering if the tune was about drug addiction or a dream.

At the heart of the 1960s drug culture was the new hippie movement, which was portrayed with fanciful idealism in *Hair,* which had recently lost the Tony Award for best Broadway musical to *1776.* Its consolation prize was a Grammy for best cast show album. *Hair* spent 59 weeks in the LP charts, 13 of them at number one, and spawned a number of single hits, one of which would win the top Grammy next year.

Dual award winner of last year Aretha Franklin was at her professional peak in 1968, having scored Nine Top 10 singles over the previous two years, and now returned to reclaim the r&b vocal laurels for "Chain of Fools." The recording was from her *Lady Soul* album, which was such a popular and critical hit that its success landed her on the cover of *Time* magazine.

The writer of the single that earned Franklin her first two Grammys, "Respect," was awarded the male vocal

Motown's only Grammy during the 1960s was an r&b prize for the Temptations' "Cloud Nine."

r&b honors for "(Sittin' on) The Dock of the Bay," the number-six song of the year. By the late 1960s, Otis Redding commanded considerable respect as a singer and songwriter and was famous in France and England for his grainy, gutsy style. In 1967, he finally came to the attention of the mainstream American music world when he wowed a dozing audience at the Monterey Pop Festival, the first major rock fete ever held. With Steve Cropper, Redding wrote "Dock of the Bay" in gratitude for the response he received in California, but three days after he taped it in a Memphis recording studio, he died at the age of 26 when his private twin-engine plane crashed into a frozen lake near Madison, Wisconsin, killing four members of his backup group, in addition to Redding, his valet and the pilot. The tune spent 16 weeks on the charts, including four weeks at number one. It was the first time that an artist ever held that rank posthumously.

It was aboard a plane that Johnny Cash wrote his hit 1955 single "Folsom Prison Blues." Cash had been killing time while waiting for a flight out of Memphis one day when he ducked into a movie theater and saw a stirring documentary about the jailhouse. Soon after he recorded his bluesy salute, the tune took off to number four on the country charts and Cash went to the prison to perform it for its inmates. The response was such a success that he returned in 1968 to make an album recording.

"By doing a prison concert, we were letting inmates know that somewhere in the free world was somebody who cared for them as human beings," Cash wrote in his autobiography, *Man in Black*. *Johnny Cash at Folsom Prison* became the number-one country album for 10 weeks and earned him the best male country vocal performance Grammy. *Folsom* also won Best Album Notes.

The trophy for best female country vocal performance went to Jeannie C. Riley, a former Nashville secretary and demo singer who was unknown to music buyers prior to the success of "Harper Valley P.T.A." The song by journeyman deejay Tom T. Hall was nominated for Record and Song of the Year and was based on an actual showdown he once witnessed between a southern widow and the P.T.A. board in her small town over her short skirts and independent ways. The recording premiered at number 81 in the pop rankings, then zoomed up to number 7 a week later—the largest leap in the history of the charts. After it settled in at number one, Riley was suddenly a star, if a short-lived one. The losing nominee for Grammy's Best New Artist said, "I soon found out people thought that's what I was really like," referring to the saucy heroine of her song. "I was just tryin' to tell a story." After failing to get into the Top 40 again, Riley eventually quit the pop field in favor of the gospel circuit. "Harper Valley P.T.A.," however, continued to survive in pop culture—as a 1980 TV film starring Barbara Eden and a brief weekly TV series the following year.

A hit feature movie that incorporated existing music into its score helped to bring singer Lester Flatt and banjo player Earl Scruggs into the popular mainstream. Flatt & Scruggs had been a favorite of country audiences since the 1940s when they first recorded "Foggy Mountain Breakdown," but when it was revived for the Warren Beatty/Faye Dunaway movie *Bonnie and Clyde,* it introduced the song to a whole new generation of music lovers and brought the duo the prize for best country group performance.

Miles Davis once said of Bill Evans (1963 Grammy winner for *Conversations with Myself*), "He plays the piano the way it should be played." Evans and his trio took a romantic approach to jazz, emphasizing strong harmonies interrupted by innovative improvisations. The first recording of their many performances at the Montreux Jazz Festival in Switzerland became a quick success and earned them the Grammy for small-group instrumental performance.

"Classical Gas" was "half flamenco, half Flatt & Scruggs and half classical."

Duke Ellington acknowledged a special Grammy tribute last year to his late arranger-composer Billy Strayhorn. This year he accepted a large-group jazz performance award for *And His Mother Called Him Bill,* Ellington's salute to the memory of the man with whom he had worked since 1939 and wrote such memorable music as *Perfume Suite*. The Duke's latest LP included Strayhorn's final composition, "Blood Count."

In the comedy category, Bill Cosby won the laugh laurels for a fifth year in a row for *To Russell, My Brother, Whom I Slept With,* in which Cosby taunts his sibling bed partner, saying, "I don't want you touchin' my body because you're not really my brother anyway. You were brought here by the police. They said, 'Take care of this boy until he starts lying.' And I'm gonna tell the police that you have *lied* and you'll go back to jail!" After the squabble intensifies in the recording, the boys break the bed and tell their angry father, "Some man came in here, started jumpin' on the bed, Dad. . . . We told him, 'You better cut it out!' and he broke it and ran out the window laughin'."

While there was no Classical Album of the Year award this year, there were still several standout LPs, including conductor Pierre Boulez's first recording with the Cleveland Orchestra, which nabbed the orchestral performance award. "This is the most lucid and illuminating performance of [Debussy's] *Images* that I know," wrote a reviewer in *High Fidelity*, "and the *Danses* are equally accomplished." The chamber music performance prize went to conductor Vittorio Negri and others behind a two-set recording of works by two innovative Italian composers. *High Fidelity* wrote: "The music recorded on both discs brilliantly recaptures the excitement that must have been in the air when the two galleries of the basilica of St. Mark's resounded to the bold new creations of Andrea Gabrieli and his even more illustrious nephew Giovanni."

Vladimir Horowitz garnered his eighth career Grammy for a recording of a TV special during which he performed works by Chopin, Schumann and Scriabin.

The award for Best Opera Recording went for a performance of a work Stendhal once called "the union of an exquisite ear with an impassioned heart"— Mozart's *Così Fan Tutte*. "It is the first truly comprehensive recording," *High Fidelity* noted, offering special praise to its American cast of vocalists that included Leontyne Price. Together they demonstrated, it said, "how far American singers have come in our time." This was the first occasion in six years, however, that Price would not win a Grammy. Instead, the vocalist award went to Spanish soprano Montserrat Caballé for her renditions of arias by Rossini.

While "smooth" music reigned at the Grammy Awards this year, the ceremonies in New York, Los Angles, Nashville and Chicago were also

"There was rarely a prize in the pop field for anyone over 30," *Variety* observed.

"smoothly functioning affairs," wrote *Variety*, adding, "The prize winners were just as frequently in Nashville or the Coast as New York, and various indications point to an even more complete departure in the future." The new L.A. venue was the Century Plaza Hotel, which accommodated 1,500 people, the largest in the event's 11-year history, *Variety* reported.

Variety caught a number of the old guard artists slipping out of the Grammy ceremony early once it became obvious that most of the awards were going to younger artists. Among them was 1961 and 1963 Song of the Year honoree Johnny Mercer, who told the publication, "I take my hat off to some of this music being written today, especially by Jimmy Webb. I'm hopeful, too, that they'll depart more and more from that deafening, metallic sound and get back to the sweeter things."

The fact that N.A.R.A.S. delayed the announcement of the winner of Grammy's most esteemed trophy—Record of the Year—till the "Best on Record" broadcast outraged many, particularly the crowd out in L.A.

"Dumb? You bet it is," commented the *Los Angeles Times*. "The audience booed" the announcement of the delay, the paper reported, adding, "Fortunately, nobody threw anything. This was probably because the waiters had wisely cleared the tables." The *L.A. Times* reporter, Wayne Warga, also noted that a number of the banquet attendees knew who the recipients were going to be before the voting results were announced. "In my pocket—and quite a few others judging from the men's room chatter," Warga wrote, "was the list of winners, handed me before the show began."

The cast of the Emmy-winning TV comedy series *Laugh-In* provided lots of entertainment. Ruth Buzzi asked, "If Yoko Ono and John Lennon have a baby, will it be a Japanese Beatle?"

The "Best on Record" TV program was put together by *Laugh-In* producer George Schlatter, but reviews were no laughing matter. According to *Variety*, it was a "weakly produced and unimaginative anticlimax to the in-person Grammy Awards earlier this year." While performers Dionne Warwick and the Los Angeles company of *Hair* "were able to project artistry," the Beatles were dismissed as "wooden," the Temptations were "lacking [their] normal spontaneity" and the creativity demonstrated by all the performers "wasn't mixed with the smallest degree of musical astuteness." The omission of jazz and classical artists caused outcries from those music fans.

• 1968 •

Awards were bestowed on March 12, 1969, for the eligibility period of November 2, 1967, to November 1, 1968, at the Century Plaza Hotel in Los Angeles, the Americana Hotel in New York, the Drake Hotel in Chicago and a dinner site in Nashville.

ALBUM OF THE YEAR
• *By the Time I Get to Phoenix*, Glen Campbell. Capitol.
Bookends, Simon & Garfunkel. Columbia.
Feliciano! José Feliciano. RCA.
Magical Mystery Tour, Beatles. Capitol.
A Tramp Shining, Richard Harris. Dunhill.

RECORD OF THE YEAR
• "Mrs. Robinson," Simon & Garfunkel. Columbia.
"Harper Valley P.T.A.," Jeannie C. Riley. Plantation.
"Hey Jude," Beatles. Capitol.
"Honey," Bobby Goldsboro. United Artists.
"Wichita Lineman," Glen Campbell. Capitol.

SONG OF THE YEAR
(Songwriter's Award)
• "Little Green Apples," Bobby Russell.

"Harper Valley P.T.A.," Tom T. Hall.
"Honey," Bobby Russell.
"Hey Jude," John Lennon, Paul McCartney.
"Mrs. Robinson," Paul Simon.

BEST NEW ARTIST
• José Feliciano
Cream
Gary Puckett & the Union Gap
Jeannie C. Riley
O. C. Smith

BEST CONTEMPORARY POP VOCAL PERFORMANCE, MALE
• José Feliciano, "Light My Fire." RCA.
Glen Campbell, "Wichita Lineman." Capitol.
Bobby Goldsboro, "Honey." United Artists.
Richard Harris, "MacArthur Park." Dunhill.
O. C. Smith, "Little Green Apples." Columbia.

BEST CONTEMPORARY POP VOCAL PERFORMANCE, FEMALE
• Dionne Warwick, "Do You Know the Way to San Jose." Scepter.
Aretha Franklin, "I Say a Little Prayer." Atlantic.

Mary Hopkins, "Those Were the Days." Capitol.

Merrilee Rush, "Angel of the Morning." Bell.

Barbra Streisand, *Funny Girl*. Columbia.

BEST CONTEMPORARY POP VOCAL PERFORMANCE BY A DUO OR GROUP

• Simon & Garfunkel, "Mrs. Robinson." Columbia.

Beatles, "Hey Jude." Capitol.

Blood, Sweat & Tears, "Child Is Father to the Man." Columbia.

Lettermen, "Goin' out of My Head/Can't Take My Eyes off You." Capitol.

Sergio Mendes & Brasil '66, "Fool on the Hill." A&M.

Gary Puckett & the Union Gap, *Woman, Woman*. Columbia.

BEST CONTEMPORARY POP PERFORMANCE BY A CHORUS

• Alan Copeland Singers, "Mission Impossible/Norwegian Wood." ABC.

Ray Charles Singers, "MacArthur Park." Command.

Ray Conniff Singers, "Honey." Columbia.

Percy Faith Chorus & Orchestra, "Angel of the Morning." Columbia.

Johnny Mann Singers, "This Guy's in Love with You." Liberty.

BEST CONTEMPORARY POP PERFORMANCE, INSTRUMENTAL

• Mason Williams, "Classical Gas." Warner Brothers.

José Feliciano, "Here, There and Everywhere." RCA.

Hugh Masekela, "Grazing in the Grass." Uni.

Hugo Montenegro, "The Good, the Bad and the Ugly." RCA.

Wes Montgomery, "Eleanor Rigby." A&M.

BEST RHYTHM & BLUES VOCAL PERFORMANCE, MALE

• Otis Redding, "(Sittin' on) The Dock of the Bay." Volt.

Marvin Gaye, "I Heard It Through the Grapevine." Tamla/Motown.

Joe Simon, "(You Keep Me) Hangin' On." Sound Stage 7.

Johnnie Taylor, "Who's Making Love." Stax.

Stevie Wonder, "For Once in My Life." Tamla/Motown.

BEST RHYTHM & BLUES VOCAL PERFORMANCE, FEMALE

• Aretha Franklin, "Chain of Fools." Atlantic.

Barbara Acklin, "Love Makes a Woman." Brunswick.

Erma Franklin, "Piece of My Heart." Shout.

Etta James, "Security." Cadet.

Ella Washington, "He Called Me Baby." Sound Stage 7.

BEST RHYTHM & BLUES PERFORMANCE BY A DUO OR GROUP (VOCAL OR INSTRUMENTAL)

• Temptations, "Cloud Nine." Gordy.

Archie Bell & the Drells, "Tighten Up." Atlantic.

Sam & Dave, "I Thank You," Stax.

Peggy Scott, Jo Jo Benson, "Pickin' Wild Mountain Berries." Plantation.

Sweet Inspiration, "Sweet Inspiration." Atlantic.

BEST RHYTHM & BLUES SONG
(Songwriter's Award)

• "(Sittin' on) The Dock of the Bay," Otis Redding, Steve Cropper. Volt.

"Chain of Fools," Don Lovay. Atlantic.

"I Wish It Would Rain," Norman Whitfield, Barrett Strong, Roger Penzabene. Gordy/Motown.

"Pickin' Wild Mountain Berries," Edward Thomas, Bob McRee, Clifton Thomas. Plantation.

"Who's Making Love," Homer Banks, Bettye Crutcher, Raymond Jackson, Donald Davis. Stax.

BEST INSTRUMENTAL JAZZ PERFORMANCE BY A SMALL GROUP OR SOLOIST WITH SMALL GROUP

- Bill Evans Trio, *Bill Evans at the Montreux Jazz Festival*. Verve.

Dave Brubeck, Gerry Mulligan, *Compadres*. Columbia.

Gary Burton, *Gary Burton Quartet in Concert*. RCA.

Miles Davis, Herbie Hancock, *Miles in the Sky*. Columbia.

Eddie Harris, *The Electrifying . . . Eddie Harris*. Atlantic.

Jazz for a Sunday Afternoon, Vol. 1, various artists. Solid State.

BEST INSTRUMENTAL JAZZ PERFORMANCE BY A LARGE GROUP OR SOLOIST WITH LARGE GROUP

- Duke Ellington, *And His Mother Called Him Bill*. RCA.

Don Ellis, *Electric Bath*. Columbia.

Erroll Garner, "Up in Erroll's Room." Verve.

Woody Herman, *Concerto for Herd*. Verve.

Wes Montgomery, *Down Here on the Ground*. A&M.

Buddy Rich, "Mercy, Mercy." World Pacific.

BEST COUNTRY SOLO VOCAL PERFORMANCE, MALE

- Johnny Cash, "Folsom Prison Blues." Columbia.

Glen Campbell, "I Wanna Live." Capitol.

Henson Cargill, "Skip a Rope." Monument.

Roger Miller, "Little Green Apples." Smash.

Porter Wagoner, "The Carroll County Accident." RCA.

BEST COUNTRY SOLO VOCAL PERFORMANCE, FEMALE

- Jeannie C. Riley, "Harper Valley P.T.A." Plantation.

Lynn Anderson, "Big Girls Don't Cry." Chart.

Jan Howard, "My Son." Decca.

Dottie West, "Country Girl." RCA.

Tammy Wynette, "D-I-V-O-R-C-E." Epic.

BEST COUNTRY PERFORMANCE BY A DUO OR GROUP (VOCAL OR INSTRUMENTAL)

- Flatt & Scruggs, "Foggy Mountain Breakdown." Columbia.

Everly Brothers, "It's My Time." Warner Bros.

Bill Wilbourne, Kathy Morrison, "The Lovers." United Artists.

Nashville Brass, "Mountain Dew." RCA.

Tompall & the Glaser Brothers, "Through the Eyes of Love." MGM.

BEST COUNTRY SONG
(Songwriter's Award)

- "Little Green Apples," Bobby Russell.

"D-I-V-O-R-C-E," Curly Putman, Bobby Braddock.

"Harper Valley P.T.A.," Tom T. Hall.

"Honey," Bobby Russell.

"Skip a Rope," Glenn Tubb, Jack Moran.

BEST SACRED PERFORMANCE

- Jake Hess, "Beautiful Isle of Somewhere." RCA.

Anita Bryant, "How Great Thou Art." Columbia.

Jim Bohi, "I'll Fly Away." Supreme.

Ralph Carmichael, *102 Strings, Vol. 2*. Word.

George Beverly Shea, "Whispering Hope." RCA.

Elvis Presley, *You'll Never Walk Alone*. RCA.

BEST GOSPEL PERFORMANCE

- Happy Goodman Family, *The Happy Gospel of the Happy Goodmans*. Word.

Blackwood Brothers Quartet, *Yours Faithfully*. RCA.

Florida Boys Quartet, *The Florida Boys Sing Kinda Country*. Word.

Oak Ridge Boys, *A Great Day*. Heartwarming.

Thrasher Brothers, *For Goodness Sake*. Anchor.

BEST SOUL GOSPEL PERFORMANCE

- Dottie Rambo, "The Soul of Me." Heartwarming.

James Cleveland & Angelic Choir, "Bread of Heaven," Parts 1 & 2. Savoy.

Staple Singers, "Long Walk to D.C." Stax.

Swan Silvertones, "Only Believe." Scepter.

Davis Sisters, "Wait a Little Longer." Savoy.

Willa Dorsey, "Willa Dorsey: The World's Most Exciting Gospel Singer." Word.

BEST FOLK PERFORMANCE

- Judy Collins, "Both Sides Now." Elektra.

Bob Dylan, "John Wesley Harding." Columbia.

Incredible String Band, "The Hangman's Beautiful Daughter." Elektra.

Irish Rovers, "The Unicorn." Decca.

Gordon Lightfoot, "Did She Mention My Name." United Artists.

Peter, Paul & Mary, "Late Again." Warner Bros.

BEST INSTRUMENTAL THEME
(Composer's Award)

- "Classical Gas," Mason Williams. Warner Bros.

"The Good, the Bad and the Ugly," Hugo Montenegro, Ennio Morricone. RCA.

"The Odd Couple," Neal Hefti. Dot.

"Rosemary's Baby," Christopher Komeda. Dot.

"Theme from *The Fox*," Lalo Schifrin. Warner Bros./Seven Artists.

BEST INSTRUMENTAL ARRANGEMENT

- Mike Post, "Classical Gas" (Mason Williams). Warner Bros.

Al Capps, "Baroque-A-Nova" (Mason Williams). Warner Bros.

Michel Legrand, "The Windmills of Your Mind" (Michel Legrand). United Artists.

Hugo Montenegro, "The Good, the Bad and the Ugly" (Hugo Montenegro). RCA.

Don Sebesky, "Scarborough Fair" (Wes Montgomery). A&M.

BEST SCORE FROM AN ORIGINAL CAST SHOW ALBUM

- *Hair*, Gerome Ragni, James Rado, Galt MacDermot. RCA.

George M! George M. Cohan. Columbia.

The Happy Time, Fred Ebb, John Kander. RCA.

Jacques Brel Is Alive and Well and Living in Paris, Jacques Brel. Columbia.

Your Own Thing, Hal Hester, Danny Apolinar. RCA.

BEST ORIGINAL SCORE WRITTEN FOR A MOTION PICTURE OR TV SPECIAL
(Composer's Award)

- *The Graduate*, Paul Simon, Dave Grusin.

Bonnie and Clyde, Charles Strouse.

The Fox, Lalo Schifrin.

The Odd Couple, Neal Hefti.

Valley of the Dolls, André Previn.

BEST ARRANGEMENT ACCOMPANYING VOCALIST(S)

- Jim Webb, "MacArthur Park" (Richard Harris). Dunhill.

Dave Grusin, "Fool on the Hill" (Sergio Mendes & Brasil '66). A&M.

Al de Lory, "Wichita Lineman" (Glen Campbell). Capitol.

George Tipton, "Light My Fire" (José Feliciano). RCA.

Torrie Zito, "Yesterday I Heard the Rain" (Tony Bennett). Columbia.

BEST CLASSICAL PERFORMANCE, ORCHESTRA
(Conductor's Award)

- Pierre Boulez conducting the New Philharmonia Orchestra, *Boulez Conducts Debussy*. Columbia.

Leonard Bernstein conducting the New York Philharmonic, *Mahler: Symphony No. 6 in A Minor and Symphony No. 9 in D Major*. Columbia.

Nikolaus Harnoncourt conducting the Concentus Musicus of Vienna, *Bach: 4 Suites for Orchestra*. Telef.

Erich Leinsdorf conducting the Boston Symphony, *Prokofiev: Romeo and Juliet*. RCA.

Seiji Ozawa conducting the Toronto Symphony, *Messiaen: Turangalîla; Takemitsu: November Steps*. RCA.

Seiji Ozawa conducting the Chicago Symphony, *Stravinsky: Rite of Spring*. RCA.

André Previn conducting the London Symphony, *Rimsky-Korsakov: Shéhérazade*. RCA.

BEST CHAMBER MUSIC PERFORMANCE

• E. Power Biggs with the Edward Tarr Brass Ensemble and Gabrieli Consort; Vittorio Negri, conductor, *Gabrieli: Canzoni for Brass, Winds, Strings and Organ*. Columbia.

Boston Symphony Chamber Players, *Works by Mozart, Brahms, Schubert, Poulenc, Haieff, Villa-Lobos, Colgrass*. RCA.

Julian Bream and the Cremona String Quartet, *Julian Bream and His Friends*. RCA.

Guarneri Quartet, *Beethoven: The 5 Middle Quartets*. RCA.

Jascha Heifetz, Gregor Piatigorsky, William Primrose, Leonard Pennario, *Mozart: Quintet K. 515; Mendelssohn: Trio No. 2 in C Minor*. RCA.

Eugene Istomin, Isaac Stern, Leonard Rose, *Beethoven: Trio No. 3 in C Minor; Mendelssohn: Trio No. 1 in D Minor*. Columbia.

Walter Trampler, Ronald Turini, *Hindemith: Sonata for Viola and Piano*. RCA.

BEST CLASSICAL PERFORMANCE, INSTRUMENTAL SOLOIST(S) (WITH OR WITHOUT ORCHESTRA)

• Vladimir Horowitz, *Horowitz on Television*. Columbia.

Arthur Grumiaux (Markevitch conducting the Concertgebouw Orchestra), *Berg: Concerto for Violin and Orchestra*. Philips.

Julian Bream, *Dances of Dowland*. RCA.

Jacob Lateiner (Leinsdorf conducting the Boston Symphony), *Carter: Concerto for Piano*. RCA.

John Ogdon (Revenaugh conducting the Royal Philharmonic), *Busoni: Concerto for Piano with Male Chorus*. Angel.

Artur Rubinstein (Giulini conducting the Chicago Symphony), *Schumann: Concerto in A Minor for Piano and Orchestra*. RCA.

Alexis Weissenberg (Prêtre conducting the Chicago Symphony), *Rachmaninov: Concerto No. 3 in D Minor for Piano and Orchestra*. RCA.

BEST OPERA RECORDING

• *Mozart: Così Fan Tutte*, Erich Leinsdorf conducting the New Philharmonia Orchestra and Ambrosian Opera Chorus (solos: Price, Troyanos, Raskin, Milnes, Shirley, Flagello). RCA.

Berg: Lulu, Karl Böhm conducting the Orchestra of German Opera, Berlin (solos: Lear, Fischer-Dieskau). Deutsche Grammophon.

Ginastera: Bomarzo, Julius Rudel conducting the Opera Society of Washington (solos: Novoa, Turner, Penagos, Simon). Columbia.

Strauss: Elektra, Georg Solti conducting the Vienna Philharmonic (solos: Nilsson, Resnik, Collier, Krause, Stolze). London.

Wagner: Das Rheingold, Herbert von Karajan conducting the Berlin Philharmonic (solos: Fischer-Dieskau, Stolze, Mitalvela, Veasey, Grobe, Keleman, Dominguez). Deutsche Grammophon.

BEST CHORAL PERFORMANCE (OTHER THAN OPERA)

• Vittorio Negri conducting the Gregg Smith Singers; Texas Boys' Choir,

George Bragg, director; Edward Tarr Ensemble (with E. Power Biggs), *The Glory of Gabrieli*. Columbia.

Colin Davis conducting the John Alldis Choir and BBC Symphony, *Mozart: Requiem*. Philips.

Eugen Jochum conducting the Schoenberg Children's Chorus; Chorus and Orchestra of German Opera, Berlin, *Orff: Carmina Burana*. Deutsche Grammophon.

Abraham Kaplan conducting the Camerata Singers; Leonard Bernstein conducting the New York Philharmonic, *Haydn: The Creation*. Columbia.

Joseph Keilberth conducting the Bavarian Symphony Chorus and Orchestra, *Pfitzner: Von Deutscher Seele*. Deutsche Grammophon.

John McCarthy conducting the Ambrosian Singers; Morton Gould conducting the Royal Philharmonia, *Shostakovich: Symphony No. 2 in C Major; Symphony No. 3 in E Flat Major*. RCA.

Charles Munch conducting the Bavarian Radio Chorus and Symphony, *Berlioz: Requiem*. Deutsche Grammophon.

Stephen Simon conducting the Vienna Jeunesse Chorus and Vienna Volksoper Orchestra (solos: Shirley-Quirk, Endich, Brooks, Young), *Handel: Solomon*. RCA.

BEST CLASSICAL PERFORMANCE, VOCAL SOLOIST

• Montserrat Caballé (Cillario conducting the RCA Italiana Opera Orchestra and Chorus), *Rossini Rarities*. RCA.

Janet Baker (Barbirolli conducting the Halle Orchestra), *Mahler: Kindertotenlieder and Songs of a Wayfarer*. Angel.

Victoria de los Angeles (ARS Musicae Ensemble of Barcelona), *Songs of Andalucia*. Angel.

Dietrich Fischer-Dieskau (Jorg Demus, pianist), *Schumann: Songs*. Deutsche Grammophon.

Gerard Souzay (Dalton Baldwin, pianist), *Songs of Poulenc*. RCA.

Shirley Verrett (Prêtre conducting the RCA Italiana Opera Orchestra), *Verrett in Opera*. RCA.

BEST ENGINEERED RECORDING, CLASSICAL

• Gordon Parry, *Mahler: Symphony No. 9 in D Major* (Solti conducting the London Symphony). London.

Bernard Keville, *Messiaen: Turangalîla; Takemitsu: November Steps* (Ozawa conducting the Toronto Symphony). RCA.

Bernard Kevill, *Stravinsky: Rite of Spring* (Ozawa conducting the Chicago Symphony). RCA.

Michael Moran, *Rachmaninov: Concerto No. 3 in D Minor for Piano and Orchestra* (Weissenberg/Prêtre conducting the Chicago Symphony). RCA.

Gordon Parry, Kenneth Wilkenson, *Britten: Billy Budd* (Britten conducting the London Symphony; solos: Glossop, Pears, Shirley-Quirk, Brannigan). London.

Anthony Salvatore, *Prokofiev: Romeo and Juliet* (Leinsdorf conducting the Boston Symphony). RCA.

Anthony Salvatore, *Verdi: Ernani* (Schippers conducting the RCA Italiana Opera Orchestra and Chorus). RCA.

BEST COMEDY RECORDING

• *To Russell, My Brother, Whom I Slept With*, Bill Cosby. Warner Bros.

W. C. Fields Original Voice Tracks from Great Movies. Decca.

Flip Wilson, You Devil You, Flip Wilson. Atlantic.

Hello Dummy! Don Rickles. Warner Bros.

Rowan and Martin's Laugh-In, Dan Rowan, Dick Martin. Epic.

BEST SPOKEN WORD RECORDING

• *Lonesome Cities*, Rod McKuen. Warner Bros.

The Canterbury Pilgrims, Martin Starkie. Deutsche Grammophon.
I Have a Dream, Rev. Martin Luther King, Jr. 20th.
Kennedy-Nixon: The Great Debates, 1960. Columbia.
Murder in the Cathedral, Paul Scofield. Caedmon.

BEST ENGINEERED RECORDING

• Joe Polito, Hugh Davies, "Wichita Lineman" (Glen Campbell). Capitol.
Richard Bogert, *The Good, the Bad and the Ugly* (Hugo Montenegro). RCA.
Jerry Boys, Peter Vince, *Man of La Mancha* (original London cast). Decca.
Doug Brand, *Rotary Connection Trip 1* (Rotary Connection). Concept.
Dave Wiechman, *Daktari* (Shelly Manne). Atlantic.

BEST ALBUM COVER

• John Berg, Richard Mantel, art directors; Horn/Griner Studio, photography, *Underground* (Thelonious Monk). Columbia.

Sam Antupit, art director; Pete Turner, photography, *Road Song* (Wes Montgomery). A&M.
John Berg, Bob Cato, art directors; Ron Coro, designer; Don Huntstein, photographer, *Ives: Holidays Symphony* (Bernstein conducting the New York Philharmonic). CBS.
Bob Cato, art director and graphic design, *Wow* (Moby Grape). Columbia.
William S. Harvey, art director; Gene Szafran, graphic design, *Rhinoceros* (Rhinoceros). Elektra.

BEST ALBUM NOTES
(Annotator's Award)

• Johnny Cash, *Johnny Cash at Folsom Prison* (Johnny Cash). Columbia.
Stan Cornyn, *Francis A. and Edward K.* (Francis Albert Sinatra, Edward Kennedy Ellington). Reprise.
Miles Kreuger, *Ethel Waters on Stage and Screen 1925–40*. Columbia.
Richard Oliver, *Anthology of Indian Music, Vol. One* (Ravi Shankar, Ali Akbar Khan, Balachander). World Pacific.
Pete Seeger, *Pete Seeger's Greatest Hits* (Pete Seeger). Columbia.

• 1969 •

Aquarius: Sign of the Times

In the final year of the turbulent 1960s, as rock music ruled the record charts and roared defiantly during Woodstock, vanguards of the old music sound still made occasional forays into the Top 40. Conservative Grammy voters embraced them like old comrades, no doubt wondering, sadly with Peggy Lee, "Is That All There Is?"

But there was enough of the old guard left to form a considerable force to take on the new music at the Grammys.

Lee's "Is That All There Is?" was up for Record of the Year along with Henry Mancini's version of "A Time for Us (Love Theme from *Romeo and Juliet*)"—both reflecting traditional N.A.R.A.S. tastes. Rock & roll was represented by "Spinning Wheel," performed by Blood, Sweat & Tears, one of the two Grammy-winning groups of 1969 that also participated in Woodstock (Crosby, Stills & Nash did, too). The Recording Academy's strong Confederate contingent also made a run at the top award with Johnny Cash's "A Boy Named Sue." None would take the top prize, however, because, towering above all of them, was the 5th Dimension, the perfect N.A.R.A.S. compromise choice that last proved its might when the group swept the awards in 1967 with Record of the Year champ "Up, Up and Away."

The 5th Dimension was now at its professional apogee. When two of its most celebrated singers—Marilyn McCoo and Billy Davis—decided to settle down by getting married, the wedding ceremony became a high-profile media event that took place, of course, aboard a floating hot-air balloon. The group's "Aquarius/Let the Sunshine In" single was the top-selling disc of the year and proved

1967 Record of the Year champs, the 5th Dimension, returned to claim the prize for "Aquarius/Let the Sunshine in," a medley from *Hair*.

the easy victor of Record of the Year honors, in addition to earning its singers the award for Best Contemporary Vocal Performance by a Group.

The record was a medley of two songs from last year's Grammy-winning best original cast show album *Hair,* a groovy, idealized vision of the hippie '60s. *Hair* was nonetheless beloved by the record-buying public (becoming the top-selling LP of 1969) and spawned several successful singles. On May 10, 1969, the 5th Dimension's "Aquarius/Let the Sunshine In" was number one on the charts, followed by the Cowsills' rendition of the "Hair" single at number two. The show's other pop hits were "Good Morning Starshine," sung by Oliver, and "Easy to Be Hard" by Three Dog Night.

"Aquarius/Let the Sunshine In" was from the 5th Dimension's *Age of Aquarius* LP, which spent 30 weeks in the best-sellers and included such other hits as "Wedding Bell Blues" (which topped the charts for three weeks the same month that

McCoo and Davis were married). It was also a strong contender for Album of the Year in a tight race involving the Beatles' *Abbey Road, Johnny Cash at San Quentin* (with Cash's humorous hit "A Boy Named Sue"), one of the most eagerly awaited debut album releases ever (*Crosby, Stills & Nash*) and one of the most critically acclaimed rock & roll discs of the decade, *Blood, Sweat & Tears.*

Blood, Sweat & Tears was the "top contender in the Grammy sweepstakes" this year, according to *Variety*. The *L.A. Times* identified its artists as "a jazz-rock outfit that has wide appeal among both a younger, rock-oriented audience and the older, big band-oriented members of N.A.R.A.S." As its name suggested, Blood, Sweat & Tears was a mature music group. Its sound was serious, full of bluesy horns, intricate arrangements and vocals that tapped underground influences such as 19th-century black spirituals. Its first album, *Child Is Father to the Man,* debuted in 1968 and was a brilliant artistic effort spearheaded by lead singer Al Kooper. When Kooper quit the troupe in 1969, he was replaced by David Clayton-Thomas, who contributed works such as "Spinning Wheel," which was nominated for Record and Song of the Year. The band's subsequent *BS&T* LP ("one of the all-time best-selling albums on the Columbia label," noted *Variety*) also included innovative works like the instrumental "Variations on a Theme by Eric Satie" as well as hits like "And When I Die" and "You've Made Me So Very Happy."

Blood, Sweat & Tears headed into the Grammy ceremony *very* happy, having 10 nominations, 4 more than its nearest rival, the 5th Dimension. (Burt Bacharach and Quincy Jones came in third with 5 bids each.) "There were no stunning upsets in the Grammy winners," *Variety* said, reporting that *BS&T* easily took the

album laurels and Best Contemporary Instrumental Performance for "Variations." "Spinning Wheel" garnered the prize for Best Arrangement Accompanying Vocalist(s).

What overrode "Spinning Wheel" for Song of the Year was "Games People Play" by Joe South, a leading session guitarist and songwriter who would also pen such popular songs during his career as "Walk a Mile in My Shoes" and "Rose Garden." "In 'Games People Play,'" the *L.A. Times* reported, "South, a 27-year-old singer-writer from Atlanta, weaves a timely, almost universal message in language that is as straightforward as its rock accompaniment: 'Oh, the games people play, now / Every night and every day, now / Never meaning what they say, now / Never saying what they mean.'" Although South was a losing nominee for a best contemporary vocal performance award for his own version of the song that he recorded for Capitol, King Curtis's rendition took Best Rhythm & Blues Instrumental Performance. "Games" also won the newly reinstated award for Best Contemporary Song.

Realizing that it had cut back too many awards last year, N.A.R.A.S. reinstated five of them, including best song honors for contemporary and r&b works, Best Recording for Children, Classical Album of the Year and separate prizes for country group vocal and instrumental performances, which had been combined in 1968. The contemporary pop categories now dropped the "pop" designation and then, strangely, welcomed back an old-style singer who was hardly in tune with the newest music sound but who still had a pop hit.

"The N.A.R.A.S. balloting went with traditional, mainline pop music," said the *L.A. Times*, "in naming Peggy Lee as best female vocal performer" for "Is That All There Is?" Peggy Lee's victory would

> The ceremony was plagued by "a bad case of the gremlins," *Variety* said.

turn out to be a swan song for the Grammy tastes of yore. She was old guard *establishment*. She had performed with Benny Goodman ("I Got It Bad and That Ain't Good"), written music with Duke Ellington ("I'm Gonna Go Fishin'") and crooned in old movies like *Pete Kelly's Blues,* for which she was Oscar-nominated in 1955.

Another Top 40, easy-listening tune took the prize for contemporary choral work: "A Time for Us (Love Theme from *Romeo and Juliet*)" by the Percy Faith Orchestra & Chorus. Henry Mancini's rendition of the music from the hit movie by director Franco Zeffirelli was up for three Grammys, including Record of the Year. It ended up with only one—for Best Instrumental Arrangement, bringing Mancini his 18th Grammy, the most of any artist to date. Since "A Time for Us" was written by Larry Kusik, Eddie Snyder and Nino Rota—and not Mancini—it's ironic that it has turned out to be the composer-arranger's only number-one career hit. (His 1961 Record of the Year, "Moon River," only reached number 11 at its peak.) "A Time for Us" ended at number 15 in the year's overall rankings, an impressive achievement considering the resistance it initially experienced in the pop world. "It was very soft for its time," Mancini once said. "Some of the big [radio stations] refused to put it on until it became number one, because it wasn't a hard rocker."

The old guard's "chairman," Frank Sinatra, was nominated for best contemporary male vocal performance for "My Way," but lost to singer-songwriter Harry Nilsson, who was also the author of such hits as "One" for Three Dog Night and "Cuddly Toy" for the Monkees. Nilsson won his Grammy for his version of Fred Neil's "Everybody's Talkin'," which was used in the Oscars' 1969 Best Picture, *Midnight Cowboy* and won the Best Instrumental Theme award for British composer John Barry—at both the Oscars and the Grammys.

Crosby, Stills & Nash's premiere LP

Atlantic Records

Crosby, Stills & Nash lost their bid for Album of the Year, but won Best New Artist over Led Zepplin, Chicago and Oliver.

was eagerly awaited because the untried new trio was made up of proven talent. David Crosby had formerly been with the Byrds, Stephen Stills with Buffalo Springfield and Graham Nash with the Hollies. Together they achieved a seasoned sound that was distinguished by perfect-pitch harmonies. Their eponymous LP lost the Album of the Year contest, but the group still nabbed Best New Artist over Chicago, Led Zeppelin, Oliver and the Neon Philharmonic.

In the r&b category, Aretha Franklin stretched her winning streak to a third year when she took a vocal performance award for "Share Your Love with Me." The male prize for r&b singing went to Joe Simon for "The Chokin' Kind," his first million-seller after a career of lesser hits like "Teenager's Prayer" and "Nine Pound Steel." One of soul's longest-lasting troupes, the Isley Brothers, won their one and only Grammy (Best R&B Vocal Performance by a Duo or Group) for "It's Your Thing." The Isley Brothers had been recording on the Tamla/Motown label prior to 1969 but had now revived their own T-Neck label and added some of their younger brothers to the act.

"Color Him Father" was hailed as Best R&B Song. Written by Richard Spencer, it was recorded by the Winstons (a group that vanished like a puff of smoke in less than a year) and reached number seven on the pop charts and number two in the r&b rankings.

"A Boy Named Sue," written by Shel Silverstein, was the winner of the revived Best Country Song award. "Sue" was a ditty about a boy cursed with a girl's name that Johnny Cash added at the last minute to his concert act being recorded at San Quentin Prison, a follow-up to his popular Folsom Prison session, which earned him two Grammys last year. As a single release, "Sue" was an instant number-one hit on both the pop and c&w charts and also earned the country crooner a Grammy for best male vocal country performance. Cash won a prize for Best Album Notes, too, although not for his latest jailhouse jamboree LP, but for Bob Dylan's *Nashville Skyline*. Cash and Dylan were close friends. Dylan, in fact, came to a "guitar pull" at Cash's home a week before the San Quentin concert to help Cash prepare for the event. During his prison gig, Cash performed Dylan's "Wanted Man."

"A Boy Named Sue" beat another classic for Best Country Song—a tune cowritten by Tammy Wynette that would become her signature song. Wynette had been popular for her feminist anthems "I Don't Wanna Play House" and "D-I-V-O-R-C-E," but in 1969 she married famed country singer George Jones and suddenly seemed to have a change of heart about female independence. Her latest hit was "Stand By Your Man," which she cowrote with her producer at Epic, Billy Sherrill (1966 Grammy winner for "Almost Persuaded"). Its new, back-stepping message caused an uproar in the women's rights movement, but Wynette stood by her work, too, which quickly became the biggest-selling single ever recorded by a country artist and earned her the Grammy for female country vocals. She did not stand by her man too long, however. Jones had a drinking problem (he once drove 10 miles on a lawn mower to buy a bottle of liquor after Wynette hid his car keys), and "Mr. and Mrs. Country Music" d-i-v-o-r-c-e-d in 1975.

The Best Country Instrumental Performance went to the Nashville Brass and its trumpet player/leader, Danny Davis, who formed the group as a country equivalent to Herb Alpert & the Tijuana Brass. Waylon Jennings & the Kimberleys covered the Richard Harris hit of last year, "MacArthur Park," to take the prize for Best Country Vocal Performance by a Duo or Group.

Joni Mitchell gave the year's Best Folk Performance on her *Clouds* LP, which she recorded, troubador style, with only her guitar for accompaniment. The newly reinstated category for Best Recording for Children went to folk performers Peter, Paul & Mary for *Peter, Paul and Mommy*. The 42 winners of best soul gospel prize, the Edwin Hawkins Singers, were known as the Northern California State Youth Choir before they recorded "Oh Happy Day" for a religious congress in Cleveland. It was then discovered by a San Francisco deejay, who introduced the tune to the airwaves.

Burt Bacharach entered the Grammy race with two nominations for Song of the Year—for "I'll Never Fall in Love Again" and his Oscar-winning tune from *Butch Cassidy and the Sundance Kid,* "Raindrops Keep Fallin' on My Head." "Raindrops," recorded by B. J. Thomas, lost the top Grammy prize, but *Butch Cassidy* still took Best Original Score Written for a Motion Picture or TV Special. Bacharach's latest Broadway musical, *Promises, Promises,* won him the laurels for Best Cast Show Album.

Nineteen sixty-six Grammy winner Wes Montgomery returned to claim a new statuette for *Willow Weep for Me,* which was voted best large-group jazz performance. The small-group honors went to Quincy Jones, who was inspired to write his victorious "Walking in Space" work by the breakthroughs then occurring in the NASA space program.

In the classical categories, Walter Carlos bagged three Grammys for his controversial *Switched-on Bach* LP, which introduced the popular Moog synthesizer to the music industry. Carlos was a friend of its creator, Dr. Robert A. Moog, and was largely responsible for convincing the inventor to attach his name to it. The Moog not only made synthetic imitations of all kinds of instrumental sounds, it created new ones, too. "Purists are going to blast hell out of it," *High Fidelity* predicted when its reviewer first heard the Moog interpretations of such Bach selections as *The Well-Tempered Clavier* and the third Brandenburg Concerto.

A blast from the purists came as expected, but the outcry was accompanied by an astounding commercial reaction, too. *Switched-on Bach* became the number-one-selling classical album for 94 weeks and remained on the charts for 310 weeks. As of 1972, only one other classical album had ever sold more copies: Van Cliburn's recording of Tchaikovsky's First Piano Concerto. *Switched-on Bach* was the easy victor of the Classical Album of the Year award and also earned best performance by an instrumental soloist and best engineered classical recording.

Pierre Boulez and the Cleveland Orchestra won the orchestral performance honors for Debussy's *Images pour Orchestre*—"an exceptional record by any standard," said *High Fidelity*. The magazine also approved of the winner of the chamber music laurels: "a triple-star brass ensemble drawn from three of the leading American symphony orchestras, five Clevelanders, seven Philadelphians and seven Chicagoans," who performed works by Giovanni Gabrieli. Pianist Artur Rubinstein had also been nominated in the chamber music lineup, but

After a half dozen losses in years past, Peggy Lee finally won a Grammy for "Is That All There Is?", which was also a Record of the Year nominee.

noticed a mistake on the Grammy ballot when he received his in the mail. He fired off a heated letter to N.A.R.A.S., saying, "I'm flattered to be nominated year after year, but the next time your Trustees select me as nominee, I would appreciate it if you would instruct the proper department to spell my name correctly."

The choral honors went to four-time past Grammy winners the Swingle Singers for a work written by Luciano Berio with them in mind—"expertly played and brilliantly recorded," wrote *High Fidelity* of *Sinfonia*. The magazine was less enthusiastic about the winner of Best Opera Recording, saying "there are things to praise and curse" about Herbert von Karajan and the Berlin Philharmonic's five-LP stereo version of Wagner's *Siegfried* segment of the *Ring* cycle. The vocalist performance award went to Leontyne Price, who sang a range of works by Samuel Barber, though "the record is not successful," *High Fidelity* wrote, claiming that the selections just didn't "add up to much of a statement."

Price was tied with Henry Mancini and Bill Cosby for having had the longest winning streak in Grammy history prior to 1969: five years (1963–67 for Price, 1960–64 for Mancini and 1964–68 for Cosby). This year Cosby surpassed the other two by taking a sixth in a row. (His record would later be topped by Aretha Franklin and Sir Georg Solti.) His precedent-setting win was for Best Comedy Recording *The Best of Bill Cosby*, which included such classic routines as "Noah and the Ark," "Revenge" and a visit with a drunken "Lone Ranger."

Cosby was the emcee of the Los Angeles ceremony held at the Century Plaza Hotel, where he was joined by winners Harry Nilsson, Burt Bacharach and Peggy Lee. His best gags of the night were about his past failure to start up a record company.

The New York ceremony at Alice Tully Hall suffered from what *Variety* called "a bad case of the gremlins." The "casual, slow-paced production" was suddenly jolted by disaster when "the amplifying system blew out during Brenda Lee's performance of 'Johnny One Time' and the songstress was stranded on stage with a dead mike for the last half of the song. It took almost a half hour to repair the electronics, a long stage wait during which the music biz trade in the audience became rather restless."

• 1969 •

Awards were bestowed on March 11, 1970, for the eligibility period of November 2, 1968, to November 1, 1969, at ceremonies held at the Century Plaza Hotel in Los Angeles, Alice Tully Hall in New York, and at dinners held in Nashville and Chicago.

ALBUM OF THE YEAR
• *Blood, Sweat and Tears*, Blood, Sweat & Tears. Columbia.
Abbey Road, Beatles. Apple.
The Age of Aquarius, 5th Dimension. Soul City.
Crosby, Stills and Nash, Crosby, Stills & Nash. Atlantic.
Johnny Cash at San Quentin, Johnny Cash. Columbia.

RECORD OF THE YEAR
• "Aquarius/Let the Sunshine In," 5th Dimension. Soul City.
"A Boy Named Sue," Johnny Cash. Columbia.
"Is That All There Is?" Peggy Lee. Capitol.
"A Time for Us (Love Theme from *Romeo and Juliet*)," Henry Mancini. RCA.

"Spinning Wheel," Blood, Sweat & Tears. Columbia.

SONG OF THE YEAR
(Songwriter's Award)
• "Games People Play," Joe South.
"I'll Never Fall in Love Again," Burt Bacharach, Hal David.
"Raindrops Keep Fallin' on My Head," Burt Bacharach, Hal David.
"Spinning Wheel," David Clayton Thomas.
"A Time for Us (Love Theme from *Romeo and Juliet*)," Larry Kusik, Eddie Snyder, Nino Rota.

BEST NEW ARTIST
• Crosby, Stills & Nash
Chicago
Led Zeppelin
Oliver
Neon Philharmonic

BEST CONTEMPORARY VOCAL PERFORMANCE, MALE
• "Everybody's Talkin'," Harry Nilsson. United Artists.
"Games People Play," Joe South. Capitol.
"Guitarzan," Ray Stevens. Monument.

"My Way," Frank Sinatra. Warner Bros.
"Raindrops Keep Fallin' on My Head,"
B. J. Thomas. Scepter.

BEST CONTEMPORARY VOCAL
PERFORMANCE, FEMALE
• "Is That All There Is?" Peggy Lee.
Capitol.
"Johnny One Time," Brenda Lee.
Decca.
"Put a Little Love in Your Heart," Jackie
DeShannon. Liberty/United Artists.
"Son of a Preacher Man," Dusty Spring-
field. Atlantic.
"This Girl's in Love with You," Dionne
Warwick. Scepter.
"With Pen in Hand," Vikki Carr. Liberty.

BEST CONTEMPORARY VOCAL
PERFORMANCE BY A GROUP
• 5th Dimension, "Aquarius/Let the
Sunshine In." Soul City.
Beatles, *Abbey Road*. Apple.
Blood, Sweat & Tears, *Blood, Sweat
and Tears*. Columbia.
Crosby, Stills & Nash, *Crosby, Stills and
Nash*. Atlantic.
Neon Philharmonic, *Morning Girl*.
Warner Bros.

BEST CONTEMPORARY
PERFORMANCE BY A CHORUS
• Percy Faith Orchestra & Chorus,
"Love Theme from *Romeo and
Juliet*." Columbia.
Brooks Arthur Ensemble, "MacArthur
Park." Verve.
Ray Charles Singers, "Slices of Life."
Command.
Ray Conniff & the Singers, "Jean."
Columbia.
Living Voices, "Angel of the Morning."
RCA.

BEST CONTEMPORARY SONG
(Songwriter's Award)
• "Games People Play," Joe South.
"In the Ghetto," Mac Davis.
"Jean," Rod McKuen.
"Raindrops Keep Fallin' on My Head,"
Burt Bacharach, Hal David.

"Spinning Wheel," David Clayton
Thomas.

BEST CONTEMPORARY
INSTRUMENTAL PERFORMANCE
• "Variations on a Theme by Erik
Satie," Blood, Sweat & Tears.
Columbia.
"Area Code 615," Area Code 615. Poly-
dor.
"A Time for Us (Love Theme from
Romeo and Juliet)," Henry Mancini.
RCA.
Midnight Cowboy, Ferrante & Teicher.
Liberty/United Aritists.
"With Love," Boots Randolph. Monu-
ment.

BEST RHYTHM & BLUES SONG
(Songwriter's Award)
• "Color Him Father," Richard Spencer.
"Backfield in Motion," Herbert McPher-
son, Melvin Harden.
"I'd Rather Be an Old Man's Sweet-
heart," Clarence Carter, George Jack-
son, Raymond Moore.
"It's Your Thing," Rudolph Isley, O.
Kelly Isley, Jr., Ronnie Isley.
"Only the Strong Survive," Kenny Gam-
ble, Leon Huff, Jerry Butler.

BEST RHYTHM & BLUES VOCAL
PERFORMANCE, MALE
• Joe Simon, "The Chokin' Kind."
Sound Stage.
Ray Charles, "Doing His Thing." Tan-
gerine.
Jerry Butler, *Ice Man Cometh*. Mercury.
B. B. King, *Live and Well*. ABC.
Lou Rawls, "Your Good Thing (Is
About to End)." Capitol.

BEST RHYTHM & BLUES VOCAL
PERFORMANCE, FEMALE
• Aretha Franklin, "Share Your Love
with Me." Atlantic.
Ruth Brown, "Yesterday." Skye.
Gloria Taylor, "You Gotta Pay the
Price." Silver Fox.
Tina Turner, *The Hunter*. Blue
Thumb.

Dee Dee Warwick, "Foolish Fool." Mercury.

BEST RHYTHM & BLUES VOCAL PERFORMANCE BY A DUO OR GROUP

- Isley Brothers, "It's Your Thing." T-Neck.
Gladys Knight & the Pips, "Friendship Train." Motown.
Mel & Tim, "Backfield in Motion." Scepter.
Peggy Scott, Jo Jo Benson, "Soulshake." SSS.
Winstons, "Color Him Father." Metromedia.

BEST RHYTHM & BLUES INSTRUMENTAL PERFORMANCE

- King Curtis, "Games People Play." Atco.
Albert Collins, "Trash Talkin'." Imperial.
Richard "Groove" Holmes, "Workin' on a Groovy Thing." World Pacific.
Ike Turner, "A Black Man's Soul." Pompeii.
Junior Walker & the All Stars, "What Does It Take." Soul.

BEST INSTRUMENTAL JAZZ PERFORMANCE BY A SMALL GROUP OR SOLOIST WITH SMALL GROUP (7 OR FEWER)

- Wes Montgomery, *Willow Weep for Me*. Verve.
Eubie Blake, *The 86 Years of Eubie Blake*. Columbia.
Miles Davis, *In a Silent Way*. Columbia.
Bill Evans, Jeremy Steig, *What's New*. Verve.
Stephane Grappelli, Stuff Smith, Sven Asmussen, Jean Luc-Ponty, *Violin Summit*. Prestige.
Herbie Mann, *Memphis Underground*. Atlantic.
Oscar Peterson, *The Great Oscar Peterson on Prestige*. Prestige.

BEST INSTRUMENTAL JAZZ PERFORMANCE BY A LARGE GROUP OR SOLOIST WITH LARGE GROUP (8 OR MORE)

- Quincy Jones, "Walking in Space." A&M.
Count Basie, *Standing Ovation*. Paramont.
Don Ellis, *The New Don Ellis Band Goes Underground*. Columbia.
Woody Herman, *Light My Fire*. Cadet.
Thad Jones, Mel Lewis, *Central Park North*. Solid State.
Gary McFarland, *America the Beautiful*. Skye.
Buddy Rich Orchestra, *Buddy and Soul*. World Pacific.
Bob Wilber, *The Music of Hoagy Carmichael*. Monmouth.

BEST COUNTRY SONG
(Songwriter's Award)

- "A Boy Named Sue," Shel Silverstein.
"All I Have to Offer You Is Me," Dallas Frazier, A. L. Owens.
"Stand By Your Man," Tammy Wynette, Billy Sherrill.
"The Things That Matter," Don Sumner.
"You Gave Me a Mountain," Marty Robbins.

BEST COUNTRY VOCAL PERFORMANCE, MALE

- Johnny Cash, "A Boy Named Sue." Columbia.
Clay Hart, "Spring." Metromedia.
Bobby Lewis, "From Heaven to Heartache." United Artists.
Charley Pride, "All I Have to Offer You Is Me." RCA.
Jerry Reed, "Are You from Dixie." RCA.

BEST COUNTRY VOCAL PERFORMANCE, FEMALE

- Tammy Wynette, "Stand By Your Man." Epic.
Lynn Anderson, "That's a No No." Chart.
Jeannie C. Riley, "Back Side of Dallas." Plantation.

Connie Smith, "Ribbon of Darkness." RCA.

Diana Trask, "I Fall to Pieces." ABC-Paramount.

BEST COUNTRY VOCAL PERFORMANCE BY A DUO OR GROUP

• Waylon Jennings, Kimberlys, "MacArthur Park." RCA.

Jack Greene, Jeanie Seely, "Wish I Didn't Have to Miss You." Decca.

Tompall & the Glaser Brothers, "California Girl." MGM

Porter Wagoner, Dolly Parton, "Just Someone I Used to Know." RCA.

Dottie West, Don Gibson, "Rings of Gold." RCA.

BEST COUNTRY INSTRUMENTAL PERFORMANCE

• Danny Davis & the Nashville Brass, *The Nashville Brass Featuring Danny Davis Play More Nashville Sounds*. RCA.

Tommy Allsup & the Nashville Survey, *The Hits of Charley Pride*. Metromedia.

Floyd Cramer, "Lovin' Season." RCA.

Bob Dylan, "Nashville Skyline Rag." Columbia.

Chet Atkins, *Solid Gold '69*. RCA.

BEST SACRED PERFORMANCE

• Jake Hess, "Ain't That Beautiful Singing." RCA.

Tennessee Ernie Ford, "Holy, Holy, Holy." Capital.

Bill Gaither Trio, "He Touched Me." Heartwarming.

George Beverly Shea, "I Believe." RCA.

Connie Smith, Nat Stuckey, "Whispering Hope." RCA.

BEST GOSPEL PERFORMANCE

• Porter Wagoner, Blackwood Brothers, "In Gospel Country." RCA.

Happy Goodman Family, "This Happy House." Word.

LeFevres, "The Best Is Yet to Come." Canaan.

Oak Ridge Boys, "It's Happening." Heartwarming.

Singing Rambos, "This Is My Valley." Heartwarming.

BEST SOUL GOSPEL PERFORMANCE

• Edwin Hawkins Singers, *Oh Happy Day*. Buddah.

James Cleveland, Southern California Choir, *Come On and See About Me*. Savoy.

Cassietta George, *Cassietta*. Audio Gospel.

Mahalia Jackson, *Guide Me, O Thou Great Jehovah*. Columbia.

Sister Rosetta Tharpe, *Precious Memories*. Savoy.

BEST FOLK PERFORMANCE

• Joni Mitchell, *Clouds*. Warner Bros.

Joan Baez, "Any Day Now." Vanguard.

Judy Collins, "Bird on a Wire." Elektra.

Donovan, "Atlantis." Epic.

Peter, Paul & Mary, "Day Is Done." Warner Bros.

Pete Seeger, "Young vs. Old." Columbia.

BEST INSTRUMENTAL ARRANGEMENT

• Henry Mancini, "A Time for Us (Love Theme from *Romeo and Juliet*)" (Mancini). RCA.

Arthur Ferrante, Lou Teicher, "Midnight Cowboy" (Ferrante & Teicher). Liberty.

Dick Halligan, "Variations on a Theme by Eric Satie" (Blood, Sweat & Tears). Columbia.

Quincy Jones, "Walking in Space" (Quincy Jones). A&M.

BEST INSTRUMENTAL THEME
(Composer's Award)

• *Midnight Cowboy*, John Barry.

"Groovy Grubworm," Harlow Wilcox, Bobby Warren.

"MacKenna's Gold," Quincy Jones.

"Memphis Underground," Herbie Mann.

"Quentin's Theme," Robert Cobert.

BEST SCORE FROM AN ORIGINAL CAST SHOW ALBUM

- *Promises, Promises*, Burt Bacharach, Hal David. Liberty.
- *Dames at Sea*, George Haimsohn, Robin Miller, Jim J. Wise. Columbia.
- *Oh! Calcutta!* Robert Dennis, Stanley Walden, Peter Schickle. Aidart.
- *1776*, Herman Edwards. Columbia.
- *Zorba*, John Kander, Fred Ebb. Capitol.

BEST ORIGINAL SCORE WRITTEN FOR A MOTION PICTURE OR TV SPECIAL (Composer's Award)

- *Butch Cassidy and the Sundance Kid*, Burt Bacharach. A&M.
- *The Lost Man*, Quincy Jones. Uni.
- *MacKenna's Gold*, Quincy Jones. RCA.
- *Me, Natalie*, Henry Mancini. Columbia.
- *Yellow Submarine*, John Lennon, Paul McCartney, George Harrison, George Martin. Capitol.

BEST ARRANGEMENT ACCOMPANYING VOCALIST(S)

- Fred Lipsius, "Spinning Wheel" (Blood, Sweat & Tears). Columbia.
- Bill Holman, Bob Alcivar, Bones Howe, "Aquarius/Let the Sunshine In" (5th Dimension). Soul City.
- Al Kooper, Fred Lipsius, "You've Made Me So Very Happy" (Blood, Sweat & Tears). Columbia.
- Randy Newman, "Is That All There Is?" (Peggy Lee). Capitol.
- Torrie Zito, "I've Gotta Be Me" (Tony Bennett). Columbia.

ALBUM OF THE YEAR, CLASSICAL

- *Switched-on Bach (Virtuoso Electronic Performance of Branden Concerto No. 3, Air on a G String, Jesu, Joy of Man's Destiny, etc.*, performed on Moog synthesizer), Walter Carlos. Columbia.
- *Berio: Sinfonia*, Luciano Berio conducting the New York Philharmonic and Swingle Singers. Columbia.
- *Boulez Conducts Berg (3 Pieces for Orchestra, Chamber Concerto, Altenberg Lieder)*, Pierre Boulez conducting the BBC Symphony (solos: Barenboim, Gawriloff, Lukomska). Columbia.
- *Boulez Conducts Debussy, Vol. 2, Images pour Orchestre*, Pierre Boulez conducting the Cleveland Orchestra. Columbia.
- *Gabrieli: Antiphonal Music of Gabrieli (Canzoni for Brass Choirs)*, Philadelphia, Cleveland and Chicago Brass Ensembles. Columbia.
- *Strauss: Also Sprach Zarathustra*, Zubin Mehta conducting the Los Angeles Philharmonic. London.

BEST CLASSICAL PERFORMANCE, ORCHESTRA (Conductor's Award)

- Pierre Boulez conducting the Cleveland Orchestra, *Boulez Conducts Debussy, Vol. 2, Images pour Orchestre*. Columbia.
- Pierre Boulez conducting the BBC Symphony, *Bartók: Music for Strings, Percussion and Celesta*. Columbia.
- Jean Martinon conducting the Chicago Symphony, *Ravel: Rapsodie Espagnole; Mother Goose Suite; Alborada del Gracioso; Introduction and Allegro*. RCA.
- Zubin Mehta conducting the Los Angeles Philharmonic, *Strauss: Also Sprach Zarathustra*. London.
- George Szell conducting the Cleveland Orchestra, *Wagner: Great Orchestral Highlights from "Der Ring des Nibelungen."* Columbia.

BEST CHAMBER MUSIC PERFORMANCE

- Philadelphia, Cleveland and Chicago Brass Ensembles, *Gabrieli: Antiphonal Music of Gabrieli (Canzoni for Brass Choirs)*. Columbia.
- Julian Bream, George Malcolm, *Bach and Vivaldi Sonatas for Lute and Harpsichord*. RCA.
- Borodin Quartet, *Shostakovich: String Quartets (Complete)*. Seraphim.

Jacqueline Du Pré, Daniel Barenboim, *Brahms: Sonatas in E Minor and F Major for Cello and Piano*. Angel.

Grumiaux Trio, *Beethoven: Trios for Strings*. Philips.

Itzhak Perlman, Vladimir Ashkenazy, *Prokofiev: Sonatas for Violin and Piano*. RCA.

Artur Rubinstein and Guarneri Quartet, *Brahms: Quartets for Piano and Strings (3); Schumann: Quintet in E Flat Major for Piano and Strings*. RCA.

BEST CLASSICAL PERFORMANCE, INSTRUMENTAL SOLOISTS(S) (WITH OR WITHOUT ORCHESTRA)

- Walter Carlos, Moog synthesizer, *Switched-on Bach*. Columbia.

Edward Druzinsky, harp (Martinon conducting the Chicago Symphony), *Ravel: Introduction and Allegro for Harp and Strings*. RCA.

Emil Gilels, *Gilels at Carnegie Hall*. Melyd.

John Kirkpatrick, *Ives: Sonata No. 2 ("Concord Mass")*. Columbia.

Mstislav Rostropovich, cello (von Karajan conducting the Berlin Philharmonic), *Dvořák: Concerto in B Minor for Cello*. Deutsche Grammophon.

Henryk Szeryng, *Bach: Sonatas and Partitas for Solo Violin*. Deutsche Grammophon.

BEST OPERA RECORDING

- *Wagner: Siegfried*, Herbert von Karajan conducting the Berlin Philharmonic (solos: Thomas, Stewart, Stolze, Dernesch, Keleman, Dominguez, Gayer, Ridderbush). Deutsche Grammophon.

Cavalli: L'Ormindo, Raymond Leppard conducting the London Philharmonic (solos: Wakefield, van Bork, Howells, Berbie, Cuenod; Glyndebourne Festival Opera). Argo.

Mozart: The Marriage of Figaro, Karl Böhm conducting the Chorus and Orchestra of German Opera (solos: Prey, Mathis, Janowitz, Fischer-Dieskau). Deutsche Grammophon.

Strauss: Ariadne auf Naxos, Rudolf Kempe conducting the Dresden State Opera (solos: Janowitz, King, Zylis-Gara, Geszty, Adam). Angel.

Strauss: Salome, Erich Leinsdorf conducting the London Symphony (solos: Caballé, Milnes, Lewis, Resnik, King). RCA.

Verdi: Otello, Sir John Barbirolli conducting the New Philharmonia Orchestra and Chorus (soloists: McCracken, Fischer-Dieskau, Jones, Di Stasio). Angel.

Verdi: La Traviata, Lorin Maazel conducting the Orchestra and Chorus of Deutsche Opera Berlin (solos: Lorengar, Aragall, Fischer-Dieskau). London.

BEST CHORAL PERFORMANCE (OTHER THAN OPERA)

- Ward Swingle, choral master; Luciano Berio conducting the New York Philharmonic and Swingle Singers, *Berio: Sinfonia*. Columbia.

Colin Davis conducting the John Alldis Choir and London Symphony Orchestra and Chorus, *Berlioz: Romèo et Juliette*. Philips.

Hans Gillesberger conducting the Vienna Boys' Choir and Chorus Viennensis; Nikolaus Harnoncourt conducting the Concentus Musicus, *Bach: Mass in B Minor*. Telefunken.

Hans Werner Henze conducting the Choirs of North German Radio, Berlin Radio, Boys' Chorus of St. Nicolai and North German Radio Symphony, *Henze: The Raft of the Frigate "Medusa."* Deutsche Grammophon.

Frederick Jackson, choral master, London Philharmonic Choir; Adrian Boult conducting the London Philharmonic, *Vaughan Williams: Symphony No. 1 ("A Sea Symphony")*. Angel.

Gregg Smith conducting the Gregg Smith Singers, *Billings: The Continental Harmony*. Columbia.

Edmund Walters conducting the Royal Liverpool Philharmonic Choir; Charles Groves conducting the Royal Liverpool Philharmonic Orchestra, *Delius: Songs of Sunset*. Angel.

BEST CLASSICAL PERFORMANCE, VOCAL SOLOIST

- Leontyne Price (Schippers conducting the New Philharmonia), *Barber: Two Scenes from "Antony and Cleopatra"; Knoxville: Summer of 1915*. RCA.
Dietrich Fischer-Dieskau (Gerald Moore, accompanist), *Richard Strauss: 19 Early Songs*. Angel.
Marilyn Horne (Lewis conducting the Vienna Cantata Orchestra), *Bach and Handel Arias (*excerpts from *Magnificat, Christmas Oratorio, St. Matthew Passion, Messiah, Rodelinda)*. London.
Christa Ludwig, Walter Berry (Gerald Moore, accompanist), *A Most Unusual Song Recital* (Beethoven, Rossini, Brahms, Reger, R. Strauss). Seraphim.
Halina Lukomska (from *Boulez Conducts Berg*, Boulez conducting the London Symphony), *Berg: Altenberg Lieder*. Columbia.
Sherrill Milnes (from *Brahms: Requiem*, Leinsdorf conducting the Boston Symphony), *Brahms: 4 Serious Songs*. RCA.
Peter Pears, Dietrich Fischer-Dieskau, *Britten: Holy Sonnets of Donne; Songs and Proverbs of Blake*. London.
Elisabeth Schwarzkopf, Dietrich Fischer-Dieskau (Szell conducting the London Symphony), *Mahler: Des Knaben Wunderhorn*. Angel.
Beverly Sills (Mackerras conducting the Royal Philharmonic), *Scenes and Arias from French Opera*. Westminster.

BEST ENGINEERED RECORDING, CLASSICAL

- Walter Carlos, *Switched-on Bach* (Walter Carlos). Columbia.

Edwin Begley, *Mahler: Symphony No. 1* (Ormandy conducting the Philadelphia Symphony). RCA.
Edward T. Graham, Arthur Kendy, *Boulez Conducts Debussy, Vol. 2, Images pour Orchestre* (Boulez conducting the Cleveland Orchestra). Columbia.
Edward T. Graham, Milton Cherin, *Gabrieli: Antiphonal Music of Gabrieli (Canzoni for Brass Choirs)* (Philadelphia, Cleveland and Chicago Brass Ensembles). Columbia/Odyssey.
Paul Goodman, *Khachaturian: Symphony No. 3; Rimsky-Korsakov: Russian Easter Overture* (Stokowski conducting the Chicago Symphony). RCA.
Fred Plaut, Ed Michalski, *Berio: Sinfonia* (Berio conducting the New York Philharmonic and Swingle Singers). Columbia.

BEST COMEDY RECORDING

- *The Best of Bill Cosby*, Bill Cosby. Uni.
Berkeley Concert, Lenny Bruce. Warner Bros.
Don Rickles Speaks! Don Rickles. Warner Bros.
Laugh-In '69. Warner Bros.
W. C. Fields on Radio. Columbia.

BEST RECORDING FOR CHILDREN

- *Peter, Paul and Mommy*, Peter, Paul & Mary. Warner Bros.
Yellow Submarine, Richard Wolfe Children's Chorus. RCA.
Chitty Chitty Bang Bang, Do-Re-Mi Chorus. Kapp.
Folk Tales of the Tribes of Africa, Eartha Kitt. Caedmon.
For All My Little Friends, Tiny Tim. Warner Bros.

BEST SPOKEN WORD RECORDING

- *We Love You, Call Collect*, Art Linkletter & Diane. Word/Capitol.
The Great White Hope, James Earl Jones. Tetra.

Home to the Sea, Jesse Pearson, narrator. Warner Bros.

Man on the Moon, Walter Cronkite. Warner Bros.

Robert F. Kennedy: A Memorial. Columbia.

BEST ENGINEERED RECORDING

• Geoff Emerick, Phillip McDonald, *Abbey Road* (Beatles). Apple.

Roy Halee, Fred Catero, *Blood, Sweat and Tears* (Blood, Sweat and Tears). Columbia.

Lee Herschberg, Larry Cox, Chuck Britz, *Velvet Voices and Bold Brass* (Anita Kerr Quartet). Para.

Bones Howe, *Age of Aquarius* (5th Dimension). Soul City.

Bruce Swedien, Doug Brand, Hans Wurman, Chuck Lishon, *Moog Groove* (Electronic Concept Orchestra). Limelight.

BEST ALBUM COVER

• Evelyn J. Kelbish, painting; David Stahlberg, graphics, *America the Beautiful* (Gary McFarland). Skye.

Gary Burden, art director; Henry Diltz, photographer, *Richard Pryor* (Richard Pryor). Dove.

David Juniper, art director; *Led Zeppelin II* (Led Zeppelin). Atlantic.

Tom Lazarus, art director; Gene Brownell, photographer; Bill Gordon, design, *Pidgeon* (Pidgeon). Decca.

Bob Seideman, art director and photographer, *Blind Faith* (Blind Faith). Atco.

BEST ALBUM NOTES
(Annotator's Award)

• Johnny Cash, *Nashville Skyline* (Bob Dylan). Columbia.

Joan Baez, *David's Album* (Joan Baez). Vanguard.

John Dodds II, *Chicago Mess Around* (Johnny Dodds). Milestone.

John Hartford, *John Hartford* (J. Hartford). RCA.

Rex Reed, *Mabel Mercer and Bobby Short at Town Hall*. Atlantic.

• 1970 •
Troubled Times

The first complete sweep of the top prizes occurred on a Grammy night that was also historic for a second reason—the awards ceremony was broadcast live on national television for the first time ever.

The ABC telecast originated from the Hollywood Palladium, where Andy Williams presided over the presentation of 17 of the year's 43 awards, the balance having been bestowed at an off-the-air ceremony held earlier in the day. Two revolving stages were installed to accommodate Grammy's first prime-time TV spectacle, and a host of celebrity talent pitched in as presenters, including Herb Alpert, Burt Bacharach, Duke Ellington, Three Dog Night, Tammy Wynette, the 5th Dimension, Henry Mancini and Bobby Sherman. The Grammys suddenly seemed to be in the same league as the Oscars, Emmys and Tonys, and the record academy wanted to put on a show to prove it.

The Grammycast did not disappoint, at least in terms of the drama surrounding the award results. It was now a fairly common occurrence for two of the three top categories—Record, Song and Album of the Year—to go to the same artist. It had happened six times in the past 12 years, but never before had anyone won the Triple Crown. Then came the folky rock team of Simon & Garfunkel, who last proved their favored status with N.A.R.A.S. voters in 1968 by winning Record of the Year for "Mrs. Robinson."

Variety finally flagged the news of Grammy winners in a banner headline now that the ceremony was broadcast live nationwide.

Their latest collaboration—and one that would be remembered as the duo's last LP of studio recordings as a duo act—was the milestone album and single release *Bridge Over Troubled Water*.

Bridge began the night with the most nominations—seven—and won six awards, incuding Record, Album and Song of the Year (Simon alone won the prize for songwriting). *Bridge*'s victory also spanned the categories for Best Contemporary Song, Best Arrangement Accompanying Vocalist(s) and Best Engineered Recording.

Bridge was the early favorite to sweep the awards, since the LP was the top seller of the year and the single ended up fourth in the rankings. *Bridge* was also embraced as an anthem of the equally troubled times. The year 1970 marked the student killings at Kent State University and Janis Joplin's drug overdose. "I'm embarrassed to say I burst into tears when I wrote and first sang the line 'Like a bridge over troubled water, I will lay me down,' " Paul Simon later told *Playboy* magazine, remembering the song's sentimental importance in 1970. "Now it's been sung so many times I have no feeling whatsoever for it." The year was an equally troubling time for Simon & Garfunkel. Although they would periodically team up for special concerts and charity benefits in the future, the duo ended their partnership soon after *Bridge*'s release.

"Bridge [may have] swept the top honors," wrote the *L.A. Times*, "but it was ex-Beatle Paul McCartney, in a rare public appearance, who created the most excitement" at the ceremony. "Though the event was strictly black tie, McCartney strolled in wearing a blue suit, red flower shirt open at the neck, and white tennis shoes."

Like Simon & Garfunkel, the Beatles broke up in 1970 but still had a bounty of nominations (six) for their farewell LP, *Let It Be*. They won only one award—for Best Original Score written for a Motion Picture or TV Special—after losing Record and Song of the Year nods (in a close contest, according to the *Washington Post*) to "Bridge." But "there were shrieks of surprise" from the audience when the winner of best film score was announced, the *Times* reported. "With Linda at his side, McCartney raced up to the podium to accept the award from actor John Wayne, saying only, 'Thank you.' "

Variety columnist Army Archerd added, "Paul McCartney kept his word, returned to the press tent after the awards—and, as expected, had to plough his way thru a mob to reach his car with (expectant) wife Linda. McCartney, informally attired (would you believe sneakers?), admitted, 'I didn't know whether they'd let me in.' "

John Lennon once said about *Let It Be:* "This is us with our trousers off." The album was from the Beatles film that documented the group's breakup and included such hit singles as "Get Back."

The movie ended with their last public concert—held on the rooftop of their Apple Records headquarters in London (the neighbors called the cops to break it up)—and with Lennon's parting words, "I'd like to say thank you very much on behalf of the group and myself, and I hope we passed the audition."

The Beatles and Simon & Garfunkel were up for Best Contemporary Vocal Performance by a Duo, Group or Chorus but lost to Grammy's best new artists, the Carpenters, who first came to fame after covering the Beatles' "Ticket to Ride" in 1969. Brother and sister Richard and Karen Carpenter were often criticized for lacking passion in their singing, but they were nonetheless expert voicesmiths who specialized in melodic ballads such as their winning "Close to You," also a Record of the Year nominee that came in number five in the year's chart rankings (just behind "Bridge Over Troubled Water"). *Close to You* was also a best-selling LP for an impressive 53 weeks, although it proved a loser as an Album of the Year nominee.

The "Close to You" single was written by Burt Bacharach and Hal David for Dionne Warwick, who recorded it first, but without much success. Warwick still reigned in the pop charts, though, with another Bacharach/David tune, "I'll Never Fall in Love Again"—from the Broadway musical *Promises, Promises*, which won last year's Grammy for best cast show album. "I'll Never Fall in Love Again" also earned Warwick the laurels for best female contemporary vocal performance, a prize she won once before, in 1968, for singing Bacharach and David's "Do You Know the Way to San Jose." Of her first 37 singles, Bacharach and David wrote all but 4 and produced all but 2. In 1971, however, she made a break with them to jump to Warner Bros., where she knew only periodic success after that.

Paul Simon became the first winner of Grammy's Triple Crown.

Winner of the award for best contemporary male singing went to Ray Stevens, who had turned down the chance to make the first recording of Bacharach/David's "Raindrops Keep Fallin' on My Head" (which rose to become the number-one song of 1970 with B. J. Thomas vocals). Stevens was a pop country singer known for humorous ditties like 1962's "Ahab the Arab." When he wrote his Grammy-winning "Everything Is Beautiful," he accentuated its seriousness by adding a chorus that sounded like a church choir. "Everything Is Beautiful" won a second Grammy when gospel belter Jake Hess gave it an even more religious lilt, earning him Best Sacred Performance.

Gospel-trained Aretha Franklin picked up her fourth Grammy in a row for best r&b vocal performance for "Don't Play That Song," which ended up number 11 in the year's chart, the exact same ranking it had when it was performed in 1962 by Ben E. King. But in this version, Lady Soul gave it her signature eruptions of joy, rage, pain and sorrow. The swings of feeling must have been easy for her to muster in 1970, considering the personal tragedies she suffered in private life. Her marriage to manager Ted White had just broken up and she had recently been arrested for drunk driving and disorderly conduct.

When B. B. ("Blues Boy") King took the equivalent r&b vocal honors for men for "The Thrill Is Gone," it was a crowning achievement. For 20 years, King had been known primarily to black audiences. In 1969, however, he was the toast of the Newport Jazz Festival, appeared on *The Tonight Show,* toured with the Rolling Stones and then ventured across Europe and Australia with his own band.

The r&b group vocal prize went to the Delfonics for what *Rolling Stone* once called their "landmark" hit "Didn't I (Blow Your Mind This Time)," which was written by Thom Bell, its producer, and William Hart, one of the three members of the pop/soul vocal trio from Pennsyl-

The Carpenters beat Elton John for Best New Artist and the Beatles and Simon & Garfunkel for the award for best contemporary vocals.

vania. "Didn't I" was up for Best R&B Song along with such other heavy hitters as Stevie Wonder's "Signed, Sealed, Delivered," but both lost to "Patches," by Ronald Dunbar and General Johnson.

The two jazz categories welcomed back two past winners this year, including pianist and composer Bill Evans (Grammy victor for 1963's *Conversations with Myself* and 1968's *Bill Evans at the Montreux Jazz Festival*). His latest work, *Alone,* reaped him Best Jazz Performance by a Small Group or Soloist with Small Group. Miles Davis had won once before, too—in 1960 for *Sketches of Spain.* He now took the prize for large-group performance for *Bitches Brew,* the most commercially successful work of his career and one that also finally achieved what Davis had been attempting for years: a critically applauded fusion of jazz and rock.

The Best Country Song of the year was the one ranked highest on the c&w charts: "My Woman, My Woman, My Wife" by Marty Robbins, who last won a Grammy for his 1960 performance of "El Paso." He wrote "My Woman" for his wife of 15 years, Marizona Baldwin. It soon became one of the 50 Top 10 country hits of his career and one of the 14 that reached number one. (Twenty-four crossed over to the pop charts. Only Johnny Cash, Kenny Rogers and Glen Campbell have bettered his record.) Six weeks after its release, Robbins was named the 1960s' Artist of the Decade by the Country Music Association.

Last year's winner of Song of the Year, Joe South ("Games People Play"), had another crossover hit this year with "Rose Garden," which was also known as "I Never Promised You a Rose Garden." The song landed at number one in the pop charts for a week and spent five weeks at number one on the country rankings. Its success was due in large part to its crystal-voiced, guitar-strumming singer Lynn Anderson who easily took the prize for best female country vocal performance. Anderson was the daughter of Liz Anderson, a notable c&w vocalist for RCA and the wife of producer Glenn Sutton, who was also the coauthor of the 1966 Grammy sweeper "Almost Persuaded." She credited her success not with talent or connections, however, but with the message of the song. " 'Rose Garden' was perfectly timed," she told the Associated Press. "We were just coming out of the Vietnam years and a lot of people were trying to recover. The song's message was that you can make something out of nothing. You can take it and go ahead."

The male vocal country performance prize went to Ray Price, who won for a tune that would become one of his trademark songs, "For the Good Times." Price had had more than 50 hits in the Top 10 on the country charts—11 of which crossed over to the pop rankings—but "Good Times" was his first song to reach number one in the pop lineup. It also represented a brief period of his career during which he dropped the honky-tonk trappings of country music (including fiddle, banjo and steel guitar) in favor of violins and a more symphonic sound.

Winners of the prize for best duo or group vocal performance were husband and wife Johnny Cash and June Carter, for "If I Were a Carpenter," one of their five joint Top 40 hits. (Another was "Jackson," for which they won their last Grammy together in 1967.)

In 1970, Chet Atkins declared in an ad in *Billboard* that renowned session guitarist Jerry Reed was "one of the greatest undeveloped talents I have ever known." Atkins was vice-president of the country music division of RCA Records at the time and hoped to make Reed a star. "If Jerry doesn't make it big in the near future," he continued, "I will probably quit my job, because if that is true, I do not know talent." Atkins's job was secure thanks in large part to his own initiative. In 1970, he and Guitar Man Reed teamed up for a popular LP, *Me and Jerry,* which earned them the Grammy for best instrumental performance, which Atkins had last won in 1967.

The Best Gospel Performance went to the controversial Oak Ridge Boys for "Talk About the Good Times." The Tennessee quartet may have been approved by Grammy voters, but they were losing popularity with the broader spectrum of the religiously devout in 1970 as they added pop/rock qualities to their sound, let their hair grow long and made sexually suggestive movements onstage.

Texas blues guitarist Aaron "T-Bone" Walker, who helped to modernize country music by introducing more jazzy and electric elements, garnered Best Ethnic or Traditional Recording for "Good Feelin'."

Flip Wilson finally ended Bill Cosby's six-year reign over the comedy category when his *The Devil Made Me Buy This Dress* bested the champ's latest nominated LP, *Live at Madison Square Garden.* Wilson was the star of his own hit

> John Lennon said about *Let It Be*: "This is us with our trousers off."

TV variety series that premiered in 1970 and he produced popular humor albums like *Flippin'* and *Flip Wilson, You Devil You.* Typical of his routines on record was his version of Christopher Columbus's discovery of America, in which Spain's Queen Isabella, a Ray Charles fan, hands Columbus a traveler's check to get him to America. "You gonna find Ray Charles? He in America?" she asks. "Damn right," Columbus answers. "That's where all those records come from."

Only once before, in 1967, did the same LP win both Classical Album of the Year and Best Opera Recording. Now the honors were shared by the first complete version of Berlioz's *Les Troyens,* with Colin Davis conducting the Chorus and Orchestra of the Royal Opera House and featuring tenor Jon Vickers and soprano Berit Lindholm (neither of whom was nominated for the vocalist's laurel, although both received rave notices; mezzo-soprano Janet Baker *was* nominated for her excerpts from the same work in a separate recording). During his lifetime, Berlioz had been forced to scale back his four-hour opera into two parts before its first performance. In 1969, the halves were combined and carefully reintegrated. "Now, more than a hundred years after its completion," wrote *High Fidelity,* "the opera's fortunes have clearly turned for the better" thanks to this "marvelous" recording.

Germany's most famous baritone, Dietrich Fischer-Dieskau, ended up taking the vocal honors for the most ambitious accomplishment of his career: a 25-disc, two-volume set of 400 songs by Schubert. "The result is, without question, an extraordinary panorama of Schubert's achievements as a Lied composer," *High Fidelity* said.

Among the losing nominees for best album was the winner of the orchestral honors: conductor Pierre Boulez and the Cleveland Orchestra's performance of Stravinsky's latest (1967) rendition of *Le Sacre du Printemps. High Fidelity* called

Conductor Pierre Boulez scored his fifth career Grammy for Stravinsky's *Le Sacre du Printemps.*

it "a reading of great authority and panache that Boulez gives us, and a worthy replacement for his earlier version in the front line of *Rite* recordings."

Another losing nominee for best classical LP was a winner of the soloist's award for violinist David Oistrakh and cellist Mstislav Rostropovich—Brahms's Double Concerto, the first concerto in music history to pair those two musical instruments. The teaming of the artists was hailed as "heaven-ordained" by critics. Violinist Isaac Stern teamed up with cellist Leonard Rose and pianist Eugene Istomin for their best chamber music performance of Beethoven's complete piano trios. *High Fidelity*'s reviewer called their interpretation "occasionally touched by Romantic nuances, but more classical than anything else, hence the closest to what I take to be the style Beethoven himself intended for this music."

The recipients of the choral laurels were the Gregg Smith Singers and Columbia Chamber Ensemble performing *New Music of Charles Ives,* which included "Duty" and "Vita" among what *High Fidelity* called the "masterpieces made available here in superb performances, superbly recorded."

Despite "minor flubs," *Variety* noted that Grammy's TV debut was "a handsome show emceed by Andy Williams. Emanating from the Palladium for live airing in east and midwest and tape delay here [L.A.], Grammy Awards show avoided the customary self-congratulatory fever and concentrated on music and entertainment.

"Performances of five nominees for song of the year were mini-specials, Anne Murray chanting an exciting 'Fire and Rain'; Aretha Franklin playing and singing 'Bridge Over Troubled Water'; Osmond Bros. whipping up 'Everything Is Beautiful'; a tremendous 'Let It Be' by Dionne Warwick; Carpenters giving out a fine 'We've Only Just Begun.' "

Banter included Andy Williams telling John Wayne, "Lawrence Welk is backstage talking to Three Dog Night." Wayne demanded: "What about?"

Variety described some of the "minor flubs": "Presenters Zsa Zsa Gabor and Bob Newhart lost their routine somewhere midpoint." There was also a major fiasco: "Not all of the drama was seen on TV, however, for just as the show ended there was a near-tragedy. A TV light hanging over the center of the auditorium exploded, with pieces showering on the audience. The dress of Mrs. Howard (Shelley) Stark, wife of the vice president of ABC Records, caught fire. The flames were quickly smothered as L.A. and Palladium firemen rushed to her assistance."

Another *Variety* writer did not like the show, claiming it "made nobody happy except Columbia Records," which won nearly half of the awards (18), compared to 4 for its nearest rival, RCA.

Other "raps were also heard from the classical disc departments," *Variety* added. "They point out that not a single Grammy Award in a classical category was made on the national TV hookup."

Rev. Martin Luther King, Jr., reaped a Grammy posthumously for *Why I Oppose the War in Vietnam*, winner of Best Spoken Word Recording over Apollo astronauts and Bill Cosby.

Variety had predicted that music "pace-setter" James Taylor would do well this year, but was clearly disappointed when he won none, despite five nominations, including ones for Record, Song and Album of the Year. "This omission," it said, "was ascribed to the failure of the young members of the industry to participate in the work of N.A.R.A.S. Efforts to bring new talent into N.A.R.A.S. have not resulted in much success. In one case, a representative of the new generation was placed on the N.A.R.A.S. council, but he never showed up. These types, it's been pointed out, are distinctly anti-organizational."

After the show, *Variety*'s Archerd noted, "John Wayne was surprised when reporters asked howcum he was at the Grammys. He reminded them he was the original 'Singin' Sam,' but couldn't take it, quit and a fella named Gene Autry got his film start."

• 1970 •

The first live telecast of the awards was aired by ABC from the Hollywood Palladium in Los Angeles on March 16, 1971, for the awards eligibility period of November 2, 1969, to October 15, 1970.

ALBUM OF THE YEAR
• *Bridge Over Troubled Water*, Simon & Garfunkel. Columbia.
Chicago, Chicago. Columbia.
Close to You, Carpenters. A&M.

Déja Vu, Crosby, Stills, Nash & Young. A&M.
Elton John, Elton John. Uni.
Sweet Baby James, James Taylor. Warner Bros.

RECORD OF THE YEAR
• "Bridge Over Troubled Water," Simon & Garfunkel. Columbia.
"Close to You," Carpenters. A&M.
"Everything Is Beautiful," Ray Stevens. Barnaby.
"Fire and Rain," James Taylor. Warner Bros.
"Let It Be," Beatles. Apple.

SONG OF THE YEAR
(Songwriter's Award)
• "Bridge Over Troubled Water," Paul Simon.
"Everything Is Beautiful," Ray Stevens.
"Fire and Rain," James Taylor.
"Let It Be," John Lennon, Paul McCartney.
"We've Only Just Begun," Roger Nichols, Paul Williams.

BEST NEW ARTIST
• Carpenters
Elton John
Melba Moore
Anne Murray
Partridge Family

BEST CONTEMPORARY VOCAL PERFORMANCE, MALE
• Ray Stevens, "Everything Is Beautiful." Barnaby.
Joe Cocker, *Mad Dogs and Englishmen*. A&M.
Brook Benton, "Rainy Night in Georgia." Cotillion.
Elton John, *Elton John*. Uni.
James Taylor, *Sweet Baby James*. Warner Bros.

BEST CONTEMPORARY VOCAL PERFORMANCE, FEMALE
• Dionne Warwick, "I'll Never Fall in Love Again." Scepter.

Bobbie Gentry, *Fancy*. Capitol.
Anne Murray, "Snowbird." Capitol.
Linda Ronstadt, *Long Long Time*. Capitol.
Diana Ross, "Ain't No Mountain High Enough." Motown.

BEST CONTEMPORARY VOCAL PERFORMANCE BY A DUO, GROUP OR CHORUS
• Carpenters, "Close to You." A&M.
Beatles, "Let It Be." Apple.
Chicago, *Chicago*. Columbia.
Jackson 5, "ABC." Motown.
Simon & Garfunkel, "Bridge Over Troubled Water." Columbia.

BEST CONTEMPORARY SONG
(Songwriter's Award)
• "Bridge Over Troubled Water," Paul Simon.
"Everything Is Beautiful," Ray Stevens.
"Fire and Rain," James Taylor.
"Let It Be," John Lennon, Paul McCartney.
"We've Only Just Begun," Roger Nichols, Paul Williams.

BEST CONTEMPORARY INSTRUMENTAL PERFORMANCE
• Henry Mancini, *Theme from "Z" and Other Film Music*. RCA.
Assembled Multitude, "Overture from *Tommy*." Atlantic.
Vincent Bell, *"Airport* Love Theme." Decca.
Jimi Hendrix, "Star Spangled Banner." Cotillion.
Quincy Jones, "Soul Flower." United Artists.

BEST RHYTHM & BLUES SONG
(Songwriter's Award)
• "Patches," Ronald Dunbar, General Johnson.
"Didn't I (Blow Your Mind This Time)," Thom Bell, William Hart. Philly Groove.
"Groovy Situation," Russell Lewis, Herman Davis.

"Signed, Sealed, Delivered," Stevie Wonder, Lee Garrett, Syreeta Wright, Lulu Hardaway.

"Somebody's Been Sleeping in My Bed," Greg Perry, General Johnson, Angelo Bond.

BEST RHYTHM & BLUES VOCAL PERFORMANCE, MALE

• B. B. King, "The Thrill Is Gone." ABC.

Clarence Carter, "Patches." Atlantic.

Wilson Pickett, "Engine No. 9." Atlantic.

Edwin Starr, "War." Gordy.

Stevie Wonder, "Signed, Sealed, Delivered." Tamla/Motown.

BEST RHYTHM & BLUES VOCAL PERFORMANCE, FEMALE

• Aretha Franklin, "Don't Play That Song." Atlantic.

Esther Phillips, "Set Me Free." Atlantic.

Nina Simone, *Black Gold*. RCA.

Candi Staton, "Stand By Your Man." Fame.

Dee Dee Warwick, "She Didn't Know." Atco.

BEST RHYTHM & BLUES PERFORMANCE BY A DUO OR GROUP (VOCAL OR INSTRUMENTAL)

• Delfonics, "Didn't I (Blow Your Mind This Time)." Philly Groove.

Four Tops, "It's All in the Game." Motown.

100 Proof, "Somebody's Been Sleeping in My Bed." Buddah.

Presidents, "5-10-15-20 (25-30 Years of Love)." Buddah.

Charles Wright & the Watts 103rd Street Rhythm Band, "Express Yourself." Warner Bros.

BEST JAZZ PERFORMANCE BY A SMALL GROUP OR SOLOIST WITH SMALL GROUP (7 OR FEWER)

• Bill Evans, *Alone*. MGM.

Gary Burton, *Good-Vibes*. Atlantic.

John Coltrane, *Coltrane Legacy*. Atlantic.

Erroll Garner, *Feeling Is Believing*. Octave.

Herbie Hancock, *Fat Albert Rotunda*. Warner Bros.

Milt Jackson Quintet with Ray Brown, *That's the Way It Is*. Impulse.

Les McCann, Eddie Harris, *Swiss Movement*. Atlantic.

BEST JAZZ PERFORMANCE BY A LARGE GROUP OR SOLOIST WITH LARGE GROUP (8 OR MORE)

• Miles Davis, *Bitches Brew*. Columbia.

Paul Desmond, *Bridge Over Troubled Water*. A&R.

Duke Ellington, *Duke Ellington, 70th Birthday Concert*. Solid State.

Don Ellis, *Don Ellis at Fillmore*. Columbia.

Johnny Hodges, *Three Shades of Blue*. Flying Dutchman.

Quincy Jones, *Gula Matari*. A&M.

Thad Jones, Mel Lewis, *Consummation*. Blue Note.

World's Greatest Jazzband, *Live at the Roosevelt Grill*. Atlantic.

BEST COUNTRY SONG
(Songwriter's Award)

• "My Woman, My Woman, My Wife," Marty Robbins.

"The Fightin' Side of Me," Merle Haggard.

"Hello Darlin'," Conway Twitty.

"Is Anybody Goin' to San Antone," Glenn Martin, Dave Kirby.

"Wonder Could I Live There Anymore," Bill Rice.

BEST COUNTRY INSTRUMENTAL PERFORMANCE

• Chet Atkins, Jerry Reed, *Me and Jerry*. RCA.

Chet Atkins, "Yestergroovin'." RCA.

Danny Davis & the Nashville Brass, "You Ain't Heard Nothin' Yet." RCA.

Merle Haggard & the Stranger, "Street Singer." Capitol.

Jerry Smith, "Drivin' Home." Decca.

BEST COUNTRY VOCAL PERFORMANCE, MALE

- Ray Price, "For the Good Times." Columbia.

Johnny Cash, "Sunday Morning Coming Down." Columbia.

Merle Haggard, *Okie from Muskogee*. Capitol.

Charley Pride, *Charley Pride's 10th Album*. Columbia.

Jerry Reed, "Amos Moses." RCA.

BEST COUNTRY VOCAL PERFORMANCE, FEMALE

- Lynn Anderson, "Rose Garden." Columbia.

Wanda Jackson, "A Woman Lives for Love." Capitol.

Dolly Parton, "Mule Skinner Blues." RCA.

Jean Shepard, "Then He Touched Me." Capitol.

Tammy Wynette, "Run, Woman, Run." Epic.

BEST COUNTRY VOCAL PERFORMANCE BY A DUO OR GROUP

- Johnny Cash, June Carter, "If I Were a Carpenter." Columbia.

Jack Blanchard, Misty Morgan, "Tennessee Birdwalk." Wayside.

Statler Brothers, "Bed of Roses." Mercury.

Waylon Jennings, Jessi Colter, "Suspicious Minds." RCA.

Porter Wagoner, Dolly Parton, "Daddy Was an Old-Time Preacher Man." RCA.

BEST SACRED PERFORMANCE, MUSICAL

- Jake Hess, "Everything Is Beautiful." RCA.

Pat Boone, "Rapture." Supreme.

Ralph Carmichael Orchestra and Chorus, "The Centurion." Light.

Mormon Tabernacle Choir, Richard Condie conducting, "God of Our Fathers." Columbia.

George Beverly Shea, "There Is More to Life." RCA.

BEST GOSPEL PERFORMANCE (OTHER THAN SOUL GOSPEL)

- Oak Ridge Boys, "Talk About the Good Times." Heartwarming.

Wendy Bagwell & the Sunliters, "Talk About the Good Times." Canaan.

Florida Boys, *The Many Moods of the Florida Boys*. Canaan.

LeFevres, *Moving Up*. Canaan.

Thrasher Brothers, "Fantastic Thrashers at Fantastic Caverns." Canaan.

BEST SOUL GOSPEL PERFORMANCE

- Edwin Hawkins Singers, "Every Man Wants to Be Free." Buddah.

James Cleveland, "Amazing Grace." Savoy.

Andrae Crouch, "Christian People." Liberty.

Jessy Dixon, "Hello Sunshine." Savoy.

Myrna Summers, "God Gave Me a Song." Cotillion.

BEST ETHNIC OR TRADITIONAL RECORDING (INCLUDING TRADITIONAL BLUES)

- "Good Feelin'," T-Bone Walker. Polydor.

Black Music of South America, David Lewisohn. Nonesuch.

Folk Fiddling from Sweden, Bjorn Stabi, Ole Hjorth. Nonesuch.

I Do Not Play No Rock and Roll, Mississippi Fred McDowell. Capitol.

Sail On, Muddy Waters. Chess.

"Shree Rag," Ali Akbar Khan, accompanied by Shankar Ghosh. Tabla. Connoisseur Society.

BEST INSTRUMENTAL ARRANGEMENT

- Henry Mancini, "Theme from *Z*" (Mancini). RCA.

Miles Davis, *Bitches Brew* (Miles Davis). Columbia.

Quincy Jones, "Gula Matari" (Quincy Jones). A&M.

Fred Selden, "The Magic Bus Ate My Donut" (Don Ellis). Columbia.

Tom Sellers, "Overture from *Tommy*" (Assembled Multitude). Atlantic.

Lalo Schifrin, "Theme from *Medical Center*" (Lalo Schifrin). MGM.

BEST INSTRUMENTAL COMPOSITION
(Composer's Award)

• Alfred Newman, *"Airport* Love Theme."

Miles Davis, "Bitches Brew."

Quincy Jones, "Gula Matari."

Henry Mancini, "Theme from *Sunflower*."

Lalo Schifrin, "Theme from *Medical Center*."

BEST SCORE FROM AN ORIGINAL CAST SHOW ALBUM

• *Company*, Stephen Sondheim, composer. Columbia.

Applause, Charles Strouse, Lee Adams, composers. ABC.

Coco, Alan Jay Lerner, André Previn, composers. Para.

Joy, Oscar Brown, Jr., Jean Pace, Sivuca, composers. RCA.

Purlie, Gary Geld, Peter Udell, composers. Ampex.

BEST ORIGINAL SCORE WRITTEN FOR A MOTION PICTURE OR TV SPECIAL
(Composer's Award)

• *Let It Be*, John Lennon, Paul McCartney, George Harrison, Ringo Starr. Apple.

Airport, Alfred Newman. Decca.

Darling Lili, Johnny Mercer, Henry Mancini. RCA.

*M*A*S*H*, Johnny Mandel. Columbia.

The Sterile Cuckoo, Fred Karlin. Paramount.

BEST ARRANGEMENT ACCOMPANYING VOCALIST(S)

• Paul Simon, Art Garfunkel, Jimmie Haskell, Ernie Freeman, Larry Knechtel, "Bridge Over Troubled Water" (Simon & Garfunkel). Columbia.

Richard Carpenter, "Close to You" (Carpenters). A&M.

Dick Halligan, "Lucretia MacEvil" (Blood, Sweat & Tears). Columbia.

Ray Stevens, "Everything Is Beautiful" (Ray Stevens). Barnaby.

ALBUM OF THE YEAR, CLASSICAL

• *Berlioz: Les Troyens*, Colin Davis conducting the Royal Opera House Orchestra and Chorus (solos: Vickers, Veasey, Lindholm). Philips.

Beethoven Edition 1970, Herbert von Karajan conducting the Berlin Philharmonic (solos: Oistrakh, Anda, Kempf, Goossens, Leitner, etc.). Deutsche Grammophon.

Brahms: Double Concerto (Concerto in A Minor for Violin and Cello), George Szell conducting the Cleveland Orchestra (solos: Oistrakh, Rostropovich). Angel.

Ives: Three Places in New England; Ruggles: Sun Treader, Michael Tilson Thomas conducting the Boston Symphony. Deutsche Grammophon.

Shostakovich: Symphony No. 13, Eugene Ormandy conducting the Philadelphia Symphony (R. Page directing the Male Chorus of the Mendelssohn Club of Philadelphia; solo: Krause). RCA.

Stravinsky: Le Sacre du Printemps, Pierre Boulez conducting the Cleveland Orchestra. Columbia.

BEST CLASSICAL PERFORMANCE, ORCHESTRA
(Conductor's Award)

• Pierre Boulez conducting the Cleveland Orchestra, *Stravinsky: Le Sacre du Printemps*. Columbia.

Carlo Maria Giulini conducting the Chicago Symphony, *Berlioz: Roméo et Juliette*. Angel.

Eugene Ormandy conducting the Philadelphia Symphony, *Mahler: Symphony No. 2 in C Minor ("Resurrection")*. RCA.

Seiji Ozawa conducting the Chicago Symphony, *Bartók: Concerto for Orchestra*. Angel.

Georg Solti conducting the Chicago Symphony, *Mahler: Symphony No. 6 in A Minor*. London.

George Szell conducting the Cleveland Orchestra, *Bruckner: Symphony No. 8 in C Minor*. Columbia.

George Szell conducting the Cleveland Orchestra, *Dvořák: Symphony No. 8 in G Major*. Angel.

Michael Tilson Thomas conducting the Boston Symphony, *Ives: Three Places in New England; Ruggles: Sun Treader*. Deutsche Grammophon.

BEST CLASSICAL PERFORMANCE, CHAMBER MUSIC (INCLUDING CHAMBER ORCHESTRA)

• Eugene Istomin, Isaac Stern, Leonard Rose, *Beethoven: The Complete Piano Trios*. Columbia.

Boston Symphony Chamber Players, *Schubert: Trio No. 1 in B Flat Major; Milhaud: Pastorale for Oboe, Clarinet and Bassoon; Hindemith: Kleine Lammer-Musik*. RCA.

Benjamin Britten conducting the English Chamber Orchestra and Ambrosian Singers, *Salute to Percy Grainger*. London.

Composers Quartet, *Carter: Quartets Nos. 1 and 2 for Strings*. Nonesuch.

Guarneri Quartet, *Beethoven: The 5 Late Quartets*. RCA.

Sviatoslav Richter, David Oistrakh, *Franck: Sonata in A Major for Violin and Piano; Brahms: Sonata No. 3 in D Minor*. Angel.

Gunther Schuller, *Ives: Calcium Light Night*. CBS.

BEST CLASSICAL PERFORMANCE, INSTRUMENTAL SOLOIST(S) (WITH OR WITHOUT ORCHESTRA)

• David Oistrakh, Mstislav Rostropovich (Szell conducting the Cleveland Orchestra), *Brahms: Double Concerto (Concerto in A Minor for Violin and Cello)*. Angel.

Walter Carlos, *The Well-Tempered Synthesizer*. Columbia.

Glenn Gould, *Bach: The Well-Tempered Clavier, Book 2, Nos. 9–16*. CBS.

Vladimir Horowitz, *Schumann: Kreisleriana*. Columbia.

Ivan Moravec, *Beethoven: Sonatas No. 26, Op. 81a ("Les Adieux"), and No. 15, Op. 28 ("Pastoral")*. Connoisseur Society.

David Oistrakh (Szell conducting the Cleveland Orchestra), *Brahms: Concerto in D Major for Violin*. Angel.

Mstislav Rostropovich (Britten, conductor), *Britten: Suites for Cello (2)*. London.

Van Cliburn (Ormandy conducting the Philadelphia Symphony), *Chopin: Concerto No. 1 in E Minor for Piano*. RCA.

Alexis Weissenberg (Ormandy conducting the Philadelphia Symphony), *Bartók: Concerto No. 2 for Piano*. RCA.

BEST OPERA RECORDING

Berlioz: Les Troyens, Colin Davis conducting the Royal Opera House Orchestra and Chorus (solos: Vickers, Veasey, Lindholm). Philips.

Debussy: Pelléas et Mélisande, Pierre Boulez conducting the Orchestra of Royal Opera House (solos: McIntyre, Shirley, Soederstroem, David, Ward, etc.). Columbia.

R. Strauss: Der Rosenkavalier, Georg Solti conducting the Vienna Philharmonic (solos: Crespin, Minton, Donath, Jungwirth). London.

Verdi: Il Trovatore, Zubin Mehta conducting the New Philharmonia Orchestra, Ambrosian Opera Chorus (solos: Price, Domingo, Milnes, Cossotto). RCA.

Wagner: Götterdämmerung, Herbert von Karajan conducting the Berlin Philharmonic, Deutsche Oper Chorus (solos: Brilioth, Stewart, Keleman, Dernesch, Janowitz, Ludwig, Chookasian). Deutsche Grammophon.

BEST CHORAL PERFORMANCE (OTHER THAN OPERA)

- Gregg Smith conducting the Gregg Smith Singers and Columbia Chamber Ensemble, *New Music of Charles Ives*. Columbia.

Arthur Oldham conducting the London Symphony Orchestra Chorus; Pierre Boulez conducting the London Symphony, *Mahler: Das Klagende Lied*. Columbia.

Robert E. Page directing the Male Chorus of the Mendelssohn Club of Philadelphia; Eugene Ormandy conducting the Philadelphia Symphony, *Shostakovich: Symphony No. 13*. RCA.

Reinhold Schmid, Helmut Froschauer conducting the Vienna Singverein; Herbert von Karajan conducting the Berlin Philharmonic, *Haydn: The Creation*. Deutsche Grammophon.

Gregg Smith conducting the Ithaca College Concert Choir; Robert Craft conducting the Columbia Symphony, *The New Stravinsky*. Columbia.

Lorna Cooke de Varon directing the New England Conservatory Chorus; Katherine Edmonds Pusztai conducting the Children's Chorus of the New England Conservatory; Seiji Ozawa conducting the Boston Symphony, *Orff: Carmina Burana*. RCA.

David Willcocks conducting the Bach Choir and New Philharmonia, *Vaughan Williams: Five Tudor Portraits*. Angel.

BEST CLASSICAL PERFORMANCE, VOCAL SOLOIST

- Dietrich Fischer-Dieskau (Gerald Moore, accompanist), *Schubert: Lieder*. Deutsche Grammophon.

Janet Baker (Gibson conducting the London Symphony), "Death of Cleopatra" final scenes, *Berlioz: Les Troyens*. Angel.

Marilyn Horn (Lewis, conductor), *Mahler: Kindertotenlieder; Wagner: Wesendonck Lieder*. London.

Christa Ludwig, Walter Berry (Bernstein conducting the New York Philharmonic), *Mahler: Des Knaben Wunderhorn*. Columbia.

Leontyne Price (Downes conducting the London Symphony), *Prima Donna, Vol. 3*. RCA.

Beverly Sills (Ceccato conducting the London Philharmonic), *Mozart and Strauss Arias*. Audio Treasury.

BEST ENGINEERED RECORDING, CLASSICAL

- Fred Plaut, Ray Moore, Arthur Kendy, *Stravinsky: Le Sacre du Printemps* (Boulez conducting the Cleveland Orchestra). Columbia.

Walter Carlos, *The Well-Tempered Synthesizer* (Walter Carlos). Columbia.

Paul Goodman, *Shostakovich: Symphony No. 6 and Age of Gold* (Stokowski conducting the Chicago Symphony). RCA.

Gunter Hermanns, *Ives: Three Places in New England; Ruggles: Sun Treader* (Thomas conducting the Boston Symphony). Deutsche Grammophon.

Bernard Keville, *Shostakovich: Symphony No. 13* (Ormandy conducting the Philadelphia Symphony). RCA.

Gordon Parry, James Locke, *R. Strauss: Der Rosenkavalier* (Solti conducting the Vienna Philharmonic; solos: Crespin, Minton). London.

Carson C. Taylor, *Brahms: Double Concerto (Concerto in A Minor for Violin and Cello)* (Szell conducting the Cleveland Orchestra; solos: Oistrakh, Rostropovich). Angel.

BEST COMEDY RECORDING

- *The Devil Made Me Buy This Dress*, Flip Wilson. Little David.

The Begatting of the President, Orson Welles. Mediarts.

Daddy Played First Base, Homer & Jethro. RCA.

I Am the President, David Frye. Elektra.

Live at Madison Square Garden, Bill Cosby. Uni.

BEST SPOKEN WORD RECORDING

- *Why I Oppose the War in Vietnam,* Rev. Martin Luther King, Jr. Black Forum.

Everett Dirksen's America, Everett Dirksen. Bell.

Grover Henson Feels Forgotten, Bill Cosby. Uni.

In the Beginning (Apollo 8, 11, 12 astronauts, Presidents Kennedy and Nixon). Creative Sound.

Poems and Ballads from 100-Plus American Poets (Ambrose, Dryden, Hecht, Molloy, Seeger). Scholastic.

The Soft Sea, Jesse Pearson. Warner Bros.

BEST RECORDING FOR CHILDREN

- *Sesame Street* (*Sesame Street* TV cast), Children's Television Workshop. Columbia.

Aristocats, Tutti Camarata, musical producer (Camarata, Holloway, Harris, Lester, Mike Sammes Singers). Disneyland.

A Boy Named Charlie Brown (soundtrack). Columbia.

Rubber Duckie, Jim Henson. Columbia.

Susan Sings Songs from "Sesame Street," Loretta Long. Scepter.

BEST ENGINEERED RECORDING

- Roy Halee, *Bridge Over Troubled Water* (Simon & Garfunkel). Columbia.

Ray Gerhardt, Dick Bogert, *Close to You* (Carpenters). A&M.

Peter Klemt, *The Kaempfert Touch* (B. Kaempfert & Orchestra). Decca.

Armin Steiner, *Tap Root Manuscript* (Neil Diamond). Uni.

Derek Vernals, Adrian Martins, Robin Thompson, *To Our Children's Children's Children* (Moody Blues). Threshold.

BEST ALBUM COVER
(Art Director's Award)

- Robert Lockart, design; Ivan Nagy, photography, *Indianola Mississippi Seeds* (B. B. King). ABC.

John Berg, Nick Fasciano, *Chicago* (Chicago). Columbia.

John Berg, Philip Hays, Lloyd Ziff, *The World's Greatest Blues Singer* (Bessie Smith). Columbia.

Ed Thrasher, Dave Bhang, *Hand Made* (Mason Williams). Warner Bros.

Desmond Strobel, John Craig, *The Naked Carmen* (various). Mercury.

Peter Whorf, Martin Donald, Christopher Whorf, *Mason Proffit* (Mason Proffit). Paper Tiger.

Peter Whorf, Christopher Whorf, Fred Poore, *Schubert: "Unfinished" Symphony; Beethoven: Fifth Symphony* (Rodzinski conducting the Philharmonic Symphony Orchestra of London). Westminster Gold.

Woody Woodward, art director; William E. McEuen, photographer; Dean O. Torrance, album design, *Uncle Charlie and His Dog Teddy* (Nitty Gritty Dirt Band). United Artists.

BEST ALBUM NOTES
(Annotator's Award)

- Chris Albertson, *The World's Greatest Blues Singer* (Bessie Smith). Columbia.

Billy Edd Wheeler, *As I See It* (Jack Moran). Athena.

Ralph J. Gleason, *Bitches Brew* (Miles Davis). Columbia.

Rod McKuen, *Hold Back the World* (Alexander's Greyhound Brass). Stanyan.

Anthony d'Oberoff, *I Do Not Play No Rock and Roll* (Mississippi Fred McDowell). Capitol.

Rex Reed, *Judy. London. 1969.* (Judy Garland). Juno.

James Goodfriend, *Sixteen All Time Greatest Hits* (Bill Monroe & the Blue Grass Boys). Columbia.

Arthur Knight, *They Shoot Horses, Don't They?* (John Green Orchestra). ABC.

• 1971 •

Carole King, Grammy Queen

Last year Simon & Garfunkel set a new Grammy record by sweeping all three top awards: Album, Record and Song of the Year. Now a new rookie artist pulled off a coup by seizing *more* than the Triple Crown.

Carole King was little known to the public before producing one of the most popular and critically lauded LPs of the era. *Tapestry* turned out to be not only the best-selling album of 1971, but it swept Grammy's three highest prizes *plus* the female pop vocals performance laurels—thereby topping Simon & Garfunkel's accomplishment (the duo lost the duo/group vocals award last year to the Carpenters).

Prior to her new stature as a vocalist, Carole King had already proved herself as the most successful female songwriter in music history, having composed eight number-one hit records, including "Will You Love Me Tomorrow?" for the Shirelles and "Hi-De-Ho" for Blood, Sweat & Tears. She wrote or cowrote all twelve numbers on *Tapestry,* including "It's Too Late" (Record of the Year), "You've Got a Friend" (Song of the Year) and "Tapestry" (vocal performance award).

The new queen of the Grammys could not, however, be on hand for her big night at the Felt Forum at New York's Madison Square Garden, where the ceremony was broadcast on ABC-TV to a national audience for the second year in a row. Instead, King remained in Los Angeles while her producer Lou Adler accepted her four trophies (one for each of four nominations) on her behalf. "The reason Carole is not here is that she just had a baby and is home learning to be

Carole King topped Paul Simon's 1970 Triple Crown victory by adding the pop vocals prize to *Tapestry*'s wins for best record, song and album.

mother of the year," he told the audience cheerfully.

King was not nominated for Record of the Year for "You've Got a Friend" because she never released it as a single. Roberta Flack and Donny Hathaway did, however, and were now up for Grammy's best r&b duo performance prize for their own version of it. King's real-life friend James Taylor recorded it, too (on *Mud Slide Slim and the Blue Horizon*), and was nominated for Record of the Year as well as the one trophy he would take this year: Best Pop Vocal Performance, Male (changed from the "contemporary" classification of last year). As good friends as King and Taylor were, though (she played piano on his *Sweet Baby James* album and toured 27 cities with him as his opening act in early 1971), she has always insisted that "Friend" was not Taylor-made. " 'You've Got a Friend' was not written for James," she once said. "It was one of those moments when

I sat down at the piano and it wrote itself from some place other than me."

Winner of the year's Best New Artist prize, Carly Simon, was similar in spirit and music style to Taylor and King and also happened to be personally close to them (she would become Mrs. James Taylor eight months after the Grammy-cast). Simon had two hit albums out in 1971—*Carly Simon* (with its number-10-ranked single "That's the Way I've Always Heard It Should Be") and *Antici-pation* (the title track of which reached number 13 as a single). Together, she, Taylor and King were leaders of a new '70s sound. The counterculture revolution of the 1960s had championed music that was usually loud, electric and shocking. King, Taylor and Simon represented a more mature and introspective approach, producing guitar-strumming tunes full of longing, love and a new adult sense of disillusionment.

Simon and Taylor were not present on Grammy night, choosing instead to take a leisurely drive together along the scenic coastal road between Los Angeles and San Francisco. At dusk, the lovers found accommodations and pulled off for the night, never even bothering to turn on a radio. They learned of their double victories the next morning when they found a note tacked to their door that read "You won!" It was from their manager, who tracked them down during the night after calling every hotel he could locate along U.S. Route 1.

Rock music was also expected to do well at this year's Grammys—even according to Richard and Karen Carpenter, last year's winners of the group vocals honors, who returned to reclaim the category with their self-titled album that included such hits as "For All We Know" and "Rainy Days and Mondays."

"We were really surprised," Richard said, picking up the award. "We both felt [Three Dog Night's] 'Joy to the World' would be the easy winner." Commenting on the Carpenters' victory, *Variety* har-rumphed, "As usual, the N.A.R.A.S. vote completely brushed off the hard rock sound."

Harder-sounding music nonetheless triumphed when Isaac Hayes and his score to the film *Shaft* picked up the sec-ond-most prizes of the night (three): Best Original Score Written for a Motion Pic-ture or TV special (beating *Love Story,* much to the surprise of N.A.R.A.S.'s crit-ics), Best Instrumental Arrangement and Best Engineered Recording. When Hayes picked up his first of the three, the audience at the Felt Forum ceremony gave him a one-minute standing ovation.

Shaft had started out with the most Grammy nominations of the year (eight), a number that amounted to a generous reflection of what music industry insid-ers thought of Hayes. He was clearly one of their own. As a session sax and piano player, he'd worked for Otis Redding and other soul greats in the 1960s. He was also an accomplished songwriter, pen-ning "Soul Man" and "Hold On, I'm Comin'" for Sam and Dave and "B-A-B-Y" for Carla Thomas. Hayes started singing his own material in 1967, but it wasn't until his *Hot Buttered Soul* LP (1969) that he became widely known as a performer. *Shaft* turned him into a super-star. Backstage at the Grammys, he told reporters that winning "made all the hard work worthwhile." Four weeks later, "Theme from *Shaft*" won Best Song at the Oscars, too.

One of the five awards that Hayes lost was for best male r&b performance, which went to three-time past Grammy champ Lou Rawls ("A Natural Man"), who also beat B. B. King, Marvin Gaye and Stevie Wonder, triggering some con-troversy. ("Rawls is considered more of a pop than a r&b performer," *Variety* insisted.) Clasping his fourth statuette at the podium, Rawls said, "There was some heavy, heavy competition and I'm real surprised and truly honored."

After Ike and Tina Turner recorded "Proud Mary," Tina announced that she was now a rock & roll singer instead of an r&b vocalist. She did not, however, refuse the r&b award for best vocal performance by a group when it went to her and Ike for the same single, a cut from the last album they did for Liberty Records, *Workin' Together*.

There was no surprise over the winner of the year's Best Rhythm & Blues Song, "Ain't No Sunshine," which had reached number three at its peak on the pop singles charts in 1971. "Sunshine" was written by the same artist who sang it—Bill Withers, a losing nominee for Best New Artist. The soul singer from West Virginia had moved to California in 1967 to pursue a recording career, started making music for Sussex records in 1970 and made his first professional appearance in 1971 at the age of 33.

Lady Soul, Aretha Franklin, held on to the laurels for best female r&b vocal performance for the fifth year in a row when she covered Simon & Garfunkel's "Bridge Over Troubled Water." The one-time gospel singer gave the 1970 Grammy-winning tune an inspired reading, too, which included a two-minute intro of just instrumental mood-setting music and Franklin's call-and-response interchange with her backup singers.

Another repeat winner from last year was Paul McCartney, who claimed Best Arrangement Accompanying Vocalist(s) for "Uncle Albert/Admiral Halsey" from his second solo album, *Ram*. (McCartney once told an interviewer that he actually did have an Uncle Albert, "who used to quote the Bible to everyone when he got drunk. It was the only time he ever read the Bible.")

Chicago bluesman Muddy Waters, who had made a profound influence on McCartney and the other Beatles back in the early '60s, was now demonstrating how rock & roll in turn affected his creative work on *They Call Me Muddy Waters*, winner of the year's Best Ethnic or Traditional Recording. Waters's real name was McKinley Morganfield. He acquired the nickname because he liked to play in the muddy creeks back on the Mississippi Delta farm where he grew up.

Los Angeles Public Library

Bill Withers accepted his Grammy for Best R&B Song "Sunshine" from Isaac Hayes who won three awards for his filmscore to *Shaft*.

Three-time past Grammy winner Bill Evans returned from last year to claim two more, both for *The Bill Evans Album*, a two-disc set that featured the jazz pianist and composer's original works. Evans's career was on the upswing in 1971, buoyed by the additions in his private life of a new wife and child. He formed a new trio, too, which included Eddie Gomez on bass and Marty Morrell on drums. Previously, the jazz Grammys were separated into categories for large and small groups (or soloist with large or small group), but when a third slot was added by N.A.R.A.S., it caused the honors to be split into three areas—soloist, group and big-band performance—the first two of which were won by Evans.

The big-band prize went to Duke Ellington and his orchestra for their performance of one of the Duke's late masterpieces, "New Orleans Suite," his tribute to such greats as Louis Armstrong and Mahalia Jackson, both of whom died last year. Armstrong and Jackson were honored this year with the Recording Academy's Bing Crosby Award.

Singer-songwriter Kris Kristofferson was a newcomer to the country and pop charts when he began the Grammy race with the second-most nominations of the year (five). Three were for writing three contenders for Best Country Song: "Help Me Make It Through the Night," "Me and Bobby McGee" and "For the Good Times." The winner was "Help Me," which was also a nominee for Song of the Year, as was "Bobby McGee." Kristofferson was inspired to write "Help Me" after reading an interview with Frank Sinatra in which Ol' Blue Eyes talked candidly about using the comforts of a woman or a bottle to get through the darkest hours of a day. "Help Me" became a brilliant success. It was named Single of the Year by the Country Music Association and sold more than 2 million copies when it was recorded by Sammi Smith, who beat former Grammy winners Tammy Wynette, Jody Miller and Lynn Anderson (plus future winner Dolly Parton) for the best female country vocal performance award.

Best song "You've Got a Friend" was not (James) Taylor-made.

Kristofferson recorded "Help Me" on his 1971 debut album as well as "Me and Bobby McGee," which was covered—and immortalized—by Janis Joplin, a losing nominee (posthumously) for best female pop vocal performance. Joplin died from a heroin overdose in October 1970.

The other two country categories went to two winners from last year: Chet Atkins and Jerry Reed. Atkins took the instrumental performance prize for his album *Snowbird* as his third Grammy. Reed took the male vocal performance laurels for singing a song of his own that was written as a fluke. In the early 1970s, Reed was a popular supporting TV star on *The Glen Campbell Goodtime Hour*. One day when he couldn't remember his next line on the program, he ad-libbed, saying, "When you're hot, you're hot!" The audience roared with approval and Reed had a song idea that would become a classic party tune.

Singer Charley Pride was not only one of the first blacks to break the color barrier in country & western music, he was voted Entertainer of the Year (and Male Vocalist of the Year) by the Country Music Association in 1971 in addition to being honored for Grammy's Best Sacred Performance for *Did You Think to Pray* as well as the year's Best Gospel Performance with "Let Me Live." Best Soul Gospel Performance was given to Shirley Caesar, who scored a country and pop hit as well with her *Put Your Hand in the Hand of the Man from Galilee*.

Bill Cosby was nominated again in the comedy album category (*When I Was a Kid*) but failed to reclaim the prize, which went instead to Lily Tomlin's *This Is a Recording*. Cosby still kidded around, however, in a more serious way to win Best Recording for Children for *Bill Cosby Talks to Kids About Drugs*.

The choice for Classical Album of the Year and for best instrumental solo performance was *Horowitz Plays Rachmaninov*, the now 10-time Grammy winner's tribute to the composer who once promised never again to play his Third Concerto after hearing a young Vladimir Horowitz perform it to perfection in the early '20s (a vow Rachmaninov nonetheless broke in 1939). In this recording, which included Etudes Tableaux, Opp. 33 and 39, plus Preludes for Piano, Opp. 23 and 32, "Horowitz's extra voltage and insight are manifest in innumerable ways," said *High Fidelity*. The same magazine was less kind about the winner of the orchestral laurels, guest conductor Carlo Maria Giulini and the Chicago Symphony for Mahler's Symphony No. 1 in D. "Giulini views the world from a narrow, Italian viewpoint that tends to reduce nearly everything to theatrics and to the strong display of rudimentary emotions," it said. "This is a position quite at odds with the personality of Mahler."

The fact that conductor Colin Davis and the London Symphony Orchestra would someday perform Berlioz's *Requiem* was considered "inevitable" by *High Fidelity,* which applauded the outcome: "This performance elucidates more dimensions of the work than any to date," it said, "and it has been recorded with considerable success by Philips engineers" at London's Westminster Cathedral. The album was awarded the engineering prize as a result, as well as the choral honors for the Wandsworth School Boys' Choir and the London Symphony Chorus. The Juilliard Quartet received the chamber music award for quartets by Ravel and Debussy. "There will always be competing ideas about how to play these two quartets, but in this release the Juilliard once again establishes itself as the leading proponent of the objective approach," said *High Fidelity.*

In 1962, when Leontyne Price recorded *Aida* with Georg Solti and the Rome Opera House Orchestra and Chorus, the LP was named Grammy's Classical Album of the Year. In honor of the opera's 100th anniversary, Price again recorded it, this time with Erich Leinsdorf and the London Symphony Orchestra (as well as Placido Domingo singing Radames), reprising the top opera album honors. "The new RCA set captures her somewhere near peak form," *High Fidelity* said, "singing with memorable beauty and relevance. Comparing her present performance with the one she made nine years ago, one notes a definite maturing of the voice, a certain caution now and then where she was formerly more free; but there is a compensating degree of command, of mastery not always present in the earlier version." Price, however, failed to be nominated for the vocal honors for her portrayal of the Ethiopian princess. Instead, she was nominated—and triumphed—for her tribute to Robert Schumann, including his *Widmung* and *Frauenliebe und Leben.*

Charley Pride was doubly blessed with honors for both Best Sacred and Best Gospel Performances.

Three weeks before the awards ceremony, serious Grammy-bashing began. Under the headline "That Yrly. Debate Already On Over Grammy Awards," *Variety* quoted record exec David Geffen saying, "The Grammy Awards mean nothing to me. There are a lot of better records out every year that never get nominated." Past Grammy grabber Henry Mancini (the award's biggest winner with 20 statuettes) rallied to the prize's defense, saying, "The thing I like about the Grammys is that they always give the new people a shot."

Come awards night, harmony seemed to reign again.

"The disc industry Grammy Awards shows are getting better," *Variety* said in its wrap-up coverage. The program "was marked by solid entertainment, attractive production values, sharp timing and an ingratiating emcee stint by Andy Williams. . . . The only sour note in the show was a nasty remark by Leonard Bernstein, who said he was leaving the proceedings to go home and watch *West Side Story* on another network."

West Side Story was being shown at the same time on NBC that the Grammys were being aired on ABC. "The film figured to swamp the Grammy Awards show in the ratings anyway," said *Variety*, "and did."

Fifteen hundred people packed the Felt Forum to be on hand to witness the awards despite having to battle a horrid New York night of rain and sleet. Presenters included Ed Sullivan, the Temptations, Richard Harris, the Carpenters, Roberta Flack and the 5th Dimension. In Los Angeles, 1,200 people watched the ceremony on closed-circuit TV at a party held at the Century Plaza Hotel.

Some complaints were also heard. "Once again there was a notable absence of rock music in the major citations," the *New York Times* observed. "If anything, both the nominees and the winners were dominated by representatives from what can best be described as the music business Establishment."

Variety agreed, adding the following complaint: "Such acts as the Rolling Stones, Grand Funk Railroad, Rod Stewart and the Faces, Elton John, Cat Stevens, Allman Bros., Alice Cooper, Traffic, Sly and the Family Stone, Jefferson Airplane were not even in contention."

Nonetheless, this year's awards did usher in what *Variety* called "a new generation of artists, typified by such names as Carole King, James Taylor, the Carpenters, Isaac Hayes and Kris Kristofferson." Lily Tomlin was another example of emerging new talent carrying the day, as was composer Stephen Schwartz, who reaped the best original cast show album award for *Godspell,* beating works by such stage veterans as Richard Rodgers and Stephen Sondheim. *Godspell* represented the perfect marriage of the popular light folk/rock tastes of "the new generation" and conservative (religious) values of the older one.

Nonetheless, discontent lingered.

Throughout Motown's artistic and sales heyday over the past decade, the upstart, independent label managed to win only a single Grammy: for the Temptations' 1968 release "Cloud Nine."

When it failed again to win any awards this year, Motown's president, Suzanne De Passe, told *Variety,* "There have been mutterings behind the scenes for years to the effect that the Grammys were ridiculous, were basically unfair, and may even be crooked. I haven't the slightest doubt that big blocs of votes are placed by individual companies and that even the trading of votes by several companies is commonplace. What chance does an honest label or artist have if they control only their own vote? It's wrong. It's disgusting. It must be changed."

One N.A.R.A.S. leader dismissed her charges as "absurd, vicious and malicious," noting that award winners were spread among 20 labels.

Still, the biggest record companies won the most awards: RCA led with seven Grammys, followed by Columbia with five.

> *They Call Me Muddy Waters* showed r&r's influence on modern blues.

• 1971 •

The awards ceremony was broadcast on ABC from New York's Felt Forum at Madison Square Garden on March 14, 1972, for the awards eligibility period of October 16, 1970, to October 15, 1971.

ALBUM OF THE YEAR
• *Tapestry*, Carole King. Ode.
All Things Must Pass, George Harrison. Apple.
Carpenters, Carpenters. A&M.

Jesus Christ Superstar (London stage production). Decca.
Shaft, Isaac Hayes. Enterprise.

RECORD OF THE YEAR
• "It's Too Late," Carole King. Ode.
"Joy to the World," Three Dog Night. Dunhill.
"My Sweet Lord," George Harrison. Apple.
"Theme from *Shaft*," Isaac Hayes. Enterprise.
"You've Got a Friend," James Taylor. Warner Bros.

SONG OF THE YEAR
(Songwriter's Award)
• "You've Got a Friend," Carole King.
"Help Me Make It Through the Night," Kris Kristofferson.
"It's Impossible," Sid Wayne, Armando Manzanero.
"Me and Bobby McGee," Kris Kristofferson, Fred Foster.
"Rose Garden," Joe South.

BEST NEW ARTIST
• Carly Simon
Chase
Emerson, Lake & Palmer
Hamilton, Joe Frank & Reynolds
Bill Withers

BEST POP VOCAL PERFORMANCE, MALE
• James Taylor, "You've Got a Friend." Warner Bros.
Perry Como, "It's Impossible." RCA.
Neil Diamond, "I Am . . . I Said." Uni.
Gordon Lightfoot, "If You Could Read My Mind." Reprise.
Bill Withers, "Ain't No Sunshine." Sussex.

BEST POP VOCAL PERFORMANCE, FEMALE
• Carole King, "Tapestry." Ode.
Joan Baez, "The Night They Drove Old Dixie Down." Vanguard.
Cher, "Gypsys, Tramps and Thieves." Kapp.

Janis Joplin, "Me and Bobby McGee." Columbia.
Carly Simon, "That's the Way I've Always Heard It Should Be." Elektra.

BEST POP VOCAL PERFORMANCE BY A DUO, GROUP OR CHORUS
• Carpenters, *Carpenters*. A&M.
Bee Gees, "How Can You Mend a Broken Heart." Atco.
London stage cast, *Jesus Christ Superstar* (Andrew Lloyd Webber, Geoffrey Mitchell, Alan Doggett, Horace James). Decca.
Sonny & Cher, "All I Ever Need Is You." Kapp.
Three Dog Night, "Joy to the World." Dunhill.

BEST POP INSTRUMENTAL PERFORMANCE
• Quincy Jones, *Smackwater Jack*. A&M.
Burt Bacharach, *Burt Bacharach*. A&M.
Michel Legrand, "Theme from *Summer of '42*." Warner Bros.
Henry Mancini, "Theme from *Love Story*." RCA.
Peter Nero, "Theme from *Summer of '42*." Columbia.

BEST RHYTHM & BLUES SONG
(Songwriter's Award)
• "Ain't No Sunshine," Bill Withers.
"If I Were Your Woman," Clay McMurray, Laverne Ware, Pamela Sawyer.
"Mr. Big Stuff," Joseph Broussard, Ralph Williams, Carol Washington.
"Never Can Say Goodbye," Clifton Davis.
"Smiling Faces Sometimes," Norman Whitfield, Barrett Strong.

BEST RHYTHM & BLUES VOCAL PERFORMANCE, MALE
• Lou Rawls, "A Natural Man." MGM.
Marvin Gaye, "Inner City Blues (Make Me Wanna Holler)." Tamla/Motown.
Isaac Hayes, "Never Can Say Goodbye." Enterprise.

B. B. King, "Ain't Nobody Home." ABC.
Stevie Wonder, "We Can Work It Out."
  Tamla/Motown.

BEST RHYTHM & BLUES VOCAL PERFORMANCE, FEMALE
• Aretha Franklin, "Bridge Over Troubled Water." Atlantic.
Janis Joplin, *Pearl*. Columbia.
Jean Knight, "Mr. Big Stuff." Stax.
Freda Payne, *Contact*. Invictus.
Diana Ross, "I Love You (Call Me)."
  Motown.

BEST RHYTHM & BLUES PERFORMANCE BY A DUO OR GROUP (VOCAL OR INSTRUMENTAL)
• Ike & Tina Turner, "Proud Mary."
  United Artists.
Roberta Flack, Donny Hathaway,
  "You've Got a Friend." Atlantic.
Isaac Hayes, "Theme from *Shaft*."
  Enterprise.
Gladys Knight & the Pips, "If I Were
  Your Woman." Soul.
Staple Singers, "Respect Yourself." Stax.

BEST JAZZ PERFORMANCE BY A SOLOIST
• Bill Evans, *The Bill Evans Album*.
  Columbia.
Larry Coryell, *Gypsy Queen*. Flying
  Dutchman.
Dizzy Gillespie, *Portrait of Jenny*. Perception.
Earl Hines, *Quintessential Recording
  Session*. Chiaroscuro.
Carmen McRae, *Carmen McRae*. Mainstream.
Jimmy Rushing, *The You and Me That
  Used to Be*. RCA.
Phil Woods, *Phil Woods and His European
  Rhythm Machine at the Frankfurt
  Jazz Festival*. Embryo.

BEST JAZZ PERFORMANCE BY A GROUP
• Bill Evans Trio, *The Bill Evans
  Album*. Columbia.
Gary Burton, Keith Jarrett, *Gary Burton
  and Keith Jarrett*. Atlantic.

Miles Davis, *Miles Davis at the Fillmore*. Columbia.
Roy Eldridge, *The Nifty Cat*. Master
  Jazz.
Dizzy Gillespie, Bobby Hackett, Mary
  Lou Williams, *Giants*. Perception.
Herbie Hancock, *Mwandishi*. Warner
  Bros.
Phil Woods, *Phil Woods and His European
  Rhythm Machine at the Frankfurt
  Jazz Festival*. Embryo.

BEST JAZZ PERFORMANCE BY A BIG BAND
• Duke Ellington, "New Orleans Suite."
  Atlantic.
Count Basie, *Afrique*. Flying Dutchman.
Buddy Rich, *A Different Drummer*. RCA.
Maynard Ferguson, *Maynard Ferguson—M.F. Horn*. Columbia.
Woody Herman, *Woody*. Cadet.

BEST COUNTRY SONG (Songwriter's Award)
• "Help Me Make It Through the
  Night," Kris Kristofferson.
"Easy Loving," Freddie Hart.
"For the Good Times," Kris Kristofferson.
"Me and Bobby McGee," Kris Kristofferson, Fred Foster.
"Rose Garden," Joe South.

BEST COUNTRY VOCAL PERFORMANCE, MALE
• Jerry Reed, "When You're Hot, You're
  Hot." RCA.
Freddie Hart, "Easy Loving." Capitol.
Johnny Paycheck, "She's All I Got."
  Columbia.
Ray Price, "I Won't Mention It Again."
  Columbia.
Charley Pride, "Kiss an Angel Good
  Mornin'." RCA.

BEST COUNTRY VOCAL PERFORMANCE, FEMALE
• Sammi Smith, "Help Me Make It
  Through the Night." Mega.
Lynn Anderson, "How Can I Unlove
  You." Columbia.

Jody Miller, "He's So Fine." Epic.
Dolly Parton, "Joshua." RCA.
Tammy Wynette, "Good Lovin'." Epic.

BEST COUNTRY VOCAL PERFORMANCE, DUO OR GROUP

• Conway Twitty, Loretta Lynn, "After the Fire Is Gone." Decca.
Roy Acuff with the Nitty Gritty Dirt Band, "I Saw the Light." United Artists.
Johnny Cash, June Carter, "No Need to Worry." Columbia.
Tompall & the Glaser Brothers, "Rings." MGM.
Porter Wagoner, Dolly Parton, "Better Move It on Home." RCA.

BEST COUNTRY INSTRUMENTAL

• Chet Atkins, *Snowbird*. RCA.
Bakersfield Brass, *Rose Garden*. Capitol.
Floyd Cramer, *For the Good Times*. RCA.
Danny Davis & the Nashville Brass, *Ruby, Don't Take Your Love to Town*. RCA.
Jerry Kennedy, *Jerry Kennedy Plays: With All Due Respect to Kris Kristofferson*. Mercury.

BEST SACRED PERFORMANCE, MUSICAL

• Charley Pride, *Did You Think to Pray*. RCA.
Pat Boone Family, *Pat Boone Family*. Word.
Anita Bryant, *Abide with Me*. Word.
Dolly Parton, *Golden Streets of Glory*. RCA.
George Beverly Shea, "Amazing Grace." RCA.

BEST SOUL GOSPEL PERFORMANCE

• Shirley Caesar, *Put Your Hand in the Hand of the Man from Galilee*. Hob.
Blind Boys of Alabam, *The Five Blind Boys of Alabama*. Hob.
Dottie Rambo, *Pass Me Not*. Heartwarming.

Valerie Simpson, *There Is a God*. Tamla/Motown.
Clara Ward, *Great Moments in Gospel*. Hob.

BEST GOSPEL PERFORMANCE (OTHER THAN SOUL GOSPEL)

• Charley Pride, "Let Me Live." RCA.
Blackwood Brothers, *He's Still King of Kings*. RCA.
Imperials, *Time to Get It Together*. Impact.
Hovie Lister with the Statesmen, *Put Your Hand in the Hand*. Skylite.
Oak Ridge Boys, *Jesus Christ, What a Man*. Impact.

BEST ETHNIC OR TRADITIONAL RECORDING (INCLUDING TRADITIONAL BLUES)

• *They Call Me Muddy Waters*, Muddy Waters. Chess.
18th Century Traditional Music of Japan, Keiko Matsuo. Everest.
The Esso Trinidad Steel Band, Esso Trinidad Steel Band. Warner Bros.
Javanese Court Gamelan, Javanese Players. Nonesuch.
Message to the Young, Howlin' Wolf. Chess.
Mississippi Fred McDowell, Mississippi Fred McDowell. Everest.
Stormy Monday Blues, T-Bone Walker. Blues-Time.

BEST INSTRUMENTAL COMPOSITION (Composer's Award)

• Michel Legrand, "Theme from *Summer of '42*." Warner Bros.
Duke Ellington, "New Orleans Suite." Atlantic.
Isaac Hayes, "Theme from *Shaft*." Enterprise.
Francis Lai, "Theme from *Love Story*." Paramount.
Chuck Mangione, "Hill Where the Lord Hides." Mercury.

BEST SCORE FROM AN ORIGINAL CAST SHOW ALBUM

• *Godspell*, Stephen Schwartz. Bell.
Follies, Stephen Sondheim. Capitol.

The Rothschilds, Jerry Bock, Sheldon Harnick. Columbia.
Touch, Kenn Long, Jim Crazier. Ampex.
Two by Two, Richard Rodgers, Martin Charnin. Columbia.

BEST ORIGINAL SCORE WRITTEN FOR A MOTION PICTURE OR TV SPECIAL
(Composer's Award)
• *Shaft*, Isaac Hayes. Stax.
Bless the Beasts and Children, Barry DeVorzon, Perry Botkin, Jr. A&M.
Friends, Elton John, Bernie Taupin. Paramount.
Love Story, Francis Lai. Paramount.
Ryan's Daughter, Maurice Jarre. MGM.

BEST INSTRUMENTAL ARRANGEMENT
• Isaac Hayes, Johnny Allen, "Theme from *Shaft*." Enterprise.
Michel Colombier, "Earth." A&M.
Michel Legrand, "Theme from *Summer of '42*." Warner Bros.
Joshua Rifkin, "Nightingale II." Elektra.
Don Sebesky, "The Rite of Spring" (Hubert Laws). CTI.

BEST ARRANGEMENT ACCOMPANYING VOCALIST(S)
• Paul McCartney, "Uncle Albert/Admiral Halsey" (Paul & Linda McCartney). Apple.
Burt Bacharach, Pat Williams, "Long Ago Tomorrow" (B. J. Thomas). Scepter.
Richard Carpenter, "Superstar" (Carpenters). A&M.
Michel Colombier, "Freedom and Fear" (Bill Medley). A&M.
David Van Depitte, "What's Going On" (Marvin Gaye). Tamla/Motown.

ALBUM OF THE YEAR, CLASSICAL
• *Horowitz Plays Rachmaninov* (études tableaux, piano music, sonatas) (solo: Vladimir Horowitz). Columbia.
Berlioz: Requiem, Colin Davis conducting the London Symphony; Russell Burgess conducting the Wandsworth School Boys' Choir; Arthur Oldham conducting the London Symphony Chorus. Philips.
Boulez Conducts Boulez: Pli Selon Pli, Pierre Boulez conducting the BBC Symphony. Columbia.
Crumb: Ancient Voices of Children, Arthur Weisberg conducting the Contemporary Chamber Ensemble (solos: DeGaetani, Dash). Nonesuch.
Haydn: Symphonies Nos. 65–72 (Vol. 1), Antal Dorati conducting the Philharmonia Hungarica. London.
Janáček: Sinfonietta; Lutoslawski: Concerto for Orchestra, Seiji Ozawa conducting the Chicago Symphony. Angel.
Mahler: Symphony No. 1 in D Major, Carlo Maria Giulini conducting the Chicago Symphony. Angel.
Penderecki: Utrenja, the Entombment of Christ, Eugene Ormandy conducting the Philadelphia Orchestra; Robert Page directing the Temple University Choirs. RCA.
Shostakovich: Symphony No. 14, Eugene Ormandy conducting the Philadelphia Orchestra (solos: Curtin, Estes). RCA.
Tippett: The Midsummer Marriage, Colin Davis conducting the Royal Opera House Orchestra, Covent Garden. Philips.

BEST CLASSICAL PERFORMANCE, ORCHESTRA
(Conductor's Award)
• Carlo Maria Giulini conducting the Chicago Symphony, *Mahler: Symphony No. 1 in D Major*. Angel.
Pierre Boulez conducting the BBC Symphony, *Boulez Conducts Boulez: Pli Selon Pli*. Columbia.
Pierre Boulez conducting the Cleveland Orchestra, *Boulez Conducts Ravel*. Columbia.
Antal Dorati conducting the Philharmonia Hungarica, *Haydn: Symphonies Nos. 65–72 (Vol. 1)*. London.
Bernard Haitink conducting the London Philharmonic, *Holst: The Planets*. Philips.

Jascha Horenstein conducting the London Symphony, *Mahler: Symphony No. 3 in D Minor*. Nonesuch.

Eugene Ormandy conducting the Philadelphia Orchestra, *Respighi: The Fountains of Rome; The Pines of Rome*. Columbia.

André Previn conducting the London Symphony, *Vaughan Williams: Symphony No. 4 in F Minor*. RCA.

BEST CLASSICAL PERFORMANCE, INSTRUMENTAL SOLOIST(S) (WITH ORCHESTRA)

• Julian Bream (Previn conducting the London Symphony), *Villa-Lobos: Concerto for Guitar*. RCA.

Kyung-Wha Chung (Previn conducting the London Symphony), *Sibelius: Concerto in D Minor for Violin; Tchaikovsky: Concerto in D Major for Violin*. London.

Van Cliburn (Ormandy conducting the Philadelphia Orchestra), *Rachmaninov: Rhapsody on a Theme of Paganini; Liszt: Concerto No. 2 in A Major*. RCA.

Jacqueline Du Pré (Barenboim conducting the Chicago Symphony), *Dvořák: Concerto in B Minor for Cello*. Angel.

Igor Kipnis (Marriner conducting the London Strings), *Bach: Complete Concertos for Harpsichord and Orchestra*. Columbia.

Yehudi Menuhin (Walton conducting the New Philharmonia), *Walton: Concerto for Violin and Orchestra; Concerto for Viola and Orchestra*. Angel.

David Oistrakh, Mstislav Rostropovich, Sviatoslav Richter (von Karajan conducting the Berlin Philharmonic), *Beethoven: Triple Concerto (Concerto in C Major for Violin, Piano and Cello, Op. 56)*. Angel.

Henryk Szeryng (Kubelik conducting the Bavarian Symphony), *Berg: Concerto for Violin and Orchestra; Martinon: Concerto for Violin*. Deutsche Grammophon.

Paul Zukofsky (Thomas conducting the Boston Symphony), *W. Schuman: Concerto for Violin*. Deutsche Grammophon.

BEST CLASSICAL PERFORMANCE, INSTRUMENTAL SOLOIST(S) (WITHOUT ORCHESTRA)

• Vladimir Horowitz, *Horowitz Plays Rachmaninov* (études tableaux, piano music, sonatas). Columbia.

Stephen Bishop, *Bartók: Mikrokosmos, Vol. 6; Out of Doors Suite; Sonatina*. Philips.

Aldo Ciccolini, *Satie: Piano Music of Erik Satie, Vol. 5*. Angel.

Van Cliburn, *Barber: Sonata for Piano; Prokofiev: Sonata No. 6 in A Major*. RCA.

Alicia de Larrocha, *Alicia de Larrocha Plays Spanish Piano Music of the 20th Century*. London.

Glenn Gould, *Bach: The Well-Tempered Clavier, Book 2, Vol. 3, Preludes and Fugues 17–24*. Columbia.

Joshua Rifkin, *Piano Rags by Scott Joplin*. Nonesuch.

Artur Rubinstein, *The Brahms I Love*. RCA.

Rudolf Serkin, *Beethoven: Sonata No. 29 in B Flat, Op. 106 ("Hammerklavier")*. Columbia.

BEST CHAMBER MUSIC PERFORMANCE

• Juilliard Quartet, *Debussy: Quartet in G Minor; Ravel: Quartet in F Major*. Columbia.

Beaux Arts Trio, *Dvořák: Piano Trios (Complete)*. Philips.

Jan DeGaetani, Michael M. Dash (Arthur Weisberg conducting the Contemporary Chamber Ensemble), *Crumb: Ancient Voices of Children*. Nonesuch.

Nikolaus Harnoncourt conducting the Concentus Musicus, *Fux-Schmelzer: Music in the Hapsburg Palace*. Telefunken.

Jascha Heifetz, Brooks Smith, *Schubert: Fantaisie in C Major for Violin (and Piano) Op. 159*. RCA.

Jean-Pierre Rampal, Isaac Stern, Alexander Schneider, Leonard Rose, *The Mozart Quartets for Flute*. Columbia.

Paul Zukofsky, Gilbert Kalish, Charles Russo, Robert Sylvester (New York String Quartet), *Ives: Chamber Music*. Columbia.

BEST OPERA RECORDING

• *Verdi: Aida*, Erich Leinsdorf conducting the London Symphony; John Alldis Choir (solos: Price, Domingo, Milnes, Bumbry, Raimondi). RCA.

Massenet: Manon, Julius Rudel conducting the New Philharmonia and Ambrosian Opera Chorus (solos: Sills, Gedda, Souzay, Bacquier). Audio Treasury.

Mozart: The Magic Flute, Georg Solti conducting the Vienna Philharmonic (solos: Prey, Lorengar, Burrows, Fischer-Dieskau, Deutekom, Talvela). London.

Puccini: Il Tabarro, Erich Leinsdorf conducting the New Philharmonia; John Alldis Choir (solos: Price, Domingo, Milnes). RCA.

Tippett: The Midsummer Marriage, Colin Davis conducting the Orchestra of Royal Opera House, Covent Garden (solos: Remedios, Carlyle, Burrows, Harwood). Philips.

Verdi: Don Carlo, Carlo Maria Giulini conducting the Orchestra of Royal Opera House, Covent Garden, and Ambrosian Opera Chorus (solos: Domingo, Caballé, Raimondi, Milnes, Verrett). Angel.

Wagner: Die Meistersinger von Nürnberg, Herbert von Karajan conducting the Dresden State Opera Orchestra and Choruses of Dresden State Opera and Leipzig Radio (solos: Adam, Donath, Kollo, Evans, Schreider). Angel.

Wagner: Parsifal, Pierre Boulez conducting the Bayreuth Festival Orchestra and Chorus (solos: Stewart, Ridderbusch, Crass, King, Jones, McIntyre). Deutsche Grammophon.

BEST CLASSICAL PERFORMANCE, VOCAL SOLOIST

• Leontyne Price (Garvey, accompanist), *Leontyne Price Sings Robert Schumann*. RCA.

Janet Baker, Dietrich Fischer-Dieskau, *An Evening of Duets*. Angel.

Cathy Berberian (Berio conducting the BBC Symphony), *Berio: Epifanie*. RCA.

Phyllis Curtin, Simon Estes (Ormandy conducting the Philadelphia Orchestra), *Shostakovich: Symphony No. 14*. RCA.

Dietrich Fischer-Dieskau (Peters conducting the Vienna Haydn Orchestra), *Haydn and Mozart Arias*. London.

Evelyn Lear, Thomas Stewart, *Ives: American Scenes/American Poets*. Columbia.

Elisabeth Schwarzkopf (Furtwängler, accompanist), *Wolf: Songs (Salzburg Festival 1953)*. Seraphim.

BEST CHORAL PERFORMANCE (OTHER THAN OPERA)

• Colin Davis conducting the London Symphony; Russell Burgess conducting the Wandsworth School Boys' Choir; Arthur Oldham conducting the London Symphony Chorus, *Berlioz: Requiem*. Philips.

Wolfgang Fromme conducting the Collegium Vocale of Cologne, *Stockhausen: Stimmung*. Deutsche Grammophon.

Robert Page directing the Temple University Choirs; Eugene Ormandy conducting the Philadelphia Orchestra, *Penderecki: Utrenja, the Entombment of Christ*. RCA.

Ensti Pohjola conducting the Helsinki University Men's Choir; Paavo Berglund conducting the Bournemouth Symphony, *Sibelius: Kullervo, Op. 7*. Angel.

Gennady Rozhdestvensky conducting the Moscow Radio Chorus and Moscow Radio Symphony, *Prokofiev: Seven, They Are Seven*. Melodia/Angel.

Roger Wagner conducting the Los Angeles Master Chorale; Zubin Mehta conducting the Los Angeles Philharmonic, *Verdi: 4 Sacred Pieces*. London.

BEST ENGINEERED RECORDING, CLASSICAL

- Vittorio Negri, *Berlioz: Requiem* (Davis conducting the London Symphony; Burgess conducting the Wandsworth School Boys' Choir; Oldham conducting the London Symphony). Philips.

Marc J. Aubort, *Crumb: Ancient Voices of Children* (Weisberg conducting the Contemporary Chamber Ensemble; solos: Jan DeGaetani, Michael Dash). Nonesuch.

Paul Goodman, *Tchaikovsky: 1812 Overture; Beethoven: Wellington's Victory* (Ormandy conducting the Philadelphia Orchestra). RCA.

Gunter Hermanns, *Holst: The Planets* (Steinberg conducting the Boston Symphony). Deutsche Grammophon.

Gordon Parry, *Beethoven: Egmont—Complete Incidental Music* (Szell conducting the Vienna Philharmonic). London.

Carson C. Taylor, *Janáček: Sinfonietta* (Ozawa conducting the Chicago Symphony). Angel.

Carson C. Taylor, *Mahler: Symphony No. 1 in D Major* (Giulini conducting the Chicago Symphony). Angel.

BEST SPOKEN WORD RECORDING

- *Desiderata*, Les Crane. Warner Bros.
Hamlet, Richard Chamberlain. RCA.
I Can Hear It Now—The Sixties, Walter Cronkite. Columbia.
Long Day's Journey into Night, Stacy Keach, Robert Ryan, Geraldine Fitzgerald. Caedmon.
Will Rogers' U.S.A. James Whitmore. Columbia.

BEST COMEDY RECORDING

- *This Is a Recording*, Lily Tomlin. Polydor.

Ajax Liquor Store, Hudson & Landry. Dore.
Cheech and Chong, Cheech & Chong. Ode.
Flip: The Flip Wilson Show, Flip Wilson. Little David.
When I Was a Kid, Bill Cosby. Uni.

BEST RECORDING FOR CHILDREN

- *Bill Cosby Talks to Kids About Drugs*, Bill Cosby. Uni.
"Sesame Street," "Rubber Duckie" and Other Songs from "Sesame Street," Richard Wolfe Children's Chorus. Camden.
Sex Explained for Children, Dr. Stanley Daniels. Carapan.
The Story of Shéhérazade, Julie Harris. Caedmon.
Willy Wonka and the Chocolate Factory, Golden Orchestra and Chorus (Peter Moore, conductor). Golden.

BEST ENGINEERED RECORDING

- Dave Purple, Henry Bush, Ron Capone, "Theme from *Shaft*" (Isaac Hayes). Enterprise.
Ray Gerhardt, Dick Bogert, *Carpenters* (Carpenters). A&M.
Bones Howe, *The 5th Dimension Live!* (5th Dimension). Bell.
Larry Levine, Roger Roche, *Wings* (Michel Colombier). A&M.
Armin Steiner, "Stones" (Neil Diamond). Uni.

BEST ALBUM COVER
(Art Director's Award)

- Gene Brownell, Dean O. Torrance, *Pollution* (Pollution). Prophesy.
John Berg, Robert Lockart, Norman Seeff, *B, S & T 4* (Blood, Sweat & Tears). Columbia.
Vincent J. Biondi, design; Susan Obrant, illustration, *The Music of Erik Satie: Through a Looking Glass* (Camarata Contemporary Chamber Orchestra). Dream.
Acy Lehman, design; Nick Sangiamo, photographer, *Bark* (Jefferson Airplane). Grunt.

Norman Seeff, John Van Hamersveld, *Black Pearl* (Jimmy McGriff). United Artists.

Ed Thrasher, John Van Hamersveld, *Hot Platters* (various). Warner Bros.

Ed Thrasher, art director; Terry Paul, photographer, *Sharepickers* (Mason Williams). Warner Bros.

Craig Braun, design; Andy Warhol, photographer, *Sticky Fingers* (Rolling Stones). Rolling Stones.

BEST ALBUM NOTES
(Annotator's Award)
• Sam Samudio, *Sam Hard and Heavy* (Samudio). Atlantic.

Colman Andrews, *Miles Davis*. United Artists.

Don Demicheal, *The Genius of Louis Armstrong*. Columbia.

Nat Hentoff, *Louis Armstrong July 4, 1900–July 6, 1971*. RCA.

James Lyons, *Music of Varèse* (Simonovitch conducting the Paris Instrumental Ensemble). Angel.

Joshua Rifkin, *Piano Rags by Scott Joplin* (Rifkin). Nonesuch.

George T. Simon, *This Is Benny Goodman*. RCA.

Tom West, *Honky Tonkin' with Charlie Walker*. Epic.

• 1972 •

Saving *Face* and *Bangla Desh*

"The [N.A.R.A.S.] voting membership is getting younger and younger," an academy official announced prior to the Grammycast when citing the results of a recent membership study, "and each year the nominations get more with it."

When the year's award winners were revealed, Warner Bros. Records President Joe Smith agreed: "The records and artists that won were outstanding as far as both artistic contributions and sales."

Aretha Franklin and Don McClean were the early Grammy front-runners with four nominations each, followed by Neil Diamond, Roberta Flack, Nilsson, Donna Fargo and Michel Legrand, all with three bids apiece. The top prizes were expected to be split between McClean's "American Pie" and Diamond's "Song Sung Blue," although Gilbert O'Sullivan's "Alone Again (Naturally)" and Flack's "The First Time Ever I Saw Your Face" were also given strong chances. All four tunes were up for both Record and Song of the Year. In the contest for best album, the conclusion seemed foregone: Pundits predicted that, surely, the *American Pie* LP would get its just desserts.

"American Pie" was McLean's musical elegy to what he perceived as the decline of rock & roll. It was the year's best-selling single and had a passionate following among tuned-in young music lovers who studied its cryptic lyrics for hidden meaning. When it failed to win *any* awards, the shock was only surpassed by the surprise of what won Album of the Year instead: a three-disc LP that showcased serious rockers shunned in the past (Bob Dylan and Eric Clapton, among them) and had received only a single nomination.

The Concert for Bangla Desh was the

Roberta Flack's best record victor "The First Time Ever I Saw Your Face" was popularized by the hit Clint Eastwood film *Play Misty for Me*.

first of the cause-oriented, fund-raising works that would involve a host of name artists and score top Grammys in future years, such as 1985 Record and Song of the Year "We Are the World" (famine relief for Africa) and 1986 Song of the Year "That's What Friends Are For" (AIDS research and awareness).

Bangla Desh was organized by ex-Beatle George Harrison to raise relief money for the war-torn and famine-plagued Asian nation. The show employed the talents of Dylan (in his first U.S. appearance in three years; he was greeted by a screaming, 10-minute ovation), Eric Clapton, Leon Russell, Ringo Starr, Billy Preston, Klaus Voormann and Ravi Shankar (Harrison's sitar instructor during his flirtation with Eastern religion) in a historic UNICEF benefit at New York City's Madison Square Garden. The other two Beatles were also invited, but Paul McCartney refused because of a lawsuit he had pending to dissolve the Beatles officially, and John Lennon declined on the basis that his invitation clearly excluded a performance by his wife, Yoko Ono. Highlights of the concert included Dylan singing "Just Like a Woman" and "Blowin' in the Wind" and Harrison and Clapton's rendition of the Beatles' "While My Guitar Gently Weeps."

The Grammy ceremony became a source of controversy when it was held this year at the Tennessee Auditorium in Nashville. ABC had broadcast the first two live Grammy shows, which had taken place in Los Angeles and New York, but disapproved of the switch to Nashville and refused to participate. NBC declined, too, but CBS picked up the option reluctantly and only after considerable prodding by N.A.R.A.S. officials. When the telecast received favorable press notices and pulled an amazing 53 percent TV audience share, ABC realized its mistake. CBS already held the broadcast rights on an exclusive basis. Obviously jealous, the alphabet web quickly went about setting up the rival, new American Music Awards produced by Dick Clark, who was also the host of the TV music series *American Bandstand.*

In addition to staging another polished ceremony and the triumph of *Bangla Desh,* what made the Grammys so "with it" this year was the winner of both Record and Song of the Year—a tune that was rescued from near obscurity after it was recorded three years earlier. "The First Time Ever I Saw Your Face" was a track from Roberta Flack's 1969 debut album, *First Take,* appropriately named since all eight songs were recorded in only 10 hours. Long after the album's release,

Flack was still crooning a living in Washington, D.C., nightspots when she got a phone call one day from Clint Eastwood, who was filming *Play Misty for Me* and needed a haunting love melody to underscore the film's eerie theme of an obsessed fan stalking a radio deejay. "Film fans ran from the theaters to record stores asking for the song," *Billboard* reported, "which Atlantic quickly rushed into their hands after slicing 66 seconds from its five minute, 21 second length to accommodate Top 40 radio airplay. At 33 years old, after being involved with music for 24 years, Roberta Flack scored her first commercial success." "First Time" became the year's second-best-selling single right behind losing Record of the Year nominee "American Pie."

Roberta Flack picked up another Grammy when the ballad "Where Is the Love" won the pop group vocal award for her and Donny Hathaway, who was once billed as the nation's youngest gospel singer when he made his debut public performance in Chicago at the age of three. Flack was not on hand to accept either honor. The *Washington Post* noted that she was in Washington, D.C., "conducting a program of Hall Johnson spirituals by the Frederick Wilkerson Choir at the Kennedy Center Concert Hall."

In the running for Best New Artist was a formidable lineup this year—America, Harry Chapin, the Eagles, Loggins & Messina and John Prine. After losing the pop group vocals statuette to Flack and Hathaway, America nabbed the consolation prize for new emerging talent.

America was a folk/rock trio that met in a school for children of U.S. servicemen stationed in London. They had a huge British following thanks to their popular performances at London's Roadhouse club, but were unknown back home before "A Horse with No Name" reached number one for three weeks on

Miffed over CBS's success with the Grammys, ABC created the American Music Awards.

the U.S. singles charts and ended up ranked ninth for the year.

The most famous acceptance speech in the history of the Grammys was given this year by Helen Reddy when she picked up the trophy for best female pop vocal performance for "I Am Woman," her spirited celebration of womanhood that became an anthem for feminists. The Australian-born vocalist cowrote the tune with Ray Burton after searching for a tune "that reflected the positive sense of self that I felt I'd gained from the women's movement," she once told *Billboard*. When she was rewarded with the Grammy, she said, "I want to thank everyone concerned at Capitol Records, my husband and manager, Jeff Wald, because he makes my success possible, and God because She makes everything possible." Following the broadcast, Reddy was flooded with protest letters from religious fundamentalists.

> ## Helen Reddy thanked God "because She makes everything possible."

The 1969 Grammy winner for "Everybody's Talkin'," Nilsson (who had dropped his first name, Harry, in professional circles), took the male pop vocal performance award again, this time for 1972's fourth-best-selling single, "Without You." *Bangla Desh*'s Billy Preston won a second trophy when the onetime gospel singer snagged the laurels for best pop instrumental performance for "Outa-Space." A second instrumental prize was introduced this year for performances "with vocal coloring" and went to Isaac Hayes, the singer and sax and piano player of *Black Moses* who had picked up two Grammys last year for his *Shaft* soundtrack.

In the 10 years that the Temptations had been performing, they had three number-one hits—"My Girl," "Just My Imagination" and "I Can't Get Next to You"—but won only a single Grammy: for 1968's "Cloud Nine." Their fourth and last chart-topper, "Papa Was a Rolling Stone," rolled through the Grammys nabbing three awards: Best R&B Vocal Performance, Duo, Group or Chorus; Best R&B Instrumental Performance; and Best R&B Song. Despite its success as Grammy's biggest-winning song of 1972, it wasn't nominated for Record of the Year, which caused some griping among music pundits.

A song that displaced "I Am Woman" at number one on the pop singles charts garnered the r&b male vocals prize for Billy Paul, causing some controversy. "Me and Mrs. Jones," a soul tune called "middle of the road (almost 1940s style)" by *Variety*, was challenged for being classified as an R&B single. "Why?" *Variety* asked. "Because the singer of the record, Billy Paul, is black?"

Aretha Franklin was nominated in three categories—r&b, soul gospel and pop—losing only the prize for pop music when it went to Helen Reddy. Franklin nabbed the soul gospel trophy for "Amazing Grace," which she performed with Rev. James Cleveland serving as pianist plus conductor of the Southern California Community Choir. She also held on to the r&b female vocal category for an amazing sixth year in a row, this time for her LP *Young, Gifted and Black*. The Blackwood Brothers returned for their fourth Grammy for *L-O-V-E*, named Best Gospel Performance. Also returning was Elvis Presley, who took the inspirational kudos for another of his religious albums, *He Touched Me*.

Despite failing health, Duke Ellington, at the age of 72, continued to record and was honored with a ninth statuette for his big-band performance of "Togo Brava Suite." It was the last Grammy that the esteemed Duke would win in his lifetime, although he would be awarded two more posthumously in 1976 and 1979.

Two Grammy first-timers took the other two jazz accolades. Classically trained vibraphone player Gary Burton garnered the soloist honors for *Alone at*

Last, an LP recording of his 1971 performance at Switzerland's Montreux Jazz Festival. Trumpeter Freddie Hubbard and his troupe took the group prize for *First Light,* which contained several of Hubbard's lyrical ballad renditions in addition to his controversial jazz interpretations of such pop hits as Paul McCartney's "Uncle Albert/Admiral Halsey."

The Best Country Song of the year was a number-one c&w hit for five weeks that subsequently crossed over to the pop charts. "Kiss an Angel Good Mornin' " was written by Ben Peters (about his newborn daughter Angela) and was sung by double Grammy winner of last year Charley Pride, who this year returned to take one more for best country male vocal performance for his LP *Charley Pride Sings Heart Songs.*

It was the year's top-selling country song that reaped the female vocal prize for former schoolteacher Donna Fargo, who also wrote "Happiest Girl in the Whole U.S.A.," winner of the Single of the Year accolades from both the Country Music Association and the Academy of Country Music. ("Happiest Girl" and Fargo's "Funny Face" were both losers of the Grammy country song award.)

The Country Music Association's Vocal Group of the Year, the Statler Brothers, previous winners of two Grammys in 1965, came back to claim further N.A.R.A.S. honors when their "Class of '57" (about a graduating class facing the disillusionment of early adulthood) brought them N.A.R.A.S.'s group vocal prize, too. The instrumental trophy went to harmonica and guitar player Charlie McCoy, for *The Real McCoy.*

Comedian George Carlin first gained fame as a frequent *Tonight Show* guest in the late 1960s. His popularity grew in the 1970s as he became more irreverent, grew his hair long (some said so that he could look like a *Doonesbury* comic strip character) and even got arrested in 1972 for giving a public performance of his infamous "Seven Words You Can Never Use on Television" routine. (The charges were

Apple Records

Album of the Year winner *The Concert for Bangla Desh* featured a wide range of guest artists in the first major rock concert benefit.

later dropped.) He finally won a Grammy for *FM & AM,* which included a parody of the TV show *Let's Make a Deal,* an impression of Ed Sullivan and a skit called "The 11 O'Clock News" in which Carlin delivered such grabber headlines as "Good Humor Man Slays 10," "Pen Pal Stabs Pal with Pen" and "Jacques Cousteau Dies in Bathtub Accident."

"The happiest by-product of this year's balloting involved the actual choices among the classical winners," the *L.A. Times* reported. *Mahler: Symphony No. 8,* with Sir Georg Solti conducting the Chicago Symphony, swept three of them and was, the *Times* added, an "eminently defensible choice": Classical Album of the Year, best choral performance and Best Engineered Recording. The orchestra traveled to Austria to tape the symphony at Vienna's Sofiensaal. "And Solti?" asked *High Fidelity.* "He carries it to the highest pitch of exaltation and excitement."

Solti also recorded Mahler's Symphony No. 7 this year (traveling only 150 miles from Chicago to do so, to the Krannert Center at the University of Illinois at Champaign-Urbana) and picked up the Grammy for orchestral honors that eluded him for Mahler's Eighth, for which he was not even nominated. The result was an achievement in "clarity and refinement" that amounted, said *High Fidelity,* to "the best-sounding Mahler Seventh we have."

"The grand old man of the keyboard did take the predictable laurels," the *L.A. Times* said of Artur Rubinstein when he seized his fifth career Grammy for *Brahms: Concerto No. 2.* "If Rubinstein wins one prize, [Vladimir] Horowitz cannot be far behind," the paper added. "True to form, he defeated all potential threats in the recital category with his all-Chopin album," which included Polonaise No. 6 in A Flat and *Polonaise-Fantaisie.* (It was Horowitz's eleventh win.) The chamber music honors went to guitarists Julian Bream and John Williams for their selections by Lawes, Carulli, Albéniz and Granados.

The year's best opera prize was claimed by conductor Colin Davis, the BBC Symphony and the Chorus of Covent Garden for *Benvenuto Cellini,* Berlioz's first opera and his last to be recorded on disc. "Davis is, of course, the premier Berlioz conductor of his day, and his sense of pacing, his ability to achieve orchestra clarity, his eye for the long-range shape are much in evidence," said *High Fidelity.* Tenor Nicholai Gedda performed the lead role, but the vocalist award went to baritone Dietrich Fischer-Dieskau for *Die Schöne Magelone* by Brahms.

This year's Grammy ceremony was hosted by Andy Williams, who *Variety* said did "a fine job." *Variety* also applauded Charley Pride's performance of "Kiss an Angel Good Morning," Helen Reddy's "I Am Woman" and Donna Fargo's "Happiest Girl in the Whole U.S.A." Otherwise, the paper slammed the TV show for being "smooth and glossy on the outside and bland all the way through." A snafu occurred when a smoke machine went berserk and obscured Curtis Mayfield while he performed "Freddy's Dead" through a thick, eerie mist.

The program had other dramatic

Sir Georg Solti and the Chicago Symphony Orchestra received three awards, including best classical album, for Mahler's *Symphony No. 8.*

moments. "We lost power eight minutes before air time," producer Pierre Cossette remembered years later in an interview with *TV Guide.* "I got on the phone with Joe Hamilton [Carol Burnett's husband and producer of the Grammy show] and asked him what *Carol Burnett Show* he wanted to rerun. Then a minute before air time, the power went on."

The broadcast out of Nashville included time for only 11 winners, "leaving the other 36 to a $25 roast beef dinner crowd in Los Angeles, which plodded through dozens of no-shows, then sat down or left for a two-color (purple and green) closed-circuit TV feed from Nashville," complained *Rolling Stone.*

While the award results were certainly more "with it" this year, there were still the usual oversights that caused the predicted "chorus of complaints." Among the artists who were passed up for nominations was Sarah Vaughan (who sang two Michel Legrand hits on the telecast, including his Song of the Year nominee "The Summer Knows" and his Grammy-winning "What Are You Doing the Rest of Your Life?"; Legrand also won an award for his theme to the hit TV film *Brian's Song*). Also overlooked were Al Green ("the top selling singles artist of 1972," said the *L.A. Times*), previous winners Paul Simon and Carole King (both of whom had more hit music this year) and "some of the rock artists whose work was widely acclaimed in 1972—including David Bowie, Procol Harum and Cat Stevens," the *Times* added.

N.A.R.A.S. had made a serious effort to improve the nominee lineup in advance of the voting by forming an advisory committee of sixteen record company presidents in addition to a National Screening Committee that "met in a New York hotel suite and spent nine hours trying to sort out the 4,000 'pre-nominations' and place them in proper categories before the ballot for final nominations," *Rolling Stone* pointed out. "But by the nature of the business (last year, as one example, over 4,200 albums were released), and by the nature of popular music, the committee had an impossible job. . . .

"Aside from the omissions," *Rolling*

Stone added, "the most embarrassing aspect of this year's balloting was the Album of the Year nomination received by the *Jesus Christ Superstar* Broadway cast album. It was the original London [studio] cast album that received both the sales and critical attention. The obvious assumption is that lots of N.A.R.A.S. voters confused this album with the original."

The jazz awards also suffered the blues, particularly since jazz was not performed on the Grammycast. Furthermore, "a hassle over the definition of jazz has led to jazz flutist Herbie Mann's resignation" from the record academy, *Variety* reported. "Mann was unhappy over the jazz category for N.A.R.A.S.'s Grammy Awards in which the music was to be judged by the 'intention' of the performer."

• 1972 •

The awards ceremony was broadcast on CBS from Nashville's Tennessee Auditorium on March 3, 1973, for the awards eligibility period of October 16, 1971, to October 15, 1972.

ALBUM OF THE YEAR

- *The Concert for Bangla Desh*, George Harrison, Ravi Shankar, Bob Dylan, Leon Russell, Ringo Starr, Billy Preston, Eric Clapton, Klaus Voormann, others. Apple.

American Pie, Don McLean. United Artists.

Jesus Christ Superstar (Broadway cast). Decca.

Moods, Neil Diamond. Uni.

Nilsson Schmilsson, Nilsson. RCA.

RECORD OF THE YEAR

- "The First Time Ever I Saw Your Face," Roberta Flack. Atlantic.

"Alone Again (Naturally)," Gilbert O'Sullivan. MAM/London.

"American Pie," Don McLean. United Artists.

"Song Sung Blue," Neil Diamond. Uni.

"Without You," Nilsson. RCA.

SONG OF THE YEAR
(Songwriter's Award)

- "The First Time Ever I Saw Your Face," Ewan MacColl.

"Alone Again (Naturally)," Gilbert O'Sullivan.

"American Pie," Don McLean.

"Song Sung Blue," Neil Diamond.

"The Summer Knows," Marilyn & Alan Bergman, Michel Legrand.

BEST NEW ARTIST

- America

Harry Chapin

Eagles

Loggins & Messina

John Prine

BEST POP VOCAL PERFORMANCE, MALE

- Nilsson, "Without You." RCA.

Mac Davis, "Baby, Don't Get Hooked on Me." Columbia.

Sammy Davis, Jr., "Candy Man."
MGM.
Don McLean, "American Pie." United
Artists.
Gilbert O'Sullivan, "Alone Again (Natu-
rally)." MAM/London.

BEST POP VOCAL PERFORMANCE, FEMALE

• Helen Reddy, "I Am Woman." Capi-
tol.
Roberta Flack, *Quiet Fire*. Atlantic.
Aretha Franklin, "Day Dreaming."
Atlantic.
Carly Simon, *Anticipation*. Elektra.
Barbra Streisand, "Sweet
Inspiration/Where You Lead."
Columbia.

BEST POP VOCAL PERFORMANCE BY A DUO, GROUP OR CHORUS

• Roberta Flack, Donny Hathaway,
"Where Is the Love." Atlantic.
America, "A Horse with No Name."
Warner Bros.
Bread, *Baby I'm-a Want You*. Elektra.
New Seekers, "I'd Like to Teach the
World to Sing (in Perfect Harmony)."
Elektra.
Seals & Crofts, "Summer Breeze."
Warner Bros.

BEST POP INSTRUMENTAL PERFORMANCE BY AN INSTRUMENTAL PERFORMER

• Billy Preston, "Outa-Space." A&M.
Apollo 100, "Joy." Mega.
Doc Severinsen, *Doc*. RCA.
Pipes & Drums & Military Band of the
Royal Scots Dragoon Guards, *Amaz-
ing Grace*. RCA.
Mahavishnu Orchestra with John
McLaughlin, *The Inner Mounting
Flame*. Columbia.

BEST POP INSTRUMENTAL PERFORMANCE WITH VOCAL COLORING

• Isaac Hayes, *Black Moses*. Enterprise.
Cy Coleman, "Theme from *The Garden
of the Finzi Continis*." London.

Emerson, Lake & Palmer, *Pictures
at an Exhibition*. Cotillion/
Atlantic.
Quincy Jones, "Money Runner."
Reprise.
Henry Mancini, Doc Severinsen, *Brass
on Ivory*. RCA.
Santana, *Caravanserai*. Columbia.

BEST RHYTHM & BLUES SONG (Songwriter's Award)

• "Papa Was a Rolling Stone," Barrett
Strong, Norman Whitfield.
"Back Stabbers," Leon Huff, Gene
McFadden, John Whitehead.
"Everybody Plays the Fool," Rudy
Clark, J. R. Bailey, Kenny
Williams.
"Freddie's Dead," Curtis Mayfield.
"Me and Mrs. Jones," Ken Gamble,
Leon Huff, Cary Gilbert.

BEST RHYTHM & BLUES VOCAL PERFORMANCE, MALE

• Billy Paul, "Me and Mrs. Jones."
Philadelphia International.
Ray Charles, "What Have They Done to
My Song Ma." Tangerine.
Curtis Mayfield, "Freddie's Dead." Cur-
tom.
Joe Simon, "Drowning in the Sea of
Love." Spring.
Joe Tex, "I Gotcha." Dial/Mercury.

BEST RHYTHM & BLUES VOCAL PERFORMANCE, FEMALE

• Aretha Franklin, *Young, Gifted and
Black*. Atlantic.
Merry Clayton, "Oh, No Not My Baby."
Ode.
Esther Phillips, *From a Whisper to a
Scream*. Kudu/CTI.
Candi Staton, "In the Ghetto." Fame.
Betty Wright, "Clean Up Woman."
Alston/Atlantic.

BEST RHYTHM & BLUES VOCAL PERFORMANCE BY A DUO, GROUP OR CHORUS

• Temptations, "Papa Was a Rolling
Stone." Gordy/Motown.

Gladys Knight & the Pips, "Help Me Make It Through the Night." Soul/Motown.

Harold Melvin & the Blue Notes, "If You Don't Know Me by Now." Philadelphia International.

Spinners, "I'll Be Around." Atlantic.

Staple Singers, "I'll Take You There." Stax.

BEST RHYTHM & BLUES INSTRUMENTAL PERFORMANCE

• Temptations, Paul Riser, "Papa Was a Rolling Stone." Gordy/Motown.

Crusaders, *Crusaders I*. Blue Thumb.

King Curtis, "Everybody's Talkin'." Atco.

Isaac Hayes, "Let's Stay Together," Enterprise.

Curtis Mayfield, "Junkie Chase." Curtom.

BEST JAZZ PERFORMANCE BY A SOLOIST

• Gary Burton, *Alone at Last*. Atlantic.

Freddie Hubbard, *The Hub of Hubbard*. MPS/BASF.

Tom Scott, *Great Scott*. A&M.

Sonny Stitt, *Tune-Up!* Cobblestone.

McCoy Tyner, *Sahara*. Milestone.

BEST JAZZ PERFORMANCE BY A GROUP

• Freddie Hubbard, *First Light*. CTI.

George Benson, *White Rabbit*. CTI.

Joe Farrell, *Outback*. CTI.

Chuck Mangione, *The Chuck Mangione Quartet*. Mercury.

McCoy Tyner, *Sahara*. Milestone.

Weather Report, *I Sing the Body Electric*. Columbia.

BEST JAZZ PERFORMANCE BY A BIG BAND

• Duke Ellington, "Togo Brava Suite." United Artists.

Kenny Clark, Francy Boland Big Band, *All Smiles*. MPS/BASF.

Don Ellis, *Connection*. Columbia.

Maynard Ferguson, *M.F. Horn Two*. Columbia.

Gerry Mulligan, *The Age of Steam*. A&M.

BEST COUNTRY SONG (Songwriter's Award)

• "Kiss an Angel Good Mornin'," Ben Peters.

"Delta Dawn," Alex Harvey, Larry Collins.

"Funny Face," Donna Fargo.

"Happiest Girl in the Whole U.S.A.," Donna Fargo.

"Woman (Sensuous Woman)," Gary S. Paxton.

BEST COUNTRY VOCAL PERFORMANCE, MALE

• Charley Pride, *Charley Pride Sings Heart Songs*. RCA.

Merle Haggard, "It's Not Love (but It's Not Bad)." Capitol.

Waylon Jennings, "Good Hearted Woman." RCA.

Jerry Lee Lewis, "Chantilly Lace." Mercury.

Charlie Rich, "I Take It on Home." Epic.

BEST COUNTRY VOCAL PERFORMANCE, FEMALE

• Donna Fargo, "Happiest Girl in the Whole U.S.A." Dot.

Skeeter Davis, "One Tin Soldier." RCA.

Loretta Lynn, "One's on the Way." Decca.

Dolly Parton, "Touch Your Woman." RCA.

Tanya Tucker, "Delta Dawn." Columbia.

Tammy Wynette, "My Man." Epic.

BEST COUNTRY VOCAL PERFORMANCE BY A DUO OR GROUP

• Statler Brothers, "Class of '57." Mercury.

Mother Maybelle Carter, Earl Scruggs, Doc Watson, Roy Acuff, Merle Travis, Jimmy Martin, Nitty Gritty Dirt Band, *Will the Circle Be Unbroken*. United Artists.

Johnny Cash, June Carter, "If I Had a Hammer." Columbia.

George Jones, Tammy Wynette, "Take Me." Epic.

Conway Twitty, Loretta Lynn, *Lead Me On*. Decca.

BEST COUNTRY INSTRUMENTAL PERFORMANCE

• Charlie McCoy, *The Real McCoy*. Monument.

Chet Atkins, *Chet Atkins Picks on the Hits*. RCA.

Chet Atkins, Jerry Reed, *Me and Chet*. RCA.

Danny Davis & the Nashville Brass, *Flowers on the Wall*. RCA.

Lester Flatt, "Foggy Mountain Breakdown." RCA.

BEST INSPIRATIONAL PERFORMANCE

• Elvis Presley, *He Touched Me*. RCA.

Little Jimmy Dempsey, *Award Winning Guitar*. Skylite.

Merle Haggard, *Land of Many Churches*. Capitol.

Danny Lee & the Children of Truth, *Spread a Little Love Around*. RCA.

Eugene Ormandy conducting the Philadelphia Orchestra and Chorus, *The Greatest Hits of Christmas*. RCA.

Pipes & Drums & Military Band of the Royal Scots Dragoon Guards, "Amazing Grace," track. RCA.

Ray Stevens, "Love Lifted Me." Barnaby.

BEST SOUL GOSPEL PERFORMANCE

• Aretha Franklin, "Amazing Grace." Atlantic.

B.C. & M. Choir, *My Sweet Lord*. Creed.

Aretha Franklin, James Cleveland, "Precious Memories," track. Atlantic.

Edwin Hawkins Singers, "Jesu." Buddah.

Clara Ward, "Last Mile of the Way." Nashboro.

BEST GOSPEL PERFORMANCE (OTHER THAN SOUL GOSPEL)

• Blackwood Brothers, *L-O-V-E*. RCA.

Wendy Bagwell & the Sunliters, *By Your Request*. Canaan.

Oak Ridge Boys, *Light*. Heartwarming.

Rambos, *Soul in the Family*. Heartwarming.

Thrasher Brothers, *America Sings*. Canaan.

BEST ETHNIC OR TRADITIONAL RECORDING (INCLUDING TRADITIONAL BLUES)

• *The London Muddy Waters Session*, Muddy Waters. Chess.

Blues Piano Orgy, Little Brother Montgomery, Roosevelt Sykes, Sunnyland Slim, Speckled Red, Otis Spann, Curtis Jones. Delmark.

Lightnin' Strikes, Lightnin' Hopkins. Tradition/Everest.

Live at Soledad Prison, John Lee Hooker. ABC.

Walking the Blues, Otis Spann. Barnaby.

BEST INSTRUMENTAL COMPOSITION
(Composer's Award)

• Michel Legrand, "Brian's Song." Bell.

Don Ellis, "Theme from *The French Connection*." Columbia.

Henry Mancini, "Brass on Ivory." RCA.

Billy Preston, Joe Greene, "Outa-Space." A&M.

Nino Rota, "Theme from *The Godfather*." Paramount.

BEST INSTRUMENTAL ARRANGEMENT

• Don Ellis, "Theme from *The French Connection*" (Don Ellis). Columbia.

Richard Carpenter, "Flat Baroque" (Carpenters). A&M.

Quincy Jones, "Money Runner" (Quincy Jones). Reprise.

Henry Mancini, "Theme from *The Mancini Generation*" (Henry Mancini). RCA.

Don Sebesky, "Lonely Town" (Freddie Hubbard). CTI.

BEST SCORE FROM AN ORIGINAL CAST SHOW ALBUM
(Composer's Award)

• *Don't Bother Me I Can't Cope*, Micki Grant. Polydor.

Ain't Supposed to Die a Natural Death, Melvin Van Peebles. A&M.

Grease, Warren Casey, Jim Jacobs. MGM.

Sugar, Jule Styne, Bob Merrill. United Artists.

Two Gentlemen of Verona, John Guare, Galt MacDermott. ABC.

BEST ORIGINAL SCORE WRITTEN FOR A MOTION PICTURE OR TV SPECIAL
(Composer's Award)

• *The Godfather*, Nino Rota. Paramount.

"$" Soundtrack, Quincy Jones. Reprise.

The Garden of the Finzi Continis, Manuel DeSica. RCA.

Nicholas and Alexandra, Richard Rodney Bennett. Bell.

Superfly, Curtis Mayfield. Curtom.

BEST ARRANGEMENT ACCOMPANYING VOCALIST(S)

• Michel Legrand, "What Are You Doing the Rest of Your Life" (Sarah Vaughan). Mainstream.

Thom Bell, "Betcha by Golly, Wow" (Stylistics). Avco.

Michel Legrand, "The Summer Knows" (Sarah Vaughan). Mainstream.

Don Sebesky, "Day by Day" (Jackie & Roy). CTI.

Don Sebesky, "Lazy Afternoon" (Jackie & Roy). CTI.

ALBUM OF THE YEAR, CLASSICAL

• *Mahler: Symphony No. 8 in E Flat Major ("Symphony of a Thousand")*, Georg Solti conducting the Chicago Symphony, Vienna Boys' Choir, Vienna State Opera Chorus, Vienna Singverein Chorus and soloists. London.

Berlioz: Benvenuto Cellini, Colin Davis conducting the BBC Symphony; Chorus of Covent Garden (solos: Gedda, Eda-Pierre, Soyer, Berbie). Philips.

Bernstein: Mass, Leonard Bernstein conducting ensemble orchestra and the Norman Scribner and Berkshire Boys' Choir. Columbia.

Brahms: Concerto No. 2 in B Flat Major for Piano, Eugene Ormandy conducting the Philadelphia Orchestra (solo: Rubinstein). RCA.

Horowitz Plays Chopin (Polonaise in A Flat Major Introduction and Rondo, Op. 16, etc.) (solo: Horowitz). Columbia.

Wagner: Tannhauser, Georg Solti conducting the Vienna Philharmonic (solos: Kolio, Dernesch, Ludwig, Braun, Sotin). London.

BEST CLASSICAL PERFORMANCE, ORCHESTRA
(Conductor's Award)

• Georg Solti conducting the Chicago Symphony, *Mahler: Symphony No. 7 in E Minor*. London.

Pierre Boulez conducting the New York Philharmonic, *Boulez Conducts Bartók: The Miraculous Mandarin and Dance Suite*. Columbia.

Antal Dorati conducting the Philharmonia Hungarica, *Haydn: Symphonies (Complete), Vols. 4 and 5*. London.

Eugene Ormandy conducting the Philadelphia Orchestra, *Glière: Ilya Murometz (Symphony No. 3)*. RCA.

Maksim Shostakovich conducting the Moscow Radio Symphony, *Shostakovich: Symphony No. 15*. Melodiya/Angel.

Leopold Stokowski conducting the London Symphony, *Ives: Orchestral Set No. 2*. London.

Michael Tilson Thomas conducting the Boston Symphony, *Stravinsky: The Rite of Spring (Le Sacre du Printemps)*. Deutsche Grammophon.

Herbert von Karajan conducting the Berlin Philharmonic, *Schumann: Symphonies (4)*. Deutsche Grammophon.

BEST CHAMBER MUSIC PERFORMANCE

• Julian Bream, John Williams, *Julian and John* (selections by Lawes, Carulli, Albéniz, Granados). RCA.

Guarneri Quartet, *Schubert: Quartet No. 13 in A Minor*. RCA.

Igor Kipnis, Thurston Dart, *Music for Two Harpsichords* (Mozart, Byrd, Farnably, etc.). Columbia.

La Salle Quartet, *String Quartets of the New Viennese School*. Deutsche Grammophon.

David Oistrakh, Sviatoslav Richter, *Shostakovich: Sonata for Violin and Piano*. Melodiya/Angel.

Artur Rubinstein, Guarneri Quartet, *Dvořák: Quintet in A Major for Piano*. RCA.

Isaac Stern, Alexander Zakin, *Bartók: Sonatas Nos. 1 and 2 for Violin and Piano*. Columbia.

John Williams, Rafael Puyana, *Music for Guitar and Harpsichord* (works by Straube, Ponce, Dodgson). Columbia.

BEST CLASSICAL PERFORMANCE, INSTRUMENTAL SOLOIST (WITH ORCHESTRA)

• Artur Rubinstein (Ormandy conducting the Philadelphia Orchestra), *Brahms: Concerto No. 2 in B Flat Major for Piano*. RCA.

Philippe Entremont (Boulez conducting the Cleveland Orchestra), *Ravel: Concerto in D Major for Left Hand*. Columbia.

Heinz Holliger (de Waart conducting the New Philharmonia), *Strauss: Concerto in D Major for Oboe*. Philips.

David Oistrakh (Berlin Philharmonic), *Mozart: Complete Works for Violin and Orchestra*. Angel.

E. Power Biggs (Peress conducting the Columbia Brass Percussion Ensemble), *Music for Organ, Brass and Percussion*. Columbia.

Barry Tuckwell (Marriner conducting the Academy of St. Martin-in-the-Fields), *Mozart: The 4 Horn Concertos*. Angel.

BEST CLASSICAL PERFORMANCE, INSTRUMENTAL SOLOIST (WITHOUT ORCHESTRA)

• Vladimir Horowitz, *Horowitz Plays Chopin*. Columbia.

Laurindo Almeida, *The Art of Laurindo Almeida*. Orion.

Rudolf Firkusny, *Janáček: Piano Works (Complete)*. Deutsche Grammophon.

William Masselos, *Schumann: Davidsbundlertanze; Brahms: Sonata No. 1*. RCA.

Arturo Beneditti Michelangeli, *Debussy: Images, Books 1 and 2, Children's Corner Suite*. Deutsche Grammophon.

Itzhak Perlman, *Paganini: The 24 Caprices*. Angel.

Rafael Puyana, *Couperin: Harpsichord Pieces*. Philips.

Charles Rosen, *Beethoven: The Late Sonatas for Piano*. Columbia.

BEST OPERA RECORDING

• *Berlioz: Benvenuto Cellini*, Colin Davis conducting the BBC Symphony; Chorus of Covent Garden (solos: Gedda, Eda-Pierre, Soyer, Berbie). Philips.

Britten: Owen Wingrave, Benjamin Britten conducting the English Chamber Orchestra (solos: Baker, Pears, Luson, Harper). London.

Mussorgsky: Boris Godunov, Herbert von Karajan conducting the Vienna Philharmonic, Vienna Boys' Choir, Vienna State Opera Chorus (solos: Ghiaurov, Vishnevskaya, Spiess, Talvela, Maslennikov). London.

Strauss: Der Rosenkavalier, Leonard Bernstein conducting the Vienna State Opera Chorus; Vienna Philharmonic (solos: Ludwig, Berry, Popp, Jones). Columbia.

Wagner: Der Ring des Nibelungen, Wilhelm Furtwängler conducting the Rome Symphony; RAI Chorus (solos: Mödl, Suthaus, Frantz). Seraphim.

Wagner: Tannhäuser, Georg Solti conducting the Vienna Philharmonic (solos: Kollo, Dernesch, Ludwig, Braun, Sotin). London.

BEST CLASSICAL PERFORMANCE CHORAL (OTHER THAN OPERA)

• Georg Solti conducting the Vienna State Opera Chorus, Vienna Singverein Chorus, Vienna Boys' Choir, Chicago Symphony, soloists, *Mahler: Symphony No. 8 in E Flat Major ("Symphony of a Thousand")*. London.

Leonard Bernstein conducting ensemble orchestra and the Norman Scribner and Berkshire Boys' Choirs, *Bernstein: Mass*. Columbia.

Charles Groves conducting the London Philharmonic Choir and Orchestra, *Delius: A Mass of Life*. Angel.

Raymond Leppard conducting the Glyndebourne Opera Chorus, Ambrosian Singers, English Chamber Orchestra, *Monteverdi: Madrigals, Books 8–10*. Philips.

E. Power Biggs, Gregg Smith Singers, Texas Boys' Choir, Gregg Smith; Vittorio Negri conducting the Tarr Brass Ensemble, *The Glory of Venice (Gabrielli in San Marco—Music for Multiple Choirs, Brass and Organ)*. Columbia.

André Previn conducting the London Symphony Chorus and Orchestra, *Prokofiev: Alexander Nevsky*. Angel.

BEST CLASSICAL PERFORMANCE, VOCAL SOLOIST

• Dietrich Fischer-Dieskau (Richter, accompanist), *Brahms: Die Schöne Magelone*. Angel.

Janet Baker (Barbirolli conducting the London Symphony), *Elgar: Sea Pictures*. Angel.

Jan DeGaetani (Kalish, accompanist), *Songs by Stephen Foster*. Nonesuch.

Anna Moffo (Robert Casadesus, accompanist), *Songs of Debussy*. RCA.

Birgit Nilsson (Davis conducting the London Symphony), *Wagner: Wesendonck Lieder*. Philips.

Leontyne Price (Cleva conducting the London Symphony), *5 Great Operatic Scenes (Verdi: La Traviata, Don Carlo; Tchaikovsky: Onegin; Strauss: Ariadne, etc.)*. RCA.

BEST ENGINEERED RECORDING, CLASSICAL

• Gordon Parry, Kenneth Wilkinson, *Mahler: Symphony No. 8 ("Symphony of a Thousand")* (Solti conducting the Chicago Symphony). London.

Paul Goodman, *Glière: Ilya Murometz (Symphony No. 3)* (Ormandy conducting the Philadelphia Orchestra). RCA.

Edward Graham, Raymond Moore, *Boulez Conducts Bartók: The Miraculous Mandarin (Complete) and Dance Suite* (Boulez conducting the New York Philharmonic; Hugh Ross directing Schola Cantorum). Columbia.

Hans Lauterslager, *Berlioz: Benvenuto Cellini* (Davis conducting the BBC Symphony, Chorus of Covent Garden). Philips.

Raymond Moore, Edward Graham, *Boulez Conducts Stravinsky (Petrushka)* (Boulez conducting the New York Philharmonic). Columbia.

Gordon Parry, James Lock, Colin Moorfoot, *Wagner: Tannhäuser* (Solti conducting the Vienna Philharmonic). London.

Don Puluse, *Bernstein: Mass* (Bernstein conducting the choirs and orchestra). Columbia.

BEST SPOKEN WORD RECORDING

• *Lenny*, original cast. Blue Thumb.

Angela Davis Speaks, Angela Davis. Folkways.

Cannonball Adderley Presents Soul Zodiac, Rick Holmes, narrator. Capitol.

The Word, Rod McKuen. Discus/Stanyan.

Yevtushenko, Yevgeny Yevtushenko. Columbia.

BEST COMEDY RECORDING

• *FM & AM*, George Carlin. Little David.

All in the Family, Carroll O'Connor, Jean Stapleton, Sally Struthers, Robert Reiner. Atlantic.

Big Bambu, Cheech & Chong. Ode.

Geraldine, Flip Wilson. Little David.

BEST RECORDING FOR CHILDREN

• *The Electric Company*, Lee Chamberlin, Bill Cosby, Rita Moreno. Warner Bros.

Kukla, Fran and Ollie, Kukla, Fran & Ollie. RCA/Camden.

The Muppet Alphabet Album, Muppets (Jim Henson). Columbia Children's Album.

Sesame Street II, original TV cast. Warner Bros.

Snoopy, Come Home, Robert B. & Richard M. Sherman, composers. Columbia.

BEST ENGINEERED RECORDING

• Armin Steiner, *Moods* (Neil Diamond). Uni.

Robin Cable, Ken Scott, Phillip MacDonald, *Son of Schmilsson* (Nilsson). RCA.

Eddy Offord, *Fragile* (Yes). Atlantic.

Ken Scott, *Honky Chateau* (Elton John). Uni.

Armin Steiner, *Baby I'm-a Want You* (Bread). Elektra.

BEST ALBUM COVER
(Art Director's Award)

• Acy Lehman, art director; Harvey Dinnerstein, artist, *The Siegel-Schwall Band* (Siegel-Schwall Band). Wooden Nickel.

Hipgnosis, design; Poe, photographer, *Flash* (Flash). Capitol.

Ron Levine, Pacific Eye & Ear, Robert Rodriguez, *Five Dollar Shoes* (Five Dollar Shoes). Neighborhood/Famous.

Bill Levy, Fred Marcellino, *Virgin (The Mission)*. Paramount.

Aaron Schumaker for Tumbleweed Graphics, *Chief* (Dewey Terry). Tumbleweed.

Norman Seeff, *Historical Figures and Ancient Heads* (Canned Heat). United Artists.

Ed Thrasher, Chris Wolf, art directors; Dave Willardson, illustrator; John & Barbara Casado, graphics, *Sunset Ride* (Zephyr). Warner Bros.

Wilkes & Braun, Inc., & Sound Packaging Corp., album design; Robert Otter, photographer, *School's Out* (Alice Cooper). Warner Bros.

BEST ALBUM NOTES, CLASSICAL
(Annotator's Award)

• James Lyons, *Vaughan Williams: Symphony No. 2 ("A London Symphony")* (Previn conducting the London Symphony). RCA.

David Cairns, *Berlioz: Benvenuto Cellini* (Davis conducting the BBC Symphony). Philips.

Tom Eastwood, *Julian and John* (Julian Bream, John Williams). RCA.

Karolynne Gee, *Michael Rabin—in Memoriam* (Michael Rabin). Seraphim.

H. C. Robbins Landon, *Haydn: Symphonies (Complete), Vols. 4 and 5* (Dorati conducting the Philharmonia Hungarica). London.

Sacheverell Sitwell, *John Ogdon Plays Alkan* (John Ogdon). RCA.

Dr. Ursula Von Rauchhaupt, *String Quartets of the New Viennese School* (La Salle Quartet). Deutsche Grammophon.

BEST ALBUM NOTES
(Annotator's Award)

• Tom T. Hall, *Tom T. Hall's Greatest Hits* (Tom T. Hall). Mercury.

Michael Brooks, *Super Chief* (Count Basie). Columbia.

Albert Goldman, *Lenny Bruce/Carnegie Hall* (Lenny Bruce). United Artists.

Charles Mingus, *Let My Children Hear Music* (Charles Mingus). Columbia.

Dan Morgenstern, *Bunny Berigan, His Trumpet and His Orchestra, Vol. 1* (Bunny Berigan). Vintage.

• 1973 •

A Comeback for Flack

Suspense spun around the Record of the Year contest.

Last year's winner, Roberta Flack, was back with her latest chart-topper, "Killing Me Softly with His Song." It was up against "You're So Vain" by past Grammy fave Carly Simon (1971's Best New Artist) and Charlie Rich's first country hit, "Behind Closed Doors," which had the backing of N.A.R.A.S.'s sizable Nashville vote. The race also included a sentimental favorite: the previously un-Grammyed Jim Croce, who died in a plane crash the previous September and was now competing with "Bad, Bad Leroy Brown." All four contenders faced the artist with the most bids this year (six), Stevie Wonder ("You Are the Sunshine of My Life"), who was also overdue for a Grammy tribute, having lost on four occasions in the past.

Four of the best record nominees were also up for Song of the Year, the one exception being "Leroy Brown," which was replaced on the songwriter's lineup by the top-selling single of 1973, Tony Orlando & Dawn's "Tie a Yellow Ribbon Round the Ole Oak Tree," which had strong appeal among N.A.R.A.S.'s most conservative voters.

The winner of both dead-heat races turned out to be "Killing Me Softly with His Song."

Roberta Flack may have snatched three of the top laurels, but it turned out to be Stevie Wonder who really made a killing on Grammy night by winning the most awards. Like Croce, Wonder had sentiment on his side because of a tragedy he'd suffered just months earlier. The Motown star had been in a car crash near Winston-Salem, North Carolina, while making a concert tour of the South,

Presenter Alice Cooper, left, posed backstage with Stevie Wonder, who'd survived a recent car crash to emerge triumphant with four Grammys.

and received multiple head injuries that left him in a coma for four days. He had been sleeping in the passenger seat when the car collided with a truck carrying a load of logs, a few of which tumbled off and crashed into the car's windshield.

On Grammy night, the artist's mother, Lula Hardaway, was with him and helped her blind son up to the podium to accept his trophies. She told the ceremony crowd, "I can only thank God he's alive to accept these awards."

Wonder dedicated his first victory of the night to her. "I would like for you all not to give this to me, but to my mother," he said, also thanking his brother Calvin, who rescued him from the wrecked car. The trophy was one of his two rhythm & blues prizes (best song and best male vocal performance) for the chart-topping single "Superstition." Wonder had written it originally for ex-Yardbird guitarist Jeff Beck, who recorded it—in a bluesy style—but not as a single. A frustrated Wonder then went ahead and made his own pop-rock version for the radio airwaves and release as a single to record stores.

Wonder won a third Grammy when he received the honors for best pop male vocal performance for "You Are the Sunshine of My Life," a million-selling single on which he performed most of the instrumentals in addition to doing the singing. Accepting the honor, he said, "I would like to thank all of you for making this night the sunshine of my life."

"Superstition" and "Sunshine" were both from his hit *Talking Book* LP, which, strangely, was not nominated for Album of the Year. Wonder's follow-up album, *Innervisions,* was, however, and included such classics as "Higher Ground," "Living for the City" and "Don't You Worry 'bout a Thing." When *Innervisions* nabbed both the LP prize and Best Engineered Recording, it crowned a night of success that was a vindication for Wonder, who had recently become the first music star to produce his own albums for Motown. It was also his first LP to feature work exclusively written and sung by him. Wonder's victory came close to making another breakthrough, too: At age 23, he was now the second-youngest artist to receive the Album of the Year award. (Barbra Streisand was 22 when she won in 1963.) "I hope that all of you know I am fantastically grateful," he said in his thank-you remarks.

Gladys Knight & the Pips also proved their r&b to pop appeal when they, like Wonder, reaped Grammys in both fields. Also like Wonder, the group had been working for Motown for more than a decade and its members felt they didn't have enough control over their careers. Knight and the Pips made their break from the Detroit label in 1973, but not before scoring one last single success with "Neither One of Us (Wants to Be the First to Say Goodbye)." The disc hit number two in the best-sellers and earned them the prize for Best Pop Vocal Performance by a Duo, Group or Chorus.

After saying goodbye to Motown, Knight and the Pips signed up with Buddah Records and hit the top of the charts with "Midnight Train to Georgia," which brought them the r&b group vocals prize, too.

Another of the r&b awards went to jazz great Ramsey Lewis, whose keyboard cover of the 1965 pop song "Hang On Sloopy" (originally performed by the McCoys) earned him the r&b instrumental performance trophy. The r&b prize for female vocals went to Aretha Franklin for "Master of Eyes," making Lady Soul officially Lady Grammy, too. Franklin's seventh victory set the new record for Grammy's longest winning streak when it surpassed the six-year reign of comedian Bill Cosby (1964–69).

> Best New Artist Bette Midler billed herself as "trash with flash."

Aretha Franklin's latest recordings were being produced by three-time past Grammy champ Quincy Jones, who now picked up the prize for Best Instrumental Arrangement for "Summer in the City," which he also sang. The instrumental performance statuette for pop music was claimed by Brazilian-born pianist Eumir Deodato for "Also Sprach Zarathustra," his hipped-up interpretation of the Richard Strauss masterwork that was used—in its original, more tame version—in the 1968 blockbuster movie *2001: A Space Odyssey*.

The victories by Flack, Wonder, Knight, Lewis, Franklin and Jones were popular with even the grumpiest of Grammy critics because all of the winners were veteran artists who were widely respected in the music industry. The choice of Grammy's Best New Artist, on the other hand, represented the "Trash with Flash" contingent of musicdom: a self-proclaimed "broad" who also called herself "the last of the truly tacky ladies." The bawdy Bette Midler also had lots of talent that lifted her to celebrity status when her *The Divine Miss M* album soared up the charts in 1973. Midler's tackiness would catch up with her on Grammy night, however. The award was bestowed to an obviously embarrassed Midler by, of all people, Karen Carpenter, whom she often lampooned in her comedy skits. The bawdiness of her best-selling debut LP, *The Divine Miss M* no doubt contributed to its loss in the Album of the Year race.

Class prevailed in the jazz lineup when Woody Herman heard huzzahs for *Giant Steps,* winner of Best Jazz Performance by a Big Band. *Steps* had been performed masterfully once before—by the same sax-playing legend who wrote it, John Coltrane—but Herman and his backup players gave it a new interpretation when they added such enhancements as a heavy dose of tenor clarinet. In the group performance category, Supersax, a new band known for its sassy interpretations of Charlie "Yardbird" Parker compositions, was acknowledged for its first album, *Supersax Plays Bird.*

Art Tatum, who died in 1956, left behind some private tapes of 1941 Harlem jam sessions. The tapes were discovered and put on vinyl, making Tatum eligible for his posthumous prize for Best Jazz Performance by a Soloist. Tatum's *God Is in the House* LP also garnered Best Album Notes.

British-born, Australian-raised Olivia Newton-John was a serious fan of country music, having spent countless hours as a child listening to her father's Tennessee Ernie Ford albums. When the unlikely country singer reaped a c&w performance Grammy, however, for "Let Me Be There" (her first American hit, which reached number six in the weekly Hot 100), the victory was somewhat controversial. Newton-John conceded in her acceptance remarks, "It's probably the first time an English person won an award over Nashville people." But it would not be the last.

N.A.R.A.S. and the Country Music Association agreed on several picks this

Cavalier, pot-puffing Cheech & Chong copped the Best Comedy Recording laurels for *Los Cochinos*.

year: Both honored Charlie Rich and his hit song "Behind Closed Doors" with multiple wins, including best male singer and Best Country Song. It was written by Kenny O'Dell for Rich, who took it to number one on the country and pop charts—a considerable achievement, since some radio stations refused to play the song because they thought it was "dirty."

Nineteen seventy-one Grammy winner Kris Kristofferson, who once had a serious drinking problem, teamed up with his new wife, Rita Coolidge, for his Grammy booty this year: best duo performance for "From the Bottle to the Bottom."

"Dueling Banjos," from the hit film *Deliverance,* won the trophy for instrumentals. The bluegrass pop tune actually pitted a guitar, played by Steve Mandell, against a banjo, handled Earl Scruggs style by Eric Weissberg.

Guitarist Doc Watson had been celebrated during his career for his agile flatpicking of the blues on the Folkways label, but he switched to United Artists Records in 1973 and released *Then and Now,* winner of Best Ethnic or Traditional Recording.

Best Instrumental Composition was

awarded to the score of the Bernardo Bertolucci film *Last Tango in Paris,* which was composed by the Argentina-born music writer and sax/clarinet player Gato Barbieri (who also appeared in the movie). *Last Tango* was not up for the Best Album of Original Score Written for a Motion Picture prize, however, which went to Neil Diamond for *Jonathan Livingston Seagull,* the film adaptation of Richard Bach's megaselling book of pop philosophy about an independently minded seagull who flies against the flock. Diamond had a hit single ("Be") from the score that took him a year to write. Actor Richard Harris lost the Grammy he was expected to win in 1968 for "MacArthur Park," but made up for it this year with 1973's Best Spoken Word Recording of the book version of *Jonathan Livingston Seagull.*

Stephen Sondheim, who won a statuette in 1970 for best stage score *Company,* was now honored for *A Little Night Music,* a musical based on the Ingmar Bergman film *Smiles of a Summer Night.*

The cavalier, pot-puffing duo Cheech & Chong topped nominees such as past victors Bill Cosby and George Carlin for the comedy laurels with their *Los Cochinos* album, which charted for 29 weeks (climbing to number two at its highest point). Typical of their humor was a *Los Cochinos* parody of a radio commercial hyping a treatment for venereal disease that intentionally sounded similar to a well-known ad for cleaning out household sewage pipes: "Hey, there, swinging bachelors! Tired of the steady drip, drip, drip of gonorrhea? Then Peter-Rooter could be just the thing you're looking for!"

When the engineers at Columbia Records went about recording Grammy's Classical Album of the Year, Béla Bartók's Concerto for Orchestra (performed by the New York Philharmonic under the baton of Pierre Boulez), they did so "in the round." Twenty-six micro-phones were placed in a circular performance space in order to catch each note and nuance for a stereo disc intended to be technologically state-of-the-art. The feat succeeded, earning the sound staff an engineering Grammy and Boulez the orchestral performance prize. *High Fidelity* reported: "Here, the music's textures are subtly emphasized, enhanced and clarified by the manner in which Boulez deploys his forces, and the interweaving thematic lines gain much from the fact that they can be related to precise sources in the surrounding space."

Vladimir Horowitz returned for a third year in a row to take the soloist honors (without orchestra). His latest recital recording was of music by Alexander Scriabin, including two Op. Poems and Etudes, Op. 8, Nos. 2, 8, 10 and 11. "This is certainly one of the finest performances available of any Scriabin work," *High Fidelity* said. The award for soloist with orchestral accompaniment went to Russian-born pianist Vladimir Ashkenazy for *Beethoven: Concertos (5) for Piano and Orchestra.*

The same publication was less enchanted with Grammy's choice for the choral laurels: André Previn and Arthur Oldham conducting the London Symphony Orchestra Chorus in Sir William Walton's *Belshazzar's Feast.* While *High Fidelity* claimed it was "a rousing, brilliant performance," it back-stepped in adding slights at both Walton and Previn: "It is the kind of work that makes a great impression on one hearing, but leaves nothing for the second, and that is precisely the kind of music in which André Previn excels." Gunther Schuller and the New England Conservatory Ragtime Ensemble gave the year's Best Chamber Music Performance with Scott Joplin's *The Red Back Book.*

A loser of the trophy for best classical album won best opera: *Carmen,* with

> "Sondheim is the genius who keeps taking musical theater to new places."

Leonard Bernstein conducting Marilyn Horne and the Metropolitan Opera Orchestra. "Not since 1959, when RCA recorded the new production of Verdi's *Macbeth*, have the forces of the Metropolitan Opera taken part in a complete studio recording," *High Fidelity* wrote. "However, Deutsche Grammophon's increasing activity on the American scene, and their particular interest in the Met . . . found a logical continuation in a complete *Carmen*"—a "big" performance, it added, that was "newsworthy and freshly studied."

Leontyne Price had been the voice on a celebrated version of *Carmen* in 1964. Price proved herself again this year by winning Grammy number nine for an album of Puccini arias she performed "with a freedom and a radiance that precious few other sopranos today could match," *High Fidelity* said.

Just prior to the Grammycast, the artist with the most awards so far, Henry Mancini, gave away five new statuettes: entries into N.A.R.A.S.'s newly established Hall of Fame, which honored music and recordings made before the Grammys were first given away for 1958. The first admissions were Coleman Hawkins's "Body and Soul," Nat King Cole's "The Christmas Song," Paul Whiteman and George Gershwin's recording of "Rhapsody in Blue," Louis Armstrong's "West End Blues" and Bing Crosby's "White Christmas."

A controversy erupted before the Grammy ceremony when the Hollywood Palladium was oversold. The *L.A. Times* publicly bemoaned N.A.R.A.S.'s "delicate, ego-bruising" plight of having to decide who would get in, and then, once inside—and even more important—who would be seated at the front tables. The latter was decided by lottery.

Variety said, "It was a flashy, name-splashed layout originating from the Hollywood Palladium, which was rigged like one of the old Busby Berkeley sound stages. . . . Andy Williams was back as host and handled his assignment with his customary ingratiating casualness, including

André Previn shared the choral Grammy with Arthur Oldham for Walton's *Belshazzar's Feast*.

his vocalizing of the five songs nominated for the best song of the year.

"Winners evidently had been told to keep their acceptance speeches short, and they did, but this may have deprived the show of drama badly needed. There were a few such touches, but too few. One was the ovation given four-Grammy winner Stevie Wonder and his poignant tribute to the late Jim Croce. In a later appearance, Wonder's touching expression of appreciation brought from Williams the observation, 'Most of us see with our eyes, Stevie sees with his heart.' "

The Grammycast had a major—and brand-new—problem. "Many of the awards and the winning artists were seen just a couple of weeks ago on the [first] American Music Awards show" on ABC, *Variety* noted. "Stevie Wonder, Roberta Flack, and Tony Orlando & Dawn were among those on both shows, so the Grammy Awards couldn't escape that *déjà vu* feeling."

The American Music Awards were

established, in part, because when ABC refused to televise last year's Nashville show, CBS picked up the broadcast option and scored a huge ratings hit.

But there was actually more to it than that. Various members of the music industry thought N.A.R.A.S. did a poor job of naming each year's best music and wanted an alternative accolade. Few of Grammy's choices, critics claimed, were in tune with what the public obviously loved—and bought (an ironic accusation, since the Grammys had been plagued from 1958 on with allegations that they deferred too often to the pop charts). The American Music Awards, however, would rely on the rankings in a large way to determine

America's "favorite" artists and recordings, while N.A.R.A.S. chose to name the year's "best" talent and recordings.

How did the results compare? Most of the A.M.A. choices were different but still went to artists favored by N.A.R.A.S. in the past: Helen Reddy, the Carpenters, Charley Pride and Lynn Anderson were all big winners at the first awards ceremony. Other initial winners: Stevie Wonder and Roberta Flack (Favorite Male and Female Artists, Soul and R&B), "Superstition" (Favorite Soul/R&B Single) and "Behind Closed Doors" (Favorite Country Single). The Grammys and the American Music Awards were now at war, and both of them were fighting for the same music.

• 1973 •

The ceremony was broadcast on CBS from the Hollywood Palladium on March 2, 1974, for the awards eligibility period of October 16, 1972, through October 15, 1973.

ALBUM OF THE YEAR
• *Innervisions*, Stevie Wonder. Tamla/Motown.
Behind Closed Doors, Charlie Rich. Epic/Columbia.
The Divine Miss M, Bette Midler. Atlantic.
Killing Me Softly, Roberta Flack. Atlantic.
There Goes Rhymin' Simon, Paul Simon. Columbia.

RECORD OF THE YEAR
• "Killing Me Softly with His Song," Roberta Flack. Atlantic.
"Bad, Bad Leroy Brown," Jim Croce. ABC.
"Behind Closed Doors," Charlie Rich. Epic/Columbia.
"You Are the Sunshine of My Life," Stevie Wonder. Tamla/Motown.
"You're So Vain," Carly Simon. Elektra.

SONG OF THE YEAR
(Songwriter's Award)
• "Killing Me Softly with His Song," Norman Gimbel, Charles Fox.
"Behind Closed Doors," Kenny O'Dell.
"Tie a Yellow Ribbon Round the Ole Oak Tree," Irwin Levine, L. Russell Brown.
"You Are the Sunshine of My Life," Stevie Wonder.
"You're So Vain," Carly Simon.

BEST NEW ARTIST
• Bette Midler
Eumir Deodato
Maureen McGovern
Marie Osmond
Barry White

BEST POP VOCAL PERFORMANCE, MALE
• Stevie Wonder, "You Are the Sunshine of My Life." Tamla/Motown.
Perry Como, "And I Love You So." RCA.
Jim Croce, "Bad, Bad Leroy Brown." ABC.
Elton John, "Daniel." MCA.

Paul Simon, *There Goes Rhymin' Simon.*
Columbia.

BEST POP VOCAL PERFORMANCE, FEMALE

- Roberta Flack, "Killing Me Softly with His Song." Atlantic.
Bette Midler, "Boogie Woogie Bugle Boy." Atlantic.
Anne Murray, "Danny's Song." Capitol.
Diana Ross, "Touch Me in the Morning." Motown.
Carly Simon, "You're So Vain." Elektra.

BEST POP VOCAL PERFORMANCE BY A DUO, GROUP OR CHORUS

- Gladys Knight & the Pips, "Neither One of Us (Wants to Be the First to Say Goodbye)." Soul/Motown.
Carpenters, "Sing." A&M.
Dawn Featuring Tony Orlando, "Tie a Yellow Ribbon Round the Ole Oak Tree." Bell.
Paul McCartney & Wings, "Live and Let Die." Apple/Capitol.
Seals & Crofts, "Diamond Girl." Warner Bros.

BEST POP INSTRUMENTAL PERFORMANCE

- Eumir Deodato, "Also Sprach Zarathustra (*2001*)." CTI.
Quincy Jones, *You've Got It Bad Girl.* A&M.
Mahavishnu Orchestra, "Bird of Fire." Columbia.
Billy Preston, "Space Race." A&M.
Edgar Winter, "Frankenstein." Epic/Columbia.

BEST RHYTHM & BLUES VOCAL PERFORMANCE, MALE

- Stevie Wonder, "Superstition." Tamla/Motown.
Marvin Gaye, *Let's Get It On.* Motown.
Al Green, "Call Me (Come Back Home)." Hi/London.
Eddie Kendricks, "Keep On Truckin'." Tamla/Motown.
Barry White, "I'm Gonna Love You Just a Little More Baby." 20th Century.

BEST RHYTHM & BLUES VOCAL PERFORMANCE, FEMALE

- Aretha Franklin, "Master of Eyes." Atlantic.
Etta James, *Etta James.* Chess.
Ann Peebles, "I Can't Stand the Rain." Hi/London.
Esther Phillips, *Alone Again (Naturally).* Kudu/CTI.
Sylvia, "Pillow Talk." Vibration.

BEST RHYTHM & BLUES VOCAL PERFORMANCE BY A DUO, GROUP OR CHORUS

- Gladys Knight & the Pips, "Midnight Train to Georgia." Buddah.
O'Jays, "Love Train." Philadelphia International/Columbia.
Spinners, "Could It Be I'm Falling in Love." Atlantic.
Staple Singers, "Be What You Are." Stax.
War, "The Cisco Kid." United Artists.

BEST RHYTHM & BLUES INSTRUMENTAL PERFORMANCE

- Ramsey Lewis, "Hang On Sloopy." Columbia.
Donald Byrd, *Black Byrd.* Blue Note/United Artists.
Crusaders, *2nd Crusade.* Blue Thumb.
Manu Dibango, *Soul Makossa.* Atlantic.
Young-Holt Unlimited, "Yes We Can Can." Atlantic.

BEST RHYTHM & BLUES SONG
(Songwriter's Award)

- "Superstition," Stevie Wonder.
"The Cisco Kid," War.
"Family Affair," Sylvester Stewart.
"Love Train," Ken Gamble, Leon Huff.
"Midnight Train to Georgia," Jim Weatherly.

BEST JAZZ PERFORMANCE BY A SOLOIST

- Art Tatum, *God Is in the House.* Onyx.
Clifford Brown, *The Beginning and the End.* Columbia.

Ray Brown (Milt Jackson Quintet), "The Very Thought of You." Impulse/ABC.

Freddie Hubbard, "In a Mist." CTI.

Hubert Laws, *Morning Star*. CTI.

BEST JAZZ PERFORMANCE BY A GROUP

• Supersax, *Supersax Plays Bird*. Capitol.

Cannonball Adderley Quintet, *Inside Straight*. Fantasy.

Chick Corea, Return to Forever, *Light as a Feather*. Polydor.

Jim Hall, Ron Carter, *Alone Together*. Milestone.

Oregon, *Music of Another Present Era*. Vanguard.

BEST JAZZ PERFORMANCE BY A BIG BAND

• Woody Herman, *Giant Steps*. Fantasy.

Don Ellis, *Soaring*. Mps/Basf.

Gil Evans, *Svengali*. Atlantic.

Oliver Nelson, *Swiss Suite*. Flying Dutchman.

Randy Weston, *Tanjah*. Polydor.

BEST COUNTRY VOCAL PERFORMANCE, MALE

• Charlie Rich, "Behind Closed Doors." Epic/Columbia.

Tom T. Hall, "(Old Dogs, Children and) Watermelon Wine." Mercury.

Kris Kristofferson, "Why Me." Monument.

Charley Pride, "Amazing Love." RCA.

Johnny Russell, "Rednecks, White Socks & Blue Ribbon Beer." RCA.

BEST COUNTRY VOCAL PERFORMANCE, FEMALE

• Olivia Newton-John, "Let Me Be There." MCA.

Barbara Fairchild, "Teddy Bear Song." Columbia.

Marie Osmond, "Paper Roses." MGM.

Dottie West, "Country Sunshine." RCA.

Tammy Wynette, "Kids Say the Darndest Things." Epic/Columbia.

BEST COUNTRY VOCAL PERFORMANCE BY A DUO OR GROUP

• Kris Kristofferson, Rita Coolidge, "From the Bottle to the Bottom." A&M.

Dolly Parton, Porter Waggoner, "If Teardrops Were Pennies." RCA.

Statler Brothers, *Carry Me Back*. Mercury.

Conway Twitty, Loretta Lynn, "Louisiana Woman, Mississippi Man." MCA.

Tammy Wynette, George Jones, "We're Gonna Hold On." Epic/Columbia.

BEST COUNTRY INSTRUMENTAL PERFORMANCE

• Eric Weissberg, Steve Mandell, "Dueling Banjos." Warner Bros.

Chet Atkins, "Fiddlin' Around." RCA.

Chet Atkins, *Superpickers*. RCA.

Danny Davis & the Nashville Brass, *I'll Fly Away*. RCA.

Charlie McCoy, *Good Time Charlie*. Monument.

BEST COUNTRY SONG
(Songwriter's Award)

• "Behind Closed Doors," Kenny O'Dell.

"Country Sunshine," Billy Davis, Dottie West.

"The Most Beautiful Girl," Rory Bourke, Billy Sherrill, Norris Wilson.

"(Old Dogs, Children and) Watermelon Wine," Tom T. Hall.

"Why Me," Kris Kristofferson.

BEST INSPIRATIONAL PERFORMANCE

• Bill Gaither Trio, *Let's Just Praise the Lord*. Impact/Heartwarming.

Anita Bryant, *Anita Bryant . . . Naturally*. Myrrh/Word.

Roy Rogers & Dale Evans, *In the Sweet By and By*. Word.

George Beverly Shea, *There's Something About That Name*. RCA.

Connie Smith, *All the Praises*. RCA.

BEST SOUL GOSPEL PERFORMANCE

• Dixie Hummingbirds, "Loves Me Like a Rock." ABC.

James Cleveland, "Down Memory Lane." Savoy.

Jessy Dixon, "He Ain't Heavy." Gospel/Savoy.

Edwin Hawkins Singers, *New World*. Buddah.

Swan Silvertones, *You've Got a Friend*. Hob/Scepter.

BEST GOSPEL PERFORMANCE (OTHER THAN SOUL GOSPEL)

• Blackwood Brothers, *Release Me (from My Sin)*. Skylite.

Andrae Crouch, *Just Andrae*. Light/Word.

The Imperials, *Live*. Impact/Heartwarming.

Oak Ridge Boys, *Street Gospel*. Heartwarming.

Statesmen, *I Believe in Jesus*. Artistic.

BEST ETHNIC OR TRADITIONAL RECORDING

• *Then and Now*, Doc Watson. United Artists.

Blues at Montreux, King Curtis, Champion Jack Dupree. Atlantic.

Can't Get No Grindin', Muddy Waters. Chess.

John Lee Hooker's Detroit (1948–1952), John Lee Hooker. United Artists.

Leadbelly (Live in Concert), Leadbelly. Playboy.

BEST INSTRUMENTAL COMPOSITION
(Composer's Award)

• Gato Barbieri, "Last Tango in Paris."

Manu Dibango, "Soul Makossa."

Billy Preston, "Space Race."

Thus van Leer, Jan Akkerman, "Hocus Pocus."

Edgar Winter, "Frankenstein."

BEST INSTRUMENTAL ARRANGEMENT

• Quincy Jones, "Summer in the City" (Quincy Jones). A&M.

Chick Corea, "Spain" (Chick Corea, Return to Forever). Polydor.

Lee Holdridge, "Prologue/Crunchy Granola Suite" (Neil Diamond). MCA.

Bill Holman, "The Daily Dance" (Stan Kenton & His Orchestra). Creative World.

Bob James, "Easy Living/Ain't Nobody's Business If I Do (Medley)" (Grover Washington, Jr.). Kudu/CTI.

BEST ARRANGEMENT ACCOMPANYING VOCALIST(S)

• George Martin, "Live and Let Die" (Paul McCartney & Wings). Apple/Capitol.

Tom Baird, Gene Page, "Touch Me in the Morning" (Diana Ross). Motown.

Richard Carpenter, "Sing" (Carpenters). A&M.

Dave Grusin, "Lady Love" (Jon Lucien). RCA.

Dave Grusin, "Rashida" (Jon Lucien). RCA.

Gene Puerling, "Michelle" (Singers Unlimited). MPS/BASF.

BEST SCORE FROM AN ORIGINAL CAST SHOW ALBUM
(Composer's Award)

• *A Little Night Music*, Stephen Sondheim. Columbia.

Cyrano, Anthony Burgess, Michael J. Lewis. A&M.

Man from the East, Stomu Yamashita. Island/Capitol.

Pippin, Stephen Schwartz. Motown.

Seesaw, Cy Coleman, Dorothy Fields. Buddah.

BEST ALBUM OF ORIGINAL SCORE WRITTEN FOR A MOTION PICTURE OR TV SPECIAL
(Composer's Award)

• *Jonathan Livingston Seagull*, Neil Diamond. Columbia.

Last Tango in Paris, Gato Barbieri. United Artists.

Live and Let Die, Paul & Linda McCartney, George Martin. United Artists.

Pat Garrett and Billy the Kid, Bob Dylan. Columbia.

Sounder, Taj Mahal. Columbia.

ALBUM OF THE YEAR, CLASSICAL

• *Bartók: Concerto for Orchestra*,
Pierre Boulez conducting the New
York Philharmonic. Columbia.

*Beethoven: Concertos (5) for Piano and
Orchestra*, Georg Solti conducting
the Chicago Symphony (solo:
Vladimir Ashkenazy). London.

Bizet: Carmen, Leonard Bernstein con-
ducting the Metropolitan Opera
Orchestra, Manhattan Opera Chorus
(solos: Marilyn Horne, James
McCracken, Adriana Maliponte, Tom
Krause). Deutsche
Grammophon/Polydor.

Joplin: The Red Back Book, Gunther
Schuller conducting the Conservatory Ragtime Ensemble. Angel/Capi-
tol.

Prokofiev: Romeo and Juliet, Lorin
Maazel conducting the Cleveland
Orchestra. London.

*Puccini: Heroines (La Bohème, La Ron-
dine, Tosca, Manon Lescaut)*, Esward
Downes conducting the New Philharmonia (solo: Leontyne Price). RCA.

*Rachmaninov: The Complete Rachmani-
nov—Vols. 1–3*, (solo: Sergei Rachmaninov). RCA.

*Rachmaninov: Concerto No. 2 in C
Minor for Piano*, Eugene Ormandy
conducting the Philadelphia Orchestra (solo: Artur Rubinstein). RCA.

BEST CLASSICAL PERFORMANCE, ORCHESTRA
(Conductor's Award)

• Pierre Boulez conducting the New
York Philharmonic, *Bartók: Concerto for Orchestra*. Columbia.

Leonard Bernstein conducting the New
York Philharmonic, *Holst: The Planets*. Columbia.

Lorin Maazel conducting the Cleveland
Orchestra, *Prokofiev: Romeo and
Juliet*. London.

Eugene Ormandy conducting the
Philadelphia Orchestra, *Sibelius:
Symphony No. 2 in D Major*. RCA.

Seiji Ozawa conducting the Boston
Symphony, *Berlioz: Symphonie Fan-
tastique*. Deutsche
Grammophon/Polydor.

Seiji Ozawa conducting the San Fran-
cisco Symphony (Seigel-Schwall
Band), *Russo: 3 Pieces for Blues
Band and Orchestra*. Deutsche
Grammophon/Polydor.

André Previn conducting the London
Symphony, *Prokofiev: Romeo and
Juliet (Complete)*. Angel/Capitol.

Georg Solti conducting the Chicago
Symphony, *Beethoven: Symphony
No. 9 in D Minor*. London.

BEST CHAMBER MUSIC PERFORMANCE

• Gunther Schuller, New England Ragtime Ensemble, *Joplin: The Red
Back Book*. Angel/Capitol.

Janet Baker, Dietrich Fischer-Dieskau,
Schubert: Duets. Deutsche Gram-
mophon/Polydor.

Julian Bream, Melos Ensemble of London, David Atherton, *Bennett: Concerto for Guitar and Chamber
Ensemble*. RCA.

Cleveland Quartet, *Brahms: Quartets
for Strings (Complete)*. RCA.

Concord String Quartet, *Rochberg:
Quartet No. 3 for Strings*. Nonesuch.

Artur Rubinstein, Guarneri Quartet,
*Dvořák: Piano Quartet in E Flat
Major, Op. 87*. RCA.

Western Wind Vocal Ensemble, *Early
American Vocal Music*. Nonesuch.

BEST CLASSICAL PERFORMANCE, INSTRUMENTAL SOLOIST(S) (WITH ORCHESTRA)

• Vladimir Ashkenazy (Solti conducting
the Chicago Symphony), *Beethoven:
Concertos (5) for Piano and Orchestra*. London.

Stephen Bishop (Davis conducting the
London Symphony), *Mozart: Concertos No. 21 in C Major and No. 25
in C Major*. Philips/Mercury.

Aldo Ciccolini (Baudo conducting the
Orchestre de Paris), *Saint-Saëns:
Concertos for Piano (Complete)*.
Seraphim/Capitol.

Emil Gilels (Jochum conducting the Berlin Philharmonic), *Brahms: Concertos No. 1 in D Minor for Piano and Orchestra and No. 2 in B Flat Major for Piano and Orchestra.* Deutsche Grammophon/Polydor.

Artur Rubinstein (Ormandy conducting the Philadelphia Orchestra), *Rachmaninov: Concerto No. 2 in C Minor for Piano.* RCA.

John Williams (Previn conducting the London Symphony), *Previn: Concerto for Guitar and Orchestra; Ponce: Concierto del Sur for Guitar and Orchestra.* Columbia.

Pinchas Zukerman (Zukerman conducting the English Chamber Orchestra), *Vivaldi: The Four Seasons.* Columbia.

BEST CLASSICAL PERFORMANCE, INSTRUMENTAL SOLOIST(S) (WITHOUT ORCHESTRA)

• Vladimir Horowitz, *Scriabin: Horowitz Plays Scriabin.* Columbia.
Julian Bream, *The Woods So Wild.* RCA.
Alfred Brendel, *Schubert: Sonata in B Flat, Op. 960.* Philips/Mercury.
Virgil Fox, *Heavy Organ at Carnegie Hall.* RCA.
Glenn Gould, *Bach: French Suites, 1–4.* Columbia.
Maurizio Pollini, *Chopin: Etudes.* Deutsche Grammophon/Polydor.
Sviatoslav Richter, *Bach: The Well-Tempered Clavier.* Melodiya/Angel.

BEST OPERA RECORDING

• *Bizet: Carmen*, Leonard Bernstein conducting the Metropolitan Opera Orchestra and Manhattan Opera Chorus (solos: Horne, McCracken, Maliponte, Krause). Deutsche Grammophon/Polydor.
Delius: A Village Romeo and Juliet, Meredith Davies conducting the Royal Philharmonic and John Alldis Choir (solos: Tear, Harwood). Angel/Capitol.
Puccini: Turandot, Zubin Mehta conducting the London Philharmonic;

John Alldis Choir and Wandsworth School Choir (solos: Sutherland, Pavarotti, Caballé, Ghiaurov, Krause, Pears). London.
Wagner: Der Ring des Nibelungen, Karl Böhm conducting the Bayreuth Festival Orchestra (solos: Nilsson, Rysanek, Burmaister, Windgassen, King, Wohlfart, Adam, Stewart, Talvela, Greindl, Neidlinger). Philips/Mercury.
Wagner: Parsifal, Georg Solti conducting the Vienna Philharmonic, Vienna State Opera Chorus, Vienna Boys' Choir (solos: Kollo, Ludwig, Fischer-Dieskau, Frick, Keleman, Hotter). London.
Wagner: Tristan und Isolde, Herbert von Karajan conducting the Berlin Philharmonic (solos: Vickers, Dernesch). Angel/Capitol.

BEST CLASSICAL CHORAL PERFORMANCE, (OTHER THAN OPERA)

• Arthur Oldham conducting the London Symphony Orchestra Chorus; André Previn conducting the London Symphony, *Walton: Belshazzar's Feast.* Angel/Capitol.
Helmuth Froschauer conducting the Vienna Singverein; Herbert von Karajan conducting the Berlin Philharmonic, *Bach: St. Matthew Passion.* Deutsche Grammophon/Polydor.
Eugen Jochum conducting the Netherlands Radio Chorus and Concertgebouw Orchestra (solos: Giebel, Höffgen, Häfliger, Ridderbusch), *Beethoven: Missa Solemnis.* Philips.
Raymond Leppard conducting the Glyndebourne Opera Chorus, *Monteverdi: Madrigals, Books 3 and 4.* Philips.
Norman Scribner directing Norman Scribner Choir; Leonard Bernstein conducting the Orchestra, *Haydn: Mass in Time of War (Leonard Bernstein's Concert for Peace).* Columbia.
Herbert von Karajan conducting the Chorus of the Deutsche Opera,

Berlin, and Berlin Philharmonic, *Haydn: The Seasons*. Angel/Capitol.

David Willcocks conducting the Choir of King's College, Cambridge; Benjamin Britten conducting the London Symphony, *Elgar: The Dream of Gerontius*. London.

BEST CLASSICAL PERFORMANCE, VOCAL SOLOIST

• Leontyne Price (Downes conducting the New Philharmonia), *Puccini: Heroines (La Bohème, La Rondine, Tosca, Manon Lescaut)*. RCA.

Janet Baker (Gerald Moore, accompanist), *Schubert: Songs*. Seraphim/Capitol.

Cathy Berberian (Berio conducting the London Sinfonietta), *Berio: Recital 1 ("For Cathy")*. RCA.

Placido Domingo (Santi conducting the New Philharmonia), *La Voce d'Oro*. RCA.

Heather Harper (Boulez conducting the BBC Symphony), *Berg: 7 Early Songs*. Columbia.

Marilyn Horne (Lewis conducting the Royal Philharmonic), *Marilyn Horne Sings Rossini (Excerpts from "Siege of Corinth" and "La Donna del Lago")*. London.

Yvonne Minton, Rene Kollo (Solti conducting the Chicago Symphony), *Mahler: Das Lied von der Erde*. London.

Martti Talvela (Irwin Gage, accompanist), *Martti Talvela—A Lieder Recital (Schumann)*. London.

BEST ENGINEERED RECORDING, CLASSICAL

• Edward T. Graham, Raymond Moore, *Bartók: Concerto for Orchestra* (Boulez conducting the New York Philharmonic). Columbia.

Paul Goodman, *Bach's Greatest Fugues* (Ormandy conducting the Philadelphia Orchestra). RCA.

Edward T. Graham, Larry Keyes, *Holst: The Planets* (Bernstein conducting the New York Philharmonic). Columbia.

Gunther Hermanns, *Bizet: Carmen* (Bernstein conducting the Metropolitan Opera Orchestra and soloists). Deutsche Grammophon/Polydor.

Jack Law, Colin Moortoot, Gordon Parry, *Prokofiev: Romeo and Juliet* (Maazel conducting the Cleveland Orchestra). London.

Tony Salvatore, *Puccini: Heroines* (Downes conducting the New Philharmonia; solo: Leontyne Price). RCA.

Hans Schweigmann, *Berlioz: Symphonie Fantastique* (Ozawa conducting the Boston Symphony). Deutsche Grammophon/Polydor.

Kenneth Wilkinson, Gordon Parry, *Wagner: Parsifal* (Solti conducting the Vienna Philharmonic and soloists). London.

BEST ALBUM NOTES, CLASSICAL
(Annotator's Award)

• Glenn Gould, *Hindemith: Sonatas for Piano (Complete)* (Glenn Gould). Columbia.

Misha Donat, *Berio: Recital 1 ("For Cathy")* (Berio conducting the London Sinfonietta; solo: Berberian). RCA.

Tom Eastwood, *The Woods So Wild* (Julian Bream). RCA.

Irving Kolodin, *Dvořák: Piano Quartet in E Flat Major, Op. 87* (Guarneri Quartet; solo: Artur Rubinstein). RCA.

Harvey Phillips, *Bizet: Carmen* (Bernstein conducting the Metropolitan Opera Orchestra; solos: Horne, McCracken, Maliponte, Krause). Deutsche Grammophon.

Alan Rich, *Rachmaninov: Concerto No. 2 in C Minor for Piano* (Ormandy conducting the Philadelphia Orchestra; solo: Rubinstein). RCA.

H. C. Robbins Landon, *Haydn: Symphonies Nos. 36 and 48* (Dorati conducting the Philharmonia Hungarica). London.

H. C. Robbins Landon, *Haydn: Symphonies No. 20 in C Major and No.*

35 in B Flat Major (Dorati conducting the Philharmonica Hungarica). London.

Erik Smith, *Bach: Brandenburg Concertos* (Marriner conducting the Academy of St. Martin-in-the-Fields). Philips/Mercury.

Clair Van Ausdall, *Debussy: La Mer/Prélude à l'Après-Midi d'un Faune; Ravel: Daphnis et Chloé, Suite No. 2* (Ormandy conducting the Philadelphia Orchestra). RCA.

BEST SPOKEN WORD RECORDING

• *Jonathan Livingston Seagull,* Richard Harris. Dunhill/ABC.
America, Why I Love Her, John Wayne. RCA.
Slaughterhouse Five, Kurt Vonnegut, Jr. Caedmon.
Songs and Conversations, Billie Holiday. Paramount.
Witches, Ghosts and Goblins, Vincent Price. Caedmon.

BEST COMEDY RECORDING

• *Los Cochinos*, Cheech & Chong. Ode/A&M.
Fat Albert, Bill Cosby. MCA.
Occupation: Foole, George Carlin. Little David/Atlantic.
Richard Nixon: A Fantasy, David Frye. Buddah.
Lemmings, National Lampoon. Banana/Blue Thumb.
Child of the 50s, Robert Klein. Brut/Buddah.

BEST RECORDING FOR CHILDREN

• *Sesame Street Live, Sesame Street* cast. Columbia.
Free to Be . . . You and Me, Marlo Thomas & Friends. Bell.
The Little Prince, Peter Ustinov. Argo.
Multiplication Rock, Bob Dorough, Grady Tate, Blossom Dearie. Capitol.
Songs from "The Electric Company" TV Show. Disneyland.

BEST ENGINEERED RECORDING (OTHER THAN CLASSICAL)

• Robert Margouleff, Malcolm Cecil, *Innervisions* (Stevie Wonder). Tamla/Motown.
Alan Parsons, *The Dark Side of the Moon* (Pink Floyd). Harvest/Capitol.
David Hentschel, *Goodbye Yellow Brick Road* (Elton John). MCA.
Donn Landee, "Long Train Runnin' " (Doobie Brothers). Warner Bros.
Robin Geoffrey Cable, Bill Schnee, *No Secrets* (Carly Simon). Elektra.

BEST ALBUM PACKAGE
(Art Director's Award)

Wilkes & Braun, Inc., *Tommy* (London Symphony/Chambre Choir). Ode/A&M.
John Berg, *Chicago VI* (Chicago). Columbia.
Hipgnosis, *Houses of the Holy* (Led Zeppelin). Atlantic.
Jim Ladwig/AGI, *Ooh La La* (Faces). Warner Bros.
Ode Visuals, Inc., *Los Cochinos* (Cheech & Chong). Ode/A&M.
Pacific Eye & Ear, *Billion Dollar Babies* (Alice Cooper). Warner Bros.
Mike Salisbury, *The World of Ike and Tina* (Ike & Tina Turner). United Artists.
Al Steckler, *Chubby Checker's Greatest Hits* (Chubby Checker). Abkco.

BEST ALBUM NOTES (OTHER THAN CLASSICAL)
(Annotator's Award)

• Dan Morgenstern, *God Is in the House* (Art Tatum). Onyx.
Stan Cornyn, *Ol' Blue Eyes Is Back* (Frank Sinatra). Reprise/Warner Bros.
Chet Flippo, *Lonesome, On'ry and Mean* (Waylon Jennings). RCA.
William Ivey, *This Is Jimmie Rodgers* (Jimmie Rodgers). RCA.
Lionel Newman, *Remember Marilyn* (Marilyn Monroe). 20th Century.

• 1974 •

Honestly, Marvin!

Roberta Flack was back *again* as a Record of the Year nominee ("Feel Like Makin' Love"), competing against two music veterans overdue for the honor—Joni Mitchell ("Help Me") and Elton John ("Don't Let the Sun Go Down on Me")—plus a Barbie-faced, first-time contender, Olivia Newton-John, who wooed voters with "I Honestly Love You."

At last year's Grammy, the Australian-born Newton-John triggered a lot of hootin' and hollerin' down in the N.A.R.A.S. Nashville chapter when she won in a country category. Now the sweet-seeming vocalist struck back with a double wollop, seizing the laurels for both Record of the Year and best female pop vocalist. The victories were also a vindication for the tune, which competed for Song of the Year award. A&M Records at first resisted its release as a single when Newton-John included it on her *If You Love Me, Let Me Know* LP, but, as its cowriter Jeffry Barry once pointed out, pretty soon "radio demanded it."

Any ruckus that the latest wins by Newton-John might have caused were quickly drowned out by another hubbub on Grammy night. The victory that "raised the most eyebrows" and "was a bit shaky," according to *Variety,* was the selection of Best New Artist—Marvin Hamlisch. *Variety* added, "Hamlisch has emerged as one of the top film score writers and also plays excellent piano, but his name doesn't have the b.o. [box office] charisma of the other contenders."

The other nominees included Phoebe Snow and Bad Company. When the winner was announced, *Rolling Stone* reported that the vote result "drew disap-

"White bread" and black soul: 1974 best record victor Olivia Newton-John with 1973 and 1974 album champ Stevie Wonder (with wife, right).

Los Angeles Public Library

proving grumbles from those among the 2,000 people assembled in the Uris [Theater in New York] who felt that the industry old guard was trying to play it safe." In the past, the Best New Artist award traditionally went to winners known primarily as performance artists. Hamlisch was mostly regarded as a composer, although when he performed "The Entertainer" on piano, the single became the 40th-best-seller of the year. Grammy's best record, "I Honestly Love You," by comparison, came in at number 50.

At the previous year's Oscars, Hamlisch won an unprecedented three music awards for contributing to the scores of two Robert Redford films, *The Way We Were* (costarring past Grammy winner Barbra Streisand) and Oscar's Best Picture, *The Sting,* which teamed Redford with Paul Newman. Streisand's rendition of "The Way We Were" was the top-selling single of 1974, while the score to *The Sting* launched a nationwide revival of interest in the music of ragtime composer Scott Joplin, who wrote "The Entertainer."

At the Grammys, Hamlisch picked up two golden statuettes for "The Way We Were": Song of the Year and best film score. "The Entertainer" also earned him the prize for Best Pop Instrumental Performance. When he accepted the accolade for Best New Artist, Hamlisch thanked Joplin, calling him "the real new artist of the year."

The Grammy grumbles over Hamlisch seem surprising in retrospect, given that he was enjoying an amazing awards romp in the mid-1970s thanks to his crossover success in most areas of show business. His *A Chorus Line* musical opened in New York at Joe Papp's Public Theater a few months after this year's Grammy ceremony, then, by summertime, was moved to Broadway, where it would reap a staggering nine trophies at the Tony Awards. *A Chorus Line* would also nab a Pulitzer Prize and eventually become the longest-running musical in Broadway history, a record that would be surpassed by *Cats* in 1997.

Tied with Hamlisch for the most victories was last year's Grammy sweeper Stevie Wonder, who was now back in the race with *Fulfillingness' First Finale,* his first number-one-ranked LP since *Little Stevie Wonder—The 10-Year-Old Genius* in 1963. *Variety* reported that he had "the inside track for Grammy honors again this year with seven nominations, three as a performer, two as a songwriter and two as a producer."

When Wonder won the pop vocals award, he received a standing ovation. He told the crowd that he planned to give the statuette to Mercer Ellington in honor of his late father, Duke, "since Mr. Ellington

Variety reported "considerable discontent in the jazz groove."

contributed more music than I ever could in a thousand years," Wonder said.

Among *Fulfillingness*'s hit singles was "Boogie on Reggae Woman," which earned Wonder the trophy for best r&b vocals. "Living for the City," a late-breaking release from last year's Album of the Year, *Innervisions,* won Best Rhythm & Blues Song.

When Wonder won this year's Album of the Year award, he became the first artist to win it two years in a row. The newest honor was bestowed on him by last year's Best New Artist, Bette Milder, who strolled out onstage wearing a mischievous grin, a skimpy dress and a 45-rpm record for a hat. "It's 'Come Go with Me' by the Dell-Vikings," she said about her headgear. "It was a great record, but it's a better *hat.*"

Midler then tossed out one more of her ongoing barbs at long-time target Karen Carpenter. "A year ago, Miss Karen Carpenter crowned me Best New Artist," said Midler, who hadn't worked much in the past year, "and if that ain't the kiss of death, I don't know what is!" When Wonder accepted his award from her, he said, graciously acknowledging their first meeting, "I've been listening to your records for some time, and I've been trying to figure out how to get to you."

Paul McCartney, who won four previous Grammys for his work with the Beatles, plus one for his work with Wings, came soaring back to reclaim the honor for best pop group vocals for the single "Band on the Run." The album of the same name was recorded in Nigeria under dire conditions. Two of Wings' musicians failed to show up for the taping, leaving McCartney alone with his wife, Linda (a singer who didn't play an instrument), and guitarist Denny Laine. "I took control on that album," McCartney once told *Musician* magazine. "I played the drums myself, the bass myself, a lot of guitar with Denny, did a lot of the vocals myself. So it was almost a solo album." The dedicated Wings technicians who also showed up received Grammy's Best Engineered Recording award.

In 1972, Aretha Franklin set a Grammy winning streak that surpassed Bill Cosby's earlier record of six consecutive victories. This year Lady Soul added an eighth—an r&b vocals award for her cover of the 1968 Marvin Gaye/Tammi Terrell hit "Ain't Nothing Like the Real Thing"—which ended her string of consecutive triumphs. Her record would hold for nearly a decade, however, until Sir Georg Solti would overtake it with 10 straight wins in the classical categories between 1974 and 1983.

In the other r&b slots, the kudos for group vocals went to Rufus featuring Chaka Khan for "Tell Me Something Good," which was written by Stevie Wonder. Rock critic Dave Marsh once wrote of Wonder's contribution to the troupe: "What he gave them wasn't just a son-of-'Superstition' hit, it was role defining, establishing, in one fell swoop, Chaka as a demanding, tough 'n' sultry siren, and Rufus as one of the premier black rock bands of the Seventies, designations to which they've devoted the rest of their careers."

When the TV program *Soul Train* asked a group of session musicians at Philadelphia's Sigma Sound Studios to come up with a theme song, they were dealing with professionals who had contributed to such hits as the O'Jays' "Love Train" and Billy Paul's 1972 Grammy winner, "Me and Mrs. Jones." The group called themselves MFSB (Mother, Father, Sister, Brother) and gave the TV show producers "TSOP (The Sound of Philadelphia)," winner of the award for best instrumental performance. It was produced by Thom Bell, the first-time recipient of the newly introduced Grammy for Producer of the Year. Bell had previously overseen works by the Stylistics and the Spinners and had more Top 10 singles (11) in 1974 than any other producer.

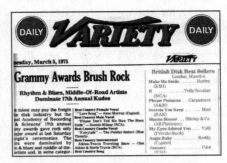

"Rock talent may pay the freight for the disk industry," *Variety* noted, "but the N.A.R.A.S.'s Grammys gave rock only one major award."

When the Grammy nominations came out this year, *Variety* reported "considerable discontent in the jazz groove. . . . Missing from the nominations are such exponents of 'fusion jazz,' a blend of rock and jazz, as Chick Corea, Mahavishnu Orchestra, Weather Report, Bill Cobham and Herbie Hancock." One fusionist, Chuck Mangione, *was* in the lineup, but *Variety* insisted that "the 'new' jazz practitioners are consistently passed over in favor of the traditionalists."

The soloist performance award went this year to a man who was not only one of jazz's foremost traditionalists (having been one of its pioneers) but also one of its long-deceased icons, topping newer talent such as fellow nominees Freddie Hubbard and Keith Jarrett. The prize lauded alto sax legend Charlie "Yardbird" Parker, who died in 1955 of a heart seizure one week after performing at Birdland, the famed Manhattan club named after him. The award acknowledged his early "Bird" recordings, never before released, which included works with Jay McShann's 1940 Kansas City band as well as a 1942 Harlem jam session. The victory gave the Grammys this year a special "note of dignity," said *Rolling Stone.*

The magazine added: "In the pretelecast award ceremony, the late Charlie Parker was finally named [a] winner . . . for the album *First Recordings* . . . . His daughter Kim delivered a short but emotional acceptance speech that drew a few gasps. 'This is *very* weird,' she said. 'Bird's still getting awards and somebody else is still getting all his money!' "

Another jazz great, keyboardist Oscar Peterson, received his first Grammy (best group performance), sharing it with guitarist Joe Pass and Danish bass player Niels Pedersen for their LP *The Trio.* A winner from last year, Woody Herman, returned to reclaim the big-band laurels for *Thundering Herd.* Herman had had a series of "Herd" bands throughout his career, the first of which was Herman's Herd, then came First, Second and Third Herd.

In the country categories, the recipient of last year's prize for best male country vocalist, Charlie Rich, took the winner of this year's Best Country Song, to the top of the c&w chart. "A Very Special Love Song" was written for him by Billy Sherrill (writer of 1966's Best Country Song, "Almost Persuaded") and Norris Wilson. Wilson told *Billboard* about the genesis of the tune: "We needed something for Charlie and he [Sherrill] said, 'Let's write for him a very special love song.' "

Three-time past Grammy champ Chet Atkins teamed up with fellow guitarist Merle Travis for this year's instrumental performance trophy, which they won for *The Atkins-Travis Traveling Show.* Atkins first heard Travis play years earlier on a radio broadcast out of Cincinnati and was inspired by his amazing two-finger technique, now known as "Travis picking." Atkins developed a three-finger style (between them, noted pundits, they had one whole hand) and

the twosome often paired up for concert appearances.

Although the jazz awards were criticized this year for going to traditionalists, "the country music awards," noted *Variety,* "are criticized for ignoring the traditionalists. Current winners—Anne Murray, Ronnie Milsap and the Pointer Sisters—are still considered outsiders in Nashville."

Later in their career, the Pointer Sisters became famous for their pop singles, but in 1974 they made their first attempt at country music and won their first Grammy (best country group vocals) for "Fairytale," beating such other name nominees as the Statler Brothers, Willie Nelson and Tracy Nelson (no relation), Bobby Bare and son, and last year's championship team of Kris Kristofferson and Rita Coolidge. *Variety* identified them as "a black group specializing in campy versions of vintage material," but Nashville suddenly took the Pointer Sisters seriously enough after their Grammy triumph to invite them to be the first black women's group to perform at the Grand Ole Opry.

"There are only two things I know about Canada," Elton John once said. "Hockey and Anne Murray." (John came up with scratch at the Grammys again this year, despite three noms, including bids for Record and Album of the Year.) Murray, the singer of the 1969 hit single "Snowbird," was raised in Nova Scotia, where she often listened to what she called the country-flavored music of Brenda Lee, Elvis Presley and Buddy Knox. Now she overtook Nashville divas Dolly Parton, Dottie West, Tammy Wynette and Tanya Tucker for the vocals award for "Love Song."

Ronnie Milsap was another relative newcomer when he beat out headliners Charley Pride, Glen Campbell, Roy Clark and Waylon Jennings for the male vocalist honors. (Milsap was so new to the business that he heard his name mispronounced "Mislap"—"repeatedly," whined *Rolling Stone*—by presenter Burl Ives at the ceremony.) "Please Don't Tell Me

How the Story Ends" was written for him by Kris Kristofferson, who penned it one night while mulling over a love relationship that he knew was doomed. Milsap had come to prominence only one year earlier with his hit single "I Hate You." Previous to that, he was a backup artist for Elvis Presley, playing piano for Presley's "Gentle on My Mind" and singing harmony on "Kentucky Rain." In honor of his mentor, Milsap taped "Please Don't Tell Me" on Elvis's birthday, in a recording studio that the King often used.

Presley had won his first Grammy in 1967 for giving the year's Best Sacred Performance on his *How Great Thou Art* LP and also won in 1972 for Best Inspirational Performance with *He Touched Me*. In what *Rolling Stone* and others now called "a strange twist," Presley came back to take the inspirational performance award again, this time for a live performance album recording of *How Great Thou Art*. The Oak Ridge Boys won Best Gospel Performance for "The Baptism of Jesse Taylor," while the backup talent for Aretha Franklin's 1972 Best Soul Gospel Performance of "Amazing Grace"—James Cleveland & the Southern California Community Choir—won the soul gospel trophy all for themselves this year for their cover of Elvis Presley's classic "In the Ghetto."

Richard Pryor had been known to black club audiences for some time, but he was suddenly catching on with liberal whites by the mid-1970s when Grammy's laugh laurels took a notable shift in preference. Previous winners were usually sassy but sweet (Bill Cosby and Vaughn Meader), but now the Grammys were suddenly applauding the kind of biting political punishment and gross scatological humor that came into the mainstream. Pryor was a master at it, and particularly skillful at rages full of four-letter words. He won his first Grammy for *That Nigger's Crazy,* which lampooned the ways that whites flee burning houses (they "just panic," he says, "fall over each other, choke to death and shit") and blacks make love ("Niggers

Marvin Hamlisch's victory as Best New Artist drew "disapproving grumbles" from the audience.

make noise. 'God damn! Move now, bitch!' ").

Just as in 1972, conductor Georg Solti was the sweepstakes winner in the classical categories. Two were for Berlioz's *Symphonie Fantastique,* performed under Solti's baton by the Chicago Symphony, which was Classical Album of the Year, in addition to best orchestral performance. "No other performance of this much-played score moves more surely, more forcefully, more eloquently than this," said *High Fidelity*. The recording was made at the University of Illinois at Champaign-Urbana and achieved such audio perfection that it also earned the engineering honors. "The sound is fully as spectacular as the performance," the magazine added.

High Fidelity was less moved by the year's Best Opera Recording, which brought Solti his third golden gramophone of the year (and eighth of his career). Solti led tenor Placido Domingo, soprano Montserrat Caballé and the London Philharmonic in Puccini's *La Bohème,* a feat of "technical mastery," it said, but added, "Those who love this score on account of its emotional generosity will find themselves fobbed off with good taste instead." The reviewer dismissed Caballé's performance as "chilling in its impersonality and unspontaneousness" and noted that Domingo "sounds tired." Neither singer was nominated for the soloist salute, which went to last year's winner, Leontyne Price, for her tribute to Richard Strauss, including operatic excerpts from *Guntram* and *Der Rosenkavalier* as well as his *Four Last Songs*. Again, *High Fidelity* was not pleased: Price, it said, "is not at home in this music." The slam was outrageous because the same magazine claimed she was "in excellent voice" when she won this same Grammy for singing Strauss in 1965.

As in the Album of the Year category, music by Berlioz was the source of another classical Grammy win: the choral laurels for *The Damnation of Faust*, conducted by Colin Davis and sung by the London Symphony Orchestra Chorus, the Ambrosian Singers and the Wandsworth School Boys' Choir ("not entirely homogenous in sound," said *High Fidelity*). Cellist Pierre Fournier, violinist Henryk Szeryng and pianist Artur Rubinstein shared the prize for chamber music for their execution of several trios by Brahms and Schumann.

> ## Georg Solti launched a new, record-setting winning streak.

The soloist performance kudos went to Russian musician David Oistrakh, who died in 1974, for Shostakovich's Violin Concerto No. 1, a performance that came about through Oistrakh's close collaboration with the composer's son. Renowned pianist Madame Alicia de Larrocha won the soloist prize (without orchestra) for her rendition of Isaac Albéniz's magnum opus, *Iberia,* a high note in music that *High Fidelity* said "cannot be minimized. . . . This is proportioned playing, pretty wonderful to experience."

"For the 17th consecutive year, Latin music was ignored at the N.A.R.A.S. awards ceremonies," *Billboard* reported when the Grammy ceremony was over, noting, "Latin music on discs consistently outsells jazz, classical and most recordings of the spoken word, categories that have their own competition." (The issue was then being explored by the record academy and would result in the creation of a Best Latin Recording prize next year.)

"Jackson Browne and Bruce Springsteen continued to go unnoticed," *Rolling Stone* groused.

"It's Grammy time so it's gripe time again," *Variety* reported when the nominations were announced. "A widespread sentiment in the disc industry, not only limited to the losers, is that the Grammy nominations represent a strictly commercial, play-it-safe name roster. Wherever there's a choice between a genuinely innovative talent and a best-selling one, there's no doubt about the outcome—the bestseller wins every time. Squawks to the effect that powers behind the Grammy Awards are old fogeys who play it safe by picking only commercial successes are flatly rejected by a spokesman for N.A.R.A.S."

When the winners were announced, *Variety* reported, "Rock talent may pay the freight for the disc industry, but the Grammy Awards gave rock only one major award [McCartney's "Band on the Run"]. The winners were dominated by rhythm & blues, middle-of-the-road artists, and, in some categories, there were some winners who raised questions about the judgment of the academy voters."

Variety noted that academy leaders are "standing pat," adding, "They believe that the awards were a rather good representation of the top 1974 recordings and represented a good test of the industry's ability to judge itself."

Two thousand people attended the Grammy galas held in New York at Broadway's Uris Theater (from which the ceremony was broadcast) and the Americana Hotel. A concurrent, nontelevised ceremony was held at the Beverly Wilshire Hotel in Los Angeles. The Uris was no doubt chosen for the TV show because it was the site of the first full production of the Scott Joplin ("The Entertainer") opera *Treemonisha,* produced in 1974 by the Houston Grand Opera company. Andy Williams again acted as Grammycast host, with award presentations made by Ann-Margret, John Lennon, Paul Simon, Rudy Vallee, David Bowie, Kate Smith and Sarah Vaughan.

"Nobody could argue with Wonder's four awards (one less than last year)," the often quarrelsome *Rolling Stone* said afterward, also noting that Wonder's limo was stormed by jubilant fans after the ceremony was over. "It began to get ugly out on the street," the magazine observed. "Even venerable old Kate Smith narrowly escaped with her makeup intact."

• 1974 •

The awards ceremony was broadcast by CBS from the Uris Theater in New York on March 1, 1975. A concurrent, nontelevised ceremony was held at the Beverly Wilshire Hotel in Los Angeles. Awards were bestowed for the eligibility period October 16, 1973, to October 15, 1974.

ALBUM OF THE YEAR
• *Fulfillingness' First Finale*, Stevie
  Wonder. Tamla/Motown.
Back Home Again, John Denver. RCA.
Band on the Run, Paul McCartney &
  Wings. Apple/Capitol.
Caribou, Elton John. MCA.
Court and Spark, Joni Mitchell. Asylum.

RECORD OF THE YEAR
• "I Honestly Love You," Olivia New-
  ton-John. MCA.
"Don't Let the Sun Go Down on Me,"
  Elton John. MCA.
"Feel Like Makin' Love," Roberta
  Flack. Atlantic.
"Help Me," Joni Mitchell. Asylum.
"Midnight at the Oasis," Maria Muldaur.
  Reprise/Warner Bros.

SONG OF THE YEAR
(Songwriter's Award)
• "The Way We Were," Marilyn & Alan
  Bergman, Marvin Hamlisch.
"Feel Like Makin' Love," Eugene
  McDaniels.
"I Honestly Love You," Jeff Barry, Peter
  Allen.

"Midnight at the Oasis," David Nichtern.
"You and Me Against the World," Paul
  Williams, Ken Ascher.

BEST NEW ARTIST
• Marvin Hamlisch
Bad Company
Johnny Bristol
David Essex
Graham Central Station
Phoebe Snow

BEST POP VOCAL PERFORMANCE, MALE
• Stevie Wonder, *Fulfllingness' First
  Finale*. Tamla/Motown.
Harry Chapin, "Cat's in the Cradle."
  Elektra.
Elton John, "Don't Let the Sun Go
  Down on Me." MCA.
Dave Loggins, "Please Come to
  Boston." Epic/Columbia.
Billy Preston, "Nothing from Nothing."
  A&M.

BEST POP VOCAL PERFORMANCE, FEMALE
• Olivia Newton-John, "I Honestly
  Love You." MCA.
Roberta Flack, "Feel Like Makin'
  Love." Atlantic.
Carole King, "Jazzman." Ode.
Cleo Laine, *Cleo Laine Live at Carnegie
  Hall*. RCA.
Joni Mitchell, "Court and Spark." Asy-
  lum.

BEST POP VOCAL PERFORMANCE BY A DUO, GROUP OR CHORUS

- Paul McCartney & Wings, "Band on the Run." Apple/Capitol.

Quincy Jones, "Body Heat." A&M.

Steely Dan, "Rikki Don't Lose That Number." ABC.

Stylistics, "You Make Me Feel Brand New." Avco.

Dionne Warwick, Spinners, "Then Came You." Atlantic.

BEST POP INSTRUMENTAL PERFORMANCE

- Marvin Hamlisch, "The Entertainer." MCA.

Herbie Hancock, *Head Hunters*. Columbia.

Quincy Jones, "Along Came Betty." A&M.

Love Unlimited Orchestra, *Rhapsody in White*. 20th Century.

Rick Wakeman, *Journey to the Center of the Earth*. A&M.

BEST RHYTHM & BLUES SONG
(Songwriter's Award)

- "Living for the City," Stevie Wonder.

"Dancing Machine," Harold Davis, Don Fletcher, Dean Parts.

"For the Love of Money," Ken Gamble, Leon Huff, Anthony Jackson.

"Rock Your Baby," Henry Wayne Casey, Richard Finch.

BEST RHYTHM & BLUES VOCAL PERFORMANCE, MALE

- Stevie Wonder, "Boogie on Reggae Woman." Tamla/Motown.

Johnny Bristol, "Hang On in There Baby." MGM.

Marvin Gaye, *Marvin Gaye—Live*. Tamla/Motown.

Eddie Kendricks, "Boogie Down." Tamla/Motown.

George McCrae, "Rock Your Baby." T.K.

BEST RHYTHM & BLUES VOCAL PERFORMANCE, FEMALE

- Aretha Franklin, "Ain't Nothing Like the Real Thing." Atlantic.

Shirley Brown, "Woman to Woman." Truth/Stax.

Thelma Houston, "You've Been Doing Wrong for So Long." Motown.

Millie Jackson, "If Loving You Is Wrong I Don't Want to Be Right." Spring.

Etta James, "St. Louis Blues." Chess.

Ann Peebles, "(You Keep Me) Hangin' On." Hi/London.

Tina Turner, *Tina Turns the Country On!* United Artists.

BEST RHYTHM & BLUES VOCAL PERFORMANCE BY A DUO, GROUP OR CHORUS

- Rufus, "Tell Me Something Good." ABC.

Jackson 5, "Dancing Machine." Motown.

Gladys Knight & the Pips, "I Feel a Song (in My Heart)." Buddah.

O'Jays, "For the Love of Money." Philadelphia International/Epic.

Spinners, "Mighty Love." Atlantic.

BEST RHYTHM & BLUES INSTRUMENTAL PERFORMANCE

- MFSB, "TSOP (The Sound of Philadelphia)." Philadelphia International/Epic.

Average White Band, "Pick Up the Pieces." Atlantic.

Crusaders, *Scratch*. Blue Thumb.

Kool & the Gang, *Light of Worlds*. De-Lite.

Billy Preston, "Struttin'." A&M.

BEST JAZZ PERFORMANCE BY A SOLOIST

- Charlie Parker, *First Recordings!* Onyx.

Freddie Hubbard, *High Energy*. Columbia.

Keith Jarrett, *Solo Concerts*. ECM/Polydor.

Hubert Laws, *In the Beginning*. CTI.

McCoy Tyner, *Naima*. Milestone.

BEST JAZZ PERFORMANCE BY A GROUP

- Oscar Peterson, Joe Pass, Niels Pedersen, *The Trio*. Pablo.

Bill Evans, *The Tokyo Concert*. Fantasy.

Freddie Hubbard, *High Energy*. Columbia.

Supersax, *Salt Peanuts*. Capitol.

McCoy Tyner, *Sama Layuca*. Milestone.

BEST JAZZ PERFORMANCE BY A BIG BAND

- Woody Herman, *Thundering Herd*. Fantasy.

Les Hooper Big Band, *Look What They've Done*. Creative World.

Chuck Mangione, Hamilton Philharmonic Orchestra, *Land of Make Believe*. Mercury.

Don Sebesky, *Giant Box*. CTI.

Pat Williams, *Threshold*. Capitol.

BEST COUNTRY SONG
(Songwriter's Award)

- "A Very Special Love Song," Norris Wilson, Billy Sherrill.

"Fairytale," Anita Pointer, Bonnie Pointer.

"If We Make It Through December," Merle Haggard.

"I'm a Ramblin' Man," Ray Pennington.

"Paper Roses," Janice Torre, Fred Spielman.

BEST COUNTRY VOCAL PERFORMANCE, MALE

- Ronnie Milsap, "Please Don't Tell Me How the Song Ends." RCA.

Glen Campbell, "Bonaparte's Retreat." Capitol.

Roy Clark, *The Entertainer*. Dot.

Waylon Jennings, "I'm a Ramblin' Man." RCA.

Charley Pride, *Country Feelin'*. RCA.

BEST COUNTRY VOCAL PERFORMANCE, FEMALE

- Anne Murray, "Love Song." Capitol.

Dolly Parton, "Jolene." RCA.

Tanya Tucker, "Would You Lay with Me (In a Field of Stone)." Columbia.

Dottie West, "Last Time I Saw Him." RCA.

Tammy Wynette, "Woman to Woman." Epic.

BEST COUNTRY VOCAL PERFORMANCE BY A DUO OR GROUP

- Pointer Sisters, "Fairytale." Blue Thumb.

Bobby Bare, Bobby Bare, Jr., "Daddy What If." RCA.

Kris Kristofferson, Rita Coolidge, "Loving Arms." A&M.

Willie Nelson, Tracy Nelson, "After the Fire Is Gone." Atlantic.

Statler Brothers, "Whatever Happened to Randolph Scott." Mercury.

BEST COUNTRY INSTRUMENTAL PERFORMANCE

- Chet Atkins, Merle Travis, *The Atkins-Travis Traveling Show*. RCA.

Floyd Cramer, *The Young and the Restless*. RCA.

Danny Davis & the Nashville Brass, *Nashville Brass in Blue Grass Country*. RCA.

Charlie McCoy, *The Nashville Hit Man*. Monument.

Charlie McCoy, Barefoot Jerry, "Boogie Woogie." Monument.

BEST INSPIRATIONAL PERFORMANCE

- Elvis Presley, *How Great Thou Art*. RCA.

Tennessee Ernie Ford, *Make a Joyful Noise*. Capitol.

Bill Gaither Trio, *Thanks for Sunshine*. Impact.

Sister Janet Mead, "The Lord's Prayer." A&M.

Bill Pursell, *Listen*. Word.

BEST GOSPEL PERFORMANCE (OTHER THAN SOUL GOSPEL)

- Oak Ridge Boys, "The Baptism of Jesse Taylor." Columbia.

Wendy Bagwell & the Sunliters, *The Carpenter's Tool*. Canaan.

Blackwood Brothers, *There He Goes*. Skylite.

Imperials, *Follow the Man with the Music*. Impact.

LeFevres, *Stepping on the Clouds*. Canaan.

BEST SOUL GOSPEL PERFORMANCE

- James Cleveland & the Southern California Community Choir, *In the Ghetto*. Savoy.
Five Blind Boys, *My Desire*. Peacock/ABC.
Edwin Hawkins Singers, *Edwin Hawkins Singers Live*. Buddah.
Ike Turner, "Father Alone." United Artists.
Ike & Tina Turner, *The Gospel According to Ike and Tina*. United Artists.

BEST ETHNIC OR TRADITIONAL RECORDING

- *Two Days in November*, Doc & Merle Watson. United Artists.
The Back Door Wolf, Howlin' Wolf. Chess.
Big Daddy, Bukka White. Biograph.
Catalyst, Willie Dixon. Ovation.
London Revisited, Muddy Waters, Howlin' Wolf. Chess.

BEST INSTRUMENTAL ARRANGEMENT

- Pat Williams, "Threshold" (Pat Williams). Capitol.
Les Hooper, "Circumvent" (Les Hooper Big Band). Creative World.
Les Hooper, "Look What They've Done" (Les Hooper Big Band). Creative World.
Bob James, "Night on Bald Mountain" (Bob James). CTI.
Don Sebesky, "Firebird/Birds of Fire" (Don Sebesky). CTI.

BEST INSTRUMENTAL COMPOSITION
(Composer's Award)

- Mike Oldfield, "Tubular Bells (Theme from *The Exorcist*)."
Benny Golson, "Along Came Betty."
Herbie Hancock, Paul Jackson, Bernie Maupin, Harvey Mason, "Chameleon."
Barry White, "Barry's Theme."
Barry White, "Rhapsody in White."

BEST SCORE FROM AN ORIGINAL CAST SHOW ALBUM
(Composer's Award)

- *Raisin*, Judd Woldin, Robert Brittan. Columbia.
Let My People Come, Earl Wilson, Jr., Phil Oesterman. Libra.
The Magic Show, Stephen Schwartz. Bell.
Over Here, Richard M. Sherman, Robert B. Sherman. Columbia.
The Rocky Horror Picture Show, Richard O'Brien. Ode.

BEST ALBUM OF ORIGINAL SCORE WRITTEN FOR A MOTION PICTURE OR TV SPECIAL
(Composer's Award)

- *The Way We Were*, Marvin Hamlisch, Alan and Marilyn Bergman. Columbia.
Death Wish, Herbie Hancock. Columbia.
QB VII, Jerry Goldsmith. ABC.
Serpico, Mikis Theodorakis. Paramount/ABC.
The Three Musketeers, Michel Legrand. Bell.

BEST ARRANGEMENT ACCOMPANYING VOCALIST(S)

- Joni Mitchell, Tom Scott, "Down to You" (Joni Mitchell). Asylum.
Michael Gibbs, "Smile of the Beyond" (Carol Shive; Mahavishnu Orchestra with the London Symphony). Columbia.
Chuck Mangione, "Land of Make Believe" (Chuck Mangione, Hamilton Philharmonic). Mercury.
Gene Puerling, Les Hooper, "We've Only Just Begun" (Singers Unlimited). MPS/BASF.
Gene Puerling, "Where Is Love" (Singers Unlimited). MPS/BASF.

ALBUM OF THE YEAR, CLASSICAL

- *Berlioz: Symphonie Fantastique*, Georg Solti conducting the Chicago Symphony. London.
Berlioz: The Damnation of Faust, Colin Davis conducting the London Symphony Orchestra and Chorus, Ambrosian Singers, Wandsworth School Boys' Choir (solos: Gedda, Bastin, Veasey, Van Allan). Philips.
Ives: The 100th Anniversary, various artists. Columbia.

Mahler: Symphony No. 2 in C Minor ("Resurrection"). Leonard Bernstein conducting the London Symphony; Edinburgh Festival Chorus (solos: Baker, Armstrong). Columbia.

Schumann: Faust, Benjamin Britten conducting the English Chamber Orchestra (solos: Fischer-Dieskau, Pears, Shirley-Quirk). London.

Snowflakes Are Dancing, Isao Tomita. RCA.

Weber: Der Freischutz, Carlos Kleiber conducting the Dresden State Orchestra; Leipzig Radio Chorus (solos: Mathis, Janowitz, Schreier, Adam, etc.). Deutsche Grammophon.

BEST CLASSICAL PERFORMANCE, ORCHESTRA
(Conductor's Award)
• Georg Solti conducting the Chicago Symphony, *Berlioz: Symphonie Fantastique*. London.

Leonard Bernstein conducting the New York Philharmonic, *Bernstein Conducts Ravel*. Columbia.

Leonard Bernstein conducting the London Symphony, *Mahler: Symphony No. 2 in C Minor*. Columbia.

André Previn conducting the London Symphony, *Holst: The Planets*. Angel.

José Serebrier conducting the London Philharmonic, *Ives: Symphony No. 4*. RCA.

Herbert von Karajan conducting the Berlin Philharmonic, *Bartók: Concerto for Orchestra*. Angel.

BEST CHAMBER MUSIC PERFORMANCE, INSTRUMENTAL OR VOCAL
• Artur Rubinstein, Henryk Szeryng, Pierre Fournier, *Brahms: Trios (Complete); Schumann: Trio No. 1 in D Minor*. RCA.

Julian Bream, John Williams, *Julian and John, Vol. 2 (Albéniz, Giuliani, Granados, etc.)*. RCA.

Aaron Copland conducting the Columbia Chamber Orchestra, *Copland: Appalachian Spring*. Columbia.

Ralph Grierson with George Sponholtz and the Southland Stingers, *Joplin: Palm Leaf Rag*. Angel.

Juilliard Quartet, *Beethoven: Late Quartets*. Columbia.

Tokyo String Quartet, *Haydn: String Quartets, Op. 50, Nos. 1 and 2*. Deutsche Grammophon.

Paul Zukofsky, Gilbert Kalish, *Ives: Violin Sonatas Nos. 1–4*. Nonesuch.

BEST CLASSICAL PERFORMANCE, INSTRUMENTAL SOLOIST(S) (WITH ORCHESTRA)
• David Oistrakh (M. Shostakovich conducting the New Philharmonic), *Shostakovich: Violin Concerto No. 1*. Angel.

Claudio Arrau (Inbal conducting the London Philharmonic), *Chopin: Variations on "Là ci darem la mano"; Fantasy on Polish Airs, Op. 13; Andante Spianato and Grande Polonaise Brillante in E Flat, Op. 22*. Philips.

Alfred Brendel (Haitink conducting the Concertgebouw Orchestra), *Brahms: Piano Concerto No. 2 in B Flat Major*. Philips.

Norbert Hauptmann (von Karajan conducting the Berlin Philharmonic), *Strauss: Horn Concerto No. 2 in E Flat Major*. Deutsche Grammophon.

Kyung-Wha Chung (Previn conducting the London Symphony), *Walton: Violin Concerto; Stravinsky: Violin Concerto in D Major*. London.

Itzhak Perlman (Previn conducting the London Symphony), *Bartók: Violin Concerto No. 2*. Angel.

Barry Tuckwell (Marriner conducting the Academy of St. Martin-in-the-Fields), *Weber: Concertino in E Minor for Horn and Orchestra*. Angel.

André Watts (Leinsdorf conducting the London Symphony), *Liszt: Todtentanz for Piano and Orchestra; Franck: Symphonic Variations for Piano and Orchestra*. Columbia.

BEST CLASSICAL PERFORMANCE, INSTRUMENTAL SOLOIST(S) (WITHOUT ORCHESTRA)

- Alicia de Larrocha, *Albéniz: Iberia*. London.
- David Burge, *Crumb: Makro Kosmos*. Nonesuch.
- Glenn Gould, *Bach: French Suites, Vol. 2, Nos. 5 and 6*. Columbia.
- Vladimir Horowitz, *Beethoven: Piano Sonatas No. 21 in C Major ("Waldstein") and No. 23 in F Minor ("Appassionata")*. Columbia.
- Alfons and Aloys Kontarsky, *Ravel and Debussy: Music for 2 Pianos/4 Hands*. Deutsche Grammophon.
- Itzhak Perlman, *Perpetual Motion*. Angel.
- Isao Tomita, *Snowflakes Are Dancing*. RCA.

BEST OPERA RECORDING

- *Puccini: La Bohème*, Georg Solti conducting the London Philharmonic (solos: Caballé, Domingo, Milnes, Blegen, Raimondi). RCA.
- *Humperdinck: Hänsel und Gretel*, Kurt Eichhorn conducting the Bavarian Radio Orchestra (solos: Moffo, Ludwig, Fischer-Dieskau). RCA.
- *Mozart: Così Fan Tutte*, Georg Solti conducting the London Philharmonic (solos: Lorengar, Berganza, Berbie, Davies, Krause, Bacquier). London.
- *Mozart: Don Giovanni*, Colin Davis conducting the Chorus and Orchestra Royal Opera House, Covent Garden (solos: Wixell, Ganzarolli, Arroyo, Te Kanawa, Freni, Burrows). Philips.
- *Pfitzner: Palestrina*, Rafael Kubelik conducting the Bavarian Radio Chorus and Orchestra (solos: Donath, Fassbaender, Gedda, Fischer-Dieskau, Prey). Deutsche Grammophon.
- *Verdi: I Vespri Siciliani*, James Levine conducting the New Philharmonia; John Alldis Choir (solos: Arroyo, Domingo, Milnes, Raimondi). RCA.
- *Weber: Der Freischütz*, Carlos Kleiber conducting the Dresden State Orchestra; Leipzig Radio Chorus (solos: Mathis, Janowitz, Schreier, Adam, Crass, Weikl). Deutsche Grammophon.

BEST CLASSICAL PERFORMANCE CHORAL, (OTHER THAN OPERA)

- Colin Davis conducting the London Symphony Orchestra and Chorus, Ambrosian Singers, Wandsworth School Boys' Choir (solos: Gedda, Bastin, Veasey, Van Allan), *Berlioz: The Damnation of Faust*. Philips.
- John Alldis, chorus master, London Philharmonic Choir; Sir Adrian Boult conducting the orchestra, *Vaughan Williams: Dona Nobis Pacem*. Angel.
- Sir Adrian Boult conducting the London Philharmonic Choir and Orchestra, *Holst: Choral Symphony*. Angel.
- Jozef Bok, chorus master, Chorus of National Philharmonic Warsaw; Wladyslaw Skoraczewski, chorus master, Pioneer Choir; Andrzej Markowski conducting the Symphony Orchestra of National Philharmonic, *Penderecki: Utrenja*. Philips.
- Russell Burgess conducting the Aldeburgh Festival Singers, Wandsworth School Choir; Benjamin Britten conducting the English Chamber Orchestra, *Schumann: Faust*. London.
- Rudolf Kempe conducting the Royal Philharmonic and Brighton Festival Chorus, *Janáček: Glagolitic Mass (Slavonic Mass)*. London.
- Eugene Ormandy conducting the Philadelphia Orchestra; Robert Page directing the Temple University Choirs, *Rachmaninov: The Bells*. RCA.
- Aleksander Sveshnikov conducting the USSR Russian Chorus, *Rachmaninov: Vespers (Mass), Op. 37*. Melodiya/Angel.

BEST CLASSICAL PERFORMANCE, VOCAL SOLOIST

- Leontyne Price, *Leontyne Price Sings Richard Strauss*. RCA.

Elly Ameling, *Schubert: Goethe-Lieder*. Philips.

Martina Arroyo, *There's a Meeting Here Tonight*. Angel.

Janet Baker, *Brahms: Alto Rhapsody*. Angel.

Cathy Berberian, *Cathy Berberian at the Edinburgh Festival*. RCA.

Jan DeGaetani, *Crumb: Night of the Four Moons*. Columbia.

Julius Eastman, *Davies: 8 Songs for a Mad King*. Nonesuch.

Marilyn Horne, *French and Spanish Songs*. London.

Sherrill Milnes, *Amazing Grace (Agnus Dei, Bless the Lord, O My Soul, etc.)*. RCA.

Birgit Nilsson, Helge Brilioth, *Wagner: Duets from "Parsifal" and "Die Walküre."* Philips.

BEST ENGINEERED RECORDING, CLASSICAL

• Kenneth Wilkinson, *Berlioz: Symphonie Fantastique* (Solti conducting the Chicago Symphony). London.

Marc Aubort, Joanna Nickrenz, *Percussion Music* (New Jersey Percussion Ensemble). Nonesuch.

Paul Goodman, Robert Auger, *Ives: Symphony No. 4* (Serebrier conducting the London Philharmonic). RCA.

Bud Graham, Ray Moore, *Bernstein: Candide* (original cast). Columbia.

Anthony Salvatore, *Puccini: La Bohème* (Solti conducting the London Philharmonic; solos: Domingo, Caballé). RCA.

Isao Tomita, *Snowflakes Are Dancing* (Isao Tomita). RCA.

Stanley Tonkel, Ray Moore, Milt Cherin, *Copland: Appalachian Spring* (Copland conducting the Columbia Chamber Players). Columbia.

BEST ALBUM NOTES, CLASSICAL

• Rory Guy, *Korngold: The Classic Erich Wolfgang Korngold* (solo: Hoeischer; Mattes, conductor). Angel.

David Cairns, *Berlioz: The Damnation of Faust* (Davis conducting the London Symphony). Philips.

Deryck Cooke, *Mahler: Symphony No. 10* (Morris conducting the New Philharmonia Orchestra). Philips.

Donald Garvelmann, *Scriabin: Piano Music (Complete), Vol. 2* (Ponti). Vox.

George Jellinek, *Humperdinck: Hänsel und Gretel* (Eichhorn conducting the Bavarian Radio Orchestra; solos: Moffo, Donath). RCA.

Irving Kolodin, *Verdi: I Vespri Siciliani* (Levine conducting the New Philharmonia). RCA.

Christopher Palmer, *Herrmann: Citizen Kane* (Gerhardt conducting the National Philharmonic). RCA.

Wolfram Schwinger, *Weber: Der Freischütz* (Kleiber, conductor). Deutsche Grammophon.

Erik Smith, *Mozart: Don Giovanni* (Davis conducting the Royal Opera House Chorus and Orchestra). Philips.

Clair W. Van Ausdall, *Rachmaninov: The Bells and 3 Russian Songs* (Ormandy, conductor; Temple University Choirs). RCA.

BEST COMEDY RECORDING

• *That Nigger's Crazy*, Richard Pryor. Partee/Stax.

Booga! Booga! David Steinberg. Columbia.

Cheech and Chong's Wedding Album, Cheech & Chong. Ode.

Mind over Matter, Robert Klein. Brut/Buddah.

Missing White House Tapes, National Lampoon. Blue Thumb.

BEST SPOKEN WORD RECORDING

• *Good Evening*, Peter Cook, Dudley Moore. Island.

An Ear to the Sounds of Our History, Eric Sevareid. Columbia.

"Autumn," Rod McKuen. Stanyan/Warner Bros.

Senator Sam at Home, Sam Ervin. Columbia.

Watergate, Vol. 3: "I Hope the President is Forgiven" (John W. Dean III testifies), compiled by Don Molner. Folkways.

BEST RECORDING FOR CHILDREN

- *Winnie-the-Pooh and Tigger Too*, Sebastian Cabot, Sterling Holloway, Paul Winchell. Disneyland.

America Sings, Burl Ives, others. Disneyland.

Eli Wallach Reads Isaac Bashevis Singer, Eli Wallach. Newbery.

New Adventures of Bugs Bunny, Vol. 2, Mel Blanc. Peter Pan.

Robin Hood, various artists, narrated by Roger Miller. Disneyland.

BEST ENGINEERED RECORDING
(OTHER THAN CLASSICAL)

- Geoff Emerick, *Band on the Run* (Paul McCartney & Wings). Apple/Capitol.

Rik Pekkonen, Peter Granet, *Southern Comfort* (Crusaders). Blue Thumb.

Bill Schnee, *Lincoln Mayorga and Distinguished Colleagues, Vol. 3* (Lincoln Mayorga). Sheffield.

Ken Scott, John Jansen, *Crime of the Century* (Supertramp). A&M.

Tommy Vicari, Larry Forkner, *Powerful People* (Gino Vannelli). A&M.

BEST ALBUM PACKAGE
(Art Director's Award)

- Ed Thrasher, Christopher Whorf, *Come and Gone* (Mason Proffit). Warner Bros.

John Berg, *Santana's Greatest Hits* (Santana). Columbia.

Eddie Biscoe, *Ride 'Em Cowboy* (Paul Davis). Bang.

Ron Coro, *On Stage* (Loggins & Messina). Columbia.

Bob Defrin, Basil Pao, *Is It In* (Eddie Harris). Atlantic.

Herb Greene, *That's a Plenty* (Pointer Sisters). Blue Thumb.

Ode Visuals, *Cheech and Chong's Wedding Album* (Cheech & Chong). Ode.

Ethan A. Russell, *Quadrophenia* (Who). MCA.

BEST ALBUM NOTES
(Annotator's Award)
(Tie)

- Charles R. Townsend, *For the Last Time* (Bob Wills & His Texas Playboys). United Artists.
- Dan Morgenstern, *The Hawk Flies* (Coleman Hawkins). Milestone.

Rudy Behlmer, *50 Years of Film Music* (original motion picture soundtrack recordings). Warner Bros.

Ralph J. Gleason, *The Pianist* (Duke Ellington). Fantasy.

J. R. Young, *The World Is Still Waiting for the Sunrise* (Les Paul, Mary Ford). Capitol.

PRODUCER OF THE YEAR

- Thom Bell

Rick Hall

Billy Sherrill

Lenny Waronker

Stevie Wonder

• 1975 •
Homecoming Night

The rock music of the recent past had been daring but not danceable. By mid-decade, a new sound that had bodies bobbing under swirling lights at downtown dance clubs suddenly shook up the music scene: disco.

Four disco acts led the Grammy race with the most nominations (five each): Earth, Wind & Fire; the Silver Connection; Van McCoy & the Soul City Symphony; and K.C. & the Sunshine Band.

"The newcomers," noted *Variety,* competed against "the comebackers"—some of rock's past music heroes who were experiencing career rallies. Singer-songwriter Janis Ian had retired in 1967 at the age of 19 after giving away the fortune she made from her hit protest song "Society's Child (Baby I've Been Thinking)" to needy friends and charities. Her 1975 album *Between the Lines* marked a triumphant return and brought Ian the second-most Grammy nominations this year—four—including bids for Record, Album and Song of the Year. Most music pundits considered Ian the Grammy derby's clear front-runner.

Also returning was Paul Simon, who seemed determined to show the crazed teenage disco set that, at age 34, he was *Still Crazy After All These Years.*

Simon won seven Grammys as part of the Simon & Garfunkel duo, which broke up in 1970 after sweeping the Grammys with Album, Record and Song of the Year *Bridge Over Troubled Water*. But now he was back with three bids, including one for Album of the Year and two for best pop vocals. In the LP contest, Simon was pitted against Janis Ian (the sentimental favorite), the Eagles (the hottest pop band in America), Elton John (long overdue for

Best album champ Paul Simon (right) with producer Phil Ramone: "I'd like to thank Stevie Wonder for not releasing an album this year."

Grammy attention) and Linda Ronstadt (a darling of N.A.R.A.S. voters who appreciated safe rock with lots of vocal craftsmanship). A *Rolling Stone* reporter sized up the album lineup thus: "As an artist, rather than a commercial force or a pleasant entertainer, Paul Simon stands out like Kareem Abdul Jabbar in a kindergarten. But I'll bet he doesn't win."

Simon shocked everyone—and pulled off his music comeback officially—when he seized the LP laurels and told the crowd gathered at the Hollywood Palladium for the Grammycast, "I'd like to thank Stevie Wonder for not releasing an album this year."

Still Crazy represented an artistic departure for Simon. The LP had a jazzy beat and more complex themes and included a collaboration with a new emerging artist (Phoebe Snow on "Gone at Last") as well as an old colleague (Art Garfunkel on "My Little Town," which Garfunkel also included in his 1975

Breakaway album). The former duo still had creative differences, but they teamed up now and then for events like a presidential fund-raiser for George McGovern in 1972. At this year's Grammys, they teamed up for the pop duo/group honors for "My Little Town" but lost to the Eagles, who had been usurped in 1972 for the Best New Artist award by America. Simon nonetheless took his ninth career Grammy for best male vocal pop performance for *Still Crazy*.

There was no greater shocker, however, than what *Variety* called the "surprising choice" for Song of the Year: "Send in the Clowns," the popular tune from Stephen Sondheim's *A Little Night Music* that Judy Collins rendered in folksy soprano on her critically acclaimed comeback album *Judith*. The good news came with some bad for the victorious Sondheim. Whereas the original Broadway recording of *A Little Night Music* was voted best original cast show album in 1973, the London cast version lost the same award this year to *The Wiz,* written by Charlie Smalls. Smalls beat out last year's Grammy grabber Marvin Hamlisch, who was competing for *A Chorus Line.*

Janis Ian had attempted a comeback in 1974 with her *Stars* LP, which did reach the bottom rungs of the album charts, but none of its individual songs caught on. When *Between the Lines* was released one year later, its "At Seventeen" single soared up the rankings, having been discovered by young female record buyers who adopted it as their anthem of teenage angst. While Ian ended up losing her bids for Record, Song and Album of the Year, she still picked up the prize for best female pop vocal performance.

Grammy grousers considered this year's contest for Record of the Year to be one of the weakest in memory. ("It's a mellow year," *Variety* declared about the

1975 Grammy contest.) "At Seventeen" was pitted against Barry Manilow's "Mandy," Glen Campbell's "Rhinestone Cowboy," "Lyin' Eyes" by the Eagles and "Love Will Keep Us Together" by the Captain & Tennille. (Paul Simon, surprisingly was overlooked in the runoff.)

Written by Neil Sedaka and Howard Greenfield, "Love Will Keep Us Together" was the top-selling single of 1975. The Captain & Tennille's debut album of the same name was number four in the year's LP charts and also included their first hit single, "The Way I Want to Touch You," which they produced, manufactured and distributed themselves in order to break into the pop field.

> "As an artist, Paul Simon stands out like Kareem Abdul Jabbar in a kindergarten."

The Captain & Tennille were married to each other and bore a passing resemblance to the Carpenters, a comparison that made them bristle noticeably. They had both worked together for a while as side artists for the Beach Boys (Toni Tennille was the group's only "Beach Girl," playing the piano and doing backup vocals; the Captain—Daryl Dragon, son of famed orchestra conductor Carmen Dragon—did arrangements) before striking out on their own with "Touch You." When they ended up with the top Grammy of 1975, the *Los Angeles Herald Tribune* was miffed: "Giving 'Love Will Keep Us Together' the Record of the Year award was almost ridiculous. It is a nice, well produced and highly listenable little record, but hardly the best of the year."

"Touch You" came out in 1974, so the Captain & Tennille were not considered for the Best New Artist prize. But the night's leader in total Grammy nominations—K.C. & the Sunshine Band—was, and was also expected, to take the award easily.

Twenty-five-year-old Natalie Cole ended up causing the second major surprise of awards night when she became the first black ever voted Best New Artist.

Her 1975 debut album, *Inseparable,* was released exactly 10 years after the death of her father, legendary Grammy-winning Nat King Cole, and included the song for which she would also win best female rhythm & blues vocal performance, "This Will Be." By winning the r&b award, Cole officially ended Aretha Franklin's eight-year monopoly of the category, a fitting victory, since Cole's producers had been hyping her around the music world as "the next Aretha Franklin."

The victories, noted the *Washington Post,* "gave her budding show business career an auspicious boost," even though Cole's success, like Ian's, would prove to be temporary. Despite the fact that Cole continued to produce LPs that brushed the bottom rungs of the album charts through the rest of the 1970s, her career went into decline during the 1980s as she battled problems with alcohol and drugs, only to rebound in the early 1990s when she returned to the Grammys, sober and triumphant, with victories for best record and album.

The winners of the pop vocals group honors, the Eagles, had three hit songs in 1975: "One of These Nights," "Best of My Love" and "Lyin' Eyes." Since their debut in 1972, the new act had three successful albums (*The Eagles, Desperado* and *On the Border*), but it wasn't until the 1975 release of *One of These Nights* that the Eagles were finally flying high as the most popular rockers on the charts. The difference: They shucked off the country accent of their earlier work.

For the male r&b vocal award, Ray Charles came back with "Living for the City" to claim his tenth trophy. Noted the *L.A. Times:* "He thus trails only Henry Mancini (20 Grammys), Vladimir Horowitz (12), and Roger Miller (11) on the all-time list," adding, "Stevie Wonder and Aretha Franklin also have 10." Like other winners this year, Charles was experiencing a comeback of sorts. He toured 12 European cities in 1975, in addition to making his yearly sweep of the United States, and, said the critics

"Grammy choices were once again slanted against the hard rock sector," *Variety* reported.

approvingly, he seemed to have recaptured his old sense of humor in his music.

The swinging disco set may have had their collective feet knocked out from under them in the top award categories, but they rose up to take the rest of the r&b slots. Of K.C. & the Sunshine Band's five nominations, three were for Best Rhythm & Blues Song. Two of the contending tunes were hits—"That's the Way (I Like It)" and "Get Down Tonight"—but the group prevailed with "Where Is the Love." The *New York Times* applauded: "In person, they are one of the most exciting groups performing today. This is no insecure Caucasian kid mimicking black inflections, exhorting a crowd to 'put your hands together.' Raised in the Pentecostal Church, K.C. has assimilated black music as if he were born to it."

The *New York Times* once called "The Hustle" by Van McCoy & the Soul City Symphony (winner, Best Pop Instrumental Performance) "the biggest dance record of the 1970s." "It was completely different from the you-do-your-thing-and-I-do-mine dances," McCoy once told *Essence.* "It was people dancing together again." In early 1975, the step was just catching on among the disco set and McCoy wanted to give them something tailor-made. He wrote the tune in less than an hour and added it at the last minute to his *Disco Baby* LP. New York's club deejays discovered it, a single was released and it zoomed to number one. After that, McCoy tried to recapture the success of "The Hustle" with more disco works and then by branching out into other music dimensions, but without luck. "It's tough to follow a record like 'The Hustle,'" he told *Billboard.* "It sold 10 million copies and was a complete accident. How do you top it?" He never did. McCoy died in 1979 of a heart attack at the age of 35.

The r&b instrumental award went to the newly formed Silver Convention, for "Fly, Robin, Fly." The Convention was an invention of noted disco producer Michael Kunze, who worked in Munich, where he also developed other such rising stars as Donna Summer. "Silver" was short for the name of the band's leader, songwriter and arranger Silvester Levay. When Levay penned "Fly, Robin, Fly," it was originally entitled "Run, Rabbit, Run." A half hour before his troupe was to tape it, however, he heard a song called "Run Rabbit" on Armed Forces Network Radio and made the word changes at the last minute. "Robin" then flew up the U.S. charts to number one after seven weeks.

Earth, Wind & Fire was an r&b group led by Maurice White, a former drummer for the Ramsey Lewis Trio, who was fast becoming a new dean of disco now that he and his band abandoned their jazz-flavored efforts of the late 1960s and early '70s for a funky new beat. By 1975, White had a message for the young movers and shakers tearing up the dance floors downtown: You, too, can be a star—or even a "Shining Star," the title of Earth, Wind & Fire's first dance hit, which also earned them the r&b group performance Grammy. The group beat not only K.C. & the Sunshine Band (for "Get Down Tonight") but also the Pointer Sisters and the Average White Band.

It was the producer behind the Average White Band who won Grammy's second annual Producer of the Year prize. Arif Mardin was actually having a better-than-average year on the job: He also produced Judy Collins's *Judith* LP, "Jive Talkin'" by the Bee Gees and Richard

Harris's reading of Kahlil Gibran's *The Prophet,* which was up for best spoken word recording. (Harris lost to James Whitmore as Harry Truman in *Give 'Em Hell Harry,* which Whitmore often performed to critical raves on the stage.)

Chicago bluesman Muddy Waters had remained loyal to the Chess record label since the days of his earliest hits such as "I'm Ready" and "Rolling Stone" (after which the rock band took its name) in the late 1940s and early '50s. But in 1973, he broke away from Chess, sued for back royalties and switched to Blue Sky, where his work took on more of a rock & roll sound. His latest LP, *The Muddy Waters Woodstock Album,* won him the category of Best Ethnic or Traditional Recording for a third time.

Dizzy Gillespie had never won a Grammy, but he made up for it this year when he claimed the soloist honors for finessing his trumpet on *Oscar Peterson and Dizzy Gillespie.* Gillespie was also nominated in the group category but lost to Chick Corea and his Return to Forever band for one of their less critically regarded LPs. (*No Mystery,* griped *Rolling Stone,* "is no pleasure either.") But Corea's win was an important victory for the jazz fusion genre. When he and other fusion vanguards like Weather Report and Herbie Hancock failed to be nominated last year, *Variety* had reported "considerable discontent in the jazz groove."

Two jazzmen who had worked for Gillespie in the past shared the trophy for big-band performance: alto sax player and onetime Gillespie sideman Phil Woods and Michel Legrand (former Gillespie arranger) and his orchestra. Their winning work, "Images," also earned Legrand the Best Instrumental Composition award. Besides being a jazz artist, Legrand was known for writing popular film scores to such hits as *Summer of '42* (1971) and the TV movie *Brian's Song* (1972), both of which earned him past Grammys. This year the category prize for original score went to a victor who would claim it more than a dozen times in the future—John

Williams, composer of the music from *Jaws*. Williams beat out the man who had won more Grammys than anyone else: Henry Mancini, who was up for *The Return of the Pink Panther*.

For the past several years, a consensus had been forming within the record academy for the addition of a new category for Latin music. Finally, a *Billboard* headline proclaimed: "N.A.R.A.S. says 'Sí' to Latin Grammy, Wins Loud Olé." The eventual award recipient was Eddie Palmieri, one of salsa's leading and most innovative artists. His victorious *Sun of Latin Music* LP had a daring mix of both south- and north-of-the-border sounds, including Palmieri's interpretation of the new disco beat using trumpets, trombones, violins, flutes and baritone sax.

Every year since 1969, Dolly Parton had been nominated for a Grammy (four times as best female country vocalist, twice for group performances) and now was up for the female singing honor. But she lost again, this time to the Arizona-born Linda Ronstadt for "I Can't Help It (If I'm Still in Love with You)," thus suggesting that Nashville outsiders were still showing considerable pull, just like last year when the Pointer Sisters took the group vocals prize.

Ronstadt was less of an outsider, though, than many believed. Her first hits may have been mainstream pop singles like 1966's "Different Drum," written by Mike Nesmith of the Monkees, and 1970's "Long, Long Time" (her first Grammy nomination), but during lulls in her early career, she explored country music, too, with singing engagements at the Grand Ole Opry and appearances on Johnny Cash's television show.

B. J. Thomas had never been on country music charts before landing there with Grammy's Best Country Song of 1975, "(Hey, Won't You Play) Another Somebody Done Somebody Wrong Song," which also crossed over to become a pop hit. The tune was written in 20 minutes by producers Chips Moman and Larry Butler, the latter of whom objected strongly

Critics called the Captain and Tennille's "Love Will Keep Us Together" "a nice, highly listenable little record, but hardly the best of the year."

to Moman's desire to have the Oklahoma-born Thomas record it. Once the song leapt up the charts, Butler told *Billboard* about his objection, "I'm glad Chips talked me out of it."

Willie Nelson lost his bid for a Grammy last year but now claimed the male singing laurels for "Blue Eyes Crying in the Rain," which almost didn't get released when it was included in his self-produced *Red Headed Stranger* LP. Columbia Records "thought it was underproduced, too sparse, all those things," Nelson told *Billboard*. "Even though they didn't like it, they had already paid me a bunch of money for it, so they had to release it under my contract." To win his Grammy, Nelson beat Waylon Jennings, John Denver, Ray Stevens, Freddy Fender and Glen Campbell. Campbell had three nominations this year (and five Grammys under his belt from 1967 and '68) but came up with scratch.

The Pointer Sisters were again up for the group prize (for "Live Your Life Before You Die") but lost to a duo they surpassed last year—Kris Kristofferson and Rita Coolidge, who now rallied with "Lover Please." Kristofferson had won Grammys twice before: for performing with Coolidge in 1973 for "From the Bottle to the Bottom" and for writing 1971's Best Country Song, "Help Me Make It Through the Night." Four-time past winner Chet Atkins held on to the instrumental category (he won it last year with Merle Travis) for his own guitar rendition of Scott Joplin's "The Entertainer," which had earned pianist Marvin Hamlisch the pop instrumental prize in 1974.

For a second year in a row, Richard Pryor got the last laugh for Best Comedy Recording. In his latest winning LP, *Is It Something I Said?*, he lampooned cocaine abuse (a problem dogging Pryor's personal life at the time), insisting, "I must've snorted up Peru. I could've bought Peru, all the shit I snorted!"

Just as in other categories on Grammy night, there was a homecoming quality to the classical field. The triple winner of last year, conductor Georg Solti, returned to reclaim the Classical Album of the Year award for his and the Chicago Symphony's recording of all nine Beethoven symphonies. *High Fidelity* gave the musical effort a mixed review. Symphony No. 1, it said, "is one of the better Firsts on modern records," also approving of this version of the Fourth ("the playing throughout has wonderful spirit and solidarity") and Seventh ("the prize of the cycle"). However, "Solti makes some serious errors of judgment" on the others, it added, asserting, for example, that his Symphony No. 9 is "for people who prefer a sonic blast to music."

Also returning were pianist Artur Rubinstein, violinist Henryk Szeryng and cellist Pierre Fournier, who took the chamber music category last year with their renditions of Brahms and Schumann trios and this year were lauded for their trios by Schubert. ("This set is even better," *High Fidelity* wrote, adding that their joint accomplishment "definitely qualifies as one of the phonograph's classic achievements.") In the soloist categories, pianist Alicia de Larrocha came back for a second consecutive Grammy for performing two Ravel concertos and Fauré's *Fan-*

taisie for Piano and Orchestra. (*High Fidelity*'s reviewer called it "marvelous . . . a major release.") Seven-time past winner Pierre Boulez and the New York Philharmonic reaped the orchestral honors for their critically praised rendition of Ravel's ballet *Daphnis et Chloé.*

Violinist Nathan Milstein last recorded Bach's solo sonatas and partitas 20 years earlier, but when he attempted them again, he told *Musical America*, "This time I must make them as good as I can. I will never do them again." "He has done them colossally," *High Fidelity* said upon his completion of the task that also earned him his only career Grammy. The choral performance award went to the Cleveland Orchestra Chorus and Boys' Choir under the choral direction of Michael Tilson Thomas for what the same publication called their "extraordinary" and "first rate" performance of Carl Orff's *Carmina Burana.*

Eddie Palmieri won the new Latin award for his daring mix of salsa and disco.

On one occasion in the past, a version of Mozart's *Così Fan Tutte* won Best Opera Recording—in 1968 with Erich Leinsdorf conducting the New Philharmonia Orchestra and Ambrosian Opera Chorus. Now it was back as the year's top opera with last year's Grammy winner Colin Davis conducting the Chorus and Orchestra of the Royal Opera House in London's Covent Garden, with soprano Montserrat Caballé as Fiordiligi and mezzo-soprano Janet Baker as Dorabella. Davis, said *High Fidelity,* gave Mozart's classic "a sense of theatrical pulse," while Caballé's voice "has never been more ravishing," although Baker proved "disappointing." Neither diva was nominated for her Mozart performance, but Baker nonetheless "refined her singing in certain details" enough to take the vocalist solo honors for Mahler's *Kindertotenlieder,* despite heavy competition from Placido Domingo and the winner of the award for the past two years, Leontyne Price, both of whom were nominated together for their *Verdi and Puccini Duets.*

This year's Grammy nominations, *Variety* reported, were "accompanied by a chorus of gripes, squawks and the sounds of crushed sour grapes. The Grammy choices were once again slanted against the hard rock sector of the disc biz and elevated to the fore such acts as Janis Ian, Morris Albert, Brecker Bros., Linda Ronstadt, Paul Simon, Captain and Tenille, among others. Among the missing were Bob Dylan, who was even brushed off by the Grammy nominations several years ago when he was at the crest of his career, and Bruce Springsteen, who made the biggest press splash of 1975."

The *L.A. Times* added: "Because a Latin music category was added this year, N.A.R.A.S. is obviously not averse to altering its awards structure. . . . It is time to establish a category to honor contemporary/rock artists. . . . The alternative is simply a continued inability to recognize artistry in a field that represents the heartbeat of pop music. If N.A.R.A.S. can find a place among its 48 categories for the man who wrote the liner notes for [Dylan's] *Blood on the Tracks,* you'd think it could find a way to at least consider the man who made the album."

"As award shows go, this was a good

Capitol Records

Natalie Cole, the 25-year-old daughter of the late Nat King Cole, became the first African-American performer to win the Best New Artist award.

one," *Variety* said in its review of the Grammycast. The ceremony at the Hollywood Palladium again employed Andy Williams as host ("Williams had the good nature to kid about his own less than daring, commercially bent image," said the *L.A. Times*) and included performances by Natalie Cole, Paul Simon, Janis Ian and Barry Manilow. "Despite the inevitable grumbling, this year's Grammy ceremony was a well-paced, intelligently designed, satisfying production," the *Times* added. "At eighteen, then, the Grammy has definitely come of age."

• 1975 •

The awards ceremony was broadcast on CBS from the Hollywood Palladium on February 28, 1976, for the eligibility period October 16, 1974, to October 15, 1975.

ALBUM OF THE YEAR
• *Still Crazy After All These Years*, Paul Simon. Columbia.
Between the Lines, Janis Ian. Columbia.
Captain Fantastic and the Brown Dirt Cowboy, Elton John. MCA.

Heart Like a Wheel, Linda Ronstadt. Capitol.
One of These Nights, Eagles. Asylum.

RECORD OF THE YEAR
• "Love Will Keep Us Together," Captain & Tennille. A&M.
"At Seventeen," Janis Ian. Columbia.
"Lyin' Eyes," Eagles. Asylum.
"Mandy," Barry Manilow. Arista.
"Rhinestone Cowboy," Glen Campbell. Capitol.

SONG OF THE YEAR
(Songwriter's Award)
- "Send in the Clowns," Stephen Sondheim.

"At Seventeen," Janis Ian.

"Feelings," Morris Albert.

"Love Will Keep Us Together," Neil Sedaka, Howard Greenfield.

"Rhinestone Cowboy," Larry Weiss.

BEST NEW ARTIST
- Natalie Cole

Morris Albert

Amazing Rhythm Aces

Brecker Brothers

K.C. & the Sunshine Band

BEST POP VOCAL PERFORMANCE, MALE
- Paul Simon, *Still Crazy After All These Years*. Columbia.

Morris Albert, "Feelings." RCA.

Elton John, *Captain Fantastic and the Brown Dirt Cowboy*. MCA.

Glen Campbell, "Rhinestone Cowboy." Capitol.

Neil Sedaka, "Bad Blood." Rocket/MCA.

BEST POP VOCAL PERFORMANCE, FEMALE
- Janis Ian, "At Seventeen." Columbia.

Judy Collins, "Send in the Clowns." Elektra.

Olivia Newton-John, "Have You Never Been Mellow." MCA.

Helen Reddy, "Ain't No Way to Treat a Lady." Capitol.

Linda Ronstadt, *Heart Like a Wheel*. Capitol.

BEST POP VOCAL PERFORMANCE BY A DUO, GROUP OR CHORUS
- Eagles, "Lyin' Eyes." Asylum.

Captain & Tennille, "Love Will Keep Us Together." A&M.

Gladys Knight & the Pips, "The Way We Were/Try to Remember." Buddah.

Simon & Garfunkel, "My Little Town." Columbia.

Singers Unlimited, *A Capella 2*. MPS.

BEST POP INSTRUMENTAL PERFORMANCE
- Van McCoy & the Soul City Symphony, "The Hustle." Avco.

Chuck Mangione, *Chase the Clouds Away*. A&M.

Mike Post, "The Rockford Files." MGM.

The Ritchie Family, "Brazil." 20th Century.

Tom Scott & the L.A. Express, *Tom Cat*. Ode.

BEST RHYTHM & BLUES SONG
(Songwriter's Award)
- "Where Is the Love," H. W. Casey, Richard Finch, Willie Clarke, Betty Wright.

"Ease on Down the Road," Charlie Smalls.

"Get Down Tonight," H. W. Casey, Richard Finch.

"That's the Way (I Like It)," H. W. Casey, Richard Finch.

"Walking in Rhythm," Barney Perry.

BEST RHYTHM & BLUES VOCAL PERFORMANCE, MALE
- Ray Charles, "Living for the City." Crossover.

Al Green, "L-O-V-E (Love)." Hi/London.

Major Harris, "Love Won't Let Me Wait." Atlantic.

Isaac Hayes, *Chocolate Chip*. Hot Buttered Soul.

Ben E. King, "Supernatural Thin, Part I." Atlantic.

BEST RHYTHM & BLUES VOCAL PERFORMANCE, FEMALE
- Natalie Cole, "This Will Be." Capitol.

Gloria Gaynor, *Never Can Say Goodbye*. MGM.

Gwen McCrae, "Rockin' Chair." Cat/T.K.

Esther Phillips, *What a Diff'rence a Day Makes*. Kudo/ CTI.

Shirley (& Company), "Shame, Shame, Shame." Vibration.

BEST RHYTHM & BLUES VOCAL PERFORMANCE BY A DUO, GROUP OR CHORUS

- Earth, Wind & Fire, "Shining Star." Columbia.

Average White Band, *Cut the Cake*. Atlantic.

K.C. & the Sunshine Band, "Get Down Tonight." T.K.

Ohio Players, *Fire*. Mercury.

Pointer Sisters, "How Long (Betcha' Got a Chick on the Side)." Blue Thumb.

BEST RHYTHM & BLUES INSTRUMENTAL PERFORMANCE

- Silver Convention, "Fly, Robin, Fly." Midland/RCA.

Brecker Brothers, "Sneakin' Up Behind You." Arista.

B.T. Express, "Express." Scepter.

Herbie Hancock, "Hang Up Your Hangups." Columbia.

Van McCoy & the Soul City Symphony, *Disco Baby*. Avco.

BEST JAZZ PERFORMANCE BY A SOLOIST

- Dizzy Gillespie, *Oscar Peterson and Dizzy Gillespie*. Pablo.

John Coltrane, "Giant Steps." Atlantic.

Jim Hall, *Concierto*. CTI.

Phineas Newborn, Jr., *Solo Piano*. Atlantic.

Phil Woods, *Images*. Gryphon/RCA.

BEST JAZZ PERFORMANCE BY A GROUP

- Return to Forever Featuring Chick Corea, *No Mystery*. Polydor.

Count Basie, *Basie Jam*. Pablo.

John Coltrane Quartet, "Giant Steps." Atlantic.

Dizzy Gillespie Quartet, *Dizzy Gillespie's Big 4*. Pablo.

Supersax, *Supersax Plays Bird with Strings*. Capitol.

BEST JAZZ PERFORMANCE BY A BIG BAND

- Phil Woods with Michel Legrand & His Orchestra, *Images*. Gryphon/RCA.

Thad Jones, Mel Lewis, *Potpourri*. Philadelphia International.

Clark Terry, *Clark Terry's Big B-A-D Band Live at the Wichita Jazz Festival*. Vanguard.

North Texas State University Lab Band. Leon Breeden, director, *Lab '75*. NTSU.

Bill Watrous & the Manhattan Wildlife Refuge, *The Tiger of San Pedro*. Columbia.

BEST COUNTRY SONG
(Songwriter's Award)

- "(Hey, Won't You Play) Another Somebody Done Somebody Wrong Song," Chips Moman, Larry Butler.

"Before the Next Teardrop Falls," Vivian Keith, Ben Peters.

"Blue Eyes Crying in the Rain," Fred Rose.

"I'm Not Lisa," Jessi Colter.

"Thank God I'm a Country Boy," John Martin Sommers.

BEST COUNTRY VOCAL PERFORMANCE, MALE

- Willie Nelson, "Blue Eyes Crying in the Rain." Columbia.

Glen Campbell, "Country Boy (You Got Your Feet in L.A.)." Capitol.

John Denver, "Thank God I'm a Country Boy." RCA.

Freddy Fender, "Before the Next Teardrop Falls." Dot/ABC.

Waylon Jennings, "Are You Sure Hank Done It This Way?" RCA.

Ray Stevens, "Misty." Barnaby.

BEST COUNTRY VOCAL PERFORMANCE, FEMALE

- Linda Ronstadt, "I Can't Help It (If I'm Still in Love with You)." Capitol.

Jessi Colter, "I'm Not Lisa." Capitol.

Emmylou Harris, "If I Could Only Win Your Love." Reprise.

Loretta Lynn, "The Pill." MCA.

Dolly Parton, "Jolene," track from *In Concert*. RCA.

BEST COUNTRY VOCAL PERFORMANCE BY A DUO OR GROUP

- Kris Kristofferson, Rita Coolidge, "Lover Please." Monument.
- Asleep at the Wheel, *Texas Gold*. Capitol.
- Pointer Sisters, "Live Your Life Before You Die." Blue Thumb.
- Statler Brothers, "I'll Go to My Grave Loving You." Mercury.
- Conway Twitty, Loretta Lynn, "Feelins." MCA.

BEST COUNTRY INSTRUMENTAL PERFORMANCE

- Chet Atkins, "The Entertainer." RCA.
- Asleep at the Wheel, "Fat Boy Rag." Capitol.
- Chet Atkins, Jerry Reed, "Colonel Bogey." RCA.
- Vassar Clements, *Vassar Clements*. Mercury.
- Charlie McCoy, *Charlie My Boy*. Monument.

BEST INSPIRATIONAL PERFORMANCE

- Bill Gaither Trio, *Jesus, We Just Want to Thank You*. Impact.
- Larry Hart, "Amazing Grace." Cam.
- Anita Kerr, *Gentle as Morning*. Word.
- Ray Price, *This Time Lord*. Myrrh.
- Speers, *Something Good Is About to Happen*. Heartwarming.

BEST GOSPEL PERFORMANCE (OTHER THAN SOUL GOSPEL)

- Imperials, *No Shortage*. Impact.
- Johnny Cash, *Johnny Cash Sings Precious Memories*. Columbia.
- Happy Goodman Family, *Happy Goodman Family Hour*. Canaan.
- Connie Smith, *Connie Smith Sings Hank Williams Gospel*. Columbia.
- Statler Brothers, *Holy Bible—New Testament*. Mercury.

BEST SOUL GOSPEL PERFORMANCE

- Andrae Crouch & the Disciples, *Take Me Back*. Light.
- James Cleveland, Charles Fold Singers, "Jesus Is the Best Thing." Savoy.
- James Cleveland, Southern California Community Choir, *To the Glory of God*. Savoy.
- James Cleveland with Voices of Tabernacle, *God Has Smiled on Me*. Savoy.
- 21st Century, *The Storm Is Passing Over*. Creed.

BEST ETHNIC OR TRADITIONAL RECORDING

- *The Muddy Waters Woodstock Album*, Muddy Waters. Chess.
- *I Got What It Takes*, Koko Taylor. Alligator.
- *Memphis Blues*, Memphis Slim. Olympic.
- *Music of Guatemala*, San Lucas Band. ABC/Command.
- *Wake Up Dead Man*, Bruce Jackson. Rounder.

BEST LATIN RECORDING

- *Sun of Latin Music,* Eddie Palmieri. Coco.
- *Afro-Indio*, Mongo Santamaria. Fania.
- *Barretto*, Ray Barretto. Fania.
- *Fania All-Stars Live at Yankee Stadium, Vol. 1*, Fania All-Stars. Fania.
- *The Good, the Bad and the Ugly*, Willie Colon. Fania.
- *Paunetto's Point*, Bobby Paunetto. Pathfinder.
- "Quieres Ser Mi Amante," Camilo Sesto. Pronto.

BEST INSTRUMENTAL ARRANGEMENT

- Mike Post, Pete Carpenter, "The Rockford Files" (Mike Post). MGM.
- Randy Brecker, "Some Skunk Funk" (Brecker Brothers). Arista.
- Alan Broadbent, "Children of Lima" (Woody Herman). Fantasy.
- Thad Jones, "Living for the City" (Thad Jones, Mel Lewis). Philadelphia International.
- Ron McClure, "No Show" (Blood, Sweat & Tears). Columbia.
- Herbert Spencer, "Theme from *Jaws*" (John Williams). MCA.

BEST INSTRUMENTAL COMPOSITION
(Composer's Award)
- Michel Legrand, "Images."
- Silvester Levay, Stephan Praeger, "Fly, Robin, Fly."
- Chuck Mangione, "Chase the Clouds Away."
- Van McCoy, "The Hustle."
- Mike Post, Pete Carpenter, "The Rockford Files."

BEST CAST SHOW ALBUM
Composer's Award
- *The Wiz*, Charlie Smalls. Atlantic.
- *Chicago*, John Kander, Fred Ebb. Artist.
- *A Chorus Line*, Marvin Hamlisch, Edward Kleban. Columbia.
- *A Little Night Music* (London cast), Stephen Sondheim. RCA.
- *Shenandoah*, Gary Geld, Peter Udell. RCA.

BEST ALBUM OF ORIGINAL SCORE WRITTEN FOR A MOTION PICTURE OR TV SPECIAL
(Composer's Award)
- *Jaws*, John Williams. MCA.
- *Murder on the Orient Express*, Richard Rodney Bennett. Capitol.
- *Nashville*, Carradine, Blakley, Baskin, Reicheg, Gibson, Black. ABC.
- *The Return of the Pink Panther*, Henry Mancini. RCA.
- *The Wind and the Lion*, Jerry Goldsmith. Artista.

BEST ARRANGEMENT ACCOMPANYING VOCALIST(S)
- Ray Stevens, "Misty" (Ray Stevens). Barnaby.
- Gene Puerling, "April in Paris" (Singers Unlimited). MPS.
- Gene Puerling, "Autumn in New York" (Singers Unlimited). MPS.
- Gene Puerling, "Killing Me Softly with His Song" (Singers Unlimited). MPS.
- Mel Tormé, "Gershwin Medley" (Mel Tormé). Atlantic.

ALBUM OF THE YEAR, CLASSICAL
- *Beethoven: Symphonies (9) Complete*, Sir Georg Solti conducting the Chicago Symphony. London.
- *Beethoven: Symphony No. 5 in C Minor*, Carlos Kleiber conducting the Vienna Philharmonic. Deutsche Grammophon.
- *Mozart: Così Fan Tutte*, Colin Davis conducting the Royal Opera House, Covent Garden (solos: Caballé, Baker, Gedda, Ganzarolli, Cotrubas, Van Allen). Philips.
- *Orff: Carmina Burana*, Michael Tilson Thomas conducting the Cleveland Orchestra; Robert Page directing the Cleveland Orchestra Chorus and Boys' Choir (solos: Blegen, Riegel, Bindery). Columbia.
- *Penderecki: Magnificat*, Kryzysztof Penderecki conducting the Polish Radio National Symphony and Chorus. Angel.
- *Ravel: Daphnis et Chloé (Complete)*, Pierre Boulez conducting the New York Philharmonic; Camarata Singers. Columbia.
- *Rossini: The Siege of Corinth*, Thomas Schippers conducting the London Symphony and Ambrosian Opera Chorus (solos: Sills, Verrett, Díaz, Theyard). Angel.

BEST CLASSICAL PERFORMANCE, ORCHESTRA
(Conductor's Award)
- Pierre Boulez conducting the New York Philharmonic, *Ravel: Daphnis et Chloé*. Columbia.
- Colin Davis conducting the Concertgebouw Orchestra, Amsterdam, *Berlioz: Symphonie Fantastique*. Philips.
- Carlos Kleiber conducting the Vienna Philharmonic, *Beethoven: Symphony No. 5 in C Minor*. Deutsche Grammophon.
- Rafael Kubelik conducting the Boston Symphony, *Bartók: Concerto for Orchestra*. Deutsche Grammophon.

James Levine conducting the Chicago
Symphony, *Mahler: Symphony No. 4
in G Major*. RCA.

Seiji Ozawa conducting the New Philharmonic Orchestra, *Beethoven:
Symphony No. 9 in D Minor*. Philips.

Sir Georg Solti conducting the Chicago
Symphony, *Beethoven: Symphonies
(9) Complete*. London.

Herbert von Karajan conducting the
Berlin Philharmonic, *Mahler: Sym-
phony No. 5 in C Sharp Minor*.
Deutsche Grammophon.

BEST OPERA RECORDING

• *Mozart: Così Fan Tutte*, Colin Davis
conducting the Chorus and Orchestra
of the Royal Opera House, Covent
Garden (solos: Caballé, Baker,
Gedda, Ganzarolli, Van Allen,
Cotrubas). Philips.

Dallapiccola: Il Prigioniero, Antal
Dorati conducting the National Sym-
phony Orchestra of Washington,
D.C.; Paul Traver directing the Uni-
versity of Maryland Chorus (solos:
Mazzieri, Barrers, Emili). London.

Korngold: Die Tote Stadt, Erich Leinsdorf conducting the Munich Radio
Orchestra, Bavarian Radio Chorus
(solos: Kollo, Neblett, Prey, Luxon).
RCA.

Rossini: The Barber of Seville, James
Levine conducting the London Sym-
phony and John Alldis Choir (solos:
Sills, Milnes, Gedda). Angel.

Rossini: The Siege of Corinth, Thomas
Schippers conducting the London
Symphony Orchestra and Ambrosian
Opera Chorus (solos: Sills, Verrett,
Díaz). Angel.

Schoenberg: Moses und Aron, Michael
Gielen conducting the Orchestra and
Chorus of the Austrian Radio (solos:
Reich, Devos, Csapo, Obrowsky,
Lucas). Philips.

Vaughan Williams: Sir John in Love,
Meredith Davis conducting the New
Philharmonia Orchestra; John Alldis
Choir (solos: Herincx, Palmer, Tear).
Angel.

BEST CHORAL PERFORMANCE (OTHER THAN OPERA)

• Robert Page directing the Cleveland
Orchestra Chorus and Boys' Choir;
Michael Tilson Thomas conducting
the Cleveland Orchestra (solos: Ble-
gen, Binder, Riegel), *Orff: Carmina
Burana*. Columbia.

Leonard Bernstein conducting the Westminster Choir and New York Philharmonic, *Haydn: Harmoniemesse*.
Columbia.

Pierre Boulez conducting the BBC
Symphony Chorus, Goldsmith's
Choral Union, Gentlemen of London
Philharmonic Choir, BBC Symphony
(solos: Napier, Minton Thomas),
Schoenberg: Gurrelieder. Columbia.

Tadeusz Dobrzanski, chorus master, Polish Radio Chorus of Krakow; Palka
and Wietrzny, chorus masters,
soloists and Boys' Chorus from
Krakow; Kryzysztof Penderecki conducting the Philharmonic Chorus,
Polish Radio National Symphony,
Penderecki: Magnificat. Angel.

John McCarthy directing the Ambrosian
Singers; Riccardo Muti conducting
the New Philharmonia Orchestra,
*Cherubini: Requiem in D Minor for
Male Chorus and Orchestra*. Angel.

John Oliver, chorus master, Tanglewood
Festival Chorus; Theodore Marier,
chorus master, Boston Boys' Choir;
Seiji Ozawa conducting the Boston
Symphony Orchestra, *Berlioz: La
Damnation de Faust*. Deutsche
Grammophon.

Herbert von Karajan conducting the
Vienna Singverein and Berlin Philharmonic, *Beethoven: Missa Solemnis*. Angel.

BEST CHAMBER MUSIC PERFORMANCE (INSTRUMENTAL OR VOCAL)

• Artur Rubinstein, Henryk Szeryng,
Pierre Fournier, *Schubert: Trios No.
1 in B Flat Major, Op. 99, and No. 2
in E Flat Major, Op. 100 (The Trios)*.
RCA.

Concord Quartet, *Ives: Quartets Nos. 1 and 2*. Nonesuch.

Ralph Grierson, Artie Kane, *Gershwin: Gershwin's Wonderful* (Side 1: "American in Paris," 3 preludes). Angel.

Heinz Holliger, Christiane Jaccottet, Marcal Cervera, *Baroque Oboe Recital: Works by Bach, Couperin and Marais*. Philips.

Jaime Laredo, Ruth Laredo, Jeffery Solow, *Ravel: Trio for Violin, Cello and Piano*. Columbia.

Itzhak Perlman, André Previn, *Joplin: "The Easy Winners" and Other Ragtime Music of Scott Joplin*. Angel.

Jean Pierre Rampal, Claude Bolling, *Bolling: Suite for Flute and Piano*. Columbia.

Mstislav Rostropovich, Vasso Devetzi, *R. Strauss: Sonata in F for Cello & Piano*. Angel.

BEST CLASSICAL PERFORMANCE, INSTRUMENTAL SOLOIST(S) (WITH ORCHESTRA)

• Alicia de Larrocha (De Burgos conducting the London Philharmonic [Fauré]; Foster conducting the London Philharmonic [Ravel]), *Ravel: Concerto for Left Hand; Concerto for Piano in G Major; Fauré: Fantaisie for Piano and Orchestra*. London.

Maurice André (von Karajan conducting the Berlin Philharmonic), *4 Trumpet Concertos by Vivaldi, Telemann, Mozart, Hummel*. Angel.

Julian Bream (Gardiner conducting the Monteverdi Orchestra), *Berkeley: Guitar Concerto; Rodrigo: Concierto de Aranjuez for Guitar*. RCA.

Alfred Brendel (Marriner conducting the Academy of St. Martin-in-the-Fields), *Mozart: Concertos No. 18 in B Flat Major and No. 27 in B Flat Major for Piano and Orchestra*. Philips.

Lynn Harrell (Levine conducting the London Symphony), *Dvořák: Concerto in B Minor for Cello*. RCA.

Murray Perahia (Marriner conducting the Academy of St. Martin-in-the-Fields), *Mendelssohn: Concertos No. 1 in G Minor for Piano and No. 2 in D Minor for Piano*. Columbia.

Itzhak Perlman (Martinon conducting the Orchestre de Paris), *Saint-Saëns: Introduction and Rondo Capriccioso; Havanaise; Chausson: Poème; Ravel: Tzigane*. Angel.

Peter Serkin (Schneider conducting the English Chamber Orchestra), *Mozart: Concertos for Piano and Orchestra Composed in 1784 (6) (Nos. 14–19)*. RCA.

BEST CLASSICAL PERFORMANCE, INSTRUMENTAL SOLOIST(S) (WITHOUT ORCHESTRA)

• Nathan Milstein, *Bach: Sonatas and Partitas for Violin Unaccompanied*. Deutsche Grammophon.

Vladimir Ashkenazy, *Chopin: Etudes, Opp. 10 and 25*. London.

Alicia de Larrocha, *Falla: Music of Falla* ("Three-Cornered Hat," "El Amor Brujo," etc.). London.

Arturo Benedetti Michelangeli, *Schumann: Carnaval, Op. 9*. Angel.

Peter Serkin, *Messiaen: 20 Regards sur l'Enfant Jésus*. RCA.

John Williams, *Bach: Suites for Lute*. Columbia.

BEST CLASSICAL PERFORMANCE, VOCAL SOLOIST

• Janet Baker (Bernstein conducting the Israel Philhamonic), *Mahler: Kindertotenlieder*. Columbia.

Elly Ameling (Baldwin, accompanist), *Schumann: Frauenliebe und Leben*. Philips.

Victoria de los Angeles (Jacquillat conducting the Lamoureux Concerts Orchestra), *Canteloube: Songs of the Auvergne, Album 2*. Angel.

Cleo Laine (Nash Ensemble, Howarth/Hymas, piano), *Cleo Laine Sings Pierrot Lunaire and Songs by Ives*. RCA.

Joan Morris (Bolcom, accompanist), *After the Ball (A Treasury of Turn-of-the-Century Popular Songs)*.

Leontyne Price, Placido Domingo (Santi conducting the New Philharmonic), *Verdi and Puccini Duets (Othello, Ballo en Maschera, Manon Lescaut, Madama Butterfly)*. RCA.

Elisabeth Schwarzkopf (Parsons, accompanist), *Schumann: Frauenliebe und Leben, Op. 42*. Angel.

BEST ENGINEERED RECORDING, CLASSICAL

• Gordon Parry, Colin Moorfoot, *Ravel: Daphnis et Chloé* (Maazel conducting the Cleveland Orchestra). London.

Bud Graham, Ray Moore, Milton Cherin, *Ravel: Daphnis et Chloé (Complete)* (Boulez conducting the New York Philharmonic). Columbia.

Edward Graham, Raymond Moore, *Orff: Carmina Burana* (Thomas conducting the Cleveland Orchestra, Cleveland Chorus and Boys' Choir, Page; solos: Blegen, Riegel, Binder). Columbia.

James Lock, Kenneth Wilkinson, *Stravinsky: The Rite of Spring* (Solti conducting the Chicago Symphony). London.

H. P. Schweigmann, *Beethoven: Symphony No. 5 in C Minor* (Kleiber conducting the Vienna Philharmonic). Deutsche Grammophon.

Heinz Wildhagen, *Bartók: Concerto for Orchestra* (Kubelik conducting the Boston Symphony). Deutsche Grammophon.

Kenneth Wilkinson, *Beethoven: Symphonies (9) (Complete)* (Solti conducting the Chicago Symphony). London.

BEST ALBUM NOTES, CLASSICAL
(Annotator's Award)

• Gunther Schuller, *Footlifters (A Century of American Marches—Sousa, Joplin, Ives)* (Gunther Schuller conducting the All-Star Band). Columbia.

Rudi Blesh, *Joplin: The Complete Works of Scott Joplin* (Dick Hyman). RCA.

Laszlo Eosze, *Kodály: Orchestral Works* (Antal Dorati conducting the Hungarian Philharmonic). London.

Rory Guy, Itzhak Perlman, *Joplin: The Easy Winners* (solos: Itzhak Perlman, André Previn). Angel.

Rory Guy, *Gershwin: Gershwin's Wonderful* (solos: Ralph Grierson, Artie Kane). Angel.

James H. Moore, *Gagliano: La Dafne* (Vorwerk conducting the Musica Pacifica). ABC/Command.

Christopher Palmer, *Korngold: Die Tote Stadt* (Leinsdorf conducting the Munich Radio Orchestra; solos: Kollo, Neblett, Prey, Luxon). RCA.

Judith Robison, *The English Harpsichord* (Byrd, Farnaby, etc.) (solo: Igor Kipnis). Angel.

H. C. Robbins-Landon, *Haydn: Symphonies 93–104* (Dorati conducting the Philharmonia Hungarica). London.

BEST COMEDY RECORDING

• *Is It Something I Said?* Richard Pryor. Reprise.

An Evening with Wally Londo Featuring Bill Slaszo, George Carlin. Little David.

Matching Tie and Handkerchief, Monty Python. Arista.

Modern Scream, Lily Tomlin. Polydor.

A Star Is Bought, Albert Brooks. Asylum.

BEST SPOKEN WORD, DOCUMENTARY OR DRAMA RECORDING

• *Give 'Em Hell Harry*, James Whitmore. United Atrists.

The Autobiography of Miss Jane Pittman, Claudia McNeil. Caedmon.

Immortal Sherlock Holmes Mercury Theater on the Air, Orson Welles. Radiola.

The Prophet, Richard Harris. Atlantic.

Talk About America, Alistair Cooke. Pye.

To Kill a Mockingbird, Maureen Stapleton. Miller-Brody.

BEST RECORDING FOR CHILDREN

• *The Little Prince*, Richard Burton, narrator (featuring Jonathan Winters, Billy Simpson). Pip.

Bert and Ernie Sing-Along, Bert & Ernie. Cra.

Merry Christmas from Sesame Street, Sesame Street cast. Cra.

Mr. Popper's Penguins, Jim Backus. Newbery.

Really Rosie, Carole King. Ode.

Sesame Street Monsters, Jim Henson's Sesame Street Monsters. Cra.

BEST ENGINEERED RECORDING (OTHER THAN CLASSICAL)

• Brooks Arthur, Larry Alexander, Russ Payne, *Between the Lines* (Janis Ian). Columbia.

Chuck Johnson, Freddie Piro, Billy Taylor, Tom Trefethen, Alan Parson, *Ambrosia* (Ambrosia). 20th Century.

Bill Schnee, *I've Got the Music in Me* (Thelma Houston, Pressure Cooker). Sheffield.

Eric Stewart, *The Original Soundtrack* (10cc). Mercury.

Tommy Vicari, *Storm at Sun-Up* (Gino Vannelli). A&M.

BEST ALBUM PACKAGE
(Art Director's Award)

• Jim Ladwig, *Honey* (Ohio Players). Mercury.

Agi, *Physical Graffiti* (Led Zeppelin). Swan Song/Atlantic.

Gary Burden, *One of These Nights* (Eagles). Asylum.

Gene Christensen, *Playing Possum* (Carly Simon). Elektra.

Bob Defrin, *Solo Piano* (Phineas Newborn, Jr.). Atlantic.

Mick Haggerty, *Steppin'* (Pointer Sisters). Blue Thumb.

Hipgnosis, *Wish You Were Here* (Pink Floyd). Columbia.

John Kosh, *Atlantic Crossing* (Rod Stewart). Warner Bros.

William E. McEuen, *Dream* (Nitty Gritty Dirt Band). United Artists.

BEST ALBUM NOTES
(Annotator's Award)

• Pete Hamill, *Blood on the Tracks* (Bob Dylan). Columbia.

Ralph J. Gleason, *The Real Lenny Bruce* (Lenny Bruce). Fantasy.

Benny Green, *The Tatum Solo Masterpieces* (Art Tatum). Pablo.

Tom T. Hall, *Greatest Hits, Vol. 2* (Tom T. Hall). Mercury.

George T. Simon, *A Legendary Performer* (Glenn Miller & His Orchestra). RCA.

PRODUCER OF THE YEAR

• Arif Mardin

Peter Asher

Gus Dudgeon

Dennis Lambert, Brian Potter

Bill Szymczyk

• 1976 •

Still a Wonder

When Paul Simon accepted the Grammy last year for 1975's top LP, *Still Crazy After All These Years*, and thanked Stevie Wonder for not releasing a new album, the half-jest turned out to be prophetically ironic.

Stevie Wonder's previous two LPs, *Innervisions* (1973) and *Fulfillingness' First Finale* (1974), had both won Album of the Year. His next work, *Songs in the Key of Life,* took more than two years to make and was causing such frenzied anticipation throughout the music industry that Wonder took to wearing a T-shirt in public that read "We're almost finished!" When *Songs in the Key of Life* finally came out in 1976, it became only the third album in chart-keeping history to debut at number one (following the lead set by Elton John's *Captain Fantastic* and *Rock of the Westies*). It also came in first in the *Village Voice*'s annual survey of music critics judging the year's best albums and then scored the year's most Grammy nominations—seven.

L.A. Times critic Robert Hilburn wrote prior to the awards telecast: "If Stevie Wonder's *Songs in the Key of Life* wins the Grammy that it deserves tonight as the year's best album, Wonder will have brought the nation's normally feuding pop critics and the Grammy voters together in a rare alliance. While critics often ridicule the Grammy Awards as too conservative, Grammy voters frequently dismiss the critics as too esoteric and rock-oriented. But a Wonder victory will soften the arguments. At least momentarily."

As predicted, it turned out to be another Wonder-ous year at the Grammys. Stevie Wonder actually received two awards for Album of the Year (as both its

Stevie Wonder tied Frank Sinatra's record for having the most best album wins (three) when *Songs in the Key of Life* prevailed as predicted.

singer-songwriter and its producer) and became only the second artist in Grammy history to win the LP prize three times. Sinatra won in 1959, 1965 and 1966.

Songs in the Key of Life also snagged the artist prizes for Producer of the Year and best pop male vocal performance. The album's first single release, "I Wish," brought him the statuette for best r&b male vocal performance. N.A.R.A.S. may have given Motown artists only one award throughout the entire decade of the 1960s (for the Temptations' "Cloud Nine" in 1968), but the academy was now burying one of its most supreme talents under an avalanche of them. Wonder was now the second-biggest winner in Grammy history. "While Mancini has been accumulating his 20 Grammys since the record industry competition was initiated in 1958," the *L.A. Times* noted, "Wonder's 15 awards have all come in the last four years. It's the most impressive concentrated show in the history of the awards."

Wonder couldn't be on hand at the Grammy show at the Hollywood Palladium because he was attending a music festival in Lagos, Nigeria, but the producers arranged for a live satellite hookup that would enable him to perform for the TV audience and accept his prizes with live thank-you remarks beamed from Africa. The transmission, however, was weak, fuzzy and garbled.

The snafu caused an embarrassing delay on the Grammycast as technicians scrambled to solve the problem and host Andy Williams panicked. Williams ended up committing the worst gaffe in Grammycast history when, in obvious desperation, he asked the blind artist at one point, "Can you *see* us?!" (It was a bad year for Williams. He had been scheduled to appear at the off-air ceremony to announce the Grammy nominations nearly two months earlier, but was replaced by Natalie Cole when he was called out of town to attend the manslaughter trial of his ex-wife, Claudine Longet, in Aspen, Colorado. Williams was the only host the awards ceremony had known since it was first aired in 1971, but he would not be invited back next year. The official explanation: The singer no longer represented the mainstream of American music.)

Strangely, not one of Stevie Wonder's seven nominations was for Record of the Year, although *Songs in the Key of Life*'s two number-one-ranked single releases, "I Wish" and "Sir Duke," were both considered strong possibilities. Instead, the contest turned out to be a tight one involving Paul Simon's "50 Ways to Leave Your Lover" (from his 1975 Album of the Year, *Still Crazy After All These Years;* "50 Ways" was released as a single after last year's eligibility period); "Afternoon Delight" by the hottest new pop group in the country, Starland Vocal Band; Barry

Manilow's "I Write the Songs" (the year's sixth-hottest single); "If You Leave Me Now" by Chicago (which had never won a Grammy despite three earlier nominations); and "This Masquerade" by jazz guitarist George Benson, who was considered a long shot, since the platter barely made it into *Billboard*'s annual Hot 100, having ended up at number 94.

When "This Masquerade" prevailed, the announcement was met with gasps and cheers. Its win marked the first time since the victory of "Up, Up and Away" in 1967 that the Record of the Year choice was not a number-one-ranked pop single. ("Up, Up and Away" only got up the weekly charts as far as number 7; "This Masquerade" reached number 10.) N.A.R.A.S. voters had been smarting for years from the accusation that they picked winners based purely on popular success, and now Benson's triumph disproved that. The outpouring also expressed voters' regard for a critically acclaimed artist who had toiled in the jazz and r&b fields since the 1950s without broad recognition. Some of his most recent, low-profile work, in fact, had been with Stevie Wonder on *Songs in the Key of Life*. (Obviously, Wonder's influence rubbed off. When "This Masquerade" was released, more than one critic commented that it sounded like a Stevie Wonder ballad.) Not everyone was in tune with its selection as the year's top platter, though. *L.A. Times* music critic Robert Hilburn dismissed it as a lightweight, "misguided" choice.

"This Masquerade" was from Benson's *Breezin'* LP, a losing nominee for Album of the Year that nonetheless became the biggest-selling jazz album ever, going platinum (marking a million in sales) soon after its release and eventually selling nearly 4 million copies. It scored big at the Grammys, too. In addition to its Record of the Year single, *Breezin'* took the prize for Best Pop

> **Strangely, album winner Stevie Wonder wasn't nominated for Record of the Year.**

Instrumental Performance, while its "Theme from *Good King Bad*" track earned Benson Best R&B Instrumental Performance. *Breezin'* was also hailed as the Best Engineered Recording.

Benson tied Stevie Wonder for having the most nominations this year—seven. *Variety* noted that Benson was "the only artist whose work was nominated in all three major categories" of Album, Record and Song of the Year.

Although "I Write the Songs" lost as Record of the Year, it prevailed as Song of the Year. The tune was written by former Beach Boy Bruce Johnston and not, as is commonly assumed, by the vocalist who took it to the Top 10, singer-songwriter Barry Manilow, who also performed it on the Grammycast. Manilow was not even the first artist to record it. The Captain & Tennille (last year's big Grammy winners, who reaped no nominations this year) had included the song on their debut album but never released it as a single.

The choice of Best New Artist was a favorite target of Grammy bashers, since the group would score only one memorable song and then fade from the limelight.

The Starland Vocal Band was called a clone of the Mamas & the Papas because both were comprised of two men and two women who displayed an obvious mastery of four-part harmonies. The band's initial two members, Bill and Taffy Danoff, had toured with John Denver (Bill Danoff and Denver wrote "Take Me Home, Country Roads" together) and so had solid music backgrounds, as did singer-pianist Jon Carroll and vocalist Margot Chapman, both of whom had worked with the Danoffs years before they signed up with Starland. It was Bill Danoff who wrote the group's first and only number-one hit—"Afternoon Delight," which was a losing contender for both Record and Song of the Year. The song had a sexually suggestive quality that helped it become so popular, but the lyrics had actually been inspired by the nickname of a memorable gourmet lunch

Warner Bros.

George Benson's "This Masquerade" was the first best-record winner in nearly a decade not to top the charts. The audience cheered its victory.

that Danoff had one day in Washington, D.C. "So Bill ate it—the food that is," his wife, Taffy, once told a concert audience, "and went home and explained to me what an 'Afternoon Delight' *should* be!"

Starland Vocal Band began the Grammy contest with five nominations, the same number as Benson, and ended up with one prize in addition to Best New Artist, an arranging award for "Afternoon Delight." The group received no further bids after 1976. It did have two moderately successful singles in the late 1970s ("Hail! Hail! Rock and Roll" and "Loving You with My Eyes") but disbanded in 1980. Soon thereafter, Bill and Taffy Danoff got divorced and Carroll and Chapman got married.

The jazz/rock band Chicago had had five number-one-ranked albums in the seven years it had been on the scene, but had never won a Grammy, a point that astonished many, since Chicago seemed like perfect N.A.R.A.S. fare. With their strong melodies and a jazzy sound, they were both hip and safe. This year they had five nominations, including Record of the Year contender "If You Leave Me Now," which ended up bringing them the prizes for Best Pop Vocal Performance by a Duo, Group or Chorus and Best Arrangement Accompanying Vocalist(s). The group's *Chicago X* LP won Best Album Package.

When Linda Ronstadt won her first Grammy last year, it was in a c&w category, but now she confused N.A.R.A.S. voters with her newest LP, *Hasten Down the Wind,* which included both

News of the Grammy winners was dwarfed by a headline touting a fight among Emmy leaders.

country and pop rock selections. Voters opted to put her in the pop lineup this time, where she was competing—just like last year, ironically—against country music's newest queen, Emmylou Harris (for "Here, There and Everywhere"). When she beat Harris a second time, Ronstadt obviously felt bad about it. "Competition is for race horses, not artists," she said backstage after receiving her Grammy, quoting George Bernard Shaw. "It doesn't mean I'm the best. It just means I won. I think Emmylou Harris is best. I'm not going to give [the Grammy] back, though."

Ronstadt also topped last year's Best New Artist, Natalie Cole, in the pop vocal category, but, for a second year in a row, Cole snagged the laurels for best female r&b vocal performance. Suddenly, it looked like Cole could be launching another winning streak in the category that Aretha Franklin had ruled for eight years before her. Cole's "Sophisticated Lady (She's a Different Lady)" overtook Franklin's "Something He Can Feel" this year and also beat out "Love Hangover" by Diana Ross, who had been nominated for a Grammy three times in the past as a soloist and twice as a member of the Supremes, but never won.

After studying est in the mid-1970s, the husband and wife vocal team of Marilyn McCoo and Billy Davis, Jr., decided to break away from the six-time Grammy-winning 5th Dimension in 1975 to try to make it on their own as a duo. Est "freed me to do what I really wanted," McCoo told *Essence* magazine. "Like Billy, I wanted to try new things." Their second single, "You Don't Have to Be a Star (to Be in My Show)," topped the rankings for two weeks and earned them the r&b group vocals honor. Soon after the Grammycast, McCoo and Davis had their own weekly variety TV show. When it went off the air after just six weeks, however, McCoo signed up to be the host of *Solid Gold* in its second season.

Rock vocalist Boz Scaggs had been active in the music scene as early as the late 1950s when he worked with the young Steve Miller's band, the Marksmen. He veered after that between singing and writing rock and r&b ballads, but then he finally experienced his first pop success with his 1976 album *Silk Degrees,* which sold 5 million copies. *Silk Degrees* was nominated in four categories, but Scaggs emerged as victor only once—when he was named with David Paich as the writing talent behind the Best Rhythm & Blues Song, "Lowdown," a hit single from the album.

Two jazz greats who hadn't been heard from at the Grammys since the early

1960s both came back with strong victories. In 1976, N.A.R.A.S. introduced a new category exclusively for jazz singers, and Ella Fitzgerald made a dramatic comeback to claim it over Sarah Vaughan and Ray Charles for her duet album with jazz guitarist Joe Pass, thus marking her first Grammy win since 1962. Count Basie's last Grammy was in 1963, but he returned to seize the Best Jazz Performance by a Soloist trophy for his keyboard virtuosity on his collaborative LP with sax player Zoot Sims. Past Grammy grabber Duke Ellington died of lung cancer in May 1974 but was honored posthumously for best big-band performance for a collection of his famous *Suites*.

Fusionists had done poorly in the jazz lineup until a few years ago, but now they seemed to hold sway as Chick Corea's overhauled Return to Forever band came back to reclaim the group performance honors that it won last year for the first time. Its 1975 LP *No Mystery* had fared poorly with the critics, but the latest, *The Leprechaun,* got gushing reviews as Corea tested his new team's talents with a wide range of sounds. "My own personal ideal is combining all the most beautiful forms of music—classical, rock and jazz—into a form that doesn't go over people's heads," Corea told *Rolling Stone.* "I guess you could call it a contemporary hybrid." Corea also won Best Instrumental Arrangement for one of its best tracks, "Leprechaun's Dream." Fusionist composer and trumpet player Chuck Mangione had been nominated on six earlier occasions but finally picked up his first trophy for Best Instrumental Composition, *Bellavia.*

Country singer Emmylou Harris may have been trounced twice in two years by Linda Ronstadt, but she topped seven-time past loser Dolly Parton and two-time past champ Tammy Wynette to be named best female country vocalist for *Elite*

Hotel, an album that included a three-song tribute to her mentor, singer-bandleader Gram Parsons, for whom she had worked as a backup vocalist till his death in 1973. Nineteen seventy-four Grammy winner Ronnie Milsap had recently been named the Country Music Association's Male Vocalist of the Year for a second time and now snagged his second N.A.R.A.S. award for his male response to Tammy Wynette's 1969 Grammy-winning "Stand By Your Man." "(I'm a) Stand By My Woman Man" hit the top of the country charts the previous August, but it was dangerously close in musical notes to the Wynette classic and incurred a lawsuit.

Milsap beat Larry Gatlin in the male vocalist category, but Gatlin rebounded when his "Broken Lady" was named Best Country Song over "Dropkick Me, Jesus" by Paul Craft. (" 'Broken Lady' was the only country song nominated in more than one category," *Variety* noted.) For a third year in a row, Chet Atkins held on to the instrumental performance laurels when he won for his collaboration with fellow guitarist Les Paul. Their *Chester and Lester* LP was hailed by the critics for its fun spirit, chatty interludes and a well-messed jazz-country quality. Also championing an experimental sound was the winner of the group vocal honors, the Amazing Rhythm Aces, the Memphis band with the heavy r&b lilt that was honored for "The End Is Not in Sight (The Cowboy Tune)." John Hartford, a former banjo player for Glen Campbell and the winner of Grammy's Best Country Song of 1967 for "Gentle on My Mind," reaped Best Ethnic or Traditional Recording for *Mark Twang.*

Two-time past winner of the gospel laurels Mahalia Jackson died in 1972 but received one last Grammy for *How I Got Over,* a posthumous collection of some of her 1954 radio performances and the songs she sang before a black church con-

> A victorious Linda Ronstadt insisted, "Competition is for race horses, not artists," but she kept her award.

gregation on a TV show in 1963. ("How I Got Over" was one of the classic songs in Jackson's repertoire.) Also winning a third Grammy were the Oak Ridge Boys for their single "Where the Soul Never Dies." Eddie Palmieri held on to the Best Latin Recording prize, created only one year earlier, for *Unfinished Masterpiece.*

Comedian Richard Pryor made a triumphant return this year, too. Pryor once said that Bill Cosby's success had inspired him to move to New York from Peoria, Illinois, where he grew up, and try to make it in the comedy field. Now it looked like Pryor was challenging Cosby's six-year winning streak by scoring his third straight win. This one was for *Bicentennial Nigger,* which admiring critics called his masterpiece and detractors labeled his most obscene and humorless LP yet. Pryor taped it in front of an audience full of celebrities whom the comedian singled out for barbs, including Natalie Cole ("She can sing her ass off!" the comic cries). His six-minute salute to the nation's bicentennial was full of ire over black people's lot in contemporary America: "We're celebrating 200 years of white folks kickin' ass," he says. "How long will this bullshit go on?"

Shortly before his 90th birthday, Artur Rubinstein took on a Herculean task: a five-disc recording of Beethoven's five Concertos for Piano and Orchestra that not only claimed Classical Album of the Year but earned him a third instrumental soloist award in a row.

"It came as no surprise," *Billboard* insisted when Vladimir Horowitz reaped the other soloist instrumental prize, bringing his Grammy total to 13 awards, making him the awards' third-biggest winner behind Henry Mancini and Stevie Wonder. Horowitz was lauded for the recording of some of his concerts in 1975–76 that included sonatas by Schumann and Scriabin. "They sound marvelously true, quite exceptional," wrote *High Fidelity.*

The orchestral honors went to Georg Solti and the Chicago Symphony for their rendition of Richard Strauss's *Also*

Loser Sarah Vaughan (right) congratulated Ella Fitzgerald on her first jazz win since 1962.

Sprach Zarathustra, "a distinctively individual, unexpectedly romantic interpretation," said *High Fidelity,* "with the Chicagoans at their Solti-led best."

High Fidelity gave its Prix Mondial Award this year to the same recipient of the Grammy for chamber music, the late David Munrow, who conducted the Early Music Consort in a three-disc set titled *The Art of Courtly Love,* which featured works by the 14th-century French composer and poet Guillaume de Machaut and his musical followers. The choral laurels were bestowed to director Arthur Oldham of the London Symphony Chorus and André Previn for leading that orchestra in Rachmaninov's *The Bells.* Singing in Russian, the chorus, said *High Fidelity,* "is in splendid form," but added that Previn's conducting "doesn't run away with the field."

For the first time ever, the Grammy for Best Opera Recording went to an American work when conductor Lorin Maazel led the Cleveland Orchestra and Chorus in the first complete recording of George Gershwin's *Porgy and Bess,* with baritone Willard White as Porgy and soprano Leona Mitchell as Bess. "Nearly all the voices are good, the pacing is lively, the execution meticulous," opined *High*

Fidelity. "There's no doubt that all of this makes the opera too long, that cuts should be made (and were, even in the first production)—but for once we should hear it all." The operatic vocal category included some unlikely contenders this year— among them, Barbra Streisand singing works by Debussy and Canteloube and veteran movie-star ghost singer Marni Nixon (who, among other credits, sang the vocals for Audrey Hepburn in the 1964 film version of *My Fair Lady*) tackling Schoenberg—but the prize was claimed by another American diva, Beverly Sills, for *Music of Victor Herbert*.

The Grammycast included musical performances by Barry Manilow, Sarah Vaughan, Wild Cherry (a losing nominee for Best New Artist), the Starland Vocal Band and Marilyn McCoo and Billy Davis, Jr. Some of its better comic interludes came when presenter Bette Milder admonished the audience, "In the music business, you're as good as your last 2-point-40 minutes." The fiasco of losing the satellite hookup to Stevie Wonder in Africa was almost made up for by successful live satellite transmissions of the awards ceremony for the first time ever to viewers in the Far East.

• 1976 •

The awards ceremony was broadcast on CBS from the Hollywood Palladium on February 19, 1977, for the awards eligibility period of October 16, 1975, to September 30, 1976.

ALBUM OF THE YEAR
• *Songs in the Key of Life*, Stevie Wonder. Tamla/Motown.
Breezin', George Benson. Warner Bros.
Chicago X, Chicago. Columbia.
Frampton Comes Alive, Peter Frampton. A&M.
Silk Degrees, Boz Scaggs. Columbia.

RECORD OF THE YEAR
• "This Masquerade," George Benson. Warner Bros.
"Afternoon Delight," Starland Vocal Band. Windsong/RCA.
"50 Ways to Leave Your Lover," Paul Simon. Columbia.
"I Write the Songs," Barry Manilow. Arista.
"If You Leave Me Now," Chicago. Columbia.

SONG OF THE YEAR
(Songwriter's Award)
• "I Write the Songs," Bruce Johnston.
"Afternoon Delight," Bill Danoff.

"Breaking Up Is Hard to Do," Neil Sedaka, Howard Greenfield.
"This Masquerade," Leon Russell.
"The Wreck of the Edmund Fitzgerald," Gordon Lightfoot.

BEST NEW ARTIST
• Starland Vocal Band
Boston
Dr. Buzzard's Original "Savannah" Band
Brothers Johnson
Wild Cherry

BEST POP VOCAL PERFORMANCE, MALE
• Stevie Wonder, *Songs in the Key of Life*. Tamla/Motown.
George Benson, "This Masquerade," track. Warner Bros.
Gordon Lightfoot, "The Wreck of the Edmund Fitzgerald." Reprise.
Lou Rawls, "You'll Never Find Another Love Like Mine." Philadelphia International.
Boz Scaggs, *Silk Degrees*. Columbia.

BEST POP VOCAL PERFORMANCE, FEMALE
• Linda Ronstadt, *Hasten Down the Wind*. Asylum.

Natalie Cole, *Natalie*. Capitol.

Emmylou Harris, "Here, There and Everywhere." Reprise.

Joni Mitchell, *The Hissing of Summer Lawns*. Asylum.

Vicki Sue Robinson, "Turn the Beat Around." RCA.

BEST POP VOCAL PERFORMANCE BY A DUO, GROUP OR CHORUS

• Chicago, "If You Leave Me Now." Columbia.

Elton John, Kiki Dee, "Don't Go Breaking My Heart." Rocket/MCA.

England Dan & John Ford Coley, "I'd Really Love to See You Tonight." Big Tree.

Starland Vocal Band, "Afternoon Delight." Windsong/RCA.

Queen, "Bohemian Rhapsody." Elektra.

BEST POP INSTRUMENTAL PERFORMANCE

• George Benson, *Breezin'*. Warner Bros.

Jeff Beck, *Wired*. Epic.

Brecker Brothers Band, *Back to Back*. Arista.

Walter Murphy & the Big Apple Band, *A Fifth of Beethoven*. Private Stock.

Stevie Wonder, "Contusion." Tamla/Motown.

BEST RHYTHM & BLUES SONG
(Songwriter's Award)

• "Lowdown," Boz Scaggs, David Paich.

"Disco Lady," Harvey Scales, Al Vance, Don Davis.

"Love Hangover," Pam Sawyer, Marilyn McLeod.

"Misty Blue," Bob Montgomery.

"(Shake, Shake, Shake) Shake Your Booty," H. W. Casey, Richard Finch.

BEST RHYTHM & BLUES VOCAL PERFORMANCE, MALE

• Stevie Wonder, "I Wish." Tamla/Motown.

Marvin Gaye, *I Want You*. Tamla/Motown.

Lou Rawls, "Groovy People." Philadelphia International.

Boz Scaggs, "Lowdown." Columbia.

Joe Simon, "I Need You, You Need Me." Spring.

Johnnie Taylor, "Disco Lady." Columbia.

BEST RHYTHM & BLUES VOCAL PERFORMANCE, FEMALE

• Natalie Cole, "Sophisticated Lady (She's a Different Lady)." Capitol.

Aretha Franklin, "Something He Can Feel." Atlantic.

Dorothy Moore, "Misty Blue." Malaco.

Melba Moore, "Lean On Me." Buddah.

Diana Ross, "Love Hangover." Motown.

BEST RHYTHM & BLUES VOCAL PERFORMANCE BY A DUO, GROUP OR CHORUS

• Marilyn McCoo, Billy Davis, Jr., "You Don't Have to Be a Star (to Be in My Show)." ABC.

Earth, Wind & Fire, *Gratitude*. Columbia.

K.C. & the Sunshine Band, "(Shake, Shake, Shake) Shake Your Booty." T.K.

Spinners, "Rubberband Man." Atlantic.

Wild Cherry, "Play That Funky Music." Epic.

BEST RHYTHM & BLUES INSTRUMENTAL PERFORMANCE

• George Benson, "Theme from *Good King Bad*." CTI.

Brass Construction, *Brass Construction*. United Artists.

Crusaders, "Keep That Same Old Feeling." Blue Thumb.

Marvin Gaye, "After the Dance." Tamla/Motown.

Herbie Hancock, "Doin' It." Columbia.

Stanley Turrentine, "Hope That We Can Be Together Soon." Fantasy.

BEST JAZZ VOCAL PERFORMANCE

• Ella Fitzgerald, *Fitzgerald and Pass . . . Again*. Pablo.

Ray Charles, Cleo Laine, *Porgy and Bess*. RCA.

Irene Kral, *Where Is Love?* Choice.
Quire, *Quire*. RCA.
Sarah Vaughan, *More Sarah Vaughan Live in Japan*. Mainstream.

BEST JAZZ PERFORMANCE BY A SOLOIST

• Count Basie, *Basie and Zoot*. Pablo.
Jim Hall, *Commitment*. Horizon/A&M.
Jaco Pastorius, "Donna Lee." Epic.
Art Tatum, *Works of Art*. Jazz.
Clark Terry, *Clark Terry and His Jolly Giants*. Vanguard.
Phil Woods, *The New Phil Woods Album*. RCA.

BEST JAZZ PERFORMANCE BY A GROUP

• Chick Corea, *The Leprechaun*. Polydor.
Count Basie, Zoot Sims, *Basie & Zoot*. Pablo.
Paul Desmond Quartet, *The Paul Desmond Quartet Live*. Horizon/A&M.
Bill Evans Trio, *Since We Met*. Fantasy.
Jaco Pastorius, *Jaco Pastorius*. Epic.

BEST JAZZ PERFORMANCE BY A BIG BAND

• Duke Ellington, *The Ellington Suites*. Pablo.
Toshiko Akiyoshi–Lew Tabackin Big Band, *Long Yellow Road*. RCA.
Dizzy Gillespie, Machito, *Afro-Cuban Jazz Moods*. Pablo.
Thad Jones, Mel Lewis, *New Life*. Horizon/A&M.
Phil Woods, *The New Phil Woods Album*. RCA.

BEST COUNTRY SONG

(Songwriter's Award)
• "Broken Lady," Larry Gatlin.
"The Door Is Always Open," Bob McDill, Dickey Lees.
"Dropkick Me, Jesus," Paul Craft.
"Every Time You Touch Me (I Get High)," Charlie Rich, Billy Sherrill.
"Hank Williams, You Wrote My Life," Paul Craft.

BEST COUNTRY VOCAL PERFORMANCE, MALE

• Ronnie Milsap, "(I'm a) Stand By My Woman Man." RCA.
Mac Davis, *Forever Lovers*. Columbia.
Larry Gatlin, "Broken Lady." Monument.
Waylon Jennings, *Are You Ready for the Country*. RCA.
Willie Nelson, "I'd Have to Be Crazy." Columbia.

BEST COUNTRY VOCAL PERFORMANCE, FEMALE

• Emmylou Harris, *Elite Hotel*. Reprise.
Crystal Gayle, "I'll Get Over You." United Artists.
Dolly Parton, *All I Can Do*. RCA.
Mary Kay Place, *Tonite! At the Capri Lounge Loretta Naggers*. Columbia.
Tammy Wynette, " 'Til I Can Make It on My Own." Epic.

BEST COUNTRY VOCAL PERFORMANCE BY A DUO OR GROUP

• Amazing Rhythm Aces, "The End Is Not in Sight (The Cowboy Tune)." ABC.
Asleep at the Wheel, "Route 66." Capitol.
George Jones, Tammy Wynette, "Golden Ring." Epic.
Loretta Lynn, Conway Twitty, "The Letter." MCA.
Statler Brothers, "Your Picture in the Paper." Mercury.

BEST COUNTRY INSTRUMENTAL PERFORMANCE

• Chet Atkins, Les Paul, *Chester and Lester*. RCA.
Ace Cannon, "Blue Eyes Crying in the Rain." Hi.
Floyd Cramer, "I'm Thinking Tonight of My Blue Eyes." RCA.
Danny Davis & the Nashville Brass, *Texas*. RCA.
Marshall Tucker Band, "Long Hard Ride." Capricorn.

BEST INSPIRATIONAL PERFORMANCE
- Gary S. Paxton, *The Astonishing, Outrageous, Amazing, Incredible, Unbelievable, Different World of Gary S. Paxton*. Newpax.

Pat Boone, *Something Super Natural*. Lamb & Lion.

Sonny James, "Just a Closer Walk with Thee." Columbia.

Willie Nelson, "Amazing Grace." Columbia.

Ray Price, *Precious Memories*. Word.

Charley Pride, *Sunday Morning with Charley Pride*. RCA.

Charlie Rich, *Silver Linings*. Epic.

Stevie Wonder, "Have a Talk with God." Tamla/Motown.

BEST GOSPEL PERFORMANCE (OTHER THAN SOUL GOSPEL)
- Oak Ridge Boys, "Where the Soul Never Dies." Columbia.

Blackwood Brothers, *Learning to Lean*. Skylight.

Florida Boys, *Here They Come*. Canaan.

Imperials, *Just Because*. Impact.

Speers, *Between the Cross and Heaven (There's a Whole Lot of Living Going On)*. Heartwarming.

BEST SOUL GOSPEL PERFORMANCE
- Mahalia Jackson, *How I Got Over*. Columbia.

Inez Andrews, *War on Sin*. Songbird.

James Cleveland & the Charles Fold Singers, *Touch Me, Vol. 2*. Savoy.

James Cleveland & the Southern California Community Choir, *Give It to Me*. Savoy.

Andrae Crouch & the Disciples, *This Is Another Day*. Light.

BEST ETHNIC OR TRADITIONAL RECORDING
- *Mark Twang*, John Hartford. Flying Fish.

Bagpipe Marches and Music of Scotland, Shotts & Dykehead Caledonia Pipe Band. Olympic.

Beware of the Dog, Hound Dog Taylor. Alligator.

If You Love These Blues, Play 'Em as You Please, Michael Bloomfield. Guitar Player.

Proud Earth, Chief Dan George, Arliene Nofchissey Williams, Rick Brosseau. Salt City.

BEST LATIN RECORDING
- *Unfinished Masterpiece*, Eddie Palmieri. Coco.

Cocinando la Salsa, Joe Cuba. Tico.

El Maestro, Johnny Pacheco. Fania.

La Gormé, Eydie Gormé. Gala.

"Salsa" Soundtrack, Fania All-Stars. Fania.

Sofrito, Mongo Santamaria. Vaya.

BEST INSTRUMENTAL ARRANGEMENT
- Chick Corea, "Leprechaun's Dream" (Chick Corea). Polydor.

Stanley Clarke, "Life Is Just a Game" (Stanley Clarke). Emperor/Atlantic.

Bob James, "Westchester Lady" (Bob James). CTI.

Henry Mancini, John Williams, Herb Spencer, Al Woodbury, "The Disaster Movie Suite" (Henry Mancini conducting the London Symphony). RCA.

Claus Ogerman, "Saudade do Brazil" (Antonio Carlos Jobim). Warner Bros.

BEST ARRANGEMENT ACCOMPANYING VOCALIST(S)
- Jimmie Haskell, James William Guercio, "If You Leave Me Now" (Chicago). Columbia.

Robert Farnon, "Sentimental Journey" (Singers Unlimited.) MPS.

Clare Fischer, "Green Dolphin Street" (Singers Unlimited). MPS.

Paul McCartney, "Let 'Em In" (Wings). Capitol.

Claus Ogerman, "Boto (Porpoise)" (Antonio Carlos Jobim). Warner Bros.

BEST ARRANGEMENT FOR VOICES
- Starland Vocal Band, "Afternoon Delight" (Starland Vocal Band). Windsong/RCA.

Christian Chevallier, "Ain't Misbehavin'"
(Quire). RCA.
Earth, Wind & Fire, "Can't Hide Love"
(Earth, Wind & Fire). Columbia.
Gene Puerling, "I Get Along Without You
Very Well" (Singers Unlimited). MPS.
Queen, "Bohemian Rhapsody" (Queen).
Elektra.

BEST INSTRUMENTAL COMPOSITION

• *Bellavia*, Chuck Mangione.
"Contusion," Stevie Wonder.
Earth, Wind & Fire, Maurice White,
Skip Scarbrough.
"Leprechaun's Dream," Chick Corea.
"Midnight Soul Patrol," Quincy Jones,
Louis Johnson, Dave Grusin.
"The White Dawn," Henry Mancini.

BEST CAST SHOW ALBUM
(Composer's Award)

• *Bubbling Brown Sugar*, Razaf, Good-
man, Sampson, Webb, Strayhorn,
Holgate, Kemp, Lopez, Rogers,
Williams, Mills, Parish, Ellington,
Hines, Sissle, Blake, Pinkard, Waller,
Overstreet, Higgins, Herzog, Web-
ster, Holiday. H&L.
My Fair Lady, 20th anniversary produc-
tion, Alan Jay Lerner, Frederick
Loewe. Columbia.
Pacific Overtures, Stephen Sondheim.
RCA.
Rex, Richard Rodgers, Sheldon Harnick.
RCA.
Side by Side by Sondheim, Stephen
Sondheim. RCA.

BEST ALBUM OF ORIGINAL SCORE
WRITTEN FOR A MOTION PICTURE
OR TV SPECIAL

• *Car Wash*, Norman Whitfield. MCA.
The Omen, Jerry Goldsmith.
Tattoo/RCA.
One Flew Over the Cuckoo's Nest, Jack
Nitzsche. Fantasy.
Rich Man, Poor Man, Alex North.
MCA.
Taxi Driver, Bernard Herrmann. Arista.
Three Days of the Condor, Dave Grusin.
Capitol.

ALBUM OF THE YEAR,
CLASSICAL

• *Beethoven: The 5 Piano Concertos*,
Daniel Barenboim conducting the
London Philharmonic (solo: Rubin-
stein). RCA.
The Art of Courtly Love (music by
Machaut and his contemporaries),
David Munrow conducting the Early
Music Consort of London. Seraphim.
Bizet: Carmen, Sir Georg Solti conduct-
ing the London Philharmonic (solos:
Troyanos, Domingo, Kanawa, van
Dam). London.
Gershwin: Porgy and Bess, Lorin
Maazel conducting the Cleveland
Orchestra (solos: Mitchell, White).
London.
Gershwin: Rhapsody in Blue (with 1925
piano roll), Michael Tilson Thomas
conducting the Columbia Jazz Band;
Gershwin: An American in Paris,
Michael Tilson Thomas conducting
the New York Philharmonic. Colum-
bia.
Horowitz Concerts 1975/76 (Schumann,
Scriabin) (solo: Horowitz). RCA.
Joplin: Treemonisha, Gunther Schuller
conducting the original cast orchestra
and chorus (solos: Balthrop, Allen,
White). Deutsche Grammophon.
*Arturo Toscanini, the Philadelphia
Orchestra* (first release of the historic
1941–42 recording, Schubert,
Debussy, Berlioz, Respighi, etc.),
Arturo Toscanini conducting the
Philadelphia Orchestra. RCA.

BEST CLASSICAL PERFORMANCE,
ORCHESTRAL
(Conductor's Award)

• Sir Georg Solti conducting the
Chicago Symphony, *Strauss: Also
Sprach Zarathustra*. London.
Pierre Boulez conducting the New York
Philharmonic, *Falla: The Three-Cor-
nered Hat (Boulez Conducts Falla)*.
Columbia.
James Levine conducting the Chicago
Symphony, *Brahms: Symphony No. 1
in C Minor*. RCA.

Jean Martinon conducting the Orchestre de Paris, *Ravel: Daphnis et Chloé (Complete)*. Angel.

Jean Martinon conducting the Orchestra National of the Orft, *Berlioz: Symphonie Fantastique*. Angel.

Zubin Mehta conducting the Los Angeles Philharmonic, *The Fourth of July! Ives: Symphony No. 2, Variations on "America"; Copland: Appalachian Spring; Bernstein: Overture to "Candide"; Gershwin: An American in Paris*. London.

Sir Georg Solti conducting the London Philharmonic, *Elgar: Symphony No. 2 in E Flat Major*. London.

Michael Tilson Thomas conducting the Columbia Jazz Band (with Gershwin 1925 piano roll), *Gershwin: Rhapsody in Blue*. Columbia.

BEST CHAMBER MUSIC PERFORMANCE (INSTRUMENTAL OR VOCAL)

• David Munrow conducting the Early Music Consort of London, *The Art of Courtly Love* (Machaut and his contemporaries). Seraphim.

The Cleveland Quartet, *Barber: Quartet for Strings, Op. 11; Ives: Quartet No. 2 for Strings (Two American Masterpieces)*. RCA.

Glenn Gould, Philadelphia Brass Ensemble, *Hindemith: Sonatas for Brass and Piano (Complete)*. Columbia.

Jascha Heifetz, Gregor Piatigorsky, *The Heifetz-Piatigorsky Concerts (Dvořák:* Trio in F Minor for Piano with Leonard Pennario; Stravinsky: Suite Italienne for Violin and Cello; Gliere: Duo for Violin and Cello, etc.). Columbia.

Thomas Igloi, Alberni Quartet, *Schubert: Quintet in C, Op. 163*. CRD.

Fitzwilliam Quartet, *Shostakovich: Quartet No. 14 in F Sharp Major*. L'Oiseau-Lyre.

Prague String Quartet, *Dvořák: Quartets, Opp. 96 and 105*. Deutsche Grammophon.

Jacqueline du Pré, Daniel Barenboim, *Beethoven: Sonatas for Cello (Complete)*. Angel.

Tashi (Peter Serkin, Fred Sherry, Ida Kavafian, Richard Stoltzman), *Messiaen: Quartet for the End of Time*. RCA.

BEST CLASSICAL PERFORMANCE, INSTRUMENTAL SOLOIST(S) (WITH ORCHESTRA)

• Artur Rubinstein, piano (Barenboim conducting the London Philharmonic), *Beethoven: The Five Piano Concertos*. RCA.

Vladimir Ashkenazy, piano (Previn conducting the London Symphony), *Prokofiev: The 5 Piano Concertos*. London.

Stephen Bishop, piano (David conducting the London Symphony), *Bartók: Concertos for Piano Nos. 1 and 3*. Philips.

Aldo Ciecolini, piano (Martinon conducting the Orchestre de Paris), *Ravel: Concerto in G Major for Piano and Orchestra and Concerto in D Major for Left Hand*. Angel.

Nathan Milstein, violin (Jochum conducting the Vienna Philharmonic), *Brahms: Concerto in D Major for Violin*. Deutsche Grammophon.

Mstislav Rostropovich, cello (von Karajan conducting the Berlin Philharmonic), *Strauss: Don Quixote*. Angel.

BEST CLASSICAL PERFORMANCE, INSTRUMENTAL SOLOIST(S) (WITHOUT ORCHESTRA)

• Vladimir Horowitz, piano, *Horowitz Concerts 1975/76* (Schumann, Scriabin). RCA.

Vladimir Ashkenazy, piano, *Rachmaninov: 23 Preludes*. London.

Lazar Berman, piano, *Liszt: Legendary Soviet Pianist Lazar Berman Plays Liszt*. Everest.

Alfred Brendel, piano, *Schubert: Sonata in A Minor, Op. 42; Hungarian Melody in B Minor (D. 817)*. Philips.

Itzhak Perlman, violin, *Itzhak Perlman Plays Fritz Kreisler*. Angel.

Maurizio Pollini, piano, *Chopin: Préludes, Op. 28*. Deutsche Grammophon.

Andrés Segovia, guitar, *The Intimate Guitar—2* (Bach, Sor, Albéniz, Molleds, San Sebastian, Samazeuilh). RCA.

André Watts, piano, *Watts by George: André Watts Plays George Gershwin* ("Rhapsody in Blue," preludes for piano (3), 13 songs from the Gershwin songbook). Columbia.

BEST OPERA RECORDING

- *Gershwin: Porgy and Bess*, Lorin Maazel conducting the Cleveland Orchestra and Chorus (solos: Mitchell, White). London.
Bizet: Carmen, Sir Georg Solti conducting the London Philharmonic (solos: Troyanos, Domingo, Te Kanawa, van Dam). London.
Joplin: Treemonisha, Gunther Schuller conducting the original cast orchestra and chorus (solos: Balthrop, Allen, White). Deutsche Grammophon.
Massenet: Thais, Lorin Maazel conducting the New Philharmonia Orchestra, John Alldis Choir (solos: Sills, Milnes, Gedda). Angel.
Schoenberg: Moses und Aron, Pierre Boulez conducting the BBC Symphony, BBC Symphony Singers, Orpheus Boys' Choir (solos: Reich, Cassilly, Angus, Palmer, Hermann). Columbia.
Verdi: Macbeth, Claudio Abbado conducting the Chorus and Orchestra of La Scala (solos: Verrett, Domingo, Ghiaurov). Deutsche Grammophon.

BEST CLASSICAL PERFORMANCE, CHORAL

- Arthur Oldham, chorus master, London Symphony Chorus; André Previn conducting the London Symphony, *Rachmaninov: The Bells*. Angel.

Leonard Bernstein conducting the Choeurs de Radio France, Orchestre National de France and Orchestre Philharmonique de Radio France (Burrows, tenor), *Berlioz: Requiem*. Columbia.

Sir Adrian Boult conducting the London Philharmonic Chorus and London Philharmonic Orchestra, *Elgar: The Kingdom, Op. 51*. Connoisseur Society.

Dom Jean Claire conducting the Choir of the Monks of Saint-Pierre de Solesmes Abbey, *Gregorian Chant*. London.

Colin Davis conducting the BBC Singers and Choral Society and BBC Symphony, *Tippett: A Child of Our Time*. Philips.

Romano Gandolfi, chorus master, Chorus of La Scala, Milan; Claudio Abbado conducting the Orchestra of La Scala, Milan, *Verdi: Opera Choruses* (from *Nabucco, Il Trovatore, Otello, Aida*, etc.). Deutsche Grammophon.

Walter Hagen-Groll, chorus master, New Philharmonia Chorus; Carlo Maria Giulini conducting the London Philharmonic, *Beethoven: Missa Solemnis*. Angel.

Phillip Ledger conducting the Kings College Choir, Cambridge, *Bernstein: Chichester Psalms; Britten: Rejoice in the Lamb*. Angel.

Franz Müller, chorus master, Netherlands Radio Chorus; Jean Fournet conducting the Rotterdam Philharmonic, *Fauré: Requiem*. Philips.

BEST CLASSICAL PERFORMANCE, VOCAL SOLOIST

- Beverly Sills (Kostelanetz conducting the London Symphony), *Music of Victor Herbert* ("Kiss in the Dark," "Italian Street Song," "Kiss Me Again," etc.). Angel.

Janet Baker, James King (Haitink conducting the Concertgebouw Orchestra), *Mahler: Das Lied von der Erde*. Philips.

Carlo Bergonzi (Santi conducting the New Philharmonia, Gardelli conducting the Royal Philharmonic), *Carlo Bergonzi Sings Verdi*. Philips.

Dietrich Fischer-Dieskau (Sviatoslav Richter, accompanist), *Wolf: Mörike Lieder*. Deutsche Grammophon.

Jan DeGaetani (Gilbert Kalish, accompanist), *Ives: Songs*. Nonesuch.

Margaret Price (Lockhart conducting the English Chamber Orchestra), *Mozart: Arias* ("La Clemenza di Tito," "Die Entführung aus dem Serail," "Nozze di Figaro," etc.). RCA.

Marni Nixon (Leonard Stein, accompanist), *Schoenberg: 9 Early Songs; The Cabaret Songs of Arnold Schoenberg*. RCA.

Barbra Streisand (Ogerman conducting the Columbia Symphony), *Classical Barbra* (Debussy: *Beau Soir*; Canteloube: *Berceuse*; Wolf: *Verschwiegene*, etc.). Columbia.

BEST ENGINEERED RECORDING, CLASSICAL

• E. T. "Bud" Graham, Ray Moore, Milt Cherin, *Gershwin: Rhapsody in Blue*, George Gershwin (1925 piano roll) and Thomas conducting the Columbia Jazz Band. Columbia.

Patrick Gleason, Skip Shimmin, Neil Schwartz, Seth Dworken, *Beyond the Sun: An Electronic Portrait of Holst's "The Planets."* Mercury.

Paul Goodman, *Brahms: Symphony No. 1 in C Minor*, James Levine conducting the Chicago Symphony. RCA.

E. T. "Bud" Graham, Ray Moore, Milton Cherin, *Falla: The Three-Cornered Hat (Boulez Conducts Falla)*, Boulez conducting the New York Philharmonic (solo: de Gaetani). Columbia.

James Lock, Arthur Lilley, Colin Moorfoot, Michael Mailes, *Gershwin: Porgy and Bess*, Maazel conducting the Cleveland Orchestra (solos: Mitchell, White). London.

James Lock, Colin Moorfoot, Jack Law, *Mahler: Symphony No. 2 in C Minor* (*"Resurrection"*), Mehta conducting the Vienna Philharmonic. London.

James Lock, *Strauss: An Alpine Symphony*, Mehta conducting the Los Angeles Philharmonic. London.

Christopher Parker, *Britten: 4 Sea Interludes and Passacaglia from "Peter Grimes*," Previn conducting the London Symphony. Angel.

Klaus Scheibe, *Saint-Saëns: Symphony No. 3 in C Minor ("Organ")*, Barenboim conducting the Chicago Symphony. Deutsche Grammophon.

BEST COMEDY RECORDING

• *Bicentennial Nigger*, Richard Pryor. Warner Bros.

Bill Cosby Is Not Himself These Days, Rat Own, Rat Own, Rat Own, Bill Cosby. Capitol.

Goodbye Pop, National Lampoon. Epic.

Sleeping Beauty, Cheech & Chong. Ode.

You Gotta Wash Your Ass, Redd Foxx. Atlantic.

BEST SPOKEN WORD RECORDING

• *Great American Documents*, Orson Welles, Henry Fonda, Helen Hayes, James Earl Jones. CBS.

Asimov: Foundation: The Psychohistorians, William Shatner. Caedmon.

Dickens: A Tale of Two Cities, James Mason. Caedmon.

Fahrenheit 451, Ray Bradbury. Listening Library.

Hemingway: The Old Man and the Sea, Charlton Heston. Caedmon.

BEST RECORDING FOR CHILDREN

• *Prokofiev: Peter and the Wolf; Saint Saëns: Carnival of the Animals*, Hermione Gingold, narrator; Bohm conducting the Vienna Philharmonic. Deutsche Grammophon.

The Adventures of Ali and His Gang vs. Mr. Tooth Decay, Muhammed Ali & His Gang. St. John's Fruits & Vegetables.

Dickens' Christmas Carol, Mickey Mouse and Scrooge McDuck. Disneyland.

Snow White and the Seven Dwarfs, original soundtrack. Buena Vista.
"Winnie-the-Pooh for President (Campaign Song)," Sterling Holloway, Larry Groce. Disneyland.

BEST ENGINEERED RECORDING (OTHER THAN CLASSICAL)

• Al Schmitt. *Breezin'* (George Benson). Warner Bros.
Jay Lewis, *The Dream Weaver* (Gary Wright). Warner Bros.
Ron Hitchcock, *The King James Version* (Harry James & His Big Band). Sheffield Lab.
Alan Parsons, Tom Trefethen, *Somewhere I've Never Travelled* (Ambrosia). 20th Century.
Alan Parsons, *Tales of Mystery and Imagination, Edgar Allan Poe* (Alan Parsons Project). 20th Century.

BEST ALBUM PACKAGE
(Art Director's Award)

• John Berg, *Chicago X* (Chicago). Columbia.
Ron Coro, Nancy Donald, *Silk Degrees* (Boz Scaggs). Columbia.
Hipgnosis, Hardie, *Presence* (Led Zeppelin). Swan Song.
Acy Lehman, *Coney Island Baby* (Lou Reed). RCA.

J. Stelmach, *Schumann: Symphony No. 1 in B Flat, Op. 38; Manfred: Overture, Op. 115* (Charles Munch conducting the Boston Symphony). RCA.
Roland Young, *Bellavia* (Chuck Mangione). A&M.
Roland Young, *The End of the Beginning* (Richie Havens). A&M.
Roland Young, *Mirrors* (Peggy Lee). A&M.

BEST ALBUM NOTES
(Annotator's Award)

• Dan Morgenstern, *The Changing Face of Harlem*, Savoy Sessions (various artists). Savoy.
George R. Marek, *Beethoven: The Five Piano Concertos* (Baremboim conducting the London Philharmonic; solo: Rubinstein). RCA.
Douglas B. Green, *The Blue Sky Boys* (Bill & Earl Bolick). RCA.
Francis Robinson, *Caruso: A Legendary Performer* (Enrico Caruso). RCA.
Mort Goode, *The Complete Tommy Dorsey, Vol. 1–1935*. RCA.

PRODUCER OF THE YEAR

• Stevie Wonder
Richard Perry
Lennie Waronker
Joe Wissert

• 1977 •

Pop Goes California

Considering how well African-American artists like Stevie Wonder, Roberta Flack and George Benson did at recent Grammys, *Variety* noted a distinct color difference when this year's bids came out: "The most striking thing about the pop nominations is the complete absence of black performers." Another trend was noted when the winners were named. They were all based in California or else tied to Hollywood films.

Typical were the winners of Record of the Year. The *L.A. Times* said that the Eagles used California "as a metaphor for the nation [when singer and drummer Don Henley and vocalist Glen Frey] wrote about the pursuit of the American dream, '70s style, using their own experiences in rock to convey the innocence ('New Kid in Town'), temptations ('One of These Nights') and disillusionments ('The Sad Cafe') of that pursuit."

The Eagles won two Grammys in 1977: Record of the Year for "Hotel California" and Best Arrangement for Voices for "New Kid in Town." Despite their earlier assurance that they would be on hand for the Grammycast at Los Angeles's Shrine Auditorium, the Eagles skipped the event at the last minute, causing considerable confusion backstage when it came time for the group to perform on the show. When the *Times* reached the group later by phone in Malibu where they were rehearsing their next studio album, *The Long Run,* Henley said with typical Californian flipness, "The whole idea of a contest to see who is 'best' just doesn't appeal to us. It's all a matter of personal taste."

Fleetwood Mac was the other leading purveyor of California rock, and its megahit *Rumours* easily took the Album

Variety credited Grammy's increasing hipness to "an influx of younger blood into N.A.R.A.S.".

of the Year award as predicted by most Grammy watchers. *Rumours* sold a staggering 10 million copies, spent an unprecedented 31 weeks at number one in the charts and was the first group album to have four Top 10 hits: "Go Your Own Way," "Dreams," "Don't Stop" and "You Make Loving Fun." "We can't even try to top what we've done with *Rumours*," guitarist Lindsey Buckingham told reporters backstage at the Grammys.

The LP prize was bestowed to them by the recently reunited Crosby, Stills & Nash, who were also leaders of the California pop movement and past winners of Grammy's Best New Artist award in 1969. (This time the trio appeared on the Grammycast dressed in conformist coats and ties in sharp contrast to the scruffy garb they wore back in 1969. "We were jive then . . . in our hippie phase," Graham Nash told the *Times* later. "I think it's different now. There's nothing wrong with putting on a suit.") Fleetwood Mac's award was accepted by Buckingham, who expressed his pleasure by reminiscing with the viewing audience, "I can remember being 11 years old and watching the Grammys on TV."

For the first time in Grammy history, there was a tie for Song of the Year, and both winners happened to be related to recent Hollywood films. Both tunes also won Best Original Song in separate years at the Oscars thanks to a difference in eligibility periods between the two awards.

Barbra Streisand was bored one day while receiving a guitar lesson on the set of *A Star Is Born,* the film she was making with Kris Kristofferson, when she launched her career as a songwriter. "I just started to fool around with chords," she told biographer James Spada. "Instead of 'A Star Is Born,' a song was born! It just came out of absolute impatience."

Singer-songwriter Paul Williams wrote the lyrics to "Love Theme from *A Star Is Born* (Evergreen)" and Streisand recorded it soon thereafter for both the film score and a single version that became her biggest-selling hit since she topped the music charts with "The Way We Were," Grammy's Song of the Year in 1974.

"Miss Streisand also was the surprise victor in the pop female singer category," noted the *New York Times* when she overtook nominees Linda Ronstadt, Dolly Parton, Carly Simon and Debby Boone. The *L.A. Times* added: "The awards broke a long Grammy dry spell for Streisand, perhaps the most respected female singer in pop. They were her first since 1965 when she was named best singer for *My Name Is Barbra.*"

"Love Theme from *A Star Is Born* (Evergreen)" had been released in early 1977, so it was not considered a strong contender at the time of the Grammy race one year later. "I thought we were forgotten," Streisand said, accepting the

best song honor, "so I really am shocked." The nervous, first-time winner Paul Williams joined her at the podium and thanked his "doctor for giving me the fantastic Valium."

The second winner of Song of the Year was the top-selling song of 1977, the biggest seller in the history of Warner Bros. Records, and the first single since Guy Mitchell's "Singing the Blues" in 1956 to spend 10 weeks ranked number one in the weekly charts. The song was "You Light Up My Life," written by Joe Brooks for a little-noticed film of the same name that he produced, directed and wrote about a disillusioned young woman trying to make it as a singer in Hollywood.

Brooks accepted his songwriter's prize with obvious relish, saying, "This song was turned down by every firm that is out there tonight. Some turned it down twice. This is so sweet."

The megahit single version of "You Light Up My Life" was sung by the winner of Grammy's Best New Artist award, Debby Boone, daughter of crooner Pat Boone. Debby Boone was only 20 years old when she topped the year's chart, just as her father had done with "Two Hearts" 22 years earlier, at exactly the same age. "You Light Up My Life" was written as a love ballad, but Boone, who was then the lead singer of a family gospel quartet comprised of her and her sisters, decided to sing it like a prayer.

Among the singers Boone beat for Best New Artist was 19-year-old heartthrob Andy Gibb, whose older brothers, the Bee Gees, were Grammy nominees for the pop group vocal honors. When they won it, the victory proved a good omen for next year's Grammy Awards.

The Bee Gees had the year's number-two-ranked song, "How Deep Is Your Love," which stayed in the Top 10 for an unprecedented 17 continuous weeks. It was an advance release from the sound-

The Eagles snubbed the Grammy show at the last minute.

track to the definitive film about disco delirium, *Saturday Night Fever,* which would come back for more Grammy gold next year, including the Album of the Year prize.

In the pop male vocals category, the trophy went to the 1971 winner for "You've Got a Friend," James Taylor, whose latest hit was "Handy Man," written in part by Otis Blackwell, who also penned "Don't Be Cruel" and "Return to Sender" for Elvis Presley. Taylor's producer, Peter Asher of Columbia Records, who was also behind the recent surge in Linda Ronstadt's career, took the Producer of the Year award.

Disco hits ruled the r&b categories. Thelma Houston had been toiling at Dunhill and then at Motown for nearly 10 years before she finally reached the top of the charts. ("You release a record and you say, 'this is it,' but it isn't," she once told the *L.A. Times,* describing her frustration during her early career.) Then producer Hal Davis suggested she remake a onetime middling hit for Harold Melvin & the Blue Notes. "Don't Leave Me This Way" ended up number eight in the year-end rankings and earned her the female r&b vocal award.

Success was also a long time coming for the victor of the group vocals prize, the Emotions, a trio of sisters who had been performing since the 1950s, initially as a gospel group called the Hutchinsons (Wanda, Sheila and Jeanette), then the Heavenly Sunbeams. The siblings turned to recording secular songs in the 1960s, but their record company, Stax/Volt, folded within a few years. They were rescued professionally by Maurice White of Earth, Wind & Fire, who cowrote and produced the song that proved a five-week chart-topper for them as well as a dance club standard, "Best of My Love."

Singer-songwriter Leo Sayer kept the discos hopping with the year's Best Rhythm & Blues Song, "You Make Me Feel Like Dancing," which he wrote with Vini Poncia, who had previously penned "Do I Love You" for the Ronettes.

Warner Bros.

The mega-selling Fleetwood Mac disc *Rumours* was the easy winner of Grammy's best LP prize.

"Dancing" was from Sayer's fourth album, *Endless Flight,* but it was his first number-one-ranked single. Also adept at making the young set boogie were the Brothers Johnson, who had been discovered by Quincy Jones, the producer of the group's next four albums. The first of the lot, *Look Out for No. 1,* sold a million copies in 1976, followed by 1977's *Right on Time,* which was certified gold three days after its release. (Single hits include "I'll Be Good to You," written by Jones.) *Right on Time* included the brothers' grateful salute to Jones, a track called "Q," which earned them the r&b instrumental performance prize.

The sole r&b champ who was not a disco star was an artist who twice before captured the award for male vocals. Lou Rawls had won in 1967 for "Dead End Street" and again in 1971 for "Natural Man." His career had been at low ebb during most of the 1970s before he signed up with Philadelphia International Records (a division of Epic) in 1976 and scored a string of hits beginning with "You'll Never Find Another Love Like Mine" the same year. His latest r&b award was for his 1977 Philadelphia International album *Unmistakably Lou.*

The biggest champ in terms of the most Grammys won this year was John

Williams, composer of the score to *Star Wars,* Hollywood's highest-grossing film to date, having earned a record $200 million at the box office by the end of 1977. ("There wasn't much doubt of the *Star Wars* phenomenon spreading to the record industry," the *L.A. Herald Tribune* commented in its Grammy coverage.) Williams's outer-space symphonics were performed under his baton by the London Symphony Orchestra and garnered him three awards: Best Instrumental Composition, Best Pop Instrumental Performance and best original score written for a motion picture. Adding to its success, Williams's score performed amazingly well on the album charts for orchestra music, spending two weeks at number two and selling more than 2 million copies.

The big-band laurels in jazz were claimed by last year's winner of the soloist award, Count Basie, for his and his orchestra's latest LP, *Prime Time.* Alto sax player Phil Woods had won the big-band award with Michel Legrand in 1975 for their *Images* album and now returned for the group performance prize for *The Phil Woods Six—Live from the Showboat.* Oscar Peterson had won the group honor in 1974 for his collaboration with Joe Pass and Niels Pedersen, but now took the soloist award for *The Giants.* Fusion singer Al Jarreau (*Look to the Rainbow*) garnered the new category for jazz vocals that was introduced in 1976 and won that year by the diva of the older-style scatting, Ella Fitzgerald.

"Don't It Make My Brown Eyes Blue" dominated the country music field in 1977, taking the Grammy's Best Country Song award as well as the equivalent prize from the Country Music Association. "Brown Eyes Blue" was written by Richard Leigh, who literally had his inspiration at his feet when he scripted it—his brown-eyed dog Amanda, who, ironically, would actually end up with one blue eye years later when she developed a cataract after being hit in the head with a rock hurled by a frightened garbage collector.

"Brown Eyes Blue" made its vocalist an overnight sensation when the song crossed over from the country charts to the number-two slot in the pop lineup. Crystal Gayle, who actually had blue eyes, had only minor success before that. She toured the honky-tonk circuit with her sister, Loretta Lynn, in the early 1970s and finally scored a minor hit with "I'll Get Over You" (Gayle's first Grammy bid in 1976) after she signed with United Artists. But it wasn't until the release of her *We Must Believe in Magic* LP and its "Brown Eyes Blue" single in 1977 that she achieved nearly the same celebrity status as her sister. *Magic* became the first country album to be certified platinum (marking a million copies in sales), and "Brown Eyes Blue" earned her the best female country vocalist Grammy as well as the Female Vocalist of the Year designation from both the Country Music Association and the Academy of Country Music. "I was in a category with four great singers," Gayle said backstage at the Grammycast, referring to fellow nominees Janie Fricke, Emmylou Harris, Barbara Mandrell and Dolly Parton. "But I knew it was a special song from the first time I heard it."

A losing nominee for Best Country Song, "Lucille," still made its performer, Kenny Rogers, Grammy's best male country vocalist. Rogers had been the leader of the First Edition, but when the group disbanded in 1975, he struck out on a solo career. A few minor hits followed. Then the singer was wrapping up his *Kenny Rogers* album one day when he learned that he still had 15 minutes of studio time left. "Lucille" was added at the last minute—and made Rogers a country/pop superstar.

Serendipity also played a part in the success of the Kendalls, winners of the country group vocals prize. "Heaven's Just a Sin Away" was released as the throwaway "B" side to only the second single issued by the harmony-singing father-daughter team of Royce and Jeannie Kendall. Hargus "Pig" Robbins spent more than a decade as an obscure session pianist for Chet Atkins at RCA's country division and working with other artists like Bob Dylan (*Blonde on Blonde*, 1966). When he won the instrumental performance Grammy for his *Country Instrumentalist of the Year* LP, Robbins ironically beat his boss, Atkins, who had won the award in the previous three years and was nominated twice this year.

Nearly all of the winners of the religious awards were repeats from previous years, including the Imperials (*Sail On*), the Oak Ridge Boys ("Just a Little Talk with Jesus") and the San Francisco gospel group the Edwin Hawkins Singers (*Wonderful!*). Pianist-singer James Cleveland had won before, too, and now reaped one more for the recording of his recent concert at Carnegie Hall. Cleveland performed one of the concert selections on the Grammycast and thus became the first gospel artist to be featured on the show. B. J. Thomas had been nominated for a pop vocalist Grammy in 1968 and sang 1975's Best Country Song, "(Hey, Won't You Play) Another Somebody Done Somebody Wrong Song," but finally claimed his first trophy for 1977's Best Inspirational Performance for his all-gospel LP *Home Where I Belong*. Thomas started recording gospel extensively in 1976 after having a religious experience that he claimed saved him from his earlier life of drug abuse.

Ever since the Latin category was introduced in 1975, it had been dominated by salsa artist Eddie Palmieri. Palmieri wasn't nominated this year, but Latin music's El Rey ("the King"), Tito Puente, was, and he was clearly the odds-on favorite to win. Instead, the award went to one of his former band members of the 1950s, Mongo Santamaria (for *Dawn*), the Afro-Cuban percussionist, bandleader and composer who became one of the leading Latin musicians of the 1960s after gaining notice for fusing the Latin beat with jazz and r&b sounds.

Richard Pryor's three-year winning

World Wide Photo

Barbara Steisand was "shocked" to win the pop vocals award for "Evergreen," which also tied for Song of the Year with "You Light Up My Life."

streak in the comedy category came to an end when the prize was claimed by the wild and crazy Steve Martin, who was fast becoming the hottest comedian in the country thanks to his frequent appearances on TV's *Saturday Night Live*. On his victorious *Let's Get Small* LP, which went platinum despite crushing reviews from the critics, Martin bordered on tastelessness when he described a visit to the Turd Museum ("They got some real great shit there") and insulted female smokers ("Virginia Slims, that's a woman's cigarette. What do they have, little breasts on 'em or something?"). Martin was actually at his funniest when he received his Grammy at the Shrine Auditorium. For his acceptance speech, he sang a few bars of "The Impossible Dream."

Grammy's classical album of the year involved a host of celebrity talent recorded at a fete held on May 18, 1976, that was billed as the "Concert of the Century" to mark the 85th anniversary of Carnegie Hall. The two-disc live recording included performances by Leonard Bernstein and the New York Philharmonic (Beethoven's *Leonore* Overture No. 3), Yehudi Menuhin and Isaac Stern (Bach's Concerto in D Minor for Two Violins) and Vladimir Horowitz and Dietrich Fischer-Dieskau (Schumann's *Diechterliebe*). It also featured the Philharmonic's Oratorio Society, as well as the Carnegie Hall audience itself, when, at the end of the evening, everyone was asked to join in singing the joyous "Hallelujah Chorus" from Handel's *Messiah*.

Carlo Maria Giulini won his only previous Grammy in 1971 when he conducted the Chicago Symphony Orchestra in Mahler's Symphony No. 1. He reclaimed the orchestra honors again now for another guest appearance with the Chicago players, this time performing Mahler's Symphony No. 9 in a recording ("with a rich and characterful sound," said *High Fidelity*) that was also nominated for Classical Album of the Year. Pianist Artur Rubinstein won a Grammy for the fourth consecutive year for his third career recording of Beethoven's Sonata for Piano No. 18 and Schumann's *Fantasiestücke*. In his latest version, actually taped in 1976, the maestro "displays certain frailties," said *High Fidelity,* "as indeed he always has, but few are traceable to advanced age. In the Beethoven sonata there were actually more finger slips in his previous recording," taped in 1963. Itzhak Perlman reaped the honors for soloist with orchestra accompaniment for his rendition of Vivaldi's *The Four Seasons,* which the critics called "pure magic."

In the early 1950s, the Juilliard Quartet taped Schoenberg's Quartets for Strings and then repeated its effort in 1977 to win the chamber music laurels. "Intensity certainly was the keynote of those earlier Juilliard performances," said *High Fidelity*, "and the remarkable, wonderful thing about the new ones is that they have relaxed (and, in places,

---

"Brown Eyes Blue" made the blue-eyed Crystal Gayle a superstar.

---

broadened) without becoming in any way less propulsive or committed." The magazine was less taken with Georg Solti's latest Grammy-winning album, Verdi's *Requiem* (best classical choral performance), which he and the Chicago Symphony Chorus and Orchestra had last recorded a decade earlier. Both versions, said *High Fidelity,* lacked "a sense of unfolding spiritual drama."

Janet Baker joined Leontyne Price for the vocals on Solti's *Requiem* but got an equally bad review from *High Fidelity*. When Baker won the vocal soloist prize for a collection of arias by Bach, however, the magazine said she "sounds far more solid and secure than she has on recent recordings." For a second year in a row, Gershwin's *Porgy and Bess* won Best Opera Recording, this latest (and also complete) version executed by the Houston Grand Opera company. The troupe took its production to New York in July 1977, then on a 16-week national tour. *High Fidelity* called it "a lively, moving, theatrically vivid re-creation of Catfish Row."

Variety declared that this year's Grammy nominations "reflect the academy members coming to terms with popular tastes to the greatest extent in the history of the awards. The list of categories can be seen as the result of an influx of younger blood into the N.A.R.A.S. roster. Example of change in tone of nominees and their music can be seen by comparing even last year's nominations with present set. Current nominees lean toward harder brand of rock than recent years, though most pop division nominees' disks could be safely programmed on 'adult' stations, again in a direct reflection of current chart performance."

The Grammy ceremony included music performances by Debby Boone, Crystal Gayle, Ronnie Milsap, Dancing Machine and host John Denver.

The *New York Times* took issue with some of its interludes of weak humor, production flubs and more: "The awards telecast was fraught with mistakes, clumsiness and vulgarity. Halfway through the proceedings the audience had stopped even trying to laugh at the jokes John Denver, the host, was asked to recite, and the cameras kept making furtive sorties to celebrities in the hall, several of whom were caught with expressions on their faces that denoted horror, embarrassment or cynicism."

On the occasion of its historic 20th birthday, the Grammys gave its fans a precedent-setting present. For the first time ever, the ceremony was open to the general public. The *L.A. Herald Tribune* noted, "Half of the 6,000 Shrine Auditorium seats were occupied by non-music industry people."

Boston Pops

John Williams was the year's biggest winner, earning three awards for his score to *Star Wars*.

• 1977 •

The ceremony was broadcast on CBS from the Los Angeles Shrine Auditorium on February 23, 1978, for the awards eligibility period of October 1, 1976, to September 30, 1977.

ALBUM OF THE YEAR
• *Rumours*, Fleetwood Mac. Warner Bros.
Aja, Steely Dan. ABC.
Hotel California, Eagles. Asylum.
J T, James Taylor. Columbia.
Star Wars, John Williams conducting the London Symphony. 20th Century.

RECORD OF THE YEAR
• "Hotel California," Eagles. Asylum.
"Blue Bayou," Linda Ronstadt. Asylum.
"Don't It Make My Brown Eyes Blue," Crystal Gayle. United Artists.
"Love Theme from *A Star Is Born* (Evergreen)," Barbra Streisand. Columbia.
"You Light Up My Life," Debby Boone. Warner Bros./Curb.

SONG OF THE YEAR
(Songwriter's Award)
(Tie)
• "Love Theme from *A Star Is Born* (Evergreen)," Barbra Streisand, Paul Williams.
• "You Light Up My Life," Joe Brooks.
"Don't It Make My Brown Eyes Blue," Richard Leigh.
"Hotel California," Don Felder, Don Henley, Glenn Frey.
"Nobody Does It Better," Marvin Hamlisch, Carole Bayer Sager.
"Southern Nights," Allen Toussaint.

BEST NEW ARTIST
• Debby Boone
Stephen Bishop
Shaun Cassidy
Foreigner
Andy Gibb

BEST POP VOCAL PERFORMANCE, MALE

- James Taylor, "Handy Man." Columbia.
- Stephen Bishop, "On and On." ABC.
- Andy Gibb, "I Just Want to Be Your Everything." RSO.
- Engelbert Humperdinck, "After the Lovin' ". Epic.
- Leo Sayer, "When I Need You." Warner Bros.

BEST POP VOCAL PERFORMANCE, FEMALE

- Barbra Streisand, "Love Theme from *A Star Is Born* (Evergreen)." Columbia.
- Debby Boone, "You Light Up My Life." Warner Bros./Curb.
- Dolly Parton, "Here You Come Again." RCA.
- Linda Ronstadt, "Blue Bayou." Asylum.
- Carly Simon, "Nobody Does It Better." Elektra.

BEST POP VOCAL PERFORMANCE BY A DUO, GROUP OR CHORUS

- Bee Gees, "How Deep Is Your Love." RSO.
- Crosby, Stills & Nash, *CSN*. Atlantic.
- Eagles, *Hotel California*. Asylum.
- Fleetwood Mac, *Rumours*. Warner Bros.
- Steely Dan, *Aja*. ABC.

BEST POP INSTRUMENTAL PERFORMANCE

- London Symphony, John Williams, conductor, *Star Wars*. 20th Century.
- Bill Conti, "Gonna Fly Now (Theme from *Rocky*)." United Artists.
- Barry De Vorzon, "Nadia's Theme (*The Young and the Restless*)." Arista.
- Maynard Ferguson, "Gonna Fly Now (Theme from *Rocky*)." Columbia.
- Meco, "*Star Wars* Theme/Cantina Band." Millennium.

BEST RHYTHM & BLUES SONG

(Songwriter's Award)
- "You Make Me Feel Like Dancing," Leo Sayer, Vini Poncia.
- "Best of My Love," Maurice White, Al McKay.

"Brick House," Milan Williams, Walter Orange, Thomas McClary, William King, Lionel Richie, Ronald LaPread.
"Don't Leave Me This Way," Kenny Gamble, Leon Huff, Carry Gilbert.
"Easy," Lionel Richie.

BEST RHYTHM & BLUES VOCAL PERFORMANCE, MALE

- Lou Rawls, *Unmistakably Lou*. Philadelphia International/Epic.
- Marvin Gaye, "Got to Give It Up (Part 1)". Motown.
- B. B. King, "It's Just a Matter of Time." ABC.
- Joe Tex, "Ain't Gonna Bump No More (With No Big Fat Woman)." Epic.
- Johnny "Guitar" Watson, "A Real Mother for Ya." DJM

BEST RHYTHM & BLUES VOCAL PERFORMANCE, FEMALE

- Thelma Houston, "Don't Leave Me This Way." Motown.
- Natalie Cole, "I've Got Love on My Mind." Capitol.
- Aretha Franklin, "Break It to Me Gently." Atlantic.
- Dorothy Moore, "I Believe You." Malaco.
- Diana Ross, "Your Love Is So Good for Me," track. Motown.

BEST RHYTHM & BLUES VOCAL PERFORMANCE BY A DUO, GROUP OR CHORUS

- Emotions, "Best of My Love," track. Columbia.
- Commodores, "Easy." Motown.
- Heatwave, "Boogie Nights." Epic.
- Gladys Knight & the Pips, "Baby Don't Change Your Mind," track. Buddah.
- Rufus featuring Chaka Khan, *Ask Rufus*. ABC.

BEST RHYTHM & BLUES INSTRUMENTAL PERFORMANCE

- Brothers Johnson, "Q," track. A&M.
- Blackbyrds, "The Unfinished Business," track. Fantasy.
- Brecker Brothers, "Funky Sea, Funky Dew." Arista.

Salsoul Orchestra, "Getaway." Salsoul.
Stuff, *More Stuff.* Warner Bros.

BEST JAZZ VOCAL PERFORMANCE

- Al Jarreau, *Look to the Rainbow.* Warner Bros.
João Gilberto, *Amoroso.* Warner Bros.
Irene Kral, *Kral Space.* Catalyst.
Carmen McRae, *Carmen McRae at the Great American Music Hall.* Blue Note/United Artists.
Helen Merrill, *Helen Merrill—John Lewis.* Mercury.

BEST JAZZ INSTRUMENTAL PERFORMANCE BY A SOLOIST

- Oscar Peterson, *The Giants.* Pablo.
John Coltrane, *Afro Blue Impressions.* Pablo.
Hank Jones, *'Bop Redux.* Muse.
Jaco Pastorius, *Heavy Weather.* Columbia
Phil Woods, *The Phil Woods Six—Live from the Showboat.* RCA.

BEST JAZZ INSTRUMENTAL PERFORMANCE BY A GROUP

- Phil Woods, *The Phil Woods Six—Live from the Showboat.* RCA.
John Coltrane, *Afro Blue Impressions.* Pablo.
Tommy Flanagan Trio, *Eclypso.* Inner City.
Dexter Gordon, *Homecoming, Live at the Village Vanguard.* Columbia.
Mel Lewis, *Mel Lewis and Friends.* Horizon/A&M.

BEST JAZZ PERFORMANCE BY A BIG BAND

- Count Basie & His Orchestra, *Prime Time.* Pablo.
Woody Herman, *The 40th Anniversary, Carnegie Hall Concert.* RCA.
North Texas State University Lab Band, Leon Breeden, director, *Lab '76.* NTSU Lab Jazz.
Buddy Rich, *Buddy Rich Plays and Plays and Plays.* RCA/ Gryphon.
Toshiko Akiyoshi–Lew Tabackin Big Band, *Road Time.* RCA.

BEST COUNTRY SONG (Songwriter's Award)

- "Don't It Make My Brown Eyes Blue," Richard Leigh.
"Desperado," Glenn Frey, Don Henley.
"It Was Almost Like a Song," Archie Jordan, Hal David.
"Lucille," Roger Bowling, Hal Bynum.
"Luckenbach, Texas," Bobby Emmons, Chips Moman.

BEST COUNTRY VOCAL PERFORMANCE, MALE

- Kenny Rogers, "Lucille." United Artists.
Larry Gatlin, "I Don't Wanna Cry." Monument.
Waylon Jennings, "Luckenbach, Texas." RCA.
Ronnie Milsap, "It Was Almost Like a Song." RCA.
Jerry Jeff Walker, "Mr. Bojangles." MCA.

BEST COUNTRY VOCAL PERFORMANCE, FEMALE

- Crystal Gayle, "Don't It Make My Brown Eyes Blue." United Artists.
Janie Fricke, "What're You Doing Tonight." Columbia.
Emmylou Harris, "Making Believe." Warner Bros.
Barbara Mandrell, "After the Lovin'," track. ABC/Dot.
Dolly Parton, "(Your Love Has Lifted Me) Higher and Higher," track. RCA.

BEST COUNTRY PERFORMANCE BY A DUO OR GROUP WITH VOCAL

- Kendalls, "Heaven's Just a Sin Away." Ovation.
Asleep at the Wheel, *The Wheel.* Capitol.
George Jones, Tammy Wynette, "Near You." Epic.
Loretta Lynn, Conway Twitty, *Dynamic Duo.* MCA.
Oak Ridge Boys, *Y'All Come Back Saloon.* ABC/Dot.

BEST COUNTRY INSTRUMENTAL PERFORMANCE

- Hargus "Pig" Robbins, *Country Instrumentalist of the Year*. Elektra.
Asleep at the Wheel, "Ragtime Annie," track. Capitol.
Chet Atkins, *Me and My Guitar*. RCA.
Chet Atkins, Floyd Cramer, Danny Davis, *Chet, Floyd and Danny*. RCA.
Jerry Reed, "West Bound and Down," track. MCA.

BEST GOSPEL PERFORMANCE, CONTEMPORARY OR INSPIRATIONAL

- Imperials, *Sail On*. Dayspring/Word.
Reba Rambo Gardner, *Reba/Lady*. Greentree.
Larry Hart & the Soul Singers, *Hart and Soul*. Genesis.
Michael Omartian, *Adam Again*. Myrrh/ Word.
Gary S. Paxton, *More from the Astonishing, Outrageous, Amazing, Incredible, Unbelievable Gary S. Paxton*. New Pax.
Evie Tornquist, *Mirror*. Word.

BEST GOSPEL PERFORMANCE, TRADITIONAL

- Oak Ridge Boys, "Have a Little Talk with Jesus." Rockland Road.
Blackwood Brothers, *Bill Gaither Songs*. Skylite.
Cathedral Quartet, *Then and Now*. Canaan.
LeFevres, *Till He Comes*. Canaan.
Rambos, *Naturally*. Heartwarming.
Speers, *Cornerstone*. Heartwarming.

BEST SOUL GOSPEL PERFORMANCE, CONTEMPORARY

- Edwin Hawkins & the Edwin Hawkins Singers, *Wonderful!* Birthright.
Danniebelle, *He Is King*. Light.
Jessy Dixon, "Born Again." Light.
Larnelle Harris, *More*. Word.
Mighty Clouds of Joy, "God Is Not Dead," track. ABC.

BEST SOUL GOSPEL PERFORMANCE, TRADITIONAL

- James Cleveland, *James Cleveland Live at Carnegie Hall*. Savoy.
James Cleveland & the Greater Metropolitan Church of Christ Choir, *The Lord Is My Life*. Savoy.
Rev. Cleavant Derricks & Family, *Satisfaction Guaranteed*. Canaan.
Five Blind Boys of Mississippi, "I'm Just Another Soldier." Jewel.
Savannah Choir & Rev. Isaac Douglas, *Stand Up For Jesus*. Creed.

BEST INSPIRATIONAL PERFORMANCE

- B. J. Thomas, *Home Where I Belong*. Myrrh/Word.
Salome Bey, Clinton Derricks-Carroll, Sheila Ellis, Delores Hall, William Hardy, Jr., Hector Jaime Mercado, Stanley Perryman, Mabel Robinson, William Thomas, Jr., *Your Arm's Too Short to Box with God*. ABC.
Quincy Jones, James Cleveland conducting the Wattsline Choir, "O Lord, Come By Here," track. A&M.
Carol Lawrence, *Tell All the World About Love*. Word.
Ray Price, *How Great Thou Art*. Word.

BEST ETHNIC OR TRADITIONAL RECORDING

- *Hard Again*, Muddy Waters. Blue Sky/CBS.
Blues Hit Big Town, Junior Wells. Delmark.
Right Place, Wrong Time, Otis Rush. Bullfrog.
Things That I Used to Do, Joe Turner. Pablo.
What Happened to My Blues, Willie Dixon. Ovation.

BEST LATIN RECORDING

- *Dawn*, Mongo Santamaria. Vaya.
Fire Works, Machito Orchestra with Lalo Rodriguez. Dutch Timeless.
La Leyenda, Tito Puente. Tico/Fania.
Muy Amigos/Close Friends, Eydie Gormé, Danny Rivera. Gala/Coco.

Tomorrow: Barretto Live, Ray Barretto Band. Atlantic.

BEST INSTRUMENTAL ARRANGEMENT
• Harry Betts, Perry Botkin, Jr., Barry De Vorzon, "Nadia's Theme (*The Young and the Restless*)" (Barry De Vorzon). Arista.
Chick Corea, "Musicmagic" (Return to Forever). Columbia.
Crusaders, "Free as the Wind" (Crusaders). ABC.
Bob James, "Scheherazade" (Hubert Laws). CTI.
Herb Spencer, "*Roots* Mural Theme" (Quincy Jones). A&M.

BEST INSTRUMENTAL COMPOSITION
(Composer's Award)
• "Main Title from *Star Wars*," John Williams.
"Birdland," Joe Zawinul.
"Bond '77/*James Bond* Theme," Marvin Hamlisch.
"Gonna Fly Now (Theme from *Rocky*)," Bill Conti, Carol Connors, Ann Robbins.
"*Roots* Medley (Motherland, *Roots* Mural Theme)," Quincy Jones, Gerald Fried.

BEST ARRANGEMENT FOR VOICES
• Eagles, "New Kid in Town" (Eagles). Asylum.
Fleetwood Mac, "Go Your Own Way" (Fleetwood Mac). Warner Bros.
Heatwave, "All You Do Is Dial" (Heatwave). Epic.
Quincy Jones, James Cleveland, John Mandel, "O Lord, Come By Here" (Quincy Jones). A&M.
Jim Seals, "Baby, I'll Give It to You" (Seals & Crofts). Warner Bros.

BEST ARRANGEMENT ACCOMPANYING VOCALIST(S)
• Ian Freebairn-Smith, "Love Theme from *A Star Is Born* (Evergreen)" (Barbra Streisand). Columbia.
Richard Carpenter, "Calling Occupants of Interplanetary Craft" (Carpenters). A&M.

Claus Ogerman, "Besame Mucho" (João Gilberto). Warner Bros.
Claus Ogerman, "Nature Boy" (George Benson). Warner Bros.
Seawind, "The Devil Is a Liar" (Seawind). CTI.

BEST CAST SHOW ALBUM
(Composer's Award)
• *Annie*, Charles Strouse, Martin Charnin. Columbia.
Guys and Dolls, Frank Loesser. Motown.
I Love My Wife, Cy Coleman, Michael Stewart. Atlantic.
Starting Here, Starting Now, Richard Maltby, Jr., David Shire. RCA.
Your Arm's Too Short to Box with God, Micki Grant, Alex Bradford. ABC.

BEST ALBUM OF ORIGINAL SCORE WRITTEN FOR A MOTION PICTURE OR TV SPECIAL
(Composer's Award)
• *Star Wars*, John Williams. 20th Century.
Rocky, Bill Conti. United Artists.
The Spy Who Loved Me, Marvin Hamlisch. United Artists.
A Star Is Born, Kenny Ascher, Alan & Marilyn Bergman, Rupert Holmes, Leon Russell, Barbra Streisand, Donna Weiss, Paul Williams, Kenny Loggins. Columbia.
You Light Up My Life, Joe Brooks. Arista.

ALBUM OF THE YEAR, CLASSICAL
• *Concert of the Century* (recorded live at Carnegie Hall May 18, 1976) (solos: Leonard Bernstein, Vladimir Horowitz, Isaac Stern, Mstislav Rostropovich, Dietrich Fischer-Dieskau, Yehudi Menuhin, Lyndon Woodside). Columbia.
Gershwin: Porgy and Bess, John De Main conducting the Houston Grand Opera Production (solos: Dale, Smith, Shakesnider, Lane, Brice, Smalls). RCA.
Haydn: Orlando Paladino, Antal Dorati conducting the Orchestre de Cham-

bre de Lausanne (solos: Auger, Ameling, Killebrew, Ahnsjo, Luxon, Trimarchi, Shirley). Philips.
Mahler: Symphony No. 9 in D Major, Carlo Maria Giulini conducting the Chicago Symphony. Deutsche Grammophon.
Parkening and the Guitar (solo: Christopher Parkening). Angel.
Ravel: Boléro; Debussy: La Mer and l' Après-Midi d' un Faune, Sir Georg Solti conducting the Chicago Symphony. London.

BEST CLASSICAL PERFORMANCE, ORCHESTRA
(Conductor's Award)
• Carlo Maria Giulini conducting the Chicago Symphony, *Mahler: Symphony No. 9 in D Major*. Deutsche Grammophon.
Pierre Boulez conducting the New York Philharmonic, *Bartók: The Wooden Prince*. Columbia.
Herbert von Karajan conducting the Berlin Philharmonic, *Bruckner: Symphony No. 8 in C Minor*. Deutsche Grammophon.
James Levine conducting the Chicago Symphony, *Mahler: Symphony No. 3 in D Minor*. RCA.
André Previn conducting the London Symphony, *Tchaikovsky: Swan Lake*. Angel.
Sir Georg Solti conducting the Chicago Symphony, *Ravel: Boléro*. London.

BEST CHAMBER MUSIC PERFORMANCE (INSTRUMENTAL OR VOCAL)
• Juilliard Quartet, *Schoenberg: Quartets for Strings (Complete)*. Columbia.
Emanuel Ax, Cleveland Quartet, *Dvořák: Quintet for Piano in A Major, Op. 81*. RCA.
Pezzo Elegiaco, Vladimir Horowitz, Isaac Stern, Mstislav Rostropovich, *Rachmaninov: Sonata for Cello and Piano in G Minor, Op. 19, Andante; Tchaikovsky: Trio for Piano in A Minor, Op. 50*. Columbia.

Guarneri Quartet, *Bartók: Quartets for Strings (6)*. RCA.
David Munrow conducting the Early Music Consort of London, *A Contemporary Elizabethan Concert* (Dowland, Williams, Purcell, etc.). Angel.
Prague String Quartet, *Dvořák: Quartets No. 8 in E Major, Op. 80, and No. 10 in E Flat Major, Op. 51*. Deutsche Grammophon.
Ravi Shankar, Yehudi Menuhin, Jean-Pierre Rampal, Martine Geliot, Alla Rakha, *Improvisations, West Meets East, Album 3*. Angel.

BEST CLASSICAL PERFORMANCE, INSTRUMENTAL SOLOIST(S) (WITH ORCHESTRA)
• Itzhak Perlman, violin (Perlman conducting the London Philharmonic), *Vivaldi: The Four Seasons*. Angel.
Lazar Berman, piano (Abbado conducting the London Symphony), *Rachmaninov: Concerto for Piano No. 3 in D Minor*. Columbia.
Alfred Brendel, piano (Haitink conducting the London Philharmonic), *Beethoven: Concertos for Piano (5)*. Philips.
Jacqueline Du Pré, cello (Barenboim conducting the Philadelphia Orchestra), *Elgar: Concerto for Cello, Op. 85*. Columbia.
Alicia de Larrocha, piano (De Burgos conducting the Royal Philharmonic), *Concertos from Spain* (Surinach: *Piano Concerto* Montsalvage; *Concerto Breve*). London.
Maurizio Pollini, piano (Böhm conducting the Vienna Philharmonic), *Beethoven: Concerto for Piano No. 4 in G Major*. Deutsche Grammophon.
Mstislav Rostropovich, cello (Bernstein conducting the Orchestre National de France), *Schumann: Concerto for Cello and Orchestra in A Minor; Bloch: Schelomo*. Angel.
Solomon, piano (Dobrowen, conductor), *Brahms: Concerto for Piano No. 2 in B Flat Major, Op. 83*. Vox.

BEST CLASSICAL PERFORMANCE, INSTRUMENTAL SOLOIST(S) (WITHOUT ORCHESTRA)

- Artur Rubinstein, piano, *Beethoven: Sonata for Piano No. 18 in E Flat Major, Op. 31, No. 3; Schumann: Fantasiestücke, Op. 12*. RCA.
- Daniel Adni, piano, *Grainger: Piano Music of Percy Grainger*. Seraphim.
- Michel Beroff, piano, *Messiaen: 20 Regards de l'Enfant Jésus*. Connoisseur Society.
- Alicia de Larrocha, piano, *Granados: Goyescas*. London.
- Glenn Gould, piano, *Bach: The English Suites (Complete)*. Columbia.
- Igor Kipnis, harpsichord, *Bach: Partitas for Harpsichord No. 1 in B Flat Major and No. 2 in C Minor*. Angel.
- Itzhak Perlman, violin, *Itzhak Perlman Plays Fritz Kreisler: Album 2*. Angel.

BEST OPERA RECORDING

- *Gershwin: Porgy and Bess*, John De Main conducting the Houston Grand Opera Production (solos: Albert, Dale, Smith, Shakesnider, Lane, Brice, Smalls). RCA.
- *Haydn: Orlando Paladino*, Antal Dorati conducting the Orchestre de Chambre de Lausanne (solos: Auger, Ameling, Killbrew, Ahnsjo, Luxon, Shirley, Trimarchi). Philips.
- *Janáček: Katya Kabanova*, Charles Mackerras conducting the Vienna Philharmonic (solos: Söderström, Kniplova). London.
- *Mussorgsky: Boris Godunov*, Jerzy Semkow conducting the Polish National Radio Symphony Orchestra and Chorus (solos: Talvela, Gedda). Angel.
- *Puccini: Tosca*, Colin Davis conducting the Chorus and Orchestra of the Royal Opera House, Covent Garden (solos: Caballé, Carreras, Wixell, Ramey). Philips.
- *Wagner: Die Meistersinger von Nürnberg*, Eugen Jochum conducting the Deutsche Oper Berlin Orchestra and Chorus (solos: Fischer-Dieskau, Domingo, Ludwig, Ligendza). Deutsche Grammophon.
- *Wagner: The Flying Dutchman*, Sir Georg Solti conducting the Chicago Symphony Orchestra and Chorus (solos: Bailey, Martin, Talvela, Kollo, Krenn, Jones). London.
- *Weill: Threepenny Opera*, Stanley Silverman conducting the original cast of the New York Shakespeare Festival (solos: Julia, Alexander, Greene). Columbia.

BEST CLASSICAL PERFORMANCE CHORAL (OTHER THAN OPERA)

- Sir Georg Solti, conductor, Margaret Hillis, choral director, Chicago Symphony Chorus and Orchestra, *Verdi: Requiem*. RCA.
- Serge Baudo conducting the Stephen Caillat Chorus and Orchestre de Paris, *Roussel: Psalm 80*, for tenor, chorus and orchestra. Connoisseur Society.
- Colin Davis conducting the John Alldis Choir; London Symphony, *Berlioz: L'Enfance du Christ*. Philips.
- Rafael Kubelik conducting the Chorus of Bavarian Radio and Bavarian Radio Symphony, *Dvořák: Stabat Mater*. Deutsche Grammophon.
- Philip Ledger conducting the King's College Choir, Cambridge; Academy of St. Martin-in-the-Fields, *Purcell: Funeral Music for Queen Mary*. Angel.
- Herbert von Karajan conducting the Vienna Singverein; Berlin Philharmonic, *Bruckner: Te Deum*. Deutsche Grammophon.
- David Willcocks conducting the King's College Choir, Cambridge; Academy of St. Martin-in-the-Fields, *Britten: Saint Nicholas*. Seraphim.

BEST CLASSICAL PERFORMANCE, VOCAL SOLOIST

- Janet Baker (Marriner conducting the Academy of St. Martin-in-the-Fields), *Bach: Arias*. Angel.

Elly Ameling (de Waart conducting the Rotterdam Philharmonic), *Schubert on Stage*. Philips.

Dietrich Fischer-Dieskau (Ponti, accompanist), *Ives: Songs*. Deutsche Grammophon.

Donald Gramm (Hassard, accompanist), *But Yesterday Is Not Today* (songs by Barber, Bowles, Copland, Chanler, etc.). New World.

Luciano Pavarotti (Adler conducting the National Philharmonic), *Luciano Pavarotti—O Holy Night* ("O Holy Night," "Sanctus," "Ave Maria," etc.). London.

Elisabeth Söderström (Ashkenazy, accompanist), *Rachmaninov: Songs, Vol. 2*. London.

Frederica von Stade (de Waart conducting the Rotterdam Philharmonic), *Rossini/Mozart: Opera Arias*. Philips.

Gerard Souzay (Baldwin, accompanist), *Fauré: Songs (Complete)*. Connoisseur Society.

Galina Vishnevskaya, soprano, Mark Reshetin, bass (Rostropovich conducting the Moscow Philharmonic), *Shostakovich: Symphony No. 14*. Columbia.

BEST ENGINEERED RECORDING, CLASSICAL

• Kenneth Wilkinson, *Ravel: Boléro* (Solti conducting the Chicago Symphony). London.

Paul Goodman, Anthony Salvatore, *Gershwin: Porgy and Bess* (De Main conducting the Houston Grand Opera). RCA.

Bud Graham, Ray Moore, Milt Cherin, *Bartók: The Wooden Prince* (Boulez conducting the New York Philharmonic). Columbia.

Klaus Scheibe, *Mahler: Symphony No. 9 in D Major* (Giulini conducting the Chicago Symphony). Deutsche Grammophon.

Heinz Wildhagen, *Mahler: Symphony No. 2 in C Minor ("Resurrection")* (Abbado conducting the Chicago Symphony). Deutsche Grammophon.

S. J. W. Witteveen, Dick van Dijk, *Berlioz: L'Enfance du Christ* (Davis conducting the London Symphony). Philips.

BEST SPOKEN WORD, DOCUMENTARY OR DRAMA RECORDING

• *The Belle of Amherst*, Julie Harris. Credo.

Alex Haley Tells the Story of His Search for Roots, Alex Haley. Warner Bros.

For Colored Girls Who Have Considered Suicide/When the Rainbow Is Enuf (original cast), Ntozake Shange, writer. Buddah.

J. R. R. Tolkien: The Silmarillion of Beren and Luthien, read by Christopher Tolkien. Caedmon.

The Truman Tapes, Harry Truman speaking with Ben Gradus. Caedmon.

BEST COMEDY RECORDING

• *Let's Get Small*, Steve Martin. Warner Bros.

Are You Serious??? Richard Pryor. Laff.

The Ernie Kovacs Album, Ernie Kovacs. Columbia.

On the Road, George Carlin. Little David.

Saturday Night Live, NBC's *Saturday Night Live* cast. Arista.

BEST RECORDING FOR CHILDREN

• *Aren't You Glad You're You*, Sesame Street cast & Muppets. Sesame Street.

A Charlie Brown Christmas, various (written by Charles M. Schulz). Charlie Brown Records.

Dope! The Dope King's Last Stand, various artists (Lily Tomlin, Muhammad Ali, Jimmy Carter, etc.). Cornucopia.

Russell Hoban: The Mouse and His Child, read by Peter Ustinov. Caedmon.

The Sesame Street Fairy Tale Album, Jim Henson's Muppets. Sesame Street.

BEST ENGINEERED RECORDING
(OTHER THAN CLASSICAL)

- Roger Nichols, Elliot Scheiner, Bill Schnee, Al Schmitt, *Aja* (Steely Dan). ABC.
- Ken Caillat, Richard Dashut, *Rumours* (Fleetwood Mac). Warner Bros.
- Val Garay, *Simple Dreams* (Linda Ronstadt). Asylum.
- Val Garay, *J T* (James Taylor). Columbia.
- Bill Schnee, *Discovered Again!* (Dave Grusin). Sheffield Lab.

BEST ALBUM PACKAGE
(Art Director's Award)

- John Berg, *Love Notes* (Ramsey Lewis). Columbia.
- Glen Christensen, *Hejira* (Joni Mitchell). Asylum.
- Kosh, *Simple Dreams* (Linda Ronstadt). Asylum.
- Kosh, *Singin'* (Melissa Manchester). Arista.
- MPL/Hipgnosis, *Wings over America* (Wings). Capitol.
- Paula Scher, *Ginseng Woman* (Eric Gale). Columbia.

Paula Scher, *Yardbirds Favorites* (Yardbirds). Epic.

Abie Sussman, Bob Defrin, *Color As a Way of Life* (Lou Donaldson). Cotillion/Atlantic.

BEST ALBUM NOTES
(Annotator's Award)

- George T. Simon, *Bing Crosby: A Legendary Performer*. RCA.
- Chris Albertson, *Stormy Blues* (Billie Holiday). Verve/Polydor.
- Michael Brooks, *The Lester Young Story, Vol. 1*. Columbia.
- George T. Simon, *Guy Lombardo: A Legendary Performer*. RCA.
- Patrick Snyder, *Jefferson Airplane— Flight Log* (Jefferson Airplane). Grunt/RCA.

PRODUCER OF THE YEAR

- Peter Asher
- Bee Gees, Albhy Galuten, Karl Richardson
- Kenneth Gamble & Leon Huff
- Richard Perry
- Bill Szymczyk

• 1978 •

Bee Gees Fever

"**J**ust call it Grammy Night with the Bee Gees," predicted the *L.A. Herald Examiner*—and most other media sources—ahead of time.

The Australian-born Bee Gees were the new kings of American disco and they ruled the Grammy race with the most nominations: six. Their bids were for their contribution to the biggest-selling album in music history to date—*Saturday Night Fever*—the soundtrack to the hit film about a shy, working-class teen, portrayed by John Travolta, who comes roaring to life each weekend when he hits the dance floor at a Brooklyn disco. The LP included the works of multiple artists but was dominated by six Bee Gees tunes, of which three reached number one on the charts: "Stayin' Alive" (nominated for Record and Song of the Year), the film's title number, "Night Fever," and "How Deep Is Your Love," which earned the Aussie trio the award for best pop group singing last year when the song was released as a single prior to the movie and album debut.

The rival Los Angeles newspaper also believed that the disco fever would be catchy. " 'Stayin' Alive' should win the Grammy as the best record of 1978," wrote Robert Hilburn in the *L.A. Times*. "That's a prediction, and a value judgment. The Bee Gee–dominated *Saturday Night Fever* soundtrack also should win a Grammy as the year's best album. That's just a prediction." Hilburn, like many other rock purists, was rooting instead for an LP that shocked everyone when it was included in the album competition—*Some Girls* by the Rolling Stones, marking the rock group's first Grammy nomination ever. Also up for best album

"We're the happiest three brothers in the world!" roared Barry Gibb (center) after the Bee Gees received five awards, including Album of the Year.

race was *Running on Empty* by first-time nominee Jackson Browne.

Despite such weighty competition, *Saturday Night Fever* took the Album of the Year award without a sweat, thus becoming the first film score to hold the honor. It was also the first collaborative LP to win since *The Concert for Bangla Desh* in 1972. When the miniature golden gramophones were passed out to the winners, they were bestowed on 16 producers and 10 of the top disco artists of the day. In addition to the Bee Gees, the other music talent included Yvonne Elliman, K.C. & the Sunshine Band, Kool & the Gang, Ralph MacDonald, MFSB, Walter Murphy, Tavares, the Trammps and David Shire. But just as the Bee Gees dominated the platter, they also dominated Grammy night. "Each mention of the group's name drew whoops of delight and shrieks from those sections of the balcony set aside for the general public," the *Times* observed.

The Bee Gees earned one Grammy for the album prize, a second for being among its producers and a third as Producer of the Year, which they shared with coproducers Albhy Galuten and Karl Richardson. (Barry Gibb, Galuten and Richardson were also behind the score to the other current hit John Travolta movie, *Grease,* which was also competing for Album of the Year.) Two more Grammys followed: Best Arrangement for Voices (for "Stayin' Alive") and a repeat of the award the Bee Gees reaped last year for best pop group vocals. Only four other artists had ever won five or more trophies in one year: Henry Mancini, Roger Miller, Paul Simon and Stevie Wonder.

"It's just great—unbelievable!" Barry Gibb roared backstage. "We're the happiest three brothers in the world."

The Bee Gees were considered the front-runners to nab the Record and Song of the Year awards, but this year's disco party was partially spoiled by a contender who wasn't even in attendance. Billy Joel didn't think he had a chance to win, so he skipped the ceremony in favor of fulfilling a concert obligation in Paris. Producer Phil Ramone went in his place, although he had to fight his way out of a snowstorm in Amsterdam to do it. "Billy wasn't the kind of mild and mellow act that always won the Grammys in those days," Ramone later recalled, "so we didn't take his nominations that seriously. When I heard his name called, I didn't think it was real."

"Billy busted up the Bee Gees' year! I can't believe it!" Ramone boomed backstage to the press after the double victory. "I was sitting there like a schnook when they announced Billy's song ["Just the Way You Are"]. I never thought we'd win."

After Joel's victories, the biggest shock on awards night was the winner of Best New Artist. When this year's Grammy bids were announced, *Variety* applauded "the academy's growing attention to music which falls into the hard rock category, reflected most strongly in N.A.R.A.S.'s nominees for new artist of the year, where the contenders are the Cars, Elvis Costello, Chris Rea, A Taste of Honey and Toto."

"Either the Cars or Toto [seem] to be the most likely winner," the *L.A. Times*

Billy Joel halted a complete Bee Gees sweep by pulling off upsets in the Record and Song of the Year categories with "Just the Way You Are."

Los Angeles Public Library

forecast. A few other media sources rooted for Elvis Costello. The choice turned out to be the black disco band A Taste of Honey, named after Herb Alpert's 1965 Grammy Record of the Year. The group would turn out to have only one hit, "Boogie Oogie Oogie," in its first incarnation, but its victory "served to emphasize the widespread appeal of disco music over the past year," said the *Herald Examiner.* (Stripped down from four members to two by the 1980s, A Taste of Honey would rebound with one more successful single, "Sukiyaki.") They were also only the second winners of the Best New Artist prize to be black (Natalie Cole preceded them in 1975). When asked about the color breakthrough backstage by a reporter for the *Times,* bass player and vocalist Hazel Payne shot back, "Don't get us involved in a racial thing!" Keyboardist Perry Kibble added, "If we weren't exceptional, we wouldn't have won!"

Another Grammy shocker was lurking in the male pop vocal category. *Variety* noted that it was "interesting that none of the five nominees—Gerry Rafferty, Barry Manilow, Gino Vannelli, Jackson Browne and Dan Hill—has ever been nominated before." Jackson Browne was considered the front-runner for *Running on Empty.* "Am I surprised at winning a Grammy for 'Copacabana'?" a victorious Barry Manilow said to reporters backstage after he pulled off an upset. "I sure am. I didn't even think it would be a hit single." The *L. A. Times* described "Copacabana (At the Copa)" as "a fluffy Latin-disco piece" from Manilow's triple-platinum contender for Album of the Year, *Even Now.*

Anne Murray had won a country vocalist Grammy in 1974 for her *Love Song* LP but retired soon afterward in order to devote herself full-time to her recent marriage and newborn baby. By 1978, she was back in the business and in Grammy contention, too, for "You Needed Me," which was also voted Song of the Year by the Academy of Country Music. But she was competing in the Grammy's female pop vocalist category against some formidable nominees: Olivia Newton-John, Carly Simon, Barbra Streisand and Donna Summer. When Murray prevailed, the *Times* said the win "came as something of a pleasant surprise over a field consisting entirely of soft-pop entries." Disco's reigning diva, Donna Summer, was the only one of the entries who hadn't won a Grammy yet, but she compensated for her loss to Murray—and further demonstrated disco's considerable pull—by picking up the r&b vocals honor over Aretha Franklin, Natalie Cole, Chaka Khan and Alicia Bridges. Summer's "Last Dance" was so popular that it was the year's only serious challenger to the status of the Bee Gees' "Night Fever" as the ultimate anthem of the disco set. In fact, "Last Dance" was part of the score to the *Saturday Night Fever* clone *Thank God It's Friday,* a film about a night at a fictitious Hollywood dance club called Zoo Disco.

Instead of expressing joy or gratitude

backstage after winning, Summer was visibly upset as she lobbied for the genre to have its own award. "Disco has sold millions and millions of records and has rejuvenated this industry," she ranted to reporters. "It's changing radio programming tremendously, as much as rock did in the late '60s. Winning the award was a thrill, but it would be even more of a thrill to win a Grammy in the first disco category." Next year Summer would see part of her wish fulfilled, with ironic consequences.

"Last Dance," written by Paul Jabara, won Best Rhythm & Blues Song, even though it had its doubters. (Referring to the president of Casablanca Records, Jabara said flippantly to the *Herald Examiner* reporter backstage, "Neil Bogart told me I probably wouldn't win. A lot he knows. Got a match?") Jabara's tune even beat the Bee Gees this year for Best Original Song at the Oscars, which caused some resentment among the *Saturday Night Fever* gang. (Ray Charles had served as the film's special musical material director and said after the Bee Gees' sweep at the N.A.R.A.S. awards, "I'm certainly glad that the Bee Gees and 'Stayin' Alive' were recognized by at least *some* professional academy.")

Earth, Wind & Fire was among the losers of Best R&B Song (for "Fantasy") and also lost its bid for the pop vocal group laurels to the Bee Gees, but nonetheless the group prevailed with its other three nominations: best r&b vocal performance by a group (*All 'n' All*), Best R&B Instrumental Performance ("Runnin' "), and an arrangement award for its founder, vocalist, drummer and arranger, Maurice White. The title track of *All 'n' All* was another movie excerpt—from the disastrous *Sgt. Pepper's Lonely Hearts Club Band,* a farfetched and overly fanciful dramatization of the Beatles classic that starred a host of rock celebrities, including members of Earth, Wind & Fire and the Bee Gees. The film was produced by Robert Stigwood, the same force behind *Saturday Night Fever* and *Grease.*

George Benson was the sole nondisco winner in the r&b lineup. He earned the male vocal award for his cover of the Drifters' hit "On Broadway," a single release from his *Weekend in L.A.* LP that was made at Los Angeles's Roxy Theater in late 1977 where he performed "It's All in the Game" and "The Greatest Love of All." The noted jazz guitarist only started singing on his records after he signed up with Warner Bros. in 1975.

Jazz fusion vocal acrobat Al Jarreau held on to the jazz singing slot for a second year in a row. His new album, *All Fly Home,* topped works by Ray Charles, Mel Tormé and Sarah Vaughan. Among the nominees in the instrumental soloist category was a former Grammy champ who hadn't been heard from in some time— Stan Getz, who won both Album of the Year (*Getz/Gilberto*) and Record of the Year ("The Girl from Ipanema") in 1964. Getz hadn't even been nominated since 1967, when he lost to the Cannonball Adderley Quartet in the jazz group instrumental category. Now he was usurped for the soloist honors by last year's winner, Oscar Peterson, who was lauded for the album recording of his 1977 performance at Switzerland's Montreux Jazz Festival.

Getz and pianist Jimmy Rowles were up for this year's group instrumental award but lost to 1976 winner Chick Corea for *Friends,* on which Corea collaborated with drummer Steve Gadd, reed player Joe Farrell and bassist Eddie Gomez. The big-band prize went to a team that epitomized the genre's old-style traditions—the Thad Jones–Mel Lewis Orchestra—for *Live in Munich,* the last LP by the full 18-member group. Jones quit in 1978 to work with the Danish Radio Big Band in Copenhagen, while Lewis continued to lead the orchestra, as he had for the previous 20 years, in its weekly Monday night gigs at New York's Village Vanguard jazz club.

When Dolly Parton left Nashville in 1976 for a recording career in Hollywood, she tried to reassure her outraged c&w fans by telling them, "I'm not leaving

Donna Summer called winning the r&b prize a "thrill," but pressed for a new disco award. She'd get her wish at next year's Grammys—but lose.

country. I am just taking it with me." She had been nominated for a Grammy on 10 unsuccessful occasions in the past—last year in both the pop and country categories—but was given little chance of winning this year when she popped up again in the country category. When she prevailed for her *Here You Come Again* album over last year's popular winner, Crystal Gayle, the *New York Times* said the triumph proved that "Miss Parton has hardly lost her hold on her country fans for all her recent pop endeavors." Parton may have "gone Hollywood" recently, but she was nowhere in evidence at the Los Angeles Shrine Auditorium on Grammy night. "Eyes searched the hall when Dolly Parton won," noted the *Herald Examiner,* "but she didn't show."

Prior to his death in 1977, the only Grammys that Elvis Presley received were for three religious recordings, but he was now given one last chance at a secular prize when he was nominated posthumously as best male country vocalist for a song called "Softly As I Leave You." But the King was up against two formidable opponents: Willie Nelson and Johnny Paycheck. When Nelson won, Paycheck was observed in the audience waving an arm in the air and shouting,

"Way to go, Willie!," even though Nelson was nowhere near enough to hear him. "Eyes searched the hall again," the *Herald Examiner* observed, "this time for Willie Nelson, who also stayed home." Nelson was honored for his rendition of "Georgia on My Mind," which last earned a Grammy in 1960 for Ray Charles.

Nelson was widely known as the reigning outlaw of country music, but he picked a poor time to dodge the ceremony for the music establishment's highest award. After Grammycast presenters Tanya Tucker and Glen Campbell sang the list of nominees for country's best vocal duo or group, the winners were revealed to be Nelson and Waylon Jennings for "Mammas, Don't Let Your Babies Grow Up to Be Cowboys," written and initially recorded by Ed Bruce in 1976. Bruce had actually composed the song for Nelson and Jennings, but when he sensed a hit in the works, he wanted his own chance at stardom with it first. When his single failed, he passed the song on to Nelson and Jennings, who included it on their *Waylon and Willie* LP that spent more than three years on the country album charts.

"Cowboys" and another country classic, "Take This Job and Shove It," were both up for Best Country Song, but lost to "The Gambler," written by Don Schlitz, who was a computer operator working the graveyard shift at Vanderbilt University in 1976 when he sold the tune to Capitol. The song hadn't yet been given its definitive performance by Kenny Rogers; again its songwriter, like "Cowboys" composer Ed Bruce, wanted to make the original recording. Shortly after it failed to make the country charts, Rogers took it to the top of the rankings when he covered it and would go on to pick up the Grammy for best country vocal performance next year.

The Best Country Instrumental Performance category contained a number of "safe" choices, including Roy Clark and Doc Watson, but N.A.R.A.S. voters shocked Grammy watchers when they picked the controversial group Asleep at the Wheel for "One O'Clock Jump." Asleep at the Wheel members hailed originally from Berkeley, California, but moved to Austin, Texas, during the early part of their career to specialize in performing music they labeled country rock and western swing, the latter of which was defined by *Rolling Stone* as "hillbilly music's answer to jazz."

In the lineup of six religious awards, winners included the returning 1975 champs, Andrae Crouch & the Disciples, for *Live in London*. Formed in 1965, the group specialized in combining gospel music with rock, jazz and soul influences to achieve a mainstream sound enjoyed by Stevie Wonder, the Crusaders and other artists who appeared on their albums. The religious awards had doubled in number over the past three years, welcoming victories in the new categories by a host of newcomers to the N.A.R.A.S. awards, including the Happy Goodman Family (*Refreshing*), Larry Hart ("What a Friend") and the Mighty Clouds of Joy (*Live and Direct*).

The singer whose group trounced the Beatles in 1965 for the group vocals award, causing one of the most spirited outcries in Grammy history—Anita Kerr—was now up for Best Inspirational Performance for *Precious Memories*. This time she took a trouncing herself when last year's winner, B. J. Thomas, proved invincible for *Happy Man*. Chicago bluesman Muddy Waters also reprised his 1977 victory for Best Ethnic or Traditional Recording for *I'm Ready*.

Last year Tito Puente was expected to prevail for Best Latin Recording but lost to his former band member from the 1950s, Mongo Santamaria. The famed

> After losing 10 times, Dolly Parton skipped this year's ceremony— and won.

multi-instrumentalist, composer and bandleader now avenged the loss when he was honored for *Homenaje a Beny Moré,* his salute to the Cuban singer and bandleader Beny Moré that included vocals by Hector Lavoe and others. When the album proved to be a commercial success, Puente followed it up with a second hit volume in 1979 and a third in 1985.

Film score composer and conductor John Williams won his first Grammy for *Jaws* in 1975, then three more last year for *Star Wars.* He brought his total tally to an even half dozen when he picked up two for his work for director Steven Spielberg's *Close Encounters of the Third Kind:* top film score and Best Instrumental Composition.

Variety noted that the Grammycast was "enlivened principally by the antics of comic Steve Martin," who returned from last year to take the comedy laurels for *A Wild and Crazy Guy.* The LP showcased some of Martin's best work, including his famous "King Tut" skit and hit song, but it was his routine at the Grammycast when he accepted the prize that brought him the most laughs. He walked up to the podium, dressed appropriately in formal attire, but without wearing his tuxedo pants. After the audience laughter died down, he referred to the heavy use of four-letter words on his album, saying, "This is the pattern of my life. To win a Grammy for an album that was banned by K-Mart." A stagehand then appeared next to Martin and handed him his trousers, fully pressed and still draped over a hanger as if they had just arrived from the cleaners. "It's about time!" Martin fumed.

The choice of Classical Album of the Year was Brahms's Concerto for Violin and Orchestra in D Major performed by Itzhak Perlman and Carlo Maria Giulini conducting the Chicago Symphony Orchestra, both of whom also reaped

> ### The *Washington Post* rooted for Nixon to win Best Spoken Word Recording.

Grammys last year. "There have been many distinguished recordings of the Brahms violin concerto," *High Fidelity* wrote, "but this one easily takes its place among the best. Conceptually, [Perlman's and Giulini's] is an extremely broad, majestic interpretation."

In many of the other categories, 1978 turned out to be the year of Beethoven, since three awards went to performances of his works. Perlman picked up an additional Grammy (best chamber music) for his rendering of Beethoven's Sonatas for Violin and Piano with Vladimir Ashkenazy, which got mixed reviews (*High Fidelity* referred to both its "dragging tempos" and "radiant, sunny, gentle reading"). The same publication was more enthusiastic about the victor of the choral laurels: the Chicago Symphony and Chorus performance (under the direction of Sir Georg Solti and choral master Margaret Hillis) of *Missa Solemnis:* "[Solti's] vocal and instrumental forces are outstanding."

Herbert von Karajan once estimated that he and the Berlin Philharmonic had performed Beethoven's nine symphonies hundreds of times since he became the orchestra's conductor in 1955. In a published interview included with Deutsche Grammophon's eight-disc set of the complete works (a losing nominee for Classical Album of the Year that still took the orchestral honors), von Karajan mused on some of the different approaches he has used throughout his career. Referring to Symphony No. 7, the maestro said, "Of course, when we were young, the generation before us conducted it *much* slower. And I knew it was wrong, but I couldn't get out of this because of the inner content of the music. Then both things were joined: the right tempo and the content of it."

Pianist Vladimir Horowitz picked up both soloist awards this year for recordings that celebrated the 50th anniversary of his American debut. *High Fidelity* referred to the "presumably studio-made Liszt B minor Sonata filled out with two late Fauré pieces (confusingly, even misleadingly, billed under the rubric *The Horowitz Concerts, 1977–78*) and a recording derived from his first performance with orchestra in 25 years, the Rachmaninov Third Concerto featured in the New York Philharmonic's January 8 [1978] pension-fund concert. . . . On both records we are hearing the pianist still in the process of getting these fearsome works back into his fingers and his blood."

Critics generally applauded the orchestration work of the winning Best Opera Recording: excerpts from Lehar's *The Merry Widow* with Julius Rudel conducting the New York City Opera Chorus and Orchestra and with Beverly Sills singing the lead role. Lambasted, though, were the new English lyrics such as "with girls in this oasis, I'm on a first name basis" and Sills's singing, which *High Fidelity* called "so tremulous as to be embarrassing." Sills was not nominated in the vocals category, which was claimed instead by Luciano Pavarotti for his *Hits from Lincoln Center,* topping other nominees Maria Callas, Marilyn Horne and Dietrich Fischer-Dieskau.

The *New York Times* complained last year about production snafus and bad camera work at the Grammycast but hailed this year's show as a "tasteful, smoothly run affair." The *L.A. Herald Examiner* concurred, calling it "a large-scale opulent presentation that served as a vivid reminder of how huge the business of popular music has become. The two-hour broadcast was crammed with 10 flashy production numbers."

Complaints came this year instead from the *Washington Post,* which took particular issue with host John Denver performing the tunes nominated for best record ("he sang them all with no style at all"). It also noted that "an audible sigh of relief swept across the audience as Orson Welles beat out former president Richard Nixon in the Best Spoken Recording category." Welles was nominated for a new LP recording of his timeless performance in the classic film *Citizen Kane,* whereas Nixon was up for the album release of his confessional interviews with former talk show host David Frost. The *Post* obviously had no love for the ex-president, having contributed to his downfall through its vigorous coverage of the Watergate scandal, and recently lampooned his N.A.R.A.S. nomination with an editorial that said: "If Mr. Nixon wins the Grammy, we fully expect to see television ads for *Richard Nixon's Greatest Hits.* There will be . . . the classic non-swan song 'You Won't Have Richard Nixon to Kick Around Any More' . . . or the heartwarming 'I Am Not a Crook,' televised live from Disneyland. . . . In short, the man is ready for stardom, and ready for his Grammy. May we say—for what must surely be the first time—we hope Mr. Nixon wins."

• 1978 •

The awards ceremony was broadcast on CBS from the Shrine Auditorium in Los Angeles on February 15, 1979, for the awards eligibility period of October 1, 1977, through September 30, 1978.

ALBUM OF THE YEAR

• *Saturday Night Fever* (soundtrack), Bee Gees, David Shire, Yvonne Elli-man, Tavares, Kool & the Gang, K.C. & the Sunshine Band, MFSB, Trammps, Walter Murphy, Ralph MacDonald. RSO.

Even Now, Barry Manilow. Arista.

Grease (soundtrack), John Travolta, Olivia Newton-John, Frankie Valli, Frankie Avalon, Stockard Channing, Jeff Conaway, Cindy Bullens,

Sha-Na-Na, Louis St. Louis. Arista.

Running on Empty, Jackson Browne. Asylum.

Some Girls, Rolling Stones. Rolling Stones.

RECORD OF THE YEAR

• "Just the Way You Are," Billy Joel. Columbia.

"Baker Street," Gerry Rafferty. United Artists.

"Feels So Good," Chuck Mangione. A&M.

"Stayin' Alive," Bee Gees. RSO.

"You Needed Me," Anne Murray. Capitol.

SONG OF THE YEAR
(Songwriter's Award)

• "Just the Way You Are," Billy Joel.

"Stayin' Alive," Barry Gibb, Robin Gibb, Maurice Gibb.

"Three Times a Lady," Lionel Richie.

"You Don't Bring Me Flowers," Neil Diamond, Alan Bergman, Marilyn Bergman.

"You Needed Me," Randy Goodrum.

BEST NEW ARTIST

• A Taste of Honey

Cars

Elvis Costello

Chris Rea

Toto

BEST POP VOCAL PERFORMANCE, MALE

• Barry Manilow, "Copacabana (At the Copa)." Arista.

Jackson Browne, *Running on Empty*. Asylum.

Dan Hill, "Sometimes When We Touch." 20th Century.

Gerry Rafferty, "Baker Street." United Artists.

Gino Vannelli, "I Just Wanna Stop." A&M.

BEST POP VOCAL PERFORMANCE, FEMALE

• Anne Murray, "You Needed Me." Capitol.

Olivia Newton-John, "Hopelessly Devoted to You." RSO.

Carly Simon, "You Belong to Me." Elektra.

Barbra Streisand, "You Don't Bring Me Flowers," solo version; track. Columbia.

Donna Summer, "MacArthur Park." Casablanca.

BEST POP VOCAL PERFORMANCE BY A DUO, GROUP OR CHORUS

• Bee Gees, *Saturday Night Fever*. RSO.

Commodores, "Three Times a Lady." Motown.

Earth, Wind & Fire, "Got to Get You into My Life." Columbia.

Roberta Flack, Donny Hathaway, "The Closer I Get to You." Atlantic.

Steely Dan, "FM (No Static at All)." MCA.

BEST POP INSTRUMENTAL PERFORMANCE

• Chuck Mangione, *Children of Sanchez*. A&M.

Chet Atkins, Les Paul, *Guitar Monsters*. RCA.

Henry Mancini, "*The Pink Panther* Theme ('78)." United Artists.

Zubin Mehta conducting the Los Angeles Philharmonic, "*Star Wars*" and "*Close Encounters of the Third Kind*." London.

John Williams, *Close Encounters of the Third Kind* (soundtrack). Arista.

BEST RHYTHM & BLUES SONG
(Songwriter's Award)

• "Last Dance," Paul Jabara.

"Boogie Oogie Oogie," Perry Kibble, Janice Johnson.

"Dance, Dance, Dance," Bernard Edwards, Kenny Lehman, Nile Rogers.

"Fantasy," Maurice White, Eddie de Barrio, Verdine White.
"Use ta Be My Girl," Kenneth Gamble, Leon Huff.

BEST RHYTHM & BLUES VOCAL PERFORMANCE, MALE
- George Benson, "On Broadway." Warner Bros.

Peter Brown, "Dance with Me." T.K.
Ray Charles, "I Can See Clearly Now." Atlantic.
Teddy Pendergrass, "Close the Door." Philadelphia International.
Lou Rawls, *When You Hear Lou, You've Heard It All*. Philadelphia International/Columbia.

BEST RHYTHM & BLUES VOCAL PERFORMANCE, FEMALE
- Donna Summer, "Last Dance." Casablanca.

Alicia Bridges, "I Love the Nightlife." Polydor.
Natalie Cole, "Our Love." Capitol.
Aretha Franklin, *Almighty Fire*. Atlantic.
Chaka Khan, "I'm Every Woman." Warner Bros.

BEST RHYTHM & BLUES VOCAL PERFORMANCE BY A DUO, GROUP OR CHORUS
- Earth, Wind & Fire, *All 'n' All*. Columbia.

A Taste of Honey, "Boogie Oogie Oogie." Capitol.
Commodores, *Natural High*. Motown.
O'Jays, "Use ta Be My Girl," track. Columbia.
Diana Ross, Michael Jackson, "Ease on down the Road." MCA.

BEST RHYTHM & BLUES INSTRUMENTAL PERFORMANCE
- Earth, Wind & Fire, "Runnin'," track. Columbia.

Average White Band, "Sweet and Sour," track. Atlantic.
Brothers Johnson, "Streetwave," track. A&M.

Crusaders, *Images*. ABC.
Stanley Clarke, *Modern Man*. Nemperor.

BEST JAZZ VOCAL PERFORMANCE
- Al Jarreau, *All Fly Home*. Warner Bros.

Ray Charles, *True to Life*. Atlantic.
Eddie Jefferson, *The Main Man*. Inner City.
Irene Kral, *Gentle Rain*. Choice.
Mel Tormé, *Together Again, for the First Time*. Gryphon/Century.
Sarah Vaughan, *How Long Has This Been Going On*. Pablo.

BEST JAZZ INSTRUMENTAL PERFORMANCE BY A SOLOIST
- Oscar Peterson, *Montreux '77, Oscar Peterson Jam*. Pablo.

Al Cohn, *Heavy Love* (Al Cohn, Jimmy Rowles). Xanadu.
Stan Getz, *Stan Getz Gold*. Inner City.
Dexter Gordon, *Sophisticated Giant*. Columbia.
Woody Shaw, *Rosewood*. Columbia.

BEST JAZZ INSTRUMENTAL PERFORMANCE BY A GROUP
- Chick Corea, *Friends*. Polydor.

Al Cohn, Jimmy Rowles, *Heavy Love*. Xanadu.
Stan Getz, Jimmy Rowles, *The Peacocks*. Columbia.
Woody Shaw Concert Ensemble, *Rosewood*. Columbia.
Phil Woods Quintet, *Song for Sisyphus*. Gryphon/Century.

BEST JAZZ INSTRUMENTAL PERFORMANCE BY A BIG BAND
- Thad Jones, Mel Lewis, *Live in Munich*. Horizon/A&M.

Rob McConnell & the Boss Brass, *Big Band Jazz*. Umbrella.
Toshiko Akiyoshi–Lew Tabackin Big Band, *Insights*. RCA.
Dexter Gordon & Orchestra, *Sophisticated Giant*. Columbia.
Thad Jones, *Thad Jones Greetings and Salutations*. Biograph.

BEST COUNTRY SONG
(Songwriter's Award)
- "The Gambler," Don Schlitz.
"Every Time Two Fools Collide," Jan Dyer, Jeffrey Tweel.
"Let's Take the Long Way Around the World," Archie Jordan, Naomi Martin.
"Mammas, Don't Let Your Babies Grow Up to Be Cowboys," Ed & Patsy Bruce.
"Take This Job and Shove It," David A. Coe.

BEST COUNTRY VOCAL PERFORMANCE, MALE
- Willie Nelson, "Georgia on My Mind." Columbia.
Waylon Jennings, *I've Always Been Crazy*. RCA.
Ronnie Milsap, "Let's Take the Long Way Around the World." RCA.
Elvis Presley, "Softly As I Leave You." RCA.
Johnny Paycheck, "Take This Job and Shove It." Epic.
Kenny Rogers, *Love or Something Like It*. United Artists.

BEST COUNTRY VOCAL PERFORMANCE, FEMALE
- *Here You Come Again*, Dolly Parton. RCA.
Crystal Gayle, "Talkin' in Your Sleep." United Artists.
Emmylou Harris, *Quarter Moon in a Ten Cent Town*. Warner Bros.
Barbara Mandrell, "Sleeping Single in a Double Bed." ABC.
Anne Murray, "Walk Right Back." Capitol.

BEST COUNTRY VOCAL PERFORMANCE BY A DUO OR GROUP
- Waylon Jennings, Willie Nelson, "Mammas, Don't Let Your Babies Grow Up to Be Cowboys." RCA.
Jim Ed Brown, Helen Cornelius, "If the World Ran Out Of Love Tonight." RCA.
Oak Ridge Boys, "Cryin' Again." ABC.

Charlie Rich with Janie Fricke, "On My Knees." Epic.
Kenny Rogers, Dottie West, "Anyone Who Isn't Me Tonight." United Artists.
Statler Brothers, "Do You Know You Are My Sunshine." Mercury.

BEST COUNTRY INSTRUMENTAL PERFORMANCE
- Asleep at the Wheel, "One O'Clock Jump," track. Capitol.
Roy Clark, Buck Trent, *Banjo Bandits*. ABC.
Danny Davis & the Nashville Brass, *Cookin' Country*. RCA.
Roy Clark, "Steel Guitar Rag," track. Dot/ABC.
Doc Watson, Merle Watson, "Under the Double Eagle." United Artists.

BEST GOSPEL PERFORMANCE, CONTEMPORARY OR INSPIRATIONAL
- Larry Hart, "What a Friend," track. Genesis.
Evie, *Come On, Ring Those Bells*. Word.
Imperials, *Imperials Live*. Dayspring.
Barry McGuire, *Cosmic Cowboy*. Sparrow.
Barry McGuire, *Destined to Be Yours*. Greentree.
Reba, *The Lady Is a Child*. Greentree/Heartwarming.

BEST GOSPEL PERFORMANCE, TRADITIONAL
- Happy Goodman Family, *Refreshing*. Canaan.
Blackwood Brothers, *His Amazing Love*. Skylite Sing.
Cathedral Quartet, *Sunshine and Roses*. Canaan.
George Beverly Shea, *The Old Rugged Cross*. Word.
J. D. Sumner & the Stamps Quartet, *Elvis' Favorite Gospel Songs*. RCA.

BEST SOUL GOSPEL PERFORMANCE, CONTEMPORARY
- Andrae Crouch & the Disciples, *Live in London*. Light.

Shirley Caeser, "Reach Out and Touch," track. Hob/Roadshow.
Danniebelle, Choralerna, *Danniebelle Live in Sweden with Choralerna*. Sparrow.
Walter Hawkins, *Love Alive II*. Light.
Highland Park Community Choir, Inc., "Because He's Jesus," track. Davida.
Loleatta Holloway, "You Light Up My Life." Gold Mine.

BEST SOUL GOSPEL PERFORMANCE, TRADITIONAL
• Mighty Clouds of Joy, *Live and Direct*. ABC.
James Cleveland & the Charles Fold Singers, directed by Charles Fold, *Tomorrow*. Savoy.
James Cleveland & the Salem Inspirational Choir, directed by Doretha Wade, *I Don't Feel Noways Tired*. Savoy/ABC.
Rev. Isaac Douglas, featuring the San Francisco Community Singers, 21st Century Singers, *Special Appearance*. Creed/Nashboro.
Gladys McFadden, Loving Sisters, "Amazing Grace," track. ABC.

BEST INSPIRATIONAL PERFORMANCE
• B. J. Thomas, *Happy Man*. Myrrh.
Boones, *First Class*. Lamb & Lion.
Tennessee Ernie Ford, *He Touched Me*. Word.
Larry Hart, *Goin' up in Smoke*. Genesis.
Anita Kerr, *Precious Memories*. Word.
Billy Preston, *Behold*. Myrrh.

BEST ETHNIC OR TRADITIONAL RECORDING
• *I'm Ready*, Muddy Waters. Blue Sky.
Chicago Blues at Home, Louis Myers, John Littlejohn, Eddie Taylor, Jimmy Rogers, Johnny Shines, Homesick James Williamson, Bob Myers. Advent.
Clifton Chenier and His Red Hot Louisiana Band in New Orleans, Clifton Chenier. Dixieland/Jubilee.
I Hear Some Blues Downstairs, Fenton Robinson. Alligator.

U.S.A., Memphis Slim & His House Rockers, featuring Matt "Guitar" Murphy. Pearl.

BEST LATIN RECORDING
• *Homenaje a Beny Moré*, Tito Puente. Tico.
"Coro Miyare," track, Fania All Stars. Columbia.
La Raza Latina, Orchestra Harlow. Fania.
Laurindo Almeida Trio, Laurindo Almeida. Dobre.
Lucumi, Macumba, Voodoo, Eddie Palmieri. Epic.
Mongo a la Carte, Mongo Santamaria. Vaya.

BEST INSTRUMENTAL ARRANGEMENT
• Quincy Jones, Robert Freedman, "Main Title (Overture Part One)," *The Wiz* original soundtrack. MCA.
Alan Broadbent, "Aja" (Woody Herman Band). Century.
Chick Corea, "Mad Hatter Rhapsody" (Chick Corea). Polydor.
Joe Roccisano, "Green Earrings" (Woody Herman Band). Century.
Tom Tom 84, "Runnin' " (Earth, Wind & Fire). Columbia.

BEST ARRANGEMENT FOR VOICES
• Bee Gees, "Stayin' Alive" (Bee Gees). RSO.
Quincy Jones, Valerie Simpson, Nick Ashford, "Stuff Like That" (Quincy Jones). A&M.
Gene Puerling, "Cry Me a River" (Singers Unlimited). MPS/Capitol.
Ira Shankman, "High Clouds" (Vocal Jazz Inc.). Grapevine.
McCoy Tyner, "Rotunda" (McCoy Tyner). Milestone.

BEST INSTRUMENTAL COMPOSITION
• "Theme from *Close Encounters of the Third Kind*," John Williams.
"The Captain's Journey," Lee Ritenour.
"Consuelo's Love Theme," Chuck Mangione.

"End of the Yellow Brick Road," Quincy Jones, Nick Ashford, Valerie Simpson.

"Friends," Chick Corea.

BEST CAST SHOW ALBUM
(Composer's Award)
• *Ain't Misbehavin'*, Thomas "Fats" Waller and others. RCA Red Seal.
The Best Little Whorehouse in Texas, Carol Hall. MCA.
Beatlemania, John Lennon, Paul McCartney, George Harrison, Ringo Starr. RCA Red Seal.
The King and I, Richard Rodgers, Oscar Hammerstein II. RCA Red Seal.
On the Twentieth Century, Adolph Green, Betty Comden, Cy Coleman. Columbia.

BEST ALBUM OF ORIGINAL SCORE WRITTEN FOR A MOTION PICTURE OR TV SPECIAL
(Songwriter's Award)
• *Close Encounters of the Third Kind*, John Williams. Arista.
Battlestar Galactica, Stu Phillip, John Tartaglia, Sue Collins, Glen Larson. MCA.
Holocaust: The Story of the Family Weiss, Morton Gould. RCA Red Seal.
Midnight Express, Giorgio Moroder, Chris Bennett, David Castle, William Hayes, Oliver Stone. Casablanca.
Revenge of the Pink Panther, Henry Mancini, composer; Leslie Bricusse, lyricist. United Artists.

BEST ARRANGEMENT ACCOMPANYING VOCALIST(S)
• Maurice White, "Got to Get You into My Life" (Earth, Wind & Fire). RSO.
Chick Corea, "Falling Alice" (Chick Corea). Polydor.
Tom Tom 84, "Fantasy" (Earth, Wind & Fire). Columbia.
Robert Freedman, "It Happens Very Softly" (Andrea Marcovicci). Take Home Tunes.

William Pursell, "We Three Kings" (Christmas Festival Choracle and Orchestra). National Geographic.

ALBUM OF THE YEAR, CLASSICAL
• *Brahms: Concerto for Violin in D Major*, Carlo Maria Giulini conducting the Chicago Symphony (solo: Itzhak Perlman). Angel.
Bach: Mass in B Minor, Neville Marriner conducting the Academy of St. Martin-in-the-Fields. Philips.
Beethoven: Symphonies (9) (Complete), Herbert von Karajan conducting the Berlin Philharmonic. Deutsche Grammophon.
Dvořák: Symphony No. 9 in E Minor ("New World"), Carlo Maria Giulini conducting the Chicago Symphony. Deutsche Grammophon.
Mahler: Symphony No. 4 in G Major, Claudio Abbado conducting the Vienna Philharmonic. Deutsche Grammophon.
Nielsen: Maskarade, John Frandsen conducting the Danish Radio Symphony Orchestra and Chorus (solos: Hansen, Landy, Johansen, Plesner, Bastian, Sorens). Unicorn.
Rachmaninov: Concerto No. 3 in D Minor for Piano (Horowitz Golden Jubilee), Vladimir Horowitz with Eugene Ormandy conducting the New York Philharmonic. RCA.
Sibelius: Symphonies (Complete), Colin Davis conducting the Boston Symphony. Philips.

BEST CLASSICAL PERFORMANCE, ORCHESTRA
(Conductor's Award)
• Herbert von Karajan conducting the Berlin Philharmonic, *Beethoven: Symphonies (9) (Complete)*. Deutsche Grammophon.
Claudio Abbado conducting the Vienna Philharmonic, *Mahler: Symphony No. 9 in D Major*. Deutsche Grammophon.
Pierre Boulez conducting the New York Philharmonic, *Varèse: Amériques;*

Arcana; Ionisation (Boulez Conducts Varèse). Columbia.

Carlo Maria Giulini conducting the Chicago Symphony, *Bruckner: Symphony No. 9 in D Minor*. Angel.

Neville Marriner conducting the Concertgebouw Orchestra, *Holst: The Planets*. Philips.

Kurt Masur conducting the Leipzig Gewandhaus Orchestra, *Mendelssohn: Symphonies (5) (Complete)*. Vanguard.

Zubin Mehta conducting the New York Philharmonic, *Stravinsky: The Rite of Spring*. Columbia.

André Previn conducting the Chicago Symphony, *Shostakovich: Symphony No. 5*. Angel.

André Previn conducting the London Symphony Orchestra, *Messiaen: Turangalîla Symphony*. Angel.

Leonard Slatkin conducting the St. Louis Symphony, *Rachmaninov: Symphony No. 1 in D Minor*. Candide.

BEST CHAMBER MUSIC PERFORMANCE (INSTRUMENTAL OR VOCAL)

• Itzhak Perlman, Vladimir Ashkenazy, *Beethoven: Sonatas for Violin and Piano (Complete)*. London.

Melos Quartet with Mstislav Rostropovich, *Schubert: Quintet in C Major for Strings*. Deutsche Grammophon.

David Munrow conducting the David Munrow Recorder Consort, members of the Early Music Consort of London, *The Art of the Recorder*. Angel.

Itzhak Perlman, Pincas Zukerman, *Duets for 2 Violins*. Angel.

Artur Rubinstein, members of the Guarneri Quartet, *Mozart: Quartets for Piano and Strings*. RCA.

Tokyo String Quartet, *Bartók: Quartet No. 2 for Strings, Op. 17; Quartet No. 6*. Deutsche Grammophon.

John Williams, Carlos Bonell, Brian Gascoigne, Morris Pert, Keith Marjoram, *John Williams and Friends*. Columbia.

BEST CLASSICAL PERFORMANCE, INSTRUMENTAL SOLOIST(S) (WITH ORCHESTRA)

• Vladimir Horowitz, piano (Ormandy conducting the Philadelphia Orchestra), *Rachmaninov: Concerto No. 3 in D Minor for Piano (Horowitz Golden Jubilee)*. RCA.

Emanuel Ax, piano (Ormandy conducting the Philadelphia Orchestra), *Chopin: Concerto No. 2 in F Minor for Piano*. RCA.

Arnold Jacobs, tuba (Barenboim conducting the Chicago Symphony), *Vaughan Williams: Concerto for Tuba*. Deutsche Grammophon.

Itzhak Perlman, violin (Giulini conducting the Chicago Symphony), *Brahms: Concerto for Violin in D Major*. Angel.

Murray Perahia, piano (Perahia conducting the English Chamber Orchestra), *Mozart: Concertos for Piano No. 21 in C Major and No. 9 in E Flat Major*. Columbia.

Mstislav Rostropovich, cello (Giulini conducting the London Philharmonic), *Dvořák: Concerto for Cello in B Minor; Saint-Saëns: Concerto for Cello No. 1 in A Minor*. Angel.

BEST CLASSICAL PERFORMANCE, INSTRUMENTAL SOLOIST(S) (WITHOUT ORCHESTRA)

• Vladimir Horowitz, piano, *The Horowitz Concerts 1977/78*. RCA.

Claudio Arrau, piano, *Liszt: 12 Transcendental Etudes and 3 Etudes de Concert*. Philips.

Alfred Brendel, piano, *Bach: Italian Concerto; Choral Prelude; Prelude S922; Chromatic Fantasy and Fugue; Fantasy and Fugue*. Philips.

Paul Jacobs, piano, *Debussy: Preludes for Piano, Books I and II*. Nonesuch.

Maurizio Pollini, piano, *Beethoven: The Late Piano Sonatas*. Deutsche Grammophon.

Charles Rosen, piano, *Beethoven: Variations on a Waltz by Diabelli*. Peters.

Rudolf Serkin, piano, *Rudolf Serkin on Television*. Columbia.

BEST OPERA RECORDING

• *Lehár: The Merry Widow*, Julius Rudel conducting the New York City Opera Orchestra and Chorus (solos: Sills, Titus). Angel.

Charpentier: Louise, Julius Rudel conducting the Chorus and Orchestra of the Paris Opera (solos: Sills, Gedda). Angel.

Mozart: La Clemenza di Tito, Colin Davis conducting the Orchestra and Chorus of the Royal Opera House, Covent Garden (solos: Baker, Popp, Minton, von Stade, Burrows). Philips.

Nielsen: Maskarade, John Frandsen conducting the Danish Radio Symphony Orchestra and Chorus (solos: Hansen, Landy, Johansen, Plesner, Bastian, Sorensen). Unicorn.

Puccini: La Fanciulla del West, Zubin Mehta conducting the Chorus and Orchestra of the Royal Opera House, Covent Garden (solos: Neblett, Domingo, Milnes). Deutsche Grammophon.

Shostakovich: The Nose, Gennady Rozhdestvensky conducting the Chorus and Orchestra of the Moscow Chamber Opera with soloists. Columbia.

R. Strauss: Salome, Herbert von Karajan conducting the Berlin Philharmonic (solos: Behrens, van Dam). Angel.

Verdi: La Traviata, Carlos Kleiber conducting the Bavarian State Opera Chorus and Orchestra (solos: Cotrubas, Domingo, Milnes). Deutsche Grammophon.

BEST CLASSICAL PERFORMANCE, CHORAL (OTHER THAN OPERA)

• Sir Georg Solti, conductor, Margaret Hillis, choral director, Chicago Symphony Orchestra and Chorus, *Beethoven: Missa Solemnis*. London.

Maurice Abravanel conducting the Utah Chorale and Symphony Orchestra, *Bloch: Sacred Service*. Angel.

Leonard Bernstein, conductor, Joseph Flummerfelt, choral director, Westminster Choir and New York Philharmonic, *Haydn: Mass No. 9 in D Minor ("Lord Nelson Mass")*. Columbia.

Leonard Bernstein conducting the Trinity Boys' Choir, English Bach Festival Chorus, English Bach Festival Orchestra, *Stravinsky: Les Noces and Mass*. Deutsche Grammophon.

Neville Marriner conducting the Chorus and Academy of St. Martin-in-the-Fields, *Bach: Mass in B Minor*. Philips.

Riccardo Muti, conductor, Norbert Balatsch, choral director, New Philharmonia Chorus and Orchestra, *Vivaldi: Gloria in D Major and Magnificat*. Angel.

Leonard Slatkin, conductor, Thomas Peck, choral director, St. Louis Symphony Chorus and Orchestra, *Prokofiev: Alexander Nevsky*. Candide.

Sir Georg Solti, conductor, John Alldis, choral director, London Philharmonic Choir and Orchestra, *Walton: Belshazzar's Feast*. London.

BEST CLASSICAL PERFORMANCE, VOCAL SOLOIST

• Luciano Pavarotti (various accompanists), *Luciano Pavarotti, Hits from Lincoln Center*. London.

Teresa Berganza (Asensio conducting the English Chamber Orchestra), *Teresa Berganza, Favorite Zarzuela Arias*. Zambra.

Maria Callas (various conductors and orchestras), *Maria Callas/The Legend: The Unreleased Recordings*. Angel.

Dietrich Fischer-Dieskau (Kubelik conducting the Bavarian Radio Orchestra), *Wagner: Arias*. Angel.

Marilyn Horne (Bernstein conducting the Orchestre National de France), *Ravel: Shéhérazade*. Columbia.

Christa Ludwig (Böhm conducting the Vienna Philharmonic), *Brahms: Alto Rhapsody*. Deutsche Grammophon.

Galina Vishnevskaya (Rostropovich conducting the London Philharmonic), *Mussorgsky: Songs and Dances of Death*. Angel.

On Stage, Lily Tomlin. Arista.
Sex and Violins, Martin Mull. ABC.
The Wizard of Comedy, Richard Pryor. Laff.

BEST ENGINEERED RECORDING, CLASSICAL

- Bud Graham, Arthur Kendy, Ray Moore, *Varèse: Amériques; Arcana; Ionisation (Boulez Conducts Varèse)* (Boulez conducting the New York Philharmonic). Columbia.
- Marc Aubort, *Prokofiev: Alexander Nevsky* (Slatkin conducting the St. Louis Symphony and Chorus). Candide.
- Paul Goodman, *Berlioz: Symphonie Fantastique* (Ormandy conducting the Philadelphia Orchestra). RCA.
- Gunter Hermann, *Beethoven: Symphonies (9) (Complete)* (von Karajan conducting the Berlin Philharmonic). Deutsche Grammophon.
- Gunter Hermann, *Bruckner: Symphony No. 5 in B Flat Major* (von Karajan conducting the Berlin Philharmonic). Deutsche Grammophon.
- Chris Parker, *Messiaen: Turangalîla Symphony* (Previn conducting the London Symphony). Angel.
- Jack Renner, *Fredrick Fennell, Cleveland Symphonic Winds*. Telarc.
- Doug Sax, Bud Wyatt, *Wagner: Die Walküre: Ride of the Valkyries; Tristan: Prelude Act 1; Götterdämmerung: Siegfried's Funeral Music; Siegfried: Forest Murmurs* (Leinsdorf conducting the Los Angeles Philharmonic). Sheffield Lab.
- *Bach: Mass in B Minor*, Marriner conducting the Chorus and Academy of St. Martin-in-the-Fields. Philips.
- *Holst: The Planets*, Marriner conducting the Concertgebouw Orchestra. Philips.

BEST COMEDY RECORDING

- *A Wild and Crazy Guy*, Steve Martin. Warner Bros.
- *The Rutles (All You Need Is Cash)*, Rutles. Warner Bros.

BEST SPOKEN WORD RECORDING

- *Citizen Kane* (original motion picture soundtrack), Orson Welles. Mark 56.
- *John Steinbeck: The Grapes of Wrath* (excerpts), read by Henry Fonda. Caedmon.
- *The Nixon Interviews with David Frost*, Richard Nixon, David Frost. Polydor.
- *Roots* (original soundtrack for TV). Warner Bros.
- *Wuthering Heights*, Dame Judith Anderson, Claire Bloom, James Mason, George Rose, Gordon Gould. Caedmon.

BEST RECORDING FOR CHILDREN

- *The Muppet Show*, Muppets. Arista.
- *Charlie Brown's All-Stars* (TV special). Charlie Brown Productions.
- *The Hobbit* (soundtrack), Orson Bean, John Huston, Hans Conried. Buena Vista/Disneyland.
- *Peter and the Wolf*, David Bowie, Eugene Ormandy conducting the Philadelphia Orchestra. RCA.
- *Sesame Street Fever*, Muppets, Robin Gibb. Sesame Street.

BEST ENGINEERED RECORDING (OTHER THAN CLASSICAL)

- Roger Nichols, Al Schmitt, "FM (No Static at All)" (Steely Dan). MCA.
- George Massenberg, *All 'n' All* (Earth, Wind & Fire). Columbia.
- John Neal, *Close Encounters of the Third Kind* (John Williams). Arista.
- Alan Parsons, *Pyramid* (Alan Parsons Project). Arista.
- Allen Sides, John Neal, *A Tribute to Ethel Waters* (Diahann Carroll). Orinda.
- Bruce Swedien, *Sounds . . . and Stuff Like That* (Quincy Jones). A&M.

BEST ALBUM PACKAGE
(Art Director's Award)

- Johnny Lee, Tony Lane, *Boys in the Trees* (Carly Simon). Elektra.
- John Berg, Paula Scher, *Heads* (Bob James). Columbia.
- Ron Coro, *The Cars* (Cars). Elektra.
- Ron Coro, Johnny Lee, *Out of the Woods* (Oregon). Elektra.
- Gribbitt/Tim Bryant, *Last Kiss* (Fandango). RCA.
- Tony Lane, *Bruce Roberts* (Bruce Roberts). Elektra.
- Juni Osaki, *Children of Sanchez* (Chuck Mangione). A&M.
- Barbara Wojirsch, *Non-Fiction* (Steve Kuhn). ECM.

BEST ALBUM NOTES
(Annotator's Award)

- Michael Brooks, *A Bing Crosby Collection, Vols. 1 and 2*. Columbia.
- Irving Kolodin, Bill Bender, *Beethoven: Symphonies (9)* (von Karajan conducting the Berlin Philharmonic). Polydor.
- Leonard Feather, *Ellington at Carnegie Hall 1943*. Prestige.

- Alan Lomax, *Georgia Sea Island Songs* (various artists). New World.
- Dan Morgenstern, *The Individualism of Pee Wee Russell*. Savoy.
- Phil David Baker, R. D. Darrell, *Works of Carpenter/Gilbert/Weiss/Powell* (Los Angeles Philharmonic). New World.

BEST HISTORICAL REPACKAGE ALBUM

- *Lester Young Story, Vol. 3*. Columbia.
- *A Bing Crosby Collection, Vols. 1 and 2*. Columbia.
- *The First Recorded Sounds 1888 to 1929* (Edison). Mark 56.
- *The Greatest Group of Them All* (Ravens). Savoy.
- *La Divina* (Maria Callas). Angel.

PRODUCER OF THE YEAR

- Bee Gees, Albhy Galuten, Karl Richardson
- Peter Asher
- Quincy Jones
- Alan Parsons
- Phil Ramone

• 1979 •

Gotta Rock . . . As Disco Rolls Out

Midway through the 1979 awards show, Grammy watchers couldn't believe their bugged-out eyes. There, at center stage, was rock rebel leader Bob Dylan, dressed in a virgin white tuxedo, performing before the same music establishment that had all but snubbed him for the past decade and a half. Dylan did win a Grammy for his partial contribution to 1972's Album of the Year, *The Concert for Bangla Desh,* but he never won one for any of his solo artistic accomplishments. Now, at the Grammy ceremony, the music establishment audience gave Dylan a standing ovation as he finished singing "Gotta Serve Somebody," a song that must have sounded to some like a surrender.

The times, as Dylan had sung years earlier, were certainly a-changing.

So were the Grammys. N.A.R.A.S.— finally, said its critics—set up special awards for rock & roll music as well as disco, jazz fusion and the classical producer of the year, bringing the year's tally to an all-time high of 57 categories. The inclusion of several new Grammys for rock marked an enormous battle won, even though the victory was diminished by the fact that the new prizes would be bestowed off the air just prior to the Grammycast.

Ever since the awards were created in 1958, N.A.R.A.S. failed to recognize rock music adequately. When the academy did make an occasional effort to give the genre its own awards, as it did in 1959 and again from 1961 to 1966, the prizes often went astray. Nat King Cole won the statuette for 1959's best performance by a Top 40 artist (which was designated an r&r award till just a few weeks before the Grammy show) for a song that never made the Top 40. The winner of best male

Doobie Brothers' best record and song "What a Fool Believes" was described as "carefully crafted, gorgeously sung, beautifully arranged."

contemporary (r&r) vocal performance of 1965 was country crooner Roger Miller for "King of the Road." Finally, just after a prize went to a real rocker—Paul McCartney for his vocal performance of the Beatles' "Eleanor Rigby" in 1966— the category was dropped altogether. Now rock awards were not only back, but back in the right hands. The first new best male rock vocal performance prize was bestowed to a grateful—and surprised— Bob Dylan. "I didn't expect this," the legendary rocker said, accepting it, "and I want to thank the Lord."

Dylan, raised a Jew, declared himself a "born again" Christian at a time when an evangelical movement was sweeping the country—and the Grammys. More than seven winners thanked Jesus or God in their acceptance speeches on awards night. Dylan would lose his passion for Christianity after the early 1980s, but for now he embraced his new faith with public fervor. The "Somebody" he "gotta serve" was God. When the *L.A. Times* asked about the heavy emphasis on Christian messages on his latest album (*Slow Train Coming*), Dylan replied: "I know what some people have been saying, but this is no fad. It's the future. We're just laying the foundation."

Winner of the best female rock vocal award also claimed to be "born again," although she was hardly a rocker in the same sense as Dylan. It was Donna Summer, who won for her "Hot Stuff" single from *Bad Girls*. Critics wondered: If the queen of the decadent disco movement was recently saved, too, could the collapse of the dance craze be far behind?

Summer began the Grammy race with five nominations. She was the clear front-runner to take Album of the Year, as well as the new trophy for Best Disco Recording—a category for which she lobbied heavily at last year's awards.

"All together, Summer had a single or album in the national Top 10 for 36 of 52 weeks in 1979," reported *L.A. Times* music critic Robert Hilburn. "For 13 of those weeks, she had two singles in the Top 10. In a field of hit-makers, she was the biggest hit-maker. Plus, I may be idealistic, but I think Summer also has one other thing going for her: She made the best album."

Also up for Album of the Year was the artist who tied Summer in total nominations—Kenny Rogers, whose *The Gambler* and its title track were contenders for the LP honor and Record of the Year. Billy Joel's *52nd Street* was in the album race, too, but was considered a long shot, since Joel won Record of the Year last year for "Just the Way You Are."

Some of Summer's most serious competition came from a group of old pros— also born again, in the professional

Capitol Records

Grammycast host Kenny Rogers lost his bids for best record and album, but still got lucky with the country vocals gold for "The Gambler."

sense. Wrote the *L. A. Herald Examiner:* "Although the Doobie Brothers have been a successful rock band for close to 15 years, it's only in the past few years, with the addition of songwriter-singer Michael McDonald, that the group has attained massive popularity by broadening their original hard-rock stance into a smoother, brisker romantic pop style." The Doobies had the most nominations in all—six. Their *Minute by Minute* LP and title track were up for Album and Song of the Year as well as the pop group vocals award; "What a Fool Believes" was contending for Record and Song of the Year plus Best Arrangement Accompanying Vocalist(s).

The *L.A. Times* predicted that the Record of the Year winner would be "I Will Survive," the triumphant disco standard that was also a comeback song for Gloria Gaynor, who was once officially crowned "Queen of the Discos" at a coronation ceremony held in New York by the National Association of Discotheque Disc Jockeys for her debut album, *Never Can Say Goodbye,* in 1975. (Soon afterward, Gaynor's career went into decline as she was eclipsed by Donna Summer.) "I'm no disco fan," the *Times*'s Hilburn wrote about "I Will Survive," "but this *Rocky*-like slice of self-affirmation transcends that usually narrow genre. The only thing that worries me about its chances is the possibility of a disco backlash."

All of the top categories resulted in surprise choices.

Album of the Year turned out to be *52nd Street,* Billy's Joel's salute to the onetime Tin Pan Alley of New York, which included such powerful songs of self-reliance as "My Life" (a nondisco equivalent to "I Will Survive," said the critics). Joel's producer, Phil Ramone, "seemed just as stunned this time as he was last year when Joel walked off with the award for Record of the Year," observed the *L.A. Herald Examiner*. Ramone spoke again on behalf of his absent singer, saying, "I didn't feel we were going to win this year either. I'm proud of the album and I know Billy is, too—but this year, I'm shocked!"

The Record and Song of the Year honors went to the stylized, soul/rock ballad "What a Fool Believes," about former lovers who run into each other, triggering old feelings of love and longing that were always stronger on his part than hers. The victories of "Fool" were hailed by the *Herald Examiner* as signaling "a return to normalcy" for rock music. They were also even hailed by normally cynical rock critics like Dave Marsh, who wrote, "For once the Grammys spent its accolades where they were deserved. Carefully crafted, gorgeously sung, beautifully arranged, and pristinely recorded, 'What a Fool Believes' holds up as one of the finest samples of seventies L.A. pop."

The Doobies also earned the awards for arrangement and pop group vocals. "I speak for the band when I say that this is a form of acceptance we never got

before," Doobie savior Michael McDonald told reporters as he pushed his way through a sea of TV cameras. "To be nominated was great. To be picked was even better." McDonald cowrote "Fool" with non-Doobie Kenny Loggins. Loggins remembered to reporters: "I met Michael at the front door of the house and we were writing from the first moment we met. I feel great about this."

Gloria Gaynor's "I Will Survive" picked up Best Disco Recording, topping Donna Summer's *Bad Girls* and Michael Jackson's "Don't Stop Till You Get Enough," both strong contenders. Summer's loss was ironic considering the category was created, to a large extent, thanks to her impassioned lobbying for it at last year's ceremony after she won an r&b award. Her victory this year, for a disco song in the rock & roll lineup instead of the disco slot, made the scenario even more bizarre. Worse, Gaynor's Best Disco Recording winner, "I Will Survive," would turn out to be the genre's death knell at the Grammys. Disco may have been so influential just last year that *Saturday Night Fever* proved contagious at the Grammys, but this year the *Herald Examiner* reported "a real disco backlash." The *Washington Post* added: "No funeral marches were played, but the death of disco was solemnly commemorated. It was not that disco records didn't win any prizes, just that no fuss was made about them." Soon after the Grammycast, N.A.R.A.S. announced that the new disco category would be dropped.

When Michael Jackson ended up with the accolade for best r&b male vocal performance, it marked the first victory for an artist who would one day win more Grammys in a year than anyone else (in 1983—for *Thriller*). "Don't Stop Till You Get Enough" was from Jackson's first solo album (*Off the Wall*) since breaking away from his brothers' group

> "No funeral marches were played, but the death of disco was solemnly" observed.

act in 1978. "He wasn't at all sure that he could make a name for himself on his own," Quincy Jones told the French magazine *Actuel* about Jackson years later. "And me, too. I had my doubts," Jackson told *Melody Maker.* The result, produced by Jones, nearly soared off the charts when *Off the Wall* sold 9 million copies.

The backlash against disco helped to welcome back a number of past winners in other categories. Dionne Warwick hadn't won a Grammy since 1970's "I'll Never Fall in Love Again" and hadn't had a hit record since 1974's "Then You Came." Now, noted *Variety,* she "scored the coup of the evening by besting Donna Summer in two categories, r&b and pop female vocals." Both victories were for comeback hits: the Barry Manilow–produced "I'll Never Love This Way Again" (best female pop vocal performance) and "Deja Vu" (best female r&b vocal performance). "Warwick's two awards," declared the *Herald Examiner,* "restored this balladeer's place in the pop pantheon."

Herb Alpert hadn't won a Grammy since 1966, when he snagged two for "What Now My Love." Now he was facing formidable opposition for Best Pop Instrumental Performance in the person of John Williams, whose latest super-film-score composition was "Theme from *Superman* (Main Title)." Williams, who recently picked up the baton at the Boston Pops, would win the film score honors again this year as well as Best Instrumental Composition for *Superman* (following up on his previous Grammy winners, *Jaws, Star Wars* and *Close Encounters of the Third Kind*), but he yielded to Alpert in the pop instrumental slot. Alpert's "Rise" was a dance number written by Randy Badazz, Alpert's cousin. It might have proved to be only a middling hit in the discos if it hadn't been adopted by the soap opera *General Hospital* to underscore some of the steamy scenes between the show's hot couple, Luke and Laura. Thereafter, "Rise" rose fast to number one on the singles charts.

The "Liszt of jazz" Oscar Peterson snagged the instrumental soloist's laurels for *Jousts.*

Other returning Grammy greats included Earth, Wind & Fire for Best Rhythm & Blues Song "After the Love Has Gone," which peaked at number two on the weekly singles charts, and Paul McCartney's group Wings. McCartney was making news in 1979 by calling for a concert to benefit the victims of war-ravaged Cambodia. His fans thought that meant a Beatles reunion and began fueling a frenzy of speculation worldwide. It was something of an anticlimax, then, when McCartney and his Wings, instead of the old Fab Four, took center stage at London's Hammersmith Odeon Theater for the relief concert in December. There they performed the definitive version of "Rockestra Theme," the recording of which earned them the Grammy for best rock instrumental performance.

The Eagles came back, too—but for their swan song at the Grammys and as a professional singing group. Their award was for best group rock vocal performance for their last number-one-ranked single, "Heartache Tonight." Soon thereafter the Eagles fell victim to inner-group feuding. "I knew the Eagles were over halfway through [the final album] *The Long Run,*" band member Glenn Frey told the *L.A. Times*. The group used the excuse of having to rehearse for *The Long Run* for not showing up as promised at the 1977 Grammy Awards.

The Eagles beat out three of the five nominees also in line for Best New Artist: Dire Straits, the Knack and the Blues Brothers (the comic duo formed by *Saturday Night Live*'s John Belushi and Dan Aykroyd). Dire Straits was considered a strong contender for top newcomer, but so were two other nominees—Rickie Lee Jones and comedian Robin Williams.

The media were rooting for singer-songwriter Rickie Lee Jones, who was considered a kind of Joni Mitchell for the dawning 1980s. She was up for four Grammys in all, including Song of the Year for "Chuck E.'s in Love," but she won only the Best New Artist prize.

The new award for Best Jazz Fusion Performance was claimed by a group that was used as a frequent example of previously snubbed talent: Weather Report, led by keyboardist Joe Zawinul and sax player Wayne Shorter, both of whom had once worked as sidemen for Miles Davis. Weather Report's *8:30* album was a two-disc set that included three sides of concert performances and one side of studio recordings that together chronicled the band's career since it was formed in 1971.

A loser in the new fusion category, Chick Corea, nonetheless proved a winner of the same award he and his band took last year for best jazz group instrumental performance. This time he was teamed with vibraphonist Gary Burton for *Duet*. Among other jazz champs from last year, pianist Oscar Peterson reprised the soloist honors for *Jousts*. Ella Fitzgerald last won the vocals prize in 1976 but came back again, topping Sarah Vaughan, for *Fine and Mellow*. Duke Ellington died in 1974 but was awarded a posthumous Grammy for recordings made of a performance he and his band gave at the Crystal Ballroom in Fargo, North Dakota, in 1940.

Time-Life Records commemorated the 20th year since Billie Holiday's death by issuing some of her classic works,

earning the label the prize for Best Historical Reissue.

The title of 1979's Best Country Song almost contributed to it not getting recorded: "You Decorated My Life" by Debbie Hupp and Bob Morrison. Kenny Rogers was among those who didn't like the sound of it, but after initial reluctance, he finally caved in and performed the tune on vinyl. Then the tune hit number one on the country chart and number seven on the pop lineup.

Rogers was at the peak of his career when he was asked to host the Grammycast, which he did to mixed notices. (The *Washington Post* said his performance proved that more than disco was dead.) Of Rogers's five Grammy nominations, including bids for Album and Record of the Year, his only victory was for best male country vocal performance for last year's Best Country Song, "The Gambler." (The song and Rogers also reaped two Academy of Country Music Awards this year and three prizes from the Country Music Association.) Quincy Jones was expected to be named Producer of the Year for his work with Michael Jackson, but, in a major upset, Rogers's producer, Larry Butler, snatched the accolade instead.

The kudos for female country vocals went to Emmylou Harris exclusively despite the fact that her *Blue Kentucky Girl* LP also included contributions from two other country divas, who, like Harris, moved to Hollywood recently—Dolly Parton and Linda Ronstadt.

The Charlie Daniels Band wasn't taken seriously as country talent in the early part of its career because of its crossover rock appeal, but when it added a heavy fiddle sound to "The Devil Went Down to Georgia," the band nabbed the laurels for group vocals and thereby reclaimed their country status. The father-son guitar-picking team of Doc and Merle Watson snagged the prize for instrumental performance ("Big Sandy/Leather Britches"), which they last shared in 1974.

Given the importance that Christianity

was playing at this year's awards, the religious categories took on a special priority. Grammycast host Kenny Rogers even told the audience his belief that "gospel is the backbone to all the music in our society."

The Mississippi-born gospel quartet the Blackwood Brothers won five awards between 1966 and 1973 but hadn't won since. Now they nabbed best traditional gospel performance for *Lift Up the Name of Jesus*. The Imperials won a religious prize for a third time in five years for *Heed the Call* (Best Gospel Performance, Contemporary or Inspirational), and B. J. Thomas came back for a third year in a row in the category of Best Inspirational Performance for *You Gave Me Love (When No One Gave Me a Prayer)*.

The two soul gospel winners were also repeats from last year. N.A.R.A.S. voters again found the heavenly harmonies of the Mighty Clouds of Joy irresistible when they honored the group for *Changing Times*. The Clouds had enormous crossover appeal: They frequently shared a concert bill with an unlikely mix of talent that included Earth, Wind & Fire, the Rolling Stones, Andrae Crouch and the artist the group beat twice this year to win the Grammy—double nominee Rev. James Cleveland. Crouch won the contemporary soul gospel performance prize for *I'll Be Thinking of You,* a selection from which he performed on the Grammycast, receiving rave reviews and a standing ovation.

Chicago bluesman Muddy Waters returned, too—for his third Grammy in a row for Best Ethnic or Traditional Recording. His latest LP, *Muddy "Mississippi" Waters Live,* earned him the sixth—and last—Grammy of his career. Waters would reap no more before his death of a heart attack in 1983.

Another three-year winning streak was marked in the children's recording category by Jim Henson's Muppets for their score to *The Muppet Movie.* (Curiously, it beat out three Sesame Street recordings, including *Sesame Disco!,* a follow-up to last year's losing—but hilarious—nominee *Sesame Street Fever.*) The Best Latin Recording was an eponymous album by Irakere, the folk-jazz fusion group from Cuba.

The Ages of Man won an Emmy in 1966 for being the Outstanding Single Dramatic Program of the Year and featured John Gielgud quoting Shakespearean verse on the subject of aging. Its transposition from TV to vinyl this year brought it the Grammy for best spoken word recording.

Had Robin Williams won his bid to be Best New Artist, he would have become only the second comedian to hold the honor (following Bob Newhart in 1960). Instead, he won a Grammy for Best Comedy Recording for his album *Reality . . . What a Concept,* which showcased Williams testing the limits of sanity and taste through rantings of improvisational humor.

When Billy Joel won best album, his producer was just as "shocked" as last year.

The winner of Best Cast Show Album challenged the theatrical tastes of Broadway in 1979 in startling new ways. *Sweeney Todd* was Stephen Sondheim's bizarre and highly experimental musical, starring George Hearn and Angela Lansbury, about a murderous barber in 19th-century London whose victims become the fillings of his girlfriend's meat pies. Since the show was also arguably an operetta, it won best engineered classical recording but wasn't nominated for any other classical awards for which it should have been eligible, such as Best Opera Recording.

Sir Georg Solti and the Chicago Symphony Orchestra last won the Classical Album of the Year prize in 1975 for their recording of all nine Beethoven symphonies. This year they reclaimed the prize (now called Best Classical Album), as well as the orchestral honors, for tackling Brahms's four symphonic works, although they did not achieve the same critical praise that they did before from *High Fidelity*. The publication complained that the orchestra "everywhere sounds big" and blamed Solti's conducting and London Records' "gargantuan brass." It added: "The Chicago's recent Brahms series under James Levine sounds crisper, brighter" by comparison.

Solti conducted another work by Brahms to win the choral laurels with choral conductor Margaret Hillis and the Chicago Symphony Chorus. "Solti recorded the Brahms *German Requiem* once before," *High Fidelity* noted, "an early-Fifties Capitol album that constituted the sole commercial documentation of his tenure with the Frankfurt Opera. . . . The new version is also outstanding." James Mallinson, Solti's producer at London Records, was hailed as the first winner of the new Classical Producer of the Year award.

For a fourth year in a row, Vladimir Horowitz reaped a soloist award for works he'd never recorded before: Liszt's *Mephisto Waltz*, Schumann's *Humoreske* and Rachmaninov's *Barcarolle* and *Humoresque*. The award for soloist with orchestral accompaniment went to Grammy newcomer Maurizio Pollini for Bartók Concertos Nos. 1 and 2. *High Fidelity* said, "Soloist and conductor are at one with each other and with the music." The chamber music prize went to Copland's *Appalachian Spring* with Dennis Russell Davies conducting the St. Paul Chamber Orchestra in a bravura performance that was recorded with superior electronic equipment.

High Fidelity wrote of the Best Opera Recording: Tenor "Jon Vickers' *Peter Grimes* [by Benjamin Britten] is the closest identification of an operatic performer and role in recent memory, and it's doubly fortunate that Philips has gotten it down on disc." Vickers failed to be nominated for best classical vocalist. Instead the award went to Luciano Pavarotti, who was beginning to emerge as a superstar in the late 1970s with a burdensome schedule of professional appearances. "The steady overexploitation of Pavarotti's voice during the past few years," wrote *High Fidelity*, "has impaired its once considerable attractiveness and the ease with which he used to produce his brilliant high notes."

The Grammy show took place once again at the Shrine Auditorium in Los Angeles and proved, said the *Herald Examiner,* to be "an evening in which pop music vanquished both disco and country." Presenters and performers included George Benson, Johnny Cash, the Charlie Daniels Band, the Doobie Brothers, Bob Dylan, James Galway, Kenny Loggins, Dionne Warwick, Debby Boone, George Burns, Natalie Cole, Deborah Harry, Isaac Hayes, Quincy Jones and Kris Kristofferson. James Galway performed a flute solo. Sarah Vaughan and Joe Williams each sang a jazz song.

A highlight of the show was Neil Diamond and Barbra Streisand's performance of Record of the Year nominee "You Don't Bring Me Flowers," which was touching in more ways than one. "Streisand stroked Diamond's cheek at the climax of the song," noted the *Herald Examiner,* "to screams from their fans."

• 1979 •

The awards ceremony was broadcast on CBS from the Los Angeles Shrine Auditorium on February 27, 1980, for the eligibility period October 1, 1978, to September 30, 1979.

ALBUM OF THE YEAR
• *52nd Street*, Billy Joel. Columbia.
Bad Girls, Donna Summer. Casablanca.
Breakfast in America, Supertramp. A&M.

The Gambler, Kenny Rogers. United Artists.

Minute by Minute, Doobie Brothers. Warner Bros.

RECORD OF THE YEAR

- "What a Fool Believes," Doobie Brothers. Warner Bros.
"After the Love Has Gone," Earth, Wind & Fire. ARC/CBS.
"The Gambler," Kenny Rogers. United Artists.
"I Will Survive," Gloria Gaynor. Polydor.
"You Don't Bring Me Flowers," Barbra Streisand, Neil Diamond. Columbia.

SONG OF THE YEAR
(Songwriter's Award)
- "What a Fool Believes," Kenny Loggins, Michael McDonald.
"After the Love Has Gone," David Foster, Jay Graydon, Bill Champlin.
"Chuck E.'s in Love," Rickie Lee Jones.
"Honesty," Billy Joel.
"I Will Survive," Dino Fekaris, Freddie Perren.
"Minute by Minute," Lester Abrams, Michael McDonald.
"Reunited," Dino Fekaris, Freddie Perren.
"She Believes in Me," Steve Gibb.

BEST NEW ARTIST

- Rickie Lee Jones
Blues Brothers
Dire Straits
Knack
Robin Williams

BEST POP VOCAL PERFORMANCE, MALE

- Billy Joel, *52nd Street*. Columbia.
Robert John, "Sad Eyes." EMI-America.
Kenny Rogers, "She Believes in Me." United Artists.
Rod Stewart, "Do Ya Think I'm Sexy?" Warner Bros.
James Taylor, "Up on the Roof." Columbia.

BEST POP VOCAL PERFORMANCE, FEMALE

- Dionne Warwick, "I'll Never Love This Way Again." Arista.
Gloria Gaynor, "I Will Survive," track. Polydor.
Rickie Lee Jones, "Chuck E.'s in Love," track. Warner Bros.
Melissa Manchester, "Don't Cry Out Loud." Arista.
Donna Summer, *Bad Girls*. Casablanca.

BEST POP PERFORMANCE BY A DUO OR GROUP WITH VOCAL

- Doobie Brothers, *Minute by Minute*. Warner Bros.
Commodores, "Sail On," track. Motown.
Little River Band, "Lonesome Loser." Capitol.
Barbra Streisand, Neil Diamond, "You Don't Bring Me Flowers." Columbia.
Supertramp, *Breakfast in America*. A&M.

BEST POP INSTRUMENTAL PERFORMANCE

- Herb Alpert, "Rise." A&M.
Chuck Mangione, *An Evening of Magic*. A&M.
Zubin Mehta, New York Philharmonic, *Manhattan* (music from the film), side 2. CBS.
Frank Mills, "Music Box Dancer," track. Polydor.
John Williams, "Theme from *Superman* (Main Title)," track. Warner Bros.

BEST ROCK VOCAL PERFORMANCE, MALE

- Bob Dylan, "Gotta Serve Somebody." Columbia.
Joe Jackson, "Is She Really Going Out with Him?" A&M.
Robert Palmer, "Bad Case of Loving You (Doctor, Doctor)." Island/Warner Bros.
Rod Stewart, "Blondes (Have More Fun)," track. Warner Bros.
Frank Zappa, "Dancin' Fool." Zappa.

BEST ROCK VOCAL PERFORMANCE, FEMALE

- Donna Summer, "Hot Stuff." Casablanca.

Cindy Bullens, "Survivor." United Artists.

Rickie Lee Jones, "The Last Chance Texaco," track. Warner Bros.

Bonnie Raitt, "You're Gonna Get What's Coming," track. Warner Bros.

Carly Simon, "Vengeance." Elektra.

Tanya Tucker, *TNT*. MCA.

BEST ROCK PERFORMANCE BY A DUO OR GROUP WITH VOCAL

- Eagles, "Heartache Tonight." Asylum.

Blues Brothers, *Briefcase Full of Blues*. Atlantic.

Cars, *Candy-O*. Elektra.

Dire Straits, "Sultans of Swing." Warner Bros.

Knack, "My Sharona." Capitol.

Styx, *Cornerstone*. A&M.

BEST ROCK INSTRUMENTAL PERFORMANCE

- Wings, "Rockestra Theme," track. Columbia.

Allman Brothers Band, "Pegasus," track. Capricorn.

Dixie Dregs, *Night of the Living Dregs*. Capricorn.

Neil Larsen, "High Gear." A&M.

Frank Zappa, "Rat Tomago," track. Zappa.

BEST RHYTHM & BLUES SONG
(Songwriter's Award)

- "After the Love Has Gone," David Foster, Jay Graydon, Bill Champlin.

"Ain't No Stoppin' Us Now," Gene McFadden, John Whitehead, Jerry Cohen.

"Deja Vu," Isaac Hayes, Adrienne Anderson.

"Reunited," Dino Fekaris, Freddie Perren.

"We Are Family," Nile Rodgers, Bernard Edwards.

BEST RHYTHM & BLUES VOCAL PERFORMANCE, MALE

- Michael Jackson, "Don't Stop Till You Get Enough." Epic.

George Benson, "Love Ballad," track. Warner Bros.

Ray Charles, "Some Enchanted Evening." Atlantic.

Isaac Hayes, "Don't Let Go." Polydor.

Elton John, "Mama Can't Buy You Love." MCA.

Smokey Robinson, "Cruisin'." Motown.

BEST RHYTHM & BLUES VOCAL PERFORMANCE, FEMALE

- Dionne Warwick, "Deja Vu." Arista.

Natalie Cole, *I Love You So*. Capitol.

Minnie Ripperton, *Minnie*. Capitol.

Amii Stewart, "Knock on Wood." Ariola.

Donna Summer, "Dim All the Lights." Casablanca.

Anita Ward, "Ring My Bell." Juana.

BEST RHYTHM & BLUES VOCAL PERFORMANCE BY A DUO, GROUP OR CHORUS

- Earth, Wind & Fire, "After the Love Has Gone." ARC/CBS.

Commodores, *Midnight Magic*. Motown.

McFadden & Whitehead, "Ain't No Stoppin' Us Now." Philips International.

Peaches & Herb, "Reunited." Polydor.

Sister Sledge, "We Are Family." Atlantic.

BEST RHYTHM & BLUES INSTRUMENTAL PERFORMANCE

- Earth, Wind & Fire, "Boogie Wonderland." ARC/CBS.

Herbie Hancock, "Ready or Not," track. Columbia.

Hubert Laws, "Land of Passion," track. Columbia.

Harvey Mason, "Wave," track. Arista.

Junior Walker, "Wishing on a Star," track. Whitfield/Warner Bros.

BEST DISCO RECORDING

- "I Will Survive," Gloria Gaynor. Polydor.

"Boogie Wonderland," Earth, Wind &
Fire, Emotions. ARC/CBS.
Bad Girls, Donna Summer. Casablanca.
"Do Ya Think I'm Sexy?" Rod Stewart.
Warner Bros.
"Don't Stop Till You Get Enough,"
Michael Jackson. Epic.

BEST JAZZ FUSION PERFORMANCE
(VOCAL OR INSTRUMENTAL)
• Weather Report, *8:30*. ARC/CBS.
George Benson, *Livin' Inside Your Love*.
Warner Bros.
Chick Corea Group, *Chick Corea/Secret
Agent*. Polydor.
Don Sebesky with Jazz Quintet &
Soloists & Symphony Orchestra,
*Three Works for Jazz Soloists and
Symphony Orchestra*. Gryphon.
Stanley Turrentine, *Betcha*. Elektra.

BEST JAZZ VOCAL PERFORMANCE
• Ella Fitzerald, *Fine and Mellow*.
Pablo.
Helen Humes, *Sneakin' Around*. Classic
Jazz.
Eddie Jefferson, *The Live-liest*. Muse.
Sarah Vaughan, *I Love Brazil*. Pablo.
Joe Williams, *Prez and Joe*.
GNP/Crescendo.

BEST JAZZ INSTRUMENTAL
PERFORMANCE BY A SOLOIST
• Oscar Peterson, *Jousts*. Pablo.
Pepper Adams, *Reflectory*. Muse.
Paul Desmond, *Paul Desmond*. Artists
House.
Dexter Gordon, *Manhattan Symphonie*.
Columbia.
Zoot Sims, *Warm Tenor*. Pablo.

BEST JAZZ INSTRUMENTAL
PERFORMANCE BY A GROUP
• Gary Burton, Chick Corea, *Duet*.
ECM/Warner Bros.
Arnett Cobb, *Arnett Cobb and the Muse
All Stars/Live at Sandy's*. Muse.
Bill Evans, Toots Thielemans, *Affinity*.
Warner Bros.
Dizzy Gillespie, Count Basie, *The
Gifted Ones*. Pablo.

Great Jazz Trio (Hank Jones, Buster
Williams, Tony Williams), *Love for
Sale*. Inner City.
Zoot Sims, *Warm Tenor*. Pablo.

BEST JAZZ INSTRUMENTAL
PERFORMANCE BY A BIG BAND
• Duke Ellington, *At Fargo, 1940 Live*.
Book-of-the-Month.
Toshiko Akiyoshi–Lew Tabackin Big
Band, *Kogun*. RCA.
Louie Bellson & the Explosion, *Note
Smoking*. Discwasher.
Thad Jones, Mel Lewis, Umo, *Thad
Jones/Mel Lewis and Umo*. RCA.
Mel Lewis & the Jazz Orchestra, *Natu-
rally*. Telarc.

BEST COUNTRY SONG
(Songwriter's Award)
• "You Decorated My Life," Bob Morri-
son, Debbie Hupp.
"All the Gold in California," Larry Gatlin.
"Blue Kentucky Girl," Johnny Mullins.
"Every Which Way but Loose," Steve
Dorff, Milton Brown, Snuff Garrett.
"If I Said You Have a Beautiful Body
Would You Hold It Against Me,"
David Bellamy.

BEST COUNTRY VOCAL
PERFORMANCE, MALE
• Kenny Rogers, "The Gambler."
United Artists.
Willie Nelson, "Whiskey River."
Columbia.
Charley Pride, *Burgers and Fries/When
I Stop Leaving (I'll Be Gone)*. RCA.
Eddie Rabbitt, "Every Which Way but
Loose." Elektra.
Hank Williams, Jr., *Family Tradition*.
Elektra.

BEST COUNTRY VOCAL
PERFORMANCE, FEMALE
• Emmylou Harris, *Blue Kentucky Girl*.
Warner Bros.
Crystal Gayle, *We Should Be Together*.
United Artists.
Brenda Lee, "Tell Me What It's Like."
MCA.

Barbara Mandrell, *Just for the Record*. MCA.

Billie Jo Spears, "I Will Survive." United Artists.

BEST COUNTRY PERFORMANCE BY A DUO OR GROUP WITH VOCAL

- Charlie Daniels Band, "The Devil Went Down to Georgia." Epic.

Bellamy Brothers, "If I Said You Have a Beautiful Body Would You Hold It Against Me." Warner Bros.

Larry Gatlin & the Gatlin Brothers Band, "All the Gold in California." Columbia.

Willie Nelson, Leon Russell, "Heartbreak Hotel." Columbia.

Kenny Rogers, Dottie West, "All I Ever Need Is You." United Artists.

BEST COUNTRY INSTRUMENTAL PERFORMANCE

- Doc & Merle Watson, "Big Sandy/ Leather Britches," track. United Artists.

Vassar Clements, Doug Jernigan, Jesse McReynolds, Buddy Spicher, *Nashville Jam*. Flying Fish.

Floyd Cramer, *In Concert*. RCA.

Lester Flatt's Nashville Grass, *Fantastic Pickin'*. CMH.

Nashville Super Pickers, *Live from Austin City Limits*. Flying Fish.

Osborne Brothers, *Bluegrass Concerto*. CMH.

BEST GOSPEL PERFORMANCE, CONTEMPORARY OR INSPIRATIONAL

- Imperials, *Heed the Call*. Dayspring.

Andrus, Blackwood & Co., *Following You*. Greentree.

Amy Grant, *My Father's Eyes*. Myrrh.

Dan Peek, *All Things Are Possible*. MCA/Songbird.

Evie Tornquist, *Never the Same*. Word.

BEST GOSPEL PERFORMANCE, TRADITIONAL

- Blackwood Brothers, *Lift Up the Name of Jesus*. Skylite.

Dottie Rambo Choir, *A Choral Concert of Love*. Heartwarming.

Mercy River Boys, *Breakout*. Canaan.

Rex Nelon Singers, *Feelings*. Canaan.

Cathedral Quartet, *You Ain't Heard Nothing Yet!* Canaan.

BEST SOUL GOSPEL PERFORMANCE, CONTEMPORARY

- Andrae Crouch, *I'll Be Thinking of You*. Light.

Cassietta George, *Cassietta in Concert*. Audio Arts.

Rev. Jesse L. Jackson, Walter Hawkins & Family, Edwin Hawkins, Push Choir, Jackie Verdell, Danniebelle, Bili Thedford, Jessy Dixon, Andrae Crouch, *Push for Excellence*. Myrrh.

Myrna Summers, *Give Me Something to Hold On To*. Savoy.

Bili Thedford, *More Than Magic*. Good News.

Kevin Yancy directing Fountain of Life Joy Choir, "Thank You." Gospel Roots.

BEST SOUL GOSPEL PERFORMANCE, TRADITIONAL

- Mighty Clouds of Joy, *Changing Times*. Epic.

Willie Banks & the Messengers, *For the Wrong I've Done*. HSE.

James Cleveland & the Southern California Community Choir, *It's a New Day*. Savoy.

James Cleveland & Triboro Mass Choir, Albert Jamison, director, *In God's Own Time*. Savoy.

Troy Ramey & the Soul Searchers, *Try Jesus*. Nashboro.

BEST INSPIRATIONAL PERFORMANCE

- B. J. Thomas, *You Gave Me Love (When Nobody Gave Me a Prayer)*. Myrrh.

Pat Boone, *Just the Way I Am*. Lamb & Lion.

Mike Douglas, *I'll Sing This Song for You*. Word.

Willie Nelson, Leon Russell, "I Saw the Light," track. Columbia.

Noel Paul Stookey, *Band and Bodyworks*. New World.

BEST ETHNIC OR TRADITIONAL RECORDING

- *Muddy "Mississippi" Waters Live*, Muddy Waters. Blue Sky/CBS.

The Chieftains 7, Chieftains. Columbia.

Ice Pickin', Albert Collins. Alligator.

Laugh Your Blues Away, Uncle Dave Macon. Rounder.

Living Chicago Blues, Vol. 1, Jimmy Johnson Blues Band, Eddie Shaw & the Wolf Gang, Left Hand Frank & His Blues Band. Alligator.

Living Chicago Blues, Vol. 3, Lonnie Brooks Blues Band, Pinetop Perkins & Sons of the Blues. Alligator.

New England Traditional Fiddling. John Edwards Memorial Foundation.

New Orleans Jazz and Heritage Festival, Eubie Blake, Charles Mingus, Roosevelt Sykes, Clifton Chenier. Flying Fish.

So Many Roads, Otis Rush. Delmark.

BEST LATIN RECORDING

- *Irakere*, Irakere. Columbia.

Cross Over, Fania All Stars. Columbia.

Eternos, Celia Cruz & Johnny Pacheco. Vaya.

Touching You, Touching Me, Airto Moreira. Warner Bros.

BEST INSTRUMENTAL COMPOSITION
(Composer's Award)

- "Theme from *Superman* (Main Title)," John Williams.

"Ambiance," Marian McPartland.

"Angela (Theme from *Taxi*)," Bob James.

Central Park, Chick Corea.

Rise, Andy Armer, Randy Badazz.

BEST INSTRUMENTAL ARRANGEMENT

- Claus Ogerman, "Soulful Strut" (George Benson). Warner Bros.

Jeremy Lubbock, Harvey Mason, "Wave" (Harvey Mason). Arista.

Claus Ogerman, "Lazy Afternoon" (Freddie Hubbard). CBS.

Don Sebesky, "Sebastian's Theme" (Don Sebesky). Gryphon.

John Serry, "Sabotage" (John Serry). Chrysalis.

BEST ALBUM OF ORIGINAL SCORE WRITTEN FOR A MOTION PICTURE OR TV SPECIAL
(Composer's Award)

- *Superman*, John Williams. Warner Bros.

Alien, Jerry Goldsmith. RCA.

Apocalypse Now, Carmine Coppola, Francis Coppola. Elektra.

Ice Castles, Alan Parsons, Eric Woolfson, Marvin Hamlisch, composers; Carole Bayer Sager, lyricist. Arista.

The Muppet Movie, Paul Williams, Kenny Ascher, composers and lyricists. Atlantic.

BEST CAST SHOW ALBUM

- *Sweeney Todd*, Stephen Sondheim, composer and lyricist. RCA.

Ballroom, Billy Goldenberg, composer; Alan & Marilyn Bergman, lyricists. Columbia.

The Grand Tour, Jerry Herman, composer and lyricist; Columbia.

I'm Getting My Act Together and Taking It on the Road, Gretchen Cryer, Nancy Ford, composers. Columbia.

They're Playing Our Song, Marvin Hamlisch, composer; Carole Bayer Sager, lyricist. Casablanca.

BEST ARRANGEMENT ACCOMPANYING VOCALIST(S)

- Michael McDonald, "What a Fool Believes" (Doobie Brothers). Warner Bros.

Jerry Hey, David Foster, "After the Love Has Gone" (Earth, Wind & Fire). ARC/CBS.

Byron Olson, "Everything Must Change" (Benard Ighner). Alfa.

Artie Butler, Barry Manilow, "I'll Never Love This Way Again" (Dionne Warwick). Arista.

Richard Evans, "Round Midnight" (Richard Evans). Horizon.

Tom Tom 84, "September" (Earth, Wind & Fire). ARC/CBS.

BEST CLASSICAL ALBUM

- *Brahms: Symphonies (4) (Complete)*, Sir Georg Solti conducting the

Chicago Symphony Orchestra. London.

Britten: Peter Grimes, Colin Davis conducting the Orchestra and Chorus of the Royal Opera House, Covent Garden (solos: Vickers, Harper, Summers). Philips.

The Horowitz Concerts 1978/79 (solo: Vladimir Horowitz). RCA.

Mussorgsky-Ravel: Pictures at an Exhibition; Stravinsky: The Firebird Suite, Riccardo Muti conducting the Philadelphia Orchestra. Angel.

Shostakovich: Lady Macbeth of Mtsensk, Mstislav Rostropovich conducting the London Philharmonic; Ambrosian Opera Chorus (solos: Vishnevskaya, Gedda). Angel.

Webern: The Complete Works of Anton Webern, Vol. 1, Pierre Boulez conducting the London Symphony Orchestra, Frankfurt Radio Orchestra and Julliard String Quartet. Columbia.

BEST CLASSICAL ORCHESTRAL RECORDING
(Conductor's Award)

• *Brahms: Symphonies (4) (Complete)* Sir Georg Solti conducting the Chicago Symphony. London.

Holst: The Planets, Sir Georg Solti conducting the London Philharmonic. London.

Ives: Three Places in New England, Dennis Russell Davies conducting the St. Paul Chamber Orchestra. Sound 80.

Mahler: Symphony No. 4 in G Major, André Previn conducting the Pittsburgh Symphony. Angel.

Rachmaninov: Symphonies No. 2 in E Minor and No. 3 in A Minor, Leonard Slatkin conducting the St Louis Symphony. Vox Box.

Sibelius: Four Legends from the "Kalevala," Eugene Ormandy conducting the Philadelphia Orchestra. Angel.

Zelenka: Orchestral Works (Complete), Alexander Van Wijnkoop conducting the Camerata Bern; Dr. Andreas

Holschneider, producer. Deutsche Grammophon.

BEST CHAMBER MUSIC PERFORMANCE (INSTRUMENTAL OR VOCAL)

• Dennis Russell Davies conducting the St. Paul Chamber Orchestra, *Copland: Appalachian Spring*. Sound 80.

Pierre Boulez, Daniel Barenboim, Pinchas Zukerman; Pay and Ensemble Inter-Contemporain, *Berg: Chamber Concerto for Piano and Violin; 4 Pieces for Clarinet and Piano*. Deutsche Grammophon.

Michael Debost, James Galway, *Telemann: 6 Sonatas for 2 Flutes*. Seraphim.

Fitzwilliam Quartet, *Shostakovich: Quartets Nos. 5 and 6*. L'Oiseau-Lyre.

Yoshikazu Fukumura conducting the Koto Flute, Ransom Wilson and the New Koto Ensemble of Tokyo, *Vivaldi: 4 Flute Concertos*. Angel.

Tokyo Quartet, *Debussy: Quartet in G Minor; Ravel: Quartet in F*. Columbia.

Itzhak Perlman, Lynn Harrell, Pinchas Zukerman, *Dohnányi: Serenade, Op. 10; Beethoven: Serenade, Op. 8*. Columbia.

Pinchas Zukerman, Claude Bolling with Max Hediguer, Marcel Sabiani, *Bolling: Suite for Violin and Jazz Piano*. Columbia.

BEST CLASSICAL PERFORMANCE, INSTRUMENTAL SOLOIST(S) (WITH ORCHESTRA)

• Maurizio Pollini (Abbado conducting the Chicago Symphony), *Bartók: Concertos for Piano Nos. 1 and 2*. Deutsche Grammophon.

Maurice André (Lopez-Cobos conducting the London Philharmonic), *Trumpet Concertos by Haydn, Telemann, Albinoni and Marcello*. Angel.

James Galway (Gerhardt conducting the National Philharmonic), *"Annie's Song" and Other Galway Favorites*. RCA.

Anne-Sophie Mutter (von Karajan conducting the Berlin Philharmonic), *Mozart: Concertos for Violin No. 3 in G Major and No. 5 in A Major.* Deutsche Grammophon.

Isaac Stern, Jean-Pierre Rampal (Jerusalem Music Center Chamber Orchestra), *Isaac Stern and Jean-Pierre Rampal Play Vivaldi and Telemann.* Columbia.

Barry Tuckwell (English Chamber Orchestra), *Horn Concertos by Joseph Haydn and Michael Haydn.* Angel.

Krystian Zimerman (Giulini conducting the Los Angeles Philharmonic), *Chopin: Concerto for Piano No. 1 in E Minor.* Deutsche Grammophon.

BEST CLASSICAL PERFORMANCE, INSTRUMENTAL SOLOIST(S) (WITHOUT ORCHESTRA)

• Vladimir Horowitz, *The Horowitz Concerts 1978/79.* RCA.

Julian Bream, *Villa-Lobos: Etudes (12) and Suite Populaire Brasilienne.* RCA.

Glenn Gould, *Bach: Toccatas, Vol. 1.* Columbia.

Paul Jacobs, *Debussy: Estampes, Images, Books 1 and 2.* Nonesuch.

Igor Kipnis, *Scarlatti: Sonatas (12).* Angel.

Ursula Oppens, *Rzewski: The People United Will Never Be Defeated.* Vanguard.

Maurizio Pollini, *Boulez: Sonata for Piano No. 2.* Deutsche Grammophon.

Artur Rubinstein, *Franck: Prelude, Chorale and Fugue for Piano*; Bach-Busoni: Chaconne; Mozart: Rondo in A Minor. RCA.

Rosalyn Tureck, *Bach: Goldberg Variations.* Columbia.

BEST OPERA RECORDING

• *Britten: Peter Grimes*, Colin Davis conducting the Orchestra and Chorus of the Royal Opera House, Covent Garden (solos: Vickers, Harper, Summers). Philips.

Hindemith: Mathis der Maler, Rafael Kubelik conducting the Bavarian Radio Symphony and Bavarian Radio Chorus (solos: Fischer-Dieskau, King). Angel.

Shostakovich: Lady Macbeth of Mtsensk, Mstislav Rostropovich conducting the London Philharmonic, Ambrosian Opera Chorus (solos: Vishnevskaya, Gedda). Angel.

Verdi: Otello, James Levine conducting the National Philharmonic (solos: Domingo, Scotto, Milnes). RCA.

Verdi: Rigoletto, Julius Rudel conducting the Philharmonia Orchestra and Ambrosian Opera Chorus (solos: Sills, Kraus, Milnes). Angel.

BEST CLASSICAL PERFORMANCE, CHORAL (OTHER THAN OPERA)

• Sir Georg Solti, conductor, Margaret Hillis, choral director, Chicago Symphony and Chorus, *Brahms: A German Requiem.* London.

Maurice Abravanel, conductor, Newell B. Wright, choral director, Utah Chorale and Utah Symphony, *Stravinsky: Symphony of Psalms.* Angel.

Daniel Barenboim conducting the Chorus of the Orchestre de Paris and the Orchestre de Paris, *Berlioz: La Damnation de Faust.* Deutsche Grammophon.

Leonard Bernstein conducting the Radio Chorus of the N.O.S. Hilversum and Concertgebouworkest, *Beethoven: Missa Solemnis.* Deutsche Grammophon.

Lorin Maazel, conductor; Robert Page, choral director, Cleveland Orchestra and Chorus, *Berlioz: Requiem.* London.

John Oliver conducting the Tanglewood Festival Chorus, *American Music for Chorus.* Deutsche Grammophon.

André Previn conducting the London Symphony Chorus; Richard Hickox, chorus master; St. Clement Danes School Boys' Choir; Keith Walters, choral director; London

Symphony, *Britten: Spring Symphony*. Angel.

Jerzy Semkow, conductor, Thomas Peck, choral director, St. Louis Symphony Chorus and Orchestra, *Beethoven: Choral Fantasy; Elegiac Song; Calm Sea and Prosperous Voyage.* Candide.

BEST CLASSICAL PERFORMANCE, VOCAL SOLOIST

- Luciano Pavarotti (Bologna Orchestra), *O Sole Mio (Favorite Neapolitan Songs).* London.
Elly Ameling (Baldwin, accompanist), *Mozart: Lieder.* Philips.
Victoria de los Angeles (Moore, accompanist), *Victoria de los Angeles in Concert.* Angel.
Dietrich Fischer-Dieskau (Richter, accompanist), *Schubert: Lieder.* Deutsche Grammophon.
Jan de Gaetani (Dunkel, Anderson, Kalish, accompanists), *Ravel: Chansons Madécasses.* Nonesuch.
Yevgeny Nesterenko (Shenderovich, Krainev, accompanists), *Mussorgsky: Songs.* Columbia/Melodiya.
Leontyne Price (Garvey, accompanist), *Lieder by Schubert and Richard Strauss.* Angel.
Frederica von Stade (Katz, accompanist), *Frederica von Stade Song Recital.* Columbia.

BEST ENGINEERED RECORDING, CLASSICAL

- Anthony Salvatore, *Sondheim: Sweeney Todd*, original cast. RCA.
Marc Aubort, Joanna Nickrenz, *Rachmaninov: Symphonies Nos. 2 and 3* (Slatkin conducting the St. Louis Symphony). Vox Box.
Klaus Hiemann, *Bartók: Concertos for Piano Nos. 1 and 2* (Abbado conducting the Chicago Symphony; solo: Pollini). Deutsche Grammophon.
Klaus Hiemann, *Prokofiev: Scythian Suite; Lieutenant Kijé* (Abbado conducting the Chicago Symphony). Deutsche Grammophon.

Tom Jung, *Copland: Appalachian Spring; Ives: Three Places in New England* (Davies conducting the St. Paul Chamber Orchestra). Sound 80.
John Kurlander, *Hindemith: Concert Music for Strings and Brass*; *Symphonic Metamorphosis on Themes by Weber* (Ormandy conducting the Philadelphia Orchestra). Angel.
John Kurlander, *Sibelius: Four Legends from the "Kalevala"* (Ormandy conducting the Philadelphia Orchestra). Angel.
Vittorio Negri, *Britten: Peter Grimes* (Davis conducting the Royal Opera House, Covent Garden; solos: Vickers, Harper, Summers). Philips.
Jack Renner, *Mussorgsky-Ravel: Pictures at an Exhibition* (Maazel conducting the Cleveland Orchestra). Telarc.
Jack Renner, *Stravinsky: The Firebird Suite; Borodin: Prince Igor* (Shaw conducting the Atlanta Symphony Orchestra and Chorus). Telarc.
Isao Tomita, *The Bermuda Triangle* (Isao Tomita). RCA.

CLASSICAL PRODUCER OF THE YEAR

- James Mallinson
Marc Aubort & Joanna Nickrenz
Andrew Kazdin
Paul Myers
Vittorio Negri
Thomas Z. Shepard
Robert Woods

BEST SPOKEN WORD, DOCUMENTARY OR DRAMA RECORDING

- *The Ages of Man (Readings from Shakespeare),* Sir John Gielgud. Caedmon.
Apocalypse Now, original motion picture soundtrack. Elektra.
An American Prayer, Jim Morrison. Elektra.
The Ox-Bow Incident, Henry Fonda. Caedmon.
Stare with Your Ears, Ken Nordine. Snail.

Orson Welles/Helen Hayes at Their Best, Orson Welles, Helen Hayes. Mark 56.

BEST COMEDY RECORDING

• *Reality . . . What a Concept*, Robin Williams. Casablanca.
Comedy Is Not Pretty, Steve Martin. Warner Bros.
I Need Your Help, Barry Manilow, Ray Stevens. Warner Bros.
"Rubber Biscuit," track, Blues Brothers. Atlantic.
Wanted, Richard Pryor. Warner Bros.

BEST RECORDING FOR CHILDREN

• *The Muppet Movie*, Jim Henson, creator. Atlantic.
Anne Murray Sings for the Sesame Street Generation, Anne Murray. Sesame Street.
Sesame Disco! Jim Henson, creator. Sesame Street.
The Stars Come Out on Sesame Street, Jim Henson, creator. Sesame Street.
You're in Love, Charlie Brown. Charlie Brown.

BEST ENGINEERED RECORDING

• Peter Henderson, *Breakfast in America* (Supertramp). A&M.
Gary Loizzo, *Cornerstone* (Styx). A&M.
Alan Parsons, *Eve* (Alan Parsons Project). Arista.
Lee Herschberg, Lloyd Clifft, Tom Knox, Roger Nichols, *Rickie Lee Jones* (Rickie Lee Jones). Warner Bros.
Phil Edwards, *Just Friends* (LA-4). Concord Jazz.

BEST ALBUM PACKAGE
(Art Director's Award)

• Mike Doud, Mick Haggerty, *Breakfast in America* (Supertramp). A&M.
John Berg, *Ramsey* (Ramsey Lewis). Columbia.

Lynne Dresse Breslin, *With Sound Reason* (Sonny Fortune). Atlantic.
Ron Coro/Johnny Lee, *Near Perfect/Perfect* (Martin Mull). Elektra.
Peter Corriston, *Morning Dance* (Spyro Gyra). Infinity.
John Gillespie, *Fear of Music* (Talking Heads). Sire.
Hipgnosis, *In Through the Out Door* (Led Zeppelin). Swan Song.
Tony Lane, *Chicago 13* (Chicago). Columbia.
Michael Ross, *Look Sharp!* (Joe Jackson). A&M.

BEST ALBUM NOTES
(Annotator's Award)

• Bob Porter, James Patrick, *Charlie Parker: The Complete Savoy Sessions*. Savoy.
Melvin Maddocks, *Billie Holiday (Giants of Jazz)*. Time-Life.
Dan Morgenstern, Stanley Dance, *Duke Ellington (Giants of Jazz)*. Time-Life.
Dick Schory, *The Magical Music of Walt Disney*. Ovation.
Richard M. Sudhalter, *Hoagy Carmichael, a Legendary Performer and Composer*. RCA.

BEST HISTORICAL REISSUE

• *Billie Holiday (Giants of Jazz)*. Time-Life.
Duke Ellington (Giants of Jazz). Time-Life.
The Magical Music of Walt Disney. Ovation.
One Never Knows, Do One? The Best of Fats Waller. Book-of-the-Month.
A Tribute to E. Power Biggs. Columbia.

PRODUCER OF THE YEAR

• Larry Butler
Mike Chapman
Quincy Jones
Ted Templeman
Maurice White

• 1980 •

Cross Sails Away

When the nominations came out, *Variety* sized up this year's race with the banner headline: FAMILIAR FACES DOMINATE GRAMMYS. Most pundits foresaw a showdown between two of them in the top categories for Album and Record of the Year: Sinatra and Streisand.

Sinatra was tied with Stevie Wonder for having won the most Album of the Year prizes (three), but now he was expected to pull ahead as supreme champ with a victory for *Trilogy,* a three-disc retrospective of his formidable career. Seventeen years had passed since Streisand last won the LP honor, and now she was back in the race with *Guilty,* which included her megahit duet with Bee Gees member Barry Gibb, who last shared in the Album of the Year honors for 1978's *Saturday Night Fever.* But more than anything, Streisand wanted her "Woman in Love" single to take the Record of the Year trophy, an accolade that had eluded her on four occasions in the past. Her toughest competition was expected to be Sinatra's "Theme from *New York, New York,"* which was considered the front-runner because the Grammys were being held in Manhattan for the first time in five years. "New Yorkers are notoriously sentimental about their town," wrote the *L.A. Times,* "so you can imagine how wild the audience will go over Sinatra and that tune at New York's Radio City Music Hall."

Then came the biggest upset—and the most thorough sweep by a debut artist— in Grammy history.

As fans gathered in the cold, gusty air outside Radio City shortly before the show, no one seemed to notice the arrival

Christopher Cross (at left, with producer Michael Omartian) is the only artist to win all four top awards. His multiple victories marked the biggest Grammy upset ever.

of the six-foot, two-inch, 200-plus-pound Christopher Cross. "The kids in the crowd seemed to be on the lookout for Barbra Streisand and Barry Gibb, who received the biggest screams of the evening," noted the *Los Angeles Herald Examiner.* (Dionne Warwick, on the other hand, got "squeals.")

Later on, at the Grammy ceremony, as Cross began winning awards, he was still ignored back in the pressroom, where photographers and reporters waited restlessly for either Streisand or Sinatra to burst into their midst with an armful of the golden gramophones, thereby giving them the page-one photos they needed for their newspapers back home. However, when Cross and his self-titled album and hit song "Sailing" finally sailed through with wins for Best New Artist, Best Arrangement Accompanying Vocalist(s) (which he shared with his producer-arranger, Michael Omartian) and Record, Album and Song of the Year, chaos erupted among the media as they scrambled to make up for previously lost photo and Q&A opportunities. " 'Who the hell is this guy?' rang out more than once," reported the *Washington Post* about the press reaction to the artist who only a year earlier was playing a fraternity party in Austin, Texas.

"Familiar Faces" may have dominated the noms, but Cross nailed the veterans on awards night.

Only twice before had anyone ever swept the Triple Crown of best record, album and song awards: Paul Simon in 1970 and Carole King in 1971. Since both artists were established music names, neither qualified for Grammy's fourth-highest honor of Best New Artist. When Cross ended up claiming that prize, too, it was a grand slam that had never before occurred.

Prior to making it big, Cross worked for ten years in a band that played covers of the latest hits to Texas bar crowds. "When disco came in, we were a disco band," he told the *Washington Post*. "My material was in my guitar case, but people didn't want to hear it." Cross eventually got Warner Bros. executives to listen to it after he sent them a demo tape. They, in turn, not only signed him up but built him up to be a huge star. Cross became the warm-up act at Fleetwood Mac and the Eagles concerts and was booked extensively on TV talk shows. The record company was rewarded with its best-selling album of the year (3 million copies) and hit singles "Sailing" (number one on the weekly charts), "Ride Like the Wind" (number two) and "Never Be the Same" (number nine).

What made his music so special? "I dunno," Cross told reporters backstage at the Grammys. "People just like it, I guess. It's a little bit of pop and a little bit of rock. Nothing really new." Critics were irate. Robert Hilburn of the *L.A. Times* was among those who claimed Cross's "music is so plain that it's a wonder

N.A.R.A.S. voters even remembered his name" when it came time to vote. But the N.A.R.A.S. crowd not only knew their winner, they cheered him with a standing ovation as the rookie claimed his last prize of the night—Album of the Year—from Diana Ross, a longtime Grammy loser who was nominated in the r&b categories this year but got snubbed again. Cross would be nominated for more awards next year for his partial contribution to the theme song to the hit film *Arthur* (he'd lose the Grammy but win the Oscar). Soon thereafter he would fade from the pop charts—and from the Warner Bros. list of artists. For the next decade, he tried to make a comeback by financing his albums independently but without much success. He told *TV Guide* in 1990, "I always feel a little left out when the Grammys come around. They've never asked me to come back or to present an award. These days, I don't even watch them."

The last singer to win Album of the Year for a debut LP was Barbra Streisand in 1963. This year the only Grammy she nabbed was for best pop group vocals, which she shared with Barry Gibb for their "Guilty" single. Streisand had been considered a cinch to nab the female pop vocals award, but, as Christopher Cross's victories foretold, it would be a night of endless upsets.

Streisand lost to 1973's Best New Artist, Bette Midler, who had a string of flop albums following her earlier Grammy victory but now saw her fate change in 1980 with "The Rose." Said the *L.A. Times:* "This Golden Globe–winning ballad from her smash dramatic film debut brought her back to the top."

Christopher Cross led this year's Grammy race with the most nominations (five), but *Variety* noted that he "was denied a clean sweep" when he lost the prize for best male pop vocals to Kenny Loggins, last year's winner of Song of the Year who cowrote "What a Fool Believes" for the Doobie Brothers. Loggins's new victory for "This Is It" was considered one of the biggest shockers on Grammy night, since he also topped Sinatra, Kenny Rogers and Grammy-cast host Paul Simon (who remarked slyly, "Not to take anything away from Kenny Rogers, but Kenny was host of this show last year and won.") *Down Beat* complained that Loggins was nominated in both the pop and rock categories, but he lost his rock bid ("I'm Alright") to 1979's winner of Album of the Year, Billy Joel, in yet another upset.

Joel won for *Glass Houses,* his musical statement that insisted he was a rock artist despite being pegged as a pop singer in recent years. N.A.R.A.S. may have agreed with Joel by giving him the rock award, but few pundits approved. The closest *Glass Houses* came to r&r, they argued, was the title (not the music) of its hit single, "It's Still Rock and Roll to Me." Joel's win was also considered astonishing because he beat rock legend Paul McCartney, longtime losing nominee Jackson Browne and a never-before-nominated Bruce Springsteen, who was considered the front-runner. Joel's producer, Phil Ramone, received the Producer of the Year prize, which caused even further controversy because it probably should have gone to him last year when Joel won Album of the Year.

"Quincy Jones was edged out for the third consecutive year," groused *Billboard,* "despite having been named the No. 1 pop producer of 1980 on *Billboard*'s year-end chart recaps."

The rest of the prizes went to bona fide rockers but were still considered shockers. When Pat Benatar won the female vocal laurels for her *Crimes of Passion* LP, she was so stunned, she startled the audience by shrieking "Holy shit!" (Marianne Faithfull was expected to win the prize for *Broken English.*) Benatar's acceptance remarks didn't have to be bleeped on TV, though, since, just like last year, the prizes were bestowed in an off-the-air ceremony held a few hours before the prime-time Grammycast (a continuing sore point to sensitive rock fans, since the awards were finally introduced on a permanent basis last year).

The group prize was supposed to be an overdue tribute to the British rockers of Queen ("Another One Bites the Dust"), but instead it went to purveyors of hard rock for the blue-collar set—Bob Seger & the Silver Bullet Band (*Against the Wind*). British rock lovers had to be satisfied instead with the winners of the instrumental performance award—the Police. In their rookie years, the Police explored the combination of pop/rock sounds with reggae rhythm, which explained the title of their winning album, *Regatta de Blanc* (White Reggae).

Diana Ross's startling loss of a Grammy in the r&b vocal category nonetheless had an element of justice to it. She was beaten by Stephanie Mills, whose first big break in show business came at age 15 when she landed the role of Dorothy in the Broadway musical *The Wiz.* Mills played the part onstage for five years but was passed over for the film role in favor of superstar Ross, who was clearly more than 20 years too old for the part. Yet Ross was considered the

Stephanie Mills's shocking defeat of Diana Ross redressed an old score.

• 309 •

favorite to take the Grammy, too, because her song, "Upside Down," turned out to be the biggest solo hit of her career. But as popular as the tune was, it still didn't score as many N.A.R.A.S. votes as Mills's "Never Knew Love Like This Before," which was also named Best R&B Song over "Upside Down." On vinyl, Mills took the song to soaring emotional heights, far surpassing Ross's singsong delivery on "Upside Down."

Another loser of Best R&B Song, "Shining Star," ended up earning the r&b group vocals prize for the Manhattans. (This "Shining Star" was different from the song of the same name that brought Earth, Wind & Fire a Grammy in 1975, but it did have the same soulful sound executed in falsetto voice.) The remaining two r&b awards went to George Benson, whose best instrumental performance for "On Broadway," a track from his *Give Me the Night* album, also brought him the male vocal award. *Variety* called Benson "the artist who batted a thousand" on Grammy night when his third nomination this year also came through: best jazz vocals for "Moody's Mood," another track from *Give Me the Night,* which was produced by Quincy Jones.

Jones may have lost the Producer of the Year prize to Phil Ramone, but he ended up winning a statuette for Best Instrumental Arrangement for "Dinorah, Dinorah," another track on Benson's album. While most music critics cheered the LP, they howled over its competing in both r&b and jazz categories at the Grammys.

The female jazz vocal prize was presented again to last year's winner, Ella Fitzgerald (*A Perfect Match/Ella and Basie*), bringing her career tally to ten. Count Basie got his own Grammy (his seventh) for best big-band instrumental performance for *On the Road.*

"None of the jazz awards were given on stage," *Down Beat* grumbled. "The winners were merely run through, quickly and all but unintelligibly, within a list of 'other winners' (including the Best Recording for Children and Best Comedy

Los Angeles Public Library

Variety noted Cross "was denied a clean sweep" by last year's winner of best song, Kenny Loggins, who took the pop vocals statuette for "This Is It."

Recording) by Harry Chapin and Judy Collins—both respected artists but neither known for their jazz chops." Time was reserved, however, for a performance by Chuck Mangione and the Manhattan Transfer of a medley of some of the fusion works contending for Grammys this year, including Mangione's "Give It All You Got" (which lost Best Instrumental Composition to John Williams's "The Empire Strikes Back," also the winner of best film score) and the Manhattan Transfer's "Birdland," which won the new award for jazz fusion performances. "Birdland" also garnered Best Arrangement for Voices.

When legendary jazz pianist Bill Evans died in 1980, he left behind two LPs with farewell titles that would both earn posthumous awards: *I Will Say Goodbye* (best soloist instrumental performance) and *We Will Meet Again* (best group instrumental performance). Throughout his career, Evans liked to keep his groups to only two or three players, but he employed a quintet for *We Will Meet Again* that was comprised of bass, drums, his piano and two horns. The horns marked a dramatic departure for Evans's trademark sound and it thrilled the critics.

The success of the latest John Travolta movie, *Urban Cowboy,* helped to popularize a number of country hits that earned Grammys. In what the *New York Times* called "something of an upset," Anne Murray reaped the female vocal honors for "Could I Have This Dance," which was originally intended as a duet with Kenny Rogers to underscore the film's wedding scene. When negotiations with Rogers's managers dragged on too long, however, Murray recorded both the male and female parts herself and the producers liked the solo version enough to drop their talks with Rogers. *Urban Cowboy* was filmed at Gilley's, a Houston bar billed as "the largest honky tonk in the world" where patrons were prone to forget their woes by swilling Texas brew and riding the saloon's mechanical bull. Mickey Gilley's Urban Cowboy Band won the instrumental performance prize for "Orange Blossom Special/Hoedown."

Andrew Lloyd Webber took two prizes for the U.S. recording of *Evita.*

Texas talent ruled the rest of the country categories, too. Roy Orbison won his first Grammy (vocal duo honors, shared with two-time past winner Emmylou Harris) for "That Lovin' You Feelin' Again," which was also from a motion picture—*Roadie,* starring music artists Orbison, Meat Loaf, Blondie and Hank Williams, Jr.

Another legendary Texan received his first Grammy this year when George Jones won the male vocal prize for "He Stopped Loving Her Today," about a man who dies early in life, leaving his sweetheart behind. The song's success marked "the climax to a stirring comeback year," according to the *New York Times.* Jones had recently tackled his alcoholism and other personal problems but apparently did not expect a first Grammy to cap off his new good fortune. "He was already backstage with his tie off when the award was announced," the *Washington Post* noted. When he returned to the press-

room later on, award in hand, Jones told reporters, "I want to thank all the fans and friends who stood by us. I also want to thank God. This has been the greatest year of my life."

Texan Willie Nelson had won three performance Grammys in the past, but none for composition prior to this year's acknowledgment for Best Country Song "On the Road Again," which he wrote for the film *Honeysuckle Rose* (later retitled *On the Road Again* for video release), in which he starred as a journeyman country crooner.

The religious awards welcomed back a host of talent from Grammy years past, including B. J. Thomas, Andrae Crouch and others in an ensemble performance on the album *The Lord's Prayer.* The Blackwood Brothers returned from last year to reclaim the best traditional gospel performance prize for *We Come to Worship.* Rev. James Cleveland had won twice before but now shared his third with the Charles Fold Singers for *Lord, Let Me Be an Instrument.*

Last year a "born again" Bob Dylan won a rock & roll Grammy for his religious song "Gotta Serve Somebody," but now he and his *Saved* LP were competing directly in the Best Inspirational Performance category where they belonged. Dylan lost, however, to Best New Artist of 1977, Debby Boone, for *With My Song I Will Praise Him.*

The recipient of the Best Latin Recording award was Cal Tjader and his sextet (for *La Onda Va Bien*). Tjader was an American known for his jazz work with the likes of Stan Getz and Charlie Byrd, who also performed Latin music with such past Grammy champs as Eddie Palmieri and Mongo Santamaria.

Rodney Dangerfield got plenty of respect on Grammy night when *No Respect* reaped Best Comedy Recording. The disc was a compilation of new material plus old one-liners that were recorded at his New York nightclub: "The other night I felt like having a few drinks. I went over to the bartender and said, 'Surprise me.' He showed me a naked picture of my wife. . . . Ain't got no sex life . . . She cut me down to once a month. I'm lucky. Two guys I know she cut out completely." Dangerfield hammed it up at the Grammys, too. While up at the podium he looked panicked as he clasped his first golden gramophone and told the audience, "There's a guy in my neighborhood who's waiting to melt mine down."

The prize for Best Cast Show Album triggered squabbling when N.A.R.A.S. allowed theatrical revivals to compete. *Down Beat* was irked that a new staging of the 1943 classic *Oklahoma!* was nominated. Andrew Lloyd Webber's *Evita,* starring Patti LuPone, won over such formidable competition as *Barnum, One Mo' Time* and *A Day in Hollywood/A Night in the Ukraine.*

Among the classical kudos, *Stereo Review* took issue with "the lopsided distribution, with three awards going to the opera *Lulu* (best album, best opera, best engineering) and four to Itzhak Perlman (chamber music, soloist with orchestra twice—a tie with himself!—and soloist without orchestra). Yes, Perlman is undeniably a superb violinist and the Deutsche Grammophon recording of *Lulu* is a landmark of sorts, but weren't there some other fine classical recordings made during the year? There were, but they lacked the advantage of exposure: *Lulu* was broadcast on public television, and Perlman is a veteran TV talk-show guest who even appears on *Sesame Street.*"

Deutsche Grammophon's *Lulu* was the first complete performance ever attempted of the opera by Alban Berg, who died in 1935. The production starred Teresa Stratas as Lulu and featured instrumental accompaniment by Pierre Boulez conducting the Paris Opera Orchestra. Berg's work also figured into the four Grammys awarded to Perlman, who was honored for performances of works by Shostakovich and Moszkowski,

Three-time past champ Willie Nelson claimed Best Country Song for "On the Road Again."

too. "Israeli-American violinist Itzhak Perlman may soon need an extension built onto his mantelpiece," *Billboard* said. "Perlman's Grammy Awards collection grew dramatically last week in the most impressive sweep by a classical artist in the ceremony's history."

Sir Georg Solti and the Chicago Symphony Orchestra won the orchestral honors for Bruckner's Sixth Symphony, but took some heat from *High Fidelity:* "Solti has evinced a disturbing tendency to stress sound over content. Such is again the case: As virtuosic display, his Sixth is astounding; as music-making, it is appalling." The magazine also blasted conductor Carlo Maria Giulini for leading the Philharmonia Orchestra in a performance of Mozart's *Requiem,* which was the recipient of the choral laurels for the Philharmonia's chorus and its master, Norbert Balatsch. "Basses and timpani [are] the main offenders," it said about the orchestration. "The trombones are all over the place." The chorus, however, it noted, was "excellent."

Leontyne Price had been awarded 10 Grammys between 1960 and 1974 but hadn't won another one since. Now she was back to claim the vocals prize for the

Los Angeles Public Library

fifth volume of her *Prima Donna* series. *High Fidelity* wrote: "This program is an assertion that (at least in the recording studio) Leontyne Price can still sing damn near anything."

When all the gold was finally presented on Grammy night, *Variety* noted, "Kenny Rogers and Frank Sinatra, each nominated three times, went awardless. Neither was present at the Radio City Music Hall ceremonies."

Variety sized up the 23rd annual Grammy Awards thus: "The two-hour and 25-minute CBS broadcast was one of the most flawed in recent years, with technical problems plaguing the evening throughout. On the other hand, host Paul Simon, himself a victim of a technical foul-up, proved a witty emcee."

Music acts included Patti LuPone performing "Don't Cry for Me, Argentina" from *Evita,* Aretha Franklin jamming with "Can't Turn You Loose" and George Jones, noted the *Herald Examiner,* singing "a verse of 'He Stopped Loving Her Today' that climaxed in a multiple-registered, goose-pimpling final note that even raised the hair on the back of *his* head." But the most moving aspect of the entire evening was what closed the Grammy tele-cast: host Paul Simon's eloquent tribute to former Beatle John Lennon, who had been murdered at the entrance of his New York apartment building in December 1980.

Once the formal ceremony was over, the informal partying began. *People* reported on the galas around town: "Paul Simon and five-statue winner Christopher ('Sailing') Cross chose the 'official' bash at the Hilton, where tickets ran from $75 to $175. So did Michael McDonald, Chuck Mangione, Kenny Loggins and nearly 2,700 others. At CBS Records president Walter Yetnikoff's more intimate affair at the Four Seasons, Barbra Streisand liked the banana cheesecake so much she asked for a whole one to take home. Across town, Arista Records president Clive Davis had problems. Aretha Franklin, the guest of honor at his party in the 48th floor Tower Suite, turned out to be afraid of heights. She couldn't bring herself to leave the elevator, so she turned around and went home. The $300 Grand Marnier-and-strawberry cake stayed in the fridge, while guests Chris Reeve, Jane Seymour, Rodney Dangerfield and Mr. and Mrs. Bruce Sudano (a.k.a. Mrs. and Mr. Donna Summer) made do with poached bass and chocolate mousse."

• 1980 •

The awards ceremony was broadcast on CBS from New York's Radio City Music Hall on February 25, 1981, for the awards eligibility period of October 1, 1979, through September 30, 1980.

ALBUM OF THE YEAR
• *Christopher Cross*, Christopher Cross. Warner Bros.
Glass Houses, Billy Joel. Columbia.
Guilty, Barbra Streisand, Barry Gibb. Columbia.
Trilogy: Past, Present and Future, Frank Sinatra. Reprise.
The Wall, Pink Floyd. Columbia.

RECORD OF THE YEAR
• "Sailing," Christopher Cross. Warner Bros.
"Lady," Kenny Rogers. Liberty/United Artists.
"The Rose," Bette Midler. Atlantic.
"Theme from *New York, New York*," Frank Sinatra. Reprise.
"Woman in Love," Barbra Streisand. Barry Gibb. Columbia.

SONG OF THE YEAR
(Songwriter's Award)
• "Sailing," Christopher Cross.
"Fame," Michael Gore, Dean Pitchford.
"Lady," Lionel Richie

"Theme from *New York, New York*,"
John Kander, Fred Ebb.
"The Rose," Amanda McBroom.
"Woman in Love," Barry Gibb, Robin
Gibb.

BEST NEW ARTIST
• Christopher Cross
Irene Cara
Robbie Dupree
Amy Holland
Pretenders

BEST POP VOCAL
PERFORMANCE, MALE
• Kenny Loggins, "This Is It," track
from *Alive*. Columbia.
Christopher Cross, *Christopher Cross*.
Warner Bros.
Kenny Rogers, "Lady." Liberty/United
Artists.
Paul Simon, "Late in the Evening."
Warner Bros.
Frank Sinatra, "Theme from *New York,
New York*." Reprise.

BEST POP VOCAL
PERFORMANCE, FEMALE
• Bette Midler, "The Rose." Atlantic.
Irene Cara, "Fame." RSO.
Olivia Newton-John, "Magic." MCA.
Barbra Streisand, "Woman in Love."
Columbia.
Donna Summer, "On the Radio."
Casablanca.

BEST POP PERFORMANCE
BY A DUO OR GROUP
WITH VOCAL
• Barbra Streisand, Barry Gibb,
"Guilty," track from *Guilty*. Colum-
bia.
Ambrosia, "Biggest Part of Me." Warner
Bros.
Pointer Sisters, "He's So Shy." Planet.
Kenny Rogers, Kim Carnes, "Don't Fall
in Love with a Dreamer." United
Artists.
Bob Seger & the Silver Bullet Band,
"Against the Wind," track from
Against the Wind. Capitol.

BEST POP INSTRUMENTAL
PERFORMANCE
• Bob James, Earl Klugh, *One on One*.
Columbia.
Herb Alpert, "Beyond." A&M.
Doobie Brothers, "South Bay Strut,"
track from *One Step*. Warner Bros.
Henry Mancini, "Ravel's *Bolero*."
Warner Bros.
John Williams, London Symphony
Orchestra, "Yoda's Theme," track
from *The Empire Strikes Back*. RSO.

BEST ROCK VOCAL
PERFORMANCE, MALE
• Billy Joel, *Glass Houses*. Columbia.
Jackson Browne, "Boulevard." Asylum.
Kenny Loggins, "I'm Alright," theme
from *Caddyshack*. Columbia.
Paul McCartney, "Coming Up (Live at
Glasgow)." Columbia.
Bruce Springsteen, *Medley: Devil with
the Blue Dress/Good Golly Miss
Molly/Jenny Take a Ride*, track from
No Nukes. Asylum.

BEST ROCK VOCAL
PERFORMANCE, FEMALE
• Pat Benatar, *Crimes of Passion*.
Chrysalis.
Joan Armatrading, *How Cruel*. A&M.
Marianne Faithfull, *Broken English*. Island.
Linda Ronstadt, "How Do I Make You."
Asylum.
Grace Slick, *Dreams*. RCA.

BEST ROCK PERFORMANCE BY A
DUO OR GROUP WITH VOCAL
• Bob Seger & the Silver Bullet Band,
Against the Wind. Capitol.
Blondie, "Call Me." Chrysalis.
Pink Floyd, *The Wall*. Columbia.
Pretenders, "Brass in Pocket (I'm Spe-
cial)." Sire.
Queen, "Another One Bites the Dust."
Elektra.

BEST ROCK INSTRUMENTAL
PERFORMANCE
• Police, "Regatta de Blanc," track from
Regatta de Blanc. A&M.

Dixie Dregs, *Dregs of the Earth*. Arista.
Emerson, Lake & Palmer, "Peter Gunn."
Atlantic.
Jean-Luc Ponty, "Beach Girl." Atlantic.
Pretenders, "Space Invader," track from
Pretenders. Sire.

BEST RHYTHM & BLUES SONG
(Songwriter's Award)
- "Never Knew Love Like This Before,"
Reggie Lucas, James Mtume.
"Give Me the Night," Rod Temperton.
"Let's Get Serious," Lee Garrett, Stevie
Wonder.
"Shining Star," Leo Graham, Paul Rich-
mond.
"Upside Down," Bernard Edwards, Nile
Rodgers.

BEST RHYTHM & BLUES VOCAL
PERFORMANCE, MALE
- George Benson, *Give Me the Night*.
Warner Bros./Qwest.
Larry Graham, *One in a Million You*.
Warner Bros.
Jermaine Jackson, "Let's Get Serious."
Motown.
Al Jarreau, "Never Givin' Up." Warner
Bros.
Stevie Wonder, "Master Blaster (Jam-
min')." Motown/Tamla.

BEST RHYTHM & BLUES VOCAL
PERFORMANCE, FEMALE
- Stephanie Mills, "Never Knew Love
Like This Before." 20th Century.
Roberta Flack, *Roberta Flack Featuring
Donny Hathaway*. Atlantic.
Aretha Franklin, "Can't Turn You
Loose," track from *Aretha*. Arista.
Minnie Riperton, *Love Lives Forever*.
Capitol.
Diana Ross, "Upside Down." Motown.

BEST RHYTHM & BLUES VOCAL
PERFORMANCE BY A DUO OR GROUP
- Manhattans, "Shining Star." Columbia.
Commodores, *Heroes*. Motown.
Roberta Flack with Donny Hathaway,
"Back Together Again." Atlantic.
Jacksons, *Triumph*. Epic.

Gladys Knight & the Pips, *About Love*.
Columbia.
Spinners, "Cupid/I've Loved You for a
Long Time." Atlantic.

BEST RHYTHM & BLUES
INSTRUMENTAL PERFORMANCE
- George Benson, "On Broadway,"
track from *Give Me the Night*.
Warner Bros./Qwest.
Brothers Johnson, "Smilin' on Ya," track
from *Light Up the Night*. A&M.
Deodato, "Night Cruiser." Warner Bros.
B. B. King, "When I'm Wrong," track
from *Now Appearing at Ole Miss*.
MCA.
David Sanborn, "Anything You Want."
Warner Bros.

BEST JAZZ FUSION PERFORMANCE
(VOCAL OR INSTRUMENTAL)
- Manhattan Transfer, "Birdland."
Atlantic.
Earl Klugh, *Dream Come True*. United
Artists.
Chuck Mangione, *Fun and Games*.
A&M.
Pat Metheny, *American Garage*. ECM.
Spyro Gyra, *Catching the Sun*. MCA.
Patrick Williams, *An American Con-
certo*. Columbia.

BEST JAZZ VOCAL PERFORMANCE,
MALE
- George Benson, "Moody's Mood,"
track from *Give Me the Night*.
Warner Bros./ Qwest.
Bill Henderson, *Street of Dreams*. Dis-
covery.
Mark Murphy, *Satisfaction Guaranteed*.
Muse.
Slam Stewart, "Sidewalks of New York,"
track from *New York, Sounds of the
Apple*. Stash.
Mel Tormé, *Tormé/A New Album*.
Gryphon.

BEST JAZZ VOCAL PERFORMANCE,
FEMALE
- Ella Fitzgerald, *A Perfect Match/Ella
and Basie*. Pablo.

Betty Carter, *The Audience with Betty Carter*. Betcar.

Helen Humes, *Helen Humes and the Muse All Stars*. Muse.

Helen Merrill, *Chasin' the Bird*. Inner City.

Sarah Vaughan, *Sarah Vaughan: Duke Ellington Song Book One*. Pablo.

BEST JAZZ INSTRUMENTAL PERFORMANCE BY A SOLOIST

• Bill Evans, *I Will Say Goodbye*. Fantasy.

Pepper Adams (of the Helen Merrill Sextet), *Chasin' the Bird*. Inner City.

Hank Jones, *I Remember You*. Classic Jazz.

Jimmy Knapper, *Cunningbird*. Steeplechase.

Phil Woods, *The Phil Woods Quartet, Vol. 1*. Clean Cuts.

BEST JAZZ INSTRUMENTAL PERFORMANCE BY A GROUP

• Bill Evans, *We Will Meet Again*. Warner Bros.

Nick Brignola, *L.A. Bound*. Sea Breeze.

Heath Brothers, *Live at the Public Theatre*. CBS.

Hank Jones, *I Remember You*. Classic Jazz.

Bobby Shew, *Bobby Shew, Outstanding in His Field*. Inner City.

Phil Woods, *The Phil Woods Quartet, Vol. 1*. Clean Cuts.

BEST JAZZ INSTRUMENTAL PERFORMANCE BY A BIG BAND

• Count Basie & His Orchestra, *On the Road*. Pablo.

Toshiko Akiyoshi–Lew Tabackin Big Band, *Farewell*. Ascent.

Louis Bellson Big Band, *Dynamite!* Concord Jazz.

Bob Florence Big Band, *Live at Concerts by the Sea*. Trend.

Mel Lewis & the Jazz Orchestra, *Bob Brookmeyer, Composer/Arranger*. Gryphon.

Rob McConnell & the Boss Brass, *Present Perfect*. Pausa.

BEST COUNTRY SONG (Songwriter's Award)

• "On the Road Again," Willie Nelson.

"He Stopped Loving Her Today," Bobby Braddock, Curly Putman.

"I Believe in You," Roger Cook, Sam Hogin.

"Lookin' for Love," Bob Morrison, Wanda Mallette, Patti Ryan.

"Drivin' My Life Away," Eddie Rabbitt, Even Stevens, David Malloy.

BEST COUNTRY VOCAL PERFORMANCE, MALE

• George Jones, "He Stopped Loving Her Today." Epic.

George Burns, "I Wish I Was Eighteen Again." Mercury.

Johnny Lee, "Lookin' for Love." Full Moon/Asylum.

Willie Nelson, "On the Road Again." Columbia.

Eddie Rabbitt, "Drivin' My Life Away." Elektra.

BEST COUNTRY VOCAL PERFORMANCE, FEMALE

• Anne Murray, "Could I Have This Dance." Capitol.

Crystal Gayle, "If You Ever Change Your Mind." Columbia.

Emmylou Harris, *Roses in the Snow*. Warner Bros.

Barbara Mandrell, "The Best of Strangers." MCA.

Sissy Spacek, "Coal Miner's Daughter." MCA.

BEST COUNTRY PERFORMANCE BY A DUO OR GROUP WITH VOCAL

• Roy Orbison, Emmylou Harris, "That Lovin' You Feelin' Again." Warner Bros.

Charlie Daniels Band, *In America*. Epic.

Larry Gatlin & the Gatlin Brothers Band, "Take Me to Your Lovin' Place." Columbia.

Oak Ridge Boys, "Heart of Mine." MCA.

Tanya Tucker, Glen Campbell, "Dream Lover." MCA.

BEST COUNTRY INSTRUMENTAL PERFORMANCE

- Gilley's Urban Cowboy Band, "Orange Blossom Special/Hoedown," track from *Urban Cowboy*. Full Moon/Asylum.

Chet Atkins, "Dance with Me." RCA.

Ry Cooder, *The Long Riders*. Warner Bros.

Floyd Cramer, *Dallas*. RCA.

Danny Davis & the Nashville Brass, "Cotton Eyed Joe." RCA.

BEST GOSPEL PERFORMANCE, CONTEMPORARY OR INSPIRATIONAL

- Reba Rambo, Dony McGuire, B. J. Thomas, Andrae Crouch, Archers, Walter & Tramaine Hawkins, Cynthia Clawson, *The Lord's Prayer*. Light.

Andrae Crouch, "It's Gonna Rain." Light.

Amy Grant, *Never Alone*. Myrrh.

Imperials, *One More Song for You*. Dayspring.

Michael & Stormie Omartian, *The Builder*. Myrrh.

BEST GOSPEL PERFORMANCE, TRADITIONAL

- Blackwood Brothers, *We Come to Worship*. Voice Box.

Kenneth Copeland, *In His Presence*. KCP.

Rambos, *Crossin' Over*. Heartwarming.

Speers, *Interceding*. Heartwarming.

Jimmy Swaggart, *Worship*. Jim.

Lanny Wolfe Trio, *Make a Joyful Noise . . .* Impact.

BEST SOUL GOSPEL PERFORMANCE, CONTEMPORARY

- Shirley Caesar, *Rejoice*. Word.

Rance Allen Group, *I Feel Like Going On*. Stax.

Dynamic Disciples, "You Don't Know What God Has Done for Me." L. Brown.

Tramaine Hawkins, *Tramaine*. Light.

Kristle Murden, *I Can't Let Go*. Light.

BEST SOUL GOSPEL PERFORMANCE, TRADITIONAL

- James Cleveland & the Charles Fold Singers, *Lord, Let Me Be an Instrument*. Savoy.

James Cleveland & the Voices of Cornerstone, *A Praying Spirit*. Savoy.

Gospel Keynotes, *Ain't No Stopping Us Now*. Nashboro.

Dorothy Norwood, *God Can*. Savoy.

O'Neal Twins, *He Chose Me*. Savoy.

Albertina Walker with James Cleveland, *Please Be Patient with Me*. Savoy.

BEST INSPIRATIONAL PERFORMANCE

- Debby Boone, *With My Song I Will Praise Him*. Lamb & Lion.

Commodores, "Jesus Is Love," track from *Heroes*. Motown.

Bob Dylan, *Saved*. Columbia.

Willie Nelson, *Family Bible*. Songbird.

B. J. Thomas, "Everything Always Works Out for the Best." Songbird.

BEST ETHNIC OR TRADITIONAL RECORDING

- *Rare Blues*, Dr. Isaiah Ross, Maxwell Street Jimmy, Big Joe Williams, Son House, Rev. Robert Wilkins, Little Brother Montgomery, Sunnyland Slim. Takoma.

Atlanta Blues: 1933, Blind Willie McTell, Curley Weaver, Buddy Moss. John Edwards Memorial Foundation.

Boil the Breakfast Early (#9) Chieftains. Columbia.

Kidney Stew Is Fine, Eddie "Cleanhead" Vinson. Delmark.

Queen Ida & the Bon Temps Zydeco Band in New Orleans, Queen Ida. GNP/ Crescendo.

BEST LATIN RECORDING

- *La Onda Va Bien*, Cal Tjader Sextet. Concord Jazz.

Dancemania '80, Tito Puente. Tico.

Hey, Julio Iglesias. Discos CBS International.

Irakere 2, Irakere. Columbia.

Rican/Struction, Ray Barretto. Fania.

BEST INSTRUMENTAL ARRANGEMENT

- Quincy Jones, Jerry Hey, "Dinorah, Dinorah," track from *Give Me the Night* (George Benson). Warner Bros.
- Jorge Calandrelli, "Forget the Woman," track from *Morning Thunder* (Eddie Daniels). CBS.
- Dave Grusin, "Marcosinho," track from *The Hawk* (Dave Valentin). GRP.
- Bob Brookmeyer, "Skylark," track from *Bob Brookmeyer, Composer/Arranger* (Mel Lewis). Gryphon.
- Claus Ogerman, "Wave," track from *Terra Brasilis* (Antonio Carlos Jobim). Warner Bros.

BEST ARRANGEMENT ACCOMPANYING VOCALIST(S)

- Michael Omartian, "Sailing" (Christopher Cross). Warner Bros.
- Don Costa, "Theme from *New York, New York*" (Frank Sinatra). Reprise.
- David Cunningham, "Money" (Flying Lizards). Virgin.
- Rob McConnell, "Tangerine," track from *The Singers Unlimited with Rob McConnell and the Boss Brass* (Singers Unlimited). Pausa.
- Joe Puerta, Burleigh Drummond, David Pack, "Biggest Part of Me" (Ambrosia). Warner Bros.

BEST INSTRUMENTAL COMPOSITION

- "The Empire Strikes Back," John Williams.
- "An American Concerto," Patrick Williams.
- "Give It All You Got," Chuck Mangione.
- "The Imperial March (Darth Vader's Theme)," John Williams.
- "Yoda's Theme," John Williams.

BEST ARRANGEMENT FOR VOICES

- Janis Siegel, "Birdland," track from *Extensions* (Manhattan Transfer). Atlantic.
- Joe Puerta, Burleigh Drummond, David Pack, "Biggest Part of Me" (Ambrosia). Warner Bros.

Rod Temperton, "Give Me the Night" (George Benson). Warner Bros./Qwest.
Gene Puerling, "Sweet Georgia Brown," track from *Friends* (Singers Unlimited). Pausa.
Alan Paul, Jay Graydon, "Twilight Zone/Twilight Tone," track from *Extensions* (Manhattan Transfer). Atlantic.

BEST CAST SHOW ALBUM

- *Evita*, American recording. Andrew Lloyd Webber, composer; Tim Rice, lyricist. MCA.
- *Barnum*, Cy Coleman, composer; Michael Stewart, lyricist. CBS Masterworks.
- *A Day in Hollywood/A Night in the Ukraine*, Frank Lazarus, Jerry Herman, composers; Dick Vosburgh, Jerry Herman, lyricists. DRG.
- *Oklahoma!* Richard Rodgers, composer; Oscar Hammerstein II, lyricist. RCA.
- *One Mo' Time*, songs by 27 songwriters performed by blacks in vaudeville. Warner Bros.

BEST ALBUM OF ORIGINAL SCORE WRITTEN FOR A MOTION PICTURE OR TV SPECIAL

- *The Empire Strikes Back*, John Williams. RSO.
- *Fame*, Michael Gore, Anthony Evans, Paul McCrane, Dean Pitchford, Lesley Gore, Robert F. Colesberry. RSO.
- *One Trick Pony*, Paul Simon. Warner Bros.
- *Stevie Wonder's Journey Through the Secret Life of Plants*, Stevie Wonder, Michael Sembello, Stephanie Andrews, Yvonne Wright. Tamla.
- *Urban Cowboy*, J. D. Souther, Boz Scaggs, David Foster, Jerry Foster, Bill Rice, Brian Collins, Robby Campbell, Joe Walsh, Bob Morrison, Johnny Wilson, Dan Fogelberg, Bob Seger, Wayland Holyfield, Bob House, Wanda Mallette, Patti Ryan. Full Moon/Asylum.

BEST CLASSICAL ALBUM

• *Berg: Lulu (Complete)*, Pierre Boulez conducting the Orchestre de l'Opéra de Paris (solos: Teresa Stratas, Yvonne Minton, Franz Mazura, Toni Blankenheim). Deutsche Grammophon.

Bartók: Concerto for Violin and Orchestra, Zubin Mehta conducting the Los Angeles Philharmonic (solo: Pinchas Zukerman). Columbia.

Berg: Concerto for Violin and Orchestra; Stravinsky: Concerto in D Major for Violin and Orchestra, Seiji Ozawa conducting the Boston Symphony (solo: Itzhak Perlman). Deutsche Grammophon.

Bruckner: Symphony No. 6 in A Major, Sir Georg Solti conducting the Chicago Symphony. London.

Ruggles: Complete Music, Michael Tilson Thomas conducting the Buffalo Philharmonic. Columbia.

BEST CLASSICAL ORCHESTRAL RECORDING

(Conductor's Award)

• *Bruckner: Symphony No. 6 in A Major*, Sir Georg Solti conducting the Chicago Symphony. London.

Beethoven: Symphonies (9), Leonard Bernstein conducting the Vienna Philharmonic. Deutsche Grammophon.

Respighi: Feste Romane; Fountains of Rome, Michael Tilson Thomas conducting the Los Angeles Philharmonic. Columbia.

Ruggles: Complete Music, Michael Tilson Thomas conducting the Buffalo Philharmonic. Columbia.

Shostakovich: Symphony No. 5, Leonard Bernstein conducting the New York Philharmonic. Columbia.

BEST CHAMBER MUSIC PERFORMANCE (INSTRUMENTAL OR VOCAL)

• Itzhak Perlman, Pinchas Zukerman, *Music for 2 Violins (Moszkowski: Suite for 2 Violins; Shostakovich: Duets; Prokofiev: Sonata for 2 Violins)*. Angel.

Daniel Barenboim, Luben Yordanoff, Albert Tetard, Claude Desurmont, *Messiaen: Quartet for the End of Time*. Deutsche Grammophon.

Cleveland Quartet, *Beethoven: Early Quartets, Op. 18*. RCA.

Juilliard Quartet, *Schubert: Quartet No. 15 in G Major, Op. 161*. Columbia.

Pinchas Zukerman, Marc Neikrug, *Debussy: Sonata No. 3 in G Minor for Violin and Piano; Fauré: Sonata in A Major for Violin and Piano*. Columbia.

BEST CLASSICAL PERFORMANCE, INSTRUMENTAL SOLOIST(S) (WITH ORCHESTRA)

(Tie)

• Itzhak Perlman (Seiji Ozawa conducting the Boston Symphony), *Berg: Concerto for Violin and Orchestra; Stravinsky: Concerto in D Major for Violin and Orchestra*. Deutsche Grammophon.

• Itzhak Perlman, Mstislav Rostropovich (Bernard Haitink conducting the Concertgebouw Orchestra), *Brahms: Concerto in A Minor for Violin and Cello ("Double Concerto")*. Angel.

Maurice André (Maurice André conducting the Franz Liszt Chamber Orchestra), *Bach for Trumpet*. Angel.

James Galway (I Solisti di Zagreb), *Telemann: Concertos in G and C for Flute; Suite in A Minor*. RCA.

Gerard Schwarz (Gerard Schwarz conducting the Y Chamber Symphony of New York), *The Classic Trumpet Concertos of Haydn and Hummel*. Delos.

Pinchas Zukerman (Zubin Mehta conducting the Los Angeles Philharmonic), *Bartók: Concerto for Violin and Orchestra*. Columbia.

BEST CLASSICAL PERFORMANCE, INSTRUMENTAL SOLOIST(S) (WITHOUT ORCHESTRA)

• Itzhak Perlman, *The Spanish Album*. Angel.

Glenn Gould, *Bach: Toccatas, Vol. 2*. Columbia.

Ruth Laredo, *Rachmaninov: Music for Piano, Vol. 7 (Sonatas Nos. 1 and 2)*. Columbia.

Joshua Rifkin, *Digital Ragtime, Music of Scott Joplin*. Angel.

Rudolf Serkin, *Brahms: Variations and Fugue on a Theme by Handel*. Columbia.

Leo Smit, *Copland: The Complete Music for Solo Piano*. Columbia.

BEST OPERA RECORDING

• *Berg: Lulu (Complete)*, Pierre Boulez conducting the Orchestre de l'Opéra de Paris (solos: Teresa Stratas, Yvonne Minton, Franz Mazura, Toni Blankenheim). Deutsche Grammophon.

Bartók: Bluebeard's Castle, Sir Georg Solti conducting the London Philharmonic (solos: Sylvia Sass, Kolos Kovats). London.

Debussy: Pelléas et Mélisande, Herbert von Karajan conducting the Berlin Philharmonic (solos: Frederica von Stade, Richard Stilwell). Angel.

Puccini: La Bohème, James Levine conducting the National Philharmonic, Ambrosian Chorus (solos: Renata Scotto, Alfredo Kraus, Carol Neblett, Sherrill Milnes). Angel.

Weill: Silverlake, Julius Rudel conducting the New York City Opera Orchestra and Chorus (solos: Joel Grey, William Neill, Elizabeth Hynes, Jack Harrold, Elaine Bonazzi). Nonesuch.

BEST CLASSICAL PERFORMANCE, CHORAL (OTHER THAN OPERA)

• Norbert Balatsch, chorus master; Carlo Maria Giulini conducting the Philharmonia Chorus and Orchestra, *Mozart: Requiem*. Angel.

Claudio Abbado conducting the London Symphony Chorus and Orchestra, *Prokofiev: Alexander Nevsky*. Deutsche Grammophon.

Thomas Hilbish conducting the University of Michigan Chamber Choir and Chamber Ensemble, *Menotti: The Unicorn, the Gorgon and the Manticore*. University of Michigan School of Music.

John Oliver, chorus master, Tanglewood Festival Chorus; Seiji Ozawa conducting the Boston Symphony, *Schoenberg: Gurrelieder*. Philips.

Robert Shaw conducting the the Atlanta Symphony Chorus and Orchestra, *Boito: Prologue to Mefistofele*. Telarc.

BEST CLASSICAL PERFORMANCE, VOCAL SOLOIST

• Leontyne Price (Henry Lewis conducting the Philharmonic Orchestra), *Prima Donna, Vol. 5, Great Soprano Arias from Handel to Britten*. RCA.

Elly Ameling (Jorg Demus, accompanist), *Mozart: Songs*. Seraphim.

Judith Blegen (Pierre Boulez conducting the New York Philharmonic), *Berg: Lulu Suite*. Columbia.

Kiri Te Kanawa (Andrew Davis conducting the London Symphony), *R. Strauss: 4 Last Songs and Orchestral Songs*. Columbia.

Jessye Norman (Pierre Boulez conducting the New York Philharmonic), *Berg: Der Wein, Concert Aria*. Columbia.

Frederica von Stade (Andrew Davis conducting the London Philharmonic), *Mahler: Songs of a Wayfarer and Ruckert Songs*. Columbia.

BEST ENGINEERED RECORDING, CLASSICAL

• Karl-August Naegler, *Berg: Lulu (Complete)* (Pierre Boulez conducting the Orchestre de l'Opéra de Paris; solos: Teresa Stratas, Yvonne Minton, Franz Mazura, Toni Blankenheim). Deutsche Grammophon.

Almeida: First Concerto for Guitar and Orchestra (Laurindo Almeida; Elmer Ramsey conducting the Los Angeles

Orchestra de Camera). Concord Concerto.

Robert Norberg, Mitchell Tanenbaum, *Bach: The 6 Brandenburg Concertos* (Gerard Schwarz conducting the Los Angeles Chamber Orchestra). Angel.

Bud Graham, Ray Moore, *Bartók: Concerto for Violin and Orchestra* (Pinchas Zukerman; Zubin Mehta conducting the Los Angeles Philharmonic). Columbia.

Michael Gray, *Brahms: Concerto in A Minor for Violin and Cello ("Double Concerto")* (Itzhak Perlman, Mstislav Rostropovich; Bernard Haitink conducting the Concertgebouw Orchestra). Angel.

John McClure, Ed Michalski, *Shostakovich: Symphony No. 5* (Leonard Bernstein conducting the New York Philharmonic). Columbia.

CLASSICAL PRODUCER OF THE YEAR
• Robert Woods
Steven Epstein
Andrew Kazdin
John McClure
Paul Myers

BEST SPOKEN WORD, DOCUMENTARY OR DRAMA RECORDING
• *Gertrude Stein, Gertrude Stein, Gertrude Stein*, Pat Carroll. Caedmon.
Adventures of Luke Skywalker: The Empire Strikes Back, original cast with narration. RSO.
A Curb in the Sky (James Thurber), Peter Ustinov. Caedmon.
I Sing Because I'm Happy, Vols. 1 and 2, Mahalia Jackson. Folkways.
Obediently Yours/Orson Welles, Orson Welles. Mark 56.

BEST COMEDY RECORDING
• *No Respect,* Rodney Dangerfield. Casablanca.
Contractual Obligation, Monty Python. Arista.
Holy Smoke, Richard Pryor. Laff.

Live at St. Douglas Convent, Father Guido Sarducci. Warner Bros.
Live from New York, Gilda Radner. Warner Bros.

BEST RECORDING FOR CHILDREN
• *In Harmony/A Sesame Street Record*, Doobie Brothers, James Taylor, Carly Simon, Bette Midler, Muppets, Al Jarreau, Linda Ronstadt, Wendy Waldman, Libby Titus & Dr. John, Livingston Taylor, George Benson & Pauline Wilson, Lucy Simon, Kate Taylor & the Simon/Taylor Family. Sesame Street.
Big Bird's Birdtime Stories, Sesame Street Muppets and cast. Sesame Street.
Christmas Eve on Sesame Street, Sesame Street Muppets and cast. Sesame Street.
Love, Sesame Street Muppets and cast. Sesame Street.
The People in Your Neighborhood, Sesame Street Muppets. Sesame Street.

BEST ENGINEERED RECORDING
• James Guthrie, *The Wall* (Pink Floyd). Columbia.
Chet Himes, *Christopher Cross* (Christopher Cross). Warner Bros.
Bill Schnee, *Growing Up in Hollywood Town* (Lincoln Mayorga, Amanda McBroom). Sheffield Lab.
Bill Schnee, *New Baby* (Don Randi, Quest). Sheffield Lab.
Bruce Swedien. "Give Me the Night," track from *Give Me the Night* (George Benson). Warner Bros./Qwest.

BEST ALBUM PACKAGE
(Art Director's Award)
• Roy Kohara, *Against the Wind* (Bob Seger & the Silver Bullet Band). Capitol.
John Berg, *Chicago XIV* (Chicago). Columbia.
Ron Coro, Johnny Lee, *Cats* (Cats). Elektra.

Vigon Nahas Vigon, *Tusk* (Fleetwood Mac). Warner Bros.

Paula Scher, *One on One* (Bob James, Earl Klugh). Columbia.

BEST ALBUM NOTES
(Annotator's Award)

• David McClintock, *Trilogy: Past, Present and Future* (Frank Sinatra). Reprise.

David Evans, Bruce Bastin, *Atlanta Blues: 1933* (Blind Willie McTell, Curley Weaver, Buddy Moss). John Edwards Memorial Foundation.

Lorene Lortie, *Elvis Aron Presley*. RCA.

John McDonough, Richard M. Sudhalter, *Lester Young* (Giants of Jazz). Time-Life.

Dan Morgenstern, *Chicago Concert, 1956* (Louis Armstrong). Columbia.

BEST HISTORICAL REISSUE ALBUM

• *Segovia, The EMI Recordings 1927–39*. Angel.

Early History of the Phonograph Record. Mark 56.

First Edition/The Golden Age of Broadway. RCA Special Production.

The Guitarists (Giants of Jazz). Time-Life.

Songs of the Depression: Happy Days Are Here Again. Book-of-the-Month.

PRODUCER OF THE YEAR

• Phil Ramone

Quincy Jones

Michael Omartian

Queen and Mack

Stevie Wonder

• 1981 •

"John Is with Us Here Tonight"

When John Lennon was gunned down outside his New York City apartment building on a dark December morning in 1980, the tragedy echoed ominously throughout the music world.

Lennon hadn't been fully appreciated by industry insiders after he split with the Beatles. Even though he was still creating such admired solo hits as "Imagine" and "Give Peace a Chance," he was often snubbed when he embraced radical rock & roll and flirted with Asian music. "Once Lennon left the safety and prestige of the Beatles, he was relegated to the mavericks," the *Los Angeles Times* reported. "After all, wasn't he the kook who went traipsing around with Yoko Ono looking like two gurus in drag?"

N.A.R.A.S. had also failed to give the former Beatle his solo due. Lennon was the only member of the Fab Four who failed to receive a Grammy after the group busted up in 1970. Worse, he didn't even get a nomination. Now he and Ono had five bids for *Double Fantasy,* their eccentric valentine to each other that included their serious musings on a crazy world. The *L.A. Times* applauded "the quiet wisdom of songs like Lennon's 'Watching the Wheels' and Ono's moving 'Hard Times Are Over.'" Smitten record buyers turned tracks like "(Just Like) Starting Over" and "Woman" into hit singles. At the Grammys, "Starting Over" was up for Record of the Year, *Double Fantasy* for 1981's best album.

As Grammy night progressed, three Lennon/Ono bids failed to result in award victories. Then the showdown came over Album of the Year. *Double Fantasy* was pitted against Kim Carnes's *Mistaken Identity* in what critics consid-

John Lennon was dismissed as a nutty maverick after teaming up with Yoko Ono. After his death, the duo was hailed with Grammy's top award.

ered a close race, but even Carnes admitted she was rooting for the Lennons as she wept quietly in her seat as everyone waited for the announcement of the winner. ("How could you help not crying?" she later asked reporters.)

Variety reported on the scene that followed: "The most touching moment in the two-hour and 24-minute broadcast was saved until nearly the end, when Yoko Ono, accompanied by her young son, Sean, stepped to the podium to accept the Album of the Year Grammy for *Double Fantasy,* which was just climbing the charts when ex-Beatle John Lennon was murdered.

"Momentarily too overcome by the

thunderous, highly emotional ovation from the Shrine Auditorium audience to speak, Ono finally accepted the Grammy by saying she and Lennon were 'always very proud and happy that we were a part of the human race . . . that we made good music for the earth and for the universe.'"

Looking appropriately regal but emotionally racked, the widow of rock's reigning martyr added, "I think John is with us here tonight."

It was, according to the *L.A. Times,* "one of the most dramatic moments in the 24-year history of the record industry competition."

Once Ono and her son resumed their seats, Kenny Loggins and Pat Benatar read through the list of contenders for best single. Once they "got to the fourth nominated record, Lennon's '(Just Like) Starting Over,' the television camera caught Ono crying," noted the *Times.* Again, Lennon and Ono's chief competition for the year's top Grammy was Carnes, whose "Bette Davis Eyes" was both a critical and a commercial hit. The *L.A. Times* was among those that predicted "Eyes" would have it: "Over the past 23 years, the Record of the Year prize has gone to a No. 1 hit 15 times and to the No. 1 hit of the year 6 times. This wry, rock inflected smash could easily make that 16 and 7." When "Bette Davis Eyes" prevailed, the *Times* added, "It probably deserved to win. At the moment it was announced, though, Carnes's victory paled in comparison to Ono's loss."

"My mind was a little numb during the best album award," Carnes told reporters backstage later. "But when I won best record, my head sort of exploded."

Carnes was a former New Christy Minstrel who, along with her husband, musician David Ellingson, also distinguished herself as a songwriter for Frank Sinatra, Barbra Streisand, Anne Murray

NIGHT BELONGED TO QUINCY JONES

Producer Wins 5 Grammys; 'Bette Davis' Year's Top Song; 'Fantasy' Comes True

Quincy Jones lost his bid for best LP, but nabbed five Grammys, including Producer of the Year.

and other star talent. Her career as a singer was less noteworthy: Her husky voice often got her dismissed as "a female Rod Stewart," and even as late as the mid-1980s, her best songs like "What About Me" always seemed to sell best when they were recorded by other artists, like Kenny Rogers and James Ingram. Ironically, "Bette Davis Eyes"—her biggest vocal hit and also winner of Song of the Year—was written by other tunesmiths: Donna Weiss and Jackie DeShannon. Reporters asked Weiss backstage what Bette Davis herself thought about the song. She answered: "Bette thanked us for making her part of the modern world. She says she's now a big hit with her grandson." After the single won Song of the Year, Davis sent roses to the artists.

The *Washington Post* made a daring move this year when it polled a number of industry experts and asked them to handicap the top 16 awards. "There are only four shoo-ins," the group concluded: One was Carnes for best female pop vocal performance.

The winner in that category turned out to be an older music pro instead—Lena Horne. "It was a year for catching up with overlooked artists of the past," the *Post* said in its wrap-up coverage. The *L.A. Herald Examiner* declared that this year's Grammys "belonged to the legends."

Horne's career began at age 17 when she was a crooner and hoofer at New York's Cotton Club. While still in her 20s, she performed at Carnegie Hall and began starring in a string of Hollywood films that would establish her as the first great black singing screen star. At the age of 64, Horne took her act to Broadway with a one-woman concert retrospective of her work, *The Lady and Her Music,* which was met with rave notices and sold-out audiences. "It's a lifetime achievement of a legend," said producer Quincy Jones as he picked up a Grammy for the LP's second award of the night: Best Cast Show Album.

But it was Jones himself—already a legend at age 49—who turned out to be the biggest winner of the night. His latest album, *The Dude,* which included contributions from singer James Ingram, scored a total of 11 nominations (although not all for him personally), including a bid for Album of the Year. Since Jones was also established as a leading producer of other artists' works, he had three additional nominations for non-*Dude* music such as Lena Horne's LP, as well as an accolade he finally won after being overlooked for the last three years: Producer of the Year.

> When "Bette Davis Eyes" became a hit, Davis said she "became part of the modern world."

"Jones finally received the kind of recognition befitting the studio genius he is," the *Herald Examiner* declared. "Jones, in fact, has been the best record producer in the world since George Martin's days of duty with the Beatles."

"If anyone owned the 24th annual Grammy Awards, it was Quincy Jones," the same paper said. Jones won five awards in all, the last three of which were for *The Dude:* the r&b group vocal performance award, an instrumental arrangement accompanying vocals prize for *Dude* track "Ai No Corrida" and an instrumental arrangement trophy for "Velas." "You have to stay around a long time for moments like this," Jones said backstage later as he admired all five Grammys in his grasp. "Man, I've been nominated something like 60 times. I've seen four decades of change. Just my nominations had blown me away. But this," he added, holding up the golden statuettes with a smile, "this is something else. What a beautiful night."

The torrent of honors for Jones helped to contribute toward James Ingram's victory for best r&b male vocal performance for a track from *The Dude* entitled "One Hundred Ways." (The *Washington Post* called the win "a mild upset," since Ingram was "a studio artist who doesn't even have his own record out.") The prize was presented by the never-nominated James Brown, who was obviously shocked. When he opened the envelope, the godfather of soul said, "And the award goes to . . . Good God! I can't stand it!"

Ingram was also up for Best New Artist but was considered a long shot thanks to another *Washington Post* "shoo-in" who actually came through: Sheena Easton.

Easton was one of the hip young singers vanquished by music's reigning "Lady," Lena Horne, for the pop singing laurels. Easton lost to Horne for the same hit that made her seem so promising as Best New Artist: the title theme song to the latest James Bond flick, *For Your Eyes Only.* The suddenly triumphant newcomer obviously felt she had paid her dues, though. "I wanted this *sooo* much," she said in her thick Scottish brogue while clutching her Best New Artist award. "I'm glad that, at the party [after the Grammy ceremony], I don't have to be gracious to everybody."

The rest of the pop singing honors were seized by artists who also struck gold in the jazz lineup. Vocal acrobat Al Jarreau had been well known in jazz circles for a half dozen years, but now he was gaining a broader audience thanks to his popular *Breaking Away* album, which earned him the pop male vocal award plus the equivalent jazz prize for its "Blue Rondo à la Turk" track. The vocal quartet Manhattan Transfer won its first Grammy last year but now claimed two more: the jazz group vocal award for "Until I Met You (Corner Pocket)" and the group pop vocal honors for "Boy from New York City," both from their *Mecca for Moderns* LP. To win the pop prize, the Manhattan Transfer beat long-time Grammy loser Diana Ross, who was the odds-on favorite to prevail with her "Endless Love" duet with Lionel Richie, which was also considered a close contender for Record and Song of the Year.

Ten-time past Grammy grabber Ella Fitzgerald returned to claim the prize for female jazz vocals for a third year in a row, winning for her performance at Switzerland's Montreux Jazz Festival. Other artists honored for their recent work in the Alpine country were Chick Corea and Gary Burton, who had previously won the group instrumental prize in 1979 and now reprised their victory for a recording of a joint concert held in Zurich. Sax player/composer/bandleader Gerry Mulligan had been prominent in the jazz field since the late 1940s when he worked with Miles Davis and Gene Krupa ("You feel as if you're listening to the past, present, and future of jazz all at one time," Dave Brubeck once said about Mulligan's music), but he received his first Grammy this year for *Walk on the Water,* a broad sampling of his original compositions. Tenor sax player John Coltrane died in 1967 but received an instrumental award posthumously for *Bye Bye Blackbird,* the recording of a concert he performed in the mid-1960s that had not been released on disc earlier.

Sax player/singer Grover Washington, Jr.'s bid for the jazz fusion award was another of the *Washington Post*'s "shoo-ins" that came out as predicted. His victorious *Winelight* LP contained the hit single "Just the Two of Us" that lost its bids to be Record and Song of the Year but nonetheless won as Best Rhythm & Blues Song for cowriters Bill Withers, William Salter and Ralph MacDonald.

"In the rock field, the female vocalist award is a tight battle between Pat Benatar (last year's winner in the same category) and Stevie Nicks (two-Grammy winner as part of Fleetwood Mac)," the

Al Jarreau heard the roar of Grammy victory in stereo after claiming awards in both the pop and jazz categories for *Breakin' Away.*

Post reported. "Bruce Springsteen, a non-winner despite platinum raves, may finally get a thank-you in the rock male category." Six out of eight experts polled by the *Post* said Springsteen was a cinch to get it for his LP *The River*.

Benatar prevailed for her hit album *Crimes of Passion*, which featured her hit single "Hit Me with Your Best Shot." In a shocking upset, Springsteen was defeated by pop heartthrob Rick Springfield. *The New York Times* reported: "Springfield's victory over Bruce Springsteen and Rod Stewart in the rock vocal category was a characteristic example of the Grammys' tendency to reflect commercial performance more accurately than artistic accomplishment. Mr. Springsteen and Mr. Stewart both made their best albums in a number of years in 1981." Springfield was bolstered by his enormous popularity as an actor on the soap opera *General Hospital,* on which he played the character Dr. Noah Drake. "The record, you know, was just another record on the market," Springfield told reporters backstage. "But I really believe *General Hospital* gave it the hook, the kick in the rear."

The Police raided the last two rock categories, beating the Rolling Stones, who still hadn't gathered a single Grammy and were heavily favored to win finally for "Start Me Up" from *Tattoo You.* But with their critical and commercial success, *Zenyatta Mondatta,* the Police prevailed, taking the group vocal prize for the single "Don't Stand So Close to Me" and the instrumental award for "Behind My Camel," a category they also won at last year's Grammys.

The *Washington Post* foretold only one of the country prizes correctly: "In the female country category, it's an acknowledged old-timer (Dolly Parton and '9 to 5') against a veteran who's just found success this year (Juice Newton and 'Queen of Hearts'). Look for a Parton victory."

Parton received four nominations for "9 to 5," three of them for composition. She started writing songs on a film set while she was bored. "The hardest thing was the long wait between shots," Parton once said about starring in *9 to 5.* "I can't embroider or nothin' like that, so I figured if I started writing songs, it would change my mood. I was amazed at how easily I could do it."

Rick Springfield trounced "shoo-in" Bruce Springsteen.

The outcome of her writing debut was so good that the tune was picked up as the film's official theme song and was competing at the Grammys for Song of the Year, Best Country Song, best female country vocal performance and best film score. It reaped both Best Country Song and the trophy for female vocals. (It lost Best Song at the Oscars to "Fame.") The film score honors went once again to John Williams, whose victorious *Raiders of the Lost Ark* score followed previous winners *Jaws* (1975), *Star Wars* (1977), *Close Encounters of the Third Kind* (1978), *Superman* (1979) and *The Empire Strikes Back* (1980).

The victory of "9 to 5" as Best Country Song was surprising considering that its chief challenger was "Elvira," sung by the Oak Ridge Boys, which had been the biggest-selling country song ever recorded in Nashville up to that point and had also been hailed as Single of the Year

by both the Country Music Association and the Academy of Country Music. The Oak Ridge Boys had won four Grammys in the past, all for singing religious music, but when they netted the group vocals prize for "Elvira," it marked their first trophy for a country performance.

The *Washington Post* sized up the lineup for the male vocals accolade this way: "Eddie Rabbit, who is basically a pop artist recording in Nashville, is a favorite as country male, though George Jones can't be discounted." The *Los Angeles Herald Examiner* called the whole category "a powerhouse lineup including Willie Nelson, George Jones, Eddie Rabbitt (well, he sells a lot of records), Ronnie Milsap, and—the most deserving and adventurous choice—John Anderson." The winner: Milsap, for his best-selling single "(There's) No Gettin' Over Me," his third Grammy. It had been five years since Chet Atkins last snared the instrumental category, but he now reclaimed it for country music with *Country, After All These Years,* which gave him his seventh statuette in all.

Repeaters once again dominated the religious awards: Andrae Crouch (*Don't Give Up,* his fifth Grammy and fourth in a row), B. J. Thomas (*Amazing Grace,* his fifth consecutive award) and the Imperials (*Priority,* their fourth winner). Past Grammy victors J.D. Sumner and James Blackwood joined a number of other noted religious singers to take the traditional gospel performance prize for a talent roundup called *The Masters V.* Al Green would go on to win more than a half dozen Grammys over the next decade, but he reaped his first for best traditional soul gospel performance for *The Lord Will Make a Way.* Earlier in his career, Green had distinguished himself as a soul singer with such hits as "Let's Stay Together," but after he became a minister in the late 1970s, he would only perform gospel music.

B. B. King had won a Grammy back in 1970, and now he claimed a second for *There Must Be a Better World Somewhere* as Best Ethnic or Traditional Recording, "a curiously titled category usually reserved for blues artists" like King, noted the *New York Times*. Backstage, King told reporters that he was not a typical blues artist, which he described this way: "His pants are worn out and his shoes don't have laces and his cap is on backwards and he has a cigarette hanging out of the eastern corner of his lip.

"Now look at me," King added, pointing to his dapper tuxedo. "I rest my case."

"Guajira pa la Jeva" reaped Best Latin Recording for Clare Fischer, who the *New York Times* said "is hardly a Latin musician, but Fischer has made a number of Latin-tinged pop-jazz albums over the years."

The Muppets continued to dominate the children's category when *Sesame Country* trounced those cartoon rockers the Chipmunks, who had not won a Grammy since 1960. The Muppets' latest winner featured a host of celebrity c&w singers such as Glen Campbell, Loretta Lynn, Tanya Tucker and Crystal Gayle. The Chipmunks were also trounced for Best Comedy Recording by Richard Pryor, who dominated the category from 1974 to 1976 but hadn't scored another win since. This time he was honored for *Rev. Du Rite,* a spoof of how ministers use religious double talk in sermons. "I come not here to plague you with the questions of the no answers," says Pryor as Rev. Du Rite, "and you can't get to the left without the right. . . . " Most of Pryor's material on the LP was taped originally in 1976, which caused some critics to protest its eligibility. The race was also controversial because a track from Mel Brooks's film LP *History of the World Part 1* called "The Inquisition" was competing against the entire album.

N.A.R.A.S. introduced a new category in 1981 that signaled a significant change in how music was being appreciated:

Lena Horne scored a pop vocals statuette for her Broadway comeback LP *The Lady and Her Music.*

Video of the Year. To be eligible, the music videos did not simply have to be shown on the new MTV cable channel or elsewhere on TV, but they had to be produced for the consumer home video market. In noting the first winner, the *Washington Post* gave away its own "Irony and Fair Warning Award to one-time Monkee Michael Nesmith for capturing the first-ever Video Grammy for 'Elephant Parts.' Nesmith, an industry maverick, has predicted that audio-only records will be obsolete within 10 years. He received a plaque rather than the traditional Victrola-shaped award."

Back in 1972, Sir Georg Solti and the Chicago Symphony won the Classical Album of the Year award for their rendition of Mahler's Symphony No. 8. In 1981, the honor went again to Solti and the Chicago Symphony for another work by Mahler—this time the Second Symphony—bringing them also the new prize for Best Classical Orchestral Recording, which replaced the earlier performance award. Solti had conducted the work earlier in his career using the London Symphony Orchestra, but this rendition was applauded by critics for being lighter. *High Fidelity* complained of some perceptible "impatience" on Solti's part, but added, "The orchestra plays magnificently and Sir Georg conducts brilliantly."

Itzhak Perlman won only half as many Grammys as he reaped in 1980 when he claimed two this year, including the honor of Best Chamber Music Performance, which he shared with Vladimir Ashkenazy and Lynn Harrell for Tchaikovsky's Piano Trio in A Minor. He also earned the soloist's (with orchestra) award for his participation in the salute to fellow violinist Isaac Stern on the occasion of Stern's 60th birthday, which was celebrated at the New York Philharmonic's 1980 opening night. *High Fidelity* predicted Perlman fans "will be ecstatic" over the birthday tribute, which also won best engineered classical recording.

The soloist award without orchestral accompaniment went to Vladimir Horowitz (*The Horowitz Concerts 1979/80*), who lately spurned studio recordings in favor of concert performances, saying, "I could polish . . . but I prefer the excitement." For the choral prize, Neville Marriner conducted the Chorus of the Academy of St. Martin-in-the-Fields in Haydn's *Creation,* which they performed, said *High Fidelity,* with masterful "poise and buoyancy."

Throughout his conducting career, Sir Charles Mackerras had distinguished himself as one of the principal interpreters of works by Leoš Janáček. For this year's Best Opera Recording, the first-time winner used some of the world's greatest Czech singers along with his Vienna Philharmonic Orchestra to dramatize the composer's final opera, *From the House of the Dead,* which he based on Dostoyevsky's recollections of his imprisonment in a Siberian labor camp. Soon after Janáček's death in 1928, the opera suffered considerable changes at the hands of two of his students who considered it unfinished. Mackerras's rendition was the first recording of the composer's original

work. "At last it is possible to hear *House of the Dead* in all its spare, stark and uncompromising majesty," *High Fidelity* wrote, adding that Mackerras's conducting "is little short of brilliant and his stabbingly unsentimental interpretation penetrates right to the heart of the music." Mackerras's producer, James Mallinson, who also oversaw Solti's London recordings, was named Classical Producer of the Year.

Roundup celebrity concerts rarely get rave critical notices, but a notable exception occurred when Joan Sutherland, Marilyn Horne and Luciano Pavarotti shared the stage at Lincoln Center and soon thereafter also shared the soloist's performance Grammy for singing excerpts from Verdi's *Otello,* Bellini's *Norma* and Ponchielli's *La Giaconda.*

The Grammycast got good notices again this year, particularly for host John Denver, who, said The *Washington Post,* "was quite smooth, a far cry from the petrified Paul Simon last year." Entertainment included the Oak Ridge Boys singing "Elvira," Rick Springfield crooning "Jessie's Girl" and the Pointer Sisters singing the nominee list for Best New Artist ("and besting them all," added the *Post*).

The night had three notable losers, though, including Diana Ross and Lionel Richie, whose "Endless Love" duet lost all four prizes for which it was nominated. For Richie, the night was even worse: He had three additional losing bids—two for his work with the Commodores and one as Producer of the Year.

Last year's big winner, Christopher Cross, was also in evidence this year while competing for Record and Song of the Year plus best male pop vocal performance. Cross not only sang "Arthur's Theme (Best That You Can Do)," but he shared the writing credit with Peter Allen, Burt Bacharach and Carole Bayer Sager. Although it won Best Song at the Oscars, it failed to take any Grammys, and Cross—who last year became the only artist to win all four top prizes—vanished from the N.A.R.A.S. awards scene completely thereafter.

The awards ceremony was broadcast on CBS from the Shrine Auditorium in Los Angeles on February 24, 1982, for the awards eligibility period of October 1, 1980, through September 30, 1981.

ALBUM OF THE YEAR

• *Double Fantasy*, John Lennon, Yoko Ono. Geffen/Warner Bros.
Breakin' Away, Al Jarreau. Warner Bros.
The Dude, Quincy Jones. A&M.
Gaucho, Steely Dan. MCA.
Mistaken Identity, Kim Carnes. EMI-America.

RECORD OF THE YEAR

• "Bette Davis Eyes," Kim Carnes. EMI-America.
"Arthur's Theme (Best That You Can Do)," Christopher Cross. Warner Bros.
"Endless Love," Diana Ross, Lionel Richie. Motown.
"(Just Like) Starting Over," John Lennon. Geffen/Warner Bros.
"Just the Two of Us," Bill Withers, Grover Washington, Jr. Elektra/Asylum.

SONG OF THE YEAR
(Songwriter's Award)

• "Bette Davis Eyes," Donna Weiss, Jackie DeShannon.
"Arthur's Theme (Best That You Can Do)," Peter Allen, Burt Bacharach, Carole Bayer Sager, Christopher Cross.
"Endless Love," Lionel Richie.
"Just the Two of Us," Bill Withers, William Salter, Ralph MacDonald.
"9 to 5," Dolly Parton.

BEST NEW ARTIST

• Sheena Easton
Adam & the Ants
Go-Go's
James Ingram
Luther Vandross

BEST POP VOCAL PERFORMANCE, MALE

• Al Jarreau, *Breaking Away*. Warner Bros.
Christopher Cross, "Arthur's Theme (Best That You Can Do)." Warner Bros.
James Ingram, "Just Once," track. A&M.
John Lennon, "Double Fantasy" (Lennon tracks only). Geffen/Warner Bros.
Bill Withers, "Just the Two of Us," track. Elektra/Asylum.

BEST POP VOCAL PERFORMANCE, FEMALE

• Lena Horne, *Lena Horne: The Lady and Her Music Live on Broadway*. Qwest/Warner Bros.
Kim Carnes, "Bette Davis Eyes." EMI-America.
Sheena Easton, "For Your Eyes Only." Liberty.
Juice Newton, "Angel of the Morning." Capitol.
Olivia Newton-John, "Physical." MCA.

BEST POP PERFORMANCE BY A DUO OR GROUP WITH VOCAL

• Manhattan Transfer, "Boy from New York City." Atlantic.
Steely Dan, *Gaucho*. MCA.

Yoko Ono was "overcome by the thunderous, highly emotional ovation," *Variety* said.

Daryl Hall, John Oates, *Private Eyes*.
  RCA.
Pointer Sisters, "Slow Hand."
  Planet/Elektra/Asylum.
Diana Ross, Lionel Richie, "Endless
  Love." Motown.

BEST POP INSTRUMENTAL PERFORMANCE

• Mike Post Featuring Larry Carlton,
  "Theme from *Hill Street Blues*."
  Elektra/Asylum.
Louis Clark conducting the Royal Phil-
  harmonic Orchestra, *Hooked on
  Classics*. RCA.
Quincy Jones, "Velas," track. A&M.
Earl Klugh, *Late Night Guitar*. Liberty.
Lee Ritenour, *Rit* (side 2, instrumentals).
  Elektra/Asylum.

BEST ROCK VOCAL PERFORMANCE, MALE

• Rick Springfield, "Jessie's Girl." RCA.
Rick James, "Super Freak."
  Gordy/Motown.
Bruce Springsteen, *The River*. Colum-
  bia/CBS.
Rod Stewart, "Young Turks." Warner
  Bros.
Gary "U. S." Bonds, *Dedication*. EMI-
  America.

BEST ROCK VOCAL PERFORMANCE, FEMALE

• Pat Benatar, *Crimes of Passion*.
  Chrysalis.
Lulu, "Who's Foolin' Who," track. Alfa.
Stevie Nicks, "Edge of Seventeen,"
  track. Modern/Atlantic.
Yoko Ono, "Walking on Thin Ice." Gef-
  fen/Warner Bros.
Donna Summer, "Cold Love," track.
  Geffen/Warner Bros.

BEST ROCK PERFORMANCE BY A DUO OR GROUP WITH VOCAL

• Police, "Don't Stand So Close to Me."
  A&M.
Foreigner, *4*. Atlantic.
REO Speedwagon, *Hi Infidelity*.
  Epic/CBS.

Stevie Nicks with Tom Petty & the
  Heartbreakers, "Stop Draggin' My
  Heart Around." Modern/Atlantic.
Rolling Stones, "Start Me Up," track
  from *Tattoo You*. Rolling
  Stones/Atlantic.

BEST ROCK INSTRUMENTAL PERFORMANCE

• Police, "Behind My Camel," track.
  A&M.
Dregs, *Unsung Heroes*. Arista.
Robert Fripp, *The League of Gentlemen*.
  Polygram/Polydor.
Kraftwerk, "Computer World," track.
  Warner Bros.
Rush, "YYZ," track. Mercury.

BEST RHYTHM & BLUES SONG
(Songwriter's Award)

• "Just the Two of Us," Bill Withers,
  William Salter, Ralph MacDonald.
"Ai No Corrida," Chas. Jankel, Kenny
  Young.
"Lady (You Bring Me Up)," Harold
  Hudson, William King, Shirley King.
"She's a Bad Mama Jama (She's Built,
  She's Stacked)," Leon Haywood.
"When She Was My Girl," Marc Blatte,
  Larry Gottlieb.

BEST RHYTHM & BLUES VOCAL PERFORMANCE, MALE

• James Ingram, "One Hundred Ways,"
  track from Quincy Jones's *The Dude*.
  A&M.
Carl Carlton, "She's a Bad Mama Jama
  (She's Built, She's Stacked)." 20th
  Century.
Rick James, *Street Songs*.
  Gordy/Motown.
Teddy Pendergrass, "I Can't Live With-
  out Your Love." Philadelphia Interna-
  tional/CBS.
Luther Vandross, *Never Too Much*.
  Epic/CBS.

BEST RHYTHM & BLUES VOCAL PERFORMANCE, FEMALE

• Aretha Franklin, "Hold On, I'm
  Comin'," track. Arista.

Patti Austin, "Razzamatazz," track. A&M.
Chaka Khan, *What Cha' Gonna Do for Me*. Warner Bros.
Teena Marie, *It Must Be Magic*. Gordy/Motown.
Stephanie Mills, *Stephanie*. 20th Century.

BEST RHYTHM & BLUES VOCAL PERFORMANCE BY A DUO OR GROUP
• Quincy Jones, *The Dude*. A&M.
Pointer Sisters, *Black and White*. Planet/Elektra/Asylum.
Stanley Clarke, George Duke, *The Clarke/Duke Project*. Epic/CBS.
Commodores, "Lady (You Bring Me Up)." Motown.
Earth, Wind & Fire, "Let's Groove." Arc/CBS.

BEST RHYTHM & BLUES INSTRUMENTAL PERFORMANCE
• David Sanborn, "All I Need Is You." Warner Bros.
Wilton Felder, *Inherit the Wind*. MCA.
Hiroshima, "Winds of Change (Henka Non Nagare)," track. Arista.
Ahmad Jamal, "You're Welcome, Stop on By," track. 20th Century.
Noel Pointer, "East St. Louis Melody," track. Liberty.

BEST JAZZ FUSION PERFORMANCE (VOCAL OR INSTRUMENTAL)
• Grover Washington, Jr., *Winelight*. Elektra/Asylum.
Miles Davis, *The Man with the Horn*. Columbia/CBS.
Pat Metheny, Lyle Mays, *As Falls Wichita, So Falls Wichita Falls*. ECM.
Tom Scott, *Apple Juice*. Columbia/CBS.
Weather Report, *Night Passage*. ARC/CBS.

BEST JAZZ VOCAL PERFORMANCE, MALE
• Al Jarreau, "Blue Rondo à la Turk," track. Warner Bros.
Johnny Hartman, *Johnny Hartman Once in Every Life*. Bee Hive.

Jimmy Rowles, "Music's the Only Thing That's on My Mind," track. Progressive.
Mel Tormé, *Mel Tormé and Friends Recorded Live at Marty's New York City*. Finesse/CBS.
Joe Turner, *Have No Fear, Joe Turner Is Here*. Pablo.

BEST JAZZ VOCAL PERFORMANCE, FEMALE
• Ella Fitzgerald, *Digital III at Montreux*. Pablo Live.
Ernestine Anderson, *Never Make Your Move Too Soon*. Concord Jazz.
Helen Humes, *Helen*. Muse.
Etta Jones, *Save Your Love for Me*. Muse.
Janet Lawson, *The Janet Lawson Quintet*. Inner City/Music Minus One.

BEST JAZZ VOCAL PERFORMANCE BY A DUO OR GROUP
• Manhattan Transfer, "Until I Met You (Corner Pocket)," track. Atlantic.
Clare Fischer's 2 + 2, *Clare Fischer and Salsa Picante Present 2 + 2*. Pausa.
Hi-Lo's, *Now*. Pausa.
Jackie & Roy, *East of Suez*. Concord Jazz.
Mel Tormé, Janis Ian, "Silly Habits," track. Finesse/CBS.

BEST JAZZ INSTRUMENTAL PERFORMANCE BY A SOLOIST
• John Coltrane, *Bye Bye Blackbird*. Pablo.
Pepper Adams, *The Master . . . Pepper Adams*. Muse.
Pete Christlieb, *Self Portrait*. Bosco 1.
Jimmy Rowles, *Music's the Only Thing on My Mind*. Progressive.
Ira Sullivan, *The Incredible Ira Sullivan*. Stash.

BEST JAZZ INSTRUMENTAL PERFORMANCE BY A GROUP
• Chick Corea, Gary Burton, *Chick Corea and Gary Burton in Concert, Zurich, October 28, 1979*. ECM.
Al Cohn, *Nonpareil*. Concord.
Vic Dickenson, *Vic Dickenson Quintet*. Storyville.

Red Rodney Featuring Ira Sullivan, *Live at the Village Vanguard*. Muse.

Zoot Sims, *The Swinger*. Pablo.

BEST JAZZ INSTRUMENTAL PERFORMANCE BY A BIG BAND

• Gerry Mulligan and his Orchestra, *Walk on the Water*. DRG.

Toshiko Akiyoshi–Lew Tabackin Big Band, *Tanuki's Night Out*. Jazz America Marketing.

Panama Francis & the Savoy Sultans, *Panama Francis and the Savoy Sultans, Vol. 2*. Classic Jazz.

Rob McConnell & the Boss Brass, *Tribute*. Pausa.

Don Menza & His '80's Big Band, "Burnin' (Blues for Bird)," track. Realtime.

BEST COUNTRY SONG
(Songwriter's Award)

• "9 to 5," Dolly Parton.

"Elvira," Dallas Frazier.

"I Was Country When Country Wasn't Cool," Kye Fleming, Dennis W. Morgan.

"Somebody's Knockin'," Ed Penney, Jerry Gillespie.

"You're the Reason God Made Oklahoma," Larry Collins, Sandy Pinkard.

BEST COUNTRY VOCAL PERFORMANCE, MALE

• Ronnie Milsap, "(There's) No Gettin' Over Me." RCA.

John Anderson, "I'm Just an Old Chunk of Coal (But I'm Gonna Be a Diamond Someday)." Warner Bros.

George Jones, "Still Doin' Time." Epic/CBS.

Willie Nelson, *Somewhere over the Rainbow*. Columbia.

Eddie Rabbitt, "Step by Step." Elektra/Asylum.

BEST COUNTRY VOCAL PERFORMANCE, FEMALE

• Dolly Parton, "9 to 5." RCA.

Rosanne Cash, *Seven Year Ache*. Columbia/CBS.

Terri Gibbs, *Somebody's Knockin'*. MCA.

Barbara Mandrell, "I Was Country When Country Wasn't Cool." MCA.

Juice Newton, "Queen of Hearts." Capital.

BEST COUNTRY PERFORMANCE BY A DUO OR GROUP WITH VOCAL

• Oak Ridge Boys, "Elvira." MCA.

Alabama, *Feels So Right*. RCA.

David Frizzell, Shelly West, "You're the Reason God Made Oklahoma." Warner Bros.

Emmylou Harris, Don Williams, "If I Needed You." Warner Bros.

Dottie West, Kenny Rogers, "What Are We Doin' in Love." Liberty.

BEST COUNTRY INSTRUMENTAL PERFORMANCE

• Chet Atkins, *Country, After All These Years*. RCA.

Chet Atkins, Doc Watson, *Reflections*. RCA.

Johnny Gimble, *The Texas Fiddle Collection*. CMH.

Barbara Mandrell, "Instrumental Medley: Mountain Dew, Fireball Mail, Old Joe Clark, Night Train, Uncle Joe's Boogie," track. MCA.

Merle Travis, *Travis Pickin'*. CMH.

BEST GOSPEL PERFORMANCE, CONTEMPORARY OR INSPIRATIONAL

• Imperials, *Priority*. Dayspring/Word.

Archers, *Spreadin' Like Wildfire*. Songbird/MCA.

Cynthia Clawson, *Finest Hour*. Triangle/Benson.

DeGarmo & Key, *This Ain't Hollywood*. Lamb & Lion/Benson.

Amy Grant, *In Concert*. Myrrh/Word.

BEST GOSPEL PERFORMANCE, TRADITIONAL

• J. D. Sumner, James Blackwood, Hovie Lister, Rosie Rozell, Jake Hess, *The Masters V*. Skylite.

Rusty Goodman, *Escape to the Light*. Canaan/Word.

Happy Goodman Family, *Goin' Higher.*
Canaan/Word.
Rambos, *Rambo Reunion.* Heartwarm-
ing/Benson.
Lanny Wolfe Trio, *Can't Stop the
Music.* Impact/Benson.

BEST SOUL GOSPEL PERFORMANCE, CONTEMPORARY
• Andrae Crouch, *Don't Give Up.*
Warner Bros.
Al Green, "The Lord Will Make a Way,"
track. Hi-Myrrh/Word.
Edwin Hawkins, *Edwin Hawkins Live.*
Myrrh/Word.
Walter Hawkins, *Walter Hawkins: The
Hawkins Family.* Light.
Winans, *Introducing the Winans.*
Light/Lexicon.

BEST SOUL GOSPEL PERFORMANCE, TRADITIONAL
• Al Green, *The Lord Will Make a Way.*
Hi-Myrrh/Word.
Shirley Caesar, *Go.* Myrrh/Word.
James Cleveland & the Southern Cali-
fornia Community Choir, *Where Is
Your Faith.* Savoy.
Daniel Hawkins, *Daniel Hawkins.*
Light/Lexicon.
Mighty Clouds of Joy, *Cloudbust.*
Myrrh/Word.

BEST INSPIRATIONAL PERFORMANCE
• B. J. Thomas, *Amazing Grace.* Myrrh/
Word.
Crusaders with Joe Cocker, "I'm So Glad
I'm Standing Here Today," MCA.
Bob Dylan, *Shot of Love.* Columbia/CBS.
Barbara Mandrell, "In My Heart," track.
MCA.
Donna Summer, "I Believe in Jesus,"
track. Geffen/Warner Bros.
Don Williams, "Miracles." MCA.

BEST ETHNIC OR TRADITIONAL RECORDING
• *There Must Be a Better World Somewhere*, B. B. King. MCA.

Blues Deluxe, Lonnie Brooks Blues
Band, the Son Seals Blues Band,
Mighty Joe Young, Muddy Waters,
Koko Taylor & Her Blues Machine,
Willie Dixon & the Chicago Blues
Allstars. XRT/Alligator.
From the Heart of a Woman, Koko Tay-
lor. Alligator.
Frozen Alive! Albert Collins. Alligator.
Living Chicago Blues Vol. 4, A. C. Reid
& the Spark Plugs, Scotty & the Rib
Tips, Lovie Lee with Carey Bell.
Alligator.

BEST LATIN RECORDING
• "Guajira pa la Jeva," track, Clare Fischer. Pausa.
Brazilian Soul, Laurindo Almeida, Charlie Byrd. Concord Jazz Picante.
Eddie Palmieri, Eddie Palmieri. Bar-
baro.
Gozame! Pero Ya . . . , Cal Tjader. Concord Jazz Picante.
"*Summertime," Digital at Montreux,
1980*, Dizzy Gillespie, Mongo Santamaria. Pablo Live.

BEST INSTRUMENTAL COMPOSITION
(Composer's Award)
• "Theme from *Hill Street Blues*," Mike
Post.
Altered States, John Corigliano.
As Falls Wichita, So Falls Wichita Falls,
Pat Metheny, Lyle Mays.
"For an Unfinished Woman," Gerry
Mulligan.
"The Slaves," Jerry Goldsmith.

BEST ARRANGEMENT OF AN INSTRUMENTAL RECORDING
• Quincy Jones, "Velas" (Quincy
Jones), track. Johnny Mandel, syn-
thesizer and string arranger. A&M.
Toshiko Akiyoshi, "A Bit Byas'D"
(Toshiko Akiyoshi–Lew Tabackin
Big Band), track. Jazz America Mar-
keting.
Jerry Goldsmith, "The Slaves" (Jerry
Goldsmith), track. MCA.

Dave Grusin, "Mountain Dance" (Dave Grusin), track. GRP/Arista.

Billy May, "South Rampart Street Parade" (John Williams, Boston Pops), track. Philips.

BEST INSTRUMENTAL ARRANGEMENT ACCOMPANYING VOCAL(S)

• Quincy Jones, Jerry Hey, "Ai No Corrida" (Quincy Jones), track. A&M.

Greg Adams, "What Is Hip" (Tower of Power), track. Sheffield Lab.

Clare Fischer, "2 + 2 (Du, Du)," track. Pausa.

Arif Mardin, "And the Melody Still Lingers On (Night in Tunisia)" (Chaka Khan), track. Warner Bros.

Gino Vannelli, Joe Vannelli, Ross Vannelli, "Living Inside Myself" (Gino Vannelli), track. Arista.

BEST VOCAL ARRANGEMENT FOR TWO OR MORE VOICES

• Gene Puerling, "A Nightingale Sang in Berkeley Square" (Manhattan Transfer), track. Atlantic.

Clare Fischer, "2 + 2 (Du, Du)," (Clare Fischer), track. Pausa.

Bernard Kafka, Jay Graydon, "Kafka" (Manhattan Transfer), track. Atlantic.

Milcho Leviev, "(The Word of) Confirmation" (Manhattan Transfer), track. Atlantic.

Gene Puerling, "The Night We Called It a Day" (Hi-Lo's), track. Pausa.

BEST CAST SHOW ALBUM

• Lena Horne: The Lady and Her Music Live on Broadway (various composers and lyricists). Qwest/Warner Bros.

Duke Ellington's Sophisticated Ladies, Duke Ellington and other composers and lyricists. RCA.

42nd Street, Harry Warren, composer; Al Dubin, Johnny Mercer & Mort Dixon, lyricists. RCA.

The Pirates of Penzance, Arthur Sullivan, composer; William S. Gilbert, lyricist. Elektra/Asylum.

Woman of the Year, John Kander, composer; Fred Ebb, lyricist. Arista.

BEST ALBUM OF ORIGINAL SCORE WRITTEN FOR A MOTION PICTURE OR TV SPECIAL
(Composer's/Songwriter's Award)

• Raiders of the Lost Ark, John Williams. Columbia/CBS.

The Elephant Man, John Morris. 20th Century-Fox.

Endless Love, Jonathan Tunick, Lionel Richie, Thomas McClary. Mercury/Polygram.

The Jazz Singer, Neil Diamond, Gilbert Becaud, Alan Lindgren, Richard Bennett, Doug Rhone. Capitol.

9 to 5, Charles Fox, Dolly Parton. 20th Century-Fox.

BEST CLASSICAL ALBUM

• Mahler: Symphony No. 2 in C Minor, Sir Georg Solti conducting the Chicago Symphony Orchestra and Chorus (solos: Isobel Buchanan, Mira Zakai). London.

The Horowitz Concerts 1979/80, Vladimir Horowitz. RCA.

Isaac Stern 60th Anniversary Celebration, Zubin Mehta conducting the New York Philharmonic (solos: Isaac Stern, Itzhak Perlman, Pinchas Zukerman). CBS.

Live from Lincoln Center, Sutherland, Horne, Pavarotti, Richard Bonynge conducting the New York City Opera Orchestra (solos: Joan Sutherland, Marilyn Horne, Luciano Pavarotti). London.

The Unknown Kurt Weill (solo: Teresa Stratas). Nonesuch.

BEST CLASSICAL ORCHESTRAL RECORDING

• Mahler: Symphony No. 2 in C Minor, Sir Georg Solti conducting the Chicago Symphony. London.

Gershwin: Porgy and Bess (Symphonic Picture); Cuban Overture and Second Rhapsody, André Previn conducting the London Symphony. Angel.

Holst: The Planets, Simon Rattle conducting the Philharmonia Orchestra. Angel.

Mahler: Symphony No. 10 (Deryck Cooke final version), James Levine conducting the Philadelphia Orchestra. RCA.

Mozart: The Symphonies: Salzburg 1775–1783, Vol. 5, Christopher Hogwood, Jaap Schroder, conductors, Academy of Ancient Music. L'Oiseau-Lyre.

BEST CHAMBER MUSIC PERFORMANCE (INSTRUMENTAL OR VOCAL)

• Itzhak Perlman, Lynn Harrell, Vladimir Ashkenazy, *Tchaikovsky: Piano Trio in A Minor*. Angel.

Itzhak Perlman, Pinchas Zukerman, *Bartók: Duos for 2 Violins*. Angel.

Ray Still, Itzhak Perlman, Pinchas Zukerman, Lynn Harrell, *Oboe Quartets (Mozart, J. C. Bach, Karl Stamitz, Wanhal)*. Angel.

Toyko String Quartet, *Bartók: Quartets for Strings (6) (Complete)*. Deutsche Grammophon.

Guarneri Quartet, *The Complete String Quartets of Brahms and Schumann*. RCA.

BEST CLASSICAL PERFORMANCE, INSTRUMENTAL SOLOIST(S) (WITH ORCHESTRA)

• Isaac Stern, Itzhak Perlman, Pinchas Zukerman (Mehta conducting the New York Philharmonic), *Isaac Stern 60th Anniversary Celebration*. CBS.

Emanuel Ax (Ormandy conducting the Philadelphia Orchestra), *Chopin: Concerto for Piano No. 1 in E Minor*. RCA.

Stanley Drucker (Mehta conducting the New York Philharmonic), *Corigliano: Concerto for Clarinet and Orchestra*. New World.

James Galway (Dutoit conducting the Royal Philharmonic), *French Flute Concertos*. RCA.

Dylana Jenson (Ormandy conducting the Philadelphia Orchestra), *Sibelius:*

Concerto for Violin in D Minor; Saint-Saëns: Introduction and Rondo Capriccioso. RCA.

BEST CLASSICAL PERFORMANCE, INSTRUMENTAL SOLOIST(S) (WITHOUT ORCHESTRA)

• Vladimir Horowitz, *The Horowitz Concerts 1979/80*. RCA.

Itzhak Perlman (Samuel Sanders, accompanist), *Itzhak Perlman Plays Fritz Kreisler, Album 3*. Angel.

Murray Perahia, *Bartók: Sonata for Piano (1926); Improvisations on Hungarian Peasant Songs; Suite, Op. 14*. CBS.

Artur Rubinstein, *Artur Rubinstein, Schumann, Ravel, Debussy, Albéniz*. RCA.

Pinchas Zukerman (Marc Neikrug, accompanist), *Virtuoso Violin*. CBS.

BEST OPERA RECORDING

• *Janáček: From the House of the Dead*, Sir Charles Mackerras conducting the Vienna Philharmonic (solos: Jiri Zahradnicek, Vaclav Zitek, lvo Zidek). London.

Berg: Wozzeck, Christoph von Dohnányi conducting the Vienna Philharmonic and Vienna State Opera Chorus (solos: Eberhard Waechter, Anja Silia). London.

Korngold: Violanta, Marek Janowski conducting the Munich Radio Orchestra; Bavarian Radio Chorus (solos: Eva Marton, Siegfried Jerusalem). CBS.

Monteverdi: Il Ritorno d'Ulisse in Patria, Raymond Leppard conducting the London Philharmonic; Glyndebourne Chorus (solos: Frederica von Stade, Richard Stillwell). CBS.

Puccini: Le Villi, Lorin Maazel conducting the National Philharmonic; Ambrosian Opera Chorus (solos: Renata Scotto, Placido Domingo, Leo Nucci, Tito Gobbi). CBS.

Rossini: L'Italiana in Algeri, Claudio Scimone conducting the I Solisti Veneti, Chorus of Prague (solos:

Marilyn Horne, Samuel Ramey, Kathleen Battle). RCA.

Wagner: Parsifal, Herbert von Karajan conducting the Berlin Philharmonic; Chorus of Deutsche Oper Berlin (solos: Peter Hofmann, Dunja Veizovic, Kurt Moll, José van Dam, Siegmund Nimsgern, Victor von Halem). Deutsche Grammophon.

BEST CLASSICAL PERFORMANCE, CHORAL (OTHER THAN OPERA)

• Neville Marriner conducting the Chorus of the Academy of St. Martin-in-the Fields and the Academy of St. Martin-in-the-Fields, *Haydn: The Creation.* Philips.

Richard Cooke, choral conductor, London Symphony Orchestra Chorus; Eduardo Mata conducting the London Symphony, *Orff: Carmina Burana.* RCA.

Thomas Peck, choral director, St. Louis Symphony Chorus; Leonard Slatkin conducting the St. Louis Symphony, *Prokofiev: Ivan the Terrible* from *Music from the Films.* Vox Cum Laude.

Robert Shaw, conductor, Atlanta Symphony Chorus, Atlanta Boys' Choir, Atlanta Symphony, *Orff: Carmina Burana.* Telarc.

Richard Westenburg, choral conductor, Musica Sacra Chorus; Zubin Mehta conducting the New York Philharmonic, *Verdi: Requiem.* CBS.

BEST CLASSICAL PERFORMANCE, VOCAL SOLOIST

• Joan Sutherland, Marilyn Horne, Luciano Pavarotti (Richard Bonynge conducting the New York City Opera Orchestra), *Live from Lincoln Center, Sutherland, Horne, Pavarotti.* London.

Elly Ameling (Dalton Baldwin, accompanist), *Think on Me.* CBS.

Barbara Hendricks (Sir Georg Solti conducting the Chicago Symphony), *Del Tredici: Final Alice.* London.

Frederica von Stade (Seiji Ozawa conducting the Boston Symphony), *Ravel:*

Shéhérazade; Cinq Mélodies Populaires Grecques; 2 Mélodies Hébraiques; Chansons Madécasses. CBS.

Teresa Stratas (Richard Woitach, accompanist), *The Unknown Kurt Weill.* Nonesuch.

BEST ENGINEERED RECORDING, CLASSICAL

• Bud Graham, Ray Moore, Andrew Kazdin, *Isaac Stern 60th Anniversary Celebration* (Zubin Mehta conducting the New York Philharmonic; solos: Isaac Stern, Itzhak Perlman, Pinchas Zukerman). CBS.

Michael Sheady, *Holst: The Planets* (Simon Rattle conducting the Philharmonia Orchestra, Ambrosian Singers). Angel.

Paul Goodman, Jules Bloomenthal, Sydney Davis, Don Morrison, *Mahler: Symphony No. 10* (Deryck Cooke final version) (James Levine conducting the Philadelphia Orchestra). RCA.

Michael Gray, Paul Goodman, *Orff: Carmina Burana* (Eduardo Mata conducting the London Symphony; Richard Cooke conducting the London Symphony Chorus; solos: Hendricks, Aler, Hagegard). RCA.

Jack Renner, Jules Bloomenthal, Sydney Davis, Jim Wolvington, *Orff: Carmina Burana; Hindemith: Symphonic Metamorphosis of Themes by Weber* (Robert Shaw conducting the Atlanta Symphony Orchestra and Chorus, Atlanta Boys' Choir; solos: Blegen, Brown, Hagegard). Telarc.

CLASSICAL PRODUCER OF THE YEAR

• James Mallinson
Steven Epstein
Andrew Kazdin
Jay David Saks
Robert Woods

BEST SPOKEN WORD, DOCUMENTARY OR DRAMA RECORDING

• *Donovan's Brain,* Orson Welles. Radiola.

Justice Holmes' Decisions, E. G. Marshall. Caedmon.
The McCartney Interview, Paul McCartney; Vic Garbarini, interviewer. Columbia.
" 'Twas the Night Before Christmas," track, Ed McMahon. Livingsong.
Vladimir Nabokov: Lolita, James Mason. Caedmon.

BEST COMEDY RECORDING
• *Rev. Du Rite*, Richard Pryor. Laff.
Airplane! (soundtrack). Regency.
"The Inquisition," track, *Mel Brooks*. Warner Bros.
Mel Brooks' History of the World Part 1. Warner Bros.
Urban Chipmunk (Chipmunks). RCA.

BEST RECORDING FOR CHILDREN
• *Sesame Country*, Muppets, Glen Campbell, Crystal Gayle, Loretta Lynn, Tanya Tucker. Sesame Street.
Ants' hillvania, Pat Boone, various artists. Birdwing/Sparrow.
Big Bird Discovers the Orchestra, Jim Henson, creator. Sesame Street.
A Chipmunk Christmas (the Chipmunks & Santa Claus), Janice Karman, Ross Bagdasarian, writers. RCA.
The Fox and the Hound (soundtrack). Disneyland.

BEST ENGINEERED RECORDING
• Roger Nichols, Elliot Scheiner, Bill Schnee, Jerry Garsza, *Gaucho* (Steely Dan). MCA.
Bruce Swedien, *The Dude* (Quincy Jones). A&M.
Mike Stone, Kevin Elson, *Escape* (Journey). Columbia/CBS.
Alan Parsons, *Turn of a Friendly Card* (Alan Parsons Project). Arista.
Nigel Gray, *Zenyatta Mondatta* (Police). A&M.

BEST ALBUM PACKAGE
(Art Director's Award)
• Peter Carriston, *Tattoo You* (Rolling Stones). Rolling Stones.

Carla Bley, Paul McDonough, *Social Studies* (Carla Bley). ECM.
Mike Doud, *Working Class Dog* (Rick Springfield). RCA.
Bush Hollyhead, *Positive Touch* (Undertones). Harvest/Capitol.
Kosh, *Eagles Live* (Eagles). Elektra/Asylum.

BEST ALBUM NOTES
(Annotator's Award)
• Dan Morgenstern, *Erroll Garner: Master of the Keyboard.* Book-of-the-Month.
C. P. Crumpacker, *The Mario Lanza Collection.* RCA/Red Seal.
John McDonough, *Pee Wee Russell (Giants of Jazz).* Time-Life.
David Thomson, Philip W. Payne, *Fats Waller (Giants of Jazz).* Time-Life.
Dick Wellstood with Willa Rouder, Frank Kappler, *James P. Johnson (Giants of Jazz).* Time-Life.

BEST HISTORICAL ALBUM
• *Hoagy Carmichael: from "Star Dust" to "Ole Buttermilk Sky"* (Hoagy Carmichael). Book-of-the-Month.
Birmingham Quartet Anthology (various artists). Clanka/Lanka.
Miles Davis: Chronicle, The Complete Prestige Recordings (Miles Davis). Prestige.
The Quintet of the Hot Club of France (1936–1937) (Django Reinhardt, Stephane Grappelli). Inner City/Music Minus One.
The Smithsonian Collection of Classic Country Music (various artists). Smithsonian.

PRODUCER OF THE YEAR
(OTHER THAN CLASSICAL)
• Quincy Jones
Val Garay
Robert John "Mutt" Lange, Mick Jones
Arif Mardin
Lionel Richie

VIDEO OF THE YEAR

- *Michael Nesmith in Elephant Parts*,
  Michael Nesmith. Pacific Arts Video.

Eat to the Beat, Blondie.
  Chrysalis/WCI/RCA.

The First National Kidisc, various
  artists. OPA/MCA.

One-Night Stand: A Keyboard Event,
  Eubie Blake, Kenny Barron, Arthur
Blythe, Ron Carter, Stanley Clarke,
  George Duke, Charles Earland,
  Rodney Franklin, Herbie Hancock,
  Sir Roland Hanna, Bobby Hutcher-
  son, Bob James, Hubert Laws,
  Buddy Williams. CBS Video Enter-
  prises.

Paul Simon, Paul Simon. Pioneer
  Artists.

• 1982 •

A Toto Surprise

The front-runner heading into the Grammy race with seven nominations, Toto, was a group of polished L.A. session players who had worked with a broad range of music talent: Boz Scaggs, Steely Dan, Pink Floyd, Cheap Trick and Earth, Wind & Fire, among them. Prior to the Grammycast, the *L.A. Times* wisecracked, with some prophetic irony, "If everyone they've met in a studio during the last few years votes for them, it'll be a runaway, even though there's a disheartening lack of depth or daring to the group's music."

Toto had been on the music scene since 1978, when it last competed at the Grammys as a nominee for Best New Artist (losing to A Taste of Honey), but it failed to win the respect of the media. The *L.A. Herald Examiner* called the group "faceless." The *Washington Post* dismissed it as "soulless." *L.A. Times* music critic Robert Hilburn acknowledged that Toto's music possessed a certain "state-of-the-art professionalism" and even described its hit single, "Rosanna," as a "bright, romantic reflection" that was "much admired in the industry." But he also claimed that the song didn't have "any aura of greatness about it," so he dismissed its chances as a Record of the Year contender.

Hilburn considered the contest for best record to be between Willie Nelson's "Always on My Mind" (his own choice) and Paul McCartney and Stevie Wonder's duet "Ebony and Ivory" (the public's favorite). He predicted, however, that if Toto's *Toto IV* LP was named Album of the Year, a "Toto bandwagon" might be hard to stop. "If I were placing a bet" on the album contest, wrote Hilburn, "I'd be awfully tempted to go with Toto. As industry pros, N.A.R.A.S.

Critics called Toto's Record of the Year winner "Rosanna" a "bright, romantic reflection," but also blasted it as "soulless" and the "w-r-e-c-k-o-r-d of the year."

members tend to judge music by what they know best: the mechanics. Remember Christopher Cross' sweep two years ago? Rather than search for artistic reach and sociological impact, they check the components, from engineering level to sales results, to see how well everyone did their job. Toto's album ranks high by these narrow standards."

At a time when some of the most critically acclaimed *and* commercially successful artists such as Prince, Bruce Springsteen and Elton John continued to go un-Grammyed, Toto picked up five: Record of the Year, Album of the Year (winning prizes as artists and producers), the separate Producer of the Year award and Best Arrangement for Voices (for keyboardist David Paich).

Toto IV's technicians garnered the engineering award, while various group members shared in two additional accolades: Best Instrumental Arrangement Accompanying Vocal(s) ("Rosanna") and Best Rhythm & Blues Song for "Turn Your Love Around," which Toto guitarist Steve Lukather wrote with Jay Graydon and Bill Champlin.

Toto's impressive Grammy sweep proved that a bandwagon, in fact, had formed. Unfortunately, it ran up smack against vociferous media opposition.

Toto's victory for best LP, said Hilburn, "thwarted the hopes of Beatles fans for back-to-back album honors for John Lennon and Paul McCartney. Lennon's *Double Fantasy* was declared best LP last year, while McCartney's *Tug of War* was nominated in that category this time." Their best record win caused the *Herald Examiner* to quote "a longtime music industry observer" as saying, " 'Rosanna'? Record of the Year? That's right, w-r-e-c-k-o-r-d of the year. This is award-winning music?"

McCartney was not the only music veteran snubbed this year. *Variety* noted, "Paul McCartney, Stevie Wonder and Donald Fagen, all multiple nominees, were shut out." McCartney's "Ebony and Ivory" duet with Wonder ended up winning nothing. Fagen lost all three of his nominations for *The Nightfly,* including its bid for Album of the Year.

Hilburn's choice of "Always on My Mind" did come through as Song of the Year, marking the first time in more than a decade that a country tune took any of the high honors. (In 1968, "Little Green Apples" was voted top song and Glen Campbell's *By the Time I Get to Phoenix* was named best album.) "Always" also swept the c&w awards: Best Country Song (for writers Johnny Christopher, Mark James and Wayne Carson) and Best Male Country Vocal Performance for Willie Nelson. (It won the equivalent prizes at the Academy of Country Music and Country Music Association Awards, too.) For Nelson, it was his biggest hit to date: "Always" spent two weeks on top of the country charts and reached number five in the weekly pop rankings.

The success of Nelson's "Always" baffled music experts, because the song had been around for more than a decade and had failed to catch on earlier despite being recorded by a number of vocal greats. (Old songs were permitted to compete for Song of the Year as long as they had never been nominated before and there was a new recording released within the eligibility period.)

Brenda Lee was the first to release "Always" as a single in 1972. Elvis Presley took it to number 16 in the rankings the following year when it appeared on the "B" side to his "Separate Ways" platter. Several other versions followed, but it didn't click as a country classic until a reluctant Willie Nelson caved in to pleas from his wife and daughters to release his own version of it as a single. At the Grammycast, he performed it in a live piped-in broadcast from Texas that the *Herald Examiner* called one of the night's "fine and stirring performances."

The choice for Best New Artist was Men at Work, the Australian quintet made famous by its funky, new wave videos. Men at Work had the number-one-selling album of the year, *Business As Usual,* which spawned such hits as "Who Can It Be Now?" and "Down Under." The album set a new record for a debut LP spending the most time on top of the charts—15 weeks—thereby surpassing the Monkees' earlier record of 12. Men at Work performed on the Grammycast, but the *Washington Post* called their appearance "tinny, stiff and nervous."

Melissa Manchester began her career as one of Bette Midler's backup singers, the Harlettes. She had her first hit single in 1975 with "Midnight Blue" but failed to win a Grammy until she scored her biggest hit of all, "You Should Hear How She Talks About You," which earned her the female pop vocals prize.

Lionel Richie was a leading contender

> "Always on My Mind" was the first country tune to take a top honor since 1968.

for the male pop vocals award but almost didn't attend the Grammy show. "Having lost so many times" in the past, said the *L.A. Times,* "he didn't want to face another loss in person." Richie suffered an astounding seven defeats last year and only ended up attending the Grammys this year because his manager and wife talked him into it at the last minute. "I'm glad they did," Richie said later, holding his prize for "Truly," his first solo hit since leaving the Commodores in 1981. "If I had missed accepting my Grammy in person, I'd be kicking myself the rest of my life."

Joining the other first-time winners were Joe Cocker and Jennifer Warnes, recipients of the pop duo prize for "Up Where We Belong," the popular ballad from the hit movie *An Officer and a Gentleman* that won Best Song at the 1981 Oscars. "I was told it was the weirdest pairing ever," Warnes said backstage about her partnership with the notoriously wild Cocker. "But we did it and it turned out beautifully." More Oscar-winning music picked up Grammys when a dance version of the theme to *Chariots of Fire* took the pop instrumental trophy. "This inspiring anthem may be what clinched the film's Oscar triumph last spring," wrote the *L.A. Times* after *Chariots* won both Best Picture and Best Film Score for 1981.

Because of the differences in the eligibility periods for the Oscars and Grammys, the film score winner at the 1981 Oscars—John Williams's music for *E.T. The Extra-Terrestrial*—also picked up three Grammys this year: for best instrumental arrangement, Best Instrumental Composition and best film score. *Variety* noted, "Williams boosted his career tally of Grammys to 14, six fewer than all-time Grammy champ Henry Mancini."

In the rock categories, the number-one single of the year—"Eye of the Tiger"—ended up with the group vocals prize after Sylvester Stallone commissioned the Midwest rock group Survivor to write it for *Rocky III,* his latest sequel to his 1976 Best Picture winner at the Oscars. A

Impressive Number Of First-Timers Turn Up In Grammy Award Nominations

By CYNTHIA KIRK

...der and Paul McCartney — both singly and in part-... with the L.A. group Toto, ex-Steely Dan member ... country's Willie Nelson and composer-conductor John ... among this year's top contenders for Grammy ... performers garnered a hefty share of

Variety counted a "hefty" tally of 52 newcomers involved in this year's Grammy Awards derby.

Flock of Seagulls, the British new wave group that took its name from the best-selling pop-philosophy book and film *Jonathan Livingston Seagull,* snagged the rock instrumental performance prize for "D.N.A."

John Cougar had recorded four LPs before hitting it big with *American Fool,* his Album of the Year contender that sold an impressive 3 million copies. The *L.A. Times* didn't think Cougar had a chance with the sedate N.A.R.A.S. crowd, though, claiming, "His rowdy rock approach is unlikely to get much support." But his "Hurts So Good" single did earn him the rock vocals award over an equally rowdy group of also-rans that included Peter Gabriel, Don Henley, Rod Stewart—and Rick Springfield, who surprisingly trounced Bruce Springsteen last year. The female vocals prize went to Pat Benatar for a third year in a row, this time for her "Shadows of the Night" single.

In the r&b lineup, the *L.A. Times*

noted: "Critics point out that singer-song-writer Marvin Gaye—who received a standing ovation when he walked on stage during the telecast to sing 'Sexual Healing'—made some of the most acclaimed records of the '60s and '70s but had never won a Grammy." ("Politics, that's what it was, Hollywood games," Gaye once told biographer David Ritz to explain the oversight. "I refused to play those games and I suffered.") Now Gaye nabbed two Grammys for his comeback single that explored both sexual desire and spiritual feelings, but "received such recognition," Gaye said, "because of the sexual content." Holding his first Grammy backstage before a sea of reporters, he added, "This award is such an inspiration . . . 25 years I've been waiting for it." Sadly, "Sexual Healing" would be Gaye's last hit. One year after his Grammy wins, he was shot to death by his father during a family squabble.

Dreamgirls, winner of the Grammy for Best Cast Show Album, was also responsible for the victor of the female r&b vocal prize: Jennifer Holliday. In the lavish Broadway musical, obviously based on the Supremes' climb to fame, the Tony Award–winning Holliday played the equivalent of real-life Florence Ballard, who was ousted from the "Dreams." Much of the show's material was written by composer Henry Krieger especially for Holliday, including her showstopping number, "And I Am Telling You I'm Not Going," which she performed on the Grammycast last year. Her r&b award for the same song this year compensated her for the loss she suffered in the Best New Artist category.

There was a tie for the r&b group vocals accolade between the ultra-funk Cleveland group Dazz (short for "dance-able jazz") Band for their one-hit wonder, "Let It Whip," and Earth, Wind & Fire's "Wanna Be with You."

Singer/guitarist/bandleader Clarence "Gatemouth" Brown had been playing the blues since the 1940s and had received his share of critical approval along the way,

but he failed to achieve superstar status. "Few paid attention when blues giant Clarence Gatemouth Brown came proudly yet humbly to meet the press and discuss his first-ever Grammy (for best traditional blues recording)," noted the *Herald Examiner.* "In fact, there was only one reporter listening. 'It's a weird feeling,' said the 58 year-old Gatemouth, smiling. 'I've never even dreamed of this.' "

"The jazz awards left little or no cause for complaint," wrote the oft-critical jazz critic Leonard Feather in the *L.A. Times.* "There was particular reason to rejoice in both the vocal categories, since Sarah Vaughan and Mel Tormé, both of whom should have collected a roomful of Grammys by now, became winners for the first time. Ironically, Vaughan, who in the 25 years of the academy's history has made at least a dozen award-worthy albums of pure jazz, finally won with an LP that was not aimed at the jazz audience. *Gershwin Live!* is a classical album and should have been so classified." It would be the only Grammy Vaughan would win in a competitive category prior to her death in 1990. N.A.R.A.S. did give her one more—a special Lifetime Achievement Award in 1989.

"There was a touch of irony also in Tormé's victory," Feather claimed, "since last year he said, 'It is just not in the cards for me to win. How can you beat the power of a Warner Bros.?' Luckily for us and for him, bloc voting is by no means as potent a force as he believed." Singer Tormé won for what Feather called his "superb collaboration with [pianist] George Shearing," which was recorded on the Concord Jazz label. Most of Tormé's other competitors were likewise represented by small labels—except for Joe Williams's *8 to 5 I Lose,* which was recorded by Warner Bros.

The *Washington Post* called the bestowal of the rest of the jazz awards "fairly predictable": Two-time past champ Phil Woods took the group instrumental prize for *"More" Live* by his quartet; Count Basie & His Orchestra scored an eighth career Grammy for Basie for *Warm Breeze* (best big band); and the Manhattan Transfer snagged their second-in-a-row group vocal award for "Route 66," thereby monopolizing the category since it was introduced. It was the ultra-hip, harmony-singing quartet's fourth Grammy in all. First-time winners Pat Metheny and his group were among the front-runners for the fusion award thanks to critical applause for their heavily synthesized sound and the variety of material on *Offramp*.

Miles Davis had won two Grammys earlier in his career (1960, 1970), but in 1982 he hadn't made a recording in six years. In plotting his comeback, he took some chances: For his live *We Want Miles* album, Davis added guitarist Mike Stern and sax player Bill Evans. It was for his own solo work on the LP, though, that he earned his first Grammy in 12 years—an honor that he may or may not have appreciated. As the *Herald Examiner* noted, Davis accepted it "without so much as a word or grimace of acknowledgment toward the industry that he professes to loathe."

For more than a half dozen years beginning in the late 1960s, Roy Clark was the highest-paid performer in country music. He had also been named Entertainer of the Year by the Country Music Association in 1973 and was the host of the popular TV show *Hee Haw,* on which he often sang as he strummed his guitar or banjo. But as popular as Clark was, he had never before won a Grammy prior to his 1982 award for "Alabama Jubilee." Another big TV country star, Barbara Mandrell, who had her own variety show on NBC, had hit songs dating back to the 1960s, too, but she didn't win a Grammy prior to her Best Inspirational Performance trophy for *He Set My Life to Music.*

Country music's other big winners were less traditional country rockers. Juice Newton was expected to prevail in the female vocalist category last year but was upset by Dolly Parton. This time she

Mel Tormé's (right) victory for his LP with George Shearing (left) was hailed as "a reason to rejoice."

Concord Records

eclipsed Parton with "Break It to Me Gently." The ultimate country rockers of the group Alabama won their first Grammy for what *Billboard* called "a modern country classic"—*Mountain Music*. It was an important time for Alabama: The group won the Academy of Country Music's awards for Top Vocal Group and Entertainer of the Year, and *Mountain Music* went platinum.

In an effort to counteract her sugar-sweet image, Olivia Newton-John made a point of adding lots of sexually suggestive scenes to the video version of her 1981 hit song "Physical," which was taped in a fitness club. The result was an outcry from religious leaders and a Video of the Year award at the Grammys.

The Best Classical Album category was a close contest won by a recording of Bach's *Goldberg Variations,* nicknamed "The Gouldberg Variations," since the works were recorded more than once by the late pianist and posthumous winner Glenn Gould. "One of the most striking features of this landmark album is its unintentional aura of the memorial," *Fanfare* wrote, since the LP was released "almost simultaneously with Gould's death." Gould first taped the *Variations* in 1955 but wanted to give the sections more of an "arithmetical relationship," as he called it, complaining of "too much piano-playing going on" in pieces like Variation 25. For his new interpretation, he garnered the additional award for best soloist performance without orchestra.

Among the losing contenders for best classical LP was the winner of the Best Classical Orchestral Recording prize: guest conductor James Levine and the Chicago Symphony for Mahler's Symphony No. 7 ("Song of the Night"). On two occasions in the previous 10 years (1972 and 1981), the Chicago Symphony was more successful at nabbing the top LP prize for renditions of Mahler symphonies. In this version, said *Fanfare,* Levine's "phrasing is outstanding."

The choral prize went to another loser of the top LP award, *Berlioz: La Damnation de Faust,* with the Chicago Symphony performing under the baton of its resident director, Sir Georg Solti. This was the ninth year in a row that Solti won an award, which established a new Grammy record, surpassing Aretha Franklin's previous winning streak of eight consecutive r&b prizes from 1967 to 1974. (It was Solti's 19th Grammy overall.) "Kudos once more to Margaret Hillis," too, wrote *Fanfare* of the Chicago Symphony Chorus's director, who won the same award three times in the late 1970s.

The soloist laurel for orchestral accompaniment was bestowed to Itzhak Perlman, bringing his career tally to five Grammys. "Overtly spectacular does describe Itzhak Perlman's violin pyrotechnics" in this recording of Elgar's Concerto in B Minor for Violin and Orchestra, said *Fanfare.* The same publication applauded the winners of the chamber music prize, clarinetist Richard Stoltzman and pianist Richard Goode for their "expansive, clean-lined readings" of Brahms sonatas.

Best Opera Recording went to 10-time past Grammy winner Pierre Boulez for conducting the Bayreuth Festival Orchestra in Wagner's *Der Ring des Nibelungen.* Winning her 12th award was Leontyne Price for her rendition of arias from Verdi operas called "sensational" by *Fanfare.*

The Grammy ceremony, again broadcast on CBS from the Shrine Auditorium in Los Angeles, received virtually across-the-board bad reviews this year. Fewer awards were bestowed on the air despite the fact that the ceremony was stretched from two to three hours. That meant that there were "more generally dreadful musical numbers," said the *Washington Post,* "as performed by such popular entertainers as Linda Ronstadt, Willie Nelson, Lena Horne, Kenny Rogers, the Spinners, Men at Work, Gladys Knight and the Pips, Bill Monroe, Leontyne Price, the Blackwood Brothers, Crystal Gayle, Miles Davis, Alabama, Joe Cocker and Jennifer Warnes." The *L.A. Herald Examiner* dismissed the "weirdness of Joan Baez singing 'Blowin' in the Wind' with [host] John Denver," while it applauded the medley performed by Ray Charles, Jerry Lee Lewis, Little Richard and Count Basie as "an astonishing display of myth and muscle." The onetime rock hero Little Richard now considered himself "born again," however, and he refused to sing songs without a religious message. In the medley with Basie, Charles and Lewis, he changed a lyric of "What'd I Say" to "Found God in '74 / Don't sing rock & roll no more." "He was right," the *Post* commented. "Only the pencil mustache remains of the old fire."

The most damning review came from the *Herald Examiner,* which wrote: "The 25th annual Grammys was perhaps the single biggest artistic washout this ceremony has produced since its seminal days in the late '50s, when N.A.R.A.S.

> ## Marvin Gaye said, "Twenty-five years I've been waiting for it!"

virtually disavowed significant rock & roll (and most significant jazz). With the exception of a few of the r&b and obligatory blues awards, the voters settled for the blandest, most prudent definition of pop music imaginable: not just massively popular pop, the kind certified by record sales and calculated accessibility—but pop that stands for technique over meaning, and smugness over courage."

• 1982 •

The awards ceremony was broadcast on CBS from the Shrine Auditorium in Los Angeles on February 23, 1983, for the awards eligibility period of October 1, 1981, through September 30, 1982.

ALBUM OF THE YEAR

- *Toto IV*, Toto. Columbia/CBS.
American Fool, John Cougar. Riva/Polygram.
The Nightfly, Donald Fagen. Warner Bros.
The Nylon Curtain, Billy Joel. Columbia/CBS.
Tug of War, Paul McCartney. Columbia.

RECORD OF THE YEAR

- "Rosanna," Toto. Columbia.
"Always on My Mind," Willie Nelson. Columbia.
"Chariots of Fire," Vangelis. Polydor.
"Ebony and Ivory," Paul McCartney, Stevie Wonder. Columbia.
"Steppin' Out," Joe Jackson. A&M.

SONG OF THE YEAR
(Songwriter's Award)

- "Always on My Mind," Johnny Christopher, Mark James, Wayne Thompson.
"Ebony and Ivory," Paul McCartney.
"Eye of the Tiger," Frankie Sullivan, Jim Peterik.
"I.G.Y. (What a Beautiful World)," Donald Fagen.
"Rosanna," David Paich.

BEST NEW ARTIST

- Men at Work
Asia
Jennifer Holliday

Human League
Stray Cats

BEST POP VOCAL PERFORMANCE, MALE

- Lionel Richie, "Truly." Motown.
Donald Fagen, "I.G.Y. (What a Beautiful World)." Warner Bros.
Joe Jackson, "Steppin' Out." A&M.
Elton John, "Blue Eyes." Geffen/Warner Bros.
Michael McDonald, "I Keep Forgetting (Everytime You're Near)." Warner Bros.
Rick Springfield, "Don't Talk to Strangers." RCA.

BEST POP VOCAL PERFORMANCE, FEMALE

- Melissa Manchester, "You Should Hear How She Talks About You." Arista.

"Rowdy" John Cougar (Mellencamp) lost best album (*American Fool*), but rebounded with the rock vocals prize for "Hurts So Good."

Laura Branigan, "Gloria." Atlantic.
Juice Newton, "Love's Been a Little Bit
Hard on Me." Capitol.
Olivia Newton-John, "Heart Attack."
MCA.
Linda Ronstadt, "Get Closer."
Elektra/Asylum.

BEST POP PERFORMANCE BY A DUO OR GROUP WITH VOCAL

• Joe Cocker, Jennifer Warnes, "Up
Where We Belong." Island.
Chicago, "Hard to Say I'm Sorry." Full
Moon/Warner Bros.
Daryl Hall, John Oates, "Maneater."
RCA.
Paul McCartney, Stevie Wonder, "Ebony
and Ivory." Columbia.
Toto, "Rosanna." Columbia.

BEST POP INSTRUMENTAL PERFORMANCE

• Ernie Watts, "Chariots of Fire"
(theme, dance version).
Qwest/Warner Bros.
Louis Clark conducting the Royal Phil-
harmonic Orchestra, *Hooked on
Classics*. RCA.
Earl Klugh, "Crazy for You."
Liberty/Capitol.
David Sanborn, "As We Speak." Warner
Bros.
John Williams, *E.T.* (film soundtrack).
MCA.

BEST ROCK VOCAL PERFORMANCE, MALE

• John Cougar, "Hurts So Good."
Riva/Polygram.
Peter Gabriel, "Shock the Monkey."
Geffen/Warner Bros.
Don Henley, "Dirty Laundry." Elektra.
Rick Springfield, "I Get Excited." RCA.
Rod Stewart, *Tonight I'm Yours*. Warner
Bros.

BEST ROCK VOCAL PERFORMANCE, FEMALE

• Pat Benatar, "Shadows of the Night."
Chrysalis.
Kim Carnes, "Voyeur." EMI-America.

Bonnie Raitt, "Green Light." Warner
Bros.
Linda Ronstadt, "Get Closer."
Elektra/Asylum.
Donna Summer, "Protection."
Geffen/Warner Bros.

BEST ROCK PERFORMANCE BY A DUO OR GROUP WITH VOCAL

• Survivor, "Eye of the Tiger." Scotti
Brothers/CBS.
Asia, *Asia*. Geffen/Warner Bros.
J. Geils Band, "Centerfold." EMI-Amer-
ica.
Kenny Loggins, Steve Perry, "Don't
Fight It." Columbia/CBS.
Frank and Moon Zappa, "Valley Girl."
Barking Pumpkin.

BEST ROCK INSTRUMENTAL PERFORMANCE

• A Flock of Seagulls, "D.N.A." Jive/
Arista.
Dregs, "Industry Standard." Arista.
Maynard Ferguson, "Don't Stop."
Columbia.
King Crimson, "Requiem." EB/Warner
Bros.
Van Morrison, "Scandinavia." Warner
Bros.

BEST RHYTHM & BLUES SONG
(Songwriter's Award)
• "Turn Your Love Around," Jay Gray-
don, Steve Lukather, Bill Champlin.
"Do I Do," Stevie Wonder.
"It's Gonna Take a Miracle," Teddy
Randazzo, Bobby Weinstein, Lou
Staliman.
"Let It Whip," Reggie Andrews, Leon
"Ndugu" Chancler.
"Sexual Healing," Marvin Gaye, O.
Brown.
"That Girl," Stevie Wonder.

BEST RHYTHM & BLUES VOCAL PERFORMANCE, MALE
• Marvin Gaye, "Sexual Healing."
Columbia/CBS.
George Benson, "Turn Your Love
Around." Warner Bros.

Ray Parker, Jr., "The Other Woman." Arista.

Luther Vandross, "Forever, for Always, for Love." Epic/CBS.

Stevie Wonder, "Do I Do." Tamla/ Motown.

BEST RHYTHM & BLUES VOCAL PERFORMANCE, FEMALE

• Jennifer Holliday, "And I Am Telling You I'm Not Going." Geffen/Warner Bros.

Aretha Franklin, "Jump to It." Arista.

Diana Ross, "Muscles." RCA.

Patrice Rushen, "Forget Me Nots." Elektra.

Donna Summer, "Love Is in Control (Finger on the Trigger)." Geffen/ Warner Bros.

Deniece Williams, "It's Gonna Take a Miracle." Columbia.

BEST RHYTHM & BLUES VOCAL PERFORMANCE BY A DUO OR GROUP (Tie)

• Dazz Band, "Let It Whip." Motown.
• Earth, Wind & Fire, "Wanna Be with You." ARC/CBS.

Crusaders with B. B. King, Josie James, "Street Life." MCA.

Paul McCartney, Stevie Wonder, "What's That You're Doing." Columbia/CBS.

Tavares, "A Penny for Your Thoughts." RCA.

BEST RHYTHM & BLUES INSTRUMENTAL PERFORMANCE

• Marvin Gaye, "Sexual Healing." Columbia/CBS.

Eddie Murphy, "Boogie in Your Butt." Columbia/CBS.

Patrice Rushen, "Number One." Elektra/ Asylum.

Spyro Gyra, "Stripes." MCA.

Grover Washington, Jr., "Come Morning." Elektra.

BEST JAZZ FUSION PERFORMANCE (VOCAL OR INSTRUMENTAL)

• Pat Metheny Group, *Offramp*. ECM/ Warner Bros.

David Sanborn, *As We Speak*. Warner Bros.

Tom Scott, *Desire*. Elektra/Musician.

Spyro Gyra, *Incognito*. MCA.

Weather Report, *Weather Report*. Columbia.

BEST JAZZ VOCAL PERFORMANCE, MALE

• Mel Tormé, *An Evening with George Shearing and Mel Tormé*. Concord Jazz.

Dave Frisberg, *The Dave Frisberg Songbook, Vol. 1*. Omnisound Jazz.

Bill Henderson, *A Tribute to Johnny Mercer*. Discovery.

Mark Murphy, *Bop for Kerouac*. Muse.

Joe Williams, *8 to 5 I Lose*. Warner Bros.

BEST JAZZ VOCAL PERFORMANCE, FEMALE

• Sarah Vaughan, *Gershwin Live!* CBS.

Ella Fitzgerald, *A Classy Pair*. Pablo Today.

Chaka Khan, *Echoes of an Era*. Elektra/Musician.

Cleo Laine, *Smilin' Through*. Finesse.

Maxine Sullivan, *Maxine Sullivan with the Ike Isaacs Quartet*. Audiophile/Jazzology.

BEST JAZZ VOCAL PERFORMANCE BY A DUO OR GROUP

• Manhattan Transfer, "Route 66." Atlantic.

Clare Fischer & Salsa Picante with 2 + 2, "One Night in a Dream." Discovery.

Jon Hendricks & Company, *Love*. Muse.

Jackie & Roy, "High Standards." Concord Jazz.

Singers Unlimited, "Easy to Love." Pausa.

BEST JAZZ INSTRUMENTAL PERFORMANCE BY A SOLOIST

• Miles Davis, *We Want Miles*. Columbia.

Tommy Flanagan, *The Magnificent Tommy Flanagan*. Progressive.

Wynton Marsalis, *Wynton Marsalis.*
Columbia.
Jimmy Rowles, *Jimmy Rowles Plays
Duke Ellington and Billy Strayhorn.*
Columbia.
Ira Sullivan, *Night and Day.* Muse.

BEST JAZZ INSTRUMENTAL
PERFORMANCE BY A GROUP
• Phil Woods Quartet, *"More" Live.*
Adelphi.
Art Blakey & the Jazz Messengers,
Straight Ahead. Concord Jazz.
Art Farmer Quartet, *A Work of Art.* Con-
cord Jazz.
Tommy Flanagan Trio, *Giant Steps.*
Enja/London.
Dizzy Gillespie, Mitchell-Ruff Duo,
*Dizzy Gillespie: Live with the
Mitchell-Ruff Duo.* Book-of-the-
Month.

BEST JAZZ INSTRUMENTAL
PERFORMANCE BY A BIG BAND
• Count Basie & His Orchestra, *Warm
Breeze.* Pablo Today.
Bob Florence Big Band, *Westlake.* Dis-
covery.
Woody Herman Big Band, *The Woody
Herman Big Band Live at the Concord
Jazz Festival 1981.* Concord Jazz.
Mel Lewis & the Jazz Orchestra, *Make
Me Smile and Other New Works by
Bob Brookmeyer.* Finesse.
Rob McConnell & the Boss Brass, *Live
in Digital.* Dark Orchid.

BEST COUNTRY SONG
(Songwriter's Award)
• "Always on My Mind," Johnny
Christopher, Wayne Carson, Mark
James.
"I'm Gonna Hire a Wino to Decorate
Our Home," D. Blackwell.
"Nobody," Kye Fleming, Dennis W.
Morgan.
"Ring on Her Finger, Time on Her
Hands," Don Goodman, Pam Rose,
Mary Ann Kennedy.
"She Got the Goldmine (I Got the
Shaft)," Tim DuBois.

BEST COUNTRY VOCAL
PERFORMANCE, MALE
• Willie Nelson, "Always on My Mind."
Columbia/CBS.
Ronnie Milsap, "He Got You." RCA.
Jerry Reed, "She Got the Goldmine (I
Got the Shaft)." RCA.
Kenny Rogers, "Love Will Turn You
Around." EMI/Liberty-Capitol.
Ricky Skaggs, "Heartbroke." Epic/CBS.

BEST COUNTRY VOCAL
PERFORMANCE, FEMALE
• Juice Newton, "Break It to Me Gen-
tly." Capitol.
Rosanne Cash, "Ain't No Money."
Columbia.
Emmylou Harris, *Cimarron.* Warner Bros.
Dolly Parton, "I Will Always Love You."
RCA.
Sylvia, "Nobody." RCA.

BEST COUNTRY PERFORMANCE BY A
DUO OR GROUP WITH VOCAL
• Alabama, *Mountain Music.* RCA.
Waylon Jennings, Willie Nelson, "(Sit-
tin' on) The Dock of the Bay." RCA.
Oak Ridge Boys, "Bobbie Sue." MCA.
Gram Parsons, Emmylou Harris, "Love
Hurts." Sierra.
Whites, "You Put the Blue in Me." Elek-
tra/Curb.

BEST COUNTRY INSTRUMENTAL
PERFORMANCE
• Roy Clark, "Alabama Jubilee."
Churchill.
Albert Coleman's Atlanta Pops Orches-
tra, *Just Hooked on Country.*
Epic/CBS.
Joe Maphis, *The Joe Maphis Flat-Pick-
ing Spectacular.* CMH.
Poco, "Feudin'." MCA.
Doc & Merle Watson, "Below Freez-
ing." Flying Fish.

BEST GOSPEL PERFORMANCE,
CONTEMPORARY
• Amy Grant, *Age to Age.* Myrrh/Word.
Andrae Crouch, *My Tribute.* Light/Lexi-
con.

Imperials, *Stand By the Power*. Dayspring/Word.

Sandi Patti, *Lift Up the Lord*. Impact/Benson.

Reba Rambo, *Lady Live*. Light/Lexicon.

BEST GOSPEL PERFORMANCE, TRADITIONAL

• Blackwood Brothers, *I'm Following You*. Voice Box.

Cathedrals, *Something Special*. Canaan/Word.

Masters V, *O, What a Savior*. Skylite/Sing.

Rex Nelon Singers, *Feeling at Home*. Canaan/Word.

Dottie Rambo, *Makin' My Own Place*. HeartWarming/Benson.

BEST SOUL GOSPEL PERFORMANCE, CONTEMPORARY

• Al Green, "Higher Plane." Myrrh/Word.

Andrae Crouch, "Finally." Light/Elektra/Asylum.

Larnelle Harris, *Touch Me, Lord*. Impact/Benson.

Edwin Hawkins, *Edwin Hawkins Live with the Oakland Symphony Orchestra*. Myrrh/Word.

Mighty Clouds of Joy, *Miracle Man*. Myrrh/Word.

BEST SOUL GOSPEL PERFORMANCE, TRADITIONAL

• Al Green, "Precious Lord." Myrrh/Word.

Andrae Crouch, "We Need to Hear from You." Light/Elektra/Asylum.

Jessy Dixon, *Jesus Is Alive and Well*. Light/Lexicon.

Mighty Clouds of Joy, *Miracle Man*. Myrrh/Word.

Ben Moore, *He Believes in Me*. Priority/CBS.

BEST INSPIRATIONAL PERFORMANCE

• Barbara Mandrell, *He Set My Life to Music*. MCA/Songbird.

Kansas, "Crossfire." Kirshner/CBS.

Oak Ridge Boys, "Would They Love Him Down in Shreveport." MCA.

Leontyne Price, "God Bless America." RCA.

B. J. Thomas, "Miracle." Myrrh/Word.

BEST TRADITIONAL BLUES RECORDING

• *Alright Again*, Clarence "Gatemouth" Brown. Rounder.

Genuine Houserocking Music, Hound Dog Taylor & the HouseRockers. Alligator.

He Was a Friend of Mine, Eddie "Cleanhead" Vinson, Roomful of Blues. Muse.

The New Johnny Otis Show, Johnny Otis. Alligator.

Sippie, Sippie Wallace. Atlantic.

BEST ETHNIC OR TRADITIONAL FOLK RECORDING

• *Queen Ida and the Bon Temps Zydeco Band on Tour*, Queen Ida. GNP Crescendo.

In the Tradition, Boys of the Lough. Flying Fish.

Live in America, John Renbourn Group. Flying Fish.

Metropolis, Klezmorim. Flying Fish.

Reggae Sunsplash '81: A Tribute to Bob Marley, various artists. Elektra.

Tennessee: Folk Heritage—The Mountains, various artists. Tennessee Folklore Society.

BEST LATIN RECORDING

• *Machito and His Salsa Big Band '82*, Machito. Timeless.

Rhythm of Life, Ray Barretto. Fania.

Canciones del Solar de los Aburidos, Willie Colon/Rubén Blades. Fania.

Escenas de Amor, José Feliciano. Motown Latino.

Momentos, Julio Iglesias. Disco CBS International.

BEST INSTRUMENTAL COMPOSITION

• "Flying (Theme from *E.T. The Extra-Terrestrial*)," John Williams.

"Adventure on Earth," John Williams. MCA, publisher.

"Are You Going with Me," Pat Metheny, Lyle Mays.

Desire, Tom Scott.

"In the Presence and Absence of Each Other, Parts 1, 2 and 3," Claus Ogerman.

BEST ARRANGEMENT ON AN INSTRUMENTAL RECORDING

• John Williams, "Flying (Theme from *E.T. The Extra-Terrestrial*)" (John Williams). MCA.

Les Hooper, "Pavane" (Les Hooper Big Band). Jazz Hounds.

Earl Klugh, Ronnie Foster, Clare Fischer, "Balladina" (Earl Klugh). EMI/Liberty.

Pat Metheny, Lyle Mays, "Are You Going with Me" (Pat Metheny Group). ECM.

Claus Ogerman, "Pavane pour une Infante Defunte" (Claus Ogerman featuring Jan Akkerman). Jazzman.

BEST ARRANGEMENT FOR VOICES

• David Paich, "Rosanna" (Toto). Columbia.

Al Capps, "Route 66" (Manhattan Transfer). Warner Bros.

Donald Fagen, "Ruby Baby" (Donald Fagen). Warner Bros.

Clare Fischer, "One Night (In a Dream)" (Clare Fischer & Salsa Picante with 2 + 2). Discovery.

Gene Puerling, "Lullaby of Birdland" (Singers Unlimited). Pausa.

BEST CAST SHOW ALBUM

• *Dreamgirls*, Henry Krieger, composer; Tom Eyen, lyricist. Geffen/Warner Bros.

Cats, Andrew Lloyd Webber, Richard Stilgoe, Trevor Nunn, composers; poems by T. S. Eliot. Geffen/Warner Bros.

Joseph and the Amazing Technicolor Dreamcoat, Andrew Lloyd Webber, composer; Tim Rice, lyricist. Chrysalis.

Merrily We Roll Along, Stephen Sondheim, composer and lyricist. RCA.

Nine, Maury Yeston, composer and lyricist. Columbia/CBS.

BEST ALBUM OF ORIGINAL SCORE WRITTEN FOR A MOTION PICTURE OR A TV SPECIAL
(Composer's/Songwriter's Award)

• *E.T. The Extra-Terrestrial*, John Williams, composer. MCA.

The French Lieutenant's Woman, Carl Davis, composer. DRG.

On Golden Pond, Dave Grusin, composer. MCA.

Ragtime, Randy Newman, composer. Elektra.

Victor/Victoria, Henry Mancini, composer; Leslie Bricusse, lyricist. MGM/Polygram.

BEST INSTRUMENTAL ARRANGEMENT ACCOMPANYING VOCAL(S)

• Jerry Hey, David Paich, "Rosanna" (Toto). Columbia.

Les Hooper, "Easy to Love" (Singers Unlimited). Pausa.

Rob Mounsey, Donald Fagen, "I.G.Y. (What a Beautiful World)" (Donald Fagen). Warner Bros.

Marty Paich, "Only a Miracle" (Kenny Loggins). Columbia.

Stevie Wonder, Paul Riser, "Do I Do" (Stevie Wonder). Tamla/Motown.

BEST CLASSICAL ALBUM

• *Bach: The Goldberg Variations*, Glenn Gould. CBS.

Berlioz: La Damnation de Faust, Sir Georg Solti conducting the Chicago Symphony Orchestra and Chorus (solos: Frederica von Stade, Kenneth Riegel, José van Dam). London.

Debussy: La Mer; Prelude à l'Après-Midi d'un Faune; Danses Sacrée et Profane, Leonard Slatkin conducting the St. Louis Symphony; Frances Tietov, harp. Telarc.

Mahler: Symphony No. 7 in E Minor ("Song of the Night"), James Levine conducting the Chicago Symphony. RCA.

Stravinsky: The Recorded Legacy, Igor Stravinsky; Robert Craft conducting the various orchestras, ensembles, solo artists. CBS.

BEST CLASSICAL ORCHESTRAL RECORDING
(Conductor's Award)

• Mahler: Symphony No. 7 in E Minor ("Song of the Night"), James Levine conducting the Chicago Symphony. RCA.

Debussy: La Mer; Prelude à l'Après-Midi d'un Faune; Danses Sacrée et Profane, Leonard Slatkin conducting the Chicago Symphony. Telarc.

Holst: The Planets, Herbert von Karajan conducting the Berlin Philharmonic. Deutsche Grammophon.

Mozart: Symphonies, Vol. 1 (The Early Works), Christopher Hogwood conducting the Academy of Ancient Music. L'Oiseau-Lyre.

R. Strauss: Death and Transfiguration; Don Juan; Salome, Dance of the Seven Veils, Eduardo Mata conducting the Dallas Symphony. RCA.

BEST CHAMBER MUSIC PERFORMANCE

• Richard Stoltzman, Richard Goode, Brahms: The Sonatas for Clarinet and Piano, Op. 120. London.

Cleveland Quartet with Pinchas Zuckerman, Bernard Greenhouse, Brahms: The String Sextets (B Flat Major, Op. 18, and G Major, Op. 36). RCA.

James Galway, Kung-Wha Chung, Phillip Moll, Moray Welsh, Bach: Trio Sonatas (BWV 1038, 1039, 1079). RCA.

Guarneri Quartet, Borodin: Quartet No. 2 in D Major; Dohnányi: Quartet No. 2 in D Flat Major, Op. 15. RCA.

Lynn Harrell, Vladimir Ashkenazy, Brahms: Sonatas for Cello and Piano No. 1 in E Minor, Op. 38, and No. 2 in F Major, Op. 99. RCA.

BEST CLASSICAL PERFORMANCE, INSTRUMENTAL SOLOIST(S) (WITH ORCHESTRA)

• Itzhak Perlman (Daniel Barenboim conducting the Chicago Symphony), Elgar: Concerto for Violin in B Minor. Deutsche Grammophon.

Vladimir Ashkenazy (Vladimir Ashkenazy conducting the Philharmonia), Mozart: Concerto for Piano No. 22 in E Flat Major, K. 482 (Ashkenazy Plays and Conducts Mozart). London.

Alicia de Larrocha (Charles Dutoit conducting the Royal Philharmonic), Schumann: Concerto for Piano in A Minor; Rachmaninov: Concerto for Piano No. 2 in C Minor, Op. 18. London.

Rudolf Serkin (Seiji Ozawa conducting the Boston Symphony), Beethoven: Concerto for Piano No. 4 in G Major, Op. 58. Telarc.

Joseph Silverstein (Seiji Ozawa conducting the Boston Symphony), Vivaldi: The Four Seasons. Telarc.

BEST CLASSICAL PERFORMANCE, INSTRUMENTAL SOLOIST(S) (WITHOUT ORCHESTRA)

• Glenn Gould, Bach: The Goldberg Variations. CBS.

Emanuel Ax, Schumann: Humoreske, Op. 20; Fantasiestücke, Op. 12. RCA.

Vladimir Horowitz, Horowitz at the Met (Scarlatti, Chopin, Liszt, Rachmaninov). RCA.

Ruth Laredo, Barber: Sonata for Piano, Op. 26; Souvenirs, Op. 28; Nocturne, Op. 33. Nonesuch.

Alicia de Larrocha, Granados: Danzas Españolas. London.

Ronald Smith, The Alkan Project (Etudes, Op. 39, in All the Minor Keys). Arabesque.

Isao Tomita, Grofé-Tomita: Grand Canyon Suite; Anderson-Tomita: Syncopated Clock. RCA.

BEST OPERA RECORDING

- *Wagner: Der Ring des Nibelungen*, Pierre Boulez conducting the Bayreuth Festival Orchestra (solos: Gwyneth Jones, Jeannine Altmeyer, Orton Wenkel, Peter Hofmann, Manfred Jung, Siegfried Jerusalem, Heinz Zednik, Donald McIntyre, Matti Salminen, Hermann Becht). Philips.
- *Fauré: Penelope*, Charles Dutoit conducting the Orchestre Philharmonique de Monte Carlo (solos: Jessye Norman, Alain Vanzo, Philippe Huttenlocher). Erato.
- *Janáček: The Cunning Little Vixen*, Sir Charles Mackerras conducting the Vienna Philharmonic Orchestra and Vienna State Opera Chorus (solos: Lucia Popp, Eva Randova, Dalibor Jedlicka). London.
- *Puccini: Tosca*, James Levine conducting the Philharmonia Orchestra and Ambrosian Opera Chorus (solos: Renata Scotto, Placido Domingo, Renato Bruson). Angel.
- *Puccini: Turandot*, Herbert von Karajan conducting the Vienna Philharmonic Orchestra, Vienna State Opera Chorus and Vienna Boys' Choir (solos: Placido Domingo, Katia Ricciarelli, Piero de Palma, Ruggero Raimondi, Barbara Hendricks, Gottfriedl Hornik). Deutsche Grammophon.
- Weinberger: *Schwanda the Bagpiper*, Heinz Wallberg conducting the Munich Radio Orchestra, Bavarian Radio Chorus (solos: Lucia Popp, Siegfried Jerusalem, Hermann Prey, Gwendolyn Killebrew, Sigmund Nimsgern). CBS.

BEST CHORAL PERFORMANCE (OTHER THAN OPERA)

- Margaret Hillis, chorus master, Chicago Symphony Orchestra Chorus; Sir George Solti conducting the Chicago Symphony Orchestra, *Berlioz: La Damnation de Faust*. London.

Norbert Balatsch, chorus master, Vienna State Opera Chorus; Bernard Haitink conducting the Vienna Philharmonic Orchestra (solos: Gundula Janowitz, Tom Krause), *Brahms: German Requiem*. Philips.

Nicholas Cleobury, chorus master, City of Birmingham Symphony Orchestra Chorus; Simon Rattle conducting the City of Birmingham Symphony Orchestra, *Janáček: Glagolitic Mass*. Angel.

Laszlo Heltay, chorus master, Chorus of the Academy of St. Martin-in-the-Fields; Neville Marriner conducting the Academy of St. Martin-in-the-Fields (solos: Dietrich Fischer-Dieskau, Edith Mathis, Siegfried Jerusalem), *Haydn: The Seasons*. Philips.

Thomas Peck, chorus master, St. Louis Symphony Chorus; Leonard Slatkin conducting the St. Louis Symphony Orchestra, Rachmaninov: "The Bells" and "Russian Songs" (from album *Rachmaninov Orchestral Music*). Vox Cum Laude.

Gerhard Schmidt-Gaden, choral conductor, Tolzer Knabenchor; Nikolaus Harnoncourt conducting the Concentus Musicus Wien, *Bach: Cantatas, Vol. 30 (Nos. 120–23)*. Telefunken.

Robert Shaw conducting the Atlanta Symphony Orchestra Chorus and Atlanta Symphony Orchestra (solo: Sylvia McNair), *Poulenc: Gloria for Soprano, Choir and Orchestra (G Major)*. Telarc.

BEST CLASSICAL PERFORMANCE VOCAL SOLOIST

- Leontyne Price (Zubin Mehta conducting the Israel Philharmonic), *Verdi: Arias (Leontyne Price Sings Verdi)*. London.
- Elly Ameling (Dalton Baldwin, accompanist), *Fauré: La Bonne Chanson; Debussy: Chansons de Bilitis and Ariettes Oubliées*. CBS.

Kiri Te Kanawa (Gyorgy Fischer conducting the Vienna Chamber Orchestra), *Mozart: Concert Arias (Andromeda, Il Burbero di Buon Core, Artaserse, Idomeneo, Cerere Placata)*. London.

Jessye Norman (Daniel Barenboim conducting the Orchestre de Paris), *Berlioz: La Mort de Cléopâtre.* Deutsche Grammophon.

Frederica von Stade (Martin Katz, accompanist), *Frederica von Stade Live!* CBS.

BEST ENGINEERED RECORDING, CLASSICAL

• Paul Goodman, *Mahler: Symphony No. 7 in E Minor ("Song of the Night")* (James Levine conducting the Chicago Symphony Orchestra). RCA.

Paul Goodman, *Dvořák: Symphony No. 9 in E Minor ("From the New World")* (James Levine conducting the Chicago Symphony Orchestra). RCA.

Gunter Hermanns, *Holst: The Planets* (Herbert von Karajan conducting the Berlin Philharmonic). Deutsche Grammophon.

James Lock, Simon Eadon, *Berlioz: La Damnation de Faust* (Sir Georg Solti conducting the Chicago Symphony Orchestra and Chorus; solos: Frederica von Stade, Kenneth Riegel, José van Dam). London.

Stan Tonkel, John Johnson, Ray Moore, Martin Greenblatt, Bud Graham, *Bach: The Goldberg Variations* (solo: Glenn Gould). CBS.

CLASSICAL PRODUCER OF THE YEAR

• Robert Woods
Steven Epstein
Glenn Gould, Samuel Carter
James Mallinson
Jay David Saks

BEST SPOKEN WORD, DOCUMENTARY OR DRAMA RECORDING

• *Raiders of the Lost Ark: The Movie on Record*, actual dialogue, music, and sound effects. Columbia.

Charles Dickens' Nicholas Nickleby, Roger Rees. Caedmon.

Foundation's Edge, Isaac Asimov. Caedmon.

No Man's Island, Sir John Gielgud, Sir Ralph Richardson. Caedmon.

2010: Odyssey Two, Arthur C. Clarke. Caedmon.

BEST COMEDY RECORDING

• *Live on the Sunset Strip,* Richard Pryor. Warner Bros.

Eddie Murphy, Eddie Murphy. Columbia/CBS.

Great White North, Bob & Doug McKenzie. Mercury/Polygram.

A Place for My Stuff, George Carlin. Atlantic.

The Steve Martin Brothers, Steve Martin. Warner Bros.

BEST RECORDING FOR CHILDREN

• *In Harmony 2*, Billy Joel, Bruce Springsteen, James Taylor, Kenny Loggins, Carly & Lucy Simon, Teddy Pendergrass, Crystal Gayle, Lou Rawls, Deniece Williams, Janis Ian, Dr. John. CBS.

Animals and Other Things, Candle with the Agapeland Singers. Birdwing/Sparrow.

Best of Friends, Smurfs. Sessions/Starland.

The Chipmunks Go Hollywood, Chipmunks. RCA.

Here Comes Garfield, Lou Rawls, Desiree Goyette. CBS/Epic.

I Am God's Project, Birdwing Kids Korus. Birdwing/Sparrow.

BEST ENGINEERED RECORDING (OTHER THAN CLASSICAL)

• Al Schmitt, Tom Knox, Greg Ladanyi, David Paich, Steve Porcaro, Dick Gall, Bruce Heigh, *Toto IV* (Toto). Columbia.

Neil Dorfsman, *Love Over Gold* (Dire Straits). Warner Bros.

Roger Nichols, Daniel Lazerus, Elliot Scheiner, *The Nightfly* (Donald Fagen). Warner Bros.

Alan Parsons, *Eye in the Sky* (Alan Parsons Project). Arista.

George Tutko, Don Gehman, Mark Stabbeds, *American Fool* (John Cougar). Riva/Polygram.

BEST ALBUM PACKAGE
(Art Director's Award)
• Kosh with Ron Larson, *Get Closer* (Linda Ronstadt). Elektra/Asylum.

Jules Bates, *Nothing to Fear* (Oingo Boingo). A&M.

Mick Haggerty, Ginger Canzoneri, *Vacation* (Go-Go's). IRS.

Denise Minobe, Ron Coro, *We Are One* (Pieces of a Dream). Elektra.

George Osaki, *Ongaku-Kai Live in Japan* (Crusaders). Crusaders/MCA.

BEST ALBUM NOTES
(Annotator's Award)
• John Chilton, Richard Sudhalter, *Bunny Berigan (Giants of Jazz)* (Bunny Berigan). Time-Life.

Gary Giddins, *Duke Ellington 1941* (Duke Ellington & His Orchestra). Smithsonian Collection.

Thornton Hagert, *An Experiment in Modern Music: Paul Whiteman at Aeolian Hall* (Paul Whiteman). Smithsonian Collection.

William Ivey, summary and glossary, *The Greatest Country Music Recordings of All Time* (various artists). Franklin Mint Recording Society.

William Ivey, Bob Pinson, *60 Years of Country Music* (various artists). RCA.

Robert Palmer, *Young Blood* (Coasters). Atlantic/ Deluxe.

BEST HISTORICAL ALBUM
• *The Tommy Dorsey/Frank Sinatra Sessions Vols, 1, 2, and 3* (Tommy Dorsey, Frank Sinatra). RCA.

Bartók at the Piano, 1920–1945 (Béla Bartók). Hungaroton.

Bunny Berigan (Giants of Jazz) (Bunny Berigan). Time-Life.

An Experiment in Modern Music: Paul Whiteman at Aeolian Hall (Paul Whiteman). RCA.

Minstrels and Tunesmiths: The Commercial Roots of Early Country Music (various artists). John Edwards Memorial Foundation.

PRODUCER OF THE YEAR (OTHER THAN CLASSICAL)
• Toto
David Foster
Quincy Jones
Gary Katz
John Cougar Mellencamp, Don Gehman

VIDEO OF THE YEAR
• *Olivia Physical*, Olivia Newton-John. MCA Video.

Fun and Games, various artists. OPA/RCA Video.

The Tales of Hoffmann, Royal Opera conducted by Georges Prêtre with Placido Domingo. Pioneer Artists.

The Tubes Video, Tubes. Pioneer Artists.

Visions: Elton John, Elton John. Embassy Home Entertainment.

• 1983 •

The Michael Jackson Show

Grammy night was a genuine thriller in every way.

Heading into the event, *Variety* reported, "Michael Jackson's *Thriller* album, which already has earned a spot in music history with more than 23 million copies sold, has set a record for Grammy Award nominations with 12 bids for the gold."

Thriller had just become the biggest-selling album in music history to date, having topped the sales record formerly held by Grammy's 1978 Album of the Year, *Saturday Night Fever*. *Thriller* also spun off huge-selling singles, seven of which became Top 10 hits, three more than any previous album.

At the time of the 1983 Grammys, a fan-driven frenzy surrounded Jackson that hadn't been seen since Beatlemania swept America nearly 20 years earlier. Jackson, in fact, even *looked* like a Beatle as he entered the Shrine Auditorium for the Grammy show dressed in a sequined Sgt. Pepper commodore's coat. Curiously, one of his dozen bids was for "The Girl Is Mine," a duet he performed with ex-Beatle Paul McCartney, but Grammy night would prove to be his alone when "The Girl" resulted in one of his few losses.

As Jackson took his seat in the front row of the auditorium for the Grammy ceremony, 60 million Americans watched him on television, a number surpassed that year only by the Super Bowl audience. Viewers in more than 25 other countries were tuned in, too.

Actor Mickey Rooney captured the spirit of the evening when he said early on in the ceremony, "It's a pleasure doing *The Michael Jackson Show*."

World Wide Photo

Sixty million viewers tuned in for a genuine Thriller of a Grammycast to see Michael Jackson and Quincy Jones sweep up 12 awards between them, including the top prize for Album of the Year.

Jackson's only previous Grammy win had been an r&b award for "Don't Stop Till You Get Enough" in 1979. Now he seemed to be taking that same advice to heart as he set a new record for most victories in a single year—eight.

The previous record was held by Roger Miller, who nabbed six in 1965, most of them for "King of the Road." Jackson's eight were for Album of the Year, Record of the Year ("Beat It"), Best New Rhythm & Blues Song ("Billie Jean," which triumphed over another Jackson song), Producer of the Year (along with last year's victor, Quincy Jones), best children's recording (for an LP version of the hit movie *E.T. The Extra-Terrestrial*, also produced by Jones) and a never-before-seen sweep across three groups of categories. Jackson ended up with the male vocal performance awards for pop, rock *and* r&b (for *Thriller*, "Beat It," and "Billie Jean," respectively). *Thriller* also won the prize for Best Engineered Recording.

As Jackson picked up his first award of the night, he looked shy and nervous as he hid behind sunglasses and whispered into the podium microphone: "I just want to say thank you and I love you all." Later on, as his booty increased, he became emboldened and assumed a kingly command of the ceremonies as he invited his sisters La Toya, Rebie and Tricia up to the stage and removed his shades for the benefit of a legendary film star (and unlikely fan) watching at home, saying, "Katharine, this is for you." The gesture and remark were directed to Katharine Hepburn, who had recently admonished Jackson for wearing sunglasses at the American Music Awards.

Jackson probably would have swept the two awards for music videos, too (increased from last year's one), since the videos for "Billie Jean," "Beat It" and "Thriller" were big hits on MTV, but they weren't qualified to compete this year because they hadn't been available for commercial sale before the eligibility cut-off period in September. Instead, Best Video, Short Form award and Best Video Album were nabbed by Duran Duran, "not too surprisingly," *Variety* noted, since the British pop stars were also MTV favorites.

When "Beat It" took Record of the Year, it beat the number-one song in *Billboard*'s Hot 100: "Every Breath You Take" by the Police. "Every Breath" was written by lead vocalist Sting, who stung Jackson by copping the Song of the Year award in what the *Washington Post* called an "upset that caught the experts by surprise." All the experts except one, that is. *L.A. Times* pundit Paul Grein predicted the winner correctly. He explained: "Ballads traditionally have an edge in this category. Besides, the presence of 'Billie Jean' and 'Beat It' may split the Jackson vote." Grein also foresaw the Police's seizure of the laurels for best rock group vocals for *Synchronicity*, but not the

> **Jackson's eight victories in one year set a new record.**

added prize it got for best pop group vocal performance ("Every Breath").

That award, Grein believed, would go to Culture Club, which was most pundits' choice to nab Best New Artist. The British pop act was competing against four other British nominees. When it prevailed as expected, its success marked the third consecutive year that the category was claimed by international artists.

Culture Club's victory was considered such a foregone conclusion that N.A.R.A.S. flew Joan Rivers, a nominee for Best Comedy Recording, to London to interview the group and its cross-dressing lead singer, Boy George (whose real name is George O'Dowd), for the U.S. TV audience via satellite. Early in the show, Rivers toyed with George playfully, saying, "You look like Brooke Shields on steroids!" George obviously enjoyed the ribbing and giggled in response. When accepting the prize for Best New Artist, he tossed a kiss at the camera and said, "Thank you, America. You've got good taste, style and you know a good drag queen when you see one!" *Variety* noted that the comment "elicited the loudest laughter" on Grammy night.

Irene Cara, who lost the Best New Artist award to Christopher Cross in 1980, now returned to the Grammy race with nominated music from *Flashdance,* the hit film starring Jennifer Beals about a factory welder by day who works as sexy dancer by night. "Coming closest to Michael Jackson's sweep is the *Flashdance* soundtrack, which garnered nine nominations," *Variety* noted. Cara's "Flashdance . . . What a Feeling" was a contender for Record of the Year, competing against another of the movie's singles, "Maniac," which was also up for Song of the Year.

Linda Ronstadt was expected to win the kudos for best female pop vocals, but Cara pulled off an upset in the category with "What a Feeling," which had just won Best Song at the Oscars. She co-wrote the tune with Giorgio Moroder and Keith Forsey, so when *Flashdance* won the Grammy for best film score, Cara shared the victory with a long list of other talent that included composer Michael Boddicker, who thanked Michael Jackson "for not writing a song for the movies." The team overcame *Star Wars* and *Superman* composer John Williams, who had dominated the category for seven out of the previous eight years and was nominated this year for *Return of the Jedi*.

Sting (left) of the Police shocked the experts when he won the Song of the Year Award for "Every Breath You Take," beating Michael Jackson's "Beat It."

The trophy for Best Cast Show Album went to the Broadway production of Andrew Lloyd Webber's *Cats*. The musical's London cast recording had been nominated last year but lost to Broadway's *Dreamgirls*.

Unlike Williams, singer Pat Benatar extended her winning streak by taking a fourth Grammy in a row for best female rock vocal performance for "Love Is a Battlefield" when she fought off a serious challenge from Stevie Nicks.

The last time that dance music was so big at the Grammys, in the late 1970s, Chaka Khan was repeatedly passed over for prizes. This year she scored three of them: best r&b vocal performance for her self-titled album (topping last year's winner, Jennifer Holliday, who was expected to return), an arrangement award with Arif Mardin for one of the LP's tracks and, as a member of Rufus, the r&b group vocal trophy for "Ain't Nobody," their last Top 10 hit together.

Disco's unexpected resurgence had an equally unexpected follower in jazz keyboardist and composer Herbie Hancock, who upset his purist fans when his dance-tinged "Rockit" soared up the charts and became one of the most popular videos on MTV. Hancock recorded it with members of the rock band Material and earned the accolade for Best R&B Instrumental Performance. When he and the band performed it on the Grammycast, *Variety* called the segment "particularly electrifying."

In the area of Best Traditional Blues Recording, two-time past winner B. B. King was hailed for his *Blues 'n' Jazz*, which *Rolling Stone* called "outstanding" because it "showcases some of King's finest vocal performances against exciting big-band arrangements." The Best Ethnic or Traditional Folk Recording award, which was traditionally claimed by blues artists, went to Clifton Chenier & His Red Hot Louisiana Band, known principally for fusing Cajun music with r&b sounds in works such as the group's victorious *I'm Here*.

The jazz lineup welcomed back a host of past winners such as the Pat Metheny Group, last year's winner for fusion vocals who now held on to the category with *Travels,* a new two-disc set of live material. The velvet-voiced Mel Tormé reclaimed the male singing category with *Top Drawer,* while the Manhattan Transfer's "Why Not!" won the group vocals prize for a fourth year in a row. Ella Fitzgerald became the seventh-most-honored Grammy recipient when she picked up her 12th, the female jazz vocal trophy for *The Best Is Yet to Come*. The Phil Woods Quartet made a comeback, too, in the group instrumental slot for its live recordings of performances at the Village Vanguard, New York's historic jazz club.

One of the few newcomers to the jazz awards was Wynton Marsalis, a 22-year-old trumpet virtuoso who pulled off a Grammy first by being nominated—and winning—in both the jazz and classical categories for *Think of One* (showcasing works by Thelonious Monk, Duke Ellington and himself) and a separate album of music by Haydn, Mozart and Hummel. The novelty of Marsalis being considered for both genres was enough for N.A.R.A.S. to invite him to perform on the show. When he won the jazz prize, Marsalis thanked his mother and father (noted jazz pianist Ellis Marsalis) "for putting up with me all these years practicing and making that noise on the trumpet" and his band members, who included his brother, saxophonist Branford.

The writer of the year's Best New Country Song, "Stranger in My House," was an unlikely hit songwriter: Mike Reid was a onetime tackle for the Cincinnati Bengals who got the idea for the song one day while having an argument with his wife. She worked nights; he worked days. "With our schedules, we weren't seeing a lot of each other," Reid said. "I told her, 'Living with you is like having a stranger in my house.' As soon as I said it, I thought, 'That's a great title for a song!' So I left the room and wrote it down. Then I went back and continued the argument."

Ronnie Milsap was nominated for the male country vocals honors for his hit version of "Stranger" but lost to Lee Greenwood for "I.O.U." Greenwood was a relative newcomer to big-time country music. He finally had his first gold album, *Somebody's Gonna Love You,* just four days before the Grammycast. The Country Music Association voted Greenwood Male Vocalist of the Year.

The winner of the female vocal honors was Anne Murray for "A Little Good News," which celebrated a positive reading of the daily newspapers with lyrics like "Nobody O.D.-ed, nobody died in vain." The song got extraordinary media coverage when Vice President George Bush referred to it in his political speeches. The Country Music Association named it Song of the Year.

For a second year in a row, Alabama (*The Closer You Get*) reaped the group vocals prize. "It all goes back to our fans," one band member told the press backstage.

Donna Summer lost her bid for best female pop vocals to Irene Cara but made up for the loss by claiming Best Inspirational Performance for "He's a Rebel." With previous victories in the r&b lineup for "Last Dance" and in rock for "Hot Stuff," Summer joined Michael Jackson to become one of the few artists to win in three different award classifications.

Other religious slots welcomed such first-time champs as Sandra Crouch (twin sister of five-time past winner Andrae), who garnered the female soul gospel performance prize for *We Sing Praises.* Before Amy Grant branched out successfully into pop music in the early '90s, she recorded gospel music almost exclusively and won her second of many Grammys for religious fare this year for "Ageless Medley." Al Green (*I'll Rise Again*) picked up his fourth award and third in a row, while Barbara Mandrell returned from last year to pick up a new trophy for her duet with Bobby Jones, "I'm So Glad I'm Standing Here Today."

A movement had been growing within N.A.R.A.S. in the recent past for more categories for Latin music. Now the former slot for Best Latin Recording was scrapped in favor of three new performance categories: Latin Pop (claimed by José Feliciano, Grammy's Best New Artist of 1968, for *Me Enamore*), Mexican-American (going to the rock/Tex-Mex fusion band Los Lobos of Los Angeles for "Anselma") and Tropical Latin (won by 1978 Latin Grammy winner Tito Puente for *On Broadway*).

The winner of Best Comedy Record-

> Boy George thanked America for knowing "a good drag queen when you see one."

ing was the target of protests from the gay community. On *Eddie Murphy: Comedian,* the *Saturday Night Live* performer made jokes about AIDS, conjured up scenes of buggery between Jackie Gleason and Art Carney and said to the audience, "Faggots are not allowed to look at my ass while I'm on stage. That's why I keep movin' while I'm up here." The award's presenters were Rodney Dangerfield, who won the prize in 1980, and Cyndi Lauper, next year's Best New Artist. Said the *Washington Post:* "Lauper, with her customized pink hair and wearing sequins on her face and clay fruits around her neck, squeaked and squealed like Betty Boop as Dangerfield told her, with utmost respect, 'You look like a rainbow, my dear.'"

Prior to the announcement of the winners of the classical awards, Sir Georg Solti was only one award shy of tying Henry Mancini's record for having the most total Grammys (20). Solti was in London on the night of the Grammycast where he waited eagerly by the phone for news of the voting results. "When the appointed hour had passed and no call came," according to N.A.R.A.S. membership magazine *Grammy Pulse,* "he resigned himself to the idea of not winning and set about the task of consoling his children. 'I didn't expect I would win anything, but I was still very sad. I said to my children, "All right, papa didn't win anything. Bad luck, I can't win every year."' Three hours later, the news of his four new Grammy wins came over the BBC radio. "You can imagine how tremendously happy I was." The next day, he said, he received a telegram from Mancini that read, "I relinquish with pleasure my leadership to you."

Solti's wins marked the 10th year in a row that he had been Grammy-honored, thereby establishing the longest winning streak in the awards' history. Two of Solti's Grammys were for con-

> ## Georg Solti emerged as Grammy's biggest winner.

ducting Mahler's Symphony No. 9 in D Major, one of which marked the third time the maestro was honored with the prize for the year's top classical LP for a Mahler symphony (the others being for No. 8 in 1972 and No. 2 in 1981). Solti's second trophy of 1983 was awarded for his orchestra's performance of Mahler's Ninth. (The same prize was awarded for the same work in 1977, when Carlo Maria Giulini acted as guest conductor of Solti's Chicago Symphony.) *Fanfare* called this newest version "praiseworthy" and "the best-played Ninth on records." It also won Best Engineered Recording.

Solti's third award was for the choral performance in Haydn's *Creation.* His fourth accolade was in the category of Best Opera Recording, which resulted in a tie between Solti's reading of Mozart's *The Marriage of Figaro*—called "effervescent" by the critics—and the soundtrack to director Franco Zeffirelli's 1982 film version of Verdi's *La Traviata* starring Teresa Stratas, Placido Domingo and Cornell MacNeil. The score was the handiwork of James Levine conducting the Metropolitan Opera Orchestra, which also provided the music for Leontyne Price and Marilyn Horne, who shared the accolade for best soloist vocals.

Last year's winner of Best Classical Album, the late pianist Glenn Gould, won the prize for soloist work (without orchestra) for what *Gramophone* called his "masculine" and "sturdy" renditions of Beethoven sonatas that "may offend drawing-room susceptibilities." The chamber music award was shared by the exuberant Russian cellist Mstislav Rostropovich and veteran Brahms pianist Rudolf Serkin for their Brahms sonatas. "There are times, especially in the E Minor Sonata, when these two temperaments mesh beautifully," said *Fanfare.* On the F Major Sonata, it added, "the collaboration is less successful."

Once again, the Grammy show was broadcast on CBS from the Shrine Auditorium with John Denver serving as host. But there was a key difference this year: The telecast reaped its biggest viewership ever with a 30.8 rating/45 share.

There were other key differences, too. "For the first time, the awards show used music videos rather than album-cover stills or live shots of the nominees when running down the contenders in several musical categories," *Variety* reported. "Live on stage at the Shrine, Herbie Hancock's performance of his Grammy-winning number 'Rockit,' proved particularly electrifying, as did the appearance of Eurythmics vocalist Annie Lennox, her carrot-red hairdo abandoned for a pompadour and sideburns hair style which suggested slender versions of Wayne Newton and Vegas-era Elvis Presley." Given the added prominence at the show of drag queen Boy George and a mascara-laden Michael Jackson, the *Washington Post* said, "Anyone tuning in without an awareness of The New Androgyny was in for a shock."

"The Grammys show had its failings, some unavoidable," griped the *New York Times*. "Two major groups—the Police and Duran Duran—were not on hand to receive their awards."

Variety reported that Jackson established a new nominations record by racking up a dozen bids.

Among the night's highlights was the bestowal of a Lifetime Achievement Award to Chuck Berry, who accepted the honor shouting, "Long live rock & roll!" Backstage, he hugged his prize and added, "Man, I wouldn't give this up for anything. I'd kill for this."

• 1983 •

The awards ceremony was broadcast on CBS from the Shrine Auditorium in Los Angeles on February 28, 1984, for the awards eligibility period of October 1, 1982, through September 30, 1983.

ALBUM OF THE YEAR
• *Thriller*, Michael Jackson. Epic/CBS.
Flashdance (soundtrack), Irene Cara, Shandi, Helen St. John, Karen Kamon, Joe Esposito, Laura Branigan, Donna Summer, Cycle V, Kim Carnes, Michael Sembello. Casablanca/Polygram.

An Innocent Man, Billy Joel. Columbia.
Let's Dance, David Bowie. EMI-America.
Synchronicity, Police. A&M.

RECORD OF THE YEAR
• "Beat It," Michael Jackson. Epic/CBS.
"All Night Long (All Night)," Lionel Richie. Motown.
"Every Breath You Take," Police. A&M.
"Flashdance . . . What a Feeling," Irene Cara. Casablanca/Polygram.
"Maniac," Michael Sembello. Casablanca/Polygram.

NEW SONG OF THE YEAR
(Songwriter's Award)
- "Every Breath You Take," Sting.
"All Night Long (All Night)," Lionel Richie.
"Beat It," Michael Jackson.
"Billie Jean," Michael Jackson.
"Maniac," Michael Sembello, Dennis Matkosky.

BEST NEW ARTIST
- Culture Club
Big Country
Eurythmics
Men Without Hats
Musical Youth

Twenty-two-year-old Wynton Marsalis became the first artist to win awards in the jazz and classical categories. He thanked his parents "for putting up with me all those years practicing."

BEST POP VOCAL PERFORMANCE, MALE
- Michael Jackson, *Thriller*. Epic/CBS.
Billy Joel, "Uptown Girl," track from *An Innocent Man*. Columbia.
Prince, *1999*. Warner Bros.
Lionel Richie, "All Night Long (All Night)." Motown.
Michael Sembello, "Maniac." Casablanca/Polygram.

BEST POP VOCAL PERFORMANCE, FEMALE
- Irene Cara, "Flashdance . . . What a Feeling." Casablanca/Polygram.
Sheena Easton, "Telefone (Long Distance Love Affair)." EMI-America.
Linda Ronstadt, *What's New*. Asylum.
Donna Summer, "She Works Hard for the Money." Mercury.
Bonnie Tyler, "Total Eclipse of the Heart." Columbia.

BEST POP PERFORMANCE BY A DUO OR GROUP WITH VOCAL
- Police, "Every Breath You Take." A&M.
Culture Club, "Do You Really Want to Hurt Me." Virgin/Epic.
James Ingram, Patti Austin, "How Do You Keep the Music Playing." Qwest/Warner Bros.
Michael Jackson, Paul McCartney, "The Girl Is Mine." Epic/CBS.

Kenny Rogers, Dolly Parton, "Islands in the Stream." RCA.

BEST POP INSTRUMENTAL PERFORMANCE
- George Benson, "Being with You," track from *In Your Eyes*. Warner Bros.
Herb Alpert, "Blow Your Own Horn," instrumental tracks from album. A&M.
Larry Carlton, *Friends*. Warner Bros.
Joe Jackson, "Breakdown," track from *Mike's Murder*. A&M.
Helen St. John, "Love Theme from *Flashdance*," track from *Flashdance*. Casablanca/Polygram.

BEST ROCK VOCAL PERFORMANCE, MALE
- Michael Jackson, "Beat It." Epic/CBS.
David Bowie, "Cat People (Putting Out Fire)," track from *Let's Dance*. EMI America.
Phil Collins, "I Don't Care Anymore," track from *Hello I Must Be Going*. Atlantic.
Bob Seger, *The Distance*. Capitol.
Rick Springfield, "Affair of the Heart." RCA.

BEST ROCK VOCAL PERFORMANCE, FEMALE
- Pat Benatar, "Love Is a Battlefield." Chrysalis.

Joan Armatrading, *The Key*. A&M.
Kim Carnes, *Invisible Hands*. EMI-
America.
Stevie Nicks, *Stand Back*.
Modern/Atlantic.
Bonnie Tyler, *Faster Than the Speed of
Night*. Columbia.

BEST ROCK PERFORMANCE BY A
DUO OR GROUP WITH VOCAL
• Police, *Synchronicity*. A&M.
Big Country, "In a Big Country." Mer-
cury/Polygram.
Huey Lewis & the News, *Heart and
Soul*. Chrysalis.
Talking Heads, "Burning Down the
House." Sire/Warner Bros.
ZZ Top, *Eliminator*. Warner Bros.

BEST ROCK INSTRUMENTAL
PERFORMANCE
• Sting, Brimstone & Treacle, track
from *Brimstone and Treacle*. A&M.
Allan Holdsworth, "Road Games," track
from *Road Games*. Warner Bros.
Rainbow, "Anybody There."
Mercury/Polygram.
Pete Townshend, "Unused Piano:
Quadrophenia," track from *Scoop*.
Atlantic.
Stevie Ray Vaughan & Double Trouble,
"Rude Mood," track from *Texas
Flood*. Epic/CBS.

BEST NEW RHYTHM & BLUES SONG
(Songwriter's Award)
• "Billie Jean," Michael Jackson.
"Ain't Nobody," Hawk Wolinski.
"Electric Avenue," Eddy Grant.
"P.Y.T. (Pretty Young Thing)," James
Ingram, Quincy Jones.
"Wanna Be Startin' Somethin'," Michael
Jackson.

BEST RHYTHM & BLUES VOCAL
PERFORMANCE, MALE
• Michael Jackson, "Billie Jean."
Epic/CBS.
Marvin Gaye, *Midnight Love*. Columbia.
James Ingram, "Party Animal."
Qwest/Warner Bros.

Jeffrey Osborne, *Stay with Me Tonight*.
A&M.
Prince, "International Lover," track from
1999. Warner Bros.

BEST RHYTHM & BLUES VOCAL
PERFORMANCE, FEMALE
• Chaka Kahn, *Chaka Khan*. Warner
Bros.
Aretha Franklin, *Get It Right*. Arista.
Jennifer Holliday, *Feel My Soul*. Geffen/
Warner Bros.
Patti LaBelle, "The Best Is Yet to Come,"
track from Grover Washington, Jr.'s
The Best Is Yet to Come. Elektra.
Stephanie Mills, *Merciless*.
Casablanca/Polygram.
Deniece Williams, *I'm So Proud*.
Columbia.

BEST RHYTHM & BLUES VOCAL
PERFORMANCE BY A DUO OR
GROUP
• Rufus & Chaka Khan, "Ain't
Nobody." Warner Bros.
DeBarge, *In a Special Way*. Gordy/
Motown.
Earth, Wind & Fire, "Fall in Love with
Me." Columbia.
Shalamar, "Dead Giveaway."
Solar/Elektra/Asylum.
Weather Girls, "It's Raining Men."
Columbia.

BEST RHYTHM & BLUES
INSTRUMENTAL PERFORMANCE
• Herbie Hancock, "Rockit." Columbia.
James Brown, "Today," track from
Bring It On. Churchill.
Gap Band, "Where Are We Going?"
track from *Gap Band V Jammin'*.
Total Experience.
Quincy Jones, Jerry Hey, "Billie Jean."
Epic/CBS.
Kashif, "The Mood," track from *Kashif*.
Arista.

BEST JAZZ FUSION PERFORMANCE
(VOCAL OR INSTRUMENTAL)
• Pat Metheny Group, *Travels*.
ECM/Warner Bros.

Miles Davis, *Star People*. Columbia.
Spyro Gyra, *City Kids*. MCA.
Weather Report, *Procession*. Columbia.
Yellowjackets, *Mirage à Trois*. Warner Bros.

BEST JAZZ VOCAL PERFORMANCE, MALE

• Mel Tormé, *Top Drawer*. Concord Jazz.
Mose Allison, *Lessons in Living*. Elektra/Musician.
Dave Frishberg, *The Dave Frishberg Songbook, Vol. 2*. Omnisound.
Jon Hendricks, *Cloudburst*. Enja/Polygram.
Jimmy Witherspoon, *Jimmy Witherspoon Sings the Blues with Panama Francis and the Savoy Sultans*. Muse.

BEST JAZZ VOCAL PERFORMANCE, FEMALE

• Ella Fitzgerald, *The Best Is Yet to Come*. Pablo Today.
Ernestine Anderson, *Big City*. Concord Jazz.
Betty Carter, *Whatever Happened to Love?* Bet-Car.
Sue Raney, *Sue Raney Sings the Music of Johnny Mandel*. Discovery.
Sarah Vaughan, *Crazy and Mixed Up*. Pablo.

BEST JAZZ VOCAL PERFORMANCE BY A DUO OR GROUP

• Manhattan Transfer, "Why Not!" track from *Bodies and Souls*. Atlantic.
Jackie Cain, Roy Kral, *A Stephen Sondheim Collection*. Finesse.
L.A. Jazz Choir, *Listen*. Mobile Fidelity Sound.
L.A. Voices, *Supersax and L.A. Voices*. Columbia.
Rare Silk, *New Weave*. Polydor.

BEST JAZZ INSTRUMENTAL PERFORMANCE BY A SOLOIST

• Wynton Marsalis, *Think of One*. Columbia.
Art Blakey, *Keystone 3*. Concord Jazz.

Chick Corea, *Trio Music*. ECM/Warner Bros.
Sonny Stitt, *The Last Stitt Sessions, Vol. 1*. Muse.
Phil Woods, *At the Vanguard*. Antilles.

BEST JAZZ INSTRUMENTAL PERFORMANCE BY A GROUP

• Phil Woods Quartet, *At the Vanguard*. Antilles/Island.
Art Blakey & the Jazz Messengers, *Keystone 3*. Concord Jazz.
Herbie Hancock, *Quartet*. Columbia.
Philly Joe Jones/Dameronia, *To Tadd with Love*. Uptown.
Wynton Marsalis, *Think of One*. Columbia.
Red Rodney, Ira Sullivan Quintet, *Sprint*. Elektra/Musician.

BEST JAZZ INSTRUMENTAL PERFORMANCE BY A BIG BAND

• Rob McConnell & the Boss Brass, *All in Good Time*. Dark Orchid.
Count Basie Big Band, *Farmers' Market Barbecue*. Pablo.
Louie Bellson Big Band, *The London Gig*. Pablo.
Gil Evans, *Priestess*. Antilles/Island.
Bob Florence Limited Edition, *Soaring*. Bosco.

BEST NEW COUNTRY SONG
(Songwriter's Award)

• "Stranger in My House," Mike Reid.
"Baby I Lied," Deborah Allen, Rory Bourke, Rafe Van Hoy.
"I.O.U.," Kerry Chater, Austin Roberts.
"Lady Down on Love," Randy Owen.
"A Little Good News," Tommy Rocco, Charlie Black, Rory Bourke.

BEST COUNTRY VOCAL PERFORMANCE, MALE

• Lee Greenwood, "I.O.U." MCA.
Ray Charles, "Born to Love Me." Columbia.
Earl Thomas Conley, "Holding Her and Loving You." RCA.

Vern Gosdin, "If You're Gonna Do Me Wrong (Do It Right)." Compleat/Polygram.
Ronnie Milsap, "Stranger in My House." RCA.
Kenny Rogers, "All My Life." Liberty.

BEST COUNTRY VOCAL PERFORMANCE, FEMALE
• Anne Murray, "A Little Good News." Capitol.
Deborah Allen, "Baby I Lied." RCA.
Crystal Gayle, "Baby What About You." Warner Bros.
Emmylou Harris, *Last Date*. Warner Bros.
Dolly Parton, *Burlap and Satin*. RCA.

BEST COUNTRY PERFORMANCE BY A DUO OR GROUP WITH VOCAL
• Alabama, *The Closer You Get*. RCA.
Larry Gatlin & the Gatlin Brothers Band, "Houston (Means I'm One Day Closer to You)." Columbia.
Merle Haggard, Willie Nelson, *Pancho and Lefty*. Epic/CBS.
Willie Nelson, Waylon Jennings, *Take It to the Limit*. Columbia.
Oak Ridge Boys, *American Made*. MCA.

BEST COUNTRY INSTRUMENTAL PERFORMANCE
• New South (Ricky Skaggs, Jerry Douglas, Tony Rice, J. D. Crowe, Todd Philips), "Fireball," track from *Bluegrass*. Sugar Hill.
Chet Atkins, "Tara Theme," track from *Work It Out with Chet Atkins*. Columbia.
Roy Clark, "Wildwood Flower." Churchill.
Albert Coleman's Atlanta Pops, "Classic Country I," track from *Classic Country*. Epic/CBS.
Earl Scruggs, "Roller Coaster," track from *Top of the World*. Columbia.
Doc & Merle Watson, *Doc and Merle Watson's Guitar Album*. Flying Fish.

BEST GOSPEL PERFORMANCE, MALE
• Russ Taff, *Walls of Glass*. Myrrh/Word.
Dion, *Chariots of Fire*. Light/Lexicon.
Dion, *I Put Away My Idols*. Dayspring/Word.
Phil Driscoll, *I Exalt Thee*. Sparrow/Birdwing.
Michael W. Smith, *Michael W. Smith Project*. Reunion/Word.

BEST GOSPEL PERFORMANCE, FEMALE
• Amy Grant, "Ageless Medley." Myrrh/Word.
Cynthia Clawson, "Come Celebrate Jesus," track from *Forever*. Priority.
Sandi Patti, "The Gift Goes On." Impact/Benson.
Michele Pillar, *Reign on Me*. Sparrow/Birdwing.
Sheila Walsh, *War of Love*. Sparrow/Birdwing.

BEST GOSPEL PERFORMANCE BY A DUO OR GROUP
• Sandi Patti, Larnelle Harris, "More Than Wonderful," track from *More Than Wonderful*. Impact/Benson.
Gaither Vocal Band, "No Other Name but Jesus," track from *Passin' the Faith Along*. Dayspring/Word.
Imperials, *Side by Side*. Myrrh/Word.
Mylon LeFevre & Broken Heart, *More*. Myrrh/Word.
Masters V, *The Masters V Featuring: Hovie Lister, J. D. Sumner, James Blackwood, Jake Hess, Shaun Neilsen*. Skylite.
White Heart, *White Heart*. Myrrh/Word.

BEST SOUL GOSPEL PERFORMANCE, MALE
• Al Green, *I'll Rise Again*. Myrrh/Word.
Solomon Burke, "Precious Lord, Take My Hand," track from *Take Me, Shake Me*. Savoy.
Morris Chapman, *Longtime Friends*. Myrrh/Word.

Thomas A. Dorsey, "Take My Hand, Precious Lord," track from *Say Amen Somebody*. DRG.

Leon Patillo, "Cornerstone," track from *Live Experience*. Myrrh/Word.

BEST SOUL GOSPEL PERFORMANCE, FEMALE

• Sandra Crouch, *We Sing Praises*. Light/Lexicon.

Vanessa Bell Armstrong, *Peace Be Still*. Onyx International/Benson.

Shirley Caesar, *Jesus, I Love Calling Your Name*. Myrrh/Word.

Tramaine Hawkins, *Determined*. Light/Lexicon.

Candi Staton, *Make Me an Instrument*. Beracah.

Albertina Walker, *God Is Able to Carry You Through*. Savoy.

BEST SOUL GOSPEL PERFORMANCE BY A DUO OR GROUP

• Bobby Jones & New Life with Barbara Mandrell, "I'm So Glad I'm Standing Here Today," track from *Come Together*. Myrrh/Word.

Clark Sisters, *Sincerely*. New Birth/Benson.

Sandra Crouch, Andrae Crouch, "Glad I Heard Your Voice," track from *We Sing Praises*. Light/Lexicon.

Jean Johnson, Sandra Crouch, Linda McCrary, Andrae Crouch, "He's Worthy," track from *We Sing Praises*. Light/Lexicon.

Winans, *Long Time Comin'*. Light/Lexicon.

BEST INSPIRATIONAL PERFORMANCE

• Donna Summer, "He's a Rebel," track from *She Works Hard for the Money*. Mercury/Polygram.

Linda Hopkins, "Precious Lord," track from *How Blue Can You Get*. Palo Alto.

Cristy Lane, "I've Come Back (To Say I Love You One More Time)," track from *Footprints in the Sand*. LS/Liberty.

Leontyne Price, *Noel! Noel!* London.

B. J. Thomas, *Peace in the Valley*. Myrrh/Word.

BEST TRADITIONAL BLUES RECORDING

• *Blues 'n' Jazz*, B. B. King. MCA.

Blues Train, Big Joe Turner & Roomful of Blues. Muse.

One More Mile, Clarence "Gatemouth" Brown. Rounder.

San Francisco '83, Albert King. Fantasy.

"Texas Flood," track from *Texas Flood*, Stevie Ray Vaughan & Double Trouble. Epic/CBS.

BEST ETHNIC OR TRADITIONAL FOLK RECORDING

• *I'm Here*, Clifton Chenier & His Red Hot Louisiana Band. Alligator.

The Grey Fox, Chieftains. DRG.

Raga Mishra Piloo, Ravi Shankar, Ali Akbar Khan. Angel.

Renaissance of the Celtic Harp, Alan Stivell. Rounder.

Synchro System, King Sunny Ade. Mango/Island.

BEST LATIN POP PERFORMANCE

• José Feliciano, *Me Enamore*. TPL.

Placido Domingo, "Besame Mucho," track from *My Life for a Song*. CBS Masterworks.

Lani Hall, *Lani*. A&M.

Menudo, *Una Aventura Llamada Menudo*. Raff.

José Luis Rodriguez, *Ven*. Discos CBS International

BEST TROPICAL LATIN PERFORMANCE

• Tito Puente & His Latin Ensemble, *On Broadway*. Concord Picante.

Ray Barretto, Celia Cruz, Adalberto Santiago, *Tremendo Trio*. Fania.

Rubén Blades, *El Que la Hace la Paga*. Fania-Vaya.

Willie Colon, *Corazón Guerrero*. Fania.

Mongo Santamaria, *Mongo Magic*. Roulette.

BEST MEXICAN-AMERICAN PERFORMANCE

- Los Lobos, "Anselma," track from
  . . . And a Time to Dance. Slash.

Los Bukis, Yo Te Necesito. Profono.

Chelo, "A Cambio de Que," track from
Otro Mas. Musart.

Vicente Fernandez, La Diferencia. CBS.

Juan Gabriel, Todo. Ariola.

BEST INSTRUMENTAL COMPOSITION

- "Love Theme from Flashdance,"
  Giorgio Moroder.

"An Actor's Life," Dave Grusin.

"Dream Hunter," Michael Sembello,
Dan Sembello.

"Rockit," Herbie Hancock, B. Laswell,
M. Beinhorn.

"The Thorn Birds Theme," Henry
Mancini.

BEST INSTRUMENTAL ARRANGEMENT

- Dave Grusin, "Summer Sketches '82,"
  track from Dave Grusin and the
  N.Y./L.A. Dream Band (Dave Grusin
  & the N.Y./L.A. Dream Band). GRP.

Toshiko Akiyoshi, "Remembering Bud,"
track from European Memoirs
(Toshiko Akiyoshi–Lew Tabackin
Big Band). Ascent.

Bob Florence, "Afternoon of a Prawn,"
track from Soaring (Bob Florence).
Bosco.

Rob McConnell, "I Got Rhythm," track
from All in Good Time. (Rob McConnell & the Boss Brass). Dark Orchid.

Patrick Williams, "Too Hip for the
Room," track from Dreams and
Themes (Patrick Williams). PCM.

BEST INSTRUMENTAL ARRANGEMENT ACCOMPANYING VOCAL(S)

- Nelson Riddle, "What's New," track
  from What's New (Linda Ronstadt).
  Asylum/Elektra.

David Foster, Jay Graydon, Jeremy Lubbock, "Mornin'," track from Jarreau
(Al Jarreau). Warner Bros.

Jerry Hey, Al Jarreau, Tom Canning, Jay
Graydon, "Step by Step," track from
Jarreau (Al Jarreau). Warner Bros.

Arif Mardin, "Be Bop Medley," track
from Chaka Khan (Chaka Khan).
Warner Bros.

Lionel Richie, James Anthony
Carmichael, "All Night Long (All
Night)" (Lionel Richie). Motown.

BEST VOCAL ARRANGEMENT FOR TWO OR MORE VOICES

- Arif Mardin, Chaka Khan, "Be Bop
  Medley," track from Chaka Khan
  (Chaka Khan). Warner Bros.

Todd Buffa, "Red Clay," track from New
Weave (Rare Silk). Polydor.

Jeremy Lubbock, "The Night That
Monk Returned to Heaven," track
from Bodies and Souls (Manhattan
Transfer). Atlantic.

Alan Paul, "Code of Ethics," track from
Bodies and Souls (Manhattan Transfer). Atlantic.

Janis Siegel, "Down South Camp
Meetin'," track from Bodies and
Souls (Manhattan Transfer). Atlantic.

BEST CAST SHOW ALBUM

- Cats (Complete Original Broadway
  Cast Recording), Trevor Nunn,
  Richard Stilgoe, lyricists.
  Geffen/Warner Bros.

La Cage aux Folles, Jerry Herman, composer and lyricist. RCA.

Little Shop of Horrors, Alan Menken,
composer; Howard Ashman, lyricist.
Geffen/Warner Bros.

On Your Toes, Richard Rodgers, composer; Lorenz Hart, lyricist. Poly-
dor/Polygram.

Zorba, John Kander, composer; Fred
Ebb, lyricist. RCA.

BEST ALBUM OF ORIGINAL SCORE WRITTEN FOR A MOTION PICTURE OR TV SPECIAL

(Composer's Award)

- Flashdance, Giorgio Moroder, Keith
  Forsey, Irene Cara, Shandi Sinna-
  mon, Ronald Magness, Douglas
  Cotler, Richard Gilbert, Michael
  Boddicker, Jerry Hey, Phil Ramone,
  Michael Sembello, Kim Carnes,

Duane Hitchings, Craig Krampf, Dennis Matkosky. Casablanca/Polygram.

Gandhi, Ravi Shankar, George Fenton. RCA.

Star Wars—Return of the Jedi, John Williams. RSO/Polygram.

Stayin' Alive, Frank Stallone, Bruce Stephen Foster, R. Freeland, V. DiCola, T. Marolda, Joe Bean Esposito, Randy Bishop, Tommy Faragher, Barry Gibb, Maurice Gibb, Robin Gibb. RSO/Polygram.

Tootsie, Dave Grusin. Warner Bros.

BEST CLASSICAL ALBUM

• *Mahler: Symphony No. 9 in D Major*, Sir Georg Solti conducting the Chicago Symphony. London.

Haydn: Concerto for Trumpet and Orchestra in E Flat Major; L. Mozart: Concerto for Trumpet and Orchestra in D Major; Hummel: Concerto for Trumpet and Orchestra in E Flat Major, Raymond Leppard conducting the National Philharmonic Orchestra (solo: Wynton Marsalis). CBS.

Leontyne Price and Marilyn Horne in Concert at the Met, James Levine conducting the Metropolitan Opera Orchestra (solos: Leontyne Price, Marilyn Horne). RCA.

Verdi: Falstaff, Carlo Maria Giulini conducting the Los Angeles Philharmonic and Los Angeles Master Chorale (solos: Renato Bruson, Katia Ricciarelli, Leo Nucci, Barbara Hendricks, Lucia Valentini Terrani, Dalmacio Gonzalez, Brenda Boozer). Deutsche Grammophon.

Vivaldi: The Four Seasons and Concerto for 4 Violins, Op. 3, No. 10; Bach: Double Concerto, BWV 1043; Mozart: Sinfonia Concertante, K. 364, Zubin Mehta conducting the Israel Philharmonic Orchestra (solos: Itzhak Perlman, Isaac Stern, Shlomo Mintz, Pinchas Zukerman, Ivry Gitlis, Ida Haendel). Deutsche Grammophon.

BEST CLASSICAL ORCHESTRAL RECORDING

• *Mahler: Symphony No. 9 in D Major*, Sir Georg Solti conducting the the Chicago Symphony Orchestra. London.

Beethoven: Symphony No. 5 in C Minor, Op. 67, Carlo Maria Giulini conducting the Los Angeles Philharmonic Orchestra. Deutsche Grammophon.

Bernstein: West Side Story Symphonic Dances and *Candide Overture*; *Barber: Adagio for Strings; W. Schuman: American Festival Overture*, Leonard Bernstein conducting the Los Angeles Philharmonic Orchestra. Deutsche Grammophon.

Del Tredici: In Memory of a Summer Day (Child Alice, Part One), Leonard Slatkin conducting the St. Louis Symphony Orchestra. Nonesuch.

Mozart: The Symphonies, Vol. 6, Christopher Hogwood conducting the Academy of Ancient Music (solo: Jaap Schroder). L'Oiseau-Lyre.

BEST CHAMBER MUSIC PERFORMANCE

• Mstislav Rostropovich, Rudolf Serkin, *Brahms: Sonata for Cello and Piano in E Minor, Op. 38, and Sonata in F Major, Op. 99*. Deutsche Grammophon.

The Philip Glass Ensemble (Michael Riesman, conductor), *Glass: The Photographer*. CBS.

Nancy Allen and the Tokyo String Quartet with Ransom Wilson and David Shifrin, *Ravel: Introduction and Allegro*. Angel.

Juilliard String Quartet, *Bartók: The String Quartets (6)*. CBS.

La Salle Quartet, *Zemlinsky: The String Quartets*. Deutsche Grammophon.

Itzhak Perlman, Lynn Harrell, Vladimir Ashkenazy, *Beethoven: Trio No. 6 in B Flat, Op. 97 ("Archduke")*. Angel.

BEST CLASSICAL PERFORMANCE, INSTRUMENTAL SOLOIST(S) (WITH ORCHESTRA)

• Wynton Marsalis (Leppard conducting the National Philharmonic Orchestra), *Haydn: Concerto for Trumpet and Orchestra in E Flat Major; L. Mozart: Concerto for Trumpet and Orchestra in D Major; Hummel: Concerto for Trumpet and Orchestra in E Flat Major*. CBS.

Leonard Bernstein (Bernstein conducting the Los Angeles Philharmonic Orchestra), *Gershwin: Rhapsody in Blue*. Deutsche Grammophon.

Itzhak Perlman (Levine conducting the Vienna Philharmonic), *Mozart: Concertos for Violin and Orchestra No. 3 in G Major, K. 216, No. 5 in A Major, K. 219*. Deutsche Grammophon.

Rudolf Serkin (Ozawa conducting the Boston Symphony Orchestra), *Beethoven: Concerto for Piano No. 3 in C Minor, Op. 37*. Telarc.

Simon Standage (Pinnock directing the English Concert), *Vivaldi: The Four Seasons*. Archiv.

Isaac Stern, Pinchas Zukerman, Itzhak Perlman, Shlomo Mintz, Ivry Gitlis, Ida Haendel (Mehta conducting the Israel Philharmonic Orchestra), *Vivaldi: The Four Seasons and Concerto for 4 Violins, Op. 3, No. 10*. Deutsche Grammophon.

Richard Stoltzman (Schneider conducting the Mostly Mozart Festival Orchestra), *Weber: Concerto for Clarinet No. 1 in F Minor, Op. 73; Rossini: Theme and Variations for Clarinet and Orchestra; Mozart: Andante in C, K. 315* . RCA.

BEST CLASSICAL PERFORMANCE, INSTRUMENTAL SOLOIST(S) (WITHOUT ORCHESTRA)

• Glenn Gould, *Beethoven: Sonatas No. 12 in A Flat Major, Op. 26, and No. 13 in E Flat Major, Op. 27, No. 1*. CBS.

Emil Gilels, *Beethoven: Sonatas for Piano No. 15 in D Major, Op. 28 ("Pastoral"), and No. 3 in C Major, Op. 2, No. 3*. Deutsche Grammophon.

Vladimir Horowitz, *Horowitz in London*. RCA.

Shlomo Mintz, *Paganini: Caprices (24)*. Deutsche Grammophon.

Ivo Pogorelich, *Ravel: Gaspard de la Nuit; Prokofiev: Sonata for Piano No. 6 in A Major, Op. 82*. Deutsche Grammophon.

BEST OPERA RECORDING
(Tie)

• *Verdi: La Traviata (Original Soundtrack)*, James Levine conducting the Metropolitan Opera Orchestra and Chorus (solos: Teresa Stratas, Placido Domingo, Cornell MacNeil). Elektra.

• *Mozart: Le Nozze di Figaro*, Sir Georg Solti conducting the London Philharmonic Orchestra (solos: Kiri Te Kanawa, Lucia Popp, Samuel Ramey, Thomas Allen, Kurt Moll, Frederica von Stade). London.

Verdi: Aida, Claudio Abbado conducting La Scala Opera Orchestra and Chorus (solos: Katia Ricciarelli, Placido Domingo, Elena Obraztsova, Leo Nucci, Nicolai Ghiaurov, Ruggero Raimondi). Deutsche Grammophon.

Verdi: Falstaff, Carlo Maria Giulini conducting the Los Angeles Philharmonic and Los Angeles Master Chorale (solos: Renato Bruson, Leo Nucci, Katia Ricciarelli, Barbara Hendricks, Lucia Valentini Terrani). Deutsche Grammophon.

Wagner: Tristan und Isolde, Leonard Bernstein conducting the Chorus and Orchestra of the Bavarian Radio Symphony (solos: Peter Hoffman, Hildegard Behrens, Yvonne Minton). Philips.

Wagner: Tristan und Isolde, Carlos Kleiber conducting the Dresden State Orchestra and Leipzig Radio Chorus (solos: René Kollo, Margaret Price, Brigitte Fassbaender). Deutsche Grammophon.

BEST CHORAL PERFORMANCE (OTHER THAN OPERA)

• Margaret Hillis, choral director, Chicago Symphony Orchestra Chorus; Sir Georg Solti conducting the Chicago Symphony Orchestra, *Haydn: The Creation*. London.

Gunter Jena, choral conductor, North German Radio Chorus, Hamburg, *The Brahms Edition: Choral Works a Capella (Complete)*. Deutsche Grammophon.

Herbert von Karajan conducting the Vienna Singverein and Vienna Philharmonic, *Haydn: The Creation*. Deutsche Grammophon.

Raymond Leppard conducting the NDR Choir and Knabenchor Hannover; NDR Symphony Orchestra, *Bach: St. Matthew Passion*. Angel.

Trevor Pinnock conducting the Choir of Westminster Abbey and English Concert, *Handel: Coronation Anthems*. Archiv.

BEST CLASSICAL PERFORMANCE, VOCAL SOLOIST

• Leontyne Price, Marilyn Horne (Levine conducting the Metropolitan Opera Orchestra), *Leontyne Price and Marilyn Horne in Concert at the Met*. RCA.

Dietrich Fischer-Dieskau (Daniel Barenboim, accompanist), *The Brahms Edition: Lieder (Complete)*. Deutsche Grammophon.

Kiri Te Kanawa (Davis conducting the London Symphony Orchestra), *Mozart Opera Arias*. Philips.

Jessye Norman (Daniel Barenboim, accompanist), *The Brahms Edition: Lieder*. Deutsche Grammophon.

Frederica von Stade (Jean-Philippe Collard, accompanist), *Fauré: 18 Songs*. Angel.

BEST ENGINEERED RECORDING, CLASSICAL

• James Lock, *Mahler: Symphony No. 9 in D Major* (Sir Georg Solti conducting the Chicago Symphony Orchestra). London.

Marc J. Aubort, *Del Tredici: In Memory of a Summer Day (Child Alice, Part One)* (Leonard Slatkin conducting the St. Louis Symphony Orchestra (solo: Phyllis Bryn-Julson). Nonesuch.

Paul Goodman, William King, *Leontyne Price and Marilyn Horne in Concert at the Met* (James Levine conducting the Metropolitan Opera Orchestra (solos: Leontyne Price, Marilyn Horne). RCA.

Gunter Hermanns, *R. Strauss: Metamorphoses; Death and Transfiguration* (Herbert von Karajan conducting the Berlin Philharmonic). Deutsche Grammophon.

James Lock, John Dunkerley, *Haydn: The Creation* (Sir Georg Solti conducting the Chicago Symphony Orchestra; Chicago Symphony Orchestra Chorus, Margaret Hillis, choral director). London.

Klaus Scheibe, *Verdi: Falstaff* (Carlo Maria Giulini conducting the Los Angeles Philharmonic and Los Angeles Master Chorale (solos: Renato Bruson, Leo Nucci, Katia Ricciarelli, Barbara Hendricks, Lucia Valentini Terrani, Dalmacio Gonzalez, Brenda Boozer). Deutsche Grammophon.

CLASSICAL PRODUCER OF THE YEAR

• Marc J. Aubort, Joanna Nickrenz

Andrew Cornall

Steven Epstein

Dr. Steven Paul

Jay David Saks

BEST COMEDY RECORDING

• *Eddie Murphy: Comedian*, Eddie Murphy. Columbia.

Bill Cosby Himself, Bill Cosby. Motown.

Monty Python's the Meaning of Life, Monty Python. MCA.

Throbbing Python of Love, Robin Williams. Casablanca/Polygram.

What Becomes a Semi-Legend Most? Joan Rivers. Geffen/Warner Bros.

BEST SPOKEN WORD OR NONMUSICAL RECORDING

• *Copland: Lincoln Portrait*, William Warfield. Mercury/Phillips.

Everything You Always Wanted to Know About Home Computers, Steve Allen, Jayne Meadows. Casablanca/Polygram.

Jane Fonda's Workout Record for Pregnancy, Birth and Recovery, Jane Fonda, Femmy De Lyser. Columbia.

Old Possum's Book of Practical Cats, Sir John Gielgud, Irene Worth. Caedmon.

The Robots of Dawn, Isaac Asimov. Caedmon.

BEST RECORDING FOR CHILDREN
• *E.T. The Extra-Terrestrial*, Michael Jackson, narration and vocals. MCA.

Born to Add, Sesame Street Muppets. Sesame Street Records.

"Born to Add," track from *Born to Add*, Bruce Stringbean & the Sesame Street Band. Sesame Street Records.

The Music Machine Part II, Candle. Birdwing/Sparrow.

Rocky Mountain Holiday, John Denver, Muppets. Sesame Street Records.

BEST ENGINEERED RECORDING (OTHER THAN CLASSICAL)
• Bruce Swedien, *Thriller* (Michael Jackson). Epic/CBS.

Tommy Vicari, Thom Wilson, James Gallagher, Peter Chaiken, *Bossa Nova Hotel* (Michael Sembello). Warner Bros.

Jay Graydon, Ian Eales, Eric Prestis, *Jarreau* (Al Jarreau). Warner Bros.

Gary Loizzo, Will Rascati, Rob Kingsland, *Kilroy Was Here* (Styx). A&M.

Allan Sides, *Target* (Tom Scott). Atlantic.

BEST ALBUM PACKAGE
(Art Director's Award)
• Robert Rauschenberg, *Speaking in Tongues*, limited edition version (Talking Heads). Sire/Warner Bros.

Bob Defrin, Lynn Dreese Breslin, *Records* (Foreigner). Atlantic.

Bill Levy, Murry Whiteman, *One Night with a Stranger* (Martin Briley). Mercury/ Polygram.

Michael Ross, *The Key* (Joan Armatrading). A&M.

Richard Seireeni, *Nothing but the Truth* (Mac McAnally). Geffen/Warner Bros.

BEST ALBUM NOTES
(Annotator's Award)
• Orrin Keepnews, *The "Interplay" Sessions* (Bill Evans). Milestone.

Lester Bangs, *The Fugs Greatest Hits, Vol. 1* (Fugs). Adelphi.

Peter Guralnick, *The Okeh Sessions* (Big Maybelle). Epic/CBS.

Richard B. Hadlock, *Giants of Jazz/Joe Sullivan* (Joe Sullivan). Time-Life.

John McDonough, *Seven Come Eleven* (Benny Goodman). Columbia.

BEST HISTORICAL ALBUM
• *The Greatest Recordings of Arturo Toscanini Symphonies, Vol. 1*, Arturo Toscanini. Franklin Mint.

Back in the Saddle Again: American Cowboy Songs, various country & western artists. Charlie Seemann, producer. New World.

The Complete Blue Note Recordings of Thelonious Monk, Thelonious Monk. Mosaic.

Kings of New Orleans Jazz, various artists. Franklin Mint.

The Motown Story: The First 25 Years, various artists. Motown.

PRODUCER OF THE YEAR (OTHER THAN CLASSICAL)
• Quincy Jones, Michael Jackson

James Anthony Carmichael, Lionel Richie

Jay Graydon

Quincy Jones

Phil Ramone

BEST VIDEO, SHORT FORM
• *Girls on Film/Hungry Like the Wolf*, Duran Duran. EMI Music Video/Sony.

Bill Wyman, Bill Wyman. Sony/Ripple.

A Flock of Seagulls, A Flock of Seagulls. Arista/Zomba/Sony.

Rod Stewart: Tonight He's Yours, Rod Stewart. Sony/Embassy Home Entertainment.

Videosyncracy, Todd Rundgren. Sony/Alchemedia.

BEST VIDEO ALBUM

• *Duran Duran*, Duran Duran. Thorn EMI Video; Disc-Pioneer Artists.

Alice Cooper "The Nightmare," Alice Cooper. Warner Home Video.

Grace Jones: A One Man Show, Grace Jones. Island Pictures/Vestron Video.

Olivia in Concert, Olivia Newton-John. MCA Home Video.

Rolling Stones: Let's Spend the Night Together, Rolling Stones. Embassy Home Entertainment.

Word of Mouth, Toni Basil. Chrysalis.

• 1984 •
Proud Tina's Triumphant Return

It was "one of the most dramatic come-backs in music history," declared *Variety*.

Back in the 1960s and '70s, Tina Turner's "wild, hip-shaking stance with the Ike and Tina Turner Revue helped to define the concept of sex and soul," the *L.A. Times* once noted. The singing duo got married in 1958, made their debut in the pop charts in 1960 with "A Fool in Love" and followed up their early recording success with numerous hits like "Proud Mary," which earned them an r&b Grammy in 1971.

But despite the dream-come-true quality of their public career, Tina Turner later related in her autobiography that her private life was a hellish nightmare. Ike frequently beat her with shoe stretchers, telephones and coat hangers, she said, resulting in facial bruises and broken bones that she had to cover up with heavy makeup before stepping out onstage to perform. She attempted suicide by taking 50 Valium in 1968 but was rescued in time and rushed to a nearby hospital, where her stomach was pumped. Finally, on Independence Day, 1976, Ike nailed her in the backseat of a limo in Dallas, beating her for the last time. Carrying only 36 cents and a gasoline credit card, she jumped out of the vehicle and at last struck out for a life on her own. But solo success was elusive. Turner struggled for years on the concert trail, where she earned barely enough to retire old debts. Then came the release of her *Private Dancer* album, eight years after she jilted Ike, and suddenly she was a reigning star again. "Talk about hard climbs!" gasped the *L.A. Times*.

Private Dancer spent an impressive 71 weeks on the album charts and revealed the new Turner as being proud

Tina Turner capped off her dramatic career comeback with three awards, including best record. The excited LP champ Lionel Richie said, "It's heart attack time!"

and even defiant ("Better Be Good to Me"), cool and aloof ("What's Love Got to Do with It") and even, at age 45, still sexy after all these years ("Private Dancer"). When all three songs became Top 10 hits, Turner was back in the headlines, too, and a surprise favorite on MTV for her saucy videos.

Turner's dramatic comeback was heralded by four Grammy triumphs, including three for Turner herself: Record of the Year and best female pop vocal performance for "What's Love Got to Do with It" plus best female rock vocal performance for "Better Be Good to Me." The fourth award was also for "What's Love Got to Do With It," hailed as Song of the Year, thus reaping gold for its songwriters, Graham Lyle and Terry Britten.

Described by the *New York Times* as "two sensational legs topped by an explosion of hair," Turner was greeted with several standing ovations throughout Grammy night as she performed "What's

Love" on the air and accepted the first two of her three prizes. Then came the presentation of the evening's highest honor, which was bestowed by a music superstar who still hadn't won a Grammy. "Diana Ross, swathed in a gown that looked like an enormous bow," noted the *Times,* presented "the Record of the Year award to Tina Turner, but the superstar was lost in the hustle and bustle of the occasion." A grateful Turner told the crowd gathered at Los Angeles's Shrine Auditorium, "I've been waiting so long for this!"

"Turner missed duplicating Michael Jackson's achievement of last year—winning in the pop, rock and r&b vocal categories—by one award," *Variety* reported. "Ironically, given Turner's past complaints about the American record industry's racial stereotyping, she missed the vocal hat trick by losing in the r&b female vocal category to Chaka Khan." Khan prevailed for the Prince-scripted tune "I Feel for You."

A minor controversy surrounded the fact that the number-one-selling song of the year, Prince's "When Doves Cry," was missing from the lineup of Record of the Year nominees. But "His Purpleness" was still considered the front-runner in the race for Album of the Year for the top-selling LP of 1984—the soundtrack to his movie *Purple Rain,* which became the biggest-grossing rock film ever made. Bruce Springsteen had been snubbed by the Grammys repeatedly in years past, but now he was also in the runoff with *Born in the U.S.A.,* number one in the *Village Voice's* annual Critics' Poll of the year's top 100 LPs (*Purple Rain* came in at number two, *Private Dancer* at number five). *Private Dancer* was nominated, too, and certainly couldn't be discounted. Neither could Lionel Richie's *Can't Slow Down,* which appealed to the more conservative N.A.R.A.S. voters with hummable hits like Song of the Year nominee "Hello." The fifth contender was *She's So Unusual* by Cyndi Lauper, the odds-on favorite to nab Best New Artist. All five LPs represented the most progressive

lineup ever offered to Grammy voters and came about as a result of N.A.R.A.S.'s recent, highly successful drive to recruit more young members. "Richie is the kind of mainstream pop artist that Grammy voters have traditionally favored," said the *L.A. Times,* sizing up the contest, "but Prince has a narrow edge."

N.A.R.A.S.'s traditional contingent ended up prevailing on behalf of Richie's *Can't Slow Down* when the youth vote split between Prince and Springsteen. It was a long-overdue triumph in a major category for one of pop's leading hit makers. On three recent occasions, Richie had lost twin bids for Record and Song of the Year—in 1980, 1981 and 1983—and had also lost twice as Producer of the Year. His defeat at the 1981 awards ceremony, in fact, was humiliating when *all seven* of his nominations proved fruitless. He finally won a pop vocals Grammy in 1984 for "Truly," but it was a modest victory compared to all his losses in the top categories. Vindication finally came with the LP laurels in 1984 and the added bonus of snagging the Producer of the Year award, which he shared with James Anthony Carmichael—and also with Chicago's producer, David Foster, when the category experienced its first tie ever. Backstage, Richie told reporters, "It's heart attack time now. If you knew how many times I've sat out in that audience hearing the names of those other winners, wondering why. I don't want to wonder tonight. I just want to enjoy it."

It was considered such a foregone conclusion by some music pundits that Prince would dominate this year's awards that the *L.A. Times* wrote: "Memo to Prince: Call your tailor. Order a purple tux. Just as last year was Michael Jackson's year at the Grammys, this figures to be Prince's year. Prince has never won a Grammy, but then he's never had an album stay at No. 1 for 24 weeks either. His Grammy time has come."

The prophesy proved partially true, but, as *Variety* noted, "Prince had to settle for less prestigious awards" when he

failed to sweep the top categories. He
scored three consolation prizes: the honors for best film score, the kudos for best
rock group vocals for *Purple Rain* and
the prize for writing the Best New R&B
Song, "I Feel for You." As he did at the
American Music Awards, Prince performed on the Grammycast, rocking the
Shrine Auditorium with an eight-and-a-
half minute version of "Baby, I'm a Star"
that ended with a dramatic exit down the
hall's center aisle to his purple limo waiting outside. "If he had won best album
later in the show, he wouldn't have been
there to accept it," the *L.A. Times*
observed.

One prediction that did not go wrong
was Cyndi Lauper's victory as Best New
Artist, her only win of the night despite
nominations for Album of the Year (*She's
So Unusual*), Song of the Year ("Time
After Time") and Record of the Year
("Girls Just Want to Have Fun"). "I never
really thought I could be anything," Lauper told reporters backstage later. "But I
always thought if you really meant to do
something and worked really hard that
you could achieve anything. It's all a matter of what you have up here [pointing to
her head] and in here [pointing to her
heart]." Soon afterward, the rocker ran
into fellow winner Tina Turner backstage
and told her, "You're my idol!" She then
gave Turner a kiss and asked her teasingly,
"Was it as good for you as it was for me?"

While Springsteen failed to be recognized by N.A.R.A.S. with a Grammy in
the past, he proved he bore no ill will
when he joined the Recording Academy
as a member of its New York chapter this
year. Yet the big question remained:
Would the Boss perform on the Grammycast? The *New York Times* reported:
"Right up to air time, an element of suspense was generated over the question of
whether Bruce Springsteen would compromise his artistic principles by becoming involved in such a glittering occasion.
He didn't." Springsteen did show up in
person, however, sporting long hair, sideburns and a long-ribboned bow tie to

Fanfare said Placido Domingo's performance in
Best Opera *Carmen* was the most "dramatically
responsive of the three he has recorded."

dress up his tux—and so was on hand to
accept the prize for best male rock vocal
performance for "Dancing in the Dark."

"It was so satisfying to finally see
Springsteen receive his first Grammy that
fans of the most acclaimed rock figure
since Bob Dylan probably even forgave
the Recording Academy for his loss three
years ago to soap opera heartthrob Rick
Springfield," commented the *L.A. Times*.

Throughout the night, as more awards
redressed past oversights like Springsteen and Prince and others recognized
hot new artists, critics proclaimed that
the Grammys at last were in tune with the
frontline music of the day. Phil Collins
had his first number-one hit and his first
Grammy (pop vocals) with "Against All
Odds (Take a Look at Me Now)," the title
song to the popular Jeff Bridges/Rachel
Ward film about a man who goes to Mexico to track down a friend's runaway girlfriend. Collins's victory seemed to come
against all odds itself when he topped
such veterans as conominees Kenny Loggins, Lionel Richie and Stevie Wonder.

The theme to the hit movie *Ghostbusters* reaped Best Pop Instrumental
Performance for Ray Parker, Jr. (again

eclipsing Stevie Wonder). The British "classical rock" band Yes had been hitting the charts since 1968 but finally earned its first Grammy for Best Rock Instrumental Performance of "Cinema," a track from *90125*. The Pointer Sisters had won their first Grammy for country music in 1974, but now they were ruling the pop rankings with "Jump (for My Love)" and won the pop group vocals prize.

Trinidad-born Billy Ocean had a minor hit in 1976 with "Love Really Hurts Without You," but he came back strong in 1984 with "Caribbean Queen (No More Love on the Run)," which brought him the male r&b vocals trophy. Doobie Brother Michael McDonald became the first white person to win in an r&b category since the Champs in 1958 when he shared this year's duo/group vocals award with 1981 Grammy champ James Ingram for "Yah Mo B There." Jazz keyboardist Herbie Hancock upset his die-hard fans last year when he released one of his first dance music albums, *Future Shock,* winning him the r&b instrumental prize for its "Rockit" track. Now he reprised the victory with another r&b LP, *Sound-System.*

Jazz trumpeter Wynton Marsalis made Grammy history last year when he became the first artist to win awards in both classical and nonclassical categories. Shocking the experts this year, he did it again by taking the jazz solo instrumental laurels for *Hot House Flowers* (which failed to capture the same critical praise that his triumphant *Think of One* LP did last year) and the classical soloist's award (with orchestra) for performing works by Handel, Purcell, Torelli, Fasch and Molter. For the third straight year, the group headed by 30-year-old jazz guitarist Pat Metheny held on to the fusion performance prize (*First Circle*), while the jazz slots welcomed a first-time winner when the band headed by drummer Art Blakey garnered the group instrumental honors for the track "New York Scene."

Jazz artists had performed on every Grammycast since 1977, and their omis-

Three-time past champ Emmylou Harris picked up a new vocalist Grammy for "In My Dreams."

sion this year triggered a revolt inside the record academy. Musician, composer and critic Leonard Feather resigned from N.A.R.A.S. a week after the show. Other artists, reported the *L.A. Times,* "are tossing their $45 renewal notices in the nearest trash can." Feather wrote in the *Times:* "Last year, jazz managed to snare three-and-a-half minutes in a three-and-a-half hour program; this time around, not a single jazz nominee got to play or sing a note. Not even Joe Williams, who at 66 won his long overdue first Grammy."

Williams won the only trophy given out this year for vocals (for *Nothin' but the Blues*), since N.A.R.A.S. elected to recombine the three awards for male, female and duo/group that had been given away over the previous three years. The *Times* noted, "Joe Williams appeared overjoyed at winning. The veteran of the Count Basie Band dodged the perennial age question, saying with a grin, 'I'm old enough to enjoy this and young enough to want some more. It feels marvelous. I'm glad it happened before the pipes went. I think I'll keep going as long as I can stay in tune.'"

The legendary (and eight-time past winner) Count Basie died in 1984, but still he proved to be a formidable presence at the Grammys when he snagged a jazz award for the last album of his career, *88 Basie Street,* featuring works by Sammy Nestico as well as some of his own compositions such as "Contractor's Blues" and "Sunday at the Savoy." Basie also joined artists Chick Webb, Tommy Dorsey, Benny Goodman and others on *Big Band Jazz,* winner of Best Historical Album and Best Album Notes. In addition, Basie's 1955 recording of "April in Paris" was inducted this year into the N.A.R.A.S. Hall of Fame along with Gene Autry's "Rudolph, the Red-Nosed Reindeer" and other classics.

A posthumous prize was awarded in the country categories, too, to the winner of Best Country Song "City of New Orleans" writer Steve Goodman, who died of leukemia in September. Goodman had written it in the early 1970s about a Chicago train called City of New Orleans that was being shut down due to a shortage of riders. Arlo Guthrie recorded the first hit version of it in 1972, while Willie Nelson brought it to the upper rungs of the charts again in 1984. In what *Variety* called "one of the most touching moments" of the Grammy ceremony, Goodman's trophy was accepted on his behalf by his nine-and-a-half-year-old daughter, Sarah.

Five-time past Grammy victor Nelson was nominated for best male vocals for "New Orleans" but lost to another country great, Merle Haggard, who scored his first win ever for "That's the Way Love Goes," a tune he'd recorded nearly a half dozen times earlier in his career, but never before to his complete satisfaction. The mother-daughter team of Naomi and Wynonna Judd became first-time champs when they won the duo singing laurels for the song written for them by Kenny O'Dell, "Mama He's Crazy," which they called their "country foundation" since it

> "Dancing in the Dark" finally brought Springsteen his first Grammy.

became their first hit platter. The song was a losing nominee for Best Country Song.

Emmylou Harris scored the fourth Grammy of her career for "In My Dreams." Ricky Skaggs took honors last year along with other name talent like Tony Rice billing themselves as the New South Group, but came back to claim a solo honor for his instrumental work on "Wheel Hoss," a track from *Country Boy.* Skaggs was being honored with multiple prizes in the mid-1980s. This was the third year in a row that he won the Country Music Association's instrumental award. Next year C.M.A. would name him Entertainer of the Year.

All of the following past winners for religious recordings returned with new prizes: Donna Summer ("Forgive Me"), Amy Grant ("Angels"), 1974's Best New Artist Debby Boone ("Keep the Flame Burning" with Phil Driscoll), Andrae Crouch ("Always Remember") and Shirley Caesar and Al Green ("Sailin' on the Sea of Your Love"). (Caesar claimed an additional Grammy for her *Sailin'* LP version.) On the Grammycast, host John Denver called gospel the root of most other forms of music and introduced a brief film that paid tribute to the genre. *Billboard* noted, "Crouch whisked the glitzy crowd away to a small Southern church during a well-produced gospel feature, an imaginary trip buoyed by stellar performances from pop staples, the Clark Sisters, the Rev. James Cleveland and others."

Like the jazz lineup, the award for Best Mexican-American Performance became the focus of controversy when, noted *Variety,* "a group calling itself the Mexican-American Recording Artists handed out protest fliers outside the Shrine, noting that many Mexican-Americans were eligible for the honor, including Vikki Carr (the group had her name misspelled) and Santana." "None of the nominees is Mexican-

American (or Chicano)," reported the *L.A. Times*. "Brazilian Roberto Carlos sings in Portuguese (although his nominated song is in Spanish); Raphael and Luis Miguel are from Spain; Sheena Easton is Scottish; Juan Gabriel and Yolanda Del Rio are Mexican citizens. None of the nominated songs by the performers is in English or even reflects the bilingual abilities of most Mexican-American performers." The cowinner, noted the *L.A. Times,* was "Sheena Easton, who has made news lately as the first performer to crack the top five in the pop, black, country and dance/disco charts." When she accepted the prize at the off-the-air ceremony prior to the Grammycast, *Variety* reported that Easton "confessed that she 'just learned to sing in Spanish a few years ago.'" She shared the award with Luis Miguel for "Me Gustas Tal Como Eres."

In the other Latin slots, two-time past winner Eddie Palmieri nabbed the tropical Latin laurels for *Palo Pa Rumba* and Placido Domingo took the pop category for "Always in My Heart." Like Wynton Marsalis, Domingo crossed over the genre lines to win a classical prize as a principal soloist for Best Opera Recording *Carmen*.

Winner of Best Ethnic or Traditional Folk Recording went to an artist who didn't begin performing professionally until age 60. Ninety-year-old singer and guitar player Elizabeth Cotten (*Elizabeth Cotten Live!*) was known for her unconventional method of plucking her instrument: Using two fingers of her left hand, she played her guitar upside down. "With her gray hair pulled back in a bun, she walked slowly into the press area, leaning heavily on a gnarled cane," noted the *L.A. Times*. "She was probably the first performer not asked what she thought of Prince. Asked how she learned her unusual left-handed guitar technique, Cotten answered, 'Jesus showed me how. He taught me how to play guitar in a dream.'"

A new category was introduced this year for Best Reggae Recording, which was claimed by the vocal trio Black Uhuru (*Anthem*), called "the first impor-

tant reggae group of the Eighties" by *Rolling Stone*.

During his sweepstakes victory last year, Michael Jackson failed to win a video award because none of his videos had been released commercially during the Grammy eligibility period. This year he made up for it by scoring Best Video Album for *Making Michael Jackson's "Thriller,"* while David Bowie's self-titled video won him the short-form prize. Jackson's only other nomination this year was in the r&b categories for "Tell Me I'm Not Dreaming," his duet with brother Jermaine. The Jacksons' hugely successful *Victory* came up with scratch in 1984.

Weird Al Yankovic reaped Best Comedy Recording for his parody of Jackson's "Beat It" called "Eat It," which conjured up a mother telling her child: "Just eat it. Eat it. Get yourself an egg and beat it. Have some more chicken. Have some more pie. It doesn't matter if it's boiled or fried. . . ." After winning, Yankovic was asked by reporters what he was going to do to celebrate. Looking underwhelmed, the comic responded flippantly, "I thought I'd get some free food and then go home and take a shower."

Past Grammy grabber John Williams nabbed a new one for his official score to the Olympic Games held in Los Angeles, tying for Best Instrumental Composition with Randy Newman, who contributed the music to the Robert Redford baseball film *The Natural*. The tie that earned Williams his 15th statuette left him tied with Stevie Wonder as Grammy's fifth-biggest overall winner.

Composer Stephen Sondheim picked up Grammy's Best Cast Show Album award for his latest Broadway musical, *Sunday in the Park with George,* which also earned a Pulitzer Prize.

Curiously, the winner of Best Classical Album was another show score—to the Oscars' Best Picture *Amadeus*. Mozart's music was brought to a wider-than-usual audience by Neville Marriner conducting the Academy of St. Martin-in-the-Fields, but the liberties taken with the composer's masterpieces in order to make them work in the context of a popular drama did not make its Grammy victory popular with classical music purists. The film's producer, John Strauss, told the N.A.R.A.S. membership magazine, *Grammy Pulse*, that the editing was necessary so that Mozart's music could "reach beyond the normal classical music record-buying public."

A loser of the laurels for best LP rebounded when conductor Leonard Slatin and the St. Louis Symphony won the orchestral honors for their recording of Prokofiev's Symphony No. 5 in B Flat, which also snagged the engineering award. Its critical reviews were schizophrenic. *Fanfare* called it "unconvincing" and added, "Slatin makes us aware of his own interposition; he doesn't fix attention on the music, but on his manipulation of it." *High Fidelity* gave it the highest praise, calling the recording "one of the greatest this world has ever received."

> Joe Williams said, "I'm old enough to enjoy this and young enough to want some more."

Another loser of the best album prize turned up as winner of the choral awards: Brahms's *A German Requiem* performed by the Chicago Symphony Orchestra and Chorus with conductor James Levine and choral director Margaret Hillis (earning her a sixth Grammy in the category). *High Fidelity* dismissed it as "melodramatically overwrought," however, and *Fanfare* said, "Levine tends to extremes of tempo that tire with repeated hearings."

Cellist Yo-Yo Ma was gaining wide critical praise as of 1984 and capped it off with his first Grammy when he won the soloist (without orchestra) trophy for a compilation of suites by Bach that the critics hailed for Ma's display of technical skill. The Juilliard Quartet reaped the chamber music prize for their last installment of all of Beethoven's quartets, which was cheered by *Fanfare* as "dramatic, often highly intense music-making."

Between 1960 and 1965, N.A.R.A.S. bestowed an award for new classical compositions, but then dropped it only to reintroduce the category in 1984. The new winner was Samuel Barber, who had won once before, in 1964 for *Concerto,* and now was honored for his opera *Antony and Cleopatra.*

The year's Best Opera Recording marked a third victory in the category for Bizet's *Carmen,* which had been honored previously for recordings by Herbert von Karajan and the Vienna Philharmonic Orchestra and Chorus in 1964 and then again in 1973 by Leonard Bernstein conducting the Metropolitan Opera Orchestra and Chorus. The 1984 winner was performed by Lorin Maazel conducting the French National Symphony Orchestra with soprano Julia Migenes-Johnson in the lead and tenor Placido Domingo as Don José. *Fanfare* called this version far superior to the "strange, eccentric, unidiomatic one Maazel presided over in 1971," giving the credit to the new cast. Migenes-Johnson, it said "makes deft, intelligent use of her small voice," while Domingo's performance was called "the most dramatically responsive and best sung of the three he has recorded." The album was the score to a 1984 French film that critic Leonard Maltin has called "overbaked and unbelievably inept," adding, "Still, opera buffs will enjoy the music— if they keep their eyes closed."

Neither Migenes-Johnson nor Domingo was up for the soloist accolade, which went to Jessye Norman, José van Dam and Heather Harper for *Songs of Maurice Ravel. Fanfare* was most appreciative of Norman, who, it said, "really cuts loose."

Leonard Bernstein was honored with the academy's Lifetime Achievement Award. *Variety* noted, "He rushed his acceptance speech, he told the crowd, so that Tina Turner, next up on the production's sked, could perform."

After the Grammy show concluded, the *L.A. Times* applauded the Recording Academy's new hipness. "The evening's main winner was the N.A.R.A.S.," it said. "After years of being ridiculed by pop and rock critics for being too conservative in its choices, the academy came up this year with its most impressive set of nominees and with a ceremony that clearly elevated rock performers to equal status with more mainstream artists. In fact, 1984 may go down as the year in which rock and roll was finally welcomed to the Grammy club—as such acclaimed rock figures as Prince, Bruce Springsteen and Cyndi Lauper were almost constant subjects of attention during the three-hour-plus program."

The New York Times added: "Significantly, the show that once wouldn't recognize rock music, opened up with the driving 'Heart of Rock & Roll' by Huey Lewis & the News, followed by a reminder from John Denver, once again

the genial and unflappable host, that 30 years ago to the very month Bill Haley & the Comets altered the future of popular music with 'Rock Around the Clock.' It may have been a long time coming, but the Grammy Awards seem to have caught up with a bigger slice of reality. Maybe one of these years, they will even let the fans screaming in the balcony come downstairs and mingle with the power brokers and current idols.

"The production numbers covered an extraordinary range of music," the *Times* continued, "from Kenny Loggins and 'Footloose' to Julia Megenes-Johnson slinking suggestively through an aria from Bizet's *Carmen* [and] a synthesizer session led by Stevie Wonder."

Variety thought the Grammycast was a bit stiff: "The awards show, which logged in at about 15 minutes past its three-hour timeslot, was a bit on the stodgy side, especially in comparison to last month's American Music Awards, although, as usual, it was not without its moments."

• 1984 •

The awards ceremony was broadcast on CBS from the Shrine Auditorium in Los Angeles on February 26, 1985, for the awards eligibility period of October 1, 1983, to September 30, 1984.

ALBUM OF THE YEAR
• *Can't Slow Down*, Lionel Richie. Motown.
Born in the U.S.A., Bruce Springsteen. Columbia/CBS.
Private Dancer, Tina Turner. Capitol.
Purple Rain, Prince & the Revolution. Warner Bros.
She's So Unusual, Cyndi Lauper. Portrait.

RECORD OF THE YEAR
• "What's Love Got to Do with It," Tina Turner. Capitol.
"Dancing in the Dark," Bruce Springsteen. Columbia/CBS.

"Girls Just Want to Have Fun," Cyndi Lauper. Portrait.
"Hard Habit to Break," Chicago. Full Moon/Warner Bros.
"The Heart of Rock & Roll," Huey Lewis & the News. Chrysalis.

SONG OF THE YEAR
(Songwriter's Award)
• "What's Love Got to Do with It," Graham Lyle, Terry Britten.
"Against All Odds (Take a Look at Me Now)," Phil Collins.
"Hello," Lionel Richie.
"I Just Called to Say I Love You," Stevie Wonder.
"Time After Time," Cyndi Lauper, Rob Hyman.

BEST NEW ARTIST
• Cyndi Lauper
Sheila E.

Frankie Goes to Hollywood
Corey Hart
Judds

BEST POP VOCAL PERFORMANCE, MALE

- Phil Collins, "Against All Odds (Take a Look at Me Now)." Atlantic.
Kenny Loggins, "Footloose." CBS.
Lionel Richie, "Hello." Motown.
John Waite, "Missing You." EMI-America.
Stevie Wonder, "I Just Called to Say I Love You." Motown.

BEST POP VOCAL PERFORMANCE, FEMALE

- Tina Turner, "What's Love Got to Do with It." Capitol.
Sheila E., "The Glamorous Life." Warner Bros.
Sheena Easton, "Strut." EMI-America.
Cyndi Lauper, "Girls Just Want to Have Fun." Portrait.
Deniece Williams, "Let's Hear It for the Boy." Columbia/CBS.

BEST POP PERFORMANCE BY A DUO OR GROUP WITH VOCAL

- Pointer Sisters, "Jump (for My Love)." Planet.
Cars, "Drive." Elektra/Asylum.
Chicago, "Hard Habit to Break." Warner Bros.
Wham! "Wake Me Up Before You Go-Go." Columbia/CBS.
Yes, "Owner of a Lonely Heart." Atco.

BEST POP INSTRUMENTAL PERFORMANCE

- Ray Parker, Jr., "Ghostbusters," track from *Ghostbusters* soundtrack. Arista.
Earl Klugh, *Nightsongs*. Capitol.
Steve Mitchell, Richard Perry, Howie Rice, "Jump (For My Love)." Planet.
Randy Newman, *The Natural*. Warner Bros.
Stevie Wonder, "I Just Called to Say I Love You." Motown.

BEST ROCK VOCAL PERFORMANCE, MALE

- Bruce Springsteen, "Dancing in the Dark." Columbia/CBS.
David Bowie, "Blue Jean." EMI-America.
Billy Idol, "Rebel Yell." Chrysalis.
Elton John, "Restless," track from *Breaking Hearts*. Geffen.
John Cougar Mellencamp, "Pink Houses." Riva.

BEST ROCK VOCAL PERFORMANCE, FEMALE

- Tina Turner, "Better Be Good to Me." Capitol.
Lita Ford, *Dancin' on the Edge*. Mercury.
Bonnie Tyler, "Here She Comes." CBS.
Wendy O. Williams, *Wow*. Passport/Jem.
Pia Zadora, "Rock It Out." MCA/Curb.

BEST ROCK PERFORMANCE BY A DUO OR GROUP WITH VOCAL

- Prince & the Revolution, *Purple Rain*. Warner Bros.
Cars, *Heartbeat City*. Elektra.
Genesis, *Genesis*. Atlantic.
Van Halen, "Jump." Warner Bros.
Yes, *90125*. Atco.

BEST ROCK INSTRUMENTAL PERFORMANCE

- Yes, "Cinema," track from *90125*. Atco.
Genesis, "Second Home by the Sea," track from *Genesis*. Atlantic.
Lionel Hampton, "Vibramatic." Glad-Hamp.
Edward Van Halen, "Donut City," track from *The Wild Life* soundtrack. MCA.
Stevie Ray Vaughan & Double Trouble, "Voodoo Chile (Slight Return)," track from *Couldn't Stand the Weather*. Epic.

BEST NEW RHYTHM & BLUES SONG (Songwriter's Award)

- "I Feel for You," Prince.
"Caribbean Queen (No More Love on the Run)," Keith Diamond, Billy Ocean.

"Dancing in the Sheets," Bill Wolfer,
Dean Pitchford.
"The Glamorous Life," Sheila E.
"Yah Mo B There," James Ingram,
Michael McDonald, Rod Temperton,
Quincy Jones.

BEST RHYTHM & BLUES VOCAL PERFORMANCE, MALE

• Billy Ocean, "Caribbean Queen (No
More Love on the Run)." Jive/Arista.
James Ingram, *It's Your Night*. Qwest.
Jeffrey Osborne, *Don't Stop*. A&M.
Jeffrey Osborne, "In the Name of Love."
Polydor.
Stevie Wonder, "The Woman in Red,"
track from *Woman in Red* sound-
track. Motown.

BEST RHYTHM & BLUES VOCAL PERFORMANCE, FEMALE

• Chaka Khan, "I Feel for You." Warner
Bros.
Patti Austin, *Patti Austin*. Qwest.
Shannon, *Let the Music Play*. Mirage.
Tina Turner, "Let's Stay Together."
Capitol.
Deniece Williams, "Let's Hear It for the
Boy." CBS.

BEST RHYTHM & BLUES VOCAL PERFORMANCE BY A DUO OR GROUP

• James Ingram, Michael McDonald,
"Yah Mo B There." Qwest.
Jermaine Jackson, Michael Jackson,
"Tell Me I'm Not Dreamin' (Too
Good to Be True)," track from *Jer-
maine Jackson*. Arista.
Kashif, Al Jarreau, "Edgartown
Groove," track from *Send Me Your
Love*. Arista.
Joyce Kennedy, Jeffrey Osborne, "The
Last Time I Made Love." A&M.
Shalamar, "Dancing in the Sheets."
Columbia/CBS.

BEST RHYTHM & BLUES INSTRUMENTAL PERFORMANCE

• Herbie Hancock, *Sound-System*.
Columbia/CBS.

Stanley Clarke, "Time Exposure," track
from *Time Exposure*. Epic.
Crusaders, *Ghetto Blaster*. MCA.
Sheila E., "Shortberry Strawcake," track
from *The Glamorous Life*. Warner
Bros.
Grover Washington, Jr., *Inside Moves*.
Elektra.

BEST JAZZ FUSION PERFORMANCE (VOCAL OR INSTRUMENTAL)

• Pat Metheny Group, *First Circle*.
ECM.
Miles Davis, *Decoy*. Columbia/CBS.
Spyro Gyra, *Access All Areas*. MCA.
Earl Klugh, *Wishful Thinking*. Capitol.
David Sanborn, *Backstreet*. Warner
Bros.

BEST JAZZ VOCAL PERFORMANCE

• Joe Williams, *Nothin' but the Blues*.
Delos.
Lorez Alexandria, *Harlem Butterfly*.
Discovery.
Carmen McRae, *You're Lookin' at Me*.
Concord Jazz.
Sue Raney, *Ridin' High*. Discovery.
Mel Tormé, *An Evening at Charlie's*.
Concord Jazz.

BEST JAZZ INSTRUMENTAL PERFORMANCE BY A SOLOIST

• Wynton Marsalis, *Hot House Flowers*.
Columbia/CBS.
Pepper Adams, Kenny Wheeler, *Live at
Fat Tuesday's*. Uptown.
Tommy Flanagan, *Thelonica*. Enja.
Zoot Sims, *Quietly There*. Pablo.
Ira Sullivan, *Ira Sullivan . . . Does It All*.
Muse.

BEST JAZZ INSTRUMENTAL PERFORMANCE BY A GROUP

• Art Blakey & the Jazz Messengers,
"New York Scene." Concord Jazz.
Clare Fischer, *Whose Woods Are These*.
Discovery.
Frank Foster, Frank Wess, *Two for the
Blues*. Pablo.
Philly Joe Jones, *Dameronia; Look Stop
Listen*. Uptown.

Phil Woods, Chris Swansen, *Piper at the Gates of Dawn*. Sea Breeze.

BEST JAZZ INSTRUMENTAL PERFORMANCE BY A BIG BAND

- Count Basie & His Orchestra, *88 Basie Street*. Pablo.

Toshiko Akiyoshi Jazz Orchestra, *Ten Gallon Shuffle*. Ascent.

Carla Bley Band, "Misterioso," track from *That's the Way I Feel Now*. A&M.

Bob Florence Limited Edition, *Magic Time*. Trend.

Woody Herman Big Band, *World Class*. Concord Jazz.

BEST COUNTRY SONG
(Songwriter's Award)

- "City of New Orleans," Steve Goodman.

"All My Rowdy Friends Are Coming Over Tonight," Hank Williams, Jr.

"Faithless Love," John David Souther.

"God Bless the U.S.A.," Lee Greenwood.

"Mama He's Crazy," Kenny O'Dell.

BEST COUNTRY VOCAL PERFORMANCE, MALE

- Merle Haggard, "That's the Way Love Goes." Epic.

Lee Greenwood, "God Bless the U.S.A." MCA.

Willie Nelson, "City of New Orleans." Columbia/CBS.

Ricky Skaggs, *Country Boy*. Epic.

Hank Williams, Jr., "All My Rowdy Friends Are Coming Over Tonight." Warner Bros./Curb.

BEST COUNTRY VOCAL PERFORMANCE, FEMALE

- Emmylou Harris, "In My Dreams." Warner Bros.

Janie Fricke, "Your Heart's Not in It." Columbia/CBS.

Crystal Gayle, "The Sound of Goodbye." Warner Bros.

Anne Murray, *Heart Over Mind*. Capitol.

Dolly Parton, "Tennessee Homesick Blues." RCA.

BEST COUNTRY PERFORMANCE BY A DUO OR GROUP WITH VOCAL

- Judds (Wynonna & Naomi), "Mama He's Crazy." RCA.

Alabama, "If You're Gonna Play in Texas (You Gotta Have a Fiddle in the Band)." RCA.

Barbara Mandrell, Lee Greenwood, "To Me." MCA.

Anne Murray, Dave Loggins, "Nobody Loves Me Like You Do." Capitol.

Willie Nelson, Julio Iglesias, "As Time Goes By," track from *Without a Song*. Columbia/CBS.

BEST COUNTRY INSTRUMENTAL PERFORMANCE

- Ricky Skaggs, "Wheel Hoss," track from *Country Boy*. Epic/CBS.

Chet Atkins, *East Tennessee Christmas*. Columbia/CBS.

Carlton Moody & the Moody Brothers, "Cotton-Eyed Joe." Lamon.

Doc & Merle Watson, "Twin Sisters," track from *Down South*. Sugar Hill.

Whites, "Move It on Over," track from *Forever You*. MCA.

BEST GOSPEL PERFORMANCE, MALE

- Michael W. Smith, *Michael W. Smith 2*. Reunion/Word.

Bob Bailey, *I'm Walkin'*. Light/Lexicon.

Phil Driscoll, *Celebrate Freedom*. Sparrow.

Leon Patillo, "J.E.S.U.S.," track from *The Sky's the Limit*. Myrrh/Word.

Steve Taylor, *Meltdown*. Sparrow.

BEST GOSPEL PERFORMANCE, FEMALE

- Amy Grant, "Angels," track from *Straight Ahead*. Myrhh/Word.

Debby Boone, *Surrender*. Lamb & Lion/Sparrow.

Sandi Patti, *Songs from the Heart*. Impact/Benson.

Michele Pillar, *Look Who Loves You Now*. Sparrow.

Kathy Troccoli, *Heart and Soul*. Reunion/Word.

BEST GOSPEL PERFORMANCE BY A DUO OR GROUP

- Debby Boone, Phil Driscoll, "Keep the Flame Burning," track from *Surrender*. Lamb & Lion/Sparrow.
- Steve Camp, Michele Pillar, "Love's Not a Feeling," track from *Fire and Ice*. Sparrow.
- Mylon LeFevre, Broken Heart, *Live Forever*. Myrrh/Word.
- New Gaither Vocal Band, *New Point of View*. Dayspring/Word.
- Petra, *Not of This World*. Starsong/Word.

BEST SOUL GOSPEL PERFORMANCE, MALE

- Andrae Crouch, "Always Remember," track from *No Time to Lose*. Light/Lexicon.
- Mel Carter, *Willing*. Onyx International/Benson.
- Rev. James Cleveland, "The Prayer," track from *I'm Giving My Life Up to You*. Savoy.
- Jessy Dixon, *Sanctuary*. Power Disc/Benson.
- Al Green, *Trust in God*. Myrrh/Word.

BEST SOUL GOSPEL PERFORMANCE, FEMALE

- Shirley Caesar, *Sailin'*. Myrrh.
- Kristle Edwards, "Jesus, Come Lay Your Head on Me," track from *No Time to Lose*, Andrae Crouch album. Light.
- Danniebelle Hall, *Unmistakably Danniebelle*. Onyx International.
- Tata Vega, "Oh, It Is Jesus," track from *No Time to Lose*, Andrae Crouch album. Light.
- Albertina Walker, *The Impossible Dream*. Savoy.

BEST SOUL GOSPEL PERFORMANCE BY A DUO OR GROUP

- Shirley Caesar, Al Green, "Sailin' on the Sea of Your Love," track from *Sailin'*. Myrrh.
- Shirley Caesar, Anne Caesar Price, "Rejoice," track from *Sailin'*, Shirley Caesar album. Myrrh.

Edwin Hawkins, *Angels Will Be Singing*. Birthright/Word.

Richard Smallwood Singers, *Psalms*. Onyx International/Benson.

BeBe & CeCe Winans, *Lord Lift Us Up*. PTL.

BEST INSPIRATIONAL PERFORMANCE

- Donna Summer, "Forgive Me," track from *Cats Without Claws*. Geffen/Warner Bros.
- Philip Bailey, *The Wonders of His Love*. Myrrh/Word.
- Pat Boone, *What I Believe*. Lamb & Lion/Sparrow.
- Lisa Whelchel, *All Because of You*. Nissi.
- Deniece Williams, "Whiter Than Snow," track from *Let's Hear It for the Boy*. CBS.

BEST ETHNIC OR TRADITIONAL FOLK RECORDING

- *Elizabeth Cotten Live!* Elizabeth Cotten. Arhoolie.
- Good Rockin', Rocking Dopsie. GNP-Crescendo.
- *On a Saturday Night*, Queen Ida. GNP-Crescendo.
- *100% Fortified Zydeco*, Buckwheat Zydecko. Black Top/Rounder.
- *Open Road*, Boys of the Lough. Flying Fish.

BEST TRADITIONAL BLUES RECORDING

- *Blues Explosion*, John Hammond, Stevie Ray Vaughan & Double Trouble, Sugar Blue, Koko Taylor & the Blues Machine, Luther "Guitar Junior" Johnson, J. B. Hutto & the New Hawks. Atlantic.
- *Guitar Slinger*, Johnny Winter. Alligator.
- *I'm in a Phone Booth, Baby*, Albert King. Fantasy.
- *Kansas City Here I Come*, Joe Turner. Pablo.
- *You've Got Me Loving You*, Bobby Bland. MCA.

BEST LATIN POP PERFORMANCE

• Placido Domingo, *Always in My Heart (Siempre en Mi Corazón).* CBS-Masterworks.

Maria Conchita, *Maria Conchita.* A&M.

José Feliciano, *Como Tu Quieres.* RCA.

Johnny, *Invitame.* RCA.

José José, *Secretos.* Ariola-America.

Menudo, *Evolucion.* RCA.

BEST TROPICAL LATIN PERFORMANCE

• Eddie Palmieri, *Palo Pa Rumba.* Musica Latina.

Rubén Blades, *Buscando America.* Elektra.

Willie Colon, *Criollo.* RCA.

El Gran Combo, *Breaking the Ice.* Combo/Rico.

Poncho Sanchez, *Bien Sabroso!* Concord Jazz.

Los Socios del Ritmo, *¡Y Ahora! "Coniff."* Ariola.

BEST MEXICAN-AMERICAN PERFORMANCE

• Sheena Easton, Luis Miguel, "Me Gustas Tal Como Eres." Top Hits.

Roberto Carlos, "Concavo y Convexo," track from *Roberto Carlos.* CBS International.

Yolanda Del Rio, *Un Amor Especial.* RCA.

Juan Gabriel, *Recuerdos II.* Ariola-America.

Raphael, *Eternamente Tuyo.* CBS International.

BEST REGGAE RECORDING

• *Anthem*, Black Uhuru. Island.

Captured Live, Peter Tosh. EMI-America.

King Yellowman, Yellowman. Columbia/CBS.

"Reggae Night," Jimmy Cliff. Columbia/CBS.

"Steppin' Out," Steel Pulse. Elektra.

BEST INSTRUMENTAL COMPOSITION
(Composer's Award)
(Tie)

• "The Natural," track from *The Natural*, Randy Newman.

• "Olympic Fanfare and Theme," track from *The Official Music of the XXIIIrd Olympiad at Los Angeles*, John Williams.

The A-Team, Mike Post, Peter Carpenter.

"Ghostbusters" (main title theme), Elmer Bernstein.

Hot House Flowers, Wynton Marsalis.

BEST ARRANGEMENT ON AN INSTRUMENTAL

• Quincy Jones, Jeremy Lubbock, "Grace (Gymnastics Theme)," track from *The Official Music of the XXIIIrd Olympiad at Los Angeles* (Quincy Jones). CBS.

Stewart Copeland, "Brothers on Wheels," track from *Rumble Fish Soundtrack* (Stewart Copeland). A&M.

Robert Freedman, "Stardust," track from *Hot House Flowers* (Wynton Marsalis). CBS.

Henry Mancini, "Cameo for Flute . . . for James," track from *In the Pink* (James Galway, Henry Mancini). RCA.

Don Sebesky, "Waltz for Debbie," track from *Full Cycle* (Don Sebesky). Crescendo.

BEST VOCAL ARRANGEMENT FOR TWO OR MORE VOICES

• Pointer Sisters, "Automatic," track from *Break Out* (Pointer Sisters). Planet.

David Foster, "What About Me?" track from *What About Me?* (Kenny Rogers, Kim Carnes, James Ingram). RCA.

David Foster, Peter Cetera, "Hard Habit to Break," track from *Chicago 17* (Chicago). Full Moon/Warner Bros.

Richard Greene, Gunnar Madsen, "Helter Skelter," track from *The Bobs* (Bobs). Kaleidoscope.

Trevor Rabin, Chris Squire, "Leave It" (Yes). Atco/Atlantic.

BEST CAST SHOW ALBUM

• *Sunday in the Park with George* (Broadway cast), Stephen Sondheim, composer and lyricist. RCA.

Doonesbury, Elizabeth Swados, com-
poser; Garry Trudeau, lyricist. MCA.
My One and Only. Atlantic.
A Stephen Sondheim Evening. RCA.
Sugar Babies, Jimmy McHugh, Arthur
Malvin, Dorothy Fields, George
Oppenheim, Harold Adamson,
music and lyrics. Broadway Enter-
tainment.

BEST ALBUM OF ORIGINAL SCORE
WRITTEN FOR A MOTION PICTURE
OR TV SPECIAL
(Composer's Award)
• *Purple Rain*, Prince & the Revolution,
John L. Nelson, Lisa & Wendy.
Against All Odds, Phil Collins, Stevie
Nicks, Peter Gabriel, Stuart Adamson,
Mike Rutherford, August Darnell,
Michel Colombier, Larry Carlton.
Footloose, Bill Wolfer, Dean Pitchford,
Kenny Loggins, Tom Snow, Sammy
Hagar, Michael Gore, Eric Carmen,
Jim Steinman.
Ghostbusters, Ray Parker, Jr., Kevin
O'Neal, Brian O'Neal, Bobby Alessi,
David Immer, Tom Bailey, Graham
Russell, David Foster, Jay Graydon,
Diane Warren & the Doctor Mick
Smiley, Elmer Bernstein.
Yentl, Michel Legrand, Alan Bergman,
Marilyn Bergman.

BEST INSTRUMENTAL ARRANGEMENT
ACCOMPANYING VOCAL(S)
• David Foster, Jeremy Lubbock, "Hard
Habit to Break" (Chicago). Full
Moon/Warner Bros.
Laurie Anderson, "Gravity's Angel,"
track from *Mister Heartbreak* (Lau-
rie Anderson). Warner Bros.
Thomas Dolby, "Mulu the Rain Forest,"
track from *The Flat Earth* (Thomas
Dolby). Capitol.
Reggie Griffin, Arif Mardin, "I Feel for
You," track from *I Feel for You*
(Chaka Khan). Warner Bros.
Michel Legrand, "Papa, Can You Hear
Me?" track from *Yentl*, original
soundtrack (Barbra Streisand). CBS.

BEST CLASSICAL ALBUM
• *Amadeus* (soundtrack), Neville Mar-
riner conducting the Academy of
St. Martin-in-the-Fields; Ambrosian
Opera Chorus; Choristers of
Westminster Abbey; soloists.
Fantasy.
Beethoven: The 5 Piano Concertos,
James Levine conducting the
Chicago Symphony (solo: Alfred
Brendel). Philips.
Brahms: A German Requiem, James
Levine conducting the Chicago Sym-
phony Orchestra and Chorus (solos:
Kathleen Battle, Hakan Hagegard).
RCA.
*Prokofiev: Symphony No. 5 in B Flat,
Op. 100*, Leonard Slatkin conduct-
ing the St. Louis Symphony.
RCA.
*Wynton Marsalis, Edita Gruberova:
Handel, Purcell, Torelli, Fasch,
Molter*, Raymond Leppard conduct-
ing the English Chamber Orchestra
(solos: Wynton Marsalis, Edita
Gruberova). CBS.

BEST CLASSICAL ORCHESTRAL
RECORDING
• *Prokofiev: Symphony No. 5 in B
Flat, Op. 100*, Leonard Slatkin con-
ducting the St. Louis Symphony.
RCA.
Amadeus (soundtrack), Neville Marriner
conducting the Academy of St. Mar-
tin-in-the-Fields. Fantasy.
Berlioz: Symphony Fantastique, Op. 14,
Claudio Abbado conducting the
Chicago Symphony. Deutsche Gram-
mophon.
*Gould: Burchfield Gallery and Apple
Waltzes*, Morton Gould conducting
the American Symphony. RCA.
Mahler: Symphony No. 4 in G Major,
Sir George Solti conducting the
Chicago Symphony. London.
*Schubert: Symphony No. 9 in C Major
("The Great")*, James Levine con-
ducting the Chicago Symphony.
Deutsche Grammophon Archive.

BEST CHAMBER MUSIC PERFORMANCE

- Juilliard String Quartet, *Beethoven: The Late String Quartets*. CBS.
- The Cleveland Quartet with Emanuel Ax, *Brahms: Piano Quintet in F Minor, Op. 34*. RCA.
- Chick Corea, Gary Burton, Ikwhan Bae, Carol Shive, Karen Dreyfus, Fred Sherry, *Corea: Lyric Suite for Sextet*. ECM.
- Guarneri Quartet, Pinchas Zukerman, *Brahms: The String Quintets in F & G*. RCA.
- Itzhak Perlman, Daniel Barenboim, *Mozart: Violin Sonatas K. 301–4*. Deutsche Grammophon.

BEST CLASSICAL PERFORMANCE, INSTRUMENTAL SOLOIST(S) (WITH ORCHESTRA)

- Wynton Marsalis, Edita Gruberova (Leppard conducting the English Chamber Orchestra), *Wynton Marsalis, Edita Gruberova: Handel, Purcell, Torelli, Fasch, Molter*. CBS.
- Emanuel Ax (Levine conducting the Chicago Symphony), *Brahms: Piano Concerto No. 1 in D Minor*. RCA.
- Julian Bream (Gardiner conducting the Chamber Orchestra of Europe), *Rodrigo: Concierto de Aranjuez, Invocation and Dance; 3 Spanish Pieces (Music of Spain, Vol. 8)*. RCA.
- Alfred Brendel (Levine conducting the Chicago Symphony), *Beethoven: The 5 Piano Concertos*. Philips.
- Itzhak Perlman (Barenboim conducting the Orchestre de Paris), *Wieniawski: Violin Concerto No. 2 in D Minor, Op. 22; Saint-Saëns: Violin Concerto No. 3 in B Minor, Op. 61*. Deutsche Grammophon.

BEST CLASSICAL PERFORMANCE, INSTRUMENTAL SOLOIST(S) (WITHOUT ORCHESTRA)

- Yo-Yo Ma, *Bach: The Unaccompanied Cello Suites*. CBS.

Julian Bream, *Music of Spain, Vol. 7: A Celebration of Andrés Segovia*. RCA.
Emil Gilels, *Beethoven: Piano Sonata No. 29 in B Flat Major, Op. 106 ("Hammerklavier")*. Deutsche Grammophon.
Glenn Gould, *R. Strauss: Glenn Gould Plays Strauss (Sonata; 5 Pieces, Op. 3)*. CBS.
Alicia de Larrocha, *Schubert: Piano Sonata in B Flat Major, D. 960*. London.

BEST OPERA RECORDING

- *Bizet: Carmen* (film soundtrack), Lorin Maazel conducting the Orchestre National de France; Choeurs et Maîtrise de Radio France (solos: Julia Migenes-Johnson, Faith Esham, Placido Domingo, Ruggero Raimondi). Erato.
- *Britten: The Turn of the Screw*, Sir Colin Davis conducting the members of the Royal Opera House Orchestra, Covent Garden (solos: Helen Donath, Heather Harper, Robert Tear). Philips.
- *Janáček: Jenufa*, Sir Charles Mackerras conducting the Vienna Philharmonic (solos: Elisabeth Söderström, Peter Dvorsky, Wieslav Ochman, Eva Randova). London.
- *Mozart: Don Giovanni*, Bernard Haitink conducting the London Philharmonic; Glyndebourne Chorus (solos: Thomas Allen, Carole Vaness, Richard Van Allan, Maria Ewing, Elizabeth Gale, Keith Lewis, John Rawnsley, Dimitri Kavrakos). Angel.
- *Verdi: Ernani*, Riccardo Muti conducting the Coro e Orchestra del Teatro alla Scala (solos: Placido Domingo, Mirella Freni, Renato Bruson, Nicolai Ghiaurov). Angel.

BEST CHORAL PERFORMANCE (OTHER THAN OPERA)

- Margaret Hillis, choral conductor, Chicago Symphony Chorus; James Levine conducting the Chicago Symphony, *Brahms: A German Requiem.* RCA.

Riccardo Chailly conducting the Cleveland Orchestra Chorus; Cleveland Orchestra, *Prokofiev: Alexander Nevsky, Op. 78.* London.

Riccardo Chailly conducting the RSO Berlin Chorus; RSO Berlin Orchestra, *Orff: Carmina Burana.* London.

Christopher Hogwood conducting the Westminster Cathedral Boys' Choir; Chorus and Orchestra of the Academy of Ancient Music, *Mozart: Requiem.* L'Oiseau-Lyre.

Simon Rattle conducting the City of Birmingham Orchestra Chorus and Boys of Christ Church Cathedral, Oxford; City of Birmingham Symphony, *Britten: War Requiem.* Angel.

BEST CLASSICAL PERFORMANCE, VOCAL SOLOIST

• Jessye Norman, José van Dam, Heather Harper (Boulez conducting the members of the Ensemble Intercontemporain and BBC Symphony), *Ravel: Songs of Maurice Ravel.* CBS.

Dame Janet Baker (Geoffrey Parsons, accompanist), *Mahler's Songs of Youth.* Hyperion.

Hakan Hagegard, Kathleen Battle (James Levine, accompanist), *Brahms: Songs of Brahms.* RCA.

Kiri Te Kanawa (Solti conducting the Chicago Symphony), *Mahler: Symphony No. 4 in G Major, 4th Movement.* London.

Jessye Norman (Maazel conducting the Wiener Philharmonic), *Mahler: Symphony No. 2 in C Minor ("Resurrection").* CBS.

BEST NEW CLASSICAL COMPOSITION (Composer's Award)

• *Antony and Cleopatra,* Samuel Barber.

"Apple Waltzes," Morton Gould.

"Magabunda (4 Poems of Agueda Pizzaro)," Joseph Schwantner.

"The Perfect Stranger," Frank Zappa.

"Winter Cantata," Vincent Persichetti.

BEST ENGINEERED RECORDING, CLASSICAL

• Paul Goodman, *Prokofiev: Symphony No. 5 in B Flat, Op. 100* (Slatkin conducting the St. Louis Symphony). RCA.

Tony Faulkner, Ray Moore, *Wynton Marsalis, Edita Gruberova: Handel, Purcell, Torelli, Fasch, Molter* (Leppard conducting the English Chamber Orchestra; solo: Marsalis, Editz Gruberova). CBS.

Paul Goodman, *Brahms: A German Requiem* (Levine conducting the Chicago Symphony Orchestra and Chorus; solos: Battle, Hagegard). RCA.

Paul Goodman, *Brahms: Piano Concerto No. 1 in D Minor* (Levine conducting the Chicago Symphony; solo: Ax). RCA.

James Lock, John Dunkerley, *Mahler: Symphony No. 4 in G Major* (Solti conducting the Chicago Symphony; solo: Te Kanawa). London.

CLASSICAL PRODUCER OF THE YEAR

• Steven Epstein

Marc Aubort, Joanna Nickrenz

Jay David Saks

Robert E. Woods

Thomas Z. Shepard

BEST COMEDY RECORDING

• "Eat It," track from *Weird Al Yankovic in 3-D,* Weird Al Yankovic. Rock 'n' Roll.

Here and Now, Richard Pryor. Warner Bros.

Hurt Me Baby, Make Me Write Bad Checks! Rick Dees. No-o-o Budget.

Rappin' Rodney, Rodney Dangerfield. RCA.

The 3 Faces of Al (Nick Danger), Fireside Theatre. Rhino.

BEST SPOKEN WORD OR NONMUSICAL RECORDING

• *The Words of Gandhi,* Ben Kingsley. Caedmon.

Heart Play (Unfinished Dialogue), John Lennon, Yoko Ono. Polydor.

Our Time Has Come, Rev. Jesse Jackson. MCA.
The Real Thing (Broadway cast), Jeremy Irons, Glenn Close. Nonesuch.
The Story of Indiana Jones and the Temple of Doom (dialogue and music from the film). Buena Vista.

BEST RECORDING FOR CHILDREN
• *Where the Sidewalk Ends*, Shel Silverstein. CBS.
Agapeland at Play with Holly Heart, Holly Heart. Birdwing/Sparrow.
Flashbeagle. Charlie Brown Records.
Jim Henson's Muppets Present Fraggle Rock. Muppet Music.
Kids Praise 4, Singsational Servants. Maranatha!/Word.
The Muppets Take Manhattan (film soundtrack). Warner Bros.

BEST ENGINEERED RECORDING (OTHER THAN CLASSICAL)
• Humberto Gatica, *Chicago 17* (Chicago). Full Moon/Warner Bros.
Nigel Green, *Heartbeat City* (Cars). Elektra.
Calvin Harris, *Can't Slow Down* (Lionel Richie). Motown.
Steven Miller, *Aerial Boundaries* (Michael Hedges). Windham Hill.
Phil Thornalley, *Into the Gap* (Thompson Twins). Arista.

BEST ALBUM PACKAGE
(Art Director's Award)
• Janet Perr, *She's So Unusual* (Cyndi Lauper). Portrait.
Bill Johnson, Virginia Team, Jeff Morris, *Willie Nelson* (Willie Nelson). CBS.
Bill Levy, *Every Man Has a Woman* (John Lennon, Harry Nilsson, Eddie Money, Rosanne Cash, others). Polydor.
Henry Marquez, *No Brakes* (John Waite). EMI-America.
Andy Summers, Michael Ross, *Bewitched* (Andy Summers, Robert Fripp). A&M.

BEST ALBUM NOTES
(Annotator's Award)
• Gunther Schuller, Martin Williams, *Big Band Jazz* (Paul Whiteman, Fletcher Henderson, Chick Webb, Tommy Dorsey, Count Basie, Benny Goodman, others). Smithsonian.
Glenn Hinson, *Virginia Traditions Work Songs* (field recordings 1936–80, various artists). Blue Ridge.
Grover Sales, *Amadeus (Original Soundtrack Recording)* (Neville Marriner conducting the Academy of St. Martin-in-the-Fields). Fantasy.
James Sundquist, *An Anthology of Sacred Carols for Classical Guitar* (James Sundquist). Eagle.
Z Factor, Lorene Lortie, *A Golden Celebration* (Elvis Presley). RCA.

BEST HISTORICAL ALBUM
• *Big Band Jazz* (Paul Whiteman, Fletcher Henderson, Chick Webb, Tommy Dorsey, Count Basie, Benny Goodman, others). Smithsonian.
Cotton Club Stars (various). Stash.
A Golden Celebration (Elvis Presley). RCA.
History Speaks: Franklin Delano Roosevelt (Franklin Delano Roosevelt, introduction by Clifton Fadiman). Book-of-the-Month.
World's First Entertainment Recordings 1889–1896 (various). Mark 56.

PRODUCER OF THE YEAR (OTHER THAN CLASSICAL)
(Tie)
• David Foster
• Lionel Richie, James Anthony Carmichael
Robert John "Mutt" Lange, Cars
Michael Omartian
Prince & the Revolution

BEST VIDEO, SHORT FORM

- *David Bowie*, David Bowie. Sony/Picture Music.
- *Ashford and Simpson*, Ashford & Simpson. Sony/Picture Music.
- *Phil Collins*, Phil Collins. Sony/Philip Collins.
- *Rubber Rodeo Scenic Views*, Rubber Rodeo. Sony/Polygram.
- *Thomas Dolby*, Thomas Dolby. Sony/Picture Music.
- *Twist of Fate*, Olivia Newton-John. MCA Home Video.

BEST VIDEO ALBUM

- *Making Michael Jackson's "Thriller,"* Michael Jackson. Vestron Music Video.
- *Billy Joel Live from Long Island*, Billy Joel. CBS/Fox Video.
- *Eurythmics Sweet Dreams*, Eurythmics. RCA Video/Zoetrope.
- *Heartbeat City*, Cars. Warner Home Video.
- *Serious Moonlight*, David Bowie. Music Media.
- *We're All Devo*, Devo. Pioneer Artist.

• 1985 •

A "World"-Wide Victory

The last time America's music elite rallied for such an important social cause, it resulted in Grammy's 1972 Album of the Year, *The Concert for Bangla Desh*. Now other top awards were in store for a work of music by artists who pitched in to help the starving millions of Africa.

"We Are the World" was written by Lionel Richie and Michael Jackson in only two and a half hours. ("We didn't really write this song. It came through us," Richie told reporters backstage at the Grammys. Jackson also claimed divine intervention, saying that God chose him and Richie to write it.) Producer Quincy Jones recruited 45 top music artists to sing the tune, a roster of rock royalty that included Paul Simon, Bruce Springsteen, Stevie Wonder, Bob Dylan, Hall & Oates, Diana Ross, Smokey Robinson and Tina Turner. Immediately following the 1985 American Music Awards, Jones summoned them all to A&M's recording studios at 10 P.M. where he instructed them "to check [their] egos at the door" and get to work. By eight o'clock the next morning, the job was done.

The result was described by the *New York Times* as "an uplifting, all-star, Hollywood-produced ballad that was born to sweep the Grammys."

"We Are the World" became the biggest-selling single in music history to date, raised $60 million for famine relief and won four awards: Record and Song of the Year, best group pop vocal performance and best short-form music video. In accepting the record award, Jones thanked "the generation that changed 'I, Me, My' to 'We, You, Us.'" Richie also singled out the music-buying public in his acceptance remarks, saying that "the

Contributors to best record "We Are the World" included (from left) Dionne Warwick, Stevie Wonder, Quincy Jones, Michael Jackson and Lionel Richie.

Wide World Photo

most important thing was, when we called, you responded, and we thank you for it." A soft-spoken Michael Jackson, dressed in a black military jacket studded with rhinestones, whispered into the podium microphone: "When you leave here, remember the children."

Variety reported, "This year's Grammys will be remembered for the crowning salute it gave to 'We Are the World.' Those who have claimed that the music industry is 'caused out' by activist/humanitarian projects like Farm Aid, Sun City et al., are clearly wrong."

Whereas the single version of "We Are the World" was considered the likely winner of its top honors, the also-nominated LP of the same name was not. Instead, the race for Album of the Year was considered a close contest between Phil Collins, Dire Straits and Sting. When Collins's *No Jacket Required* prevailed, *Variety* noted, "Collins, who sincerely confessed backstage that he had hoped, at best, to come away with one trophy [out of his five nominations], scored a major upset, at least in the eyes of the Grammy press crew, in the album category, besting such highly acclaimed fare as Dire Straits' *Brothers in Arms* and Sting's *The Dream of the Blue Turtles*."

The *New York Times* cheered, saying, "As both a songwriter and an instrumentalist, Collins is especially adept at sustaining a mood of suspense, often heavily tinged with menace. His shadowy song lyrics are suffused with lurking suspicion, dread and the suggestion of passions so pent-up they could explode violently, though they never do." *No Jacket* spun off five hit singles, including "Don't Lose My Number" and "Sussudio," and spent seven weeks on top of the album charts. It achieved that rank only four weeks after its release, which was faster than it took Michael Jackson's *Thriller* (Grammy's 1983 Album of the Year) to reach the same lofty height.

Collins won three Grammys in all, including Producer of the Year (with Hugh Padgham) and best male pop vocal performance for *No Jacket Required*. At the Grammys, a jacket *was* recommended attire for men, even for superstar winners like Collins. "Am I glad I bought this tux!" he said early in the evening. By the time he picked up the Album of the Year award, the thrice-lauded Collins added, "I've run out of things to say, to be honest."

Variety called this year's Grammy celebration "a virtual stag party," since "all the leading nominees in the high-profile pop categories were male." Dire Straits' music received the second-most nominations of the year: eight. The British rock band ended up with three awards, including an engineering prize and the laurels for rock group vocals for "Money for Nothing," which was a losing nominee for Record and Song of the Year. "Money" was somewhat controversial: Music critics and gay groups protested its disparaging reference to a "little faggot" in its lyrics, and Warner Bros. edited the phrase out of later releases. The third honor went to Dire Straits' singer-guitarist, Mark Knopfler, who shared the

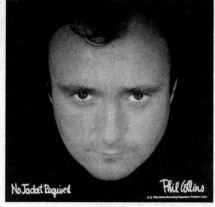

Phil Collins "scored a major upset," *Variety* said, by winning best album for *No Jacket Required*, a work full of suspense and "tinged with menace."

country instrumental laurels with guitarist Chet Atkins for "Cosmic Square Dance," a track from Atkins's *Stay Tuned*.

Former Eagle Don Henley's "The Boys of Summer" was another loser of Record and Song of the Year, but it garnered the consolation prize of best male rock vocals. Back in the pressroom, reporters plugged Henley with questions about the single, but he seemed more eager to talk about the musical score he was then writing for the Martin Scorsese film *The Color of Money*.

Tina Turner held on to the female rock vocal honors that she won last year for a song ("One of the Living") from the film in which she also starred, *Mad Max: Beyond Thunderdome*. She triumphed over, among others, Pat Benatar, who had monopolized the category for four years prior to Turner. As expected, the rock instrumental laurels went to U.K. guitarist Jeff Beck for "Escape," a track from his album *Flash*. Prior to his wild experiments with rock on recent LPs, Beck was known mostly for his mastery of r&b/pop music.

Also as expected, Sade (pronounced Shah-*day*) reaped the Best New Artist prize over John Lennon's son Julian and Katrina & the Waves. The Nigerian-born British pop star was red-hot at Grammy time. She'd been dubbed the "Queen of Cool" in a recent cover story by *Time* magazine and she already had two hit albums, *Diamond Life* and *Promise,* which sold a combined total of 12 million copies worldwide.

The Best New Artist category was the source of controversy when Whitney Houston was barred from competing due to a technicality. One N.A.R.A.S. spokesman declared: "The rule that disqualified Whitney is perfectly clear. . . . An artist is not eligible if [he or she had a previous] label credit or album credit." Houston had made earlier minor contributions to albums by Jermaine Jackson and Teddy Pendergrass. In her defense, *Billboard* noted that former Best New Artist Carly Simon had recorded an album with her sister prior to her 1971 win and asked, "Didn't last year's winner, Cyndi Lauper, receive credit as the lead singer on the Blue Angel album, for which she deserved, and got, considerable acclaim and attention?"

Roseanne Cash won a Grammy for a song about losing a Grammy.

Houston, the daughter of famed gospel singer Cissy Houston, was a sudden pop superstar in 1985–86. Her eponymous LP set the record for becoming the biggest-selling album by a debut artist. It was also the top seller of 1986 and a losing nominee for Grammy's Album of the Year. As a consolation, one of its hit singles, "Saving All My Love for You," earned her the female pop vocals prize, which was bestowed by another relative of Houston's who was also a famous singing star—cousin Dionne Warwick. "Warwick bounced up and down in obvious delight as she read Whitney Houston's name as winner," noted the *Herald Examiner.* Houston said in her acceptance remarks, "Oh, my goodness. I must thank God, who makes it all possible for me!"

It was the number-one-selling album of 1985 that brought Jan Hammer, a former keyboard artist for the Mahavishnu Orchestra, the honors for Best Instrumental Composition and Best Pop Instrumental Performance. Hammer's theme song to the hit TV detective series *Miami Vice* was the first all-instrumental number-one single hit since Vangelis's "Theme from *Chariots of Fire,*" and the album spent the longest time ever at number one for a score to a TV show (11 weeks), surpassing the previous record set by Grammy's first Album of the Year winner, *The Music from Peter Gunn* (1958) by Henry Mancini. Hammer missed attending the Grammy show because he was at his home in upstate New York "still working on this week's *Miami Vice* music," he said in a message passed on by his publicist.

Aretha Franklin had monopolized the female r&b vocals category for eight years between 1967 and 1974, but had only returned once since, in 1981, for "Hold On, I'm Comin'." Now she was back with "Freeway of Love," which also nabbed Best Rhythm & Blues Song for writers Narada Michael Walden and Jeffrey Cohen. Stevie Wonder, who had reaped 15 Grammys in just four years during the mid-1970s but hadn't won a single golden statuette since, rebounded with the r&b male vocal award for *In Square Circle.* One of the album's biggest hits was "Part-Time Lover," which Wonder sang on the Grammy show in what the *Herald Examiner* called "a passionate performance."

When the Commodores snagged the r&b group vocals accolade for "Nightshift," the *Washington Post* called it "a particularly sweet victory [since] the veteran group had been virtually written off after the departure of Lionel Richie" in 1981. The *Herald Examiner* noted "Lead singer J.D. Nicholas thanked, among others, former lead singer Lionel Richie for leaving the group so Nicholas could take his place."

Ever since 1973, jazz was the only music genre in which the nominations weren't determined by the N.A.R.A.S. membership. Instead, they were selected by craft committees set up in various chapter cities. "The argument against the craft committee approach was that it was elitist and resulted in many of the same familiar names being nominated time and again," *Billboard* said. This year N.A.R.A.S. returned the vote to academy members on a one-year trial basis, resulting in bids for some unlikely jazz artists like Sting and Barry Manilow. *Billboard* complained, "Manhattan Transfer is all over the place. A total of six selections from the group's star-studded *Vocalese* album, plus the album itself, are nominated in the male, female and group vocal categories. Both Dizzie Gillespie and James Moody are nominated in the instrumental soloist category for their contributions to individual tracks."

Vocalese led with the most nominations this year, 12, although the Manhattan Transfer ended up with only one, the group vocals prize. The album's "Another Night in Tunisia" track earned the male singing honors for guest artists Jon Hendricks and Bobby McFerrin. (The jazz singing awards were again broken down into male, female and group categories after being combined into one prize last year.) McFerrin also shared in the award for arrangement.

Despite the new voting procedure, familiar names among past winners continued to spring up: Alto sax player David Sanborn reaped the instrumental fusion accolade for *Straight to the Heart,* and trumpeter Wynton Marsalis returned to claim both the soloist and group instrumental awards for *Black Codes from the Underground.* Cleo Laine, the British-born singer of jazz, pop, classical and show tune music, gave a historic appearance at Carnegie Hall in 1973, resulting in a best-selling, live two-disc album that reaped her a Grammy nomination for pop vocals in 1974. Laine returned 10 years later with *Cleo at Carnegie* and won the 1985 female jazz vocal prize. The soundtrack to the Francis Ford Coppola film *The Cotton Club,* filled mostly with masterworks by Duke Ellington, snagged the

Cellist Yo-Yo Ma won two prizes for his "truthful interpretations" of works by Brahms and Elgar.

big-band instrumental award for John Barry and Bob Wilber.

"Last year, of course, jazz was snubbed on the Grammys with no performances or artists featured in the three-hour telecast," *Variety* recalled. This year N.A.R.A.S. made up for the omission with an eight-minute segment that *Variety* called "the musical triumph of the night, an all-star jam/chorus that lifted the Shrine crowd out of its seats for two standing ovations, the only ones generated by music during the three-hour show. It included such instrumental and vocal luminaries as Dizzy Gillespie, Buddy Rich, Herbie Hancock, Joe Williams and Sarah Vaughan."

The country categories welcomed back a past Grammy star when songwriter Jimmy Webb won the prize for Best Country Song. *Billboard* remarked: "His 'Highwayman' was declared best country song 18 years after 'Up, Up and Away' [which he wrote] walked away with the Grammy for Song of the Year and 17 years after Webb's last Grammy, for arranging Richard Harris's 'MacArthur Park.'"

Another returning champ was three-time past winner Ronnie Milsap, who seized the male vocal laurels for what the

Washington Post called "his smooth piece of nostalgia," "Lost in the Fifties Tonight (In the Still of the Night)," which lost its bid for Best Country Song but did win the Song of the Year award from the Academy of Country Music. The tune was a tribute to the "doo-wop" era of country music in the 1950s and was based on "In the Still of the Nite" by Freddy Parris. The mother-daughter duo of Wynonna and Naomi Judd scored such success with their Grammy-winning performance of "Mama He's Crazy" last year that RCA gave them a full album project in 1985 with *Why Not Me,* which earned them their second statuette.

When Johnny Cash's daughter Rosanne lost her bid for best female country vocal performance at the 1982 awards, she left the Shrine Auditorium depressed. She later said, "I was drivin' down Hollywood Boulevard and I was very tongue-in-cheek,

> Bloc voting caused the classical awards to be dismissed as "a bad joke."

saying, 'I got my new dress, I got my new shoes / I don't know why you don't want me,' just writing this little ditty and being very sarcastic. So when I went home and I showed Rodney [Crowell] what I had, he said, 'This is good enough to make into a real song. Why don't we write it together?' So we did." "I Don't Know Why You Don't Want Me" lost its bid for Best Country Song, but at last won her the female vocal award for 1985. While accepting the trophy, Cash said, "I wrote it out of self pity. How ironic to win with it!"

For the fourth year in a row Amy Grant (*Unguarded*) was awarded a gospel Grammy, while other comeback veterans included Shirley Caesar ("Martin"), Larnelle Harris (two awards for tracks from *I've Just Seen Jesus*) and Jennifer Holliday ("Come Sunday"). A quartet of brothers who would come to sweep the religious awards in future years, the Winans, took their first this year for *Tomorrow* plus an additional trophy for their member Marvin

for the album's track "Bring Back the Days of Yea and Nay."

The category of Best Mexican-American Performance caused a controversy last year when leading Mexican-American artists like Vikki Carr failed to be nominated over dubious other contenders. Carr, who had never won a Grammy before, finally prevailed this year for *Simplemente Mujer.*

"The award for Best Latin Pop Performance stayed distinctly within the family," commented the *Herald Examiner.* "It went to Lani Hall [*Es Fácil Amar*], who received it from her husband, Herb Alpert, head of A&M Records, for which Hall records." There was a tie for the prize of Best Tropical Latin Performance between Eddie Palmieri (*Solito*) and Tito Puente & His Latin Ensemble (*Mambo Diablo*), but, in an embarrassing flub, only Puente was named as a winner on the Grammycast.

A new category for Best Polka Recording was introduced this year and went to noted accordian player Frank Yankovic. "Yankovic, 70, thanked 'least but not last' all the musicians who helped him on his winning album, *70 Years of Hits*," said the *Herald Examiner.* The one-year-old award for Best Reggae Recording was bestowed for 1985 to singer Jimmy Cliff, noted for tingeing his music with r&b influences and strong political messages. The purveyor of "swamp blues," Rockin' Sydney, was hailed for Best Ethnic or Traditional Folk Recording for "My Toot Toot."

Soon after comedian Whoopi Goldberg was discovered by stage and screen director Mike Nichols, she was given her own Broadway show, the LP recording of which earned her the kudos for best comedy album. Going for strong gut reactions from her audience, Goldberg portrayed a series of down-and-out characters and brainless stereotypes in the show, including a junkie and an irritating California

1985

Valley Girl she called Surfer Chick. Surfer Chick peppered her conversation with a grating amount of "you knows" and "okay" while she described an abortion she gave herself using a coat hanger, saying, "You have to take the paper off because you never know where it's been."

Other Broadway shows were honored, too. August Wilson's dramatic tribute to a legendary American blues singer in *Ma Rainey's Black Bottom* snagged Best Spoken Word or Nonmusical Recording. When the score to a revival of *West Side Story* was named Best Cast Show Album over such newer competition as the Tony Award–winning *Big River* by Roger Miller, *High Fidelity* denounced its victory as "ludicrous." *West Side Story* had won numerous prizes in the past, including jazz awards for André Previn in 1960 and Stan Kenton in 1961 as well as the 1961 honors for best film score. The original Broadway production was never honored, however, because the show opened a year before the Grammys were inaugurated.

This year the film score laurels were awarded to the music from the Eddie Murphy comedy *Beverly Hills Cop,* beating out the music from *Back to the Future,* which was written in part by Huey Lewis. Huey Lewis & the News had four nominations in 1985, including Record of the Year nominee "The Power of Love," but reaped only one statuette, for their "Heart of Rock 'n' Roll" video (the song lost its bid for Record of the Year in 1984). "That puts the group in company with David Bowie and Duran Duran, who have also won Grammys for their videos, but not yet for their records," noted *Billboard.*

The *Los Angeles Times* denounced the classical awards as "ridiculous" and *Billboard* called them "a bad joke" when a controversy erupted over an accusation of bloc voting. Writing in a *Billboard* guest column, CBS Masterworks Senior Vice-President Joseph Dash added: "N.A.R.A.S. was embarrassed by a stuff-the-ballot-box campaign that swung an incredible preponderance of classical Grammy nominations and awards of the Atlanta Symphony. In

Variety called this year's Grammys "a virtual stag party" when the nominations were announced.

August, 1985, the Atlanta chapter of N.A.R.A.S. offered members of the Atlanta Symphony Orchestra and Chorus a 'pro-rated,' three-month N.A.R.A.S. membership for $10 that would enable them to cast Grammy ballots. With Atlanta chapter membership swelling 62 percent after the offer—from 265 to 430—those recordings received 12 Grammy nominations, including (according to published reports) four of the original five nominations for classical album of the year."

Robert Shaw conducting the Atlanta Symphony Orchestra and Chorus won three awards for a recording of Berlioz's *Requiem*: Best Classical Album, best vocal soloist performance (for John Aler) and Best Choral Performance. The album was also named Best Engineered Recording. Shaw and the symphony took the additional prize for Best Classical Orchestral Recording for their reading of Fauré's *Pelléas et Mélisande.*

When Sir Georg Solti set out to record Schoenberg's *Moses und Aron,* he told his musicians among the Chicago Symphony Orchestra and singers such as Franz Mazura (as Moses) and Philip Langridge (as Aron) to "play and sing as if you were performing Brahms." The dynamic and highly romanticized version of the classic earned them the opera recording award, bringing Solti his 24th Grammy. (He had won continuously from 1972 to 1983 but failed to win in 1984.)

Cellist Yo-Yo Ma reaped two awards: for best soloist with orchestra for concertos by Edward Elgar and William Walton and Best Chamber Music Performance for sonatas by Brahms. He shared the chamber music honors with pianist Emanuel Ax, who, critics complained, overpowered Yo-Yo Ma's playing. Reviewers nonetheless applauded the Brahms LP. Pianist Vladimir Ashkenazy had recorded Ravel works such as the "Pavane pour une Infante Défunte" earlier in his career but showed much more artistic range in a new release that earned him the laurels for best soloist without orchestra.

A new category was added this year for Best New Classical Artist, which went to Chicago Pro Musica, a group composed of saxophonist Robert Black, pianist-composer Easley Blackwood and nine members of the Chicago Symphony Orchestra. ("These people are good!" Fanfare roared.) The category reinstated last year for new classical compositions was won by Andrew Lloyd Webber, who had snagged previous Grammys for his Broadway shows *Evita* in 1980 and *Cats* in 1983. His latest victory was for *Requiem,* a paean to his recently deceased father that featured music by the English Chamber Orchestra (with Lorin Maazel as conductor) and vocals by Lloyd Webber's wife, Sarah Brightman, Placido Domingo and the choir at Britain's Winchester Cathedral, where the performance was recorded. Some critics dismissed the work as being derivative of Verdi and Fauré, while others called it the apogee of the music writer's career. Webber called it "the most personal of all my compositions."

"Major surprises in this year's Grammy nominations had to do with who wasn't nominated," *Variety* said when the bids came out, noting the low profiles or virtual snubs of Prince, Bruce Springsteen, Madonna, Tears for Fears and Wham! "Voters weighed in heavily on the side of pop-rock in the prestigious genre-wide categories of record, album

and song of the year. No country, and a lone, pop-oriented r&b entry made it to the finals for any of those awards."

One of the vocalists on "We Are the World," Kenny Rogers, acted as the Grammycast host at the Shrine Auditorium in Los Angeles despite having just had throat surgery. (Dionne Warwick was standing by ready to intercede on his behalf, in the event his pipes failed on the show.) Performers included Sting, Huey Lewis & the News and the Norwegian group a-ha, which was a losing nominee for Best New Artist. Whitney Houston's performance of "Saving All My Love for You" on the TV program was so good that she won an Emmy Award for Outstanding Individual Performance in a Variety or Music Program.

Grammycast viewership was down 15 percent from last year. The show scored its second-lowest rating in 10 years: 20.3 rating/32 share. *Variety* noted, "For the fourth time in five years, the Grammys failed to equal the ratings strength of ABC's American Music Awards, which posted a 20.5/30 last month."

N.A.R.A.S. made a special point this year of trying to redress a much older, embarrassing rock oversight when it bestowed a Lifetime Achievement Award on the Rolling Stones.

The *Herald Examiner* noted: "Although the Stones have been making popular music for more than 20 years, and have in fact made many of the most consequential works in all of rock 'n' roll, they had never before received a Grammy—and, given that this particular citation was something of a consolation prize, chances are they will never receive *another* one.

"If the Grammy folks were trying to apologize for the unconscionable way the band had been overlooked (if not purposely disregarded) in the past, it backfired on them. Mick Jagger and crew were wonderfully irreverent and vain—as if they knew that we knew how ludicrous this moment was, and all there was to do was to be mock-gracious about it.

" 'Thank you,' said Jagger, 'to all the people who stood by us through the thick and thin over the years. And,' he added, using a vulgar British expression addressed to those who refused to take them seriously, 'the joke is on you.' "

• 1985 •

The awards ceremony was broadcast on CBS from the Shrine Auditorium in Los Angeles on February 25, 1986, for the awards eligibility period of October 1, 1984, through September 30, 1985.

ALBUM OF THE YEAR
• *No Jacket Required*, Phil Collins. Atlantic.
Brothers in Arms, Dire Straits. Warner Bros.
The Dream of the Blue Turtles, Sting. A&M.
We Are the World, USA for Africa, various artists. Columbia/CBS.
Whitney Houston, Whitney Houston. Arista.

RECORD OF THE YEAR
• "We Are the World," USA for Africa. Columbia/CBS.
"Born in the U.S.A.," Bruce Springsteen. Columbia/CBS.
"The Boys of Summer," Don Henley. Geffen.
"Money for Nothing," Dire Straits. Warner Bros.
"The Power of Love," Huey Lewis & the News. Chrysalis.

SONG OF THE YEAR
(Songwriter's Award)
• "We Are the World," Michael Jackson, Lionel Richie.
"The Boys of Summer," Don Henley, Mike Campbell.
"Everytime You Go Away," Daryl Hall.
"I Want to Know What Love Is," Mick Jones.
"Money for Nothing," Mark Knopfler, Sting.

BEST NEW ARTIST
• Sade
a-ha
Freddie Jackson
Katrina & the Waves
Julian Lennon

BEST POP VOCAL PERFORMANCE, MALE
• Phil Collins, *No Jacket Required*. Atlantic.
Glenn Frey, "The Heat Is On." MCA.
Sting, *The Dream of the Blue Turtles*. A&M.
Stevie Wonder, "Part-Time Lover." Tamla/Motown.
Paul Young, "Everytime You Go Away." Columbia/CBS.

BEST POP VOCAL PERFORMANCE, FEMALE
• Whitney Houston, "Saving All My Love for You." Arista.
Pat Benatar, "We Belong." Chrysalis.
Madonna, "Crazy for You." Geffen.
Linda Ronstadt, *Lush Life*. Elektra.
Tina Turner, "We Don't Need Another Hero (Thunderdome)." Capitol.

BEST POP PERFORMANCE BY A DUO OR GROUP WITH VOCAL
• USA for Africa, "We Are the World." Columbia/CBS.
Philip Bailey, Phil Collins, "Easy Lover." Columbia/CBS.
Foreigner, "I Want to Know What Love Is." Atlantic.
Huey Lewis & the News, "The Power of Love." Chrysalis.
Mr. Mister, "Broken Wings" track from *Welcome to the Real World*. RCA.

BEST POP INSTRUMENTAL PERFORMANCE

- Jan Hammer, "*Miami Vice* Theme." MCA.

Harold Faitermeyer, "Axel F." MCA.

David Foster, "Love Theme from *St. Elmo's Fire*." Atlantic.

Dave Grusin, Lee Ritenour, *Harlequin*. GRP.

Spyro Gyra, "Shake Down." MCA.

BEST ROCK VOCAL PERFORMANCE, MALE

- Don Henley, "The Boys of Summer." Geffen.

Bryan Adams, *Reckless*. A&M.

John Fogerty, *Centerfield*. Warner Bros.

Mick Jagger, "Just Another Night." Columbia/CBS.

John Cougar Mellencamp, *Scarecrow*. Mercury.

BEST ROCK VOCAL PERFORMANCE, FEMALE

- Tina Turner, "One of the Living." Capitol.

Pat Benatar, "Invincible (Theme from *The Legend of Billie Jean*)." Chrysalis.

Nona Hendryx, "Rock This House," track from *The Heat*. RCA.

Cyndi Lauper, "What a Thrill," track from *The Goonies* soundtrack. Epic/CBS.

Melba Moore, "Read My Lips," track from *Read My Lips*. Capitol.

BEST ROCK PERFORMANCE BY A DUO OR GROUP WITH VOCAL

- Dire Straits, "Money for Nothing." Warner Bros.

Bryan Adams, Tina Turner, "It's Only Love," track from *Restless* (Bryan Adams). A&M.

Heart, *Heart*. Capitol.

Eurythmics, "Would I Lie to You?" RCA.

Starship, "We Built This City." Grunt.

BEST ROCK INSTRUMENTAL PERFORMANCE

- Jeff Beck, "Escape," track from *Flash*. Epic/CBS.

Jon Butcher Axis, "The Ritual," track from *Along the Axis*. Capitol.

Big Guitars from Texas, "Guitar Army," track from *Trash, Twang & Thunder*. Jungle.

Yngwie Malmsteen, *Rising Force*. Polydor.

Northern Star, "Back to Earth," track from *Northern Star I*. Dead Pidgeon.

Stevie Ray Vaughan & Double Trouble, "Say What!" track from *Soul to Soul*. Epic/CBS.

BEST RHYTHM & BLUES SONG (Songwriter's Award)

- "Freeway of Love," Narada Michael Walden, Jeffrey Cohen.

"New Attitude," Sharon Robinson, Jon Gilutin, Bunny Hull.

"Nightshift," Walter Orange, Dennis Lambert, Franne Golde.

"Through the Fire," David Foster, Tom Keane, Cynthia Weil.

"You Give Good Love," LaLa.

BEST RHYTHM & BLUES VOCAL PERFORMANCE, MALE

- Stevie Wonder, *In Square Circle*. Tamla/Motown.

Philip Bailey, *Chinese Wall*. Columbia/CBS.

Freddie Jackson, "You Are My Lady." Capitol.

Al Jarreau, "High Crime," track from *High Crime*. Warner Bros.

Luther Vandross, *The Night I Fell in Love*. Epic/CBS.

BEST RHYTHM & BLUES VOCAL PERFORMANCE, FEMALE

- Aretha Franklin, "Freeway of Love." Arista.

Whitney Houston, "You Give Good Love." Arista.

Chaka Khan, *I Feel for You*. Warner Bros.

Patti LaBelle, "New Attitude." MCA.

Teena Marie, "Lovergirl," track from *Starchild*. Epic/CBS.

BEST RHYTHM & BLUES VOCAL PERFORMANCE BY A DUO OR GROUP

- Commodores, "Nightshift." Gordy/Motown.

Ashford & Simpson, *Solid*. Capitol.

Eurythmics, Aretha Franklin, "Sisters Are Doin' It for Themselves," track from *Be Yourself Tonight* (Eurythmics). RCA. Also track from *Who's Zoomin' Who?* (Aretha Franklin). Arista.

Daryl Hall, John Oates, David Ruffin, Eddie Kendrick, "The Way You Do the Things You Do/My Girl." RCA.

Pointer Sisters, *Contact*. RCA.

BEST RHYTHM & BLUES INSTRUMENTAL PERFORMANCE

- Ernie Watts, *Musican*. Qwest.

Five Star, "First Avenue." RCA.

Paul Hardcastle, *Rain Forest*. Profile.

Jeff Lorber, "Pacific Coast Highway," track from *Step by Step*. Arista.

Barney Rachabane, "Caribbean Queen." Jive/Arista.

Sly & Robbie, "Bass and Trouble," track from *Language Barrier*. Island.

Dave Valentin, "Love Light in Flight," track from *Jungle Garden*. GRP.

BEST JAZZ VOCAL PERFORMANCE, MALE

- Jon Hendricks, Bobby McFerrin, "Another Night in Tunisia," track from *Vocalese* (Manhattan Transfer). Atlantic.

George Benson, "Beyond the Sea," track from *20/20*. Warner Bros.

David Frishberg, *Live at Vine Street*. Fantasy.

Mark Murphy, *Mark Murphy Sings Nat's Choice, The Nat "King" Cole Songbook, Vol. 1*. Muse.

Alan Paul, "Oh Yes, I Remember Clifford," track from *Vocalese* (Manhattan Transfer). Atlantic.

BEST JAZZ VOCAL PERFORMANCE, FEMALE

- Cleo Laine, *Cleo at Carnegie the 10th Anniversary Concert*. DRG.

Cheryl Bentyne, "Meet Benny Bailey," track from *Vocalese* (Manhattan Transfer). Atlantic.

Tania Maria, *Made in New York*. Manhattan.

Flora Purim, "20 Years Blue," track from *Humble People* (Flora Purim & Airto). George Wein Collection/Concord Jazz.

Janis Siegel, "Sing Joy Spring," track from *Vocalese* (Manhattan Transfer). Atlantic.

Maxine Sullivan, *The Great Songs from the Cotton Club*. Stash.

BEST JAZZ VOCAL PERFORMANCE BY A DUO OR GROUP

- Manhattan Transfer, *Vocalese*. Atlantic.

Manhattan Transfer, Jon Hendricks, "Ray's Rockhouse," track from *Vocalese* (Manhattan Transfer). Atlantic.

Manhattan Transfer, Four Freshmen, "To You," track from *Vocalese* (Manhattan Transfer). Atlantic.

Barry Manilow, Sarah Vaughan, "Blue," track from *2:00 A.M. Paradise Cafe*. Arista.

Phil Mattson & the P.M. Singers, *Night in the City*. Dark Orchid.

Rare Silk, *American Eyes*. Palo Alto.

University of Northern Colorado Vocal Jazz I, *Hot IV*. Eaglear.

BEST JAZZ INSTRUMENTAL PERFORMANCE BY A SOLOIST

- Wynton Marsalis, "Black Codes from the Underground," track from *Black Codes from the Underground*. Columbia/CBS.

Miles Davis, "Human Nature," track from *Unknown*. Columbia/CBS.

Dizzy Gillespie, "Sing Joy Spring," track from *Vocalese* (Manhattan Transfer). Atlantic.

Stanley Jordan, *Magic Touch*. Blue Note.

James Moody, "Meet Benny Bailey," track from *Vocalese* (Manhattan Transfer). Atlantic.

BEST JAZZ INSTRUMENTAL PERFORMANCE BY A GROUP

- Wynton Marsalis Group, *Black Codes from the Underground*. Columbia/CBS.

Chick Corea, Steve Kujala, *Voyage*. ECM.

Keith Jarrett, *Standards, Vol. 2*. ECM.

Sting, "The Dream of the Blue Turtles," track from *The Dream of the Blue Turtles*. A&M.

Various artists, *One Night with Blue Note*. Blue Note.

BEST JAZZ INSTRUMENTAL PERFORMANCE BY A BIG BAND

- John Barry, Bob Wilber, *The Cotton Club* (film soundtrack). Geffen.

Toshiko Akiyoshi–Lew Tabackin Big Band, *March of the Tadpoles*. Ascent.

Louie Bellson, *Don't Stop Now!* Bosco.

Lionel Hampton, *Ambassador at Large*. Glad Hamp.

George Russell & the Living Time Orchestra, *The African Game*. Blue Note.

BEST JAZZ FUSION PERFORMANCE (VOCAL OR INSTRUMENTAL)

- David Sanborn, *Straight to the Heart*. Warner Bros.

Miles Davis, *You're Under Arrest*. Columbia/CBS.

Stanley Jordan Group, *Magic Touch*. Blue Note.

Wayne Shorter, *Atlantis*. Columbia/CBS.

Spyro Gyra, *Alternating Currents*. MCA.

Weather Report, *Sportin' Life*. Columbia/CBS.

BEST COUNTRY SONG
(Songwriter's Award)

- "Highwayman," Jimmy L. Webb.

"Baby's Got Her Blue Jeans On," Bob McDill.

"Desperados Waiting for a Train," Guy Clark.

"Forty Hour Week (For a Livin')," Dave Loggins, Lisa Silver, Don Schlitz.

"I Don't Know Why You Don't Want Me," Rosanne Cash, Rodney Crowell.

"Lost in the Fifties Tonight (In the Still of the Night)," Mike Reid, Troy Seals, Fred Parris.

"Love Is Alive," Kent M. Robbins.

BEST COUNTRY VOCAL PERFORMANCE, MALE

- Ronnie Milsap, "Lost in the Fifties Tonight (In the Still of the Night)." RCA.

Lee Greenwood, "I Don't Mind the Thorns (If You're the Rose)." MCA.

Mel McDaniel, "Baby's Got Her Blue Jeans On." Capitol.

Willie Nelson, "Forgiving You Was Easy." Columbia/CBS.

Ricky Skaggs, "You Make Me Feel Like a Man." Epic/CBS.

BEST COUNTRY VOCAL PERFORMANCE, FEMALE

- Rosanne Cash, "I Don't Know Why You Don't Want Me." CBS.

Janie Fricke, "She's Single Again." Columbia/CBS.

Emmylou Harris, *The Ballad of Sally Rose*. Warner Bros.

Dolly Parton, *Real Love*. RCA.

Juice Newton, "You Make Me Want to Make You Mine." RCA.

BEST COUNTRY PERFORMANCE BY A DUO OR GROUP WITH VOCAL

- Judds, *Why Not Me*. RCA.

Alabama, "Can't Keep a Good Man Down." RCA.

Forester Sisters, *The Forester Sisters*. Warner Bros.

Waylon Jennings, Willie Nelson, Johnny Cash, Kris Kristofferson, "Highwayman." Columbia/CBS.

Marie Osmond, Dan Seals, "Meet Me in Montana." Capitol.

Dolly Parton, Kenny Rogers, "Real Love," track from *Real Love*. RCA.

BEST COUNTRY INSTRUMENTAL PERFORMANCE

- Chet Atkins, Mark Knopfler, "Cosmic Square Dance," track from *Stay Tuned* (Chet Atkins). Columbia/CBS.

Vassar Clements, John Hartford, Dave Holland, *Vassar Clements, John Hartford, Dave Holland*. Rounder.

Charlie McCoy, "Lasso the Moon," track from *Rustlers' Rhapsody and Other Songs*. Warner Bros.

Earl Scruggs, "Folsom Prison Blues," track from *American-Made, World-Played*. Columbia/CBS.

Doc & Merle Watson, "Windy and Warm," track from *Pickin' the Blues*. Flying Fish.

BEST GOSPEL PERFORMANCE, MALE

- Larnelle Harris, "How Excellent Is Thy Name," track from *I've Just Seen Jesus*. Benson.

James Blackwood, *Fifty Golden Years*. Skylite/Sing.

Phil Driscoll, *Power of Praise*. Sparrow.

Steve Green, *He Holds the Keys*. Sparrow.

Russ Taff, *Medals*. Myrrh/Word.

BEST GOSPEL PERFORMANCE, FEMALE

- Amy Grant, *Unguarded*. Myrrh/Word.

Debby Boone, *Choose Life*. Lamb & Lion/Sparrow.

Sandi Patti, *Hymns Just for You*. Benson.

Leslie Phillips, *Black and White in a Grey World*. Myrrh/Word.

Sheila Walsh, *Don't Hide Your Heart*. Sparrow.

BEST GOSPEL PERFORMANCE BY A DUO OR GROUP

- Larnelle Harris, Sandi Patti, "I've Just Seen Jesus," track from *I've Just Seen Jesus*. Benson.

De Garmo & Key, *Commander Sozo and the Charge of the Light Brigade*. Power Disc/Benson.

The Imperials, *Let the Wind Blow*. Myrrh/Word.

Petra, *Beat the System*. Star Song.

Randy Stonehill, Amy Grant, "I Could Never Say Goodbye." Myrrh/Word.

BEST SOUL GOSPEL PERFORMANCE, MALE

- Marvin Winans, "Bring Back the Days of Yea and Nay," track from *Tomorrow*. Light.

Howard McCrary, *So Good*. Good News.

Douglas Miller, *Unspeakable Joy*. Light.

Philip Nicholas, "Stop Your Searchin' (Try God!)," track from *Dedicated*. Command.

Rev. Marvin Yancy, *Heavy Load*. Nashboro.

BEST SOUL GOSPEL PERFORMANCE, FEMALE

- Shirley Caesar, "Martin." Rejoice/Word.

Vanessa Bell Armstrong, *Chosen*. Onyx International.

Vernessa Mitchell, "Blessed Assurance," track from *This Is My Story*. Command.

Dorothy Norwood, "Lift Him Up," track from *Lift Him Up*. Savoy.

Deleon Richards, *Deleon*. Myrrh/Word.

BEST SOUL GOSPEL PERFORMANCE BY A DUO OR GROUP

- Winans, *Tomorrow*. Light.

Sandra Crouch & Friends, *We're Waiting*. Light.

Sandra Crouch, Jean Johnson, "Completely Yes," track from *We're Waiting*. Light.

Edwin Hawkins with Music & Arts Seminar Mass Choir, *Have Mercy*. Birthright.

Carvin Winans, Michael Winans, "Tomorrow," track from *Tomorrow*. Light.

BEST INSPIRATIONAL PERFORMANCE

- Jennifer Holliday, "Come Sunday," track from *Say You Love Me*. Geffen.

Pat Boone, *16,000 Faces*. B.P.I.

Glen Campbell, *No More Night*. Word.

Kool & the Gang, "You Are the One," track from *Emergency*. De-Lite.

Barbara Mandrell, *Christmas at Our House*. MCA.

BEST TRADITIONAL BLUES RECORDING

- B. B. King, "My Guitar Sings the Blues," track from *Six Silver Strings*. MCA.

Bobby Bland, *Members Only*. Malaco.

Roy Buchanan, *When a Guitar Plays the Blues*. Alligator.

Koko Taylor, *Queen of the Blues*. Alligator.

Big Joe Turner with Knocky Parker & His Houserockers, *Big Joe Turner with Knocky Parker and His Houserockers*. Southland.

Joe Turner, Jimmy Witherspoon, *Patcha, Patcha, All Night Long*. Pablo.

Johnny Winter, *Serious Business*. Alligator.

BEST ETHNIC OR TRADITIONAL FOLK RECORDING

- "My Toot Toot," Rockin' Sidney. Maison de Soul.

Live at the San Francisco Blues Festival, Clifton Chenier. Arhoolie.

Souvenirs, Dewey Balfa. Swallow.

Turning Point, Buckwheat Zydeco. Rounder.

Zydeco Gris Gris, BeauSoleil. Swallow.

BEST LATIN POP PERFORMANCE

- Lani Hall, *Es Fácil Amar*. A&M.

José Feliciano, *Yo Soy Tuyo*. RCA.

José Feliciano, José José, "Por Ella," track from *Yo Soy Tuyo*. RCA.

José José, *Reflexiones*. Ariola-America.

Lucia Mendez, *Solo una Mujer*. Ariola-America.

BEST TROPICAL LATIN PERFORMANCE

(Tie)

- Tito Puente & His Latin Ensemble, *Mambo Diablo*. Concord Jazz.
- Eddie Palmieri, *Solito*. Musica Latina International.

Rubén Blades, *Mucho Mejor*. Fania/Musica Latina International.

Bonny Cepeda y Orquesta, *Noche de Discotheque*. RCA.

Celia Cruz, Johnny Pacheco, *De Nuevo*. Vaya/Musica Latina International.

Mongo Santamaria & His Latin Jazz Orchestra, *Free Spirit, Espirito Libre*. Tropical Budda.

BEST MEXICAN-AMERICAN PERFORMANCE

- Vikki Carr, *Simplemente Mujer*. Discos CBS International.

Rocio Durcal, *Canta a Juan Gabriel*. Ariola-America.

Los Humildes, *13 Aniversario/13 Album/13 Exitos*. Profono Internacional.

Santiago Jiminez, Jr., *Santiago Strikes Again*. Arhoolie.

Maria de Lourdes, *Mujer Importante*. RCA.

Juan Valentin, *20 Exitos Romanticos con Juan Valentin*. Musart.

BEST REGGAE RECORDING

- Jimmy Cliff, *Cliff Hanger*. Columbia/CBS.

The Blue Riddim Band, *Alive in Jamaica*. Flying Fish.

Burning Spear, *Resistance*. Heartbeat/Rounder.

Melody Makers Featuring Ziggy Marley, *Play the Game Right*. EMI-America.

Judy Mowatt, *Working Wonders*. Shanachie.

BEST POLKA RECORDING

- *70 Years of Hits*, Frank Yankovic. Cleveland International/CBS.

Brass with Class, Brass Release. LeMans.

Polka Fireworks, Eddie Blazonczyk's Versatones. Bel Aire.

Polskie Czucie Polish Feelings, L'il Wally & Orchestra. Jay Jay.

Simply Polkamentary, Lenny Gomulka & the Chicago Push. Chicago Polkas.

BEST ARRANGEMENT ON AN INSTRUMENTAL

- Dave Grusin, Lee Ritenour, "Early A.M. Attitude," track from *Harlequin* (Dave Grusin, Lee Ritenour). GRP.

George Russell, *The African Game*
(George Russell & the Living Time
Orchestra). Blue Note.

Toshiko Akiyoshi, "March of the Tadpoles," track from *March of the Tadpoles* (Toshiko Akiyoshi–Lew
Tabackin Big Band). Ascent.

Chip Davis, "Stille Nacht (Silent
Night)," track from *Mannheim
Steamroller Christmas* (Mannheim
Steamroller). American Gramophone.

William D. Bruhn, "Suite of Dances
from 'Pacific Overtures,'" track from
Sondheim (Symphony Orchestra conducted by Paul Gemignani). Book-
of-the-Month.

BEST INSTRUMENTAL ARRANGEMENT ACCOMPANYING VOCAL(S)

• Nelson Riddle, "Lush Life," track
from *Lush Life* (Linda Ronstadt).
Asylum.

David Foster, "Through the Fire,"
(Chaka Khan). Warner Bros.

Frank Foster, Ralph Burns, "Beyond the
Sea (La Mer)," track from *20/20*
(George Benson). Warner Bros.

Dave Grusin, Lee Ritenour, "Harlequin,"
track from *Harlequin* (Dave Grusin,
Lee Ritenour). GRP.

Peter Wolf, "Why Do People Fall in
Love," track from *Copolin' Out*
(Dennis Edwards, Thelma Houston).
Gordy/Motown.

BEST VOCAL ARRANGEMENT FOR TWO OR MORE VOICES

• Cheryl Bentyne, Bobby McFerrin,
"Another Night in Tunisia" (Manhattan Transfer). Atlantic.

Dennis Lambert, "Nightshift" (Commodores). Motown.

Phil Mattson, "I Hear Music," track
from *Night in the City* (Phil Mattson
& the P.M. Singers). Dark Orchid.

Alan Paul, "Ray's Rockhouse," track
from *Vocalese* (Manhattan Transfer).
Atlantic.

Janis Siegel, Dennis Wilson, "Blee Blop
Blues," track from *Vocalese* (Manhattan Transfer). Atlantic.

BEST INSTRUMENTAL COMPOSITION

• "*Miami Vice* Theme," Jan Hammer
"Axel F," Harold Faitermeyer.
"Back to the Future," Alan Silvestri.
"Love Theme from *St. Elmo's Fire*,"
David Foster.
"With Bells On," Thad Jones.

BEST CAST SHOW ALBUM

• *West Side Story*, Stephen Sondheim,
lyricist; Leonard Bernstein, composer and conductor. Deutsche
Grammophon.

Big River, Roger Miller, composer and
lyricist. MCA.

*Greatest Hits from "Leader of the
Pack,"* Ellie Greenwich, Jeff Barry,
Phil Spector, George "Shadow" Mor-
ton, songwriters. Elektra.

The Tap Dance Kid, Robert Lorick, lyricist; Henry Krieger, composer. Polydor.

Very Warm for May, Oscar Hammerstein
II, lyricist; Jerome Kern, composer.
AEI.

BEST ALBUM OF ORIGINAL SCORE WRITTEN FOR A MOTION PICTURE OR TV SPECIAL
(Composer's Award)

• *Beverly Hills Cop*, Sharon Robinson,
John Gilutin, Bunny Hull, Hawk,
Howard Hewett, Micki Free, Keith
Forsey, Harold Faltermeyer, Allee
Willis, Dan Sembello, Marc Benno,
Richard Theisen. MCA.

Back to the Future, John Colla, Chris
Hayes, Huey Lewis, Lindsey Buck-
ingham, Alan Silvestri, Eric Clapton,
Sean Hopper. MCA.

A Passage to India, Maurice Jarre. Capitol.

St. Elmo's Fire, David Foster, John Parr,
Billy Squier, John & Dino Elefante,
Jon Anderson, Fee Waybill, Steve
Lukather, Richard Marx, Jay Gray-
don, Stephen A. Kipner, Peter Beck-
ett, Cynthia Weil. Atlantic.

Witness, Maurice Jarre. Varèse Sarabande.

BEST CLASSICAL ALBUM

• *Berlioz: Requiem*, Robert Shaw conducting the Atlanta Symphony Orchestra and Chorus (solo: John Aler). Telarc.

Berlioz: Les Nuits d'Eté; Fauré: Pelléas et Mélisande, Robert Shaw conducting the Atlanta Symphony Orchestra (solo: Elly Ameling). Telarc.

Dvořák: Symphony No. 7 in D Minor, James Levine conducting the Chicago Symphony Orchestra. RCA Red Seal.

Gershwin: Rhapsody in Blue; Second Rhapsody for Orchestra with Piano; Prelude for Piano; Short Story; Violin Piece; For Lily Pons; Sleepless Night; Promenade, Michael Tilson Thomas; conducting the Los Angeles Philharmonic Orchestra. CBS Masterworks.

Handel: Messiah, Robert Shaw conducting the Atlanta Symphony Orchestra and Chorus (solos: Kaaren Erickson, Sylvia McNair, Alfreda Hodgson, Jon Humphrey, Richard Stilwell). Telarc.

Mahler: Symphony No. 7 in E Minor, Claudio Abbado conducting the Chicago Symphony Orchestra. Deutsche Grammophon.

Mozart: Violin and Piano Sonatas K. 296, 305, 306 (solos: Itzhak Perlman, Daniel Barenboim). Deutsche Grammophon.

Prokofiev: Cinderella (Suite), Leonard Slatkin conducting the St. Louis Symphony Orchestra. RCA Red Seal.

Respighi: Pines of Rome; The Birds; Fountains of Rome, Louis Lane conducting the Atlanta Symphony Orchestra. Telarc.

BEST CLASSICAL ORCHESTRAL RECORDING
(Conductor's Award)

• *Fauré: Pelléas et Mélisande*, Robert Shaw conducting the Atlanta Symphony Orchestra. Telarc.

Dvořák: Symphony No. 7 in D Minor, James Levine conducting the

Chicago Symphony Orchestra. RCA Red Seal.

Liszt: A Faust Symphony, James Conlon conducting the Rotterdam Philharmonic Orchestra. Erato-Editions.

Prokofiev: Cinderella (Suite), Leonard Slatkin conducting the St. Louis Symphony Orchestra. RCA Red Seal.

Respighi: Pines of Rome; The Birds; Fountains of Rome, Louis Lane conducting the Atlanta Symphony Orchestra. Telarc.

BEST NEW CLASSICAL ARTIST

• Chicago Pro Musica
Sarah Brightman
Rosalind Plowright
Esa-Pekka Salonen
Brian Slawson

BEST CHAMBER MUSIC PERFORMANCE

• Emanuel Ax, Yo-Yo Ma, *Brahms: Cello and Piano Sonatas in E Major and F Major*. RCA.

Daniel Barenboim, Pinchas Zukerman, Jacqueline Du Pré, *Tchaikovsky: Piano Trio in A Minor*. Angel.

Itzhak Perlman, Jorge Bolet, Juilliard String Quartet, *Chausson: Concerto for Violin, Piano and String Quartet, Op. 21*. CBS Masterworks.

Itzhak Perlman, Samuel Sanders, *Dvořák: Sonatina in G and 4 Romantic Pieces; Smetana: From My Homeland*. Angel.

André Previn, Vienna Wind Soloists, *Mozart: Piano and Wind Quintet in E Flat; Beethoven: Piano and Wind Quintet in E Flat*. Telarc.

BEST CLASSICAL PERFORMANCE, INSTRUMENTAL SOLOIST(S) (WITH ORCHESTRA)

• Yo-Yo Ma (Previn conducting the London Symphony Orchestra), *Elgar: Cello Concerto, Op. 85; Walton: Concerto for Cello and Orchestra*. CBS Masterworks.

James Galway (Chung conducting the Royal Philharmonic Orchestra), *James Galway Plays Khachaturian (Concerto for Flute and Orchestra, Spartacus, Masquerade and Gayaneh).* RCA.

Itzhak Perlman (Mehta conducting the Israel Philharmonic Orchestra), *Khachaturian: Violin Concerto in D Minor.* Angel.

André Previn (Previn conducting the Pittsburgh Symphony Orchestra), *Gershwin: Rhapsody in Blue.* Philips.

Andras Schiff (Dorati conducting the Concertgebouw Orchestra), *Schumann: Piano Concerto in A Minor; Chopin: Piano Concerto No. 2 in F Minor.* London.

Michael Tilson Thomas (Thomas conducting the Los Angeles Philharmonic), *Gershwin: Second Rhapsody for Orchestra with Piano.* CBS Masterworks.

BEST CLASSICAL PERFORMANCE, INSTRUMENTAL SOLOIST(S) (WITHOUT ORCHESTRA)

- Vladimir Ashkenazy, *Ravel: Gaspard de la Nuit, Pavane pour une Infante Défunte, Valses Nobles et Sentimentales.* London.

Claudio Arrau, *Chopin: 4 Scherzos; Polonaise; Fantaisie, Op. 61.* Philips.

Julian Bream, *"Guitarra": The Guitar in Spain (Mudarra, Guera, Boccherini, Sor, Tarrega, Albeniz, Falla, Turina, etc.).* RCA Red Seal.

François-René Duchable, *Chopin: Piano Sonatas No. 2 in B Flat Minor and No. 3 in B Minor.* Erato-Editions.

Michael Tilson Thomas, *Gershwin: Preludes for Piano; Short Story; Violin Piece; For Lily Pons; Sleepless Night; Promenade.* CBS Masterworks.

BEST OPERA RECORDING

- *Schoenberg: Moses und Aron,* Sir Georg Solti conducting the Chicago Symphony Orchestra and Chorus (solos: Franz Mazura, Philip Langridge). London.

Leoncavallo: Pagliacci (soundtrack), Georges Prêtre conducting the Coro e Orchestra del Teatro alla Scala, Milan (solos: Teresa Stratas, Placido Domingo, Juan Pons, Alberto Rinaldi, Florindo Andreolli). Polygram Classics/Philips.

Puccini: Manon Lescaut, Giuseppe Sinopoli conducting the Philharmonia Orchestra and Chorus of the Royal Opera House, Covent Garden (solos: Mirella Freni, Placido Domingo, Renato Bruson, Kurt Rydi, Robert Gambill). Deutsche Grammophon.

Stravinsky: The Rake's Progress, Riccardo Chailly conducting the London Sinfonietta and London Sinfonietta Chorus (solos: Philip Langridge, Cathryn Pope, Samuel Ramey, Sarah Walker, John Dobson). London.

Wagner: Der Fliegende Holländer (The Flying Dutchman), Herbert von Karajan conducting the Berlin Philharmonic Orchestra and Vienna State Opera Chorus (solos: José van Dam, Dunja Vejzovic, Kurt Moll, Peter Hofmann). Angel.

BEST CHORAL PERFORMANCE (OTHER THAN OPERA)

- Robert Shaw conducting the Atlanta Symphony Chorus and Orchestra (solo: John Aler), *Berlioz: Requiem.* Telarc.

Daniel Barenboim conducting the Choeurs et Orchestre de Paris (solos: Ann Murray, Kathleen Battle, David Rendall, Matti Salminen), *Mozart: Requiem.* Angel.

Herbert von Karajan conducting the Konzertvereinigung Wiener Staatsopernchor, Chor der Nationaloper Sofia, Wiener Philharmoniker (solos: Anna Tomowa-Sintow, Agnes Baltsa, José Carreras, José van Dam), *Verdi: Requiem.* Deutsche Grammophon.

Ton Koopman conducting the Choeur "The Sixteen" and Amsterdam Baroque Orchestra (solos: James Bowman, Paul Elliott, Gregory Rein-

hart), *Handel: Messiah*. Erato-
Editions.
Lorin Maazel conducting the English
Chamber Orchestra and Winchester
Cathedral Choir (solos: Placido
Domingo, Sarah Brightman, Paul
Miles-Kingston), *Lloyd Webber:
Requiem*. Angel.

BEST CLASSICAL PERFORMANCE, VOCAL SOLOIST
• John Aler (Shaw conducting the
Atlanta Symphony Orchestra and
Chorus), *Berlioz: Requiem*. Telarc.
Elly Ameling (Shaw conducting the
Atlanta Symphony Orchestra),
Berlioz: Les Nuits d'Eté. Telarc.
Placido Domingo, Pilar Lorengar (Na-
varro conducting the ORF Symphonie
orchester), *Zarzuela Arias and Duets
(Arias Only)*. CBS Masterworks.
Marilyn Horne (Foster conducting the
Orchestre Philharmonique de Monte
Carlo), *Marilyn Horne Sings (Offen-
bach, Cherubini, Saint-Saëns, etc.)*.
Erato-Editions.
Kiri Te Kanawa (Tate conducting the
English Chamber Orchestra), *Can-
teloube: Chants d'Auvergne, Vol. 2;
Villa-Lobos: Bachianas Brasileiras
No. 5*. London.
Frederica von Stade (Ozawa conducting
the Boston Symphony Orchestra),
*Berlioz: Les Nuits d'Eté; Debussy: La
Damoiselle Elue*. CBS Masterworks.

BEST CONTEMPORARY COMPOSITION
(Composer's Award)
• *Requiem*, Andrew Lloyd Webber.
Harmonium for Large Orchestra and
Chorus, John Adams.
Satyagraha, Philip Glass.
Serenade No. 3 for Piano and Chamber
Orchestra, George Perle.
Violin Concerto, Robert Starer.

BEST ENGINEERED RECORDING, CLASSICAL
• Jack Renner, *Berlioz: Requiem* (Shaw
conducting the Atlanta Symphony

Orchestra and Chorus; solo: John
Aler). Telarc.
Paul Goodman, *Dvořák: Symphony No.
7 in D Minor* (Levine conducting the
Chicago Symphony Orchestra). RCA
Red Seal.
Paul Goodman, Thomas MacCluskey,
*Tchaikovsky: The Nutcracker (Com-
plete)* (Slatkin conducting the St.
Louis Symphony Orchestra). RCA.
James Lock, *Mahler: Symphony No. 1 in
D Major* (Solti conducting the Chi-
cago Symphony Orchestra). London.
Paul Goodman, *Prokofiev: Cinderella
(Suite)* (Slatkin conducting the St.
Louis Symphony Orchestra). RCA
Red Seal.
Jack Renner, *Berlioz: Les Nuits d'Eté;
Fauré:* Pelléas et Mélisande (Shaw
conducting the Atlanta Symphony
Orchestra; solo: Elly Ameling).
Telarc.
Jack Renner, *Respighi: Pines of Rome;
The Birds; Fountains of Rome* (Lane
conducting the Atlanta Symphony
Orchestra). Telarc.

CLASSICAL PRODUCER OF THE YEAR
• Robert E. Woods
Steven Epstein
James Mallinson
David Mottley
Jay David Saks

BEST COMEDY RECORDING
• *Whoopi Goldberg (Original Broadway
Show Recording)*, Whoopi Goldberg.
Geffen.
"Born in East L.A.," Cheech & Chong.
MCA.
Dare to Be Stupid, Weird Al Yankovic.
Rock 'n' Roll/CBS.
"Honeymooners Rap," Joe Piscopo.
Columbia/CBS.
"You Look Marvelous," Billy Crystal.
A&M.

BEST SPOKEN WORD OR NONMUSICAL RECORDING
• *Ma Rainey's Black Bottom* (Broadway
cast). Manhattan.

The Adventures of Huckleberry Finn by Mark Twain, Dick Cavett. Listen for Pleasure.
Catch-22 by Joseph Heller, Alan Arkin. Listen for Pleasure.
The Spy Who Came in from the Cold by John Le Carré, John Le Carré. Listen for Pleasure.
Zuckerman Bound by Philip Roth, Philip Roth. Caedmon.

BEST RECORDING FOR CHILDREN
• *Follow That Bird* (film soundtrack), Jim Henson's Muppets and the Sesame Street cast. RCA.
Bullfrogs and Butterflies, Part II, Candle and the Agapeland Singers. Birdwing/Sparrow.
E.T.A. Hoffman, Tchaikovsky, Nutcracker, Christopher Plummer, narrator; Michael Tilson Thomas conducting the Philharmonia Orchestra. Caedmon.
Prokofiev: Peter and the Wolf, Dudley Moore, John Williams & the Boston Pops Orchestra. Philips.
The Velveteen Rabbit, Meryl Streep, narrator; George Winston, piano. Dancing Cat.
We Are the World, Children of the World. Starborn.

BEST ENGINEERED RECORDING (OTHER THAN CLASSICAL)
• Neil Dorfsman, *Brothers in Arms* (Dire Straits). Warner Bros.
Jeff Hendrickson, *Crazy from the Heat* (David Lee Roth). Warner Bros.
Don Murray. *Harlequin* (Dave Grusin, Lee Ritenour). GRP.
Pete Smith, Jim Scott. *The Dream of the Blue Turtles* (Sting). A&M.
Paul Wickliffe, Chieli Minucci, Paul Wickliffe, *Modern Manners* (Special EFX). GRP.

BEST ALBUM PACKAGE
(Art Director's Award)
• Kosh, Ron Larson, *Lush Life* (Linda Ronstadt). Asylum.

Jeffrey Kent Ayeroff, Jeri McManus, *Hunting High and Low* (a-ha). Warner Bros.
Renee Hardaway, Johnny Lee, *In Square Circle* (Stevie Wonder). Tamla/Motown.
Virginia Team, *Highwayman* (Waylon Jennings, Willie Nelson, Johnny Cash, Kris Kristofferson). Columbia/CBS.
Murry Whiteman, Bill Levy, Stan Watts, *Dangerous Moments* (Martin Briley). Mercury.

BEST ALBUM NOTES
(Annotator's Award)
• Peter Guralnick, *Sam Cooke Live at the Harlem Square Club* (Sam Cooke). RCA.
Lenny Kaye, *Bleecker and MacDougal: The Folk Scene of the 1960's* (Judy Collins, Tom Paxton, Phil Ochs, others). Elektra.
Lenny Kaye, *Crossroads: White Blues in the 1960's* (Koener, Ray and Glover, Paul Butterfield Blues Band, Lovin' Spoonful, others). Elektra.
James R. Morris, J. R. Taylor, Dwight Blocker Bowers, *American Popular Song* (Fred Astaire, Bing Crosby, Judy Garland, Ella Fitzgerald, others). Smithsonian/CBS Special Products.
Neil Tesser, *The Girl from Ipanema: The Bossa Nova Years* (Stan Getz). Verve.

BEST HISTORICAL ALBUM
• *RCA/Met—100 Singers, 100 Years* (Melba, Schumann-Heink, Caruso, Price, Verrett, Domingo, 94 others). RCA Red Seal.
American Popular Song (Fred Astaire, Lena Horne, Nat King Cole, Sarah Vaughan, others). Smithsonian/CBS Special Products.
Bill Evans: The Complete Riverside Recordings (Bill Evans). Riverside.
Billie Holiday on Verve 1946–1959 (Billie Holiday). Verve.

The Human Orchestra (Rhythm Quartets in the Thirties) (Mills Brothers, Ink Spots, Four Blackbirds, others). Clanka Lanka.

PRODUCER OF THE YEAR (OTHER THAN CLASSICAL)

• Phil Collins, Hugh Padgham
David Foster
Don Henley, Danny Kortchmar, Greg Ladanyi
Mark Knopfler, Neil Dorfsman
Narada Michael Walden

BEST MUSIC VIDEO, SHORT FORM

• *We Are the World, the Video Event*, USA for Africa. Tom Trbovich, director. RCA/Columbia Pictures Home Video.
The Daryl Hall and John Oates Video Collection, 7 Big Ones, Daryl Hall & John Oates. Mick Haggerty, C. D. Taylor, directors. RCA/Columbia Pictures Home Video.

Do They Know It's Christmas? Band Aid. Dave Bridges, Rob Wright, directors. Vestron Video.
No Jacket Required, Phil Collins. Jim Vulcich, director. Atlantic Video.
Private Dancer, Tina Turner. Brian Grant, director. Sony/Pioneer.

BEST MUSIC VIDEO, LONG FORM

• *Huey Lewis and the News: The Heart of Rock 'n' Roll*, Huey Lewis & the News. Bruce Gowers, director. Warner Home Video.
The Police Synchronicity Concert, Police. Godley & Creme, directors. A&M Video/I.R.S. Video.
Prince and the Revolution Live, Prince & the Revolution. Paul Becher, director. Warner Music Video.
Tina Live, Private Dancer Tour, Tina Turner. David Mallet, director. Sony/Picture Music/Capitol.
Wham! The Video, Wham! CBS/Fox Video.

• 1986 •

Anthems Against AIDS and Apartheid

The 29th annual Grammy Awards show opened with nominee Paul Simon and the South African music group Ladysmith Black Mambazo performing "Diamonds on the Soles of Her Shoes" from his Album of the Year contender, *Graceland*. "Mr. Simon then sat in the audience for more than three hours," observed the *New York Times*, "watching others beat him out in a number of awards categories."

But not in one of the biggest ones. At evening's close, presenters Whoopi Goldberg and Don Johnson summoned Simon back up to the stage to collect the trophy for best LP.

Graceland was Simon's third best album winner (following *Bridge Over Troubled Water* in 1970 and *Still Crazy After All These Years* in 1975), an accomplishment matched only by Frank Sinatra and Stevie Wonder in past years. It was a hugely controversial disc, however, since it contained tribal rhythms that Simon discovered while visiting South Africa in defiance of an international boycott. He was lambasted for his trip by media such as the *Village Voice* and threatened with censure by the United Nations Committee Against Apartheid.

But Simon was actually a critic of apartheid and, in deference to the boycott, refused to perform while in Johannesburg. He told *Esquire* that his album was "a motion toward helping. It exposes a culture, a people. I'm trying to be in the dialogue." On Grammy night, Simon felt vindicated and he expressed his appreciation to his collaborators, who had valiantly survived "one of the most repressive regimes on the planet today," he said.

The *Washington Post* was among

Anti-AIDS fund-raiser and best song winner "That's What Friends Are For" featured from left, Dionne Warwick, Stevie Wonder and Gladys Knight.

those predicting that *Graceland*'s title track would nab Song of the Year. "Other strong contenders include [Steve] Winwood's 'Higher Love,'" it added, "and [Peter] Gabriel's 'Sledgehammer,' a witty take on sexual double entendres that criminally failed to make the best music video category." Then the paper added as an afterthought, "If there's a left-field choice, it's the sentimental 'That's What Friends Are For.'"

Reflecting the same spirit as "We Are the World," the famine fund-raiser that won both best song and record last year, "Friends" had already generated $1 million for victims of AIDS. It was written by Burt Bacharach and wife Carol Bayer Sager and was performed by Dionne Warwick, Elton John, Stevie Wonder and Gladys Knight. When it prevailed as best song, the victory brought Elton John his first Grammy after 14 past losses. The win also marked the first time that Bacharach won Song of the Year despite five bids dating back to "Wives and Lovers" in 1963. "Friends" also made friends again of Bacharach and Warwick, who had a falling-out 10 years earlier after Warwick filed a lawsuit accusing the songwriter of breach of contract. Prior to that, Bacharach and partner Hal David were responsible for Warwick's reaching the pop charts an amazing 33 times.

It was Sager who patched things up between writer and artist—and she was also the one who suggested that the proceeds from their new joint effort go to AIDS research. Elizabeth Taylor, a noted AIDS activist, had dropped by the recording studio one day at the invitation of Stevie Wonder, thus giving Sager the idea. While accepting the songwriter's prize, Bacharach said, "Of all the songs that I have written, it's the one song that, when I hear it on the radio or in performance, I still get a little teary."

Despite a career spanning 20 years, Steve Winwood had never been nominated for a Grammy, but now he rallied by scoring the most nominations for 1986 (five—compared to four for second-placed Simon, Gabriel and Wynton Marsalis). After being trounced in the Album and Song of the Year categories, Winwood managed to pull off the biggest upset of the night when he garnered Record of the Year for "Higher Love," his first number-one-ranked single. The song also earned him the pop vocal honors, while its album, *Back in the High Life,* was named Best Engineered Recording. The artist, called a "rock survivor" by *Variety,* was nonplussed and even somewhat ungracious about the award. He told reporters: "I didn't care about winning a Grammy early in my career. When I first started out, I wouldn't even have come to the awards. The idea of approval by one's peers didn't matter to a 19-year-old singer. It still doesn't."

Peter Gabriel turned out to be the night's big loser when his four bids resulted in scratch. Janet Jackson had three nominations and came up with the same result, including a loss, like Gabriel, in the race for Album of the Year for her multiplatinum *Control.* Jackson's producers, however, prevailed as Producer of the

Year. *The New York Times* wrote: "Jimmy Jam and Terry Lewis looked almost mean and forbidding in their fedoras and shades, but turned out to be pussycats, quickly noting that 'we want to thank our moms, first of all.'"

Part of the reason for Jackson's defeat was reflected in *Variety*'s headline after the show: "Grammys Rock with the Ages: Disk Vets Dominate Awards." This year's ceremony, agreed the *New York Times,* "provided a somewhat surprising picture of an industry drifting into middle age, if not already long there." Simon, Bacharach, Warwick and Winwood were all part of music's new old guard and they were soon joined by another seasoned talent, Barbra Streisand. The 1963 Album of the Year winner was also among those who failed to win this year's LP laurels. Still, her nomination in the category was significant, since it amounted to her seventh, thereby putting her right behind Frank Sinatra, leader of the *original* old guard, who held the record for most best album bids (eight).

Streisand took the pop vocal laurels for a project that was considered chancy for any veteran artist trying to stay hip—*The Broadway Album,* a collection of her favorite show tunes, most of which were written by Stephen Sondheim (winner of this year's Best Musical Cast Show Album, *Follies*). It was Streisand's eighth Grammy and it amounted to a shocking victory, since Madonna was expected to take the prize for "Papa Don't Preach." In her acceptance remarks, Streisand referred to the trouble she had in convincing her producers to let her record yet another LP of old show music. "It was a struggle to make this album," she said, then expressed her surprise that people bought it. The platter's success, she added, was a "reaffirmation of the stature and quality of this timeless material." One of the reasons people purchased the album was its hauntingly beautiful rendition of *West Side Story*'s "Somewhere," which Streisand had rearranged to accommodate a new bridge she wanted near the end. The brilliant result earned its arranger, David Foster, a Grammy, too.

Among more fledgling talent, the winner of Best New Artist was no surprise. "This award should have Bruce Hornsby's name already engraved on it," the *Washington Post* said prior to the show about the lead artist of the Range, since the former pianist for Sheena Easton's band "has once again opened up radio to the sound of piano-powered pop. . . . Long shots [in this category] include the dreadful corporate rockers Glass Tiger, one-hit wonder Nu Schooz and Timbuk 3 (a clever Texas-based tech duo probably still in shock at having been nominated in the first place)." Accepting the award, Hornsby thanked "the large Hornsby clan out in Virginia" and "my big brother and our head cheerleader, Huey Lewis," who produced his hit single "The Way It Is."

In the rock categories, another one of the old pros, Tina Turner, proved her staying power by holding on to the female vocal laurels for a third year running for "Back Where You Started." The male honors went, as predicted, to the British white soul singer Robert Palmer for Record and Song of the Year nominee "Addicted to Love." Palmer wrote the tune after the melody came to him in his sleep one night and he woke up to hum it into a tape recorder. "In the morning, I listened to it and knew I'd caught one," he told *People*.

Eurythmics joined the Grammys in the past when Annie Lennox made a gender-bending appearance at the 1983 awards show. Now they stunned Grammy watchers by pulling off an upset in the rock group vocals category for "Missionary Man" to win their only career trophy. The Fabulous Thunderbirds had been the odds-on favorite to take the prize for "Tuff Enuff" and their chief competition was expected to come from "Sun City," a joint cry against South Africa by 45 artists that was orchestrated by Steve Van Zandt.

N.A.R.A.S. made a bold move this year to embrace more avant-garde works by introducing a category for New Age music that was claimed by Andreas Vollenweider

Variety called Record of the Year champ Steve Winwood ("Higher Love") "a rock survivor."

for *Down to the Moon.* The only problem was that most of the artists nominated for it, like Vollenweider, "reject the New Age tag as constrictive and misleading," said the *Washington Post*.

The Art of Noise Featuring Duane Eddy won the laurels for best rock instrumental performance for "Peter Gunn," the same music that brought Henry Mancini Grammy's first Album of the Year award in 1958.

"Oh, my Grammy! Oh, my Grammy!" Anita Baker shrieked backstage as she tried to calm down following her double upset in the r&b categories. Janet Jackson was supposed to grab the female vocals prize—plus Best Rhythm & Blues Song—for "What Have You Done for Me Lately," but she was eclipsed for both by Baker, who prevailed for "Sweet Love" and its album, *Rapture*.

James Brown made a startling comeback when he snared the male r&b award 21 years after winning it the first time. The *Washington Post* was among those that predicted he'd rebound for his latest hit, "Living in America," while other sources such as *Billboard* foresaw a win by Luther Vandross ("Give Me the Reason"). After the artist known as Soul Brother Number 1 won, N.A.R.A.S. membership magazine *Grammy Pulse* noted, "Brown couldn't make the Grammy show because he was in the middle of a European tour that took in a couple of Iron Curtain dates and Turkey!"

In the contest for group vocal honors, the Chicago Bears football team was given a presumbaly serious bid for "The Super Bowl Shuffle," a tongue-in-cheek promotion for their role in the biggest sports showdown of the year that proved funnier as a video than as a straightforward song. "If this wins and 'Sun City' doesn't [in the rock categories]," said the *Post*, "we'll know things haven't changed as much as some people have hoped." When Prince prevailed for "Kiss," he became the fourth artist—following Michael Jackson, Donna Summer and Tina Turner—to win awards for both r&b and r&r. "The other three acts all won in r&b first and later in rock," observed *Billboard*. "Prince did it the other way around."

In the jazz lineup, surprises consisted of a victory by the creamy-voiced Diane Schuur, who nabbed her first Grammy for *Timeless*. Benny Goodman died the previous June but scored the first nomination of his career for *Let's Dance* in the big-band competition. The category ended up being claimed by the Tonight Show Band with Doc Severinsen for the group's eponymous LP. "No one hears the band play [on *The Tonight Show Starring Johnny Carson*] for more than 20 seconds at a time," Severinsen said. "This proves we can do it."

When trumpet wunderkind Wynton Marsalis entered the Grammy race with four bids, some critics predicted he'd finally get a public lesson in humility. He did on three of those four accounts but still salvaged a win (best group instrumental prize) for *J Mood*. Marsalis shared one of

his defeats with his saxophonist brother, Branford, when the prize for best instrumental soloist was claimed by three-time past champ Miles Davis for *Tutu*.

Nineteen eighty-five winner Bobby McFerrin turned out to be the star of the jazz prizes this year when he bested Mel Tormé and Joe Williams for the male vocals trophy and then gave a memorable acceptance speech. To win, McFerrin had performed what the *L.A. Herald Examiner* called some "sublime vocalizing" on the score to the celebrated jazz film *'Round Midnight,* starring tenor sax player Dexter Gordon as a character loosely based on jazz greats Bud Powell and Lester Young. To express his thanks at the Grammy ceremony, McFerrin sang what the *Herald Examiner* called "some charming scat doodlings."

Variety reported, "While country nominations reflected the popularity of 'new wave' country artists like Dwight Yoakam and Steve Earle, familiar names won in all categories."

A controversy erupted when Ronnie Milsap repeated his 1985 victory for male vocals—for the same music. Last year he won for the title track to *Lost in the Fifties Tonight;* this year he was hailed for the whole LP. (The single had been released in advance of the album and fell into an earlier Grammy eligibility period.) The victory was startling because the prize was expected to go to one of country music's young lions, Randy Travis.

The female country vocals prize was bestowed on first-time champ Reba McEntire for "Whoever's in New England," her first number-one-ranked single, from her first gold album. The song title refers to the musings of a jealous housewife whose husband takes frequent business trips to Boston.

The biggest winner in the country categories was "Grandpa (Tell Me 'bout the

> Ronnie Milsap repeated his 1985 Grammy victory— for the same music.

Good Old Days)," the Judds' number-one-ranked single that won them the best duo vocals prize for a third year in a row. It also won Best Country Song for tunesmith Jamie O'Hara, who, ironically, never knew his own grandparents. Like Robert Palmer's "Addicted to Love," "Grandpa" came to O'Hara in his sleep. "I woke up one morning and that's the song that came out," he once said. "'Grandpa' was a gift that songwriters get every once in a while if you're putting in your work."

Singer Deniece Williams lost her first Grammy bid in 1984 but now she snagged two golden gramophones in the religious categories, both for tracks from her album *So Glad I Know*. She shared one of the gospel prizes with Sandi Patti, with whom she performed "They Say." Patti reaped an additional Grammy for *Morning Like This*.

The Latin awards were again the target of criticism when *Billboard* blasted the Recording Academy for the failure of El Gran Combo to be nominated, calling the group "the undisputed tropical leader in popularity, record sales and world geographical musical diffusion."

Still, the winners were less controversial than in past years: 1968's Best New Artist José Feliciano reaped the accolade for Best Latin Pop Performance for "Lelolai," a track from *Te Amare*, while the Mexican-American award went to Flaco Jimenez, the Tex-Mex accordionist and songwriter and son of Santiago Jimenez. Recipient of the tropical Latin prize was veteran singer Rubén Blades, who was certainly a tropical talent himself, being of Cuban–St. Lucian descent.

Albert Collins, Robert Cray and Johnny Copeland shared the new prize for Best Traditional Blues Recording, *Showdown!*, a reunion album for the trio. Prior to launching their solo careers, Cray and Copeland had been protégés of Collins, who was known as a "cold blues" singer because he was, in his own words, "like something cold in the ice box."

The new blues prize was a replacement in part for the old award for Best

This year's Grammys "belonged to veterans like Paul Simon and Barbara Streisand," *Variety* noted.

Ethnic or Traditional Folk Recording, which had usually gone to blues artists. Folk music was now given two new honors. Grammy's first Best Traditional Folk Recording was *Riding the Midnight Trail* by flat-picker and three-time past winner Doc Watson. The equivalent kudos for a contemporary work went to an LP tribute to the late folk/country artist Steve Goodman by the likes of John Hartford, Richie Havens and the Nitty Gritty Dirt Band.

There was a tie in the category introduced just last year for polka: *Another Polka Celebration* by Eddie Blazonczyk's Versatones and *I Remember Warsaw* by Jimmy Sturr & His Orchestra. *Grammy Pulse* said the two winners "had no problems about the tie. 'We've been friends for years,' said Sturr. 'People think there's a competition between Eddie and myself, but that's not so.' Sturr said after the Grammy ceremony: 'These two Grammys will bring more unity to the polka field.' "

Bill Cosby once ruled Grammy's comedy field by winning eight awards over the nine years between 1964 and 1972 but thereafter scored none until this year. Now he rebounded with *Those of You with or without Children, You'll Understand*.

As a member of the Police, Sting lost the long-form video award last year to Huey Lewis & the News, but he came back to claim it for *Bring On the Night,* a compilation of excerpts from his similarly named and critically acclaimed "rockumentary" film about his newest band. Dire Straits may have lost its bid for Album of the Year last year for *Brothers in Arms,* but the music now brought the rock group the short-form video prize, beating out works by Paul McCartney and the Pointer Sisters.

Vladimir Horowitz reigned over the classical categories when his *Studio Recordings* reaped Best Classical Album, Best Engineered Recording and the soloist's award, which now combined the two previously bestowed for artists performing with and without orchestral accompaniment.

Over the previous 12 years of his career, the 81-year-old Horowitz spurned recording in a studio in favor of making tapes at home or during public performances. His return caused some awkward problems, however, particularly when his piano was shipped to the studio after suffering what *Gramophone* called "a precarious descent from a second floor window." But the reviewer quickly added: "Let me say at once that the [album's] sound quality could scarcely be bettered."

Studio Recordings includes two sonatas each by Scarlatti and Liszt, a Scriabin étude and additional works by Schubert and Schumann. *Stereo Review* said the outcome "can be described without hyperbole as one of the high points of his recording activity," while *Gramophone* called it "a graphic reminder of the last great believer in the divine right of keyboard kings." Horowitz's producer, Thomas Frost, was voted Classical Producer of the Year.

Losers in the best album competition included cellist Yo-Yo Ma and pianist Emanuel Ax, who nonetheless received the chamber music kudos (repeating their win of last year) for Beethoven's Cello and Piano Sonata No. 4 in C Major. Sir Georg Solti missed out last year but returned to claim the orchestral prize for his Chicago Symphony Orchestra's performance of Liszt's *A Faust Symphony.* Critics hailed it as being superior even to Sir Thomas Beecham's 1959 recording with the Royal Philharmonic Orchestra, which had previously been considered the definitive reading.

James Levine headed up the Chicago Symphony Orchestra and Chorus for the year's Best Choral Performance: Orff's *Carmina Burana.* "As a performance, it is a satisfactory, rather than a memorable version," *Gramophone* wrote. The renowned 70-year old Polish composer Witold Lutoslawski won Best Contemporary Composition for his Symphony No. 3, which he had been commissioned to write by the Chicago Symphony Orchestra and Sir Georg Solti. The Chicagoans performed it for the first time in September 1983; its premiere recording came in 1986 by the Los Angeles Philharmonic Orchestra under the baton of Esa-Pekka Salonen.

In Leonard Bernstein's *Candide* (which he called his "valentine to European music"), the composer lampooned the simpleminded optimism of Voltaire's France by satirizing the sacred operatic conventions that existed then and now. *Candide* bombed when it debuted on Broadway in 1956, mostly due to Lillian Hellman's ponderous libretto, but it was reworked in subsequent years, most successfully so in 1973 when director Hal Prince overhauled it for another New York production. John Mauceri served as the conductor for Prince's revision, but in 1982, he went to work editing the various versions into his own opera house rendition that stressed strong entertainment

> **Leonard Bernstein called *Candide* his "valentine to European music."**

qualities and equally demonstrative vocals. Critics cheered it as the best of all possible recordings and, while *Candide* lost out as a Best Classical Album contender, it won Best Opera Recording.

Kathleen Battle's victory over Marilyn Horne, Luciano Pavarotti, Frederica von Stade and Teresa Stratas for the vocalist's laurels was offset somewhat by the bad reviews she received for her triumphant roundup of Mozart arias. *Fanfare* did say that her singing was "superb" and blamed the "non-electric results of this recital [on André] Previn's lackluster conducting." *Gramophone* referred to her "fluent, silvery instrument" as sounding "rather thin and characterless," adding, "Battle simply doesn't carry the vocal guns or conviction."

When this year's Grammy nominations came out, *Variety* noted, "The academy snubbed such acts as the Bangles, Huey Lewis & the News, Bon Jovi and Lionel Richie despite the fact that each logged a platinum-plus album in 1986."

Reporting on the actual ceremony, *Variety* said, "Grammy Awards, aired by CBS live from the Shrine, were hosted smoothly by comic Billy Crystal and featured 14 performances, including turns by Whitney Houston, Anita Baker, Janet Jackson, Simply Red, Luther Vandross and Paul Simon." Dionne Warwick, Stevie Wonder and Gladys Knight hooked up for a version of "That's What Friends Are For" that the critics called even more soulful than the recording.

The ceremony ended on a touching note—the production of "a particularly impassioned version" of "Stand By Me,"

First-time nominee Diane Schuur garnered the female jazz vocalist award for *Timeless*.

Los Angeles Public Library

said the *Herald Examiner,* that was led by former Drifter Ben E. King and gathered momentum as numerous other artists joined in, at first from backstage and then from the audience. Eventually, more than 150 people swelled the stage, at which point, added the *Post,* "the song seemed to degenerate into 'Don't Stand So Close to Me,' or, in a few instances, 'Don't Stand in Front of Me.' "

The *Herald Examiner* was less cynical: "It seemed as if we were witnessing something a bit more special than a mere star-studded grand finale—that, in fact, we were witnessing an invitation to take part in a heartfelt but risky experiment in fraternity—and with voices so lovely and rhythms so undeniable leading the way, who could resist such a call? With moments like these, clearly the 29th Annual Grammys show set new standards against which its future performances will have to be judged."

• 1986 •

The awards ceremony was broadcast on CBS from the Shrine Auditorium in Los Angeles on February 24, 1987, for the awards eligibility period of October 1, 1985, to September 30, 1986.

ALBUM OF THE YEAR
• *Graceland*, Paul Simon. Warner Brothers.
Back in the High Life, Steve Winwood. Island.

The Broadway Album, Barbra Streisand. Columbia/CBS.
Control, Janet Jackson. A&M.
So, Peter Gabriel. Daniel Lanois, Peter Gabriel, producers. Geffen.

RECORD OF THE YEAR

• "Higher Love," Steve Winwood. Island.
"Addicted to Love," Robert Palmer. Island.
"Greatest Love of All," Whitney Houston. Arista.
"Sledgehammer," Peter Gabriel. Geffen.
"That's What Friends Are For," Dionne Warwick, Elton John, Gladys Knight, Stevie Wonder. Arista.

SONG OF THE YEAR
(Songwriter's Award)

• "That's What Friends Are For," Burt Bacharach, Carole Bayer Sager.
"Addicted to Love," Robert Palmer.
"Graceland," Paul Simon.
"Higher Love," Steve Winwood, Will Jennings.
"Sledgehammer," Peter Gabriel.

BEST NEW ARTIST

• Bruce Hornsby & the Range
Glass Tiger
Nu Shooz
Simply Red
Timbuk 3

BEST POP VOCAL
PERFORMANCE, MALE

• Steve Winwood, "Higher Love." Island.
Peter Cetera, "Glory of Love (Theme from *Karate Kid II*)." Full Moon.
Kenny Loggins, "Danger Zone." Columbia/CBS.
Michael McDonald, "Sweet Freedom (Theme from *Running Scared*)." MCA.
Paul Simon, *Graceland*. Warner Bros.

BEST POP VOCAL
PERFORMANCE, FEMALE

• Barbra Streisand, *The Broadway Album*. Columbia/CBS.

Cyndi Lauper, "True Colors." Portrait/CBS.
Madonna, "Papa Don't Preach." Sire.
Tina Turner, "Typical Male." Capitol.
Dionne Warwick, *Dionne and Friends*. Arista.

BEST POP PERFORMANCE BY A DUO
OR GROUP WITH VOCAL

• Dionne Warwick, Elton John, Gladys Knight & Stevie Wonder, "That's What Friends Are For." Arista.
Peter Cetera, Amy Grant, "The Next Time I Fall." Warner Bros.
Patti LaBelle, Michael McDonald, "On My Own." MCA.
Mike & the Mechanics, "All I Need Is a Miracle." Atlantic.
Simply Red, "Holding Back the Years." Elektra.

BEST POP INSTRUMENTAL
PERFORMANCE (ORCHESTRA,
GROUP OR SOLOIST)

• Harold Faltermeyer, Steve Stevens, "*Top Gun* Anthem," track from *Top Gun* (film soundtrack). Columbia/CBS.
Stanley Clarke, "Overjoyed," track from *Hideaway*. Epic/CBS.
David Foster, *David Foster*. Atlantic.
Genesis, "The Brazilian," track from *Invisible Touch*. Atlantic.
Tonight Show Band with Doc Severinsen, "Johnny's Theme (*The Tonight Show* theme)," track from *The Tonight Show Band with Doc Severinsen*. Amherst.

BEST ROCK VOCAL
PERFORMANCE, MALE

• Robert Palmer, "Addicted to Love." Island.
John Fogerty, *Eye of the Zombie*. Warner Bros.
Peter Gabriel, "Sledgehammer." Geffen.
Billy Idol, "To Be a Lover." Chrysalis.
Eddie Money, "Take Me Home Tonight." Columbia/CBS.

BEST ROCK VOCAL PERFORMANCE, FEMALE

• Tina Turner, "Back Where You Started," track from *Break Every Rule*. Capitol.

Pat Benatar, "Sex As a Weapon." Chrysalis.

Cyndi Lauper, "911," track from *True Colors*. Portrait/CBS.

Stevie Nicks, "Talk to Me." Modern.

Bonnie Raitt, "No Way to Treat a Lady." Warner Bros.

BEST ROCK PERFORMANCE BY A DUO OR GROUP WITH VOCAL

• Eurythmics, "Missionary Man." RCA.

Artists United Against Apartheid, "Sun City." Manhattan.

Fabulous Thunderbirds, "Tuff Enuff." CBS Associated.

Rolling Stones, "Harlem Shuffle." Columbia/CBS.

ZZ Top, *Afterburner*. Warner Bros.

BEST ROCK INSTRUMENTAL PERFORMANCE (ORCHESTRA, GROUP OR SOLOIST)

• Art of Noise Featuring Duane Eddy, "Peter Gunn," track from *In Visible Silence*. China/Chrysalis.

Fabulous Thunderbirds, "Down at Antones," track from *Tuff Enuff*. CBS Associated.

Eric Johnson, "Zap," track from *Tones*. Reprise.

Alan Parsons Project, "Where's the Walrus?" track from *Stereotomy*. Arista.

Yes, "Amazing Grace," track from *90125 Live: The Solos*. Atlantic.

BEST RHYTHM & BLUES SONG
(Songwriter's Award)

• "Sweet Love," Anita Baker, Louis A. Johnson, Gary Bias.

"Give Me the Reason," Luther Vandross, Nat Adderley, Jr.

"Kiss," Prince & the Revolution.

"Living in America," Dan Hartman, Charlie Midnight.

"What Have You Done for Me Lately," James Harris III, Terry Lewis, Janet Jackson.

BEST RHYTHM & BLUES VOCAL PERFORMANCE, MALE

• James Brown, "Living in America." Scotti Brothers/CBS.

Al Jarreau, "Since I Fell for You," track from *Double Vision* (Bob James, David Sanborn). Warner Bros.

Oran "Juice" Jones, "The Rain." Def-Jam/CBS.

Billy Ocean, "Love Zone." Jive/Arista.

Luther Vandross, "Give Me the Reason." Epic/CBS.

BEST RHYTHM & BLUES VOCAL PERFORMANCE, FEMALE

• Anita Baker, *Rapture*. Elektra.

Aretha Franklin, "Jumpin' Jack Flash." Arista.

Janet Jackson, *Control*. A&M.

Chaka Khan, *Destiny*. Warner Bros.

Patti LaBelle, *Winner in You*. MCA.

BEST RHYTHM & BLUES VOCAL PERFORMANCE BY A DUO OR GROUP

• Prince & the Revolution, "Kiss." Paisley Park.

Ashford & Simpson, *Real Love*. Capitol.

Cameo, "Word Up." Atlanta Artists.

Chicago Bears Shufflin' Crew, "The Super Bowl Shuffle." Red Label.

Run D.M.C., *Raising Hell*. Profile.

Sade, *Promise*. Portrait/CBS.

BEST RHYTHM & BLUES VOCAL INSTRUMENTAL PERFORMANCE (ORCHESTRA, GROUP OR SOLOIST)

• Yellowjackets, "And You Know That," track from *Shades*. MCA.

Stanley Clarke, "The Boys of Johnson Street," track from *Hideaway*. Epic/CBS.

Billy Cobham, "Zanzibar Breeze," track from *Power Play*. GRP.

Kenny G., *Duotones*. Arista.

Kashif, "Movie Song," track from *Condition of the Heart*. Arista.

BEST JAZZ VOCAL PERFORMANCE, MALE

- Bobby McFerrin, " 'Round Midnight," track from 'Round Midnight soundtrack. Columbia/CBS.

Grady Tate, "She's out of My Life," track from Go for Whatcha Know. Blue Note.

Mel Tormé, An Elegant Evening. Concord Jazz.

Joe Williams, I Just Want to Sing. Delos International.

Jimmy Witherspoon, Midnight Lady Called the Blues. Muse.

BEST JAZZ VOCAL PERFORMANCE, FEMALE

- Diane Schuur, Timeless. GRP.

Etta James (Etta James, Eddie "Cleanhead" Vinson), Blues in the Night. Fantasy.

Flora Purim, "Esquinas," track from The Magicians, Flora Purim and Airto. Crossover.

Sue Raney, Flight of Fancy. Discovery.

Maxine Sullivan, Uptown. Concord Jazz.

BEST JAZZ VOCAL PERFORMANCE BY A DUO OR GROUP

- 2 + 2 Plus (Clare Fischer & His Latin Jazz Sextet), Free Fall. Discovery.

Jackie Cain, Roy Kral, Bogie. Fantasy.

Four Freshmen, Fresh! Pausa.

L.A. Jazz Choir, From All Sides. Pausa.

Arthur Prysock, Betty Joplin, "Teach Me Tonight," track from A Rockin' Good Way. Milestone.

BEST JAZZ INSTRUMENTAL PERFORMANCE BY A SOLOIST

- Miles Davis, Tutu. Warner Bros.

Eddie Daniels, Breakthrough. GRP.

Dizzy Gillespie, Closer to the Source. Atlantic.

Branford Marsalis, Royal Garden Blues. Columbia/CBS.

Wynton Marsalis, "Insane Asylum," track from J Mood. Columbia/CBS.

BEST JAZZ INSTRUMENTAL PERFORMANCE BY A GROUP

- Wynton Marsalis, J Mood. Columbia/CBS.

Art Blakey & the Jazz Messengers, Art Blakey and the Jazz Messengers Live at Sweet Basil. GNP Crescendo.

Gerry Mulligan, Scott Hamilton, Soft Lights and Sweet Music. Concord Jazz.

Keith Jarrett, Gary Peacock, Jack DeJohnette, Standards Live. ECM.

Teddy Wilson, Benny Carter, Red Norvo, Louis Bellson, Remo Palmier, George Duvivier, Freddie Green, Swing Reunion. Book-of-the-Month.

BEST JAZZ INSTRUMENTAL PERFORMANCE BY A BIG BAND

- Tonight Show Band with Doc Severinsen, The Tonight Show Band with Doc Severinsen. Amherst.

Benny Goodman & His Orchestra, Let's Dance. Music-Masters.

Lionel Hampton & His Orchestra, Sentimental Journey. Atlantic.

Woody Herman & His Big Band, 50th Anniversary Tour. Concord Jazz.

Mel Lewis Orchestra, 20 Years at the Village Vanguard. Atlantic.

BEST JAZZ FUSION PERFORMANCE (VOCAL OR INSTRUMENTAL)

- Bob James, David Sanborn, Double Vision. Warner Bros..

Chick Corea, The Chick Corea Elektric Band. GRP.

Lee Ritenour, Earth Run. GRP.

Clare Fischer & His Latin Jazz Sextet, Free Fall. Discovery.

Lyle Mays, Lyle Mays. Geffen.

BEST COUNTRY SONG
(Songwriter's Award)

- "Grandpa (Tell Me 'bout the Good Old Days)," Jamie O'Hara.

"Daddy's Hands," Holly Dunn.

"Guitar Town," Steve Earle.

"Guitars, Cadillacs," Dwight Yoakam.

"Whoever's in New England," Quentin Powers, Kendall Franceschi.

BEST COUNTRY VOCAL PERFORMANCE, MALE

- Ronnie Milsap, *Lost in the Fifties Tonight*. RCA.
Steve Earle, *Guitar Town*. MCA.
Randy Travis, "Diggin' Up Bones." Warner Bros.
Hank Williams, Jr., "Ain't Misbehavin'." Warner Bros.
Dwight Yoakam, *Guitars, Cadillacs, Etc., Etc.* Reprise.

BEST COUNTRY VOCAL PERFORMANCE, FEMALE

- Reba McEntire, "Whoever's in New England." MCA.
Holly Dunn, "Daddy's Hands." MTM.
Crystal Gayle, "Cry." Warner Bros.
Emmylou Harris, "Today I Started Loving You Again." Warner Bros.
Kathy Mattea, "Love at the Five & Dime." Mercury.

BEST COUNTRY PERFORMANCE BY A DUO OR GROUP WITH VOCAL

- Judds, "Grandpa (Tell Me 'bout the Good Old Days)." RCA.
Alabama, "She and I." RCA.
Everly Brothers, *Born Yesterday*. Mercury.
Gatlin Brothers, "She Used to Be Somebody's Baby." Columbia/CBS.
Carl Perkins, Jerry Lee Lewis, Roy Orbison, Johnny Cash, *Class of '55*. America Record Corp.

BEST COUNTRY INSTRUMENTAL PERFORMANCE (ORCHESTRA, GROUP OR SOLOIST)

- Ricky Skaggs, "Raisin' the Dickens," track from *Love's Gonna Get Ya*. Epic/CBS.
Jerry Douglas, *Under the Wire*. MCA Master Series.
Albert Lee, *Speechless*. MCA Master Series.
New Grass Revival, "Seven by Seven," track from *New Grass Revival*. EMI America.
Mark O'Connor, *Meanings Of*. Warner Bros.

BEST GOSPEL PERFORMANCE, MALE

- Philip Bailey, *Triumph*. Myrrh/Word.
Steve Green, *For God and God Alone*. Sparrow.
Larnelle Harris, *From a Servant's Heart*. Benson.
Michael W. Smith, *The Big Picture*. Reunion.
BeBe Winans, "It's Only Natural," track from *Kaleidoscope* (Keith Thomas). Dayspring/Word.

BEST GOSPEL PERFORMANCE, FEMALE

- Sandi Patti, *Morning Like This*. Word.
Cynthia Clawson, *Immortal*. Dayspring/Word.
Teri DeSario, *Voices in the Wind*. Dayspring/Word.
Sheila Walsh, *Shadowlands*. Myrrh/Word.
Deniece Williams, *So Glad I Know*. Sparrow.

BEST GOSPEL PERFORMANCE BY A DUO, GROUP, CHOIR OR CHORUS

- Sandi Patti, Deniece Williams, "They Say," track from *So Glad I Know*. Sparrow.
CeCe Winans, Carman, "Our Blessed Saviour Has Come," track from *A Long Time Ago . . . in a Land Called Bethlehem*. Benson.
DeGarmo & Key, *Street Light*. Power Disc/Benson.
First Call, *Undivided*. Dayspring/Word.
Petra, *Back to the Street*. Star Song/Word.

BEST SOUL GOSPEL PERFORMANCE, MALE

- Al Green, "Going Away." A&M.
Derrick Brinkley, *Glorious Day*. Tyscot.
Daryl Coley, *Just Daryl*. The First Epistle.
Rodney Friend, *Worthy*. Command.
Howard Smith, *Totally Committed*. Light.

BEST SOUL GOSPEL PERFORMANCE, FEMALE

- Deniece Williams, "I Surrender All," track from *So Glad I Know*. Sparrow.

Shirley Caesar, *Celebration*. Rejoice/Word.
Candi Staton, *Sing a Song*. Beracah.
Tramaine, *The Search Is Over*. A&M.
Albertina Walker, *Spirit*. Rejoice/Word.

BEST SOUL GOSPEL PERFORMANCE BY A DUO, GROUP, CHOIR OR CHORUS

• Winans, *Let My People Go*. Qwest.
James Cleveland & the Southern California Community Choir, *James Cleveland and the Southern California Community Choir*. King James.
Dorothy Norwood, Rev. F. C. Barnes, Rev. Janice Brown, Albertina Walker, Rev. James Cleveland, *Dorothy Norwood and Friends*. AIR.
Albertina Walker, Shirley Caesar, *Jesus Is Mine*. Rejoice/Word.
Winans with Vanessa Bell Armstrong, "Choose Ye," track from *Let My People Go*. Qwest.

BEST TRADITIONAL FOLK RECORDING

• *Riding the Midnight Train*, Doc Watson. Sugar Hill.
Caught in the Act, Queen Ida. GNP/Crescendo.
Hot Steppin' with Rockin' Sidney, Rockin' Sidney. ZBC.
20th Anniversary Concert, New Lost City Ramblers with Elizabeth Cotton, Pete Seeger, Highwood String Band. Flying Fish.
Waitin' for My Ya Ya, Buckwheat Zydecko. Rounder.

BEST CONTEMPORARY FOLK RECORDING

• *Tribute to Steve Goodman*, Arlo Guthrie, John Hartford, Richie Havens, Bonnie Koloc, Nitty Gritty Dirt Band, John Prine, others. Red Pajamas.
German Afternoons, John Prine. Oh Boy.
I'm Alright, Loudon Wainwright III. Rounder.
Last of the True Believers, Nanci Griffith. Philo.

No Easy Walk to Freedom, Peter, Paul & Mary. Gold Castle.

BEST TRADITIONAL BLUES RECORDING

• *Showdown!* Albert Collins, Robert Cray, Johnny Copeland. Alligator.
Jealous, John Lee Hooker. Pausa.
Live! Backstage Access, Willie Dixon. Pausa.
Live from Chicago, Mr. Superharp Himself! James Cotton. Alligator.
Pressure Cooker, Clarence "Gatemouth" Brown. Alligator.

BEST LATIN POP PERFORMANCE

• José Feliciano, "Lelolai," track from *Te Amare*. RCA.
José José, "Pruebame." Ariola.
Pandora, "Como Te Va Mi Amor," track from *Pandora*. Odeon.
Danny Rivera, *Inolvidable Tito . . . a Mi Me Pasa lo Mismo Que a Usted*. DNA/Puerto Rico.
Yuri, "Yo Te Pido Amor," track from *Yo Te Pido Amor*. Odeon.

BEST TROPICAL LATIN PERFORMANCE

• Rubén Blades, *Escenas*. Elektra.
Mario Bauza, Graciela, *Afro-Cuban Jazz*. Caiman.
Willie Colon, *Especial No. 5*. Sonotone.
Celia Cruz, Tito Puente, *Homenaje a Beny Moré, Vol. 3*. Vaya/Musica Latina International.
Willie Rosario, *Nueva Cosecha*. Bronco.

BEST MEXICAN-AMERICAN PERFORMANCE

• Flaco Jiminez, *Ay Te Dejo en San Antonio*. Arhoolie.
Rafael Buendia, *Y . . . Zas!* Ariola.
Steve Jordan, *Turn Me Loose*. RCA.
Los Tigres del Norte, *El Otro México*. Profono International.
Salvador Torres, "Unidos Cantemos." Mas.
Juan Valentin, *Juan Valentin*. Musart.
Los Yonics, "Corazón Vacío." Profono.

BEST REGGAE RECORDING
- *Babylon the Bandit*, Steel Pulse. Elektra.
- *Brutal*, Black Uhuru. RAS.
- "Club Paradise," Jimmy Cliff. Columbia/CBS.
- *Linton Kwesi Johnson in Concert with the Dub Band*, Linton Kwesi Johnson & the Dub Band. Shanachie.
- *Rasta Philosophy*, Itals. Nighthawk.

BEST POLKA RECORDING
(Tie)
- *Another Polka Celebration*, Eddie Blazonczyk's Versatones. Bel Aire.
- *I Remember Warsaw*, Jimmy Sturr & His Orchestra. Starr.
- *America's Favorites*, Frank Yankovic. Smash.
- *By Special Request*, Walter Ostanek (cassette). CBS/Select.
- *Thank You Dear and Give Her Roses*, Hank Haller Ensemble. Haller.

BEST NEW AGE RECORDING
- *Down to the Moon*, Andreas Vollenweider. FM/CBS.
- *Canyon*, Paul Winter. Living Music.
- *Rendezvous*, Jean-Michel Jarre. Polydor-Dreyfus.
- *Windham Hill Records Sampler '86*, various artists. Windham Hill.
- *A Winter's Solstice*, various artists. Windham Hill.

BEST ARRANGEMENT ON AN INSTRUMENTAL
- Patrick Williams, "Suite Memories," track from *Someplace Else*. Soundwings.
- Jorge Calandrelli, "The First Letter," track from *The Color Purple* soundtrack. Qwest.
- Jorge Calandrelli, "Solfeggietto Metamorphosis," track from *Breakthrough*. GRP.
- Bill Meyers, "AM/PM," track from *Images*. Spindletop.
- Don Sebesky, "Cherokee," track from *Moving Lines*. Doctor Jazz.

BEST INSTRUMENTAL ARRANGEMENT ACCOMPANYING VOCAL(S)
- David Foster, "Somewhere," track from *The Broadway Album* (Barbra Streisand). Columbia/CBS.
- Jorge Calandrelli, "Forget the Woman," track from *The Art of Excellence*. Columbia/CBS.
- Clare Fischer, "Free Fall," track from *Free Fall*. Discovery.
- Jeremy Lubbock, "A Time for Love," track from *Timeless*. GRP.
- Rob McConnell, "Duke Ellington Medley," track from *Mel Tormé–Rob McConnell & the Boss Brass*. Concord Jazz.

BEST INSTRUMENTAL COMPOSITION
(Composer's Award)
- *Out of Africa* (film soundtrack), John Barry.
- *Aliens* (film soundtrack), James Horner.
- "Earth Run," track from *Earth Run*, Lee Ritenour, Dave Grusin.
- "Elektric City," track from *The Chick Corea Elektric Band*. Chick Corea.
- "J Mood," track from *J Mood*, Wynton Marsalis.
- "Top Gun Anthem," track from *Top Gun* (film soundtrack), Harold Faltermeyer.
- *Young Sherlock Holmes* (film soundtrack), Bruce Broughton.

BEST MUSICAL CAST SHOW ALBUM
- *Follies in Concert*, Stephen Sondheim, composer and lyricist. RCA.
- *Me and My Girl*, Douglas Furber, R. Butler, lyricists; Nod Gay, composer. Manhattan.
- *The Mystery of Edwin Drood* (Broadway recording), Rupert Holmes, composer and lyricist. Rupert Holmes, producer. Polydor.
- *Song and Dance*, Andrew Lloyd Webber, composer; Don Black, Richard Maltby, Jr., lyricists. RCA.
- *Sweet Charity*, Dorothy Fields, lyricist; Cy Coleman, composer. EMI America.

BEST CLASSICAL ALBUM

- *Horowitz: The Studio Recordings, New York 1985*, Vladimir Horowitz. Deutsche Grammophon.

Beethoven: Cello and Piano Sonata No. 4 in C and Variations, Yo-Yo Ma, Emanuel Ax. CBS Masterworks.

Beethoven: Symphony No. 9 in D Minor, Robert Shaw conducting the Atlanta Symphony Orchestra and Chorus (solos: Benita Valente, Jerry Hadley, Florence Kopleff, John Cheek). Pro Arte.

Bernstein: Candide, John Manuceri conducting the New York City Opera Chorus and Orchestra (solos: Erie Mills, David Eisler, John Lankston, Joyce Castle, Scott Reeve, Jack Harrold, James Billings, Maris Clement). New World.

Copland: Billy the Kid and Rodeo (Complete Ballets), Leonard Slatkin conducting the St. Louis Symphony Orchestra. Angel.

Mendelssohn: Symphonies No. 3 in A Minor ("Scottish") and No. 4 in A ("Italian"), Sir Georg Solti conducting the Chicago Symphony Orchestra. London.

Pleasures of Their Company (Bach, Gounod, Villa-Lobos), Kathleen Battle, Christopher Parkening. Angel.

BEST CLASSICAL ORCHESTRAL RECORDING
(Conductor's Award)

- *Liszt: A Faust Symphony*, Sir Georg Solti conducting the Chicago Symphony Orchestra. London.

Beethoven: Symphony No. 9 in D Minor ("Choral"), Robert Shaw conducting the Atlanta Symphony Chorus and Orchestra. Pro Arte.

Copland: Billy the Kid and Rodeo (Complete Ballets), Leonard Slatkin conducting the St. Louis Symphony Orchestra. Angel.

Respighi: Pines of Rome; Fountains of Rome; Roman Festival, Riccardo Muti conducting the Philadelphia Orchestra. Angel.

Vaughan Williams: Sinfonia Antarctica, Bernard Haitink conducting the London Philharmonic Orchestra. Angel.

BEST OPERA RECORDING

- *Bernstein: Candide*, John Mauceri conducting the New York City Opera Chorus and Orchestra (solos: Erie Mills, Maris Clement, David Eisler, John Lankston, Joyce Castle, Scott Reeve, Jack Harrold, James Billings). New World.

Mozart: The Marriage of Figaro, Sir Neville Marriner conducting the Academy of St. Martin-in-the-Fields (solos: Barbara Hendricks, Ruggero Raimondi, Lucia Popp, Agnes Baltsa, Robert Lloyd, Felicity Palmer, Aldo Baldin). Phillips Classics.

Verdi: Don Carlos, Claudio Abbado conducting La Scala Opera Chorus and Orchestra (solos: Placido Domingo, Katia Ricciarelli, Lucia Valentini-Terrani, Ruggero Raimondi, Nicolai Ghiaurov). Deutsche Grammophon.

Verdi: Otello, Lorin Maazel conducting the Orchestra e Coro del Teatro alla Scala (solos: Placido Domingo, Katia Ricciarelli, Justino Diaz). Angel.

Verdi: Un Ballo in Maschera, Sir Georg Solti conducting the National Philharmonic Orchestra (solos: Luciano Pavarotti, Margaret Price, Renato Bruson, Kathleen Battle, Christa Ludwig). London.

BEST CHAMBER MUSIC PERFORMANCE

- Yo-Yo Ma, Emanuel Ax, *Beethoven: Cello and Piano Sonata No. 4 in C and Variations*. CBS Masterworks.

Benny Goodman, Berkshire String Quartet, Fritz Maag, Leon Pammers, *Benny Goodman: Private Collection*. Musicmasters.

Lynn Harrell, Vladimir Ashkenazy, *Rachmaninov: Cello and Piano Sonata*. London.

Members of the Chicago Symphony winds, vocalists, *Mozart: Music for*

Basset Horns (Divertimenti, Notturni, Adagios). CBS Masterworks.
Itzhak Perlman, Vladimir Ashkenazy, *Brahms: Violin and Piano Sonatas No. 1 in G, No. 2 in A and No. 3 in D Minor; Hungarian Dances.* Angel.

BEST CLASSICAL PERFORMANCE, INSTRUMENTAL SOLOIST(S) (WITH OR WITHOUT ORCHESTRA)

• Vladimir Horowitz, *Horowitz: The Studio Recordings, New York 1985.* Deutsche Grammophon.
Claudio Arrau (Davis conducting the Dresden State Orchestra), *Beethoven: Piano Concerto No. 5 in E Flat ("Emperor").* Philips Classics.
Dale Clevenger (Abbado conducting the Chicago Symphony), *Mozart: Horn Concertos.* Deutsche Grammophon.
Adolph Herseth (Abbado conducting the Chicago Symphony), *Haydn: Trumpet Concerto in E Flat.* Deutsche Grammophon.
Wynton Marsalis (Salonen conducting the Philharmonia Orchestra), *Tomasi: Concerto for Trumpet and Orchestra; Jolivet: Concerto No. 2 for Trumpet; Concertino for Trumpet, String Orchestra and Piano.* CBS Masterworks.
Andras Schiff, *Bach: The Well-Tempered Clavier, Book I.* London.

BEST CHORAL PERFORMANCE (OTHER THAN OPERA)

• James Levine conducting the Chicago Symphony Chorus and Orchestra; Margaret Hillis, choral director, *Orff: Carmina Burana.* Deutsche Grammophon.
John Eliot Gardiner conducting the Monteverdi Choir and English Baroque Soloists, *Bach: Mass in B Minor.* Archiv.
Herbert von Karajan conducting the Vienna Singverein and Wiener Philharmoniker; Heimuth Froschauer, chorus master, *Beethoven: Missa Solemnis.* Deutsche Grammophon.

Riccardo Muti conducting the Westminster Choir and Philadelphia Orchestra; Joseph Flummerfelt, choral director, *Berlioz: Roméo et Juliette.* Angel.
Robert Shaw conducting the Atlanta Symphony Chorus and Orchestra, *Choral Masterpieces.* Telarc.

BEST CLASSICAL PERFORMANCE, VOCAL SOLOIST

• Kathleen Battle (Previn conducting the Royal Philharmonic Orchestra), *Kathleen Battle Sings Mozart.* Angel.
Marilyn Horne (Davis conducting the English Chamber Orchestra), *Beautiful Dreamer (The Great American Songbook).* London.
Luciano Pavarotti (Chiaramello conducting the Orchestra del Teatro Communale di Bologna), *Passione Pavarotti (Favorite Neapolitan Love Songs).* London.
Frederica von Stade (de Almeida conducting the Royal Philharmonic Orchestra), *Canteloube: Chants d'Auvergne, Vol. 2; Triptyque.* CBS Masterworks.
Teresa Stratas (Schwarz conducting the Chamber Symphony), *Stratas Sings Weill.* Nonesuch.

BEST CONTEMPORARY COMPOSITION
(Composer's Award)

• Symphony No. 3, Witold Lutoslawski.
Septet, Chick Corea.
Company, Philip Glass.
Mountain Songs (A Cycle of American Folk Music), Robert Beaser.
Symphony No. 1, Ellen Taafe Zwilich.

BEST ENGINEERED RECORDING, CLASSICAL

• Paul Goodman, *Horowitz: The Studio Recordings, New York 1985,* Vladimir Horowitz. Deutsche Grammophon.
Marc Aubort, *Copland: Billy the Kid and Rodeo (Complete Ballets)*

(Slatkin conducting the St. Louis Symphony Orchestra). Angel.

Paul Goodman, *Bernstein: Candide* (Mauceri conducting the New York City Opera Chorus and Orchestra). New World.

James Lock, *Liszt: A Faust Symphony* (Solti conducting the Chicago Symphony). London.

Michael Sheady, *Respighi: The Pines of Rome, The Fountains of Rome, Roman Festivals* (Muti conducting the Philadelphia Orchestra). Angel.

CLASSICAL PRODUCER OF THE YEAR
• Thomas Frost
Marc Aubort, Joanna Nickrenz
Steven Epstein
Jay David Saks
Robert Woods

BEST COMEDY RECORDING
• *Those of You with or without Children, You'll Understand*, Bill Cosby. Geffen.
Bob and Ray: A Night of Two Stars Recorded Live at Carnegie Hall, Bob Elliott, Ray Goulding. Radioart.
I Have a Pony, Steven Wright. Warner Bros.
Mud Will Be Flung Tonight! Bette Midler. Atlantic.
Playin' with Your Head, George Carlin. Eardrum.
"Twist and Shout," Rodney Dangerfield, track from *Back to School* (film soundtrack). MCA.

BEST SPOKEN WORD OR NONMUSICAL RECORDING
• *Interviews from the Class of '55, Recording Sessions*, Carl Perkins, Jerry Lee Lewis, Roy Orbison, Johnny Cash, Sam Phillips, Rick Nelson, Chips Moman. America Record.
Gulliver, Sir John Gielgud. Soundwings.
Hardheaded Boys, Bill Cosby. Nicetown.
Interview with the Vampire, F. Murray Abraham. Random House Audiobooks.

The Stories of Ray Bradbury, Ray Bradbury. Random House Audiobooks.

BEST RECORDING FOR CHILDREN
• *The Alphabet*, Sesame Street Muppets. Golden Books.
A Child's Gift of Lullabyes, Tanya Goodman. JABA.
"Itsy Bitsy Spider," Carly Simon. Arista.
A Light in the Attic, Shel Silverstein. Columbia/CBS.
One-Minute Bedtime Stories, Shari Lewis. Caedmon.

BEST ENGINEERED RECORDING (OTHER THAN CLASSICAL)
• Tom Lord Alge, Jason Corsaro, *Back in the High Life* (Steve Winwood). Island.
Humberto Gatica, *David Foster* (David Foster). Atlantic.
Mike Shipley, *Dog Eat Dog* (Joni Mitchell). Geffen.
Don Murray, *GRP Live in Session* (various artists). GRP.
Jason Corsaro, Eric "ET" Thorngren, *Riptide* (Robert Palmer). Island.

BEST ALBUM PACKAGE
(Art Director's Award)
• *Tutu*, Eiko Ishioka. Warner Bros.
Songs Unspoken, Buddy Jackson. Meadowlark.
Stereotomy, Andrew Ellis, Colin Chambers. Arista.
True Stories, Michael Hodgson, Jeffrey Kent Ayeroff. Sire.
The Voice: The Columbia Years 1943–1952 (Frank Sinatra), John Berg. Columbia/CBS.

BEST ALBUM NOTES
(Annotator's Award)
• Gary Giddins, Wilfred Sheed, Jonathan Schwartz, Murray Kempton, Andrew Sarris, Cameron Crowe, *Biograph*. Columbia/CBS.
Richard Freed, Peter Eliot Stone, *Virtuosi*. Smithsonian.

David Hall, John Stratton, Tom Owen, Robert Tuggle, David Hamilton, *The Mapleson Cylinders*. Rodgers & Hammerstein Archives.

Stephen Holden, Frank Conroy, *The Voice: The Columbia Years 1943–1952* (Frank Sinatra). Columbia/ CBS.

Lenny Kaye, *Elektrock the Sixties*. Elektra.

BEST HISTORICAL ALBUM

• *Atlantic Rhythm and Blues 1947–1974, Vols. 1–7*, various artists. Atlantic.

Biograph, Bob Dylan. Columbia/CBS.

The Complete Keynote Collection (334 jazz performances from the 1940s). Keynote.

The Mapleson Cylinders, various Metropolitan Opera artists. Rodgers & Hammerstein Archives.

The Voice: The Columbia Years 1943–1952, Frank Sinatra. Columbia/CBS.

PRODUCER OF THE YEAR (OTHER THAN CLASSICAL)

• Jimmy Jam, Terry Lewis
David Foster
Michael Omartian
Paul Simon
Russ Titelman, Steve Winwood

BEST MUSIC VIDEO, SHORT FORM

• *Dire Straits Brothers in Arms*, Dire Straits. Various directors. Warner Reprise Video.

Brother Where You Bound, Supertramp. Rene Daalder, director. A&M Video.

Runaway, Louis Cardenas. Cayce B. Redding, director. Allied Artists.

Rupert and the Frog Song, Paul McCartney. Various directors. Pioneer Arists.

So Excited, Pointer Sisters. Richard Perry, director. RCA/Columbia Pictures Home Video.

BEST MUSIC VIDEO, LONG FORM

• *Bring On the Night*, Sting. Michael Apted, director. Karl-Lorimar Home Video.

Frank Sinatra: Portrait of an Album, Frank Sinatra. Emil G. Davidson, director. MGM/UA Home Video.

90125 Live, Yes. Steven Soderbergh, director. Atlantic Video.

Pete Townshend: White City, The Music Movie, Pete Townshend. Richard Lowenstein, director. Vestron Music Video.

Sun City, Artists United Against Apartheid. Godley & Creme, Hart Perry, Jonathan Demme, directors. Karl-Lorimar Home Video.

• 1987 •
"A Night Loaded with Shockers"

Just three years after Michael Jackson made Grammy history by nabbing the most awards in a single year (eight, seven of them for *Thriller*), he was back with five bids for his megahit *Bad*. Jackson faced formidable foes in his latest Album of the Year showdown: Prince and Whitney Houston were both overdue and all three contenders had to take on the fiesty Irish pub band U2 that had music pundits drunk with praise. When *Bad* turned out to have *really* bad luck with Grammy voters—winning only an engineering prize, and nothing for Jackson—one press account called the snub "the biggest surprise of the night."

And that was saying something, considering that *Variety* called it "a night loaded with shockers."

The leading jaw-dropper was in the Record of the Year race, which included Suzanne Vega ("Luka"), Los Lobos ("La Bamba," their cover of the Richie Valens song), U2 ("I Still Haven't Found What I'm Looking For") and Steve Winwood and Paul Simon with nominations that looked like they had gone astray from last year. Winwood's "Back in the High Life Again" was the title track from the same album that featured his 1986 Record of the Year winner, "Higher Love." "Graceland" was from Simon's 1986 Album of the Year winner of the same name. Since both songs were released late as singles, they fell into this year's eligibility period and now competed for best record even though they were considered old news. *Billboard* cheered the progressive lineup: "This is the first year that all five of the acts nominated in the Record of the Year category have rock credentials." U2 was favored.

"If one name belongs at the head of the latest Grammy class, it has to be U2," *Variety* reported when the nominations were announced.

Vega was considered the dark horse to watch.

Then came what *Variety* called the night's chief "jolt." The winner: "Graceland," which gave Simon the most triumphs for best record (three), following his previous victories in 1968 for "Mrs. Robinson" and 1970 for "Bridge Over Troubled Water," both with ex-partner Art Garfunkel. The reaction to the success of "Graceland" was hardly jubilant, however. Calling the result "a major surprise," the *Washington Post* added, "Though widely admired as an album cut, the single never got off the ground. It peaked at No. 81 on the Hot 100, marking the first time that a Record of the Year winner has failed to crack the Top 40. Since Simon was in Brazil, his absence and the crowd's tepid response to the award sounded a disconcertingly sour note."

The fact that U2 was favored to take the prize was strange, considering that foreigners seldom did well in the top award categories. Nearly 90 percent of the past winners of Record, Song and Album of the Year had been Americans.

The sole exceptions over 30 years of Grammy history were the Beatles, Bee Gees, Sting, Phil Collins, João Gilberto and Domenico Modugno.

When this year's nominations were announced, *Variety* singled out the Irish rockers as likely Grammy favorites this year, even though they were not the sole front-runner, having tied Michael Jackson and Emmylou Harris for the most bids (four). "If one name belongs at the head of the latest Grammy class, it has to be U2, the socially conscious, spiritually tinged rockers with the surging, yearning sound who broke into the commercial mainstream last year with *The Joshua Tree*," *Variety* said. The album was named after the California desert town where 1970s country rocker Gram Parsons died. The actual gnarled tree, like its biblical namesake hero, is reputed to point the way to the Promised Land. The album received passionate critical praise and sold 4.5 million copies as of Grammy night.

> "My nomination must have been a fluke," Frank Zappa said.

Early on during the ceremony, the news that the band won the award for rock vocals was met with thunderous applause. By evening's end, they would also shake up the Grammy's once stodgy image by nabbing the trophy for Album of the Year.

U2 member the Edge (guitarist David Evans) got solemn as he accepted the first honor. The *Washington Post* noted that he thanked "Bishop Tutu, Martin Luther King and the alternative rock programming of college radio where U2 first received major airplay." The newspaper was only giving its readers a bit of Evans's "bit of a list." He also thanked, among others, Bob Dylan, Walt Disney, John the Baptist, Jimi Hendrix, Dr. Ruth Westheimer, Morris the Cat, Flannery O'Connor, Batman and Robin, "sumo wrestlers throughout the world, and, of course, Ronald Reagan."

"We set out to make music—soul music," Bono (vocalist Paul Hewson) added. "Soul music is not about being black or white or whether you use a drum machine. It's a decision to reveal and not conceal." He also made reference to the band's reputation for being politically outspoken, at first with a joke: "It really is hard to carry the weight of the world on your shoulders . . . [saving] the whales . . . organizing summit meetings between world leaders, but we enjoy our work." He then turned politically relevant: "It's hard, however, when 50 million people are watching not to take the opportunity to talk about things like South Africa, what's happening there."

U2 was also nominated for Song of the Year but came up against another one of this year's shockers. "Also startling," said *Variety,* "was presentation of Song of the Year honors to 'Somewhere Out There,' " a tune from the animated film *An American Tail* about 19th-century Russian mice immigrating to the United States. "Somewhere" earned prizes for first-time-winning songwriters James Horner, Barry Mann and Cynthia Weil, two of whom (Mann and Weil) had been part, as *Song Talk* noted, "of the original New York Brill Building school of songwriting from the 1950s." The tune had recently lost its bid for the Oscars' Best Song award to "Take My Breath Away" from *Top Gun,* but made up for it with the additional Grammy for Best Song Written Specifically for a Motion Picture or TV. The *Washington Post* observed a lack of enthusiasm over its chief victory as Song of the Year, though: "It didn't seem to be a popular choice with the crowd, which greeted the announcement with but a smattering of polite applause."

The actual Grammy Awards ceremony had its share of surprises, too, when Little Richard joined Buster Poindexter as a presenter of the year's Best New Artist prize and sparked the "most spontaneous and electric moment of the night," according to *Variety*. After he opened the envelope and saw the winner's name, Little Richard delayed the news to tease the audience, saying, "And the winner is . . . me!" He then launched into a tirade that was part playful and part serious, shouting at the N.A.R.A.S. voters, "I have never received nuthin'! You never gave me no Grammys and I've been singing for years! I am the *architect* of rock & roll! I am the *originator*!" Instead of a statuette, the Grammy crowd gave him a standing ovation and roared its approval. Backstage later, Little Richard told reporters, "I am not bitter, but I would like to have one to look at."

Variety added, "Actual winner of the new artist award was Jody Watley," the former *Soul Train* dancer who was also the vocalist for Shalamar from 1977 to 1984 and now had such solo hits as "Looking for a New Love," which landed at number 20 in 1987's Hot 100. When she accepted the award, The *Washington Post* noted that she "thanked God after her label MCA and her manager, but before her video director and her attorney."

Album of the Year loser Whitney Houston thanked "Almighty God" first of all when she accepted the trophy for best pop vocals for her fourth number-one single, "I Wanna Dance with Somebody (Who Loves Me)." She then mentioned her record company and its founder, Clive Davis. "I love you, Clive!" she cried. "I love you, Arista!" Backstage, she made a sly reference to her current hit single when she told reporters, "I can't tell you how I feel. It's *so emotional!*" Her producer, Narada Michael Walden, took the prize for Producer of the Year. Walden was such a popular choice that rival contender Quincy Jones (nominated for Jackson's *Bad*) told Walden that he'd voted for him, too.

Clips from Sting's critically acclaimed "rockumentary" *Bring On the Night* won a video award last year. Now the album release earned him the trophy for male pop vocals, although he was not present at the ceremony to accept it.

Winners of the kudos for group singing

Bruce Springsteen's *Tunnel of Love* failed to snag a nomination for best album, but it won the rock vocalist's award for "the Boss" for a second time.

were on hand, however: former Righteous Brother Bill Medley and Jennifer Warnes for the Oscar-winning song of 1987 "(I've Had) The Time of My Life," from the film *Dirty Dancing*, about a spoiled teenager who falls in love with a dancer while at a summer resort in the 1960s.

Warnes won this same Grammy in 1982 for her duet with Joe Cocker in the Oscar-winning "Up Where We Belong," which was used in the film *An Officer and a Gentleman*. *Grammy Pulse* reminded its readers: "Bill Medley was nominated (his only one until this year) for a Grammy Award in 1964 [Best Rock & Roll Recording]. Then he was one-half of the Righteous Brothers and their song was 'You've Lost That Lovin' Feeling' (written incidentally by Barry Mann and Cynthia Weil)," authors of Song of the Year "Somewhere

Out There." When accepting his statuette, Medley thanked God, too, "for 26 wonderful years." Backstage, he told reporters: "It's been a long way back for me and I'm grateful. I had a lot of voice problems for about 10 years starting in the 1970s that kept me out of the business. Now I'd like to get back and do some rock & roll, some rhythm & blues . . . jump back in the fast lane and get to work, pay the rent."

Springsteen fans were upset that his *Tunnel of Love* wasn't up for 1987's Album of the Year, but the Boss nonetheless snagged an impressive four nominations. When he ended up with one award, for best rock vocal for *Tunnel*, he became the first male artist to win twice in the rock categories since they were introduced in 1979. The categories for male and female rock vocals were combined this year because N.A.R.A.S. said there weren't enough female rockers to merit a separate competition.

One of Springsteen's three losing bids was for Best Rock Instrumental Performance, which was claimed by an electric rocker who loved to shock his fans with outrageous titles like "Why Does It Hurt When I Pee?" Frank Zappa's victorious work was *Jazz from Hell,* which he discussed with The *Cleveland Plain Dealer* one week before the Grammycast: "My nomination must have been an accident. Either that or a lot of people have a perverse sense of humor. I'm convinced that nobody ever heard [it]. I have no ambiguous feelings about the Grammys at all. I know they're fake. I find it difficult to believe that Whitney Houston is the answer to all of America's music needs."

Another veteran music great won his first Grammy when Smokey Robinson nabbed an r&b performance prize, thereby making up for having been overlooked— along with all other Motown artists except the Temptations—by N.A.R.A.S. voters throughout the 1960s when he first gained fame with the Miracles. Robinson struck out on a solo career in 1972. He often wrote his own material, including the 1970 classic hit "Tears of a Clown," and

was once called the best living poet in America by Bob Dylan. Interestingly, Robinson now finally earned a Grammy for a single he didn't compose, "Just to See Her," a losing nominee for Best Rhythm & Blues Song written by Jimmy George and Lou Pardini. The victorious r&b song turned out to be "Lean on Me" by first-time Grammy winner Bill Withers—15 years after the tune was a hit. (The song qualified for an award this year since it failed to be nominated for any in the past and there was a new recording this year, performed by Club Nouveau.)

Aretha Franklin set a new Grammy record by becoming the female artist with the most Grammys (surpassing Leontyne Price's tally of 13) when she picked up 2 more for her album *Aretha,* bringing her career tally to 14. It was the 11th time she won the female r&b slot, and a track she shared with George Michael, "I Knew You Were Waiting (for Me)," earned them both the award for group vocals. Michael had had the number-one song in 1985's Hot 100 ("Careless Whisper") and again in 1987 ("Faith"), but his soul credits were dubious prior to his successful matchup with Lady Soul. He said in a statement issued after the Grammycast: "Winning the r&b category with Aretha validates the tremendous influence r&b music has had on my music, songwriting and creative process. Not bad for a Brit with soul."

Alto sax player David Sanborn had won three jazz Grammys in the past, but, like George Michael, also insisted that his music was heavily tinged with r&b. The proof came when he scored the r&b instrumental accolade for "Chicago Song."

Lots of jazz artists competed outside the jazz awards this year. Larry Carlton, noted *Billboard,* "is almost certainly the first musician in Grammy history to cop nominations in the jazz, fusion and pop-instrumental categories in one year." (He ended up with the pop instrumental kudos for "Minute by Minute," topping fellow jazzmen Dave Grusin and Chick Corea.) The fusion award went to a three-time past winner, the Pat Metheny Group, for *Still Life (Talking)*, beating both Sanborn and Carlton. Trumpeter Wynton Marsalis came back, too, when *Marsalis Standard Time—Vol. 1* brought him his eighth award in just five years.

Diane Schuur nabbed the female vocals award for a second consecutive year when she won for an album that had topped the jazz chart for nearly four months prior to Grammy night—*Diane Schuur and the Count Basie Orchestra,* also winner of a statuette for its arrangements. Mercer Ellington and the Duke Ellington Orchestra seized the big-band laurels for *Digital Duke.* Mercer had been the band's leader since his father's death in 1974.

At last year's Grammys, Bobby McFerrin won the male vocals award for his contribution to the film *'Round Midnight.* A follow-up recording, *The Other Side of 'Round Midnight,* again rewarded McFerrin with the same jazz prize, while Dexter Gordon himself was also honored with the instrumental soloist trophy.

> **"You never gave me no Grammys!"** fumed Little Richard.

The album became the most lauded musical work of the year when it won a third award, which went to Gordon, Herbie Hancock, Wayne Shorter, Ron Carter and Billy Higgins as composers. *Billboard* objected to it early on when the full list of 1987's contenders was first announced: "The oddest nomination—possibly of all time—for Best Instrumental Composition is 'Call Sheet Blues' from the *The Other Side of 'Round Midnight* soundtrack, which is not really a composition at all, but a spontaneously improvised blues [session]." *'Round Midnight* was the title of an original music work by Thelonious Monk, who died in 1982. Monk had recorded exclusively on the Riverside label between 1955 and 1961. The complete set of his Riverside recordings was voted Grammy's Best Historical Album and also won Best Album Notes.

Reed player, composer and teacher Yusef Lateef turned 76 this year and finally won his first Grammy. *Yusef Lateef's Little Symphony* was named Best New Age Performance instead of being honored in a jazz slot, where some critics said it belonged. The nonjazz classification made some sense: Lateef's work was infused with strong Middle Eastern influences and he always objected to being labeled a jazzman despite his long career association with the genre and its greats, including Dizzy Gillespie and Cannonball Adderley. Accepting his prize, the veteran artist noted, "I've been at this 50 years this month!"

K. T. Oslin was described as a "veteran newcomer" by the *Washington Post* when the 45-year-old singer snagged the country vocals accolade for the title track to her debut album, *'80s Ladies.* (The LP features three types of women for the decade: "the smart one, the pretty one and the borderline fool," in the words of one RCA official.) Prior to her solo LP, Oslin had worked on the periphery of the limelight doing backup vocals and other side work. Accepting her first Grammy, she invoked God and called herself "a heathen," saying, "He didn't have a lot of time to personally supervise me."

Though defeated last year, Randy Travis came back to claim the male singing laurels for *Always and Forever,* his megahit album that spent a remarkable 43 weeks at the top of the country LP charts and then became the first country album to crack the top 20 of the pop rankings since Kenny Rogers's *Eyes That See in the Dark* did so in 1983. Accepting his prize, the onetime Nashville cook and dishwasher said, "The Grammy was the farthest thing from my mind when I got into the music business. I never thought about winning one."

Travis was the artist who sang this year's Best Country Song, which was so popular that it was also hailed as Single of the Year by the Country Music Association and the Academy of Country Music: "Forever and Ever, Amen," by Paul Overstreet and Don Schlitz. Schlitz had won the same songwriting Grammy nine years earlier when he scripted "The Gambler," which became a standard for Kenny Rogers. Only two other songwriters had won the category twice: Roger Miller and Billy Sherrill.

Kenny Rogers hadn't won a Grammy himself in eight years, but now he rallied to score a victory he shared with Ronnie Milsap in the new category of Best Country Vocal Performance Duet, for "Make No Mistake, She's Mine." The tune was written by 1981 Record of the Year winner Kim Carnes ("Bette Davis Eyes"; Carnes and Rogers first worked together when they were both members of the New Christy Minstrels), who originally used "he's" instead of "she's" when she and Barbra Streisand recorded the original version in 1985. Soon thereafter, Rogers was touring with Milsap and needed a song they could sing together, so he picked "Mistake" and cleared the gender switch with Carnes.

"To no one's surprise, long-time-getting-around-to-that-project and longer-time friends Dolly Parton, Linda Ronstadt and Emmylou Harris took the group vocal Grammy for *Trio*," reported the *Washington Post*, noting that the LP "also crossed over into the Album of the Year category." The *L.A. Times* described *Trio* as "a warm and endearing collection of country-flavored tunes."

Asleep at the Wheel had been asleep at the Grammys after 1978 when they last won the same award they took this year for "String of Pars" (best country instrumental). "It feels great. It feels amazing," band member Ray Benson said. "It's like you've been down 10 to nothing in the ninth inning—and winning. When we won our first Grammy [in 1978 for 'One O'Clock Jump'], we were working in a bar in Texas and hadn't got paid for the evening. Then the news came over the

radio that we'd won. It's sometimes difficult keeping a band together. We are the Grateful Dead of country music."

The Grammys for religious performances went to a number of past winners, including Al Green ("Everything's Gonna Be Alright") and Larnelle Harris (*The Father Hath Provided*). Last year's double winner Deniece Williams returned for one more for "I Believe in You." Newcomers included southern rocker Melon LeFevre and Broken Heart for *Crack the Sky*.

Winans siblings scored two victories, including the group soul gospel prize for the single "Ain't No Need to Worry," which was overseen by Grammy's Producer of the Year, Narada Michael Walden, and sung by the Winans along with Anita Baker. "They worked side by side kicking each other and just pushing it and made it happen," Walden once said about their collaboration. When sister CeCe Winans garnered the award for female soul gospel vocals, she said at the Grammy ceremony, "Thank you, Jesus, number one. He is wonderful. He is my life."

"First of all, I thank God and then Paul Simon," said Joseph Shalalala, founder of the black South African a cappella group Ladysmith Black Mambazo, when he accepted the statuette for Best Traditional Folk Recording *Shaka Zulu*. Simon showcased the group on *Graceland* and produced *Shaka Zulu*.

Folk/country singer and guitarist Steve Goodman died of leukemia in 1984 (the same year he won Best Country Song for "City of New Orleans"), leaving behind *Unfinished Business*, which garnered Best Contemporary Folk Recording. New Orleans music guru Professor Longhair passed away in 1980 but now won the traditional blues prize for *Houseparty New Orleans Style*.

A third winner was honored posthumously when Peter Tosh's *No Nuclear War* was named Best Reggae Recording. Whenever Tosh performed in a traditional mode, critics cheered the music's adherence to classic reggae sound, but he was also often applauded for experimenting with daring fusion elements like those included on his triumphant LP.

Robert Cray shared in the traditional blues award last year but now picked up the equivalent trophy for contemporary recordings alone for *Strong Persuader*. Jimmy Sturr & His Orchestra also tied for a Grammy last year but claimed the whole Best Polka Recording trophy by themselves for *A Polka Just for Me*. "This is our 62nd album," Sturr said upon accepting the honor. "We started recording in Nashville 10 years ago. Before that we worked in New York and there's no question about it. Nashville helped our sound."

The Spanish Sinatra, Julio Iglesias, had gained such an enormous worldwide following as of 1987 that he was listed in *The Guinness Book of World Records* as being the world's most popular recording artist for selling 100 million copies of 60 albums in five languages. Iglesias proved popular with N.A.R.A.S. voters, too, when he picked up a Grammy for Best Latin Pop Performance (*Un Hombre Solo*). Los Tigres del Norte snared the Mexican-American laurels for *Gracias! América sin Fronteras,* while five-time past winner Eddie Palmieri was hailed for Best Tropical Latin Performance (*La Verdad—The Truth*).

When the original Broadway version of *Les Misérables* was voted Best Musical Cast Show Album, it was considered surprising for more than just the fact that critics had preferred a recording of the earlier London production. Curiously, it beat odds-on favorite *The Phantom of the Opera* by Andrew Lloyd Webber, who had won four previous Grammys. Also shocking was that 15-time past champ John Williams lost the film score laurels, along with fellow Grammy veteran Henry Mancini, to Ennio Morricone for his music to director Brian De Palma's film adaptation of the popular 1960s TV series *The Untouchables*.

Garrison Keillor had established himself as a superstar on the radio for spinning engaging yarns about the sleepy but some-

When Vladimir Horowitz won best classical disc for his Moscow recordings, "he simply smiled and carried [the Grammy] away, saying nothing."

Deutsche Grammophon

times scandalous goings-on in the fictitious town of Lake Wobegon, Minnesota. Keillor had recently canceled the show after 13 years on the air, but when excerpts were collected onto a disc, *Lake Wobegon Days* was voted best spoken word recording.

Winner of 1979's Best Comedy Recording (*Reality . . . What a Concept*) Robin Williams made a comeback with *A Night at the Met*. But Williams wasn't on hand to accept the statuette himself, so it was claimed for him by low-key comedian Steven Wright, who told the Grammy audience, "He couldn't be here, so we'll go look for him."

For the second year in a row, a recording by Vladimir Horowitz won both Best Classical Album and the laurels for best instrumental soloist without orchestra. The pianist's latest victories were for *Horowitz in Moscow,* a historic recording of the virtuoso's triumphant return to the land of his birth after an absence of more than 60 years. "He was also given a President's Special Merit Award from the Academy," the *Washington Post* noted. "Horowitz looked somewhat dazed by his gaudy surroundings, saying in his still-thick Russian accent, 'Thank you, thank you very much. I am so very happy that classical music still has an appreciation.' When he won the album award, he simply smiled and carried it away, saying nothing."

Horowitz's double victory brought his Grammy total to 22, a career tally second only to that of Sir Georg Solti, whose number of statuettes increased to 26 this year when *Beethoven: Symphony No. 9 in D Minor* was hailed as Best Orchestral Recording. Solti and the Chicago Symphony gave the classic a slower-than-usual reading, which the critics applauded for its qualities of spaciousness.

Recordings taped over a five-year period of Beethoven's complete piano trios earned Itzhak Perlman, Lynn Harrell and Vladimir Ashkenazy the chamber music prize. Perlman claimed a second Grammy when his *Mozart: Violin Concertos Nos. 2 and 4 in D* brought him the soloist award for orchestral accompaniment.

At the end of World War II, conductor Robert Shaw commissioned Paul Hindemith to compose a requiem for those who had died during the conflict. Taking his title from Walt Whitman's classic poem memorializing the slain Abraham Lincoln, Hindemith responded with *When Lilacs Last in the Dooryard Bloom'd (A Requiem for Those We Loved)*, a performance of which earned Shaw and his Altanta Symphony Orchestra and Chorus the Grammy for Best Choral Performance.

Kathleen Battle led the classical Grammys this year with five nominations. She ended up with two awards when Strauss's *Ariadne auf Naxos* was hailed as Best Opera Recording (Battle gave an "excellent" performance as Zerbinetta, said the critics) and the soloist vocal kudos for her *Salzburg Recital*.

The year's Best Contemporary Composition was Cello Concerto No. 2 by Polish composer Krzysztof Penderecki, who had recently "returned to melody," as he once put it, describing his break with the more avant-garde experimentations of his earlier years.

The Grammys returned to New York City after a six-year absence for its 30th annual ceremony, which was held at Radio City Music Hall. Once again the Big Apple welcomed the gala with a warm reception that included a party for the nominees at the mayor's Gracie Mansion. Also, noted the *New York Times,* "During the broadcast, the Spectacolor computerized billboard in Times Square flashed award winners' names moments after the on-stage announcements. Police officers ringed the Music Hall as a red carpet was rolled up the Avenue of the Americas."

The CBS broadcast "surged to the best rating for a Grammycast since 1985," *Variety* reported, citing its score of a 21.3 rating/33 share, which was a hike of 16 percent over last year's viewership. "For just the second time in seven years, the Grammys have topped the American Music Awards broadcast of the same year." This year's American Music Awards had its ratings spoiled by the preemption of President Ronald Reagan's State of the Union speech.

• 1987 •

The awards ceremony was broadcast on CBS from New York's Radio City Music Hall on March 2, 1988, for the awards eligibility period of October 1, 1986, to September 30, 1987.

ALBUM OF THE YEAR
• *The Joshua Tree*, U2. Island.
Bad, Michael Jackson. Epic.
Sign o' the Times, Prince. Paisley Park.
Trio, Dolly Parton, Linda Ronstadt, Emmylou Harris. Warner Bros.
Whitney, Whitney Houston. Arista.

RECORD OF THE YEAR
• "Graceland," Paul Simon. Warner Bros.
"Back in the High Life Again," Steve Winwood. Island.

"I Still Haven't Found What I'm Looking For," U2. Island.
"La Bamba," Los Lobos. Slash.
"Luka," Suzanne Vega. A&M.

SONG OF THE YEAR
(Songwriter's Award)
- "Somewhere Out There," James Horner, Barry Mann, Cynthia Weil.
"Didn't We Almost Have It All," Michael Masser, Will Jennings.
"I Still Haven't Found What I'm Looking For," U2.
"La Bamba," adapted by Ritchie Valens.
"Luka," Suzanne Vega.

BEST NEW ARTIST
- Jody Watley
Breakfast Club
Cutting Crew
Terence Trent D'Arby
Swing Out Sister

BEST POP VOCAL PERFORMANCE, MALE
- Sting, *Bring On the Night*. A&M.
Michael Jackson, *Bad*. Epic.
Al Jarreau, *"Moonlighting* Theme." MCA.
Elton John, "Candle in the Wind." MCA.
Bruce Springsteen, "Brilliant Disguise." Columbia/CBS.

BEST POP VOCAL PERFORMANCE, FEMALE
- Whitney Houston, "I Wanna Dance with Somebody (Who Loves Me)." Arista.
Belinda Carlisle, "Heaven Is a Place on Earth." MCA.
Carly Simon, *Coming Around Again.* Arista.
Barbra Streisand, *One Voice*. Columbia/CBS.
Suzanne Vega, "Luka." A&M.

BEST POP PERFORMANCE BY A DUO OR GROUP WITH VOCAL
- Bill Medley, Jennifer Warnes, "(I've Had) The Time of My Life," track from *Dirty Dancing*. BMG Music/RCA.
Heart, "Alone." Capitol.
Los Lobos, "La Bamba." Slash.
Linda Ronstadt, James Ingram, "Somewhere Out There." MCA.
Swing Out Sister, "Breakout." Mercury.

BEST POP INSTRUMENTAL PERFORMANCE
- Larry Carlton, "Minute by Minute." MCA.
Herb Alpert, *Keep Your Eye on Me* (instrumental tracks only). A&M.
Art of Noise, "Dragnet," track from *In No Sense? Nonsense!* China/Chrysalis.
Chick Corea Elektric Band, "Light Years," track from *Light Years*. GRP.
Dave Grusin, "It Might Be You," track from *Cinemagic*. GRP.

BEST ROCK VOCAL PERFORMANCE, SOLO
- Bruce Springsteen, *Tunnel of Love*. Columbia/CBS.
Joe Cocker, "Unchain My Heart." Capitol.
Richard Marx, "Don't Mean Nothing." Manhattan.
Bob Seger, "Shakedown." MCA.
Tina Turner, "Better Be Good to Me," track from *The Prince's Trust 10th Anniversary Birthday Party*. A&M.

BEST ROCK PERFORMANCE BY A DUO OR GROUP WITH VOCAL
- U2, *The Joshua Tree*. Island.
Georgia Satellites, "Keep Your Hands to Yourself." Elektra.
Heart, *Bad Animals*. Capitol.
Los Lobos, *By the Light of the Moon*. Slash.
Yes, *Big Generator*. Atco.

BEST ROCK INSTRUMENTAL PERFORMANCE (ORCHESTRA, GROUP OR SOLOIST)
- Frank Zappa, *Jazz from Hell*. Barking Pumpkin.

Herbie Hancock, Dweezil Zappa, Terry Bozzio, "Wipe Out," track from *Back to the Beach* soundtrack. Columbia/CBS.

Bruce Springsteen & the E Street Band, "Paradise by the 'C,'" track from *Live 1975–85*. Columbia/CBS.

Stevie Ray Vaughan, Dick Dale, "Pipeline." Columbia/CBS.

Stevie Ray Vaughan & Double Trouble, "Say What!" track from *Live Alive*. Epic.

BEST RHYTHM & BLUES SONG (Songwriter's Award)
• "Lean on Me," Bill Withers.
"Casanova," Reggie Calloway.
"Just to See Her," Jimmy George, Lou Pardini.
"Skeletons," Stevie Wonder.
"U Got the Look," Prince.

BEST RHYTHM & BLUES VOCAL PERFORMANCE, MALE
• Smokey Robinson, "Just to See Her." Motown.
Jonathan Butler, "Lies." Jive.
Michael Jackson, "Bad." Epic.
Wilson Pickett, "In the Midnight Hour," track from *American Soul Man*. Motown.
Stevie Wonder, "Skeletons." Motown.

BEST RHYTHM & BLUES VOCAL PERFORMANCE, FEMALE
• Aretha Franklin, *Aretha*. Arista.
Natalie Cole, *Everlasting*. Manhattan.
Whitney Houston, "For the Love of You," track from *Whitney*. Arista.
Jody Watley, "Looking for a New Love." MCA.
Nancy Wilson, *Forbidden Lover*. Columbia/CBS.

BEST RHYTHM & BLUES VOCAL PERFORMANCE BY A DUO OR GROUP
• Aretha Franklin, George Michael, "I Knew You Were Waiting (for Me)," track from *Aretha*. Arista.
LeVert, *Casanova*. Atlantic.

Club Nouveau, "Lean on Me." King Jay/Warner Bros.
Prince, Sheena Easton, "U Got the Look." Paisley Park.
Whispers, "Rock Steady." Solar/Elektra.

BEST RHYTHM & BLUES INSTRUMENTAL PERFORMANCE (ORCHESTRA, GROUP OR SOLOIST)
• David Sanborn, "Chicago Song." Warner Bros.
Herb Alpert, "Diamonds," instrumental version. A&M.
Jonathan Butler, "Going Home," track from *Jonathan Butler*. Jive.
Najee, *Najee's Theme*. EMI-America.
Stanley Turrentine, "Boogie on Reggae Woman," track from *Wonderland*. Blue Note.

BEST JAZZ VOCAL PERFORMANCE, MALE
• Bobby McFerrin, "What Is This Thing Called Love," track from *The Other Side of 'Round Midnight*. Blue Note.
Billy Eckstine, *Billy Eckstine Sings with Billy Carter*. Emarcy.
Dave Frishberg, *Can't Take You Nowhere*. Fantasy
Arthur Prysock, *This Guy's in Love with You*. Milestone.
Joe Williams, *Every Night*. Verve.

BEST JAZZ VOCAL PERFORMANCE, FEMALE
• Diane Schuur, *Diane Schuur and the Count Basie Orchestra*. GRP.
Ella Fitzgerald, *Easy Living*. Pablo.
Carmen McRae, *Any Old Time*. Denon.
Janis Siegel, *At Home*. Atlantic.
Sarah Vaughan, *Brazilian Romance*. FM.

BEST JAZZ INSTRUMENTAL PERFORMANCE BY A SOLOIST
• Dexter Gordon, *The Other Side of 'Round Midnight*. GRP.
Michael Brecker, *Michael Brecker*. MCA/Impulse.
Eddie Daniels, *To Bird with Love*. GRP.

Branford Marsalis, "Cottontail," track from *Digital Duke* (Duke Ellington Orchestra). GRP.

Wynton Marsalis, *Marsalis Standard Time, Vol. 1*. Columbia/CBS.

BEST JAZZ INSTRUMENTAL PERFORMANCE BY A GROUP

• Wynton Marsalis, *Marsalis Standard Time, Vol. 1*. Columbia/CBS.

Michael Brecker, *Michael Brecker*. MCA/Impulse.

Larry Carlton, *Last Nite*. MCA.

Chick Corea, Miroslav Vitous, Roy Haynes, *Trio Music, Live in Europe*. FCM.

Eddie Daniels, *To Bird with Love*. GRP.

BEST JAZZ INSTRUMENTAL PERFORMANCE BY A BIG BAND

• Duke Ellington Orchestra conducted by Mercer Ellington, *Digital Duke*. GRP.

Louis Bellson & His Jazz Orchestra, *Louis Bellson and His Jazz Orchestra*. Musicmasters.

Woody Herman & His Big Band, *Woody's Gold Star*. Concord Jazz.

Tonight Show Band with Doc Severinsen, *The Tonight Show Band with Doc Severinsen Vol. 2*. Amherst.

Patrick Williams's New York Band, *10th Avenue*. Soundwings.

BEST JAZZ FUSION PERFORMANCE (VOCAL OR INSTRUMENTAL)

• Pat Metheny Group, *Still Life (Talking)*. Geffen.

George Benson, Earl Klugh, *Collaboration*. Warner Bros.

Larry Carlton, *Discovery*. MCA.

David Sanborn, *A Change of Heart*. Warner Bros.

Yellowjackets, *Four Corners*. MCA.

BEST COUNTRY SONG
(Songwriter's Award)

• "Forever and Ever, Amen," Paul Overstreet, Don Schlitz.

"All My Ex's Live in Texas," Sanger D. Shafer, Lyndia J. Shafer.

" '80s Ladies," K. T. Oslin.

"I'll Still Be Loving You," Mary Ann Kennedy, Pat Bunch, Pam Rose.

"Tellin' Me Lies," Linda Thompson, Betsy Cook.

BEST COUNTRY VOCAL PERFORMANCE, MALE

• Randy Travis, *Always and Forever*. Warner Bros.

George Strait, "All My Ex's Live in Texas." MCA.

Hank Williams, Jr., *Born to Boogie*. Curb/Warner Bros.

Steve Earle, *Exit O*. MCA.

Dwight Yoakum, *Hillbilly Deluxe*. Reprise.

BEST COUNTRY VOCAL PERFORMANCE, FEMALE

• K. T. Oslin, " '80s Ladies," track from *'80s Ladies*. BMG Music/RCA.

Rosanne Cash, *King's Record Shop*. Columbia/CBS.

Emmylou Harris, *Angel Band*. Warner Bros.

Reba McEntire, "The Last One to Know." MCA.

Tanya Tucker, "Love Me Like You Used To." Capitol.

BEST COUNTRY PERFORMANCE BY A DUO OR GROUP WITH VOCAL

• Dolly Parton, Linda Ronstadt, Emmylou Harris, *Trio*. Warner Bros.

Desert Rose Band, *The Desert Rose Band*. MCA.

Judds, *Heartland*. BMG Music/RCA.

O'Kanes, "Can't Stop My Heart from Loving You." Columbia/CBS.

Restless Heart, "I'll Still Be Loving You," track from *Wheels*. BMG Music/RCA.

BEST COUNTRY VOCAL PERFORMANCE, DUET

• Ronnie Milsap, Kenny Rogers, "Make No Mistake, She's Mine." BMG Music/RCA.

Glen Campbell, Emmylou Harris, "You Are," track from *Still Within the Sound of My Voice*. MCA.

Glen Campbell, Steve Wariner, "The Hand That Rocks the Cradle." MCA.

Crystal Gayle, Gary Morris, "Another World." Warner Bros.

Michael Martin Murphey, Holly Dunn, "A Face in the Crowd." Warner Bros.

BEST COUNTRY INSTRUMENTAL PERFORMANCE (ORCHESTRA, GROUP OR SOLOIST)

• Asleep at the Wheel, "String of Pars," track from *Asleep at the Wheel*. Epic.

Jerry Douglas, *Changing Channels*. MCA Master Series.

Stephane Grappelli, Vassar Clements, *Together at Last*, cassette. Flying Fish.

Albert Lee, *Gagged but Not Bound*. MCA.

Bill Monroe, "The Old Brown Country Barn," track from *Bluegrass '87*. MCA.

BEST GOSPEL PERFORMANCE, MALE

• Larnelle Harris, *The Father Hath Provided*. Benson.

Steve Green, *Joy to the World*. Sparrow.

Dallas Holm, *Against the Wind*. Dayspring/Word.

Leon Patillo, *Brand New*. Sparrow.

Wayne Watson, *Watercolour Ponies*. Dayspring/Word.

BEST GOSPEL PERFORMANCE, FEMALE

• Deniece Williams, "I Believe in You," track from *Water Under the Bridge*. Columbia/CBS.

Debby Boone, "The Name Above All Names," track from *Friends for Life*. Benson.

Terri Gibbs, "Turnaround." Canaan/Word.

Debbie McClendon, "Count It All Joy." Star Song.

Kathy Troccoli, "Images." Reunion.

BEST GOSPEL PERFORMANCE BY A DUO, GROUP, CHOIR OR CHORUS

• Mylon LeFevre, Broken Heart, *Crack the Sky*. Myrrh/Word.

Bill Gaither Trio, *Welcome Back Home*. Star Song.

Mr. Mister, "Healing Waters," track from *Go On*. BMG Music/RCA.

Petra, *This Means War!* Star Song.

Stryper, *To Hell with the Devil*. Enigma.

BEST SOUL GOSPEL PERFORMANCE, MALE

• Al Green, "Everything's Gonna Be Alright," track from *Soul Survivor*. A&M.

Jessy Dixon, *The Winning Side*. Power Disc/Benson.

Wintley Phipps, *Wintley Phipps*. Word.

Keith Pringle, *All to You*. Muscle Shoals.

BeBe Winans, "Call Me," track from *BeBe and CeCe Winans*. Sparrow.

BEST SOUL GOSPEL PERFORMANCE, FEMALE

• CeCe Winans, "For Always," track from *BeBe and CeCe Winans*. Sparrow.

Shirley Caesar, "The Lord Will Make a Way," track from *Her Very Best*. Rejoice/Word.

Della Reese, "You Gave Me Love," track from *Della Reese and Brilliance*. Air.

Lynette Hawkins Stephens, *Baby Sis*. Birthright.

Vickie Winans, *Be Encouraged*. Light.

BEST SOUL GOSPEL PERFORMANCE BY A DUO, GROUP, CHOIR OR CHORUS

• Winans, Anita Baker, "Ain't No Need to Worry." Qwest.

Clark Sisters, *Heart and Soul*. Rejoice/Word.

Edwin Hawkins & the Music and Arts Seminar Mass Choir, *Give Us Peace*. Birthright.

BeBe and CeCe Winans, *BeBe and CeCe Winans*. Sparrow.

Winans, *Decisions*. Qwest.

BEST TRADITIONAL FOLK RECORDING

• *Shaka Zulu*, Ladysmith Black Mambazo. Warner Bros.

Belizaire the Cajun, Michael Doucet, BeauSoleil. Arhoolie.
Celtic Wedding, Chieftains. Red Seal.
Mbube Roots, Zulu Choral Music from South Africa, Bantu Glee Singers, Crocodiles, Shooting Stars, others. Rounder.
Zulu Men's Singing Competition, various artists. Rounder.

BEST CONTEMPORARY FOLK RECORDING

• *Unfinished Business*, Steve Goodman. Red Pajamas.
Annual Waltz, John Hartford. MCA.
"Asimbonanga," track from *Recently*, Joan Baez. Gold Castle.
More Love Songs, Loudon Wainwright III. Rounder.
The Washington Squares, Washington Squares. Gold Castle.

BEST TRADITIONAL BLUES RECORDING

• *Houseparty New Orleans Style*, Professor Longhair. Rounder.
Cold Snap, Albert Collins. Alligator.
Live from Chicago, an Audience with the Queen, Koko Taylor. Alligator.
"Old Maid Boogie," Eddie "Cleanhead" Vinson, track from *The Late Show* (Etta James). Fantasy.
Take Me Back, James Cotton. Blind Pig.

BEST CONTEMPORARY BLUES RECORDING

• *Strong Persuader*, Robert Cray Band. Mercury/Hightone.
After All, Bobby Bland. Malaco.
Glazed, Earl King, Roomful of Blues. Black Top/ Rounder.
On a Night Like This, Buckwheat Zydecko. Island.
"Standing on the Edge of Love," B. B. King, track from *The Color of Money* soundtrack. MCA.

BEST LATIN POP PERFORMANCE

• Julio Iglesias, *Un Hombre Solo*. Discos CBS International.

Maria Conchita Alonso, "Otra Mentira Más." A&M.
Braulio, "En Bancarrota," track from *Lo Bello y lo Prohibido*. Discos CBS International.
Emmanuel, *Solo*. BMG Music/RCA.
José José, *Siempre Contigo*. Ariola.
Lunna, *Lunna*. A&M.
Luis Miguel, *Luis Miguel '87, Soy Como Quiero Ser*. WEA Latina.
Yolandita Monge, *Laberinto de Amor*. Discos CBS International.
Danny Rivera, *Amar o Morir*. DNA.

BEST TROPICAL LATIN PERFORMANCE

• Eddie Palmieri, *La Verdad—The Truth*. Fania/Musica Latina International.
Ray Barretto, *Aquí Se Puede*. Fania/Musica Latina International.
Ruben Blades, *Agua de Luna* (Moon Water). Elektra.
Caribbean Express, *Caribbean Express*. A&M.
Celia Cruz, Willie Colon, *The Winners*. Vaya/Musica Latina International.
Hector Lavoe, *Strikes Back*. Fania/Musica Latina International.

BEST MEXICAN-AMERICAN PERFORMANCE

• Los Tigres del Norte, *Gracias! América sin Fronteras*. Profono International.
Antonio Aguilar, *15 Exitos con Tambora, Vol. 2*. Musart.
Chavela y Su Grupo Express, *El Rey del Barrio*. Profono International.
Los Diablos, *Celebración*. Discos CBS International.
Little Joe, *Timeless*. Discos CBS International.

BEST REGGAE RECORDING

• *No Nuclear War*, Peter Tosh. EMI America.
Hold On to Love, Third World. Columbia/CBS.
People of the World, Burning Spear. Slash.
UB40 CCCP (Live in Moscow), UB40. A&M.

BEST POLKA RECORDING

- Jimmy Sturr & His Orchestra, *A Polka Just for Me*. Starr.
- Eddie Blazonczyk's Versatones, *Let's Celebrate Again*. Bel-Aire.
- Lenny Gomulka, Dick Pillar, *In Polka Unity*. Steljo.
- Walt Groller & His Orchestra, *It's Polkamatic*. Chalet.
- Kryger Brothers, *Polka Mania*. Starr.

BEST NEW AGE PERFORMANCE

- Yusef Lateef, *Yusef Lateef's Little Symphony*. Atlantic.
- Paul Horn, *Traveler*. Golden Flute/Global Pacific.
- Kitaro, "The Field," track from *The Light of the Spirit*. Geffen.
- Montreux, "Sweet Intentions," track from *Sign Language*. Windham Hill.
- Patrick O'Hearn, *Between Two Worlds*. Private Music.
- Liz Story, "Reconciliation," track from *Part of Fortune*. Novus.

BEST INSTRUMENTAL COMPOSITION

- "Call Sheet Blues," track from *The Other Side of 'Round Midnight*, Dexter Gordon, Wayne Shorter, Herbie Hancock, Ron Carter, Billy Higgins.
- "The Blues in Three," track from *The Glass Menagerie*, Henry Mancini.
- *Bolling: Suite No. 2 for Flute and Jazz Piano Trio*, Claude Bolling.
- "Jazz from Hell," track from *Jazz from Hell*, Frank Zappa.
- "Minuano (Six Eight)," track from *Still Life (Talking)*, Pat Metheny, Lyle Mays.

BEST ARRANGEMENT ON AN INSTRUMENTAL

- Bill Holman, "Take the 'A' Train," track from *The Tonight Show Band with Doc Severinsen, Vol. 2*. Amherst.
- Jorge Calandrelli (strings arranged by Jorge Calandrelli, Dori Caymmi, Christian Chevalier), "Any Time, Any Season," track from *Any Time, Any Season*. Innovation.

Michael Convertino, "Main Title," track from *Children of a Lesser God*. GNP/Crescendo.

Dave Grusin, "The Heart Is a Lonely Hunter," track from *Cinemagic*. GRP.

Patrick Williams, "Jive Samba," track from *10th Avenue*. Soundwings.

BEST MUSICAL CAST SHOW ALBUM

- *Les Misérables* (Broadway cast), Herbert Kretzmer, lyricist; Claude-Michel Schonberg, composer. Geffen.
- *Me and My Girl* (Broadway cast), L. Arthur Rose, Douglas Furber, lyricists. Noel Gay, composer.
- *My Fair Lady* (Kiri Te Kanawa, Jeremy Irons, others), Alan Jay Lerner, lyricist; Frederick Loewe, composer. London.
- *The Phantom of the Opera* (London cast), Charles Hart with Richard Stilgoe, lyricists; Andrew Lloyd Webber, composer. Polydor.
- *South Pacific* (Kiri Te Kanawa, José Carreras, others), Oscar Hammerstein II, lyricist; Richard Rodgers, composer. FM.

BEST ALBUM OF ORIGINAL INSTRUMENTAL BACKGROUND SCORE WRITTEN FOR A MOTION PICTURE OR TV

Composer's Award

- *The Untouchables* (film soundtrack), Ennio Morricone. A&M.
- *An American Tail* (film soundtrack), James Horner. MCA.
- *The Glass Menagerie* (film soundtrack), Henry Mancini. MCA.
- *The Princess Bride*, Mark Knopfler. Warner Bros.
- *The Witches of Eastwick* (film soundtrack), John Williams. Warner Bros.

BEST SONG WRITTEN SPECIFICALLY FOR A MOTION PICTURE OR TV

- "Somewhere Out There," James Horner, Barry Mann, Cynthia Weil. MCA.

"(I've Had) The Time of My Life,"
Frankie Previte, John Denicola, Donald Markowitz. BMG Music/RCA.
"*Moonlighting* Theme," Al Jarreau, Lee Holdridge. MCA.
"Nothing's Gonna Stop Us Now" (from *Mannequin* soundtrack), Diane Warren, Albert Hammond. Grunt.
"Who's That Girl," Madonna, Patrick Leonard. Sire.

BEST INSTRUMENTAL ARRANGEMENT ACCOMPANYING VOCAL(S)

• Frank Foster, "Deedles' Blues," track from *Diane Schuur and the Count Basie Orchestra*. GRP.
Randy Kerber, "Over the Rainbow," track from *One Voice*. Columbia/CBS.
Henry Mancini, "It Might As Well Be Spring," track from *The Hollywood Musicals*. Columbia/CBS.
Van Dyke Parks, Bill Ginn, "A Singer Must Die," track from *Famous Blue Raincoat*. Cypress.
Jack Walrath, "I'm So Lonesome I Could Cry," track from *Master of Suspense*. Blue Note.

BEST CLASSICAL ALBUM

• *Horowitz in Moscow*, Vladimir Horowitz. Deutsche Grammophon.
Adams: The Chairman Dances; Christian Zeal and Activity; 2 Fanfares for Orchestra; Tromba Iontana; Short Ride in a Fast Machine; Common Tones in Simple Time, Edo de Waart conducting the San Francisco Symphony. Elektra/Nonesuch.
Beethoven: Symphony No. 9 in D Minor ("Choral"), Sir Georg Solti conducting the Chicago Symphony Orchestra. London.
Fauré: Requiem, Op. 48; Duruflé: Requiem, Op. 9, Robert Shaw conducting the Atlanta Symphony Chorus and Orchestra. Telarc.
Hanson: Symphony No. 2 ("Romantic"); Barber: Violin Concerto, Leonard Slatkin conducting the St. Louis Symphony. Angel.

BEST ORCHESTRAL RECORDING (Conductor's Award)

• *Beethoven: Symphony No. 9 in D Minor ("Choral")*, Sir Georg Solti conducting the Chicago Symphony Orchestra. London.
Berg, Webern, Schoenberg: Orchestral Pieces, James Levine conducting the Berlin Philharmonic. Deutsche Grammophon.
Copland: Symphony No. 3; Quiet City, Leonard Bernstein conducting the New York Philharmonic. Deutsche Grammophon.
Hanson: Symphony No. 2 ("Romantic"), Leonard Slatkin conducting the St. Louis Symphony. Angel.
Holst: The Planets, Charles Dutoit conducting the Montreal Symphony Orchestra. London.

BEST CHAMBER MUSIC PERFORMANCE (INSTRUMENTAL OR VOCAL)

• Itzhak Perlman, Lynn Harrell, Vladimir Ashkenazy, *Beethoven: The Complete Piano Trios*. Angel.
Beaux Arts Trio, *Dvořák: Piano Trio in E Minor ("Dumky"); Mendelssohn: Piano Trio in D Minor*. Philips Classics.
Kronos Quartet, *White Man Sleeps (Music by Volans, Ives, Hassell, Coleman, Johnson, Bartók)*. Elektra/Nonesuch.
Murray Perahia, members of the Amadeus Quartet, *Brahms: Piano Quartet No. 1 in G Minor*. CBS Masterworks.
Jean-Pierre Rampal, Isaac Stern, Salvatore Accardo, Mstislav Rostropovich, *Mozart: The Flute Quartets (K. 285, 285A, 285B, 298)*. CBS Masterworks.

BEST CLASSICAL PERFORMANCE, INSTRUMENTAL SOLOIST(S) (WITH ORCHESTRA)

• Itzhak Perlman (James Levine conducting the Vienna Philharmonic),

Mozart: Violin Concertos No. 2 in D and No. 4 in D. Deutsche Grammophon.

Dale Clevenger (Franz List Chamber Orchestra), *Mozart: Horn Concertos Nos. 1–4; Rondo; Fragment*. CBS Masterworks.

Wynton Marsalis (Donald Hunsberger conducting the Eastman Wind Ensemble), *Carnaval (Works by Arban, Clarke, Levy, Paganini, Rimsky Korsakov, Bellstedt)*. CBS Masterworks.

Elmar Oliveira (Leonard Slatkin conducting the St. Louis Symphony), *Barber: Violin Concerto, Op. 14*. Angel.

Murray Perahia (Bernard Haitink conducting the Concertgebouw Orchestra), *Beethoven: Piano Concerto No. 5 in E Flat ("Emperor")*. CBS Masterworks.

BEST CLASSICAL PERFORMANCE, INSTRUMENTAL SOLOIST(S) (WITHOUT ORCHESTRA)

• Vladimir Horowitz, piano, *Horowitz in Moscow*. Deutsche Grammophon.

Itzhak Perlman, violin (Samuel Sanders, accompanist), *My Favorite Kreisler*. Angel.

Murray Perahia, *Beethoven: Piano Sonatas No. 17, Op. 31; No. 18, Op. 31; No. 26, Op. 81A*. CBS Masterworks.

Andras Schiff, piano, *Bach: The Well-Tempered Clavier, Book 2*. London.

Peter Serkin, piano, *Stravinsky, Wolpe, Lieberson (Stravinsky: Serenade in A and Sonata; Wolpe: Form IV: Broken Sequences, Pastorale, Pascaglia; Lieberson: Bagatelles)*. New World.

BEST OPERA RECORDING

• *R. Strauss: Ariadne auf Naxos*, James Levine conducting the Vienna Philharmonic (solos: Anna Tomowa-Sintow, Kathleen Battle, Agnes Baltsa, Gary Lakes, Hermann Prey). Deutsche Grammophon.

Mozart: Die Entführung aus dem Serail, Sir Georg Solti conducting the Vienna Philharmonic Orchestra and Chorus (solos: Edita Gruberova, Kathleen Battle, Gosta Winbergh, Heinz Zednik, Martti Talvela). London.

Mozart: Don Giovanni, Herbert von Karajan conducting the Berlin Philharmonic Orchestra and Chorus (solos: Samuel Ramey, Anna Tomowa-Sintow, Agnes Baltsa, Kathleen Battle, Gosta Winbergh, Ferruccio Furlanetto, Alexander Malta, Paata Burchuladze). Deutsche Grammophon.

Mozart: The Marriage of Figaro, Riccardo Muti conducting the Vienna Philharmonic and Chorus (solos: Thomas Allen, Margaret Price, Kathleen Battle, Jorma Hynninen, Ann Murray, Kurt Rydl). Angel.

Verdi: Macbeth, Riccardo Chailly conducting the Orchestra e Coro del Teatro Communale di Bologna (solos: Leo Nucci, Shirley Verrett, Samuel Ramey, Veriano Luchetti, Antonio Barasorda). London.

BEST CHORAL PERFORMANCE (OTHER THAN OPERA)

• Robert Shaw conducting the Atlanta Symphony Chorus and Orchestra, *Hindemith: When Lilacs Last in the Dooryard Bloom'd (A Requiem for Those We Loved)*. Telarc.

John Eliot Gardiner conducting the Monteverdi Choir and English Baroque Soloists, *Bach: St. John Passion*. Archiv.

Sir Charles Mackerras conducting the Prague Philharmonic Chorus and Czech Philharmonic Orchestra; Lubomir Matl, chorus master, *Janáček: Glagolitic Mass*. Supraphon.

André Previn conducting the Brighton Festival Chorus and Royal Philharmonic Orchestra; Laszlo Heltay, chorus master, *Tippett: A Child of Our Time*. RPO Records.

Klaus Tennstedt conducting the London Philharmonic Choir and Orchestra, Richard Cooke, chorus master; Tiffin School Boys' Choir, Neville Creed, chorus master, *Mahler: Symphony No. 8 in E Flat ("Symphony of a Thousand")*. Angel.

Michael Tilson Thomas conducting the Mormon Tabernacle Choir and Utah Symphony; Jerold D. Ottley, choral director, *Copland: Old American Songs; Canticle of Freedom; Four Motets*. CBS Masterworks.

BEST CLASSICAL PERFORMANCE, VOCAL SOLOIST

• Kathleen Battle (James Levine, accompanist), *Kathleen Battle, Salzburg Recital (Fauré, Handel, Mendelssohn, Mozart, Purcell, Strauss, Spirituals)*. Deutsche Grammophon.

Elly Ameling (Rudolf Jansen, accompanist), *Soire Française (Debussy, Fauré, Poulenc, Franck, Canteloube, Roussel, Chausson, Messiaen, etc.)*. Philips Classics.

Arleen Auger (Yale Cellos of Aldo Parisot), *Villa-Lobos: Bachianas Brasileiras No. 5 for Soprano and Orchestra of Violincellos*. Delos Intl.

Marni Nixon (Keith Clark conducting members of the Pacific Symphony Orchestra, *Copland: 8 Poems of Emily Dickinson*. Reference Recordings.

Jessye Norman (Geoffrey Parsons, accompanist), *R. Strauss: Lieder (Including "Malven")*. Philips Classics.

BEST CONTEMPORARY COMPOSITION
(Composer's Award)

• Cello Concerto No. 2, Krzysztof Penderecki.

The Chairman Dances, John Adams.

Piano Concerto, Milton Babbitt.

A Sudden Rainbow, Joseph Schwanter.

Symphony No. 5, Roger Sessions.

The Mask of Time, Michael Tippett.

BEST ENGINEERED RECORDING, CLASSICAL

• Jack Renner, *Fauré: Requiem, Op. 48; Duruflé: Requiem, Op. 9* (Shaw conducting the Atlanta Symphony Chorus and Orchestra; solos: Judith Blegen, James Morris). Telarc.

Thomas Frost, *Horowitz in Moscow* (solo: Vladimir Horowitz). Deutsche Grammophon.

John Pellowe, James Lock, *Beethoven: Symphony No. 9 in D Minor ("Choral")* (Solti conducting the Chicago Symphony Orchestra). London.

John Pellowe, *Tchaikovsky: 1812 Overture; Romeo and Juliet; The Nutcracker Suite* (Solti conducting the Chicago Symphony Orchestra). London.

Jack Renner, *Hindemith: When Lilacs Last in the Dooryard Bloom'd (A Requiem for Those We Loved)* (Shaw conducting the Atlanta Symphony Orchestra and Chorus, soloists). Telarc.

CLASSICAL PRODUCER OF THE YEAR

• Robert Woods

Steven Epstein

Thomas Frost

Michael Haas

Jay David Saks

BEST COMEDY RECORDING

• *A Night at the Met*, Robin Williams. Columbia/CBS.

The Best of Bob and Ray Vol. 1, Bob Elliott, Ray Goulding. Radioart.

Polka Party! Weird Al Yankovic. CBS Associated/Rock 'n' Roll.

The World According to Me! Jackie Mason. Warner Bros.

Would Jesus Wear a Rolex? Ray Stevens. MCA.

BEST SPOKEN WORD OR NONMUSICAL RECORDING

• *Lake Wobegon Days*, Garrison Keillor. PHC.

Lauren Bacall by Myself, Lauren Bacall. Random House Audiobooks.

"Lincoln Portrait," Katharine Hepburn, track from *Aaron Copland: Lincoln Portrait and Other Works*. Telarc.

Star Trek IV: The Voyage Home, read by Leonard Nimoy, George Takei. Simon & Schuster Audio Works.

Whales Alive, Leonard Nimoy. Living Music.

BEST RECORDING FOR CHILDREN

• *The Elephant's Child*, Jack Nicholson, Bobby McFerrin. Windham Hill.

Bullfrogs and Butterflies (Part III). Sparrow.

The Emperor and the Nightingale, Glenn Close, Mark Isham. Windham Hill.

Everything Grows, Raffi. Shoreline/A&M.

Lullaby for Teddy, Barbara Fairchild. Jaba.

BEST ENGINEERED RECORDING (OTHER THAN CLASSICAL)

• Bruce Swedien, Humberto Gatica, *Bad*. Epic.

Don Murray, Keith Grant, engineers; Josiah Gluck, Dave Grusin, mixers, *Cinemagic* (cassette). GRP.

Ben Harris, Kyle Lehning, Joe Bogen, *Heart and Soul*. BMG Music/RCA.

Andrew Jackson, *A Momentary Lapse of Reason*. Columbia/CBS.

Tom Jung, *Neon* (cassette). Digital Music Projects.

Al Schmitt, *Reflections*. Soundwings.

BEST ALBUM PACKAGE (Art Director's Award)

• Bill Johnson, *King's Record Shop*. Columbia/CBS.

Peter Barrett, *Shaka Zulu*. Warner Bros.

Bruce Licher, *Echelons*. Independent Project.

Ron Scarselli, *Document*. I.R.S.

Joe Stelmach, *Duke Ellington: The Webster Blanton Band*. BMG Music/RCA.

BEST ALBUM NOTES (Annotator's Award)

• Orrin Keepnews, *Thelonious Monk: The Complete Riverside Recordings*. Riverside.

Peter Guralnick, *The Complete Sun Sessions*. BMG Music/RCA.

Nolan Porterfield, *Jimmie Rodgers on Record: America's Blue Yodeler*. Smithsonian Collection of Recordings.

Mark Tucker, *Singers and Soloists of the Swing Bands*. Smithsonian Collection of Recordings.

Charles K. Wolfe, *The Bristol Sessions*. Country Music Foundation.

BEST HISTORICAL ALBUM

• *Thelonious Monk: The Complete Riverside Recordings*, Thelonious Monk. Riverside.

The Bristol Sessions, Carter family, Jimmie Rodgers, others. Country Music Foundation.

The Gershwin Collection, Ella Fitzgerald, Johnny Mathis, Andy Williams, others. Teledisc USSA.

The Otis Redding Story, Otis Redding. Atlantic.

Singers and Soloists of the Swing Bands, Louis Armstrong, Benny Goodman, Frank Sinatra, others. Smithsonian Collection of Recordings.

PRODUCER OF THE YEAR (OTHER THAN CLASSICAL)

• Narada Michael Walden
Emilio & the Jerks
Quincy Jones, Michael Jackson
Daniel Lanois, Brian Eno
John Mellencamp, Don Gehman

BEST PERFORMANCE MUSIC VIDEO

• *The Prince's Trust All-Star Rock Concert*. David G. Croft, director. MGM Home Video.

Cyndi Lauper in Paris, Cyndi Lauper. Andy Morahan, director. CBS Music Video Enterprises.

Horowitz in Moscow, Vladimir Horowitz. Brian Large, director. Camivideo.

One Voice, Barbra Streisand. Dwight Hemion, director. CBS/Fox Video Music.

Spontaneous Inventions, Bobby McFerrin. Bud Schaetzle, director. PMI/HBO/Pioneer Artists.

BEST CONCEPT MUSIC VIDEO

• *Land of Confusion*, Genesis. John Lloyd, Jim Yukich, directors. Atlantic Video.

Control, the Videos, Part II, Janet Jackson. Dominic Sena, director. A&M Video.

David Lee Roth, David Lee Roth. Pete Angelus, David Lee Roth, directors. Warner Reprise Video.

Day In, Day Out, David Bowie. Julien Temple, director. Picture Music International/Sony.

Kate Bush: The Whole Story, Kate Bush. Picture Music International/Sony Software.

"To no one's surprise, nouveau folkie Tracy Chapman collected more Grammy nominations than anyone else," *Variety* reported on the success of the artist it called "the year's biggest musical media darling." Prior to awards night, the *L.A. Times* even declared that Chapman "could be headed for the biggest Grammy sweep ever by a new artist— surpassing even Christopher Cross' five-Grammy blow-out of 1980." She was favored in all six categories in which she was nominated: Album, Record and Song of the Year, Best New Artist, best female pop vocalist and Best Contemporary Folk Recording. The only race she had to worry about, said the pundits, was for best record. "There will be considerable sentiment to give Michael Jackson the award to take some of the sting out of his Grammy shut out last year," the *Times* added, claiming that the chances of other contenders were "slim."

Chapman was beloved by the media because of the critical praise that followed her "Fast Car" single, which zoomed up the pop charts thanks to heavy radio airplay and the popularity of its video on MTV. The song was an anthem for the forgotten underclass in the prosperous Reagan America of the late 1980s. It captured the voice of a convenience store worker who lives in a homeless shelter and yearns for escape, singing to her lover: "You got a fast car / And I got a plan to get us out of here. . . . / You leave tonight or live and die this way."

The *New York Times* called Chapman's work "resoundingly adult music, soft and temperate and literate." The *L.A. Times* added, "If Chapman doesn't win

Wide World Photo

"To the surprise of just about everyone, it was one-man-band Bobby McFerrin who came closest to sweeping," *Variety* said.

Best New Artist, the Grammys shouldn't even bother renting a hall."

When she ended up taking the prizes for new artist, pop vocals and contemporary folk, *Rolling Stone* gasped, "The Grammys seemed to be saluting the political, dangerous and—*gulp!*—hip."

But pundits had to swallow hard when she lost her other three Grammy bids.

Variety reported, "To the surprise of just about everyone, it was one-man-band Bobby McFerrin who came closest to sweeping. McFerrin's upset over Chapman's 'Fast Car' in the best song competition was particularly unexpected as the prize in the recent past has gone to such socially conscious tunes as 'We Are the World.' "

Variety called McFerrin a "Grammy perennial," since he'd won five awards over the previous three years. Now his pop hit "Don't Worry, Be Happy" won Record and Song of the Year in addition to the prize for best male pop vocals. He nabbed a fourth Grammy when he took the male jazz vocals prize for "Brothers," a track from Rob Wasserman's *Duets*.

"The multiple triumph of Bobby McFerrin was at once surprising, gratifying and puzzling," the *L.A. Times* wrote later about the artist known as a "vocal Cuisinart" in the jazz world for his uncanny ability to imitate the sounds of an entire band. "Here is an artist whose jazz credentials are impeccable, but who, over the past decade, has broadened his scope and his audience by developing into a unique entertainer and comedic personality."

"Don't Worry, Be Happy" was not only Grammy's Record and Song of the Year, it was the bouncy, feel-good song of the year and "the first a cappella track ever to reach number one on the pop charts," noted *Variety*. It sold 10 million single copies as of Grammy night after being introduced on McFerrin's *Simple Pleasures* album and in the Tom Cruise movie *Cocktail*. The upbeat song was so popular that Vice President George Bush even tried to appropriate it for his presidential campaign, but he was turned down by McFerrin. Its victory as Record of the Year marked the first time that a song from a film reaped the honor since Roberta Flack's "The First Time Ever I Saw Your Face" did so, being featured in Clint Eastwood's *Play Misty for Me*.

"I think it was so popular because it went to the spirit," McFerrin told reporters backstage about his song's huge success. "People wanted something uplifting and jovial and funny."

Curiously, other jazz music also performed well in Grammy's pop categories.

"Upsets seemed to be one of the prevailing themes" of this year's awards, *Variety* declared. "The Beach Boys, heavily favored to win their first Grammy ever with 'Kokomo,' nominated for Best Pop Performance by a Duo or Group with Vocal, were beaten out by another set of veterans, Manhattan Transfer." Frank Zappa was nominated again in the rock instrumental category, which

he won last year, but now he got zapped by the Mexican-born, fusion guitarist Carlos Santana with *Blues for Salvador*. Mike Post (*Music from "L.A. Law" and Otherwise*) was the front-runner for Best Pop Instrumental Performance, but he was surpassed by alto sax player David Sanborn (*Close-Up*), the winner of three jazz Grammys in the past.

More crossover triumphs followed when six-time jazz honoree Chick Corea claimed the r&b instrumental category for a track from *GRP Super Live in Concert*. Furthermore, the *L.A. Times* added: "Roger Kellaway, a distinguished jazz composer, was a winner for best instrumental arrangement, another nonjazz department, for an album called *Memos from Paradise* by the jazz clarinetist Eddie Daniels. [What these] victories add up to may well indicate a powerful trend. Never before in the 31-year history of the Grammy Awards have two top divisions been won by a jazz artist, and never before have so many jazz-related musicians been honored in so many nonjazz categories."

Prior to the Grammycast, the *L.A. Times* sized up some of the top nonjazz contenders, saying, "This year's big surprise was the failure of British pop sensation George Michael to nab more than two nominations. Michael had figured to be among the leaders because his *Faith* album received generally favorable reviews and sold more than six million copies."

Variety suggested that Michael's "nonappearance in the Record of the Year category can probably be attributed to the fact that the five singles from *Faith* divided his vote."

Michael ended up losing his bid for best male pop vocals to McFerrin, but he surpassed both McFerrin and Tracy Chapman to score an upset for Album of the Year. Perhaps Grammy pundits didn't have faith in his chances because he got his start in the music business as one-half of the bubblegum-pop group Wham! After he broke with partner Andrew Ridgeley and went solo, some critics stuck by him.

Stephen Holden of the *New York Times* wrote, "If asked to nominate the one contemporary pop star most likely to be as successful 10 years from now as today, I'd cast my vote for George Michael. [He] has everything a pop star requires for longevity . . . [including] extraordinary skills as a songwriter, arranger and producer."

"To no one's surprise, nouveau folkie Tracy Chapman collected more nominations that anyone else," earning six, *Variety* reported.

"Prognosticators had been favoring Rod Stewart to pick up his first Grammy," *Variety* reported when eyeing the race for best male rock vocalist. Just like the still-Grammyless Beach Boys, however, Stewart continued to be snubbed by N.A.R.A.S. voters when an upset was scored by white British soul singer Robert Palmer ("Simply Irresistible"), who last won the category in 1986 for "Addicted to Love." *Variety* noted a curious thing about Palmer and his Grammy rivals, which included Joe Cocker, Robbie Robertson and Eric Clapton in addition to Stewart: "The men vying for solo honors in rock—historically the domain of the young—are distinguished by their age. The youngest among them, Robert Palmer, just turned 40."

With the exception of last year when male and female rock vocals categories were combined, Tina Turner and Pat Benatar had virtually monopolized the female slot since it was reintroduced in 1979 and now were pitted against each other along with three critically acclaimed rookies: Toni Childs, Melissa Etheridge and Sinéad O'Connor. When the vote for the newcomers split, Turner emerged triumphant for *Tina Live in Europe*.

Another past Grammy favorite proved strong when U2 returned from last year to take the rock instrumental category again, this time for "Desire," from the group's concert documentary film *U2: Rattle and Hum*. The Irish rockers also won Best Per-

formance Music Video for "Where the Streets Have No Name," the lead song on their 1987 Album of the Year, *The Joshua Tree*. Weird Al Yankovic snared the Best Concept Music Video award for "Fat," his parody of Michael Jackson's "Bad." Since Jackson's only nomination was for Record of the Year ("Man in the Mirror"), he was shut out for a second year in a row.

For months before this year's Grammy race, *Variety* reported on the growing clamor for new categories covering rap and hard rock/metal, "two genres that have generated megabucks in recent years, but received little respect from the diskery biz establishment." When both were added, Metallica was widely favored to win the metal prize. *Variety* noted "a few scattered boos from the crowd asembled in Los Angeles' Shrine Auditorium" when an upset was scored by what the *New York Times* called "the long-running, long-irrelevant band Jethro Tull," the British rock group named after the inventor of the steel drill. Lead singer Ian Anderson wasn't in attendance at the Grammy ceremony to accept the prize, so *Rolling Stone* asked Metallica's James Hetfield what he thought of Tull's victory. "Maybe it would have excited me ten years ago," he answered.

Metallica was nevertheless invited to perform on the Grammycast. "The thrash band Metallica emerged from a dry-ice cloud to perform a stunning version of 'One,'" *Rolling Stone* noted. "As Metallica leader James Hetfield sang the line

'Hold my breath as I wish for death,' the stodgy Grammy voters must have been nodding in agreement." The *L.A. Times* said Metallica "shook the Shrine Auditorium chandelier with a performance unlike anything ever seen or heard on a Grammy show."

The new award for Best Rap Performance ended up shaking up the Grammy gala, too, when a protest was lodged by D.J. Jazzy Jeff & the Fresh Prince, who won it for "Parents Just Don't Understand."

The duo were invited to be presenters at the ceremony, but they joined three of the other four contenders in a boycott because the new rap prize was being bestowed at the off-air ceremony held prior to the telecast. A spokesman for the artists charged that rap music was being "treated like a stepchild" and "ghettoized." Grammycast producer Pierre Cossette countered: "The problem is arithmetic. When you have 76 categories and you only [have time] to put 12 on the air, you've got 64 unhappy groups of people." Only loser Kool Moe Dee agreed to accept the award if he won. After both the on- and off-the-air ceremonies were over, winner Fresh Prince (Will Smith) could be found at MTV's party at the L.A. club Cat & Fiddle, where he told *Rolling Stone,* "They're giving us the award, but they're giving it to us under the table."

A curious coincidence occurred in the r&b lineup when Anita Baker repeated her dual victories of 1986 by again being named best female r&b vocalist in addition to sharing in the writer's prize for Best R&B Song, "Giving You the Best That I Got," which was also a contender for Record and Song of the Year. Gladys Knight & the Pips added to their previous Grammy stash (two in 1973 and a third for Knight's contribution to 1986 Song of the Year "That's What Friends Are For")

> ## Jethro Tull's victory was met with "scattered boos," noted *Variety.*

by garnering the gold for best r&b group vocal performance.

In the race for best male r&b singing, *Variety* reported that Luther Vandross was favored to win the first Grammy of his career. Vandross had lost all six of his earlier bids (including one for 1981's Best New Artist) and now lost again—to a performer who lost Best New Artist last year: Terence Trent D'Arby.

D'Arby's victory was a shocker considering the drumming he was getting in the media after he smugly declared his album *Introducing the Hardline According to Terence Trent D'Arby* "the most brilliant debut album from any artist this decade." He even said it was a better work than the Beatles' *Sgt. Pepper's Lonely Hearts Club Band,* winner of Grammy's 1967 Album of the Year. *Rolling Stone* came to his defense after the Grammycast, however, using the opportunity to bash N.A.R.A.S. voters: "The victory of the one certifiably hip winner—Terence Trent D'Arby for best male r&b vocal—can probably be attributed to the fact that he performed at last year's ceremony and thus was familiar to the constituents."

Losers of this year's Best New Artist prize, Take 6, still scored a dramatic coup by winning two other Grammys: a gospel award for their eponymous debut album and the jazz group vocals award for one of its tracks, "Spread Love." In the latter, the young black sextet urged listeners, "Spread love instead of spreading lies." Other tracks were more overtly religious, with titles such as "Get Away, Jordan" and "David and Goliath."

One of jazz's reigning veterans was honored for the first time when the female vocals prize went to Betty Carter (*Look What I Got!*), who was once called "the only real jazz singer" by fellow jazz diva Carmen McCrae. (McCrae, who had never won a Grammy either, was one of the nominees who lost to Carter. A duet

LP, featuring both McCrae *and* Carter, lost the group vocals prize to Take 6.) Carter had been performing since the late 1940s when she toured with Lionel Hampton, but was not as widely known as McCrae, Ella Fitzgerald, Sarah Vaughan and other thrushes of the genre, since she seldom made recordings. She started her own label in 1971, Bet-Car, but issued only a few releases before signing with Verve in 1987.

For decades, the Chicago blues scene was ruled by Muddy Waters, Howlin' Wolf and Willie Dixon. Waters and Wolf died years ago, but Dixon was still going strong at age 72 and was hailed with his first Grammy (Best Traditional Blues Recording) for *Hidden Charms.*

Just prior to his death in 1988, Gil Evans, along with his Monday Night Orchestra, recorded a tribute to Bud Powell and Charlie "Yardbird" Parker— *Bud and Bird*—that earned them the big-band jazz kudos. Sax legend and onetime Grammy winner John Coltrane had died two decades earlier, but *Blues for Coltrane: A Tribute to John Coltrane* now reaped the jazz group instrumental performance award for McCoy Tyner, Pharoah Sanders, David Murray, Cecil McBee and Roy Haynes. The prize for best solo instrumental work was bestowed on fusion reedman Michael Brecker for *Don't Try This at Home.* Trumpet player Wynton Marsalis was nominated against both Brecker and the group paying homage to Coltrane, but he came up Grammyless for the first time since his winning streak began in 1983. Wynton's brother, sax player Branford, also lost in both competitions.

The Grammys' penchant for burying fallen music greats with laurels was shown in the country awards when Roy Orbison, who died in 1988, was honored in the vocal collaboration category for his "Cryin'" duet with k. d. lang.

After a three-year winning streak that

> ### The Grammyless Beach Boys lost both bids for "Kokomo."

ended in 1986, the mother-daughter duo the Judds staged a comeback in country music's duo/group vocal category for a track from their *Greatest Hits* album, "Give a Little Love." Also returning was Randy Travis (*Old 8 x 10*), who reclaimed the honors he won last year for best male vocalist. Another repeater from 1987 was the "western swing" band from Austin, Texas, Asleep at the Wheel, which held on to the country instrumental slot with "Sugarfoot Rag."

K. T. Oslin won her first Grammy last year but surpassed that success by doing in the country categories exactly what Anita Baker did in the r&b lineup: She won both the female vocal honors and best song. Her triumph for "Hold Me," a track from *This Woman,* made Grammy history with two other, non-country victories. Never before had all three best song awards (Song of the Year, Best R&B Song and Best Country Song) gone to the artists who both sang *and* wrote the work. Curiously, all three artists also won Grammys for their performances.

In addition to new categories for rap and heavy metal music, N.A.R.A.S. introduced a slot for Best Bluegrass Recording, which was won by veteran singer, bandleader and mandolin player Bill Monroe. The Kentucky native had been performing since the mid-1920s and was known as the father of bluegrass music, as *Rolling Stone* once noted, "not because he invented that variant of country & western, but because he was its most adventurous pioneer."

As usual, the religious categories welcomed back a chorus of past victors, including three four-time champs: Amy Grant (*Lead Me On*), Larnelle Harris (*Christmas*) and the Winans (*The Winans Live at Carnegie Hall*), who claimed the gospel prizes for, respectively, best female, male and group performances. Last year CeCe Winans won a Grammy.

This year it was her brother BeBe's turn to claim the male soul gospel award for "Abundant Life." CeCe was nominated for the female soul gospel prize but lost to Aretha Franklin (*One Lord, One Faith, One Baptism*), who bolstered her lead over all other female Grammy winners by bringing her total to 15 trophies.

Newcomer Roberto Carlos was the winner of Best Latin Pop Performance for his eponymous LP, while 1986 victor of the tropical Latin kudos, Rubén Blades, returned to reclaim the prize (*Antecedente*). Linda Ronstadt had previously won Grammys in both the pop and country fields, but now she crossed over into a third genre when she received the year's Best Mexican-American Performance award for *Canciones de Mi Padre*.

Jimmy Sturr & His Orchestra (*Born to Polka*) held on to the Best Polka Recording accolade for a third year in a row. Jamaica's native-music king, Bob Marley, died in 1981, but his legacy was continued by his son Ziggy (*Conscious Party*), who won Best Reggae Recording for his debut album with the Melody Makers.

Comedian Robin Williams scored two Grammy victories with prizes for the Best Recording for Children (*Pecos Bill*, which he narrated) and Best Comedy Recording (*Good Morning, Vietnam,* a collection of Williams's rantings as an army deejay in the hit film). Composer Stephen Sondheim had won the award for Best Musical Cast Show Album four times in the past: *Company* (1970), *A Little Night Music* (1973), *Sweeney Todd* (1979) and *Sunday in the Park with George* (1984). Now he returned triumphant with *Into the Woods,* his new Broadway show based loosely on Grimms' fairy tales.

The trio of composing talent behind the Oscars' Best Picture, *The Last Emperor* (Ryuichi Sakamoto, David Byrne and Cong Su), prevailed over past winners John Williams and Maurice Jarre to reap the film score accolade.

Of the two songs from *Cocktail* considered for other Grammys this year (the Beach Boys' "Kokomo" and Record of

Luciano Pavarotti in Concert earned the tenor a fourth career prize as best classical vocalist.

the Year "Don't Worry, Be Happy"), only "Kokomo" was in the lineup for Best Song Written Specifically for a Motion Picture or TV. The Beach Boys lost again, however, when the trophy was snatched by 1985 Album of the Year winner Phil Collins for "Two Hearts," from the movie *Buster,* in which Collins made his film acting debut. He had previously acted on the stage when his mother helped him to land the role of the Artful Dodger in a London production of *Oliver!* when Collins was 15 years old.

Serious discord erupted in the classical categories when Robert Shaw and the Atlanta Symphony Orchestra and Chorus won five awards, leading to accusations of bloc voting. One of the most suspicious award results was Atlanta's producer Robert Woods being named Classical Producer of the Year for a fifth time in 10 years. "Insidious . . . the question of bloc voting," *Billboard* commented. "Regional loyalties seem to be the functional culprit. There really is no other way to explain the lopsided Grammy results for the Atlanta Symphony Orchestra, its releasing labels and producer. Does anyone doubt that the small but active Atlanta academy chapter [with 300 members] votes its municipal pride? Something is wrong."

"It takes very few votes to win a classical Grammy, because the number of people who vote is small," explained

Joseph Dash, a CBS Masterworks executive. "N.A.R.A.S. should do something as soon as possible, before the value of a Grammy is reduced to zero."

Ironically, considering the uproar, Shaw and his team picked up three of their Grammys (Best Classical Album, the choral performance prize and engineering laurels) for a work that critics considered one of their finest recordings: *Verdi's Requiem and Operatic Choruses*, featuring choruses from *Aida, Don Carlo* and other classics. They also picked up the Best Orchestral Recording prize for *Ned Rorem's String Symphony, Sunday Morning and Eagles* in addition to the kudos for producer Woods.

Vladimir Horowitz had won Best Classical Album the previous two years and this year was a losing nominee (for *Horowitz Plays Mozart*), but at least he picked up the consolation prize of the soloist honors with orchestra for a concerto on the LP. Critics noted that the 85-year-old artist performed well on the LP despite a noticeable decline of his powers due to age. The soloist's prize without orchestral backup was awarded to two-time past champ Alicia de Larrocha for works by Isaac Albéniz, which earned her rave reviews. Several sources even declared it to be one of Decca's best piano recordings ever.

Sir Georg Solti nabbed 2 more awards to solidify his status as all-time Grammy champ, with 28 awards, for the year's Best Opera Recording (Wagner's *Lohengrin*) and the chamber music honors for a joint recording of works by Bartók and Brahms on which he played piano along with Murray Perahia.

An album performance of John Adams's *Nixon in China* by the Orchestra of St. Luke's was "an inevitable nominee" for Best Opera Recording but also "a trendy longshot," according to the *L.A. Times,* correctly predicting its defeat. Still, *Nixon* earned its writer the consolation prize of Best Contemporary Composition. *Opera News* said of its recording, "Though the opera itself is a media event,

"The Beach Boys were beaten out by another set of veterans, Manhattan Transfer," *Variety* noted.

and the visual elements are sorely missed here, this is a brilliant execution of the score."

When the Grammy race began this year, *Variety* observed, "Notable by their absence from the list of nominees in 76 categories are Bruce Springsteen and Guns N' Roses. GN'R, especially, made its mark this year, selling 6 million copies of the *Appetite for Destruction* album. Though that disc was ineligible for consideration because it was released in July 1987, the hit singles 'Sweet Child o' Mine' and 'Welcome to the Jungle' had been expected to score in some categories, at the very least in the new hard rock/metal division.

"Drawing attention among the jazz nominees is Peggy Lee, whose appearance in the best female vocal performance derby, for her *Miss Peggy Lee Sings the Blues* album, makes her one of five contenders this year to have also been nominated in 1958, the year the awards started. The other longevity kings are Henry Mancini, Leonard Bernstein, Vladimir Horowitz and Isaac Stern."

Variety was startled by the inclusion of two "oddball picks" as Best New Artist nominees, claiming that "the soft-gospel group Take 6 and defrocked Miss America-turned-recording-star Vanessa Williams came out of left field. Shut out were such acclaimed new acts as Keith

Sweat, Al B. Sure!, Sinéad O'Connor and Edie Brickell and New Bohemians."

When the Grammy ceremony at the Los Angeles Shrine Auditorium was over, *Variety* reported, "The evening's most unusual moments were proved by female rock nominee Sinéad O'Connor, who performed wearing combat boots, ripped jeans and black halter top to go with her shaven head, and rapper Kool Moe Dee, who chided the record academy in rhyme for not presenting the new rap award" on TV. Billy Crystal was host of the ceremony.

Rolling Stone described the aftermath: "When the show was over, everyone stumbled out of L.A.'s Shrine Auditorium and into their limousines (except for O'Connor, who refuses to ride in a limo) and took off to the parties."

Out on the town later, Huey Lewis was overheard telling Olivia Newton-John, "This year's awards just weren't that exciting." Apparently, TV viewers agreed. It may have been a great night for McFerrin's "Don't Worry, Be Happy," but *Variety* reported, "CBS had little reason to be happy" when the Grammycast experienced its worst TV ratings ever, netting a 16 rating/26 share, down 24 percent from last year.

• 1988 •

Winners were announced at the Shrine Auditorium, Los Angeles, on February 22, 1989, for the eligibility period of October 1, 1987, through September 30, 1988.

ALBUM OF THE YEAR

• *Faith*, George Michael. Columbia/CBS.
  . . . Nothing Like the Sun, Sting. A&M.
  Roll with It, Steve Winwood. Virgin.
  Simple Pleasures, Bobby McFerrin. EMI/Manhattan.
  Tracy Chapman, Tracy Chapman. Elektra.

RECORD OF THE YEAR

• "Don't Worry, Be Happy," Bobby McFerrin. EMI/Manhattan.
  "Fast Car," Tracy Chapman. Elektra.
  "Giving You the Best That I Got," Anita Baker. Elektra.
  "Man in the Mirror," Michael Jackson. Epic.
  "Roll with It," Steve Winwood. Virgin.

SONG OF THE YEAR
(Songwriter's Award)

• "Don't Worry, Be Happy," Bobby McFerrin.
  "Be Still My Beating Heart," Sting.

"Fast Car," Tracy Chapman.
"Giving You the Best That I Got," Anita Baker, Skip Scarborough, Randy Holland.
"Piano in the Dark," Brenda Russell, Jeff Hall, Scott Cutler.

BEST NEW ARTIST

• Tracy Chapman
  Rick Astley
  Toni Childs
  Take 6
  Vanessa Williams

BEST POP VOCAL PERFORMANCE, MALE

• Bobby McFerrin, "Don't Worry, Be Happy." EMI/Manhattan.
  Phil Collins, "A Groovy Kind of Love." Atlantic.
  George Michael, "Father Figure." Columbia.
  Sting, "Be Still My Beating Heart." A&M.
  Steve Winwood, "Roll with It." Virgin.

BEST POP VOCAL PERFORMANCE, FEMALE

• Tracy Chapman, "Fast Car." Elektra.
  Taylor Dayne, *Tell It to My Heart.* Arista.

Whitney Houston, "One Moment in
Time." Arista.
Joni Mitchell, *Chalk Mark in a Rain
Storm*. Geffen.
Brenda Russell, *Get Here*. Elektra.

BEST POP VOCAL PERFORMANCE BY
A DUO OR GROUP WITH VOCAL

• Manhattan Transfer, *Brasil*. Altantic.
Beach Boys, "Kokomo." Elektra.
Escape Club, "Wild, Wild West."
Atlantic.
Gloria Estefan & Miami Sound
Machine, "Anything for You." Epic.
Brenda Russell, Joe Esposito, "Piano in
the Dark," track from *Get Here*. A&M.

BEST POP INSTRUMENTAL
PERFORMANCE

• David Sanborn, *Close-Up*. Reprise.
Kenny G, *Silhouette*. Arista.
M/A/R/R/S, "Pump Up the Volume." 4th
& Broadway/Island.
Mike Post, *Music from "L.A. Law" and
Otherwise*. Polydor.
Joe Satriani, "Always with Me, Always
with You." Relativity.

BEST ROCK VOCAL PERFORMANCE,
MALE

• Robert Palmer, "Simply Irresistible."
EMI/Manhattan.
Eric Clapton, "After Midnight." Polydor.
Joe Cocker, *Unchain My Heart*. Capitol.
Robbie Robertson, *Robbie Robertson*.
Geffen.
Rod Stewart, "Forever Young." Warner
Bros.

BEST ROCK VOCAL PERFORMANCE,
FEMALE

• Tina Turner, *Tina Live in Europe*.
Capitol.
Pat Benatar, "All Fired Up." Chrysalis.
Toni Childs, "Don't Walk Away," track
from *Union*. A&M.
Melissa Etheridge, "Bring Me Some
Water," track from *Melissa
Etheridge*. Island.
Sinéad O'Connor, *The Lion and the
Cobra*. Chrysalis.

BEST ROCK PERFORMANCE BY A
DUO OR GROUP WITH VOCAL

• U2, "Desire." Island.
INXS, *Kick*. Atlantic.
Joan Jett & the Blackhearts, "I Hate
Myself for Loving You." Blackheart.
Little Feat, *Let It Roll*. Warner Bros.
Midnight Oil, "Beds Are Burning."
Columbia/CBS.

BEST ROCK INSTRUMENTAL
PERFORMANCE

• Carlos Santana, *Blues for Salvador*.
Columbia/CBS.
Jeff Healey Band, "Hideaway," track
from *See the Light*. Arista.
Jimmy Page, "Writes of Winter," track
from *Outrider*. Geffen.
Joe Satriani, *Surfing with the Alien*. Rel-
ativity.
Frank Zappa, *Guitar*. Rykodisc.

BEST HARD ROCK/METAL
PERFORMANCE (VOCAL OR
INSTRUMENTAL)

• Jethro Tull, *Crest of a Knave*.
Chrysalis.
AC/DC, *Blow Up Your Video*. Atlantic.
Jane's Addiction, *Nothing's Shocking*.
Warner Bros.
Metallica, *And Justice for All*. Elektra.
Iggy Pop, "Cold Metal." A&M.

BEST RHYTHM & BLUES SONG
(Songwriter's Award)

• "Giving You the Best That I Got,"
Anita Baker, Skip Scarborough,
Randy Holland.
"Any Love," Luther Vandross, Marcus
Miller.
"Don't Be Cruel," Babyface, L. A. Reid,
Daryl Simmons.
"I'll Always Love You," Jimmy George.
"Just Got Paid," Johnny Kemp, Gene
Griffin.

BEST RHYTHM & BLUES VOCAL
PERFORMANCE, MALE

• Terence Trent D'Arby, *Introducing the
Hardline According to Terence Trent
D'Arby*. Columbia/CBS.

Teddy Pendergrass, *Joy*. Elektra.
Al B. Sure, "Nite and Day." Warner
Bros.
Luther Vandross, *Any Love*. Epic.
Stevie Wonder, *Characters*. Motown.

BEST RHYTHM & BLUES VOCAL PERFORMANCE, FEMALE

• Anita Baker, "Giving You the Best
That I Got." Elektra.
Taylor Dayne, "I'll Always Love You."
Arista.
Pebbles, "Girlfriend." MCA.
Karyn White, "The Way You Love Me."
Warner Bros.
Vanessa Williams, "The Right Stuff."
Wing.

BEST RHYTHM & BLUES PERFORMANCE BY A DUO OR GROUP WITH VOCAL

• Gladys Knight & the Pips, "Love
Overboard." MCA.
Robert Cray Band, "Acting This Way,"
track from *Don't Be Afraid of the
Dark*. Mercury.
E.U., "Da'Butt," track from *School
Daze* (film soundtrack). EMI.
Jets, "Rocket 2 U." MCA.
New Edition, "If It Isn't Love." MCA.

BEST RHYTHM & BLUES INSTRUMENTAL PERFORMANCE

• Chick Corea, "Light Years," track
from *GRP Super Live in Concert,
Vols. 1 and 2*. GRP.
Gerald Albright, "So Amazing."
Atlantic.
Cornell Dupree & Who It Is, *Coast to
Coast*. Antilles New Directions.
George Howard, *Reflections*. MCA.
Paul Jackson, Jr., *I Came to Play*.
Atlantic.
Doc Powell, "What's Going On," track
from *Love Is Where It's At*. Mercury.

BEST RAP PERFORMANCE

• D.J. Jazzy Jeff & the Fresh Prince,
"Parents Just Don't Understand,"
track from *He's the DJ, I'm the Rapper*. Jive.

J.J. Fad, "Supersonic."
Ruthless/Atlantic.
Kool Moe Dee, "Wild, Wild West,"
track from *How Ya Like Me Now*.
Jive.
L.L. Cool J, "Going Back to Cali."
Columbia.
Salt-n-Pepa, "Push It." Next Plateau.

BEST JAZZ VOCAL PERFORMANCE, MALE

• Bobby McFerrin, "Brothers," track
from *Rob Wasserman*'s *Duets*.
MCA.
Mose Allison, *Ever Since the World
Ended*. Blue Note.
João Gilberto, *Live in Montreux*. Elek-
tra.
Mark Murphy, *September Ballads*. Mile-
stone.
Mel Tormé, *A Vintage Year*. Concord
Jazz.

BEST JAZZ VOCAL PERFORMANCE, FEMALE

• Betty Carter, *Look What I Got!*
Verve.
Lena Horne, *The Men in My Life*. Three
Cherries Records.
Rickie Lee Jones, "Autumn Leaves,"
track from Rob Wasserman's *Duets*.
MCA.
Peggy Lee, *Miss Peggy Lee Sings the
Blues*. Musicmasters.
Carmen McRae, *Fine and Mellow*. Con-
cord Jazz.

BEST JAZZ VOCAL PERFORMANCE BY A DUO OR GROUP

• Take 6, "Spread Love." Reprise.
Jackie Cain, Roy Krat, *One More Rose*.
Audiophile.
Cunninghams, *Strings 'n' Swing "I
Remember Bird."* Discovery.
Lena Horne, Joe Williams, "I Won't
Leave You Again," track from *The
Men in My Life*. Three Cherries
Records.
Carmen McRae, Betty Carter, *The Car-
men McRae–Betty Carter Duets*.
Great American Music Hall.

BEST JAZZ INSTRUMENTAL PERFORMANCE BY A SOLOIST

- Michael Brecker, *Don't Try This at Home*. MCA-Impulse.

Miles Davis, *Music from Siesta*. Warner Bros.

Branford Marsalis, *Random Abstract*. Columbia/CBS.

Wynton Marsalis, *The Wynton Marsalis Quartet Live at Blues Alley*. Columbia/CBS.

Rob Wasserman, *Duets*. MCA.

BEST JAZZ INSTRUMENTAL PERFORMANCE BY A GROUP

- McCoy Tyner, Pharoah Sanders, David Murray, Cecil McBee, Roy Haynes, *Blues for Coltrane: A Tribute to John Coltrane*. MCA-Impulse.

Chick Corea Elektric Band, "Amnesia," track from *Eye of the Beholder*. GRP.

Keith Jarrett Trio, *Still Live*. ECM.

Branford Marsalis Quartet, *Random Abstract*. Columbia/CBS.

Wynton Marsalis Quartet, *The Wynton Marsalis Quartet Live at Blues Alley*. Columbia/CBS.

BEST JAZZ INSTRUMENTAL PERFORMANCE BY A BIG BAND

- Gil Evans & the Monday Night Orchestra, *Bud and Bird*. Intersound.

Gene Harris All-Star Big Band, *Tribute to Count Basie*. Concord Jazz.

Woody Herman's Thundering Herd, *Ebony*. RCA Victor.

Bill Holman Band, *Bill Holman Band*. JVC.

Illinois Jacquet & His Big Band, *Jacquet's Got It!* Atlantic Jazz.

BEST JAZZ FUSION PERFORMANCE

- Yellowjackets, *Politics*. MCA.

David Benoit, *Every Step of the Way*. GRP.

Lyle Mays, *Sweet Dreams*. Geffen.

John Patitucci, *John Patitucci*. GRP.

Tom Scott, "Amaretto," track from *Streamlines*. GRP.

BEST COUNTRY SONG (Songwriter's Award)

- *Hold Me*, K. T. Oslin. RCA.

"Chiseled in Stone," Vern Gosdin, Max D. Barnes. Columbia.

"I Couldn't Leave You If I Tried," Rodney Crowell. Columbia/CBS.

"She's No Lady," Lyle Lovett. Curb/MCA.

"Streets of Bakersfield," Homer Joy. Reprise.

BEST COUNTRY VOCAL PERFORMANCE, MALE

- Randy Travis, *Old 8 x 10*. Warner Bros.

Rodney Crowell, *Diamonds and Dirt*. Columbia/CBS.

Lyle Lovett, *Pontiac*. MCA.

Dan Seals, "Addicted." Capitol.

Dwight Yoakam, *Buenas Noches from a Lonely Room*. Reprise.

BEST COUNTRY VOCAL PERFORMANCE, FEMALE

- K. T. Oslin, "Hold Me," track from *This Woman*. RCA.

Emmylou Harris, "Back in Baby's Arms," track from *Planes, Trains and Automobiles—Original Motion Picture Soundtrack*. MCA.

k. d. lang, "I'm Down to My Last Cigarette." Sire.

Reba McEntire, *Reba*. MCA.

Tanya Tucker, "Strong Enough to Bend." Capitol.

BEST COUNTRY VOCAL PERFORMANCE BY A DUO OR GROUP WITH VOCAL

- Judds, "Give a Little Love," track from *Greatest Hits*. RCA.

Forrester Sisters, *Sincerely*. Warner Bros.

Highway 101, *Highway 101—2*. Warner Bros.

Oak Ridge Boys, "Gonna Take a Lot of River." MCA.

Restless Heart, *Big Dreams in a Small Town*. RCA.

BEST COUNTRY VOCAL COLLABORATION

- Roy Orbison, k. d. lang, "Crying." Virgin.

Earl Thomas Conley, Emmylou Harris, "We Believe in Happy Endings," track from Earl Thomas Conley's *The Heart of It All*. RCA.

Rodney Crowell, Rosanne Cash, "It's Such a Small World." Columbia/CBS.

k. d. lang, Brenda Lee, Loretta Lynn, Kitty Wells, "Honky Tonk Angels' Medley," track from k. d. lang's *Shadowland*. Sire.

Dwight Yoakam, Buck Owens, "Streets of Bakersfield." Reprise.

BEST COUNTRY INSTRUMENTAL PERFORMANCE

- Asleep at the Wheel, "Sugarfoot Rag," track from *Western Standard Time*. Epic.

Johnny Gimble, "Still Fiddlin' Around." MCA.

Leo Kottke, "Busy Signal," track from *Regards from Chuck Pink*. Private Music.

Carlton Moody & the Moody Brothers, "The Great Train Song Medley," track from *Do the Sugar Foot Rag*. Lamon.

Mason Williams & Mannheim Steamroller, "Country Idyll," track from *Classical Gas*. American Gramophone.

BEST GOSPEL PERFORMANCE, MALE

- Larnelle Harris, *Christmas*. Benson.

Steven Curtis Chapman, *Real Life Conversations*. Sparrow.

Steve Green, *Find Us Faithful*. Sparrow.

Michael W. Smith, *I 2 (Eye)*. Reunion.

Russ Taff, *Russ Taff*. Myrrh.

BEST GOSPEL PERFORMANCE, FEMALE

- Amy Grant, *Lead Me On*. A&M.

Margaret Becker, *The Reckoning*. Sparrow.

Sandi Patti, "Almighty God," track from *Make His Praise Glorious*. Word.

Deniece Williams, "Do You Hear What I Hear?" track from *Christmas—Various Artists*. Sparrow.

Delores Winans, "Precious Is the Name," track from *Ron Winans Family and Friends Choir*. Selah Records.

BEST GOSPEL PERFORMANCE BY A DUO, GROUP, CHOIR OR CHORUS

- Winans, *The Winans Live at Carnegie Hall*. Qwest.

DeGarmo & Key, *D&K*. Power Disc/Benson.

First Call, *An Evening in December, Vol. 2*. Dayspring/Word.

Whites, *Doing It by the Book*. Canaan/Word.

BeBe & CeCe Winans, "Silent Night, Holy Night," track from *Christmas—Various Artists*. Sparrow.

BEST SOUL GOSPEL PERFORMANCE, MALE

- BeBe Winans, "Abundant Life," track from *Ron Winans Family and Friends Choir*. Selah Records.

Walter Hawkins, solo tracks from *Special Gift*. Birthright.

Richard Smallwood, "You Did It All," track from *Visions*. Word.

Marvin Winans, "Dancin' in the Spirit," track from *Ron Winans Family and Friends Choir*. Selah Records.

Melvin Williams, *Back to the Cross*. Light.

BEST SOUL GOSPEL PERFORMANCE, FEMALE

- Aretha Franklin, *One Lord, One Faith, One Baptism*. Arista.

Vanessa Bell Armstrong, "Pressing On." Jive.

Shirley Caesar, *Live . . . in Chicago*. Rejoice.

Tramaine Hawkins, *The Joy That Floods My Soul*. Sparrow.

CeCe Winans, "I Have a Father," track from *Ronald Winans Family and Friends Choir*. Selah Records.

BEST SOUL GOSPEL PERFORMANCE BY A DUO, GROUP, CHOIR OR CHORUS

• Take 6, *Take 6*. Reprise
Clark Sisters, *Conqueror*. Rejoice/Word.
Aretha Franklin, Mavis Staples, "Oh Happy Day." Arista.
Edwin Hawkins, *That Name*. Birthright.
New Jersey Mass Choir, *Hold Up the Light*. Light.
Ronald Winans Family & Friends Choir, *Ron Winans Family and Friends Choir*. Selah Records.

BEST TRADITIONAL FOLK RECORDING

• *Folkways: A Vision Shared—A Tribute to Woody Guthrie and Leadbelly*, various artists. Columbia/CBS.
Irish Heartbeat, Van Morrison, Chieftains. Mercury.
Journey of Dreams, Ladysmith Black Mambazo. Warner Bros.
Le Mystère des Voix Bulgares, Bulgarian State Radio & Television Female Vocal Choir. Elektra/Nonesuch.
"Pretty Boy Floyd," track from *Folkways: A Vision Shared*, Bob Dylan. Columbia/CBS.

BEST CONTEMPORARY FOLK RECORDING

• *Tracy Chapman*, Tracy Chapman. Elektra.
"Emergency," track from *Live at Carnegie Hall*, Sweet Honey in the Rock. Flying Fish.
Homeland—A Collection of Black South African Music, various South African artists. Rounder.
John Prine Live, John Prine. Oh Boy.
Short Sharp Shocked, Michelle Shocked. Mercury.

BEST TRADITIONAL BLUES RECORDING

• *Hidden Charms*, Willie Dixon. Bug/Capitol.

Ain't Nothin' but a Party, Johnny Copeland. Rounder.
Live at Antone's Nightclub, James Cotton. Antone's Records.
Saturday Night Zydeco, Rockin' Dopsie. Maison de Soul.
The Story of My Life, Guitar Slim Jr. Orleans.

BEST CONTEMPORARY BLUES RECORDING

• "Don't Be Afraid of the Dark," the Robert Cray Band. Mercury.
Blues You Can Use, Bobby Bland. Malaco.
"Low-Commotion," track from *Get Rhythm*, Ry Cooder. Warner Bros.
Seven Year Itch, Etta James. Island.
Talk to Your Daughter, Robben Ford. Warner Bros.

BEST BLUEGRASS RECORDING (VOCAL OR INSTRUMENTAL)

• *Southern Flavor*, Bill Monroe. MCA.
Drive, Bela Fleck. Rounder.
Fifteenth Anniversary Celebration, Live at the Kennedy Center, Seldom Scene & Their Very Special Guests. Sugar Hill.
Home Is Where the Heart Is, David Grisman. Rounder.
New Moon Rising, Peter Rowan & the Nashville Bluegrass Band. Sugar Hill.

BEST LATIN POP PERFORMANCE

• Roberto Carlos, *Roberto Carlos*. Discos CBS International.
Dyango, *Cae la Noche*. EMI.
José José, *Soy Así*. Ariola.
José Luis Perales, *Sueno de Libertad*. Discos CBS International.
Raphael, *Las Apariencias Enganan*. Discos CBS International.

BEST TROPICAL LATIN PERFORMANCE

• Rubén Blades, Son del Solar, *Antecedente*. Elektra.
Oscar D'Leon, *La Salsa Soy Yo*. TH-Rodven U.S.A.
Pete Escovedo, *Mister E*. Crossover.

Johnny Pacheco, Pete "El Conde" Rodriguez, *Salsobita*. Fania.

Eddie Santiago, *Sigo Astrevido*. TH-Rodven U.S.A.

BEST MEXICAN-AMERICAN PERFORMANCE

• Linda Ronstadt, *Canciones de Mi Padre*. Elektra.

Los Bukis, *Si Me Recuerdas*. Melody.

Los Freddy's, *Vida Nueva*. EMI.

Flaco Jimenez, *Flaco's Amigos*. Arhoolie.

José Javier Solis, *No Me Olvidaras*. Profono.

Los Tigres del Norte, *Idolos del Pueblo*. Fonovisa.

Pio Trevino & Majic, *Quiero Verte Otra Vez*. Discos CBS International.

Los Yonics, *Petalo y Espinas*. Fonovisa.

BEST REGGAE RECORDING

• *Conscious Party*, Ziggy Marley & the Melody Makers. Virgin.

"Breakfast in Bed," track from *UB40*. UB40, Chrissie Hynde. A&M.

Hanging Fire, Jimmy Cliff. Columbia/ CBS.

Toots in Memphis, Toots (Hibbert). Mango/Island.

UB40, UB40. A&M.

BEST POLKA RECORDING

• *Born to Polka*, Jimmy Sturr & His Orchestra. Starr.

All Aboard It's Polka Time, Walter Ostanek & His Band. World Renowned Sounds.

Join the Polka Generation, Lenny Gomulka's Chicago Push. World Renowned Sounds.

Let's Have a Party, Stas Bulanda's Average Polka Band. Chicago Polkas.

Sounds from a Polka Party, Jimmy Weber & the Sounds. World Renowned Sounds.

BEST NEW AGE PERFORMANCE

• Shadowfax, *Folksongs for a Nuclear Village*. Capitol.

Suzanne Ciani, *Neverland*. Private Music.

Mark Isham, *Castalia*. Virgin.

Steve Khan, Rob Mounsey, *Local Color*. Denon.

Paul Winter, "Down in Belgorod," track from *Earthbeat*. Living Music.

BEST ARRANGEMENT ON AN INSTRUMENTAL

• Roger Kellaway, "Memos from Paradise," track from *Memos from Paradise* (Eddie Daniels). GRP.

David Balakrishnan, "A Night in Tunisia," track from *Turtle Island String Quartet* (Turtle Island String Quartet). Windham Hill.

Bill Barber, Bill Berg, Jimmy Johnson & Dick Oatts, "Jazz Patrol," track from *The Further Adventures of Flim and the BB's* (Flim & the BB's). DMP.

John Dankworth, "Caravan," track from *Misty* (John Dankworth conducting the London Symphony Orchestra). Pro Arte.

Henry Mancini, "Suite from *The Thorn Birds*," track from *Premier Pops* (Henry Mancini & R.P.O. Pops). Denon.

BEST INSTRUMENTAL COMPOSITION

• "The Theme from *L.A. Law*," track from *Music from "L.A. Law" and Otherwise*, Mike Post (Mike Post). Polydor.

Central City Sketches (side 2), Benny Carter, composer, and conducting the American Jazz Orchestra. Musicmasters.

"Eternal Child," track from *Eye of the Beholder*, Chick Corea (Chick Corea Elektric Band). GRP.

"Olympic Spirit," track from 1988 Summer Olympics album *One Moment in Time*, John Williams (John Williams). Arista.

"Winter Games," track from *The Symphony Sessions*, David Foster (Vancouver Symphony). Atlantic.

BEST MUSICAL CAST SHOW ALBUM

- *Into the Woods*, Bernadette Peters, Joanna Gleason, Chip Zien, Tom Aldredge, Robert Westenberg. Stephen Sondheim, music and lyrics. RCA.

Anything Goes, Patti LuPone, Bill McCutcheon, Howard McGillian, others. Cole Porter, composer and lyricist. RCA.

Chess, David Carroll, Philip Casnoff, Judy Kuhn, others. Benny Andersson, Bjorn Ulvaeus, composers; Tim Rice, lyricist. RCA Victor.

Of Thee I Sing/Let 'Em Eat Cake, Maureen McGovern, Larry Kert, Jack Gilford. Michael Tilson Thomas conducting the New York Choral Artists & Orchestra of St. Luke's. George & Ira Gershwin. CBS.

Show Boat, Frederica von Stade, Jerry Hadley, Teresa Stratas, Nancy Culp, Lillian Gish, others. John McGlinn conducting the London Sinfonietta. Jerome Kern, composer; Oscar Hammerstein, lyricist. Angel.

BEST ALBUM OF ORIGINAL INSTRUMENTAL BACKGROUND SCORE WRITTEN FOR A MOTION PICTURE OR TV

- *The Last Emperor*, Ryuichi Sakamoto, David Byrne, Cong Su. Virgin.

Empire of the Sun, John Williams. Warner Bros.

Fatal Attraction, Maurice Jarre. GNP-Crescendo.

Tucker: The Man and His Dream, Joe Jackson. A&M.

Who Framed Roger Rabbit, Alan Silvestri. Walt Disney Records.

BEST SONG WRITTEN SPECIFICALLY FOR A MOTION PICTURE OR TV

- "Two Hearts," track from *Buster*, Phil Collins, Lamont Dozier (Phil Collins). Atlantic.

"Century's End," track from *Bright Lights, Big City*, Donald Fagen. Warner Bros.

"Cry Freedom," track from *Cry Freedom*, George Fenton & Jonas Gwangwa. MCA.

"Kokomo," track from *Cocktail*, Mike Love, Terry Melcher, John Philips, Scott Mackenzie (Beach Boys). Elektra.

"One Moment in Time," track from 1988 Summer Olympics Album *One Moment in Time*, Albert Hammond, John Bettis (Whitney Houston). Arista.

BEST INSTRUMENTAL ARRANGEMENT ACCOMPANYING VOCAL(S)

- Jonathan Tunick, "No One Is Alone," track from *Cleo Sings Sondheim* (Cleo Laine). RCA.

Henry Mancini, "Volare," track from *Volare* (Luciano Pavarotti). London.

Marcus Miller, "Funny," track from *Other Roads* (Boz Scaggs). Columbia/CBS.

Mike Renzi, "I Wish I'd Met You," track from *Men in My Life* (Lena Horne, Sammy Davis, Jr.). Three Cherries Records.

Thomas Dolby & the Lost Toy People, "The Key to Her Ferrari," track from *Aliens Ate My Buick* (Thomas Dolby). EMI/Manhattan.

BEST CLASSICAL ALBUM

- *Verdi: Requiem and Operatic Choruses*, Robert Shaw conducting the Atlanta Symphony Orchestra and Chorus. Telarc.

Horowitz Plays Mozart (Piano Concerto No. 23 in A and Piano Sonata No. 13 in B Flat), Vladimir Horowitz, piano; Carlo Maria Giulini conducting La Scala Opera Orchestra. Deutsche Grammophon.

Mahler: Symphony No. 2 in C Minor ("Resurrection"), Leonard Bernstein conducting the New York Philharmonic. Deutsche Grammophon.

Rorem: String Symphony; Sunday Morning; Eagles, Robert Shaw conducting the Atlanta Symphony Orchestra for "String Symphony";

Louis Lane conducting the Atlanta Symphony Orchestra for "Sunday Morning," "Eagles." New World.

Wagner: Lohengrin, Sir Georg Solti conducting the Vienna State Opera Choir and Vienna Philharmonic (solos: Placido Domingo, Jessye Norman, Eva Randova, Siegmund Nimsgern, Hans Sotin, Dietrich Fischer-Dieskau). London.

BEST ORCHESTRAL RECORDING
(Conductor's Award)

• *Rorem: String Symphony,* Robert Shaw conducting the Atlanta Symphony Orchestra; *Sunday Morning, Eagles,* Louis Lane conducting the Atlanta Symphony. New World.

Beethoven: Symphony No. 9 in D Minor, Roger Norrington conducting the London Classical Players. Angel.

Bruckner: Symphony No. 7 in E, Sir Georg Solti conducting the Chicago Symphony Orchestra. London.

Copland: Appalachian Spring (Complete); Letter from Home; John Henry; Cortège Macabre from Grohg, Leonard Slatkin conducting the St. Louis Symphony Orchestra. Angel.

Mahler: Symphony No. 2 in C Minor ("Resurrection"), Leonard Bernstein conducting the New York Philharmonic. Deutsche Grammophon.

BEST CHAMBER MUSIC PERFORMANCE (INSTRUMENTAL OR VOCAL)

• Murray Perahia, Sir Georg Solti, pianos; David Corkhill, Evelyn Glennie, percussion, *Bartók: Sonata for 2 Pianos and Percussion; Brahms: Variation on a Theme by Joseph Haydn for 2 Pianos.* CBS Masterworks.

Guarneri Quartet, *Dvořák: String Quartet in F ("American Quartet"); Smetana: String Quartet in E Minor ("From My Life").* Philips.

Kim Kashkashian, viola; Robert Levin, piano, *Hindemith: Viola Sonata Op.*

11, No. 4; Violin Sonata, 4; Op. 25, No. 4; Violin Sonatas, 1937). ECM.

Gidon Kremer, violin; Martha Argerich, piano, *Beethoven: Violin-Piano Sonatas No. 4 in A, Op. 23, and No. 5 in F, Op. 24.* Deutsche Grammophon.

James Levine, piano; Ensemble Wien-Berlin, *Mozart: Quintet in E Flat for Piano and Winds, K. 452; Beethoven: Quintet in E Flat for Piano and Winds, Op. 16.* Deutsche Grammophon.

BEST CLASSICAL PERFORMANCE, INSTRUMENTAL SOLOIST(S) (WITH ORCHESTRA)

• Vladimir Horowitz, piano (Carlo Maria Giulini conducting La Scala Opera Orchestra), *Mozart: Piano Concerto No. 23 in A.* Deutsche Grammophon.

Gary Gray, clarinet (Harry Newstone conducting the Royal Philharmonic Orchestra), *The Art of Gary Gray (Copland: Clarinet Concerto; Lutoslawski: Dance Preludes for Clarinet and Orchestra; Arnold: Clarinet Concerto No. 1; etc.).* Unicorn/ Kanchana Records.

Zoltan Kocsis, piano (Ivan Fischer conducting the Budapest Festival Orchestra), *Bartók: Works for Piano and Orchestra (Concerto No. 1, Concerto No. 2, Rhapsody for Piano and Orchestra, etc.).* Philips.

Wynton Marsalis, trumpet (Raymond Leppard conducting the English Chamber Orchestra), *Baroque Music for Trumpets (Vivaldi, Telemann, Pachelbel, Haydn, von Biber).* CBS Masterworks.

Itzhak Perlman, violin (Zubin Mehta conducting the Israel Philharmonic Orchestra), *Bruch: Scottish Fantasy and Violin Concerto No. 2 in D Minor.* Angel.

Isaac Stern, violin (Lorin Maazel conducting the Orchestre National de France), *Dutilleux: L'Arbre des Songes—Concerto for Violin and Orchestra.* CBS Masterworks.

Isaac Stern, violin; Yo-Yo Ma, cello (Claudio Abbado conducting the Chicago Symphony Orchestra), *Brahms: Double Concerto in A Minor, Op. 102.* CBS Masterworks.

BEST CLASSICAL PERFORMANCE, INSTRUMENTAL SOLOIST(S) (WITHOUT ORCHESTRA)

• Alicia de Larrocha, piano, *Albéniz: Iberia; Navarra; Suite Espagnola.* London.

Alfred Brendel, piano, *Liszt: Années de Pèlerinage, Second Year: Italy.* Philips.

Vladimir Horowitz, piano, *Mozart: Piano Sonata No. 13 in B Flat, K. 333.* Deutsche Grammophon.

Keith Jarrett, piano. *Bach: The Well-Tempered Clavier, Book I.* ECM.

Maurizio Pollini, piano, *Schubert: The Late Piano Sonatas (D. 958, 959, 960); 3 Piano Pieces, D. 946; Allegretto, D. 915.* Deutsche Grammophon.

BEST OPERA RECORDING

• *Wagner: Lohengrin,* Sir Georg Solti conducting the Vienna State Opera Choir and Vienna Philharmonic (solos: Placido Domingo, Dietrich Fischer-Dieskau, Siegmund Nimsgern, Jessye Norman, Eva Randova, Hans Sotin). London.

Adams: Nixon in China, Edo de Waart conducting the Orchestra of St. Luke's (solos: Sanford Sylvan, James Maddalena, Thomas Hammons, John Duykers, Carolann Page). Elektra/Nonesuch.

Bellini: Norma, Richard Bonynge conducting the Welsh National Opera Orchestra and Chorus (solos: Joan Sutherland, Luciano Pavarotti, Montserrat Caballé, Samuel Ramey). London.

Bernstein, Wadsworth: A Quiet Place, Leonard Bernstein conducting the Austrian Radio Symphony (solos: Chester Ludgin, Beverly Morgan, John Brandstetter, Peter Kazaras,

Jean Kraft, Wendy White). Deutsche Grammophon.

Mozart: Idomeneo, Sir John Pritchard conducting the Vienna Philharmonic Orchestra and Chorus (solos: Luciano Pavarotti, Agnes Baltsa, Lucia Popp, Edita Gruberova, Leo Nucci). London.

Puccini: La Bohème, Leonard Bernstein conducting the Chorus and Orchestra of Santa Cecilia (solos: Angelina Reaux, Jerry Hadley, Barbara Daniels, Thomas Hampson). Deutsche Grammophon.

BEST CHORAL PERFORMANCE (OTHER THAN OPERA)

• Robert Shaw conducting the Atlanta Symphony Orchestra and Chorus, *Verdi: Requiem and Operatic Choruses.* Telarc.

Helmuth Froschauer, chorus master; Herbert von Karajan conducting the Vienna Singverein and Vienna Philharmonic, *Mozart: Requiem.* Deutsche Grammophon.

John Eliot Gardiner conducting the Monteverdi Choir, the English Baroque Soloists, *Bach: Christmas Oratorio.* Archiv.

Margaret Hillis, choral director; Sir Georg Solti conducting the Chicago Symphony Chorus and Orchestra, *Bach: St. Matthew Passion.* London.

Trevor Pinnock conducting the English Concert Choir and English Concert, *Vivaldi: Gloria; Scarlatti: Dixit Dominus.* Archiv.

BEST CLASSICAL PERFORMANCE, VOCAL SOLOIST

• Luciano Pavarotti, tenor (Emerson Buckley conducting the Symphonic Orchestra of Amelia Romagna "Arturo Toscanini") *Luciano Pavarotti in Concert* (arias from *Lucia di Lammermoor, Rigoletto, La Bohème, Fedora, Turandot*). CBS Masterworks.

Arleen Auger, soprano (Dalton Baldwin, accompanist), *Love Songs* (Copland,

R. Strauss, Poulenc, Mahler, Schumann, Gounod, Schubert). Delos.

Jan DeGaetani, mezzo-soprano (Gilbert Kalish, accompanist), *Songs of America* (Stephen Foster, Elliott Carter, Ruth Crawford, Milton Babbitt, George Crumb, Carrie Jacobs-Bond, Irving Fine, Sergius Kagen). Elektra/Nonesuch.

Christa Ludwig, soprano (James Levine, accompanist), *Schubert: Winterreise.* Deutsche Grammophon.

Jessye Norman, soprano (Geoffrey Parsons, accompanist), *Handel, Schubert, Schumann: Lieder (Jessye Norman—Live at Hohenems).* Philips Classics.

BEST CONTEMPORARY COMPOSITION

• John Adams, *Nixon in China* (Edo de Waart conducting the Orchestra of St. Luke's). Elektra/Nonesuch.

Leonard Bernstein, Stephen Wadsworth, *A Quiet Place* (Leonard Bernstein conducting the Austrian Radio Symphony Orchestra; soloists). Deutsche Grammophon.

William Bolcom, *Symphony No. 4* (Slatkin conducting the St. Louis Orchestra; Joan Morris, mezzo-soprano). New World.

Ned Rorem, *String Symphony* (Robert Shaw conducting the Atlanta Symphony Orchestra). New World.

Karlheinz Stockhausen, *Amour* (Suzanne Stephens, clarinet). Deutsche Grammophon.

BEST ENGINEERED RECORDING, CLASSICAL

• Jack Renner, *Verdi: Requiem and Operatic Choruses* (Robert Shaw conducting the Atlanta Symphony Chorus and Orchestra). Telarc.

Simon Eadon, *Bruckner: Symphony No. 7 in E* (Sir Georg Solti conducting the Chicago Symphony Orchestra). London.

Cees Heijkoop, Willem van Leeuwen, Volker Strauss, *Beethoven: The 9*

Symphonies (Complete) (Bernard Haitink conducting the Concertgebouw Orchestra). Philips Classics.

Jack Renner, *Beethoven: Missa Solemnis; Mozart: Great C Minor Mass* (Robert Shaw conducting the Atlanta Symphony Chorus and Orchestra, soloists). Telarc.

Klaus Scheibe, *Mahler: Symphony No. 2 ("Resurrection")* (Leonard Bernstein conducting the New York Philharmonic). Deutsche Grammophon.

CLASSICAL PRODUCER OF THE YEAR

• Robert Woods
Andrew Cornall
Steven Epstein
Thomas Frost
Joanna Nickrenz

BEST COMEDY RECORDING

• *Good Morning, Vietnam*, Robin Williams. A&M.

Even Worse, Weird Al Yankovic. Scotti Bros./Rock 'n' Roll Records.

Fontaine: Why Am I Straight? Whoopie Goldberg. MCA.

Jonathan Winters Finally Captured, Jonathan Winters. Dove Books on Tape.

What Am I Doing in New Jersey? George Carlin. Eardrum.

BEST SPOKEN WORD OR NONMUSICAL RECORDING

• "Speech by Rev. Jesse Jackson, July 27," track from Aretha Franklin's *One Lord, One Faith, One Baptism*, Rev. Jesse Jackson. Arista.

A Christmans Carol (Charles Dickens), Sir John Gielgud. Bantam Audio Publishing.

A Prairie Home Companion: The 2nd Annual Farewell Performance, various artists, Garrison Keillor. Minnesota Public Radio.

The Screwtape Letters (C. S. Lewis), John Cleese. Audio Literature.

Winters' Tales (Jonathan Winters), Jonathan Winters. Sound Editions.

BEST RECORDING FOR CHILDREN

- *Pecos Bill*, Robin Williams, narrator; Ry Cooder, music. Windham Hill.
- *The Bible: The Amazing Book*, Candle. Sparrow.
- *The Legend of Sleepy Hollow*, Glenn Close, narrator; Tim Story, music. Windham Hill.
- *Peter and the Wolf/Carnival of the Animals, Part II*, Weird Al Yankovic, narrator; Wendy Carlos, music. Epic.
- *The Tailor of Gloucester*, Meryl Streep, narrator; Chieftains, music. Windham Hill.
- *The Tale of Peter Rabbit, . . .* , Meryl Streep, narrator; Lyle Mays, music. Windham Hill.

BEST ENGINEERED RECORDING (OTHER THAN CLASSICAL)

- Tom Lord Alge, *Roll with It* (Steve Winwood). Virgin.
- John Archer, *Through the Lens* (Checkfield). American Gramaphone.
- Ray Bardani, John Potoker, *Provision* (Scritti Politti). Warner Bros.
- Mick Guzauski, *Facets* (Doc Severinsen). Amherst.
- George Massenburg, *Let It Roll* (Little Feat). Warner Bros.
- Elliot Scheiner, *Soul Searchin'* (Glenn Frey). MCA.

BEST ALBUM PACKAGE
(Art Director's Award)

- Bill Johnson, *Tired of the Runnin'* (O'Kanes). Columbia/CBS.
- Andrew Reid, *Bete Noire* (Bryan Ferry). Reprise.
- Jeri Heiden, *Brian Wilson* (Brian Wilson). Sire.
- Bruce Licher, *Our Beloved Revolutionary Sweetheart* (Camper Van Beethoven). Virgin.
- Henry Marquez, *Picture This* (Valentine Brothers). EMI America.

BEST ALBUM NOTES
(Annotator's Award)

- Anthony DeCurtis, *Crossroads* (Eric Clapton). Polydor.

John Edward Hasse, *The Classic Hoagy Carmichael* (Hoagy Carmichael & others). Indiana Historical Society.
Miles Kreuger, *Show Boat* (Frederica von Stade, Jerry Hadley, Teresa Stratas, Nancy Culp, Lillian Gish & others; John McGlinn conducting the London Sinfonietta). Angel.
Dan Morgenstern, *The Complete Commodore Jazz Recordings, Vol. 1*. Mosaic.
Vaughn Webb, *Virginia Traditions: Southwest Virginia Blues*. BRI.

BEST HISTORICAL ALBUM

- *Crossroads*, Eric Clapton. Polydor.
- *The Classic Hoagy Carmichael*, Hoagy Carmichael & others. Indiana Historical Society.
- *The Complete Commodore Jazz Recordings, Vol. 1*, various artists. Mosaic.
- *Djangologie USA*, Django Reinhartdt. Disques Swing.
- *The Erteguns' New York—New York Cabaret Music*, various artists. Atlantic.

PRODUCER OF THE YEAR (OTHER THAN CLASSICAL)

- Neil Dorfsman
- Thomas Dolby
- David Kershenbaum
- L. A. Reid, Babyface
- Narada Michael Walden

BEST PERFORMANCE MUSIC VIDEO

- *Where the Streets Have No Name*, U2. Meiert Avis, director. Island.
- *Check It Out*, John Cougar Mellencamp. Jonathon Dark, director. Polygram Music Video-U.S.
- *Glass Spider*, David Bowie. David Mallet, director. MPI Home Video.
- *Stevie Nicks: Live at Red Rocks*, Stevie Nicks. Marty Callner, director. Sony Video Software.
- *The Symphony Sessions*, David Foster. Tony Greco, director. Atlantic Records Video.

BEST CONCEPT MUSIC VIDEO

- *Fat*, Weird Al Yankovic. Jay Levey, director. Rock 'n' Roll/Epic.
Get a Job, Hampton String Quartet. Sara Nichols, director. RCA.
Storytelling Giants, Talking Heads. David Byrne, director. Warner Reprise Video.
This Note's for You, Neil Young. Julien Temple, director. Reprise/Warner Bros.
When We Was Fab, George Harrison. Godley & Creme, directors. Warner Bros.

• 1989 •

Bonnie Raitt Gets "Real"—Milli Vanilli "Phony Baloney!"

It was "a real miracle," Bonnie Raitt said of the shocking outcome of this year's Grammys.

For 20 years, stardom had eluded the veteran country-rock and blues artist who the *New York Times* once said "always seemed to be 'too good' a singer—too self-effacing, too subtle, too 'real'—to become a major pop star." The daughter of noted Broadway singer John Raitt had quit college in 1969 to explore new musical directions in the smoky, dim-lit clubs of New York and Boston where she developed a faithful following—and eventually a serious drinking problem. Her albums sold well but never climbed higher than 25th in the pop charts, so she was dropped by Warner Bros. after 15 years.

But once she sobered up and Capitol signed her up to record again, *Variety* reported on the amazing career resurrection that followed: "Bonnie Raitt stole the show and the hearts of the audience at the 32nd annual Grammy Awards. To the astonishment of critics and fans alike, Raitt defeated Don Henley, Tom Petty, Fine Young Cannibals and the Traveling Wilburys for the coveted Album of the Year trophy and pulled something of an upset in the female pop vocal performance category as well. Her other wins were for Best Female Rock Vocal Performance and Best Traditional Blues Recording for her 'I'm in the Mood' collaboration with John Lee Hooker on his Chameleon album *The Healer*."

"Had I been asked three years ago to evaluate the chances of Ms. Raitt's winning four Grammy Awards with an album that would sell over two million copies, I would have shaken my head and said 'impossible,'" wrote critic Stephen

"The impossible has happened," said *The New York Times* when Bonnie Raitt nabbed four prizes, including best album and a blues award she shared with John Lee Hooker (right).

Holden in the *New York Times* after her sweep. "Now the impossible has happened. [But] Ms. Raitt's late-blooming success is anything but accidental. *Nick of Time* captures and defines a moment in her generation's self-awareness."

Nick of Time expressed the 40-year-old's new sober views on love and getting older. It may have sold a million copies prior to the Grammycast, signaling a dramatic comeback for her, but it was ranked only 40th on the LP charts at its highest and was considered "a l-o-n-g shot" for Album of the Year by the *L.A. Times*.

The *L.A. Times* had predicted that the Fine Young Cannibals' *The Raw and the Cooked* would prevail, while other Grammy pundits foresaw a romp by the self-titled album by the Traveling Wilburys, a group comprised of rock vets George Harrison, Bob Dylan, Jeff Lynne, Tom Petty and the late Roy Orbison. But Raitt capped off her surprising career rally with one of the biggest upsets in Grammy history.

Raitt scored a Grammy for each of her four nominations, becoming only the fourth female artist ever to win Album of the Year, following earlier triumphs by Judy Garland, Barbra Streisand and Carole King. After her first few victories, Raitt told the viewing audience, "I'm so transported!" Finally stunned by her fourth win for the year's top LP, she said, "I can only take so much of this! Wake me when it's over!

"I'd like to thank God for bringing me to this at a time when I can really appreciate it," she added in a more somber voice, noting that *Nick of Time* was "my first sober album. I made a lot of changes in my life, but I don't take responsibility for that." She credited "divine intervention" instead. Then she smiled proudly at the audience and said, "My sobriety means I'm going to feel *great* tomorrow!"

Soon after the show, one record store executive reported, "Business absolutely exploded." Never before had the Grammys made such an impact on a winner's career. *Nick of Time* jumped to number 22 from 40th place in the trade paper's album chart, then up to number 6, then to first place for nearly a month, thereby doubling the LP's pre-Grammy sales. The *Washington Post* said her Grammy success proved that "good things happen to good people, although sometimes only in good time. Maybe that's why Raitt, 40, called her album *Nick of Time*."

Surveying the candidates in the Record of the Year category, the *L.A. Times* openly addressed the artist it was sure would clinch it for "We Didn't Start the Fire." "Billy Joel, get that tux pressed," the paper ordered.

Joel was competing against Grammy's Best New Artist of 1973, Bette Midler, who was up for "Wind Beneath My Wings," a ballad she sang in her hit movie *Beaches*. The *L.A. Times* blew it off: "'Wind Beneath My Wings' is the kind of single that would have won hands-down

in the early 1970s, but no longer." *L.A. Times* music editor Robert Hilburn picked Don Henley's "The End of the Innocence" to sail through. "The worst case scenario," he wrote, "is a Midler or Joel victory." He added, "'Wind Beneath My Wings' is a hopelessly leaden melodrama, while 'We Didn't Start the Fire' is shallow and irritating. Either record on a jukebox should be enough to empty a room."

Variety reported on the shocking outcome: "Despite the much-applauded profusion of rock nominations this year, the Recording Academy's traditionally favored ballads again snagged several of the top prizes," including Record of the Year for Bette Midler's "Wind Beneath My Wings."

In her acceptance speech, Midler told the audience, "I'm stunned and I'm flabbergasted," then roared, "Hey, Bonnie Raitt, I got one, too!" "Wind" swept the category of Song of the Year, too, for its writers, Larry Henley and Jeff Silbar. Backstage, Henley told reporters, "I'd like to thank Bonnie Raitt for not being in my category."

What *Variety* called "the biggest disgrace in Grammy history" occurred over the naming of this year's Best New Artist—Milli Vanilli—a pop act from West Germany that had previously won the equivalent honor at the American Music Awards (plus two other prizes) and the 1989 Juno Award for Best International Album (*Girl You Know It's True*) bestowed by the Canadian Academy of Recording Arts and Sciences.

Milli's Grammy victory was ominous from the beginning. The *Washington Post* noted that the news of their win "played better in the balcony (where the fans sit) than it did in the mezzanine seats occupied by industry folk."

When Milli Vanilli (translation: "positive energy" in Turkish) first hit the pop scene, *Time* magazine wrote, "Unheard of. Milli Vanilli, a dance-music duo that sounds like Alvin and the Chipmunks and speaks English like the two Teutonic muscleheads on *Saturday Night Live,* has done something boggling. The group, scorned by critics and adored by clubgoers and devotees of MTV, has scored three No. 1 singles off its debut album. The Millis appear in their videos snazzily dressed, or half dressed, whirling like cotton candy around a spool. Their lighter-than-airhead lyrics and freeze-dried hip-hop rhythms combine pop and pap in tunes for instant consumption and rapid oblivion."

Milli Vanilli was more than just the flavor of the week. *Girl* sold as briskly as fast food, racking up 7 million copies in sales in the United States and 12 million worldwide. Nothing seemed to dent the pair's enormous popularity, not even the results of *Rolling Stone*'s annual Critics' Picks Poll, which voted Milli the worst band of 1989 and *Girl* the worst album. ("We don't listen to what the critics say," Milli member Rob Pilatus told the *L.A. Times*. "It's not important what they think of us.") And not even the persistent rumor that the "dreadlocked duo," as they were nicknamed in the press, didn't really sing their own music—a stinging allegation that would be proved true.

Soon after their Grammy Awards triumph, the seemingly invincible Rob Pilatus and Fabrice Morvan, who had never sung professionally before, insisted that they do the vocals on their next album. When producer Frank Farian refused, they fired him. Then Farian retaliated by admitting the deception publicly, and suddenly Milli Vanilli had to face the music.

The outcry that followed was horrific—and hilarious. "Milli Vanilli, Phony Baloney," roared a headline in the *New York Post*. "For Sham, Silli Vanilli!" countered a headline in the *New York Daily News*. N.A.R.A.S. President Michael Greene said that the academy trustees "were just livid about the situation," adding, "It was fraud and we're appalled by it."

At a quickly called press conference in New York, Pilatus pleaded for sympathy. "We were living together in the projects, with two other musicians in Munich," he told reporters. "We had nothing to eat, and

"Bonnie Raitt stole the show and the hearts [of Grammy watchers] after years of relative obscurity," said *Variety*.

we were unhappy. We wanted to be stars. And suddenly this guy [Farian] gave us a chance and we took it." Pitalus insisted that he and Morvan had informed Arista executives of the hoax early on (a charge denied by Arista) but also admitted they had "made a pact with the devil" for fame, which spawned new headlines the next day proclaiming "The Devil Made Them Do It." "But we don't understand that it's us, the two little guys from Germany, the victims, who have to play suddenly the role of the crooks," he added. The reporters present goaded the twosome into proving that they could really sing by insisting they perform "Girl You Know It's True" on the spot. "The performance, with their trademark dreadlocks shaking," noted *Time,* "only proved once more that looking good was what they did best."

Pilatus and Morvan might not have suffered such open scorn had it not been for some smug remarks they made earlier in their career. "Musically, we are more talented than any Bob Dylan," Pilatus once boasted. "Musically, we are more talented than Paul McCartney. Mick Jagger, his lines are not clear. He don't know how he should produce a sound. I'm the new modern rock & roll. I'm the new Elvis."

Shortly after the press conference, N.A.R.A.S. ended the affair officially by stripping Milli Vanilli of its award based on the admission that *Girl*'s album credits had been falsified.

Elsewhere in the pop field, Michael Bolton topped Prince, Billy Joel, Richard Marx and Roy Orbison for the best male pop vocal Grammy for "How Am I Supposed to Live Without You." (Prince's bid was considered an oddity because his *Batman* music was mostly instrumental.) Bolton's career dated back to the late 1970s when he was the lead singer of the pop/rock group Blackjack before breaking away on a solo path in 1983. In his acceptance remarks, he acknowledged that his recent success made him seem like an overnight sensation, but he added, "It was more like 3,642 nights."

The British band Fine Young Cannibals was expected to devour the pop group vocal laurels for "She Drives Me Crazy" but was upset by the U.S. duo of Aaron Neville and Linda Ronstadt for "Don't Know Much," which they also sang on the Grammycast. (The performance was "quite good," opined the *Washington Post*.) "Don't Know Much" was a single from the Neville Brothers' *Yellow Moon*. Another track, "Healing Chant," earned all four brothers (Aaron, Arthur, Charles and Cyril) the instrumental trophy. In her acceptance speech, Ronstadt thanked her partner's mother, saying, "She gave us not only Aaron, but all the Neville Brothers, and that's a pretty great musical contribution." Ronstadt's and the Nevilles' producer, Peter Asher, repeated his 1977 victory as Producer of the Year.

Former Eagle Don Henley made up for his loss in the Record and Song of the Year categories by rallying to claim the best male rock vocal performance honors for *The End of the Innocence,* which he won only moments after performing the title track on the show. "Great," he said, smiling, upon accepting the award. "You sing a song, you win an award."

> *Variety* called Milli Vanilli "the biggest disgrace in Grammy history."

The Traveling Wilburys rebounded from their defeat for Album of the Year, too, to receive the rock group accolade, giving Tom Petty and Jeff Lynne each their first Grammy. Petty had been nominated seven times in previous years; Lynne, never.

Both Henley and Petty began the award race with four nominations, but *Variety* claimed that both rockers were "virtually swept aside by the wave of balladeer winners" at this year's Grammys. Completely snubbed were the Rolling Stones, still Grammyless thanks to the Wilburys' victory in the rock group category.

Former Yardbird Jeff Beck had teamed up in the past with other artists such as Donovan, but now he earned the prize for Best Rock Instrumental Performance for *Jeff Beck's Guitar Shop with Terry Bozzio and Tony Hymas*.

"Metallica avenged what many saw as an injustice last year when it lost out to Jethro Tull in the hard rock/metal category with a win in the newly separated metal division for its Elektra single 'One,'" *Variety* reported.

N.A.R.A.S. was pressured to allow the winners of the hard-rock kudos, the black rock group Living Colour, to compete for Best New Artist, which might have averted the Milli Vanilli scandal had the group won, but the academy refused on the basis that individual band members had made partial past contributions to works by other artists. Living Colour took its revenge on fellow nominees Guns N' Roses, Metallica and Mötley Crüe for "Cult of Personality." Its victory over Guns N' Roses was particularly sensitive, since, as the *Washington Post* noted, "Living Colour and Guns N' Roses [had] opened for the Rolling Stones in Los Angeles and exchanged harsh words both on and off the stage."

The *Post* also noted that Guns N' Roses was the target of another group at the Grammys: "Outside the auditorium, the

Los Angeles chapter of the Guardian Angels protested the nomination of two groups they said promoted 'hate music.'" Public Enemy was the other band singled out and was competing for the Best Rap Performance award, which it lost to the British-born, New York City–raised Young MC for "Bust a Move." In sharp contrast to last year when four of the five nominees boycotted the awards show because the rap prize was bestowed off the telecast, the *L.A. Times* wrote, "On the rap front, it's smiles all around this year." The Grammycast even included time for a rap number, which was performed by last year's winners and this year's losing contenders, D.J. Jazzy Jeff & the Fresh Prince.

The British soul dance group Soul II Soul lost its Best New Artist bid to Milli Vanilli but garnered two awards in consolation: the r&b group vocal honors for "Back to Life," which they shared with vocalist Caron Wheeler, and the r&b instrumental laurels for "African Dance." Winner of the male r&b vocals prize, Bobby Brown, had been labeled a "hot new act" by the *Washington Post* and was expected by some to be a likely Best New Artist contender, but N.A.R.A.S. disqualified him because of his previous work as a member of the New Edition.

Anita Baker won the female r&b award for the third time in four years, thereby reigning over the category much like Aretha Franklin did in the 1960s and '70s. Baker's victory over Franklin, Natalie Cole, Janet Jackson and last year's Best New Artist nominee Vanessa Williams was confusing to some, since Baker won this year for the album of the same name as the song that she won for in 1988, "Giving You the Best That I Got." But the single was released prior to the LP, causing the two to fall in different eligibility periods.

Confusion reigned to a lesser extent over the winner of Best R&B Song, "If You Don't Know Me by Now," which had been covered recently by Simply Red. *Billboard* explained: "The Grammy for Best R&B Song went to a recycled 1972 oldie for the second time in three years.

Milli Vanilli was stripped of the Best New Artist prize when the duo was unmasked as lip-synching frontmen. They told the press they had "made a pact with the devil" for fame.

Wide World Photo

Kenny Gamble and Leon Huff's 'If You Don't Know Me by Now' won this year; Bill Withers' 'Lean on Me' won two years ago." Older songs were permitted to compete if they had never been nominated before and had new recordings made.

Last year jazz artists invaded traditionally nonjazz categories to score major triumphs, but now the opposite happened to some degree. When Dr. John and 1979 Best New Artist Rickie Lee Jones won the duo/group jazz vocals award for "Makin' Whoopee," the *L.A. Times* pointed out that they were "two names more commonly associated with pop and rock."

The male jazz vocal winner was the source of some rumblings, too, when rookie, Sinatra-styled crooner Harry Connick, Jr., prevailed over Dr. John, George Benson and others for his score to the film *When Harry Met Sally, . . .* which starred Billy Crystal and Meg Ryan. His songs included works by jazz greats George Gershwin and Duke Ellington, but many music critics considered Connick more of a pop-leaning cabaret singer because he also performed lots of Broadway standards.

Another first-time champ emerged to claim the jazz kudos for show tunes when Ruth Brown was honored as best female vocalist for *Blues on Broadway,* besting the *L.A. Times*'s pick of Diane Schuur for "The Christmas Song." Brown may have been known for decades in the jazz world as Miss Rhythm, but she had never before been nominated despite a formidable career that included gigs with such greats as Thelonious Monk and Miles Davis. Trumpet legend Davis won two awards this year, too—for solo and big-band instrumentals, both for *Aura*—in addition to being honored with N.A.R.A.S.'s Lifetime Achievement Award.

In the group instrumental category, the *Times* observed, "It's brother against brother—Wynton vs. Branford Marsalis," but ended up picking the winner right when it forecast a victory for the Chick Corea Akoustic Band and its self-titled LP. The paper was less fortunate predicting the victor of the fusion prize when four-time past champ the Pat Metheny Group prevailed with *Letter from Home*. The *Times* had said, "We see [Larry] Carlton's effort—his first since recovering from a gunshot assault outside his Hollywood Hills home—as the one left standing after this Grammy title fight."

Stevie Vaughan, the younger brother of blues guitarist Jimmie, proved he was also a gifted picker at Switzerland's Montreux Jazz Festival in 1982 and earned subsequent critical acclaim. He reaped his first Grammy over veteran nominee B. B. King for *In Step,* which lost its bid for the Best Rock Instrumental Performance honors but was voted Best Contemporary Blues Recording.

Considering the country music credentials of Bonnie Raitt and the winners of Song of the Year (Larry Henley and Jeff Silbar), *Billboard* ran the following headline after this year's Grammy ceremony: "Nashville the Biggest Winner of All." The trade paper cited the Nashville roots of the recipients of the religious awards, too, such as the Winans clan. CeCe Winans won the female gospel prize for "Don't Cry"; brother BeBe reaped the male honors for "Meantime"; and another brother, Daniel, who was

> "k. d. lang scares the hell out of country radio."

working with choir accompaniment, snagged the soul gospel group laurels for "Let Brotherly Love Continue." The doo-wop sextet and double champs from last year, Take 6, took one more in 1989 for "The Savior Is Waiting." The only non-Nashville artist to win was Al Green ("As Long As We're Together"), who marked his seventh win over the past eight years.

Randy Travis's previous two-year reign over the male country vocals category came to an end when a double loser from last year, Lyle Lovett, rebounded with *Lyle Lovett and His Large Band*. In 1988, k. d. lang shared the duet/group award with the late Roy Orbison, but she now surpassed such past champs as Emmylou Harris and Dolly Parton to claim the female singing prize for *Absolute Torch and Twang*. The *Post* called her triumph "something of a surprise," since, as *Billboard* put it, "the image lang projects scares the living hell out of country radio. She doesn't have her hair piled on top of her head. She doesn't look like the rest of them and that intimidates people."

Once she was backstage with reporters, *Variety* reported, "Canadian country chanteuse k. d. lang" was "radiant" as she told the media that her Grammy success proved that "all my work in progressive country isn't in vain. After not having radio acceptance, and meeting resistance in some aspects of the country market, it feels like I am finally making progress. I'm elated."

Lang was teamed up with Dwight Yoakam for the vocal collaboration honors but lost to a duo with sentiment on its side. "Country legend Hank Williams, who died in 1953—five years before the inception of the Grammys—shared a Grammy with his son, Hank Williams, Jr., on 'There's a Tear in My Beer,'" *Billboard* wrote, noting that the younger Hank achieved the task by singing along with an old tape of his dad crooning, too. "It was the first Grammy for both artists, though senior was awarded a Lifetime Achievement Award in 1987."

"There's a Tear in My Beer" was in the race for Best Country Song but lost to "After All This Time" by Rodney Crowell. Crowell began writing the tune about his relationship with wife Rosanne Cash in 1978 but didn't complete it until seven years later when he happened to come across some old notes for it.

A follow-up tribute to the broad heritage of country music swept the remaining two categories—instrumental music and duo/group vocals—for the Nitty Gritty Dirt Band's *Will the Circle Be Unbroken, Vol. 2.* The band had recruited a host of country legends to perform on the first volume, including Ray Acuff, Merle Haggard and Doc Watson. Virtually all of them returned for the sequel, which also snagged Best Bluegrass Recording.

Jimmy Sturr & His Orchestra, which recorded in Nashville, stretched its monopoly over Best Polka Recording for a fourth consecutive year. Several other (non-Nashville) past champs came back for additional prizes, too, when 1968 Best New Artist José Feliciano was hailed for Best Latin Pop Performance ("Cielito Lindo") and the Tex-Mex/rock fusion band Los Lobos nabbed Best Mexican-American Performance (*La Pistola y el Corazón*), which it last won in 1983.

The veteran Afro-Cuban singer Celia Cruz, also known as the Queen of Salsa, had contributed to Tito Puente's 1978 Best Latin Recording *Homenaje a Beny Moré*, but she didn't receive her own first Grammy until 1989 for her Best Tropical Latin Performance *Ritmo en el Corazón.* She shared the prize with Ray Barretto, the legendary Congo drummer, composer, arranger and bandleader. Bob Marley's son Ziggy repeated his victory of last year when *One Bright Day* was named Best Reggae Recording.

Indigo Girls was a hot new singing and guitar-strumming duo act from Georgia that lost its bid for Best New Artist but won Best Contemporary Folk Recording for its eponymous debut LP.

"After Bonnie Raitt, the next biggest Grammy winner was something of a dark horse to grab the spotlight," *Variety* reported. "Multitalented jazz composer/arranger/artist Dave Grusin won three awards." He received an arrangement prize for "Suite from *The Milagro Beanfield War*" (a film directed by Robert Redford) and two more (best film score and another arranger's award) for his contributions to the Jeff Bridges, Beau Bridges and Michelle Pfeiffer film *The Fabulous Baker Boys*, about the travails of a gypsy lounge act. "Both albums are on GRP Records, of which Grusin is part owner," *Variety* noted.

Baker Boys pulled an upset over Danny Elfman's *Batman* score (and nominated works by John Williams and Peter Gabriel), but Elfman reaped the consolation for Best Instrumental Composition for "The *Batman* Theme." Prince lost both of his Grammy bids for *Batman* but had contributed only a few songs to the blockbuster film starring Michael Keaton. Grammy's 1971 Best New Artist, Carly Simon, contributed only one song to director Mike Nichols's film *Working Girl,* but "Let the River Run" won both the Oscar and the Grammy as best film song.

The late *Saturday Night Live* comic Gilda Radner wasn't nominated for the comedy laurels this year but was hailed instead for *It's Always Something,* which was named Best Spoken Word or Non-musical Recording.

The winner of Best Comedy Recording became known in the music world as Professor Peter Schickele soon after the renowned composer began spoofing the great masters on recordings such as *P.D.Q. Bach: 1712 Overture and Other Musical Assaults. The New York Times* called his work "the greatest comedy-in-music act before the public today."

"Jackson siblings Michael and Janet cornered the video categories," *Variety* reported. Over the past two years, Michael Jackson had lost all of his nominations for his mega-hit *Bad* album, but this year at least he picked up best short-form music video for *Leave Me Alone.* His sister Janet nabbed the first Grammy of her career when she won the long-form video prize for *Rhythm Nation.*

"The classical Grammys produced a bumper crop of surprises this year," the *L.A. Times* reported. Following last year's accusations of bloc voting by the Atlanta Symphony Orchestra, an 11-member committee was established to come up with a final ballot instead of letting N.A.R.A.S. members determine the lineup as they had in the past. Missing were such usual Grammy favorites as Sir Georg Solti, Itzhak Perlman and Luciano Pavarotti. "Last year the fat cats won in all categories," the *Times* reported. "This time around, the mix is so catholic that the outcome is hearteningly unclear."

Despite the procedural overhaul, Robert Shaw and the Atlanta Symphony Orchestra and Chorus ended up winning three awards, including a sixth Classical Producer of the Year prize for Robert Woods and two (Best Engineered Recording and Best Choral Performance) for the team's reading of Benjamin Britten's *War Requiem.* "Bloc voting from the Atlanta classical contingent no doubt contributed" to their sweep, said the *L.A. Times.*

"For the past two decades, the performance practice of the Bartók quartets has been defined by recordings of the Juilliard Quartet," *High Fidelity* wrote of the Juilliard recording that earned the quartet the 1965 Grammy for best chamber music performance. Now a new and highly acclaimed version by the Emerson String Quartet reaped the same prize plus Best Classical Album.

"It is against the Juilliard's standard that the Emerson Quartet must be measured," *High Fidelity* added, "and the Emerson fares so well that future recordings may well be judged against *it.* The results are spectacular, yielding no less than a redefinition of the standards for Bartók quartet performance." The *L.A. Times* had called its chances for reaping best classical LP "tenuous" in a category usually "dominated by big-budget, big-

"Hey, Bonnie Raitt, I got one, too!" Bette Midler said when "Wind Beneath My Wings" won best record over works by Don Henley and Billy Joel.

name symphonies and operas" and predicted "the best album prize may go to Herbert von Karajan [*Bruckner: Symphony No. 8 in C Minor*], who in spite of being the most formidable (and best selling) podium personage of our time, has never been a major player in the Grammy sweepstakes. His chances are improved by the In Memoriam Factor (he recently died)."

Von Karajan was also competing for the orchestral laurels, but as the *L.A. Times* noted, "memorial sentiment did not help [his] final recording, nor did 25 weeks on the best-seller charts boost Gerard Schwarz and the Seattle Symphony past Leonard Bernstein's Mahler Third in the Orchestral category." Some critics blasted Bernstein and the New York Philharmonic's victorious interpretation as too exaggerated.

In the category honoring soloists' work without orchestra, four of the five contenders were pianists. Andras Schiff prevailed for his recording of Bach's *English Suites,* which was reviewed favorably for its ease of delivery. The competition for the soloist honors with orchestra was comprised of artists all performing works written in the twentieth century—a rare occurrence—and was won, as predicted, by cellist Yo-Yo Ma for his interpretations of works by Samuel Barber and Benjamin Britten. "Ma's celebrity, rather than his coupling of tough-nut concertos . . . should make him the winner," the *Times* had forecast.

On two previous occasions, the Best Opera Recording Grammy was bestowed for performances of Wagner's *Ring* cyle: Sir Georg Solti and the Vienna Philharmonic won in 1966 for *Die Walküre* and Pierre Boulez and the Bayreuth Festival Orchestra were honored for their ambitious performance of the full cycle in 1982. This year's winner was *Die Walküre* with James Levine conducting the Metropolitan Opera Orchestra, starring Gary Lakes, Kurt Moll, James Morris, Jessye Norman and Hildegard Behrens.

"The Met's *Walküre* is another mandatory purchase for Wagnerites, as well as an ideal set for those just starting a *Ring* collection," declared *Stereo Review*. "This cast upsets the widespread notion that great Wagnerian voices disappeared with Birgit Nilsson and Jon Vickers. Levine fuses these individual performances into a gripping representation of the opera as a whole." The *New York Times* added, "It ranks with the best this opera has received: grand yet exciting, pungent and full of character." Soprano Dawn Upshaw pulled an upset over Placido Domingo and Kathleen Battle to take the vocal soloist kudos. "Hers is a quintessentially American sound," said *Opera News,* "ideal for Samuel Barber's *Knoxville: Summer of 1915,* a classic of gentle nostalgia."

Winner of the year's Best Contemporary Composition was *Different Trains* by Steve Reich, a champion of minimalist style who preferred to write for small chamber-size groups. "*Different Trains* represents the very apex of his creative output so far," commented *Hi-Fi News & Record Review*.

When the Grammy nominations were announced in mid-January, *Variety* noted that Fine Young Cannibals was "the lone relatively 'new' act nominated in any of the three core categories, adding fuel to critics' charges that the academy's approximately 7,000 voting members are an irrepressibly stodgy group. Conspicuously absent from the bids is Madonna, who despite releasing a double-platinum album failed to make the grade in even one category. Other big-selling absentees include Rod Stewart and Roxette."

When the race was over, *Variety* reported on the Grammycast: "The ceremony, held at the Shrine Auditorium for the second year in a row, was hosted by comedian Garry Shandling after three timer Billy Crystal opted to appear on the Oscars this year instead." Viewership jumped 18 percent over last year, scoring an 18.9 rating/31 share.

In its review of the telecast, *Variety* blasted Shandling, saying that he "appeared completely detached from most of the categories and brought little spontaneity or élan to his role, often betraying no glimmer of recognition: had he *heard* of any of these acts? It was an utterly sanguine Grammycast where winners thanked their lawyers, managers and mothers and then went home." The reviewer complained that there were "too few emotional highs to punctuate the unrelenting boredom. Where were Guns N' Roses when you need them?"

The fact that Paul McCartney was being lauded with a Lifetime Achievement Award was announced weeks before the show, triggering the rumor that the Grammys would be the showcase for the long-awaited Beatles reunion, since George Harrison was up for two awards, too, as part of the Traveling Wilburys. But Harrison declined to attend the ceremony and McCartney told the *L.A. Times,* "Rumors of a Beatles reunion are not possible because John [Lennon] is dead."

The Grammys gave a Trustees Award to Dick Clark, the creator of the rival American Music Awards and former host of the TV show *American Bandstand*. Nat

King Cole and Vladimir Horowitz were given posthumous Liftetime Achievement Awards.

Horowitz's widow, Wanda Toscanini Horowitz, didn't feel well enough to travel to California to accept the honor, so N.A.R.A.S. President Michael Greene flew to New York to present it to her at her brownstone on Manhattan's Upper East Side.

A curious writer for the *New Yorker* tagged along to record Mrs. Horowitz's reaction to the tribute. "You know, [Vladimir] used to say to me, 'I'm celebrated but not popular,'" she said. "He wanted to be popular. Not because he wanted to be a star, but because he wanted to know that he had really communicated with people. And my husband won more than Henry Mancini. He was proud of that."

• 1989 •

The awards ceremony was broadcast on CBS from the Shrine Auditorium in Los Angeles on February 22, 1990 for the eligibility period of October 1, 1988, through September 30, 1989.

ALBUM OF THE YEAR
• *Nick of Time*, Bonnie Raitt. Capitol.
The End of the Innocence, Don Henley. Geffen.
Full Moon Fever, Tom Petty. MCA.
The Raw and the Cooked, Fine Young Cannibals. I.R.S./MCA.
Traveling Wilburys, Vol. 1, Traveling Wilburys. Wilbury.

RECORD OF THE YEAR
• "Wind Beneath My Wings," Bette Midler. Atlantic.
"The End of the Innocence," Don Henley. Geffen.
"The Living Years," Mike & the Mechanics. Atlantic.
"She Drives Me Crazy," Fine Young Cannibals. I.R.S./MCA.
"We Didn't Start the Fire," Billy Joel. Columbia/CBS.

SONG OF THE YEAR
(Songwriter's Award)
• "Wind Beneath My Wings," Larry Henley, Jeff Silbar.
"Don't Know Much," Barry Mann, Cynthia Weil, Tom Snow.
"The End of the Innocence," Don Henley, Bruce Hornsby.

"The Living Years," Mike Rutherford, Brian A. Robertson.
"We Didn't Start the Fire," Billy Joel.

BEST NEW ARTIST
• Milli Vanilli (award revoked)
Neneh Cherry
Indigo Girls
Soul II Soul
Tone Loc

BEST POP VOCAL PERFORMANCE, MALE
• Michael Bolton, "How Am I Supposed to Live Without You." Columbia/CBS.
Billy Joel, "We Didn't Start the Fire." Columbia/CBS.
Roy Orbison, "You Got It." Virgin.
Richard Marx, "Right Here Waiting." EMI.
Prince, *Batman* (film soundtrack). Warner Bros.

BEST POP VOCAL PERFORMANCE, FEMALE
• Bonnie Raitt, "Nick of Time," track from *Nick of Time*. Capitol.
Paula Abdul, "Straight Up." Virgin.
Gloria Estefan, "Don't Wanna Lose You." Epic.
Bette Midler, "Wind Beneath My Wings." Atlantic.
Linda Ronstadt, *Cry Like a Rainstorm, Howl Like the Wind*. Elektra.

BEST POP VOCAL PERFORMANCE BY A DUO OR GROUP WITH VOCAL

• Linda Ronstadt, Aaron Neville, "Don't Know Much." Elektra.
B-52's, "Love Shack." Reprise.
Fine Young Cannibals, "She Drives Me Crazy." I.R.S./MCA.
Mike & the Mechanics, "The Living Years." Atlantic.
Simply Red, "If You Don't Know Me by Now." Elektra.

BEST POP INSTRUMENTAL PERFORMANCE

• Neville Brothers, "Healing Chant," track from *Yellow Moon*. A&M.
Kenny G, "Breadline Blues," track from *Happy Anniversary, Charlie Brown*. GRP.
Earl Klugh, *Whispers and Promises*. Warner Bros.
Paul Shaffer, "Late Night," track from *Coast to Coast*. Capitol.
Andreas Vollenweider, "Dancing with the Lion." Columbia/CBS.

BEST ROCK VOCAL PERFORMANCE, MALE

• Don Henley, *The End of the Innocence*. Geffen.
Joe Cocker, "When the Night Comes." Capitol.
Tom Petty, "Free Fallin'," track from *Full Moon Fever*. MCA.
Lou Reed, *New York*. Sire.
Neil Young, *Freedom*. Reprise.

BEST ROCK VOCAL PERFORMANCE, FEMALE

• Bonnie Raitt, *Nick of Time*. Capitol.
Pat Benatar, "Let's Stay Together." Chrysalis.
Melissa Etheridge, *Brave and Crazy*. Island.
Cyndi Lauper, "I Drove All Night." Epic.
Tina Turner, *Foreign Affair*. Capitol.

BEST ROCK PERFORMANCE BY A DUO OR GROUP WITH VOCAL

• Traveling Wilburys, *Traveling Wilburys, Vol. 1*. Wilbury.

Living Colour, "Glamour Boys." Epic.
Rolling Stones, "Mixed Emotions." Rolling Stones/Columbia.
U2, *Rattle and Hum*. Island.
U2, B. B. King, "When Love Comes to Town." Island.

BEST ROCK INSTRUMENTAL PERFORMANCE

• Jeff Beck, Terry Bozzio, Tony Hymas, *Jeff Beck's Guitar Shop with Terry Bozzio and Tony Hymas*. Epic.
Steve Morse, *High Tension Wires*. MCA.
Joe Satriani, "The Crush of Love," track from *Dreaming #11*. Relativity Records.
Andy Summers, "A Piece of Time," track from *The Golden Wire*. Private Music.
Stevie Ray Vaughan & Double Trouble, "Travis Walk," track from *In Step*. Epic.

BEST HARD ROCK PERFORMANCE (VOCAL OR INSTRUMENTAL)

• Living Colour, "Cult of Personality." Epic.
Aerosmith, "Love in an Elevator." Geffen.
Great White, "Once Bitten, Twice Shy." Capitol.
Guns N' Roses, *GN'R Lies*. Geffen.
Motley Crue, "Dr. Feelgood." Elektra.

BEST METAL PERFORMANCE (VOCAL OR INSTRUMENTAL)

• Metallica, "One." Elektra.
Dokken, *Beast from the East*. Elektra.
Faith No More, *The Real Thing*. Slash/Reprise.
Soundgarden, *Ultramega O.K.* SST Records.
Queensryche, "I Don't Believe in Love." EMI.

BEST RHYTHM & BLUES SONG (Songwriter's Award)

• "If You Don't Know Me by Now," Kenny Gamble, Leon Huff.
"Every Little Step," L. A. Reid, Babyface.

"Miss You Much," James Harris III, Terry Lewis.
"Superwoman," L. A. Reid, Babyface, Daryl Simmons.
"When a Man Loves a Woman," Calvin Lewis, Andrew Wright.

BEST RHYTHM & BLUES VOCAL PERFORMANCE, MALE

• Bobby Brown, "Every Little Step." MCA.
Al Jarreau, *Heart's Horizon*. Reprise.
Prince, "Batdance." Warner Bros.
Smokey Robinson, "We've Saved the Best for Last." Arista.
Luther Vandross, "She Won't Talk to Me." Epic.

BEST RHYTHM & BLUES VOCAL PERFORMANCE, FEMALE

• Anita Baker, *Giving You the Best That I Got*. Elektra.
Natalie Cole, *Good to Be Back*. EMI.
Aretha Franklin, *Through the Storm*. Arista.
Janet Jackson, "Miss You Much." A&M.
Vanessa Williams, "Dreamin'," Wing/Polygram.

BEST RHYTHM & BLUES PERFORMANCE BY A DUO OR GROUP WITH VOCAL

• Soul II Soul, "Back to Life." Virgin.
Aretha Franklin, James Brown, "Gimme Your Love." Arista.
Aretha Franklin, Whitney Houston, "It Isn't, It Wasn't, It Ain't Never Gonna Be." Arista.
Deniece Williams, Natalie Cole, "We Sing Praises," track from *Special Love*. Sparrow.
BeBe & CeCe Winans, "Celebrate New Life." Capitol.

BEST RHYTHM & BLUES INSTRUMENTAL PERFORMANCE

• Soul II Soul, "African Dance," track from *Keep On Movin'*. Virgin.
Gerald Albright, *Bermuda Nights*. Atlantic.
Babyface, "It's No Crime." Solar/Epic.

Omar Hakim, "Constructive Criticism," track from *Rhythm Deep*. GRP.
Stix Hooper, "I Can't Get Enough of Your Love," track from *Lay It on the Line*. Artful Balance.

BEST RAP PERFORMANCE

• Young MC, "Bust a Move." Delicious Vinyl.
De La Soul, "Me Myself and I." Tommy Boy.
D.J. Jazzy Jeff & the Fresh Prince, "I Think I Can Beat Mike Tyson." Jive/RCA.
Public Enemy, "Fight the Power." Motown.
Tone Loc, "Funky Cold Medina." Delicious Vinyl.

BEST JAZZ FUSION PERFORMANCE

• Pat Metheny Group, *Letter from Home*. Geffen.
Larry Carlton, *On Solid Ground*. MCA.
Terri Lyne Carrington, *Real Life Story*. Verve Forecast.
Miles Davis, *Amandla*. Warner Bros.
John Patitucci, *On the Corner*. GRP.
Joe Sample, *Spellbound*. Warner Bros.

BEST JAZZ VOCAL PERFORMANCE, MALE

• Harry Connick, Jr., *When Harry Met Sally . . .* Columbia/CBS.
George Benson, *Tenderly*. Warner Bros.
Dr. John, *In a Sentimental Mood*. Warner Bros.
Lou Rawls, *At Last*. Blue Note/Capitol.
Joe Williams, *In Good Company*. Verve.

BEST JAZZ VOCAL PERFORMANCE, FEMALE

• Ruth Brown, *Blues on Broadway*. Fantasy.
Dee Dee Bridgewater, *Live in Paris*. Impulse.
Anita O'Day, *In a Mellow Tone*. Deutsche Grammophon.
Diane Schuur, "The Christmas Song," track from *GRP Christmas Collection*. GRP.
Janis Siegel, *Short Stories*. Atlantic.

BEST JAZZ VOCAL PERFORMANCE BY A DUO OR GROUP

- Dr. John, Rickie Lee Jones, "Makin' Whoopee." Warner Bros.
- Ray Charles, Lou Rawls, "Save the Bones for Henry Jones," track from *Just Between Us*. Columbia/CBS.
- James Moody, Dizzy Gillespie, "Get the Booty," track from *Sweet and Lovely*. Novus/RCA.
- Take 6, "Like the Whole World's Watching," track from *Steve Dorff and Friends*. Reprise.
- Joe Williams, Marlena Shaw, "Is You Is or Is You Ain't My Baby," track from *In Good Company*. Verve.

BEST JAZZ INSTRUMENTAL PERFORMANCE BY A SOLOIST (ON A JAZZ RECORDING)

- Miles Davis, *Aura*. Columbia/CBS.
- Chick Corea, "Sophisticated Lady," track from *Chick Corea Akoustic Band*. GRP.
- Wynton Marsalis, *The Majesty of the Blues*. Columbia/CBS.
- John Patitucci, "Bessie's Blues," track from *Chick Corea Akoustic Band*. GRP.
- André Previn, *After Hours*. Telarc.

BEST JAZZ INSTRUMENTAL PERFORMANCE BY A GROUP

- Chick Corea Akoustic Band, *Chick Corea Akoustic Band*. GRP.
- Branford Marsalis, *Trio Jeepy*. Columbia/CBS.
- Wynton Marsalis, *The Majesty of the Blues*. Columbia/CBS.
- André Previn, Joe Pass, Ray Brown, *After Hours*. Telarc.
- Yellowjackets, *The Spin*. MCA.

BEST JAZZ INSTRUMENTAL PERFORMANCE BY A BIG BAND

- Miles Davis, *Aura*. Columbia/CBS.
- Count Basie Orchestra conducted by Frank Foster, *The Legend, The Legacy*. Denon.
- Duke Ellington Orchestra conducted by Mercer Ellington, *Music Is My Mistress*. MusicMasters.
- Mel Lewis Jazz Orchestra, *The Definitive Thad Jones*. MusicMasters.
- McCoy Tyner Big Band, *Uptown/Downton*. Milestone.

BEST COUNTRY SONG
(Songwriter's Award)

- "After All This Time," Rodney Crowell. Columbia.
- " A Better Man," Clint Black, Hayden Nicholas. RCA.
- "Luck in My Eyes," k. d. lang, Ben Mink. Sire.
- "She Don't Love Nobody," John Hiatt. MCA/Curb.
- "There's a Tear in My Beer," Hank Williams, Sr. Curb.

BEST COUNTRY VOCAL PERFORMANCE, MALE

- Lyle Lovett, *Lyle Lovett and His Large Band*. MCA.
- Clint Black, *Killin' Time*. RCA.
- Rodney Crowell, "After All This Time." Columbia.
- Randy Travis, "It's Just a Matter of Time." Warner Bros.
- Keith Whitley, "I'm No Stranger to the Rain." RCA.

BEST COUNTRY VOCAL PERFORMANCE, FEMALE

- k. d. lang, *Absolute Torch and Twang*. Sire.
- Rosanne Cash, "I Don't Want to Spoil the Party." Columbia.
- Emmylou Harris, *Bluebird*. Reprise.
- Kathy Mattea, *Willow in the Wind*. Mercury.
- Dolly Parton, "Why'd You Come in Here Looking Like That." Columbia/CBS.

BEST COUNTRY VOCAL PERFORMANCE BY A DUO OR GROUP WITH VOCAL

- Nitty Gritty Dirt Band, *Will the Circle Be Unbroken, Vol. 2*. Universal.

Desert Rose Band, "She Don't Love Nobody." MCA/Curb.

Highway 101, "Honky Tonk Heart." Warner Bros.

Judds, "Young Love." RCA.

Restless Heart, "Big Dreams in a Small Town." RCA.

BEST COUNTRY VOCAL COLLABORATION

• Hank Williams, Jr., Hank Williams, Sr., "There's a Tear in My Beer." Curb.

Chris Hillman, Roger McGuinn, "You Ain't Goin' Nowhere." Universal.

Nitty Gritty Dirt Band with Johnny Cash, Roy Acuff, Ricky Skaggs, Levon Helm, Emmylou Harris, "Will the Circle Be Unbroken," track from *Will the Circle Be Unbroken, Vol. 2.* Universal.

Buck Owens, Ringo Starr, "Act Naturally." Capitol.

Dwight Yoakam, k. d. lang, "Sin City," track from *Just Lookin' for a Hit.* Reprise.

BEST COUNTRY INSTRUMENTAL PERFORMANCE

• Randy Scruggs, Nitty Gritty Dirt Band, "Amazing Grace," track from *Will the Circle Be Unbroken, Vol. 2.* Universal.

Asleep at the Wheel, "Black and White Rag." Asleep at the Wheel Music.

Jerry Douglas, "If You've Got the Money (Honey, I've Got the Time)," track from *Plant Early.* MCA Master Series.

John Hartford, "All I Got Is Gone Away," track from *Down on the River.* Flying Fish.

New Grass Revival, "Big Foot," track from *Friday Night in America.* Capitol.

BEST GOSPEL PERFORMANCE, MALE

• BeBe Winans, "Meantime," track from BeBe & CeCe Winans's *Heaven.* Capitol.

Eddie DeGarmo, *Feels Good to Be Forgiven.* Forefront/Benson.

Larnelle Harris, *I Can Begin Again.* Benson.

Wintley Phipps, *A Love Like This.* Coral/Word.

Michael W. Smith, "Holy, Holy, Holy," track from *Our Hymns.* Word.

Russ Taff, "Farther On," track from *The Way Home.* Myrrh/Word.

BEST GOSPEL PERFORMANCE, FEMALE

• CeCe Winans, "Don't Cry," track from *Heaven.* Capitol/Sparrow.

Margaret Becker, *Immigrant's Daughter.* Sparrow.

Debby Boone, *Be Thou My Vision.* Lamb & Lion/Benson.

Amy Grant, " 'Tis So Sweet to Trust in Jesus," track from *Our Hymns* (various artists). Word.

Sandi Patti, "Forever Friends." Word.

Deniece Williams, "Healing," track from *Special Love.* Sparrow.

BEST GOSPEL PERFORMANCE BY A DUO, GROUP, CHOIR OR CHORUS

• Take 6, "The Savior Is Waiting," track from *Our Hymns* (various artists). Word.

First Call, "O Sacred Head Now Wounded," track from *Our Hymns* (various artists). Word.

Mylon & Broken Heart, *Big World.* Star Song.

Petra, *On Fire!* Star Song.

BeBe & CeCe Winans, "Heaven." Capitol/Sparrow.

BEST SOUL GOSPEL PERFORMANCE, MALE OR FEMALE

• Al Green, "As Long As We're Together." A&M.

Albertina Walker, *My Time Is Not Over.* Word.

Beau Williams, *Wonderful.* Light.

Daniel Winans, "You Got a Choice to Make," track from *Brotherly Love.* Rejoice/Word.

Vickie Winans, *Total Victory.* Light.

BEST SOUL GOSPEL PERFORMANCE BY A DUO, GROUP, CHOIR OR CHORUS

- Daniel Winans & Choir, "Let Brotherly Love Continue," track from *Brotherly Love*. Rejoice.

Rev. Milton Brunson & the Thompson Community Singers, *Available to You*. Rejoice.

Commissioned, *Will You Be Ready?* Light.

L.A. Mass Choir, *Can't Hold Back*. Light.

Minister Thomas Whitfield & the Thomas Whitfield Company, *And They Sang a Hymn*. Sound of Gospel/King James.

BEST TRADITIONAL FOLK RECORDING

- *Le Mystère des Voix Bulgares, Vol. 2*, Bulgarian State Radio & Television Female Choir. Elektra/Nonesuch.

A la Veille Facon, Cajun Tradition. Swallow.

American Indian Dance Theatre, various American Indian tribes; Broadway Limited.

Blind Dog, Norman & Nancy Blake. Rounder.

Now That's a Good Tune, Masters of Traditional Missouri Fiddling. Grey Eagle.

BEST CONTEMPORARY FOLK RECORDING

- *Indigo Girls*, Indigo Girls. Epic.

"Bamboleo," Gipsy Kings. Elektra.

Bayou Cadillac, BeauSoleil. Rounder.

Crossroads, Tracy Chapman. Elektra.

Old Friends, Guy Clark. Sugar Hill.

BEST TRADITIONAL BLUES RECORDING

- "I'm in the Mood," track from John Lee Hooker's *The Healer*, John Lee Hooker, Bonnie Raitt. Chameleon Music Group.

Ginger Ale Afternoon, Willie Dixon. Varèse Sarabande.

The Healer, John Lee Hooker. Chameleon Music Group.

"If I Can't Sell It, I'll Keep Sittin' on It," track from *Blues on Broadway*, Ruth Brown. Fantasy.

Memphis Blues: The Paris Sessions, Memphis Slim. Stash.

BEST CONTEMPORARY BLUES RECORDING

- *In Step*, Stevie Ray Vaughan & Double Trouble. Epic.

King of the Blues: 1989, B. B. King. MCA.

Live from Austin, Delbert McClinton. Alligator.

Midnight Run, Bobby Blue Bland. Malaco.

"Wang Dang Doodle," track from Paul Shaffer's *Coast to Coast*, Koko Taylor. Capitol.

BEST BLUEGRASS RECORDING

- "The Valley Road," track from *Will the Circle Be Unbroken, Vol. 2*, Bruce Hornsby, Nitty Gritty Dirt Band. Universal.

At the Old Schoolhouse, Johnson Mountain Boys. Rounder.

Heartbreak Hotel, Doug Dillard Band. Flying Fish.

The Masters, Eddie Adcock, Kenny Baker, Josh Graves, Jesse McReynolds. CMH.

Bill Monroe and the Bluegrass Boys Live at the Opry, Bill Monroe & the Bluegrass Boys. MCA.

Two Highways, Alison Kraus, Union Station. Rounder.

BEST LATIN POP PERFORMANCE

- José Feliciano, "Cielito Lindo." EMI.

Chayanne, *Chayanne*. CBS Discos International.

Dyango, *Suspiros*. Capitol EMI Latin.

Miguel Gallardo, *America*. Philips/Polygram Latino.

José Luis Rodriguez, "Baila Mi Rumba." Mercury.

BEST TROPICAL LATIN PERFORMANCE

- Celia Cruz, Ray Baretto, *Ritmo en el Corazón*. Fania.

Ray Barretto, *Irresistible*. Fania.
Willie Colon, *Top Secrets/Altos Secretos*. Fania.
Eddie Palmieri, "Azúcar," track from *Sueno*. Intuition/Capitol.
Wilfrido Vargas, *Animation*. Sonotone Music Corp.

BEST MEXICAN-AMERICAN PERFORMANCE

• Los Lobos, *La Pistola y el Corazón*. Warner Bros./Slash.
Narciso Martinez, *The Father of Tex-Mex Conjunto*. Folklyric.
Emilio Navaira & Rio Band, *Emilio Navaira and Rio Band*. CBS Discos International.
Peter Rubalcava, *Amanecer*. NALR.
Los Tigres del Norte, *Corridos Prohibidos*. Fonovisa, Inc.

BEST REGGAE RECORDING

• *One Bright Day*, Ziggy Marley & the Melody Makers. Virgin.
I.D., Wailers Band. Atlantic.
Liberation, Bunny Wailer. Shanachie.
Live in Paris, Burning Spear. Slash.
Serious Business, Third World. Mercury.

BEST POLKA RECORDING

• *All in My Love for You*, Jimmy Sturr & His Orchestra. Starr.
Any Time Is Polka Time, Walter Ostanek & His Band. World Renowned Sounds.
Moldie Oldie Golden Goodies, Gene Mendalski & the G-Men. Starr.
Penn Ohio Polka Pals Souvenir Edition, Penn Ohio Polka Pals. Marjon.
Polkaholic, Gordon Hartmann. HG Records.

BEST NEW AGE PERFORMANCE

• Peter Gabriel, *Passion—Music for "The Last Temptation of Christ."* Geffen.
Enya, "Orinoco Flow (Sail Away)." Geffen.
Mark Isham, *Tibet*. Windham Hill.
Andreas Vollenweider, *Dancing with the Lion*. Columbia/CBS.

Paul Winter, "Icarus," track from *Wolf Eyes*. Living Music.

BEST INSTRUMENTAL COMPOSITION

• "The *Batman* Theme," Danny Elfman (Sinfonia of London Orchestra). Warner Bros.
"Field of Dreams," track from *Field of Dreams* soundtrack, James Horner (James Horner). Novus.
"Letter from Home," track from *Letter from Home*, Pat Metheny (Pat Metheny Group). Geffen.
"Morning Sprite," track from *Chick Corea Akoustic Band*, Chick Corea (Chick Corea Akoustic Band). GRP.
"Suite from *The Milagro Beanfield War*," track from *Migration*, Dave Grusin (Dave Grusin). GRP.
"*Who Framed Roger Rabbit* Suite," track from *Screen Themes*, Alan Silvestri (John Scott). Varese Sarabande.

BEST ARRANGEMENT ON AN INSTRUMENTAL

• Dave Grusin, "Suite from *The Milagro Beanfield War*," track from *Migration* (Dave Grusin). GRP.
Frank Foster, "The Count Basie Remembrance Suite," track from *The Legend, the Legacy* (Count Basie Orchestra). Denon.
Les Hooper, "Anything Goes," track from *Anything Goes* (Les Hooper). ITI.
Thad Jones, "Three in One," track from *The Definitive Thad Jones* (Mel Lewis Jazz Orchestra). MusicMasters.
Maxine Roach, "Extensions," track from *Max Roach Presents the Uptown String Quartet* (Uptown String Quartet). Philips.

BEST MUSICAL CAST SHOW ALBUM

• *Jerome Robbins' Broadway*, Jason Alexander, Debbie Shapiro, Robert La Fasse, others. RCA Victor.
Aspects of Love, London cast. Andrew Lloyd Webber, composer; Don

Black, Charles Hart, lyricists. Polydor.

Broadway The Hard Way, Frank Zappa. Barking Pumpkin.

Sarafina! The Music of Liberation, Broadway cast. Mbongeni Ngema, Hugh Masekela. RCA Victor.

Sondheim: Pacific Overtures, James Holmes conducting the English National Opera. RCA Victor.

BEST ALBUM OF ORIGINAL INSTRUMENTAL BACKGROUND SCORE WRITTEN FOR A MOTION PICTURE OR TV

• *The Fabulous Baker Boys*, Dave Grusin. GRP.

Batman, Danny Elfman (Sinfonia of London Orchestra). Warner Bros.

Field of Dreams, James Horner. Novus.

Indiana Jones and the Last Crusade, John Williams. Warner Bros.

Passion (music for *The Last Temptation of Christ*), Peter Gabriel. Geffen.

BEST SONG WRITTEN SPECIFICALLY FOR A MOTION PICTURE OR TV

• "Let the River Run," from *Working Girl* film soundtrack, Carly Simon (Carly Simon). Arista.

"Angel of Harlem," from *Rattle and Hum* film soundtrack, Bono & U2 (U2). Island.

"The Girl Who Used to Be Me," from *Shirley Valentine* film soundtrack, Alan & Marilyn Bergman, Marvin Hamlisch (Patti Austin). GRP.

"I Love to See You Smile," from *Parenthood* film soundtrack, Randy Newman (Randy Newman). Reprise.

"Partyman," from *Batman* film soundtrack, Prince (Prince). Warner Bros.

BEST INSTRUMENTAL ARRANGEMENT ACCOMPANYING VOCAL(S)

• Dave Grusin, "My Funny Valentine," from *The Fabulous Baker Boys* film soundtrack (Michele Pfeiffer). GRP.

Frank Foster, "Bring on the Raindrops," track from *The Legend, the Legacy* (Carmen Bradford). Denon.

Janet Jackson, Terry Lewis, Jimmy Jam, "Rhythm Nation," track from *Rhythm Nation 1814* (Janet Jackson). A&M.

Don Sebesky, "Carlotta's Heart," track from *Working Girl* film soundtrack (Carly Simon). Arista.

Marc Shaiman, "It Had to Be You," track from *When Harry Met Sally . . .* film soundtrack (Harry Connick, Jr.). Columbia/CBS.

BEST CLASSICAL ALBUM

• *Bartók: 6 String Quartets*, Emerson String Quartet. Deutsche Grammophon.

Bruckner: Symphony No. 8 in C Minor, Herbert von Karajan conducting the Vienna Philharmonic. Deutsche Grammophon.

Busoni: Piano Concerto in C (with Male Chorus), Christoph von Dohnányi conducting the Cleveland Orchestra. Garrick Ohlsson, piano. Telarc.

Hanson: Symphonies No. 1 in E Minor ("Nordic") and No. 2 ("Romantic"); Elegy in Memory of Serge Koussevitsky, Gerard Schwarz conducting the Seattle Symphony. Delos International.

Wagner: Die Walküre, James Levine conducting the Metropolitan Opera Orchestra (solos: Lakes, Moll, Morris, Norman, Behrens, Ludwig). Deutsche Grammophon.

BEST ORCHESTRAL PERFORMANCE
(Conductor's Award)

• Leonard Bernstein conducting the New York Philharmonic, *Mahler: Symphony No. 3 in D Minor*. Deutsche Grammophon.

Charles Dutoit conducting the Montreal Symphony Orchestra, *Bartók: Concerto for Orchestra; Music for Strings, Percussion and Celesta*. London.

Herbert von Karajan conducting the Vienna Philharmonic, *Bruckner:*

Symphony No. 8 in C Minor.
Deutsche Grammophon.
Orpheus Chamber Orchestra, *Copland:
Appalachian Spring; Short Sym-
phony; 3 Latin American Sketches;
Quiet City.* Deutsche Grammophon.
Gerard Schwarz conducting the Seattle
Symphony, *Hanson: Symphonies No.
1 in E Minor ("Nordic") and No. 2
("Romantic"); Elegy in Memory of
Serge Koussevitsky.* Delos Interna-
tional.

**BEST CHAMBER MUSIC PERFORMANCE
(INSTRUMENTAL OR VOCAL)**

• Emerson String Quartet, *Bartók: 6
String Quartets.* Deutsche Gram-
mophon.
Emanuel Ax, piano; Isaac Stern, violin;
Yo-Yo Ma, cello, *Shostakovich: Trio
No. 2 for Violin, Cello and Piano in
E Minor, Op. 67; and Sonata for
Cello and Piano in D Minor.* CBS
Masterworks.
Guarneri Quartet, *Beethoven: String
Quartet No. 13 in B Flat; Grosse
Fuge in B Flat.* Philips Classics.
Shlomo Mintz, violin; Yefim Bronfman,
piano, *Prokofiev: Violin Sonatas No.
1 in F Minor and No. 2 in D.*
Deutsche Grammophon.
Anne-Sophie Mutter, violin; Mstislav
Rostropovich, cello; Bruno Giuranna,
viola, *Beethoven: String Trios (E
Flat, Op. 3; Serenade in D, Op. 8; G,
Op. 9, No. 1; D, Op. 9, No. 2; C, Op.
9, No. 3).* Deutsche Grammophon.

**BEST CLASSICAL PERFORMANCE,
INSTRUMENTAL SOLOIST(S) (WITH
ORCHESTRA)**

• Yo-Yo Ma, cello (David Zinman con-
ducting the Baltimore Symphony
Orchestra), *Barber: Cello Concerto,
Op. 22; Britten: Symphony for Cello
and Orchestra, Op. 68.* CBS Master-
works.
Gidon Kremer, violin (Charles Dutoit
conducting the Boston Symphony),
Gubaidulina: Offertorium. Deutsche
Grammophon.

Robert McDuffie, violin (Leonard
Slatkin conducting the St. Louis
Symphony Orchestra), *W. Schuman:
Violin Concerto; Bernstein: Serenade
for Violin, Strings and Percussion
(After Plato's "Symposium").* Angel.
Viktoria Mullova, violin (André Previn
conducting the Royal Philharmonic
Orchestra), *Shostakovich: Violin
Concerto No. 1; Prokofiev: Violin
Concerto No. 2.* Philips Classics.
David Shifrin, clarinet (Gerard Schwarz
conducting the New York Chamber
Symphony), *Copland: Clarinet Con-
certo.* Angel.

**BEST CLASSICAL PERFORMANCE,
INSTRUMENTAL SOLOIST(S)
(WITHOUT ORCHESTRA)**

• Andras Schiff, piano, *Bach: English
Suites, BWV 806–11.* London.
Rudolf Firkusny, piano, *Martinu: Piano
Sonata No. 1; Les Ritournelles; Fan-
tasie et Toccata.* RCA Victor Red
Seal.
Richard Goode, piano, *Beethoven: The
Late Piano Sonatas (Opp. 101, 106,
109, 110, 111).* Elektra/Nonesuch.
Janos Starker, cello (Chingeo Neriki,
accompanist), *Popper: Romantic
Cello Favorites.* Delos International.
Krystian Zimerman, piano, *Chopin: 4
Ballades (Opp. 23, 38, 47, 52); Bar-
carolle, Op. 60; Fantasie, Op. 49.*
Deutsche Grammophon.

BEST OPERA RECORDING

• *Wagner: Die Walküre,* James Levine
conducting the Metropolitan Opera
Orchestra (solos: Lakes, Moll, Morris, Norman, Behrens, Ludwig).
Deutsche Grammophon.
Berg: Wozzeck, Claudio Abbado conducting the Vienna Philharmonic
(solos: Grundheber, Raffeiner, Langridge, Zednik, Haugland, Behrens).
Deutsche Grammophon.
Gershwin: Porgy and Bess, Simon Rattle conducting the London Philharmonic and Glyndebourne Chorus
(solos: White, Haymon, Evans,

Blackwell, Hubbard, Clarey, Baker). Angel.

R. Strauss: Elektra, Seiji Ozawa conducting the Boston Symphony Orchestra (solos: Ludwig, Behrens, Secunde, Ulfung, Hynninen). Philips Classics.

Tchaikovsky: Eugene Onegin, James Levine conducting the Dresden State Orchestra (solos: Freni, von Otter, Lang, Allen, Shicoff, Burchuladze, Senechal). Deutsche Grammophon.

BEST CHORAL PERFORMANCE (OTHER THAN OPERA)

• Robert Shaw conducting the Atlanta Symphony Orchestra and Chorus; Atlanta Boys' Choir, *Benjamin Britten: War Requiem*. Telarc.

Stephen Darlington conducting the Christ Church Cathedral Choir, *Vaughan Williams: Choral Music (Oxford Elegy, Flos Campi, etc)*. Nimbus.

John Eliot Gardiner conducting the Monteverdi Choir and English Baroque Soloists. *Handel: Jephtha*. Philips Classics.

Trevor Pinnock conducting the English Concert Choir and English Concert. *Handel: Messiah*. Archiv.

Leonard Slatkin conducting the London Philharmonic Choir and Orchestra; Richard Cooke, choral. *Elgar: The Kingdom*. RCA Victor Red Seal.

BEST CLASSICAL PERFORMANCE, VOCAL SOLOIST

• Dawn Upshaw, soprano (David Zinman conducting the Orchestra of St. Luke's), *Knoxville: Summer of 1915* (music by Barber, Menotti, Harbison, Stravinsky). Elektra/Nonesuch.

Kathleen Battle, soprano (James Levine, accompanist), *Schubert: Lieder*. Deutsche Grammophon.

Placido Domingo, tenor (Julius Rudel, accompanist), *Puccini: The Unknown Puccini*. Deutsche Grammophon.

Placido Domingo, tenor; Kathleen Battle, soprano (James Levine conduct-

ing the Metropolitan Opera Orchestra), *Live in Tokyo 1988*. Deutsche Grammophon.

William Sharp, baritone (Steven Blier, accompanist), *William Sharp, Baritone*. New World.

BEST CONTEMPORARY COMPOSITION

• Steve Reich, *Different Trains* (Kronos Quartet). Elektra/Nonesuch.

Sofia Gubaidulina, *Offertorium* (Gidon Kremer, violin; Charles Dutoit conducting the Boston Symphony Orchestra). Deutsche Grammophon.

Witold Lutoslawski, *Chain 2* (Anne-Sophie Mutter, violin; Witold Lutoslawski conducting the BBC Symphony Orchestra). Deutsche Grammophon.

Witold Lutoslawski, *Partita* (Anne-Sophie Mutter, violin; Witold Lutoslawski conducting the BBC Symphony Orchestra). Deutsche Grammophon.

Arvo Part, *Passio* (Paul Hillier conducting the Hilliard Ensemble and Western Wind Choir; solos: Michael George, John Potter). ECM.

BEST ENGINEERED RECORDING, CLASSICAL

• Jack Renner, *Britten: War Requiem* (Robert Shaw conducting the Atlanta Symphony Orchestra and Chorus and Atlanta Boys' Choir). Telarc.

John Dunkerley, *Bartók: Concerto for Orchestra; Music for Strings, Percussion and Celesta* (Charles Dutoit conducting the Montreal Symphony Orchestra). London.

John Eargle, *Hanson: Symphonies No. 1 in E Minor ("Nordic") and No. 2 ("Romantic"); Elegy in Memory of Serge Koussevitsky* (Gerard Schwarz conducting the Seattle Symphony). Delos International.

Wolfgang Mitlehner, *Wagner: Die Walküre* (James Levine conducting the Metropolitan Opera Orchestra and soloist). Deutsche Grammophon.

Karl-August Naegler, Helmut Burk, *Mahler: Symphony No. 3 in D Minor* (Leonard Bernstein conducting the New York Philharmonic; New York Choral Artists and Brooklyn Boys' Chorus; solo: Ludwig). Deutsche Grammophon.

CLASSICAL PRODUCER OF THE YEAR

• Robert Woods
Wolf Erichson
Michael Haas
Patti Laursen
Elizabeth Ostrow

BEST COMEDY RECORDING

• *P.D.Q. Bach: 1712 Overture and Other Musical Assaults*, Professor Peter Schickele, Greater Hoople Area Off-Season Philharmonic. Telarc.
Dice, Andrew Dice Clay. Geffen.
Motherhood: The Second Oldest Profession, Erma Bombeck. McGraw-Hill-Areille.
"Wild Thing," Sam Kinison. Warner Bros.
Without You I'm Nothing, Sandra Bernhard. Enigma.

BEST SPOKEN WORD OR NONMUSICAL RECORDING

• *It's Always Something*, Gilda Radner. Simon & Schuster Audio.
All I Really Need to Know I Learned in Kindergarten, Robert Fulghum. Sound Editions.
It's Always Something, Gilda Radner. Simon & Schuster.
I Want to Grow Hair, I Want to Grow Up, I Want to Go to Boise, Erma Bombeck. Caedmon.
Sir John Gielgud Reads Alice in Wonderland, Sir John Gielgud, narrator. Nimbus.
The War of the Worlds 50th Anniversary Production, Jason Robards, Steve Allen, Douglas Edwards. Otherworld Media.

BEST RECORDING FOR CHILDREN

• *The Rock-A-Bye Collection, Vol. 1*, Tanya Goodman. Jaba Records.

Bullfrogs and Butterflies—I've Been Born Again, various artists. Tony Salerno, Ron Kreuger, Frank Hernandez, producers. Anthony Paul Productions.
A Disney Spectacular (48 Favorite Disney Songs), Eric Kunzel conducting the Cincinnati Pops Orchestra. Telarc.
Oliver and Company/Story and Songs from the Motion Picture, various artists. Walt Disney.
Raffi in Concert with the Rise and Shine Band, Raffi. Shoreline/A&M.
Thumbelina, Kelly McGillis, reading; Mark Isham, music. Windham Hill.

BEST ENGINEERED RECORDING (OTHER THAN CLASSICAL)

• George Massenburg, *Cry Like a Rainstorm, Howl Like the Wind* (Linda Ronstadt). Elektra.
Bill Bottrell, *Like a Prayer* (Madonna). Sire.
Mike Campbell, Don Smith, Bill Botrell, *Full Moon Fever* (Tom Petty). MCA.
Neil Dorfsman, *Flowers in the Dirt* (Paul McCartney). Capitol.
Josiah Gluck, *Happy Anniversary, Charlie Brown* (Patti Austin, Dave Brubeck, Dave Grusin, Lee Ritenour.) GRP.
Don Murray, Ed Rak, *Migration* (Dave Grusin). GRP.

BEST ALBUM PACKAGE
(Art Director's Award)

• Roger Gorman, *Sound + Vision* (David Bowie album). Rykodisc.
Bill Burks, Tommy Steele, *Foreign Affair* (Tina Turner). Capitol.
Tom Recchion, *Batman* (Prince). Warner Bros.
Tommy Steele, *Monster* (Fetchin Bones). Capitol.
Jimmy Wachtel, *World in Motion* (Jackson Browne). Elektra.

BEST ALBUM NOTES
(Annotator's Award)

• Phil Schaap, *Bird: The Complete Charlie Parker on Verve* (Charlie Parker). Verve.

Dwight Blocker Bowers, *American Musical Theater—Shows, Songs and Stars* (various artists). Smithsonian Collection.

Gene Lees, *The Complete Fantasy Recordings* (Bill Evans). Fantasy.

Howard Wright Marshall, Amy E. Skillman, *Now That's a Good Tune* (Masters of Traditional Missouri Fiddling). Grey Eagle.

Martin Williams, Dick Katz, Francis Davis, *Jazz Piano* (various artists, 1898–1964). Smithsonian Collection.

BEST HISTORICAL ALBUM

• *Chuck Berry—The Chess Box.* Chess/MCA.

American Musical Theater—Shows, Songs and Stars (various artists). Smithsonian Collection.

Blue Note 50th Anniversary Collection, Vols. 1–5, 1939–1989 (various jazz artists). Blue Note.

Jazz Piano (various artists, 1989–1964). Smithsonian Collection.

Nat King Cole and the King Cole Trio (Nat King Cole & the King Cole Trio). Savoy Jazz.

PRODUCER OF THE YEAR (OTHER THAN CLASSICAL)

• Peter Asher

Emilio Estefan, Jr., Jorge Casas, Clay Ostwald

Jimmy Jam, Terry Lewis, Janet Jackson

L.A. Reid, Babyface

Prince

Tears for Fears, David Bascombe

BEST MUSIC VIDEO, SHORT FORM

• *Leave Me Alone*, Michael Jackson. Jim Blashfield, director. Epic.

The Living Years, Mike & the Mechanics. Atlantic.

Orinoco Flow (Sail Away), Enya. Michael Geoghegan, director. Geffen.

Something to Hold On To, Trevor Rabin. Jeff Stein, director. Elektra.

There's a Tear in My Beer, Hank Williams, Jr., Hank Williams, Sr. Ethan Russell, director. Warner Bros./Curb.

BEST MUSIC VIDEO, LONG FORM

• *Rhythm Nation*, Janet Jackson. Dominic Sena, Jonathan Dayton, Valerie Faris, directors. A&M.

Hangin' Tough, New Kids on the Block. Doug Nichol, director. CBS Music Video.

In Concert—Delicate Sound of Thunder, Pink Floyd. Wayne Isham, director. CBS Music Video.

Moonwalker, Michael Jackson. Colin Chilvers, Dennis Jones, Michael Jackson, Jerry Kramer, Frank DiLeo, directors. CBS Music Video.

Savage, Eurythmics. Sophie Muller, director. Virgin Video.

• 1990 •

Quincy Jones: Top of the Pops

It was a " 'Block' buster" year, declared *Variety*'s banner headline when past Grammy grabber Quincy Jones returned to nab six new awards for his Album of the Year champ *Back on the Block,* thereby becoming the most honored pop artist in Grammy history.

"The veteran producer/songwriter/ engineer/performer is now the leading nonclassical Grammy winner of all time with 25 trophies, topping the 20 won by Henry Mancini," *Variety* reported. "Jones still trails Sir Georg Solti's total of 28 lifetime Grammys."

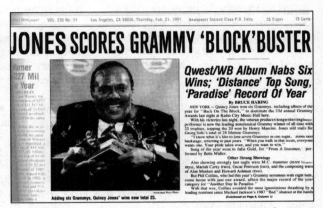

After winning six trophies for *Back on the Block,* Quincy Jones became "the leading nonclassical Grammy winner of all time," *Variety* reported.

Quincy Jones had received his first award for arranging jazz for Count Basie in 1963 and subsequently picked up prizes for jazz instrumental performance ("Walking in Space" in 1969), r&b group vocal performance (*The Dude* in 1981) and producing (1985 Record of the Year "We Are the World" and 1983 Album of the Year *Thriller*).

Given his diverse background, Jones tried to pull it all together when he produced *Back on the Block.* The album spanned four decades of black musical traditions, including bebop, soul, r&b, funk, hip-hop and rap. Jones recruited an equally broad array of talents for the task such as Sarah Vaughan, Ella Fitzgerald, Dizzy Gillespie, Ray Charles, George Benson, Chaka Khan, James Ingram, Kool Moe Dee and Ice-T. In the album notes, he wrote, "These colleagues and I

have taken a journey through every influence and everyone that I love in music . . . and we've worked together to bridge generations and traverse musical boundaries."

The result: In addition to the gold for best album, *Back on the Block* earned Jones his third Producer of the Year award, Best Jazz Fusion Performance ("Birdland," with cowinners Dizzy Gillespie, Miles Davis and others), Best Arrangement on an Instrumental ("Birdland," with Ian Prince and others), Best Rap Performance by a Duo or Group ("Back on the Block," with his son, Quincy Jones III, Melle Mel, et. al.) and Best Instrumental Arrangement Accompanying Vocal(s) ("The Places You Find Love," with Siedah Garrett, Chaka Khan). The half dozen awards tied him with Roger Miller for having the second-most victories in a single year. Miller earned his six in 1965 for "King of the Road" and *The Return of Roger Miller*. Michael Jackson surpassed Miller in 1983 with eight for his and Quincy Jones's *Thriller*.

"Pray for peace on earth," Jones said when he accepted the Album of the Year honor, "and when we get peace on earth, let's take care of the earth."

Back on the Block also reaped an engineering trophy plus the r&b duo/group vocal award. The latter acknowledgment marked the return of two past Grammy favorites for "I'll Be Good to You": Chaka Khan, who'd been missing in the awards lineup since the early 1980s, and Ray Charles, who scored his first new Grammy in 15 years.

In the contest for best album, Quincy Jones beat Phil Collins, who won the category in 1985 for *No Jacket Required* and now led this year's Grammy derby with the most nominations. *Variety* noted that, despite eight bids, he "came home with just one award, albeit the major Record of the Year category for 'Another Day in Paradise.'" The *L.A. Times* described the song as "a timely statement about social indifference in the homeless age, with a lush undisturbing arrangement that may be meant as irony."

Collins's consciousness-raising song was also up for Song of the Year but lost to "From a Distance," a ballad sung by Bette Midler that was considered potential trouble for "Paradise" in the record lineup, since Collins was seen as the early front-runner and Midler won last year for "Wind Beneath My Wings."

"From a Distance" became a hit during the Desert Storm military action just weeks prior to the Grammy ceremony when U.S. troops joined United Nations forces in ousting Iraqi soldiers from Kuwait. Americans took the song to heart because of its comforting promise that "God is watching us" during turbulent times. When sung by country/folk singer Nanci Griffith five years earlier, the same tune topped the record charts in Northern Ireland when it was embraced as a source of comfort by warring Catholics and Protestants.

Accepting the Song of the Year award, writer Julie Gold gushed, "I'm on top of the world, living a dream! To our soldiers, we pray for your speedy return." Then she added, echoing Quincy Jones, "We pray for peace on earth."

Variety reported Gold "had a limo bring her parents and brother up from Philadelphia for the show. 'It's harder to get tickets to the Grammys than to be nominated,' she said. 'Believe me, I know!'"

Bette Midler was the favorite to snag the pop vocal laurels for "From a Distance" but lost to this year's Best New Artist, Mariah Carey, for "Vision of Love." Carey suffered losses in the Record, Song and Album of the Year categories, but her double win, *Variety* said, "capped off her meteoric rise to the top." The only other artists ever nominated in all of Grammy's top four slots (including Best New Artist) were Tracy Chapman in 1988, who, like Carey, nabbed only the newcomer's kudos, and Christopher Cross, who swept all four categories in 1980.

Backstage, *Variety* observed, "Mariah Carey looked like a deer trapped in the headlights of an oncoming car as she clutched her Grammy and faced the howling press mob. Perhaps age has something to do with it. The two-time Grammy winner will turn 21 next month."

Roy Orbison died of a heart attack in 1988 and lost a posthumous Grammy bid last year to Michael Bolton, but now he was back in the music race with what *Variety* called "a live version remake of his 1964 classic 'Oh, Pretty Woman.'" When he beat a new stellar lineup that included Bolton, Phil Collins, Billy Joel, James Ingram and the still-Grammyless Rod Stewart, the award was accepted by

---

Sinéad O'Connor became the first artist ever to refuse a Grammy.

---

his widow, Barbara, who thanked the academy, remarking "how magnificently you have remembered him. Thanks for loving Roy."

Last year Linda Ronstadt and Aaron Neville pulled off an upset over Britain's Fine Young Cannibals to garner the duo/group pop vocals award. The pair now achieved another surprise victory with their latest hit, "All My Life." The vanquished this time included Wilson Phillips, the pop group comprised of Carnie and Wendy Wilson (daughters of Beach Boy Brian Wilson) and Chynna Phillips (daughter of John and Michelle Phillips of the Mamas & the Papas). Wilson Phillips had been viewed as the probable victor because the trio was also competing for Album and Song of the Year, in addition to Best New Artist.

The only Grammy that veteran rocker Eric Clapton ever won was for his partial contribution to 1972 Album of the Year *The Concert for Bangla Desh*. He'd been nominated on two other occasions (most recently losing to Robert Palmer in 1988) but finally prevailed all on his own by giving the year's best male rock vocal performance in "Bad Love." Billy Idol had been expected to take the category with a large sympathy vote for "Cradle of Love," since he'd recently recovered from a serious motorcycle accident.

Yet another upset occurred when a Canadian newcomer to the pop charts slunk past the younger sister of Michael Jackson for the female rock honors. The *L.A. Times* had predicted it would be the other way around, saying, "Janet Jackson's 'Black Cat' is likely to edge past Alannah Myles' 'Black Velvet.'" Jackson had been nominated seven times before, but the only award she won was last year for her *Rhythm Nation* video.

Variety revealed, "Myles admitted she was surprised at upsetting the likes of Janet Jackson, Tina Turner, Stevie Nicks and Melissa Etheridge to capture the rock vocal female trophy. 'I was up against people who at one point in my career were my idols.'"

Mariah Carey lost her bids for Record, Song and Album of the Year, but won Best New Artist and best pop vocal performance for "Vision of Love."

Variety reported on one repeater returning from last year: "Metallica's powerful performance on 1989 Grammy telecast may have been remembered in the voting, as its version of Queen's 'Stone Cold Crazy,' a cut from the Elektra anniversary compilation *Rubaiyat*, triumphed in the metal performance category." The all-star LP celebrated the label's 40th anniversary.

Like Rod Stewart, the Rolling Stones still hadn't won a Grammy, but they were expected to prevail for the rock group laurels over INXS and the Red Hot Chili Peppers. Instead, another previously un-Grammyed group, Aerosmith, shocked them all and grabbed the gold with "Janie's Got a Gun."

Last year Grammy watchers were stunned when Aerosmith lost the hard-rock category to Living Colour. Now they were out of the race and Living Colour returned to reclaim the honor for *Time's Up*. Guitarist Vernon Reid accepted the award by dedicating it to "all the bar bands, all the acts who are struggling to make it." The *New York Times* noted: "He was wearing a Sinéad O'Connor T-shirt, but his words suggested a willingness to participate in just the commercial process Ms. O'Connor professes to abhor."

What the *Times* was talking about was a growing brouhaha over Irish rock singer O'Connor, whose hit cover of a Prince song, "Nothing Compares 2 U," was one of the most critically acclaimed singles of 1990 and a nominee for Grammy's Record of the Year.

O'Connor had four nominations but issued an announcement prior to the Grammycast saying that she wouldn't accept any awards if she won. When she ended up winning the new prize for Best Alternative Music Performance for her album, ironically titled *I Do Not Want What I Haven't Got* she became the first artist in Grammy history to refuse an award.

O'Connor appeared on Arsenio Hall's late-night TV talk show shortly after making her announcement and elaborated, "I've said that if I win, I won't accept it and I wouldn't want it near me. As far as I'm concerned, it represents everything I despise about the music industry." In a separate interview with the *L.A. Times,* she accused N.A.R.A.S. of "false and materialistic values." The *Times* added: "She thinks the [Grammy] ceremony honors commercial success more than pop artistry." O'Connor said she wanted America's leading music artists to ignore the pop charts and concentrate instead on probing "the reasons why this world is now at war, why [it] abuses its children and why people are homeless and are starving."

She had caused a controversy last summer when she refused to allow the national anthem to be played at one of her concerts and then suffered the ire of patriotic fans. Probably because the gulf war was going on concurrently with the Grammy show and feelings of national pride were running high, the backlash this time was stinging. A leading radio and TV programmer told the *Times,* "I think she must be from another planet. How she equates an awards ceremony with all the ills of the world is beyond my comprehension." California disc jockey Rick Dees reported a flood of telephone calls from listeners outraged by her

stance. He said, "I had no idea of the venom that is out there for this girl."

Rock critic Dave Marsh was more compassionate, writing, "I think it's an honorable thing to do, but not a helpful thing. I'd rather see her show up at the Grammys and make an anti-war statement."

O'Connor tried to cope with the growing chorus of denouncements by insisting that she was attacking the music industry in general and didn't mean to single out the Grammys. But she clearly had. She'd recently attended the MTV awards show as well as the American Music Awards ceremony, although she claimed she would boycott both in the future, too. The brouhaha finally died down soon after the Grammycast, which went on without her.

Another breakout star of the year, M.C. Hammer, also proved triumphant at the Grammys when he scored three, making him the second-biggest winner after Quincy Jones. Hammer lost his bids for Album and Record of the Year but made up for the defeats with the year's Best Rhythm & Blues Song ("U Can't Touch This," written with James Miller), Best Rap Solo Performance for the same song and the best long-form best music video for *Please Hammer Don't Hurt 'Em, the Movie*. When he won the latter prize, *Variety* noted, "The Who failed to win its first Grammy."

Please Hammer Don't Hurt 'Em was the best-selling LP of the year and was, commented the *L.A. Times,* "the album that made rap safe for mainstream America—and you don't get any more mainstream than Grammy voters. Eight million album buyers can't be wrong." In his acceptance remarks, Hammer mentioned the Persian Gulf crisis and dedicated his victories to the American soldiers who are "putting their lives on the line for us."

After losing nine previous Grammy

> **After losing nine times, Luther Vandross finally struck gold.**

bids dating back to 1981, Luther Van-dross finally struck gold when he took the r&b male vocals award for "Here and Now." Janet Jackson was favored to take the r&b female vocal kudos for "Alright" but was upset by Anita Baker (*Compositions*), who had now swept the category for the fourth time in five years.

A curious double victory occurred when the Vaughan Brothers' *Family Style* crossed over two genres to win awards as contemporary blues and rock instrumental music. *Variety* reported on some backstage buzz: "Jimmie Vaughan said there were no outtakes from the recording sessions [with his late brother Stevie Ray Vaughan] that might find their way into the market."

After not having won a N.A.R.A.S. prize since 1983, the veteran Grammy queen Ella Fitzgerald, at age 72, made a triumphant comeback to claim the female jazz vocal laurels for *All That Jazz,* marking her 13th win. Pianist Oscar Peterson, now 65, hadn't won a Grammy since 1979, but he scored two this year for *The Legendary Oscar Peterson Trio Live at the Blue Note*: both the soloist and group jazz instrumental performance awards.

Last year's champ Harry Connick, Jr., reprised his victory in the male jazz singing slot (for his best-selling *We Are in Love,* another controversial mix of jazz and show tunes), topping previous Grammy champs George Benson, Jon Hendricks, Bobby McFerrin and Tony Bennett. *Variety* reported on the winner mingling backstage with reporters: "Connick seemed almost apologetic about accepting the Grammy. 'I'm not a jazz singer. I can list a bunch of jazz singers for you. But they chose to honor me and I accepted.' "

Benson's album *Big Boss Band* won the big-band instrumental trophy for the Count Basie Orchestra for its track "Basie's Bag."

Considering that Kathy Mattea had recently swept the Country Music Association Awards for the second year in a row, it wasn't surprising when the young West

M.C. Hammer lost best record and album, but still claimed three consolation prizes, beating the Who, which failed to win its first Grammy.

Wide World Photo

Virginian thrush bested K. T. Oslin, Reba McEntire and others for the female country vocals kudos for "Where've You Been," which was also hailed as Best Country Song, bringing laurels to its writers, Jon Vezner and Don Henry. After her victory, Mattea told *Entertainment Weekly,* "It's like, OK, what do you do now? Do you try to make these albums that sound like the other ones so you can keep winning these awards, or do you go for expressing your more artistic side?" She soon opted, the magazine added, "to follow her heart into more personal, seemingly less commercial territory" with her next album, *Time Passes By,* which would earn her another nomination next year.

Two songs popularized by Garth Brooks were close contenders for Best Country Song, and one, "Friends in Low Places," was supposed to earn Brooks his first male vocal performance Grammy. The statuette ended up going to another award rookie, Vince Gill, for "When I Call Your Name," a song he wrote with Tim DuBois. He told reporters backstage, "This is the first time I got to come." Gill, now 34, had been working in near obscurity as a sideman and solo artist throughout the 1980s and then he said his career "went nuts in the last two years. I don't know why. It's the same four chords it's always been." The Country Music Association named him Male Vocalist of the Year and awarded him the Song of the Year prize for "When I Call Your Name."

The *L.A. Times* predicted the Judds would claim the duo/group performance category because, it said, "By now all the voters have learned of Naomi Judd's forced retirement from concerts due to health reasons." But the winner turned out to be the Kentucky Headhunters ("the scariest things in country music," according to its rhythm guitarist, Richard Young) for *Pickin' on Nashville. Time* magazine described the band thus: "The KenHeads blend whimsy, old-time picking and some refried hippie riffs with the dynamism of a rock band from some Ozark Olympus."

More traditional talent won out in the instrumental performance category when Chet Atkins and Mark Knopfler scored for "So Soft, Your Goodbye." They also picked up the vocal collaboration honors for "Poor Boy Blues," beating, according to the *Times,* "the Mt. Rushmore of country music"—the Highwaymen, comprised of Waylon Jennings, Willie Nelson, Kris Kristofferson and Johnny Cash.

Despite her youth, 19-year-old upstart Alison Krauss took the laurels for Best Bluegrass Recording for *I've Got That Old Feeling. Time* magazine commented: "She's come a long way from being just another kid with a violin case. The bluegrass field has been tough for ladies, especially ones so young, but Krauss has had lots of practice. The old pro from Champaign, Illinois, recorded her first album at 14."

As usual, the religious awards were claimed by a host of returning veterans, including Take 6 (*So Much 2 Say,* Best Contemporary Soul Gospel Album), Sandi Patti (*Another Time . . . Another Place,* Best Pop Gospel Album) and Rev. James Cleveland, who died a few weeks before the Grammy ceremony (*Having Church,* Best Gospel Album by a Choir or Chorus). Among the newcomers was the veteran Christian rock band Petra, which performed its own original material on recordings such as *Beyond Belief,* winner

Lifetime Achievement honoree Johnny Cash appeared backstage with wife June Carter Cash.

of Best Rock/Contemporary Gospel Album.

The writers of the music used in the hit animated Disney film *The Little Mermaid*—Howard Ashman and Alan Menken—garnered two Grammys: Best Recording for Children for the movie soundtrack and the best film song award for the popular single "Under the Sea."

Among the new categories added in recent years was Best New Age Performance, which was earned this year by one of the genre's most popular artists, keyboardist Mark Isham, for his self-titled album.

In the classical field, a secret committee continued to select the nominees in order to prevent bloc voting. The target of those accusations in the past—the Atlanta Symphony Orchestra and Chorus—did receive one Grammy this year, however, when they were awarded the choral laurels for works by Walton and Bernstein.

But it turned out to be Leonard Bernstein's big year at the Grammys, as forecast. "The recent passing of America's beloved, heart-on-sleeve, good-cause-associated, conductor-composer-educator—and [his Ives] recording's sheer beauty—will overwhelm the membership," the *L.A. Times* had predicted.

Bernstein and the New York Philharmonic garnered Best Classical Album for their recording of Charles Ives's Symphony No. 2 and other works such as "Central Park in the Dark," which were taped live during a performance at New York's Avery Fisher Hall.

Bernstein led the Chicago Symphony Orchestra in a recording of Shostakovich's Symphonies Nos. 1 and 7 and reaped the orchestral performance accolade over such competition as his Best Classical Album and another Chicago Symphony recording with Grammy grabber Sir Georg Solti holding the baton. "Here Bernstein is in his element!" *American Record Guide* gushed over the Shostakovich program.

"Bernstein will also be the sentimental favorite for Best Contemporary Composition, with his 'Arias and Barcarolles,'" "the *L.A. Times* predicted correctly, too. The work's strange title came from a comment once made by President Dwight Eisenhower after he heard Bernstein play a Mozart concerto. He said, "I like music with a theme, not all them arias and barcarolles."

The classical Grammys continued their memorial note when *The Last Recording* of the late Vladimir Horowitz, which contained works by Chopin, Haydn, Liszt and Wagner, brought him the trophy for best soloist performance without orchestra. "Horowitz had an autumnal last period in which he was constantly looking at new literature and playing it in a relaxed, charming manner," the *New York Times* commented on this LP. "Gone were the neuroticism and outsize dynamics that could surge into his playing. In this kind of performance he gives the feeling that now he is no longer out to prove anything, that he is merely having a good time playing the piano. His patented kind of electricity is still there."

Violinist Itzhak Perlman scored two awards, including the soloist (with orchestra) honors for works by Shostakovich and Glazunov. He also snagged the chamber music prize, sharing it with pianist Daniel Barenboim for three Brahms violin sonatas. The *L.A. Times* foresaw the latter victory but maintained that the "thrilling" program of Bartók's *Contrasts* performed by Richard Goode and Richard and Lucy Stoltzman really *should* win instead.

The winner of Best Opera Recording was intimately related to last year's winner. Both were part of James Levine's first American production of Wagner's *The Ring of Nibelung,* which was staged at the Metropolitan Opera. *Die Walküre* won the 1989 kudos; this year it went to the *Das Rheingold* installment. "This is a gripping performance, both dramatically and musically," *Opera News* wrote.

Carreras, Domingo, Pavarotti in Concert, a recording commonly known as "The Three Tenors," brought the vocalist kudos to a triumverate of talent: José Carreras, Placido Domingo and Luciano Pavarotti. The *L.A. Times* did not approve, writing, "It finds Placido and Luciano bawling their golden lungs out and Carreras straining with his now-limited equipment to match their decibel output and endeavoring (with sporadic success) to sing on pitch. The recording has been declared a 'crossover hit.' "

Considering the number of veteran artists who won in most of the award categories this year, *Variety* declared, "the Grammys' reputation for honoring the hidebound over the fresh remains intact." Most races, it said, had "predictable results as the academy's penchant for sentimentalism and old school ways held sway."

The ceremony, hosted again by comedian Garry Shandling, was held in New York for the fifth time overall and the first time since 1988. At Radio City Music Hall, *Variety* said Shandling seemed out of place, adding, "His biggest gaffe: Calling Wilson Phillips a 'he.' "

"Nielsen ratings appeared oblivious to the site change," *Variety* reported. "CBS won the 8 P.M. to 11 P.M. slot with an 18.8

rating and 31 share, almost identical to last year's 18.9/31."

Variety added, "There was a general shrugging of shoulders over mini-controversies surrounding no-shows Sinéad O'Connor and Public Enemy—the former objected to the 'commerciality' of the music industry and the Grammys, while the latter protested the exclusion of the rap performance of a duo or group category (in which PE was nominated) from the televised portion.

"Evening's one unforeseen moment, and the most talked-about, was Lifetime Achievement winner Bob Dylan's rocked-up version of his 'Masters of War' and his obscure acceptance speech." After Dylan was given the accolade by actor Jack Nicholson, he quoted his father, saying, "It's possible to be so defiled in this world that even your mother and father won't know you. But God will always believe in your own ability to mend your own ways."

• 1990 •

The awards ceremony was broadcast on CBS from Radio City Music Hall in New York City on February 20, 1991, for the eligibility period of October 1, 1989, through September 30, 1990.

ALBUM OF THE YEAR
- *Back on the Block*, Quincy Jones. Qwest.
. . . *But Seriously*, Phil Collins. Atlantic.
Mariah Carey, Mariah Carey. Columbia/CBS.
Please Hammer Don't Hurt 'Em, M.C. Hammer. Capitol.
Wilson Phillips, Wilson Phillips. SBK.

RECORD OF THE YEAR
- "Another Day in Paradise," Phil Collins. Atlantic.
"From a Distance," Bette Midler. Atlantic.
"Nothing Compares 2 U," Sinéad O'Connor. Ensign/Chrysalis.
"U Can't Touch This," M.C. Hammer. Capitol.
"Vision of Love," Mariah Carey. Columbia/CBS.

SONG OF THE YEAR
(Songwriter's Award)
- "From a Distance," Julie Gold.
"Another Day in Paradise," Phil Collins.
"Hold On," Chynna Phillips, Glen Ballard, Carnie Wilson.

"Nothing Compares 2 U," Prince.
"Vision of Love," Mariah Carey, Ben Margulies.

BEST NEW ARTIST
- Mariah Carey
Black Crowes
Kentucky Headhunters
Lisa Stansfield
Wilson Phillips

BEST POP VOCAL PERFORMANCE, MALE
- Roy Orbison, "Oh Pretty Woman," track from *A Black and White Night Live*. Virgin.
Michael Bolton, "Georgia on My Mind." Columbia/CBS.
Phil Collins, "Another Day in Paradise." Atlantic.
James Ingram, "I Don't Have the Heart." Warner Bros.
Billy Joel, *Storm Front*. Columbia/CBS.
Rod Stewart, "Downtown Train." Warner Bros.

BEST POP VOCAL PERFORMANCE, FEMALE
- Mariah Carey, "Vision of Love." Columbia/CBS.
Whitney Houston, "I'm Your Baby Tonight." Arista.
Bette Midler, "From a Distance." Atlantic.

Sinéad O'Connor, "Nothing Compares 2 U." Ensign/Chrysalis.

Lisa Stansfield, "All Around the World." Arista.

Janet Jackson, "Black Cat." A&M.

Stevie Nicks, "Whole Lotta Trouble." Modern/Atlantic.

Tina Turner, "Steamy Windows." Capitol.

BEST POP PERFORMANCE BY A DUO OR GROUP WITH VOCAL

• Linda Ronstadt with Aaron Neville, "All My Life." Elektra.

B-52's, "Roam." Reprise.

Heart, "All I Wanna Do Is Make Love to You." Capitol.

Bruce Hornsby & the Range, "Across the River." RCA.

Wilson Phillips, "Hold On." SBK.

Righteous Brothers, "Unchained Melody" (1990 rerecording). Curb.

BEST POP INSTRUMENTAL PERFORMANCE

• Angelo Badalamenti, *"Twin Peaks* Theme," track from *Twin Peaks Soundtrack*. Warner Bros.

Phil Collins, "Saturday Night and Sunday Morning," track from . . . *But Seriously*. Atlantic.

Kenny G, "Going Home," track from *Live*. Arista.

Quincy Jones, various artists, "Setembro (Brazilian Wedding Song)," track from *Back on the Block*. Qwest.

Stanley Jordan, "What's Goin' On," track from *Cornucopia*. Blue Note.

BEST ROCK VOCAL PERFORMANCE, MALE

• Eric Clapton, "Bad Love." Reprise/Duck.

Joe Cocker, "You Can Leave Your Hat On." Capitol.

Billy Joel, "Cradle of Love." Chrysalis.

Jon Bon Jovi, "Blaze of Glory," track from *Blaze of Glory*. Mercury.

Neil Young, "Rockin' in the Free World." Reprise.

BEST ROCK VOCAL PERFORMANCE, FEMALE

• Alannah Myles, "Black Velvet." Atlantic.

Melissa Etheridge, "The Angels." Island.

BEST ROCK PERFORMANCE BY A DUO OR GROUP WITH VOCAL

• Aerosmith, "Janie's Got a Gun." Geffen.

INXS, "Suicide Blonde." Atlantic.

Midnight Oil, *Blue Sky Mining*. Columbia/CBS

Red Hot Chili Peppers, "Higher Ground." EMI.

Rolling Stones, "Almost Hear You Sigh." Columbia/CBS.

BEST ROCK INSTRUMENTAL PERFORMANCE

• Vaughan Brothers, "D/FW," track from *Family Style*. Epic Associated.

Allman Brothers Band, "True Gravity," track from *Seven Turns*. Epic.

Eric Johnson, *Ah Via Musicom*. Capitol.

Joe Satriani, *Flying in a Blue Dream*. Relativity.

Steve Vai, *Passion and Warfare*. Relativity.

BEST HARD ROCK PERFORMANCE

• Living Colour, *Time's Up*. Epic.

AC/DC, *The Razors Edge*. Atco.

Faith No More, "Epic." Slash/Reprise.

Jane's Addiction, *Ritual de lo Habitual*. Warner Bros.

Mötley Crüe, "Kickstart My Heart." Elektra.

BEST METAL PERFORMANCE

• Metallica, "Stone Cold Crazy," track from *Rubaiyat*. Elektra.

Anthrax, *Persistence of Time*. Island.

Megadeth, *Rust in Peace*. Capitol.

Judas Priest, *Painkiller*. Columbia.

Suicidal Tendencies, *Lights . . . Camera . . . Revolution*. Epic.

BEST ALTERNATIVE MUSIC PERFORMANCE

• Sinéad O'Connor, *I Do Not Want What I Haven't Got*. Ensign/Chrysalis.

Laurie Anderson, *Strange Angels*. Warner Bros.

Kate Bush, *The Sensual World*. Columbia/CBS.

Replacements, *All Shook Down*. Sire/Reprise.

World Party, *Goodbye Jumbo*. Chrysalis/Ensign.

BEST RHYTHM & BLUES SONG
(Songwriter's Award)

• "U Can't Touch This," James Miller, M.C. Hammer.

"Alright," Janet Jackson, James Harris III, Terry Lewis.

"Here and Now," Terry Steele, David L. Elliott.

"I'll Be Good to You," George Johnson, Louis Johnson, Sonora Sam.

"My, My, My," L. A. Reid, Babyface, Daryl Simmons.

BEST RHYTHM & BLUES VOCAL PERFORMANCE, MALE

• Luther Vandross, "Here and Now." Epic.

Babyface, "Whip Appeal." Solar/Epic.

Tevin Campbell, "Round and Round." Warner Bros./Paisley Park.

Johnny Gill, *Johnny Gill*. Motown.

Al B. Sure!, "Missunderstanding." Warner Bros.

BEST RHYTHM & BLUES VOCAL PERFORMANCE, FEMALE

• Anita Baker, *Compositions*. Elektra.

Regina Belle, "Make It Like It Was." Columbia/CBS.

Janet Jackson, "Alright." A&M.

Patti LaBelle, "I Can't Complain." MCA.

Pebbles, "Giving You the Benefit." MCA.

BEST RHYTHM & BLUES PERFORMANCE BY A DUO OR GROUP WITH VOCAL

• Ray Charles, Chaka Khan, "I'll Be Good to You." Qwest.

After 7, "Can't Stop." Virgin.

Al B. Sure!, James Ingram, El DeBarge, Barry White, "The Secret Garden (Sweet Seduction Suite)." Qwest.

En Vogue, *Born to Sing*. Atlantic.

Was (Not Was), "Papa Was a Rolling Stone." Chrysalis.

BEST RAP SOLO PERFORMANCE

• M.C. Hammer, "U Can't Touch This." Capitol.

Big Daddy Kane, "I Get the Job Done." Cold Chillin'/Reprise.

Monie Love, "Monie in the Middle." Warner Bros.

Queen Latifah, *All Hail the Queen*. Tommy Boy.

Vanilla Ice, "Ice Ice Baby." SBK.

BEST RAP PERFORMANCE BY A DUO OR GROUP

• Ice-T, Melle Mel, Big Daddy Kane, Kool Moe Dee, "Back on the Block," track from Quincy Jones's *Back on the Block*. Warner Bros.

Digital Underground, "The Humpty Dance." Tommy Boy.

D.J. Jazzy Jeff & the Fresh Prince, *And in This Corner . . .* Jive/RCA.

Public Enemy, *Fear of a Black Planet*. Def Jam/Columbia.

West Coast Rap All-Stars, "We're All in the Same Gang." Warner Bros.

BEST JAZZ VOCAL PERFORMANCE, MALE

• Harry Connick, Jr., *We Are in Love*. Columbia/CBS.

Tony Bennett, *Astoria: Portrait of the Artist*. Columbia/CBS.

George Benson, *Big Boss Band*. Warner Bros.

Jon Hendricks, *Freddie Freeloader*. Denon.

Bobby McFerrin, "Scrapple from the Apple," track from *The Many Faces of Bird*. Verve.

BEST JAZZ VOCAL PERFORMANCE, FEMALE

• Ella Fitzgerald, *All That Jazz*. Pablo.

Betty Carter, *Droppin' Things*. Verve.

Peggy Lee, *The Peggy Lee Songbook—There'll Be Another Spring*. Music-Masters.

Carmen McRae, *Carmen Sings Monk.*
Novus.
Dianne Reeves, "I Got It Bad and That
Ain't Good," track from *Echos of
Ellington Vol. 1.* Verve.

BEST JAZZ INSTRUMENTAL
PERFORMANCE BY A SOLOIST

• Oscar Peterson, *The Legendary Oscar
Peterson Trio Live at the Blue Note.*
Telarc.
George Benson, "Basie's Bag," track
from *Big Boss Band.* Warner Bros.
Miles Davis, *The Hot Spot.* Antilles.
Stan Getz, *Anniversary.* Emarcy.
Branford Marsalis, *Crazy People Music.*
Columbia/CBS.

BEST JAZZ INSTRUMENTAL
PERFORMANCE BY A GROUP

• Oscar Peterson Trio, *The Legendary
Oscar Peterson Trio Live at the Blue
Note.* Telarc.
Art Blakey, Dr. John, David "Fathead"
Newman, *Bluesiana Triangle.* Wind-
ham Hill.
Branford Marsalis Quartet Featuring
Terence Blanchard, "Again Never,"
track from *Mo' Better Blues.* Colum-
bia/CBS.
Wynton Marsalis Group, *Standard Time,
Vol. 3—The Resolution of Romance.*
Columbia/CBS.
Max Roach, Dizzy Gillespie, *Max and
Dizzy—Paris 1989.* A&M.

BEST JAZZ INSTRUMENTAL
PERFORMANCE BY A BIG BAND

• Count Basie Orchestra, "Basie's Bag,"
track from George Benson's *Big
Boss Band.* Warner Bros.
Louie Bellson, *Airmail Special.* Music-
Masters.
Bob Florence Limited Edition, *Treasure
Chest.* USA Music Group.
Lionel Hampton and His Big Band,
Cookin' in the Kitchen. Glad Hamp.
Mel Lewis Jazz Orchestra, *The Defini-
tive Thad Jones, Vol. 2, Live from
the Village Vanguard.* MusicMas-
ters.

BEST JAZZ FUSION PERFORMANCE

• Quincy Jones, various artists, "Bird-
land," track from *Back on the Block.*
Qwest/Warner Bros.
Chick Corea Elektric Band, *Inside Out.*
GRP.
Stan Getz, *Apasionado.* A&M.
Lee Ritenour, *Stolen Moments.* GRP
Spyro Gyra, *Fast Forward.* GRP.

BEST COUNTRY SONG
(Songwriter's Award)

• "Where've You Been," Jon Vezner,
Don Henry.
"Come Next Monday," K. T. Oslin,
Rory Michael Bourke, Charlie Black.
"The Dance," Tony Arata.
"Friends in Low Places," DeWayne
Blackwell, Earl Bud Lee.
"When I Call Your Name," Vince Gill,
Tim DuBois (Vince Gill).

BEST COUNTRY VOCAL
PERFORMANCE, MALE

• Vince Gill, "When I Call Your Name."
MCA.
Garth Brooks, "Friends in Low Places."
Capitol/Nashville.
Doug Stone, "I'd Be Better Off (In a
Pine Box)." Epic.
Randy Travis, "Hard Rock Bottom of
Your Heart." Warner Bros.
Dwight Yoakam, "Turn It On, Turn It
Up, Turn Me Loose." Reprise.

BEST COUNTRY VOCAL
PERFORMANCE, FEMALE

• Kathy Mattea, "Where've You Been."
Mercury.
Mary-Chapin Carpenter, "Quittin'
Time." Columbia/CBS.
Carlene Carter, *I Fell in Love.* Reprise.
Reba McEntire, "You Lie." MCA.
K. T. Oslin, "Come Next Monday."
RCA.

BEST COUNTRY PERFORMANCE BY A
DUO OR GROUP WITH VOCAL

• Kentucky Headhunters, *Pickin' on
Nashville.* Mercury.
Alabama, "Jukebox in My Mind." RCA.

Judds, "Love Can Build a Bridge."
Curb/RCA.
Restless Heart, "Fast Movin' Train." RCA.
Shenandoah, "Ghost in This House."
Columbia/CBS.

BEST COUNTRY VOCAL COLLABORATION

• Chet Atkins, Mark Knopfler, "Poor
Boy Blues." Columbia/CBS.
Waylon Jennings, Willie Nelson, Kris
Kristofferson, Johnny Cash, *High-
wayman 2*. Columbia/CBS.
Randy Travis, George Jones, "A Few
Ole Country Boys." Warner Bros.
Randy Travis, B. B. King, "Waiting on
the Light to Change," track from
Heroes and Friends. Warner Bros.
Keith Whitley, Lorrie Morgan, "Till a
Tear Becomes a Rose." RCA.

BEST COUNTRY INSTRUMENTAL PERFORMANCE

• Chet Atkins, Mark Knopfler, "So Soft
Your Goodbye," track from *Neck and
Neck*. Columbia/CBS.
Asleep at the Wheel, "Pedernales
Stroll," track from *Keepin' Me Up
Nights*. Arista.
Foster & Lloyd, "Whoa," track from
Version of the Truth. RCA Victor.
David Grisman, *Dawg '90*. Acoustic
Disc.
Wild Rose, "Wild Rose," track from
Breaking New Ground. Capitol.

BEST ROCK/CONTEMPORARY GOSPEL ALBUM

• *Beyond Belief*, Petra. Dayspring/Word.
Crank It Up, Mylon & Broken Heart.
Star Song.
Find Me in These Fields, Phil Keaggy.
Myrrh/Word.
Phase II, Eddie Degarmo.
Forefront/Benson.
The Secret of Time, Charlie Peacock.
Sparrow Records.

BEST POP GOSPEL ALBUM

• *Another Time . . . Another Place*,
Sandi Patti. A&M/Word.

Go West Young Man, Michael W. Smith.
Reunion.
God Is Good, First Call. Myrrh.
More to This Life, Steven Curtis Chap-
man. Sparrow.
Warriors, Phil Driscoll. Word.

BEST SOUTHERN GOSPEL ALBUM

• *The Great Exchange*, Bruce Carroll.
Word.
He's Still in the Fire, Speers. Home
land.
Let the Redeemed Say So, Nelons.
Canaan/Word.
The Reunion, Happy Goodman Family.
Word/Epic.
Victory Road, J. D. Sumner & the
Stamps. River Song/Benson.

BEST TRADITIONAL SOUL GOSPEL ALBUM

• *Tramaine Hawkins Live*, Tramaine
Hawkins. Sparrow.
Bringing It Back Home, Clark Sisters.
Word/Word Inc.
I Remember Mama, Shirley Caesar.
Word/Word Inc.
Mom and Pop Winans, Mom & Pop
Winans. Sparrow.
*Ron Winans Presents Family and
Friends Choir II*, Ron Winans Family
& Friends Choir. Selah.

BEST CONTEMPORARY SOUL GOSPEL ALBUM

• *So Much 2 Say*, Take 6. Reprise.
Face to Face, Edwin Hawkins. Lection/
Polygram.
*He's Right on Time/Live from Los Ange-
les*, Daryl Coley. Sparrow.
Portrait, Richard Smallwood Singers.
Word.
Return, Winans. Warner Bros./Qwest.

BEST GOSPEL ALBUM BY A CHOIR OR CHORUS

• *Having Church*, Rev. James Cleveland
& the Southern California Community Choir; Rev. James Cleveland,
choir director. Savoy.

He's Worthy, Dr. Jonathan Greer & the
Cathedral of Faith Choirs; Maurice
Culpepper, choir director. Savoy.
Hold On, Help Is on the Way, Georgia
Mass Choir; James Bignon, choir
director. Savoy.
Love Alive IV, Love Center Mass Choir;
Walter Hawkins, choir director.
Malaco.
Open Our Eyes, Rev. Milton Brunson &
the Thompson Community Singers;
Rev. Milton Brunson, choir director.
Word/Word Inc.

BEST TRADITIONAL FOLK RECORDING

• **On Praying Ground**, Doc Watson.
Sugar Hill.
**Brazil Forro: Music for Maids and Taxi
Drivers**, Toinho de Alagoas, Duda da
Passira, Jose Orlando, Heleno Dos
Oito Baixos. Rounder.
Classic Tracks, Ladysmith Black Mam-
bazo. Shanachie.
Let's Get Cajun, Basin Brothers. Flying
Fish.
Old Time Duets, Whitstein Brothers.
Rounder.
**Partisans of Vilna: Songs of World War
II Jewish Resistance**, various artists.
Flying Fish.

BEST CONTEMPORARY FOLK RECORDING

• **Steady On**, Shawn Colvin. Colum-
bia/CBS.
Days of Open Hand, Suzanne Vega.
A&M.
"Hammer and a Nail," track from
Nomads, Indians, Saints, Indigo
Girls. Epic.
Helpless Heart, Maura O'Connell.
Warner Bros.

BEST TRADITIONAL BLUES RECORDING

• **Live at San Quentin**, B. B. King.
MCA.
"Coming to Town," track from **The Hot
Spot**, John Lee Hooker, Earl Palmer,
Tim Drummond, Miles Davis, Roy
Rogers. Antilles.

Little Milton, **Too Much Pain** . . .
Malaco.
Standing My Ground, Clarence "Gatemouth" Brown. Alligator.
" 'Tain't Nobody's Bizness If I Do,"
track from the **Black and Blue** cast
recording, Ruth Brown, Linda Hopkins. Deutsche Grammophon.

BEST CONTEMPORARY BLUES RECORDING

• **Family Style**, Vaughan Brothers. Epic
Associated.
Jump for Joy, Koko Taylor. Alligator.
Midnight Stroll, the Robert Cray Band
Featuring the Memphis Horns. Mer-
cury.
"Red Hot & Blue," track from **Red, Hot
and Blue**, B. B. King, Lee Atwater.
Curb.
Stickin' to My Guns, Etta James. Island.

BEST BLUEGRASS RECORDING

• **I've Got That Old Feeling**, Alison
Krauss. Rounder.
The Boys Are Back in Town, Nashville
Bluegrass Band. Sugar Hill.
"Darlin' Boy," track from **Let It Fly**, Dil-
lards. Vanguard.
Grassroots to Bluegrass, Mac Wiseman.
CMH.
Take It Home, Hot Rize. Sugar Hill.

BEST LATIN POP PERFORMANCE

• José Feliciano, "Por Qué Te Tengo
Que Olvidar?" track from **Nina**. Cap-
ital/EMI Latin.
Duncan Dhu, **Autobiografiá**.
Sire/Warner Bros.
Ana Gabriel, **Quien Como Tu**. CBS Dis-
cos International.
Luis Miguel, **20 Anos**. WEA Latina.
Isabel Pantoja, "Se Me Enamora el
Alma," track from **Se Me Enamora el
Alma**. RCA.

BEST TROPICAL LATIN PERFORMANCE

• Tito Puente, "Lambada Timbáles,"
track from **Goza Mi Timbal**. Concord
Picante.

Willie Colon, *Color Americano*. CBS
Discos International.
Luis Enrique, "Amiga," track from *Los
Principes de la Salsa*. CBS Discos
International.
Tito Puente, Millie P., *Tito Puente Presents Millie P*. RMM.
Poncho Sanchez, "Mama Guela," track
from *Chile con Soul*. Concord
Picante.

BEST MEXICAN-AMERICAN PERFORMANCE

• Texas Tornados, "Soy de San Luis,"
track from *Texas Tornados*. Reprise.
Los Diablos, *Nuestro Tiempo*. WEA
Latina.
Vicente Fernadez, *Las Clásicas de José
Alfredo Jiménez*. CBS Discos International.
Santiago Jimenez, Jr., *Familia y Tradición*. Rounder.
Mazz, "Amor con Amor," track from *No
Te Olvidare*. Capitol/EMI Latin.

BEST REGGAE RECORDING

• *Time Will Tell—A Tribute to Bob Marley*, Bunny Wailer. Shanachie.
An Hour Live, Toots & the Maytals.
Sunsplash.
Make Place for the Youth, Andrew Tosh.
Tomato.
Mek We Dweet, Burning Spear.
Mango/Island.
Now, Black Uhuru. Mesa.

BEST POLKA RECORDING

• *When It's Polka Time at Your House*,
Jimmy Sturr & His Orchestra. Starr.
Everybody Polka, Eddie Blazonczyk's
Versatones. Bel-Aire.
Fiddle Faddle, Polka Family Band.
Polka Family Band.
Grand Illusion, Toledo Polkamotion.
World Renowned Sounds.
Sounds from the Heart, Jimmy Weber &
the Sounds. World Renowned
Sounds.

BEST NEW AGE PERFORMANCE

• Mark Isham, *Mark Isham*. Virgin.

Acoustic Alchemy, "Caravan of
Dreams," track from *Reference Point*.
GRP.
Michael Hedges, *Taproot*. Windham
Hill.
Mannheim Steamroller, *Yellowstone—
The Music of Nature*. American
Gramaphone.
Mysterious Voices of Bulgaria, *Balkan*.
Virgin.
Paul Winter, *Earth: Voices of a Planet*.
Living Music.

BEST INSTRUMENTAL COMPOSITION

• "Change of Heart," Pat Metheny.
"The Chief," Pat Metheny.
"Going Home," Kenny G, Walter
Aranasieff.
"One Last Pitch (Take Two)," Harry
Connick, Jr., and Joe Livingston.
"The Sinister Minister," Bela Fleck.

BEST ARRANGEMENT ON AN INSTRUMENTAL

• Quincy Jones, Ian Prince, Rod Temperton, Jerry Hey, "Birdland," track
from *Back on the Block* (Quincy
Jones, various artists). Qwest/Warner
Bros.
John Clayton, "Brush This," track from
The Groove Shop (Clayton-Hamilton
Jazz Orchestra). Capri.
Chick Corea, "Tale of Daring, Chapters
1–4," track from *Inside Out* (Chick
Corea Elektric Band). GRP.
Henry Mancini, "Monster Movie Music
Suite," track from *Mancini in Surround—Mostly Monsters, Murders
and Mys* (Henry Mancini & the
Mancini Pops Orchestra). RCA Victor.
John Williams, "Born on the Fourth of
July" (John Williams). MCA.

BEST MUSICAL CAST SHOW ALBUM

• *Les Misérables, the Complete Symphonic Recording*, Gary Morris,
Philip Quast, Kaho Shimada, Tracey
Shayne and various casts. Alain Boublil, Herbert Kretzmer, lyricists;

Claude Michel Schonberg, composer. Relativity.

Anything Goes, Kim Criswell, Cris Groenendaal, Jack Gilford, Frederica von Stade and cast. Cole Porter, lyricist and composer. Angel.

Black and Blue, Ruth Brown, Linda Hopkins and original Broadway cast. Various lyricists and composers; Deutsche Grammophon.

City of Angels, James Naughton, Gregg Edelman and original Broadway cast. Cy Coleman, composer. David Zippel, lyrics. Columbia/CBS.

Gypsy, Tyne Daly and original Broadway cast. Stephen Sondheim, lyricist; Jule Style, composer. Elektra-Nonesuch.

BEST INSTRUMENTAL COMPOSITION WRITTEN FOR A MOTION PICTURE OR TV

• *Glory*, James Horner. Virgin.

Dick Tracy Original Score, Danny Elfman. Sire/Warner Bros.

"Driving Miss Daisy—End Titles," track from *Driving Miss Daisy Original Soundtrack*, Hans Zimmer. Varèse Sarabande.

The Little Mermaid—Original Motion Picture Soundtrack (instrumental score), Alan Menken (various artists). Walt Disney.

Soundtrack from Twin Peaks, Angelo Badalamenti (Angelo Badalamenti). Warner Bros.

BEST SONG WRITTEN SPECIFICALLY FOR A MOTION PICTURE OR TV

• "Under the Sea," track from *The Little Mermaid Original Soundtrack*, Alan Menken, Howard Ashman. Walt Disney.

"Blaze of Glory," track from the motion picture *Young Guns II*, Jon Bon Jovi. Mercury.

"Kiss the Girl," track from *The Little Mermaid Original Soundtrack*, Howard Ashman, Alan Menken. Walt Disney.

"More," track from *Dick Tracy*, Stephen Sondheim. Sire/Warner Bros.

"Sooner or Later," track from *I'm Breathless*, Stephen Sondheim. Sire/Warner Bros.

BEST INSTRUMENTAL ARRANGEMENT ACCOMPANYING VOCAL(S)

• Jerry Hey, Glen Ballard, Cliff Magness, Quincy Jones, "The Places You Find Love" (Siedah Garrett and Chaka Khan on the Quincy Jones track from *Back on the Block*). Qwest/Warner Bros.

Jorge Calandrelli, "Body and Soul," track from *Astoria: Portrait of the Artist* (Tony Bennett). Columbia/CBS.

George Duke, "Fumilayo," track from *Never Too Far* (Dianne Reeves). EMI.

Mark Shaiman, Harry Connick, Jr., "Recipe for Love," track from *We Are in Love* (Harry Connick, Jr.). Columbia/CBS.

Mervyn Warren, Cedric Dent, "Come Sunday," track from *Bigger World* (Donna McElroy). Reprise.

BEST CLASSICAL ALBUM

• *Ives: Symphony No. 2; The Gong on the Hook and Ladder (Fireman's Parade on Main Street); Central Park in the Dark; The Unanswered Question*, Leonard Bernstein conducting the New York Philharmonic. Deutsche Grammophon.

Adams: Fearful Symmetries; The Wound-Dresser, John Adams conducting the Orchestra of St. Luke's (Sanford Sylvan, baritone). Elektra/Nonesuch.

Carreras, Domingo, Pavarotti in Concert, José Carreras, Placido Domingo, Luciano Pavarotti, tenors; Zubin Mehta conducting the Orchestra del Maggio Musicale Fiorentino and Orchestra del Teatro dell'Opera di Roma. London.

Hanson: Symphonies Nos. 3 and 6; Fantasy Variations on a Theme of Youth, Gerard Schwarz conducting the Seattle Symphony and New York Chamber Symphony (Carol Rosenberger, piano). Delos International.

The Last Recording (Chopin, Hayden, Liszt, Wagner), Vladimir Horowitz, piano. Sony Classical.

Rachmaninov: Vespers, Robert Shaw conducting the Robert Shaw Festival Singers. Telarc.

BEST ORCHESTRAL PERFORMANCE (Conductor's Award)

• Leonard Bernstein conducting the Chicago Symphony Orchestra, *Shostakovich: Symphonies No. 1, Op. 10, and No. 7 ("Leningrad"), Op. 60*. Deutsche Grammophon.

Leonard Bernstein conducting the New York Philharmonic, *Ives: Symphony No. 2; The Gong on the Hook and Ladder (Fireman's Parade on Main Street); Central Park in the Dark; The Unanswered Question*. Deutsche Grammophon.

Gerard Schwarz conducting the Seattle Symphony Orchestra, *Hanson: Symphonies Nos. 3 and 6*. Delos International.

Leonard Slatkin conducting the St. Louis Symphony Orchestra, *Shostakovich: Symphony No. 8, Op. 65*. RCA Victor Red Seal.

Sir Georg Solti conducting the Chicago Symphony Orchestra, *Beethoven: Symphonies No. 7 in A and No. 8 in F*. London.

BEST CHAMBER MUSIC OR OTHER SMALL ENSEMBLE PERFORMANCE

• Itzhak Perlman, violin; Daniel Barenboim, piano, *Brahms: The 3 Violin Sonatas (No. 1, Op. 78; No. 2, Op. 100; No. 3, Op. 108)*. Sony Classical.

Mona Golabek, piano; Andres Cardenes, violin; Jeffrey Solow, cello, *Arensky: Piano Trio No. 2 in D Minor; Tchaikovsky: Piano Trio in A Minor*. Delos International.

Juilliard String Quartet: Benita Valente, Jan DeGaetani, Jon Humphrey, Thomas Paul, *Haydn: The Seven Last Words of Christ*. Sony Classical.

Kronos Quartet, *Crumb: Black Angels; Tallis: Spem in Alium; Marta: Doom. A Sigh; Ives: They Are There!; Shostakovich: Quartet No. 8*. Elektra/Nonesuch.

Richard Stoltzman, clarinet; Richard Goode, piano; Lucy Chapman Stoltzman, violin, *Bartók: Contrasts; Stravinsky: L'Histoire du Soldat—Suite; Ives: Largo; Songs*. RCA Victor Red Seal.

BEST CLASSICAL PERFORMANCE, INSTRUMENTAL SOLOIST(S) (WITH ORCHESTRA)

• Itzhak Perlman, violin (Zubin Mehta conducting the Israel Philharmonic), *Shostakovich: Violin Concerto No. 1 in A Minor; Glazunov: Violin Concerto in A Minor, Op. 82*. Angel.

Paul Crossley, piano (Esa-Pekka Salonen conducting the London Sinfonietta), *Stravinsky: Works for Piano and Orchestra (Concerto for Piano and Orchestra, Capricco for Piano and Orchestra, etc.)*. Sony Classical.

Garrick Ohlsson, piano (Gerard Schwarz conducting the Seattle Symphony), *Lazarof: Tableaux (After Kandinsky) for Piano and Orchestra*. Delos International.

Carol Rosenberger, piano (Gerard Schwarz conducting the New York Chamber Symphony), *Hanson: Fantasy Variations on a Theme of Youth*. Delos International.

Rolf Smedvig, trumpet (Jahja Ling conducting the Scottish Chamber Orchestra), *Trumpet Concertos (Hayden, Hummel, Tartini, Torelli, Bellini)*. Telarc.

BEST CLASSICAL PERFORMANCE, INSTRUMENTAL SOLOIST (WITHOUT ORCHESTRA)

• Vladimir Horowitz, piano, *The Last Recording (Chopin, Haydn, Liszt, Wagner)*. Sony Classical.

Alicia de Larrocha, piano, *Mozart: Piano Sonatas K. 283, 331, 332, 333*. RCA Victor Red Seal.

Midori, violin, *Paganini: 24 Caprices for Solo Violin, Op. 1*. CBS Masterworks.

Ursula Oppens, piano, *Carter: Night Fantasies; Adams: Phrygian Gates*. Music & Arts Program of America.

Mitsuko Uchida, piano, *Debussy: 12 Piano Etudes*. Philips Classics.

BEST OPERA RECORDING

• *Wagner: Das Rheingold*, James Levine conducting the Metropolitan Opera Orchestra (solos: Morris, Ludwig, Jerusalem, Wlaschiha, Moll, Zednik, Rootering). Deutsche Grammophon.

Mussorgsky: Boris Godunov, Mstislav Rostropovich conducting the National Symphony Orchestra (solos: Raimondi, Vichnevskaia, Gedda, Plishka, Riegel, Tesarowicz). Erato.

Prokofiev: The Love for Three Oranges, Kent Nagano conducting the Orchestra of the Opéra de Lyon and Chorus (solos: Bacquier, Viala, Gautier, Dubosc, Bastin). Virgin Classics.

Verdi: Attila, Riccardo Muti conducting the Orchestra e Coro del Teatro alla Scala, (solos: Ramey, Studer, Shicoff, Zancaro). Angel.

Weill: The Threepenny Opera, John Mauceri conducting the RIAS Berlin Sinfonietta Berlin (solos: Lemper, Kollo, Milva, Adori, Denesch). London.

BEST CHORAL PERFORMANCE (OTHER THAN OPERA)

• Robert Shaw conducting the Atlanta Symphony Chorus and Orchestra, *Walton: Belshazzar's Feast; Bernstein: Chichester Psalms; Missa Brevis*. Telarc.

John Eliot Gardiner conducting the Monteverdi Choir, London Oratory Junior Choir and English Baroque Soloists, *Bach: St. Matthew Passion*. Archiv.

Bernard Haitink conducting the London Philharmonic Choir and Orchestra, *Vaughan Williams: Symphony No. 1 ("Sea Symphony")*. Angel.

Nicholas McGegan conducting the U.C. Berkeley Chamber Chorus, Philip Brett, choral conductor, and Philharmonia Baroque Orchestra, *Handel: Susanna*. Harmonia Mundi.

Robert Shaw conducting the Robert Shaw Festival Singers, *Rachmaninov: Vespers*. Telarc.

BEST CLASSICAL VOCAL PERFORMANCE

• José Carreras, Placido Domingo, Luciano Pavarotti, tenors (Zubin Mehta conducting the Orchestra del Maggio Musicale Fiorentino and Orchestra del Teatro dell'Opera di Roma), *Carreras, Domingo, Pavarotti in Concert*. London.

Elly Ameling, soprano (Graham Johnson, accompanist), *Schubert: The Complete Songs, Vol. 7*. Hyperion.

Jan DeGaetani, mezzo-soprano (David Effron conducting the Eastman Chamber Ensemble), *Berlioz: Les Nuits d'Eté, Op. 7; Mahler: 5 Wunderhorn Songs and 5 Ruckert Songs*. Bridge.

Thomas Hampson, baritone (Geoffry Parsons, accompanist), *Songs from "Des Knaben Wunderhorn" (Mahler, Brahms, Schumann, Loewe, Strauss, Zemlinsky, von Weber)*. Teldec.

Sanford Sylvan, baritone (John Adams conducting the Orchestra of St. Luke's), *Adams: The Wound-Dresser*. Elektra/Nonesuch.

BEST CONTEMPORARY COMPOSITION

• *Arias and Barcarolles*, Leonard Bernstein.

The Wound-Dresser, John Adams.

Tableaux (After Kandinsky) for Piano and Orchestra, Henri Lazarof.

Salome Dances for Peace, Terry Riley.

Symphony No. 2, Ellen Taaffe Zwillich.

BEST ENGINEERED RECORDING, CLASSICAL

• Jack Renner, *Rachmaninov: Vespers*, Robert Shaw conducting the Robert Shaw Festival Singers. Telarc.

Bud Graham, *Mahler: Symphony No. 8 in E Flat ("Symphony of a Thousand")*, Lorin Maazel conducting the Vienna Philharmonic; Vienna State Opera Chorus; Vienna Boys' Chorus; ORF Chorus and Arnold Schoenberg Choir. Sony Classical.

William Hoekstra, *Shostakovich: Symphony No. 8, Op. 65*, Leonard Slatkin conducting the St. Louis Symphony Orchestra. RCA Victor Red Seal.

Karl-August Naegler, *Shostakovich: Symphonies No. 1, Op. 10, and No. 7 ("Leningrad"), Op. 60*, Leonard Bernstein conducting the Chicago Symphony Orchestra. Deutsche Grammophon.

Judith Sherman, *Crumb: Black Angels; Tallis: Spem in Alium; Marta: Doom. A Sigh; Ives: They Are There!; Shostakovich: Quartet No. 8*, Kronos Quartet. Elektra/Nonesuch.

CLASSICAL PRODUCER OF THE YEAR
• Adam Stern
Michael Fine
Judith Sherman
Hans Weber
Max Wilcox

BEST COMEDY RECORDING
• *P.D.Q. Bach: Oedipus Tex and Other Choral Calamities*, Professor Peter Schickele. Telarc.
The Best of Bob and Ray: Selections from a Career, Vol. 4, Bob Elliott, Ray Goulding. Radioart.
The Best of Comic Relief '90, various artists. Rhino.
Jonathan Winters into the . . . '90s, Jonathan Winters. Dove Books on Tape.
More News from Lake Wobegon, Garrison Keillor. PHC.

BEST SPOKEN WORD OR NONMUSICAL RECORDING
• *Gracie: A Love Story*, George Burns (George Burns). Simon and Schuster Audio.

"Diane . . ." The Twin Peaks Tapes of Agent Cooper, Kyle Maclachlan. Simon and Schuster Audio.
Jimmy Stewart and His Poems, Jimmy Stewart (Jimmy Stewart). Sound Editions.
A Prairie Home Companion: The 4th Annual Farewell Performance, Garrison Keillor. Minnesota Public Radio.
Profiles in Courage (John F. Kennedy), John F. Kennedy, Jr. Harper Audio.

BEST RECORDING FOR CHILDREN
• *The Little Mermaid* (selections from film soundtrack), Howard Ashman, Alan Menken, composers. Disneyland.
Doc Watson Sings Songs for Little Pickers, Doc Watson. Alacazam.
How the Leopard Got His Spots, Danny Glover, narrator; Ladysmith Black Mambazo, music. Windham Hill.
The Little Mermaid (selections from film soundtrack), Roy Dotrice, narrator. Dove Books on Tape.
The Rock-A-Bye Collection, Vol. 2, various artists. Jaba.

BEST ENGINEERED RECORDING (OTHER THAN CLASSICAL)
• Bruce Swedien, *Back on the Block* (Quincy Jones). Qwest/Warner Bros.
Steve Churchyard, Dan Marnien, *Bedtime Stories* (David Baerwald). A&M.
Scott Hendricks, *Holdin' a Good Hand* (Lee Greenwood). Capitol.
Don Murray, *Love Is Gonna Getcha* (Patti Austin). GRP.
Hugh Padgham, *. . . But Seriously* (Phil Collins). Atlantic.

BEST ALBUM PACKAGE
(Art Director's Award)
• Len Peltier, Jeffrey Gold, Suzanne Vega, *Days of Open Hand* (Suzanne Vega). A&M.
Carol Bobolts, Anita Baker, Jim Ladwig, *Compositions* (Anita Baker). Elektra.

Jeri Heiden, *Behind the Mask* (Fleetwood Mac). Warner Bros.

Vaughan Oliver, *Bossanova* (Pixies). Elektra.

Tom Recchion, *Songs for Drella* (Lou Reed, John Cale). Sire/Warner Bros.

BEST ALBUM NOTES
(Annotator's Award)
• Dan Morgenstern, *Brownie: The Complete Emarcy Recordings of Clifford Brown* (Clifford Brown). Emarcy.

Mary Katherine Aldin, Robert Palmer, *Muddy Waters—The Chess Box* (Muddy Waters). MCA/Chess.

Gary Giddons, *Art Pepper: The Complete Galaxy Recordings* (Art Pepper). Galaxy/Fantasy.

Robert Palmer, *Bo Diddley—The Chess Box* (Bo Diddley). MCA-Chess.

David Perry, *The Jack Kerouac Collection* (Jack Kerouac). Rhino.

BEST HISTORICAL ALBUM
• *Robert Johnson: The Complete Recordings*, Robert Johnson. Columbia/CBS.

Beethoven: Symphonies 1–9 and Leonore Overture No. 3, Arturo Toscanini conducting the NBC Symphony Orchestra. RCA Victor Gold Seal.

Brownie: The Complete Emarcy Recordings of Clifford Brown, Clifford Brown. Emarcy.

The Jack Kerouac Collection, Jack Kerouac. Rhino.

Verdi: Aida, Falstaff, Requiem, Te Deum, Va, Pensiero, Hymn of the Nations, Arturo Toscanini conducting the NBC Symphony Orchestra. RCA Victor Gold Seal.

PRODUCER OF THE YEAR
(OTHER THAN CLASSICAL)
• Quincy Jones
Glen Ballard
Phil Collins, Hugh Padgham
Mick Jones, Billy Joel
Arif Mardin

BEST MUSIC VIDEO, SHORT FORM
• *Opposites Attract*, Paula Abdul. Michael Patterson, Candice Reckinger, directors. Virgin.

All I Want, Lighting Seeds. Tarsem, director. MCA.

Another Day in Paradise, Phil Collins. Jim Yukich, director. Atlantic.

Nothing Compares 2 U, Sinéad O'Connor. John Maybury, director. Chrysalis/Ensign Records.

Oh Father, Madonna. David Fincher, director. Sire.

BEST MUSIC VIDEO, LONG FORM
• *Please Hammer Don't Hurt 'Em, the Movie*, M.C. Hammer. Rupert Wainwright, director. Fragile Films.

Bernstein in Berlin, Beethoven: Symphony No. 9, Leonard Berstein. Humphrey Burton, director. Deutshe Grammophon.

Live—Featuring the Rock Opera Tommy, Who. R. Daltry, P. Townshend, J. Entwistle. Larry Jordan, director. CMV Enterprises.

The Singles Collection, Phil Collins. Jim Yukich, director. Atlantic.

We Too Are One Too, Eurythmics. Sophie Muller, director. Arista Records.

An *Unforgettable* Sweep

It was, said virtually every press account the next day, an unforgettable night for Natalie Cole.

Grammy's Best New Artist of 1975 made a triumphant return to the awards when *Unforgettable* and its title track brought her golden statuettes for Album and Record of the Year, marking only the eighth time in the Grammys' 34-year history that the two top trophies went to the same artist and the fifth time that a solo female artist reaped the top album honor. *Unforgettable* also brought her the new award for Best Traditional Pop Performance in addition to earning separate prizes for engineering, arrangement, Producer of the Year David Foster and Song of the Year laurels for the tune's writer, Irving Gordon.

COLE'S HOT ON GRAMMY NIGHT

'Unforgettable' nabs 7 nods; R.E.M., Raitt bag 3 each

BY BRUCE HARING

Natalie Cole's "Unforgettable" Elektra album racked up seven Grammys.

"It's been an incredible, incredible time," a victorious Natalie Cole said. "I thank my dad for leaving me such a wonderful, wonderful legacy."

Cole crafted *Unforgettable* as a tribute to her father, Nat King Cole, who died of lung cancer in 1965. She covered 22 of his classic works and, on the album's final—and title—track, joined him in an intimate duet by splicing her new 1991 rendition into the original tape of his Top 20 hit that was recorded exactly 40 years earlier. Listeners heard father and daughter croon together lovingly, "Unforgettable, that's what you are. . . . "

The old-fashioned ballad was an unlikely hit in the rock era, but "Unforgettable" climbed to number 14 on the singles charts and proved irresistible to N.A.R.A.S.'s notoriously conservative voters. When Natalie accepted the trophy for Record of the Year, she referred to her new pop success, saying, "It's been an incredible, incredible time. I thank my dad for leaving me such a wonderful, wonderful legacy." She had just bounced back from a long struggle with drug and alcohol problems and thanked her husband "for believing in me when I was having a hard time believing in myself."

But Natalie Cole's "much anticipated coronation" at the Grammys, as *Variety* called it, was cause for an equally predictable revolt among music's young guard that was sure to follow. The *L.A. Times* warned: "Although the series of awards [was] cheered by the Grammy audience, they—and other choices—are bound to renew grumbling by Grammy critics who believe the 7,000 member N.A.R.A.S. tends to honor mainstream best sellers rather than the maverick forces that reshape pop music."

The winner of Song of the Year took aim at those mavericks when he accepted his statuette. The victory of a 40-year-old ballad upset—and confused—some Grammy watchers, but N.A.R.A.S. rules permitted all tunes to compete as long as new recordings were released within the eligibility period and the work was never before nominated. Songwriter Irving Gordon took obvious glee in the victory of his old chestnut as the 77-year-old expressed his thanks for the award, saying, "In a youth-oriented culture, it's nice to have a middle-aged song do something. It's nice to have a song come out that doesn't scream, yell and have a nervous breakdown while it talks about tenderness. It's nice to have a song accepted where you don't get a hernia when you sing it."

Gordon's speech amounted to what the *L.A. Times* called "the worst nightmare of the progressive wing of the academy," not only for its slap at modern music but because Gordon accepted his award from Michael Bolton, who'd just sung a howling rendition of his hit version of the Percy Sledge tune "When a Man Loves a Woman," for which he won the laurels for best male pop vocal performance. "I realized after I said it, what I had gotten myself into," Gordon told the *Times*. "I'm of a different generation, into a different kind of music." He apologized profusely to Bolton as the singer escorted him offstage, but Bolton proved gracious, saying, "No, no, no . . . I voted for you."

Backstage, Bolton told reporters, "I happen to be very happy for him that he won. But as to how in touch Mr. Gordon is with today's music, I can't speak for him. I can say I don't get a hernia when I sing."

In its harsh review of the awards ceremony, *Variety* pointed out that the Grammy show was an inappropriate place for the slam against rock: "The fact is, the academy's industry stalwarts have been slow to honor anything other than antiseptic, traditional compositions and performances, and this year was, for the most part, no exception."

According to the *New York Daily News,* the night's biggest "shocker" turned out to be the selection of Marc Cohn ("Walking in Memphis") as Best

New Artist over Boyz II Men. Cohn had three nominations in all but lost to Gordon in the Song of the Year category and to Bolton in the pop vocals contest. The introspective singer-songwriter and his 14-member band, the Supreme Court, were discovered, coincidentally, by Grammy's Best New Artist of 1971, Carly Simon, and then subsequently given broad exposure when asked to perform at Caroline Kennedy's wedding.

"Cohn said he was surprised at his win but said it was a good example of how Atlantic's been behind his record," *Variety* reported.

Having just swept the MTV Music Video Awards, R.E.M. led with the most Grammy nominations (seven), including ones for Record, Album and Song of the Year. "The Georgia-based quartet, which blends enticing, folk-flavored rock-roots music with teasingly elusive lyrics, was the class of the alternative/college rock scene in the 1980s," the *L.A. Times* noted.

"Losing My Religion" won R.E.M. the short-form music video prize and the group pop vocals honors. *Out of Time,* the album that took the group to the top of the LP charts for the first time, reaped the prize for Best Alternative Music Album. Considering that *Out of Time* was also up for Album of the Year, the *Washington Post* called the potential combination "a nice double, suggesting you can have your cake and eat it, too." *Out of Time,* however, was certainly an alternative choice compared to the eventual winner, *Unforgettable,* although critic Robert Hilburn of the *L.A. Times* grumbled about Grammy voters, "They should have saluted Nirvana." Hilburn was nonetheless a R.E.M. fan: Early on, he was among those who believed "Losing My Religion" could beat Cole's "Unforgettable" for Record of the Year.

Most other Grammy watchers had considered a Bryan Adams song to be the strongest alternative to Natalie Cole's "Unforgettable" for the highest honors. Adams had the second-most nominations of the year (six), most of them for his blockbuster hit "(Everything I Do) I Do It for You," which was included in the Kevin Costner film *Robin Hood: Prince of Thieves* and became the biggest-selling single since Grammy's 1985 Record of the Year winner, "We Are the World." The Canadian rocker pulled off only one victory, however, for "Everything" as best film song.

In third place with the most bids (five) was 1989 Grammy champ Bonnie Raitt, who ended up with three trophies, including best pop and rock vocals honors. By the time the veteran country rocker picked up the third Grammy—the rock duo/group singing laurels, which she shared with Delbert McClinton for "Good Man, Good Woman"—she gasped while up at the podium, "Man, oh, man . . . I've had enough already!"

Variety called the vote result predictable when the new category for Best Rock Song was claimed by four-time past Grammy winner Sting for "Soul Cages," triumphing over considerable competition from Bryan Adams, Tom Petty and Metallica. Metallica held on to the metal performance award for a surprising third year in a row, this time for its eponymous album. "There was so much of a howl when tired rock warhorse Jethro Tull won over the infinitely more vital Metallica [for 1989], the year that the heavy metal category was introduced to the Grammy competition, that the academy voters seem afraid to vote for anyone other than Metallica for fear of making another mistake," said the *L.A. Times.*

Variety noted that "drummer Lars Ulrich teased the crowd with his thankyou." He said, "The first thing we have to do is thank Jethro Tull for not putting out an album this year. We also have to thank the academy for giving the Grammy to Tull two years ago. Read between the lines. You know what I mean."

Van Halen took the hard-rock category with *For Unlawful Carnal Knowledge* over Guns N' Roses, which was favored by pundits. In his acceptance speech, Eddie Van Halen insisted, "Over

Georgia-based quartet R.E.M. led with the most nominations (seven) and received three awards for "Losing my Religion" and *Out of Time.*

the years, we have not lost touch with fans. We've never second guessed what they like. Our hearts are into this."

Rap was the source of an uproar again when the award for duo/group performance went to 1988 Grammy champs D.J. Jazzy Jeff & the Fresh Prince. The act had new prominence since Fresh Prince (actor Will Smith) had a new TV sitcom, *The Fresh Prince of Bel-Air,* which started in the fall of 1990 and was considered featherweight fare designed for his teenage fans.

Variety griped: "The victory further underscored the conservativeness of the Grammy voting bloc, which bypassed the street-oriented sound of Public Enemy, Naughty by Nature and Salt-N-Pepa. The academy redeemed itself somewhat in its voting for rap solo performance, which went to L.L. Cool J for his 'Mama Said Knock You Out,' which he also performed on the show."

After having been overlooked on nine previous occasions, Luther Vandross won his first Grammy last year as 1990's best r&b singer and now scored two more victories. He repeated his win in the male r&b vocals category for *Power of Love,* which he performed on the Grammycast while twirling to show off his new, slimmed-down physique. He also shared in the prize for writing the tune when it won Best Rhythm & Blues Song.

Variety reported, "Female r&b honors provided one of the night's surprises—a tie." The award was shared by two first-time winners: Lisa Fischer ("How Can I Ease the Pain"), the Brooklyn-born artist who often toured with Vandross, and Patti LaBelle (*Burnin'*), one of the queens of r&b who had been performing professionally since the mid-1960s.

Vandross, LaBelle and such past Grammy favorites as Aretha Franklin, Prince and Gladys Knight all lost in the r&b duo/group lineup to Motown's newest stars and losing nominee for Best New Artist Boyz II Men (*Cooleyhighharmony*). The four Boyz met at Philadelphia's High School of Creative and Performing Arts, where they listened to "jazz, opera, classical and everything—so that's what we sing," group member Nathan Morris told *Entertainment Weekly* soon after their victory. At the Grammycast, the Boyz squared off in what the magazine called "an a cappella duel" with the rival group Color Me Badd, which they trounced in the r&b category.

The jazz categories welcomed back lots of veteran champs, including four-time past victor Take 6 (Best Jazz Vocal Performance, *He Is Christmas*), seven-time past champ the Manhattan Transfer (contemporary jazz performance, "Sassy"), six-time past winner the Oscar Peterson Trio (jazz group instrumental, *Saturday Night at the Blue Note*) and four-time recipient Stan Getz (solo instrumental, "I Remember You"), who had died of liver cancer in June. Dizzy Gillespie, still going strong at age 74, had won once before, in 1975, and now was hailed with the prize for large-ensemble performance, which he shared

with the United Nations Orchestra for *Live at the Royal Festival Hall*.

B. B. ("Blues Boy") King began his recording career in 1951 and was still going strong, too, 40 years later when he was lauded for the year's Best Traditional Blues Album, *Live at the Apollo*. One of Chicago's leading bluesmen, Buddy Guy (actually born in Louisiana), nabbed the equivalent prize for contemporary LPs for *Damn Right, I've Got the Blues*.

One month before the Grammycast, Wynonna and Naomi Judd proved the amazing pull of country music when their pay-per-view TV special drew higher ratings than similar specials by the Rolling Stones and New Kids on the Block. This year the four-time past Grammy champs proved their own considerable pull at the awards by scoring a double victory: best country duo/group vocals and Best Country Song for "Love Can Build a Bridge." *Variety* called the Judds a "sentimental favorite," since Naomi's "career has been curtailed because of chronic hepatitis."

Among the other writers they vanquished for the song award was Mary-Chapin Carpenter, a future Grammy grabber who took her first prize, the female vocals accolade, for her Cajun-spiced Best Country Song loser, "Down at the Twist and Shout." Carpenter claimed she felt out of place in the country categories. She was a native of Washington, D.C., and an Ivy League grad (Brown, '81) who crafted her work more for the acoustic-music crowd than the country fans who embraced her early in her career. She told *Entertainment Weekly*: "It's been a real identity crisis these last few years. I never thought of myself as a country musician."

Winner of the statuette for best male country crooner was first-time recipient Garth Brooks for his history-making

> For a sixth year in a row, Jimmy Sturr snagged the polka prize.

Ropin' the Wind. Prior to *Ropin'*'s release, no other country album had ever before premiered at number one on the album charts. "Since his recording debut a short three years ago, Brooks has moved more albums with more velocity than anyone else in the history of Nashville," *Entertainment Weekly* reported, noting his impressive tally of 16 million albums sold so far. *Variety* complained that Brooks's failure to score more Grammy bids and wins was one of the "biggest disappointments" this year.

In the vocalist competition, Brooks trounced last year's winner, Vince Gill, who rallied to win a Grammy for his collaboration with Steve Wariner and Ricky Skaggs ("Restless").

John Prine originally gained fame in the early 1970s when he sang the sad tale of a Vietnam vet, "Sam Stone," and received critical praise that labeled him "the new Dylan." By the early 1980s, he had trouble getting recorded but rallied by the decade's end and now picked up the Best Contemporary Folk Album Grammy for *The Missing Years.*

In the religious categories, a number of past winners returned for further glory, including Mighty Clouds of Joy (*Pray for Me,* Best Traditional Soul Gospel Album), which hadn't won a Grammy since 1979, and brother-sister duo BeBe and CeCe Winans (*Different Lifestyles,* Best Contemporary Soul Gospel Album). BeBe Winans accepted the latter award, saying, "Look out, music industry, gospel is here to stay!" New victors included the Sounds of Blackness, which won the prize for Best Gospel Album by a Choir or Chorus for *The Evolution of Gospel.* The statuette was accepted by band member Gary Hines, who thanked "the Father, Son, the Holy Ghost and [producers] Jimmy Jam and Terry Lewis."

For the sixth year in a row, Jimmy Sturr & His Orchestra claimed the Best Polka Album statuette (*Live! At Gilley's*), leading to some controversy. *New York Daily News* columnist David Hinckley wrote, "Polka fans are not happy that

The failure of the best country crooner Garth Brooks to nab more than a single award for *Ropin' the Wind* was one of the year's biggest disappointments," *Variety* said.

they have only one award and Jimmy Sturr aways wins it."

The big news in the Hispanic awards was that pop star vocalist Vikki Carr at last won a Grammy after having been nominated only once before, in 1967, for her hit "It Must Be Him." Twenty-four years after her initial loss, she rebounded with *Cosas del Amor,* which was hailed as Best Latin Pop Album. (Carr was born of Hispanic parents in Texas, where she was originally named Florencia Bisenta de Casillas Martinez Cardona.)

Grateful Dead drummer Mickey Hart won the new award for Best World Music Album for *Planet Drum.* Reporting on Shabba Ranks's victory for *As Raw As Ever* as Best Reggae Album, *Time* magazine called him "the reigning monarch of reggae" and quoted Ranks as saying about *Raw,* "My type of work is . . . energetic, you know? When you dance to my music, you get dizzy, get crazy." As he accepted his Grammy, he said proudly, "I'm a star now."

Gospel-turned-pop-rock-star Amy Grant had won five Grammys for religious recordings between 1982 and 1988 but reaped no awards this year despite top bids in such secular categories as Record, Album and Song of the Year. Madonna had been passed up on four occasions in the past for nominations dating back to 1985, but she finally experienced her first victory when *Blonde Ambition World Tour Live* was hailed as best long-form music video.

Last year's homage to the late Leonard Bernstein in the classical categories continued this year when again he was given the honor for Best Classical Album posthumously. Conductor John Mauceri won the Grammy for Best Opera Recording in 1986 for his and director Hal Prince's opera house version of Bernstein's *Candide,* which was just one of many overhauls attempted following the original's disastrous reception on Broadway in 1956. Prior to his death, the composer made an ambitious effort to compile his own reedited version, which he performed with the London Symphony Orchestra at the Barbican in London in 1989, earning him the top LP honor when the recorded version was released two years later.

A losing contender for Best Classical Album, composer John Corigliano's Symphony No. 1, was hailed as Best Contemporary Composition and also garnered the orchestral award for conductor Daniel Barenboim and the Chicago Symphony Orchestra. Corigliano wrote the work as an elegy to fallen friends, three of whom died of AIDS. Critics said Barenboim captured the composer's broad range of emotions—from expressions of quiet grief to outbursts of rage—with passionate sensitivity.

Another loser of the LP kudos was hailed with other awards when a recording of works by Samuel Barber earned the soloist (with orchestra) performance prize for pianist John Browning and also picked up the engineering prize. Pianist and three-time past Grammy champ Alicia de Larrocha returned for the soloist (without orchestra) trophy for her updated interpretations of works by Enrique Granados, which critics considered equal in quality to versions she'd recorded more than a decade earlier. *American Record Guide* recommended the recording highly, calling it "music you may rightly call voluptuous, classic, richly colored. In the hands of this distinguished pianist, a native of Barcelona, the aura of Spain may overwhelm you."

Sir Georg Solti had won choral performance Grammys in the past for works by Berlioz, Haydn, Brahms, Beethoven, Verdi and Mahler and now scored one more for himself and the Chicago Symphony Orchestra and Chorus for Bach's *Mass in B Minor,* bringing the all-time Grammy champ to a career tally of 29. Quincy Jones remained in second place overall, with 25.

For the third year in a row, conductor James Levine dominated the Best Opera Recording category with installment recordings of his historic staging at the Metropolitan Opera of Wagner's full *The Ring of Nibelung.* This year he prevailed with *Götterdämmerung.* The vocal performance laurels were bestowed on 1989 victor Dawn Upshaw for a collection of works by Ravel, Stravinsky and others.

The Grammycast emanated for a second consecutive year from New York's Radio City Music Hall and set a new record for length: nearly four hours. *Variety* reported, "Whoopi Goldberg, making her Grammy-hosting bow, appeared more at ease than last year's minimally qualified emcee, Garry Shandling, but with little reason, for she proved just as unfamiliar with the music world and even less funny."

When this year's Grammy nominations were announced, *Variety* lingered over a few "nuggets" that included film icon "Katharine Hepburn, who weighed

> "I feel like a work in progress," Living Legend honoree Streisand said.

in with a Grammy bid for her narration on the Random House Audio autobiography *Me: Stories of My Life.*" Hepburn lost to the audio version of the critically acclaimed PBS TV series *The Civil War,* which also reaped an Emmy, while Roy Rogers got lost in the stampede of winners that took the country vocal collaboration category: Steve Wariner, Ricky Skaggs and Vince Gill.

James Brown did prevail for Best Album Notes and also received a Lifetime Achievement Award, which he accepted wordlessly before a standing ovation.

When Barbra Streisand was given a Living Legends Award, she, too, was greeted with a vertical cheer, but she acknowledged it with a brief speech during which she said, "In all honesty, I

For a third straight year, the Met's performance of Wagner's *Ring* cycle took the opera award.

don't feel like a legend. I feel more like a work in progress."

• 1991 •

The awards ceremony was broadcast on CBS from Radio City Music Hall in New York City on February 25, 1992, for the eligibility period of October 1, 1990, through September 30, 1991.

ALBUM OF THE YEAR

• *Unforgettable*, Natalie Cole. Elektra Entertainment.
Heart in Motion, Amy Grant. A&M.
Luck of the Draw, Bonnie Raitt. Capital.
Out of Time, R.E.M. Warner Bros.
The Rhythm of the Saints, Paul Simon. Warner Bros.

RECORD OF THE YEAR

• "Unforgettable," Natalie Cole (with Nat King Cole). Elektra.
"Baby Baby," Amy Grant. A&M.
"(Everything I Do) I Do It for You," Bryan Adams. A&M
"Losing My Religion," R.E.M. Warner Bros.
"Something to Talk About," Bonnie Raitt. Capitol.

SONG OF THE YEAR
(Songwriter's Award)

• "Unforgettable," Irving Gordon.
"Baby Baby," Amy Grant, Keith Thomas.
"(Everything I Do) I Do For You," Bryan Adams, Robert John "Mutt" Lange, Michael Kamen.
"Losing My Religion," Bill Berry, Peter Buck, Mike Mills, Michael Stipe.
"Walking in Memphis," Marc Cohn.

BEST NEW ARTIST

• Marc Cohn
Boyz II Men
C + C Music Factory
Color Me Badd
Seal

BEST POP VOCAL
PERFORMANCE, MALE

• Michael Bolton, "When a Man Loves a Woman." Columbia.
Bryan Adams, "(Everything I Do) I Do It for You." A&M.

Marc Cohn, "Walking in Memphis."
Atlantic.
George Michael, "Freedom 90." Columbia.
Aaron Neville, *Warm Your Heart.*
A&M.
Seal, "Crazy." Sire/Warner Bros.

BEST POP VOCAL
PERFORMANCE, FEMALE
• Bonnie Raitt, "Something to Talk
About." Capitol.
Oleta Adams, "Get Here." Fontana.
Mariah Carey, *Emotions.* Columbia.
Amy Grant, "Baby Baby." A&M.
Whitney Houston, "All the Man That I
Need." Arista.

BEST PERFORMANCE BY A DUO OR
GROUP WITH VOCAL
• R.E.M., "Losing My Religion."
Warner Bros.
Commitments, *The Commitments* (film
soundtrack). MCA.
Extreme, "More Than Words." A&M.
Jesus Jones, "Right Here, Right Now."
SBK Records.
Wilson Phillips, "You're in Love." SBK
Records.

BEST TRADITIONAL POP
PERFORMANCE
• Natalie Cole (with Nat King Cole),
"Unforgettable." Elektra.
Harry Connick, Jr., *Blue Light, Red
Light.* Columbia.
Johnny Mathis, *In a Sentimental Mood:
Mathis Sings Ellington.* Columbia.
Diane Schuur, *Pure Schuur.* GRP.
Barbra Streisand, "Warm All Over,"
track from *Just for the Record.*
Columbia.

BEST POP INSTRUMENTAL
PERFORMANCE
• Michael Kamen conducting the
Greater Los Angeles Orchestra,
Robin Hood: Prince of Thieves. Morgan Creek.
Candy Dulfer, *Saxuality.* Arista.

Kenny G, "Theme from *Dying Young*,"
track from *Dying Young* (soundtrack). Arista.
Dave Grusin, *Havana.* GRP.
John Williams conducting the Skywalker Symphony Orchestra, *John
Williams Conducts John
Williams/The Star Wars Trilogy.*
Sony Classical.

BEST ROCK SONG
(Songwriter's Award)
• "Soul Cages," Sting.
"Been Caught Stealing," Jane's Addiction.
"Can't Stop This Thing We Started,"
Bryan Adams, Robert John "Mutt"
Lange.
"Enter Sandman," James Hetfield, Lars
Ulrich, Kirk Hammett.
"Learning to Fly," Tom Petty, Jeff
Lynne.
"Silent Lucidity," Chris DeGarmo.

BEST ROCK VOCAL
PERFORMANCE, SOLO
• Bonnie Raitt, *Luck of the Draw.* Capitol.
Bryan Adams, "Can't Stop This Thing
We Started." A&M.
Eric Clapton, *24 Nights.* Reprise.
John Mellencamp, *Whenever We
Wanted.* Mercury.
Robbie Robertson, *Storyville.*
Geffen.
Bob Seger, *The Fire Inside.* Capitol.

BEST ROCK PERFORMANCE BY A
DUO OR GROUP WITH VOCAL
• Bonnie Raitt, Delbert McClinton,
"Good Man, Good Woman," track
from Bonnie Raitt's *Luck of the
Draw.* Capitol.
Jane's Addiction, "Been Caught Stealing." Warner Bros.
Tom Petty & the Heartbreakers, *Into the
Great Wide Open.* MCA.
Queensryche, "Silent Lucidity."
EMI.
R.E.M., "Radio Song." Warner Bros.

BEST HARD ROCK PERFORMANCE WITH VOCAL

- Van Halen, *For Unlawful Carnal Knowledge*. Warner Bros.
AC/DC, "Moneytalks," track from *The Razor's Edge*. Atco/Atlantic.
Alice in Chains, "Man in the Box." Columbia.
Guns N' Roses, *Use Your Illusion I*. Geffen.

BEST METAL PERFORMANCE WITH VOCAL

- Metallica, *Metallica*. Elektra.
Anthrax, *Attack of the Killer B's*. Island.
Soundgarden, *Badmotorfinger*. A&M.
Megadeth, "Hangar 18." Capitol.
Motorhead, *1916*. WTG.

BEST ROCK INSTRUMENTAL PERFORMANCE

- Eric Johnson, "Cliffs of Dover." Capitol.
Allman Brothers Band, "Kind of Bird," track from *Shades of 2 Worlds*. Epic.
Danny Gatton, *88 Elmira Street*. Elektra.
Rush, "Where's My Thing?" track from *Roll the Bones*. Atlantic.
Yes, "Masquerade," track from *Union*. Arista.

BEST ALTERNATIVE MUSIC ALBUM

- *Out of Time*, R.E.M. Warner Bros.
Doubt, Jesus Jones. SBK.
Mighty Like a Rose, Elvis Costello. Warner Bros.
Nevermind, Nirvana. DGC.
Rumor and Sigh, Richard Thompson. Capitol.

BEST RHYTHM & BLUES SONG
(Songwriter's Award)

- "Power of Love/Love Power," Luther Vandross, Marcus Miller, Teddy Vann.
"Can You Stop the Rain," Walter Afanasieff, John Bettis.
"How Can I Ease the Pain," Narada Michael Walden, Lisa Fischer.
"I Wanna Sex You Up," Dr. Freeze.
"I'll Take You There," Alvertis Isbell.

BEST RHYTHM & BLUES VOCAL PERFORMANCE, MALE

- Luther Vandross, *Power of Love*. Epic.
James Brown, *Love Over-due*. Scotti Bros.
Peabo Bryson, "Can You Stop the Rain." Columbia.
Teddy Pendergrass, "How Can You Mend a Broken Heart." Elektra.
Keith Washington, "Kissing You." Qwest/Warner Bros.
Stevie Wonder, "Gotta Have You." Motown.

BEST RHYTHM & BLUES VOCAL PERFORMANCE, FEMALE
(Tie)

- Lisa Fischer, "How Can I Ease the Pain." Elektra.
- Patti LaBelle, *Burnin'*. MCA.
Aretha Franklin, *What You See Is What You Sweat*. Arista.
Gladys Knight, *Good Woman*. MCA.
Vanessa Williams, "Runnin' Back to You." Mercury.

BEST RHYTHM & BLUES PERFORMANCE BY A DUO OR GROUP WITH VOCAL

- Boyz II Men, *Cooleyhighharmony*. Motown.
Color Me Badd, "I Wanna Sex You Up." Giant.
Aretha Franklin, Luther Vandross, "Doctor's Orders," track from Aretha Franklin's *What You See Is What You Sweat*. Arista.
Gladys Knight, Patti LaBelle, Dionne Warwick, "Superwoman." MCA.
Prince & the N.P.G., "Gett Off." Paisley Park/Warner Bros.

BEST RAP SOLO PERFORMANCE

- L.L. Cool J, "Mama Said Knock You Out." Def Jam/Columbia.
Ice-T, "New Jack Hustler (Nino's Theme)." Giant.
M.C. Hammer, "Here Comes the Hammer (Version I)." Capitol.
Monie Love, "It's a Shame (My Sister)." Warner Bros.
Queen Latifah, "Fly Girl." Tommy Boy.

BEST RAP PERFORMANCE BY A DUO OR GROUP

- D.J. Jazzy Jeff & the Fresh Prince, "Summertime." Jive/RCA.
Heavy D. & the Boyz, "Now That We Found Love." Uptown/MCA.
Naughty by Nature, "O.P.P." Tommy Boy.
Public Enemy, *Apocalypse 91 . . . The Enemy Strikes Black*. Def Jam/Columbia.
Salt-N-Pepa, "Let's Talk About Sex." Next Plateau.

BEST CONTEMPORARY JAZZ PERFORMANCE (VOCAL OR INSTRUMENTAL)

- Manhattan Transfer, "Sassy," track from *The Offbeat of Avenues*. Columbia.
Joe Sample, *Ashes to Ashes*. Warner Bros.
Claus Ogerman, Michael Brecker, *Claus Ogerman Featuring Michael Brecker*. GRP.
Bela Fleck, Flecktones, *Flight of the Cosmic Hippo*. Warner Bros.
Yellowjackets, *Greenhouse*. GRP.
Bobby McFerrin, *Medicine Music*. EMI.

BEST JAZZ VOCAL PERFORMANCE

- Take 6, *He Is Christmas*. Reprise.
Natalie Cole, "Long 'Bout Midnight," track from *Garfield*. GRP.
Shirley Horn, *You Won't Forget Me*. Verve.
Manhattan Transfer, *The Offbeat of Avenues*. Columbia.
Mel Tormé, "Ellington Medley," track from *Mel and George Do World War II*. Concord Jazz.

BEST JAZZ INSTRUMENTAL SOLO

- Stan Getz, "I Remember You," track from *Serenity*. Emarcy.
Dave Grusin, "How Long Has This Been Going On?" track from *The Gershwin Connection*. GRP.
David Sanborn, "Another Hand," track from *Another Hand*. Elektra-Musician.

Toots Thielemans, "Bluesette," track from *Cleo Laine's Jazz*. RCA Victor.
Phil Woods, "All Bird's Children," track from *All Bird's Children*. Concord Jazz.

BEST JAZZ INSTRUMENTAL PERFORMANCE, GROUP

- Oscar Peterson Trio, *Saturday Night at the Blue Note*. Telarc.
Chick Corea Akoustic Band, *Alive*. GRP.
Dave Grusin, *The Gershwin Connection*. GRP.
Lionel Hampton & the Golden Men of Jazz, *Lionel Hampton and the Golden Men of Jazz Live at the Blue Note*. Telarc.
David Sanborn, *Another Hand*. Elektra-Musician.

BEST LARGE JAZZ ENSEMBLE PERFORMANCE

- Dizzy Gillespie & the United Nation Orchestra, *Live at the Royal Festival Hall*. Enja.
Charlie Haden & the Liberation Music Orchestra, *Dream Keeper*. Blue Note.
Rob McConnell & the Boss Brass, *The Brass Is Back*. Concord Jazz.
Jay McShann, *Paris All-Star Blues (A Tribute to Charlie Parker)*. Music-Masters.
Bob Mintzer, *Art of the Big Band*. Digital Music Products, Inc.
Doc Severinsen & the Tonight Show Band, *Once More with Feeling*. Amherst.

BEST COUNTRY SONG
(Songwriter's Award)

- "Love Can Build a Bridge," Naomi Judd, John Jarvis, Paul Overstreet.
"Don't Rock the Jukebox," Alan Jackson, Roger Murrah, Keith Stegall.
"Down at the Twist and Shout," Mary-Chapin Carpenter.
"Eagle When She Flies," Dolly Parton.
"Here's a Quarter (Call Someone Who Cares)," Travis Tritt.

BEST COUNTRY VOCAL PERFORMANCE, MALE

- Garth Brooks, *Ropin' the Wind*. Capitol.
- Billy Dean, "Somewhere in My Broken Heart." Capitol.
- Vince Gill, *Pocket Full of Gold*. MCA.
- Alan Jackson, *Don't Rock the Jukebox*. Arista.
- Travis Tritt, "Here's a Quarter (Call Someone Who Cares)." Warner Bros.

BEST COUNTRY VOCAL PERFORMANCE, FEMALE

- Mary-Chapin Carpenter, "Down at the Twist and Shout." Columbia.
- Kathy Mattea, *Time Passes By*. Mercury/Polygram.
- Reba McEntire, *For My Broken Heart*. MCA.
- Tanya Tucker, "Down to My Last Teardrop," track from *What Do I Do with Me*. Capitol.
- Trisha Yearwood, "She's in Love with the Boy." MCA.

BEST COUNTRY PERFORMANCE BY A DUO OR GROUP WITH VOCAL

- Judds, "Love Can Build a Bridge." RCA.
- Alabama, "Forever's As Far As I'll Go." RCA.
- Diamond Rio, "Meet in the Middle." Arista.
- Forrester Sisters, "Men," track from *Talkin' Bout Men*. Warner Bros.
- Kentucky Headhunters, *Electric Barnyard*. Mercury.
- Texas Tornados, *Zone of Our Own*. Reprise.

BEST COUNTRY VOCAL COLLABORATION

- Steve Wariner, Ricky Skaggs, Vince Gill, "Restless" from Mark O'Connor's *The New Nashville Cats*. Warner Bros.
- Lee Greenwood, Suzy Bogguss, "Hopelessly Yours," track from *A Perfect 10*. Capitol.

Dolly Parton, Ricky Van Shelton, "Rockin' Years." Columbia.
Roy Rogers, Clint Black, "Hold On Partner." RCA.
Keith Whitley, Earl Thomas Conley, "Brotherly Love." RCA.

BEST COUNTRY INSTRUMENTAL PERFORMANCE

- Mark O'Connor, *The New Nashville Cats*. Warner Bros.
- Chet Atkins, Mark Knopfler, *Neck and Neck*. Columbia.
- Diamond Rio, "Poultry Promenade," track from *Diamond Rio*. Arista.
- Osborne Brothers, "Orange Blossom Special," track from *Hillbilly Fever*. CMH.
- Roy Rogers, Norton Buffalo, "Song for Jessica," track from *R&B*. Blind Pig.

BEST ROCK/CONTEMPORARY GOSPEL ALBUM

- *Under Their Influence*, Russ Taff. Myrrh.
- *Brave Heart*, Kim Hill. Reunion.
- *Go to the Top*, De Garmo & Key. Benson.
- *Nu Thang*, D.C. Talk. Forefront/Benson.
- *Simple House*, Margaret Becker. Sparrow.

BEST POP GOSPEL ALBUM

- *For the Sake of the Call*, Steven Curtis Chapman. Sparrow.
- *Larnelle Live (Psalms, Hymns and Spiritual Songs)*, Larnelle Harris. Benson.
- *The Me Nobody Knows*, Marilyn McCoo. Warner Alliance.
- *Michael English*, Michael English. Warner Alliance.
- *Shakin' the House . . . Live*, Carman & Commissioned (& the Christ Church Choir). Benson.

BEST SOUTHERN GOSPEL ALBUM

- *Homecoming*, Gaither Vocal Band. Star Song.
- *Hallelujah Time*, Speers. Homeland.
- *Love Will*, Talleys. Word.

Peace in the Valley, J. D. Sumner & the Stamps. River Song/Benson.
Shoulder to Shoulder, Mid-South Boys. Word.
Still Rollin', Chuck Wagon Gang. Associated Artists.

BEST TRADITIONAL SOUL GOSPEL ALBUM
• *Pray for Me*, Mighty Clouds of Joy. Word.
My Faith, Thomas Whitfield. Benson.
Thank You Mamma for Praying for Me, Jackson Southernaires. Malaco.
This Is Your Night, Williams Brothers. Blackberry.
The Truth About Christmas, Vanessa Bell Armstrong. Jive.

BEST CONTEMPORARY SOUL GOSPEL ALBUM
• *Different Lifestyles*, BeBe & CeCe Winans. Sparrow.
Look a Little Closer, Helen Baylor. Word.
Mean What You Say, Witness. Fixit/Star Song.
Phenomenon, Rance Allen Group. Bellmark.
The Promise, Ricky Dillard's New Generation Chorale. Muscle Shoals Sound Gospel.

BEST GOSPEL ALBUM BY A CHOIR OR CHORUS
• *The Evolution of Gospel*, Sounds of Blackness; Gary Hines, choir director. Perspective/A&M.
Above and Beyond, O'Landa Draper & the Associates; O'Landa Draper, choir director. Word.
Edwin Hawkins Music and Arts Seminar Chicago Mass Choir, Music & Arts Seminar Chicago Mass Choir; Edwin Hawkins, choir director. Lection/Polygram.
Hand in Hand, Christ Church Choir; Landy Gardner, choir director. Star Song.
Jesus Be Praised, Brooklyn Tabernacle Singers; Carol Cymbala, choir director. Word/Word Inc.

Rev. James Cleveland and the L.A. Gospel Messengers; L.A. Gospel Messengers; Rev. James Cleveland, choir director. Savoy.

BEST TRADITIONAL FOLK ALBUM
• *The Civil War* (soundtrack), various artists. Elektra/Nonesuch.
Alligator Man, Jimmy C. Newman, Cajun Country. Rounder.
Le Mystère des Voix Bulgares, Vol. 3, various artists. Fontana.
My Dear Old Southern Home, Doc Watson. Sugar Hill.
Solo—Oldtime Country Music, Mike Seeger. Rounder.

BEST CONTEMPORARY FOLK ALBUM
• *The Missing Years*, John Prine. Oh Boy.
Back on the Bus, Y'all, Indigo Girls. Epic.
Cajun Conja, BeauSoleil. RNA.
Interiors, Rosanne Cash. Columbia.
Jerry Garcia/David Grisman, Jerry Garcia, David Grisman. Acoustic Disc.

BEST TRADITIONAL BLUES ALBUM
• *Live at the Apollo*, B. B. King. GRP.
All My Life, Charles Brown. Bullseye Blues.
Johnnie B. Bad, Johnnie Johnson. Elektra/Nonesuch.
Mr. Lucky, John Lee Hooker. Charisma.
Mule Bone, Taj Mahal. Gramavision.

BEST CONTEMPORARY BLUES ALBUM
• *Damn Right, I've Got the Blues*, Buddy Guy. Silvertone.
Albert Collins, Albert Collins. Charisma.
Let Me In, Johnny Winter. Charisma.
Live—Simply the Best, Irma Thomas. Rounder.
Signature, Charlie Musselwhite. Alligator.

BEST BLUEGRASS ALBUM
• *Spring Training*, Carl Jackson, John Starling, Nash Ramblers. Sugar Hill.
Hillbilly Fever, Osborne Brothers. CMH.

Home of the Blues, Nashville Bluegrass Band. Sugar Hill.
Music Among Friends, Jim and Jesse McReynolds. Rounder.
Simple Pleasures, Alison Brown. Vanguard.

BEST LATIN POP ALBUM
• *Cosas del Amor*, Vikki Carr. Sony Discos International.
A Traves de Tus Ojos, Los Bukis. Fonovisa.
Amada Más Que Nunca, Daniela Romo. Capitol/EMI Latin.
. . . Con Amor Eterno, Pandora. Capitol/EMI Latin.
Flor de Papel, Alejandra Guzman. Melody.

BEST TROPICAL LATIN ALBUM
• *Bachata Rosa*, Juan Luis Guerra 4.40. Karen.
Caminando, Rubén Blades. Sony Discos International.
Luces del Alma, Luis Enrique. Sony Discos International.
The Mambo King 100th LP, Tito Puente. RMM.
A Night at Kimball's East, Poncho Sanchez. Concord Picante.

BEST MEXICAN-AMERICAN ALBUM
• *16 de Septiembre*, Little Joe. Sony Discos International.
Para Adoloridos, Los Tigres del Norte. Fonovisa.
Para Nuestra Gente, Mazz. Capitol/EMI Latin.
Porque Te Quiero, La Sombra. Fonovisa.

BEST REGGAE ALBUM
• *As Raw As Ever*, Shabba Ranks. Epic.
Gumption, Bunny Wailer. Shanachie.
Iron Storm, Black Uhuru. Mesa.
Jahmekya, Ziggy Marley & the Melody Makers. Virgin.
Victims, Steel Pulse. Elektra .
We Must Carry On, Rita Marley. Shanachie.

BEST POLKA ALBUM
• *Live! At Gilley's*, Jimmy Sturr & His Orchestra. Starr.
All Around the World, Eddie Blazonczyk's Versatones. Bel-Aire.
We Are Family, Polka Family Band. Polka Family Music.
When the Band Plays a Polka, the Dynatones. World Renowned Sounds.
A Wonderful World of Polkas and Waltzes, Walter Ostanek. World Renowned Sounds.

BEST NEW AGE ALBUM
• *Fresh Aire 7*, Mannheim Steamroller. American Gramaphone.
Borrasca, Ottmar Liebert. Higher Octave Music.
Canyon Dreams, Tangerine Dream. Miramar.
Hotel Luna, Suzanne Ciani. Private Music.
In the Wake of the Wind, David Arkenstone. Narada.

BEST WORLD MUSIC ALBUM
• *Planet Drum*, Mickey Hart. Rykodisc, Inc.
Amen, Salif Keita. Mango/Island.
Brazilian Serenata, Dori Caymmi. Qwest.
Este Mundo, Gipsy Kings. Elektra/Musician.
Txai, Milton Nascimento. Sony Music.

BEST ARRANGEMENT ON AN INSTRUMENTAL
• Dave Grusin, "Medley: Bess You Is My Woman/I Love You Porgy," track from *The Gershwin Connection* (Dave Grusin). GRP.
Peter Apfelbaum, "Candles and Stones," track from *Signs of Life* (Peter Apfelbaum & the Hieroglyphics Ensemble). Antilles.
Mike Bogle, "Got a Match?" track from *Lab 89* (University of North Texas One O'Clock Lab Band). North Texas Jazz.

Michael Kamen, "Maid Marian," track from *Robin Hood: Prince of Thieves* (film soundtrack) (Michael Kamen conducting the Greater Los Angeles Orchestra). Morgan Creek.

Henry Mancini, "The Untouchables," track from *Cinema Italiano* (Henry Mancini & Mancini Pops Orchestra). RCA Victor.

Ed Neumeister, "A Nightingale Sang in Berkeley Square," track from *To You—A Tribute to Mel Lewis* (Mel Lewis Jazz Orchestra). MusicMasters.

BEST INSTRUMENTAL COMPOSITION

• "Basque," track from *The Wind Beneath My Wings* (James Galway), Elton John.

"Blu-Bop," track from *Flight of the Cosmic Hippo* (Bela Fleck & the Flecktones), Bela Fleck, Howard Levy, Victor Wooten, Roy Wooten, composers.

"Cliffs of Dover," Eric Johnson.

"Corfu," track from *Claus Ogerman Featuring Michael Brecker*, Claus Ogerman.

"North on South St.," Herb Alpert, Greg Smith.

BEST MUSICAL SHOW ALBUM

• *The Will Rogers Follies* (Broadway cast), Betty Comden, Adolph Green, lyricists; Cy Coleman, composer. Columbia.

Assassins, Stephen Sondheim, composer. RCA Victor.

Into the Woods (London cast), Stephen Sondheim, composer. RCA Victor.

Kiss Me Kate, John McGlinn, conductor; Cole Porter, composer. Angel/EMI Classics.

The Music Man, Erich Kunzel conducting the Cincinnati Pops Orchestra. Meredith Willson, composer. Telarc.

BEST INSTRUMENTAL COMPOSITION WRITTEN FOR A MOTION PICTURE OR TV

• *Avalon*, Randy Newman.

Awakenings, Randy Newman.
Dances with Wolves, John Barry.
Edward Scissorhands, Danny Elfman.
Havana, Dave Grusin.
Robin Hood: Prince of Thieves, Michael Kamen.

BEST SONG WRITTEN SPECIFICALLY FOR A MOTION PICTURE OR TV

• "(Everything I Do) I Do It for You" from *Robin Hood: Prince of Thieves*, Bryan Adams, Robert John "Mutt" Lange, Michael Kamen.

"Gotta Have You," from *Jungle Fever*, Stevie Wonder.

Home Alone main title "Somewhere in My Memory," track from *Home Alone Soundtrack*, John Williams, Leslie Briscusse.

"You Can't Resist It," track from *Switch Soundtrack*, Lyle Lovett.

BEST INSTRUMENTAL ARRANGEMENT ACCOMPANYING VOCAL(S)

• Marty Paich, "A Medley of: For Sentimental Reasons/Tenderly/Autumn Leaves," track from *Unforgettable* (Natalie Cole). Elektra.

Arthur Morton, "Alone in the World," track from *The Russia House* (film soundtrack) (Patti Austin). MCA.

Harry Connick, Jr., "Blue Light, Red Light (Someone's There)," track from *Blue Light, Red Light* (Harry Connick, Jr.). Columbia.

Michel Legrand, "Nature Boy," track from *Unforgettable* (Natalie Cole). Elektra.

Johnny Mandel, "Unforgettable" (Natalie Cole). Elektra.

BEST CLASSICAL ALBUM

• *Bernstein: Candide*, Leonard Bernstein conducting the London Symphony Orchestra (solos: Hadley, Anderson, Ludwig, Green, Gedda, Jones, Ollmann). Deutsche Grammophon.

Barber: Symphony No. 1, Op. 9; Piano Concerto, Op. 38; Souvenirs, Op. 28, Leonard Slatkin conducting the St.

Louis Symphony Orchestra; John Browning, piano. RCA Victor Red Seal.

Carter: The 4 String Quartets; Duo for Violin and Piano, the Juilliard String Quartet; Christopher Oldfather, piano. Sony Classical.

Corigliano: Symphony No. 1, Daniel Barenboim conducting the Chicago Symphony Orchestra. Erato/Elektra International Classics.

Hanson: Symphony No. 4, Op. 34; Serenade, Op. 35; Lament for Beowulf, Op. 25; Pastorale, Op. 38; Merry Mount Serenade, Op. 35, Gerard Schwarz conducting the Seattle Symphony Orchestra, New York Chamber Symphony ("Serenade" and "Pastorale"). Delos International.

Ives: Symphonies Nos. 1 and 4; Hymns, Michael Tilson Thomas conducting the Chicago Symphony Orchestra and Chorus. Sony Classical.

BEST ORCHESTRAL PERFORMANCE
(Conductor's Award)

• Daniel Barenboim conducting the Chicago Symphony Orchestra, *Corigliano: Symphony No. 1*. Erato/Elektra International Classics.

Rafael Kubelik conducting the Czech Philharmonic Orchestra, *Smetana: Ma Vlast*. Supraphon/Denon.

James Levine conducting the Chicago Symphony Orchestra, *Holst: The Planets*. Deutsche Grammophon.

Leonard Slatkin conducting the St. Louis Symphony Orchestra, *Copland: Symphony No. 3; Music for a Great City*. RCA Victor Red Seal.

Michael Tilson Thomas conducting the Chicago Symphony Orchestra, *Ives: Symphonies Nos. 1 and 4*. Sony Classical.

BEST CHAMBER MUSIC
PERFORMANCE

• Isaac Stern, Jamime Laredo, violins; Yo-Yo Ma, cello; Emanuel Ax, piano, *Brahms: Piano Quartets, Opp. 25 and 26*. Sony Classical.

Arditti String Quartet, *Arditti II (Bartók: Quartet No. 4; Gubaidulina: Quartet No. 3; Schnittke: Quartet No. 2)*. Gramavisions.

Hilliard Ensemble, *Gesualdo: Tenebrae*. ECM New Series.

Juilliard String Quartet; Christopher Oldfather, piano, *Carter: The 4 String Quartets; Duo for Violin and Piano*. Sony Classical.

Gidon Kremer, violin; Martha Argerich, piano, *Bartók: Violin Sonata No. 1; Janáček: Violin Sonata; Messiaen: Theme and Variations for Violin and Piano*. Deutsche Grammophon.

BEST CLASSICAL PERFORMANCE, INSTRUMENTAL SOLOIST(S) (WITH ORCHESTRA)

• John Browning, piano (Leonard Slatkin conducting the St. Louis Symphony Orchestra), *Barber: Piano Concerto, Op. 38*. RCA Victor Red Seal.

Yuri Bashmet, viola (Mstislav Rostropovich conducting the London Symphony Orchestra), *Schnittke: Viola Concerto*. RCA Victor Red Seal.

Stanley Drucker, clarinet (Leonard Bernstein conducting the New York Philharmonic), *Copland: Clarinet Concerto*. Deutsche Grammophon.

Yo-Yo Ma, cello (Yuri Temirkanov conducting the Leningrad Philharmonic Orchestra), *Tchaikovsky: Variations on a Rococo Theme, Op. 33*. RCA Victor Red Seal.

Mitsuko Uchida, piano (Jeffrey Tate conducting the English Chamber Orchestra), *Mozart: Piano Concertos No. 15 in B Flat and No. 16 in D*. Philips Classics.

Pinchas Zukerman, violin/viola (Leonard Slatkin conducting the St. Louis Symphony Orchestra), *Bartók: Violin Concerto No. 2; Viola Concerto Op. Posth.; Violin Concerto No. 2 Alternative Ending*. RCA Victor Red Seal.

BEST CLASSICAL PERFORMANCE, INSTRUMENTAL SOLOIST (WITHOUT ORCHESTRA)

- Alicia de Larrocha, piano, *Granados: Goyescas; Allegro de Concierto; Danza Lenta*. RCA Victor Red Seal.

Alan Feinberg, piano, *The American Romantic (Beach, Gottschalk, Helps)*. Argo.

Rudolf Firkusny, piano, *Janáček: Piano Music (Sonata 1.x.1905; On an Overgrown Path; In the Mist)*. RCA Victor Red Seal.

Evgeny Kissin, piano, *Evgeny Kissin: Carnegie Hall Debut Concert*. RCA Victor Red Seal.

Murray Perahia, piano, *The Aldeburgh Recital (Beethoven, Rachmaninov, Schumann, Liszt)*. Sony Classical.

BEST OPERA RECORDING

- *Wagner: Götterdämmerung*, James Levine conducting the Metropolitan Opera Orchestra and Chorus (solos: Behrens, Studer, Schwarz, Goldberg, Weikl, Wlaschiha, Salminen). Deutsche Grammophon.

Debussy: Pelléas et Mélisande, Charles Dutoit conducting the Orchestre Symphonique de Montréal (solos: Henry, Alliot-Lugaz, Thau, Cachemaille, Carlson, Golfier). London.

Mozart: Idomeneo, John Eliot Gardiner conducting the English Baroque Soloists (solos: Rolf-Johnson, von Otter, McNair, Martinpelto). Archiv.

Mussorgsky: Khovanshchina, Claudio Abbado conducting the Vienna State Opera Orchestra and Concert Chorus (solos: Lipovsek, Atlantov, Burchuladze, Haugland, Kotscherga, Popov). Deutsche Grammophon.

Schubert: Fierrabras, Claudio Abbado conducting the Chamber Orchestra of Europe (solos: Studer, Mattila, Hampson). Deutsche Grammophon.

R. Strauss: Elektra, Wolfgang Sawallisch conducting the Bavarian Radio Orchestra and Chorus (solos: Studer,

Weikl, Marton, Lipovsek, Winkler). Angel/EMI Classics.

BEST PERFORMANCE OF A CHORAL WORK

- Sir Georg Solti conducting the Chicago Symphony Chorus and Orchestra; Margaret Hillis, choral director, *Bach: Mass in B Minor*. London.

John Eliot Gardiner conducting the Monteverdi Choir and English Baroque Soloists, *Beethoven: Missa Solemnis*. Archiv.

Krzysztof Penderecki conducting the North German Radio Choir, Werner Hagen, chorus master; Bavarian Radio Chorus, Hans-Peter Rauscher, chorus master; and North German Radio Symphony Orchestra, *Penderecki: Polish Requiem*. Deutsche Grammophon.

Krzysztof Penderecki conducting the Warsaw National Philharmonic Chorus and National Radio Symphony Orchestra, *Penderecki: St. Luke's Passion*. Argo.

Robert Shaw conducting the Atlanta Symphony Chorus and Orchestra, *Janáček: Glagolitic Mass; Dvořák: Te Deum*. Telarc.

BEST CLASSICAL VOCAL PERFORMANCE

- Dawn Upshaw, soprano (ensemble accompaniment), *The Girl with Orange Lips (De Falla, Ravel, Kim, Stravinsky, Delage)*. Elektra/Nonesuch.

Jan DeGaetani, mezzo-soprano (Lee Luvisi, piano; Lawrence Dutton, viola), *Jan DeGaetani in Concert, Vol. 2 (Brahms, Schumann, etc.)*. Bridge.

Thomas Hampson, baritone (Leonard Bernstein conducting the Vienna Philharmonic), *Mahler: Songs of a Wayfarer; 5 Ruckert Lieder*. Deutsche Grammophon.

Samuel Ramey, baritone (Warren Jones, accompanist), *Copland: Old American Songs; Ives: Songs*. Argo.

Cheryl Studer, soprano (Sir Neville Marriner conducting the Academy of St. Martin-in-the-Fields), *Mozart: Arias*. Philips Classics.

Sanford Sylvan, baritone (David Breitman, piano), *Beloved That Pilgrimage (Chanler: 8 Epitaphs; Barber: Hermit Songs; Copland: 12 Poems of Emily Dickinson)*. Elektra-Nonesuch.

BEST CONTEMPORARY COMPOSITION

• John Corigliano, *Symphony No. 1* (Daniel Barenboim conducting the Chicago Symphony Orchestra). Erato/Elektra International Classics.

Dominick Argento, *Te Deum* (Philip Brunelle conducting the Plymouth Festival Chorus and Orchestra). Virgin Classics.

Elliot Carter, *Oboe Concerto* (Heinz Holliger, oboe; Pierre Boulez conducting the Ensemble Intercontemporain). Erato/Elektra International Classics.

Nicholas Maw, *Odyssey* (Simon Rattle conducting the City of Birmingham Symphony Orchestra). Angel.

Arvo Part, *Miserere* (the Hilliard Ensemble; Dennis Russell Davies conducting the Orchester der Beethovenhalle Bonn). ECM.

BEST ENGINEERED RECORDING, CLASSICAL

• William Hoekstra, *Barber: Symphony No. 1, Op. 9; Piano Concerto, Op. 38; Souvenirs, Op. 28* (Leonard Slatkin conducting the St. Louis Symphony Orchestra; John Browning, piano). RCA Victor Red Seal.

Stanley Goodall, *Bartók: Music for Strings, Percussion and Celesta, etc.* (Sir Georg Solti conducting the Chicago Symphony Orchestra). London.

Gregor Zielinsky, *Bernstein: Candide* (Leonard Bernstein conducting the London Symphony Orchestra; solos: Hadley, Anderson, Ludwig, Green, Gedda, Jones, Ollmann). Deutsche Grammophon.

Lawrence Rock, *Corigliano: Symphony No. 1* (Daniel Barenboim conducting the Chicago Symphony Orchestra). Erato/Elektra International Classics.

Wolfgang Mitlehner, *Wagner: Götterdämmerung* (James Levine conducting the Metropolitan Opera Orchestra and Chorus; solos: Behrens, Studer, Schwarz, Goldberg, Weikl, Wlaschiha, Salminen). Deutsche Grammophon.

CLASSICAL PRODUCER OF THE YEAR

• James Mallinson

Steven Epstein

Thomas Frost

Jay David Saks

Hans Weber

BEST COMEDY ALBUM

• *P.D.Q. Bach: WTWP Classical Talkity-Talk Radio*, Professor Peter Schickele. Telarc.

Brand New, Jackie Mason. Columbia.

Local Man Moves to the City, Garrison Keillor. HighBridge.

Parental Advisory: Explicit Lyrics, George Carlin. Eardrum.

When You Look Like Your Passport Photo, It's Time to Go Home, Erma Bombeck. Harper Audio.

BEST SPOKEN WORD OR NONMUSICAL ALBUM

• *The Civil War*, Ken Burns. Sound Editions.

The Hitchhiker's Guide to the Galaxy, Douglas Adams. Dove Audio.

A Life on the Road, Charles Kuralt. Simon and Schuster Audioworks.

Me: Stories of My Life, Katharine Hepburn. Random House Audio.

BEST ALBUM FOR CHILDREN

• *A Cappella Kids*, Maranatha! Kids. Maranatha.

Brer Rabbit and the Wonderful Tar
  Baby, Danny Glover, narrator; Taj
  Mahal, music. Windham Hill.
The Emperor's New Clothes, John Giel-
  gud, narrator; Mark Isham, music.
  Windham Hill.
Paul Bunyan, Jonathan Winters, narra-
  tor; Leo Kottke, music. Windham
  Hill.
Prokofiev: Peter and the Wolf; A Zoo
  Called Earth/Gerald McBoing
  Boing, Dom De Luise, Peter Schick-
  ele, Carol Channing; Dino Anagnost,
  conductor. MusicMasters.

BEST ENGINEERED ALBUM (OTHER THAN CLASSICAL)

• Al Schmitt, Woody Woodruff, Armin
  Steiner, Unforgettable (Natalie Cole).
  Elektra.
Ed Cherney, Luck of the Draw (Bonnie
  Raitt). Capitol.
George Massenburg, Warm Your Heart
  (Aaron Neville). A&M.
Don Murray, Havana Soundtrack (Dave
  Grusin). GRP.
Steve Nye, Storyville (Robbie Robert-
  son). Geffen.

BEST ALBUM PACKAGE
(Art Director's Award)

• Vartan, Billie Holiday: The Complete
  Decca Recordings (Billie Holiday).
  GRP.
Geoff Gans, Beat the Boots (Frank
  Zappa). FOO-EE/Rhino.
Jeff Gold, Kim Champagne, Recycler
  (ZZ Top). Warner Bros.
Gabrielle Raumberger, Just for the
  Record (Barbra Streisand). Colum-
  bia.
Dirk Walter, Mighty Like a Rose (Elvis
  Costello). Warner Bros.

BEST ALBUM NOTES
(Annotator's Award)

• James Brown, Cliff White, Harry
  Weinger, Nelson George, Alan M.
  Leeds, Star Time (James Brown).
  Polydor.

John Bauldie, The Bootleg Series, Vols.
  1–3 (Rare and Unreleased),
  1961–1991 (Bob Dylan). Columbia.
Rob Bowman, The Complete Stax/Volt
  Singles 1959–1968. Atlantic.
Colin Escott, The Original Singles Col-
  lection . . . Plus (Hank Williams).
  Polydor.
Robert Palmer, The Birth of Soul (Ray
  Charles). Atlantic.

BEST HISTORICAL ALBUM

• Billie Holiday: The Complete Decca
  Recordings, Billie Holiday. GRP.
The Complete Caruso, Enrico Caruso.
  RCA Victor Gold Seal.
The Complete Stax/Volt Singles
  1959–1968, various artists. Atlantic.
The First 100 Years, Sir Georg Solti
  conducting the Chicago Symphony
  Orchestra. Chicago Symphony
  Orchestra.
Igor Stravinsky: The Recorded Legacy,
  Igor Stravinsky. Sony Classical.

PRODUCER OF THE YEAR (OTHER THAN CLASSICAL)

• David Foster
Walter Afanasieff, Mariah Carey
Andre Fischer
Paul Simon
Keith Thomas

BEST MUSIC VIDEO, SHORT FORM

• Losing My Religion, R.E.M. Tarsem,
  director. Warner Bros.
Calling Elvis, Dire Straits. Steve Barron,
  director. Warner Bros.
Series of Dreams, Bob Dylan. Meirt
  Avis, director. Columbia.
The Thunder Rolls, Garth Brooks. Bud
  Schaetzle, director. Capitol.
When You Wish upon a Star, Billy Joel.
  Scott Garen, director. Walt Disney.

BEST MUSIC VIDEO, LONG FORM

• Madonna: Blonde Ambition World
  Tour Live, Madonna. David Mallet,
  Mark "Aldo" Miceli, directors. Pio-
  neer LDCA, Inc.

Lifers Group World Tour Rahway Prison, That's It, Lifers Group. Penelope Spheeris, director. Hollywood.

Live at Yankee Stadium, Billy Joel. Jon Small, director. Sony Music Video.

P.O.V., Peter Gabriel. Michael Chapman and Hart Perry, directors. Virgin Music Video.

Year of the Horse, Sinéad O'Connor. Sophie Mueller, director. Chrysalis/Ensign.

• 1992 •

"Grammys Agree: Clapton Is God"

Variety predicted that this could be a divine year for "a music industry outsider."

The reference was to Eric Clapton, who reigned with the most nominations. It had been nearly 30 years since British teens scratched "Clapton is God" on the sides of London buildings during his heyday as a rock and blues maverick. Among other early disciples were progressive music critics who penned frequent hosannas to his pioneering work with Cream and Derek & the Dominoes. But by the early 1980s, Clapton descended into a personal hell of heroin and booze. When he emerged in the 1990s, sober and eager to try a career resurrection, new tragedy struck when his four-year-old son, Conor, died accidentally after falling 53 floors from a Manhattan apartment tower. Clapton poured his grief into a song, "Tears in Heaven," which he wrote for the film score to *Rush* and performed on the new *MTV Unplugged* concert program. "It's the record of someone who, after incalculable pain, is renewing himself as we listen," *Time* magazine observed.

When the awards were over, *Variety* proclaimed, "Grammys agree: Clapton is God," adding, "The legendary rock guitar/singer long deified by his fans ascended to Grammy heights, capturing six prizes, including Album, Song and Record of the Year." He also received the pop vocals prize for "Tears," the rock vocals kudos for the score to *MTV Unplugged* and Best Rock Song for a bluesy remix of his 1970 standard "Layla." The half dozen honors tied him with Quincy Jones (1990) and Roger Miller (1965) for scoring the second-most awards in one year. (Michael Jackson still led with eight, which he received for

Grammy voters finally embraced Clapton after he rebounded from substance abuse and the tragic death of his infant son.

1983.) Parallels to other artists were also obvious: The tribute was reminiscent of how N.A.R.A.S. voters embraced Bonnie Raitt and Natalie Cole after they rebounded from alcoholism.

When Clapton accepted his first award on the Grammycast, for best pop vocals, the venerated veteran seemed profoundly humbled: "I don't know what to say. I don't think I'm deserving of this. There were better songs, but I'm very grateful anyway."

Upon receiving the best album award for *Unplugged,* the music "god" admitted to being fallible: "I was convinced that this wasn't worth releasing. I really didn't want this record to come out. It's blown my mind."

The Grammy audience gave Clapton his third standing ovation of the night when he claimed the Record of the Year statuette from Tina Turner. "I'm very moved and very shaken and very emotional," he said. "The one person I want to thank is my son for the love he gave me and the song he gave me."

Prior to this year, Clapton had received only two Grammys: the rock vocals prize for "Bad Love" in 1990 and a statuette for his partial contribution to 1972's ensemble Album of the Year *The Concert for Bangla Desh.*

Billboard groused about the tardiness of his new bounty: "The sweep by Clapton aroused mixed feelings among long-time fans in attendance. Many believed he is worthy of several Grammys, but he should have been honored two decades ago. 'Tears in Heaven' and *Unplugged* are in stark contrast to the blistering guitar work that made Clapton a rock legend."

Clapton was widely expected to win best record and song, but the pundits had been divided over his chances to take best album. A national poll found radio programmers and deejays betting on U2's *Achtung Baby*; so was *TV Guide*. Grammy voters ended up giving *Achtung*'s artists the salute for rock group vocals. They also hailed U2's producers, Daniel Lanois and Brian Eno, with the Producer of the Year award, a consolation prize shared, in a first-time tie, with L. A. Reid and Babyface (Kenny Edmonds). The latter duo ruled the charts in 1992, even shattering one lofty music record, but their work failed to reap bids in any of the top recording categories. Obviously grateful for what they did get from N.A.R.A.S. voters, Babyface accepted the producer's award, saying, "We'll take a tie anytime!"

Reid and Babyface produced and wrote the number-one single of the year,

> ## Clapton believed MTV Unplugged "wasn't worth releasing."

"The End of the Road," sung by Boyz II Men, who lost the Best New Artist Grammy last year in an upset to Marc Cohn. "The End of the Road" topped the charts for 13 consecutive weeks, thereby ending the record held by Elvis Presley's "Don't Be Cruel." Many Grammy critics accused voters of being cruel for failing to give it a shot at Record or Song of the Year. *Variety* reported on its final Grammy fate: "Motown's Boyz II Men, whom many felt were slighted in the nominations, salved some ego by winning the r&b group vocals prize" for a second year in a row. "The End of the Road" also took Best R&B Song for its writers.

Some artists who did score bids in the leading Grammy races ended up with consolation awards in the pop categories. The female vocalist honors went to k. d. lang for her torch-hued "Constant Craving," which *Entertainment Weekly* called "a drastic departure from her previous country-flavored work." (Her earlier three Grammys were all in the country categories.) *Billboard* had predicted that the award would go to defrocked Miss America Vanessa Williams (a losing contender for 1988's Best New Artist) for "Save the Best for Last," which also competed for 1992's Record and Song of the Year.

Another loser in the best record and song categories won the second-most statuettes of the year, proving *Variety* partly right when it suggested before the awards showdown, "The ever-sentimental academy may have a tender spot for 'Beauty and the Beast.' "

Oscar voters fell for the title song of the Disney film last year. Record buyers did, too, turning the Celine Dion/Peabo Bryson tune into a best-seller that radio deejays and VH1 programmers also found irresistible. As "Beauty" entered the Grammy race, the *L.A. Times* was so certain that N.A.R.A.S. voters would be smitten as well that the paper predicted it would beat "Tears in Heaven" for best song because the category usually went to romantic ballads.

"Beauty" ended up with five dates in the lower categories.

Among its honors: best instrumental composition for a motion picture, Best Album for Children and best film song. When composer Alan Menken accepted them, he uttered a dire reminder of what recently killed his lyricist partner: "The message is that, running through the bloodstream of American culture, are the words of Howard Ashman and this is a man who was infected with AIDS."

When Celine Dion and Peabo Bryson accepted the pop vocals statuette for "Beauty," the French-Canadian thrush with a five-octave range obviously didn't foresee some of the heights she'd reach in her future career. "To be part of a classic, it happens only once in your life if you're lucky," she gushed to reporters backstage. "To be part of a classic at 24! Five years ago, I could't speak English!"

Music from the score of the 1987–90 TV series *Beauty and the Beast* reaped best pop instrumental performance.

Annie Lennox shared a Grammy in 1986 as part of the Eurythmics but now competed alone with her first solo work, *Diva*. It lost its bid for Album of the Year, but the VHS version earned her the long-form video prize just months after the MTV Awards hailed her for having the year's best female video.

The winner of MTV's Video of the Year award, Van Halen's *Right Now*, wasn't nominated for a Grammy, which left the field for short-form works wide open. It was claimed by Peter Gabriel, who seized the prize for *Digging in the Dirt*, which relied heavily on the use of quirky computer graphics. On the Grammycast, Gabriel chose to perform "Steam" instead (for which he'd win this same award next year) while flanked by Marilyn Monroe impersonators pretending to play saxophones.

"Arrested Development, one of the year's cutting-edge acts, surprised some

Vince Gill nabbed two prizes for "I Still Believe in You": Best Country Song and Best Vocalist.

observers by winning Best New Artist," *Variety* reported. *Entertainment Weekly* had predicted N.A.R.A.S. voters would embrace Latin heartthrob Jon Secada. The *L.A. Times* went with Billy Ray Cyrus, the country beefcake whose Record and Song of the Year contender "Achy Breaky Heart" launched a national dance craze. When the Atlanta-based rappers prevailed instead, they accepted the honor defiantly, roaring, "The type of people who supported us are warriors because they understand the need for life music in these types of times!" Arrested Development also nabbed the gold for best rap group performance.

"The changing nature of the Grammy voting bloc was reflected in several awards during the precast," *Variety* noted. "Melissa Etheridge triumphed over past Grammy winners Tina Turner and Alannah Miles for best female rock performance, winning for the track 'Ain't It Heavy,' her first Grammy. The victory was a shocker." Most pundits had agreed with how the *L.A. Times* sized up the category, insisting, "Tina Turner is an automatic vote-getter."

After having headlined the summer's Lollapalooza concert tour that featured a roundup of alternative bands, the Red Hot

Chili Peppers "pulled what purists may view as an upset by copping the hard rock prize, besting odds-on-favorite Nirvana and Pearl Jam," *Variety* said. "Bassist Flea said backstage that 'Give It Away' wasn't even a hard-rock song, noting, 'It's a funk song. We'll take it. They probably just felt sorry for us.'" In what *Variety* called "the night's most outrageous performance" on the Grammycast, the Chilis did "Give It Away" with George Clinton, the P-Funk All-Stars, lots of attitude and bizarre fashions. Flea dressed as a geisha while other men donned such wacky wear as diapers and a wedding dress.

N.A.R.A.S. voters continued to mourn for Stevie Ray Vaughan, who was killed in a helicopter crash in 1990, by giving him more prizes posthumously. His latest awards: Best Rock Instrumental Performance and Best Contemporary Blues Album for *The Sky Is Crying.*

Dr. John took the category of Best Traditional Blues Album with *Goin' Back to New Orleans,* a follow-up to *Gumbo,* his hit 1972 toast to the Mardi Gras capital.

"With perpetual winner Metallica between albums, there's an opening for Megadeth, which is fronted by former Metallica member Dave Mustaine," the *L.A. Times* predicted for the metal category, mirroring *Billboard*'s prophesy. When the surprise winner turned out to be another Lollapalooza star, Nine Inch Nails, for "Wish," *Billboard* griped, saying the victory "may have turned some heads, since the band is generally considered to be alternative or industrial."

"Eyebrows were also raised by Tom Waits' win in the alternative music category, also his first Grammy victory," *Variety* reported. "Waits, considered an offbeat songwriter but certainly not the college radio fodder that constitutes most of what is usally perceived as 'alternative' music, won for his Island album *Bone Machine,* beating out the B-52's, the Cure, Morrissey and XTC."

In the r&b categories, *Variety* reported "a mild upset" when Vanessa Williams lost the female vocals accolade to Chaka

Leonard Bernstein reaped Best Classical Album posthumously for a third consecutive year when he was hailed for Mahler's *Symphony No. 9.*

Khan, a longtime Grammy favorite who rallied to win a fifth award, her third in this category. *Time* magazine wrote of her triumphant work *The Woman I Am:* "Taking charge for the first time in her 20-year career, Khan produced the album herself and co-wrote six of its 13 songs, including the title track. Her fiery contralto is in total command on all of them."

Michael Jackson was expected to snag the male vocals prize but was upset by four-time past champ Al Jarreau (*Heaven and Earth*), who also topped Bobby Brown, Peabo Bryson and a newcomer, Tevin Campbell, who was fawned over by music critics.

"In the R&B instrumental category, the late Miles Davis won because he's Miles Davis," the *L.A. Times* reported. "Did the voters even listen to this *Doo-Bop* album—one of the lows of his career?" The work was the jazz trumpeter's last studio album before his death by pneumonia in 1991.

Sir Mix-a-Lot sailed past Grammy champ Hammer to secure the rap solo honor for "Baby Got Back," his raunchy tribute to big-butt women. Backstage, he told reporters that rap artists deserve more

Grammy categories (hard-core rap, Afro-centric rap, etc.) and threatened a revolt: "If we're making more money collectively than anyone else in the record industry, maybe we should do our own awards!"

At the outset of the Grammy contest, *Variety* declared, "Biggest surprises in the nominations came from the list of the excluded. Garth Brooks, the dominant force of the Billboard 200 for more than a year, was consigned to the country music ghetto." Worse, both of his "ghetto" bids failed. Brooks lost the award for Best Country Vocal Collaboration ("Whatcha Gonna Do with a Cowboy," sung with Chris LeDoux) to two Grammy first-timers: Travis Tritt and Marty Stuart ("The Whiskey Ain't Workin'"). In the male vocal category, 1991 champ Vince Gill rallied with *I Still Believe in You* over Brooks's megaseller *The Chase*. Gill also shared in the award for Best Country Song as the cowriter of "Believe."

Reba McIntyre swept the recent American Music Awards, but Wynonna Judd was expected to take the Grammys by storm after the triumphant launch of her solo career that resulted in her debut album, *Wynonna,* going triple platinum. Instead, last year's winner Mary-Chapin Carpenter, hit the jackpot again with "I Feel Lucky," a frisky fantasy song in which she wins the lottery and gets to pick her own paradise. Its lyrics tweaked her crooner cohorts: "Dwight Yoakam's in the corner trying to catch my eye / Lyle Lovett's right beside me with his hand upon my thigh."

N.A.R.A.S. voters continued to snub the best-selling country artists of the year when they passed over Brooks & Dunn, which hit the top of the charts with "Boot Scootin' Boogie." Now they were expected to tower over the group performance category, since it was no longer monopolized by the Judds. The void

ended up luring the return of Emmylou Harris, the five-time past Grammy champ who performed works by Bruce Springsteen, Stephen Foster and Bill Monroe on her victorious disc, *Emmylou Harris and the Nash Ramblers at the Ryman.*

Also returning was Alison Krauss & Union Station, who last won the Grammy for Best Bluegrass Album in 1990. Now they were honored for *Every Time You Say Goodbye,* which sold 100,000 copies and was hailed as Album of the Year at the International Bluegrass Music Association Awards.

Ever since Chet Atkins discovered Jerry Reed and helped him to launch a solo career, the two guitar pickers teamed up often. The latest collaboration of the Grammy veterans, *Sneakin' Around,* was hailed as Best Country Instrumental Performance.

Two upsets rocked the jazz categories.

Either the Toshiko Akiyoshi Jazz Orchestra or the GRP All-Star Big Band was expected to take the prize for large ensembles, but the category was claimed by the 15-piece band of pianist-composer McCoy Tyner, whose only previous Grammy was for his part in a 1988 ensemble Coltrane tribute. In *The Turning Point,* he again performed works by Coltrane, in addition to Duke Ellington.

The late Stan Getz was favored to repeat as winner of the laurels for best instrumental soloist, but they were snatched by a first-time champ: tenor saxophonist Joe Henderson, a jazz journeyman for 30 years, who suddenly got critics' attention with *Lush Life—The Music of Billy Strayhorn.* The LP got picked as the best jazz album of the year by the *New York Times* and its success helped to get Henderson picked by fellow sax player Bill Clinton as a performer at his presidential inauguration.

Henderson was also nominated for the instrumental honors for an individual or

---

Melissa Etheridge's victory "was a shocker," *Variety* said.

group, but the category was claimed by another Grammy first-timer, sax player Branford Marsalis, who'd recently got the gig as bandleader of *The Tonight Show*.

Six-time past champ Pat Metheny won the award for contemporary instrumental performance over the Brecker Brothers (favored by pundits) for *Secret Story,* a remembrance of his ill-fated affair with a Brazilian woman.

Famed composer and conductor Benny Carter earned the first Grammy of his career when "Harlem Renaissance Suite" was hailed as Best Instrumental Composition. It had been performed recently by the Rutgers University Orchestra in honor of his 85th birthday.

Shirley Horn was the critics' favorite to win the jazz vocalist's prize, but nine-time past Grammy champ Bobby McFerrin claimed a new one for his reading of Thelonious Monk's " 'Round Midnight," which he recorded with pianist Chick Corea.

Thirty years ago, crooner Tony Bennett won his last Grammy when he picked up the Record of the Year award for "I Left My Heart in San Francisco." His new salute to Frank Sinatra (*Perfectly Frank*) brought him the prize for Best Traditional Pop Vocal Performance in a close race against Rosemary Clooney, Bobby Short and Nancy Wilson.

Irish thrush Enya recorded as many as 140 vocal tracks on *Shepherd Moons,* her haunting hit (3 million copies sold) that earned her the prize for Best New Age Album.

Discussing a popular Irish folk group, *Variety* noted, "The Chieftains had the best of both worlds, winning for contemporary and traditional folk." The album featuring traditional works, *An Irish Evening Live at the Grand Opera House, Belfast,* included guest vocals by Roger Daltry and Nanci Griffith. On its LP of contemporary music, *Another Country,* the Irish folk group performed American country tunes.

In the Christian music categories, Petra won its second career Grammy for having the year's best contemporary rock album (*Unseen Power*).

Steven Curtis Chapman won the category of Best Pop Gospel Album for a second year in a row. He returned with *The Great Adventure,* which spent 12 weeks topping the contemporary Christian music charts.

Five-time past champ Shirley Caesar hadn't won a Grammy since 1985, but now she rebounded with the year's Best Traditional Soul Gospel Album, *He's Working It Out for You.*

Winner of Best Contemporary Soul Gospel Album was *Messiah* performed by more than 100 artists (including Stevie Wonder, Gladys Knight and Take 6) under the musical direction of Quincy Jones. The new version of Handel's masterwork, noted *Ebony,* "presents the classic 18th-century oratorio as a history of black music from pre-slavery to post hip-hop."

Edwin Hawkins directed a 500-voice choir at California's Pasedena College to win the choral award for gospel albums.

A loser of the award for Best New Artist, Jon Secada, took the consolation prize for Best Latin Pop Album for *Otro Día Más sin Verte,* which included the Spanish-language version of the title track ("Just Another Day") that made the Cuban-born crooner a pop sensation.

Linda Ronstadt had won six times in the past, including once in the Mexican-American category for 1988's *Canciones de Mi Padre.* Now she took the slot for its sequel, *Más Canciones.* She also picked up the Grammy for the year's Best Tropical Latin Album, *Frenesi,* which featured mambo dance music

Twenty-seven years after he left Brazil for Los Angeles, Sergio Mendes scored the first Grammy of his career for his homeland tribute *Brasileiro,* winner of Best World Music Album.

Canada's accordian king, Walter Ostanek, had been nominated four times in the past for Best Polka Album but failed to win while Jimmy Stuff reigned over the category. Now he finally prevailed for his 35th anniversary collection of music. The victory allowed him to achieve his "biggest goal in life," he told *Maclean's*. "I didn't think I was going to win. It was like someone hit me with a sledgehammer."

The cast recording of the Tony-winning Broadway revival of *Guys and Dolls* starring Nathan Lane nabbed the Grammy for Best Musical Show Album.

Basketball great Earvin "Magic" Johnson retired from the Los Angeles Lakers last year after it was disclosed he was playing while infected with HIV. He became a Grammy champ when *What You Can Do to Avoid AIDS* was honored in the spoken word category.

TV Guide correctly predicted that the late Leonard Bernstein would "continue his logic- and grave-defying winning streak" by claiming Best Classical Album for a third straight year. He also won Best Orchestral Performance for his recording of Mahler's Symphony No. 9 with the Berlin Philharmonic, earning his 15th and 16th career Grammys. *National Review* observed a curious analogy between the two maestros: "Mahler's contemporaries thought of him as a conductor who wrote music. Bernstein is another conductor who wrote music."

The *L.A. Times* noted that "more music by dead guys seemed to be a theme" in the classical categories when the late pianist Vladimir Horowitz, who died in 1989, won the solo instrumental laurels for *Discovered Treasures,* a new album of vault recordings that included works by Chopin, Liszt, Scarlatti and Scriabin. "Even the best contemporary composition award went to Samuel Barber (d. 1981), as the voting went retrospective with a vengeance," the *Times* added. "To be eligible for the contemporary composition award, the piece must have been first released on record during the award year, but could have been composed any time the last quarter-century. Which tells us how Barber's 1971 *The Lovers* (the

Chicago Symphony conducted by Andrew Schenk, also deceased) got into the category, but not why the voters thought it a better example of contemporary composition than Anthony Davis' powerful and topical opera 'X, the Life and Times of Malcolm X' or Witold Lutoslawski's gripping, visionary Piano Concerto."

Opera News defended *The Lovers,* calling the musical adaptation of 20 erotic poems by Chilean poet Pablo Neruda, "Barber's most ambitious composition."

Cellist Yo-Yo Ma picked up his seventh and eighth career Grammys: best solo instrumental performance for works by Prokofiev and Tchaikovsky and best chamber music, an award he shared with Emanuel Ax for *Brahms: Sonatas for Cello and Piano.*

"Sir Georg Solti continued to add to his lifetime Grammy record, winning his 30th award," *Variety* noted when the maestro was honored for conducting the Vienna Philharmonic in Strauss's *Die Frau Ohne Schatten* starring Placido Domingo. Domingo attended the Grammycast and visited the pressroom backstage. He asked reporters: "Any questions? Or is opera not of your interest?" After an awkward silence, he said, "Bye-bye."

Some pundits were rooting for Cecilia Bartoli to win the opera vocal award for *Rossini Heroines,* but three-time past champ Kathleen Battle fought her way back for a fourth victory, winning for her Carnegie Hall concert of 21 songs that included works by Handel and Gershwin.

The one classical prize presented on the Grammycast was for best choral work, which was claimed by first-time award winner Herbert Blomstedt, who conducted the San Francisco Symphony and Chorus in Orff's *Carmina Burana.* He was the sentimental favorite, having announced that he would soon retire from his post at the orchestra that he had brought "back up to the status it enjoyed during the glory

---

Beauty and the Beast claimed the year's most awards: five.

---

years of Pierre Monteux," noted *American Record Guide*. Accepting the award, Blomstedt said, "I want to thank all of my 150 volunteer singers who provide 40,000 hours of contributed time to the symphony every year, my 30 paid singers who provide a professional thrust to the group."

The Grammycast was hosted by Garry Shandling and was broadcast worldwide to 110 countries.

Variety said that "despite some impressive production values, show lacked excitement—in performances, or the kind that comes with spontaneous moments. Performers alternated between live and seemingly lip-synched presentations, with some singers—En Vogue among them—not even pretending to use a microphone. One of the most exciting moments came late in the show with the annual token jazz number, a blistering version of 'Cherokee' featuring a front line of trumpeters led by Arturo Sandoval.

"A Grammy Legend Award to Michael Jackson, seen earlier in the audience seated next to date Brooke Shields. The singer was introduced by sister Janet in deifying terms, and won a laugh by posing with her—'I hope,' he said, 'this puts to rest another rumor that has been in the press for too many years. Me and Janet really are two different people.' "

• 1992 •

The awards ceremony was broadcast on CBS from the Shrine Auditorium in Los Angeles on February 24, 1993, for the eligibility period of October 1, 1991, through September 30, 1992.

ALBUM OF THE YEAR
• *Unplugged*, Eric Clapton. Reprise.
Ingenue, k. d. lang. WB/Sire.
Diva, Annie Lennox. Arista.
Achtung Baby, U2. Island.
Beauty and the Beast (soundtrack). Disney.

RECORD OF THE YEAR
• "Tears in Heaven," Eric Clapton. Reprise.
"Achy Breaky Heart," Billy Ray Cyrus. Mercury.
"Beauty and the Beast," Celine Dion, Peabo Bryson. Epic.
"Constant Craving," k. d. lang. WB/Sire.
"Save the Best for Last," Vanessa Williams. Mercury/Wing.

SONG OF THE YEAR
(Songwriter's Award)
• "Tears in Heaven," Eric Clapton, Will Jennings.

"Achy Breaky Heart," Don Von Tress.
"Beauty and the Beast," Alan Menken, Howard Ashman.
"Constant Craving," k.d. lang, Ben Mink.
"Save the Best For Last," Wendy Waldman, Jon Lind, Phil Galdston.

BEST NEW ARTIST
• Arrested Development
Billy Ray Cyrus
Sophie B. Hawkins
Kris Kross
Jon Secada

BEST POP VOCAL PERFORMANCE, MALE
• Eric Clapton, "Tears in Heaven." Reprise.
Peter Gabriel, *US*. Geffen.
Michael Jackson, "Black or White." Epic.
Elton John, "The One." MCA.
Lyle Lovett, *Joshua Judges Ruth*. MCA.

BEST POP VOCAL PERFORMANCE, FEMALE
• k. d. lang, "Constant Craving." WB/Sire.
Mariah Carey, *MTV Unplugged EP*. Columbia.

Celine Dion, *Celine Dion*. Epic.
Annie Lennox, *Diva*. Arista.
Vanessa Williams, "Save the Best for Last." Wing/Mercury.

BEST POP PERFORMANCE BY A DUO OR GROUP WITH VOCAL

• Celine Dion, Peabo Bryson, "Beauty and the Beast." Epic.
Genesis, "I Can't Dance." Atlantic.
George Michael, Elton John, "Don't Let the Sun Go Down on Me." Columbia.
Prince & the New Power Generation, "Diamonds and Pearls." WB/Paisley Park.
Patty Smyth, Don Henley, "Sometimes Love Just Ain't Enough." MCA.

BEST TRADITIONAL POP VOCAL PERFORMANCE

• Tony Bennett, *Perfectly Frank*. Columbia.
Rosemary Clooney, *Girl Singer*. Concord Jazz.
Michael Feinstein, *Michael Feinstein Sings the Jule Styne Songbook*. Elektra Nonesuch.
Bobby Short, *Late Night at the Cafe Carlyle*. Telarc.
Nancy Wilson, *With My Lover Beside Me*. Columbia.

BEST POP INSTRUMENTAL PERFORMANCE

• Richard Kaufman conducting the Nuremberg Symphony Orchestra, "Beauty and the Beast," track from *Symphonic Hollywood*. Varese Sarabande.
Chieftains with Chet Atkins, "Tahitian Skies," track from *The Chieftains Another Country*. RCA.
Bruce Hornsby, Branford Marsalis, "Twenty-Nine to Five," track from *Coca-Cola Vol. 3*. Warner Bros.
Bob James, Earl Klugh, *Cool*. Warner Bros.
John Williams, *Hook*. Epic Soundtrax.

BEST ROCK SONG
(Songwriter's Award)
• "Layla," Eric Clapton, Jim Gordon.

"Digging in the Dirt," Peter Gabriel.
"Smells Like Teen Spirit," Kurt Cobain, Nirvana.
"Jeremy," Eddie Vedder, Jeff Ament.
"Human Touch," Bruce Springsteen.

BEST ROCK VOCAL PERFORMANCE, MALE

• Eric Clapton, *Unplugged*. Reprise.
Bryan Adams, "There Will Never Be Another Tonight." A&M.
Tom Cochrane, "Life Is a Highway." Capitol.
Peter Gabriel, "Digging in the Dirt." Geffen.
Bob Seger, "The Fire Inside." Capitol.
Bruce Springsteen, *Human Touch*. Columbia.

BEST ROCK VOCAL PERFORMANCE, FEMALE

• Melissa Etheridge, "Ain't It Heavy," track from *Never Enough*. Island.
Lita Ford, "Shot of Poison." RCA.
Alison Moyet, "It Won't Be Long." Columbia.
Alannah Myles, *Rockinghorse*. Atlantic.
Tina Turner, "The Bitch Is Back," track from *Two Rooms*. Polydor.

BEST ROCK PERFORMANCE BY A DUO OR GROUP WITH VOCAL

• U2, *Achtung Baby*. Island.
En Vogue, "Free Your Mind." EastWest Records.
Little Village, *Little Village*. Reprise.
Los Lobos, *Kiko*. WB/Slash.
Red Hot Chili Peppers, "Under the Bridge." Warner Bros.

BEST HARD ROCK PERFORMANCE WITH VOCAL

• Red Hot Chili Peppers, "Give It Away." Warner Bros.
Alice in Chains, *Dirt*. Columbia.
Faith No More, *Angel Dust*. Slash/Reprise.
Guns N' Roses "Live and Let Die." Geffen.
Nirvana, "Smells Like Teen Spirit." DGC.

Pearl Jam, "Jeremy." Epic Associ
ated.

BEST METAL PERFORMANCE
WITH VOCAL

- Nine Inch Nails, "Wish," track from
  Broken. Interscope.
- Helmet, "In the Meantime," track from
  Meantime. Interscope.
- Megadeth, *Countdown to Extinction*.
  Capitol.
- Ministry, "N.W.O." track from
  *KE*A*H***. Sire/Warner Bros.
- Soundgarden, "Into the Void (Stealth),"
  track from *Badmotorfinger/SOMMS*.
  A&M.

BEST ROCK INSTRUMENTAL
PERFORMANCE

- Stevie Ray Vaughan, Double Trouble,
  "Little Wing," track from *The Sky Is
  Crying*. Epic.
- Jeff Beck, Jed Leiber, "Hound Dog,"
  track from *Honeymoon in Las Vegas*.
  Epic Soundtrax.
- Dixie Dregs, *Bring 'Em Back Alive*.
  Capricorn.
- Santana, "Gypsy/Grajonca," track from
  Milagro. Polydor.
- Joe Satriani, *The Extremist*. Relativity.

BEST ALTERNATIVE MUSIC
ALBUM

- *Bone Machine*, Tom Waits. Island.
- *Good Stuff*, B-52's. Reprise.
- *Wish*, Cure. Elektra.
- *Your Arsenal*, Morrissey. Sire/Reprise.
- *Nonsuch*, XTC. Geffen.

BEST RHYTHM & BLUES SONG
(Songwriter's Award)

- "The End of the Road," L. A. Reid,
  Babyface, Daryl Simmons.
- "I'll Be There," Hal Davis, Berry Gordy,
  Willie Hutch, Bob West.
- "My Lovin' (You're Never Gonna Get
  It)," Thomas McElroy, Denzil Foster.
- "Jam," Michael Jackson, Rene Moore,
  Bruce Swedien, Teddy Riley.
- "Ain't 2 Proud 2 Beg," Dallas Austin,
  Lisa "Left Eye" Lopes.

BEST RHYTHM & BLUES VOCAL
PERFORMANCE, MALE

- Al Jarreau, *Heaven and Earth*.
  Reprise.
- Bobby Brown, "Humpin' Around."
  MCA.
- Peabo Bryson, "Lost in the Night."
  Columbia.
- Tevin Campbell, *T.E.V.I.N.* WB/Qwest.
- Michael Jackson, "Jam." Epic.

BEST RHYTHM & BLUES VOCAL
PERFORMANCE, FEMALE

- Chaka Khan, *The Woman I Am*.
  Warner Bros.
- Oleta Adams, "Don't Let the Sun Go
  Down on Me," track from *Two
  Rooms*. Polydor.
- Whitney Houston, "I Belong to You."
  Arista.
- Shanice, "I Love Your Smile." Motown.
- Vanessa Williams, "The Comfort Zone."
  Wing/Mercury.

BEST RHYTHM & BLUES VOCAL
PERFORMANCE BY A DUO OR
GROUP WITH VOCAL

- Boyz II Men, "The End of the Road."
  Motown.
- Arrested Development, "People Every-
  day." Chrysalis.
- Mariah Carey, Trey Lorenz, "I'll Be
  There." Columbia.
- En Vogue, *Funky Divas*. EastWest
  Records.
- Luther Vandross, Janet Jackson, "The
  Best Things in Life Are Free." Per-
  spective Records.

BEST RHYTHM & BLUES
INSTRUMENTAL PERFORMANCE

- Miles Davis, *Doo-Bop*. Warner Bros.
- Brecker Brothers, "Big Idea," track from
  Return of the Brecker Brothers. GRP.
- George Howard, "Just the Way I Feel,"
  track from *Do I Ever Cross Your
  Mind*. GRP.
- Soul II Soul, "Mood," track from *Vol.
  III Just Right*. Virgin.
- Grover Washington, Jr., "Summer Chill,"
  track from *Next Exit*. Columbia.

BEST RAP SOLO PERFORMANCE

• Sir Mix-a-Lot, "Baby Got Back," track from *Mack Daddy*. Def American/Rhyme Cartel.

Hammer, "Addams Groove." Capitol.

L.L. Cool J, "Strictly Business." Uptown/MCA.

Marky Mark, "You Gotta Believe." Interscope.

Queen Latifah, "Latifah's Had It Up 2 Here." Tommy Boy.

BEST RAP PERFORMANCE BY A DUO OR GROUP

• Arrested Development, "Tennessee." Chrysalis.

Beastie Boys, "Check Your Head." Capitol.

House of Pain, "Jump Around." Tommy Boy.

Kris Kros, "Jump." Ruffhouse/Columbia.

Public Enemy, *Greatest Misses*. Def Jam/Chaos/Columbia.

BEST CONTEMPORARY JAZZ PERFORMANCE, INSTRUMENTAL

• Pat Metheny, *Secret Story*. Geffen.

Bob Berg, *Back Roads*. Denon Records.

Brecker Brothers, *Return of the Brecker Brothers*. GRP.

Bob Mintzer, *One Music*. Digital Music Products.

David Sanborn, *Upfront*. Elektra.

BEST JAZZ VOCAL PERFORMANCE

• Bobby McFerrin, " 'Round Midnight," track from *Play—McFerrin/C. Corea*. Blue Note.

Shirley Horn, *Here's to Life*. Verve.

Abbey Lincoln, *You Gotta Pay the Band*. Verve.

Jimmy Scott, *All the Way*. Warner Bros/Sire.

Take 6, "I'm Always Chasing Rainbows," track from *Glengarry Glen Ross*. Elektra Entertainment.

BEST JAZZ INSTRUMENTAL SOLO

• Joe Henderson, "Lush Life," track from *Lush Life—The Music of Billy Strayhorn*. Verve.

Randy Brecker, "Above and Below," track from *Return of the Brecker Brothers*. GRP.

Miles Davis, "Fantasy," track from *Doo-Bop*. Warner Bros.

Stan Getz, Kenny Barron, "Soul Eyes," track from *People Time*. Verve.

Wynton Marsalis, "Blue Interlude," track from *Blue Interlude*. Columbia.

BEST JAZZ INSTRUMENTAL PERFORMANCE (INDIVIDUAL OR GROUP)

• Branford Marsalis, *I Heard You Twice the First Time*. Columbia.

Eddie Daniels, Gary Burton, *Benny Rides Again*. GRP.

Charlie Haden Quartet West, *Haunted Heart*. Verve.

Joe Henderson, *Lush Life*. Verve.

Arturo Sandoval, *I Remember Clifford*. GRP.

BEST LARGE JAZZ ENSEMBLE PERFORMANCE

• McCoy Tyner Big Band, *The Turning Point*. Verve.

Toshiko Akiyoshi Jazz Orchestra, *Carnegie Hall Concert*. Columbia.

Benny Carter Big Band, Rutgers University Orchestra, *Harlem Renaissance*. Musicmasters.

GRP All-Star Big Band, *GRP All-Star Big Band*. GRP.

Rob McConnel, Boss Brass, *Brassy and Sassy*. Concord Jazz.

BEST COUNTRY SONG
(Songwriter's Award)

• "I Still Believe in You," Vince Gill, John Barlow Jarvis.

"I Feel Lucky," Mary-Chapin Carpenter, Don Schlitz.

"Achy Breaky Heart," Don Von Tress.

"She Is His Only Need," Dave Loggins.

"The Greatest Man I Never Knew," Richard Leigh, Layng Martine, Jr.

BEST COUNTRY VOCAL PERFORMANCE, MALE

• Vince Gill, *I Still Believe in You*. MCA.

Garth Brooks, *The Chase*. Liberty.
Billy Ray Cyrus, "Achy Breaky Heart."
Mercury
Randy Travis, "Better Class of Losers."
Warner Bros.
Travis Tritt, "Lord Have Mercy on the
Working Man." Warner Bros.

BEST COUNTRY VOCAL
PERFORMANCE, FEMALE

• Mary-Chapin Carpenter, "I Feel
Lucky." Columbia.
Wynonna Judd, *Wynonna*. Curb/MCA.
Reba McEntire, "The Greatest Man I
Never Knew." MCA.
Lorrie Morgan, "Something in Red."
RCA.
Pam Tillis, "Maybe It Was Memphis."
Arista.

BEST COUNTRY PERFORMANCE
BY A DUO OR GROUP WITH
VOCAL

• Emmylou Harris, Nash Ramblers,
*Emmylou Harris and the Nash Ram-
blers at the Ryman*. Reprise.
Alabama, *American Pride*. RCA.
Brooks & Dunn, "Boot Scootin' Boo-
gie." Arista.
Kentucky Headhunters, "Only Daddy
That'll Walk the Line." Mercury.
Restless Heart, "When She Cries."
RCA.

BEST COUNTRY VOCAL
COLLABORATION

• Travis Tritt, Marty Stuart, "The
Whiskey Ain't Workin'." Warner
Bros.
Mary-Chapin Carpenter, Joe Diffie,
"Not Too Much to Ask." Columbia.
Chieftains, Nitty Gritty Dirt Band,
"Killybegs," track from *Another
Country*. RCA Victor.
Chris LeDoux, Garth Brooks, "Whatcha
Gonna Do with a Cowboy," track
from *Whatcha Gonna Do with a
Cowboy*. Liberty.
Tanya Tucker, Delbert McClinton, "Tell
Me About It," track from *Can't Run
from Yourself*. Liberty.

BEST COUNTRY INSTRUMENTAL
PERFORMANCE

• Chet Atkins, Jerry Reed, *Sneakin'
Around*. Columbia.
Asleep at the Wheel, "Black and White
Rag," track from *Greatest Hits—Live
and Kickin'*. Arista.
Chieftains, Ricky Skaggs, "Cotton-Eyed
Joe," track from *Another Country*.
RCA.
Jerry Douglas, "Ride the Wild Turkey,"
track from *Slide Rule*. Sugar Hill
Emmylou Harris, Nash Ramblers,
"Scotland," track from *Emmylou
Harris and the Nash Ramblers at the
Ryman*. Reprise.

BEST ROCK/CONTEMPORARY
GOSPEL ALBUM

• *Unseen Power*, Petra. Dayspring.
A Friend Like U, Geoff Moore, Dis-
tance. Forefront.
Not Ashamed, Newsboys. Star Song.
Pray for Rain, Pray for Rain. Vireo.
Tales of Wonder, White Heart. Star
Song.

BEST POP GOSPEL ALBUM

• *The Great Adventure*, Steven Curtis
Chapman. Sparrow.
Angels of Mercy, Susan Ashton. Sparrow.
Addicted to Jesus, Carman. Benson.
I Choose Joy, Larnelle Harris. Benson.
Faith, Hope and Love, Mylon LeFevre.
Star Song.

BEST SOUTHERN GOSPEL ALBUM

• *Sometimes Miracles Hide*, Bruce Car-
roll. Word.
Camp Meeting Live, Cathedrals.
Canaan.
Pickin' the Best . . . Live, Jeff Easter,
Sheri Easter. Benson Music Group.
Live, Florida Boys. New Haven.
70th Anniversary Celebration, Speers.
Homeland.

BEST TRADITIONAL SOUL GOSPEL
ALBUM

• *He's Working It Out for You*, Shirley
Ceasar. Word.

Standing in the Safety Zone, Fairfield
Four. Warner Bros.
Steppin' Out, Gospel Hummingbirds.
Blind Pig.
Live, Albertina Walker. Benson.
For the Rest of My Life, Mom Winans,
Pop Winans. Sparrow.

BEST CONTEMPORARY SOUL
GOSPEL ALBUM
• *Handel's Messiah—A Soulful Cele-
bration*, various artists. Reprise.
When the Music Stops, Daryl Coley.
Sparrow
Love Is Reality, Al Green. Word.
Testimony, Richard Smallwood Singers.
Sparrow.
The Lady, Vickie Winans, MCA.

BEST GOSPEL ALBUM BY A CHOIR
OR CHORUS
• *Edwin Hawkins Music and Arts Semi-
nar Mass Choir*; Music & Arts Semi-
nar Mass Choir; Edwin Hawkins,
choir director. Fixit.
*African Children's Choir—Live! in Con-
cert*, African Children's Choir;
Matthew Kalulu, choir director.
Maranatha!Music.
Only to Him, Brooklyn Tabernacle
Singers; Carol Cymbala, choir direc-
tor. Warner Alliance.
With All of My Heart, Sandra Crouch &
Friends; Sandra Crouch, choir direc-
tor. Sparrow.
Never Let Go of His Hand, Rev.
Lawrende Thomison & the Music
City Mass Choir; O'Landa Draper,
choir director. New Haven.

BEST TRADITIONAL FOLK
ALBUM
• *An Irish Evening Live at the Grand
Opera House, Belfast, with Roger
Daltrey and Nanci Griffith*, Chief-
tains. RCA Victor.
Just Gimme Somethin' I'm Used To,
Norman Blake, Nancy Blake.
Shanachie.
Grandfather's Greatest Hits, David
Holt. Highwindy Audio.

A Cathedral Concert, Le Mystère des
Voix Bulgares. Verve World.
Le Trio Cadien, D. L. Menard, Eddie
LeJeun, Ken Smith. Rounder.

BEST CONTEMPORARY FOLK ALBUM
• *Another Country*, Chieftains. RCA
Victor.
Play Me Backward, Joan Baez. Virgin.
The Criminal Under My Own Hat, T
Bone Burnett. Columbia.
Rites of Passage, Indigo Girls. Epic.
Arkansas Traveler, Michelle Shocked.
Mercury.

BEST TRADITIONAL BLUES ALBUM
• *Goin' Back to New Orleans*, Dr. John.
Warner Bros.
Someone to Love, Charles Brown. Bulls-
eye Blues.
No Looking Back, Clarence "Gate-
mouth" Brown. Alligator.
Got Love If You Want It, John Ham-
mond. Charisma.
*Roots of Rhythm and Blues: A Tribute to
the Robert Johnson Era*, various
artists. Columbia.

BEST CONTEMPORARY BLUES ALBUM
• *The Sky Is Crying*, Stevie Ray
Vaughan, Double Trouble. Epic.
I Was Warned, Robert Cray. Mercury.
Robben Ford and the Blue Line, Robben
Ford, Blue Line. GRP.
The Right Time, Etta James. Elektra
Entertainment.
Peace to the Neighborhood, Pops Sta-
ples. Charisma.

BEST BLUEGRASS ALBUM
• *Every Time You Say Goodbye*, Alison
Krauss, Union Station. Rounder.
*Larry Cordle, Glen Duncan and Lone-
some Standard Time*, Larry Cordle,
Glen Duncan, Lonesome Standard
Time. Sugar Hill.
Slide Rule, Jerry Douglas. Sugar Hill.
Bluegrass Reunion, David Grisman,
Herb Pedersen, Red Allen, Jim
Buchanan, James Kerwin, Jerry Gar-
cia. Acoustic Disc.

Scene 20—20th Anniversary Concert, Seldom Scene. Sugar Hill.

BEST LATIN POP ALBUM

• *Otro Día Más sin Verte,* Jon Secada. Capitol-EMI-Latin.
Aqua Nueva, Cristian. Fonovisa, Inc.
Calor, Julio Iglesias. Sony Discos.
Romance, Luis Miguel. WEA Latina
Ave Fenix, Raphael. Sony Discos.
El Puma en Ritmo, Jose Luis Rodriguez. Sony Discos.

BEST TROPICAL LATIN ALBUM

• *Frenesi,* Linda Ronstadt. Elektra Entertainment.
Soy Dichoso, Ray Barretto. Fania/Sonido Inc.
Amor y Control, Rubén Blades. Sony Discos.
Tributo a Ismael Rivera, Celia Cruz. Vaya/Sonido Inc.
Gracias, El Gran Combo. Combo.

BEST MEXICAN-AMERICAN ALBUM

• *Más Canciones,* Linda Ronstadt. Elektra.
Un Nuevo Comienzo, Los Diablos. BMG Int'l.
Con Sentimiento y Sabor, Los Tigres del Norte. Fonovisa.
Unsung Highways, Emilio Navaira. Capitol/EMI Latin.
I Love My Freedom, I Love My Texas, Mingo Saldivary y Sus Tremendos Cuatro Espadas. Rounder.

BEST REGGAE ALBUM

• *X-Tra Naked,* Shabba Ranks. Epic.
Breakout, Jimmy Cliff. GRS.
Rastafari Centennial/Live in Paris—Elysée Montmartre, Steel Pulse. MCA.
Committed, Third World. Mercury.
All Over the World, Wailing Souls. Chaos/Columbia.

BEST POLKA ALBUM

• *35th Anniversary,* Walter Ostanek. World Renowned Sounds.

All American Country Flavored Polkas, Eddie Blazonczyk's Versatones. Bel-Aire.
Where Were You Back Then? Lenny Gomulka & the Chicago Push. World Renowned Sounds.
Sturr-It-Up, Jimmy Sturr. Starr.
Happy Polka Days, Dick Tady Orchestra. Corjal.

BEST NEW AGE ALBUM

• *Shepherd Moons,* Enya. Reprise.
Dream, Kitaro. Geffen.
Esperanto, Shadowfax. EarthBeat.
Rockoon, Tangerine Dream. Miramar.
Dare to Dream, Yanni. Private Music.

BEST WORLD MUSIC ALBUM

• *Brasileiro,* Sergio Mendes. Elektra Entertainment.
Gipsy Kings Live, Gipsy Kings. Elektra Musician.
Kirya, Ofra Hazra. Shanachie.
Eyes Open, Youssou N'Dour. Forty Acres/Columbia.
Americas, Strunz & Farah. Mesa.

BEST ARRANGEMENT ON AN INSTRUMENTAL

• Rob McConnell, "Strike Up the Band," track from *Brassy and Sassy* (Rob McConnell & the Boss Brass). Concord Jazz.
Russ Gershon, "Bennie Moten's Weird Nightmare," track from *The Calculus of Pleasure* (Either/Orchestra). Accurate.
Michael Abene, "Airegin," track from *GRP All-Star Big Band* (GRP All-Star Big Band). GRP.
Gary Lindsay, "Cherokee," track from *I Remember Clifford* (Arturo Sandoval). GRP.
Neil Slater, "Values," track from *LAB 91* (University of North Texas One O'Clock Lab Band). North Texas Jazz.

BEST INSTRUMENTAL COMPOSITION

• "Harlem Renaissance Suite," track from *Harlem Renaissance.* Benny Carter.

"Magic Fingers," track from *UFO TOFU*, Bela Fleck.

"Blue Interlude," track from *Blue Interlude*, Wynton Marsalis.

"The Truth Will Always Be," track from *Secret Story*, Pat Metheny.

"Oblivion," track from *Symphonic Tango*, Astor Piazzolla.

BEST MUSICAL SHOW ALBUM

• *Guys and Dolls—The New Broadway Cast Recording*. Frank Loesser. RCA.

The King and I, Julie Andrews, Ben Kingsley, others. John Mauceri conducting the Hollywood Bowl Orchestra. Richard Rodgers, composer; Oscar Hammerstein, lyricist. Phillips Classics.

Crazy for You, Broadway cast. George Gershwin, composer; Ira Gershwin, lyricist. Angel.

Jelly's Last Jam, Broadway cast. Luther Henderson, Jelly Roll Morton, composers; Susan Birkenhead, lyricist. Mercury.

The Secret Garden, Broadway cast. Lucy Simon, composer; Marsha Norma, lyricist. Columbia.

BEST INSTRUMENTAL COMPOSITION WRITTEN FOR A MOTION PICTURE OR TV

• "Theme from *Beauty and the Beast*," Alan Menken.

Rush, Eric Clapton.

"Mambo Caliente," track from *The Mambo Kings*, Arturo Sandoval.

"Theme from *Northern Exposure*," track from *Northern Exposure* TV soundtrack, David Schwartz.

Hook, John Williams.

BEST SONG WRITTEN SPECIFICALLY FOR A MOTION PICTURE OR TV

• "Beauty and the Beast," from *Beauty and the Beast*, Alan Menken, Howard Ashman.

"Tears in Heaven," from *Rush*, Eric Clapton, Will Jennings.

"Now and Forever," track from *A League of Their Own*, Carole King.

"Beautiful Maria of My Soul," track from *The Mambo Kings*. Robert Kraft, Arne Glimcher.

"It's Probably Me," track from *Lethal Weapon 3,* Michael Kamen, Sting, Eric Clapton.

BEST INSTRUMENTAL ARRANGEMENT ACCOMPANYING VOCAL(S)

• Johnny Mandel, "Here's to Life," track from *Here's to Life* (Shirley Horn). Verve Forecast.

Robert Farnon, "Lush Life," track from *It's Over* (Eileen Farrell). Reference Recordings.

Bob Freedman, "Stella by Starlight," track from *Nnenna Freelon* (Nnenna Freelon). Columbia.

Jeremy Lubbock, "Guess I'll Hang My Tears Out to Dry," track from *In Tribute* (Diane Schuur). GRP.

Mervyn Warren, "Why Do the Nations So Furiously Rage?" track from *Handel's Messiah: A Soulful Celebration*. Reprise.

BEST CLASSICAL ALBUM

• *Mahler: Symphony No. 9*, Leonard Bernstein conducting the Berlin Philharmonic Orchestra. Deutsche Grammophon.

Beethoven: Symphonies (Complete), Nicholas Harnoncourt conducting the Chamber Orchestra of Europe. Teldec.

Cecilia Bartoli: Rossini Heroines, Cecilia Bartoli, soprano; Ion Marin conducting the Orchestra e Coro del Teatro la Fenice. London.

Gorecki: Symphony No. 3, David Zinman conducting the London Sinfonietta (Dawn Upshaw). Elektra Nonesuch.

R. Strauss: Die Frau Ohne Schatten, Sir Georg Solti conducting the Vienna Philharmonic; Domingo, Varady, van Dam, Behrens, Runkel, principal soloists. London.

BEST ORCHESTRAL PERFORMANCE
(Conductor's Award)

- Leonard Bernstein conducting the the Berlin Philharmonic Orchestra, *Mahler: Symphony No. 9*. Deutsche Grammophon.

Nicholas Harnoncourt conducting the Chamber Orchestra of Europe, *Beethoven: Symphonies (Complete)*. Teldec.

David Zinman conducting the London Sinfonietta (Dawn Upshaw), *Gorecki: Symphony No. 3*. Elektra Nonesuch.

Myung-Whun Chung conducting the Orchestre de l'Opéra Bastille, *Messiaen: Turangalîla Symphonie*. Deutsche Grammophon.

Leonard Slatkin conducting the St. Louis Symphony Orchestra, *W. Schuman: Symphony No. 10; New England Triptych; American Festival Overture*. RCA Victor Red Seal.

BEST CHAMBER MUSIC PERFORMANCE

- Yo-Yo Ma, cello; Emanuel Ax, piano, *Brahms: Sonatas for Cello and Piano*. Sony Classical.

Tokyo String Quartet, *Beethoven: The Late String Quartets (Opp. 127, 130, 131, 132, 133, 135)*. RCA Victor Red Seal.

Isaac Stern, Cho-Liang Lin, violins; Yo-Yo Ma, Sharon Robinson, cellos; Jaime Laredo, Michael Tree, violas, *Brahms: Sextets, Opp. 18 and 36; Theme and Variations*. Sony Classical.

Rudolf Firkusny, piano; Ridge String Quartet, *Dvořák: Piano Quintets, Opp. 81 and 5*. RCA Victor Red Seal.

Carmina Quartet, *Szymanowski: String Quartets No. 1, Op. 37, and No. 2, Op. 56; Webern: Langsamer Satz for String Quartet*. Denon.

BEST CLASSICAL PERFORMANCE, INSTRUMENTAL SOLOIST(S) (WITH ORCHESTRA)

- Yo-Yo Ma, cello (Lorin Maazel conducting the Pittsburgh Symphony Orchestra), *Prokofiev: Sinfonia Concertante; Tchaikovsky: Variations on a Rococo Theme*. Sony Classical.

Anne-Sophie Mutter, violin (Seiji Ozawa conducting the Boston Symphony Orchestra), *Bartók: Violin Concerto No. 2; Moret: En Rêve*. Deutsche Grammophon.

Geoffrey Tozer, piano (Neeme Jarvi conducting the London Philharmonic), *Medtner: Piano Concertos Nos. 1–3*. Chandos.

Alicia de Larrocha, piano (Sir Colin Davis conducting the English Chamber Orchestra), *Mozart: Piano Concertos Nos. 23 and 24*. RCA Victor Red Seal.

Horacio Gutierrez, piano (Lorin Maazel conducting the Pittsburgh Symphony Orchestra), *Rachmaninov: Piano Concertos Nos. 2 and 3*. Telarc.

BEST CLASSICAL PERFORMANCE, INSTRUMENTAL SOLOIST (WITHOUT ORCHESTRA)

- Vladimir Horowitz, piano, *Horowitz—Discovered Treasures (Chopin, Clementi, Liszt, Scarlatti, Scriabin)*. Sony Classical.

Emanuel Ax, piano, *Brahms: Variations and Fugue on a Theme by Handel, Op. 24; 6 Piano Pieces, Op. 118; 2 Rhapsodies, Op. 79*. Sony Classical.

Jean-Yves Thibaudet, piano, *Ravel: L'Oeuvre pour Piano Seul* (Complete Works for Solo Piano). London.

Yevgeny Kissin, piano, *Schubert: Fantasie in C and 4 Lieder; Brahms: Fantasien, Op. 116; Liszt: Ungarishe*. Deutsche Grammophon.

Keith Jarrett, piano, *Shostakovich: 24 Preludes and Fugues, Op. 87*. ECM.

BEST OPERA RECORDING

- *R. Strauss: Die Frau Ohne Schatten*, Sir Georg Solti conducting the Vienna Philharmonic (solos: Domino, Varady, van Dam, Behrens, Runkel, Jo). London.

Handel: Giulio Cesare, Rene Jacobs conducting the Concerto Köln (solos:

Larmore, Schlick, Fink, Rorholm, Ragin, Zanasi, Visse, Lallouette). Harmonia Mundi.

Janáček: The Cunning Little Vixen, Simon Rattle conducting the Orchestra of the Royal Opera House, Covent Garden (solos: Howell, Watson, Tear, Allen, Montague). EMI Classics.

Tchaikovsky: Pique Dame (The Queen of Spades), Seiji Ozawa conducting the Boston Symphony Orchestra (solos: Freni, Atlantov, Hvorostovsky, Forrester, Leiferkus, Ciesinski). RCA Victor Red Seal.

Wagner: Siegfried, James Levine conducting the Metropolitan Opera Orchestra (solos: Goldberg, Zednik, Morris, Behrens, Svenden, Wlaschiha, Moll, Battle). Deutsche Grammophon.

BEST PERFORMANCE OF A CHORAL WORK

• Herbert Blomstedt conducting the San Francisco Girls'/Boys' Chorus and San Francisco Symphony Orchestra, *Orff: Carmina Burana.* Decca.

Martin Pearlman conducting the Boston Baroque Chorus and Orchestra, *Handel: Messiah.* Telarc.

John Eliot Gardiner conducting the Monteverdi Choir and English Baroque Soloists. *Haydn: The Seasons.* Archiv.

Michael Tilson Thomas conducting the London Symphony Chorus and Orchestra; Malcolm Hicks, chorus master, *Janáček: Glagolitic Mass.* Sony Classical.

Riccardo Chailly conducting the Stadtischer Musikverein Düsseldorf and Radio Symphony Orchestra Berlin, *Mahler: Das Klagende Lied.* London.

BEST CLASSICAL VOCAL PERFORMANCE

• Kathleen Battle, soprano (Margo Garett, accompanist), *Kathleen Battle at Carnegie Hall (Handel, Mozart,*

Liszt, Strauss, Charpentier). Deutsche Grammophon.

Cecilia Bartoli, soprano (Ion Marin conducting the Orchestra e Coro del Teatro le Fenice), *Cecilia Bartoli: Rossini Heroines.* London.

Thomas Hampson, baritone (Sir Charles Mackerras conducting the Welsh National Opera Orchestra and Chorus), *Delius: Sea Drift.* Argo.

Marilyn Horne, mezzo-soprano (Martin Katz, accompanist), *Marilyn Horne: Rossini Recital.* RCA Victor Red Seal.

Arleen Auger, soprano (Irwin Gage, accompanist), *Wolf: Songs to the Poetry of Goethe and Morike.* Hyperion.

BEST CONTEMPORARY COMPOSITION

• *The Lovers,* Samuel Barber.
X, the Life and Times of Malcolm X, Anthony Davis.
Piano Concerto, Witold Lutoslawski.
The Protecting Veil, John Tavener.
Flute Concerto, Ellen Taaffe Zeilich.

BEST ENGINEERED RECORDING, CLASSICAL

• James Lock, James Pellowe, Jonathan Stokes, Phillip Siney, *R. Strauss: Die Frau Ohne Schatten* (Sir Georg Solti conducting the Vienna Philharmonic; solos: Domingo, Varady, van Dam, Behrens). London.

Keith O. Johnson, *Arnold: A Sussex Overture; Beckus the Dandipratt; The Smoke; The Fair Field* (Malcolm Arnold conducting the London Philharmonic Orchestra). Reference Recordings.

Mitch Heller, *Barber: The Lovers; Prayers of Kierkegaard* (Andrew Schenck conducting the Chicago Symphony Orchestra). Koch International.

John Eargle, *Hanson: Mosaics; Piano Concerto in G; Symphonies Nos. 5 and 7* (Gerard Schwarz conducting the Seattle Symphony; Carol Rosenberger, piano). Delos International.

Stanley Goodall, *Orff: Carmina Burana* (Herbert Blomstedt conducting the San Francisco Chorus, San Francisco Symphony Chorus and San Francisco Symphony Orchestra). Decca.

Michael Bishop, *Stravinsky: The Rite of Spring and Pulcinella Suite* (Yoel Levi conducting the Atlanta Symphony Orchestra). Telarc.

CLASSICAL PRODUCER OF THE YEAR
• Michael Fine
Andrew Cornall
Steven Epstein
Thomas Frost
James Mallinson

BEST COMEDY ALBUM
• *P.D.Q. Bach: Music for an Awful Lot of Winds and Percussion*, Professor Peter Schickele. Telarc.
An Evening with George Burns, George Burns. Dove Audio.
Naked Beneath My Clothes, Rita Rudner. Peguin-HB.
Jonathan Winters Is Terminator 3, Jonathan Winters. Dove Audio.
Off the Deep End, Weird Al Yankovic. Scotti Brothers.

BEST SPOKEN WORD OR NONMUSICAL ALBUM
• *What You Can Do to Avoid AIDS*, Earvin "Magic" Johnson, Robert O'Keefe. Random House AudioBooks.
Fried Green Tomatoes at the Whistle Stop Cafe, Fannie Flagg. Random House AudioBooks.
Stories, Garrison Keillor. Highbridge.
Devout Catalyst, Ken Nordine. Greatful Dead Records.
A Christmas Carol (Charles Dickens), Patrick Stewart. Simon and Schuster Audio.
This Is Orson Welles, Orson Welles, Peter Bogdanovich. Caedmon.

BEST ALBUM FOR CHILDREN
• *Beauty and the Beast,* film soundtrack, Alan Menken, Howard Ashman. Walt Disney.

Chipmunks in Low Places, John Boylan, Janice Karman, Ross Bagdasarian. Epic/Sony Kids.
Snuggle Up—A Gift of Songs for Sweet Dreams, J. Aaron Brown, David R. Lehman, Barbara Bailey Hutchinson. Jaba.
Woody's Grow Big Songs 1 and 2, Woody Guthrie, Arlo Guthrie, Nora Guthrie, Frank Fuchs. Warner Bros.
Pete Seeger's Family Concert, Pete Seeger. Sony Kids Music.

BEST ENGINEERED ALBUM (OTHER THAN CLASSICAL)
• Bruce Swedien, Teddy Riley, *Dangerous* (Michael Jackson). Epic.
Lindsey Buckingham, Richard Dashut, Kevin Killen, Greg Droman, Chris Lord-Alge, *Out of the Cradle* (Lindsey Buckingham). Reprise.
Greg Penny, Marc Ramaer, *Ingenue* (k. d. lang). Sire/Warner Bros.
Moogie Canazio, *Brasileiro* (Sergio Mendes). Elektra.
Elliot Scheiner, Walter New, *The Hunter* (Jennifer Warnes). Private Music.

BEST ALBUM PACKAGE
(Art Director's Award)
• Melanie Nissen, *Spellbound—Compact* (Paula Abdul). Capitol/Virgin.
Geoff Gans, *Queen of Soul—The Atlantic Recordings* (Aretha Franklin). Rhino.
Tommy Steele, *Too Legit to Quit* (Hammer). Capitol.
Ria Lewerke, Norman Moore, *Elvis the King of Rock 'n' Roll—The Complete 50's Masters* (Elvis Presley). RCA.
Len Peltier, *99.9 F* (Suzanne Vega). A&M.

BEST ALBUM NOTES
(Annotator's Award)
• Dave Marsh, Jerry Wexler, David Ritz, Thulani Davis, Ahmet Ertegun, Tom Down, Arif Mardin, *Queen of Soul—The Atlantic Recordings* (Aretha Franklin). Rhino.

Will Friedwald, Dick Katz, *The Complete Capitol Recordings of the Nat King Cole Trio* (Nat King Cole Trio). Mosaic.

Peter Guralnick, *Elvis the King of Rock 'n' Roll—The Complete 50's Masters* (Elvis Presley). RCA.

Pete Welding, Lawrence Cohn, *Roots n' Blues the Retrospective (1925— 1950)* (various artists). Columbia/Legacy.

Robert Kimball, Richard Sudhalter, *You're the Top: Cole Porter in the 1930s* (various artists). Koch International Classics.

BEST HISTORICAL ALBUM

• *The Complete Capitol Recordings of the Nat King Cole Trio*, Nat King Cole Trio. Mosaic.

Les Paul: The Legend and The Legacy, Les Paul. Capitol.

Elvis the King of Rock 'n' Roll—The Complete 50's Masters, Elvis Presley. RCA.

The Music of Disney—A Legacy in Song, various artists. Walt Disney.

You're the Top: Cole Porter in the 1930s, various artists. Koch Int'l Classics/Indiana Historical.

PRODUCER OF THE YEAR (OTHER THAN CLASSICAL)

(Tie)

• Daniel Lanois, Brian Eno

• L. A. Reid, Babyface
Mitchell Froom
Teddy Riley
Chris Thomas

BEST MUSIC VIDEO, SHORT FORM

• *Digging in the Dirt*, Peter Gabriel. John Downer, director. Geffen.

Free Your Mind, En Vogue. Mark Romanek, director.

Kiko and the Lavender Moon, Los Lobos. Ondrej Rudavsky, director. Warner Bros.

Church, Lyle Lovett. Matt Mahurin, director. Curb/MCA Records.

What God Wants, Roger Waters. Tony Kaye, director. Columbia.

BEST MUSIC VIDEO, LONG FORM

• *Diva*, Annie Lennox. Sophie Muller, director. 6 West Home Video.

Classic Visions 5—Gershwin, D'Albert, Strauss, Honegger, Swiss Radio Symphony Orchestra; Matthias Bamert, conductor. Adrian Marthaler, video director. RCA Victor Red Seal.

Phallus in Wonderland, Gwar. Distortion Wells, Judas Bullhorn, directors. Metal Blade.

Hammerin' Home, Hammer. Rupert Wainwright, director. Capitol/EMI Music Inc.

The Enemy Strikes Live, Public Enemy. Larry Holland, director. Sony Music.

• 1993 •
Whitney's Forgiving "Love"

She was "nervous as hell," Whitney Houston told *Variety,* but she still went through with it anyway. As the 36th annual Grammy ceremony began, she took center stage at Radio City Music Hall in New York City and sang a passionate rendition of "I Will Always Love You" to the same crowd that snubbed her eight years earlier.

N.A.R.A.S. had refused to let Houston compete for Best New Artist in 1985 even though she set a new record for having the biggest-selling album ever by a debut artist. Now she was back making music history again with a soaring ballad that hovered atop the music charts for the longest consecutive period of any single ever—14 weeks. Since the mid-1980s, she won two awards for pop vocals, but this year Grammy watchers wondered: Would voters finally embrace Houston in the upper categories?

"I Will Always Love You" competed at an earlier Grammy race, in 1982, when Dolly Parton was nominated for best female country vocalist for performing the song she wrote for the film version of *The Best Little Whorehouse in Texas.* (She lost to Juice Newton singing "Break It to Me Gently.") Houston appropriated the tune for her film debut opposite Kevin Costner in *The Bodyguard.* The critics slammed the movie ("the year's highest-profile stinker," said *USA Today*), but the score quickly muscled its way to the top

Variety called Grammy night a coronation for Whitney Houston after she reigned atop the pop charts for a record-setting 14 weeks.

of the album charts for 20 weeks, selling more than 11 million copies, which tied it with the record set by Grammy's 1978 Album of the Year, *Saturday Night Fever,* as the biggest-selling soundtrack. *The Bodyguard* was up for this year's Album of the Year award, but only the *New York Times* thought it could win. It seemed that "Love" was best poised to take its categories, including Record of the Year and best pop group vocals. ("Quite frankly, we don't even know why there are other nominees," said *Billboard.*) *Variety* noted that the song "has by now been seared into the American consciousness." One fan was so obsessed with it that irritated neighbors had her thrown in jail for playing the record too loud and too often.

As predicted, Houston reaped the Grammys for pop vocals and Record of the Year. *Variety* reported, "The run continued for Houston right up until the Grammy show's end, when producer David Foster picked up the Producer of the Year nod, clearly as a result of his work on *The Bodyguard.*

"The album also earned Foster and Houston the Album of the Year trophy." Houston gushed with gratitude as she accepted the latter, saying, "Thank you, Lord Jesus. This is so nice. Thank you, Mommy and Daddy." Next, she spoke as a mother herself when she addressed her own one-year-old daughter watching at home, saying to the TV camera, "Bobbi Kristina, I love ya. It's time to go to bed."

The artist who led with the most nominations this year (six) was 10-time past champ Sting, who had never won Record or Album of the Year. *TV Guide,* the *Los Angeles Times* and *USA Today* all predicted he'd finally snag it for *Ten Summoner's Tales* (*Billboard* and *Entertainment Weekly* picked Billy Joel's *River of Dreams*), but when his hopes were crushed by a Whitney Houston juggernaut, Sting received two consolation prizes: best long-form video for the album's VHS version (taped at Sting's English country estate) and best male pop vocal performance for its hit single, "If I Ever Lose My Faith in You." *Summoner's* also won an engineering prize. The *Village Voice* reported, "Sting's producer, Hugh Padgham, seemed amazed by his engineering award because the album was recorded in Sting's dining room. 'We always had to go outside and say, 'Stop mowing the lawn!'"

"Sting took the losses in the bigger awards in stride," *Variety* reported on his attitude backstage.

As he clutched his new award for best pop vocals, Sting was asked by reporters if it would boost his ego. He replied, "I'm glad I got it, but it won't have any real effect on how I play my music. I've never been lacking in confidence. I've always been arrogant."

Among Sting's losses was a bid for Song of the Year, an award he won in 1983 for "Every Breath You Take." The songwriter's category was considered wide open this year, since best record champ "I Will Always Love You" was barred from competing due to a rule change. Old songs were no longer eligible as a result of the flap that followed "Unforgettable" winning the best song award of 1991, 40 years after it was written.

The prize now went to Alan Menken and Tim Rice for "A Whole New World (*Aladdin*'s Theme)." At last year's Grammys, the music from the Disney cartoon hit *Beauty and the Beast* won several statuettes for Menken for having teamed up with Harold Ashman, who died of AIDS. On *Aladdin,* he was now working with Andrew Lloyd Webber's former partner, and their new music won three Grammys in addition to Song of the Year: best song written for film, best movie instrumental composition and Best Musical Album For Children.

"World" also took the duo pop vocal award for Peabo Bryson, who won the category last year for "Beauty" with Celine Dion. This time he was crooning with Regina Belle.

The movie music's success was so broad that *Variety* said, "If not for Whitney Houston's wins in several key awards, *Aladdin* music might have swept the ceremony."

Probably as a result of Houston's expected prominence at this year's awards, N.A.R.A.S. changed the rules surrounding the Best New Artist category. Previously, contenders were not permitted to have earlier album credits, although occasional exceptions were made for such artists as Carly Simon, who won in 1971. Houston was barred from competing in 1985 because she'd been a guest vocalist on Teddy Pendergrass and Jermaine Jackson recordings. Now the new rule stated that contenders need only establish their "public identity" in the awards eligibility period.

It didn't matter this year. The winner turned out to be a genuinely new talent, Toni Braxton, a minister's daughter from Maryland who also pulled off an upset in the female r&b vocalist cateogry when "Another Sad Love Song" beat Whitney Houston's "I'm Every Woman." Backstage, Braxton roared to reporters: "I can't believe I beat Whitney! She's my favorite singer!"

Another loser in the category was Janet Jackson, who was nominated for "That's the Way Love Goes." The tune ended up scoring Best R&B Song, a prize she shared with cowriters James Harris III and Terry Lewis. Luther Vandross lost two bids in the songwriter's category, but *Billboard* and the *New York Times* claimed he was certain to win best r&b male vocalist for "How Deep Is Your Love." He lost to 11-time past Grammy champ Ray Charles, who prevailed with "A Song for You."

There was a hubbub in the r&b races when past Best New Artist winner Sade was nominated in the category reserved for groups. The Nigerian-born, British-raised songstress had retired four years earlier to concentrate on a new marriage, but now she was back with *Love Deluxe,* 1993's number-12-ranked album. Its hit release "No Ordinary Love," won her a new Grammy. Backstage, she told reporters that her marriage "just didn't work out."

The biggest career comeback of the year was the return of Meat Loaf, who'd quit the music business soon after the 1978 release of *Bat Out of Hell,* which went on to become the third-best-selling album of all time. After patching things up with his songwriter, Jim Steinman, the 46-year-old singer released *Bat Out of Hell II: Back Into Hell,* which included the hit "I'll Do Anything for Love (But I Won't Do That)," earning him the rock vocalist award.

The category was controversial because only male rock artists were nominated. N.A.R.A.S. dropped a separate slot for female rockers this year, as it had in 1987 and 1991, when the obligatory minimum of 10 singers failed to put their names up for award consideration. The academy's solution was to combine men and women into one, genderless competition for all solo vocalists, but the new slot still snubbed such notable women rockers

Mary Chapin Carpenter ("Passionate Kisses") won the prize for Best Female Country Vocal Performance for a third consecutive year.

as Liz Phair, whose *Exile in Guyville* had been declared the year's best album by *Billboard* and the *New York Times.*

"No awards show is complete without a protest or two," *USA Today* reported. "This year a group of female artists including Kim Gordon of Sonic Youth and members of the Breeders stood outside the music hall and criticized the lack of an award for best female rock vocals. One sign read 'Meat Loaf Again?' The several dozen protesters chanted 'Grammy nomination boys, hear our litany: There's more to rock & roll than Mariah and Whitney.' "

Also rebounding this year were veteran rockers Aerosmith, who scored the year's number-14-ranked album (*Get a Grip*) and MTV's number-one video of the year (*Cryin'*). *Variety* reported on their appearance at the Grammys: "Best reason for wearing a tribal witch doctor mask goes to Steven Tyler of Aerosmith, who donned said mask at start of band's live perf of 'Livin' on the Edge.' Backstage, Tyler quipped, 'I met a witch doctor. He said, "Wear this and you'll win a Grammy." ' True enough, the band copped an award for rock performance."

Accepting the prize, Tyler said, "Why

do I love rock & roll? Because it gets me off. Everything I've ever loved was immoral, cheap, fattening or put hair on your palms."

Neither *Cryin'* nor *Livin' on the Edge* was nominated for best short-form video. Instead, the prize went to last year's champ—Peter Gabriel—for *Steam,* which he performed at last year's Grammy ceremony. One of the notable losers in the category was Soul Asylum's *Runaway Train,* which featured photos of scores of real-life runaway teens, more than a dozen of which ended up being reunited with their families as a result of the video's prominence. "Runaway" caught up with the consolation prize of Best Rock Song.

Rock icon Frank Zappa died of prostate cancer in late 1993, a few days short of his 53rd birthday. He was honored at this year's Grammys when band members led by guitarist Steve Vai nabbed the prize for rock instrumental performance for "Sofa," a track from *Zappa's Universe.* "Because I was the designated featured artist, I received the Grammy," Vai said as he thanked his former partner. He recalled Zappa's advice "Keep the humor in the music," and added, "We miss ya, Big Daddy!"

The Stone Temple Pilots were considered a shoo-in for a nomination as the year's Best New Artist, having won the equivalent prize at the MTV Awards. They were snubbed in that Grammy lineup, however, but rallied with their hit single "Plush" in the category for best hard-rock vocals to pull off an upset victory over AC/DC.

An upset also rocked the category of best metal performance when Ozzy Osbourne's "I Don't Want to Change the World" from his "No More Tears" tour bumped off Megadeth's "Angry Again."

U2 failed to be nominated in any rock categories and ended up with the gold for Best Alternative Music Album for *Zooropa* despite critics' cries that it wasn't alternative music. The honor was accepted by Bono, who "stunned the Grammy crowd," noted *Variety,* when he strutted out onto the stage with a defiant manner and lit cigarette, saying, "We should all continue to abuse our position and fuck up the mainstream!"

Backstage, Bono admitted to the *Village Voice* that he was drunk, but he nonetheless went back out onstage again later to present Frank Sinatra with the Grammy Legend Award. The *Village Voice* reported on his rambling, five-minute speech: "More welcome insanity was Bono's tribute to the original gangsta, Frank Sinatra, which was so over-the-top it deserved its own Grammy. As Sting, for one, looked dumbfounded, Bono recited lines like, 'Good cop, bad cop, all in the same breath . . . Frank walks like America. Cocksure. His songs are his home—and he lets you in.' "

Variety added, "Sinatra, unsure whether he'd been praised or punted, called it the 'best welcome I've ever had.' "

Choking back tears, Sinatra accepted the award as the audience gave him a lengthy standing ovation. After stalling for several moments while he gathered his thoughts, Sinatra countered, 'This is more applause than Dean had in his whole life.' "

After the playful dig at his crooner pal Martin, he proceeded to ramble a bit, too, and said, "This is like being in baseball with the bases loaded. You don't know what you're going to do."

Clearly, Sinatra was not only flustered but upset. His critically cheered *Duets* CD not only failed to be nominated for Album of the Year, but the 78-year-old singer wasn't asked to perform on the show. "That's not what they wanted tonight and I'm angry, I'm hurt," he said.

He then added, "I hope we can do this again. I'm not leaving you yet." Moments later, however, he was cut off abruptly as

---

"I'm not leaving you yet!" Sinatra vowed, then was cut off on TV.

---

the telecast switched to a commercial break. It was a move, noted *Time* magazine, "that had television audiences scratching their heads."

In its wrap-up Grammy coverage, the media nailed N.A.R.A.S. for the flub, but academy officials claimed, said *Variety*, "Sinatra's people had cut off the singer, not the show's helmer."

"He started drifting and his people wanted him out of there," producer Pierre Cossette insisted. "They were yelling, 'Go to a commercial!' and so we went."

Last year Tony Bennett won the traditional pop category for his salute to Sinatra on the album *Perfectly Frank.* Now Bennett snatched the laurels for his bow to Fred Astaire on *Steppin' Out.* Backstage, *Variety* caught the 67-year-old saloon singer taking a rap at rap music. "I'm just waiting for that second note," he said. "It's all one note."

Digable Planets, a New York hip-hop trio that lost its bid for Best New Artist, won the rap group performance prize for "Rebirth of Slick (Cool Like Dat)," which it performed on the Grammycast. "The newcomers appeared less than grateful," *Variety* observed. "DP front man, Ishmael Butler, chastised the academy during his acceptance speech for its $300 seats and $900 seats when there's (people) out there not eating at all." Backstage, one group member told reporters that their enemy is "the white infrastructure."

The Planets' Grammy victory was a major upset, since pundits predicted the accolade would go either to L.L. Cool J or to the combo of Dr. Dre and protégé Snoop Doggy Dog.

Dr. Dre rallied to claim the rap solo prize for "Let Me Ride," a release from *The Chronic,* his 3-million seller that knocked Whitney Houston's *Bodyguard* out of the top spot on the album charts. Dr. Dre had been named Top Debut Artist at the Billboard Awards in December and had also distinguished himself as a leading producer of other rappers throughout 1993.

The jazz categories embraced a num-

Tejano queen Selena became a figure of cult adoration 13 months after her Grammy victory when she was killed by the head of her fan club.

ber of past Grammy favorites, including former Best New Artist and Record and Album of the Year champ Natalie Cole, who was the best-selling jazz vocalist of the year. She was honored for *Take a Look,* but she performed "Mr. Sandman" on the Grammycast.

"Contemporary jazzman Pat Metheny may have won his eighth straight Grammy," *USA Today* reported, "but it was the first time he attended the event. 'I didn't know it was such a big deal,' he said."

Last year's victor Joe Henderson won two instrumental performance prizes for the year's best-selling jazz LP, *So Near, So Far (Musings for Miles),* his tribute to the late Miles Davis that spanned music from his first release, "Milestones," to one of his early fusion works, "Circle." On the press platform as he faced reporters backstage, the tenor saxman reveled in his newfound celebrity, saying, "I can't say I didn't like it better when things were simpler, but the view is nice from up here."

Miles Davis was honored in the ensemble category, along with Quincy Jones, for their work at the Montreux Swiss Jazz Festival, which was recorded just weeks before Davis's death.

B. B. King was acknowledged for having the year's Best Traditional Blues Album, *Blues Summit,* which included duets with John Lee Hooker, Ruth Brown, Robert Cray, Albert Collins, Lowell Fulson and Buddy Guy.

Guy was hailed in the separate category for contemporary works for *Feels Like Rain,* a collection of Marvin Gaye and James Brown songs featuring the Chicago guitarist performing with Bonnie Raitt, Paul Rodgers and Travis Tritt.

Bruce Hornsby and Branford Marsalis's Grammy for giving the year's Best Pop Instrumental Performance for "Barcelona Mona" was a sweet victory considering the struggle they had over naming the music. The piece was written for NBC's coverage of the 1992 Summer Olympics, but the peacock network thought that the Spanish hosts would find the title insulting. "So the web changed it to '29-5,' a reference to the world record long jump length," *Variety* reported. Backstage at the Grammys, "Hornsby said that the title lasted until he got into the studio to record. 'Now I get to call the shots, so I called it 'Barcelona Mona.' So I'm sure they're appalled.' "

A work recorded in Spain by the Paul Winter Consort, *Spanish Angel,* pulled off an upset in the category for new age works when it beat Yanni's megaseller *In My Time* and Tangerine Dream's comeback album, *220 Volt Live.* The six-person Consort performed original works that included a tribute to their flautist, who'd recently left them to pursue a solo career.

When this year's Grammy bids were announced, *Variety* insisted that the "country nominations yielded no surprises with Garth Brooks weighing in with a nom for best male country vocal for 'Ain't Going Down (Till the Sun Comes Up),' the first single off his *In Pieces* disc." Brooks was considered the front-runner because past Grammy grabber Vince Gill failed to make the race even though he recently swept the Country Music Association Awards. Brooks's only serious challenge seemed to come from Alan Jackson's huge hit "Chattahoochee," but Dwight Yoakam ended up scoring an upset with "Ain't That Lonely Yet," a tune described by *Entertainment Weekly* as "a big pop kiss-off to a black-hearted girlfriend."

Gill did end up sharing in the instrumental performance award along with Asleep at the Wheel, Chet Atkins and others who teamed up to do "Red Wing."

Mary-Chapin Carpenter held on to the female vocalist category for a third year in a row with "Passionate Kisses," which also earned the Best Country Song trophy for writer Lucinda Williams.

Newcomers were welcomed in the duo/group category when country music's top-selling team, Brooks & Dunn, followed up on their two-year reign at the Country Music Association Awards with their first Grammy, which they earned for "Hard Workin' Man." Neither artist appeared at the awards show to claim the trophy, however. One day before the event, Ronnie Dunn learned that his wife was pregnant, so he decided to stay home with her.

For the ninth year in a row, Reba McEntire ranked as America's best-selling female country singer, but she failed to be nominated in the solo category. Instead, she nabbed two bids for best country vocal collaboration: with Vince Gill for "The Heart Won't Lie" and with Linda Davis for "Does He Love You." "Love" prevailed.

Lots of past Grammy talent got resurrected in the religious categories.

Kathy Mattea was honored in the country competitions in 1990 but now was blessed in the religious races for *Good News,* winner of the new award for Best Southern Gospel, Country Gospel or Bluegrass Gospel Album.

> The Grammycast was long and pretentious, but not boring, *Variety* said.

Steven Curtis Chapman held on to the prize for contemporary gospel works for a third year in a row (*The Live Adventure*), while six-time past victor Shirley Caesar took the traditional soul gospel prize with an album that included more than music. In *Stand Still,* the pastor interspersed brief sermons imploring young people to spurn street violence.

The Winans earned their fifth career Grammy (Best Contemporary Soul Gospel Album) for their first new release since 1990, *All Out,* which included guest vocals by country singer Ricky Van Shelton.

First-time honorees reaped the prize for Best Rock Gospel Album—DC Talk, a group of graduates of Rev. Jerry Falwell's Liberty University whose initials stood for "decent Christian." Their dance-pop work *Free at Last* was their third album and a breakout hit that would reach platinum sales by 1995.

The big story in the Latin categories was the triumph of Selena, whose death 13 months after winning a Grammy for *Live* (Best Mexican-American Album) turned her into a cult hero.

At the time of the Grammys, 22-year-old Selena was considered the queen of Tejano music, having sold 400,000 copies of "Amor Prohibido (Forbidden Love)." When asked by the *San Jose Mercury News* to describe her work, she once said, "It's got polka in it, a little bit of country, a little bit of jazz. Fuse all those types of music together. I think that's where you get Tejano." *The New York Times* described her as a significant, emerging star: "With her pouting smile, suggestive clothing and theatrical command of a microphone, Selena was the Madonna of the Mexican American world and was an idol and heartthrob on both sides of the border." When she was shot and killed in April 1995 at a Days Inn in Corpus Christi, Texas, however, the slender beauty became an internally venerated music martyr. What made the death especially noteworthy—and eerie—was that she was murdered by the founder of her fan club.

Male heartthrob Luis Miguel last won a Grammy in 1983, but now he returned to claim the prize for Best Latin Pop Album for *Aires,* a collection of soulful love songs that was the second-best-selling Latin work of the year, topped only by Miguel's *Romance.* The latter album lost its bid in this category last year to Jon Secada's *Otro Día Más sin Verte,* but it went on to sell more than 4.5 million copies worldwide.

Gloria Estefan earned her first career Grammy for her first all-Spanish album, *Mi Tierra* (My Land), a tribute to her Cuban roots that included her hit dance single "Tradición."

Texas-born singer and songwriter Nanci Griffith took the trophy for contemporary folk music for *Other Voices/ Other Rooms,* her salute to the post-1960s folk music of Bob Dylan and Arlo Guthrie, who made guest appearances on the album.

After pulling off an upset for the traditional folk Grammy last year, the Chieftains retained the category with *The Celtic Harp,* their collaboration with the Belfast Harp Orchestra in remembrance of Edward Bunting, who hosted a legendary harpists' festival two centuries earlier.

Ex-Beatle George Harrison presented the award for Best World Music Album to Indian guitarist Vishwa Mohan Bhatt for *A Meeting by the River,* his collaboration with American picker Ry Cooder. Bhatt saluted his teacher, Ravi Shankar, who sat in the front row at the Grammy ceremony. Bhatt said, "This music is a small part of what he has given me."

The prize for Best Reggae Album *Bad Boys* was accepted by a member of Inner Circle, whom *Variety* singled out for its own award: "Best reggae outfit went to Lancelot Hall, decked in shaman hat and vest. The dreadlocked Hall said he didn't mind his reggae tunes being used for the real-life TV show *Cops* considering the current problem of police brutality against blacks. 'After meeting certain cops, we realized these guys were just human beings,' he said."

Maya Angelou, America's first poet laureate in 30 years, received the additional honor of a Grammy for Best Spoken Word or Nonmusical Album for *On the Pulse of Morning,* a work she recited at the presidential inauguration ceremony just two months earlier. *Variety* noted, "Angelou thanked President Bill Clinton for asking her to write the poem."

The new prize for Best Spoken Word Album for Children went to *Audrey Hepburn's Enchanted Tales,* a recording that featured the film star reciting such fairy tales as "Sleeping Beauty" and "Tom Thumb" to background music by Ravel, who once told the stories to her as a child.

Twenty-one years after nabbing his first Grammy gold for best comedy album, George Carlin came back for more with *Jammin' in New York.* "Before *Jammin',* I was on autopilot," he once said. "I was just a cute guy, a funny guy from the neighborhood talking about stuff. And then I formed this kind of feeling that this fucking thing sucks, this whole life experience."

Twenty-three years after it was written, *The Who's Tommy* finally premiered on Broadway but lost the Tony Award for Best Musical to *Kiss of the Spider Woman.* At the Grammys, the classic rock opera reversed the Who's fortunes to claim Best Musical Show Album.

Bartók's *The Wooden Prince* and *Cantata Profana,* performed by Pierre Boulez conducting the Chicago Symphony Orchestra and Chorus, scored four Grammys, including the laurels for orchestral and choral work, the engineering prize and Best Classical Album (Boulez's fourth victory in the top category). Earlier in his career, the French-born maestro had recorded *The Wooden Prince* when he was the music director of the New York Philharmonic, but more than just Grammy voters preferred his

latest version. "The sound is much better on this one," said *American Record Guide.*

Billboard noted an abundance of recent recordings of Berg's Violin Concerto, but insisted, "None brings it more authority than Anne-Sophie Mutter," winner of the soloist award (with orchestra). The other accolade for solo work went to John Browning for *The Complete Solo Piano Music* of Samuel Barber, who wrote his piano concerto for Browning in 1962.

Best Opera Recording was Handel's *Semele* performed by John Nelson conducting the English Chamber Orchestra and Ambrosian Opera Chorus. It was only the fourth recording of the work extant and it starred Kathleen Battle, who had recently been axed from the New York Metropolitan Opera for what some press reports called extreme diva behavior. Backstage at the Grammys, the album's producer, Steven Paul, defended Battle, saying, "She's highly professional, but she *is* a perfectionist."

Battle was not nominated for the vocalist's award, which went to Arleen Auger, who had died of a brain tumor at age 53 the previous June. The California-born soprano had captivated critics as a member of the Vienna State Opera and made headlines singing at the wedding of Britain's Prince Andrew and Sarah Ferguson.

The laurel for Best Contemporary Composition went to Elliott Carter for his three-movement, 25-minute violin concerto written in 1990 and performed on disc by Ole Bohn.

"Long, yes. Pretentious, often. But the Grammy Awards show was seldom boring," *Variety* said in its review of the ceremony.

Kenny G performed "Forever in Love," his winner of Best Instrumental Composition from the year's number-two-selling album.

"The tribute to Curtis Mayfield, fronted by musical heavyweights Bruce Springsteen, Bonnie Raitt, Steve Winwood and B. B. King, was also a program high point," *Variety* added, "as the veteran R&B artist and industry fixture looked on. Mayfield, paralyzed from the neck down, is one of the prime motivators for the creation by N.A.R.A.S. of the MusiCares program, which offers health care to members of the music industry.

"Billy Joel chimed in, during a live perf of his song 'The River of Dreams' with a stab at CBS. In between verses, he looked at his watch and said, 'Valuable advertising time going by. Dollars, dollars, dollars.' He smiled, then resumed playing."

The Grammycast was hosted by Garry Shandling for a fourth time in five years and it received a 16.1 rating/24 share—down 20 percent compared to last year—thereby becoming "the second-lowest rated version of the music special in two decades, topping only the 16.0/26 recorded in 1989," *Variety* reported. Perhaps comic David Letterman was scaring viewers away. He gave them the bird during commercial breaks.

• 1993 •

The awards ceremony was broadcast on CBS from Radio City Music Hall in New York City on March 1, 1994, for the eligibility period of October 1, 1992, through September 30, 1993.

ALBUM OF THE YEAR
• *The Bodyguard* (soundtrack), Whitney Houston. Arista.
Kamakiriad, Donald Fagen. Reprise.
River of Dreams, Billy Joel. Columbia.
Automatic for the People, R.E.M. Warner Bros.
Ten Summoner's Tales, Sting. A&M.

RECORD OF THE YEAR
• "I Will Always Love You," Whitney Houston. Arista.
"A Whole New World (*Aladdin*'s Theme)," Peabo Bryson, Regina Belle. Columbia & Walt Disney.
"The River of Dreams," Billy Joel. Columbia.
"If I Ever Lose My Faith in You," Sting. A&M.
"Harvest Moon," Neil Young. Reprise.

SONG OF THE YEAR
(Songwriter's Award)
• "A Whole New World (*Aladdin*'s Theme)," Alan Menken, Tim Rice.
"Harvest Moon," Neil Young.

"I'd Do Anything for Love (But I Won't Do That)," Jim Steinman.
"If I Ever Lose My Faith in You," Sting.
"The River of Dreams," Billy Joel.

BEST NEW ARTIST
• Toni Braxton
Belly
Blind Mellon
Digable Planets
SWV (Sisters with Voices)

BEST POP VOCAL PERFORMANCE, MALE
• Sting, "If I Ever Lose My Faith in You." A&M.
Boy George, "The Crying Game." SBK.
Billy Joel, "The River of Dreams." Columbia.
Aaron Neville, "Don't Take Away My Heaven." A&M.
Rod Stewart, "Have I Told You Lately." Warner Bros.

BEST POP VOCAL PERFORMANCE, FEMALE
• Whitney Houston, "I Will Always Love You." Arista.
Mariah Carey, "Dreamlover." Columbia.
Shawn Colvin, "I Don't Know Why." Columbia.
k. d. lang, "Miss Chatelaine." Sire/Warner Bros.

Tina Turner, "I Don't Wanna Fight." Virgin.

BEST POP PERFORMANCE BY A DUO OR GROUP WITH VOCAL

• Peabo Bryson, Regina Belle, "A Whole New World (*Aladdin*'s Theme)." Columbia & Walt Disney.

Celine Dion, Clive Griffin, "When I Fall in Love," track from *Sleepless in Seattle*. Epic Soundtrax.

R.E.M., "Man on the Moon." Warner Bros.

Barbra Streisand, Michael Crawford, "The Music of the Night," track from *Back to Broadway*. Columbia.

Vanessa Williams, Brian McKnight, "Love Is," track from *Beverly Hills, 90210* (soundtrack). Giant.

BEST TRADITIONAL POP VOCAL PERFORMANCE

• Tony Bennett, *Steppin' Out*. Columbia.

Rosemary Clooney, *Do You Miss New York?* Concord Jazz.

Michael Crawford, *A Touch of Music in the Night*. Atlantic.

Diane Schuur, *Love Songs*. GRP.

Barbra Streisand, *Back to Broadway*. Columbia.

BEST POP INSTRUMENTAL PERFORMANCE

• Bruce Hornsby, Branford Marsalis, "Barcelona Mona." RCA.

George Benson, "Got to Be There." Warner Bros.

Kenny G, "Forever in Love." Arista

James Galway conducting the Galway Pops Orchestra, "Beauty and the Beast," track from *Beauty and the Beast—Galway at the Movies*. Arista.

BEST ROCK SONG
(Songwriter's Award)

• "Runaway Train," David Pirner.

"Are You Gonna Go My Way," Lenny Kravitz, Craig Ross.

"Cryin'," Steven Tyler, Joe Perry, Taylor Rhodes.

"I'd Do Anything for Love (But I Won't Do That,)" Jim Steinman.

"Livin' on the Edge," Steven Tyler, Joe Perry, Mark Hudson.

BEST ROCK VOCAL PERFORMANCE, SOLO

• Meat Loaf, "I'd Do Anything for Love (but I Won't Do That)." MCA.

Peter Gabriel, "Steam." Geffen.

Lenny Kravitz, "Are You Gonna Go My Way," track from *Are You Gonna Go My Way*. Virgin.

Sting, "Demolition Man." A&M.

Neil Young, "All Along the Watchtower," track from *Bob Dylan—The 30th Anniversary Concert Celebration*. Columbia.

BEST ROCK PERFORMANCE BY A DUO OR GROUP WITH VOCAL

• Aerosmith, "Livin' on the Edge." Geffen.

Blind Melon, "No Rain." Capitol.

Bob Dylan, Roger McGuinn, Tom Petty, Neil Young, Eric Clapton, George Harrison, "My Back Pages," track from *Bob Dylan—The 30th Anniversary Concert Celebration*. Columbia.

Soul Asylum, "Runaway Train." Columbia.

Spin Doctors, "Two Princes." Epic/Associated.

BEST HARD ROCK PERFORMANCE WITH VOCAL

• Stone Temple Pilots, "Plush," track from *Core*. Atlantic.

AC/DC, "Highway to Hell." Atco.

Living Colour, "Leave It Alone." Sony Music.

Robert Plant, "Calling to You," track from *Fate of Nations*. Es Paranza/Atlantic.

Smashing Pumpkins, "Cherub Rock," track from *Siamese Dream*. Virgin.

BEST METAL PERFORMANCE WITH VOCAL

• Ozzy Osbourne, "I Don't Want to Change the World," track from *Live and Loud*. Epic Associated.

Iron Maiden, "Fear of the Dark," track from *A Real Live One*. Capitol.

Megadeth, "Angry Again," track from *Last Action Hero* (soundtrack). Columbia.

Suicidal Tendencies, "Institutionalized," track from *Still Cyco After All These Years*. Epic.

White Zombie, "Thunder Kiss '65." Geffen.

BEST ROCK INSTRUMENTAL PERFORMANCE

• Zappa's Universe Rock Group Featuring Steve Vai, "Sofa," track from *Zappa's Universe*. Verve.

Aerosmith, "Boogie Man," track from *Get a Grip*. Geffen.

Jeff Beck, Jed Beiber, "Hi-Heel Sneakers," track from *Frankie's House* (soundtrack). Epic.

Joe Satriani, "Speed of Light," track from *Super Mario Brothers* (soundtrack). Capitol.

Tangerine Dream, "Purple Haze," track from *220 Volt Live*. Miramar.

BEST ALTERNATIVE MUSIC ALBUM

• *Zooropa*, U2. Island.

Star, Belly. Sire/Reprise.

In Utero, Nirvana. Geffen.

Automatic for the People, R.E.M. Warner Bros.

Siamese Dream, Smashing Pumpkins. Virgin.

BEST RHYTHM & BLUES SONG
(Songwriter's Award)

• "That's the Way Love Goes," Janet Jackson, James Harris III, Terry Lewis.

"Anniversary," Raphael Wiggins, Carl Wheeler.

"Can We Talk," Babyface, Daryl Simmons.

"Heaven Knows," Luther Vandross, Reed Vertelney.

"Little Miracles (Happen Every Day)," Luther Vandross, Marcus Miller.

BEST RHYTHM & BLUES VOCAL PERFORMANCE, MALE

• Ray Charles, "A Song for You." Warner Bros.

Babyface, "For the Cool in You." Epic.

Tevin Campbell, "Can We Talk." Qwest/Warner Bros.

Teddy Pendergrass, "Voodoo." Elektra Entertainment.

Luther Vandross, "How Deep Is Your Love." Epic/LV.

BEST RHYTHM & BLUES VOCAL PERFORMANCE, FEMALE

• Toni Braxton, "Another Sad Love Song." La Face.

Aretha Franklin, "Someday We'll All Be Free," track from *Malcolm X Soundtrack*. Qwest/Reprise.

Whitney Houston, "I'm Every Woman." Arista.

Janet Jackson, "That's the Way Love Goes." Virgin.

Patti LaBelle, "All Right Now." MCA.

BEST RHYTHM & BLUES VOCAL PERFORMANCE BY A DUO OR GROUP WITH VOCAL

• Sade, "No Ordinary Love." Epic.

Boyz II Men, "Let It Snow." Motown.

Earth, Wind & Fire, "Sunday Morning," track from *Millennium*. Reprise.

En Vogue, "Give It Up, Turn It Loose," track from *Funky Divas*. EastWest America.

Tony Toni Tone, "Anniversary." Wing/Mercury.

BEST RAP SOLO PERFORMANCE

• Dr. Dre, "Let Me Ride." Interscope/Death Row.

L.L. Cool J, "Stand By Your Man." Def Jam/Columbia.

MC Lyte, "Ruffneck." First Priority/Atlantic.

Paperboy, "Ditty." Next Plateau.

Sir Mix-a-Lot, "Just da Pimpin' in Me," track from *Seattle . . . The Dark Side*. American Recordings/Rhyme Cartel.

BEST RAP PERFORMANCE BY A DUO OR GROUP

- Digable Planets, "Rebirth of Slick (Cool Like Dat)." Pendulum/Elektra.
Arrested Development, "Revolution." Chrysalis.
Cypress Hill, "Insane in the Brain." Ruffhouse/Columbia.
Dr. Dre, Snoop, "Nuthin' but a 'G' Thang." Interscope/Death Row.
Naughty by Nature, "Hip Hop Hooray." Tommy Boy.

BEST CONTEMPORARY JAZZ PERFORMANCE, INSTRUMENTAL

- Pat Metheny Group, *The Road to You*. Geffen.
Chick Corea Elektric Band II, *Paint the World*. GRP.
Fourplay, *Between the Sheets*. Warner Bros.
John Patitucci, *Another World*. GRP.
Yellowjackets, *Like a River*. GRP.

BEST JAZZ VOCAL PERFORMANCE

- Natalie Cole, *Take a Look*. Elektra.
Ernestine Anderson, *Now and Then*. Qwest/Reprise.
Shirley Horn, *Light out of Darkness*. Verve.
Bobby McFerrin, "*The Pink Panther Theme*," track from *Son of the Pink Panter* (soundtrack). RCA.
Bobby Short, Alden-Barrett Quintet, *Swing That Music*. Telarc.

BEST JAZZ INSTRUMENTAL SOLO

- Joe Henderson, "Miles Ahead," track from *So Near, So Far (Musings for Miles)*. Verve.
Benny Carter, "The More I See You," track from *Legends*. Musicmasters.
Herbie Hancock, "Brasil (Aquarela do Brasil)," track from *Kicking Cans*. Qwest/Warner Bros.
Lee Ritenour, "4 on 6," track from *Wes Bound*. GRP.
Phil Woods, "Nostalgico," track from *American Jazz Philharmonic*. GRP.

BEST JAZZ INSTRUMENTAL PERFORMANCE (INDIVIDUAL OR GROUP)

- Joe Henderson, *So Near, So Far (Musings for Miles)*. Verve.
Kenny Barron, *Sambao*. Verve.
Fred Hersch Trio, *Dancing in the Dark*. Chesky.
Joshua Redman, *Joshua Redman*. Warner Bros.
Lee Ritenour, *Wes Bound*. GRP.

BEST LARGE JAZZ ENSEMBLE PERFORMANCE

- Miles Davis, Quincy Jones, *Miles and Quincy Live at Montreux*. Warner Bros.
GRP All-Star Big Band, Tom Scott, *Dave Grusin Presents GRP All-Star Big Band Live*. GRP.
Jimmy Heath, *Little Man, Big Band*. Verve.
Rob McConnell, *The Boss Brass, Our 25th Year*. Concord Jazz.
Johnny Otis & His Orchestra, *Spirit of the Black Territory Bands*. Arhoolie.

BEST COUNTRY SONG
(Songwriter's Award)

- "Passionate Kisses," Lucinda Williams.
"Ain't That Lonely Yet," Kostas, James House.
"Chattahoochee," Alan Jackson, Jim McBride.
"Does He Love You," Sandy Knox, Billy Stritch.
"The Hard Way," Mary Chapin Carpenter.

BEST COUNTRY VOCAL PERFORMANCE, MALE

- Dwight Yoakam, "Ain't That Lonely Yet." Reprise.
Garth Brooks, "Ain't Going Down (Till the Sun Comes Up)," track from *In Pieces*. Liberty.
Alan Jackson, "Chattahoochee." Arista.
George Jones, "I Don't Need Your Rockin' Chair," track from *Walls Can Fall*. MCA.

Aaron Neville, "The Grand Tour," track from *The Grand Tour*. A&M.

BEST COUNTRY VOCAL PERFORMANCE, FEMALE

- Mary Chapin Carpenter, "Passionate Kisses." Columbia.
Emmylou Harris, "High Powered Love," track from *Cowgirl's Prayer*. Asylum.
Tanya Tucker, "Soon," track from *Soon*. Liberty.
Wynonna, "Only Love." Curb/MCA.
Trisha Yearwood, "Walkaway Joe." MCA.

BEST COUNTRY PERFORMANCE BY A DUO OR GROUP WITH VOCAL

- Brooks & Dunn, "Hard Workin' Man." Arista.
Confederate Railroad, "Trashy Women," track from *Confederate Railroad*. Atlantic.
Diamond Rio, "In a Week or Two." Arista.
Little Texas, "God Blessed Texas." Warner Bros.
Sawyer Brown, "All These Years." Curb.

BEST COUNTRY VOCAL COLLABORATION

- Reba McEntire, Linda Davis, "Does He Love You." MCA.
Clint Black, Wynonna, "A Bad Goodbye." RCA/Nashville.
Reba McEntire, Vince Gill, "The Heart Won't Lie." MCA.
Dolly Parton, Tanya Tucker, Billy Ray Cyrus, Kathy Mattea, Pam Tillis, Mary Chapin Carpenter, "Romeo." Columbia.
Ralph Stanley, Dwight Yoakam, "Miner's Prayer," track from *Saturday Night and Sunday Morning*. Freeland.

BEST COUNTRY INSTRUMENTAL PERFORMANCE

- Asleep at the Wheel, "Red Wing." Liberty.

Roy Clark, "Jingle Bells," track from *Christmas in Branson*. Laserlight Digital.
John McEuen, "The Ballad of Jed Clampett," track from *String Wizards II*. Vanguard.
Mark O'Connor, Byron Berline, "Gold Rush," track from *Heroes*. Warner Bros.
Mark O'Connor, Johnny Gimble, "Fiddlin' Around," track from *Heroes*. Warner Bros.

BEST ROCK GOSPEL ALBUM

- *Free at Last*, DC Talk. Forefront.
Heat It Up, DeGarmo & Key. Benson Music Group.
Pullin' No Punches, D.O.C. Star Song.
Crimson and Blue, Phil Keaggy. Myrrh.
Evolution, Geoff Moore & the Distance. ForeFront.

BEST POP/CONTEMPORARY GOSPEL ALBUM

- *The Live Adventure*, Steven Curtis Chapman. Sparrow.
Soul, Margaret Becker. Sparrow.
Hope, Michael English. Warner Alliance.
Le Voyage, Sandi Patti. Word.
A Beautiful Place, Wayne Watson. Dayspring/Word.

BEST SOUTHERN GOSPEL, COUNTRY GOSPEL OR BLUEGRASS GOSPEL ALBUM

- *Good News*, Kathy Mattea. Mercury.
Walk On, Bruce Carroll. Word.
Worship His Glory, Cathedrals. Canaan/Word.
Southern Classics, Gaither Vocal Band. Benson Music Group.
Sunday Morning, Ralph Stanley. Freeland.

BEST TRADITIONAL SOUL GOSPEL ALBUM

- *Stand Still*, Shirley Caesar. Word.
Live in Memphis, Canton Spirituals. Blackberry.

In Good Health, Dixie Hummingbirds. AIR.

Deep River, Five Blind Boys of Alabama Featuring Clarence Fountain. Elektra Nonesuch.

Better Days Ahead, Dorothy Norwood. Malaco.

He Keeps on Blessing Me, Albertina Walker. Benson Music Group.

BEST CONTEMPORARY SOUL GOSPEL ALBUM

• *All Out*, Winans. Warner Alliance.

Angie and Debbie, Angie & Debbie. Capitol.

Something on the Inside, Vanessa Bell Armstrong. Jive.

Start All Over, Helen Baylor. Word.

Live, Richard Smallwood Singers. Sparrow.

BEST GOSPEL ALBUM BY A CHOIR OR CHORUS

• *Live . . . We Come Rejoicing*, Brooklyn Tabernacle Choir; Carol Cymbala, choir director. Warner Alliance.

Rev. Milton Brunson Presents Tyrone Block and the Christ Tabernacle Combined Choirs, Rev. Milton Brunson, Tyrone Block & the Christ Tabernacle Combined Choirs; Tyrone Block, choir director. Word.

All the Bases, O'Landa Draper & the Associated Choir; O'Landa Draper, choir director. Word.

If You Love Me, Edwin Hawkins Music & Arts Seminar Choir; Edwin Hawkins, choir director. Fixit.

Amen! A Gospel Celebration, Erich Kunzel & the Cincinnati Pops with Jennifer Holliday, Maureen McGovern, Lou Rawls; Erich Kunzel, choir director. Telarc.

BEST TRADITIONAL FOLK ALBUM

• *The Celtic Harp*, Chieftains. RCA Victor.

Melody, Rhythm and Harmony, Le Mystère des Voix Bulgares. Mesa.

Friend of Mine, Bill Morrissey, Greg Brown. Philo.

Ancestral Voices, R. Carlos Nakai, William Eaton, Black Lodge Singers. Canyon.

Trace of Time, Steve Riley, Manou Playboys. Rounder.

Our Town, Jody Stecher, Kate Brislin. Rounder.

BEST CONTEMPORARY FOLK ALBUM

• *Other Voices/Other Rooms*, Nanci Griffith. Elektra.

La Danse de la Vie, BeauSoleil. Rhino/Forward.

Fat City, Shawn Colvin. Columbia.

Good As I Been to You, Bob Dylan. Columbia.

Spinning Around the Sun, Jimmie Dale Gilmore. Elektra.

Breaking Silence, Janice Ian. Morgan Creek.

BEST TRADITIONAL BLUES ALBUM

• *Blues Summit*, B. B. King. MCA.

Collins Mix, Albert Collins. Pointblank/Charisma.

Boom Boom, John Lee Hooker. Pointblank/Charisma.

Dancing the Blues, Taj Mahal. Private Music.

The Alligator Records 20th Anniversary Tour, various artists. Alligator.

BEST CONTEMPORARY BLUES ALBUM

• *Feels Like Rain*, Buddy Guy. Silvertone.

Mystic Mile, Robben Ford, Blue Line. Stretch.

Wake Up Call, John Mayall. Silvertone.

Muddy Mater Blues—A Tribute to Muddy Waters, Paul Rodgers. Victory Music.

Hey, Where's Your Brother? Johnny Winter. Pointblank/Charisma.

BEST BLUEGRASS ALBUM

• *Waitin' for the Hard Times to Go*, Nashville Bluegrass Band. Sugar Hill.

Stuart Duncan, Stuart Duncan. Rounder.
Blue Diamond, Johnson Mountain Boys.
    Rounder.
Tony Rice Plays and Sings Bluegrass,
    Tony Rice. Rounder.
Saturday Night (and Sunday Morning),
    Ralph Stanley. Freeland.

BEST LATIN POP ALBUM
• *Aries*, Luis Miguel. WEA Latina.
Imaginame, Maria Conchita Alonso.
    Sony Latin.
Brindo a la Vida, al Boléro, a Ti, Vikki
    Carr. Sony Latin.
Latin Street '92, Josáe Feliciano. Capi-
    tol/EMI Latin.
Algo Más Que Amor, Las Triplets. EMI
    Latin.

BEST TROPICAL LATIN ALBUM
• *Mi Tierra*, Gloria Estefan. Epic.
Hecho en Puerto Rico, Willie Colon.
    Sony Tropical.
Azúcar Negra, Celia Cruz. RMM/Sony.
First Class International, El Gran
    Combo de Puerto Rico. Combo.
Dilema, Luis Engrique. Sony Tropical.
Areito, Juan Luis Guerra, 4.40.
    Karen/BMG.

BEST MEXICAN-AMERICAN
ALBUM
• *Live*, Selena. Capitol/EMI Latin.
Lastima Que Seas Ajena, Vincente Fer-
    nandez. Sony Discos.
Corazón de Piedra, Santiago Jimenez,
    Jr. Watermelon.
Qué Paso? Little Joe. Tejano Discos.
La Garra de . . ., Los Tigres del Norte.
    Fonovisa.

BEST REGGAE ALBUM
• *Bad Boys*, Inner Circle. Big
    Beat/Atlantic.
Mystical Truth, Black Uhuru. Mesa.
The World Should Know, Burning Spear.
    Heartbeat.
Joy and Blues, Ziggy Marley, Melody
    Makers. Virgin.
Fe Real, Maxi Priest. Charisma.

BEST POLKA ALBUM
• *Accordionally Yours*, Walter Ostanek
    & His Band. WRS.
A New Batch of Polkas, Eddie Blazon-
    czyk's Versatones. Bel-Aire.
Most Requested Hits, Lenny Gomulka,
    Chicago Push. WRS.
Polka Music Fan, Polka Family Band.
    Polka Family.
Saturday Night Polka, Jimmy Sturr &
    His Orchestra. Starr.

BEST NEW AGE ALBUM
• *Spanish Angel*, Paul Winter Consort.
    American Gramaphone.
Banba, Clannad. Atlantic.
The Hours Between Night + Day,
    Ottmar Liebert, Luna Negra. Epic.
220 Volt Live, Tangerine Dream. Mira-
    mar.
In My Time, Yanni. Private Music.

BEST WORLD MUSIC ALBUM
• *A Meeting by the River*, Ry Cooder,
    V. M. Bhatt. Water Lily Acoustics.
Heat, Dust and Dreams, Johnny Clegg,
    Savuka. Capitol.
Deep Forest, Deep Forest. Epic.
A World out of Time, Vol. 2, Henry
    Kaiser, David Lindley. Shanachie.
From Blugaria with Love, Le Mystère
    des Voix Bulgares. Mesa.

BEST ARRANGEMENT ON AN
INSTRUMENTAL
• Dave Grusin, "Mood Indigo," track
    from *Homage to Duke* (Dave
    Grusin). GRP.
Michael Abene, "Oleo," track from
    *Dave Grusin Presents GRP All-Star
    Big Band Live!* GRP.
Vince Mendoza, "Buleria," track from
    *Jazzpana—The Mendoza/Mardin
    Project* (Vince Mendoza, Arif
    Mardin). Atlantic Jazz.
Arif Mardin, "Suite Fraternidad (1st and
    2nd Movements)," track from *Jaz-
    zpana—The Mendoza/Mardin Project*
    (Vince Mendoza, Arif Mardin).
    Atlantic Jazz.

Lalo Schifrin, "Dizzy Gillespie Fire-
works," track from *Jazz Meets the
Symphony* (Lalo Schifrin). Atlantic
Jazz.

BEST INSTRUMENTAL COMPOSITION
• "Forever in Love," Kenny G.
"Autumn," track from *Trio Brubeck*.
Dave Brubeck.
"Bill Evans," track from *Fictionary*.
Lyle Mays.
"Blue Miles," track from *Paint the
World*. Chick Corea.
"Half Life of Absolution," track from *The
Road to You*. Pat Metheny, Lyle Mays.

BEST MUSICAL SHOW ALBUM
• *The Who's Tommy—Original Cast
Recording*. Pete Townshend, com-
poser and lyricist. RCA Victor.
Bernstein: On the Town, various artists;
Michael Tilson Thomas, conductor.
Leonard Bernstein, composer; Betty
Comden, Adolph Green, lyricists.
Deutsche Grammophon.
*Joseph and the Amazing Technicolor
Dreamcoat*. Michael Damian and
cast. Andrew Lloyd Webber, com-
poser; Tim Rice, lyricist. Polydor.
Kiss of the Spider Woman. John Kander,
composer; Fred Ebb, lyricist. RCA
Victor.
*Sondheim: A Celebration at Carnegie
Hall*, various artists. Pete Townshend,
composer and lyricist. RCA Victor.

BEST INSTRUMENTAL COMPOSITION
WRITTEN FOR A MOTION PICTURE
OR TV
• *Aladdin*, Alan Menken.
The Age of Innocence, Elmer Bernstein.
The Firm, Dave Grusin.
Jurassic Park, John Williams.
A River Runs Through It, Mark Isham.

BEST SONG WRITTEN SPECIFICALLY
FOR A MOTION PICTURE OR TV
• "A Whole New World (*Aladdin*'s
Theme)," from *Aladdin*, Alan
Menken, Tim Rice.

"Friend Like Me," from *Aladdin*, Alan
Menken, Howard Ashman.
"I Don't Wanna Fight," from *What's
Love Got to Do with It,* Steve
DuBerry, Lulu Lawrie, Billy Lawrie.
"I Have Nothing," from *The Bodyguard*.
David Foster, Linda Thompson.
"Run to You," from *The Bodyguard*.
Allan Rich, Jud Friedman.

BEST INSTRUMENTAL
ARRANGEMENT ACCOMPANYING
VOCAL(S)
• Jeremy Lubbock, "When I Fall in
Love," track from *Sleepless in Seattle*
(Celine Dion, Clive Griffin). Epic.
David Foster, Jeremy Lubbock, "I Have
Nothing," (Whitney Houston). Arista.
Gary Hines, "Santa's Comin' to Town,"
track from *The Night Before Christ-
mas—A Musical Fantasy* (Sounds of
Blackness). Perspective.
Jeremy Lubbock, "Luck Be a Lady,"
track from *Back to Broadway* (Bar-
bra Streisand). Columbia.
Johnny Mandel, David Foster, "Some
Enchanted Evening," track from
Back to Broadway (Barbra
Streisand). Columbia.

BEST CLASSICAL ALBUM
• *Bartók: The Wooden Prince and Can-
tata Profana*, Pierre Boulez conduct-
ing the Chicago Symphony Orchestra
and Chorus; John Aler, tenor; John
Tomlinson, baritone. Deutsche
Grammophon.
*Berg: Violin Concerto; Rihm: Time
Chant*, James Levine conducting the
Chicago Symphony; Anne-Sophie
Mutter, violin. Deutsche Gram-
mophon.
*Debussy: Le Martyre de Saint-
Sébastien*, Michael Tilson Thomas
conducting the London Symphony;
McNair, Murray, Stutzmann, princi-
pal soloists; Sony Classical.
*If You Love Me (18th-Century Italian
Songs)*, Cecilia Bartoli, soprano;
Gyorgy Fischer, piano. London.

Venetian Vespers, Paul McCreesh conducting the Gabrieli Consort and Players. Archiv.

BEST ORCHESTRAL
PERFORMANCE
(Conductor's Award)

• Pierre Boulez conducting the Chicago Symphony, *Bartók: The Wooden Prince.* Deutsche Grammophon.

David Zinman conducting the Baltimore Symphony, *Barber: Adagio; Symphony No. 1; The School for Scandal; Essays.* Argo.

Pierre Boulez conducting the Cleveland Orchestra, *Debussy: Images; Printemps; Prélude à l'Après-Midi d'un Faune.* Deutsche Grammophon.

Ingo Metzmacher conducting the Ensemble Modern, *Ives: A Portrait of Charles Ives* (tracks 1–4, 6–10, 15–21, 23–25). EMI Classics.

Leonard Slatkin conducting the St. Louis Symphony, *Ives: Symphony No. 3; Three Places in New England; The Unanswered Question; Central Park in the Dark.* RCA Victor Red Seal.

BEST CHAMBER MUSIC
PERFORMANCE

• Emerson String Quartet, *Ives: String Quartets Nos. 1 and 2/Barber: String Quartet, Op. 11 (American Originals).* Deutsche Grammophon.

Itzhak Perlman, violin; Pinchas Zukerman, viola; Lynn Harrell, cello, *Beethoven: Complete String Trios, Opp. 3, 8 and 9.* EMI Classics.

Emanuel Ax, piano; Isaac Stern, violin; Jaime Laredo, viola; Yo-Yo Ma, cello, *Fauré: Piano Quartets Nos. 1 and 2.* Sony Classical.

Janos Starker, cello; Rudolf Firkusny, piano; *Martinu: Cello Sonatas Nos. 1–3.* RCA Victor Red Seal.

Girdon Kremer, violin; Martha Argerich, piano, *Prokofiev: Violin Sonatas Nos. 1 and 2; Melodies.* Deutsche Grammophon.

BEST CLASSICAL PERFORMANCE,
INSTRUMENTAL SOLOIST(S) (WITH
ORCHESTRA)

• Anne-Sophie Mutter, violin (James Levine conducting the Chicago Symphony), *Berg: Violin Concerto; Rihm: Time Chant.* Deutsche Grammophon.

Stephen Kovacevich, piano (Wolfgang Sawallisch conducting the London Philharmonic), *Brahms: Piano Concerto No. 1.* EMI Classics.

Richard Stoltzman, clarinet (Michael Tilson Thomas conducting the London Symphony), *Copland: Clarinet Concerto; Bernstein: Clarinet Sonata; Gershwin: 3 Preludes.* RCA Victor Red Seal.

Leon Fleisher, piano (Seiji Ozawa conducting the Boston Symphony), *Ravel: Piano Concerto for Left Hand/Prokofiev: Piano Concerto No. 4 for Left Hand; Britten: Piano Diversions (Left Hand).* Sony Classical.

Gil Shaham, violin (Giuseppe Sinopoli conducting the Philharmonia Orchestra), *Tchaikovsky: Violin Concerto; Sibelius: Violin Concerto.* Deutsche Grammophon.

BEST CLASSICAL PERFORMANCE,
INSTRUMENTAL SOLOIST
(WITHOUT ORCHESTRA)

• John Browning, piano, *Barber: The Complete Solo Piano Music.* MusicMasters.

Marc-Andre Hamelin, piano, *Alkan: Concerto for Solo Piano.* Music & Arts Program of America.

Andras Schiff, piano, *Bach: 6 French Suites, BWV 812–17.* London.

Richard Goode, piano, *Beethoven: Piano Sonatas Nos. 1–4, 8–12, 13–15, 19–27.* Elektra Nonesuch.

Leon Fleisher, piano, *Leon Fleisher Recital (Piano Works for Left Hand—Tackacs, Saint-Saëns, Bach, Scriabin).* Sony Classical.

BEST OPERA RECORDING

- *Handel: Semele*, John Nelson conducting the English Chamber Orchestra and Ambrosian Opera Chorus (solos: Battle, Horne, Ramey, Aler, McNair, Chance, Mackie, Doss). Philips Classics.

Adams: The Death of Klinghoffer, Kent Nagano conducting the Orchestra of the Opéra de Lyon and the London Opera Chorus (solos: Maddalena, Hammons, Sylvan, Friedman, Nadler). Elektra Nonesuch.

Britten: Gloriana, Sir Charles Mackerras conducting the Welsh National Opera Orchestra and Choir (solos: Barstow, Langridge, Opie, Kenny, Jones, Summers, Van Allan, Terfel, White). Argo.

Gluck: Iphigénie en Tauride, Riccardo Muti conducting the Orchestra e Coro del Teatro alla Scala (solos: Vaness, Allen, Winbergh, Surian, Brunet). Sony Classical.

Prokofiev: War and Peace, Valery Gergiev conducting the Kirov Orchestra and Chorus, St. Petersburg (solos: Gergalov, Prokina, Gregoriam, Borodina, Okhotnikov, Gerelo). Philips Classics.

BEST PERFORMANCE OF A CHORAL WORK

- Pierre Boulez conducting the Chicago Symphony Orchestra and Chorus; Margaret Hillis, choral director, *Bartók: Cantata Profana*. Deutsche Grammophon.

Roger Norrington conducting the London Classical Players and Schutz Choir of London, *Brahms: A German Requiem*. EMI Classics.

Michael Tilson Thomas conducting the London Symphony Orchestra and Chorus, *Debussy: Le Martyre de Saint-Sébastien*. Sony Classical.

Leonard Slatkin conducting the Philharmonia Orchestra and Chorus, *Vaughan Williams: A Sea Symphony*. RCA Victor Red Seal.

Paul McCreesh conducting the Gabrieli Consort and Players, *Venetian Vespers*. Archiv.

BEST CLASSICAL VOCAL PERFORMANCE

- Arleen Auger, soprano (Joel Revzen, accompanist), *The Art of Arleen Auger (Works of Larsen, Purcell, Schumann, Mozart)*. Koch International.

Gabriela Benackova, soprano (Rudolf Firkusny, accompanist), *Dvořák, Janáček, Martinu: Lieder*. RCA Victor Red Seal.

Sylvia McNair, soprano (John Eliot Gardiner conducting the Monteverdi Choir and English Baroque Soloists), *Exsultate Jubilate (Works of Handel, Mozart)*. Philips Classics.

Christa Ludwig, contralto (Charles Spencer, accompanist), *Farewell to Salzburg (Works of Brahms, Mahler, Schumann, Strauss)*. RCA Victor Red Seal.

Anne Sofie von Otter, soprano (Bengt Forsberg, accompanist), *Grieg: Lieder*. Deutsche Grammophon.

BEST CONTEMPORARY COMPOSITION

- Violin Concerto, Elliott Carter (Oliver Knussen conducting the London Sinfonietta; Ole Bohn, violin). Virgin Classics.

Orphee-Serenade, William Bolcom (Orpheus Chamber Orchestra). Deutsche Grammophon.

Cello Concerto, Donald Erb (Lynn Harrell, cello; Leonard Slatkin conducting the St. Louis Symphony). New World.

A Way a Lone, Toru Takemitsu (Tokyo String Quartet). RCA Victor Red Seal.

Byzantium , Michael Tippett (Sir Georg Solti conducting the Chicago Symphony; Faye Robinson, soprano). London.

BEST ENGINEERED RECORDING, CLASSICAL

- Rainer Maillard, *Bartók: The Wooden Prince and Cantata Profana* (Pierre Boulez conducting the Chicago Symphony). Deutsche Grammophon.

Henk Jansen, *Adams: The Death of Klinghoffer* (Kent Nagano conducting the Orchestra of the Opéra de Lyon). Elektra Nonesuch.

Marcus Herzog, *Debussy: Le Martyre de Saint-Sébastien* (Michael Tilson Thomas conducting the London Symphony). Sony Classical.

Jack Renner, *Haydn: The Creation* (Robert Shaw conducting the Atlanta Symphony and Chamber Chorus). Telarc.

Colin Moorfoot, *Tangazo—Music of Latin America* (Michael Tilson Thomas conducting the New World Symphony). Argo.

CLASSICAL PRODUCER OF THE YEAR

- Judith Sherman

Andrew Cornall

Michael Haas

Adam Stern

Robina G. Young

BEST SPOKEN COMEDY ALBUM

- *Jammin' in New York*, George Carlin. Eardrum/Atlantic.

Lake Wobegon U.S.A., Garrison Keillor. High Bridge.

Leslie Nielsen: The Naked Truth, Leslie Nielsen. Simon and Schuster Audioworks.

A Marriage Made in Heaven or Too Tired for an Affair, Erma Bombeck. Harper Audio.

You're Good Enough, You're Smart Enough, and Doggone It, People Like You! Al Franken. Bantam Doubleday Dell Audio.

BEST SPOKEN WORD OR NONMUSICAL ALBUM

- *On the Pulse of Morning*, Maya Angelou. Random House Audio Books.

Bound for Glory, Arlo Guthrie. Audio Literature.

Howard's End, Emma Thompson. Penguin-Highbridge.

Miles: The Autobiography, LeVar Burton. Audio Literature.

Mr. and Mrs. Bridge, Paul Newman, Joanne Woodward. Dove Audio.

BEST MUSICAL ALBUM FOR CHILDREN

- *Aladdin* (soundtrack), various artists. Walt Disney.

Barney's Favorites, Vol. 1, Barney & Friends. SBK.

The Muppet Christmas Carol (soundtrack), Muppets. Jim Henson.

Peter, Paul and Mommy, Too, Peter, Paul & Mary. Warner Bros.

Tim Burton's "The Nightmare Before Christmas" (soundtrack), various artists. Walt Disney.

BEST SPOKEN WORD ALBUM FOR CHILDREN

- *Audrey Hepburn's Enchanted Tales*, Audrey Hepburn. Dove Audio.

Aladdin Sound and Story Theater, various artists. Walt Disney.

Brer Rabbit and Boss Lion, Danny Glover, Dr. John. Rabbit Ears.

Did I Ever Tell You How Lucky You Are? (Dr. Seuss), John Cleese. Random House Audio.

The Muppet Christmas Carol Story Album, Muppets, Michael Cain, various others. Jim Henson Productions.

BEST ENGINEERED ALBUM (OTHER THAN CLASSICAL)

- Hugh Padgham, *Ten Summoner's Tales* (Sting). A&M.

Steve Hodge, Dave Rideau, *Janet* (Janet Jackson). Virgin.

Cesar Sogbe, Joe Galdo, *Lam Toro* (Baaba Maal). Mango.

Andy Wallace, Stan Katayama, G. G. Garth, *Rage Against the Machine* (Rage Against the Machine). Epic Associated.

Don Murray, *Wes Bound* (Lee Ritenour).
GRP.

BEST RECORDING PACKAGE
(Art Director's Award)
• David Lau, *The Complete Billie Holiday on Verve 1945–1959* (Billie Holiday). Verve.
David Coleman, *Live and Loud* (Ozzy Osbourne). Epic Associated.
Storm Thorgerson, Stylorouge, *Shine On* (Pink Floyd). Columbia.
Tom Recchion, Michael Stipe, Jeff Gold, Jim Ladwig, *Automatic for the People (2nd Set)* (R.E.M.). Reprise.
Kim Champagne, Jeff Gold, *14 Songs* (Paul Westerberg). Sire/Reprise.

BEST ALBUM NOTES
(Annotator's Award)
• Buck Clayton, Phil Schaap, Joel E. Siegel, *The Complete Billie Holiday on Verve 1945–1959* (Billie Holiday). Verve.
Colin Escott, *King of the Blues* (B. B. King). MCA.
Orrin Keepnews, Jim Ferguson, *The Complete Riverside Recordings* (Wes Montgomery). Riverside.
Peter Guralnick, *Elvis from Nashville to Memphis: The Essential 60's Masters I* (Elvis Presley). RCA.
Alan Lomax, Robert Palmer, *Sounds of the South—A Musical Journey from the Georgia Sea Islands to the Mississippi Delta Recorded in the Field by Alan Lomax* (various artists). Atlantic.

BEST HISTORICAL ALBUM
• *The Complete Billie Holiday on Verve 1945–1959,* Billie Holiday. Verve.
Noel Coward: The Masters' Voice—His HMV Recordings 1928–1953, Noel Coward. Angel.
Bing—His Legendary Years 1931–1957, Bing Crosby. MCA.

Frank Sinatra—The Columbia Years 1943–1952: The Complete Recordings, Frank Sinatra. Columbia/Legacy.
The Monterey International Pop Festival, various artists. Rhino.

PRODUCER OF THE YEAR (OTHER THAN CLASSICAL)
• David Foster
Walter Afanasieff
Tony Brown
Bruce Fairbairn
Jimmy Jam, Terry Lewis
Hugh Padgham

BEST MUSIC VIDEO, SHORT FORM
• *Steam,* Peter Gabriel. Stephen R. Johnson, director. Geffen.
Human Behaviour, Bjork. Michel Gondry, director. Elektra.
Beautiful Girl, INXS. Mark Pellington, director. Atlantic.
Everybody Hurts, R.E.M. Jake Scott, director. Warner Bros.
Runaway Train, Soul Asylum. Tony Kaye, director. Columbia.

BEST MUSIC VIDEO, LONG FORM
• *Ten Summoner's Tales,* Sting. Doug Nichol, director. A&M.
Canadian Brass: Home Movies, Canadian Brass. Niv Fichman, director. Rhombus Media.
Miles and Quincy Live at Montreux, Miles Davis, Quincy Jones. Gavin Taylor, Rudi Dolezal, Hannes Rossacher, directors. Reprise.
Rocky World, Daniel Lanois. Philip King, director. Warner Reprise Video.
Three Phase, Tangerine Dream. Michael Boydstun, director. Miramar.
A Celebration—A Musical Tribute to the Spirit of the Disabled American Veteran, Travis Tritt. Jack Cole, director. Warner Reprise Video.

• 1994 •
Unplugged Sets Off a Gusher

"**I**f the year belongs to anyone, it may be Bruce Springsteen," *Variety* foresaw when the nominations came out.

The 45-year-old rock legend received five bids for "Streets of Philadelphia," his haunting AIDS ballad featured in the film that won Tom Hanks an Oscar for Best Actor and the Boss one for Best Song. Now music pundits believed Springsteen was poised for the same kind of overdue Grammy coronation that Eric Clapton received two years earlier. Twice in the mid-1980s Springfield lost bids for Record of the Year ("Dancing in the Dark," "Born in the U.S.A."). Now the *Los Angeles Times* insisted, "He'll finally take home the prize."

It was so widely expected that Grammy night would belong to Springsteen that the telecast opened with him performing "Streets" while backed up by members of his old E Street Band as he sang:

*I walked the avenue till my legs felt like
  stone
I heard the voices of friends vanished
  and gone
at night I could hear the blood in my
  veins
black and whispering in the rain
on the streets of Philadelphia*

"I had tears in my eyes as I watched," Melissa Etheridge told reporters.

Best song champ Bruce Springsteen may have "led the awards charge," as *Variety* noted, but he lost best record to Sheryl Crow.

A few minutes after Springsteen left the stage, he returned to receive the first of four Grammys. It was the writer's prize for Song of the Year, which was presented to him by a playful Annie Lennox, who wore a shiny plastic minidress, Mickey Mouse ears and a dog collar. Springsteen thanked "the folks who have come up to me in restaurants and on the street who have lost their sons or their lovers or their friends to AIDS and said that the song meant something to them."

He also received the awards for best movie song, Best Rock Song and best rock vocals. He looked puzzled as he accepted the last honor. "I'm not sure this is a rock vocal," he grumbled, then thanked "all those disparaged and mysterious Grammy voters out there." He spoke with some authority on the subject. The only Grammys he'd won prior to this year were in the same rock category (1984, 1987).

"Everyone in the Western World fully expected to see him back at the podium to accept the best record award," the *L.A. Times* wrote. The odds were certainly on his side: The music that won Grammy's Song of the Year also won Record of the Year 6 out of the past 10 years.

But an upset rocked the category.

The only nominee that seemed to have a chance to beat "Streets of Philadelphia" was Boyz II Men's "I'll Make Love to You," which was picked to win by the *New York Times* and *Entertainment Weekly.* (*Billboard* and E! Entertainment network joined the *L.A. Times* in siding with Springsteen.) But instead voters embraced a 32-year-old artist who'd been toiling for years in the L.A. music scene as a backup vocalist and writer. Now after the release of her breakout debut album, *Tuesday Night Music Club* (2 million in sales), Sheryl Crow reached for music's highest honor by appealing to the thousands of N.A.R.A.S.'s California voters with feel-good lyrics full of local Los Angeles color: "*All I wanna do is have some fun . . . / till the sun comes up over Santa Monica Boulevard.*"

Crow had been dubbed "the thinking man's party girl" for the cavalier bohemian attitude of the song described by the *L.A. Times* as "an idiosyncratic adaptation of a poem about seedy bar habitués mocking the passing Joes who have actual jobs." But "All I Wanna Do" was a huge radio hit and a popular video on VH1 and MTV, which fueled the surge behind the artist who scored additional Grammys for pop vocals (in an upset over Mariah Carey's "Hero") and Best New Artist. The combination of two of those honors was ominous: The last performer to win both best record and the newcomer's prize was Christopher Cross, who soon sailed off into music oblivion after his 1980 Grammy sweep.

Crow had been the odds-on favorite to win the new artist category, but her victory in the other top slot came as a

> "This year's awards came under particular fire," *Variety* noted.

shocker even to the head of her recording label. A&M President Al Cafaro told reporters: "I was completely surprised by the Record of the Year award."

L.A. Times critic Robert Hilburn was furious about it: "It tells you how haywire the Grammy voting is that Springsteen lost to Crow. She's a spunky singer, but there's no way 'All I Wanna Do' deserves to win anything short of a Rickie Lee Jones sound-alike contest."

The music that scored the Album of the Year trophy turned out to be even *more* controversial.

Entertainment Weekly once again proved to be a lousy prognosticator when it predicted Eric Clapton's *From the Cradle* would win the honor. *The New York Times* disagreed: "Bonnie Raitt's *Longing in Their Hearts* is the most plausible choice with heartfelt, well-made new songs by a previous winner." *People* picked *The Three Tenors in Concert*, featuring José Carreras, Placido Domingo and Luciano Pavarotti in a performance at Dodger Stadium that reunited them as a follow-up to their hit 1990 joint appearance in Rome. Curiously, the same recording was *not* nominated for Classical Album of the Year but *was* in the running for the new award for Best Pop Album. (New categories were also added this year for Best Country, Rock and R&B Albums.)

The winner turned out to be the nominee backed by the *L.A. Times* and E!— Tony Bennett, who claimed the top album honor 32 years after he won the Record of the Year award for "I Left My Heart in San Francisco."

"Tony Bennett has enjoyed a remarkable career resurgence over the past two years," *Variety* observed.

Bennett was back in vogue thanks to his manager son, Danny, who orchestrated an amazing comeback. He got his dad a cameo on the hip cartoon series *The Simpsons,* a star role singing at Super

Bowl halftime and even a gig that must have shaken up the slacker crowd watching cable TV's rock music channel: Bennett hosted an *MTV Unplugged* concert that featured the 68-year-old saloon singer teamed up with Elvis Costello ("They Can't Take That Away from Me") and k. d. lang ("Moonglow"). Referring to the latter combo, *Entertainment Weekly* wisecracked, "Back when Bennett ruled the charts, who would have predicted that some day his duet with a Canadian lesbian vegetarian country recording artist might be a wise career move?"

Bennett certainly didn't think so at first, according to *Life* magazine. "Hey, what's going on?!" he griped to his son. "I'm used to playing nice rooms!" Danny retorted, "Trust me." *Life* noted that Bennett was soon the "unlikely darling of the green-haired, alternative-music crowd . . . 40 years after 5,000 girls chased him across a Brooklyn park."

An *MTV Unplugged* recording was the lucky break that earned Eric Clapton an Album of the Year award two years ago; now it worked for Bennett, too. It also earned him the laurels for best traditional pop vocalist for a third consecutive year.

"I can't believe this! I really can't believe this!" Bennett said, beaming, as he accepted the album award.

"He wasn't alone," an outraged *L.A. Times* added. Bennett's recording had not made the Top 10 list of a single notable critic weighing in on the year's best music. Now lots of Grammy gripers would soon weigh in heavily against its awards success, forcing N.A.R.A.S. to consider drastic voting reforms in the future.

Elton John had a long history of being slighted by the Grammys, especially in the top categories. Twice he suffered defeats in the Album of the Year race (1970, 1975) and once for Record of the Year (1974). Perhaps his most humiliating loss was to the Carpenters for Best New Artist of 1970. This year he had two bids for Song of the Year—"Can You Feel the Love Tonight" and "Circle of Life" from Disney's hit animated film *The Lion*

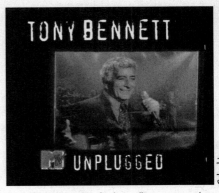

Tony Bennett's victory for best album triggered an uproar, forcing the recording academy to consider radical new voting reforms next year.

Columbia

King—but they canceled each other out in the voting. He ended up with the consolation prize for male pop vocals for "Can You Feel the Love Tonight?," which had previously won him the Golden Globe for best movie song. John's new Grammy was his first for solo performance work. He'd won a golden gramophone for his small role in the ensemble song "That's What Friends Are For," which took 1986's pop group vocals award. Other than that, the only other Grammy he'd ever won was for 1991's Best Instrumental Composition, "Basque," which was recorded by flautist James Galway.

A number of artists who'd never won a Grammy finally scored this year. For nearly three decades, Pink Floyd remained key players on the music scene despite setbacks that included the departure of their leader, Roger Waters. In mid-1994, their comeback U.S. concert tour drew more than 3 million fans. Soon afterward, the Grammy wall finally fell when they won their first award, Best Rock Instrumental Performance, for "Marooned."

Booker T and the MG's had been nominated for an award in 1967 for "Hip-Hug-Her," but the soul/rock group finally nabbed a Grammy for Best Pop Instrumental Performance for "Cruisin'," its first single release in nearly 18 years.

Among the Grammy-slighted, no artists loomed larger than the Rolling Stones, however. They'd never won a prize in a competitive category, although they *were* given an honorary Lifetime Achievement Award in 1985. Their luck finally changed this year with *Voodoo Lounge,* the British rockers' 17th platinum album and the first for their new label, Virgin. It claimed the new Grammy for Best Rock Album in an upset over *Monster* by R.E.M. The Stones also claimed a second Grammy (best short-form video) for their hit single "Love Is Strong." The video version cost more than $1 million to produce because of the elaborate computer graphics used to enlarge the rock titans to Godzilla size in a city setting. They were not on hand to accept their prizes, however, since they were performing in Japan while on a world tour.

"Few people take the Grammys seriously," David Geffen fumed.

The Producer of the Year award went to the Rolling Stones' overseer, Don Was, also the business brains behind Bonnie Raitt, who was tied with the most nominations this year (five), including bids for Record and Album of the Year. *Longing in Their Hearts* ended up winning Best Pop Album, a category *Variety* described as having an unlikely roundup of nominees: "Oddly enough, Seal is up against Lyle Lovett, Ace of Base, Raitt and the Three Tenors for the pop album award. Try finding *anyone* who owns all five of those discs."

Lyle Lovett ended up winning two Grammys, one for best pop vocal collaboration with Al Green ("Funny How Time Slips Away"). *Variety* called the victory "the first total upset" on Grammy night, adding, "They beat Tony Bennett and k. d. lang, who had performed their pop vocal collaboration 'Moonglow' right before the award. "Green, clearly surprised by the win, accepted the nod on behalf of Lovett, who was injured this week in a motorcycle accident."

Lovett's second prize was for teaming up with Asleep at the Wheel for best country duo/group vocals ("Blues for Dixie"). It was accepted by Wheel's Ray Benson, who told the Grammy crowd that his partner was "really hurting" from a broken collarbone.

"The female rock performance category, eliminated last year because of insufficient entries, is back and is particularly strong," *Variety* announced, citing the inclusion of such critics' favorites as first-time nominee Liz Phair. Claiming the slot, however, was the winner from two years ago, Melissa Etheridge, who prevailed with "Come to My Window" after having a high-flying year on the charts.

Aerosmith returned to reclaim the category for rock group performances with *Crazy* after recently sweeping the MTV Video Awards with three prizes, including Video of the Year (*Cryin'*—not nominated for the equivalent Grammy). The 40-year-old rockers beat the twenty-something Seattle grunge group Nirvana, who many pundits thought would win with a strong sympathy vote after the suicide of its frontman, Kurt Cobain.

Variety noted, "The vital music of '94, in sales and newsworthiness, continued to emerge from Seattle, and yet Soundgarden, Nirvana and Pearl Jam are relegated to the less-important categories of hard rock and alternative."

Soundgarden took the awards for both hard rock ("Black Hole Sun") and metal ("Spoonman") and they used their victories as a chance to sound off with their own Grammy gripes. Singer Chris Cornell told reporters, "It seems like from the nominations and winners that the Grammys are probably out of touch. It doesn't cover a broad spectrum and if that means younger or harder-edged styles get short shrift, tough."

The prize for alternative music went to Berkeley, California–based punk trio

Green Day for *Dookie,* which *Time* hailed as "the best rock CD of the year." *Variety* added, "Although many N.A.R.A.S. critics would have preferred that Nine Inch Nails get the honor, the nod to Green Day—which has sold more than 6 million units—may indicate the org's voters are not as far afield as some record label chiefs have suggested."

Last year's winner of the award for alternative music, U2, reaped the long-form video award for a VHS tape, using 28 cameras, of a concert they gave at a soccer stadium in Sydney, Australia, during their recent world tour.

Grammy's Best New Artist and top female r&b vocalist of 1993, Toni Braxton, held on to the r&b laurels with "Breathe Again," fending off a challenge from four-time queen of the category Anita Baker. It was an ironic victory, since Braxton got her first big career break while once standing in for a pregnant Baker when the latter couldn't make it to the recording studio to sing "Love Shoulda Brought You Home," which went on to become a hit.

Braxton's producer and the writer of "Breathe," Babyface, nabbed the male r&b crown for "When Can I See You" over previous champs Luther Vandross and Al Jarreau and a particularly strong bid by the un-Grammyed Barry White. The tune was up against two other Babyface works for Best R&B Song: "I'll Make Love to You" and "You Mean the World to Me." After "Love" prevailed, *Variety* asked the songwriter backstage if he'd won for the right one. "I wished I could have won for 'When Can I See You,' but I'll take this," he said, waving the golden gramophone.

Although Boyz II Men's rendition of "I'll Make Love to You" lost its bid for Record of the Year, it made music history. Their earlier hit "End of the Road" had set a record in 1992 for spending the most weeks topping the charts (13), a milestone soon surpassed by Whitney's Houston's "I Will Always Love You." The Boyz "Love" ended up tying the new record in 1994 by

Motown

Exposure from her TV sitcom surely helped Queen Latifah to claim the rap solo award for "U.N.I.T.Y.," a track from *Black Reign.*

remaining at number one for 14 weeks and also earned them the Grammy for Best R&B Group Performance for a third time in four years. They also grabbed more gold for Best R&B Album for their sophomore release *II,* which sold 7 million copies as of Grammy night.

In the rap categories, the *L.A. Times* reported, "This year some fairly hardcore nominees were included—but by default, since so little pop-rap is being recorded these days. So artists like Cypress Hill, Coolio and Warren G had to get nominations. It's no surprise, though, that they didn't win. Given the voting tendencies, the less-threatening female rap artists—Queen Latifah and Salt-N-Pepa—were a shoo-in for Grammys."

The *L.A. Times* predicted early on that the 25-year-old star of the TV sitcom *Living Single* would take the rap solo honor for "U.N.I.T.Y.," a single from *Black Reign,* her first album on Motown after breaking with the Tommy Boy label. The paper's reasoning: "Queen Latifah has a high TV profile and a positive image—

two of the factors that helped D.J. Jazzy Jeff and the Fresh Prince become two-time Grammy winners."

Salt-N-Pepa took the rap group gold for "None of Your Business" over 1992's Best New Artist Arrested Development ("Ease My Mind") and the duo the *New York Times* was betting on—Warren G & Nate Dogg ("Regulate").

"Country wins ran among the expected," *Variety* noted.

Mary Chapin Carpenter's prominence at this year's Grammys could be seen high up in the top category where "He Thinks He'll Keep Her" became the first country tune to compete for Record of the Year without being a Top 40 hit. In the female vocalist competition, however, she was nominated for "Shut Up and Kiss Me," taking it easily for a fourth year in a row. Both songs were from *Stones in the Road,* her fifth album and her first comprised of all self-written music. It was also a megaseller, reaching the top of the charts just two weeks after its release, and was an easy winner of the first new Best Country Album award.

Five-time past Grammy grabber Vince Gill reclaimed the male vocalist slot with "When Love Finds You," capping off his recent sweep of the Country Music Association Awards. He was hailed C.M.A.'s Entertainer of the Year for a second time and became the only artist to win the organization's male vocalist prize for four consecutive years. When he nabbed the equivalent Grammy for vocals this year, he prevailed over John Michael Montgomery's "I Swear," which had been picked to win by *Entertainment Weekly.*

"I Swear" won Best Country Song in addition to garnering a nomination in the top Song of the Year category. Montgomery's recording topped the country charts for four weeks and was hailed as best single at the C.M.A. Awards. The tune was also hailed worldwide, becoming a hit in 26 language versions.

It was the rendition sung by the multiracial male quartet All-4-One that scored the biggest success, including the Grammy for pop group vocals. The recording hovered over the pop charts for 11 weeks, tying the fourth-place record held by Elvis Presley's "Hound Dog/ Don't Be Cruel."

At the Grammycast, the two award winners teamed up. *Variety* reported, "High among the bright spots on the show was the joint performance of 'I Swear' by country singer John Michael Montgomery and r&b group All-4-One."

A new recording of the Patsy Cline classic "I Fall to Pieces" reaped the Best Country Vocal Collaboration prize for Aaron Neville and Trisha Yearwood. "We both just came into the studio and started singing, and it was like we'd been singing together for a long time," Neville told *Billboard.* "Winning a Grammy for it was so cool." *Variety* reminded readers, "The song was shunned by country radio." Backstage at the Grammys, Yearwood elaborated: "Country radio was not incredibly user-friendly on the song. The country audience probably would have gone for it, but they just didn't get the opportunity to hear it on the radio."

Chet Akins received his thirteenth career Grammy for Best Country Instrumental Performance of "Young Thing," a track from *Read My Licks,* which also featured duets with George Benson, Steve Wariner and Eric Johnson.

Johnny Cash had seven past Grammys to his credit, but he hadn't struck any new gold since 1986 while his career seemed to dip. The Man in Black now earned the prize for Best Contemporary Folk Album for *American Recordings,* his first new work in three years. It was "a dream album," he told the press, full of self-written songs and others by Kris Kristofferson and rocker Glen Danzig. *Time* noted, "Cash's voice has deepened with age. His guitar work is direct and intimate—an old cowboy strumming away around a dying campfire."

The Grammys had certainly been less generous to Bob Dylan through the years. He had two awards, one for his cameo role in 1972's Album of the Year, *The Concert for Bangla Desh,* and then a shocking victory when one of his religious songs ("Gotta Serve Somebody") claimed the first of the new rock & roll awards instituted for 1979. He now won Best Traditional Folk Album for *World Gone Wrong,* which included such soulful works as two songs by late Georgia bluesman Willie McTell and a tribute tune written in memory of him by Dylan.

The prize for Best New Age Album went to soprano saxman Paul Winter for *Prayer for the Wild Things,* on which he incorporated the wild calls of wolves, ravens, eagles and coyotes.

The year's Best Bluegrass Album was *The Great Dobro Sessions,* an ensemble collection of blues, jazz and even Beatles music by such various artists as Mike Auldridge, Oswald Kirby and Sally Van Meter.

Eric Clapton's losing nominee for Album of the Year, *From the Cradle,* rebounded to claim Best Traditional Blues Album. The work recalled his early blues heyday in London with the Bluesbreakers in the mid-1960s and was comprised of seven original works and several classics such as Willie Dixon's "Hoochi Coochie Man," Lowell Fulson's "Sinner's Prayer" and James Lane's "Blues Leave Me Alone." *Time* magazine said, "Clapton's playing lacks fire, but in its place he brings a great worldliness, something that sounds like wisdom."

Eighty-year-old Chicago guitarist and gospel singer Roebuck "Pops" Staples earned his first career Grammy for Best Contemporary Blues Album, *Father Father.*

"It wasn't exactly an adventurous year for jazz Grammy nominations," the *L.A. Times* griped, "with virtually no entries from such exciting young performers as Joshua Redman and Cyrus Chestnut. So it's no surpirse that the academy, despite its professed interest in youth, chose to honor veterans and push aside the few young performers nominated.

"Still, there's no arguing with the best

jazz instrumental performance award for Herbie Hancock, Ron Carter, Tony Williams, Wayne Shorter and Wallace Roney's *Tribute to Miles.* In an otherwise not especially distinguished list of performances, the album stands out both as a reminder of the group's golden past and as world-class contemporary jazz." All of the album artists, except Roney, had performed with Miles Davis during the 1960s. The recording was from the five artists' 1992 world tour and included such cuts as "Eighty One," "Pinocchio" and "All Blues." Backstage at the Grammys, Hancock said about making the memorial album: "It was almost painful to do it."

Lena Horne was expected to take the jazz vocals statuette, but the surprise victory of first-timer Etta James capped a celebratory occasion: her 40th anniversary in music. After years of drug and alcohol abuse, James was now sober, which inspired her to record the Grammy-winning *Mystery Lady,* a tribute to friend and idol Billie Holiday, who'd once warned her against the vices. James wrote in her autobiography, "Maybe she saw the wildness in my eyes, maybe she saw all the trouble waiting for me."

The GRP label responded to the recent reunion of brothers Michael and Randy Brecker with a major marketing push behind *Out of the Loop,* which scored several nominations and earned them the trophy for Best Contemporary Jazz Performance. Michael Brecker was also honored individually for Best Instrumental Composition for the album track "African Skies." The category was dominated by jazz artists and was expected to be won by Benny Carter. The 87-year-old sax legend Carter nonetheless claimed the separate prize for Best Jazz Instrumental Solo for "Prelude to a Kiss."

The *L.A. Times* predicted a win in the large jazz ensemble category for one of two relative newcomers, either Toshiko Akiyoshi ("Desert Lady/Fantasy") or Carla Bley ("Big Band Theory"). But the award went to the McCoy Tyner Big Band for *Journey,* which featured "Tyner's rhythmic conception bursting and rolling on the uptempo tunes even when he's laying out," according to *Down Beat*.

The Latin jazz slot was especially competitive, with the front-runner considered to be Mario Bauza (*944 Columbus*), who died in 1993. Cuban trumpeter Arturo Sandoval took it instead with *Danzón*, a collection of Afro-Cuban jazz, mariachi music and a work by Mozart with guest vocals by such stars as Gloria Estefan and Vikki Carr.

Vikki Carr nabbed her third career Grammy for *Recuerdo a Javier Solis,* a tribute to the *bolero ranchero* master. She beat last year's winner of the same category for Best Mexican-American Performance, Selena, who would be murdered one month after this year's awards ceremony.

Luis Miguel received his third Grammy and second in a row for Best Latin Pop Album (*Segundo Romance*), going *mano a mano* with such superstar nominees as six-time past Grammy champ Placido Domingo. Miguel's latest album included new ballads like "El Día Que Me Quieras" and remixes of such 1940s classics as "Nosotros" and "Delirio."

Seventy-six-year-old Israel "Cachao" Lopez was acknowledged with giving the Best Tropical Latin Performance for *Master Sessions, Vol. 1*. The *L.A. Times* cheered: "Cachao won with a truly masterful record that could've beaten anyone's, even in the Latin jazz department. The Cuban bassist and orchestra leader, arguably the real father of mambo, beat another fine work by Juan Luis Guerra in a category in which the smoking-hot Japanese salsa band Orquesta de la Luz was also nominated."

The career of veteran Jamaican reggae star Bunny Wailer dates back to the 1960s when he performed with Bob Marley's Wailers, then went solo in the mid-1970s, scoring his first Grammy in 1990 for a tribute to his old mentor. Now he won again for a collection of original Wailers recordings that Bunny selected

such as "Boderation," "Struggle" and "Power Strugglers."

Two guitar greats, Ali Farka and Ry Cooder, nabbed Best World Music Album for *Talking Timbuktu*. *Variety* noted that an "offstage announcer pronounced Ry Cooder's name as 'Randy Cowder.' Surprisingly everybody got nominee Me'shell NdegeOcello's name right."

In the religious categories, Petra earned its third career Grammy for Best Rock Gospel Album, *Wake-up Call,* which had just won the equivalent prize at the Dove Awards bestowed by the Gospel Music Association.

Andrae Crouch had won six Grammys between 1975 and 1984 but had been noticeably absent since then while the gospel singer retired in order to devote more attention to his family and church. "During that time, recording seemed secondary," he told *American Visions* magazine. In his comeback work, *Mercy* (Best Pop/Contemporary Gospel Album), he explored an adventurous new mix of reggae and African rhythms. "Africa is the cradle of civilization, where history began," he said. "This celebrates God's mercy down through the ages." Crouch was also one of three winners of Best Instrumental Arrangement Accompanying Vocal(s) for "Circle of Life."

The 23-year-old megastar of modern bluegrass, Alison Krauss, recorded many Cox Family songs during her nine-year career. On her Grammy-winning *I Know Who Holds Tomorrow* (Best Southern Gospel, Country Gospel or Bluegrass Gospel Album), she teamed up with them in a work that helped launch the brood's own recording career.

The former member of the Caravans, Albertina Walker, won Best Traditional Soul Gospel Album for *Songs of the Church—Live in Memphis,* comprised of such classic hymns as "O Lord, Remember Me."

The jazz/gospel sextet Take 6 scored their sixth Grammy, a victory for Best Contemporary Soul Gospel Album *Join the Band*. Group member David Thomas told *The Ethnic NewsWatch:* "We felt that we had taken a cappella to its furthest extent and it was time for us to move on." In their new work, they teamed up with keyboardist Herbie Hancock, saxman Gerald Albright and singers Stevie Wonder and Ray Charles.

There was a tie for winner of Best Gospel Album by a Choir or Chorus. On *Through God's Eyes,* Rev. Milton Brunson and the Thompson Community Singers recorded its 10 songs at Christ Tabernacle Baptist Church in Chicago, 6 of which were written by musical director Darius Brooks.

Billboard called cowinner *Live in Atlanta at Morehouse College* "a rousing affair" recorded by the Rev. Hezekiah Walker's Love Fellowship Crusade Choir of Brooklyn. The *New York Daily News* noted that the young group did not attend the Grammys or watch it together on TV, since most members had jobs or attended school. "A couple of us could have gone, but we had a recording on Monday," one of them said. Their business manager added, "Seven of us had just finished having prayer when we heard we won. We started jumping up and down. We hugged each other and thanked God."

Rock star Henry Rollins beat recordings of actor Kenneth Branagh performing *Hamlet* and Gregory Peck reading the Bible to take the prize for Best Spoken World or Nonmusical Album. He was honored for the audio version of his self-published book *Get in the Van: On the Road with Black Flag,* a memoir of his days as a gypsy rock artist before he set up the Rollins Band. Backstage at the Grammys, wearing only a green T-shirt and shorts, he told reporters why he deserved to beat Shakespeare and the Bible, saying, "Those are wonderful tales, but they've been told many times. I think my thing was a little fresher. I don't think anybody could stay awake for Gregory Peck reading all of the Bible."

Walt Disney's animated hit *The Lion King* reaped both prizes for children's recordings. The soundtrack was named

Best Musical Album. *Benson* TV star Robert Guillaume was among the actors performing on the read-along version that won Best Spoken Word Album for Children.

It was ironic that devilish comedian Sam Kinison should die so soon after the release of *Live from Hell,* which went on to win Best Spoken Comedy Album. There were cruel ironies involved in his death, too. The same comic who often encouraged his club audiences to drink and drive was killed in 1992 by an allegedly inebriated 17-year-old, who smashed into his vehicle, staggered out of the wreckage and exclaimed, "God! Look at my truck!"

At the Tonys, the Best Musical trophy went to Stephen Sondheim's *Passion,* about an older woman's obsession with a young solider. At the Grammys, it won Best Musical Show Album over the recordings of two other Broadway shows that won Tony's Best Musical award in other years: *Sunset Blvd.* (1995) and *Crazy for You.* (1992). This recording used an orchestra that was expanded from the Broadway production.

The Verve label won a Grammy last year for Best Historical Album for *The Complete Billie Holiday on Verve 1945–1959* and now scored two prizes for *The Complete Ella Fitzgerald Song Books on Verve*: Best Historical Album and the new award for Best Album Package, Boxed. (The CDs are contained in a plastic reproduction of a vintage 1940s radio.) Fitzgerald's *Song Books* grabbed Grammy's attention in earlier years. Her *Irving Berlin Song Book* was nominated for 1958's Album of the Year and won the vocal performance award that year; her Duke Ellington *Song Book* scored best jazz performance then, too.

Overlooking all of the Grammy categories this year, the *L.A. Times* noted, "Once again voters turned frequently to former winners. By picking up one and two awards, respectively, composer John Williams and conductor Pierre Boulez moved into a sixth-place tie with Paul

Simon and Leonard Bernstein on the list of all-time Grammy winners, with 16 awards each."

Williams won a Grammy (best film or TV instrumental composition) for his score to Oscar's Best Picture champ, *Schindler's List*.

The *L.A. Times* explained the popularity of the other 16-time victor: "As was the case when he won last year, Boulez had an advantage: his orchestra was the previously often-honored Chicago Symphony," where he was a guest conductor four weeks per year.

The *Times* accused Grammy voters of a strong preference for music out of Chicago and works by Béla Bartók and Samuel Barber in recent years when it sized up the current race for Best Classical Album: "Last year's winner, Bartók by Boulez in Chicago, is a possibility to repeat, this time with the dour Hungarian's popular *Concerto for Orchestra*. The competition is a release loaded with recent Grammy winners Thomas Hampson, John Browning and the Emerson Quartet and a certain future winner, Cheryl Studer, but you're unlikely to encounter the music in a lifetime of concert-going: *Songs of Samuel Barber*."

Two works by Barber were nominated for best album, but Boulez came through with his Bartók recording to earn his 15th and 16th career Grammys, thereby repeating his 1993 victories for Best Classical Album and Best Orchestral Performance. He scored an upset in the latter category over English conductor John Eliot Gardiner's reinterpretation of Beethoven's nine symphonies using such actual 19th-century instruments as gut-stringed violins and valveless horns.

John Eliot Gardiner nonetheless nabbed the choral performance Grammy for conducting the Orchestre Révolutionnaire et Romantique and the Monteverdi Choir. Together they staged the debut of *Messe Solennelle,* an early work by Berlioz that had been lost for nearly 150 years. The performance at London's Westminster Abbey was again faithful to the work's contemporary sound by including only period instruments without valves and steel strings.

In the competition for best instrumental soloist with orchestra, the *L.A. Times* predicted correctly that Yo-Yo Ma was the "likely champ [presenting] the redoubtable cellist in sterner stuff by the late Stephen Albert, Bloch and, yes, Bartók."

Winner of the equivalent honor for soloists without orchestral accompaniment was Emanuel Ax, who was hailed for his recording of four Haydn sonatas. The work was cheered by critics for being superior to many similar CDs that were then hitting the market, including reissues of Haydn performances by Glenn Gould and Sviatoslav Richter.

The *L.A. Times* noted that the "chamber music category is notable for a Grammy first, a super-budget entry" on the independent Naxos label. It was for a collection of Bartók's violin sonatas performed by Gyorgy Pauk. The paper predicted that the laurels would go to "the solidly entrenched Emerson Quartet" for their Dvořák works, but instead there was an upset by a recording of Beethoven and Mozart quintets by a disperse group that included members of the Chicago Symphony and Berlin Philharmonic.

The prize for Best Classical Contemporary Composition was designated for previously unrecorded music written in the past 25 years. The latest winner was expected to be the Fourth Symphony of the late Witold Lutoslawski, which was penned for Esa-Pekka Salonen and the Los Angeles Philharmonic. However, Stephen Albert's Cello Concerto took the prize in an upset.

The *L.A. Times* cried "bravo!" over this year's lineup for Best Opera Recording, calling it "a category unprecendently rich in unhackneyed marvels." It was also a close competition, causing the paper to refuse to project a winner. The laurels went to the first recording of Carlisle Floyd's first full-length opera, *Susannah,* written in 1995 and adapted from the biblical story of Susannah and the Elders. It featured Cheryl Studer in the star role, with music and backup voices by the Orchestra and Chorus of the Lyons Opera, conducted by Kent Nagano.

Cheryl Studer failed to be nominated for best vocalist, but so did the controversial megaseller *The Three Tenors,* which competed for Album of the Year. This vocalist category was devoted mostly to new opera talent. Four of the five contenders were singers who achieved star billing in the past decade: Bryn Terfel, Cecilia Bartoli, Anne Sofie von Otter and Dmitri Hvorostovky. Bartoli, a 28-year-old Italian mezzo-soprano, won for *The Impatient Lover,* a collection of Italian love songs by such non-Italian music giants as Beethoven, Schubert, Haydn and Mozart.

This year's Grammycast had the worst TV viewership ever, receiving an 11.8 rating/19 share. The previous low was a 16 rating/26 share in 1989 for the 1988 awards.

Variety's review slammed this year's show: "The telecast was best characterized by its lack of surprise or excitement. There were no magic moments . . . and the winners were laughably easy to predict, even for those who had never heard a record before. For whatever reasons, for the first several presentations, whoever performed won the next category: Bruce Springsteen, Sheryl Crow, Salt-N-Pepa, Babyface and Mary-Chapin Carpenter in order, followed by several others including Boyz II Men and Crow again. Henry Rollins was the first apparent upset in this cycle, losing to Soundgarden in the heavy metal category."

Most press accounts blasted host Paul Reiser, who was particularly off when covering for a delay as Bonnie Raitt's band got ready to perform. He finally admitted, "I'm boring myself. This has never happened before."

> " 'All I Wanna Do' was not the year's best record," the *L.A. Times* insisted.

Grammy Revolt Triggers New Reforms

This year's nominations triggered an uproar when such dubious contenders as *The Three Tenors* and Tony Bennett's *MTV Unplugged* made the lineup for Album of the Year.

"The Grammy Awards have long been accused by musicians and music journalists of being out of touch," the *New York Times* reported. "But this year, many top-ranking executives in the music industry have also turned against them."

Even Tommy Mottola, head of Sony Music, which released the Bennett album, fumed to the *L.A. Times,* "The current Grammy categories do not at all reflect what is going on in music today." Warner Music Chairman Doug Morris said, "We believe the voting process is in serious need of review."

Soon after the bids were announced, Geffen Records took out a full-page ad in *Billboard* citing the many critics' polls that agreed that the best album of the year was *Live Through This* by Courtney Love's band Hole. On the bottom of the ad, in large letters, the ad groused: "Recognized by everyone but N.A.R.A.S." Hole had not received a single Grammy nomination, not even in the lower categories.

"The Grammys clearly do not reflect excellence with regard to the music that is released each year," label founder David Geffen added. "It's getting to the point where few people in the music business take them seriously. And if they keep it up, at the rate they're going, it won't be long before they're considered completely irrelevant."

The *L.A. Times* noted a breakaway effort to form rival honors: "Some executives are so upset over the situation that they've threatened privately to withdraw support from future Grammy events. Representatives for the biggest recording conglomerates have even begun talks with a major network in hopes of launching their own awards show."

The uproar only got worse when the Grammy winners were announced. "Bennett's *MTV Unplugged* wasn't the best album of the year," *L.A. Times* music critic Robert Hilburn grumbled. "Sheryl Crow's single 'All I Wanna Do' was in no way the best record of the year. She's a spunky singer, but there's no way 'All I Wanna Do' deserves to win anything short of a Rickie Lee Jones sound-alike contest."

N.A.R.A.S. President Michael Greene publicly announced that he "got the message loud and clear" and promised to introduce reforms that would "do something about getting rid of—or at least mitigate—two things: popularity and sentimentality" in the voting process.

From now on, the academy's general membership would continue to submit ballots to nominate works for the top four awards: Album, Record, Song of the Year and Best New Artist. The final five contenders, however, would be chosen from the top 20 vote-getters by a secret committee of 25 music professionals. The final decision on who wins would then be returned to the full membership for a vote.

Curiously, the reforms did not address what the *New York Times* considered the award's chief problem, which occurs throughout its 80-plus categories: "Many experts in a particular style of music feel that votes are made in their category simply because an artist's name is familiar, rather than because of the quality of the work nominated.

"Few of the academy members interviewed for this article had heard every nominated song and album in the general categories in which they voted this year, and not one owned every nominated song or album in these categories."

• 1994 •

The awards ceremony was broadcast on CBS from the Shrine Auditorium in Los Angeles on March 1, 1995, for the eligibility period of October 1, 1993, through September 30, 1994.

ALBUM OF THE YEAR
• *MTV Unplugged*, Tony Bennett. Columbia.
The Three Tenors in Concert 1994, José Carreras, Placido Domingo, Luciano Pavarotti, Zubin Mehta. Atlantic.
From the Cradle, Eric Clapton. Reprise.
Longing in Their Hearts, Bonnie Raitt. Capitol.
Seal, Seal. ZTT/Sire/Warner Bros.

RECORD OF THE YEAR
• "All I Wanna Do," Sheryl Crow. A&M.
"I'll Make Love to You," Boyz II Men. Motown.
"He Thinks He'll Keep Her," Mary-Chapin Carpenter. Columbia.

"Love Sneakin' Up on You," Bonnie Rait. Capitol.
"Streets of Philadelphia," Bruce Springsteen. Columbia/Epic.

SONG OF THE YEAR
(Songwriter's Award)
• "Streets of Philadelphia," Bruce Springsteen.
"All I Wanna Do," David Baerwald, Bill Bottrell, Wyn Cooper, Sheryl Crow, Kevin Gilbert.
"Can You Feel the Love Tonight," Elton John, Tim Rice.
"Circle of Life," Elton John, Tim Rice.
"I Swear," Gary Baker, Frank J. Meyers.

BEST NEW ARTIST
• Sheryl Crow
Ace of Base
Counting Crows
Crash Test Dummies
Green Day

BEST POP VOCAL PERFORMANCE, MALE

- Elton John, "Can You Feel the Love Tonight." Hollywood.

Artist Formerly Known as Prince, "The Most Beautiful Girl in the World." NPG/Bellmark.

Michael Bolton, "Said I Loved You . . . but I Lied." Columbia.

Seal, "Prayer for the Dying." ZTT/Sire/Warner Bros.

Luther Vandross, "Love the One You're With," track from *Songs*. Epic/LV.

BEST POP VOCAL PERFORMANCE, FEMALE

- Sheryl Crow, "All I Wanna Do." A&M.

Mariah Carey, "Hero." Columbia.

Celine Dion, "The Power of Love." 550 Music/Epic.

Bonnie Raitt, "Longing in Their Hearts," track from *Longing in Their Hearts*. Capitol.

Barbra Streisand, "Ordinary Miracles." Columbia.

BEST POP PERFORMANCE BY A DUO OR GROUP WITH VOCAL

- All-4-One, "I Swear." Blitzz/Atlantic.

Ace of Base, "The Sign." Arista.

Crash Test Dummies, "MMM MMM MMM MMM." Arista.

Lisa Loeb & Nine Stories, "Stay (I Missed You)." RCA.

Pretenders, "I'll Stand By You." Sire/Warner Bros.

BEST POP VOCAL COLLABORATION

- Al Green, Lyle Lovett, "Funny How Time Slips Away," track from *Rhythm, Country and Blues*. MCA.

Bryan Adams, Rod Stewart, Sting, "All for Love." A&M.

Tony Bennett, k. d. lang, "Moonglow," track from *MTV Unplugged*. Columbia.

John Mellencamp, Me'shell NdegeOcello, "Wild Night." Mercury.

Luther Vandross, Mariah Carey, "Endless Love." Columbia.

BEST TRADITIONAL POP VOCAL PERFORMANCE

- Tony Bennett, *MTV Unplugged*. Columbia.

Roberta Flack, *Roberta*. Atlantic.

Willie Nelson, *Moonlight Becomes You*. Justice.

Frank Sinatra, *Duets*. Capitol.

Barbra Streisand, *The Concert*. Columbia.

BEST POP INSTRUMENTAL PERFORMANCE

- Booker T & the MG's, *Cruisin'*. Columbia.

Kenny G, *Sentimental*. Arista.

Branford Marsalis, Bruce Hornsby, "The Star Spangled Banner," track from *Baseball*. Elektra Nonesuch.

Mike Post, "Theme from *NYPD Blue*," track from *Inventions from the Blue Line*. American Gramaphone.

Alan Silvestri, "I'm Forrest . . . Forrest Gump (The Feather Theme)," track from *Forrest Gump* (soundtrack). Epic.

BEST POP ALBUM

- *Longing in Their Hearts*, Bonnie Raitt. Capitol.

The Sign, Ace of Base. Arista.

The Three Tenors in Concert 1994, José Carreras, Placido Domingo, Luciano Pavarotti, Zubin Mehta. Atlantic.

I Love Everybody, Lyle Lovett. Curb/MCA.

Seal, Seal. ZTT/Sire/Warner Bros.

BEST ROCK SONG
(Songwriter's Award)

- "Streets of Philadelphia," Bruce Springsteen.

"All Apologies," Kurt Cobain.

"Black Hole Sun," Chris Cornell.

"Come to My Window," Melissa Etheridge.

"I'm the Only One," Melissa Etheridge.

BEST ROCK VOCAL PERFORMANCE, MALE

- Bruce Springsteen, "Streets of Philadelphia." Columbia/Epic.

Beck, "Loser." DGC.

Peter Gabriel, "Red Rain," track from *Secret World Live*. Geffen.

Van Morrison, "In the Garden/You Send Me/Allegeny," track from *A Night In San Francisco*. Polydor.

Neil Young, "Philadelphia," track from *Philadelphia* (soundtrack). Epic.

BEST ROCK VOCAL PERFORMANCE, FEMALE

- Melissa Etheridge, "Come to My Window." Island.

Sheryl Crow, "I'm Gonna Be a Wheel Someday," track from *To Nowhere*. A&M.

Liz Phair, "Supernova," track from *Whip-Smart*. Matador/Atlantic.

Sam Phillips, "Circle of Fire," track from *Martinis and Bikinis*. Virgin.

Bonnie Raitt, "Love Sneakin' Up on You." Capitol.

BEST ROCK PERFORMANCE BY A DUO OR GROUP WITH VOCAL

- Aerosmith, *Crazy*. Geffen

Counting Crows, " 'Round Here," track from *August and Everything After*. DGC.

Green Day, "Basket Case," track from *Dookie*. Reprise.

Nirvana, "All Apologies," track from *In Utero*. DGC.

Pearl Jam, "Daughter," track from *Vs*. Epic Associated.

BEST HARD ROCK PERFORMANCE

- Soundgarden, "Black Hole Sun," track from *Superunknown*. A&M.

Alice in Chains, "I Stay Away," track from *Jar of Flies*. Columbia.

Beastie Boys, "Sabotage." Capitol.

Green Day, "Longview," track from *Dookie*. Reprise.

Pearl Jam, "Go," track from *Vs*. Epic Associated.

BEST METAL PERFORMANCE

- Soundgarden, "Spoonman," track from *Superunknown*. A&M.

Anthrax, Public Enemy, "Bring the Noise," track from *Live: The Island Years*. Island.

Megadeth, "99 Ways to Die," track from *The Beavis and Butt-head Experience*. Geffen.

Pantera, "I'm Broken," track from *Far Beyond Driven*. EastWest America.

Rollins Band, *Liar*. Imago.

BEST ROCK INSTRUMENTAL PERFORMANCE

- Pink Floyd, "Marooned," track from *The Division Bell*. Columbia.

Dixie Dregs, "Shapes of Things," track from *Full Circle*. Capricorn.

Rush, "Leave That Thing Alone!" track from *Counterparts*. Atlantic/Anthaem.

Santana, "Luz Amore y Vida," track from *Brothers*. Guts & Grace/Island.

Joe Satriani, "All Alone," track from *Time Machine*. Relativity.

BEST ROCK ALBUM

- *Voodoo Lounge,* Rolling Stones. Virgin.

Vs., Pearl Jam. Epic Associated.

Monster, R.E.M. Warner Bros.

Superunknown, Soundgarden. A&M.

Sleeps with Angels, Neil Young, Crazy Horse. Reprise.

BEST ALTERNATIVE MUSIC PERFORMANCE

- Green Day, *Dookie*. Reprise.

Tori Amos, *Under the Pink*. Atlantic.

Crash Test Dummies, *God Shuffled His Feet*. Arista.

Sarah McLachlan, *Fumbling Towards Ecstasy*. Arista.

Nine Inch Nails, *The Downward Spiral*. Nothing/TVT/Interscope.

BEST RHYTHM & BLUES SONG
(Songwriter's Award)

- "I'll Make Love to You," Babyface.

"Body and Soul," Rick Nowels, Ellen Shipley.

"If That's Your Boyfriend (He Wasn't Last Night)," Me'Shell NdegeOcello.

"When Can I See You," Babyface.
"You Mean the World to Me," Babyface, L. A. Reid, Daryl Simmons.

BEST RHYTHM & BLUES VOCAL PERFORMANCE, MALE

- Babyface, "When Can I See You." Epic.
Tevin Campbell, "I'm Ready." Qwest/Warner Bros.
Al Jarreau, "Wait for the Magic," track from *Tenderness*. Reprise.
Luther Vandross, "Always and Forever," track from *Songs*. Epic/ LV.
Barry White, "Practice What You Preach." A&M.

BEST RHYTHM & BLUES VOCAL PERFORMANCE, FEMALE

- Toni Braxton, "Breathe Again." LaFace Records.
Anita Baker, "Body and Soul." Elektra.
Aretha Franklin, "A Deeper Love." Arista.
Gladys Knight, "I Don't Want to Know." MCA.
Me'Shell NdegeOcello, "If That's Your Boyfriend (He Wasn't Last Night)." Maverick/Sire.

BEST RHYTHM & BLUES VOCAL PERFORMANCE BY A DUO OR GROUP WITH VOCAL

- Boyz II Men, "I'll Make Love to You." Motown.
Sade, "Please Send Me Someone to Love," track from *Philadelphia* (soundtrack). Epic.
Salt-N-Pepa, En Vogue, "Whatta Man." Next Plateau/London.
Take 6, "Biggest Part of Me." Reprise.
BeBe & CeCe Winans, "If Anything Ever Happened to You." Capitol.

BEST RHYTHM & BLUES ALBUM

- *II*, Boyz II Men. Motown.
Rhythm of Love, Anita Baker. Elektra.
I'm Ready, Tevin Campbell. Qwest/Warner Bros.
Just for You, Gladys Knight. MCA.

Plantation Lullabies, Me'Shell NdegeOcello. Maverick/Sire/Reprise.
Songs, Luther Vandross. Epic/LV.

BEST RAP SOLO PERFORMANCE

- Queen Latifah, "U.N.I.T.Y." Motown.
Coolio, "Fantastic Voyage." Tommy Boy.
Craig Mack, "Flava in Ya Ear." Bad Boy.
Snoop Doggy Dogg, "Gin and Juice." Death Row/Interscope.
Warren G, "This DJ." Violator/Ral.

BEST RAP PERFORMANCE BY A DUO OR GROUP

- Salt-N-Pepa, "None of Your Business." Next Plateau/London.
Arrested Development, "Ease My Mind." Chrysalis/ERG.
Cypress Hill, "I Ain't Goin' Out Like That." Ruffhouse/Columbia.
Heavy D & the Boyz, "Nuttin' but Love." MCA/Uptown.
Warren G & Nate Dogg, "Regulate," track from *Regulate . . . G Funk Era*. Violator/Ral.

BEST CONTEMPORARY JAZZ PERFORMANCE

- Brecker Brothers, "Out of the Loop." GRP.
Jan Garbarek Group, "Twelve Moons." ECM.
Marcus Miller, "The Sun Don't Lie." PRA.
Mike Stern, "Is What It Is." Atlantic Jazz.
Yellowjackets, "Run for Your Life." GRP.

BEST JAZZ VOCAL PERFORMANCE

- Etta James, *Mystery Lady (Songs of Billie Holiday)*. Private Music.
Dee Dee Bridgewater, *Keeping Tradition*. Verve.
Shirley Horn, *I Love You, Paris*. Verve.
Lena Horn, *We'll Be Together Again*. Blue Note.
Cassandra Wilson, *Blue Light 'Til Dawn*. Blue Note.

BEST JAZZ INSTRUMENTAL SOLO

• Benny Carter, "Prelude to a Kiss," track from *Elegy in Blue*. MusicMasters Jazz.

Michael Brecker, "African Skies," track from *Out of the Loop* (Brecker Brothers). GRP.

Chick Corea, "Lush Life," track from *Expressions*. GRP.

Charlie Haden, "Alone Together," track from *Always Say Goodbye*. Verve.

Wayne Shorter, "Pinocchio," track from *A Tribute to Miles* (various artists). Qwest/Reprise.

BEST JAZZ INSTRUMENTAL PERFORMANCE (INDIVIDUAL OR GROUP)

• Ron Carter, Herbie Hancock, Wallace Roney, Wayne Shorter, Tony Williams, *A Tribute to Miles*. Reprise/Qwest.

Benny Carter, *Elegy in Blue*. MusicMasters.

Charlie Haden Quartet West, *Always Say Goodbye*. Verve.

Joe Lovano, *Tenor Legacy*. Blue Note.

Gonzalo Rubalcaba, *Rapsodia*. Blue Note.

BEST LARGE JAZZ ENSEMBLE PERFORMANCE

• McCoy Tyner Big Band, *Journey*. Birdology/Verve.

Toshiko Akiyoshi, *Desert Lady/Fantasy*. Columbia.

Carla Bley, *Big Band Theory*. ECM.

Bob Mintzer Big Band, *Only in New York*. DMP.

Maria Schneider Jazz Orchestra, *Evanescence*. Enja.

BEST LATIN JAZZ PERFORMANCE

• Arturo Sandoval, *Danzón*. GRP.

Ray Barretto & New World Spirit, *Taboo*. Concord Picante.

Mario Bauza & the Afro-Cuban Jazz Orchestra, *944 Columbus*. Messidor.

Jerry Gonzalez & the Fort Apache Band, *Crossroads,* Milestone.

Eddie Palmieri, *Palmas*. Elektra Nonesuch/American Explorer Ser.

BEST COUNTRY SONG
(Songwriter's Award)

• "I Swear," Gary Baker, Frank J. Myers.

"How Can I Help You Say Goodbye," Burton Banks Collins, Karen Taylor Good.

"Independence Day," Gretchen Peters.

"Shut Up and Kiss Me," Mary Chapin Carpenter.

"When Love Finds You," Vince Gill, Michael Omartian.

BEST COUNTRY ALBUM

• *Stones in the Road*, Mary Chapin Carpenter. Columbia.

Tribute to the Music of Bob Wills and the Texas Playboys, Asleep at the Wheel. Liberty.

When Love Finds You, Vince Gill. MCA.

Read My Mind, Reba McEntire. MCA.

The Song Remembers When, Trisha Yearwood. MCA.

BEST COUNTRY VOCAL PERFORMANCE, MALE

• Vince Gill, "When Love Finds You." MCA.

David Ball, "Thinkin' Problem," track from *Thinkin' Problem*. Warner Bros.

John Berry, "Your Love Amazes Me," track from *John Berry*. Liberty.

John Michael Montgomery, "I Swear." Atlantic.

Dwight Yoakam, "Pocket of a Clown," track from *This Time*. Reprise.

BEST COUNTRY VOCAL PERFORMANCE, FEMALE

• Mary Chapin Carpenter, "Shut Up and Kiss Me." Columbia.

Wynonna Judd, "Is It Over Yet." Curb/MCA.

Patty Loveless, "How Can I Help You Say Goodbye." Epic.

Martina McBride, "Independence Day." RCA.

Reba McEntire, "She Thinks His Name Was John." MCA.

BEST COUNTRY PERFORMANCE BY A DUO OR GROUP WITH VOCAL

- Asleep at the Wheel, Lyle Lovett, "Blues for Dixie," track from *Tribute to the Music of Bob Wills and the Texas Playboys*. Liberty.

Diamond Rio, "Love a Little Stronger." Arista.

Alison Krauss, Union Station, "When You Say Nothing at All," track from *Keith Whitley—A Tribute*. BNA.

Mavericks, "What a Crying Shame." MCA.

Tractors, "Baby Likes to Rock It." Arista.

BEST COUNTRY VOCAL COLLABORATION

- Aaron Neville, Trisha Yearwood, "I Fall to Pieces." MCA.

Suzy Bogguss, Alison Krauss, Kathy Mattea, Crosby, Stills & Nash, "Teach Your Children," track from *Red Hot + Country*. Mercury.

Johnny Cash, Marty Stuart, Travis Tritt, "The Devil Comes Back to Georgia." Warner Bros.

George Jones, B. B. King, "Patches," track from *Rhythm Country and Blues*. MCA.

Dolly Parton, Loretta Lynn, Tammy Wynette, "Silver Threads and Golden Needles." Columbia.

BEST COUNTRY INSTRUMENTAL PERFORMANCE

- Chet Atkins, "Young Thing," track from *Read My Licks*. Columbia.

Roy Clark, Joe Pass, "Kaw-Liga," track from *Roy Clark and Joe Pass Play Hank Williams*. Buster Ann Music.

Diamond Rio, "Appalachian Dream," track from *Love a Little Stronger*. Arista.

Randy Scruggs, Earl Scruggs, Doc Watson, "Keep on the Sunny Side," track from *Red Hot + Country*. Mercury.

Marty Stuart, "Marty Stuart Visits the Moon," track from *Love and Luck*. MCA.

BEST ROCK GOSPEL ALBUM

- *Wake-up Call*, Petra. DaySpring.

To Extremes, DeGarmo & Key. Benson.

Going Public, Newsboys. Star Song.

Squint, Steve Taylor. Warner Alliance.

Strong Hand of Love—A Tribute to Mark Heard, various artists. Fingerprint-Myrrh.

BEST POP/CONTEMPORARY GOSPEL ALBUM

- *Mercy*, Andrae Crouch. Qwest/Warner Bros.

The Light Inside, Gary Chapman. Reunion.

Heaven in the Real World, Steven Curtis Chapman. Sparrow.

Beyond All the Limits, Larnelle Harris. Benson Music Group.

First Christmas, Bebe & CeCe Winans. Capitol.

BEST SOUTHERN GOSPEL, COUNTRY GOSPEL OR BLUEGRASS GOSPEL ALBUM

- *I Know Who Holds Tomorrow*, Alison Krauss, Cox Family. Rounder.

Tell It Again, Wendy Bagwell, Sunliters. Canaan.

High and Lifted Up, Cathedrals. Canaan.

The Door, Charlie Daniels. Sparrow.

Just Stopped By, Torchmen. SCD.

BEST TRADITIONAL SOUL GOSPEL ALBUM

- *Songs of the Church—Live in Memphis*, Albertina Walker. Benson.

I Will Trust in the Lord, James Moore. Malaco.

"Live" with the Georgia Mass Choir—Feel Like . . . ., Dorothy Norwood. Malaco.

In This Place, Williams Brothers. Blackberry.

Come Thou Almighty King, Timothy Wright, N.Y. Fellowship Mass Choir. Savoy.

BEST CONTEMPORARY SOUL GOSPEL ALBUM

- *Join the Band*, Take 6. Reprise.
- *Save the World*, Yolanda Adams. Tribute.
- *The Live Experience*, Helen Baylor. Word.
- *Matters of the Heart*, Commissioned. Benson.
- *To a Higher Place*, Tramine Hawkins. Columbia.

BEST GOSPEL ALBUM BY A CHOIR OR CHORUS

(Tie)

- *Through God's Eyes*, Thompson Community Singers; Milton Brunson, choir director. Word.
- *Live . . . A Celebration of Praise*, Associates; O'Landa Draper, choir director. Word.
- *Kings and Kingdoms*, Music and Arts Seminar Mass Choir; Edwin Hawkins, choir director. Intersound.
- *We Haven't Forgotten You*, Los Angeles Gospel Messengers; Kurt Carr, choir director. Savoy.
- *Live in Atlanta at Morehouse College*, Love Fellowship Crusade Choir; Hezekiah Walker, choir director. Benson.

BEST TRADITIONAL FOLK ALBUM

- *World Gone Wrong*, Bob Dylan. Columbia.
- *L'Echo*, BeauSoleil. Forward.
- *Ritual—Le Mystère des Voix Bulgares*, Bulgarian State Television Female Vocal Choir. Elektra Nonesuch.
- *Liph'Iauiniso*, Ladysmith Black Mambazo. Shanachie.
- *Wheel of Fortune*, John Renbourn, Robin Williamson. Flying Fish.
- *Third Annual Farewell Reunion*, Mike Seeger. Rounder.

BEST CONTEMPORARY FOLK ALBUM

- *American Recordings*, Johnny Cash. American.
- *Cover Girl*, Shawn Colvin. Columbia.
- *My Life*, Iris DeMent. Warner Bros.

Flyer, Nanci Griffith. Elektra.
Swamp Ophelia, Indigo Girls. Epic.

BEST TRADITIONAL BLUES ALBUM

- *From the Cradle*, Eric Clapton. Reprise.
- *Living the Blues*, James Cotton. Verve.
- *Trouble No More*, John Hammond. Pointblank/Charisma.
- *In My Time*, Charlie Musselwhite. Alligator.
- *Ain't Enough Comin' In,* Otis Rush. This Way Up/Mercury.

BEST CONTEMPORARY BLUES ALBUM

- *Father Father*, Pop Staples. Pointblank.
- *Shame + A Sin*, Robert Cray Band. Mercury.
- *Force of Nature*, Koko Taylor. Alligator.
- *Strange Pleasure*, Jimmie Vaughan. Epic.
- *Bow Wow*, Johnny "Guitar" Watson. Wilma.

BEST BLUEGRASS ALBUM

- *The Great Dobro Sessions*, various artists. Sugar Hill.
- *Flashback*, J. D. Crowe, New South. Rounder.
- *A Deeper Shade of Blue*, Del McCoury. Rounder.
- *When the Roses Bloom in Dixieland*, Osborne Brothers. Pinecastle.
- *Like We Used to Be*, Seldom Scene. Sugar Hill.

BEST LATIN POP ALBUM

- *Segundo Romance*, Luis Miguel. WEA Latina.
- *El Camino del Alma*, Cristian. Fonovisa.
- *De Mi Alma Latina*, Placido Domingo. EMI Latin/Angel.
- *Gracias por Esperar*, Juan Gabriel. Ariola.
- *Vida*, La Mafia. Sony Discos.

BEST TROPICAL LATIN ALBUM

- *Master Sessions, Vol. 1*, Cachao. Crescent Moon/Epic.

Luis Enrique, Luis Enrique. Sony Tropical.

Fogarate! Juan Luis Guerra 440. Karen/BMG.

La Aventura, Orquesta de la Luz. Ariola.

Cara de Niño, Jerry Rivera. Sony Tropical.

BEST MEXICAN-AMERICAN ALBUM

• *Recuerdo a Javier Solis*, Vikki Carr. Sony Latin.

Dime Cuando Volveras, Ramon Ayala, Los Bravos del Norte. Freddie.

Recordando a los Panchos, Vicente Fernandez. Sony Discos.

La Diferenzia, La Diferenzia. Arista/Texas.

El Bronco, Los Terribles del Norte. Freddie.

Amor Prohibido, Selena. EMI Latin.

BEST REGGAE ALBUM

• *Crucial! Roots Classics*, Bunny Wailer. Shanachie.

Rise and Shine, Aswad. Mesa.

Strongg, Black Uhuru. Mesa.

Light My Fire, Dennis Brown. Heartbeat.

Reggae Dancer, Inner Circle. Big Beat/Atlantic.

Stir It Up, various artists. Columbia.

BEST POLKA ALBUM

• *Music and Friends*, Walter Ostanek Band. WRS.

Always . . . Forever . . . and a Day, Eddie Blazonczyk's Versatones. Bel-Aire.

Your Polka Sweethearts, Happy Louie & Julcia's Polka Band. Hi-Lo.

Jan Lewan and His Orchestra, Jan Lewan. JRD.

Polka Your Troubles Away, Jimmy Sturr & His Orchestra, Johnny Karas. Rounder.

BEST NEW AGE ALBUM

• *Prayer for the Wild Things*, Paul Winter. Living Music.

Acoustic Planet, Craig Chaquico. Higher Octave Music.

Mandala, Kitaro. DOMO.

The Garden, Michael Nesmith. Rio.

Turn of the Tides, Tangerine Dream. Miramar.

BEST WORLD MUSIC ALBUM

• *Talking Timbuktu*, Ali Farka Toure, Ry Cooder. Hannibal.

Love and Liberte, Gipsy Kings. Elektra Musician.

Angelus, Milton Nascimento. Warner Bros.

The Guide (Wommat), Youssou N'Dour. Chaos/Columbia.

Sabsylma, Zap Mama. Luaka Bop/Warner Bros.

BEST ARRANGEMENT ON AN INSTRUMENTAL

• Dave Grusin, "Three Cowboy Songs," track from *The Orchestral Album* (Dave Grusin). GRP.

Richard Eddy, Arturo Sandoval, "A Mis Abuelos," track from *Danzón* (Arturo Sandoval). GRP.

Toshiko Akiyoshi, "Bebop," track from *Desert Lady-Fantasy* (Toshiko Akiyoshi Jazz Orchestra). Columbia.

Louie Bellson, "Ellington-Strayhorn Suite," track from *Black, Brown and Beige* (Louie Bellson). MusicMasters.

Nan Schwartz Mishkin, "In the Wee Small Hours of the Morning," track from *Night and Day—Celebrate Sinatra* (John Williams, Boston Pops Orchestra). Sony Classical.

BEST INSTRUMENTAL COMPOSITION

• "African Skies," Michael Brecker.

"A Mis Abuelos," Arturo Sandoval.

"Elegy in Blue," Benny Carter.

"Ellington-Strayhorn Suite," Louie Bellson.

"Evanescence," Maria Schneider.

BEST MUSICAL SHOW ALBUM

• *Passion*, original Broadway cast. Stephen Sondheim, lyricist and composer. Angel.

Andrew Lloyd Webber's Sunset Blvd., American premiere cast with Glenn Close. Don Black, Christopher Hampton, lyricists. Andrew Lloyd Webber, composer. Really Useful.

Beauty and the Beast: A New Musical. Howard Ashman, Tim Rice, lyricists; Alan Menken, composer. Walt Disney.

Crazy for You. Ira Gershwin, lyricist; George Gershwin, composer. RCA Victor.

Rodgers and Hammerstein's Carousel. Oscar Hammerstein, lyricist; Richard Rodgers, composer. Angel.

BEST INSTRUMENTAL COMPOSITION WRITTEN FOR A MOTION PICTURE OR TV

- "Schindler's List," John Williams.
"The Lion King," Hans Zimmer.
"Little Buddha," Ryuichi Sakamoto.
"The Shawshank Redemption," Thomas Newman.
"Wolf," Ennio Morricone.

BEST SONG WRITTEN SPECIFICALLY FOR A MOTION PICTURE OR TV

- "Streets of Philadelphia," Bruce Springsteen (*Philadelphia*).
"Can You Feel the Love Tonight," Elton John, Tim Rice (*The Lion King*).
"Circle of Life," Elton John, Tim Rice (*The Lion King*).
"The Day I Fall in Love," James Ingram, Clif Magness, Carole Bayer Sager (*Beethoven's 2nd*).
"I'll Remember," M. Ciccone, Patrick Leonard, Richard Page (*With Honors*).

BEST INSTRUMENTAL ARRANGEMENT ACCOMPANYING VOCAL(S)

- Andrae Crouch, Lebo Morake, Hans Zimmer, "Circle of Life," track from *The Lion King* (Carmen Twillie). Walt Disney.
Patti Austin, Jerry Hey, Bob James, Lee Ritenour, Mervyn Warren, "Ability to Swing," track from *That Secret Place* (Patti Austin). MCA/GRP.

Jeremy Lubbock, "I Can't Make You Love Me," track from *Love, Nancy* (Nancy Wilson). Columbia.

Patrick Williams, Nelson Riddle, "I've Got a Crush on You," track from *Duets* (Frank Sinatra, Barbra Streisand). Capitol.

Alan Broadbent, "Without a Word of Warning," track from *A Tribute to Bing Crosby, Paramount's Greatest Singer* (Mel Tormé). Concord Jazz.

Johnny Mandel, "Young at Heart," track from *It Could Happen to You* (Tony Bennett, Shawn Colvin). Columbia.

BEST CLASSICAL ALBUM

- *Bartók: Concerto for Orchestra: 4 Orchestral Pieces, Op. 12*, Pierre Boulez conducting the Chicago Symphony Orchestra. Deutsche Grammophon.

Barber: Secrets of the Old—The Complete Songs, Thomas Hampson, Cheryl Studer, John Browning, Emerson String Quartet. Deutsche Grammophon.

Barber: Violin Concerto; Korngold: Violin Concerto; etc., Gil Shaham, violin; André Previn conducting the London Symphony Orchestra. Deutsche Grammophon.

Debussy: Preludes (Books 1 and 2), Krystian Zimerman. Deutsche Grammophon.

Mahler: Symphony No. 2, Herbert Blomstedt conducting the San Francisco Symphony Orchestra, San Francisco Symphony Chorus, various artists. London.

BEST ORCHESTRAL PERFORMANCE (Conductor's Award)

- Pierre Boulez conducting the Chicago Symphony Orchestra, *Bartók: Concerto for Orchestra: 4 Orchestral Pieces, Op. 12*. Deutsche Grammophon.
John Eliot Gardiner conducting the Orchestre Révolutionnaire et Romantique, *Beethoven: 9 Symphonies*. Archiv Producktion.

Oliver Knussen conducting the Cleveland Orchestra, *Copland: Grohg; Hear Ye! Hear Ye!; Prelude*. Argo.

Orpheus Chamber Orchestra, *Ives: A Set of Pieces (Three Places in New England, Symphony No. 3, etc.)*. Deutsche Grammophon.

Myung-Whun Chung conducting the Orchestre de L'Opéra Bastille, *Messiaen: Eclairs sur L'Au-Dela*. Deutsche Grammophon.

BEST CHAMBER MUSIC PERFORMANCE

• Daniel Barenboim, piano; Dale Clevenger, horn; Larry Combs, clarinet; Daniele Damiano, bassoon; Hansjorg Schellenberger, oboe, *Beethoven, Mozart: Quintets*. Erato.

Gyorgy Pauk, violin; Kalman Berkes, clarinet; Jeno Jando, piano, *Bartók: Violin Sonatas Nos. 1 and 2: Contrasts*. Naxos.

Martha Argerich, piano; Mischa Maisky, cello, *Beethoven: Cello Sonatas, Opp. 69 and 102*. Deutsche Grammophon.

Juilliard String Quartet, *Debussy, Ravel, Dutilleux: Quartets*. Sony Classical.

Emerson String Quartet; Menahem Pressler, piano, *Dvořák: Piano Quintet, Op. 81; Piano Quartet, Op. 87*. Deutsche Grammophon.

BEST CLASSICAL PERFORMANCE, INSTRUMENTAL SOLOIST(S) (WITH ORCHESTRA)

• Yo-Yo Ma, cello and alto violin (David Zinman conducting the Baltimore Symphony Orchestra), *The New York Album (Works of Albert, Bartók, Bloch)*. Sony Classical.

Kwung-Wha Chung, violin (Simon Rattle conducting the City of Birmingham Symphony Orchestra), *Bartók: Violin Concerto No. 2; Rhapsodies Nos. 1 and 2*. EMI Classics.

Gil Shaham, violin (André Previn conducting the London Symphony Orchestra), "Korngold: Violin Concerto in D Major," track from *Bar-ber: Violin Concerto, Op. 14; Korngold: Violin Concerto in D Major; etc*. Deutsche Grammophon.

Yefim Bronfman, piano (Zubin Mehta conducting the Israel Philharmonic Orchestra), "Prokofiev: Piano Concerto No. 2," track from *Prokofiev; Piano Concertos Nos. 2 and 4; Overture on Hebrew Themes*. Sony Classical.

Emanuel Ax, piano (Esa-Pekka Salonen conducting the Philharmonia Orchestra), *Schoenberg, Liszt: Piano Concertos*. Sony Classical.

BEST CLASSICAL PERFORMANCE, INSTRUMENTAL SOLOIST (WITHOUT ORCHESTRA)

• Emanuel Ax, piano, *Haydn: Piano Sonatas Nos. 32, 47, 53 and 59*. Sony Classical.

Alan Feinberg, piano, *The American Innovator (Works of Adams, Ives, etc.)*. Argo.

Viktoria Mullova, violin, *Bach: Partitas for Violin Solo*. Philips Classics.

Evgeny Kissin, piano, *Chopin Recital, Vol. 1*. RCA Victor Red Seal.

Krystian Zimerman, piano, *Debussy: Preludes (Books 1 and 2)*. Deutsche Grammophon.

BEST OPERA RECORDING

• *Floyd: Susannah*, Kent Nagano conducting the Orchestra of the Opéra de Lyon (solos: Jerry Hadley, Samuel Ramey, Cheryl Studer). Virgin Classics.

Busoni: Arlecchino and Turandot, Kent Nagano conducting the Orchestra of the Opéra de Lyon (solos: Ernst Richter, Thomas Mohr, Mechthild Gessendorf, Franz-Josef Selig). Virgin Classics.

Rossini: Semiramide, Ion Marin conducting the London Symphony Orchestra, Ambrosian Opera Chorus (solos: Jennifer Larmore, Frank Lopardo, Samuel Ramey, Cheryl Studer). Deutsche Grammophon.

Shostakovich: Lady Macbeth of
Mtsensk, Myung-Whun Chung conducting the Orchestra of the Bastille
Opera, Choir of the Bastille Opera
(solos: Maria Ewing, Aage Haugland, Anatoly Kotcherga, Sergei
Larin). Deutsche Grammophon.

Wagner: Die Meistersinger von Nürn-
berg, Wolfgang Sawallisch conduct-
ing the Bavarian State Opera
Orchestra, Bavarian State Opera
Chorus (solos: Cheryl Studer, Bernd
Weikl). EMI Classics.

BEST CHORAL PERFORMANCE

• John Eliot Gardiner conducting the
Monteverdi Choir and Orchestre
Révolutionnaire et Romantique,
Berlioz: Messe Solennelle. Philips
Classics.

Nikolai Korniev conducting the St.
Petersburg Chamber Choir, Evening
Star—The Rachmaninov Vespers.
Philips Classics.

Tonu Kalijuste conducting the Estonian
Philharmonic Chamber Choir and the
Tallinn Chamber Orchestra. Part: Te
Deum; Silouans Song; etc. ECM
New Series.

Simon Rattle conducting the City of
Birmingham Symphony Chorus and
the City of Birmingham Symphony
Orchestra; Simon Halsey, choir
director, Szymanowski: Stabat Mater;
Litany to the Virgin Mary; etc. EMI
Classics.

Richard Hickox, John Scott, Stephen
Westrop conducting the London
Symphony Chorus, the Choristers of
St. Paul's Cathedral, the London
Symphony Orchestra; John Scott,
choir director; Stephen Westrop, cho-
rus master, Vaughan Williams: Dona
Nobis Pacem; Sancta Civitas. EMI
Classics.

BEST CLASSICAL VOCAL
PERFORMANCE

• Cecilia Bartoli, The Impatient Lover
(Italian Songs by Beethoven, Schubert, Mozart, etc.). London.

Bryn Terfel, An die Musik—Favorite
Schubert Songs (Die Forelle, An die
Leier, etc.). Deutsche Grammophon.

Anne Sofie von Otter, Love's Twilight—
Late Romantic Songs by Berg, Korn-
gold, R. Strauss. Deutsche
Grammophon.

Peter Screier, Mendelssohn: Lieder (Der
Mond, Reiselied, etc.). Berlin Classics.

Dmitri Hvorostovsky, Songs and Dances
of Death (Works of Mussorgsky, Rimsky-Korsakov, Borodin, etc.). Philips
Classics.

BEST CLASSICAL CONTEMPORARY
COMPOSITION

• Cello Concerto, Stephen Albert.
Concerto for Piano and Orchestra,
Gyorgy Ligeti.
Symphony No. 4, Witold Lutoslawski.
"Eclairs sur L'au-Dela," Olivier Messi-
aen.
"Fantasma/Cantos," Toru Takemitsu.

BEST ENGINEERED RECORDING,
CLASSICAL

• William Hoekstra, Copland: Music
for Films (The Red Pony, Our Town,
etc.). RCA Victor Red Seal.

William Hoekstra, Bartók: Concerto for
Orchestra; Miraculous Mandarin
(Complete). RCA Victor Red Seal.

Bud Graham, Charles Harbutt, Debussy,
Ravel, Dutilleux: Quartets. Sony
Classical.

Jack Renner, Mozart: Così Fan Tutte.
Telarc.

Mike Hatch, Szymanowski: Stabat
Mater; Litany to the Virgin Mary;
etc. EMI Classics.

CLASSICAL PRODUCER OF THE YEAR

• Andrew Cornall
Anna Barry
Wilhelm Hellweg
Judith Sherman
Max Wilcox

BEST SPOKEN COMEDY ALBUM

• Live from Hell, Sam Kinison. Priority.

Attention Butt Pirates and Lesbetarians, Judy Tenuta. Goddess.

The Jerky Boys 2, Jerky Boys. Select.

The Official Politcally Correct Dictionary and Handbook (Henry Beard and Christopher Cerf), Christopher Cerf. Dove Audio.

They're All Gonna Laugh at You, Adam Sandler. Warner Bros.

BEST SPOKEN WORD OR NONMUSICAL ALBUM

• *Get in the Van: On the Road with Black Flag,* Henry Rollins. Time Warner Audiobooks.

Baseball (Geoffrey C. Ward and Ken Burns), Ken Burns. Random House Audio.

The Bible (The New Testament), Gregory Peck. Olive Branch.

Hamlet, Kenneth Branagh. BDD Audio.

Schindler's List, Ben Kingsley. Simon and Schuster Audio.

BEST MUSICAL ALBUM FOR CHILDREN

• *The Lion King,* Mark Mancina, Jay Rifkin, Chris Thomas, Hans Zimmer. Walt Disney.

Bananaphone, Raffi, Michel Creber. Shoreline/MCA.

Little Sleepy Eyes, J. Aaron Brown, Otis Forrest, David Lehman. Jaba.

The Manhattan Transfer Meets Tubby the Tuba, Manhattan Transfer, Joseph Magee, Timothy Russell. Summit.

Return to Pooh Corner, Kenny Loggins, Terry Nelson, David Pack. Sony Wonder.

BEST SPOKEN WORD ALBUM FOR CHILDREN

• *The Lion King Read-Along,* Robert Guillaume, Ted Kryczko, Randy Thornton. Walt Disney.

Aladdin and the Magic Lamp, John Hurt, Brian Gleeson, Michey Hart, C. W. Rogers. BMG Kidz.

The Creation, Amy Grant, Bela Fleck, Brian Gleeson, Craig Rogers. BMG Kidz.

Johnny Appleseed, Garrison Keillor, Ken Hoin, Mark O'Connor. Rabbit Ears.

The Magic School Bus: Fun with Sound, John Wynne. TW Kids.

BEST ENGINEERED ALBUM (OTHER THAN CLASSICAL)

• Ed Cherney, Paul Dieter, Rik Pekkonen, *I'm Alive* (Jackson Browne). Elektra.

Andrew Jackson, *The Division Bell* (Pink Floyd). Columbia.

Ed Cherney, *Longing in Their Hearts* (Bonnie Raitt). Capitol.

Chuck Ainlay, Ed Cherney, Roger Nichols, Rik Pekkonen, Don Smith, Bob Clearmountain, *Rhythm, Country and Blues* (various artists). MCA.

Robin Barclay, Sean Chenery, Steve Fitzmaurice, Gregg Jackman, Steve MacMillin, Carmen Rizzo, Tim Weidner, Paul Wright, *Seal* (Seal). Sire.

BEST ALBUM PACKAGE (Art Director's Award)

• Buddy Jackson, *Tribute to the Music of Bob Wills and the Texas Playboys* (Asleep at the Wheel). Liberty.

Deborah Norcross, *Boingo* (Boingo). Giant.

Mary Maurer, *Jar of Flies* (Alice in Chains). Columbia.

Michael Coulson, *Secret World Live* (Peter Gabriel). Geffen.

Mark Farrow, Pet Shop Boys, David Wieo, *Very Relentless* (Pet Shop Boys). EMI.

BEST ALBUM PACKAGE, BOXED (Art Director's Award)

• Chris Thompson, *The Complete Ella Fitzgerald Song Books.* Verve.

Deborah Norcross, *Boingo.* Giant.

David Lau, *The Complete Bud Powell on Verve.* Verve.

Chris Bilheimer, Tom Recchion, Michael Stipe, *Monster (Ltd)* (R.E.M.). Warner Bros.

Geoff Gans, Coco Shinomiya, *Songs of the West* (various artists). Rhino.

BEST ALBUM NOTES
(Annotator's Award)

- Dan Morgenstern, Loren Schoenberg, *Louis Armstrong: Portrait of the Artist As a Young Man, 1923–1934.* Columbia/Legacy.

Yves Beauvais, Don Cherry, Ornette Coleman, Robert Palmer, *Beauty Is a Rare Thing—The Complete Atlantic Recordings* (Ornette Coleman). Rhino.

Francis Pandras, Celia Powell, Peter Pullman, Sonny Rollins, Horace Silver, *The Complete Bud Powell on Verve.* Verve.

Carol Cooper, Steve Greenberg, Jaime Wolf, *Otis! The Definitive.* Rhino.

Peter Guralnick, *Sam Cooke's SAR Records Story 1959–1965* (various artists). ABKCO.

BEST HISTORICAL ALBUM

- *The Complete Ella Fitzgerald Song Books on Verve.* Verve.

Andrés Segovia: A Centenary Celebration. MCA Classics.

The Complete Decca Masters (Plus) (Judy Garland). MCA.

Louis Armstrong: Portrait of the Artist As a Young Man, 1923–1934. Columbia Legacy.

The Song Is You (Tommy Dorsey, Frank Sinatra). RCA.

Songs of the West (various artists). Rhino.

PRODUCER OF THE YEAR (OTHER THAN CLASSICAL)

- Don Was
David Foster
Trevor Horn

Jimmy Jam, Terry Lewis
Brendon O'Brien

BEST MUSIC VIDEO, SHORT FORM

- *Love Is Strong*, Rolling Stones. David Fincher, director. Virgin.

Agolo, Angelique Kidjo. Michel Meyer, director. Island.

Lucas with the Lid Off, Lucas. Michel Gondry, director. Big Beat/Atlantic Group.

Fire on Babylon, Sinead O'Conner. Michel Gondry, director. Chrysalis.

Go West, Pet Shop Boys, Howard Greenhalgh, director. EMI.

Jurassic Park, Weird Al Yankovic. Scott Nordlund, Mark Osborne, directors. Scotti Bros./Imaginary Entertainment.

BEST MUSIC VIDEO, LONG FORM

- *Zoo TV—Live from Sydney*, U2. David Mallet, director. Polygram Video.

A Prokofiev Fantasy with Peter and the Wolf, Claudio Abbado conducting the Chamber Orchestra of Europe; Sting, narrator. Steve Bendelack, Roger Law, Christopher Swann, directors. Spitting Swanns Limited Production.

Devotional, Depeche Mode. Anton Corbijn, director. Warner Reprise Video.

Ravel: Boléro; Mussorgsky: Pictures at an Exhibition, Charles Dutoit conducting the Orchestre Symphonique de Montréal. Bernar Hebert, Adrian Marthaler, Barbara Willis Sweete, directors. London.

The Girlie Show—Live Down Under, Madonna. Mark "Aldo" Miceli, director. Warner Bros./Maverick Home Video.

• 1995 •

"Hipper" Grammys Gulp Down *Jagged Little Pill*

"This is not your father's Grammys," host Ellen DeGeneres promised as the show began.

The awards certainly looked younger and hipper. Although rap music had made the race for Record of the Year once before (M.C. Hammer's "U Can't Touch This" in 1990), no *hard* rap works ever did. Now competing was Coolio's "Gangsta's Paradise," which had been declared the year's best single by music critics sounding off in polls conducted by *Rolling Stone* and the *Village Voice*. It was up against "Waterfalls" by the slinky r&b/hip-hop trio TLC and "One of Us" by Kentucky-born blues-rocker Joan Osborne, whose irreverent lyrics like "What if God were just a slob like one of us?" would have been considered heretical by Grammy voters of yore. Among the grittier contenders for best album were Seattle grungers Pearl Jam, whose *Vitalogy* was considered their best work yet, and Canadian angst-belter Alanis Morissette, whose *Jagged Little Pill* was perfect for what ailed the stodgy "Grannys" if only voters would swallow hard this year.

How did the nominations become so savvy?

Variety explained, "For the first time in the academy's 38 years, a panel reviewed the selections of the 7,500 voting members. For the new artist contest and the top three categories of each genre—album, single and song—the 20 entries that received the

MORISSETTE KNOWS GRAMMYS

Canadian singer leads nods; Seal gets 3

Would *Jagged Little Pill* have been nominated for best album under the old voting system, too? If so, it's logical to assume it would have won.

most votes from the general membership were submitted to a 25-member panel that assured the nominations were an accurate reflection of the year in music."

But in order for the cool, progressive music to prevail, it had to get by the kind of megaselling ballads that usually triumph and were also nominated—Seal's "Kiss from a Rose" and Mariah Carey and Boyz II Men's "One Sweet Day." The media obviously expected the same old Grammy song this year. The *L.A. Times* picked Seal to take best record. *Billboard* and *Entertainment Weekly* sided with "One Sweet Day." All three publications agreed that Carey's *Daydream* would take best album.

Then the biggest shocker of the night occurred when *Jagged Little Pill* slashed its way through for a huge win as Album of the Year. A roar of approval greeted the news and the *L.A. Times* noted that "the excitement seemed in part a cheer for the Grammys' integrity itself."

When *Pill* gobbled up three other awards, too, the *L.A. Times* added: "The real winner was the Grammy Awards themselves. After years of seeing its annual record industry competition ridiculed for often favoring conventional, mainstream artists at the expense of pop music's most dynamic and innovative figures, N.A.R.A.S. finally threw in the towel."

USA Today added: "The coronation of anti-diva Alanis Morissette propelled the once-stodgy award show closer to its long-stated goal of hipness and timeliness."

Pill was also honored as Best Rock Album and scored two awards for its track "You Oughta Know" (Best Rock Song and best female rock vocal performance).

"You Oughta Know" was embraced as the ulitimate revenge anthem of jilted lovers everywhere, making Morissette a breakout star as it dominated the summer radio airwaves and MTV in 1995. The lyrics were stinging: *"It was a slap in the face how quickly I was replaced / Are you thinking of me when you fuck her?"* When she performed it on the Grammycast, censors bleeped the f-word.

Upon receiving the best album trophy, she said, "I accept this on behalf of anyone who's ever written a song from a very pure place. . . . This award [means] that a lot of people connected to what I wrote."

Curiously, the fearless-sounding rocker looked shy and nervous after her Grammy triumphs and she refused to go backstage to meet the press.

As of awards night, *Jagged Little Pill* sold 4 million copies. It would go on to sell 11 million more, thereby becoming the biggest-selling debut work ever by a solo artist. Only one other debut album ever sold more: Boston's self-titled LP sold 16 million copies. Some pundits wondered: Did Morissette's best album victory really signal significant Grammy

change? The *L.A. Times* insisted that it probably would have been nominated for best album under the old voting system, too. If so, that means it probably would have won, since reforms didn't affect the latter stage of Grammy voting when winners are chosen by the broad popular vote of N.A.R.A.S. members. Once in the running, *Pill* may simply have been upstoppable in the category, just like U2's *The Joshua Tree* in 1987 and the Beatles' *Sgt. Pepper's Lonely Hearts Club Band* in 1967 when both rock blockbusters blasted through the Grammys' long-standing preference for smooth mainstream pop while conquering the rest of the music world.

"You Oughta Know" wasn't eligible for best record because it wasn't released as a commercial single, but it was up for Song of the Year and Morissette was a contender for Best New Artist. When "Know" lost the songwriter's award to the same tune that took best record, *Variety* called Grammy night "an evening of mixed results for the new voting procedures. . . . For all of the attempts to contemporize the awards, the winners for the most part showed a decidedly middle-of-the-road bent. While the academy recognized some of pop's vital currents in its nominations, the awards swayed toward pop songcrafting and lilting ballads."

In short: The nominees may have been hepper, but many of the top winners sure looked (and sounded) familiar.

What won Record and Song of the Year was *very* familiar music, in fact, since it was a track from a CD that was a losing nominee for Album of the Year last year—"Kiss from a Rose" from *Seal.* The song was released as a single during an eligibility period later than the album, since it was timed to coincide with the opening of the film *Batman Forever,* which included it on its soundtrack. Its victories, said *Variety,* "proved that acad-

> Results were "mixed for the new voting system," *Variety* said.

emy voters prefer soulful, chart-topping ballads supported by elaborate and often-played music videos backed by a film's promotional campaign."

The *Kiss* video did have frequent rotation on both MTV and VH1. The *Batman* single hovered in the Top 10 on the music charts for 17 weeks.

When it won the lofty prizes of Record and Song of the Year, the victories proved to be laurels honoring an artist who had come a long, hard way. In fact, the 32-year-old British pop star Seal was homeless when he wrote "Kiss" eight years earlier.

Now that he was holding two golden statuettes for his work, Seal talked comfortably with reporters about the poverty and hardship he endured prior to his first chart hit, "Killer," in 1990. He said backstage at the Grammys: "I'm very fond of those years. I guess I was hungry. Hungry for success. Hungry for life in general. Maybe that's why I have such a great life at the moment. I really did pay my dues."

He admitted, however, that "Kiss from a Rose" "is a bit of a peculiar song. I really have no idea what the words mean. But I don't know what half of my songs are about. When we first put the album together, 'Rose' stood out not as a great song, but as a sore thumb," he added. "I wasn't proud of it at first, but in retrospect I'm very glad it made it to the album."

In the category welcoming the best newcomers of 1995, *Variety* approved of Grammy's list of contenders, saying, "The benefit of the new process was probably most clearly reflected in the Best New Artist category, an area that has produced some of the most dubious winners in years past. This year's noms went to 1995's biggest-selling act, Hootie & the Blowfish, teenage r&b phenom Brandy, hot country singer Shania Twain and the critical faves Alanis Morissette and Joan Osborne."

Morissette and Osborne lost to what *Variety* called "the retail sales success story Hootie & the Blowfish."

Just one year earlier, Grammy's

Seal's self-titled debut disc lost its bid for best album last year, but returned triumphant when its "Kiss from a Rose" track won best record of '95.

favorite newcomers were performing to a bar crowd of 300 in Texas. Now, *Variety* reported, "As expected, Hootie & the Blowfish nabbed Best New Artist as the academy seemingly rewarded the band for helping to keep retailers' cash registers ringing throughout 1995."

The Blowfish's breakthrough was the 11-million-seller *Cracked Rear View,* which wasn't eligible for a best album bid, since it was released before the eligibility period. Various spin-off singles did make the current Grammy race, however, with "Let Her Cry" ending up with the kudos for best pop vocal performance by a group, a prize bestowed by Gene Simmons of Kiss. Backstage, Blowfish frontman Darius Rucker gushed to reporters, "Winning a Grammy is one thing, but to get it from Kiss, that's *greatness.*"

In another pop music category, *Variety* reported that Annie Lennox "landed one of the evening's surprises when 'No More "I Love You's" ' took home the best female pop vocal performance. Her win seemingly split Acad voters as she toppled heavily favored Mariah Carey and newcomer Joan Osborne in the category." While accepting the statuette, Lennox admitted to the audience that she was "stunned."

Also claiming to be stunned was 1960s folk icon Joni Mitchell, who had no thank-you speech prepared when she triumphed over Lennox in a different pop music slot. *Variety* reported: "The unexpected win by Mitchell in the Best Pop Album category signaled the Academy's recognition of her longevity as an artist. Mitchell defeated Carey's *Daydream,* which had been the odds-on favorite, and Lennox's *Medusa.* The win is particularly sweet as *Turbulent Indigo* marked Mitchell's return to Warner Bros. records after a two-decade absence."

Mitchell last won a Grammy two decades earlier—in 1974. Also returning this year after a decades-long absence was Frank Sinatra, who'd won eight Grammys prior to 1967, but none since. Pundits expected him to be nominated for—and to win—Album of the Year two years ago for *Duets,* which included collaborations with Julio Iglesias, Bono, Carly Simon and Luther Vandross. But Grammy voters surprisingly snubbed it. Now, however, they hailed its sequel, *Duets II,* with the prize for Best Traditional Pop Vocal Performance. The newest work included collaborations with Linda Ronstadt ("Moonlight"), Gladys Knight ("For Once in My Life"), Patti LaBelle ("Bewitched") and Willie Nelson ("A Foggy Day"). Both albums employed technological tricks that caused some critics to grumble. "The artists recorded their contributions at different times and from different locations," *People* griped. "They don't seem to be singing together—in some cases they don't even seem to be singing the same song. Once again, what we've got is a triumph of technology over artistry."

Sinatra and friends were not nominated in the category of Best Pop Collaboration with Vocal, which enabled another respected music veteran, Van Morrison, to win his first Grammy. Morrison had worked with fellow Irishmen the Chieftains on a previous album (*Irish Heartbeat*), but it was a track from the Chieftain's 30th release, *The Long Black Veil,* that earned them a joint victory over two teams that seemed invincible in this category: Mariah Carey and Boyz II Men

("One Sweet Day") and Michael and Janet Jackson ("Scream").

"Scream" was the first single release off Michael Jackson's *HIStory: Past, Present and Future,* a losing nominee for Album of the Year. In it, Jackson finally spoke out against recent charges that he'd sexually molested a boy. "Jackson seems determined to answer his accusers and make his return a triumphant vindication," *Entertainment Weekly* noted. " 'Stop questioning me!' he snarls defiantly on 'Scream.' " The video version, shot for $7 million, employed funky Japanese animation and won the Grammy for best short-form video, but it was not received well by critics. *Newsweek* slammed it as "a jittery industrial dance number featuring sister Janet [that's] simply there to remind us that Michael's angry. The siblings wander around their own private space-world, bouncing off walls and smashing guitars like a couple of mismatched, junkie-chic androids. You want to scream back at them, 'Hey! Would you two please shut up and dance?' "

The prize for best long-form video was claimed by Peter Gabriel for *Secret World Live,* the tape of a concert he gave in Modena, Italy, during a 1994 world tour. In the long-form video, he performs music that earned him Grammys for short-form videos in years past: "Digging in the Dirt" (1992) and "Steam" (1993).

Another loser in the best album race rebounded to win a consolation prize when Pearl Jam snagged the laurels for Best Hard Rock Performance ("Spin the Black Circle") over Alice in Chains, Primus, Red Hot Chili Peppers and Van Halen. Lead singer Eddie Vedder hardly seemed grateful when he accepted the statuette, however, saying, "I don't know what this means. I don't think it means anything. My dad would have liked it. My dad died before I got to know him. So that's why I'm here. Thanks . . . I guess."

In addition to Morissette's "You Oughta Know," the song that received the most ubiquitous radio airplay during 1995 was "Run-Around" by Blues Traveler, winner of the rock group vocals prize. "We're a glorified bar band," front-man John Popper demured humbly to reporters backstage, but actually the foursome had been touring profession-ally for nearly a decade, infusing their music with a slick range of sounds span-ning rock, blues and reggae. On "Run-Around," the 350-pound Popper added a bouncy harmonica beat that had radio deejays and TV veejays hooked.

When the Grammy bids came out this year, *Variety* noted, "Veterans led the way in many of the eight rock categories as nominations went to Bob Dylan, Neil Young, the Eagles, Tom Petty, Jimmy Page and Robert Plant, U2, Van Halen, the Allman Brothers Band, King Crim-son and Santana."

Tom Petty was one of the few solo artists who came through, though, win-ning the male vocal category for "You Don't Know How It Feels," a release from *Wildflowers,* his second solo album after quitting the Heartbreakers and his first since returning to his old label, Warner Bros. It was also nominated for Best Rock Album (and picked to win by *Billboard*) but lost to Morissette's *Jagged Little Pill.* Petty's only previous Grammy was for being part of the Traveling Wilburys, which won best rock group performance of 1989.

The Allman Brothers, recently reunited, had never before won a Grammy, but now the blues-based south-ern rock group came through with the year's Best Rock Instrumental Perfor-mance ("Jessica").

Despite six nominations in past years, Nirvana still hadn't received a Grammy even though the Seattle grungers were heavily favored to win last year follow-ing the suicide of singer Kurt Cobain. Now they finally triumphed with *MTV Unplugged in New York,* which reaped the prize for alternative music. During their televised concert, they performed such hits as "Come As You Are," "On a Plain" and "All Apologies."

Nine Inch Nails pulled off a surprise victory in the metal category in 1992 and now returned to face off against three-time past champ Metallica, both nomi-nated with tracks from *Woodstock '94,* and White Zombie, which was predicted to win by the *L.A. Times.* Nine Inch Nails nailed it, however, with a concert version of "Happiness in Slavery."

The biggest news in r&b music this year was the impact felt by TLC, whose *Crazysexycool* sold 6 million copies, making the saucy trio the biggest-selling female group in music history. The frisky young women also made other headlines recently, however, thanks to their love and money woes. Group member Lisa "Left Eye" Lopez was convicted of burn-ing down her boyfriend's house. One week after their breakthrough hit "Water-falls" reached the top of the charts, TLC declared bankruptcy.

TLC got more bad ink when *USA Today* complained about their appear-ance at the Grammycast: "Unfortunately, the ghost of Milli Vanilli returned in TLC's performance of 'Waterfalls,' lip-synched in violation of Grammy rules. Show execs tap-danced to excuse it, say-ing that exceptions are made for cases 'where you can't catch your breath because of the exertion.' So why not tone down the high-stepping instead of chuck-ing live vocals?"

"Waterfalls" lost its bid for Record of the Year, but the bankrupt TLC nonethe-less grabbed Grammy gold for *Crazy-sexycool* (Best R&B Album) and "Creep" (best r&b group performance).

Five-time past Grammy champ Baby-face won the Producer of the Year award for producing *Crazysexycool* in addition to overseeing recent works by Vanessa Williams and Madonna.

The *L.A. Times* sized up the race for best female r&b vocals thus: "Toni Brax-ton is likely to win for the third year in a row—though teen star Brandy could sneak in if Braxton and Baker split the diva vote."

Anita Baker, a seven-time past Grammy victor (four wins as best r&b

singer), retired from music four years ago to concentrate on her family life. After giving birth to two boys, she was back now, and she seized the Grammy slot back, too—with "I Apologize," a track from her critically cheered new album, *Rhythm of Love*.

Also experiencing a career resurgence lately was Stevie Wonder. ("What a pleasure it is to welcome the legendary Mr. Wonder back to active duty!" *Billboard* gushed upon the release of "For Your Love.") Wonder arrived at the Grammy ceremony with his own two children in tow—son Keita and daughter Aisha—whom he brought along to watch him receive the Lifetime Achievement Award. But he also scored 2 new statuettes for "For Your Love," bringing his career count to 19 Grammys: best r&b male vocals and Best R&B Song. Backstage, he told reporters, "I wish someone else had won [the two competitive awards]. I was very much into the songs and the artists that were up." He added that he was nonetheless happy to be reaching a whole new generation of music fans with his latest work. "I feel like a child and I feel like an older man," he said. "I'm very happy."

Wonder reached millions of young people this year with his contribution to Coolio's megahit "Gangsta's Paradise," which borrowed catchy chords from Wonder's old song "Pastime Paradise." Wonder told reporters backstage that he approved of the adaptation: "I think it's a great rendition of the song. I'm behind it all the way. I think that the lyric that he did with his song and the way that he sang it brought it into the '90s."

Coolio's new words preached a pacifist message about resisting the lure of drugs and violence in the ghetto. When the new song won the Grammy for best rap solo, the L.A. braider expounded on that view, saying, "I only got one thing to say to all of my black and Latino brothers out there fighting: ain't no gangsters in paradise. So wake up and get something new in your life."

The *L.A. Times* noted, however, that

Pat Metheny's group took its eighth career Grammy for *We Live Here*, a disc declared "worthy" by *Billboard* and the *L.A. Times.*

Coolio contradicted his message of nonviolence "by stating that a 'revolution is coming' and wearing blue bandana colors associated with the Crips gang."

Since it came out after this Grammy eligibility period, Coolio's *Gangsta's Paradise* CD was not eligible for Best Rap Album, a category that went to Naughty by Nature's *Poverty's Paradise*. The twentysomething trio from East Orange, N.J., earned broad critical acclaim in 1995 for its blues and jazzy touches to hip-hop. *People* told its readers in its review of *Poverty's Paradise:* "If you're jonesing for a good, curbside view of the 'hood without leaving the couch, it don't get no better than this."

Naughty by Nature was also nominated in the rap category for duo/group performances but lost to "the queen of hip-hop soul," Mary J. Blige, and Method Man, a member of the group Wu-Tang Clan. When Blige held the statuette in hand backstage for "I'll Be There for You/You're All I Need to Get By," the obviously excited cowinner told reporters that she was eager to celebrate by hitting the party scene after the Grammy show.

When Canadian thrush Shania Twain hit the U.S. country music scene this year, she had much to celebrate, considering the impact she made. Her debut work, *The Woman in Me,* was the fastest-selling album in country music history and the biggest seller ever for a female country artist. It was also the easy winner of Best Country Album. In addition, Twain was nominated for Best New Artist (losing to Hootie & the Blowfish) plus best female country vocalist and Best Country Song ("Any Man of Mine").

Twain actually had a chance at winning the vocalist's prize, since category queen Mary Chapin Carpenter wasn't nominated. The *L.A. Times* even predicted Twain would take it for her "sassy square dance," but she was topped by a 24-year-old bluegrass fiddler and crooner who was declared the Country Artist of the Year by the *Rolling Stone* Music Critics' Poll.

Alison Krauss had just won four Country Music Association Awards, including the vocalist prize for the same work for which she won a Grammy: her cover of the old Foundations' hit "Baby, Now That I've Found You." She was also honored at both the Grammys and the C.M.A.s for "Somewhere in the Vicinity of the Heart," her collaboration with Shenandoah upon the occasion of the group's 10th anniversary.

Shenandoah, however, lost its bid for the duo/group performance prize to the Mavericks ("Here Comes the Rain"), the young country rockers from Miami who were cheered by *Entertainment Weekly* for "synthesizing '50s country and '60s pop and rock with intelligence, verve and cultural variety."

Asleep at the Wheel celebrated its 25th anniversary with a win for best country instrumental work ("Hightower"), a prize shared with Bela Fleck and Johnny Gimble. It was the western swing group's seventh victory.

"Mighty" best opera *Les Troyens* cost $1 million to produce.

The male vocalist honors went to the same artist who'd won the category three times in the recent past (1990, 1992, 1994): Vince Gill, who also just swept the equivalent category at the C.M.A.s for an unprecedented fifth time. Gill's total Grammy count so far was six, all of which were performance prizes. He'd never been honored for songwriting. That changed this year when "Go Rest High on That Mountain," which earned him the vocals award, also brought him the gold for Best Country Song. "Mountain" was his private eulogy to his brother, who'd recently died of a heart attack. "It's the first thing I've ever done that really was personal in my career," he said backstage at the Grammys about writing and performing the song. "I'm really thrilled for my mom that one of her sons could do something for her other son."

Country artists also claimed the category for Best Bluegrass Album when the Nashville Bluegrass Band was honored for *Unleashed.* In its review, *People* described the album thus: "Five kinda cornfed-lookin' guys who have been together since the 1980s perform old chestnuts and fresh pop tunes."

Old Grammy favorites once again dominated the jazz categories. The Pat Metheny Group earned its eighth career prize when *We Live Here* scored the accolade for Best Contemporary Jazz Performance. *Billboard* applauded the album in its review: "Tracks such as 'Here to Stay' and 'To the End of the World' rank among the best the group has cut. It should rule jazz radio." When the CD ended up ruling the Grammys, the *L.A. Times* declared it "a worthy winner."

The 1981 recipient of the prize for jazz vocals returned now with *An Evening with Lena Horne,* a nightclub performance taped at New York's Supper Club where she crooned such saloon standards as "Yesterday When I Was Young." *People* wrote of the recording: "If the survivor and legend, 77, sometimes wobbles and shouts rather than sings, such lapses are compensated for with dignity, tenderness and sass—few can growl like Horne." Lena Horne beat the critics' favorite in the category, Abbey Lincoln, whose *Turtle's Dream* was hailed as the best jazz album of the year by *Time*.

Among the many stars comprising the GRP All-Star Band were the Brecker Brothers, Chick Corea, Ramsey Lewis, Dave Grusin and Arturo Sandoval. Led by Tom Scott, the band's *All Blues* reaped the Grammy for large-ensemble jazz.

Tenor saxman and two-time past champ Michael Brecker beat four pianists to take the prize for best solo performance with a track from *Infinity*. The album won the additional Grammy for best group instrumental work for Brecker's collaboration with the McCoy Tyner Trio. The *L.A. Times* called the latter victory "deserving."

Brecker's win with the McCoy Tyner Trio was at the expense of Joe Henderson's salute to works by Antonio Carlos "Tom" Jobim, 67, who died of heart failure in December 1994. Jobim's music was nonetheless honored elsewhere at the Grammys when the late father of bossa nova received what *Billboard* called "a misplaced Grammy in a jazz category." The composer of Grammy's 1967 Record of the Year, "The Girl from Ipanema," had never won a Grammy during his lifetime. (The "Ipanema" gold went to singer Astrud Gilberto and saxman Stan Getz; "Ipanema" wasn't nominated for Song of the Year, which would have given Jobim his own chance for the equivalent honor.) Now Jobim won the Best Latin Jazz Performance award for *Antonio Brasileiro,* a collection of Brazilian works that went on sale in his homeland just a week before his death in a New York hospital.

In the category for contemporary blues albums, a victory was widely predicted for Buddy Guy, who'd won twice before. On *Slippin' In*, he featured new works by himself and classics by Jimmy Reed, Charles Brown, Lowell Fulsom

and Freddy King. He performed with his own group plus reunited members of Stevie Ray Vaughan's band Double Trouble.

Seventy-five-year-old Delta blues singer and guitarist John Lee Hooker first won the category for traditional blues recordings in 1989 for a track from *The Healer,* a work that rejuvenated his career. Now he claimed the gold for *Chill Out,* which featured heartfelt reflections on lost love ("Too Young") and his long career as a gypsy artist ("Talkin' the Blues").

Ramblin' Jack Elliott earned the first Grammy of his career for *South Coast,* his first studio album in 27 years. It included four songs by Woody Guthrie, his old friend and sometimes music partner. At the Grammys, Elliott told reporters that he was "shocked" it won. He also confessed that he'd never seen the awards show before. "I don't have a TV out where I live," Elliott explained.

Winner of the trophy for Best Contemporary Folk Album, Emmylou Harris, told *Variety,* "I've always pushed the boundaries and this time we went out of the ballpark."

She was referring to *Wrecking Ball,* which *Variety* noted "was hardly her usual country fare." The *L.A. Times* called it "a Nashville-based collaboration with rock producer-songwriter Daniel Lanois that pushed the boundaries of country so far that her album wound up in the contemporary folk category where Harris topped a very strong field that included Bob Dylan, the Chieftains, John Prine and Steve Earle." When Harris won, she told reporters, "I'm glad N.A.R.A.S. found a category for us."

The winner of a Latin pop Grammy in 1992, Jon Secada, rallied with *Amor,* which included such romantic works as "Es por T" and "Alma con Alma" in addition to four of his own new compositions. The *L.A. Times* insisted, "Secada won in a weak category in which only Mana's *Cuando los Angeles Lloran* stood out as an above-average work."

Gloria Estefan won her first Grammy in 1993 for her first Spanish-language album, *Mi Tierra.* Now her second Spanish release, *Abriendo Puertas* (Opening Doors), earned her the same prize for Best Tropical Latin Performance. Although it contained salsa and other Latin music, the *L.A. Times* griped over its Grammy classification, since "it's dominated by Colombia's accordion-tinged sound."

When the 55 year-old-Tex-Mex accordionist Flaco Jimenez was Grammy-honored, the *L.A. Times* also complained that it was "as the undisputed best of a pathetic Mexican-American category in which only Juan Gabriel provided serious competition." In his self-titled disc, Flaco Jimenez explored a range of sounds from traditional Tejano to Dixie country while accompanied by electric and steel guitars.

Two-time past champ Los Lobos earned the Best Pop Instrumental Performance award for "Mariachi Suite," which was featured in the film soundtrack to the Antonio Banderas film *Desperado.* Previously, Los Lobos had worked on such movies as *La Bamba* and *Mambo Kings.* Backstage at the Grammys, group frontman Cesar Rosas told the press, "Working in films keeps us off the road and allows us to be at home and work at the same time."

A new singer, musician and songwriter from Nashville, Ashley Cleveland, got recognized in the Christian categories when *Lesson of Love* was acknowledged as Best Rock Gospel Album.

Otherwise, past Grammy veterans prevailed, such as 1984 champ Michael W. Smith, who was one of the leaders of the recent surge in Christian music that saw U.S. sales rise to nearly $1 billion in 1995. In its first week of release, Smith's *I'll Lead You Home* (Best Pop/Contemporary Gospel Album) landed at number 16 on the pop charts, the highest album debut ever by Christian music. Backstage at the Grammys, Smith told reporters that the secret to his success was his refusal to do squeaky-clean music. "People want to hear about struggles," he said. "A lot of gospel tries hard to not talk about the hard times."

Working without brother BeBe for the first time, CeCe Winans not only rose to

Deutsche Grammophon

For his 70th birthday, voters gave Pierre Boulez two Grammys for "La Mer," including his fifth victory for Best Classical Album of the year.

fifth place on the gospel charts with *Alone in His Presence* but garnered the Grammy for Best Contemporary Soul Gospel Album. It included self-written music such as the title track plus works by others (Steven Curtis Chapman's "His Strength Is Perfect") and hymn classics ("Blessed Assurance").

Eleven notable country stars, including Emmylou Harris, John Berry, Martina McBride, Charlie Daniels, Alison Krauss and the Cox Family, teamed up for *Amazing Grace,* winner of Best Southern Gospel, Country Gospel or Bluegrass Gospel Album.

The singing preacher known as the Queen of Gospel, Shirley Caesar, took the prize for Best Traditional Soul Gospel Album for *Shirley Caesar Live . . . He Will Come,* a work she recorded at the Greater Bibleway Miracle Temple Worldwide Church in Atlanta. She told the press, "When I'm secluded in a studio, I have to make my own church, but with live audiences, I am really inspired to belt it out and I think I'm most effective when I'm able to let go and praise God."

The 240-voice Brooklyn Tabernacle Choir got the gold for Best Gospel Album by a Choir or Chorus for *Praise Him . . . Live!*

When it reviewed *Forest, Billboard* cheered the future winner of Best New Age Album: "Fourteen years after his first album *Autumn,* George Winston still stands alone among solo pianists. His gifted lyricism remains true."

Deep Forest explored new terrain in *Bohème,* winner of Best World Music Album. Its French-based composers, Erik Mouquet and Michel Sanchez, incorporated African, Celtic and Eastern European sounds and invited Hungarian thrush Marta Sebasteynn to sing several songs.

The Jamaican-born Brooklyn rapper Shaggy reaped a Grammy for the same song for which he recently won Record of the Year at the Tamika Reggae Awards: his Top 10 summer dance hit "Boombastic." Shaggy explained the title to *People:* "Boombastic means anythng sensational. For instance, on the record, basically, I'm a boombastic lover."

When a noted actor won the category for Best Spoken Word Album for Children for reading Prokofiev's *Peter and the Wolf, Billboard* couldn't resist noting that his TV character would probably prefer the company of his galactic enemies over human wee ones: "Well, it's probably ironic only to *Star Trek: The Next Generation* devotees, who know that the Enterprise's Capt. Jean-Luc Picard is more terrified of kids than of Romulans, Cardassians and the Borg combined."

In the spoken word category for adults, poet Maya Angelou was honored for reading from *Phenomenal Woman*:

I say
It's the fire in my eyes
And the flash of my teeth
The swing in my waist
And the joy in my feet
I'm a woman
Phenomenally.
Phenomenal woman
That's me.

Smokey Joe's Cafe lost the Tony Award for Best Musical to *Sunset Blvd.,* but a recording of its Broadway cast was honored at the Grammys as Best Musical Show Album. It marked the first Grammy win by Mike Stoller and Jerry Leiber, the composing team behind such classic tunes as "Jailhouse Rock," "Stand By Me" and "Love Potion Number 9," which were all performed in *Cafe. Variety* encountered the duo backstage at the Grammys: "Control, Mike Stoller said, was the main ingredient that allowed him and partner Jerry Leiber to assemble *Smokey Joe's Cafe.* 'We had approval,' Stoller said, 'and we wanted our show to stand on its own.' The duo's songs, written for the likes of Elvis Presley and the Drifters, 'were turned out like a daily newspaper,' Leiber said."

Bill Hollman was known mostly for his arrangements for leading postwar big bands, but he earned a Grammy for writing the title track to *A View from the Side,* winner of Best Instrumental Composition.

Recipient of Best Historical Album was *The Heifetz Collection,* a 65-disc career tribute to the violin virtuoso. It begins with Jascha Heifetz's first studio recording two weeks after his Carnegie Hall debut in 1917 (the cheering audience charged the stage) and ends with his last recording in 1972 before he retired to devote his final years to teaching and writing.

Pierre Boulez's 70th birthday was widely celebrated in 1995. He was feted at the Grammys with two nominations for Best Classical Album and two more for Best Orchestral Performance. Considering how generous the Grammys have been in the past to orchestras in Chicago and music by Bartók, most pundits predicted that the famed conductor would now win both awards for Bartók's "Divertimento" and "Dance Suite" performed by the Chicago Symphony Orchestra. Instead, he won both awards (including his fifth victory for Best Classical Album) for Debussy's "La Mer." His accompaniment was the Cleveland Orchestra, the same group that performed for him at his American debut 31 years ago.

In the race for the top trophy in classical music, the *L.A. Times* believed that "a split vote among Boulezians could give a best album victory to Berlioz's mighty opera *Les Troyens.*"

Although the "mighty" album lost, it did win consolation gold for Best Opera Recording. The first modern studio recording of the complete, four-hour opera (including a newly restored scene) was cheered by *Opera News* in its review: "Conductor Charles Dutoit, by virtue of his rare command of French style, has brought us closer to *Les Troyens* than anyone else. His Montreal Symphony plays with the fiery lightness that suits Berlioz best." The ambitious artistic undertaking was also expensive, costing $1 million. *Opera News* commented, "It will take Decca about 30 years to recoup its investment on *Troyens,* as opposed to the 10 or 15 years it might take a more typical title."

None of *Troyens*' singers was nominated for best vocalist. The category went to its only female nominee, American soprano Sylvia McNair, who acknowledged the 300th anniversary of the death of British composer Henry Purcell with performances of his works, including "If Music Be the Food of Love" and "Sweeter Than Roses." *American Record Guide* cried bravo over the result: "In point of technique, she is breathtaking."

Herbert Blomstedt was the sentimental favorite in the category for Best Choral Performance, since he had just retired as conductor of the San Francisco Symphony. He won for Brahms's *Ein Deutsches Requiem.*

The *L.A. Times* was proved right with this forecast: "The chamber music category has the perennial '90s winners, the Emerson Quartet, playing recondite Webern superbly. If anyone beats them it will be the starry trio of Emanual Ax, Yo-Yo Ma and Richard Stoltzman, with their hyper-glossy Brahms-Beethoven-Mozart collection."

Considering all the fuss that Russian fiddler Maxim Vengerov, a Grammy newcomer, was getting from admiring critics lately, he was considered the front-runner in the category for best soloist performance with an orchestra. Instead, it went to 14-time past champ Itzhak Perlman, who performed part of his victorious work, *The American Album,* on the Grammycast.

Five pianists faced off in the category for best soloists without orchestra: Either Evgeny Kissin or Murray Perahia was expected to win. The victor turned out to be Radu Lupu, who was honored for performing part of his signature repertoire: Schubert's piano sonatas.

The award for Best Contemporary Composition went to "Concert à Quatre," the last unfinished work by Olivier Messiaen, who died in April 1992. It was commissioned by Myung Whun Chung, music director of Paris's Orchestre de l'Opéra Bastille, which recently recorded the work.

Overall at this year's Grammys, *Billboard* noted a curious trend: "Indie artists prevailed in more than a dozen diverse categories. Among the biggest winners was Rounder Records bluegrass artist Alison Krauss, who took a solo award for 'Baby, Now That I've Found You' and shared a tiny Victrola with Shenandoah. The indies also ruled in a variety of other categories from jazz to historical albums: Ramblin' Jack Elliott, Jonathan Winters, Jimmy Sturr."

At the outset of this year's Grammy race, Mariah Carey had led with six nominations and it looked like Grammy's Best New Artist of 1990 was the front-runner to take both Album and Record of the Year of 1995. At the end of Grammy night, however, after winning nothing, she proved to be a trouper by stopping by the post-Grammy "victory party" set up ahead of time by hubby Tommy Mottola, who was also the president of her label, Sony Music. Few fans showed up.

Also snubbed this year was Joan

Osborne, who'd begun with five noms, including bids for best record and album.

Babyface liked the winners, though. He told *Variety,* "It's especially great to see Brandy and Alanis get recognized, but Seal really deserves it. He's had an incredible year."

Variety said in its review of the show: "This ceremony was by some standards the best Grammy telecast in years—for instance, there were no colossal embarrassments on the order of cutting Frank Sinatra off in the middle of his acceptance speech, or terminating the show halfway through the final production number due to time constraints. On the other hand, the show, hosted by comic Ellen De-Generes, lacked fire; it was nearly as smooth and sanitary as TLC's lip-synched performance.

"The comic hosted more than capably, especially considering that she's not generally identified with the music business, a handicap she was quick to disparage, enthusing that 'I have been listening to music for about two years now, and I really like a lot of it.' In truth, she was one of the few Grammy hosts ever to give the impression of familiarity with much of the nominated music.

"Show had its moments, but lacked any electrifying sequences."

Ratings jumped 24 percent over last year's viewership, reaching 14.6 rating/23 share.

• 1995 •

The awards ceremony was broadcast on CBS from the Shrine Auditorium in Los Angeles on February 28, 1996, for the eligibility period of October 1, 1994, through September 30, 1995.

ALBUM OF THE YEAR
• *Jagged Little Pill*, Alanis Morissette. Maverick Reprise.
Daydream, Mariah Carey. Columbia.
HIStory: Past, Present and Future Book I, Michael Jackson. Epic.
Relish, Joan Osborne. Blue Gorilla/Mercury.
Vitalogy, Pearl Jam. Epic.

RECORD OF THE YEAR
• "Kiss from a Rose," Seal. ZTT/Sire/Warner Bros.
"One Sweet Day," Mariah Carey, Boyz II Men. Columbia.
"Gangsta's Paradise," Coolio. MCA.
"One of Us," Joan Osborne. Blue Gorilla/Mercury.
"Waterfalls," TLC. LaFace.

SONG OF THE YEAR
(Songwriter's Award)
• "Kiss from a Rose," Seal.

"I Can Love You Like That," Maribeth Derry, Steve Diamond, Jennifer Kimball.
"One of Us," Eric Bazillian.
"You Are Not Alone," R. Kelly.
"You Oughta Know," Glen Ballard, Alanis Morissette.

BEST NEW ARTIST
• Hootie & the Blowfish
Brandy
Alanis Morissette
Joan Osborne
Shania Twain

BEST POP ALBUM
• *Turbulent Indigo*, Joni Mitchell. Reprise.
Daydream, Mariah Carey. Columbia.
Hell Freezes Over, Eagles. Geffen.
Medusa, Annie Lennox. Arista.
Bedtime Stories, Madonna. Maverick/Sire.

BEST POP VOCAL
PERFORMANCE, MALE
• Seal, "Kiss from a Rose." ZTT/Sire/Warner Bros.

Bryan Adams, "Have You Ever Really Loved a Woman?" A&M.

Michael Jackson, "You Are Not Alone." Epic.

Elton John, "Believe." Rocket/Island.

Sting, "When We Dance." A&M.

BEST POP VOCAL PERFORMANCE, FEMALE

- Annie Lennox, "No More 'I Love You's.'" Arista.

Mariah Carey, "Fantasy." Columbia.

Dionne Farris, "I Know." Columbia.

Joan Osborne, "One of Us." Blue Gorilla/Mercury.

Bonnie Raitt, "You Got It." Arista.

Vanessa Williams, "Colors of the Wind." Hollywood.

BEST POP PERFORMANCE BY A DUO OR GROUP WITH VOCAL

- Hootie & the Blowfish, "Let Her Cry." Atlantic.

All-4-One, "I Can Love You Like That." Blitzz/Atlantic.

Eagles, "Love Will Keep Us Alive," track from *Hell Freezes Over.* Geffen.

Rembrandts, "I'll Be There for You (Theme from *Friends*)." EastWest.

TLC, "Waterfalls." LaFace.

BEST TRADITIONAL POP VOCAL PERFORMANCE

- Frank Sinatra, *Duets II.* Capitol.

Julie Andrews, *Julie Andrews—Broadway—The Music of Richard Rodgers.* Philips Classics.

Rosemary Clooney, *Demi-Centennial!* Concord Jazz.

Eartha Kitt, *Back in Business.* DRG.

John Raitt, *Broadway Legend.* Angel.

BEST POP COLLABORATION WITH VOCAL

- Chieftains, Van Morrison, "Have I Told You Lately That I Love You?" RCA Victor.

John B. Featuring Babyface, "Someone to Love." Yab Um/550 Music/Epic.

Anita Baker, James Ingram, "When You Love Someone." Electra.

Mariah Carey, Boyz II Men, "One Sweet Day." Columbia.

Michael Jackson, Janet Jackson, "Scream." Epic.

BEST POP INSTRUMENTAL PERFORMANCE

- Los Lobos, "Mariachi Suite," track from *Desperado* (soundrack). Epic Soundtrax.

Allman Brothers Band, "In Memory of Elizabeth Reed," track from *2nd Set—An Evening with the Allman Brothers Band.* Epic.

Kenny G, "Have Yourself a Merry Little Christmas," track from *Miracles— The Holiday Album.* Arista.

Dave Grusin, "Yesterday," track from *(I Got No Kick Against) Modern Jazz, A GRP Artists' Celebration of the Songs of the Beatles.* GRP.

Bruce Hornsby, "Song B." RCA.

BEST ROCK ALBUM

- *Jagged Little Pill*, Alanis Morissette. Maverick/Reprise.

Forever Blue, Chris Isaak. Reprise.

Vitalogy, Pearl Jam. Epic.

Wildflowers, Tom Petty. Warner Bros.

Mirror Ball, Neil Young. Reprise.

BEST ROCK SONG
(Songwriter's Award)

- "You Oughta Know," Glen Ballard, Alanis Morissette.

"Dignity," Bob Dylan.

"Downtown," Neil Young.

"Hold Me, Thrill Me, Kiss Me, Kill Me," Bono, U2.

"Hurt," Trent Reznor.

BEST ROCK VOCAL PERFORMANCE, MALE

- Tom Petty, "You Don't Know How It Feels." Warner Bros.

Bob Dylan, "Knockin' on Heaven's Door," track from *Bob Dylan MTV Unplugged.* Columbia.

Chris Isaak, "Somebody's Crying." Reprise.

Lenny Kravitz, "Rock and Roll Is Dead." Virgin America.

Neil Young, "Peace and Love," track from *Mirror Ball*. Reprise.

BEST ROCK VOCAL PERFORMANCE, FEMALE

- Alanis Morissette, "You Oughta Know," track from *Jagged Little Pill*. Maverick/Reprise.

Toni Childs, "Lay Down Your Pain." DGC.

P. J. Harvey, "Down by the Water." Island.

Joan Osborne, "St. Teresa," track from *Relish*. Blue Gorilla/Mercury.

Liz Phair, "Don't Have Time," track from *Higher Learning—Music from the Motion Picture*. 550 Music/Epic.

BEST ROCK PERFORMANCE BY A DUO OR GROUP WITH VOCAL

- Blues Traveler, "Run-Around." A&M.

Eagles, "Hotel California." Geffen.

Dave Matthews Band, "What Would You Say," track from *Under the Table and Dreaming*. RCA.

Jimmy Page, Robert Plant, "Kashmir," track from *No Quarter*. Atlantic.

U2, "Hold Me, Thrill Me, Kiss Me, Kill Me." Atantic/Island.

BEST ROCK INSTRUMENTAL PERFORMANCE

- Allman Brothers Band, "Jessica," track from *2nd Set—An Evening with the Allman Brothers Band*. Epic.

Jeff Healey Band, "Shapes of Things," track from *Cover to Cover*. Arista.

King Crimson, "Vroom," track from *Thrak*. Virgin America.

Santana, Vernon Reid, "Every Now and Then," track from *Dance of the Rainbow Serpent*. Legacy/Columbia.

Steve Vai, "Tender Surrender," track from *Alien Love Secrets*. Relativity.

BEST HARD ROCK PERFORMANCE

- Pearl Jam, "Spin the Black Circle," track from *Vitalogy*. Epic.

Alice in Chains, "Grind." Columbia.

Primus, "Wynona's Big Brown Beaver," track from *Tales from the Punch-bowl*. Interscope.

Red Hot Chili Peppers, "Blood Sugar Sex Magik," track from *Woodstock '94*. A&M.

Van Halen "The Seventh Seal," track from *Balance*. Warner Bros.

BEST METAL PERFORMANCE

- Nine Inch Nails, "Happiness in Slavery," track from *Woodstock '94*. A&M.

S.F.W., "Gwar," track from *S.F.W.* A&M.

Megadeth, "Paranoid," track from *Nativity in Black—A Tribute to Black Sabbath*. Columbia.

Metallica, "For Whom the Bell Tolls," track from *Woodstock '94*. A&M.

White Zombie, "More Human Than Human," track from *Astro-Creep: 2000 Songs of Love, Destruction and Other Synthetic Delusions of the Electric Head*. Geffen.

BEST ALTERNATIVE MUSIC PERFORMANCE

- Nirvana, *MTV Unplugged in New York*. DGC.

Björk, *Post*. Elektra.

Foo Fighters, *Foo Fighters*. Roswell/Capitol.

P. J. Harvey, *To Bring You My Love*. Island.

Presidents of the United States of America, *The Presidents of the United States of America*. Columbia.

BEST RHYTHM & BLUES ALBUM

- *Crazysexycool*, TLC. LaFace.

My Life, Mary J. Blige. Uptown/MCA.

Brown Sugar, D'Angelo. EMI.

The Gold Experience, Artist Formally Known As Prince. Warner Bros.

The Icon Is Love, Barry White. A&M.

BEST RHYTHM & BLUES SONG
(Songwriter's Award)

- "For Your Love," Stevie Wonder.

"Brown Sugar," D'Angelo.

"Creep," Dallas Austin.
"Red Light Special," Babyface.
"You Can't Run," Babyface.

BEST RHYTHM & BLUES VOCAL PERFORMANCE, MALE

- Stevie Wonder, "For Your Love." Motown.
- D'Angelo, "Brown Sugar." EMI.
- Montell Jordan, "This Is How We Do It." RAL/PMP.
- Artist Formally Known as Prince, "I Hate You." Warner Bros.
- Barry White, "Baby's Home," track from *The Icon Is Love*. A&M.

BEST RHYTHM & BLUES VOCAL PERFORMANCE, FEMALE

- Anita Baker, "I Apologize," track from *Rhythm of Love*. Elektra.
- Brandy, "Baby." Atlantic.
- Toni Braxton, "I Belong to You." LaFace.
- Mariah Carey, "Always Be My Baby," track from *Daydream*. Columbia.
- Vanessa Williams, "The Way That You Love." Wing/Mercury.

BEST RHYTHM & BLUES VOCAL PERFORMANCE BY A DUO OR GROUP WITH VOCAL

- TLC, "Creep." LaFace.
- All-4-One, "I'm Your Man." Blitzz/Atlantic.
- Brownstone, "If You Love Me." MJJ Music/Epic.
- Terence Trent D'Arby, Booker T, MG's, "A Change Is Gonna Come," track from *The Promised Land*. Columbia.
- Take 6, "All I Need (Is a Chance)." Reprise.

BEST RHYTHM & BLUES INSTRUMENTAL PERFORMANCE

- Miles Davis, *Doo-Bop*. Warner Bros.
- Brecker Brothers, "Big Idea," track from *Return of the Brecker Brothers*. GRP.
- George Howard, "Just the Way I Feel," track from *Do I Ever Cross Your Mind*. GRP.

Soul II Soul, "Mood," track from *Vol. III Just Right*. Virgin.
Grover Washington, Jr., "Summer Chill," track from *Next Exit*. Columbia.

BEST RAP ALBUM

- *Poverty's Paradise*, Naughty by Nature. Tommy Boy.
- *E. 1999 Eternal*, Bone Thugs-N-Harmony. Ruthless.
- *Return to the 36 Chambers: The Dirty Version*, Ol' Dirty Bastard. Elektra.
- *I Wish*, Skee-Lo. Sunshine/Scotti Bros.
- *Me Against the World*, 2Pac. Interscope.

BEST RAP SOLO PERFORMANCE

- Coolio, "Gangsta's Paradise." MCA.
- Dr. Dre, "Keep Their Heads Ringin'." Priority.
- Notorious B.I.G., "Big Poppa." Bad Boy Entertainment/Arista.
- Skee-Lo, "I Wish." Sunshine/Scotti Bros.
- 2Pac, "Dear Mama." Interscope.

BEST RAP PERFORMANCE BY A DUO OR GROUP

- Method Man Featuring Mary J. Blige, "I'll Be There for You/You're All I Need to Get By." Def Jam.
- Bone Thugs-N-Harmony, "1st of Tha Month." Ruthless.
- Cypress Hill, "Throw Your Set in the Air," track from *Temple of Boom*. Ruffhouse/Columbia.
- Naughty by Nature, "Feel Me Flow." Tommy Boy.
- Tha Dogg Pound, "What Would U Do?" Death Row/Interscope.

BEST CONTEMPORARY JAZZ PERFORMANCE

- Pat Metheny Group, *We Live Here*. Geffen.
- Fourplay, *Elixir*. Warner Bros.
- Marcus Miller, *Tales*. PRA.
- Lee Ritenour, Larry Carlton, *Lee and Larry*. GRP.
- Yellowjackets, *Dreamland*. Warner Bros.

BEST JAZZ VOCAL PERFORMANCE
- Lena Horne, *An Evening with Lena Horne*. Blue Note.

Dee Dee Bridgewater, *Love and Peace: A Tribute to Horace Silver*. Verve.

Kurt Elling, *Close Your Eyes*. Blue Note.

Abbey Lincoln, *A Turtle's Dream*. Verve.

Dianne Reeves, *Quiet After the Storm*. Blue Note.

BEST JAZZ INSTRUMENTAL SOLO
- Michael Brecker, "Impressions," track from *Infinity*. Impulse!

Kenny Barron, "Take the Coltrane," track from *Wanton Spirit*. Verve.

Pete Christlieb, "But Beautiful," track from *A View from the Side*. JVC.

Eliane Elias, Herbie Hancock, "The Way You Look Tonight," track from *Solos and Duets*. Blue Note.

Charlie Haden, Hank Jones, "Go Down Moses," track from *Steal Away*. Verve.

BEST JAZZ INSTRUMENTAL PERFORMANCE (INDIVIDUAL OR GROUP)
- McCoy Tyner Trio Featuring Michael Brecker, *Infinity*. Impulse!

Kenny Barron, Roy Haynes, Charlie Haden, *Wanton Spirit*. Verve.

Charlie Haden, Hank Jones, *Steal Away*. Verve.

Joe Henderson, *Double Rainbow—The Music of Antonio Carlos Jobim*. Verve.

Fred Hersch, *I Never Told You—Fred Hersch Plays Johnny Mandel*. Varèse Sarabande Jazz.

BEST LARGE JAZZ ENSEMBLE PERFORMANCE
- GRP All-Stars Big Band, Tom Scott, *All Blues*. GRP.

Bill Holman Band, *A View from the Side*. JVC.

Joe Lovano, *Rush Hour*. Blue Note.

Mingus Big Band, *Gunslinging Birds*. Dreyfus Jazz.

Gerald Wilson Orchestra, *State Street Sweet*. MAMA Foundation.

BEST LATIN JAZZ PERFORMANCE
- Jobim, *Antonio Brasileiro*. Sony Latin Jazz.

Jerry Gonzalez & the Fort Apache Band, *Pensativo*. Milestone.

Chico O'Farrill & His Afro-Cuban Jazz Orchestra, *Pure Emotion*. Milestone.

Eddie Palmieri, *Arete*. TropiJazz.

Patato, Changuito, Orestes, *Ritmo y Candela: Rhythm at the Crossroads*. Redwood.

BEST COUNTRY ALBUM
- *The Woman in Me*, Shania Twain. Mercury Nashville.

Junior High, Junior Brown. MCG/Curb.

Music for All Occasions, Mavericks. MCA.

John Michael Montgomery, John Michael Montgomery. Atlantic Nashville.

Thinkin' About You, Trisha Yearwood. MCA.

Dwight Live, Dwight Yoakam. Reprise.

BEST COUNTRY SONG
(Songwriter's Award)
- "Go Rest High on That Mountain," Vince Gill.

"Any Man of Mine," Robert John, Mutt Lange, Shania Twain.

"Gone Country," Bob McDill.

"I Can Love You Like That," Maribeth Derry, Steve Diamond, Jennifer Kimball.

"You Don't Even Know Who I Am," Gretchen Peters.

BEST COUNTRY VOCAL PERFORMANCE, MALE
- Vince Gill, "Go Rest High on That Mountain." MCA.

John Berry, "Standing on the Edge of Goodbye," track from *Standing on the Edge*. Rounder.

Alan Jackson, "Gone Country." Arista.

John Michael Montgomery, "I Can Love You Like That," track from *John*

Michael Montgomery. Atlantic Nashville.

Dwight Yoakam, "A Thousand Miles from Nowhere," track from *Dwight Live.* Reprise.

BEST COUNTRY VOCAL PERFORMANCE, FEMALE

• Alison Krauss, "Baby, Now That I've Found You," track from *Now That I've Found You: A Collection.* Rounder.

Patty Loveless, "You Don't Even Know Who I Am." Epic.

Martina McBride, "Safe in the Arms of Love." RCA.

Pam Tillis, "Mi Vida Loca (My Crazy Life)," track from *Sweetheart's Dance.* Arista.

Shania Twain, "Any Man of Mine." Mercury Nashville.

BEST COUNTRY PERFORMANCE BY A DUO OR GROUP WITH VOCAL

• Mavericks, "Here Comes the Rain." MCA.

Brooks & Dunn, "You're Gonna Miss Me When I'm Gone." Arista.

Little Texas, "Amy's Back in Austin." Warner Bros.

Shenandoah, "Darned If I Don't (Danged If I Do)." Capitol Nashville/Liberty.

Tractors, "Trying to Get to New Orleans," track from *The Tractors.* Arista.

BEST COUNTRY VOCAL COLLABORATION

• Shenandoah, Alison Krauss, "Somewhere in the Vicinity of the Heart," track from *In the Vicinity of the Heart.* Capitol Nashville/Liberty.

Suzy Bogguss, Chet Atkins, "All My Loving," track from *Come Together—America Salutes the Beatles.* Capitol Nashville/Liberty.

George Jones, Alan Jackson, "A Good Year for the Roses." MCA.

Reba McEntire, Trisha Yearwood, Martina McBride, Linda Davis, "On My Own." MCA.

Dolly Parton, Vince Gill, "I Will Always Love You," track from *Something Special.* Columbia/Blue Eye.

BEST COUNTRY INSTRUMENTAL PERFORMANCE

• Asleep at the Wheel, "Hightower." Capitol Nashville.

Byron Berline, Earl Scruggs, Bill Monroe, "Sally Goodin," track from *Fiddle and a Song.* Sugar Hill.

Bela Fleck, "Cheeseballs in Cowtown," track from *Tales from the Acoustic Planet.* Warner Bros.

Flaco Jimenez, Lee Roy Parnell, "Cat Walk," track from *Flaco Jimenez.* Arista Texas.

Doc Watson, "Thunder Road/Sugarfoot Rag," track from *Docabilly.* Sugar Hill.

BEST ROCK GOSPEL ALBUM

• *Lesson of Love,* Ashley Cleveland. Reunion.

Big Tent Revival, Big Tent Revival. Ardent/ForeFront.

Jars of Clay, Jars of Clay. Essential/Brentwood Music.

Home Run! Geoff Moore & the Distance. ForeFront.

No Doubt, Petra. Word.

BEST POP/CONTEMPORARY GOSPEL ALBUM

• *I'll Lead You Home,* Michael W. Smith. Reunion.

The Music of Christmas, Steven Curtis Chapman. Sparrow.

Unbelievable Love, Larnelle. Benson Music Group.

Find It on the Wings, Sandi Patty. Word.

My Utmost for His Highest, various artists. Word/Myrrh.

BEST SOUTHERN GOSPEL, COUNTRY GOSPEL OR BLUEGRASS GOSPEL ALBUM

• *Amazing Grace—A Country Salute to Gospel,* various artists. Sparrow.

One Summer Evening Live, Bruce Carroll. Word.

Someday, Crystal Gayle. Intersound.
A Gospel Gathering, Ralph Stanley, Joe Isaacs. Freeland.
At the Feet of God, Jerry Sullivan, Tammy Sullivan. New Haven.

BEST TRADITIONAL SOUL GOSPEL ALBUM

• *Shirley Caesar Live . . . He Will Come*, Shirley Ceasar. Word.
No Ways Tired, Fontella Bass. Nonesuch.
I Brought Him with Me, Blind Boys of Alabama. House of Blues/Private Music.
Power, Mighty Clouds of Joy. Intersound.
Live at Jackson State University, Rev. James Moore, Mississippi Mass Choir. Malaco.

BEST CONTEMPORARY SOUL GOSPEL ALBUM

• *Alone in His Presence*, CeCe Winans. Sparrow.
More Than a Melody, Yolanda Adams. Tribute.
The Call, Anointed. Myrrh.
Motown Comes Home, various artists. Motown.
Heartsongs, Doug Williams. Blackberry.
Not in My House, Daniel Winans. Glorious Music.

BEST GOSPEL ALBUM BY A CHOIR OR CHORUS

• *Praise Him . . . Live!* Brooklyn Tabernacle Choir; Carol Cymbala, choir director. Warner Alliance.
Bible Stories, Donald Lawrence & the Tri-City Singers; Donald Lawrence, choir director. Sparrow.
Live in New York by Any Means, Hezekiah Walker & the Love Fellowship Crusade; Hezekiah Walker, choir director. Benson Music Group.
Shout, Rev. Milton Brunson & the Thompson Community Singers; Percy Bady, choir director. Word Gospel.

Show Up! New Life Community Choir Featuring John P. Kee; John P. Kee, choir director. Verity/Tyscot.

BEST TRADITIONAL FOLK ALBUM

• *South Coast*, Ramblin' Jack Elliott. Red House.
While Passing Along This Way, Norman Blake, Nancy Blake. Shanachie.
Then and Now, Ali Akbar Khan. AMMP.
The Oak and the Laurel, Laurie Lewis, Tom Rozum. Rounder.
From . . . Another Time and Place, Dave Van Ronk. Alcazar Productions.

BEST CONTEMPORARY FOLK ALBUM

• *Wrecking Ball*, Emmylou Harris. Asylum/Electra.
The Long Black Veil, Chieftains. RCA Victor.
MTV Unplugged, Bob Dylan. Columbia.
Train A Comin', Steve Earle. Winter Harvest.
Lost Dogs and Mixed Blessings, John Prine. Oh Boy.

BEST TRADITIONAL BLUES ALBUM

• *Chill Out*, John Lee Hooker. Pointblank.
Charles Brown's Cool Christmas Blues, Charles Brown. Bullseye Blues.
Them Update Blues, Lowell Fulson. Bullseye Blues.
The Last Real Texas Blues Band Featuring Doug Sahm, Last Real Texas Blues Band Featuring Doug Sahm. Antone's.
Turn It On! Turn It Up! Roomful of Blues. Bullseye Blues.

BEST CONTEMPORARY BLUES ALBUM

• *Slippin' In*, Buddy Guy. Silvertone.
The Man, Clarence "Gatemouth" Brown. Verve.
(Live '92–'93), Albert Collins & the Icebreakers. Pointblank.
Some Rainy Morning, Robert Cray. Mercury.
Blue Night, Percy Sledge. Pointblank/Sky Ranch.

BEST BLUEGRASS ALBUM

- *Unleashed*, Nashville Bluegrass Band. Sugar Hill.
- *Fiddle and a Song*, Byron Berline. Sugar Hill.
- *Beyond the City*, Cox Family. Sugar Hill.
- *Moonlighter*, Claire Lynch. Rounder.
- *$35 and a Dream*, Rose Maddox. Arhoolie Productions.

BEST LATIN POP PERFORMANCE

- Jon Secada, *Amor*. EMI-Latin/SBK.
- Adolfo Angel, Gustavo Angel, *Nuestras Canciones*. AFG Sigma.
- Rocio Durcal, *Hay Amores y Amores*. BMG-U.S. Latin.
- Julio Iglesias, *La Carretera*. Sony Latin.
- Mana, *Cuando Los Angeles Lloran*. WEA Latina.

BEST TROPICAL LATIN PERFORMANCE

- Gloria Estefan, *Abriendo Puertas*. Epic.
- Marc Anthony, *Todo a Su Tiempo*. Soho Latino.
- Cachao, *Master Sessions, Vol. 2*. Crescent Moon/Epic.
- Willie Colon & Rubén Blades, *Tras la Tormenta*. Sony Tropical.
- Celia Cruz, *Irrepetible*. RMM.

BEST MEXICAN-AMERICAN PERFORMANCE

- Flaco Jimenez, *Flaco Jimenez*. Arista Texas.
- Ramon Ayala y Sus Bravos del Norte, *Lagrimas*. Freddie.
- Juan Gabriel, *El México Que Se Nos Fue*. BMG-U.S.-Latin.
- Jaime y Los Chamacos, *. . . No Se Cansan!* Freddie.
- La Mafia, *Exitos en Vivo*. Sony Discos.

BEST REGGAE ALBUM

- *Boombastic*, Shaggy. Virgin Records America.
- *Rasta Business*, Burning Spear. Heartbeat.
- *Free Like We Want 2B*, Ziggy Marley & the Melody Makers. Elektra.

Hi-Bop Ska! The 30th Anniversary Recording, Skatalites. Shanachie.
Live It Up, Third World. Solar/Hines.

BEST POLKA ALBUM

- *I Love to Polka*, Jimmy Sturr. Rounder.
- *Better Than Ever*, Eddie Blazonczyk's Versatones. Bel-Aire.
- *Polkas for a Gloomy World*, Brave Combo. Rounder.
- *For Old Times Sake*, Lenny Gomulka & Chicago Push. Push.
- *Happiness Is Polkas and Waltzes with Walter Ostanek and Friends*, Walter Ostanek. World Renowned Sounds.

BEST NEW AGE ALBUM

- *Forest*, George Winston. Windham Hill.
- *Dream Suite*, Suzanne Ciani. Seventh Wave.
- *An Enchanted Evening*, Kitaro. Domo.
- *Trust*, Patrick O'Hearn. Deep Cave.
- *Tyranny of Beauty*, Tangerine Dream. Miramar.

BEST WORLD MUSIC ALBUM

- *Bohème*, Deep Forest. 550 Music/Epic.
- *Cesaria Evora*, Cesaria Evora. Nonesuch.
- *Firin' in Fouta*, Baaba Maal. Mango.
- *Raga Aberi*, Ravi Shankar, Zakir Hussain, Vikku Vinayakram. Music of the World.
- *The Splendid Master Gnawa Musicians of Morocco,* Splendid Master Gnawa Musicians of Morocco, Randy Weston. Antilles.

BEST ARRANGEMENT ON AN INSTRUMENTAL

- Robert Farnon, "Lament," track from *Tangence* (J. J. Johnson with the Robert Farnon Orchestra). Verve.
- Jorge Calandrelli, "Atras da Porta," track from *Symphonic Bossa Nova* (Ettore Stratta conducting the Royal Philharmonic). Teldec.
- Marcus Miller, "Come Together," track from *Tales* (Marcus Miller). PRA.

Michael Abene, "Cookin' at the Continental," track from *All Blues* (GRP All-Star Band). GRP.

Jorge Calandrelli, "Manha de Carnaval," track from *Symphonic Boss Nova* (Ettore Stratta conducting the Royal Philharmonic). Teldec.

BEST INSTRUMENTAL COMPOSITION

• "A View from the Side," Bill Holman (*A View from the Side*).

"Homage Part I," Billy Taylor (*Homage*).

"New Life," Chick Corea (*Time Warp*).

"Tales," Marcus Miller, Allen Toussaint (*Tales*).

"The Starry Night," Billy Childs (*I've Known Rivers*).

BEST MUSICAL SHOW ALBUM

• *Smokey Joe's Cafe—The Songs of Leiber and Stoller*, Broadway cast. Jerry Leiber, Mike Stoller, composers and lyricists. Atlantic Theatre.

Anyone Can Whistle—Live at Carnegie Hall, various artists. Stephen Sondheim, lyricist and composer. Columbia.

Hello, Dolly! 1994 cast with Carol Channing. Jerry Herman, lyricist and composer. Varèse Sarabande.

How to Succeed in Business Without Really Trying! Matthew Broderick and Broadway cast. Frank Loesser, lyricist and composer. RCA Victor.

Kiss of the Spider Woman, Vanessa Williams and Broadway cast. Fred Ebb, lyricist; John Kander, composer. Mercury.

BEST INSTRUMENTAL COMPOSITION WRITTEN FOR A MOTION PICTURE OR TV

• "Crimson Tide," Hans Zimmer (*Crimson Tide*).

"Batman Forever," Elliot Goldenthal (*Batman Forever*).

"Buggy Ride," Wynton Marsalis (*Joe Cool Blues*).

"The Cure," Dave Grusin (*The Cure*).

"Main Title," Howard Shore (*Ed Wood*).

BEST SONG WRITTEN SPECIFICALLY FOR A MOTION PICTURE OR TV

• "Colors of the Wind," Alan Menken, Stephen Schwartz (*Pocahontas*).

"Have You Ever Really Loved a Woman?" Bryan Adams, Michael Kamen, Robert John "Mutt" Lange (*Don Juan DeMarco*).

"Love Me Still," Bruce Hornsby, Chaka Khan (*Clockers*).

"Someone to Love," Babyface (*Bad Boys*).

"Whatever You Imagine," James Horner, Barry Mann, Cynthia Weil (*The Pagemaster*).

BEST INSTRUMENTAL ARRANGEMENT ACCOMPANYING VOCAL(S)

• Rob McConnell, "I Get a Kick out of You," track from *Velvet and Brass* (Mel Tormé, Rob McConnell). Concord Jazz.

Rene Depere, "Alegria," track from *Alegria* (Cirque du Soleil). RCA Victor.

Bobby McFerrin, "Bibbidi-Bobbidi-Boo (The Magic Song)," track from *Cinderella* (Bobby McFerrin). Walt Disney.

Jeremy Lubbock, " 'Round Midnight," track from *Self Portrait* (Carmen Lundy). JVC Music.

Tom Scott, "Stormy Monday Blues," track from *All Blues* (GRP All-Star Big Band, B. B. King). GRP.

BEST CLASSICAL ALBUM

• *Debussy: La Mer; Nocturnes; Jeux; etc.*, Pierre Boulez conducting the Cleveland Orchestra; Cleveland Orchestra Choir; Franklin Cohen, clarinet. Deutsche Grammophon.

Bartók: Divertimento; Dance Suite; etc., Pierre Boulez conducting the Chicago Symphony Orchestra. Deutsche Grammophon.

Berlioz: Les Troyens, Charles Dutoit conducting the Montreal Symphony Orchestra; Montreal Symphony Orchestra Choir; Gary Lakes, Françoise Follet, Gino Quilico, Deborah Voigt, principal soloists. London.

Music for Queen Mary (Works of Purcell, Morley, Blow, etc.), Martin Neary conducting the New London Consort; Westminster Abbey Choir. Sony Classical.

Prokofiev, Shostakovich: Violin Concerto No. 1, Mstislav Rostropovich conducting the London Philharmonic Orchestra; Maxim Vengerov, violin. Teldec.

BEST ORCHESTRAL PERFORMANCE
(Conductor's Award)

• Pierre Boulez conducting the Cleveland Orchestra, *Debussy: La Mer*. Deutsche Grammophon.

Pierre Boulez conducting the Chicago Symphony Orchestra, *Bartók: Divertimento; Dance Suite; etc*. Deutsche Grammophon.

Simon Rattle conducting the City of Birmingham Symphony Orchestra, *Elgar: Enigma Variations; Falstaff; Grania and Diarmid*. EMI Classics.

Wolfgang Sawallisch conducting the Philadelphia Orchestra, *Hindemith: Mathis der Maler—Symphonie; Symphonic Metamorphosis of Themes by C. M. von Weber; etc*. EMI Classics.

André Previn conducting the London Symphony Orchestra, *Shostakovich: Symphony No. 8*. Deutsche Grammophon.

BEST CHAMBER MUSIC PERFORMANCE

• Emanuel Ax, piano; Yo-Yo Ma, cello; Richard Stoltzman, clarinet, *Brahms, Beethoven, Mozart: Clarinet Trios*. Sony Classical.

Vermeer String Quartet, *Haydn: The Seven Last Words of Christ*. Alden Productions.

Alban Berg Quartet, *Janáček: String Quartets Nos. 1 and 2*. EMI Classics.

St. Petersburg String Quartet, *Shostakovich: String Quartets Nos. 3, 5 and 7*. Sony Classical.

Emerson String Quartet, *Webern: Works for String Quartet; String Trio, Op. 20*. Deutsche Grammophon.

BEST CLASSICAL PERFORMANCE, INSTRUMENTAL SOLOIST(S) (WITH ORCHESTRA)

• Itzhak Perlman, violin (Seiji Ozawa conducting the Boston Symphony Orchestra), *The Amerian Album (Works of Bernstein, Barber, Foss)*. EMI Classics.

Maria João Pires, piano (André Previn conducting the Royal Philharmonic Orchestra), "Chopin: Concerto for Piano and Orchestra No. 2 in F Minor, Op. 21," track from *Chopin: Piano Concerto No. 2; 24 Preludes*. Deutsche Grammophon.

Catherine Cantin, flute; Heinz Holliger, oboe; Yvonne Loriod, piano; Mstislav Rostropovich, violoncello (Myung-Whun Chung conducting the Bastille Opera Orchestra), "Messiaen: Concert à Quatre," track from *Messiaen: Concert à Quatre; Les Offrandes Oubliées; Un Sourire; etc*. Deutsche Grammophon.

Evgeny Kissin, piano (Claudio Abbado conducting the Berliner Philharmoniker), *Prokofiev: Piano Concertos Nos. 1 and 3*. Deutsche Grammophon.

Maxim Vengerov, violin (Mstislav Rostropovich conducting the London Symphony Orchestra), *Prokofiev, Shostakovich: Violin Concerto No. 1*. Teldec.

BEST CLASSICAL PERFORMANCE, INSTRUMENTAL SOLOIST (WITHOUT ORCHESTRA)

• Radu Lupu, piano, *Schubert: Piano Sonatas (B Flat Major and A Major)*. London.

Konstantin Lifschitz, piano, *Bach: Goldberg Variations*. Denon.

Stephen Kovacevich, piano, *Beethoven: Piano Sonata, Op. 31, Nos. 16–18*. EMI Classics.

Murray Perahia, piano, *Chopin: 4 Ballades (Waltzes, Nocturne, Mazurkas and Etudes)*. Sony Classical.

Evgeny Kissin, piano, *Chopin, Vol. 2 (Sonata No. 3; Mazurkas).* RCA Victor Red Seal.

BEST OPERA RECORDING

• *Berlioz: Les Troyens,* Charles Dutoit conducting the Montreal Symphony Orchestra (solos: Lakes, Pollet, Quilico, Voigt). London.

Borodin: Prince Igor, Valery Gergiev conducting the Kirov Orchestra (solos: Borodina, Gassiev, Gorchakova, Grigorian, Kit, Minjelkiev, Ognovienko). Philips Classics.

Mozart: Don Giovanni, John Eliot Gardiner conducting the English Baroque Soloists and the Monteverdi Chorus (solos: Clarkson, D'Arcangelo, Gilfry, James, Margiono, Orgonasova, Pregardien, Silvestrelli). Archiv Produktion.

Mozart: La Clemenza di Tito, Christopher Hogwood conducting the Academy of Ancient Music Orchestra (solos: Bartoli, Bonney, Cachemaille, Heilmann, Jones, Montague). L'Oiseau-Lyre.

Rossini: Tancredi, Alberto Zedda conducting the Collegium Instrumentale Brugense (solos: Micco, Jo, Lendi, Olsen, Podles, Spagnoli). Naxos.

BEST CHORAL PERFORMANCE

• Herbert Blomstedt conducting the San Francisco Symphony and Chorus, *Brahms: Ein Deutsches Requiem.* London.

Robert Shaw conducting the Robert Shaw Festival Singers, *Evocation of the Spirit (Works of Gorecki, Part, Barber, etc.).* Telarc.

Barbara Thornton conducting Sequentia, *Hildegard von Bingen: Canticles of Ecstasy.* Deutsche Harmonia Mundi.

Yuri Temirkanov conducting the St. Petersburg Philharmonic Chamber Choir, *Prokofiev: Alexander Nevsky.* RCA Victor Red Seal.

John Eliot Gardiner conducting the Monteverdi Choir and Orchestre Révolutionnaire et Romantique,

Verdi: Requiem; 4 Pezzi Sahri. Philips Classics.

BEST CLASSICAL VOCAL PERFORMANCE

• Sylvia McNair, soprano (Christopher Hogwood conducting the Academy of Ancient Music), *The Echoing Air—The Music of Henry Purcell (If Music Be the Food of Love, Sweeter Than Roses, etc.).* Philips Classics.

Sergei Leiferkus, baritone (Semion Skigin, piano), *Mussorgsky Songs (Songs and Dances of Death, The Nursery, etc.).* Conifer Classics.

Roberto Alagna, tenor (Richard Armstrong conducting the London Philharmonic), *Roberto Alagna—Operatic Arias (Works of Donizetti, Massenet, etc.).* EMI Classics.

Wolfgang Holzmair, baritone (Imogine Cooper, piano), *Schumann: Dichterliebe; Liederkreis, Op. 24; Heine-Lieder.* Philips Classics.

Bryn Terfel, baritone (Malcolm Martineau, piano), *The Vagabond (Songs by Vaughan Williams, Butterworth, etc.). Deutsche Grammophon.*

BEST CONTEMPORARY COMPOSITION

• "Concert à Quatre," Olivier Messiaen.
Chamber Symphony, John Adams.
Concerto for Violin and Orchestra, Gyorgy Ligeti.
"Of Reminiscences and Reflections," Gunther Schuller.
Symphony No. 3, Ellen Taafe Zwilich.

BEST ENGINEERED RECORDING, CLASSICAL

• Michael Mailes, Jonathan Stokes, *Bartók: Concerto for Orchestra; "Kossuth"—Symphonic Poem* (Herbert Blomstedt, conductor). London.

Tony Faulkner, *The Lily and the Lamb (Chant and Polyphony from Medieval England)* (Anonymous 4). Harmonia Mundi USA.

William Hoekstra, Larry Rock, *Orff: Carmina Burana* (Leonard Slatkin, conducter). RCA Victor Red Seal.

Tony Faulkner, *Prokofiev: Alexander Nevsky* (Yuri Temirkanov, conductor). RCA Victor Red Seal.

William Hoekstra, Larry Rock, *The Typewriter—Leroy Anderson Favorites* (Leonard Slatkin, conductor). RCA Victor Red Seal.

CLASSICAL PRODUCER OF THE YEAR

• Steven Epstein
Andrew Cornall
John Fraser
Jay David Saks
Michael Woolcock

BEST COMEDY ALBUM

• *Crank Calls*, Jonathan Winters. Audio Select.
Funk It, Martin Lawrence. EastWest America.
Games Rednecks Play, Jeff Foxworthy. Warner Bros.
God's Other Son (Don Imus), Don Imus. Simon and Schuster Audioworks.
In Goddess We Trust, Judy Tenuta. Goddess.

BEST SPOKEN WORD OR NONMUSICAL ALBUM

• *Phenomenal Woman* (Maya Angelou), Maya Angelou. Random House AudioBooks.
Guy Noir: Radio Private Eye (Garrison Keillor), Garrison Keillor, Walter Bobbie. HighBridge.
I Am Spock (Leonard Nimoy), Leonard Nimoy. Nova Audio Books.
Long Walk to Freedom (Nelson Mandela), Nelson Mandela. Time Warner AudioBooks.

BEST MUSICAL ALBUM FOR CHILDREN

• *Sleepy Time Lullabies*, J. Aaron Brown, David R. Lehman (Barbara Bailey Hutchison). Jaba.
Papa's Dream, Los Lobos, Lalo Guerrero (Los Lobos, Lalo Guerrero). Music for Little People.

John McCutcheon's Four Seasons: Summersongs, Bob Dawson, John McCutcheon. Rounder.
Pocahontas Sing-Along, Alan Menken, Stephen Schwartz. Walt Disney.
Winnie-the-Pooh's Take My Hand, Michael L. Becker, Harold J. Kleiner, Marco Marinangeli (Chieftains, Kathie Lee Gifford, various artists). Walt Disney.

BEST SPOKEN WORD ALBUM FOR CHILDREN

• *Prokofiev: Peter and the Wolf*, Dan Broatman, Martin Sauer (Patrick Stewart). Erato.
Follow the Drinking Gourd, Taj Mahal, John McCally, Doris Wilhousky (Morgan Freeman). Rabbit Ears.
Why the Dog Chases the Cat: Great Animal Stories, David Holt, Bill Mooney. High Windy Audio.
The Dairy of a Young Girl (Anne Frank), Lauren Krenzel (Winona Ryder). BDD Audio.
John Henry, B. B. King, Doris Wilhousky (Denzel Washington). Rabbit Ears.

BEST ENGINEERED ALBUM (OTHER THAN CLASSICAL)

• Dave Bianco, Richard Dodd, Stephen McLaughlin, Jim Scott, *Wildflowers* (Tom Petty). Warner Bros.
Al Schmitt, *Afterglow* (Dr. John). Blue Thumb.
Terry Date, Ulrich Wild, *Astro-Creek: 2000 Songs of Love, Destruction and Other Synthetic Delusions of the Electric Head* (White Zombie). Geffen.
Rob Jacobs, Elliot Scheiner, *Hell Freezes Over* (Eagles). Geffen.
Bruce Swedien, *HIStory: Past, Present and Future Book I* (Michael Jackson). Epic.

BEST ALBUM PACKAGE
(Art Director's Award)

• Robbie Cavolina, Joni Mitchell, *Turbulent Indigo* (Joni Mitchell). Reprise.

Gary Burden, *Mirror Ball* (Neil Young). Reprise.

Stefan Sagmeister, *Mountains of Madness* (H. P. Zinker). Energy.

Tim Stedman, *This Is Fort Apache* (various artists). MCA.

Joel Zimmerman, *Vitalogy* (Pearl Jam). Epic.

BEST ALBUM PACKAGE, BOXED
(Art Director's Award)
• Frank Zappa, Gail Zappa, *Civilization Phaze III* (Frank Zappa). Barking Pumpkin.

Blind Mellon, Jeffery Fey, Chris Jones, Tommy Steele, *Soup* (Blind Mellon). Capitol.

Mark Farrow, *Alternative* (Pet Shop Boys). EMI.

Storm Thorgerson, *Pulse* (Pink Floyd). Columbia.

Allen Weinberg, *Box of Fire* (Aerosmith). Columbia.

BEST ALBUM NOTES
(Annotator's Award)
• Rob Bowman, *The Complete Stax/Volt Soul Singles, Vol. 3: 1972–1975* (various artists). Stax.

Geoffrey Mark Fidelman, James Gavin, *Ella—The Legendary Decca Recordings* (Ella Fitzgerald). Decca Jazz.

John Fricke, *25th Anniverary—Retrospective* (Judy Garland). Capitol.

Dan Morgenstern, *I'll Be Seeing You: A Tribute to Carmen McRae*. Decca Jazz.

Dan Morgenstern, *Let's Do It: Best of the Verve Years* (Louis Armstrong). Verve.

BEST HISTORICAL ALBUM
• *The Heifetz Collection*, Jascha Heifetz, various artists. RCA Victor Gold Seal.

John Coltrane: The Heavyweight Champion: The Complete Atlantic Recordings, John Coltrane. Rhino Records/Atlantic Jazz Gallery.

Live at the BBC, Beatles. Capitol.

The R&B Box: 30 Years of Rhythm and Blues, various artists. Rhino.

Early Ellington: The Complete Brunswick and Vocalion Recordings of Duke Ellington, 1926–1931, Duke Ellington & His Orchestra. GRP.

PRODUCER OF THE YEAR
(OTHER THAN CLASSICAL)
• Babyface
Glen Ballard
Rick Chertoff
Jimmy Jam, Terry Lewis
Rick Rubin

BEST MUSIC VIDEO, SHORT FORM
• *Scream*, Michael Jackson, Janet Jackson. Mark Romanek, director. Epic.

It's Oh So Quiet, Björk. Spike Jonze, director. Elektra.

Dis Is da Drum, Herbie Hancock. Mark Dippe, director. Mercury.

What Would You Say, Dave Matthews Band. David Hogan, director. RCA.

Famine, Sinéad O'Connor. Andy Delaney, Monty Whitebloom, directors. Chrysalis.

BEST MUSIC VIDEO, LONG FORM
• *Secret World Live*, Peter Gabriel. Francois Girard, director. Geffen Home Video.

The Line, the Cross and the Curve, Kate Bush. Kate Bush, director. Columbia Music Video.

Saltimbanco, Cirque du Soleil. Jacques Payette, director. RCA Victor/BMG Classics.

The Planets, Charles Dutoit conducting the Montreal Symphony Orchestra. Barbara Willis Sweete, director. Polygram Video.

333, Green Jelly. Green Jelly, director. Zoo Entertainment.

Where'd You Hide the Body, James McMurtry. K. C. Amos, Bill Brown, Ingrid Calame, Sande Chen, Gregory E. Connor, Linda Feferman, Johannes Gamble, Nathan Hope, Pip Johnson, Brenda McIntyre, Luis Ruiz, Deborah Stratman, directors. Columbia Music Video.

• 1996 •

Garden Party

"It will be unlike any award show produced in America," Grammycast producer Pierre Cossette promised *Variety* columnist Army Archerd. "I've had this dream for years—to do it in Madison Square Garden. Now we'll have to go full-out, and yet also create an air of intimacy."

The switch of venue doubled the usual number of 6,000 seats available at New York's Radio City Music Hall or L.A.'s Shrine Auditorium, but tickets still sold out immediately at hefty prices ranging from \$250 to \$900. The ceremony turned into the most elaborate event ever staged at the Garden. N.A.R.A.S. needed the arena for nine days, which meant kicking the Knicks basketball team out, but the hoopsters were given a chartered plane to shuttle them to their newly rescheduled game sites. When the Grammy stage was finally ready for the broadcast, the set cost more than a million dollars to build, it had more than 100 tons of equipment hanging overhead and needed 75 stagehands to manage installation and scene changes.

The scale of the drama surrounding the top award competitions seemed just as immense. In fact, the two top categories looked like a trans-American border clash between U.S. music maven Babyface and the cherubic-looking Canadian diva Celine Dion.

Babyface entered this year's Grammy fight with a historic number of nominations—12, thereby tying the one-year record set by Michael Jackson in 1983. He told *Variety*, "I never expected this. Even though it's about the music and not about awards, it makes you feel good that people think highly enough of your work to nominate you. I guess it means you're appreciated."

The Grammycast, said *Variety*, "was a decidedly downbeat affair despite being held in its largest venue ever, Madison Square Garden."

One of Babyface's bids was as producer of Eric Clapton's "Change the World" (on which he also played guitar), which was favored to win Record of the Year by the *Los Angeles Times*, *TV Guide*, *USA Today* and *Billboard*. He also produced the film soundtrack to *Waiting to Exhale*, featuring the likes of Whitney Houston, CeCe Winans, Brandy and Mary J. Blige singing 15 of his songs. *TV*

Guide and the *L.A. Times* rooted for the latter to win Album of the Year.

But *Waiting* was up against Dion's *Falling Into You,* the biggest-selling new album of 1996 (Grammy's 1995 Album of the Year, *Jagged Little Pill* actually sold the most copies). Predicting that *Falling* would rise to claim best album were *Billboard, Entertainment Weekly, USA Today* and E! Entertainment network.

When Dion won, *Variety* noted the immense scope of her gratitude: "Longest acceptance speech by far was from Album of the Year winner Celine Dion, who seemingly thanked everyone she's ever met—the album credits 14 producers. Even the swell of 'get off the stage' music faded out while Dion was still conveying her seemingly limitless gratitude."

Backstage, she explained her chattiness: "I know that talent is not just enough. There are so many people responsible for my success." *Falling* also won Best Pop Album.

Considering how often Grammy voters have named romantic ballads Record of the Year in the past, some pundits believed that the album's chart-topping single, "Because You Loved Me," was this year's front-runner. When the nominations were unveiled, however, *Variety* warned: "In previous years, the love song 'Because You Loved Me' would have been considered a shoo-in. But with Clapton in the mix, combined with Babyface producing a track that spent much of the year in heavy rotation on radio and vid-channels, 'Change' could pick up the trophy."

Variety was proved prophetic when "Change the World" earned Clapton two awards, including best record, a high honor he last took three years ago when he seized Grammy's Triple Crown of Record, Song and Album of the Year with "Tears in Heaven" and *MTV Unplugged.* He also now nabbed another category he last took in 1993.

"Many of the wins followed performances of the nominated songs by the artists," *Variety* observed when reporting on Clapton's first win of the night. "Just moments after performing 'Change the World' as the opening performance of the telecast, Clapton picked up the Grammy for best male pop vocal."

"I feel this is kind of rigged," Clapton admitted in his acceptance speech. "I did the song, now I get the prize."

The Record of the Year victory was also a big win for producer Babyface, but when "Change" also won Song of the Year, as Record of the Year champs usually do, it was at his own expense. He was nominated in the category for the Whitney Houston ballad "Exhale (Shoop Shoop)" but lost to the trio of Nashville songwriters behind "Change." *Billboard* had predicted that Diane Warren's "Because You Loved Me" would win best song. "Because" ended up with the consolation prize of best movie song (it had been used in the Robert Redford film *Up Close and Personal*). Strangely, "Change" was not a contender in the latter contest, although it was eligible as part of the score to the John Travolta film *Phenomenon.*

Half of Babyface's dozen bids were split between the categories for movie tunes and Best R&B Song. He made up for his three losses in the former lineup by prevailing for one of his three noms in the latter, winning for "Exhale (Shoop Shoop)." For a second year in a row and third time overall, he was also voted Grammy's Producer of the Year.

Babyface's paltry showing of only three Grammys out of 12 nominations was a "huge surprise" to *Variety.* But the year's biggest shocker came in the Best New Artist race where the laurels were suddenly snatched by a 14-year-old Nashville nightingale who no one thought had a chance to win.

Not a single one of the national media forecasters picked LeAnn Rimes to take Best New Artist. (*Billboard* and the *L.A. Times* valued Jewel. *USA Today*: No Doubt. *TV Guide*: the Tony Rich Project. *Entertainment Weekly*: Garbage.) In fact, the *L.A. Times, Entertainment Weekly* and *USA Today* didn't even bother to mention Rimes when discussing serious contenders in their preview articles.

Apparently, the upset also surprised Rimes, who later confessed backstage to reporters, "I thought it was going to No Doubt."

The 14-year-old country star was surprising a lot of media watchers. Her album *Blue* topped the country sales chart for six months; the success of its lead single, "Blue," made her the youngest country singer ever to reach the Top 10 of the pop charts. At the Grammys, she became the youngest person to win a top award and the first country singer to win Best New Artist in 30 years.

She burst into tears when she learned that she won the newcomer's prize. She accepted it, saying, "This award means more to me than anything in this world."

Earlier in the day, she pulled off another upset—for best female country vocalist—over the usual, automatic winner in the category, Mary-Chapin Carpenter.

Rimes told reporters that they shouldn't underestimate her. "I'm not an overnight success," she reminded them. "I've been at this since I was six."

When reporters asked her how she'd celebrate her double victory, she said that she was going out to dinner, adding, "At my age, I guess that's all I can do."

"Blue" lost its bid as Song of the Year but came through as Best Country Song. It was written in 1958 by Bill Mack, who'd recently been honored as an inductee into the Disc Jockey Hall of Fame, but he told reporters, "Nothing compares to winning a Grammy."

Several past winners of Best New Artist returned this year to claim more Grammys.

N.A.R.A.S. voters' favorite newcomers of 1964, the Beatles, had won only five Grammys during their heyday. Now, 27 years after they broke up, the Fab Four were back in the race thanks to the release of a two-CD career retrospective, *The Beatles Anthology,* which included a new song, "Free As a Bird," recorded by combining the voices of the three surviving

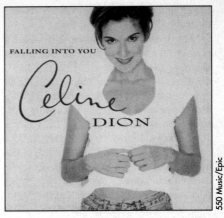

Falling Into You by chart-topping Canadian diva Celine Dion surprised some pundits by beating the *Waiting to Exhale* soundtrack for best album.

Beatles with an old tape of an unfinished song sung by deceased member John Lennon. "The Beatles are considered a shoo-in for a Grammy for their first new song in more than two decades," *Variety* reported on the race for best pop group vocals, which they did win.

Free earned the Grammy for best short-form video, too. The Beatles also reaped the prize for best long-form video for the eight-tape, 10-hour version of *Anthology* that included such never-before-released scenes as Lennon performing valiantly in a rainstorm during a 1964 concert in Sydney.

Another past winner of Best New Artist (1975) also resurrected the dead via audio trickery to win new Grammy gold. The last time Natalie Cole teamed up with her late father, Nat King Cole, on a posthumous recording, "Unforgettable," she won Record and Album of the Year of 1991. Now she won the prize for best pop collaboration for a remixed duet of his 1957 classic "When I Fall in Love."

Grammy's Best New Artist of 1993, Toni Braxton, received a shizophrenic homecoming this year. Just like the new choice for best rookie, LeAnn Rimes, Braxton was forbidden to perform on the Grammycast because she'd sung at the recent American Music Awards. She was nonetheless welcomed with two new Grammys: best r&b vocalist for "You're Makin' Me High" (beating front-runner Whitney Houston) and best female pop vocalist for "Unbreak My Heart." When she won the latter, she seemed flustered while accepting the trophy. She told reporters later, "I really, honestly felt they were going to announce Celine Dion, so I forgot to thank everybody." *Time* magazine accused her of faking it, calling Braxton's podium appearance "the worst performance by a winner pretending she didn't expect to win."

Also returning for two golden statuettes was Best New Artist of 1994 Sheryl Crow, whose new, self-titled release "proved that she is not just a one-disc wonder," insisted *Variety*. She told reporters that the double win was a vindication, "especially since I produced the album."

Sheryl Crow won Best Rock Album. Its track "If It MakesYou Happy" earned Crow the laurel for best female rock vocalist, besting odds-on favorites Bonnie Raitt and Tracy Chapman. Accepting the latter prize, she told the audience, "All I can think to do right now is to thank everyone I ever met in my entire life."

Winner of Best Rock Song was Grammy's Best New Artist of 1988, Tracy Chapman, whose "Give Me One Reason" was a losing contender for this year's Record and Song of the Year honors. *Variety* noted that the tune was from her "aptly titled *New Beginning* disc," which welcomed the former street performer back into the Top 10 of the pop charts, reaching number five. *USA Today* declared that "Give Me One Reason" had no reason to be in Grammy's rock category: "Among this year's head-scratchers was Tracy Chapman's rock song win. It's pop, it's blues, it's folkish. It's not rock."

A loser of this year's Best New Artist

> ### Hillary Clinton was "surprised that Grammys were given to tone-deaf people."

---

award, the Tony Rich Project, rebounded to win the prize for Best R&B Album for *Words,* which surely had an easier time of things since, strangely, Babyface's *Waiting to Exhale* wasn't nominated. Still, the 25-year-old Detroit native had to fend off a formidable challenge by Curtis Mayfield, who, the *L.A. Times* said, was "the sentimental favorite for two reasons: the r&b legend has never won a Grammy in regular competition, and he has been paralyzed since a 1990 accident."

The Tony Rich Project did suffer a defeat to a different veteran of the genre, Luther Vandross, who took the male r&b vocal kudos for "Your Secret Love." It was the title track to his latest album, which critics cheered for its adventurous explorations into new sounds like rap.

The top rap music of the year was made especially accessible to mainstream audiences by the r&b touches of the Fugees, a Haitian-American group from New Jersey who combined both musical genres in the year's third-best-selling album, *The Score,* which became only the second rap work ever to be nominated for Grammy's Album of the Year award (after *Please Hammer Don't Hurt 'Em* in 1990). After losing the top prize, *The Score* took Best Rap Album. It also earned the accolade for r&b group vocals for a tune that was an old Grammy favorite—"Killing Me Softly with His Song," which won Record and Song of the Year in 1973 when performed by Roberta Flack. Accepting their honors on the Grammycast, Fugees member Pras used the opportunity to appeal for peace between Los Angeles and New York City rappers, saying, "East Coast, West Coast, one love."

Variety cheered the Fugees' musical appearance on the Grammycast: "Performance highlights included two-category winners the Fugees, backed by members of Bob Marley's family and the Wailers, for a version of Marley's classic 'No Woman, No Cry.' " They performed it with Marley's wife, Rita, and son Stephen.

The Grammys honored Marley in a different category when *Hall of Fame—A Tribute to Bob Marley's 50th Anniversary* became the winner of the trophy for Best Reggae Album for former group member Bunny Wailer. It was Wailer's fifth album-length remembrance of his former mentor. An earlier effort, *Time Will Tell,* won Best Reggae Recording of 1990.

A loser in the category for Best Rap Album rebounded in the race for Best Rap Solo Performance: *Mr. Smith* by L.L. Cool J, who last won the category for 1991. His latest victory, for the album's "Hey Lover" track, proved that Grammy voters prefer that their rap soloists have TV sitcom credentials. L.L. Cool J was the star of NBC's *In the House.* Previous winners in the category included Queen Latifah of *Living Single* and *Fresh Prince* Will Smith.

Many Grammy pundits wondered if a sympathy vote would swing the rap categories to the late 2Pac, who'd been murdered in a gangland shooting during 1996. Since 2Pac had two nominations in the race for best rap group, the prognosticators were correct to predict that his votes would split in favor of Bone Thugs-N-Harmony's "Tha Crossroads," which zoomed to number one on the charts just two weeks after its release, the fastest rise since the Beatles' "Can't Buy Me Love" in 1964. "Crossroads" stressed a positive social message, being an elegy for the group's friends gunned down in Cleveland's east side ghetto. Group leader Layzie Bone recalled those violent days to the media backstage at the Grammys, saying, "I was shot in the head. It's a miracle I'm alive."

A song described as "a trip to rap's roots"—"Where It's At"—brought the prize for Best Male Rock Vocal Performance to Beck, the 26-year-old high school dropout whose breakout CD *Odelay* was clearly the critics' choice for the best of the year, even though it lost Grammy's Album of the Year award to

Celine Dion's *Falling into You.* Music critics voting in *Rolling Stone's* poll named *Odelay* the best of 1996; so did the *New York Times. Spin* declared Beck its Artist of the Year. The fact that *Odelay* made it into the Grammy best album lineup was surely a result of the new reforms in the top four categories that made the entries more hip. Backstage at the music awards, though, the artist stood up for other music that failed to get recognized, telling reporters, "There were a lot of great records this year that weren't a thousand miles within the Grammys."

Beck's victory in the rock vocals category was impressive. He beat not only Bruce Springsteen (who trounced him in the category two years ago) but also this year's best record winner, Eric Clapton. In addition, Beck scored the award for Best Alternative Music Performance, which he accepted, saying, "This is very smooth." The response by the media was less smooth, however, since critics wondered: How could the same music be both rock *and* alternative?

Strangely, the Smashing Pumpkins were up for awards in rock, alternative *and* hard-rock categories. The band began the award race with a whopping seven nominations. "It floored me!" group leader Billy Corgan told *Variety* when he heard the news. Particularly impressive was that the Pumpkins were up for Record of the Year ("1979") and Album of the Year (*Mellon Collie and the Infinite Sadness*) after being named the year's best band by the *Rolling Stone's* Critics' Poll and *Spin.*

The Pumpkins ended up with only one award—Best Hard Rock Performance—for "Bullet with Butterfly Wings," a song that resonated with fans for its powerful lyric: "Despite all my rage, I am still just a rat in a cage / And I still believe that I cannot be saved." One member of the group, keyboardist Jonathan Melvoin, had died of a heroin overdose the previous summer. The loss hit the Grammys especially hard, since the artist was the son of former N.A.R.A.S. president Michael Melvoin. Backstage at the Grammys, the press asked Pumpkins lead singer Corgan how the group endured the loss. He implied that they were mature enough to handle it, saying, "We are children of the '90s."

Variety noted that "the first significant upset" at this year's Grammys came in the category for rock group vocals, which the Pumpkins lost when it was claimed by the Dave Matthews Band for "So Much to Say." Matthews, a South African native based in Virginia, found a winning musical combination when he dared to dress up his rock sound with classical violins and jazz saxophones.

Rage Against the Machine, the year's best hard rock/metal band according to the *Rolling Stones* Critics' Poll, lost its Grammy bid for Best Hard Rock Performance, but the rap metal group rallied to take the trophy for Best Metal Performance for "Tire Me."

The rock instrumental category honored eight artists who played together at the 1990s blues festival with Stevie Ray Vaughan the day before he died in a helicopter crash. The performance award went to "SRV," a track from *A Tribute to Stevie Ray Vaughan,* which included musical contributions from Jimmie Vaughan, Eric Clapton, Bonnie Raitt, Robert Cray, B. B. King, Buddy Guy, Dr. John and Art Neville.

The biggest song on country radio in 1996 was Brooks & Dunn's "My Maria," which set a new record for being played the most times in one week: 5,779. In 1996, the duo also became the first ever to be hailed as Entertainer of the Year at both the Country Music Association and Academy of Country Music Awards. "My Maria" earned the biggest-selling duo in country music history the additional kudos of a Grammy for Best Country Performance by a Duo or Group.

"My Maria" was from the best-selling country disc of the year, *Borderline,* which lost the award for Best Country Album to Lyle Lovett's *The Road to Ensenada.*

Variety described *Ensenada* as "quirky and decidedly un-country." It was Lovett's sixth album and clearly his best yet. It was the only country album to make most critics' top 10 list of the year's best music and it marked the wily Texan's return to the country charts for the first time in more than five years.

A loser in the Best Country Album competition rallied to beat Lovett for best male country vocalist—Vince Gill ("Worlds Apart"), who claimed the category for a fifth time in seven years. He also earned his 10th career Grammy for his collaboration with Alison Krauss & Union Station ("High Lonesome Sound"). The artists teamed up again at the Grammycast. *Variety* saluted them for giving one of the ceremony's "performance highlights . . . a tribute to the late inventor of bluegrass Bill Monroe."

Monroe died of a stroke at the age of 84 in 1996, soon after the release of a new tribute work that would earn Grammy's Best Bluegrass Album—*True Life Blues: The Songs of Bill Monroe.* It showcased the contributions of 30 bluegrass and country artists, including Vassar Clements, Del McCoury, Jerry Douglas and the Nashville Bluegrass Band.

Winner of Best Traditional Blues Album was James Cotton, the blues harmonica player who played a key role in the Chicago blues revival of the 1960s and '70s. On *Deep in the Blues,* he celebrated music of his native Mississippi Delta. A salute to the Chicago heyday was the focus of the work that won Best Contemporary Blues Album: *Just Like You,* by acoustic blues artist Keb' Mo', who beat works by Buddy Guy, Bo Diddley and Clarence "Gatemouth" Brown.

In the folk categories, Pete Seeger reaped his first career Grammy for his first studio album in 17 years, *Pete,* which included 18 new and old songs performed with banjo, guitar or choir backup. He

> Rubén Blades won for his "best tropical effort in years."

was prodded into doing the recording by Paul Winter, the owner of his record label. "I've lost my voice! You can't record me!" Seeger protested. But Winter persevered. Backstage at the Grammys, Seeger told reporters, "I don't have a career. I've simply made music all my life for the fun of it. It's nice to make a living."

"The Best Contemporary Folk Album category normally wouldn't get a second glance," *Variety* reported. "But Bruce Springsteen's win for the title track to *The Ghost of Tom Joad,* which he performed during the telecast, gave the listing new visibility. In his thank you's, the Boss recalled how Columbia Records chief Don Ienner supported the effort, even though he 'sat in my studio, his dreams of mega-sales slipping down the drain.' "

Springsteen won right after he performed "Ghost" and echoed a gripe heard earlier in the Grammycast when he said, "I guess Eric Clapton was right. When you sing a song, you get the award."

"Tunnel vision prevails again," the *L.A. Times* complained when the jazz noms came out. "The Recording Academy membership never has revealed any particular desire to seek out unfamiliar music or performers. This year's choices take no chances whatsoever."

Nonetheless, the *L.A. Times* appreciated the quality of the entries: "The best contemporary jazz performance category lineup is excellent, with first-rate albums by Bob James and Kirk Whalum, Harvey Mason, Wayne Shorter, Mike Stern and T. J. Kirk." The winner was Shorter for *High Life.*

Two categories had four of the same nominees. Both slots were won by four-time past Grammy champ Michael Brecker: Music from *Tales from the Hudson,* featuring all original Brecker compositions, won two prizes for his tenor sax instrumental performances.

A Grammy first-timer was welcomed in the vocalist category: Cassandra Wilson, who had been named best female jazz singer by *Down Beat* every year since 1994. Critics went crazy over her

New Moon Daughter in 1996. *Time* magazine named it the best album of the year, calling Wilson "the queen of contemporary jazz vocalists and the true heir to Billie Holiday and Sarah Vaughan." The *New York Times* declared it one of the best albums of the decade. Wrote critic Stephen Holden: "Ms. Wilson's spellbindingly intense performances of everything from Billie Holiday's 'Strange Fruit' to U2's 'Love Is Blindness' to Hank Williams' 'I'm So Lonesome I Could Cry' reinvents the material from the ground up."

One of the genre's leading "ghost bands," the Count Basie Orchestra, led by trombonist Grover Mitchell, beat the Mingus Big Band to snag the trophy for Best Large Jazz Ensemble Performance (*Live at Manchester Craftsmen's Guild*). Both groups were having a particularly good year, according to *Down Beat:* "Orchestras playing under the names Basie and Mingus scored first and second place, respectively, in the Big Band category of *Down Beat*'s 1996 Readers' Poll, not only leaving other big-name legacy bands in the dust, but beating out jazz orchestras named after (and led by) the living."

Although not technically a jazz category, the competition for Best Instrumental Composition was dominated by such jazz greats as Wayne Shorter and Arturo Sandoval. The gold went to Herbie and Jean Hancock for "Manhattan (Island of Lights and Love)," which Herbie performed on his album *The New Standard.* Backstage at the Grammys, *Variety* noted, "Pianist Herbie Hancock paid tribute to jazz drummer Tony Williams, who died this week, for his role in the creation of jazz fusion. 'Miles Davis got credit, but Tony was the first person whose group played that kind of music,' Hancock said. 'He changed everything forever, as far as rhythm was concerned.' "

Grammy voters gave Davis generous credit this year by bestowing three awards on *The Complete Columbia Studio Recordings* of Miles Davis and Gil Evans: Best Historical Album, Best

Recording Package, Boxed, and Best Album Notes. *BusinessWeek* described the music: "The Columbia recordings, made between 1957 and 1968, showcase Davis' spare, mournful trumpet against the dense orchestral background provided by Evans' arrangements." The package contained six digitally remastered CDs filled with alternate recording takes and other never-before-released material.

There was a huge upset in the category for Best Pop Instrumental Performance when Stevie Wonder and the Smashing Pumpkins were beaten by the banjo-led jazz group Bela Fleck & the Fleckstones ("The Sinister Minister"). Fleck told *Down Beat,* "The banjo is originally an African instrument and originally a jazz instrument. A lot of people forget that the banjo really has a very natural place in jazz."

The prize for Best Latin Jazz Performance went to alto saxman Paquito D'Rivera for the Cuban exile's salute to his homeland—*Portraits of Cuba.*

Elsewhere in the Latin categories, the *L.A. Times* griped that " 'pop' means either romantic or soft, mariachi is the same as Tex-Mex, rock 'n' roll doesn't exist and, year after year, the voters seem to have lost all sense of the reality of today's Latin music. As usual, the nominees for best Latin pop performance are mostly a bunch of huge-selling romantic singers with nothing new to offer."

But the category of Best Latin Pop Performance did welcome a newcomer over several Grammy veterans: Enrique Iglesias, the 21-year-old-son of Julio. The younger Iglesias was emerging as a new teen heartthrob thanks to the gushing love songs and dramatic ballads on his self-titled CD.

Although some observers considered the new title redundant, N.A.R.A.S. changed the name of the Mexican-American category to include Tejano music. The winner was another first-time Grammy recipient: La Mafia for its fourth album, and biggest seller to date, *Un Millon de Rosas.* The *L.A. Times*

"The Beatles are considered a shoo-in," *Variety* prophesied correctly. The Fab Four took three prizes for *Anthology*'s CD and VHS versions.

described the group's sound as "tejano-cumbia-romantic pop fusion."

Billboard made this bold forecast about another race: "In the Best Tropical Latin Performance category, the hands-down nod goes to Ruben Blades' best tropical effort in years, *La Rosa de los Vientos*. But the bet here is that Albita's likable *Dicen Que* wins because her manager, Emilio Estefan Jr., is five for five so far in Latino Grammy categories." Blades ended up winning, earning his third career Grammy.

The world music category went to the Irish Chieftains for their seventh album, *Santiago,* which explored the music of the Spanish regions of Galicia and Basque, which were both once settled by ancient Celts. *People* asserted in its review of the disc, "The lands are linked to this day, as is beautifully demonstrated by the playing of the gaita, a Galician version of the bagpipes."

Discussing the nature of Irish music, 25-year-old Grammy winner Enya told reporters backstage, "A lot of it sounds melancholy, but that's a reflection of the passion of Irish cluture." She had just been honored for having the year's Best New Age Album, *The Memory of Trees,* an award she last claimed for 1992 with her last album, *Shepherd Moons.*

Riverdance, a production of Irish folk music that introduced a new interpretation of the jig called Irish stepdancing, won Best Musical Show Album over the score to the critically aclaimed Tony winner *Rent*. *Variety* cheered the cast's appearance on the Grammycast: "First show of enthusiasm came more than an hour into the program with numbers by casts of Grammy-nominated B'way musicals *Bring in 'Da Noise, Bring in 'Da Funk* and *Riverdance,* connected by a faceoff between *Funk*'s Savion Glover and Colin Dunn from category winner *Riverdance*."

Tony Bennett scored Grammys in the past for his album salutes to Sinatra (*Perfectly Frank*) and Fred Astaire (*Steppin' Out*). Now he was honored in the traditional pop category for *Here's to the Ladies,* his tribute to such great women of song as Dinah Washington, Judy Garland, Ella Fitzgerald, Billie Holiday, Barbra Streisand and Liza Minnelli. Ironically, *Ladies* beat album entries by Minnelli and three other reigning music queens—Rosemary Clooney, Bernadette Peters and Natalie Cole.

In the polka category, onetime past champ Frank Yankovic faced three-time past winner Walter Ostanek. "They'll split the Slovenian vote," predicted the also-nominated, six-time loser Lenny Gomulka to the *New York Times*. "Eddie Blazonczyk and I will split the Polish vote. That leaves Jimmy Sturr." Sturr, the *Times* added, "is known for the Eastern sound, which uses a big-band arrangement and is played faster than Slovenian or Chicago." Sturr ended up with his eighth victory out of 12 nominations when he took the category for *Polka! All Night Long!*

An unlikely name appeared among the winners for religious music—Andy Griffith, the 69-year-old actor who once trained as a classical singer while attending the University of North Carolina. Early in his showbiz career, Griffith was told during an audition that he'd never make it as a singer, so he pursued acting instead. In 1996, he finally recorded an album, *I Love to Tell the Story,* on which he applied his folksy baritone to 25 hymns. It won him the Grammy for Best Southern Gospel, Country Gospel or Bluegrass Gospel Album over works by Willie Nelson and Charlie Daniels.

Although her daughter Whitney already had five Grammys on the shelf, Cissy Houston finally earned one of her own—for Best Traditional Soul Gospel Album *Face to Face,* her first solo recording in 15 years. Houston began her singing career in the 1960s by performing gospel wth her family group, the Drinkard Sisters. Now she returned to her music roots by performing "Amazing Grace," Marvin Gaye's 1960s hit "How Sweet It Is" and six new, self-written songs while backed up by the choir and pianist from the New Hope Baptist Church of Newark, New Jersey, where she served as minister of music. "I'm not afraid to sing about God," Houston told reporters. "That's what my life is all about."

The 26-year-old hip-hop music minister out of Fort Worth, Texas, Kirk Franklin, had his recording debut in 1993 but now garnered his first Grammy for Best Contemporary Soul Gospel Album *Whatcha Lookin' 4*.

Another first-time Grammy recipient was DC Talk (the initials stand for "decent Christian"), a trio of Christian rappers-turned-grungers who met while students at Jerry Falwell's Liberty University. They were honored for Best Rock Gospel Album for *Jesus Freak,* which entered the Billboard Top 200 at number 16, making it the highest-ranked debut ever by a Christian disc. "We've made it our goal to be missionaries to our generation," group member Toby McKeehan told the media backstage at the Grammys.

Elsewhere in the religious lineup, old Grammy veterans prevailed again, including eight-time past champ Shirley Caesar, whose recording with the Outreach Convention Choir won Best Gospel Album by a Choir or Chorus. Winner of Best Pop/Contemporary Gospel Album was *Tribute: The Songs of Andrae Crouch,* which saluted the works of the seven-time past Grammy honoree.

The nonmusic categories sparked unusual notice when First Lady Hillary Clinton won Best Spoken Word or Non-musical Album for her audio rendition of her best-selling children's book *It Takes a Village.* "Each of us plays a part in every child's life," she told reporters. "As an old African proverb says, 'It takes a village to raise a child.'"

Backstage, Clinton also said that she was "surprised that Grammys were given to tone-deaf people." She added that if her husband, Bill, "really got to work on his sax, don't count him out" for winning a Grammy in the future, too.

Since the award was one of the 75 prizes bestowed prior to the evening Grammy ceremony, *Variety* noted that Clinton "was the only pre-telecast winner whose acceptance was shown during the program proper."

After Clinton received the prize in the afternoon, *USA Today* noted, "She raced back to cohost a state dinner. She left the Garden quickly, hopped an Air Force plane back to Washington and entered the White House at 8:05 P.M. clutching her Grammy."

Linda Ronstadt claimed Best Musical Album for Children for *Dedicated to the One I Love,* a recording on which she retooled familiar music by Brahms, the Beach Boys and the Beatles into children's lullabies.

Winner of Best Spoken Word Album for Children was *Stellaluna,* the best-selling story of an infant fruit bat. It had recently been declared Book of the Year by the American Booksellers Association.

Former *Saturday Night Live* comedian Al Franken beat two past Grammy favorites, Professor Peter Schickele and Stan Freberg, to claim Best Spoken Comedy Album for *Rush Limbaugh Is a Big Fat Idiot,* an audio version of Franken's best-selling book that fired liberal barbs at the blustery conservative radio and TV host.

"The Grammy Award classical nominations follow the pattern set in recent years, with their focus squarely on 20th-

"I'm not an overnight success," said 14-year-old LeAnn Rimes, who scored an upset to win Best New Artist. "I've been at this since I was 6."

century repertoire and the continuing presence of Pierre Boulez," *Billboard* reported. "With four nominations for three recordings this year, Boulez appears to be the Georg Solti of the 1990s."

Boulez began with four nominations but only scored one win, claiming the new category for works that are not quite chamber music and not orchestra: Best Small Ensemble Performance. He was honored for "Explosante-Fixe," a track from *Boulez Conducts Boulez* with the Ensemble Intercontemporain.

Boulez was nominated for Best Classical Album but lost to *Of Rage and Remembrance,* a collection of works that included Corigliano's Symphony No. 1 performed by Leonard Slatkin leading the National Symphony Orchestra, mezzo-soprano Michelle DeYoung and two male choirs. The music is known commonly as "The AIDS Symphony," since the American composer was inspired to write it after viewing the AIDS Memorial Quilt in Washington, D.C. An earlier recording of it by Daniel Barenboim leading the Chicago Symphony won the Grammy for Best Orchestral Performance of 1991.

John Corigliano won the Grammy for Best Contemporary Composition for his String Quartet, which he wrote for the final performance of the Cleveland String Quartet group, which disbanded in 1996 after 26 years. A recording of their farewell appearance earned the troupe its own prize—for Best Chamber Music Performance.

When Michael Tilson Thomas, former conductor of the London Symphony Orchestra, took over the San Francisco Symphony in 1996 from Herbert Blomstedt, he was welcomed to town like a beloved sports hero or visiting film star. *Time* noticed soon after his arrival, "Already the San Francisco Symphony has undergone a transformation. Woodwinds dance merrily, the brass resonates nobly and the strings speak as one. Tilson Thomas's wizardry is on display in a smashing new recording of Prokofiev's *Romeo & Juliet.*" The recording won the statuette for Best Orchestral Performance.

Winner of Best Opera Recording was Richard Hickox conducting the London Opera, London Symphony Chorus and City of London Sinfonia in Benjamin Britten's *Peter Grimes. American Record Guide* called this fourth commercial recording of the work "the most consistently musical. . . . Hickox's take on the score is lithe and agile, lean and taut, moving in a crescendo from strength to strength." The lead was sung by tenor Philip Langridge, who was cheered by *Opera News* for possessing a "lyrical quality and some useful edge and snarl."

Peter Grimes was not nominated for Best Classical Album, but a collection of Mozart, Wagner and Borodin arias by bass-baritone Bryn Terfel was, receiving the vocal performance award instead.

Terfel also performed on the recording that won the trophy for Best Choral Performance: Walton's oratorio *Belshazzar's Feast,* with Andrew Litton, Neville Creed and David Hill leading the Bournemouth Symphony Choir.

Another loser in the competition for Best Classical Album won a different Grammy: best instrumental soloist with orchestra. It was claimed by pianist Yefim Bronfman, the 39-year-old Russ-

ian-Israeli immigrant who performed three Bartók piano concertos.

The laurels for soloist work without orchestral accompaniment went to American pianist Earl Wild for *The Romantic Master,* which celebrated his 80th birthday by presenting signature Liszt works, some of the music he performed for the 1937 Disney film classic *Snow White* "and one of the best Beethoven Hammerklavier Sonatas you will ever hear," insisted *American Record Guide.*

Variety's review of this year's Grammys was not upbeat: "With a listless opening number, flaccid, seemingly ad-libbed hosting by comic Ellen DeGeneres, ballad-heavy performances and what seemed to be more time devoted to commercials than music, the 39th annual Grammy Awards TV show was a decidedly downbeat affair, despite event's being held in its largest venue ever, Madison Square Garden."

Variety was also clearly disappointed in the award results: "In a year when it looked like fresh faces and new sounds were finally due for Grammy recognition, key awards went instead to the mainstream pop that sells records and has traditionally earned statuettes."

USA Today also protested the voting outcome: " 'Change the World' is a charming ballad, but it's hardly worthy of best record and song awards. Celine Dion's victory is especially disappointing in light of the competition: Beck's *Odelay,* the Pumpkins' *Mellon Collie and the Infinite Sadness* and the Fugees' *The Score.* With three strong entries splitting the hip contingent, Dion's win was inevitable."

The Grammycast had its second-worst TV viewership ever: 13.4 rating/22 share. The numbers were big enough, however, to beat DeGeneres's own sitcom that aired concurrently on ABC.

Entertainment Weekly insisted that the real story this year was fashion, noting that "peekaboo duds stole the show." Among the highlights: "Sheryl Crow's Dolce and Gabbana dress designed to let everyone know that, yes, by golly, she was wearing panties. And the Marc Bouwer gown on dual-award winner Toni Braxton had everyone speculating that she probably wasn't. Also wearing titillating getups were Album of the Year winner Celine Dion, No Doubt's Gwen Stefani, the Smashing Pumpkins' D'Arcy and Jewel, whose dress by Gianfranco Ferré so clearly displayed her private parts—it became translucent under the lights—that one critic quipped, 'The show ought to have been rated TV-T&A.'"

• 1996 •

The awards ceremony was broadcast on CBS from the Shrine Auditorium in Los Angeles on February 26, 1997, for the eligibility period of October 1, 1995, through September 30, 1996.

ALBUM OF THE YEAR
• *Falling Into You*, Celine Dion. 550 Music/Epic.
Odelay, Beck. DGC.
The Score, Fugees. Ruffhouse/Columbia.
Mellon Collie and the Infinite Sadness, Smashing Pumpkins. Virgin.
Waiting to Exhale (soundtrack). Arista.

RECORD OF THE YEAR
• "Change the World," Eric Clapton. Reprise.
"Give Me One Reason," Tracy Chapman. Elektra.
"Because You Loved Me," Celine Dion. 550 Music/Epic.
"Ironic," Alanis Morissette. Maverick/Reprise.
"1979," Smashing Pumpkins. Virgin.

SONG OF THE YEAR
(Songwriter's Award)
• "Change the World," Gordon Kennedy, Wayne Kirkpatrick, Tommy Sims.
"Because You Loved Me," Diane Warren.
"Blue," Bill Mack.
"Exhale (Shoop Shoop)," Babyface.
"Give Me One Reason," Tracy Chapman.

BEST NEW ARTIST
• LeAnn Rimes
Garbage
Jewel
No Doubt
Tony Rich Project

BEST POP ALBUM
• *Falling Into You*, Celine Dion. 550 Music/Epic.
Secrets, Toni Braxton. LaFace.
New Beginning, Tracy Chapman. Elektra.
A Few Small Repairs, Shawn Colvin. Columbia.
Mercury Falling, Sting. A&M.

BEST POP VOCAL PERFORMANCE, MALE
• Eric Clapton, "Change the World," track from *Phenomenon*. Reprise.
Bryan Adams, "Let's Make a Night to Remember," track from *18 Til I Die*. A&M.
John Mellencamp, "Key West Intermezzo (I Saw You First)," track from *Mr. Happy Go Lucky*. Mercury.
Tony Rich Project, "Nobody Knows," track from *Words*. LaFace.
Sting, "Let Your Soul Be Your Pilot," track from *Mercury Falling*. A&M.

BEST POP VOCAL PERFORMANCE, FEMALE
• Toni Braxton, "Unbreak My Heart," track from *Secrets*. LaFace.
Shawn Colvin, "Get Out of This House," track from *A Few Small Repairs*. Columbia.
Celine Dion, "Because You Loved Me," track from *Falling Into You*. 550 Music/Epic.

Gloria Estefan, "Reach," track from *Destiny*. Epic.

Jewel, "Who Will Save Your Soul," track from *Pieces of You*. Atlantic.

BEST POP PERFORMANCE BY A DUO OR GROUP WITH VOCAL

- Beatles, "Free As a Bird," track from *Anthology I*. Capitol.

Gin Blossoms, "As Long As It Matters," track from *Congratulations I'm Sorry*. A&M.

Journey, "When You Love a Woman," track from *Trial By Fire*. Columbia Records.

Neville Brothers, "Fire on the Mountain," track from *Mitakuye Oyasin Oyasin/All My Relations*. A&M.

Presidents of the United States of America, "Peaches," track from *The Presidents of the United States of America*. Columbia.

Take 6, "When You Wish Upon a Star," track from *Music from the Park*. Walt Disney.

BEST POP COLLABORATION WITH VOCAL

- Natalie Cole (and Nat King Cole), "When I Fall in Love," track from *Stardust*. Elektra.

Burt Bacharach, Elvis Costello, "God Give Me the Strength," track from *Grace of My Heart*. MCA.

Brandy, Tamia, Gladys Knight, Chaka Khan, "Missing You," track from *Set It Off*. EastWest/EEG.

Whitney Houston, CeCe Winans, "Count On Me," track from *Waiting to Exhale* (soundtrack). Arista.

Frank Sinatra, Luciano Pavarotti, "My Way," track from *Sinatra 80th—Live in Concert*. Capitol.

BEST TRADITIONAL POP VOCAL PERFORMANCE

- Tony Bennett, *Here's to the Ladies*. Columbia.

Rosemary Clooney. *Dedicated to Nelson*. Concord Jazz.

Natalie Cole, *Stardust*. Elektra.

Liza Minnelli, *Gently*. Angel.

Bernadette Peters, *I'll Be Your Baby Tonight*. Angel.

BEST POP INSTRUMENTAL PERFORMANCE

- Bela Fleck & the Fleckstones, "The Sinister Minister," track from *Live Art*. Warner Bros.

Larry Mulle, Adam Clayton, "Mission: Impossible," track from *Mission: Impossible* (soundtrack). Mother/Island.

Lalo Schifrin with the London Philharmonic Orchestra, "Mission: Impossible," track from *Firebird*. Four Winds.

Smashing Pumpkins, "Mellon Collie and the Infinite Sadness," track from *Mellon Collie and the Infinite Sadness*. Virgin.

Stevie Wonder, "Kiss Lonely Goodbye (Harmonica with Orchestra)," track from *Pinocchio*. London.

BEST ROCK ALBUM

- *Sheryl Crow*, Sheryl Crow. A&M.

Crash, Dave Matthews Band. RCA.

Tragic Kingdom, No Doubt. Trauma/Interscope.

Road Tested, Bonnie Raitt. Capitol.

Broken Arrow, Neil Young with Crazy Horse. Reprise.

BEST ROCK SONG
(Songwriter's Award)

- "Give Me One Reason," Tracy Chapman.

"Cry Love," John Hiatt.

"6th Avenue Heartache," Jakob Dylan.

"Stupid Girl," Garbage.

"Too Much," Dave Matthews Band.

"Wonderwall," Noel Gallagher.

BEST ROCK VOCAL PERFORMANCE, MALE

- Beck, "Where It's At," track from *Odelay*. DGC.

Bryan Adams, "The Only Thing That Looks Good on Me Is You," track from *18 Til I Die*. A&M.

Eric Clapton, "Ain't Gone 'n Give Up on Your Love," track from *A Tribute to Stevie Ray Vaughan*. Epic.

John Hiatt, "Cry Love," track from *Walk On*. Capitol.

Bruce Springsteen, "Dead Man Walking," track from *Dead Man Walking*. Columbia.

BEST ROCK VOCAL PERFORMANCE, FEMALE

• Sheryl Crow, "If It Makes You Happy," track from *Sheryl Crow*. A&M.

Tracy Bonham, "Mother Mother," track from *The Burdens of Being Upright*. Island.

Tracy Chapman, "Give Me One Reason," track from *New Beginning*. Elektra.

Joan Osborne, "Spider Web," track from *Relish*. Blue Gorilla/Mercury.

Bonnie Raitt, "Burning Down the House," track from *Road Tested*. Capital.

BEST ROCK PERFORMANCE BY A DUO OR GROUP WITH VOCAL

• Dave Matthews Band, "So Much to Say," track from *Crash*. RCA.

Garbage, "Stupid Girl," track from *Garbage*. Almo Sounds.

Oasis, "Wonderwall," track from *(What's the Story) Morning Glory?* Epic.

Smashing Pumpkins, "1979," track from *Mellon Collie and the Infinite Sadness*. Virgin.

Wallflowers, "6th Avenue Heartache," track from *Bringing Down the Horse*. Interscope.

BEST ROCK INSTRUMENTAL PERFORMANCE

• Jimmie Vaughan, Eric Clapton, Bonnie Raitt, Robert Cray, B. B. King, Buddy Guy, Dr. John & Art Neville, "SRV Shuffle," track from *A Tribute to Stevie Ray Vaughan*. Epic.

Booker T & the MG's, "Green Onions," track from *The Concert for the Rock and Roll Hall of Fame*. Columbia.

Eric Johnson, "Pavilion," track from *Venus Isle*. Capitol.

Joe Satriani, "(You're) My World," track from *Joe Satriani*. Relativity.

Edward & Alex Van Halen, "Respect the Wind," track from *Twister*. Warner Sunset/Warner.

BEST HARD ROCK PERFORMANCE

• Smashing Pumpkins, "Bullet with Butterfly Wings," track from *Mellon Collie and the Infinite Sadness*. Virgin.

Alice in Chains, "Again," track from *Alice in Chains*. Columbia.

Rage Against the Machine, "Bulls on Parade," track from *Evil Empire*. Epic.

Soundgarden, "Pretty Noose," track from *Down on the Upside*. A&M.

Stone Temple Pilots, "Trippin' on a Hole in a Paper Heart," track from *Tiny Music . . . Songs from the Vatican Gift Shop*. Atlantic.

BEST METAL PERFORMANCE

• Rage Against the Machine, "Tire Me," track from *Evil Empire*. Epic.

Korn, "Shoots and Ladders," track from *Korn*. Immortal/Epic.

Pantera, "Suicide Note Pt. 1," track from *The Great Southern Trendkill*. East-West /EEG.

White Zombie, "I'm Your Boogie Man," track from *The Crow: City of Angels*. Miramax/Hollywood.

Rob Zombie, Alice Cooper, "Hands of Death (Burn Baby Burn)," track from *Songs in the Key of X*. Warner Bros.

BEST ALTERNATIVE MUSIC PERFORMANCE

• Beck, *Odelay*. DGC.

Tori Amos, *Boys for Pele*. Atlantic.

Tracy Bonham, *The Burdens of Being Upright*. Island.

R.E.M., *New Adventures in Hi-Fi*. Warner Bros.

Smashing Pumpkins, *Mellon Collie and the Infinite Sadness*. Virgin.

BEST RHYTHM & BLUES ALBUM

- *Words*, Tony Rich Project. LaFace.
Moving On, Oleta Adams. Fontana/Mercury.
Maxwell's Urban Hang Suite, Maxwell. Columbia.
New World Order, Curtis Mayfield, Warner Bros.
Peace Beyond Passion, Me'shell NdegeOcello. Maverick/Reprise.

BEST RHYTHM & BLUES SONG
(Songwriter's Award)

- "Exhale (Shoop Shoop)," Babyface.
"Sittin' Up in My Room," Babyface.
"You Put a Move on My Heart," Rod Temperton.
"Your Secret Love," Luther Vandross, Reed Vertelney.
"You're Makin' Me High," Babyface, Bryce Wilson.

BEST RHYTHM & BLUES VOCAL PERFORMANCE, MALE

- Luther Vandross, "Your Secret Love," track from *Your Secret Love*. Epic/LV.
D'Angelo, "Lady," track from *Brown Sugar*. EMI.
Al Green, "A Change Is Gonna Come," track from *The Concert for the Rock and Roll Hall of Fame*. Columbia.
Curtis Mayfield, "New World Order," track from *New World Order*. Warner Bros.
Tony Rich Project, "Like a Woman," track from *Words*. LaFace.

BEST RHYTHM & BLUES VOCAL PERFORMANCE, FEMALE

- Toni Braxton, "You're Makin' Me High," track from *Secrets*. LaFace.
Mary J. Blige, "Not Gon' Cry," track from *Waiting to Exhale* (soundtrack). Arista.
Brandy, "Sittin' Up in My Room," track from *Waiting to Exhale* (soundtrack). Arista.
Whitney Houston, "Exhale (Shoop Shoop)," track from *Waiting to Exhale* (soundtrack). Arista.

Tamia, "You Put a Move on My Heart," track from *Quincy Jones—Q's Jook Joint*. Qwest/Warner Bros.

BEST RHYTHM & BLUES VOCAL PERFORMANCE BY A DUO OR GROUP WITH VOCAL

- Fugees, "Killing Me Softly with His Song," track from *The Score*. Ruffhouse/Columbia.
Babyface, Tamia with Portrait, Barry White, "Show James," track from *Quincy Jones—Q's Jook Joint*. Qwest/Warner Bros.
Luke Cresswell, Fiona Wilkes, Carl Smith, Fraser Morrison, Everett Bradley, Mr. X, Melle Mel, Coolio, Yo-Yo, Chaka Khan, Charlie Wilson, Shaquille O'Neal, Luniz, "Stomp," track from *Quincy Jones—Q's Jook Joint*. Qwest/Warner Bros.
En Vogue, "Don't Let Go (Love)," track from *Set It Off*. EastWest/EEG.
Chaka Khan, Me'shell NdegeOcello, "Never Miss the Water," track from *Epiphany*. Reprise.

BEST RAP ALBUM

- *The Score*, Fugees. Ruffhouse/Columbia.
Gangsta's Paradise, Coolio. Tommy Boy Music.
Mr. Smith, L.L. Cool J. Def Jam.
Beats, Rhymes and Life, A Tribe Called Quest. Jive.
All Eyez on Me, 2Pac. Death Row/Interscope.

BEST RAP SOLO PERFORMANCE

- L.L. Cool J, "Hey Lover," track from *Mr. Smith*. Def Jam.
Busta Rhymes, "Woo-Hah! Got You All in Check," track from *The Coming*. Elektra.
Coolio, "1, 2, 3, 4 (Sumpin' New)," track from *Gangsta's Paradise*. Tommy Boy Music.
Heavy D, "Rock with You," track from *Quincy Jones—Q's Jook Joint*. Qwest/Warner Bros.

NAS, "If I Ruled the World (Imagine That)," track from *It Was Written*. Columbia.

BEST RAP PERFORMANCE BY A DUO OR GROUP

• Bone Thugs-N-Harmony, "Tha Crossroads," track from *E. 1999 Eternal*. Ruthless/Relativity.

Salt-N-Pepa, "Champagne," track from *Bulletproof*. MCA.

A Tribe Called Quest, "Ince Again," track from *Beats, Rhymes and Life*. Jive.

2Pac Featuring Dr. Dre & Roger Troutman, "California Love," track from *All Eyez on Me*. Death Row/Interscope.

2Pac Featuring KC & JoJo, "How Do U Want It," track from *All Eyez on Me*. Death Row/Interscope.

BEST CONTEMPORARY JAZZ PERFORMANCE

• Wayne Shorter, *High Life*. Verve.

Bob James, Kirk Whalum, *Joined at the Hip*. Warner Bros.

Harvey Mason, *Ratamacue*. Atlantic.

Mike Stern, *Between the Lines*. Atlantic Jazz.

T. J. Kirk, *If Four Was One*. Warner Bros.

BEST JAZZ VOCAL PERFORMANCE

• Cassandra Wilson, *New Moon Daughter*. Blue Note.

Ernestine Anderson, *Blues, Dues & Love News*. Qwest/Warner Bros.

Nnenna Freelon, *Shaking Free*. Concord Jazz.

Shirley Horn, *The Main Ingredient*. Verve.

Diana Krall, *All for You*. Impulse.

BEST JAZZ INSTRUMENTAL SOLO

• Michael Brecker, "Cabin Fever," track from *The Hudson*. Impulse.

Charlie Haden, "Now Is the Hour," track from *Now Is the Hour*. Verve.

Joe Lovano, "Duke Ellington's Sound of Love," track from *Quartets*. Blue Note.

Gonzalo Rubalcaba, "Agua de Beber," track from *Antonio Carlos Jobim and Friends*. Verve. Horace Silver, "Diggin' on Dexter," track from *The Hardbop Grandpop*. Impulse.

BEST JAZZ INSTRUMENTAL PERFORMANCE (INDIVIDUAL OR GROUP)

• Michael Brecker, *Tales from the Hudson*. Impulse.

Billy Childs, *The Child Within*. Shanachie.

Charlie Haden, *Quartet West*. Verve.

Joe Lovano, *Quartets: Live at the Village Vanguard*. Blue Note.

Horace Silver, *The Hardbop Grandpop*. Impulse.

BEST LARGE JAZZ ENSEMBLE PERFORMANCE

• Count Basie Orchestra, *Live at Manchester Craftsmen's Guild*. Jazz MCG.

Rob McConnell & the Boss Brass, *Even Canadians Get the Blues*. Concord Jazz.

Mingus Big Band, *Live in Time*. Dreyfun.

Marcus Roberts with the Lincoln Center Jazz Orchestra, *Portraits in Blue*. Sony Classical.

Maria Schneider Orchestra, *Coming About*. Enja.

BEST LATIN JAZZ PERFORMANCE

• Paquito D'Rivera, *Portraits of Cuba*. Chesky.

Ray Barretto, *My Summertime*. Owl/Blue Note.

Steve Berrios, Son Bacheche, *And Then Some!* Milestone.

Terence Blanchard, Ivan Lins, *The Heart Speaks*. Columbia.

Don Grolnick, *Medianoche*. Warner Bros.

BEST COUNTRY ALBUM

• *The Road to Ensenada*, Lyle Lovett. Curb/MCA.

Borderline, Brooks & Dunn. Arista.

High Lonesome Sound, Vince Gill. MCA.
The Trouble with the Truth, Patty Loveless. Epic.
Everybody Knows, Trisha Yearwood. MCA.
Gone, Dwight Yoakam. Reprise.

BEST COUNTRY SONG
(Songwriter's Award)
• "Blue," Bill Mack.
"Believe Me Baby (I Lied)," Angelo, Larry Gottlieb, Kim Richey.
"High Lonesome Sound," Vince Gill.
"My Wife Thinks You're Dead," Junior Brown.
"Strawberry Wine," Matraca Berg, Gary Harrison.

BEST COUNTRY VOCAL PERFORMANCE, MALE
• Vince Gill, "Worlds Apart," track from *High Lonesome Sound*. MCA.
Clint Black, "Like the Rain," track from *The Greatest Hits*. RCA/Nashville.
Junior Brown, "My Wife Thinks You're Dead," track from *Junior High*. MCG/Curb.
Lyle Lovett, "Private Conversation," track from *The Road to Ensenada*. Curb/MCA.
Dwight Yoakam, "Nothing," track from *Gone*. Reprise.

BEST COUNTRY VOCAL PERFORMANCE, FEMALE
• LeAnn Rimes, "Blue," track from *Blue*. MCG/Curb.
Mary-Chapin Carpenter, "Let Me into Your Heart," track from *Tin Cup*. Epic/Columbia.
Deana Carter, "Strawberry Wine," track from *Did I Shave My Legs for This?* Capitol/Nashville.
Alison Krauss, "Baby Mine," track from *The Best of Country/The Best of Disney*. Walt Disney.
Trisha Yearwood, "Believe Me Baby (I Lied)," track from *Everybody Knows*. MCA.

BEST COUNTRY PERFORMANCE BY A DUO OR GROUP WITH VOCAL
• Brooks & Dunn, "My Maria," track from *Borderline*. Arista/Nashville.
BR5-49, "Cherokee Boogie," track from *BR5-49*. Arista/Nashville.
Diamond Rio, "That's What I Get for Loving You," track from *IV*. Arista.
Mavericks, "All You Ever Do Is Bring Me Down," track from *Music for All Occasions*. MCA.
Texas Tornados, "Little Bit Is Better Than Nada," track from *4 Aces/Tin Cup*. Reprise/Epic.

BEST COUNTRY COLLABORATION WITH VOCAL
• Vince Gill, Alison Krauss & Union Station, "High Lonesome Sound," track from *High Lonesome Sound*. MCA.
Jeff Foxworthy, Alan Jackson, "Redneck Games," track from *Crank It Up*. Warner Bros.
Vince Gill, Faith Hill, Tim McGraw, Trisha Yearwood, Lorrie Morgan, Marty Stuart, Little Texas, Tracy Lawrence, Terri Clark, Neal McCoy, Travis Tritt, John Berry, *Hope: Country Music's Quest for a Cure*. Giant.
Lyle Lovett, Randy Newman, "Long Tall Texan," track from *The Road to Ensenada*. Curb/MCA.
Marty Stuart, Travis Tritt, "Honky Tonkin's What I Do Best," track from *Honky Tonkin's What I Do Best*. MCA.

BEST COUNTRY INSTRUMENTAL PERFORMANCE
• Chet Atkins C.G.P., "Jam Man," track from *Almost Alone*. Columbia Records.
Vassar Clements, Richard Greene, Chris Thile, Scott Nygaard, Todd Phillips, "Scotland," track from *True Life Blues: The Songs of Bill Monroe*. Sugar Hill.
Diamond Rio, "Big," track from *IV*. Arista.

Ronnie McCoury, David Grier, Start
Duncan, Craig Smith, Todd Phillips,
"Rawhide," track from *True Life
Blues: The Songs of Bill Monroe*.
Sugar Hill Records.
Steve Wariner, "The Brickyard Boogie,"
track from *No More Mr. Nice Guy*.
Arista.

BEST ROCK GOSPEL ALBUM
• *Jesus Freak*, DC Talk. ForeFront.
Bloom, Audio Adrenaline. ForeFront.
Open All Nite, Big Tent Revival. Ardent/
ForeFront.
Take Me to Your Leader, Newsboys. Star
Song.
God, Rebecca St. James. ForeFront.

BEST POP/CONTEMPORARY
GOSPEL ALBUM
• *Tribute: The Songs of Andrae Crouch*,
various artists. Warner Alliance.
Shelter, Gary Chapman. Reunion.
Signs of Life, Steven Curtis Chapman.
Sparrow.
The Message, 4 Him. Benson Music.
Life Love and Other Mysteries, Point of
Grace. Word.

BEST SOUTHERN GOSPEL,
COUNTRY GOSPEL OR BLUEGRASS
GOSPEL ALBUM
• *I Love to Tell the Story*, Andy Griffith.
Sparrow.
Steel Witness, Charlie Daniels. Spar-
row.
There's a Light Guiding Me, Doyle
Lawson, Quicksilver. Sugar Hill.
How Great Thou Art, Willie Nelson,
Bobbie Nelson. Finer Arts.
Don't Overlook Salvation, Ricky Van
Shelton. Word/Nashville.

BEST TRADITIONAL SOUL
GOSPEL ALBUM
• *Face to Face*, Cissy Houston. House
of Blues Music.
New Dawning, Walter Hawkins & the
Hawkins Family. Bellmark.
Shake the Devil Off, Dorothy Norwood.
Malaco.

Together As One, Slim & the Supreme
Angels, Mighty Clouds of Joy,
Williams Brothers, various artists.
Intersound.
Let's Go Back: Live in Chicago,
Albertina Walker. Benson.

BEST CONTEMPORARY SOUL
GOSPEL ALBUM
• *Whatcha Lookin' 4*, Kirk Franklin &
the Family. Gospo Centric.
Live in Washington, Yolanda Adams.
Tribute.
Love Brought Me Back, Helen Baylor.
Word.
Shakin' the House, Hezekiah Walker,
Yolanda Adams, Fred Hammond.
Benson.
Heart and Soul, Winans. Qwest/Warner
Bros.

BEST GOSPEL ALBUM BY A CHOIR
OR CHORUS
• *Just a Word*, Shirley Caesar's Out-
reach Convention Choir. Word
Gospel.
All Things Are Possible, Edwin Hawkins
Music & Arts Seminar. Bellmark.
Gotta Feelin', Associates. Warner
Alliance.
I'll See You in the Rapture, Mississippi
Mass Choir, Malaco.
*A New Thing . . . Experience the Full-
ness*, Full Gospel Baptist Fellowship
Mass Choir. Gospo Centric.

BEST TRADITIONAL FOLK ALBUM
• *Pete*, Pete Seeger. Living Music.
The Hobo's Last Ride, Norman and
Nancy Blake. Shanachie.
Wild Hog in the Red Brush, John Hart-
ford. Rounder.
Intoxicated Spirit, Nusrat Fateh Ali
Khan. Shanachie.
*Thuthukani Ngoxolo—Let's Develop in
Peace*, Ladysmith Black Mambazo.
Shanachie.

BEST CONTEMPORARY FOLK ALBUM
• *The Ghost of Tom Joad*, Bruce Springsteen. Columbia.

Yonder, Jerry Douglas, Peter Rowan.
Sugar Hill.
Braver Newer World, Jimmie Dale
Gilmore. Elektra.
You? Me? Us? Richard Thompson.
Capitol.
Revival, Gillian Welch. Almo.

BEST TRADITIONAL BLUES ALBUM
• *Deep in the Blues*, James Cotton.
Verve.
Found True Love, John Hammond.
Pointblank.
*You're Gonna Miss Me (When I'm Dead
and Gone)*, Muddy Waters Tribute
Band. Telarc Blues.
Come On in This House, Junior Rells
with Guest Slide Guitarists. Telarc
Blues.
Live at the Mint, Jimmy Witherspoon.
On the Spot/Private Music.

BEST CONTEMPORARY BLUES ALBUM
• *Just Like You*, Keb' Mo'. Okeh/Epic.
Sad Street, Bobby Blue Bland. Malaco.
Long Way Home, Clarence "Gatemouth"
Brown. Verve.
A Man Amongst Men, Bo Diddley. Code
Blue/Atlantic.
Live! The Real Deal, Buddy Guy with
G. E. Smith & Saturday Night Live
Band. Silvertone.
Phantom Blues, Taj Mahal. Private
Music.

BEST BLUEGRASS ALBUM
• *True Life Blues: The Songs of Bill
Monroe,* various artists. Sugar Hill.
The Cold Hard Facts, Del McCoury
Band. Rounder.
Red on Blonde, Tim O'Brien. Sugar
Hill.
Bluegrass Boy, Peter Rowan. Sugar Hill.
The Stanley Tradition, various artists.
Doobie Shea.

BEST LATIN POP PERFORMANCE
• Enrique Iglesias, *Enrique Iglesias.*
Fonovisa.
Vikki Carr, *Emociones.* Rodven/Poly-
gram.

José Feliciano, *Americano.*
Rodven/Polygram.
Luis Miquel, *Nada Es Igual.* WEA
Latina.
Marco Antonio Solis, *En Pleno Vuelo.*
Fonovisa.

BEST TROPICAL LATIN PERFORMANCE
• Rubén Blades, *La Rosa de los Vientos.*
Sony.
Albita, *Dicen Que . . .* Crescent
Moon/Epic.
Oscar D'Leon, *El Sonero del Mundo.*
RMM.
DLG, *DLG (Dark Latin Groove).* Sony
Tropical/Sir George.
Jerry Rivera, *Fresco.* Sony Tropical.
Tony Vega, *Tony Vega.* RMM.

BEST MEXICAN-AMERICAN/TEJANO MUSIC PERFORMANCE
• La Mafia, *Un Millon de Rosas.* Sony.
Ramon Ayala y Sus Bravos del Norte,
Arrancame el Corazón. Freddie.
Fandango U.S.A., 10th Anniversary.
Freddie.
Vicente Fernandez, *Vicente Fernandez y
Sus Canciones.* Sony.
Jaime y los Chamacos, *En Vivo . . .
Puro Party Live!* Freddie.

BEST REGGAE ALBUM
• *Hall of Fame—A Tribute to Bob Mar-
ley's 50th Anniversary*, Bunny
Wailer. RAS.
Mr. Cool, Gregory Isaacs. VP.
Man with the Fun, Maxi Priest. Virgin.
Lyrically Potent, Sister Carol. Heartbeat.
Greetings from Skamania, Skatalites.
Shanachie.

BEST POLKA ALBUM
• *Polka! All Night Long!* Jimmy Sturr.
Rounder.
Music, Music, Music! Eddie Blazon-
czyk's Versatones. Bel-Aire.
Irresistible You, Lennon Gomulka,
Chicago Push. Push.
Putting It All To-gether, Walter
Ostanek & Friends. World
Renowned Sounds.

Songs of the Polka King, Frank Yankovic & Friends. Cleveland International.

BEST NEW AGE ALBUM
- *The Memory of Trees*, Enya. Reprise.

Arcanum, Acoustic Alchemy. GRP.

Pianissimo II, Suzanne Ciani. Seventh Wave.

Lore, Clannad. Atlantic.

Opium, Ottmar Liebert, Luna Negra. Epic.

BEST WORLD MUSIC ALBUM
- *Santiago*, Chieftains. RCA.

Tabula Rasa, Bela Fleck, V. M. Bhatt, Jie-Bing Chen. Water Lily.

Tierra Gitana, Gipsy Kings. Nonesuch.

Legacy, Ali Akbar Khan. Triloka/AMMP.

Night Song, Nusrat Fateh Ali Khan, Michael Brook. Real World.

My People, Joe Zawinul. Escapade.

BEST INSTRUMENTAL ARRANGEMENT
- Michael Kamen, "An American Symphony" (*Mr. Holland's Opus*). Polydor.

Lalo Schifrin, "Charlie Parker: The Firebird (Medley)" (*Firebird—Jazz Meets the Symphony No. 3*). Four Winds.

Wayne Shorter, "Children of the Night" (*High Life*). Verve.

Jim McNeeley, "Sing, Sing, Sing" (*The Carnegie Hall Jazz Band*). Blue Note.

Jorge Calandrelli, "Summer" (*The Five Seasons*). Shanachie.

BEST INSTRUMENTAL COMPOSITION
- "Manhattan (Island of Lights and Love)," Herbie Hancock, Jean Hancock.

"Aaron's Song," Billy Childs.

"The Fifth Season," Jorge Calandrelli.

"Midnight in Carlotta's Hair," Wayne Shorter.

"Real McBop," Arturo Sandoval.

BEST MUSICAL SHOW ALBUM
- *Riverdance*, Will Whelan, composer and lyricist. Celtic Heartbeat/Atlantic.

Bring in 'Da Noise, Bring in 'Da Funk, original Broadway cast. Angel. Ann Duquesnay, Reg. E. Gaines, George C. Wolfe, lyricists; Ann Duquesnay, Zane Mark, Daryl Waters, composers.

Rent, original Broadway cast. Jonathan Larson, composer and lyricist. Dreamworks.

Victor/Victoria, original Broadway cast. Leslie Bricusse, lyricist; Henry Mancini, composer. Phillips Classics.

BEST INSTRUMENTAL COMPOSITION WRITTEN FOR A MOTION PICTURE OR TV
- "Independence Day," David Arnold (*Independence Day*).

"Defile and Lament," Elliot Goldenthal (*A Time to Kill*).

"Get Shorty," John Lurie (*Get Shorty*).

"The Star Maker," Ennio Morricone.

"Unstrung Heroes," Thomas Newman.

BEST SONG WRITTEN SPECIFICALLY FOR A MOTION PICTURE OR TV
- "Because You Loved Me," Diane Warren (*Up Close and Personal*).

"Count on Me," Babyface, Michael Houston, Whitney Houston (*Waiting to Exhale*).

"Exhale (Shoop Shoop)," Babyface (*Waiting to Exhale*).

"It Hurts Like Hell," Babyface (*Waiting to Exhale*).

"Moonlight," Alan Bergman, Marilyn Bergman, John Williams (*Sabrina*).

BEST INSTRUMENTAL ARRANGEMENT ACCOMPANYING VOCAL(S)
- Alan Broadbent, David Foster, Gordon Jenkins, "When I Fall in Love," track from *Stardust* (Natalie and Nat King Cole). Elektra.

Quincy Jones, Sam Nestico, "Do Nothin' Till You Hear from Me," track from *Quincy Jones—Q's Jook Joint*. Qwest/Warner Bros.

Clare Fischer, "In the Still of the Night," track from *Lost in the Stars* (Chanticleer). Teldec.

John Clayton, Jr., "Teach Me Tonight,"
track from *Stardust*. Elektra.

Take 6, "When You Wish Upon a Star,"
track from *Music from the Park* (various artists). Walt Disney.

BEST CLASSICAL ALBUM

- *Corigliano: Of Rage and Remembrance (Symphony No. 1, etc.)*, Leonard Slatkin conducting the National Symphony Orchestra; Male Choir of the Oratorio Society of Washington, D.C.; Male Chorus of the Choral Arts Society of Washington. RCA Red Victor Red Seal.

Bartók: The Miraculous Mandarin; Music for Strings, Percussion and Celesta, Pierre Boulez conducting the Chicago Symphony Orchestra. Deutsche Grammophon.

Bartók: The 3 Piano Concertos, Yefim Bronfman, piano; Esa-Pekka Salonen conducting the Los Angeles Philharmonic. Sony Classical.

Copland: Dance Symphony; Short Symphony; Organ Symphony; etc., Leonard Slatkin conducting the St. Louis Symphony Orchestra; Simon Preston, organ. RCA Victor Red Seal.

Opera Arias (Works of Mozart, Wagner, Borodin, etc.), Bryn Terfel, bass-baritone; James Levine conducting the Metropolitan Opera Orchestra. Deutsche Grammophon.

Prokofiev: Violin Concertos Nos. 1 and 2; Sonata for Solo Violin, Gil Shaham, violin; André Previn conducting the London Symphony Orchestra. Deutsche Grammophon.

BEST ORCHESTRAL PERFORMANCE
(Conductor's Award)

- Michael Tilson Thomas conducting the San Francisco Symphony, *Prokofiev: Romeo and Juliet (Scenes from the Ballet)*. RCA Victor Red Seal.

Pierre Boulez conducting the Chicago Symphony Orchestra and Chorus, *Bartók: The Miraculous Mandarin; Music for Strings, Percussion and Celesta*. Deutsche Grammophon.

Esa-Pekka Salonen conducting the Los Angeles Philharmonic, "Symphony No. 2," track from *Lutoslawski: Symphony No. 2; Chantefleurs et Chantefables; Piano Concerto*. Sony Classical.

Pierre Boulez conducting the Cleveland Orchestra, *Messiaen: Et Exspecto Resurrectionem Mortuorum; Chronochromie; etc.* Deutsche Grammophon.

Yuri Temirkanov conducting the St. Petersburg Philharmonic Orchestra, *Shostakovich: Symphony No. 7 ("Leningrad")*. RCA Victor Red Seal.

BEST CHAMBER MUSIC
PERFORMANCE

- Cleveland Quartet, "String Quartet," track from *The Farewell Recording— Corigliano: String Quartet; Haydn: Quartet in D Major*. Telarc.

Martha Argerich, piano; Gidon Kremer, violin, *Beethoven: Violin Sonatas No. 9 ("Kreutzer") and No. 10*. Deutsche Grammophon.

Anner Bylsma, violoncello; Lambert Orkis, piano, *Brahms: Cello Sonatas Nos. 1 and 2; Schumann: 5 Stücke im Volkston, Op. 102; etc.* Sony Classical.

Olaf Bar, baritone; Barbara Bonney, soprano; Kurt Streit, tenor; Anne Sofie von Otter, mezzo-soprano, *Brahms: Liebeslieder-Walzer, Op. 52; Neue Liebeslieder-Walzer, Op. 65*. EMI Classics.

Martha Argerick, piano, *Schumann: Piano Quintet; Piano Quartet; etc.* EMI Classics.

BEST SMALL ENSEMBLE
PERFORMANCE (WITH OR WITHOUT
CONDUCTOR)

- Pierre Boulez conducting the Ensemble Intercontemporair, "Explosante-Fixe," track from *Boulez Conducts Boulez*. Deutsche Grammophon.

Gidon Kremer, violin, *Hommage à Piazzolla*. Nonesuch.
Oliver Knussen, conductor, "Suns Dance," track from *Matthews: Broken Symmetry; Fourth Sonata; etc.* Deutsche Grammophon.
New Century Chamber Orchestra, *Shostakovich: Written with the Hearts of Blood*. New Albion.
Federico Maria Sardelli, conductor; Modo Antiquo, *Vivaldi: Concerti per Molti Istromenti*. Tactus.

BEST CLASSICAL PERFORMANCE, INSTRUMENTAL SOLOIST(S) (WITH ORCHESTRA)

• Yefim Bronfman, piano (Esa-Pekka Salonen conducting the Los Angeles Philharmonic), *Bartók: The 3 Piano Concertos*. Sony Classical.
Gidon Kremer, violin (Kent Nagano conducting the London Symphony Orchestra), "Violin Concerto," track from *Adams: Violin Concerto; Shaker Loops*. Nonesuch.
Gil Shaham, violin (André Previn conducting the London Symphony Orchestra), "Concerto for Violin and Orchestra No. 2," track from *Prokofiev: Violin Concertos Nos. 1 and 2; etc.* Deutsche Grammophon.
Alfred Brendel, piano (Michael Gielen conducting the SWF Symphony; Orchestra Baden-Baden), "Piano Concerto," track from *Schoenberg: Piano Concerto; The Chamber Symphonies*. Philips Classics.
Truls Mork, cello (Mariss Jansons conducting the London Philharmonic), *Shostakovich: Cello Concertos Nos. 1 and 2*. Virgin Classics.

BEST CLASSICAL PERFORMANCE, INSTRUMENTAL SOLOIST (WITHOUT ORCHESTRA)

• Earl Wild, piano, *The Romantic Master (Works of Saint-Saëns, Handel, etc.)*. Sony Classical.
Yefim Bronfman, piano, *Prokofiev: Piano Sonatas Nos. 2, 3, 5 and 9*. Sony Classical.

Evgeny Kissin, piano, *Schumann: Fantasy; Liszt: Transcendental Etudes*. RCA Victor Red Seal.
Radu Lupu, piano, *Schumann: Kinderscenen; Kreisleriana; etc.* London Records.
Alan Feinberg, piano, *Wuorinen: Third Piano Sonata; Bagatelle, Etc.; Feldman: Palais de Mari*. Koch International Classics.

BEST OPERA RECORDING

• *Britten: Peter Grimes*, Richard Hickox conducting the London Opera, London Symphony Chorus and City of London Sinfonia (solos: Langridge, Opie, Watson). Chandos.
Dallapiccola: Il Prigioniero, Esa-Pekka Salonen conducting the Eric Ericson Chamber Chorus, Swedish Radio Chorus and Swedish Radio Symphony Orchestra (solos: Bryn-Julson, Haskin, Hynninen). Sony Classical.
Gluck: Orphée et Eurydice, Donald Runnicles conducting the Orchestra and Chorus of the San Francisco Opera (solos: Hagley, Larmore, Upshaw). Teldec.
Kunzen: Holger Danske, Thomas Dausgaard conducting the Danish National Radio Symphony Orchestra and Chorus (solos: Bonde-Hansen, Inger Dam-Jensen, Henning-Jensen, Mannov, Nielsen, Paevatalu, Reuter, Rorholm). Dacapo.
Weber: Der Freischütz, Nikolaus Harnoncourt conducting the Berliner Philharmonic and Rundfunkchor Berlin (solos: Cachemaille, Holzmair, Moll, Orgonasova, Salminen, Schafer, Wottrich). Teldec.

BEST CHORAL PERFORMANCE

• Andrew Litton, conductor; Neville Creed, David Hill, chorus masters, "Belshazzar's Feast," track from *Walton: Belshazzar's Feast; Suite from Henry V; etc.* London.
Ton Koopman, conductor; Simon Schouten, chorus master, *Bach: Complete Cantatas, Col. 1 (Der Herr*

Denket an Uns, Gott Ist Mein König, etc.) Erato.

John Eliot Gardiner, conductor, *Danny Boy—Songs and Dancing Ballads by Percy Grainger*. Philips Classics.

William Christie, conductor; François Bazola, chorus master, "Requiem," track from *Mozart: Requiem; Ave Verum Corpus*. Erato.

Carlo Maria Giulini, conductor, *Schubert: Mass in E Flat*. Sony Classical.

BEST CLASSICAL VOCAL PERFORMANCE

• Bryn Terfel, bass-baritone (James Levine conducting the Metropolitan Opera Orchestra), *Opera Arias*. Deutsche Grammophon.

Lorraine Hunt, soprano (Kent Nagano conducting the Halle Orchestra), "Phaedra," track from *Britten: The Rescue of Penelope; Phaedra*. Erato.

Sanford Sylvan, baritone (David Breitman, piano; Lydian String Quartet), *Fauré: L'Horizon Chimérique*. Nonesuch.

Renee Fleming, soprano (Sir Charles Mackerras conducting the Orchestra of St. Luke's), *Visions of Love—A Collection of Mozart Arias*. London.

Jennifer Larmore, mezzo-soprano (Jesus Lopez-Cobos conducting the Orchestre de Chambre de Lausanne), *Where Shall I Fly—Handel & Mozart Arias*. Teldec.

Anne Sofie von Otter, mezzo-soprano (Bengt Forsberg, piano), *Wings in the Night—Swedish Songs*. Deutsche Grammophone.

BEST CONTEMPORARY COMPOSITION

• String Quartet, John Corigliano.
Violin Concerto, John Adams.
Fourth Sonata, Colin Marthews.
"Angel of Light," Einojuhani Rautavaara.
"Four Soundscapes," Gunther Schuller.

BEST ENGINEERED RECORDING, CLASSICAL

• William Hoekstra, Lawrence Rock, *Copland: Dance Symphony; Short Symphony; Organ Symphony; etc.* RCA Victor Red Seal.

Lawrence Rock, *Barber: Violin Concerto; Cello Concerto*. RCA Victor Red Seal.

Charles Harbutt, *Bartók: The 3 Piano Concertos*. Sony Classical.

Keith O. Johnson, *Stravinsky: The Song of the Nightingale; The Firebird Suite; etc.* Reference Recordings.

John Eargle, *Tchaikovsky: 1812 Overture; Moscow Coronation Cantata; etc.* Delos International.

CLASSICAL PRODUCER OF THE YEAR

• Joanna Nickrenz
Manfred Eicher
James Lamminson
Martin Sauer
Gary Schultz

BEST SPOKEN COMEDY ALBUM

• *Rush Limbaugh Is a Big Fat Idiot*, Al Franken. Dove Audio.
The Definitive Biography of P.D.Q. Bach, Professor Peter Schickele. Highbridge Audio.
The Rants, Dennis Miller. BDD Audio.
Stan Freberg Presents the United States of America, Vol. 2 (The Middle Years), Stan Freberg. Rhino.
What the Hell Happened to Me? Adam Sandler. Warner Bros.

BEST SPOKEN WORD OR NONMUSICAL ALBUM

• *It Takes a Village*, Hillary Rodham Clinton. Simon and Schuster Audioworks.
The Adventures of Huckleberry Finn, Garrison Keillor (Mark Twain). Penguin/Highbridge Audio.
Charles Kuralt's America, Charles Kuralt. Simon and Schuster Audioworks.
Grow Old Along with Me, The Best Is Yet to Be, Edward Asner, Ellen

Burstyn, CCH Pounder, Alfre
Woodard. Audio Literature.
*Harry S Truman: A Journey to Indepen-
dence*, Lauren Bacall, Martin Lan-
dau, Jack Lemmon, Gregory Peck
(Paul Werth). Soundelux/Mind's Eye
Audio.

BEST MUSICAL ALBUM FOR CHILDREN
• *Dedicated to the One I Love*, Linda
Ronstadt. Elektra.
*John McCutcheon's Four Seasons: Win-
tersongs*, John McCutcheon.
Rounder.
Around the World and Back Again, Tom
Chapin. Sony Wonder.
Blanket Full of Dreams, Cathy Fink,
Marcy Marxer. Rounder Kids.
*Love Songs and Lullabyes for Daddy's
Little Dreamer*, various artists. Jaba.

BEST SPOKEN WORD ALBUM FOR CHILDREN
• *Stellaluna*, David Holt. High Windy
Audio.
The Wonderful O, Melissa Manchester.
Dove Audio.
The Prince and the Pauper, Carl Reiner.
Dove Audio.
Treasure Island, Michael York. Dove
Audio.
Jumanji, Robin Williams. Houghton
Mifflin/Charlesberry.

BEST ENGINEERED ALBUM (OTHER THAN CLASSICAL)
• Francis Buckley, Al Schmitt, Bruce
Swedien, Tommy Vicari, *Q's Jook
Joint* (Quincy Jones). Qwest/Warner
Bros.
Moogie Canazio, *Oceano* (Sergio
Mendes). Verve Forecast.
Michael Krowiak, Bob Power, Rail Jon
Rogut, *Peace Beyond Passion*
(Me'shell NdegeOcello).
Maverick/Reprise.
Dave Reitzas, Elliot Scheiner, Al
Schmitt, Erik Zobler, *Stardust*
(Natalie Cole). Elektra.
Eliot Scheiner, Al Schmitt, Bill Smith,
Tambu (Toto). Columbia.

BEST RECORDING PACKAGE (Art Director's Award)
• Andy Engel, Tommy Steele, *Ultra-
Lounge (Leonard Skin Sampler)* (var-
ious artists). Capitol.
Stefan Sagmeister, *Set the Twilight Reel-
ing* (Lou Reed). Warner Bros.
Adam Jones, Kevin Willis, *Aenima*
(Tool). Zoo/Volcano.
Stefan Sagmeister, *Miracle of Science*
(Marshall Crenshaw). Razor & Tie.
Chika Azuma, Patricia Lie, *East of the
Sun: The West Coast Sessions* (Stan
Getz). Verve.

BEST RECORDING PACKAGE, BOXED (Art Director's Award)
• Chika Azuma, Arnold Levine, *The
Complete Columbia Studio Record-
ings* (Miles Davis & Gil Evans).
Columbia.
JoDee Stringham, *The Complete Reprise
Studio Recordings* (Frank Sinatra).
Reprise.
Michael Lang, David Lau, Giulio Tur-
turro, *Blues, Boogie and Bop: The
1940s Mercury Sessions* (various
artists). Polygram.
Giulio Turturro, *The Man from Ipanema*
(Antonio Carlos Jobim). Verve
Chris Bilheimer, Michael Stipe, *New
Adventures in Hi-Fi* (R.E.M.).
Warner Bros.

BEST ALBUM NOTES (Annotator's Award)
• George Avakian, Bob Belden, Bill
Kirchner, Phil Schaap, *The Complete
Columbia Studio Recordings* (Miles
Davis & Gil Evans). Columbia.
Will Friedwald, Dave Kapp, Mel Tormé,
The Mel Tormé Collection, 1944–85.
Rhino.
Lawrence Hoffman, *Mean Old World—
The Blues from 1940 to 1994* (vari-
ous artists). Smithsonian Collection
of Recordings.
Will Friedwald, *The Complete Capitol
Singles Collection* (Frank Sinatra).
Capitol Records.

Chris Albertson, *The Complete Recordings, Vol. 5: The Final Chapter* (Bessie Smith). Columbia/Legacy.

BEST HISTORICAL ALBUM
- *The Complete Columbia Studio Recordings* (Miles Davis & Gil Evans). Columbia.
The Mel Tormé Collection, 1944–1985 (Mel Tormé). Rhino.
The Complete Reprise Studio Recordings (Frank Sinatra). Reprise.
Fritz Kreisler: The Complete RCA Recordings (Fritz Kreisler). RCA Victor Gold Seal.
The Mercury Blues 'n' Rhythm Story 1945–55 (various artists). Mercury.

PRODUCER OF THE YEAR (OTHER THAN CLASSICAL)
- Babyface
David Foster
Don Gehman
Brendan O'Brien
Don Was

BEST MUSIC VIDEO, SHORT FORM
- *Free As a Bird*, Beatles. Kevin Godley, director. Capitol.

Ironic, Alanis Morissette. Stephane Sedaoui, director. Maverick.
Tonight, Tonight, Smashing Pumpkins. Jonathan Dayton, Valerie Faris, directors. Virgin.
Earth Song, Michael Jackson. Nicholas Brandt, director. MJJ Productions/Sony Music.
Walking Contradiction, Green Day. Roman Coppola, director. Warner Bros./Reprise.

BEST MUSIC VIDEO, LONG FORM
- *The Beatles Anthology*, Beatles. Geoff Wonfor, director. Capitol Video/Turner Home Entertainment.
Satie and Suzanne, Reinbert de Leeuw. Tim Southam, director. Philips Classics.
Live from London, Bon Jovi. David Mallet, director. PolyGram Video.
Blood Brothers, Bruce Springsteen. Ernie Fritz, director. Columbia Music Video.
Farewell—Live from the Universal Amphitheatre, Oingo Boingo. Scott Palazzo, director. A&M Video.

• 1997 •
Time for Dylan

"**M**aybe people need time to catch up with it," Bob Dylan once said about his music.

Although he was one of the many artists who shared the Album of the Year Award of 1972 for *The Concert for Bangla Desh,* none of Dylan's milestone solo recordings—*Blood on the Tracks, Highway 61 Revisited* or *Blonde on Blonde*—was ever nominated for the trophy.

Now the times certainly seemed to be a-changing as Dylan entered the Grammy derby as the best album front-runner with *Time Out of Mind,* his first work of new music in seven years and one that made most critics' lists of top 10 recordings of 1997. *The New York Times* described it: "Haunted by mortality, swamped with the blues and saved by orneriness, Mr. Dylan testifies to the pain of loneliness and lost youth."

When a triumphant Dylan nabbed the top gold prize at Radio City Music Hall in New York, *Variety* described it as "a win that was expected and greeted with sustained applause and a standing ovation. The album is widely considered his best work in two decades."

As the Tambourine Man accepted the honor, he said, "We got a particular type of sound on this record which you don't get every day. We didn't know what we had when we did it, but we did it anyway."

He then reminisced about seeing Buddy Holly perform, and said, "I know he was with us all the time when we were making this record in some kind of way. In the words of the immortal Robert Johnson, 'The stuff we got'll bust your brains out.' We tried to get that across."

A moment of lesser but more bizarre Grammy drama busted out just a few minutes earlier.

Variety called Bob Dylan's best album winner *Time Out of Mind* "his best work in two decades." Son Jakob won two Grammys with the Wallflowers, but skipped the ceremony.

"Dylan's album of the year win followed his performance of 'Love Sick,' during which a half-dressed intruder crashed the stage with 'Soy Bomb' printed on his bare chest," *Variety* reported. "At first, audience members thought the man dancing beside Dylan was part of the perf—until security guards tried to grab him. But the man got on stage because he was a member of Dylan's ensemble, which ringed the performer during the song."

Dylan's success may have been largely due to voters' fondness for hailing rock veterans after their youthful prime, but that penchant went to extremes in the category for best male rock artist where, *Variety* noted, "50-something rockers ruled the roost." *Time* magazine added, "The five codgers competing for best rock vocal boast an average age of 51. Bob Dylan received his first nomination before four of the five female nominees were born." The senior, 56-year-old Dylan pulled rank and took the category easily with *Time* track "Cold Irons Bound" in addition to the accolade for Best Contemporary Folk Album.

"The academy members not only voted Dylan three awards, including best album, but they also made sure they weren't ever going to be accused of overlooking a Dylan again, so they threw in two awards for Dylan's son, Jakob," the *L.A. Times* noted.

The 28-year-old Dylan's rock band, the Wallflowers, had a breakout year with 1997's seventh-best-selling CD, *Burning Down the Horse*. Both awards (rock group vocals and Best Rock Song) went to "One Headlight," a ubiquitous radio hit and the number-one video of the year for VH1. It beat another Jakob Dylan tune, "The Difference," in the rock song contest.

The younger Dylan did not attend the Grammys and his father did not visit the media backstage. "Both father and son have been reluctant to speak of their relationship since Jakob's band made a splash last year," the *L.A. Times* reported.

While Grammy pundits were in full agreement that Dylan would snag best album, there was no consensus over what would happen in the race for Record of the Year. Pop-rock divas are normally a good guess (Sheryl Crow, Bonnie Raitt, Carole King in past years), but this year the category contained three of them.

TV Guide picked Sheryl Crow to prevail again ("Every Day Is a Winding Road"), while *Entertainment Weekly* and *USA Today* forecast Paula Cole ("Where Have All the Cowboys Gone?"). Believing that the divas might split the vote, the *L.A. Times* embraced the year's feel-good ditty "MMMBop" by the Tulsa teens of Hanson, and the Associated Press and the *L.A. Daily News* bet on R. Kelly's soaring ballad "I Believe I Can Fly."

Only *Billboard* got it right: "Sunny Came Home" by Shawn Colvin, which also won Song of the Year for Colvin and former lover/current collaborator and producer John Leventhal. "This is too cool," Colvin said, accepting the best song prize.

"We've been doing this a long time, it's been a long road and this does matter."

In retrospect, the choice of Colvin seemed consistent with past female best record champs like King and Crow who were crowned with Grammys when they finally broke into the Top 10 after years of toiling in the music biz trenches. The 42-year-old native of South Dakota began performing in bars and clubs at the age of 18, then moved to New York, where she was spotted by Columbia in 1988 and given a recording contract. In the first decade of her career, she earned six Grammy nominations and one win: 1990's Best Contemporary Folk Album (*Steady On*).

Variety called Colvin's best record victory "a surprise, since that top trophy typically goes to a commercially successful work which gets seared into the nation's consciousness." But "Sunny Came Home" was one of the year's longest-charting singles and also enjoyed broad radio airplay and frequent rotation on vid channels. What was truly surprising was that the winner defied Grammy's long-standing preference for uplifting ballads. "It's about an act of vengeance," Colvin told *Variety* about the song. *Time* called it the story of "a lost soul who returns home, gathers up the kids and sets the place on fire, as a suave, sing-along chorus offers the musical equivalent of God's unmeddling sympathy."

The vote results in the leading three categories were a blow to Paula Cole, who scored the second-most nominations this year (seven) and who was the first artist since Tracy Chapman in 1988 to be nominated in all four top slots—Album, Record, Song of the Year and Best New Artist. She rebounded to claim the newcomer's prize, however, which was presented to her by the Queen of Soul. Cole said, accepting it, "This is my dream, getting this award from Aretha Franklin!"

TV Guide opined, "Cole's newfound acclaim clearly stems from her impassioned voice and piano playing, her par-

ticipation in last summer's Lilith Fair—
and maybe, just maybe, the fact that the
striking 29-year-old appears naked on the
cover of *This Fire*." *This Fire* sold nearly
a million copies as of Grammy night,
making the Massachusetts native and former backup singer for Peter Gabriel a
sudden star thanks to such hit tracks as
"Cowboys" and "I Don't Want to Wait."
When she heard the news of her multiple
Grammy bids this year, she told the *L.A.
Times,* "Being nominated makes me feel
so acknowledged. It's like I've been this
dark horse for years, and suddenly I've
been given this wonderful gift."

Cole was widely favored to win the
prize for best female pop vocals, too, but
it went instead to the artist who organized
the all-female, 32-city "Lilith Fair" tour—
Sarah McLachlan. The Canadian singer-
songwriter was honored for "Building a
Mystery" from her new album, *Surfacing,*
which also earned McLachlan the additional Grammy for Best Pop Instrumental
Performance ("Last Dance").

Another "Lilith Fair" star fared well
when Fiona Apple copped the female rock
vocals gold for "Criminal," a sassy track
(lyrics reveal "I've been a bad, bad girl")
from her debut album, *Tidal*. The 20-year-
old New York singer-songwriter proved
just as naughty at the MTV Awards when
she accepted the prize as Best New Artist.
She lost the equivalent newcomer's honor
at the Grammys but displayed the same
brashness upon receiving her rock vocals
award. *Variety* noticed, "Fiona Apple forgot to wear shoes."

Prior to the 1995 voting reforms that
gave a secret committee of 25 music
experts the power to pick the nominees
for the top four awards, it would have
been a safe bet that Elton John's "Candle
in the Wind 1997" would have scored a
bid for Record of the Year—and possibly
would have won. Like Bob Dylan, John
was overdue for a salute in the top categories and it was an opportune time for
him to take a bow: His poignant tribute to
the late Princess Diana made music history by surpassing Bing Crosby's "White

Columbia

Variety called Shawn Colvin's best record win a
surprise after prognosticators split their picks
among R. Kelly, Paula Cole and Hanson.

Christmas" to become the best-selling
single of all time (11 million copies sold
in the United States; 30 million worldwide). But the only Grammy bid that
"Candle" earned was for best male pop
vocals, which John claimed easily.

Other music veterans took second-tier
awards, too.

"Sooner or later you get old enough to
win a Grammy," said first-timer John
Fogerty, whose *Blue Moon Swamp*
pulled off an upset for Best Rock Album
over U2's *Pop* and the Rolling Stones'
Bridges to Babylon. The former lead
singer for Creedence Clearwater Revival
told reporters backstage that the credit
was not his own: "My regeneration and
rebirth is directly a result of knowing my
wife, Julie."

Two-time past champ James Taylor
also surprised Grammy watchers with the
success of his Top 10, comeback album,
Hourglass. *Variety* reported, "The
announcement that James Taylor and producer Frank Filipetti's efforts on *Hourglass* nabbed the Grammy for Best Pop
Album earned gasps from the house and
the press room. It was widely thought to

be the category's dark horse in light of its relatively low profile compared to the other nominees," such as odds-on-favorite *The Dance* by Fleetwood Mac.

Taylor was on tour and couldn't be at the ceremony. Filipetti told reporters that the artist would be "very surprised," since he "really didn't think he had a chance of winning this."

One of the biggest Grammy shockers this year came in the category of best pop group vocals, which was claimed by U.K. pop/soul band Jamiroquai for "Virtual Insanity." *Variety* reported, "The win surprised many in the house, since No Doubt's 'Don't Speak' was thought to be the front-runner in the category that featured Fleetwood Mac's 'Silver Springs' and the Rolling Stones' 'Has Anybody Seen My Baby?' " Fleetwood Mac and the Stones were both experiencing dramatic career comebacks, but they and No Doubt were all overtaken by the fleet-footed winners of the MTV Video of the Year award. "The group's been a smash with Britain's club kids since 1992, but didn't grab the U.S. market until its videos started spinning," *Newsweek* noted. *Virtual Insanity* was the video that grabbed viewers most, featuring lead singer Jason Kay dancing deftly between sliding sofas in a room where the floor won't stop moving.

Two other British imports also claimed significant victories.

Both *Rolling Stone* and *Spin* had just declared Radiohead the best band of the year when it entered the Grammy race with a heady Album of the Year nomination cheered universally by music critics. Few gave *OK Computer* a serious chance to win, though, even, apparently, the producers of the Grammycast, who did not invite the British alternative group to perform on the show. Radiohead snubbed the Grammys in return by not attending, so they were not on hand to accept their consolation award for Best Alternative Music Performance. *Variety* reported, "Lead singer Thom Yorke doesn't feel the group would fit in amid all the 'tuxedos and self-congratulation' of the evening and they don't want to end up making some ill-timed remarks à la Eddie Vedder, who ended up dismissing the Grammys when the band accepted an award in the 1996 telecast."

Radiohead beat another hot British act, the Chemical Brothers, who rallied to take the gold for Best Rock Instrumental Performance for "Block Rockin' Beats," a track from *Dig Your Own Hole*, *Entertainment Weekly*'s pick for second-best album of the year—after *OK Computer*. The magazine described the duo's brand of techno dance music: "Lurching their computers back and forth, [Tom Rowlands and Ed Simons] look like Butt-head and Garth partying in a cybercafe." *Dig Your Own Hole* became the first hardcore British dance album ever to reach the Top 20 of the U.S. pop charts.

Disco queen Donna Summer made a Grammy comeback when a category she once lobbied for heavily did the same. Back in 1979, Summer was instrumental in getting a new award introduced for Best Disco Recording, which she promptly lost to Gloria Gaynor's "I Will Survive." Disco's sudden death soon afterward left the category a casualty, too. Now it was back as Best Dance Recording and was claimed by Summer for "Carry On," her 1993 European club hit produced by her old partner Giorgio Moroder.

Producer Babyface had a relatively low profile on the music scene this year as he concentrated on the release of his own solo album, *The Day*. Grammy voters still paid notice, however, with a nomination for Album of the Year—plus seven more. When all the Grammy bids came out, *Variety* announced that he was the front-runner for a second year in a row with the banner headline "Grammy's Familiar 'Face." He told *Variety*, "I really thought that this would be a year when there wouldn't be any nominations for me, especially with all the really hot things happening this year [and] with Puffy. This felt like a quiet year for me."

Things proved fairly quiet for him on

awards day when he experienced even worse luck than he did last year. In 1996, he scored only three wins for 12 noms. Now he scored only one—the Producer of the Year award—for the third year in a row and the fourth time overall.

Variety noted a glaring omission among those who competed against Babyface: "In the producer category, some industry observers were scratching their heads over the exclusion of Sean 'Puffy' Combs, who despite being behind the boards for several of the year's biggest singles, failed to pick up a single producing nod." In all, Puffy produced 14 of the year's Top 40 hits.

Puffy had such a standout year professionally that he was favored early on to be in the running for Record and Album of the Year, too, but he was shut out of all of the top categories except for Best New Artist. Nonetheless he reaped seven bids in all—tying Paula Cole for having the second most, after Babyface.

Three of his nominations were in the race for best rap group performance, which he won with "I'll Be Missing You," his remix of Sting's 1983 Song of the Year Grammy winner, "Every Breath You Take." The words were changed to become an elegy to rap star Notorious B.I.G., who was gunned down in Los Angeles after leaving a party in 1997, and it became one of the year's biggest hits, spending the most time on the top of the charts: 11 weeks. Ironically, among the songs it towered over at the Grammys was Puffy's duet with Notorious B.I.G. on the latter's spookily titled *Life After Death* disc.

Life After Death also lost to Puffy in the race for Best Rap Album, which went to *No Way Out* (number one for four weeks) during the pretelecast ceremonies held during the afternoon.

A few hours later, once the Grammycast began, an irked loser in the rap album category interrupted the show to mouth off. Worse, he picked an awkward time to grandstand—just as Shawn Colvin approached the podium to accept her trophy for best song. *Variety* reported, "Colvin's win for Song of the Year was overshadowed by Ol' Dirty Bastard, a member of Wu-Tang Clan, who grabbed presenter Erykah Badu's live microphone and offered a protest."

Ol' Dirty Bastard said, "When it comes to the children, Wu-Tang is for the children. Puffy is good, but Wu-Tang is the best."

Colvin waited for him to step aside, then told the crowd, "I'm confused now . . . " She giggled nervously and then began her thank-yous.

Backstage later, country nominee Deana Carter fumed to the press, "The rap community needs to have a little more respect. That was incredibly disrespectful."

In the rap solo category, voters embraced a mainstream choice and past Grammy favorite—Will Smith. The win was so predictable that Grammycast producers opened the show with a blockbuster dance version of the theme to the hit film *Men in Black*. A few minutes later, when Smith accepted his third career Grammy, he petitioned for other rappers to clean up their act. He insisted, "We do have a responsibility for the ears, for what goes into the impressionable ears that listen to the music we make."

One leading r&b star recently cleaned up his act by declaring his conversion to Christianity. R. Kelly heralded the experience by writing "I Believe I Can Fly," which many pundits considered a leading contender for Record and Song of the Year. When Kelly performed "Fly" on the Grammycast, he broadcast his new religious fervor boldly by backing himself up with a bobbing church choir dressed in swaying white gowns. His pulpit-pounding performance stirred the audience into a standing ovation, which was followed by three Grammys for Kelly: best r&b

R. Kelly thanked Bugs Bunny.

male vocals, best r&b song and best tune written for a movie (*Space Jam*).

Variety was perplexed by one of his thank-you speeches, calling it one of the "weirdities and faux pas" of the night: "R. Kelly thanked Bugs Bunny in his acceptance for top male r&b vocal, giving rise to the question of Daffy demanding equal time."

Backstage, Kelly also credited his higher power, telling the press that "Fly" was a song "God wrote." He said that he was grateful for the triple win "because it's another level for me" and added that he planned to take his three statuettes home and put them "on a shelf right next to my mom's picture."

Two other r&b categories were claimed by a loser for Best New Artist— Erykah Badu, a 26-year-old Dallas native (and "Lilith Fair" star) who had critics swooning over her Afro-hued vocals tinged with soul, jazz, blues and hip-hop. *Time* named her debut disc, *Baduizm,* the best album of the year and called her "the most thrilling new voice in pop."

Variety noted, "Badu's out-of-the-box success, *Baduizm,* is particularly noteworthy, since it gave the two-year-old Universal Records its first big hit and had industry tongues wagging over her contributions to the r&b and pop music folds." *Baduizm* became such a speedy hit that it sold 3.5 million copies in only 10 months.

A track from *Baduizm* not only earned Badu the female r&b prize, but the disc pulled off an upset over Babyface's *The Day* to take Best R&B Album. *Variety* described her acceptance speech: "Badu, who has been touted as one of the industry's new musical bright spots—a reputation helped by her hit single 'On & On'—said the award was for all the artists 'who don't get heard.' "

Whitney Houston's soundtrack to *The Preacher's Wife* was also nominated in both categories, a fact that got Houston so irked she boycotted the Grammys. She insisted that the album should have been nominated in the gospel slots.

The award for best r&b vocals by a group went to Blackstreet, a revamped version of the r&b foursome who debuted in 1994. Their tune "No Diggity" was such an infectious hit that one reporter for the *Chicago Tribune* griped, "The new rap song 'No Diggity' is being played to psychotic excess on WBBM-FM. The station admits to spinning the song 66 times per week, but I've heard it aired as often as twice an hour."

Janet Jackson earned a Grammy for best long-form video in 1989 for *Rhythm Nation* and shared the short-form prize with her brother Michael in 1995 (*Scream*); but now she reaped the latter award solo for *Got Till It's Gone,* a release from *Velvet Rope,* her first album in four years. Since the r&b song and video were widely compared with Joni Mitchell's "Big Yellow Taxi," Jackson invited the folk star to accompany her by singing a chorus.

Nineteen ninety-five Album of the Year champ Alanis Morissette took the long-form honor for *Jagged Little Pill.* The 90-minute video version chronicled the life, musical performances and backstage horseplay of her and her band during a marathon tour.

The chief drama in the country categories occurred in the showdown over best female vocalist, which pitted together two Nashville divas who'd just finished thrashing things out in America's music market. The *New York Times* called the battle "one of the more complex and contentious sagas involving a pop song in recent memory."

Last year's winner of Best New Artist, LeAnn Rimes, originally recorded "How Do I Live" for the film *Con Air,* but the producers didn't like it (not enough heartbreak) and called in Trisha Yearwood. When the Yearwood version became a hit single, Rimes retaliated by releasing her own. The two faced off on the country charts and radio (Yearwood won), then in the pop market (Rimes prevailed). When both scored nominations in the female vocalist category, the *New*

York Times promised, "The year-long contest will reach a climax at the 40th annual Grammy Awards."

Since the song, written by Diane Warren, was also a contender for Song of the Year, it merited a performance on the Grammycast. But which artist should do it? Grammy producers picked Rimes. Grammy voters, however, picked Yearwood—just moments after Rimes finished singing.

Backstage, reporters asked Yearwood about the battle. "I wish that song hadn't had to go through that," she said. "But everything happens the way it's supposed to, I guess. Diane Warren's the big winner here tonight, because she wrote the song and had two number-ones with it. So everybody's happy."

Yearwood won an additional Grammy for her collaboration with Garth Brooks on "In Another's Eyes." "We've known each other for years," Yearwood told reporters.

Another country thrush, and a recent Grammy favorite, Alison Krauss, nabbed three new awards, including a startling upset in the group vocals category over the Mavericks. She and her group Union Station won for "Looking in the Eyes of Love," a track from *So Long So Wrong,* which also took Best Bluegrass Album in addition to the instrumental performance prize for its track "Little Liza Jane."

In the brawl over best male country vocalist, *USA Today* and *Billboard* both predicted that George Straight would finally snare his first award. Grammycast producers apparently thought so, too, since they invited him to perform, but he had to bow out at the last minute due to illness. Vince Gill stood in for him and sang Straight's "Carrying Your Love with Me," but then, a few moments later, the longtime Grammy favorite ended up overstepping Straight to win the award. His victory for "Pretty Little Adriana" was Gill's sixth

---

Aretha Franklin took on Pavarotti's aria and brought down the house.

---

win in the category in eight years. A few months earlier, he was voted best country vocalist for a fifth year in a row at the Country Music Association Awards.

When another past Grammy favorite returned, it marked a heartfelt reunion with his old Nashville crowd. Johnny Cash may have won eight Grammys over the past three decades, but he hadn't prevailed in the country categories since 1970. Sizing up this year's race for Best Country Album, the *L.A. Times* wrote, "A win may be viewed as a sympathy vote in light of Cash's current battle with Parkinson's disease, yet his nominated performances are so clearly superior to other nominees that nonmusical considerations are irrelevant."

He won easily for *Unchained,* which had been cheered by *Entertainment Weekly* in its review: "At 64, the Man in Black is still taking risks and retooling his style."

Winner of best country song was Bob Carlisle's "Butterfly Kisses," a father's gooey tribute to a daughter who once gave him "butterfly kisses" with her eyelashes. *Variety* noted, "The tune became a worldwide phenomenon in 1997 and was inescapable on radio." It also became inescapable in America's churches when, suddenly during the summer, the song became a hit used at thousands of weddings. Backstage at the Grammys, Carlisle said the song was "not about fatherhood, it is about gratitude and was written for the ears of a child."

America's leading Cajun band, BeauSoleil, took the laurel for Best Traditional Folk Album for its 20th anniversary disc *L'Amour ou la Folie,* a work applauded by critics for bridging traditional and contemporary music styles. A salute to traditional folk tunes originally recorded between 1927 and 1932, *Anthology of American Folk Music* has been regarded as a classic since its release in 1952. A new, expanded version recorded on six CDs picked up two Grammys: Best Historical Album and Best Album Notes.

Pundits were divided over who would win the prize for pop collaborations, with guesses split evenly between Babyface and Stevie Wonder ("How Come, How Long") and Barbra Streisand and Celine Dion ("Tell Him"). *Variety* noted, "Another upset came when John Lee Hooker and Van Morrison landed the pop collaboration with vocals Grammy for 'Don't Look Back,' the title track from Hooker's Pointblank/Virgin Records disc. The win was but one example of sentimentality taking prizes as the aging Hooker and Morrison won alongside Bob Dylan, James Taylor, Elton John and John Fogerty." *Don't Look Back* also brought the 80-year-old Hooker the kudos for Best Traditional Blues Album.

Another veteran of the genre, Taj Mahal, claimed the statuette for Best Contemporary Blues Album with *Senor Blues,* on which he covered old works by James Brown, Louis Armstrong and Marvin Gaye.

"Surprises are hard to come by in the jazz winners," the *L.A. Times* declared. "And, since the nominations included few unexpected entries it has to be considered another year in which conservatism triumphed. The only surprising result is trumpeter Randy Brecker's win over competition from heavyweights Lee Ritenour and Grover Washington Jr. in the contemporary jazz category." The victory came as no surprise to the *Chicago Tribune,* which predicted that Brecker would prevail for *Into the Sun.*

In fact, the *Tribune* displayed amazing clairvoyance when forecasting the jazz honors. In the category for large ensembles, the paper said, "The nod ought to go to *Joe Henderson Big Band.* Though the jazz industry does not lack for top-notch big-band recordings, Henderson's stands out for the translucent textures and eternal sound that distinguishes his art and his band's recordings." Other prognosticators picked the Bill Hollman Band despite the fact that Henderson was a Grammy favorite, with three past wins.

All seers foresaw the win by 24-year-old trumpet prodigy Nicholas Payton and the collaborator he met on a cruise ship at the age of 16: Doc Cheatham. Cheatham died at the age of 91 in 1997, making their final duet, "Stardust," the sentimental favorite. The *Tribune* wrote of the recording, "Listen to these trumpeters in musical dialogue and you are hearing one end of the 20th century speaking to another."

The duo was also nominated for Best Jazz Instrumental Performance but lost to Charlie Haden and Pat Metheny's bass and guitar teaming on *Beyond the Missouri Sky.*

The one race in which the *Tribune* erred was for vocals, underestimating the clout of Dee Dee Bridgewater, "whose artful tribute to Ella Fitzgerald, *Dear Ella,* marks Bridgewater as the sole and rightful heir to Fitzgerald's legacy. Unfortunately, Bridgewater probably will lose to Diana Krall whose *Love Scenes* affirms her position as the female Harry Connick, Jr." The expatriate, Paris-based singer had been making recent, high-profile returns to the States, however, including a widely lauded appearance at the Chicago Jazz Festival. Her renewed American prominence surely helped Bridgewater score the Grammy for her readings of "A-Tisket, A-Tasket," "Cotton Tail" and "Mack the Knife."

Jazz artists once again dominated the category for Best Instrumental Composition, which went to soprano saxman Wayne Shorter for "Aung San Suu Kyi," his tribute to the Burmese dissident and Nobel Peace Prize winner.

Roy Hargrove and his band Crisol garnered the gold for Best Latin Jazz Performance for their celebration of Cuban music in *Habana*. The *Tribune* noted, "The recording not only marked a historic partnership of American and Cuban musicians, but established Hargrove as something more than just a young lion of the trumpet."

"The category that will seriously put the voters' judgment to the test is best tropical performance," the *L.A. Times* wrote of the other Latin races. "One can only hope that the academy will avoid the obvious choices (the overexposed India and Albita) and instead acknowledge the humble genius of Ry Cooder, who, by taking a trip to Cuba and recording *Buena Vista Social Club,* revealed the tenderness of the Hispanic soul as no Latin artist did in 1997." Cooder prevailed for his disc that included the rarely heard work of such leading Cuban musicians as Compay Segundo and Rubén González.

Last year Enrique Iglesias pulled off an upset over his father, Julio, plus fellow heartthrob Luis Miguel to nab the vocalist's award. Now, facing only Miguel, he lost to his rival, who was honored for his third, best-selling bolero album, *Romances*.

Responding to recent clamor for it in the music industry, N.A.R.A.S. introduced a new category for Latin rock/alternative music. The *L.A. Times* insisted, "The Grammy should go to the [Los Fabulosos] Cadillacs for their masterful *Fabulosos Calavera*. But that record may just be too specialized and experimental for the average voter." The Argentine rockers snagged it anyway and the *L.A. Times* cheered: "The winners in two of the four Latin categories are actually responsible for the best records of the year in their fields. The Grammys for Ry Cooder and Fabulosos Cadillacs are a sure sign that the academy members have been keeping up with Latin popular music."

Repeating its win of last year, La Mafia held on to the category of Best Mexican-American/Tejano Music Performance for *En Tus Manos*.

Milton Nascimento, one of the leaders of the Brazilian tropicalismo music movement, earned Best World Album for *Nascimento,* his salute to his home state of Minas Gerais.

Two-time past champs Ziggy Marley & the Melody Makers hadn't reaped a victory in the reggae race since 1989

Ry Cooder's tropical winner *Buena Vista Social Club,* recorded in Cuba, "revealed the tenderness of the Hispanic soul as no Latin artist did in '97."

while they explored hip-hop and techno music. Now, revisiting the islands sound on *Fallen Is Babylon,* they returned to reclaim the award.

Also returning—for an eighth Grammy in 12 years—was the Irishman from New York State, Jimmy Sturr, who took the polka prize for *Living on Polka Time*.

The year's most successful act in Christian music, Jars of Clay, was nominated once before, in 1995, for their freshman disc. Now they were back in the Grammy derby with their second release, *Much Afraid,* which debuted at number eight on the pop charts and earned the Nashville-based group the gold for Best Pop/Contemporary Gospel Album.

A number of other Nashville artists—including Bryan White, Billy Ray Cyrus, the Cox Family and Charlie Daniels—were hailed for their contributions to *Amazing Grace 2* (Best Southern Gospel, Country Gospel or Bluegrass Gospel Album).

After winning the category last year for *Freak Show,* DC Talk returned with *Welcome to the Freak Show* to take Best Rock Gospel Album, although *Time* magazine voiced its protest that the Christian rockers, renowned for tempering their grunge sound with smooth vocal harmonies, were nominated in the wrong category.

The septuagenarian quartet renowned for rendering vocal harmonies a cappella, the Fairfield Four, took the category for traditional soul works with *I Couldn't Hear Nobody Pray.*

Take 6 took its seventh career award when it claimed the category of Best Contemporary Soul Gospel Album for *Brothers.* Last year's victor, Kirk Franklin, entered this year's Grammy race with four nominations in other categories, including Producer of the Year. He won one—for directing his Texas choir God's Property on *God's Property from Kirk Franklin's Nu Nation* in the showdown for choral gospel works. His other two bids were in the r&b categories for album track "Stomp." *USA Today* noted, "This contemporary gospel song raised the profile of the whole genre."

Over the past five years, Tony Bennett ruled the race for Best Traditional Pop Performance four times with salutes to his contemporaries such as Frank Sinatra and Fred Astaire. Now he topped Rosemary Clooney and Julie Andrews to reclaim the category with *Tony Bennett on Holiday,* his tribute to Billie Holiday. *Entertainment Weekly* applauded the disc: "His naturally laid-back phrasings remind us of Lady Day without mimicking her. The gentle spirited song set is framed by Ellington's 'Solitude' and 'God Bless the Child,' a posthumous duet with Holiday and the only questionable note here." "God Bless the Child" was nominated for Best Pop Vocal Collaboration, losing to John Lee Hooker and Van Morrison's "Don't Look Back."

The recording of the Broadway revival of the Fred Ebb/John Kander musical *Chicago* (starring Ann Reinking, Bebe Neuwirth, James Naughton and Joel Gray) scored an upset for Best Musical Show Album over the new Broadway hit *Ragtime* and Tony's Best Musical of 1997, *Titanic.* The music to Oscar's Best Picture winner in 1997, *The English Patient,* reaped the Grammy for instrumental movie compositions.

Just a few months after winning two Emmy Awards for an HBO special, former *Saturday Night Live* star Chris Rock got the last laugh in the race for Best Spoken Comedy Album over past champs Bob Newhart and Garrison Keillor. His bawdy disc *Roll with the New* continued his recent rants against Washington, D.C., Mayor Marion Barry, an admitted drug abuser. On the disc, Rock fumes, "Who ran against him that they lost? Who was so bad that they lost to a crackhead?" After the Grammy ceremony, the 31-year-old comic was asked by E! Entertainment network what he planned to do with his sudden bounty of showbiz awards. He said, "Well, eventually I'm going to sell them off for drugs."

Variety disapproved of the contenders in the category for Best New Age Album, claiming that the nominees "reflect a stilted, purist approach more indicative of the genre a decade ago," since the race snubbed top-selling works by George Winston, Jim Brickman and Yanni. Voters chose to honor Michael Hedges (*Oracle*), the late, Oklahoma-born performer and composer renowned for his two-handed guitar picking. Hedges died in 1997 at the age of 43 when his car lurched over an embankment in California.

Voters also embraced several other winners posthumously.

John Denver died the previous October when his private plane crashed into California's Monterey Bay. He'd never won a Grammy for the 14 gold albums of his career, but now he was hailed with Best Musical Album for Children for *All Aboard!,* a collection of train-themed songs, including "The Little Engine That Could" and "On the Atchison, Topeka and the Santa Fe." *Variety* reported, "The children of the late singer John Denver plan to take his Grammy for musical children's album to Aspen and put it in his house 'somewhere special,' said Denver's oldest son, John."

The late Charles Kuralt, a 10-time

Emmy champ, was once before nominated for a Grammy when the audio version of his autobiography competed for Best Spoken Word or Nonmusical Album of 1991. The veteran CBS newsman, who died of heart failure at the age of 62 in 1997, finally claimed the category posthumously with *Charles Kuralt's Spring,* his celebration of "the season of hope and promise" that included interviews with jazz musicians and a maple syrup farmer. He also won Best Spoken Word Album for Children for his reading of the A. A. Milne classic *Winnie-the-Pooh.* In its review, the *L.A. Times* praised it: "The late, much-missed Kuralt had a thick, deep voice and slow manner befitting a bear stuffed with honey. Though perfectly Pooh-like, he nevertheless changed his mood and tone subtly for each of Milne's lively critters, easily capturing the humor, silliness and endearing kindness of Christopher Robin, Tigger, Piglet and Eeyore as well."

All-time Grammy champ Sir Georg Solti died in his sleep in 1997 at the age of 84 but was remembered with two posthumous nominations for his second career recording of Wagner's only comedy, *Die Meistersinger von Nürnberg.* The late release of his 1995 performance with Ben Heppner, Karita Mattila and the Chicago Symphony Orchestra won Best Opera Recording, bringing his total Grammy tally to 31 awards. *Variety* hailed the maestro's artistic achievements in its obituary: "Solti was a powerful conductor, generating the kind of energy and excitement that sold out performances and brought audiences to their feet. His athleticism defied his years. Phrases like 'visceral intensity' were used to describe his Bartók or 'big and driving' for his Prokofiev."

Die Meistersinger von Nürnberg was considered the odds-on favorite to win Best Classical Album, too, but it was usurped by the kind of recording that seldom wins the award—music by a solo artist. Yo-Yo Ma's reading of cello concertos by Danielpour, Kirchner and Rouse was a popular choice of Grammy voters this year, also reaping the soloist laurels for Ma. It'd previously received the vote of critics, too, including the *L.A. Times,* which said in its review: "Danielpour's half-hour programmatic work is unfailingly fluent and theatrical. Ma plays like Ma—with commanding virtuosity and commitment."

The recording's producer, Stephen Epstein, was acknowledged with the Classical Producer of the Year award, fending off a serious challenge from Wolf Erichson. When the nominations came out, *Variety* warned, "Erichson, a pioneer of the genre, is the likely sentimental favorite of the category, as he has announced his intention to retire soon."

When an *L.A. Times* writer weighed the nominations, he forecast the chances of another recording competing for best disc: "For Best Classical Album there is the Emerson Quartet's celebrated set of the Beethoven String Quartets, brilliantly aggressive and captivatingly played. Given Solti, however, the voters are more likely to make it a shoo-in—appropriately, I think—for best chamber music performance, where it is also nominated." The Emerson Quartet won easily. In its review, *Fortune* magazine applauded the troupe for treating each movement "as if it's a chapter in a great novel. The cumulative impact of listening to these seven CDs ($110) in sequence is comparable to reading *Anna Karenina*—long but magnificent."

Another loser for Best Classical Album scored a victory in a different category when conductor Pierre Boulez and the Cleveland Orchestra's reading of Berlioz's *Symphonie Fantastique* and *Tristia* was hailed as Best Orchestral Performance. The *L.A. Times* noted, "Boulez has his doubts about the *Symphonie Fantastique,* which he voices in the liner notes—something about the 'container' being more interesting than the 'content'—and which are plainly evident in the performance. It all has a certain fascination, but the container is only half full.

The Cleveland Orchestra performs with a chamber music delicacy and point."

Two works by San Francisco composer John Adams were acknowledged elsewhere in the classical categories when conductor Robert Shaw and his Atlanta Symphony Orchestra and Chorus snagged the choral honors for *Harmonium.* Adams wrote the half-hour work, which includes poetry by Emily Dickinson, in the early 1990s, but it was rarely performed.

Adams was honored separately with the Grammy for Best Contemporary Composition for "El Dorado," which he described as a work of "friction" between humans and the natural world that's resolved by "re-creation and renewal."

For best soloist performance without orchestra, the kudos went to Janos Starker for Bach's Suites for Solo Cello Nos. 1–6. The *Washington Post* wrote in its review: "Janos Starker has been the interpreter of choice for this music for more than a generation, and his new disc—austere, stylistically precise and superbly controlled—shows that his interpretation has continued to grow."

Having achieved the status of global superstar over the past eight years, 31-year-old Cecilia Bartoli was lauded at the Grammys with her second prize for best vocals. On *An Italian Songbook,* the Italian mezzo performed works by such countrymen as Bellini, Donizetti and Rossini.

Conductor Claudio Abbado earned the first Grammy of his career (Best Small Ensemble Performance) for leading members of his Berliner Philharmonic in Hindemith's Kammermusik No. 1 with Finale 1921, Op. 24, No. 1.

Radio City Music Hall was chosen as the site of this year's Grammys after critics complained that last year's circus-sized production at Madison Square Garden lacked intimacy. When the nominations were announced at the music hall in January, a brouhaha erupted backstage between an aide to Mayor Rudolph Giuliani and N.A.R.A.S. President Michael

Greene over whether hizzoner would announce some of the contenders. The spat continued publicly for several weeks while the city's tabloids hyped it in inflammatory headlines ("Giuliani: Grammy Scrammy"). Meantime, out on the West Coast, the *L.A. Times* ran an exposé accusing Greene and the Recording Academy of mismanagement.

The N.A.R.A.S. headlines threatened to overshadow the awards ceremony, but the show scored an amazing jump in TV viewership. *Variety* noted, "Telecast of the Grammy awards has presented CBS with a spectacular 17.0 rating, 27 share, up 27 percent from last year's tally and the highest-rated non-Oscars awardscast in the five years since the 1993 Grammys. Coverage also towered 40 percent above ABC's rival American Music Awards which last month settled for a 12.1/18. It's the biggest Grammys-over-AMA edge since 1981."

Variety called the performance of ceremony host Kelsey Grammer "off-kilter," but added, "Grammer's ironic demeanor perfectly matched a night of sheer lunacy," referring to Ol' Dirty Bastard's outburst and the dance of the shirtless "Soy Bomb" intruder.

Variety hailed the night's best musical performance: "Aretha stepped in for the ailing Luciano Pavarotti to bring down the house in a rousing rendition of Puccini's 'Nessun Dorma,' which is sort of like Mick Jagger ripping through 'Moon River.' Except that Franklin positively aced it in the evening's only true piece of magic."

Variety also noted, "TV commercials touting Dylan's album *Time Out of Mind* and its Grammy Award win for Album of the Year began airing just hours after he was given the statuette during the ceremony. The speed with which the new TV spots were rushed to broadcasts is indicative of how much money a Grammy win, especially in a key category like Album of the Year, can add to a label's coffers. 'Our stores start putting up Grammy winners displays the morning after the

show,' said Tower Records CEO Russ
Solomon. 'Viewers will often come in
the very next day and ask for something
they saw on the show.' "

In the week after Dylan's victory, *Time
Out of Mind* leapt 95 notches on the charts
to number 27, selling 47,000 copies—four
times the number sold the previous week.

1997

• 1997 •

The awards ceremony was broadcast on
CBS from Radio City Music Hall in New
York City on February 25, 1998, for the
eligibility period of October 1, 1996,
through September 30, 1997.

ALBUM OF THE YEAR
• *Time Out of Mind*, Bob Dylan.
  Columbia.
The Day, Babyface. Epic.
This Fire, Paula Cole. Warner Bros.
Flaming Pie, Paul McCartney. Capitol.
OK Computer, Radiohead. Capitol.

RECORD OF THE YEAR
• "Sunny Came Home," Shawn Colvin.
  Columbia.
"Where Have All the Cowboys Gone?"
  Paula Cole. Warner Bros.
"Every Day Is a Winding Road," Sheryl
  Crow. A&M.
"MMMBop," Hanson. Mercury.
"I Believe I Can Fly," R. Kelly.
  Jive/Atlantic/Warner Sunset.

SONG OF THE YEAR
(Songwriter's Award)
• "Sunny Came Home," Shawn Colvin,
  John Leventhal.
"Don't Speak," Eric Stefani, Gwen Ste-
fani.
"How Do I Live," Diane Warren.
"I Believe I Can Fly," R. Kelly.
"Where Have All the Cowboys Gone?"
  Paula Cole.

BEST NEW ARTIST
• Paula Cole
Fiona Apple
Erykah Badu
Puff Daddy
Hanson

BEST POP ALBUM
• *Hourglass*, James Taylor. Columbia.
This Fire, Paula Cole. Warner Bros.
The Dance, Fleetwood Mac. Reprise.
Travelling Without Moving, Jamiroquai.
  Work Group.
Surfacing, Sarah McLachlan. Arista.

BEST POP VOCAL PERFORMANCE,
MALE
• Elton John, "Candle in the Wind
  1997." Rocket.
Babyface, "Every Time I Close My
  Eyes," track from *The Day*. Epic.
Maxwell, "Whenever Wherever What-
  ever," track from *MTV Unplugged*.
  Columbia.
Seal, "Fly Like an Eagle," track from
  Space Jam. Warner Sunset/Atlantic.
Duncan Sheik, "Barely Breathing," track
  from *Duncan Sheik*. Atlantic.

BEST POP VOCAL PERFORMANCE,
FEMALE
• Sarah McLachlan, "Building a Mys-
  tery," track from *Surfacing*. Arista.
Mariah Carey, "Butterfly," track from
  Butterfly. Columbia.
Paula Cole, "Where Have All the Cow-
  boys Gone?" track from *This Fire*.
  Warner Bros.
Shawn Colvin, "Sunny Came Home,"
  track from *A Few Small Repairs*.
  Columbia.
Jewel, "Foolish Games," track from *Bat-
man and Robin*. Warner Bros./Sunset.

BEST POP PERFORMANCE BY A DUO
OR GROUP WITH VOCAL
• Jamiroquai, "Virtual Insanity," track
  from *Travelling Without Moving*.
  Work Group.

Fleetwood Mac, "Silver Springs," track from *The Dance*. Reprise.

Hanson, "MMMBop," track from *Middle of Nowhere*. Mercury.

No Doubt, "Don't Speak," track from *Tragic Kingdom*. Trauma/Interscope.

Rolling Stones, "Has Anybody Seen My Baby?" track from *Bridges to Babylon*. Virgin.

BEST POP COLLABORATION WITH VOCAL

• John Lee Hooker, Van Morrison, "Don't Look Back," track from *Don't Look Back*. Pointblank/Virgin.

Babyface, Stevie Wonder, "How Come, How Long," track from *The Day*. Epic.

Tony Bennett (with Billie Holiday), "God Bless the Child," track from *Tony Bennett on Holiday*. Columbia.

Barbra Streisand, Bryan Adams, "I Finally Found Someone," track from *The Mirror Has Two Faces*. Columbia.

Barbra Streisand, Celine Dion, "Tell Him." 550 Music.

BEST TRADITIONAL POP VOCAL PERFORMANCE

• Tony Bennett, *Tony Bennett on Holiday*. Columbia.

Julie Andrews, *Julie Andrews Broadway/Here I'll Stay*. Philips.

Rosemary Clooney, *Mothers and Daughters*. Concord Jazz.

Bernadette Peters, *Sondheim, Etc., Live at Carnegie Hall*. Angel.

Carly Simon, *Film Noir*. Arista.

BEST POP INSTRUMENTAL PERFORMANCE

• Sarah McLachlan, "Last Dance," track from *Surfacing*. Arista.

George Benson, "Song for My Brother," track from *That's Right*. Giant Step/GRP.

Chieftains, "An Gaoth Aneas," track from *Carnival!* RCA Victor.

Kenny G, "Havana," track from *The Moment*. Arista.

Grover Washington, Jr., "Soulful Strut," track from *Soulful Strut*. Columbia.

BEST DANCE RECORDING

• "Carry On," track from *NRG Unlimited*, Donna Summer, Giorgio Moroder. Interhit.

"Da Funk," track from *Homework*, Daft Punk. Virgin.

"Ooh Ahh . . . Just a Little Bit," track from *Fresh!* Gina G. Eternal/Warner Bros.

"To Step Aside," track from *Bilingual*, Pet Shop Boys. Atlantic.

"Space Jam," track from *Space Jam*, Quad City DJ's. Warner Sunset/Atlantic.

BEST ROCK ALBUM

• *Blue Moon Swamp*, John Fogerty. Warner Bros.

Nine Lives, Aerosmith. Columbia.

The Colour and the Shape, Foo Fighters. Roswell/Capitol.

Bridges to Babylon, Rolling Stones. Virgin.

Pop, U2. Island.

BEST ROCK SONG
(Songwriter's Award)

• "One Headlight," Jakob Dylan.

"Bitch," Meredith Brooks, Shelly Peiken.

"Crash Into Me," Dave Matthews.

"Criminal," Fiona Apple.

"The Difference," Jakob Dylan.

BEST ROCK VOCAL PERFORMANCE, MALE

• Bob Dylan, "Cold Irons Bound," track from *Time Out of Mind*. Columbia.

David Bowie, "Dead Man Walking," track from *Earthling*. Virgin.

John Fogerty, "Blueboy," track from *Blue Moon Swamp*. Warner Bros.

John Mellencamp, "Just Another Day," track from *Mr. Happy Go Lucky*. Mercury.

Bruce Springsteen, "Thunder Road," track from *In Concert MTV Unplugged*. Columbia.

BEST ROCK VOCAL PERFORMANCE, FEMALE

- Fiona Apple, "Criminal," track from *Tidal*. Work Grup.
- Meredith Brooks, "Bitch," track from *Blurring the Edges*. Capitol.
- Ani Difranco, "Shy," track from *Living in Clip*. Righteous Babe.
- Abra Moore, "Four Leaf Clover," track from *Strangest Places*. Arista Austin.
- Patti Smith, "1959," track from *Peace and Noise*. Arista.

BEST ROCK PERFORMANCE BY A DUO OR GROUP WITH VOCAL

- Wallflowers, "One Headlight," track from *Bringing Down the Horse*. Interscope.
- Aerosmith, "Falling in Love (Is Hard on the Knees)," track from *Nine Lives*. Columbia.
- Fleetwood Mac, "The Chain," track from *The Dance*. Reprise.
- Matchbox 20, "Push," track from *Yourself or Someone Like You*. Lava/Atlantic.
- Dave Matthews Band, "Crash Into Me," track from *Crash*. RCA.

BEST ROCK INSTRUMENTAL PERFORMANCE

- Chemical Brothers, "Block Rockin' Beats," track from *Dig Your Own Hole*. Astralwerks.
- Robben Ford, "In the Beginning," track from *Tiger Walk*. Blue Thumb.
- Eric Johnson, "S.R.V.," track from *Venus Isle*. Capitol.
- Joe Satriani, "Summer Song," track from *G3—Live in Concert*. Epic.
- Steve Vai, "For the Love of God," track from *G3—Live in Concert*. Epic.

BEST HARD ROCK PERFORMANCE

- Rage Against the Machine, "People of the Sun," track from *Evil Empire*. Epic.
- Bush, "Swallowed," track from *Razorblade Suitcase*. Trauma/Interscope.
- Foo Fighters, "Monkey Wrench," track from *The Colour and the Shape*. Roswell/Capitol.

Nine Inch Nails, "The Perfect Drug," track from *Lost Highway*. Nothing/Interscope.
Smashing Pumpkins, "The End Is the Beginning Is the End," track from *Batman and Robin*. Warner Bros./Sunset.

BEST METAL PERFORMANCE

- Tool, "Aenema," track from *Aenima*. Zoo/Volcano.
- Corrosion of Conformity, "Drowning in a Daydream," track from *Wiseblood*. Columbia.
- Korn, "No Place to Hide," track from *Life Is Peachy*. Immortal/Epic.
- Megadeth, "Trust," track from *Cryptic Writings*. Capitol.
- Pantera, "Cemetery Gates," track from *Official Live: 101 Proof*. EastWest/EEG.

BEST ALTERNATIVE MUSIC PERFORMANCE

- Radiohead, *OK Computer*. Capitol.
- Björk, *Homogenic*. Elektra.
- David Bowie, *Earthling*. Virgin.
- Chemical Brothers, *Dig Your Own Hole*. Astralwerks.
- Prodigy, *The Fat of the Land*. Maverick/Warner Bros.

BEST RHYTHM & BLUES ALBUM

- *Baduizm*, Erykah Badu. Kedar/Universal.
- *The Day*, Babyface. Epic.
- *Share My World*, Mary J. Blige. MCA.
- *Evolution*, Boyz II Men. Motown.
- *The Preacher's Wife*, Whitney Houston. Arista.
- *Flame*, Patti LaBelle. MCA.

BEST RHYTHM & BLUES SONG
(Songwriter's Award)

- "I Believe I Can Fly," R. Kelly.
- "Honey," Mariah Carey, Sean "Puffy" Combs, K. Fareed, S. Hague, S. Jordan, R. Larkins, M. McLaren, L. Price, B. Robinson.

"No Diggity," Dr. Dre, C. Hannibal, Teddy Riley, William "Skylz" Stewart, L. Walters.

"On & On," Erykah Badu, JaBorne Jamal.

"Stomp," George Clinton, Jr., Kirk Franklin, Walter Morrison, Garry M. Shider.

BEST RHYTHM & BLUES VOCAL PERFORMANCE, MALE

• R. Kelly, "I Believe I Can Fly," track from *Space Jam*. Jive/Atlantic/Warner Sunset.

Kenny Lattimore, "For You," track from *Kenny Lattimore*. Columbia.

Curtis Mayfield, "Back to Living Again," track from *New World Order*. Warner Bros.

Usher, "You Make Me Wanna," track from *My Way*. LaFace.

Luther Vandross, "When You Call on Me/Baby That's When I Come Runnin'," track from *One Night with You*. LV/Epic.

BEST RHYTHM & BLUES VOCAL PERFORMANCE, FEMALE

• Erykah Badu, "On & On," track from *Baduizm*. Kedar/Universal.

Mariah Carey, "Honey," track from *Butterfly*. Columbia.

Whitney Houston, "I Believe in You and Me," track from *The Preacher's Wife*. Arista.

Chaka Khan, "Summertime," track from *Porgy and Bess*. Verve.

Patti LaBelle, "When You Talk About Love," track from *Flame*. MCA.

BEST RHYTHM & BLUES VOCAL PERFORMANCE BY A DUO OR GROUP WITH VOCAL

• Blackstreet, "No Diggity," track from *Another Level*. Interscope.

Az Yet Featuring Peter Cetera, "Hard to Say I'm Sorry (Remix)," track from *Az Yet*. LaFace.

Boyz II Men, "A Song for Mama," track from *Soul Food*. LaFace.

God Property Featuring Kirk Franklin & "Salt," "Stomp," track from *God's Property from Kirk Franklin's Nu Nation*. B-Rite.

Take 6, "You Don't Have to Be Afraid," track from *Brothers*. Warner-Alliance.

BEST RAP ALBUM

• *No Way Out*, Puff Daddy & the Family. Bad Boy.

Supa Dupa Fly, Missy "Misdemeanor" Elliott. EastWest/EEG.

Wyclef Jean Presents the Carnival, Wyclef Jean (Featuring Refugee All-stars). Ruffhouse/Columbia.

Life After Death, Notorious B.I.G. Bad Boy.

Wu-Tang Forever, Wu-Tang Clan. Loud/RCA.

BEST RAP SOLO PERFORMANCE

• Will Smith, "Men in Black," track from *Men in Black*. Columbia/Sony.

Busta Rhymes, "Put Your Hands Where My Eyes Could See," track from *When Disaster Strikes . . .* Elektra/EEG.

Missy "Misdemeanor" Elliott, "The Rain (Supa Dupa Fly)," track from *Supa Dupa Fly*. EastWest/EEG.

L.L. Cool J, "Ain't Nobody," track from *Beavis and Butt-head Do America*. Geffen.

Notorious B.I.G., "Hypnotize," track from *Life After Death*. Bad Boy.

BEST RAP PERFORMANCE BY A DUO OR GROUP

• Puff Daddy & Faith Evans Featuring 112, "I'll Be Missing You," track from *Tribute to Notorious B.I.G.* Bad Boy.

Puff Daddy Featuring Mase, "Can't Nobody Hold Me Down," track from *No Way Out*. Bad Boy.

Wyclef Jean Featuring Celia Cruz & Jeni Fujita, "Guantanamera," track from *Wyclef Jean Presents the Carnival*. Ruffhouse/Columbia.

Lil' Kim Featuring Da Brat, Left Eye, Missy "Misdemeanor" Elliott &

Angie Martinez, "Not Tonight," track from *Hard Core*. Undeas/Big Beat/Atlantic.

Notorious B.I.G. Featuring Mase & Puff Daddy, "Mo Money Mo Problems," track from *Life After Death*. Bad Boy.

BEST CONTEMPORARY JAZZ PERFORMANCE

- Randy Brecker, *Into the Sun*. Concord Vista.

Lee Ritenour, *Alive in L.A.* GRP.

Patrice Rushen, *Signature*. Discover/Sire.

Joe Sample, *Sample This*. Warner Bros.

Grover Washington, Jr., *Breath of Heaven*. Columbia.

BEST JAZZ VOCAL PERFORMANCE

- Dee Dee Bridgewater, *Dear Ella*. Verve.

Kurt Elling, *The Messenger*. Blue Note.

Shirley Horn, *Loving You*. Verve.

Diana Krall, *Love Scenes*. Impulse.

Mark Murphy, *Song for the Geese*. RCA Victor.

BEST JAZZ INSTRUMENTAL SOLO

- Doc Cheatham, Nicholas Payton, "Stardust," track from *Doc Cheatham and Nicholas Payton*. Verve.

Buddy DeFranco, "You Must Believe in Swing," track from *You Must Believe in Swing*. Concord Jazz.

Tommy Flanagan, "Dear Old Stockholm," track from *Sea Changes*. Alfa Jazz/Evidence.

Antonio Hart, "The Community," track from *Here I Stand*. Impulse.

Brad Mehldau, "Blame It on My Youth," track from *The Art of the Trio*. Warner Bros.

BEST JAZZ INSTRUMENTAL PERFORMANCE (INDIVIDUAL OR GROUP)

- Charlie Haden, Pat Metheny, *Beyond the Missouri Sky*. Verve.

Doc Cheatham, Nicholas Payton, *Doc Cheatham and Nicholas Payton*. Verve.

Chick Corea & Friends, *Remembering Bud Powell*. Stretch.

Kenny Garrett, *Songbook*. Warner Bros.

Joe Lovano, *Celebrating Sinatra*. Blue Note.

BEST LARGE JAZZ ENSEMBLE PERFORMANCE

- Joe Henderson Big Band, *Joe Henderson Big Band*. Verve.

Bill Holman Band, *Brilliant Corners*. JVC.

J. J. Johnson, *The Brass Orchestra*. Verve.

Anthony Wilson, *Anthony Wilson*. MAMA.

Phil Woods & the Festival Orchestra, *Celebration!* Concord Jazz.

BEST LATIN JAZZ PERFORMANCE

- Roy Hargrove's Crisol, *Habana*. Verve.

Banda Mantiqueira, *Aldeia*. Blue Jackel.

Conrad Herwig, *The Latin Side of John Coltrane*. Astor Place.

Giovanni Hidalgo, *Hands of Rhythm*. TopiJazz.

Carlos "Patato" Valdes, *Ritmo y Candela II: African Crossroads*. Round World.

BEST COUNTRY ALBUM

- *Unchained*, Johnny Cash. American.

Everything I Love, Alan Jackson. Arista Nashville.

Long Stretch of Lonesome, Patty Loveless. Epic Nashville.

Carrying Your Love with Me, George Strait. MCA Nashville.

Under the Covers, Dwight Yoakam. Warner Bros/Reprise Nashville.

BEST COUNTRY SONG
(Songwriter's Award)

- "Butterfly Kisses," Bob Carlisle, Randy Thomas.

"All the Good Ones Are Gone," Dean Dillon, Bob McDill.

"Did I Shave My Legs for This?" Deana Carter, Rhonda Hart.

"In Another's Eyes," Garth Brooks, John Peppard, Bobby Wood.

"It's Your Love," Stephony Smith.

BEST COUNTRY VOCAL PERFORMANCE, MALE

• Vince Gill, "Pretty Little Adriana," track from *High Lonesome Sound*. MCA Nashville.

Clint Black, "Something That We Do," track from *Nothin' but the Taillights*. RCA.

Johnny Cash, "Rusty Cage," track from *Unchained*. American.

Willie Nelson, "Peach Pickin' Time Down in Georgia," track from *The Songs of Jimmie Rodgers*. Columbia.

George Strait, "Carrying Your Love with Me," track from *Carrying Your Love with Me*. MCA Nashville.

BEST COUNTRY VOCAL PERFORMANCE, FEMALE

• Trisha Yearwood, "How Do I Live," track from *(Songbook)*. MCA Nashville.

Deana Carter, "Did I Shave My Legs for This?" track from *Did I Shave My Legs for This?* Capitol Nashville.

Patty Loveless, "The Trouble with the Truth," track from *The Trouble with the Truth*. Epic Nashville.

LeAnn Rimes, "How Do I Live." Curb.

Pam Tillis, "All the Good Ones Are Gone," track from *Greatest Hits*. Arista.

BEST COUNTRY PERFORMANCE BY A DUO OR GROUP WITH VOCAL

• Alison Krauss & Union Station, "Looking in the Eyes of Love," track from *So Long So Wrong*. Rounder.

Alabama, "Dancin', Shaggin' on the Boulevard," track from *Dancin' on the Boulevard*. RCA.

Diamond Rio, "How Your Love Makes Me Feel," track from *Greatest Hits*. Arista Nashville.

Kinleys, "Please," track from *Just Between You and Me*. Epic Nashville.

Mavericks, "I Don't Care (If You Love Me Anymore)." MCA.

BEST COUNTRY COLLABORATION WITH VOCAL

• Trisha Yearwood, Garth Brooks, "In Another's Eyes," track from *(Songbook)*. MCA Nashville.

Clint Black, Martina McBride, "Still Holding On," track from *Nothin' but the Taillights*. RCA.

Toby Keith, Sting, "I'm So Happy I Can't Stop Crying," track from *Dream Walkin'*. Mercury Nashville.

Patty Loveless, George Jones, "You Don't Seem to Miss Me," track from *Long Stretch of Lonesome*. Epic Nashville.

Tim McGraw, Faith Hill, "It's Your Love," track from *Everywhere*. Curb.

BEST COUNTRY INSTRUMENTAL PERFORMANCE

• Alison Krauss & Union Station, "Little Liza Jane," track from *So Long So Wrong*. Rounder.

Asleep at the Wheel, "Fat Boy Rag," track from *Back to the Future Now Live at Arizona Charlie's Las Vegas*. Epic/Lucky Dog.

Chet Atkins, Tommy Emmanuel, "Smokey Mountain Lullaby," track from *The Day Finger Pickers Took Over the World*. Columbia Nashville.

Scotty Moore, D. J. Fontana & Bill Black Combo, "Goin' Back to Memphis," track from *All the King's Men*. Sweetfish.

Lee Roy Parnell, "Mama, Screw Your Wig on Tight," track from *Every Night's a Saturday Night*. Career.

BEST ROCK GOSPEL ALBUM

• *Welcome to the Freak Show*, DC Talk. ForeFront.

All Star United, All Star United. Reunion.

Threads, Geoff Moore & the Distance. ForeFront.

Smalltown Poets, Smalltown Poets. Ardent/ForeFront.
Conspiracy No. 5, Third Day. Reunion.

BEST POP/CONTEMPORARY GOSPEL ALBUM

- *Much Afraid*, Jars of Clay. Silvertone/Essential.
Under the Influence, Anointed. Myrrh.
This Gift, Gary Chapman. Reunion.
Petra Praise 2: We Need Jesus, Petra. Word.
Star Bright, Vanessa Williams. Mercury.

BEST SOUTHERN GOSPEL, COUNTRY GOSPEL OR BLUEGRASS GOSPEL ALBUM

- *Amazing Grace 2: A Country Salute to Gospel*, various artists. Sparrow.
Keep Lookin' Up: The Texas Swing Sessions, James Blackwood & the Light Crust Doughboys. Doughboy.
Back Home in Indiana, Gaither Vocal Band. Spring House.
Light of the World, Martins. Spring-Hill.

BEST TRADITIONAL SOUL GOSPEL ALBUM

- *I Couldn't Hear Nobody Pray*, Fairfield Four. Warner Bros. Nashville.
A Miracle in Harlem, Shirley Caesar. Word Gospel.
Woman, Thou Art Loosed! Songs of Healing and Restoration, T. D. Jakes. Integrity.
Live in Charleston, Mighty Clouds of Joy. Intersound.
Live in Detroit, Vickie Winans. CGI.

BEST CONTEMPORARY SOUL GOSPEL ALBUM

- *Brothers*, Take 6. Warner-Alliance.
Come Walk with Me, Oleta Adams. Harmony.
Pray, Andrae Crouch. Warner-Alliance.
Donnie McClurkin, Donnie McClurkin. Warner-Alliance.
Grace and Mercy, Marvin Sapp. Word Gospel.

BEST GOSPEL ALBUM BY A CHOIR OR CHORUS

- *God's Property from Kirk Franklin's Nu Nation*, God's Property; Kirk Franklin, choir director. B-Rite.
He's Still Good! Rev. Milton Brunson's Thompson Community Singers; Tyrone Block, choir director. Word Gospel.
Live in London at Wembley, Love Fellowship Crusade Choir; Hezekiah Walker, choir director. Verity.
Time for Healing, Sounds of Blackness; Gary Hines, choir director. Perspective/A&M.

BEST TRADITIONAL FOLK ALBUM

- *L'Amour ou la Folie*, BeauSoleil. Rhino.
Deep Water, Hackberry Ramblers. Hot Biscuits.
There Ain't No Way Out, New Lost City Ramblers. Smithsonian Folkways.
Cajun Pride, Jo-El Sonnier. Rounder.
Heart Songs: The Old Time Country Songs of Utah Phillips, Jody Stecher, Kate Brislin. Rounder.

BEST CONTEMPORARY FOLK ALBUM

- *Time Out of Mind*, Bob Dylan. Columbia.
Keepers, Guy Clark. Sugar Hill.
The Way I Should, Iris DeMent. Warner Bros.
Shaming of the Sun, Indigo Girls. Epic.
Live on Tour, John Prine. Oh Boy.

BEST TRADITIONAL BLUES ALBUM

- *Don't Look Back*, John Lee Hooker. Pointblank/Virgin.
R + B = Ruth Brown, Ruth Brown. Bullseye Blues.
Rough News, Charlie Musselwhite. Pointblank/Virgin.
Born in the Delta, Pinetop Perkins. Telarc Blues.
Live at Buddy Guy's Legends, Junior Wells. Telarc Blues.

BEST CONTEMPORARY BLUES ALBUM

- *Senor Blues*, Taj Mahal. Private Music.
Reckless, Luther Allison. Alligator.

Sweet Potato Pie, Robert Cray Band. Mercury.
Trippin' Live. Dr. John. Surefire.
Come on Home, Boz Scaggs. Virgin.

BEST BLUEGRASS ALBUM
• *So Long So Wrong*, Alison Krauss & Union Station. Rounder.
Sales Tax Toddle, Richard Greene & the Grass Is Greener. Rebel.
Silver and Gold, Claire Lynch. Rounder.
Age of Innocence, Kate MacKenzie. Red House.
Short Life of Trouble, Ralph Stanley. Rebel.

BEST LATIN POP PERFORMANCE
• Luis Miguel, *Romances*. WEA Latina.
Cristian, *Lo Mejor de Mi*. BMG U.S. Latin.
Alejandro Fernandez, *Me Estoy Enamorando*. Sony Latin.
Enrique Iglesias, *Vivir*. Fonovisa.
Julio Islesias, *Tango*. Sony Discos.

BEST LATIN ROCK/ALTERNATIVE PERFORMANCE
• Los Fabulosos Cadillacs, *Fabulosos Calavera*. BMG U.S. Latin.
Aterciopelados, *La Pipa de la Paz*. BMG U.S. Latin.
Cafe Tacvba, *Avalancha de Exitos*. WEA Latina.
El Tri, *Cuando Tu No Estás*. WEA Latina.
Molotov, *Dónde Jugaran las Niñas?* Universal Music Latino.

BEST TROPICAL LATIN PERFORMANCE
• Ry Cooder, *Buena Vista Social Club*. World Circuit/Nonesuch.
Afro-Cuban All Stars, *A Toda Cuba le Gusta*. World Circuit/Nonesuch.
Albita, *Una Mujer Como Yo*. Crescent Moon/Epic.
India, *Sobre el Fuego*. RMM.
Olga Tanon, *Llevame Contigo*. WEA Latina.

BEST MEXICAN-AMERICAN/TEJANO MUSIC PERFORMANCE
• La Mafia, *En Tus Manos*. Sony Discos.

Ramon Ayala y Sus Bravos del Norte, *En las Alas de un Angel/Despedimos a Cornelio Reyna*. Freddie.
Alejandro Fernandez, *Muy Dentro de Mi Corazon*. Sony Discos.
Lizza Lamb, *Destino*. BMG U.S. Latin.
Los Tigres del Norte, *Jefe de Jefes*. Fonovisa.

BEST REGGAE ALBUM
• *Fallen Is Babylon*, Ziggy Marley & the Melody Makers. Elektra/EEG.
Big Up, Aswad. Mesa/Atlantic.
Appointment with His Majesty, Burning Spear. Heartbeat.
Rage and Fury, Steel Pulse. Mesa/Atlantic.
Freedom of Speech, Yellowman. RAS.

BEST POLKA ALBUM
• *Living on Polka Time*, Jimmy Sturr. Rounder.
Home Is Where the Heart Is, Lenny Gomulka & the Chicago Push. Push.
Duty Free Polkas, John Gora & Gorale. Sunshine.
Moments to Remember, Walter Ostanek. World Renowned.
Songs of the Polka King, Frank Yankovic & Friends. Cleveland International.

BEST NEW AGE ALBUM
• *Oracle*, Michael Hedges. Windham Hill.
Le Roi Est Mort, Vive le Roi! Enigma. Virgin.
Voyager, Mike Oldfield. Reprise.
Oceanic, Vangelis. EastWest.
Canyon Lullaby, Paul Winter. Living Music.

BEST WORLD MUSIC ALBUM
• *Nascimento*, Milton Nascimento. Warner Bros.
Cabo Verde, Cesaria Evora. Nonesuch.
Compas, Gipsy Kings. Nonesuch.
Passing on the Tradition, Ali Akbar Khan. AMMP.
Love Drum Talk, Babatunde Olatunji. Chesky.

BEST INSTRUMENTAL ARRANGEMENT

- Bill Holman, "Straight, No Chaser," track from *Brilliant Corners* (Bill Holman Band). JVC Music.

Michael Abene, Dave Grusin, "America," track from *Dave Grusin Pesents West Side Story*. N2K Encoded Music.

Vince Mendoza, "Don't Talk (Put Your Head on My Shoulder)," track from *Wouldn't It Be Nice—A Jazz Portrait of Brian Wilson* (various artists). Blue Note Contemporary.

Dave Grusin, "Peter Gunn," track from *Two for the Road* (Dave Grusin). GRP.

Robert Farnon, "Wild Is the Wind," track from *The Brass Orchestra* (J. J. Johnson). Verve.

BEST INSTRUMENTAL COMPOSITION
(Composer's Award)

- "Aung San Suu Kyi," Wayne Shorter.

"Canonn for Bela," J. J. Johnson.

"Earth," Bob Florence.

"Everytime I Think of You," Alan Broadbent.

"New Rochelle," Bob Mintzer.

BEST MUSICAL SHOW ALBUM

- *Chicago*, new Broadway cast. Fred Ebb, lyricist; John Kander, composer. RCA Victor.

Jekyll and Hyde, original Broadway cast. Leslie Bricusse, lyricist; Frank Wildhorn, composer. Atlantic Theater.

The Life, original Broadway cast. Ira Gasman, lyricist; Cy Coleman, composer. Sony Classical.

Ragtime, recording cast. Lynn Ahrens, lyricist; Stephen Flaherty, composer. RCA Victor.

Titanic, original Broadway cast. Maury Yeston, lyricist and composer. RCA Victor.

BEST INSTRUMENTAL COMPOSITION WRITTEN FOR A MOTION PICTURE OR TV
(Composer's Award)

- "The English Patient," Gabriel Yared, composer.

"The Lost World: Jurassic Park," John Williams, composer.

"Men in Black," Danny Elfman, composer.

"Selena," Dave Grusin, composer.

"Seven Years in Tibet," John Williams, composer.

BEST SONG WRITTEN SPECIFICALLY FOR A MOTION PICTURE OR TV

- "I Believe I Can Fly," R. Kelly (*Space Jam*).

"Father of Our Nation," Cedric Gradus Samson (*Mandela*).

"For the First Time," Jud Friedman, James Newton Howard, Allan Rich (*One Fine Day*).

"How Do I Live," Diane Warren (*Con Air*).

"A Song for Mama," Babyface (*Soul Food*).

BEST INSTRUMENTAL ARRANGEMENT ACCOMPANYING VOCAL(S)

- Slide Hampton, "Cotton Tail" (Dee Dee Bridgewater). Verve.

Arif Mardin, "Laura" (Carly Simon). Arista.

John Clayton, "My Heart Belongs to Daddy" (Dee Dee Bridgewater). Verve.

Don Sebesky, "Our Love Is Here to Stay" (John Pizzarelli). RCA.

Mike Renzi, "The Summer Knows" (Maureen McGovern). Sterling.

BEST CLASSICAL ALBUM

- *Premieres—Cello Concertos (Works of Danielpour, Kirchner, Rouse)*, Yo-Yo Ma, violoncello; David Zinman conducting the Philadelphia Orchestra. Sony Classical.

Beethoven: The String Quartets, Emerson String Quartet. Deutsche Grammophon.

Berlioz: Symphonie Fantastique; Tristia, Pierre Boulez conducting the Cleveland Orchestra. Deutsche Grammophon.

Brahms: The 4 Symphonies; Academic Festival Overture; etc., Sir Charles

Mackerras conducting the Scottish Chamber Orchestra. Telarc.

Wagner: Die Meistersinger von Nürnberg, Sir Georg Solti conducting the Chicago Symphony Orchestra and Chorus. London.

BEST ORCHESTRAL PERFORMANCE
(Conductor's Award)

• Pierre Boulez conducting the Cleveland Orchestra and Chorus, *Berlioz: Symphonie Fantastique; Tristia.* Deutsche Grammophon.

Sir Charles Mackerras conducting the Scottish Chamber Orchestra, *Brahms: The 4 Symphonies; Academic Festival Overture; etc.* Telarc.

Franz Welser-Most conducting the Philadelphia Orchestra, "Symphony in F Sharp, Op. 40," track from *Korngold: Symphony in F Sharp, Op. 40.* EMI Classics.

Christopher Lyndon-Gee conducting the Arnhem Philharmonic Orchestra, *Markevitch: Complete Orchestral Music, Vol. 1 (Le Nouvel Age; Sinfonietta in F; Cinéma Ouverture.* Marco Polo.

Riccardo Chailly conducting the Philadelphia Orchestra, *Shostakovich: The Dance Album (Moscow-Cheromushki, The Bolt, etc.).* London.

BEST CHAMBER MUSIC PERFORMANCE

• Emerson String Quartet, *Beethoven: The String Quartets.* Deutsche Grammophon.

Beaux Arts Trio, *Beaux Arts Trio Plays Turina, Granados (Turina: Trio No. 1, Op. 35, etc.; Granados: Trio, Op. 50).* Philips.

Anne-Sophie Mutter, violin; Lambert Orkis, piano, *The Berlin Recital (Works of Brahms, Debussy, Franck, Mozart).* Deutsche Grammophon.

Kronos Quartet, *Early Music— Lachryma Antiqua (Works of Machaut, Tye, Lamb, Dowland, etc.).* Nonesuch.

Jaime Laredo, viola; Cho-Liang Lin, violin; Yo-Yo Ma, cello; Sharon Robinson, cello; Isaac Stern, violin, *Schubert, Boccherini: Quintets (Schubert: Quintet in C Major, Boccherini: Quintet in E Major).* Sony Classical.

BEST SMALL ENSEMBLE PERFORMANCE (WITH OR WITHOUT CONDUCTOR)

• Claudio Abbado conducting members of the Berliner Philharmonic, "Hindemith: Kammermusik No. 1 with Finale 1921, Op. 24, No. 1," track from *Hindemith: Kammermusik Nos. 1, 4 and 5.* EMI Classics.

Sian Edwards conducting the Ensemble Modern, *Adams: Chamber Symphony; Shaker Loops; Phrygian Gates for Solo Piano.* RCA Victor Red Seal.

Reinhard Goebel conducting Musica Antiqua Koln, *Chaconne (Works of Blow, Corelli, Muffat, etc.).* Archiv Produktion.

Peter Phillips conducting the Tallis Scholars, *Ockeghem: Missa de Plus en Plus, etc.; Binchois: Missa au Travail Suis, etc.* Gimell.

Philippe Herreweghe conducting the Ensemble Vocal Européen, *Schein: The Fountains of Israel—Sacred Madrigals (O Herr, Ich Bin Dein Knecht; Ich Lasse Dich Nicht; etc.).* Harmonia Mundi.

Philip Pickett conducting the Musicians of the Globe, *Shakespeare's Musick—Songs and Dances from Shakespeare's Plays (Works of Byrd, Dowland, Holborne, Etc.).* Philips.

BEST CLASSICAL PERFORMANCE, INSTRUMENTAL SOLOIST(S) (WITH ORCHESTRA)

• Yo-Yo Ma, violoncello (David Zinman conducting the Philadelphia Orchestra), *Premieres—Cello Concertos (Works of Danielpour, Kirchner, Rouse).* Sony Classical.

Joshua Bell, violin (David Zinman conducting the Baltimore Symphony Orchestra), *Barber, Walton: Violin Concertos; Bloch: Baal Shem*. London.

Richard Goode, piano (Orpheus Chamber Orchestra), *Mozart: Piano Concertos Nos. 18 and 20*. Nonesuch.

Evelyn Glennie, percussion and marimba (Leonard Slatkin conducting the National Symphony Orchestra), "Concerto for Percussion and Orchestra," track from *Schwantner: Velocities; Concerto for Percussion and Orchestra; New Morning for the World*. RCA Victor Red Seal.

Martha Argerich, piano (Claudio Abbado conducting the Berliner Philharmonic), "Piano Concerto No. 1," track from *Tchaikovsky: Piano Concerto No. 1*. Deutsche Grammophon.

BEST CLASSICAL PERFORMANCE, INSTRUMENTAL SOLOISTS(S) (WITHOUT ORCHESTRA)

• Janos Starker, cello, *Bach: Suites for Solo Cello Nos. 1–6*. RCA Victor Red Seal.

Pierre-Laurent Aimard, piano, *Ligeti: Works for Piano (Etudes, Musica Ricercata, etc.)*. Sony Classical.

Murray Perahia, piano, *Murray Perahia Plays Handel and Scarlatti (Handel: Suite No. 5 in E Major, etc.; Scarlatti: Sonata in D Major, etc.)*. Sony Classical.

Leif Ove Andsnes, piano, *Schumann: Piano Sonata No. 1; Fantasy in C*. EMI Classics.

Arcadi Volodos, piano, *Volodos—Piano Transcriptions (Works of Bizet, Liszt, Rachmaninov-Volodos, etc.)*. Sony Classical.

BEST OPERA RECORDING

• *Wagner: Die Meistersinger von Nürnberg*, Sir Georg Solti conducting the Chicago Symphony Orchestra and Chorus (solos: Lippert, Mattila, Opie, Pape, van Dam, Vermillion). London.

Braunfels: Die Vogel, Lothar Zagrosek conducting the Deutsches Symphony Orchestra of Berlin (solos: Gorne, Holzmair, Kraus, Kwon, Wottrich). London.

Glinka: Ruslan and Lyudmila, Valery Gergiev conducting the Kirov Orchestra and Chorus (solos: Bezzubenkov, Diadkova, Gorchakova, Netrebko, Ognovienko). Philips.

Mozart: Don Giovanni, Sir Georg Solti conducting the London Philharmonic and London Voices (solos: Fleming, Murray, Pertusi, Terfel). London.

Rameau: Hippolyte et Aricie, William Christie conducting the Orchestra and Chorus of Les Arts Florissants (solos: Hunt, James, Naouri, Padmore, Panzarella). Erato.

BEST CHORAL PERFORMANCE

• Robert Shaw conducting the Altanta Symphony Orchestra and Chorus, *Adams: Harmonium; Rachmaninov: The Bells*. Telarc.

Franz Welser-Most conducting the London Philharmonic and the Mozart Chorus of Linz, *Bruckner: Messe No. 3 in F Minor; Te Deum*. EMI Classics.

Richard Hickox conducting the London Symphony Orchestra and Chorus, *Dyson: The Canterbury Pilgrims; Overture: At the Tabard Inn; In Honour of the City*. Chandos.

John Eliot Gardiner conducting the Monteverdi Chorus, *Haydn: The Creation*. Archiv Produktion.

James Paul conducting the Royal Scottish National Orchestra and Chorus; Christopher Bell, chorus master, *Paray: Mass for the 500th Anniversary of the Death of Joan of Arc*. Reference.

BEST CLASSICAL VOCAL PERFORMANCE

• Cecilia Bartoli, mezzo-soprano (James Levine, piano), *An Italian Songbook (Works of Bellini, Donizetti, Rossini)*. London.

Anne Sofie von Otter, mezzo-soprano
(Bengt Forsberg, piano), *La Bonne
Chanson—Fauré Chamber Songs
(Works of Ravel, Chausson, etc.).*
Deutsche Grammophon.
Omar Ebrahim, baritone; Rosemary
Hardy, soprano; Phyllis Bryn-Julson,
soprano; Rose Taylor, contralto
(King's Sisters; Esa-Pekka Salonen
conducting members of the Philhar-
monia Orchestra), *Ligeti: Vocal Works
(Nonsense Madrigals, Aventures, Der
Sommer, etc.).* Sony Classical.
Vesselina Kasarova, mezzo-soprano (Sir
Colin Davis conducting Staatskapelle
Dresden), *Mozart: Arias (Non So
Piu, Cosa Son; Vedrai Carino; In
Quali Eccessi, O Numi; etc.).* RCA
Victor Red Seal.
Renee Fleming, soprano (Sir Georg
Solti conducting the London Sym-
phony Orchestra), *Signatures—Great
Opera Scenes (Porgi, Amor; Dove
Sono; O Silver Moon; etc.).* London.

BEST CONTEMPORARY COMPOSITION
• "El Dorado," John Adams.
Concerto for Orchestra, Richard
Danielpour.
Second Symphony, Aaron Jay Kernis.
Concerto No. 2 for Piano and Orchestra,
Op. 36, Lowell Liebermann.
Symphony No. 5, Per Norgard.

BEST ENGINEERED RECORDING, CLASSICAL
• Michael Bishop, Jack Renner, *Cop-
land: The Music of America.* Telarc.
Tony Faulkner, Jack Renner, *Brahms:
The 4 Symphonies; Academic Festi-
val Overture; etc.* Telarc.
Richard King, *Herrmann: The Film
Scores.* Sony Classical.
Tony Faulkner, *Holst: The Planets;
Varèse: Arcana.* RCA Victor Red
Seal.
Neil Hutchinson, Krzysztof Jarosz,
James Lock, John Pellowe, *Wagner:
Die Meistersinger von Nürnberg.*
London.

CLASSICAL PRODUCER OF THE YEAR
• Stephen Epstein
Wolf Erichson
J. Tamblyn Henderson, Jr.
Andrew Keener
Judith Sherman

BEST SPOKEN COMEDY ALBUM
• *Roll with the New,* Chris Rock.
DreamWorks.
Button Down Concert, Bob Newhart.
Nick at Nite/550 Music/Sony Won-
der.
*Dirty Jokes and Beer: Stories of the
Unrefined,* Drew Carey. Simon and
Schuster Audioworks.
Garrison Keillor's Comedy Theater,
Garrison Keillor. High Bridge.
God Said Ha! Julia Sweeney. Warner
Bros.

BEST SPOKEN WORD OR NONMUSICAL ALBUM
• *Charles Kuralt's Spring,* Charles
Kuralt. Simon and Schuster
Audioworks.
Contact, Jodie Foster. Simon and Schus-
ter Audioworks.
Even the Stars Look Lonesome, Maya
Angelou. Random House Audio-
books.
Living Faith, Jimmy Carter. Random
House Audiobooks.
A Reporter's Life, Walter Cronkite. Ran-
dom House Audioworks.

BEST MUSICAL ALBUM FOR CHILDREN
• *All Aboard!* John Denver. Sony Won-
der.
Bigger Than Yourself, John
McCutcheon. Rounder Kids.
Shakin' a Tailfeather, Taj Mahal, Eric
Bibb, Linda Tillery. Music for Little
People.
Songs from a Parent to a Child, Art Gar-
funkel. Sony Wonder.
This Land Is Your Land, Arlo Guthrie.
Rounder.

BEST SPOKEN WORD ALBUM FOR CHILDREN

- *Winnie-the-Pooh*, Charles Kuralt (A. A. Milne). Penguin Audiobooks.

The Original Story of Winnie-the-Pooh, Long John Baldry (A. A. Milne). Walt Disney.

The Quite Remarkable Adventures of the Owl and the Pussycat, Eric Idle (Eric Idle). Dove Kids Audio.

The Star-Child and the Nightingale and the Rose, Gabriel Byrne (Oscar Wilde). Dove Kids Audio.

BEST ENGINEERED ALBUM (OTHER THAN CLASSICAL)

- Frank Filipetti, *Hourglass* (James Taylor). Columbia.

Bob Clearmountain, John Lowson, *Blue Moon Swamp* (John Fogerty). Warner Bros.

John Guess, Julian King, *Dream Walkin'* (Toby Keith). Mercury Nashville.

Elliot Scheiner, Al Schmitt, *Two for the Road* (Dave Grusin). GRP.

REMIXER OF THE YEAR

- Frankie Knuckles
David Morales
Mousse T.
Todd Terry
Armand Van Helden

BEST RECORDING PACKAGE
(Art Director's Award)

- Hugh Brown, Al Q, Jeff Smith, *Titanic: Music As Heard on the Fateful Voyage* (various artists). Rhino.

Stefan Sagmeister, *Fantastic Spikes Through Balloon* (Skeleton Key). Capitol.

Peter Grant, Stephanie Hughes, *Free Mars* (Lusk). Zoo/Volcano.

Johann Zambryski, *Le Roi Est Mort, Vive Le Roi!* (Enigma). Virgin.

Julian Peploe, *The Planet Sleeps* (various artists). Work Group.

BEST RECORDING PACKAGE, BOXED
(Art Director's Award)

- Hugh Brown, David Gorman, Rachel Gutek, *Beg, Scream and Shout! The Big Ol' Box of '60s Soul* (various artists). Rhino.

Patricia Lie, *The Complete Bill Evans on Verve*. Verve.

Giulio Turturro, *The Complete Ella Fitzgerald and Louis Armstrong on Verve*. Verve.

Carol Bobolts, Laurie Goldman, Jack O'Neil, *Cuba: I Am Time* (various artists). Blue Jackel.

Bryan Lasley, *Shakedown! The Texas Tapes Revisited*. Del-Fi.

BEST ALBUM NOTES
(Annotator's Award)

- John Fahey, Luis Kemnitzer, Jon Pankake, Chuck Pirtle, Jeff Place, Neil V. Rosenberg, Luc Sante, Peter Stampfel, Eric Von Schmidt, *Anthology of American Folk Music (1997 Edition Expanded)*. Smithsonian Folkways.

Robert Gordon, *Anthology* (Al Green). Right Stuff.

Ben Edmonds, Mark Kemp, Meegan Lee Ochs, Michael Ventura, *Farewells and Fantasies* (Phil Ochs). Elektra/Rhino.

Dave Alvin, James Austin, Bill Dahl, Ahmet Ertegun, David Ritz, Billy Vera, Jerry Wexler, *Ray Charles Genius and Soul: The 50th Anniversary Collection*. Rhino.

Ian Whitcomb, *Titantic: Music As Heard on the Fateful Voyage* (various artists). Rhino.

BEST HISTORICAL ALBUM

- *Anthology of American Folk Music (1997 Edition Expanded)* (various artists). Smithsonian Folkways.

Centenary Edition: 100 Years of Great Music (various artists). EMI Classics.

The Complete Bill Evans on Verve. Verve.

Cuba: I Am Time (various artists). Blue Jackel.

Ray Charles Genius and Soul: The 50th Anniversary Collection. Rhino.
Sing, Cowboy, Sing! The Gene Autry Collection. Rhino.

PRODUCER OF THE YEAR (OTHER THAN CLASSICAL)

- Babyface

Walter Afanasieff

Paula Cole

Kirk Franklin

Keith Thomas

BEST MUSIC VIDEO, SHORT FORM

- *Got Till It's Gone*, Janet Jackson. Mark Romanek, director. Virgin.

How Come, How Long, Babyface, Stevie Wonder. G. Gary Gray, director. Epic.

I Care 'bout You, Milestone. Mark Gerard, director. LaFace.

Early to Bed, Morphine. Jamie Caliri, director. DreamWorks.

Stinkfist, Tool. Adam Jones, director. Zoo/Volcano.

BEST MUSIC VIDEO, LONG FORM

- *Jagged Little Pill*, Alanis Morissette. Alanis Morissette, Steve Purcell, directors. Warner/Reprise Video/Maverick.

Letters from a Porcupine, Blind Melon. Steve MacCorkle, director. Capitol.

Forever's a Long Long Time, Orquestra Was. Don Was, director. Verve.

Live in Amsterdam—Wildest Dreams Tour, Tina Turner. David Mallet, director. Fox Lorber/WinStar Home Entertainment.

Blue Note—A Story of Modern Jazz, various artists. Julian Benedikt, director. Blue Note.

• Grammy Notes •

How Winners Are Chosen

The Grammy Awards are decided by the 9,000 voting members of the National Academy of Recording Arts & Sciences who qualify to vote by having contributed creatively or technically to at least six musical recordings. N.A.R.A.S. has 3,000 associate members as well, which include record firm executives, disc jockeys, publicists and others, but they are not permitted to vote. Membership costs $65 per year.

In 1998, 13,000 entries were submitted by N.A.R.A.S. members and 150 record companies resulting in 460 nominations in 92 categories. There is no entry fee for submissions.

To determine nominees, voters can choose five works in each category—including the top four of Record, Song, Album of the Year and Best New Artist—but then are restricted to participating in only 9 fields of music out of 22.

A secret committee of 25 music experts determines the nominees in the top four races after considering the leading 20 vote-getters submitted by academy members. National committees pick the contenders in the fields of classical and jazz music. Panels also determine the nominees for engineering, arranging, album notes and album package.

To determine winners on the second ballot, the vote is returned to the general membership. Voters make their selections for the top four awards and then are restricted to choosing winners in only 9 fields. Ballots are mailed to the accounting firm of Deloitte & Touche for tabulation.

Fast Grammy Facts

- On two occasions the award for best album went to nonmusic artists. Both were comedians. Bob Newhart won for 1960's *Button Down Mind* and Vaughn Meader for 1962's *The First Family*. Newhart beat Leontyne Price that same year to become the only nonmusic artist to win Best New Artist.

- Chicago Symphony conductor Sir Georg Solti won more awards than anyone else: 31. Quincy Jones is the biggest winner outside the classical field, having 26 Grammys.

- Sir Georg Solti also has the longest winning streak in Grammy history, having won each year from 1974 to 1983. Aretha Franklin has the second-longest victory streak, having prevailed in the r&b categories for the eight years between 1967 and 1974.

- Two artists are tied for snagging the most nominations in one year (12): Michael Jackson (1983) and Babyface (1992).

- Michael Jackson holds the record for winning the most awards in a single year, which he did in 1983, claiming seven for Album of the Year *Thriller* and one for *E.T. The Extra-Terrestrial* as Best Recording for Children. The previous record was held by Roger Miller, who won six Grammys in 1965 for "King of the Road" and *The Return of Roger Miller*. Miller remains in second place, tied with Quincy Jones (1990) and Eric Clapton (1992).

- Michael Jackson is the only winner to prevail in the vocal performance categories for pop, rock and r&b, which he did in 1983 during his *Thriller* sweep.

- Paul Simon has received Grammy's highest honor, Record of the Year, the most times (three)—for "Mrs. Robinson" in 1968, "Bridge Over Troubled Water" in 1970 and "Graceland" in 1987.

- Three artists are tied for winning Album of the Year the most times (three). Frank Sinatra won for *Come Dance with Me* in 1959, *September of My Years* in 1965 and *Sinatra: A Man and His Music* in 1966. Paul Simon won for *Bridge Over Troubled Water* in 1970, *Still Crazy After All These Years* in 1975 and *Graceland* in 1986. Stevie Wonder triumphed for *Innervisions* in 1973, *Fulfillingness' First Finale* in 1974 and *Songs in the Key of Life* in 1976. Wonder is the only artist to win for three consecutive albums.

- Only four artists have won Record, Album and Song of the Year in one year: Paul Simon for his 1970 album and its title track *Bridge Over Troubled Water;* Carole King for "It's Too Late," *Tapestry,* and "You've Got a Friend" in 1971; Eric Clapton in 1992 for "Tears in Heaven" and *MTV Unplugged;* and Christopher Cross for his self-titled album and "Sailing" in 1980. Cross also won Best New Artist, making him the only person to win all four of the top prizes.

- Christopher Cross and Sheryl Crow are the only two artists who've won Record of the Year and Best New Artist in the same year.

- The only artist who has won Record of the Year twice in a row was Roberta Flack for "The First Time Ever I Saw Your Face" in 1972 and "Killing Me Softly with His Song" in 1973. Flack was also the first solo black artist to win in one of the top categories.

- Although they have won Grammys in other top categories, none of the following artists ever received the highest honor of Record of the Year: Elvis Presley, Ella Fitzgerald, Barbra Streisand, Beatles, Bing Crosby, Judy Garland, Stevie Wonder, Rolling Stones, Aretha Franklin, Bruce Springsteen, Sting or Boyz II Men. All of the following artists have won it twice: Roberta Flack (1972, 1973), Fifth Dimenson (1967, 1969), Eric Clapton (1992, 1996) and Henry Mancini (1961, 1963). Paul Simon has won three times (1968, 1970, 1987).

- Although the Beatles never won Record of the Year, they did claim the other three of Grammy's four top awards: Album of the Year (*Sgt. Pepper's Lonely Hearts Club Band*, 1967), Song of the Year ("Michelle," 1966) and Best New Artist (1964).

- The only Grammys Elvis Presley ever won were for albums in the religious categories: *How Great Thou Art* (studio recording; Best Sacred Performance, 1967), *He Touched Me* (studio recording; Best Inspirationsal Performance, 1972) and *How Great Thou Art* (live performance recording; Best Inspirational Performance, 1974).

- The only artists to win Grammys in both the classical and nonclassical fields are Wynton Marsalis (1983 and 1984) and Ravi Shankar (1967 and 1972).

- Chet Atkins has won the most country awards (14), which he earned for instrumental performances like "The Entertainer" in 1975 and collaborative albums with Merle Travis, Les Paul, Jerry Reed and others. Roger Miller has won 11 Grammys, but only 9 of them were country prizes. In 1965, "King of the Road" won several c&w trophies, but it also scored in two "contemporary (r&r)" categories.

- The biggest winner in the jazz field is Ella Fitzgerald with 13 Grammys, followed by Duke Ellington with 11. Bill Cosby has won the most (9) for Best Comedy Recording. Leontyne Price is the top-winning opera singer with 13 trophies.

- When 14-year-old LeAnn Rimes was voted Best New Artist of 1997, she became the youngest person to win a top award. "I'm not an overnight success," she told reporters. "I've been at this since I was 6."

- Barbra Streisand was the youngest person ever to win Album of the Year. She was just 22 when her eponymous LP was named 1963's Album of the Year. (Stevie Wonder was 23 when he won 1973's Album of the Year award for *Innervisions*.)

- The only artist who has ever refused a Grammy was Sinéad O'Connor, who declined to accept her prize for Best Alternative Music Performance for *I Do Not Want What I Haven't Got* in 1990. She fumed, "I've said that if I win, I won't accept it and I wouldn't want it near me. As far as I'm concerned, it represents everything I despise about the music industry."

- The only winner ever stripped of an award was Milli Vanilli, which lost its Best New Artist designation of 1989 after it was learned that the duo did not actually sing on its recordings. In

1996, duo member Rob Pilatus was arrested by L.A. police for making "terrorist threats" after he was caught trying to break into a parked car. In 1998, he was found dead at the age of 32 in a German hotel room, the apparent victim of an accidental overdose of alcohol and prescription pills that he was taking as part of a drug withdrawal program.

- The names of winners have sometimes leaked out ahead of time. N.A.R.A.S. founding father Jim Conkling said about Grammy's earliest days, "There weren't any surprises like you have today. We had to tell the people because they were on the road and we had to bring them in." The *L.A. Times* reported that the full list of 1968's winners got passed around among attendees surreptitiously before the ceremony began.

- Two versions of the same song have won Grammys in the same year. The Fifth Dimension's rendition of "Up, Up and Away" won 1967's Record and Song of the Year plus the group contemporary vocals award. The Johnny Mann Singers won the best choral performance prize for their own recording, too. In 1994, "I Swear" won best Country Song for songwriter Gary Baker and Frank J. Myers, presumably because of the success of John Michael Montgomery's vocal version. All-4-One won a pop group vocals award for their version.

- The lowest-rated Grammycast was in 1995 (for the 1994 awards), scoring an 11.8 rating/19 share. The highest viewership was the 1984 broadcast (for the 1983 awards) when Michael Jackson's *Thriller* swept the night. It posted a 30.8 rating/45 share.

- Some of the more dubious victories in the Best New Artist category: Marc Cohn beat Boyz II Men and Seal (1991); America soared over the Eagles (1972); the Swingle Singers beat Vikki Carr (1963); the Carpenters nailed Elton John (1970) and comedian Bob Newhart got the last laugh over Leontyne Price (1960). Quite a few notable artists were losing nominees: Sonny & Cher, Led Zeppelin, Fifth Dimension, Eurythmics, Leontyne Price and Luther Vandross. Some of the most obscure winners: Starland Vocal Band, A Taste of Honey and Men at Work.

- What's a Grammy worth? Sales of Bob Dylan's *Time Out of Mind* jumped more than 400 percent the week after the 1997 Grammys, selling 41,000 copies and moving from 122nd on the charts to number 27. Bonnie Raitt's *Nick of Time* peaked at only number 22 just before winning 1989 Album of the Year, then zoomed to number 1. Sony Music President Tommy Motolla once estimated that winning a top award can increase sales of CDs by one-half million to 1 million copies.

- Not every winner reaps real gold. At the 1995 awards, Naughty by Nature's *Poverty's Paradise* actually sold fewer copies in the week after winning the first Grammy ever bestowed for Best Rap Album.

- When gauging music sales, who performs on the Grammycast seems to be just as important as who wins Grammys. Joan Osborne was nominated for four 1995 awards and lost all bids, but she performed on the telecast and saw her CD sales leap 47 percent the week after her TV performance. According to Warner Music Group, the average sales hike is between 26 percent and 34 percent for those who win or perform on the show.

Best Records, Songs, Albums and New Artists

Record of the Year Winners

(Recording Artist's Award)
1958 "Nel Blu DiPinto di Blu (Volare)," Domenico Modugno
1959 "Mack the Knife," Bobby Darin
1960 "Theme from A Summer Place," Percy Faith
1961 "Moon River," Henry Mancini
1962 "I Left My Heart in San Francisco," Tony Bennett
1963 "The Days of Wine and Roses," Henry Mancini
1964 "The Girl from Ipanema," Stan Getz, Astrud Gilberto
1965 "A Taste of Honey," Herb Alpert & the Tijuana Brass
1966 "Strangers in the Night," Frank Sinatra
1967 "Up, Up and Away," Fifth Dimension
1968 "Mrs. Robinson," Simon & Garfunkel
1969 "Aquarius/Let the Sunshine In," Fifth Dimension
1970 "Bridge Over Troubled Water," Simon & Garfunkel
1971 "It's Too Late," Carole King
1972 "The First Time Ever I Saw Your Face," Roberta Flack
1973 "Killing Me Softly with His Song," Roberta Flack
1974 "I Honestly Love You," Olivia Newton-John
1975 "Love Will Keep Us Together," Captain & Tennille
1976 "This Masquerade," George Benson
1977 "Hotel California," Eagles
1978 "Just the Way You Are," Billy Joel
1979 "What a Fool Believes," Doobie Brothers
1980 "Sailing," Christopher Cross
1981 "Bette Davis Eyes," Kim Carnes
1982 "Rosanna," Toto
1983 "Beat It," Michael Jackson
1984 "What's Love Got to Do with It," Tina Turner
1985 "We Are the World," USA for Africa
1986 "Higher Love," Steve Winwood
1987 "Graceland," Paul Simon
1988 "Don't Worry, Be Happy," Bobby McFerrin
1989 "Wind Beneath My Wings," Bette Midler
1990 "Another Day in Paradise," Phil Collins
1991 "Unforgettable," Natalie Cole (with Nat King Cole)
1992 "Tears in Heaven," Eric Clapton
1993 "I Will Always Love You," Whitney Houston
1994 "All I Wanna Do," Sheryl Crow
1995 "Kiss from a Rose," Seal
1996 "Change the World," Eric Clapton
1997 "Sunny Came Home," Shawn Colvin

Song of the Year Winners

(Songwriter's Award)
1958 "Nel Blu DiPinto di Blu (Volare)," Domenico Modugno
1959 "The Battle of New Orleans," Jimmy Driftwood
1960 "Theme from A Summer Place," Ernest Gold
1961 "Moon River," Henry Mancini, Johnny Mercer
1962 "What Kind of Fool Am I," Leslie Bricusse, Anthony Newley

1963 "The Days of Wine and Roses," Henry Mancini, Johnny Mercer

1964 "Hello, Dolly!" Jerry Herman

1965 "The Shadow of Your Smile (Love Theme from *The Sandpiper*)," Paul Francis Webster, Johnny Mandel

1966 "Michelle," John Lennon, Paul McCartney

1967 "Up, Up and Away," Jimmy L. Webb

1968 "Little Green Apples," Bobby Russell

1969 "Games People Play," Joe South

1970 "Bridge Over Troubled Water," Paul Simon

1971 "You've Got a Friend," Carole King

1972 "The First Time Ever I Saw Your Face," Ewan MacColl

1973 "Killing Me Softly with His Song," Norman Gimbel, Charles Fox

1974 "The Way We Were," Marilyn and Alan Bergman, Marvin Hamlisch

1975 "Send in the Clowns," Stephen Sondheim

1976 "I Write the Songs," Bruce Johnston

1977 (Tie:) "Love Theme from *A Star Is Born*," Barbra Streisand, Paul Williams; "You Light Up My Life," Joe Brooks

1978 "Just the Way You Are," Billy Joel

1979 "What a Fool Believes," Kenny Loggins, Michael McDonald

1980 "Sailing," Christopher Cross

1981 "Bette Davis Eyes," Donna Weiss, Jackie DeShannon

1982 "Always on My Mind," Johnny Christopher, Mark James, Wayne Carson

1983 "Every Breath You Take," Sting

1984 "What's Love Got to Do with It," Graham Lyle, Terry Britten

1985 "We Are the World," Michael Jackson, Lionel Richie

1986 "That's What Friends Are For," Burt Bacharach, Carole Bayer Sager

1987 "Somewhere Out There," James Horner, Barry Mann, Cynthia Weil

1988 "Don't Worry, Be Happy," Bobby McFerrin

1989 "Wind Beneath My Wings," Larry Henley, Jeff Silbar

1990 "From a Distance," Julie Gold

1991 "Unforgettable," Irving Gordon

1992 "Tears in Heaven" Eric Clapton

1993 "A Whole New World (*Aladdin*'s Theme)," Alan Menken, Tim Rice

1994 "Streets of Philadelphia," Bruce Springsteen

1995 "Kiss from a Rose," Seal

1996 "Change the World," Gordon Kennedy, Wayne Kirkpatrick, Tommy Sims

1997 "Sunny Came Home," Shawn Colvin, John Leventhal

Album of the Year Winners

(Recording Artist's Award)

1958 *The Music of Peter Gunn*, Henry Mancini

1959 *Come Dance with Me*, Frank Sinatra

1960 *Button Down Mind*, Bob Newhart

1961 *Judy at Carnegie Hall*, Judy Garland

1962 *The First Family*, Vaughn Meader

1963 *The Barbra Streisand Album*, Barbra Streisand

1964 *Getz/Gilberto*, Stan Getz, João Gilberto

1965 *September of My Years*, Frank Sinatra

1966 *Strangers in the Night*, Frank Sinatra

1967 *Sgt. Pepper's Lonely Hearts Club Band*, Beatles

1968 *By the Time I Get to Phoenix*, Glen Campbell

| 1969 | *Blood, Sweat & Tears*, Blood, Sweat & Tears | 1996 | *Falling Into You*, Celine Dion |
| 1970 | *Bridge Over Troubled Water*, Simon & Garfunkel | 1997 | *Time Out of Mind*, Bob Dylan |

1969	*Blood, Sweat & Tears*, Blood, Sweat & Tears
1970	*Bridge Over Troubled Water*, Simon & Garfunkel
1971	*Tapestry*, Carole King
1972	*The Concert for Bangla Desh*, George Harrison, Ravi Shankar, Bob Dylan, Leon Russell, Ringo Starr, Billy Preston, Eric Clapton, Klaus Voormann
1973	*Innervisions*, Stevie Wonder
1974	*Fulfillingness' First Finale*, Stevie Wonder
1975	*Still Crazy After All These Years*, Paul Simon
1976	*Songs in the Key of Life*, Stevie Wonder
1977	*Rumours*, Fleetwood Mac
1978	*Saturday Night Fever*, Bee Gees, other artists
1979	*52nd Street*, Billy Joel
1980	*Christopher Cross*, Christopher Cross
1981	*Double Fantasy*, John Lennon, Yoko Ono
1982	*Toto IV*, Toto
1983	*Thriller*, Michael Jackson
1984	*Can't Slow Down*, Lionel Richie
1985	*No Jacket Required*, Phil Collins
1986	*Graceland*, Paul Simon
1987	*The Joshua Tree*, U2
1988	*Faith*, George Michael
1989	*Nick of Time*, Bonnie Raitt
1990	*Back on the Block*, Quincy Jones
1991	*Unforgettable*, Natalie Cole (with Nat King Cole)
1992	*MTV Unplugged*, Eric Clapton
1993	*The Bodyguard*, Whitney Houston
1994	*MTV Unplugged*, Tony Bennett
1995	*Jagged Little Pill*, Alanis Morissette

Best New Artist Winners

1959	Bobby Darin
1960	Bob Newhart
1961	Peter Nero
1962	Robert Goulet
1963	Swingle Singers
1964	Beatles
1965	Tom Jones
1966	(no award)
1967	Bobbi Gentry
1968	José Feliciano
1969	Crosby, Stills & Nash
1970	Carpenters
1971	Carly Simon
1972	America
1973	Bette Midler
1974	Marvin Hamlisch
1975	Natalie Cole
1976	Starland Vocal Band
1977	Debbie Boone
1978	A Taste of Honey
1979	Rickie Lee Jones
1980	Christopher Cross
1981	Sheena Easton
1982	Men at Work
1983	Culture Club
1984	Cyndi Lauper
1985	Sade
1986	Bruce Hornsby & the Range
1987	Jodi Watley
1988	Tracy Chapman
1989	Milli Vanilli (revoked)
1990	Mariah Carey
1991	Mark Cohn
1992	Arrested Development
1993	Toni Braxton
1994	Sheryl Crow
1995	Hootie & the Blowfish
1996	LeAnn Rimes
1997	Paula Cole

Biggest Grammy Champs

Winners with the highest number of awards.

Sir Georg Solti	31
Quincy Jones	26
Vladimir Horowitz	25
Henry Mancini	20
Pierre Boulez	19
Stevie Wonder	19
Leonard Bernstein	16
Paul Simon (including Simon & Garfunkel)	16
John T. Williams	16
Aretha Franklin	15
Itzhak Perlman	15
Chet Atkins	14
David Foster	14
Ella Fitzgerald	13
Michael Jackson	13
Paul McCartney (including Beatles, Wings)	13
Leontyne Price	13
Robert Shaw	13
Ray Charles	12
Eric Clapton	12
Yo-Yo Ma	12
Thomas Z. Shepard	12
Sting (including Police)	12
Duke Ellington	11
Vince Gill	11
James Mallinson	11
Roger Miller	11
Babyface	10
George Harrison (including Beatles, Traveling Wilburys)	10
John Lennon (including Beatles)	10
Bobby McFerrin	10
Alan Menken	10
Pat Metheny (including Pat Metheny Group)	9
Artur Rubinstein	10
Robert Woods	10

Count Basie	9
James Blackwood (including Blackwood Brothers)	9
Shirley Caesar	9
Johnny Cash	9
Bill Cosby	9
Al Green	9
Dave Grusin	9
Margaret Hillis	9
Bonnie Raitt	9
Linda Ronstadt	9
Janis Siegel (including Manhattan Transfer)	9
Frank Sinatra	9
Ringo Starr (including Beatles)	9
Anita Baker	8
Beatles	8
George Benson	8
Blackwood Brothers	8
Natalie Cole	8
Chick Corea	8
Miles Davis	8
Art Garfunkel (including Simon & Garfunkel)	8
B. B. King	8
Erich Leinsdorf	8
James Levine	8
Manhattan Transfer	8
Wynton Marsalis	8
Pat Metheny Group	8
Phil Ramone	8
Barbra Streisand	8
Jimmy Sturr	8
Tony Bennett	7
Phil Collins (including Genesis)	7
Andrae Crouch	7
Sir Colin Davis	7
Bill Evans	7
Barry Gibbs (including Bee Gees)	7
Emmylou Harris (including Emmylou Harris & Nash Ramblers)	7

Marilyn McCoo (including Fifth Dimension)	7
Oscar Peterson	7
André Previn	7
Al Schmitt	7
Stephen Sondheim	7
Bruce Springsteen	7
Isaac Stern	7
Tina Turner (including Ike & Tina)	7
U2	7
Maurice White (including Earth, Wind & Fire)	7
Herb Alpert	6
Asleep at the Wheel	6
Emanuel Ax	6
Bee Gees	6
Michael Brecker	6
Placido Domingo	6
Earth, Wind & Fire	6
José Feliciano	6
Fifth Dimension	6
Thomas Frost	6
Edward T. Graham	6
Don Henley (including Eagles)	6
Jerry Hey	6
Robert M. Jones	6
Naomi Judd (including the Judds)	6
Chaka Khan	6
Alison Krauss (including the Cox Family and Union Station)	6
Arif Mardin	6
Ronnie Milsap	6
Ray Moore	6
Dan Morgenstern	6
Jay David Saks	6
Take 6	6
Stevie Ray Vaughan	6
Muddy Waters	6
Marvin Winans (including the Winans)	6
Laurindo Almeida	5
Vladimir Ashkenazy	5
Kathleen Battle	5

Glen Campbell	5
Mary Chapin Carpenter	5
Chieftains	5
Christopher Cross	5
Stan Getz	5
Amy Grant	5
Herbie Hancock	5
Lamelle Harris	5
Jim Henson	5
Whitney Houston	5
Al Jarreau	5
Billy Joel	5
Judds	5
Mark Knopfler (including Dire Straits)	5
Michel Legrand	5
Johnny Mandel	5
Michael McDonald (including Doobie Brothers)	5
Alanis Morissette	5
Willie Nelson	5
Oak Ridge Boys	5
Roy Orbison (including Traveling Wilburys)	5
Eddie Palmieri	5
Sandi Patti	5
Luciano Pavarotti	5
Peter, Paul & Mary	5
Police	5
Mike Post	5
Richard Pryor	5
Jack Renner	5
Lionel Richie (including Commodores)	5
David Sanborn	5
Igor Stravinsky	5
Donna Summer	5
Bruce Swedien	5
Ward Swingle (including Swingle Sisters)	5
B. J. Thomas	5
Dionne Warwick	5
Doc Watson	5
Winans	5

Grammy Losers

The following artists have never won a Grammy Award in a competitive category. Some have received special or honorary prizes.

Roy Acuff
Beach Boys
Chuck Berry
Bon Jovi
Jackson Browne
Byrds
Pablo Casals
Cher
Patsy Cline
Sam Cooke
Elvis Costello
Cream
Creedence Clearwater Revival
Jim Croce
Bing Crosby
Fats Domino
Doors
Drifters
Four Tops
Peter Frampton
Benny Goodman
Grateful Dead
Guns N' Roses
Lionel Hampton
Jimi Hendrix
Jackson Five
Jefferson Airplane
Janis Joplin
Kinks
Led Zeppelin
Bob Marley
Curtis Mayfield
Mitch Miller
Buck Owens
"Little Richard" Penniman
Liz Phair
Pretenders
Queen
Ramones
Diana Ross
Santana
Sex Pistols
Patti Smith
Cat Stevens
Rod Stewart
Supremes
Talking Heads
Tangerine Dream
Three Dog Night
Velvet Underground
Lawrence Welk
Kitty Wells
Who
Bob Wills
Neil Young

Hall of Fame

Label and year of recording are in parentheses.

Abbey Road, Beatles (Capitol, 1969)

"Ain't Misbehavin'," Thomas "Fats" Waller (Victor, 1929)

An American in Paris, George Gershwin, piano; Nat Shilkret, conductor of the Victor Symphony Orchestra (Victor, 1929)

"And the Angels Sing," Benny Goodman & His Orchestra; Martha Tilton, vocal; Ziggy Elman, trumpet (RCA Victor, 1939)

"April in Paris," Count Basie & His Orchestra (Clef, 1955)

"Artistry in Rhythm," Stan Kenton & His Orchestra (Capitol, 1945)

"A-Tisket A-Tasket," Chick Webb & His Orchestra with Ella Fitzgerald (Decca, 1938)

Bach: Goldberg Variations, Glenn Gould (Columbia, 1956)

Bach: Goldberg Variations for Harpsichord, Wanda Landowska (Victor, 1945)

Bach: Suites for Unaccompanied Cello (6), Pablo Casals (RCA Victor, 1936–39)

Bach: The Well-Tempered Clavier (Complete), Wanda Landowska (RCA Victor, 1949–54)

Bach-Stokowski: "Toccata and Fugue in D Minor," Leopold Stokowski conducting the Philadelphia Orchestra (Victrola, 1927)

"Back in the Saddle Again," Gene Autry (Vocalion, 1939)

Ballad for Americans, Paul Robeson (Victor, 1940)

Bartók: "Contrasts for Violin, Clarinet and Piano," Béla Bartók, piano; Joseph Szigeti, violin; Benny Goodman, clarinet (Columbia, 1940)

Bartók: Quartets (6) (Complete) , Juilliard Quartet (Columbia, 1950)

Beethoven: "Concerto in D Major for Violin and Orchestra, Opus 61," Jascha Heifetz, Arturo Toscanini conducting the NBC Symphony Orchestra (Victor, 1940)

Beethoven: Concertos for Piano Nos. 1–5, Artur Schnabel; Malcolm Sargent conducting the London Symphony (1, 5) and London Philharmonic (2, 3, 4) (Victor, 1955)

Beethoven: Piano Sonatas (32), Artur Schnabel (Beethoven Sonata Society/HMV, 1932–38)

Beethoven: Quartets for Strings (16) (Complete), Budapest String Quartet (Columbia, 1952)

Beethoven: Symphonies (9), Arturo Toscanini conducting the NBC Symphony Orchestra (RCA Victor, 1950–53)

"Begin the Beguine," Artie Shaw & His Orchestra (Bluebird, 1938)

"Bei Mir Bist du Schon," Andrews Sisters (Decca, 1938)

Berg: Wozzeck, Dimitri Mitropoulous conducting the New York Philharmonic Orchestra; Mack Harrell, Eileen Farrell (Columbia, 1952)

Birth of the Cool, Miles Davis (Capitol, 1957)

"Black and Tan Fantasy," Duke Ellington & His Orchestra (Victor, 1928)

"Black, Brown & Beige," Duke Ellington & His Famous Orchestra (RCA Victor, 1944)

"Blowin' in the Wind," Bob Dylan (Columbia, 1963)

"Blue Suede Shoes," Carl Perkins (Sun, 1956)

"Blue Yodel (T for Texas)," Jimmie Rodgers (Victor, 1928)

"Blueberry Hill," Fats Domino (Imperial, 1956)

"Body and Soul," Coleman Hawkins & His Orchestra (Bluebird, 1939)

"Call It Stormy Monday," T-Bone Walker (Black & White, 1948)

Carnegie Hall Jazz Concert, Benny Goodman (Columbia, 1950)

Charlie Parker with Strings, Charlie Parker (Mercury, 1950)

Chattanooga Choo Choo, Glenn Miller Orchestra with Tex Beneke & the Modernaires (Bluebird, 1941)

"Chimes Blues," King Oliver's Creole Jazz Band (Gennett, 1923)

"The Christmas Song," Nat King Cole (Capitol, 1946)

"Cocktails for Two," Spike Jones & His City Slickers (RCA Victor, 1945)

"Cool Water," Sons of the Pioneers (Decca, 1941)

"Crazy," Patsy Cline (Decca, 1961)

"Crazy Blues," Mamie Smith & Her Jazz Hounds (Okeh, 1994)

"Empty Bed Blues," Bessie Smith (Columbia, 1928)

"Everyday (I Have the Blues)," Count Basie Orchestra, Joe Williams (Clef, 1955)

"Flying Home," Lionel Hampton & His Orchestra (Decca, 1942)

"Four Brothers," Woody Herman (Columbia, 1948)

The Genius of Art Tatum, Vols. 1–13 (Clef, 1954–55)

The Genius of Ray Charles, Ray Charles (Altantic, 1960)

"Georgia on My Mind," Ray Charles (ABC-Paramount, 1960)

Gershwin: Porgy and Bess, Lehman Engel, conductor; Lawrence Winters, Camilla Williams, singers (Columbia, 1951)

Gershwin: Porgy and Bess Highlights, Vols. 1 and 2, original cast and Broadway revival cast (Decca, 1940, 1942)

Gershwin: Rhapsody in Blue, Paul Whiteman, George Gershwin (Victor, 1927)

Gershwin: Rhapsody in Blue, Oscar Levant, Eugene Ormandy conducting the Philadelphia Orchestra (Columbia, 1945)

"God Bless America," Kate Smith (Victor, 1939)

"God Bless the Child," Billie Holiday (Okeh, 1941)

"Good Vibrations," Beach Boys (Capitol, 1966)

"Heartbreak Hotel," Elvis Presley (RCA, 1956)

"Hound Dog," Elvis Presley (RCA Victor, 1956)

"How High the Moon," Les Paul, Mary Ford (Capitol, 1951)

I Can Hear It Now, Vols. 1–3, Edward R. Murrow (Columbia, 1948–50)

"I Can't Get Started," Bunny Berigan & His Orchestra (Victor, 1937)

"I Left My Heart in San Francisco," Tony Bennett (Columbia, 1962)

"If I Didn't Care," Ink Spots (Decca, 1939)

"I'll Never Smile Again," Tommy Dorsey, Frank Sinatra, Pied Pipers (Victor, 1940)

"In a Mist," Bix Beiderbecke (Okeh, 1927)

"In the Mood," Glenn Miller & His Orchestra (Bluebird, 1939)

In the Wee Small Hours, Frank Sinatra (Capitol, 1955)

"I've Got a Woman," Ray Charles (Altantic, 1954)

Jazz at Massey Hall, Dizzy Gillespie, Bud Powell, Max Roach, Charles Mingus (Debut, 1953)

Jelly Roll Morton: The Saga of Mr. Jelly Lord, 12 albums, Library of Congress Recordings, Ferdinand "Jelly Roll" Morton (Circle Sound, 1949–50)

Kind of Blue, Miles Davis (Columbia, 1959)

Leoncavallo: Pagliacci, Act 1: Vesti la Giubba, Enrico Caruso (Victrola, 1907)

"Lover Man (Oh, Where Can You Be?)," Billie Holiday (Decca, 1945)

"Mack the Knife," Louis Armstrong & the Allstars (Columbia, 1955)

Mahler: Das Lied von der Erde, Bruno Walter conducting the Vienna Philharmonic Orchestra with Kathleen Ferrier and Julius Patzak (London, 1952)

"Maybellene," Chuck Berry (Chess, 1955)

Miles Ahead, Miles Davis, Gil Evans & His Orchestra (Columbia, 1958)

"Misty," Erroll Garner Trio (Mercury, 1954)

"Mona Lisa," Nat King Cole (Capitol, 1950)

"Mood Indigo," Duke Ellington & His Orchestra (Brunswick, 1931)

"Moonlight Serenade," Glenn Miller & His Orchestra (Bluebird, 1939)

"My Blue Heaven," Gene Austin (Victor, 1928)

My Fair Lady, original Broadway cast with Rex Harrison and Julie Andrews (Columbia, 1956)

"Nobody," Bert Williams (Columbia, 1906)

Oklahoma! original Broadway cast with Alfred Drake (Decca, 1943)

"One O'Clock Jump," Count Basie & His Orchestra (Decca, 1937)

"Ornithology," Charlie Parker Sextet (Dial, 1946)

"Over the Rainbow," Judy Garland (Decca, 1939)

"Pinetop's Boogie Woogie," Pine Top Smith (Vocalion, 1928)

Puccini: Tosca, Victor de Sabata conducting the Orchestra and Chorus of Teatro alla Scala, Milan, with Maria Callas, Giuseppe DiStefano, Tito Gobbi (Angel, 1953)

Rachmaninov: "Piano Concerto No. 2 in C Minor," Sergei Rachmaninov, piano; Philadelphia Orchestra; Leopold Stokowski, conductor (Victrola, 1929)

Rachmaninov: "Rhapsody on a Theme of Paganini," Sergei Rachmaninov, piano; Philadelphia Orchestra; Leopold Stokowski, conductor (RCA Victor, 1935)

Ravel: Boléro, Maurice Ravel conducting the Lamoureux Orchestra (Brunswick, 1937)

"Rock Around the Clock," Bill Haley & the Comets (Decca, 1955)

"Roll Over Beethoven," Chuck Berry (Chess, 1956)

" 'Round About Midnight," Thelonious Monk Quintet (Blue Note, 1948)

"Rudolph, the Red-Nosed Reindeer," Gene Autry (Columbia, 1949)

"Saint Louis Blues," Bessie Smith, Louis Armstrong (Columbia, 1925)

"September Song," Walter Huston (Brunswick, 1938)

Sgt. Pepper's Lonely Hearts Club Band, Beatles (Capitol, 1967)

Show Boat, Paul Robeson, Helen Morgan, James Melton, Frank Munn, Countess Albani, Victor Young (Brunswick, 1932)

"Sing, Sing, Sing," Benny Goodman (Victor, 1937)

Singin' the Blues, Frankie Trumbauer & His Orchestra; Bix Beiderbecke, cornet (Okeh, 1927)

Sketches of Spain, Miles Davis, Gil Evans (Columbia, 1959)

"Some of These Days," Sophie Tucker (Edison, 1911)

South Pacific, Mary Martin, Ezio Pinza, original Broadway cast (Columbia, 1949)

"Star Dust," Hoagy Carmichael & His Pals (Gennett, 1927)

"Star Dust," Artie Shaw & His Orchestra (RCA Victor, 1940)

"Strange Fruit," Billie Holiday (Commodore, 1939)

Stravinsky: Le Sacre du Printemps, Pierre Monteaux conducting the Boston Symphony (RCA Victor, 1951)

"Take Five," track from Time Out, Dave Brubeck Quartet (Columbia, 1960)

"Take the 'A' Train," Duke Ellington & His Orchestra (Victor, 1941)

"Tea for Two," Art Tatum, piano solo (Decca, 1939)

"This Land Is Your Land," Woody Guthrie (Asch, 1947)

Verdi: Celeste Aida, Enrico Caruso (Victor, 1908)

Villa-Lobos: "Bachianas Brasileiras No. 5—Aria," Bidu Sayao with Heitor Villa-Lobos conducting 'cello Ensemble (Columbia, 1945)

Wagner: Tristan und Isolde, Wilhelm Furtwangler conducting the Philharmonic Orchestra and Chorus of the Royal Opera House (RCA Victor, 1953)

Weill: The Threepenny Opera, Theater de Lys Production with Lotte Lenya (MGM, 1954)

West End Blues, Louis Armstrong & His Hot Five (Okeh, 1928)

West Side Story, Carol Lawrence, Larry Kert, original Broadway cast (Columbia, 1957)

"White Christmas," Bing Crosby (Decca, 1942)

"Yesterday," Beatles (Capitol, 1965)

"Your Cheating Heart," Hank Williams (MGM, 1953)

Special Honors

Harold Arlen
Burt Bacharach & Hal David
Béla Bartók
Count Basie
Beatles
Emile Berliner
Dick Clark
Aaron Copland
Pierre Cossette
John Culshaw
Hal David
Walt Disney
Thomas A. Dorsey
Thomas A. Edison
Duke Ellington & Billy Strayhorn
Ahmet Ertegun
Nesuhi Ertegun
Christine M. Farnon
Milt Gabler
George & Ira Gershwin
Berry Gordy
Norman Granz
Oscar Hammerstein II
John Hammond
W. C. Handy
Lorenz Hart
Larry Hiller
Holland-Dozier-Holland
Eldridge R. Johnson
Quincy Jones
Jerome Kern
Goddard Lieberson
George Martin
Johnny Mercer
Robert Moog

Jerry Moss
Les Paul
Krzysztof Penderecki
Sam Phillips
Cole Porter
Frances Preston
Richard Rodgers
George T. Simon
Frank Sinatra
George Solti & John Culshaw
Leopold Stokowski
Billy Strayhorn
Paul Weston
Jerry Wexler

LEGEND AWARDS

Johnny Cash
Aretha Franklin
Michael Jackson
Billy Joel
Quincy Jones
Curtis Mayfield
Liza Minnelli
Willie Nelson
Smokey Robinson
Frank Sinatra
Barbra Streisand
Andrew Lloyd Webber

TECHNICAL GRAMMY AWARDS

Ray Dolby
Rupert Neve
Dr. Thomas G. Stockham, Jr.

INDEX

All page numbers in italics indicate victory or victories.